The **Organizational Behavior Case for Discussion** assists students in the transition from textbook learning to real-world application.

- The Humanistic Workplace (Ch. 1)
- Work Hard, or Get a Life? (Ch. 2)
- Texaco Does It Wrong and Then Does It Right (Ch. 3)
- Personality and Perception at Sears and Montgomery Ward (Ch. 4)
- Motivating Knowledge Workers (Ch. 5)
- Motivation at Mirage (Ch. 6)
- Employee Participation at Chaparral Steel (Ch. 7)
- Rewarding the Hourly Worker (Ch. 8)
- Over the Edge (Ch. 9)
- Is Big Brother Reading Your Email? (Ch. 10)
- Procter & Gamble Seeks to Innovate (Ch. 11)
- Team-Based System at Consolidated Diesel (Ch. 12)
- Leading for Change at Ford (Ch. 13)
- Leading for Change at adidas (Ch. 14)
- Encouraging Dissent at AT&T (Ch. 15)
- Disney Reorganizes to Rebound (Ch. 16)
- Microsoft Reorganizes and Reorganizes (Ch. 17)
- Defining the "Astra USA" Way (Ch. 18)
- Nissan Goes Against the Grain (Ch. 19)

**Experiencing Organizational Behavior** exercises continue students' transition to real-world application by asking them to work together to apply concepts to their own surroundings.

- Relating OB and Popular Culture (Ch. 1)
- Managing in Today's Organization (Ch. 2)
- Understanding Your Own Stereotypes and Attitudes Toward Others (Ch. 3)
- Matching Personalities and Jobs (Ch. 4)
- Relating Your Needs to the Theories of Motivation (Ch. 5)
- Understanding the Dynamics of Expectancy Theory (Ch. 6)
- Learning About Job Design (Ch. 7)
- Using Compensation to Motivate Workers (Ch. 8)
- Learning How Stress Affects You (Ch. 9)
- The Importance of Feedback in Oral Communication (Ch. 10)
- Benefits of a Group (Ch. 11)
- Using Teams (Ch. 12)
- Understanding Successful and Unsuccessful Leadership (Ch. 13)
- Learning About Ethics and Power (Ch. 14)
- Programmed and Nonprogrammed Decisions (Ch. 15)
- Understanding Organization Structure (Ch. 16)
- Studying a Real Organization (Ch. 17)
- Culture of the Classroom (Ch. 18)
- Planning a Change at the University (Ch. 19)

**Building Organizational Behavior Skills** exercises give students the opportunity to apply concepts to brief self-assessment or diagnostic activities.

- Assessing Your Own Theory X and Theory Y Tendencies (Ch. 1)
- Assessing Your Own Management Skills (Ch. 2)
- Cross-Cultural Awareness (Ch. 3)
- Assessing Your Locus of Control (Ch. 4)
- Assessing Your Own Needs (Ch. 5)
- Assessing Your Equity Sensitivity (Ch. 6)
- The Job Characteristics Inventory (Ch. 7)
- Diagnosing Poor Performance and Enhancing Motivation (Ch. 8)
- Are You Type A or Type B? (Ch. 9)
- Diagnosing Your Listening Skills (Ch. 10)
- Group Cohesiveness (Ch. 11)
- Using Teams (Ch. 12)
- Applying Vroom's Decision Tree Approach (Ch. 13)
- Are You a Charismatic Leader? (Ch. 14)
- Rational Versus Practical Approaches to Decision Making (Ch. 15)
- Making Delegation Work (Ch. 16)
- Diagnosing Organization Structure (Ch. 17)
- An Empowering Culture: What It Is and What It Is Not (Ch. 18)
- Support for Change (Ch. 19)

**Developing OB Internet Skills** exercises direct students to go to the web site of a company or organization or to search the web for information about some topic illustrating how organizations are approaching issues discussed in the chapter.

The **Integrative Running Case** at the end of each part provides an opportunity for students to discuss an actual ongoing management situation with significant organizational behavior facets.

- The AOL-Time Warner Deal (Part 1)
- The People Behind the AOL-Time Warner Deal (Part 2)
- Influence Processes at Work in the AOL-Time Warner Deal (Part 3)
- The AOL-Time Warner Deal—From Two Organizations to One (Part 4)

# Organizational Behavior

## Managing People and Organizations

Sixth Edition

Gregory Moorhead

Arizona State University

Ricky W. Griffin

Texas A&M University



Houghton Mifflin Company Boston New York

For my family: Linda, Alex, and Lindsay. — G.M.

For my daughter Ashley: Still a sweet and shining star moving boldly forward through life's big adventure. — R.W.G.

*Executive Editor:* George Hoffman
*Senior Development Editor:* Susan M. Kahn
*Editorial Assistant:* Lauren Gagliardi
*Project Editor:* Rachel D'Angelo Wimberly
*Editorial Assistant:* Claudine Bellanton
*Senior Production/Design Coordinator:* Sarah Ambrose
*Manufacturing Manager:* Florence Cadran
*Marketing Manager:* Melissa Russell

*Cover Design:* Harold Burch, Harold Burch Design, New York City

*Cover Image:* Robert Neubecker

*Back Cover Credit:* Netscape Communicator browser window copyright © 1999 Netscape Communication Corporation. Used with permission.

*Photo Credits:* **Chapter 1:** p. 4, Alex Hoester/Corbis Sygma; p. 10, Courtesy of AT &T Archives; p. 14, Greg Girard/Contact Press Images. **Chapter 2:** p. 30, Gregory Foster; p. 32, Rex Rystedt; p. 38, Alan Levenson; p. 41, Jens Wunderlich. **Chapter 3:** p. 55, © 2000 Brian Coats. All rights reserved; p. 65, AP/Wide World Photos; p. 71 Richard Schultz/Matrix International, Inc. **Chapter 4:** p. 90, Valerie Shaff; p. 93, Liane Enkelis; p. 103, Gail Albert Halaban/SABA. **Chapter 5:** p. 115, Patrick Kovarik/AFP; p. 122, Mike Nelson/AFP; p. 131, Jeffrey Lowe. **Chapter 6:** p. 142, Brown W. Cannon III; p. 145, Christian Jennings/Reuters/Archive Photos; p. 152, Michael L. Abramson. **Chapter 7:** p. 169, Ricardo Azoury/SABA; p. 177, © Tony Savino 1999; p. 182 (L): Darcy Padilla; p. 182 (R): Darcy Padilla. **Chapter 8:** p. 193, John Emerson; p. 203, Webb Chappell; p. 206, Robert Wright; p. 213, Douglas Woods. **Chapter 9:** p. 222, Toru Yamanaka-AFP; p. 229, Courtesy of The Madison Black Wolf; p. 231, Eli Reichman; p. 238, Mark Richards. **Chapter 10:** p. 250, Matty Stern/U.S. Embassy Tel Aviv, U.S. Department of State. Reprinted with permission; p. 255, Anna Curtis; p. 259, Jeffrey Mermelstein; p. 266, © Eli Reichman. **Chapter 11:** p. 283, Ken Gabrielsen; p. 287, David Stover; p. 289, Doug Knutson; p. 302, Monika Graff/The Image Works. **Chapter 12:** p. 312, Greg Kiger/Corporate Photography Group; p. 315, Lynn Johnson/ Aurora & Quanta Productions; p. 319, Will McIntyre/McIntyre Photography; p. 326, Nathaniel Welch/SABA. **Chapter 13:** p. 334, Andrew Gardner/ Life Magazine; p. 337, AP/Wide World Photos; p. 346, Liane Enkelis; p. 348, Kristine Larsen. **Chapter 14:** p. 360, D. Farber/Corbis Sygma; p. 363, David Burnett/Contact Press Images; p. 365, © 2000 Brian Coats. All rights reserved; p. 368, Wyatt McSpadden. **Chapter 15:** p. 401, Patrick Harbron; p. 409, Steve Goldstein; p. 411, AP/Wide World Photos. **Chapter 16:** p. 422, David Butow/SABA; p. 434, Marc Joseph; p. 437, Mambo/Corbis Sygma. **Chapter 17:** p. 451, Jonathan Saunders; p. 467, Richard Howard; p. 472, Tom Maday. **Chapter 18:** p. 484, Mark Richards; p. 490, T. Michael Keza; p. 496, Torin Boyd; p. 499, Reprinted with permission by Merck & Co., Inc. **Chapter 19:** p. 511, Jeffrey MacMillan/USN&WR; p. 517, Andy Freeberg; p. 522, Bernd Auers.



Printed in the U.S.A.

Library of Congress Catalog Card Number: 00-133865

ISBN: 0-618-05649-1

4 5 6 7 8 9—DOW—04 03 02

# Brief Contents

# Contents

## Part II
## Individual Processes in Organizations

# Part III
# Interpersonal Processes in Organizations

# Part IV
# Organizational Processes and Characteristics

# Preface

## The Challenge of the New Century

The dawning of a new century provides everyone with a chance to reflect on the past, as well as to look ahead to new opportunities for success. The popular press has generated a plethora of top ten lists highlighting the standouts of the past century. *Fortune* magazine described the ten best management ideas of the twentieth century: scientific management, assembly line manufacturing, the modern corporation, leadership, the management guru, labor rights, managing by the numbers, quality, reengineering, and knowledge management.[1] All of these great ideas of management deal in some way with the human side of management–organizational behavior. The great industrialists of the century, also described by *Fortune*, were Henry Ford (Ford Motor Company), Alfred P. Sloan (General Motors), Tom Watson, Jr. (IBM), and Bill Gates (Microsoft).[2] Each of these pioneers, in his own way, shaped how business operates. Each went against the standard ways of operating by making changes in established practices and developing new ways of doing business that essentially changed the world.

Concurrently with celebrating the past, attention is focusing on how to survive and thrive in the twenty-first century. Computers are finally having the impact that was predicted twenty to thirty years ago. With computers and the advances in communications technology, the Internet age is upon us. The Internet age is becoming so much more than just a faster way to communicate, however. Everything that people do now must be done faster. In organizations managers no longer have the luxury of making significant changes and sitting back to watch as the system adjusts and restabilizes, and the changes have an impact on operations. Previously, managers had the time to take measurements on the impact of the change and make more adjustments. Managers now must make a change and prepare for the next change before the first change has fully taken effect. All of the changes that organizations are making—downsizing, merging, valuing diversity, acquiring, reengineering, and going global—are now made at warp speed. For example, managers are creating new business—online stores that cannibalize their existing sales and distribution systems—before they know if Internet shopping will even work for their business. All of these changes require people to make the decisions and others to carry them out, just as the great industrialists of the twentieth century relied on people to implement the changes they made.

So, how will organizations look and operate in this new century? How does what we learned in the twentieth century apply to the twenty-first century? What do we do with ideas and theories that were developed during the last century now that we have entered the new century? As we prepared the sixth edition of *Organizational Behavior: Managing People and Organizations*, we considered what we had learned in the past and what new managers will need to know over the next few years. We realize that we cannot prepare them for every possibility and dilemma they will face in their management careers—their careers, after all, may last forty or fifty years! The world is already changing too fast for that, and it will soon change even faster.

We realize that we need to equip today's students with a perspective on managing people that allows them to create, judge, imagine, and build relationships,

*"Most managers now seem to understand that they will find competitive advantage by tapping employees' most essential humanity, their ability to create, judge, imagine, and build relationships. The champion managers of the Infotech Age will be those who do it fastest and best." — Geoffrey Colvin*[3]

rather than provide every answer to every dilemma. That perspective needs to provide a firm grasp of the fundamentals of human behavior in organizations—the basic foundations of behavior so that they can develop new answers to new problems they encounter. That perspective must provide the background of the theories and approaches; not simply so students can answer questions on an exam, but so they can go back to the basics and the fundamentals when things perplex them. One of the author's favorite coaches told him that whenever you go into a slump in shooting a basketball or hitting the golf ball you should always go back to the basics, check the fundamentals in order to get back on track. The same works for managing people in organizations. As new challenges are thrust on us from around the world by global competition, new technologies, newer and faster information processes, and customers who demand the best in quality and service, the next generation of managers will need to go back to basics and fundamentals. Then they can develop some creative new solution, process, product, or service to succeed and even gain a competitive advantage.

# The Text That Meets the Challenge

The sixth edition of *Organizational Behavior: Managing People and Organizations* takes on the new challenges of management by providing the basics in each area, bolstered by the latest research in the field, and infused with examples of what companies are doing in each area. We have made some significant changes in how the material is presented. For example, we found that students rarely read or used the chapter outlines and learning objectives that preceded each chapter. Therefore, we eliminated them and open each chapter with an introduction that weaves new previews and opening vignettes with examples of how the topic of the chapter is relevant in organizations. The chapter outlines and objectives are available on the student web site, as well as in the *Instructor's Resource Manual*, for use in planning the discussion of the chapter material. To bring the material into the Internet age we have developed an Internet exercise at the end of each chapter to provide students with an opportunity to use the Internet as a tool to learn more about the material covered in the chapter. We eliminated one of the two short cases at the end of each chapter, replacing those cases with a new, more in-depth case that is presented at the end of each part of the book. This integrative running case follows the blockbuster deal of the new millennium—the merger of AOL and Time Warner. There are many interesting aspects of that merger that make it a perfect platform for discussion of the topics in each part of this book.

The text is presented in a more dynamic and contemporary fashion than in previous editions. We use bolder colors, more pictures, different typeface styles, and quotations by real managers about real organizational situations. In addition to changing the introduction of each chapter, we now present the material in a fashion that is more like popular business periodicals. The book reads more like a contemporary business magazine, but it still contains the basic foundation material of the field. Our students have remarked how easy it is to read this book and really get into the material. (They say they never count the pages they have left to read in each chapter in this book the way they do in other texts!) In the sixth edition we use call-out quotes to emphasize bold statements made by contemporary organizational leaders who are talking about real managerial issues. In addition, we added material in the sixth edition that had not even been published in academic journals at the time we went to print (see the discussion of Vroom decision model in Chapter 13).

We have also resisted the popular trend of authors and publishers to cut the heart of the book in an effort to make it thinner. Several editions ago we cut out some material and rewrote other parts in a briefer form in an effort to reduce the mass of the book. Although those changes were favorably received, we have not gone any further in this downsizing in order to maintain the integrity of the book as truly representative of the field. We have left the meat. The basic theoretical approaches and developments that are the heart of this field are discussed in enough detail that students will understand them, yet not in so exhaustive a fashion that students are overwhelmed.

*Organizational Behavior: Managing People and Organizations*, Sixth Edition, prepares and energizes managers of the future for the complex and challenging tasks of the new century while it preserves the past contributions of the classics. It is comprehensive in its presentation of practical perspectives, backed up by the research and learning of the experts. We expect each reader to be inspired by the most exciting task of the new century: managing people in organizations.

# Content and Organization

The sixth edition of *Organizational Behavior: Managing People and Organizations* has essentially the same overall organization and topical presentation as did the previous edition. That is one of the benefits of a book in its sixth edition: we no longer have to experiment with different ways of combining the topics into chapters and parts. Based on feedback from reviewers, the current organization fits the way that many instructors prefer to approach the topics in their courses. We have, however, updated much of the research and added topics that needed attention throughout the text. Part I discusses the managerial context of organizational behavior. In Chapter 1 we describe some of the innovative things that SAS Institute Inc., a major software company, is doing for the benefit of its people and how being innovative in managing people can contribute to the bottom line. This opening case provides an effective vehicle to introduce basic concepts of the field, to discuss the importance of the study of organizational behavior, and to give a brief history of the field, and to set the stage for study of the field. In Chapter 2 we develop a managerial perspective on the field by describing how Gordon Bethune effectively integrated basic and sound management techniques with respect and consideration for the employees and led a remarkable turnaround at Continental Airlines. This chapter develops a managerial perspective on organizational behavior and describes the manager's job in terms of its functions, roles, and skills. New material on workforce expansion and information technology has been added as part of the discussion of managerial challenges. Chapter 3, new in the previous edition, was a real hit with users of the fifth edition. It combined former chapters on diversity and international issues to form a cohesive treatment of globalism and workforce diversity. In addition to the discussion of diversity programs in operation at AT&T, we have updated the data on the changing workforce and added special features on the special managerial problems of State-Owned Enterprises in China, English-only rules in the workplace, and bribery as a way of doing business internationally. The first three chapters, therefore, constitute an in-depth look at the context within which organizational behavior takes place.

Part II includes six chapters that focus on key aspects of individual processes in organizations: individual differences and perception, motivation, employee performance, and stress. Chapter 4 presents the foundations for understanding individual behavior in organizations by discussing the psychological nature of people, elements of personality, individual attitudes, perceptual processes, and creativity. We use the examples of Levi Strauss and Delta Airlines to illustrate some of the difficulties of dealing with the individuality of employees. Chapters 5 and 6 focus on the two primary categories of motivation theories: need-based approaches and process-based approaches. Although some may view this material as rather dull recitations of old theories, these two chapters are spiked with great real-world examples of how the basic approaches are meaningfully used in organizations today. Motivation techniques used by big companies such as Lucent Technologies, Ford Motor Company, and Xerox; by small companies such as TixToGo; and in places from Saudi Arabia to North America are used throughout these chapters. Chapters 7 and 8 focus on specific methods, techniques, and strategies managers use to affect individual performance in organizations. Chapter 7 makes the transition from the theories to actual organizational practice by discussing job design, employee participation, and alternative work arrangements, including an expanded section on job sharing. Included in this chapter are descriptions of jobs in such diverse areas as chicken processing, lumber work for Georgia-Pacific Corporation, and hospitality jobs at Marriott hotels. To round out our study of individual/organizational motivation and performance, Chapter 8 provides the next practical step in motivation by focusing on goal setting, performance measurement, and rewards. The chapter includes special features on actual techniques, such as accelerated reviews; pay and benefit practices at General Motors, Wal-Mart, Marriott International, and Pier 1; and merit pay in Japan. Part II closes with the very important topics of work stress and work-life balance in Chapter 9. It presents the latest research on stress at work and shows how companies are paying more attention to the individual work-life balance and the needs of their employees. Included in this chapter is a new discussion of the role of information technology in work stress.

In Part III we move from the individual aspects of organizational behavior to the more interpersonal aspects of the field, including communication, groups and teams, leadership and influence processes, and decision making. Chapter 10 describes the behavioral aspects of communication in organizations. Since most college and university business programs typically include one or two courses in communication, it is not our intent here to replicate that material. We do, however, provide an overview of the communication process, discuss important aspects of international communication, describe communication networks in organizations, and examine the impacts of computerized information processing and telecommunications in a variety of organizational settings. Chapters 11 and 12 are a two-chapter sequence on groups and teams in organizations. We believe there is too much important material to just have one chapter on these topics. Therefore, we present the basics of understanding the dynamics of small group behavior in Chapter 11 and discuss the more applied material on teams in Chapter 12. In this manner readers get to understand the more basic processes first before attacking the more complex issues in developing teams in organizations. New material on affinity groups has been added to Chapter 11, as well as examples from business—Procter & Gamble and Intel—and the business of sports—New York Yankees (the most successful sports franchise in history) and stock car racing. Chapter 12 uses diverse examples, such as Lend Lease Corporation from Australia, Consolidated Diesel Company, Dell Computers' global teams, and Novell's geek teams to illustrate the differences between groups and teams, the benefits and costs of teams, and the steps for implementing a team-based organization. We present leadership in a two-chapter sequence, examining models and concepts in Chapter 13 and influence processes in Chapter 14. Chapter 13 presents several new examples of nontraditional leaders such as Carly Fiorina, CEO at Hewlett-Packard Co., Jacques Nasser at Ford Motor Co., and Konosuke Matsushita at Matsushita Electric in its coverage of the historical views of leadership; the basic trait, behavioral, and situational views; and contemporary views. New to this chapter is a discussion of the role of gender in leadership and the newest version of the Vroom decision tree model of leadership. Closely related to leadership is the more complex topic of influence processes, discussed in Chapter 14. The chapter moves from influence-based leadership approaches—transformational and charismatic leadership—to a discussion of substitutes for leadership, and then describes power and political behavior in organizations—both highly influence related phenomena. Special features of this chapter include new leadership at McDonald's, and the charisma of Yanira Merina, the influential union organizer from El Salvador. Finally, the last chapter in Part III on Interpersonal Processes in Organizations is Chapter 15, Decision Making and Negotiation. As we did in the fifth edition, we included group decision making in this chapter in order to present a cohesive discussion of individual and group decision making. Special features in this chapter include a discussion of decisions made at Coca-Cola by Doug Ivester and his replacement, Douglas N. Daft; at AT&T by CEO Mike Armstrong; and by Yoshito Hori, a rare risk-taker and entrepreneur in Japan.

In Part IV we address more macro and system-wide aspects of organizational behavior. Chapter 16, the first of a two-chapter sequence on organization structure and design, describes the basic building blocks of organizations—division of labor, specialization, centralization, formalization, responsibility, and authority—and then presents the classical view of organizations of Weber, Fayol, and Likert. Special features describe the organization structures of Sony, Walt Disney Co., Gateway 2005, and the University of Texas Athletic Department. Chapter 17 describes more about the factors and the process through which the structure of an organization is matched to fit the demands of change, new technology, and expanding competition, including global issues and describes the restructuring process at Compaq Computer Corporation and the difficult structuring processes made necessary by the merger of Citicorp and Travelers Group. Chapter 18 moves on to the more elusive concept of organizational culture. We differentiate culture from climate and describe the classic views of culture, as described by Peters and Waterman, Deal and Kennedy, and Ouchi. We strengthened the discussion of the process of creating the organizational culture and present special features on the unusual culture of Siebel Systems; the impact of the harmful culture at Astra USA, now part of AstraZeneca; the changing culture of Boeing; and the unique ways that culture is communicated at Nike. The final chapter, Chapter 19, could really be the cornerstone of every chapter, because it presents the classical and contemporary views of organizational change. Due to the demands on organizations today, as stated earlier and by every management writer alive, change is the order of the day, the year, the decade, and the new century. The only constant in organizations today is constant change. Changes at Electronic Data Systems Corporation, Nissan Motor, DuPont, and Ford Motor Company provide powerful illustrations of the necessity and complexity of change.

# Features of the Book

The sixth edition of *Organizational Behavior: Managing People and Organizations* is guided by our continuing devotion to the preparation of the next generation of managers. This is reflected in four key elements of the book which we believe stem from this guiding principle: a strong student orientation; contemporary content; a real world, applied approach; and effective pedagogy.

## Student Orientation

We believe that students, instructors, and other readers will agree with our students' reactions to the book as being easy and even enjoyable to read, with its direct and active style. We have tried to retain the comprehensive nature of the book, while writing in a style that is active and lively and geared to the student reader. We want your students to enjoy reading the book while they learn from it. We have added new cartoons with content-rich captions to tie the humorous intent of the cartoons to the concepts in the text. All of the figures include meaningful captions, again to tie the figure directly to the concepts. The end-of-chapter features retain the popular experiential exercises and the diagnostic questionnaire, or self-assessments, and real-world cases that show how the chapter material relates to actual practice.

We have added an integrative running case at the end of each the four parts of the book, to provide a deeper and more integrative real-world example. These end-of-part cases describe the interesting management facets of the merger between American Online and Time Warner, which was announced in January 2000. We had been looking for a complex management situation that typified the Internet age for months and were profoundly grateful when AOL and Time Warner dropped this one into our laps as the book was being produced. We hope you and your students enjoy considering the issues of this merger as outlined in this case, as well as following the inevitable changes that will come as the two companies struggle to make it work.

## Contemporary Content Coverage

The sixth edition continues our tradition of presenting the most modern management approaches as expressed in the popular press and academic research. The basic structure of this book remains the same, but you will find new sections or subsections throughout, such as the discussions of workforce expansion in Chapter 2, of affinity groups in Chapter 10, of the role of gender in leadership in Chapter 13, and of the newest version of Vroom's decision tree approach to leadership in Chapter 13.

## Real World, Applied Approach

The organizations cited in the opening vignettes, examples, cases, and boxed features throughout this edition represent a blend of large, well-known organizations and smaller, less well-known organizations so that students will see the applicability of the material in a variety of organizational settings. Each chapter opens and closes with concrete examples of relevant topics from the chapter. The integrative running end-of-part case on the AOL/Time Warner merger provides a more in-depth case for class discussion. Each chapter also contains two or three boxes, selected from the five types of boxed features included in this edition. Each box has a unique, identifying icon that distinguishes it and makes it easier for students to identify.

Each "Talking Technology" box describes how a company uses advances in computer and information technology to improve its business.

Each "Mastering Change" box shows an organization rethinking its methods of operation to respond to changes in the business climate.

Each "The Business of Ethics" box explores an organization dealing with ethical issues.

Each "Working with Diversity" box describes an organization meeting the needs of its increasingly diverse workforce.

Each "World View" box shows an organization and the people in it facing an issue as the organization expands its global operations.

## Effective Pedagogy

Our guiding intent continues to be to put together a package that enhances student learning. That package includes several features of the book, many of which have already been mentioned.

- Each chapter begins with a "Management Preview" and ends with a "Synopsis."
- "Discussion Questions" at the end of each chapter stimulate interaction among students and provide a guide to complete studying of the chapter concepts.
- An "Experiencing Organizational Behavior" exercise at the end of each chapter helps students make the transition from textbook learning to real-world applications. The end-of-chapter case, "Organizational Behavior Case for Discussion" also assists in this transition.
- A "Building Organizational Behavior Skills" activity at the end of each chapter gives students the opportunity to apply a concept from the chapter to a brief self-assessment or diagnostic activity.
- A "Developing OB Internet Skills" feature encourages students to reach beyond the text to find organizations or other resources on the web that illustrate the issues discussed in the chapter.
- The "Integrative Running Case" at the end of each part examines the AOL/Time Warner merger and provides an opportunity for students to discuss a real, ongoing management situation with significant organizational behavior facets
- Figures, tables, photographs, and cartoons offer visual and humorous support for the text content. Explanatory captions for figures, photographs, and cartoons enhance their pedagogical value.
- A running marginal glossary and a complete glossary at the end of the book provide additional support in identifying and learning key concepts.

A new design reflects the significant changes in the sixth edition's content, style, and pedagogical program. The text is more colorful to reflect the dynamic nature of the behavioral and managerial challenges facing managers today. All interior photographs are new to this edition and have been specially selected to highlight the dynamic world of organizational behavior. Callout quotes, as found in many popular business magazines, have been added throughout every chapter to call special attention to what real managers are saying about managing people in organizations.

We would like to hear from you about your experiences using this book. We want to know what you like and what you do not like about it. Please write to us via email to tell us about your learning experiences with the text. You may contact us at:

Greg Moorhead
greg.moorhead@asu.edu

Ricky Griffin
rgriffin@tamu.edu

# A Complete Teaching and Learning Package

A complete package of teaching and learning support materials accompanies the sixth edition.

## For Students

A completely new **Student Web Site** provides additional information, study aids, activities, and resources to help reinforce the concepts presented in the text. The site includes: learning objectives; brief chapter outlines; chapter summaries; the Developing OB Internet Skills exercises from the text with relevant links and any necessary updates; ACE self-tests; a glossary of key terms; flash cards for reviewing the key terms; additional cases; convenient chapter links to the organizations highlighted in the text; and a resource center with links to various sites of general organizational behavior interest.

***OB in Action*, Sixth Edition** by Steven Wolff and Gail Gilmore provides additional cases and hands-on experiential exercises to help students bridge the gap between theory and practice. Working individually or with teams, students tackle problems and find solutions, using organizational theories as their foundation. The authors bring their extensive experience in both university classroom and executive training and development settings to their work in creating this new edition.

## For Instructors

The ***Instructor's Resource Manual***, revised by Bruce Barringer (University of Central Florida) includes for each chapter a synopsis, learning objectives, detailed lecture outline, suggested answers to the text questions and activities, and a supplemental mini-lecture. Also included are a section on learning and teaching ideologies, suggested course outlines, suggestions on how to use the mini-lectures, and a transition guide to help current users of the fifth edition move easily to the sixth edition.

The **Test Bank**, prepared by David Glew (The University of Tulsa), has been thoroughly revised to match changes in the new edition and contains multiple-choice, true/false, completion, matching, and essay questions for every chapter. Each question is accompanied by a text page reference and learning-level indicator. A Windows-based **Computerized Test Bank** is available to allow instructors to generate and change tests easily on the computer. A **Call-in Test Service** is also available.

The completely new password-protected **Instructor Web Site** provides several tools to help prepare and deliver lectures: downloadable files of the *Instructor's*

*Resource Manual;* downloadable PowerPoint® slides; suggested answers to the activities on the Student Web Site, and the Video Guide with videos summaries, suggested uses, and questions for discussion.

A detailed set of **PowerPoint® Slides**, available on the Instructor Web Site, combines clear, concise text and art to create a complete lecture package with more than twenty slides per chapter. Instructors can use the slides as-is or edit them. The slides can also be printed for lecture notes and class distribution.

A set of full-color **Transparencies** includes 100 images that highlight key figures and definitions from the text as well as additional images that can be used to enhance lecture presentation.

A special set of **Videos** is provided to enhance the teaching package. Focusing on key topics of organizational behavior, the videos present additional material to help bring the concepts to life. Teaching notes and suggestions are also provided.

The ***Instructor's Resource Manual*** for *OB in Action* provides requirements, objectives, background, suggested outlines and timing for each exercise, and it flags some issues that may be raised. It also includes curve balls for instructors to use when groups come to facile or premature decisions.

# Acknowledgments

Although this book bears our two names, numerous people have contributed to it. Through the years we have had the good fortune to work with many fine professionals who helped us to sharpen our thoughts about this complex field and to develop new and more effective ways of discussing it. Their contributions were essential to the development of the sixth edition. Any and all errors of omission, interpretation, and emphasis remain the responsibility of the authors.

A number of reviewers made essential contributions to the development of this and previous editions. We would like to express special thanks to them for taking the time to provide us with their valuable assistance:

Abdul Aziz, COLLEGE OF CHARLESTON
Steve Ball, CLEARY COLLEGE
Brendan Bannister, NORTHEASTERN UNIVERSITY
Greg Baxter, SOUTHEASTERN OKLAHOMA STATE UNIVERSITY
Jon W. Beard, TEXAS A&M UNIVERSITY
Mary-Beth Beres, MERCER UNIVERSITY ATLANTA
Ronald A. Bigoness, STEPHEN F. AUSTIN STATE UNIVERSITY
Allen Bluedorn, UNIVERSITY OF MISSOURI COLUMBIA
Murray Brunton, CENTRAL OHIO TECHNICAL COLLEGE
John Bunch, KANSAS STATE UNIVERSITY
Mark Butler, SAN DIEGO STATE UNIVERSITY
Richaurd R. Camp, EASTERN MICHIGAN UNIVERSITY
Anthony Chelte, WESTERN NEW ENGLAND COLLEGE
Dan R. Dalton, INDIANA UNIVERSITY BLOOMINGTON
Carla L. Dando, IDAHO STATE UNIVERSITY
T. K. Das, BARUCH COLLEGE
George deLodzia, UNIVERSITY OF RHODE ISLAND
Ronald A. DiBattista, BRYANT COLLEGE
Thomas W. Dougherty, UNIVERSITY OF MISSOURI COLUMBIA
Cathy Dubois, KENT STATE UNIVERSITY

Earlinda Elder-Albritton, DETROIT COLLEGE OF BUSINESS
Stanley W. Elsea, KANSAS STATE UNIVERSITY
Maureen J. Fleming, THE UNIVERSITY OF MONTANA-MISSOULA
Joseph Forest, GEORGIA STATE UNIVERSITY
Eliezer Geisler, NORTHEASTERN ILLINOIS UNIVERSITY
Robert Giacalone, UNIVERSITY OF RICHMOND
Lynn Harland, UNIVERSITY OF NEBRASKA AT OMAHA
Stan Harris, LAWRENCE TECH UNIVERSITY
Nell Hartley, ROBERT MORRIS COLLEGE
Peter Heine, STETSON UNIVERSITY
William Hendrix, CLEMSON UNIVERSITY
John Jermier, UNIVERSITY OF SOUTH FLORIDA
Avis L. Johnson, UNIVERSITY OF AKRON
Bruce Johnson, GUSTAVUS ADOLPHUS COLLEGE
Gwen Jones, BOWLING GREEN STATE UNIVERSITY
Robert T. Keller, UNIVERSITY OF HOUSTON
Michael Klausner, UNIVERSITY OF PITTSBURGH AT BRADFORD
Stephen Kleisath, UNIVERSITY OF WISCONSIN
David R. Lee, UNIVERSITY OF DAYTON
Richard Leifer, RENSSELAER POLYTECHNIC INSTITUTE
Peter Lorenzi, UNIVERSITY OF CENTRAL ARKANSAS
Joseph B. Lovell, CALIFORNIA STATE UNIVERSITY, SAN BERNARDINO
Patricia Manninen, NORTH SHORE COMMUNITY COLLEGE
Edward K. Marlow, EASTERN ILLINOIS UNIVERSITY
Edward Miles, GEORGIA STATE UNIVERSITY
C. W. Millard, UNIVERSITY OF PUGET SOUND
Alan N. Miller, UNIVERSITY OF NEVADA LAS VEGAS
Herff L. Moore, UNIVERSITY OF CENTRAL ARKANSAS
Robert Moorman, WEST VIRGINIA UNIVERSITY
Stephan J. Motowidlo, UNIVERSITY OF MINNESOTA
Richard T. Mowday, UNIVERSITY OF OREGON
Margaret A. Neale, NORTHWESTERN UNIVERSITY
Christopher P. Neck, VIRGINIA TECH
Linda L. Neider, UNIVERSITY OF MIAMI
Mary Lippitt Nichols, UNIVERSITY OF MINNESOTA MINNEAPOLIS
Ranjna Patel, BETHUNE-COOKMAN COLLEGE
Robert J. Paul, KANSAS STATE UNIVERSITY
Pamela Pommerenke, MICHIGAN STATE UNIVERSITY
James C. Quick, UNIVERSITY OF TEXAS AT ARLINGTON
Richard Raspen, WILKES UNIVERSITY
Joan B. Rivera, WEST TEXAS A&M UNIVERSITY
Bill Robinson, INDIANA UNIVERSITY OF PENNSYLVANIA
Hannah Rothstein, CUNY-BARUCH COLLEGE
Carol S. Saunders, UNIVERSITY OF OKLAHOMA
Mary Jane Saxton, UNIVERSITY OF COLORADO AT DENVER
Ralph L. Schmitt, MACOMB COMMUNITY COLLEGE
Randall S. Schuler, RUTGERS UNIVERSITY
Amit Shah, FROSTBURG STATE UNIVERSITY
Randall G. Sleeth, VIRGINIA COMMONWEALTH UNIVERSITY
William R. Stevens, MISSOURI SOUTHERN STATE COLLEGE
Steve Taylor, BOSTON COLLEGE

Donald Tompkins, SLIPPERY ROCK UNIVERSITY
Ahmad Tootoonchi, FROSTBURG STATE UNIVERSITY
Matthew Valle, TROY STATE UNIVERSITY AT DOTHAN
Linn Van Dyne, MICHIGAN STATE UNIVERSITY
David D. Van Fleet, ARIZONA STATE UNIVERSITY WEST
Bobby C. Vaught, SOUTHWEST MISSOURI STATE UNIVERSITY
Jack W. Waldrip, AMERICAN GRADUATE SCHOOL OF INTERNATIONAL MANAGEMENT
John P. Wanous, THE OHIO STATE UNIVERSITY
Judith Y. Weisinger, NORTHEASTERN UNIVERSITY
Albert D. Widman, BERKELEY COLLEGE

The sixth edition could never have been completed without the support of Arizona State University and Texas A&M University. Bill Glick, chair of the Management Department: Larry Penley, dean of the College of Business at Arizona State University; and A. Benton Cocanougher, dean of the Lowry Mays College and Graduate School of Business at Texas A&M University facilitated our work by providing the environment that encourages scholarly activities and contributions to the field. Several secretaries and graduate and undergraduate assistants were also involved in the development of the sixth edition. We extend our appreciation to Alex Moorhead, Phyllis Washburn and Courtney Hall, for their help in the development of the sixth edition.

We also would like to acknowledge the outstanding team of professionals at Houghton Mifflin Company who helped us prepare this book. Susan Kahn and Rachel D'Angelo Wimberly have done yeoman's work in pulling all of the parts of this book together and shepherding it through the process. George Hoffman and Melissa Russell were also key players in planning the book and supplements package from start to finish. Others who made significant contributions to this edition's team are David Cunningham, Sarah Ambrose, Florence Cadran, Marcy Kagan, Jessyca Broekman, and Claudine Bellanton.

Finally, we would like to acknowledge the daily reminders that we get from our families about the importance of our work. As we wrote each revision, our families grew and changed, just as we did. Neither of our wives is doing the same things they were when we wrote the first edition, and the children are now college students, and even graduates in some cases. But as always, they provide us with some of the best reasons for doing what we do. We now get long distance phone calls asking how the book is going and are often chastised for not meeting a deadline. With all of the changes in our lives, we devoted the time and energy to prepare this revision. Without the love and support of our families our lives would be far less enriched and meaningful. It is with all of our love that we dedicate this book to them.

G.M.

R.W.G.

Notes

1. Ann Harrington, "The Big Ideas," *Fortune*, November 22, 1999, pp. 152–154.
2. Thomas A. Stewart, Alex Taylor III, Peter Petre, and Brent Schlender, "Henry Ford Alfred P. Sloan Tom Watson Jr. Bill Gates The Businessman of the Century," *Fortune*, November 22, 1999, pp. 108–128.
3. "Managing in the Info Era," *Fortune*, March 6, 2000, pp. F-6–F-9, quote on p. F-9.

chapter

1

# An Overview of Organizational Behavior

## Management Preview

Effective management of an organization's resources is one of the most critical activities in any complex society. Human behaviors, decisions, and actions, in turn, play vital and pervasive roles throughout every aspect of both management processes and organizations. Thus, understanding human behavior in organizational settings is a fundamental necessity for all managers, including both current practitioners and those who aspire to hold management positions in the future. In this introductory chapter, we introduce you to the concept of organizational behavior and trace its development from its earliest simple ideas into a complex and multidisciplinary field capable of explaining many different forms of complex organizational phenomena. We conclude the chapter by introducing useful contextual perspectives that effectively link the field's theoretical concepts with the practical elements of organizational realities. First, though, we begin by illustrating how one organization, SAS Institute, and its leader, Jim Goodnight, have achieved remarkable success by meshing with near perfection the requirements of business and the requirements of people in ways that many other firms aspire to but which few attain. ■

SAS Institute Inc., based in rural North Carolina, is perhaps the least well known major software company in the world today. SAS creates software that helps big companies to better manage and analyze especially large quantities of data and information. For example, Marriott International uses SAS software to manage its frequent-visitor program; the U.S. government uses SAS software to compute the Consumer Price Index and other complex measures; and pharmaceutical companies like Pfizer and Merck use SAS software to compare near-infinite combinations of elements as they develop new drugs.

Because SAS is a private firm, the general public knows little about its revenues and profits. A few details are illuminating, however. The firm's founder and leader, Jim Goodnight, with a net worth of $3 billion, is listed by *Forbes* as the forty-third richest individual in the United States. (This ranking is based on Goodnight's two-thirds ownership of the company; the other third is owned by senior vice president John Sall, who still spends much of his time writing code.) SAS hires several hundred new employees each year, a clear indicator that the firm is consistently growing at a strong pace. And the firm also continues to invest in impressive—and clearly expensive—buildings and related facilities.

SAS is even more impressive under the surface. For example, even though SAS pays salaries that are merely competitive for the industry, its employees are almost fanatical in their devotion to SAS in general and to Jim Goodnight in particular. As a result, the annual employee turnover is less than 4 percent, far below that of other firms in the industry, and employees are constantly coming up with new and better ways of doing things for the company. Both insiders and outside experts agree that the key to all these factors is how Goodnight treats his employees.

*"Jim's idea is that if you hire adults and treat them like adults, then they'll behave like adults." — David Russo, head of human resources at SAS**

For example, all SAS employees get unlimited sick days and can use them to stay home and care for sick family members. In order to keep work from interfering with employees' families, SAS operates the largest child-care facility in the state; company cafeterias have baby seats and highchairs so employees can eat with their children. SAS has also adopted a seven-hour workday; the company switchboard shuts down at 5:00 P.M. each day, and the front gate is locked at 6:00. Unlike many high-tech firms in other parts of the country, Goodnight doesn't want his employees to work late or to come back to the office on the weekend.

If they want, however, they can come in early—to work out in a lavish 36,000-square-foot gym and health center. The center also offers massages several times a week, as well as classes in golf, tennis, tai chi, and African dance. Center staff even launder dirty workout clothes at the end of the day and return them clean and neatly folded. SAS provides unlimited free soda, coffee, tea, and juice, and has live piano music in the cafeteria. The company shuts down for the week between Christmas and New Year's Day each year, but everyone still gets paid. An on-site health clinic has two full-time physicians and six nurses; health insurance is free for everyone. All this comes from Jim Goodnight's most fundamental philosophy: if you treat people with dignity and respect and reward them for their contributions, they will treat you the same in return. And when this relationship can be established and maintained within the context of a business, everyone can win.[1] ■

---

Jim Goodnight's success at SAS Institute Inc. has been based on a number of different factors, including his skills as a manager and his understanding of the importance of other people. He clearly recognizes the value of control and operational systems in a successful organization. But perhaps even more importantly, he sees the value of people as a key determinant of success. Indeed, no manager can succeed without the assistance of others. Thus, any manager—whether responsible for an industrial giant like General Electric, Honda, IBM, or British Petroleum, the Boston Celtics basketball team, the Mayo Clinic, or for a local Pizza Hut restaurant—must strive to understand the people who work in the organization. This book is about those people. It is also about the organization itself and the managers who operate it. The study of organizations and of the people who work in them together constitutes the field of organizational behavior. We begin our exploration of this field with a detailed discussion of the meaning of the term "organizational behavior" and its importance to managers.

# What Is Organizational Behavior?

What exactly is meant by the term "organizational behavior"? And why should organizational behavior be studied? The answers to these two fundamental questions will both help establish our foundation for discussion and analysis and help you better appreciate why understanding the field can be of value to you in the future.

## The Meaning of Organizational Behavior

**Organizational behavior (OB)** is the study of human behavior in organizational settings, the interface between human behavior and the organization, and the organization itself.

**Organizational behavior (OB)** is the study of human behavior in organizational settings, of the interface between human behavior and the organization, and of the organization itself.[2] Although we can focus on any one of these three areas, we must remember that all three are ultimately necessary for a comprehensive understanding of organizational behavior. For example, we can study individual behavior (such as the behavior of Jim Goodnight or of one of his SAS employees) without explicitly considering the organization. But because the organization influences and is influenced by the individual, we cannot fully understand the individual's behavior without learning something about the organization. Similarly, we can study organizations (such as SAS itself) without focusing explicitly on the people within them. But again, we are looking at only a portion of the puzzle. Eventually we must consider the other pieces, as well as the whole.

Figure 1.1 illustrates an interrelated view of organizational behavior. It shows the linkages among human behavior in organizational settings, the individual-organization interface, the organization, and the environment surrounding the organization. Each individual brings to an organization a unique set of personal background and characteristics, and experiences from other organizations. In considering the people who work in organizations, therefore, a manager must look at the unique perspective each individual brings to the work setting. For example, suppose The Home Depot hires a consultant to investigate employee turnover. As a starting point, the consultant might analyze the types of people the company

**figure 1.1 The Nature of Organizational Behavior**

*The field of organizational behavior attempts to understand human behavior in organizational settings, the organization itself, and the individual-organization interface. As illustrated here, these areas are highly interrelated. Thus, although it is possible to focus on only one of these areas at a time, a complete understanding of organizational behavior requires knowledge of all three areas.*

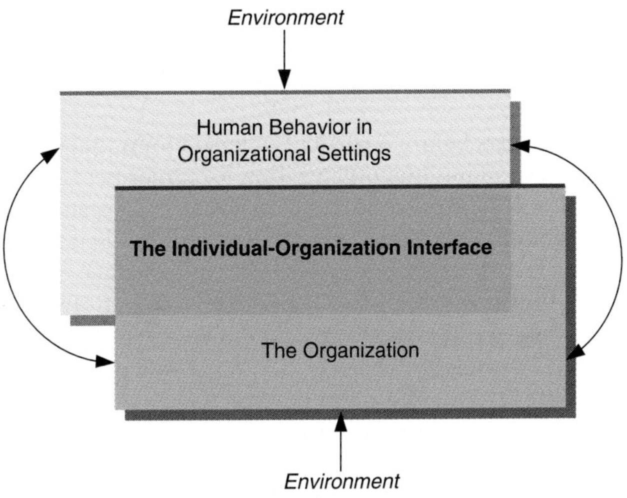

When people hear the name of a company, their first thoughts are often of a building, a product, or a company logo or slogan. But in reality, it is people who actually represent the essence of an organization. From the managers who direct a corporation in its competitive environment to the rank-and-file employees who perform basic organizational tasks to the workers who clean up at the end of the day, it is people who determine the success—or failure—of an organization. And increasingly, today's most successful organizations place a very high premium on attracting, retaining, and rewarding the best people. For example, Qualcomm, a high-flying California communications firm offers numerous innovative rewards and benefits to its employees, including access to a sand volleyball court (shown here) and unlimited accumulation of unused vacation time.

usually hires. The goal would be to learn as much as possible about the nature of the company's work force as individuals—their expectations, their personal goals, and so forth.

But individuals do not work in isolation. They come in contact with other people and with the organization in a variety of ways. Points of contact include managers, coworkers, the formal policies and procedures of the organization, and various changes implemented by the organization. Over time, the individual changes, too, as a function both of personal experiences and maturity and of work experiences and the organization. The organization, in turn, is affected by the presence and eventual absence of the individual. Clearly, then, managers must also consider how the individual and the organization interact. Thus, the consultant studying turnover at The Home Depot might next look at the orientation procedures for newcomers to the organization. The goal of this phase of the study would be to understand some of the dynamics of how incoming individuals interact with the broader organizational context.

An organization, of course, exists before a particular person joins it and continues to exist after he or she leaves. Thus, the organization itself represents a crucial third perspective from which to view organizational behavior. For instance, the consultant studying turnover would also need to study the structure and culture of The Home Depot. An understanding of factors such as the performance evaluation and reward systems, the decision-making and communication patterns, and the design of the firm itself can provide added insight into why some people choose to leave a company and others elect to stay.

Thus, the field of organizational behavior is both exciting and complex. Myriad variables and concepts accompany the interactions just described, and together these factors greatly complicate the manager's ability to understand, appreciate, and manage others in the organization. They also provide unique and important opportunities to enhance personal and organizational effectiveness.

## The Importance of Organizational Behavior

The importance of the field of organizational behavior may now be clear, but we should take a few moments to make it even more explicit. Most people are born and educated in organizations, acquire most of their material possessions from organizations, and die as members of organizations. Many of our activities are regulated by the various organizations that make up our governments. And most adults spend the better part of their lives working in organizations. Because organizations influence our lives so powerfully, we have every reason to be concerned about how and why those organizations function.

In our relationships with organizations, we may adopt any one of several roles or identities. For example, we can be consumers, employees, or investors. Since most readers of this book are either present or future managers, we will adopt a managerial perspective throughout our discussion. The study of organizational behavior can greatly clarify the factors that affect how managers manage. It is the field's job to describe the complex human context in which managers work and to define the problems associated with that realm. The value of the field of organizational behavior is that it isolates important aspects of the manager's job and offers specific perspectives on the human side of management: people as organizations, people as resources, and people as people.

Clearly, then, an understanding of organizational behavior can play a vital role in managerial work. To most effectively use the knowledge provided by this field, however, managers must thoroughly understand its various concepts, assumptions, and premises. To provide a groundwork for this understanding, we start by looking at the field's historical roots.

# The Historical Roots of Organizational Behavior

Many disciplines, such as physics and chemistry, are literally thousands of years old. Management has also been around in one form or another for centuries. For example, the writings of Aristotle and Plato abound with references to and examples of management concepts and practices. But because serious interest in the study of management did not emerge until around the turn of the twentieth century, the study of organizational behavior is only a few decades old.[3]

*"Business history lets us look at what we did right and, more important, it can help us be right the next time."* — ***Alfred D. Chandler Jr., noted business historian***[4]

One reason for the relatively late development of management as a scientific field is that few large business organizations existed until the nineteenth century.[5] Although management is just as important to a small organization as to a large one, large firms were needed to provide both a stimulus and a laboratory for management research. A second reason is that many of the first people who took an interest in studying organizations were economists who initially assumed that management practices at the organizational level are by nature efficient and effective; therefore, they concentrated on higher levels of analysis such as national economic policy and industrial structures.

Interestingly, many contemporary managers today have come to appreciate the value of history. For example, managers glean insights from Homer's *Iliad*, Machiavelli's *The Prince*, Sun Tsu's *The Art of War*, Musashi's *The Book of Five Rings*, and Chaucer's *The Canterbury Tales.* And some organizations, such as Polaroid and Wells Fargo, even have corporate historians. Others, such as Shell Oil and Coca-Cola, openly proclaim their heritage as part of their employee orientation programs and often stress their rich histories as part of their advertising and public relations activities.[6]

## The Scientific Management Era

**Scientific management**, one of the first approaches to management, focused on the efficiency of individual workers.

One of the first approaches to the study of management, popularized during the early 1900s, was **scientific management**. Scientific management was developed primarily in the United States and focused chiefly on the efficiency of individual workers. Several individuals helped develop and promote scientific management, including Frank and Lillian Gilbreth (whose lives were portrayed in a book and a subsequent movie, *Cheaper by the Dozen*), Henry Gantt, and Harrington Emerson. But Frederick W. Taylor is most closely identified with this approach.[7] Early in his life, Taylor developed an interest in efficiency and productivity. While working as a foreman at Midvale Steel Company in Philadelphia from 1878 to 1890, he became aware of a phenomenon he called soldiering—employees working at a pace much slower than their capabilities. Because most managers had never systematically studied jobs in the plant—and, in fact, had little idea how to gauge worker productivity—they were completely unaware of this practice.

To counteract the effects of soldiering, Taylor developed several innovative techniques. For example, he scientifically studied all the jobs in the Midvale plant and developed a standardized method for performing each one. He also installed a piece-rate pay system in which each worker was paid for the amount of work that individual completed during the workday rather than for the time spent on the job. (Taylor believed that money was the only important motivational factor in the workplace.) These innovations boosted productivity markedly and are the foundation of scientific management.

After leaving Midvale, Taylor spent several years working as a management consultant for industrial firms. At Bethlehem Steel Company, he developed several efficient techniques for loading and unloading rail cars. At Simonds Rolling Machine Company, he redesigned jobs, introduced rest breaks to combat fatigue, and implemented a piece-rate pay system. In every case, Taylor claimed his ideas and methods greatly improved worker output. His book *Principles of Scientific Management*, published in 1911, was greeted with enthusiasm by practicing managers and quickly became a standard reference.

*"It's [Frederick Taylor's] ideas that determine how many burgers McDonald's expects its flippers to flip or how many callers the phone company expects its operators to assist." — Robert Kanigel, Taylor's biographer*[8]

Scientific management quickly became a mainstay of business practice. Among other things, it facilitated job specialization and mass production, profoundly influencing the U.S. business system.[9] It also demonstrated to managers the importance of enhancing performance and productivity and confirmed their influence on these matters. For example, firms such as UPS still use some of the basic concepts introduced during the scientific management era today in their efforts to become ever more efficient.

Taylor had his critics, however. Labor opposed scientific management because its explicit goal was to get more output from workers. Congress investigated Taylor's methods and ideas because some argued that his incentive system would dehumanize the workplace and reduce workers to little more than drones. Later theorists recognized that Taylor's views of employee motivation were inadequate and narrow. And recently there have been allegations that Taylor falsified some of his research findings and paid someone to do his writing for him. Nevertheless, scientific management represents a key milestone in the development of management thought.[10]

## Classical Organization Theory

**Classical organization theory**, another early approach to management, focused on how organizations can be structured most effectively to meet their goals.

During the same era, another perspective on management theory and practice was also emerging. Generally referred to as **classical organization theory**, this perspective was concerned with structuring organizations effectively. Whereas scientific management studied how individual workers could be made more efficient, classical organization theory focused on how a large number of workers and managers could be organized most effectively into an overall structure. Interestingly, whereas scientific management was generally an American phenomenon, classical organization theory has a much more international heritage.

Henri Fayol (a French executive and engineer), Lyndall Urwick (a British executive), and Max Weber (a German sociologist) were major contributors to classical organization theory. Weber, the most prominent of the three, proposed a "bureaucratic" form of structure that he believed would work for all organizations.[11] Although today the term "bureaucracy" conjures up images of paperwork, red tape, and inflexibility, in Weber's model bureaucracy embraced logic, rationality, and efficiency. Weber assumed that the bureaucratic structure would always be the most efficient approach. (Such a blanket prescription represents what is now called a universal approach.) Table 1.1 summarizes the elements of Weber's ideal bureaucracy.

table 1.1
**Elements of Weber's Ideal Bureaucracy**

| Elements | Comments |
|---|---|
| **1. Rules and Procedures** | A consistent set of abstract rules and procedures should exist to ensure uniform performance. |
| **2. Distinct Division of Labor** | Each position should be filled by an expert. |
| **3. Hierarchy of Authority** | The chain of command should be clearly established. |
| **4. Technical Competence** | Employment and advancement should be based on merit. |
| **5. Segregation of Ownership** | Professional managers, rather than owners, should run the organization. |
| **6. Rights and Properties of the Position** | These should be associated with the organization, not the person who holds the office. |
| **7. Documentation** | A record of actions should be kept regarding administrative decisions, rules, and procedures. |

In contrast to Weber's views, contemporary organization theorists recognize that different organization structures may be appropriate in different situations. However, like scientific management, classical organization theory played a key role in the development of management thought, and Weber's ideas and the concepts associated with his bureaucratic structure are still interesting and relevant today. (Chapters 16 and 17 discuss contemporary organization theory.)

# The Emergence of Organizational Behavior

Rationality, efficiency, and standardization were the central themes of both scientific management and classical organization theory. The roles of individuals and groups in organizations were either ignored altogether or given only minimal attention. Indeed, the cartoon illustrates how many managers in this and earlier eras saw their employees as factors of production, just like equipment and raw materials. A few early writers and managers, however, recognized the importance of individual and social processes in organizations.[12]

## Precursors of Organizational Behavior

In the early nineteenth century, Robert Owen, a British industrialist, attempted to better the condition of industrial workers. He improved working conditions,

"Human Resources."

In earlier times, many managers saw their employees in the same way they saw equipment and materials—simply as a factor of production to be bought, exploited, and then tossed aside when its usefulness was past. Indeed, many workplaces in the early days of the twentieth century were harsh environments where overbearing supervisors pushed employees to the limits of their capabilities. Because economic need was so great and jobs so scarce, however, many workers had no choice but to accept these conditions. But enlightened managers gradually began to appreciate both the importance of human dignity at work and the value-added capabilities of people in all jobs. Thus there was a growing receptivity to the ideas that eventually fostered the field of organizational behavior.

Reference: *The New Yorker Collection 1995* Peter Steiner from cartoonbank.com. All Rights Reserved.

raised minimum ages for hiring children, introduced meals for employees, and shortened working hours. In the early twentieth century, the noted German psychologist Hugo Münsterberg argued that the field of psychology could provide important insights into such areas as motivation and the hiring of new employees. Another writer in the early 1900s, Mary Parker Follett, believed that management should become more democratic in its dealings with employees. An expert in vocational guidance, Follett argued that organizations should strive harder to accommodate their employees' human needs.[13] Indeed, as the "Working with Diversity" box clearly indicates, Follett's work, neglected in the years following

WORKING WITH DIVERSITY

## *The Mother of Them All?*

The business section of virtually any bookstore today carries literally dozens of books extolling the virtues of empowerment and cross-functional work teams and dozens of other books stressing the importance of knowledge-based leadership and organizational flexibility. Interestingly, however, many of these same "cutting-edge" ideas were also set forth around eighty years ago by a management pioneer named Mary Parker Follett.

*"People often puzzle about who is the father of management. I don't know who the father was, but* ***I have no doubt about who was the mother."*** *— Sir Peter Parker, London School of Economics chairman*

Follett was born in Quincy, Massachusetts, in 1868. After graduating from Radcliffe College, she taught political science for several years. During this period of her life, her social circle came to include a number of influential and wealthy philanthropists and business leaders. One of these leaders became enthralled with her ideas regarding wages and work structures and began providing her with a monthly stipend so that she could devote more time to pursuing her ideas and interests.

With her new freedom to explore her ideas, she began a long and serious study of organizations and how they functioned. One of her first messages involved worker participation. She warned, for example, that the bureaucratic model of organization just then coming into vogue might tend to bury the knowledge and ability of workers at lower levels in the hierarchy while simultaneously eliminating an important motivational factor, self-control.

Follett was also among the first to recognize the potential value of cross-functional work teams. She believed, for example, that authority in an organization should be distributed laterally across departments, rather than vertically up and down the hierarchy. This approach, she argued, would result in collaboration based on expertise rather than on power or position. And indeed, power itself needed rethinking, at least in Follett's view. Most managers and management experts of her day thought that managers should strive to precisely define and allocate power on the basis of hierarchical position. Follett, meanwhile, suggested that power should instead be based on knowledge and expertise—again, ideas currently popular in most modern organizations.

As her ideas began to take shape, so too did her influence. She became a widely respected authority in the field and a popular speaker to business groups. And some managers no doubt tried to implement her ideas in their own organizations. Ultimately, however, Follett's views fell from favor after her death in 1933. Most experts at that time were advocating different ideas and methods, and without Follett on the scene to personally champion her ideas, they soon fell from favor and her work fell into obscurity. But today her writings have found new favor among managers and management theorists, and Follett is winning the status and recognition as an important management pioneer that she so richly deserves.

References: Dana Wechsler Linden, "The Mother of Them All," *Forbes*, January 16, 1995, pp. 75–76 (quote on p. 76); Daniel Wren, *The Evolution of Management Theory*, 4th ed. (New York: Wiley, 1994).

her death, foreshadowed many of today's most popular and widely used management innovations.

Like Follett's perspective, the views of Owen and Münsterberg were not widely shared by practicing managers. Not until the 1930s did management's perception of the relationship between the individual and the workplace change significantly. At that time, a series of now-classic research studies led to the emergence of organizational behavior as a field of study.

## The Hawthorne Studies

The **Hawthorne studies**, conducted between 1927 and 1932, led to some of the first discoveries of the importance of human behavior in organizations.

The **Hawthorne studies** were conducted between 1927 and 1932 at Western Electric's Hawthorne plant near Chicago. (General Electric initially sponsored the research but withdrew its support after the first study was finished.) Several researchers were involved, the best known being William Dickson, chief of Hawthorne's Employee Relations Research Department, who initiated the research, and Elton Mayo and Fritz Roethlisberger, Harvard faculty members and consultants, who were called in after some of the more interesting findings began to surface.[14]

The first major experiment at Hawthorne investigated the effects of different levels of lighting on productivity. The researchers systematically manipulated the lighting of the area in which a group of women worked. The group's productivity was measured and compared with that of another group (the control group), whose lighting was left unchanged. As lighting was increased for the experimental group, productivity went up—but, surprisingly, so did the productivity of the control group. Even when lighting was subsequently reduced, the productivity of both groups continued to increase. Not until the lighting had become almost as dim as

The Hawthorne studies were a series of early experiments that focused new attention on the role of human behavior in the workplace. In one experiment involving this group of workers, for example, researchers monitored how productivity changed as a result of changes in working conditions. To the surprise of the researchers, behavioral processes apparently played a major role in the productivity gains that were achieved. These findings, in turn, served as a catalyst for other major research projects designed to learn more about the role of human behavior at work. The Hawthorne studies and subsequent research thus led directly to the emergence of organizational behavior as an important field of study in the business world.

moonlight did productivity start to decline. This led the researchers to conclude that lighting had no relationship to productivity—and it was at this point that General Electric withdrew its sponsorship of the project!

In another major experiment, a piecework incentive system was established for a nine-man group that assembled terminal banks for telephone exchanges. Scientific management would have predicted that each man would work as hard as he could to maximize his personal income. But the Hawthorne researchers instead found that the group as a whole established an acceptable level of output for its members. Individuals who failed to meet this level were dubbed "chiselers," and those who exceeded it by too much were branded "rate busters." A worker who wanted to be accepted by the group could not produce at too high or too low a level. Thus, as a worker approached the accepted level each day, he slowed down to avoid overproducing.

After a follow-up interview program with several thousand workers, the Hawthorne researchers concluded that the human element in the workplace was considerably more important than previously believed. The lighting experiment, for example, suggested that productivity might increase simply because workers were singled out for special treatment and thus perhaps felt more valued. In the incentive system experiment, being accepted as a part of the group evidently meant more to the workers than earning extra money. Several other studies supported the overall conclusion that individual and social processes are too important to ignore.

Like the work of Taylor, unfortunately, the Hawthorne studies recently have been called into question. Critics cite deficiencies in research methods and alternative explanations of the findings. Again, however, these studies played a major role in the advancement of the field and are still among its most frequently cited works.[15]

## The Human Relations Movement

The Hawthorne studies created quite a stir among managers, providing the foundation for an entirely new approach to management known as the human relations movement. The basic premises underlying the **human relations movement** were that people respond primarily to their social environment, that motivation depends more on social needs than on economic needs, and that satisfied employees work harder than unsatisfied employees. This perspective represented a fundamental shift away from the philosophy and values of scientific management and classical organization theory.

The **human relations movement**, the beginning of organizational behavior, was based on the assumption that employee satisfaction is a key determinant of performance.

The works of Douglas McGregor and Abraham Maslow perhaps best exemplified the values of the human relations approach to management.[16] McGregor is best known for his classic book *The Human Side of Enterprise*, in which he identified two opposing perspectives that he believed typified managerial views of employees. Some managers, McGregor said, subscribed to what he labeled Theory X, whose characteristics are summarized in Table 1.2. **Theory X** takes a pessimistic view of human nature and employee behavior. In many ways, it is consistent with the premises of scientific management. A much more optimistic and positive view of employees is found in Theory Y, also summarized in Table 1.2. **Theory Y**, which is generally representative of the human relations perspective, was the approach McGregor himself advocated.

**Theory X**, described by Douglas McGregor, indicates an approach to management that takes a negative and pessimistic view of workers.

**Theory Y**, also described by McGregor, reflects an approach to management that takes a more positive and optimistic perspective on workers.

In 1943, Abraham Maslow published a pioneering theory of employee motivation that became well known and widely accepted among managers. Maslow's

**table 1.2**
**Theory X and Theory Y**

| Theory X Assumptions | Theory Y Assumptions |
|---|---|
| 1. People do not like work and try to avoid it. | 1. People do not naturally dislike work; work is a natural part of their lives. |
| 2. People do not like work, so managers have to control, direct, coerce, and threaten employees to get them to work toward organizational goals. | 2. People are internally motivated to reach objectives to which they are committed. |
| 3. People prefer to be directed, to avoid responsibility, to want security; they have little ambition. | 3. People are committed to goals to the degree that they receive personal rewards when they reach their objectives. |
| | 4. People will seek and accept responsibility under favorable conditions. |
| | 5. People have the capacity to be innovative in solving organizational problems. |
| | 6. People are bright, but under most organizational conditions their potentials are underutilized. |

Reference: Douglas McGregor, *The Human Side of Enterprise* (New York: McGraw-Hill, 1960), pp. 33–34, 47–48.

theory, which we describe in detail in Chapter 5, assumes that motivation arises from a hierarchical series of needs. As the needs at each level are satisfied, the individual progresses to the next higher level.

The Hawthorne studies and the human relations movement played major roles in developing the foundations for the field of organizational behavior. Some of the early theorists' basic premises and assumptions were incorrect, however. For example, most human relationists believed that employee attitudes, such as job satisfaction, are the major causes of employee behaviors, such as job performance. As we explain in Chapter 6, however, this usually is not the case at all. Also, many of the human relationists' views were unnecessarily limited and situation specific. Thus there was still plenty of room for refinement and development in the emerging field of human behavior in organizations.

*"I have found that you can never go wrong indulging your employees."*
*— Stephen Wynn, former CEO of Mirage Resorts*[17]

## Toward Organizational Behavior: The Value of People

Organizational behavior began to emerge as a mature field of study in the late 1950s and early 1960s.[18] That period saw the field's evolution from the simple assumptions and behavioral models of the human relationists to the concepts and methodologies of a true scientific discipline. Since that time, organizational behavior as a scientific field of inquiry has made considerable strides, although there have been occasional steps backward as well. As the "Talking Technology" box indicates, organizations

TALKING TECHNOLOGY

# *Information Technology Versus the Human Touch*

People and technology have coexisted in businesses for centuries. For example, sea captains navigating cargo ships have long used various kinds of instruments to make their way between ports; skilled craftspeople have long used sewing machines, work benches and hand tools, and kilns to create fine garments, jewelry, and pottery; and manufacturing workers have used machines and assembly line configurations to produce vast quantities of automobiles, electronic equipment, and myriad other products. But workplaces today are undergoing transformations the likes of which no one has ever experienced. These transformations center around the ever-increasing array of information technology devices that more and more people are using as part of their work.

> *"Combining high tech and high touch is not easy. Technology always seems to take precedence."* — *Edward M. Hallowell, psychiatrist*

Indeed, information and communication have always been at the heart of what most managers do. Finding out what is going on, thinking about what it means and what else is going on, and then telling others what is going on are constant rituals that define much of the work of many managers. But today's cutting-edge information technology makes it possible for these managers to keep in constant touch with all of their information contacts, regardless of time or location. Need to get a quick message to someone? Send an email. Need an important document from the office? Have it faxed. Need to talk to someone right away? Use the cellular phone.

Are these good things? Certainly new information technology has enabled many managers to make decisions better and faster than ever before. And this technology also promotes more frequent communication among people, resulting in improved coordination and enhanced organizational flexibility and response times. Managers can keep in constant touch with others, and a manager's boss, colleagues, and subordinates can get in touch anytime.

But there are also trouble spots to be wary of as well. For example, information technology makes it easier than ever before for managers to suffer from information overload. One recent survey, for example, found that managers in typical large corporations send or receive an astonishing 177 messages each day. The form of these messages run the gamut from email to Post-it notes. And many managers fall into the trap of thinking that because they *can* always be in touch, they *must* always be in touch. Thus, they check their email constantly, carry their cell phones on vacation or to the golf course, and keep a pager clipped to their waist at all times.

But aside from the surface risks this information deluge brings, information technology may also be fundamentally changing the human character of work and of organizations. That is, even when making extensive use of technology, people in organizations have still worked together—face to face, interacting in various ways, and making regular "human" contact with each other. But in an era of telecommuting, home offices, and global expansion—all facilitated by information technology—some people are growing more and more isolated from their colleagues. In one big company, for example, two managers recently worked together for over six months on a joint project, talked to each other every day, and communicated extensively, but never met one another. Every single point of contact was via electronic media. Although each acknowledged the efficiency of how they had done things, each also admitted vague misgivings and a bit of emptiness in the experience.

But experts agree that they may just need to "get over it." After all, they point out, this is clearly the way organizations are headed and is representative of how more and more work will be handled in the future. But nobody really knows how this will affect organizations, managers, and workers. Thus, a growing number of these experts believe that more attention is needed to keep the human element in its rightful place in organizations. That is, their advice is that managers should indeed take advantage of new forms of information technology. But they should also make sure that human contact and interpersonal relations are not swept away in the process.

References: Anne Field, "A Living or a Life?" *Fast Company*, January–February 2000, pp. 256–267; "Balancing Acts," *Fast Company*, February–March 1999, pp. 83–90; Edward M. Hallowell, "The Human Moment at Work," *Harvard Business Review*, January–February 1999, pp. 58–66 (quote on p. 64); "Drowning in Data," *Newsweek*, April 28, 1997, p. 85.

continue to struggle with the right blend of people and technology. Overall, however, managers increasingly recognize the value of human resources and strive to better understand people and their role in complex organizations and competitive business situations.[19] Many of the ideas discussed in this book have emerged over the past two decades. We turn now to contemporary organizational behavior.

# Contemporary Organizational Behavior

Two fundamental characteristics of the field of contemporary organizational behavior warrant special discussion. Furthermore, a particular set of concepts is generally accepted as defining the field's domain.

## Characteristics of the Field

Researchers and managers who use concepts and ideas from the field of organizational behavior must recognize that it has an interdisciplinary focus and a descriptive nature; that is, it draws from a variety of other fields, and it attempts to describe behavior (rather than to prescribe how behavior can be changed in consistent and predictable ways).

**An Interdisciplinary Focus** In many ways, the subject of organizational behavior synthesizes several other fields of study. Perhaps the greatest contribution is from psychology, especially organizational psychology. Psychologists study human behavior, whereas organizational psychologists deal specifically with the behavior of people in organizational settings. Many of the concepts that interest psycholo-

Contemporary organizational behavior reinforces the need for a strong interdisciplinary focus. For example, consider these Chinese workers distributing Dell Computers in their homeland. When Dell first announced plans to make and sell computers in China, critics were aghast. After all, they noted, Asia has relatively low levels of Internet usage and puts a premium on personal relationships—something very different from Dell's computerized ordering and delivery systems. But by developing a keen and comprehensive understanding of the psychology, sociology, and anthropology of Chinese workers, Dell has prospered in Asia and can deliver a computer there in the same time as in the United States—about nine days from order to delivery.

gists, such as individual differences and motivation, are also central to students of organizational behavior. These concepts are covered in Chapters 4–9.

Sociology, too, has had a major impact on the field of organizational behavior. Sociologists study social systems such as families, occupational classes, and organizations. Because a major concern of organizational behavior is the study of organization structures, the field clearly overlaps with areas of sociology that focus on the organization as a social system. Chapters 16–19 reflect the influence of sociology on the field of organizational behavior.

Anthropology is concerned with the interactions between people and their environments, especially their cultural environment. Culture is a major influence on the structure of organizations and on the behavior of people in organizations. Culture is discussed in Chapters 3 and 18.

Political science also interests organizational behaviorists. We usually think of political science as the study of political systems, such as governments. But themes of interest to political scientists include how and why people acquire power and such topics as political behavior, decision making, conflict, the behavior of interest groups, and coalition formation. These are also major areas of interest in organizational behavior, as is reflected in Chapters 13–15.

Economists study the production, distribution, and consumption of goods and services. Students of organizational behavior share the economist's interest in areas such as labor market dynamics, productivity, human resource planning and forecasting, and cost-benefit analysis. Chapters 2, 7, and 8 most strongly illustrate these issues.

Engineering has also influenced the field of organizational behavior. Industrial engineering in particular has long been concerned with work measurement, productivity measurement, work flow analysis and design, job design, and labor relations. Obviously these areas are also relevant to organizational behavior and are discussed in Chapters 2, 7, and 12.

Most recently, medicine has come into play in connection with the study of human behavior at work, specifically in the area of stress. Increasingly, research is showing that controlling the causes and consequences of stress in and out of organizational settings is important for the well-being of both the individual and the organization. Chapter 9 is devoted to stress.

**A Descriptive Nature** A primary goal of studying organizational behavior is to describe relationships between two or more behavioral variables. The theories and concepts of the field, for example, cannot predict with certainty that changing a specific set of workplace variables will improve an individual employee's performance by a certain amount. At best, the field can suggest that certain general concepts or variables tend to be related to one another in particular settings. For instance, research might indicate that in one organization, employee satisfaction and individual perceptions of working conditions are positively related. However, we may not know if better working conditions lead to more satisfaction, if more-satisfied people see their jobs differently than dissatisfied people, or if both satisfaction and perceptions of working conditions are actually related through other variables. Also, the relationship between satisfaction and perceptions of working conditions observed in one setting may be considerably stronger, weaker, or nonexistent in other settings.

Organizational behavior is descriptive for several reasons: the immaturity of the field; the complexities inherent in studying human behavior; and the lack of valid, reliable, and accepted definitions and measures. Whether the field will ever be able to make definitive predictions and prescriptions is still an open question.

MASTERING CHANGE

## Predicting Human Behavior: Fad or Fact?

Managers would truly love to be able to predict the behaviors of their bosses, colleagues, and employees. For example, it would be great to know in advance precisely how a particular employee would respond to a raise, promotion, or reprimand. And who wouldn't like to know with certainty how the boss would take bad news or react to a request for an extension to complete a big project. But the ability to make such exact predictions continues to elude us. In fact, only technology seems to hold a possible key to the prediction puzzle.

*"Companies will choose to* ***model reality differently,*** *because we all have different assumptions about how people behave."*
*— Michael Schrage, technology consultant*

But if this is the case, it might never happen, because people are people, and machines are machines, right? Yes, of course. While most machines function in perfectly predictable, logical, rational, and precise ways, human behavior is subject to the influences of myriad individual differences and other nuances that make each and every person on earth at least subtly different from every other person. But some interesting current work has the potential to help managers use machines to better understand how and why people behave as they do.

This technology started in consumer research. Marketing researchers have found that they can construct a virtual "sample" of individuals, each imbued with ages, incomes, spending patterns, and so forth. These characteristics have, in turn, been modeled within the sample following statistical profiles of a relevant population. Thus, a consumer products firm can electronically introduce into the virtual sample two different products and then see which one sells the best.

More recently, this technology has been extended to workplace and management issues. For example, one decision managers must make is how much to invest in training employees. If a company invests too little, it will have an unproductive workforce. But if it invests too much, competitors will start systematically raiding the firm to hire its well-trained workers to leave and join them. Computer modeling tools can be used to help a firm determine the optimal range of training investment between these two extremes.

Other related applications include helping a company configure the best compensation and benefits packages for its employees, the best approach for recruiting, and the best approach for structuring teams and work groups. Will computers ever be able to precisely model and predict the behaviors of a real person? Probably not, but they seem to be getting closer and closer.

References: Anna Muoio, "Where Do Great Ideas Come From?" *Fast Company*, January–February 2000, pp. 150–167; Ray Kurzwell, "The Next Hundred Years," *Across the Board*, July/August 1999, pp. 21–26; "Playing the Game of Life," *Forbes*, April 7, 1997, pp. 100–108 (quote on p. 100).

The "Mastering Change" box describes how some experts are working on new methods for predicting human behavior in organizations. But even if these experts never succeed in their endeavors, the value of studying organizational behavior is firmly established. Because behavioral processes pervade most managerial functions and roles, and because the work of organizations is done primarily by people, the knowledge and understanding gained from the field can help managers significantly in many ways.[20]

## Basic Concepts of the Field

The central concepts of organizational behavior can be grouped into three basic categories: (1) individual processes, (2) interpersonal processes, and (3) organizational processes and characteristics. As Figure 1.2 shows, these categories provide the basic framework for this book.

figure 1.2

**The Framework for Understanding Organizational Behavior**

*Organizational behavior is an exciting and complex field of study. The specific concepts and topics that constitute the field can be grouped into three categories: individual, interpersonal, and organizational processes and characteristics. Here these concepts and classifications are used to provide an overall framework for the organization of this book.*

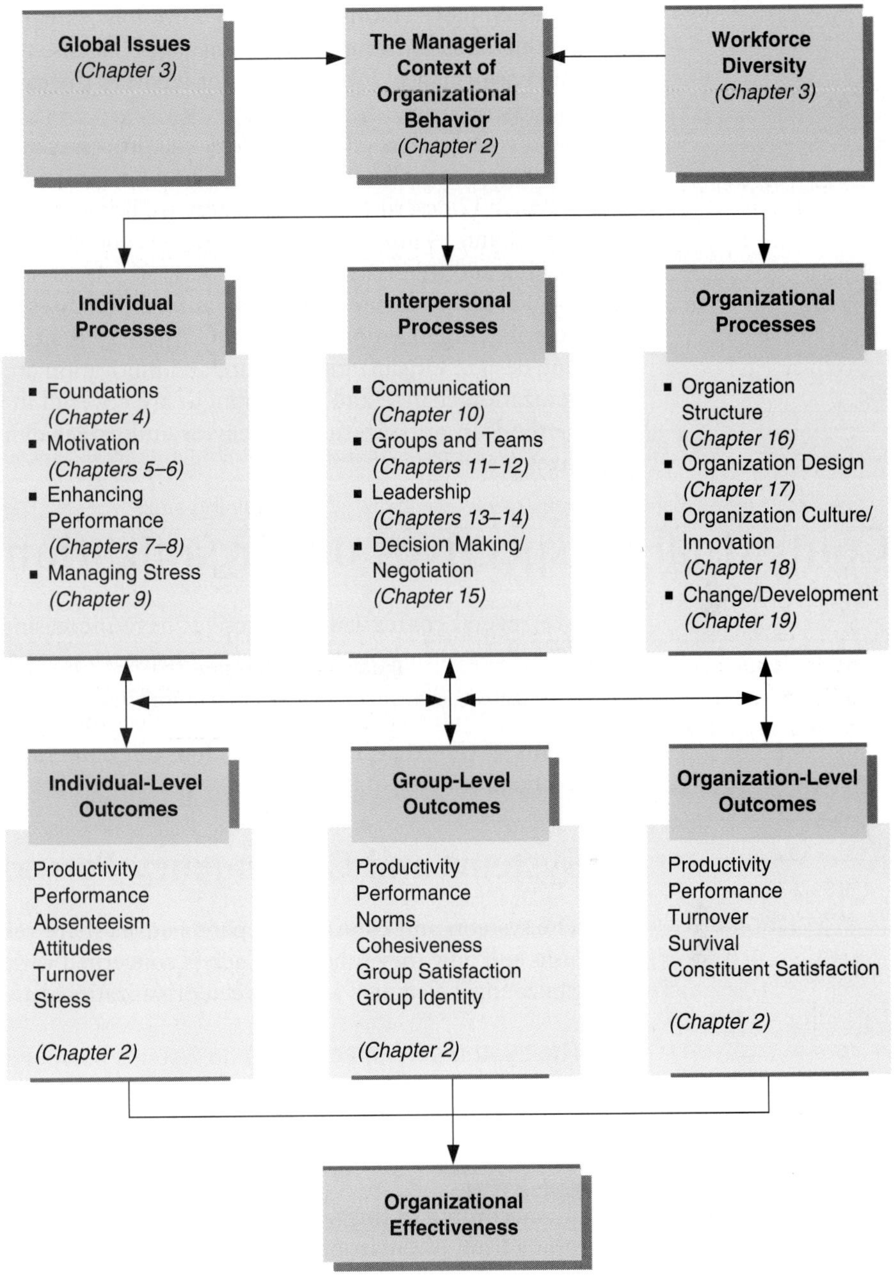


Chapter 2 develops a managerial perspective on organizational behavior and links the core concepts of organizational behavior with actual management for organizational effectiveness. Chapter 3 discusses two increasingly important areas of organizational behavior, global and workforce diversity. Together, the three chapters in Part I provide a fundamental introduction to organizational behavior.

The six chapters of Part II cover individual processes in organizations. Chapter 4 explores key individual differences in such characteristics as personality and attitudes. Chapters 5 and 6 provide in-depth coverage of an especially important topic, employee motivation in organizations. Chapters 7 and 8 are devoted to various methods and strategies that managers can use to enhance employee motivation and performance. Finally, Chapter 9 covers the causes and consequences of stress in the workplace.

Part III is devoted to interpersonal processes in organizations. Chapter 10 covers interpersonal communication, and Chapter 11 is devoted to group dynamics. Chapter 12 describes how managers are using teams in organizations today. Chapters 13 and 14 discuss leadership models and concepts. Chapter 15 covers decision making and negotiation.

Part IV is devoted to organizational processes and characteristics. Chapter 16 describes organization structure; Chapter 17 is an in-depth treatment of organization design. Organization culture and innovation are discussed in Chapter 18. Organization change and development are covered in Chapter 19. Finally, research methods in organizational behavior and career dynamics are covered in Appendixes A and B.

# Contextual Perspectives on Organizational Behavior

Several contextual perspectives have increasingly influenced organizational behavior: the systems and contingency perspectives, the interactional view, and contemporary applied perspectives. Many of the concepts and theories discussed in the chapters that follow reflect these perspectives; they represent basic points of view that influence much of our contemporary thinking about behavior in organizations.

## Systems and Contingency Perspectives

The systems and contingency perspectives share related viewpoints on organizations and how they function. Each is concerned with interrelationships among organizational elements and between organizational and environmental elements.

A **system** is a set of interrelated elements functioning as a whole.

**The Systems Perspective** The systems perspective, or the theory of systems, was first developed in the physical sciences, but it has been extended to other areas, such as management.[21] A **system** is an interrelated set of elements that function as a whole. Figure 1.3 shows a general framework for viewing organizations as systems.

According to this perspective, an organizational system receives four kinds of inputs from its environment: material, human, financial, and informational. The organization then combines and transforms the inputs and returns them to the environment in the form of products or services, employee behaviors, profits or losses, and additional information. Then the system receives feedback from the environment regarding these outputs.

As an example, we can apply systems theory to the Shell Oil Company. Material inputs include pipelines, crude oil, and the machinery used to refine petroleum. Human inputs are oil field workers, refinery workers, office staff, and other people employed by the company. Financial inputs take the form of money received from oil and gas sales, stockholder investment, and so forth. Finally, the company receives information inputs from forecasts about future oil supplies, geological surveys on potential drilling sites, sales projections, and similar analyses.

figure 1.3

**The Systems Approach to Organizations**

*The systems approach to organizations provides a useful framework for understanding how the elements of an organization interact among themselves and with their environment. Various inputs are transformed into different outputs, with important feedback from the environment. If managers do not understand these interrelations, they may tend to ignore their environment or to overlook important interrelationships within their organization.*

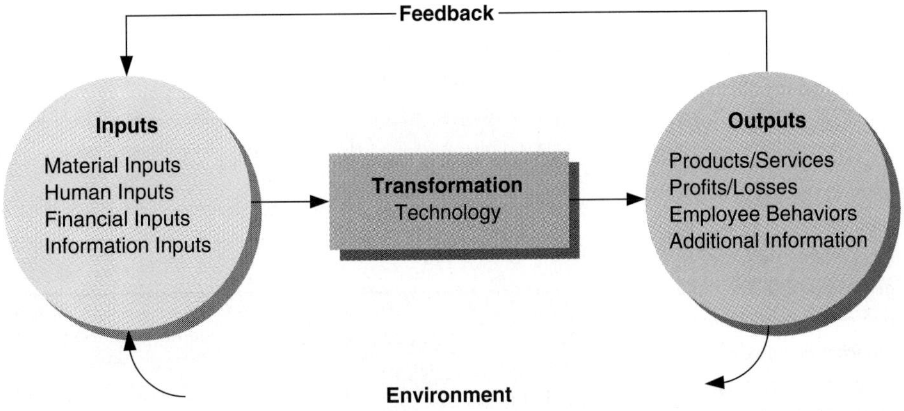


Through complex refining and other processes, these inputs are combined and transformed to create products such as gasoline and motor oil. As outputs, these products are sold to the consuming public. Profits from operations are fed back into the environment through taxes, investments, and dividends; losses, when they occur, hit the environment by reducing stockholders' incomes. In addition to having on-the-job contacts with customers and suppliers, employees live in the community and participate in a variety of activities away from the workplace, and their behavior is influenced in part by their experiences as Shell workers. Finally, information about the company and its operations is also released into the environment. The environment, in turn, responds to these outputs and influences future inputs. For example, consumers may buy more or less gasoline depending on the quality and price of Shell's product, and banks may be more or less willing to lend Shell money based on financial information released about the company.

The systems perspective is valuable to managers for a variety of reasons. First, it underscores the importance of an organization's environment. Failing to acquire the appropriate resources and to heed feedback from the environment, for instance, can be disastrous. The systems perspective also helps managers conceptualize the flow and interaction of various elements of the organization as they enter the system, are transformed by it, and then reenter the environment.[22] Many of the basic management concepts introduced in Chapter 2 rely heavily on the systems perspective.

The **contingency perspective** suggests that, in most organizations, situations and outcomes are contingent on, or influenced by, other variables.

**The Contingency Perspective** Another useful viewpoint for understanding behavior in organizations comes from the **contingency perspective**. In the earlier days of management studies, managers searched for universal answers to organizational questions. They sought prescriptions, the "one best way" that could be used in any organization under any conditions—searching, for example, for forms of leadership behavior that would always lead employees to be more satisfied and to work harder. Eventually, however, researchers realized that the complexities of human behavior and organizational settings make universal conclusions virtually impossible. They discovered that in organizations, most situations and outcomes are contingent; that is, the relationship between any two variables is likely to depend on other variables.[23]

Figure 1.4 distinguishes the universal and contingency perspectives. The universal model, shown at the top of the figure, presumes a direct cause-and-effect linkage between variables. For example, it suggests that whenever a manager

figure 1.4

**Universal Versus Contingency Approach**

*Managers once believed that they could identify the "one best way" of solving problems or reacting to situations. Here we illustrate a more realistic view, the contingency approach. The contingency approach suggests that approaches to problems and situations are contingent on elements of the situation.*

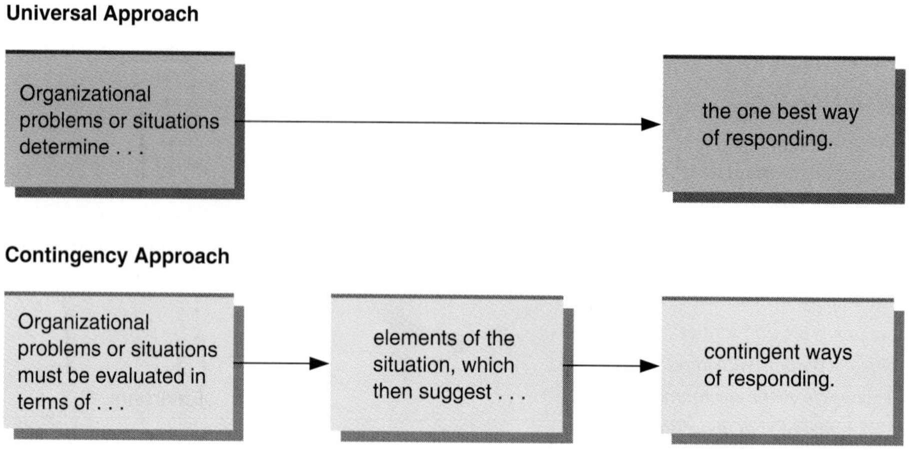


encounters a certain problem or situation (such as motivating employees to work harder), a universal approach exists (such as raising pay or increasing autonomy) that will lead to the desired outcome. The contingency perspective, on the other hand, acknowledges that several other variables alter the direct relationship. In other words, the appropriate managerial action or behavior in any given situation depends on elements of that situation.

The field of organizational behavior gradually has shifted from a universal approach in the 1950s and early 1960s to a contingency perspective. The contingency perspective is especially strong in the areas of motivation (Chapters 5–6), job design (Chapter 7), leadership (Chapters 13 and 14), and organization design (Chapter 17), but it is becoming increasingly important throughout the field.

When Ron Canion founded Compaq Computer Corporation in 1982, he focused on building expensive, complicated, high-quality computers for the business market. That formula led to enormous success for Compaq, which five years later became the fastest firm ever to enter the *Fortune* 500 list of the largest five hundred corporations in the United States. When the environment of the computer industry shifted to a more marketing-oriented business stressing affordability and user-friendliness in 1991, however, Canion was unable to shift his own thinking and management style. That is, he did not recognize that circumstances had so radically changed that a new approach to managing the firm was needed. Compaq's board of directors eventually replaced him with Eckhard Pfeiffer, a German marketing specialist. Pfeiffer quickly altered the firm's strategy and soon had it back on a fast-growth trajectory. And for the next several years Compaq grew rapidly and was the envy of the industry. But by 1999 the environment had again changed, and, like his predecessor, Pfeiffer failed to see that different strategies were needed. Thus, Compaq's board replaced him with Michael Capellas, hoping that under new leadership the firm could again get back on track. Both Canion and Pfeiffer achieved dramatic success when each was running Compaq; but each also fell from grace when the business environment shifted and the firm's leadership failed to adjust in concert. In both cases, then, appropriate managerial action depended on the environment of the computer industry and Compaq's strategies relative to that environment.[24]

**Interactionalism: People and Situations** Interactionalism is a relatively new approach to understanding behavior in organizational settings. First presented

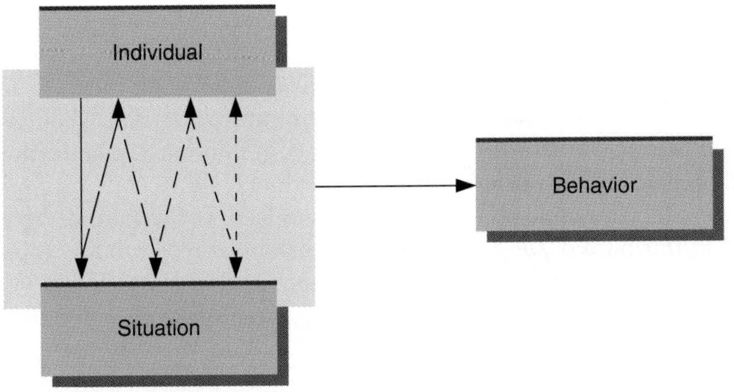


figure 1.5

**The Interactionist Perspective on Behavior in Organizations**

*When people enter an organization, their own behaviors and actions shape that organization in various ways. Similarly, the organization itself shapes the behaviors and actions of each individual who becomes a part of it. This interactionist perspective can be useful in explaining organizational behavior.*

in terms of interactional psychology, this view assumes that individual behavior results from a continuous and multidirectional interaction between characteristics of the person and characteristics of the situation. More specifically, **interactionalism** attempts to explain how people select, interpret, and change various situations.[25] Figure 1.5 illustrates this perspective. Note that the individual and the situation are presumed to interact continuously. This interaction is what determines the individual's behavior.

The interactional view implies that simple cause-and-effect descriptions of organizational phenomena are not enough. For example, one set of research studies may suggest that job changes lead to improved employee attitudes. Another set of studies may propose that attitudes influence how people perceive their jobs in the first place. Both positions probably are incomplete: Employee attitudes may influence job perceptions, but these perceptions may in turn influence future attitudes. Because interactionalism is a fairly recent contribution to the field, it is less prominent in the chapters that follow than are the systems and contingency theories. Nonetheless, the interactional view appears to offer many promising ideas for future development.

**Interactionalism** suggests that individuals and situations interact continuously to determine individuals' behavior.

## Contemporary Applied Perspectives

In recent years, books written for the so-called popular press have also had a major impact on both the field of organizational behavior and the practice of management.[26] This trend first became noticeable in the 1980s with the success of books such as William Ouchi's *Theory Z*, Thomas Peters and Robert Waterman's *In Search of Excellence*, and Terrence Deal and Allan Kennedy's *Corporate Cultures*. Each of these books spent time on the *New York Times* best-seller list and was virtually required reading for any manager who wanted to appear informed. Biographies of successful and less-than-successful executives such as Lee Iacocca, Donald Trump, and Bill Gates also received widespread attention.

*"You are what you read." — Martha Finney, business writer*[27]

More recently, other applied authors have had a similar impact. Among the most popular applied authors today are Peter Senge (*The Fifth Discipline*), Stephen Covey (*The Seven Habits of Highly Effective People*), Tom Peters (*Liberation Management: Necessary Disorganization for the Nanosecond Nineties*), and Michael Porter (*The Competitive Advantage of Nations*). These books highlight the management practices—many of them directly linked with concepts from organizational behavior—of successful firms such as Kodak, Ford, and IBM, among others. In addition, a new body of writing focusing specifically on feminist issues in management has also begun to emerge.[28]

Scott Adams, creator of the popular comic strip *Dilbert*, is also immensely popular today. Adams himself is a former communications industry worker who developed his strip to illustrate some of the absurdities of contemporary organizational life. The daily strip is routinely posted outside office doors, above copy machines, and beside water coolers in hundreds of offices. (And indeed, you may find a few of the strips posted in this book!) *The Joy of Work*, Adams's most recent book, topped best-seller lists and there is even a *Dilbert* home page on the World Wide Web. Adams's work is satirical, but it seems to reflect the actual perceptions of many people who work in organizations today.

## Synopsis

Organizational behavior is the study of human behavior in organizational settings, the interface between human behavior and the organization, and the organization itself. The study of organizational behavior is important because organizations have a powerful influence over our lives.

Serious interest in the study of management first developed around the beginning of this century. Two of the earliest approaches were scientific management (best represented by the work of Taylor) and classical organization theory (exemplified by the work of Weber).

Organizational behavior began to emerge as a scientific discipline as a result of the Hawthorne studies. McGregor and Maslow led the human relations movement that grew from those studies.

Contemporary organizational behavior attempts to describe, rather than prescribe, behavioral forces in organizations. Ties to psychology, sociology, anthropology, political science, economics, engineering, and medicine make organizational behavior an interdisciplinary field.

The basic concepts of the field are divided into three categories: individual processes, interpersonal processes, and organizational processes and characteristics. Those categories form the framework for the organization of this book.

Important contextual perspectives on the field of organizational behavior are the systems and contingency perspectives, interactionalism, and contemporary applied perspectives.

## Discussion Questions

1. Some people have suggested that understanding human behavior at work is the single most important requirement for managerial success. Do you agree or disagree with this statement? Why?
2. In what ways is organizational behavior comparable to functional areas such as finance, marketing, and production? In what ways is it different from these areas? Is it similar to statistics in any way?
3. Identify some managerial jobs that are highly affected by human behavior and others that are less so. Which would you prefer? Why?
4. Besides those cited in the text, what reasons can you think of for the importance of organizational behavior?
5. Suppose you have to hire a new manager. One candidate has outstanding technical skills but poor interpersonal skills. The other has exactly the opposite mix of skills. Which would you hire? Why?
6. Some people believe that individuals working in an organization have a basic human right to satisfaction with their work and to the opportunity to grow and develop. How would you defend this position? How would you argue against it?
7. Many universities offer a course in industrial or organizational psychology. The content of those courses is quite similar to the content of this one. Do you think that behavioral material is best

taught in a business or psychology program, or is it best to teach it in both?

8. Do you believe the field of organizational behavior has the potential to become prescriptive as opposed to descriptive? Why or why not?

9. Are the notions of systems, contingency, and interactionalism mutually exclusive? If not, describe ways in which they are related.

10. Get a recent issue of a popular business magazine such as *Business Week* or *Fortune* and scan its major articles. Do any of them reflect concepts from organizational behavior? Describe.

11. Do you read *Dilbert*? Do you think it accurately describes organization life? Are there other comic strips that reflect life and work in contemporary organizations?

# Organizational Behavior Case for Discussion

## The Humanistic Workplace

Although such frameworks as Theory X and Theory Y often present an overly simplistic view of management, there are nevertheless very clear differences that can be identified in the ways managers view their employees. Some, for example, clearly take the view that people are, at best, a necessary evil. Similar to a Theory X orientation, this view regards employees almost as a factor of production, like machines and materials, to use at the organization's whims but with little or no thought given to the human needs or preferences of the employees themselves.

Other managers, meanwhile, have come to recognize both the humanistic and business benefits of seeing employees as individuals and working to help them satisfy their own personal needs and goals. Doing so, these managers believe, is the ethical way for organizations to treat their employees. Moreover, the organization may also benefit directly in terms of reduced absenteeism, reduced employee turnover, and improved performance. And during times of marked labor shortages in some sectors of the economy, using a humanistic approach to managing can better enable the organization to attract and retain the very best people.

As a result, more and more organizations are working hard to be seen as an attractive employer, an "employer of choice," as it were, to be truly competitive today. Southwest Airlines, for example, a firm known as a casual and an interesting place to work, often treats job seekers to theme days. Interviewers may show up at the firm's recruiting center wearing pajamas or beach attire, for example, and job applicants may be asked to join in by selecting props such as nightcaps or sunglasses to wear during their interviews. Of course, in addition to selling Southwest as a fun place to work, the firm's savvy recruiters also get a firsthand opportunity to observe how the job seekers themselves might fit into its quirky corporate culture.

Other companies are playing this same game. At PeopleSoft, a leading human resource management software company, top executives perform rock music at employee meetings. Cognex, another big software developer, sponsors Ultimate Frisbee contests, Friday afternoon socials, and free movie nights, and even has a pinball and video game room for its employees. And many high-tech companies in the Silicon Valley provide jogging paths, basketball courts, gyms, and cappuccino machines for their employees.

Beyond fun and games, companies also find that taking more serious steps to be seen as attractive employers can pay dividends. For example, increasingly savvy job seekers are relying more and more on "best places to work" lists and rankings. These lists, in turn, take into account such things as pay, job security, benefits, promotion opportunities, flexibility, and communication. MBNA Corporation offers its employees on-site banking, dry cleaning, shoe repair, and hairdressing services. Virtually all Microsoft employees are eligible for stock options and thus get to share directly in the firm's successes. Continental Airlines gives all employees a bonus when the company finishes in the top five airlines in on-time arrivals. Intel gives its employees a paid eight-week sabbatical every seven years.

And many ranking services are now taking an even more focused look by evaluating firms on the basis of their attractiveness to women, single parents, and families. Deloitte & Touche is recognized for its family-friendly benefits, including flextime and telecommuting options. Merck has three on-site day-care centers for its employees. And Starbucks extends its benefit coverage to part-time workers, a boon to single parents who need to split time between work and home.

At the extreme, some firms are investing heavily in new facilities, with employee recruiting and retention as a major goal. Sprint Corporation, for example, is building a new corporate headquarters center in Overland Park, Kansas. When complete, the complex will consist of eighteen office buildings, encompassing almost 4 million square feet, spread across 200 acres. But beyond offices and administrative facilities, the Sprint complex will include a 75,000-square-foot fitness center, a 44,000-square-foot child-care center with private nursing rooms for mothers, two athletic fields, an 8-acre lake, jogging paths, and work facilities designed to optimize productivity and comfort. In addition, the site will also include banks, dry cleaners, restaurants, and a post office—all intended to make life easier for workers. And Sprint executives seem firmly convinced that the $700 million investment will pay huge dividends as a lure for attracting and keeping new employees.

### Case Questions

1. What are the advantages and disadvantages of using humanistic workplace innovations of the type described here?
2. What circumstances might cause humanistic companies to drop their current practices?
3. Can a company worry too much about being an attractive and humanistic employer?

References: Jerry Useem, "Welcome to the New Company Town," *Fortune*, January 10, 2000, pp. 62–70; Robert Levering and Milton Moskowitz, "The 100 Best Companies to Work For," *Fortune*, January 10, 2000, pp. 82–110; "Those Lists Ranking Best Places to Work Are Rising in Influence," *Wall Street Journal*, August 26, 1998, p. B1; Ronald Lieber, "Why Employees Love These Companies," *Fortune*, January 12, 1998, pp. 72–74.

## Experiencing Organizational Behavior

### Relating OB and Popular Culture

**Purpose:** This exercise will help you appreciate the importance and pervasiveness of organizational behavior concepts and processes in both contemporary organizational settings and popular culture.

**Format:** Your instructor will divide the class into groups of three to five members. Each group will be assigned a specific television program to watch before the next class meeting.

**Procedure:** Arrange to watch the program as a group. Each person should have a pad of paper and a pencil handy. As you watch the show, jot down examples of individual behavior, interpersonal dynamics, organizational characteristics, and other concepts and processes relevant to organizational behavior. After the show, spend a few minutes comparing notes. Compile one list for the entire group. (It is advisable to turn off the television set during this discussion!)

During the next class meeting, have someone in the group summarize the plot of the show and list the concepts it illustrated. The following television shows are especially good for illustrating behavioral concepts in organizational settings:

| ***Network Shows*** | ***Syndicated Shows*** |
|---|---|
| *The Practice* | *M*A*S*H* |
| *E.R.* | *Cheers* |
| *N.Y.P.D. Blue* | *Star Trek* |
| *The Drew Carey Show* | *Home Improvement* |
| *Frasier* | *L.A. Law* |
| *Spin City* | *Gilligan's Island* |

### Follow-up Questions

1. What does this exercise illustrate about the pervasiveness of organizations in our contemporary society?
2. What recent or classic movies might provide similar kinds of examples?
3. Do you think television programs from countries other than the United States would provide more or fewer examples set in organizations?

# Building Organizational Behavior Skills

## Assessing Your Own Theory X and Theory Y Tendencies

The questions below are intended to provide insights into your tendencies toward Theory X or Theory Y management styles. Answer each of the following questions on the scales by circling the number that best reflects your feelings. For example, circle a "5" for a statement if you strongly agree with it, or a "2" if you disagree with it.

1. Most employees today are lazy and have to be forced to work hard.

| 5 | 4 | 3 | 2 | 1 |
|---|---|---|---|---|
| Strongly Agree | Agree | Neither Agree Nor Disagree | Disagree | Strongly Disagree |

2. People in organizations are only motivated by extrinsic rewards such as pay and bonuses.

| 5 | 4 | 3 | 2 | 1 |
|---|---|---|---|---|
| Strongly Agree | Agree | Neither Agree Nor Disagree | Disagree | Strongly Disagree |

3. Most people do not like to work.

| 5 | 4 | 3 | 2 | 1 |
|---|---|---|---|---|
| Strongly Agree | Agree | Neither Agree Nor Disagree | Disagree | Strongly Disagree |

4. Most people today generally avoid responsibility.

| 5 | 4 | 3 | 2 | 1 |
|---|---|---|---|---|
| Strongly Agree | Agree | Neither Agree Nor Disagree | Disagree | Strongly Disagree |

5. Many employees in big companies today do not accept the company's goals but instead work only for their own welfare.

| 5 | 4 | 3 | 2 | 1 |
|---|---|---|---|---|
| Strongly Agree | Agree | Neither Agree Nor Disagree | Disagree | Strongly Disagree |

6. Most people are not innovative and are not interested in helping their employer solve problems.

| 5 | 4 | 3 | 2 | 1 |
|---|---|---|---|---|
| Strongly Agree | Agree | Neither Agree Nor Disagree | Disagree | Strongly Disagree |

7. Most people need someone else to tell them how to do their job.

| 5 | 4 | 3 | 2 | 1 |
|---|---|---|---|---|
| Strongly Agree | Agree | Neither Agree Nor Disagree | Disagree | Strongly Disagree |

8. Many people today have little ambition, preferring to stay where they are and not work hard for advancement.

| 5 | 4 | 3 | 2 | 1 |
|---|---|---|---|---|
| Strongly Agree | Agree | Neither Agree Nor Disagree | Disagree | Strongly Disagree |

9. Work is not a natural activity for most people and instead is something they feel they have to do.

| 5 | 4 | 3 | 2 | 1 |
|---|---|---|---|---|
| Strongly Agree | Agree | Neither Agree Nor Disagree | Disagree | Strongly Disagree |

10. Most employees today are not interested in utilizing their full potential and capabilities.

| 5 | 4 | 3 | 2 | 1 |
|---|---|---|---|---|
| Strongly Agree | Agree | Neither Agree Nor Disagree | Disagree | Strongly Disagree |

Instructions: Add up the responses you gave for each question. If you scored 40 or above, you have clear tendencies toward the Theory X view of management. If you scored 20 or below, you have clear tendencies toward the Theory Y view of management. If you scored between 20 and 40, your tendencies fall in between the extreme Theory X and Y viewpoints and you have a more balanced approach. [Note: This brief instrument has not been scientifically validated and is to be used for classroom discussion purposes only.]

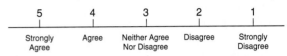

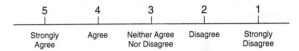

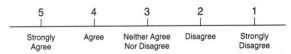

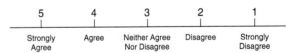

## Developing OB Internet Skills

**Introduction:** This chapter's closing case discusses how many companies are aggressively working to develop an image of being an especially good employer. Indeed, making some publication's list of the "Best Places to Work" has even become a formal goal for some companies. This exercise will help you better understand differences in how organizations attempt to portray themselves in terms of being a good place to work.

**Internet Assignment:** Identify at least six different companies for which you might conceivably be interested in working. Use a search engine to locate their corporate web sites and then visit each site. Assume the role of a potential employee seeking (1) to learn more about the company and (2) to determine how to apply for employment. Thoroughly review the information on each site that directly relates to these two goals.

**Follow-up:** Describe the strengths and weaknesses of each web site as they relate to the specific goals noted above. Finally, respond to the following instructions and/or questions:

1. Based on the web site information alone, rank the companies you studied in terms of their relative attractiveness as an employer.
2. Next, rank the companies in terms of the ease with which an interested job seeker could apply for employment.
3. Develop an explanation for differences in the two rankings you developed.
4. What advice would you give each company about its web site from the perspective of a job seeker?

chapter

# 2

# Managing People and Organizations

## Management Preview

Effective management is the key to organizational success. Of course, figuring out how to manage effectively is sometimes akin to searching for the proverbial alchemist's stone. Effective management requires a level of understanding of human behavior that is both complex and elusive, again reinforcing the need for current and future managers to be familiar with the basic concepts and processes of behavior in organizations. This chapter relates the general field of management to the more specific field of organizational behavior. We start by developing a managerial perspective on organizational behavior. Then we characterize the manager's job in terms of its functions, roles, and requisite skills. Next, we identify and discuss a variety of organizational and environmental challenges in a context of organizational behavior. We conclude by discussing how an understanding of organizational behavior can enhance the manager's ability to achieve effectiveness. First, however, we examine how one manager, Gordon Bethune, has led a remarkable turnaround at Continental Airlines by effectively integrating basic and sound management techniques with respect and consideration for the employees who work there. ■

For years Continental Airlines was a company going nowhere. The firm was wallowing in red ink and had perhaps the poorest reputation of any carrier in the airline industry. For example, the company lost $2.4 billion in 1990 alone, and many business travelers routinely refused to fly Continental. The airline also went through two bankruptcies and a succession of ineffective senior leaders. Continental's pilots and rank-and-file workers endured layoffs, wage cuts, poor benefits, and broken promises by management, and were frequently embarrassed to tell people where they worked.

But in late 1994, things began to change. The key to what would eventually become one of the biggest turnarounds in the history of U.S. business was the appointment of a new chief executive officer (CEO), Gordon Bethune. Bethune, a former navy fighter pilot and chief engineer at Boeing, had a reputation for making tough but effective decisions. He was also known to be fair and open with employees. The board of directors told him to do whatever needed to be done to make Continental competitive again.

One area that needed immediate attention was operations. Bethune frantically cut unprofitable routes and added new and more profitable ones in their place. He also overhauled the firm's ticketing and baggage handling operations, improved marketing, and updated the firm's aging fleet of aircraft. He also overhauled Continental's cash management system. But Bethune knew that operations was not the only problem area—he also knew that employee attitudes and morale were at the root of many of the company's problems.

*". . . I've never heard of a successful company that didn't have people who liked working there." — Gordon Bethune, CEO of Continental Airlines**

One of the biggest problems Bethune had to overcome was the legacy of his predecessors. Employees at Continental had endured ten CEOs in fifteen years. Many of these CEOs, had been perceived as being ineffective and as exhibiting little concern for the company's employees. As a result, many of those same employees had developed a deep-seated distrust of top managers.

One thing Bethune noticed immediately was that the primary variable-pay component in how the firm paid its pilots was based on fuel-cost savings. This arrangement, in turn, caused pilots to fly at relatively slower speeds and to be unwilling to increase airspeed to make up for lost ground time. As soon as Bethune changed this system to instead pay for on-time performance, Continental quickly moved from last to the middle of the industry in on-time performance.

Bethune then calculated that this increase in performance was saving the firm millions of dollars, because when planes are late an airline must often pay for passengers' meals and hotel rooms and for rebooking them onto other airlines. He divided the total savings by the number of employees and sent each of them a check for that amount—$65 per employee. Although not a big sum, this gesture served as an important demonstration that Bethune was willing to share success with everyone. He also announced that henceforth each employee would receive a check for $65 every month that Continental was in the top five in on-time performance, and a check for $100 when it was in the top three.

Bethune also wanted to improve communication throughout Continental. He set up a toll-free number for employees to call with complaints and problems. And he created a committee to respond to every call within forty-eight hours. He also gave employees his own personal voicemail number and returns most of these calls himself. And today, he is careful to refer to Continental's employees as his "coworkers."

Bethune also began to restore employee wages that had been previously cut. And again, Continental's employees have responded in dramatic fashion. Once the joke of the airline industry, Continental is now among the most profitable carriers in the world, and its reputation among business travelers has soared to near the top of the ratings. Indeed, the firm won the J.D. Power customer satisfaction award as the best long-haul carrier in the United States in three of the last four years, and Continental was recently listed by *Fortune* magazine as one of the one hundred best companies to work for.[1] ■

Gordon Bethune clearly recognizes that if an organization is to succeed, its managers cannot rely solely on operations alone or people alone. Instead, they must effectively meld both operations and people to ensure organizational success. In today's competitive environment, driven by such forces as globalization, technology, and downsizing, it is more important than ever for managers to hone their craft to a fine art. Whether it involves taking courses in local business programs, going through in-house training programs, or visiting other successful firms, managers are constantly seeking new ways to perform their tasks more effectively. The nature of managerial work varies from company to company and continues to evolve, but one common thread permeates virtually all managerial activity: interacting with other people. Indeed, the "typical" day for most managers is devoted almost entirely to interacting with others. Thus, the management process and the behavior of people in organizations are undeniably intertwined.

# Managerial Perspectives on Organizational Behavior

Virtually all organizations have managers with titles such as chief financial officer, marketing manager, director of public relations, vice president for human resources, and plant manager. But probably no organization has a position called "organizational behavior manager." The reason is simple: Organizational behavior is not a designated function or area. Rather, an understanding of organizational behavior is a perspective or set of tools that all managers can use to carry out their jobs more effectively.[2]

An appreciation and understanding of organizational behavior helps managers better recognize why others in the organization behave as they do.[3] For example, most managers in an organization are directly responsible for the work-related behaviors of a set of other people—their immediate subordinates. Typical managerial activities in this realm include motivating employees to work harder, ensuring that employees' jobs are properly designed, resolving conflicts, evaluating performance, and helping workers set goals to achieve rewards. The field of organizational behavior abounds with models and research relevant to each of these functions.[4]

Unless they happen to be chief executive officers (CEOs), managers also report to others in the organization (and even the CEO reports to the board of directors). In dealing with these individuals, an understanding of basic issues associated with leadership, power and political behavior, decision making, organization structure and design, and organization culture can be extremely beneficial. Again, the field of organizational behavior provides numerous valuable insights into these processes.

Managers can also use their knowledge of organizational behavior to better understand their own needs, motives, behaviors, and feelings, which will help them improve decision-making capabilities, control stress, communicate better, and comprehend how career dynamics unfold. The study of organizational behavior provides insights into all of these concepts and processes.

Managers interact with a variety of colleagues, peers, and coworkers inside the organization. An understanding of attitudinal processes, individual differences, group dynamics, intergroup dynamics, organization culture, and power and political behavior can help managers handle such interactions more effectively. Organizational behavior provides a variety of practical insights into these processes. Virtually all of the behavioral processes already mentioned are also valuable in interactions with people outside the organization—suppliers, customers, competitors, government officials,

Concepts and processes from the field of organizational behavior permeate virtually every aspect of management. Consider, for example, the success enjoyed by MindSpring Enterprises, the fourth-largest Internet service provider in the United States and widely acclaimed as one of the best-managed cyberspace companies around. MindSpring's CEO credits much of the firm's success to employees like these who are so totally dedicated to the firm that they bend over backwards to respond to customer needs and who are fiercely loyal to the company. The firm ingrains these characteristics in its employees in part by treating each and every one of them with respect and dignity and allowing all employees to share in the firm's success through profit sharing and lavish benefits programs.

representatives of citizens' groups, union officials, and potential joint venture partners. In addition, a special understanding of the environment, technology, and global issues is valuable. Again, organizational behavior offers managers many different insights into how and why things happen as they do.

Finally, these patterns of interactions hold true regardless of the type of organization. Whether a business is large or small, domestic or international, growing or stagnating, its managers perform their work within a social context. And the same can be said of managers in health-care, education, government, and student organizations such as fraternities, sororities, and professional clubs.

We see, then, that it is essentially impossible to understand and practice management without considering the numerous areas of organizational behavior. We now turn to the nature of the manager's job in more detail.

*"We spend all our time on people. The day we screw up the people thing, this company is over." — Jack Welch, CEO of General Electric*[5]

# Basic Management Functions, Roles, and Skills

There are many different ways to conceptualize the job of a contemporary manager.[6] The most widely accepted approaches, however, are from the perspectives of basic managerial functions, common managerial roles, and fundamental managerial skills.

## Fundamental Managerial Functions

Managers in all organizations engage in four basic functions. These functions are generally referred to as planning, organizing, leading, and controlling. All organizations also use four kinds of resources: human, financial, physical, and information. As illustrated in Figure 2.1, managers combine these resources through the four basic functions, with the ultimate purpose of efficiently and effectively attaining the goals of the organization. That is, the figure shows how managers apply the

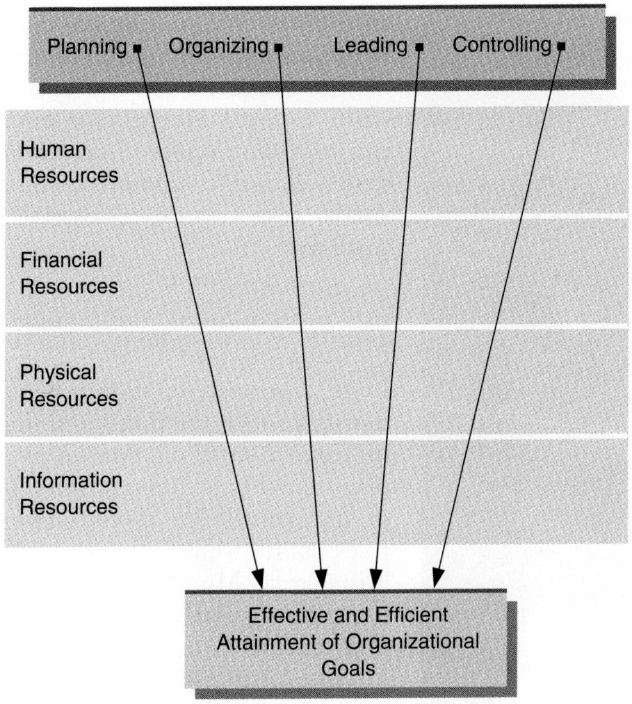


figure 2.1 **Basic Managerial Functions**

*Managers engage in the four basic functions of planning, organizing, leading, and controlling. These functions are applied to human, financial, physical, and information resources, with the ultimate goal of attaining organizational goals efficiently and effectively.*

basic functions across resources to advance the organization toward its goals.

**Planning** **Planning**, the first managerial function, is the process of determining the organization's desired future position and deciding how best to get there. The planning process at Sears, for example, includes studying and analyzing the environment, deciding on appropriate goals, outlining strategies for achieving those goals, and developing tactics to help execute the strategies. Behavioral processes and characteristics pervade each of these activities. Perception, for instance, plays a major role in environmental scanning, and creativity and motivation influence how managers set goals, strategies, and tactics for their organization. Larger organizations such as General Electric and IBM usually rely on their top management teams to handle most planning activities. In smaller firms, the owner usually takes care of planning.

**Organizing** The second managerial function is **organizing**—the process of designing jobs, grouping jobs into manageable units, and establishing patterns of authority between jobs and units. This process produces the basic structure, or framework, of the organization. For large organizations such as Sears, that structure can be extensive and complicated. Smaller firms can often function with a relatively simple and straightforward form of organization. As noted earlier, the processes and characteristics of the organization itself are a major theme of organizational behavior.

**Planning** is the process of determining an organization's desired future position and the best means of getting there.

**Organizing** is the process of designing jobs, grouping jobs into units, and establishing patterns of authority between jobs and units.

**Leading** **Leading,** the third managerial function, is the process of motivating members of the organization to work together toward the organization's goals. A Sears manager, for example, must hire people, train them, and motivate them. Major components of leading include motivating employees, managing group dynamics, and the actual process leadership. These are all closely related to major areas of organizational behavior. All managers, whether they work in a huge multinational corporation or a small neighborhood business, must understand the importance of leading.

**Leading** is the process of getting the organization's members to work together toward the organization's goals.

**Controlling** The fourth managerial function, **controlling,** is the process of monitoring and correcting the actions of the organization and its people to keep them headed toward their goals. A Sears manager has to control costs, inventory, and so on. Again, behavioral processes and characteristics are a key part of this function. Performance evaluation, reward systems, and motivation, for example,

**Controlling** is the process of monitoring and correcting the actions of the organization and its members to keep them directed toward their goals.

Management involves four basic functions, ten roles, and four fundamental skills. The work of Dan Ling, director of Microsoft Research, clearly illustrates several of these. His current challenges include doubling the size of his research lab's staff, developing mechanisms for retaining the lab's most talented employees, keeping Microsoft technology at the forefront of its industry, keeping abreast of all current developments in his field, and managing several ongoing applied and basic research programs.

all apply to control. Control is of vital importance to all businesses, but it may be especially critical to smaller ones. General Motors, for example, can withstand a loss of several thousand dollars due to poor control, but a similar loss may be devastating to a small firm.

## Basic Managerial Roles

In an organization, as in a play or a movie, a role is the part a person plays in a given situation. Managers often play a number of different roles. Much of our knowledge about managerial roles comes from the work of Henry Mintzberg.[7] Mintzberg identified ten basic managerial roles clustered into three general categories; they are listed in Table 2.1.

Key interpersonal roles are the figurehead, the leader, and the liaison.

### Interpersonal Roles

The **interpersonal roles** are primarily social in nature; that is, they are roles in which the manager's main task is to relate to other people in certain ways. The manager sometimes may serve as a *figurehead* for the organization. Taking visitors to dinner and attending ribbon-cutting ceremonies are part of the figurehead role. In the role of *leader*, the manager works to hire, train, and motivate employees. Finally, the *liaison* role consists of relating to others outside the group or organization. For example, a manager at Intel might be responsible for handling all price negotiations with a key supplier of electronic circuit boards. Obviously, each of these interpersonal roles involves behavioral processes.

Key informational roles are the monitor, the disseminator, and the spokesperson.

### Informational Roles

The three **informational roles** involve some aspect of information processing. The *monitor* actively seeks information that might be of value to the organization in general or to specific managers. The manager who transmits this information to others is carrying out the role of *disseminator*. The *spokesperson* speaks for the organization to outsiders. A manager chosen by Dell Computer to appear at a press conference announcing a new product launch or other major deal, such as a recent decision to undertake a joint venture with Microsoft, would be serving in this role. Again, behavioral processes are part of each of these roles, because information is almost always exchanged between people.

Important decision-making roles are the entrepreneur, the disturbance handler, the resource allocator, and the negotiator.

### Decision-Making Roles

Finally, there are also four **decision-making roles**. The *entrepreneur* voluntarily initiates change, such as innovations or new strategies,

table 2.1
**Important Managerial Roles**

| Category | Role | Example |
|---|---|---|
| **Interpersonal** | Figurehead | Attend employee retirement ceremony |
| | Leader | Encourage workers to increase productivity |
| | Liaison | Coordinate activities of two committees |
| **Informational** | Monitor | Scan *Business Week* for information about competition |
| | Disseminator | Send out memos outlining new policies |
| | Spokesperson | Hold press conference to announce new plant |
| **Decision-making** | Entrepreneur | Develop idea for new product and convince others of its merits |
| | Disturbance handler | Resolve dispute |
| | Resource allocator | Allocate budget requests |
| | Negotiator | Settle new labor contract |

in the organization. The *disturbance handler* helps settle disputes between various parties, such as other managers and their subordinates. The *resource allocator* decides who will get what—how resources in the organization will be distributed among various individuals and groups. The *negotiator* represents the organization in reaching agreements with other organizations, such as contracts between management and labor unions. Again, behavioral processes clearly are crucial in each of these decisional roles.

## Critical Managerial Skills

Another important element of managerial work is the skills necessary to carry out basic functions and fill fundamental roles. In general, most successful managers have a strong combination of technical, interpersonal, conceptual, and diagnostic skills.[8]

**Technical skills** are the skills necessary to accomplish specific tasks within the organization.

### Technical Skills

**Technical skills** are skills necessary to accomplish specific tasks within the organization. Assembling a computer for Dell Computer, developing a new formula for a frozen-food additive for Conagra, and writing a press release for Exxon require technical skills. Hence, these skills are generally associated with the operations employed by the organization in its production processes. For example, David Packard and Bill Hewlett, founders of Hewlett-Packard, started out their careers as engineers. They still work hard today to keep abreast of new technology—their technical skills are an important part of their success. Other examples of managers with strong technical skills include David Glass (CEO of Wal-Mart, who started his career as a store manager) and John Reed (CEO of Citicorp, who started out as a loan officer in a bank).

The manager uses **interpersonal skills** to communicate with, understand, and motivate individuals and groups.

**Interpersonal Skills** The manager uses **interpersonal skills** to communicate with, understand, and motivate individuals and groups. As we noted, managers spend a large portion of their time interacting with others, so it is clearly important that they get along with other people. As noted in our chapter opening case, Gordon Bethune, CEO of Continental Airlines, is one of the most admired business leaders in America. Part of his success is attributable to how he deals with people in the firm; he treats them with dignity and respect and is always open and direct when he talks to them.

The manager uses **conceptual skills** to think in the abstract.

**Conceptual Skills** **Conceptual skills** are the manager's ability to think in the abstract. A manager with strong conceptual skills is able to see the "big picture." That is, she or he can see opportunity where others see roadblocks or problems. For example, after Steve Wozniak and Steve Jobs built a small computer of their own design in a garage, Wozniak saw just a new toy that could be tinkered with. Jobs, however, saw far more and convinced his partner that they should start a company to make and sell the computers. Thus was born Apple Computer.

The manager uses **diagnostic skills** to understand cause-and-effect relationships and to recognize the optimal solutions to problems.

**Diagnostic Skills** Most successful managers also bring diagnostic skills to the organization. **Diagnostic skills** allow managers to better understand cause-and-effect relationships and to recognize the optimal solutions to problems. For example, when Gordon Bethune took over Continental, he immediately began searching for ways to turn the failing company around. It was his diagnostic skills that enabled him to first recognize the enormous costs being incurred by late departures and arrivals, then to identify the reasons for this problem, and, finally, to determine how to most effectively change things so as to solve the problem.

Of course, not every manager has an equal measure of these four basic types of skills. Nor are equal measures critical. As shown in Figure 2.2, for example, the optimal skills mix tends to vary with the manager's level in the organization. First-line managers generally need to depend more on their technical and interpersonal skills and less on their conceptual and diagnostic skills. Top managers tend to exhibit the reverse combination—more emphasis on conceptual and diagnostic skills and less dependence on technical and interpersonal skills. Middle managers require a more even distribution of skills.

figure 2.2

**Managerial Skills at Different Organizational Levels**

*Most managers need technical, interpersonal, conceptual, and diagnostic skills, but the importance of these skills varies by level in the organization. As illustrated here, conceptual and diagnostic skills are usually more important for top managers in organizations, whereas technical and interpersonal skills may be more important for first-line managers.*

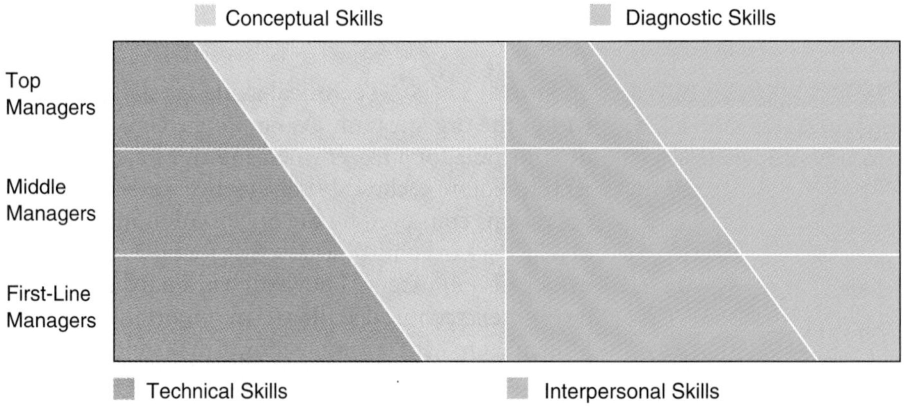

# Organizational Challenges

The field of organizational behavior has several implications for various organizational and environmental challenges. From the organizational perspective, particularly important challenges are workforce expansions and reductions, the new workplace, organization change, information technology, and new ways of organizing.

## Workforce Expansion and Reduction

One important organizational challenge involves workforce expansion and reduction. Although expansion has been the norm in recent years, reductions and downsizing dominated business headlines in the early to mid-1990s and still happen often enough to remain highly relevant to managers.

**Downsizing** is the process of purposely becoming smaller by reducing the size of the workforce or shedding divisions or businesses.

### Downsizing

**Downsizing** is purposely becoming smaller by reducing the size of the workforce or by shedding entire divisions or businesses. Downsizing became common in the mid-1980s and, as noted above, happened regularly for about ten years. For example, General Motors, IBM, and AT&T each underwent major downsizing efforts involving thousands of employees. More recently, because of declining sales of western-style boots, Justin Industries closed two of its factories, putting 260 people out of work. And growing international competition compelled Kellogg Company to recently shut down much of its oldest factory, cutting 550 jobs.[9]

Organizations going through such downsizing must be concerned about managing the effects of these cutbacks, not only for those who are let go, but for those who continue—albeit with reduced security. Moreover, as discussed more fully in the "Mastering Change" box, some firms have gone too far in their reductions and damaged their own ability to compete. We should note that downsizing sometimes has surprisingly positive results. The firm that cuts staff presumably lowers its costs. But the people who leave may find that they are happier as well. Many start their own businesses, and some find employment with companies that better meet their needs and goals. Unfortunately, others suffer the indignities of unemployment and financial insecurity.

*"I think they could try a little bit harder to bring more jobs in here. The community is going to suffer tremendously, as are we."* — ***Debra Robinson, Kellogg employee whose job was eliminated***[10]

### Expansion

In more recent years, downsizing and reductions have given way in many sectors of the economy to growth and expansion. Indeed, in some sectors, especially those involving high-technology and intensive knowledge work, such severe labor shortages exist that firms often have to pay hefty signing bonuses and provide a growing array of benefits and perks. A clear understanding of organizational behavior concepts and processes can help managers in this situation in a variety of ways. These include attracting new workers in sufficient numbers and with necessary skills and abilities, retaining both newer and older workers in the face of alternative work options, and blending newer and older workers into a harmonious and effective workforce.

MASTERING CHANGE

## *Too Much of a Good Thing?*

Throughout the 1980s and 1990s, a key watchword among U.S. companies has been downsizing. Diet metaphors abound: cut the fat, get lean, trim down. But recently, another diet metaphor has also emerged—*corporate anorexia*. The concern is that although many companies may have indeed needed to cut back a bit, some may have gone too far and cut into the muscle of their organization. And a few may have gotten so addicted to the ideas of controlling expenses, eliminating jobs, and slashing inventories that they have forgotten how to take risks, grow, innovate.

*"You can't shrink to greatness." — Jim Stanford, president of Petro-Canada, a Calgary-based oil and gas giant*

What kinds of problems can result from corporate anorexia? One potential problem is an internal attitude among survivors that only costs matter. Overburdened staff members may start only going through the motions of their work. They avoid all risks, and managers continually cut back on innovation and development as a way of cutting short-terms costs. In the long term, however, these attitudes and behaviors can be deadly for a company.

Another problem with cutting too far is that the organization may hamper its ability to compete—to do the jobs that are necessary to the firm's survival. For example, if the sales staff is cut too far, customers will eventually begin to lose touch with the firm and take their business elsewhere. A smaller engineering staff may be unable to devote adequate attention to developing and refining products, so the firm may gradually lose its presence in the marketplace. And a smaller human resource staff may not be able to adequately recruit new employees and provide the support needed to maintain and develop existing ones.

The challenge, then, is both clear—and daunting. On the one hand, managers should clearly be on the alert for inefficiencies and excess costs. But on the other hand, pruning should be done with caution, and from a long-term perspective. The key, of course, is finding this ideal balance without tipping too far in either direction.

References: "Call It Dumbsizing: Why Some Companies Regret Cost-cutting," *Wall Street Journal*, May 14, 1996, pp. A1, A6; "Some Companies Cut Costs Too Far, Suffer 'Corporate Anorexia,'" *Wall Street Journal*, July 5, 1995, pp. A1, A5 (quote on p. A5).

At the same time, managers should be somewhat cautious to avoid overexpanding too quickly. That is, if an organization hires more workers than it can sustain, as soon as economic growth slows or the firm's fortunes stall, managers may find themselves in the position of having to reduce their workforce all over again. To help buffer against this possibility, many firms, especially larger ones, are relying on temporary workers to add to their workforce and meet expansion needs without incurring too great a commitment to those workers for long-term job security. Organizational behavior concepts again help managers here deal with issues arising from blending permanent and temporary workers together in a single job setting.

## The New Workplace

As implied above, workplaces are also changing. These changes relate in part to both workforce reductions and expansion. But even more central to the idea of workplace change are such things as workforce diversity and characteristics of newer workers themselves.

**Workforce Diversity** The management of diversity is another important organizational challenge today. The term "diversity" refers to differences among people. Diversity may be reflected along numerous dimensions, but most managers tend to focus on age, gender, ethnicity, and physical abilities and disabilities.[11] For example, the average age of workers in the United States is gradually increasing. This is partly because of declining birthrates and partly because people are living and working longer. Many organizations are finding retirees to be excellent part-time and temporary employees. McDonald's has hired hundreds of elderly workers in recent years. Apple Computer has used many retired workers for temporary assignments and projects. By hiring retirees, the organization gets the expertise of skilled workers and the individuals get extra income and an opportunity to continue to use their skills.

An increasing number of women have also entered the American workforce. In 1950, only about a third of American women worked outside their homes; today almost two-thirds work part-time or full-time outside the home. Many occupations traditionally dominated by women—nursing, teaching, being a secretary—continue to be popular with females. But women have also moved increasingly into occupations previously dominated by males, becoming lawyers, physicians, and executives. Further, many blue-collar jobs are being increasingly sought by women; and women are increasingly moving into positions of business ownership as entrepreneurs and functioning as senior executives in major corporations. Similarly, more and more men are also entering occupations previously dominated by women. For example, there are more male secretaries and nurses today than ever before.

The ethnic composition of the workplace is also changing. One obvious change has been the increasing number of Latina/Latino and black Americans entering the workplace.[12] Further, many of these individuals now hold executive positions. In addition, there has been a dramatic influx of immigrant workers in the last few years. Immigrants and refugees from Central America and Southeast Asia have entered the American workforce in record numbers.

The passage of the Americans with Disabilities Act in 1990 brought to the forefront the importance of providing equal employment opportunities for people with various disabilities. As a result, organizations are attracting qualified employees from groups that they may once have ignored. Clearly, then, along just about any dimension imaginable, the workforce is becoming more diverse. Workforce diversity enhances the effectiveness of most organizations, but it also provides special challenges for managers. We return to these issues in Chapter 3.

**Characteristics of the New Workforce** Aside from its demographic composition, the workforce today is changing in other ways. During the 1980s, many people entering the workforce were what came to be called "yuppies," slang for "young urban professionals." These individuals were highly motivated by career prospects, sought employment with big corporations, and were often willing to make work their highest priority. Thus, they put in long hours and could be expected to remain loyal to the company, regardless of what happened.

Younger people entering the workforce in the 1990s, however, were frequently quite different from their predecessors. Sometimes called "Generation X," these workers were less devoted to long-term career prospects and less willing to adapt to a corporate mindset that stressed conformity and uniformity. Instead, they often sought work in smaller, more entrepreneurial firms that allowed flexibility and

Managing the new workforce takes a keen understanding of the attitudes, goals, and needs of the members of that workforce. Consider, for example, the case of Sean Suhl (shown here in the center). Suhl is chief creative officer of Lemonpop.com, an online network aimed at Generation Y. When Suhl was lured away from Digital Entertainment Network to help launch Lemonpop.com, he knew from the beginning that he needed a certain kind of talent to succeed there. To attract and keep that talent, Lemonpop.com provides everything employees like Suhl would want—a low-key and comfortable work environment, stock options, the latest technology, and the freedom to work when and where they wanted. As Suhl left Digital, he convinced some of the best and brightest people from Digital to join him, and they are now making Lemonpop.com a major player in the world of e-business.

individuality. They also put a premium on lifestyle considerations, often putting location high on their list of priorities when selecting an employer. And of course, new workers entering the workforce in the first years of this century are likely to be different still from both their counterparts in the 1980s and those in the 1990s.

Thus, managers are increasingly faced first with the challenge of creating an environment that will be attractive to today's worker. Second, managers must address the challenge of providing new and different incentives to keep people motivated and interested in their work. Finally, they must build enough flexibility in the organization to accommodate an ever-changing set of lifestyles and preferences.

*"Look, I don't go around saying this is the place for everyone. It's not. But it's definitely an environment where people who are passionate about what they do can thrive."*

***— Jeff Daniel, director of college recruiting at Trilogy Software[13]***

## Organization Change

Managers must be prepared to address organization change.[14] This has always been a concern, but the rapid, constant environmental change faced by businesses today has made change management even more critical. Simply put, an organization that fails to monitor its environment and to change to keep pace with that environment is doomed to failure.[15] But more and more managers are seeing change as an opportunity, not a cause for alarm. Indeed, some managers think that if things get too calm in an organization and people start to become complacent, managers should shake things up to get everyone energized.[16] We discuss the management of organizational change in more detail in Chapter 19.

*"Fenwick, Benton & Perkins. How may I direct your call?"*

Advances in information technology are fundamentally changing when, where, and how managers work. Rather than being confined to their offices, managers are now more than ever free to visit geographically dispersed organizational facilities, customers, and suppliers. They can check in with their offices via email and voicemail any time of the day or night, and can send and receive information back and forth with anyone else in the organization at a moment's notice. Of course, these changes may also make it more difficult than before for managers to detach themselves from their work for a proper vacation or break.



## Information Technology

New technology, especially as it relates to information, also poses an increasingly important challenge for managers. Specific forms of hardware, such as cellular telephones and facsimile machines, have made it easier than ever for managers to communicate with one another. At the same time, these innovations have increased the work pace for managers, cut into their time for thoughtful contemplation of decisions, and increased the amount of information they must process.[17]

As illustrated in the cartoon, the Internet and World Wide Web, local area networks, and the increased use of email and voicemail have changed the manager's job.[18] On the one hand, these tools make it easier to acquire, process, and disseminate information. But they also increase the risk that the manager will get distracted by superfluous information or become so wrapped up in communication as to give too little time to other important management functions. A related issue is the increased capabilities this technology provides for people to work at places other than their office.[19] Chapter 10 examines some of these issues in more depth.

## New Ways of Organizing

A final organizational challenge today is the complex array of new ways of organizing that managers can consider.[20] Recall from Chapter 1 that early organization theorists such as Max Weber advocated "one best way" of organizing. These

WORLD VIEW

## Globalizing Corporate Culture at Merrill Lynch

Merrill Lynch & Company is the largest brokerage operation in the United States. Ever since Charles Merrill and Edmund Lynch first formed the company in 1914, the firm has focused its attention on individual investors and has based its operations on customer service. Each local Merrill Lynch office is led by a manager who has been totally immersed in the company's culture. These managers start as assistants in existing offices to learn the ropes and then go through an extended series of training programs at the firm's training center in Princeton, New Jersey. One ongoing component of this training focuses on the firm's culture—where it started and how it is to be perpetuated.

In the last several years Merrill Lynch has been undergoing a major expansion into international markets. Fueled in part by opening new offices and in part by buying existing brokerage firms, Merrill Lynch has become one of the largest retail brokerage companies in the world. When this expansion started, many of the firm's competitors doubted that it would be able to transfer its culture abroad. But, so far, at least, these skeptics have been proved wrong.

*"Visit our offices, whether it be Thailand, Malaysia, South Africa, or Germany, and you will see the same plaques on the wall with those same Merrill Principles in the local language."*
*— David H. Komansky, CEO of Merrill Lynch*

Merrill Lynch knew from the beginning of its internationalization efforts that sustaining its culture would be both important and difficult. Therefore, it made the same commitment to training as it makes to its local managers—each and every Merrill Lynch office manager from foreign offices receives the same level of training as do the firm's domestic managers. And like the training provided to those domestic managers, international managers also get a continued exposure to the firm's heritage and culture. As a result, company executives say, the organization culture of any Merrill Lynch office, regardless of where it is, remains true to the spirit of the company's founders.

References: *Hoover's Handbook of American Business 2000* (Austin, Texas: Hoover's Business Press, 2000), pp. 958–959; "How Merrill Lynch Is Winning the East," *Business Week*, September 1, 1997, pp. 79–80; "Merrillizing the World," *Forbes*, February 10, 1997, pp. 146–151 (quote on p. 147).

organizational prototypes generally resembled pyramids—tall structures with power controlled at the top and rigid policies and procedures governing most activities. Now, however, many organizations seek greater flexibility and the ability to respond more quickly to their environment by adopting flat structures. These flat structures are characterized by few levels of management, broad spans of management, and fewer rules and regulations. The increased use of work teams also goes hand in hand with this new approach to organizing. Likewise, as discussed more fully in the "World View" box, international expansion must also be accompanied by changes in how a business organizes itself. We will examine these new ways of organizing in Chapters 12 and 17.

# Environmental Challenges

Managers also face numerous environmental challenges. The environmental issues most relevant to the domain of organizational behavior are competitive strategy, globalization, ethics and social responsibility, quality and productivity, and manufacturing and service technology.

## Competitive Strategy

A **competitive strategy** is an outline of how a business intends to compete with other firms in the same industry.

A firm's **competitive strategy** explains how it intends to compete with other firms in the same industry. In general, most firms adopt one of three business strategies.[21] A firm using a *differentiation strategy* attempts to make its products or services at least appear to be different from others in the marketplace. For example, Rolex has created the image that its watches are of higher quality and prestige than those offered by its competitors, so it can charge a higher price. Other firms that have successfully used this model are BMW, Calvin Klein, and Nikon.

A firm that adopts a *cost leadership strategy*, on the other hand, works aggressively to push its costs as low as possible. This allows the firm to charge a lower price for its products or services and thus gain more market share. Bic, the French firm, uses cost leadership to sell its inexpensive disposable ballpoint pens. Timex and Texas Instruments also use this strategy to sell watches and calculators, respectively.

Finally, a *focus strategy* involves targeting products or services to meet the unique needs of a specific customer group. Fiesta Mart, a Houston-based supermarket, has prospered by targeting that city's large Latina/Latino population. Customers at a Fiesta store can buy Mexican soft drinks, corn husks for wrapping tamales, and other ethnic products not readily available at other supermarkets.

A firm's managers must know its business strategy when hiring employees. For example, if the business strategy calls for differentiation, the firm will need employees who can produce higher-quality products or services and project a differentiated image. On the other hand, a cost leadership strategy dictates the need for people who can keep focused on cost cutting and who respond well to tight cost controls. Finally, a focus strategy requires people who clearly understand the target population being courted by the firm.[22]

Today's competitive environment and the relentless move toward globalization combine to make management and organizational behavior increasingly complex for today's managers. For example, Lakshmi Mittal is Chairman of Ispat International, a major steel company. Mittal travels the globe in search of troubled steel mills to buy for his firm. He then renovates them and relaunches them as a manufacturer of specialty steel products and/or as low-cost mini-mills. His efforts have made Ispat the fastest-growing steel company in the world, with annual sales of $3.5 billion. Mittal also has the responsibility of overseeing steel operations in seven countries and dealing with an incredibly diverse workforce.

## Globalization

It is no secret that the world economy is becoming increasingly global in character.[23] But often people do not realize the true magnitude of this globalization trend or the complexities it creates for managers. Consider, for example, the impact of international businesses on our daily lives. We wake to the sound of Panasonic alarm clocks made in Japan. For breakfast we drink milk from Carnation—a subsidiary of Nestlé, a Swiss firm—and coffee ground from Colombian beans. We dress in clothes sewn in

Taiwan and drive in a Japanese automobile. Along the way, we stop and buy gas imported from the Middle East by Shell, a Dutch company. Of course, U.S. citizens are not alone in experiencing the effects of globalization. Indeed, people in other countries eat at McDonald's restaurants and snack on Mars candy bars and Coca-Cola soft drinks. They drive Fords, use IBM computers, and wear Levi jeans. They use Kodak film and fly on Boeing airplanes.

The globalization trend started right after World War II. The U.S. economy emerged from the war strong and intact. U.S. businesses were the dominant worldwide suppliers in virtually all major industries. But war-torn Europe and the Far East rebuilt. Businesses there were forced to build new plants and other facilities, and their citizens turned to their work as a source of economic security. As a result, these economies grew in strength, and each developed competitive advantages. Today those advantages are being exploited to their fullest.

The situation is further confounded by the rapid change that has characterized the international arena. When the 1980s began, the Eastern bloc countries (including East Germany) were going nowhere economically, the Japanese and German economies were dominant, many observers were writing off the United States, and countries such as South Korea and Taiwan played only minor roles. As the 1990s began, however, much of the Eastern bloc had embraced capitalism and opened their markets, Japan was slowing down, the United States was coming back, Germany had unified, and South Korea and Taiwan had become powerhouses. And at the dawn of the twenty-first century, Pacific Asia is struggling to emerge from a major financial crisis, Hong Kong has become a part of China, and both China and India are emerging as economic powerhouses. Vietnam is again an important market, and the European Union and the North American Free Trade Agreement (NAFTA) have defined major new trading blocks.

*"You've got Germans and Japanese producing cars in the United States, and Koreans producing cars in Eastern Europe, and you've got Malaysia exporting cars and parts. . . . So that's why we're in the process of reinventing Ford as a global organization with a single strategic focus on consumers and shareholder value."*
*— Jacques Nasser, CEO of Ford*[24]

Managing in a global economy poses many different challenges and opportunities. For example, at a macro level, property ownership arrangements vary widely. So does the availability of natural resources and components of the infrastructure, as well as the role of government in business. For our purposes, a very important consideration is how behavioral processes vary widely across cultural and national boundaries. Values, symbols, and beliefs differ sharply among cultures. Different work norms and the role work plays in a person's life influence patterns of both work-related behavior and attitudes toward work. They also affect the nature of supervisory relationships, decision-making styles and processes, and organizational configurations. Group and intergroup processes, responses to stress, and the nature of political behaviors also differ from culture to culture.

## Ethics and Social Responsibility

Individual **ethics** are personal beliefs about what is right and wrong or good and bad.

As "The Business of Ethics," illustrates, ethics and social responsibility are also taking on increased importance. An individual's **ethics** are his or her beliefs about

THE BUSINESS OF ETHICS

## *Working Overtime*

The U.S. Congress passed the Fair Labor Standards Act (FLSA) back in 1938. Among other things, the FLSA mandated that hourly employees working in excess of 40 hours a week must be paid a premium wage of 1.5 times their normal hourly rate for those additional hours. The FLSA also exempted managerial and professional employees from this regulation. That is, because these individuals are paid salaries rather than hourly wages, they receive the same pay regardless of the number of hours they work during any given period. Although it is up to the organization itself to determine which jobs are exempt and which are not, there are a number of legal standards that have been used over the years for making these distinctions.

*"They know . . . the first to go will be the ones the boss thinks are not giving 150%. That atmosphere makes it very difficult for most people to say, 'No, I won't work the weekend.'"*
*— Alice Freedman, consultant*

Recently, however, the distinctions among exempt and nonexempt jobs have become blurred in some organizations. For example, some people worry that an organization might reclassify some of its wage-based, lower-level jobs as managerial positions and then refuse to pay overtime to those individuals. Even more extreme are charges that some organizations today are pressuring hourly employees to work "off the clock"—to work when they are not being paid at all! Sometimes this is legal, but other times it is not.

Because of corporate workforce reduction programs in recent years, some firms feel that the remaining employees need to carry a greater workload. This means working harder and being more productive. It may also mean working longer hours. In some cases, it's a matter of work spilling over into what used to be free time. At AT&T, for example, workers are encouraged to participate in the firm's "Ambassador Program" by selling AT&T products to their friends, relatives, and neighbors during nonwork hours. Employees can win prizes for their efforts but earn no additional income.

Other cases are more troubling. In the state of Washington, for example, a jury recently ruled that Taco Bell was guilty of pressuring its employees to do paperwork, such as timesheets and schedules, at home. And workers were sometimes asked to do some food preparation work after arriving at work—but before "clocking in." Mervyn's, a chain of discount stores, has been sued by a group of its lower-level managers called team coordinators. These managers charge that they were routinely ordered to work through lunch and to take paperwork home. And Albertson's, the nation's fourth-largest grocery chain, has been charged with pushing employees to work past their assigned quitting time without receiving additional wages.

In some of these cases, of course, an individual employee might simply be misinterpreting events and suggestions from the boss. In other situations, companies charge that unions are distorting things to make the business look bad. And even in cases in which the law is being broken, the actions might be the isolated tactics of only one or a few managers working outside formal organizational policies to get a bit more productivity out of their employees. But regardless of the circumstances, it does seem like some organizations today are seeking ways to get more and more work out of fewer and fewer people. And while there may be a variety of legitimate ways to do this, some managers may be crossing the line in how they are seeking to get more from their employees—without having to give anything in return.

References: "So Much for the Minimum-Wage Scare," *Business Week*, July 21, 1997, p. 19; "'Off-the-Clock' Time: More Work for No Pay," *USA Today*, April 24, 1997, p. 1B (quote on p. 1B).

An organization's **social responsibility** is its obligation to protect and contribute to the social environment in which it functions.

what is right and wrong or good and bad.[25] **Social responsibility**, meanwhile, is the organization's obligation to protect and contribute to the social environment in which it functions. Thus, the two concepts are related, but they are also distinct from each other.

Both ethics and social responsibility have taken on new significance in recent years. Scandals in organizations ranging from Royal Caribbean Cruise Lines (improper dumping of waste) to Astra (improper use of company assets for the benefit of senior managers) to various Olympics committees (bribery by government officials) have made headlines around the world. "The Business of Ethics" box highlights a growing controversy about the ethical treatment of workers. From the social responsibility angle, increasing attention has been focused on pollution and business's obligation to help clean up our environment, business contributions to social causes, and similar issues.[26]

Leadership, organization culture, and group norms—all important organizational behavior concepts—are relevant in managing these processes.[27] For example, a recent brokerage scandal at Morgan Stanley Dean Witter grew because individual brokers felt pressure from their colleagues to participate. A scandal at Beech-Nut was perpetuated because it started at the very top of the organization. But if at the first indication of a problem senior managers step forward, accept responsibility and acknowledge any clear wrongdoing, and outline changes to prevent future problems, most situations can be diffused with less impact on the firm itself and its workers. The issues are featured in a recent popular movie, *The Insider*.

## Quality and Productivity

**Quality** is the total set of features and characteristics of a product or service that determine its ability to satisfy stated or implied needs.

Another competitive challenge that has attracted much attention is quality and productivity. **Quality** is the total set of features and characteristics of a product or service that define its ability to satisfy a stated or implied need of customers or consumers.[28] Quality is an important issue for several reasons.[29] First, more and more organizations are using quality as a basis for competition. In 1999, Continental Airlines' advertising campaign stressed its high rankings in the J.D. Power survey of customer satisfaction.

Second, improving quality tends to increase productivity because making higher-quality products generally results in less waste and rework. Third, enhancing quality lowers costs. Whistler Corporation once found that it was using 100 of its 250 employees to repair defective radar detectors that were built incorrectly the first time.[30]

**Productivity** is an indicator of how much an organization is creating relative to its inputs.

Quality is also important because of its relationship to productivity. In a general sense, **productivity** is an indicator of how much an organization is creating relative to its inputs. For example, if Honda can produce a car for $11,000 while General Motors needs $13,000 to produce a comparable car, Honda is clearly more productive. Experts suggest numerous techniques and strategies for improving productivity. Many of these center around increased cooperation and participation on the part of workers. Ultimately, then, managers and workers will need to work in greater harmony and unity of purpose. The implications for organizational behavior are obvious: the more closely people work together, the more important it is to understand behavioral processes and concepts.

Indeed, many of the things organizations can do to enhance the quality of their products and services depend on the people who work for them. Motivating employees to get involved in quality improvement efforts, increasing the level of participation throughout the organization, and rewarding people on the basis of contributions to quality are common suggestions—and all rely on human behavior.[31]

## Manufacturing and Service Technology

**Technology** is the mechanical and intellectual processes used to transform inputs into products and services.

A final environmental challenge confronting managers today is the set of issues involving technology. **Technology** is the set of processes the organization uses to transform resources into goods and services. Traditionally, most businesses were manufacturers—they used tangible resources like raw materials and machinery to create tangible products such as automobiles and steel.

Managing this form of technology requires managers to keep abreast of new forms of technology and to make appropriate investments in the acquisition of new manufacturing equipment. In addition, training employees for this type of work and then evaluating their performance was a relatively straightforward undertaking.

In recent years, however, the service sector of the economy has become much more important. Indeed, services now account for well over half of the gross domestic product in the United States and play a similarly important role in many other industrialized nations as well. Service technology involves the use of both tangible resources (such as machinery) and intangible resources (such as intellectual property) to create intangible services (such as a haircut, insurance protection, or transportation between two cities). Because of the intangible properties associated with services, training and performance evaluation are obviously more complex. Many other managerial activities must also be approached in fundamentally different ways in service-based organizations.[32]

# Managing for Effectiveness

Earlier in this chapter we noted that managers work toward various goals. We are now in a position to elaborate on the nature of these goals in detail. In particular, as shown in Figure 2.3, goals—or outcomes—exist at three specific levels in an organization: individual-level outcomes, group-level outcomes, and organizational-level outcomes. Of course, it may sometimes be necessary to make tradeoffs among these different kinds of outcomes, but, in general, each is

figure 2.3

**Managing for Effectiveness**

*Managers work to optimize a variety of individual-level, group-level, and organization-level outcomes. It is sometimes necessary to make tradeoffs among the different types and levels of outcomes, but each is an important determinant of organizational effectiveness.*

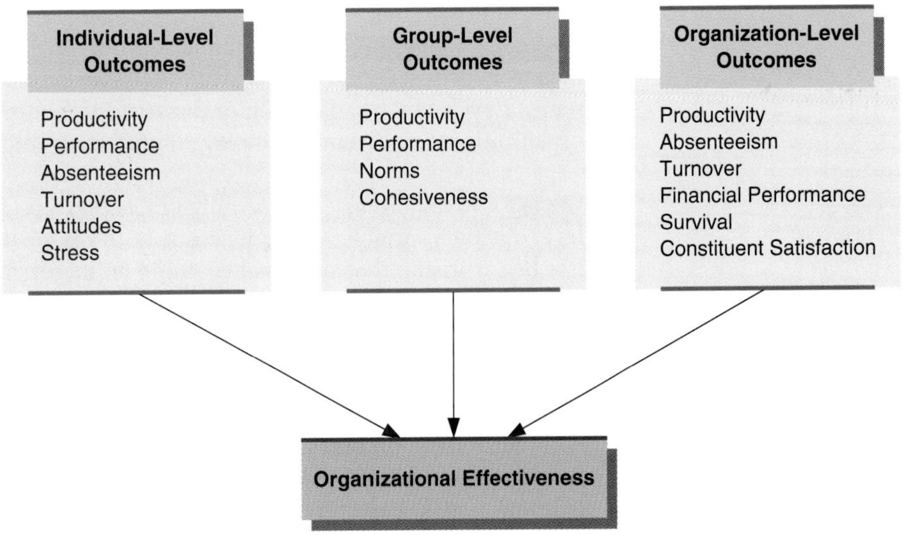

seen as a critical component of organizational effectiveness. The sections that follow elaborate on these different levels in more detail.

## Individual-Level Outcomes

Several different outcomes at the individual level are important to managers. Given the focus of the field of organizational behavior, it should not be surprising that most of these outcomes are directly or indirectly addressed by various theories and models.

**Individual Behaviors** First, several individual behaviors result from a person's participation in an organization. One important behavior is productivity. A person's productivity is an indicator of his or her efficiency and is measured in terms of the products or services created per unit of input. For example, if Bill makes 100 units of a product in a day and Sara makes only 90 units in a day, then assuming that the units are of the same quality and that Bill and Sara make the same wages, Bill is more productive than Sara.

Performance, another important individual-level outcome variable, is a somewhat broader concept. It is made up of all work-related behaviors. For example, even though Bill is highly productive, it may also be that he refuses to work overtime, expresses negative opinions about the organization at every opportunity, and will do nothing unless it falls precisely within the boundaries of his job. Sara, on the other hand, may always be willing to work overtime, is a positive representative of the organization, and goes out of her way to make as many contributions to the organization as possible. Based on the full array of behaviors, then, we might conclude that Sara actually is the better performer.

Two other important individual-level behaviors are absenteeism and turnover. Absenteeism is a measure of attendance. Although virtually everyone misses work occasionally, some people miss far more than others. Some look for excuses to miss work and call in sick regularly just for some time off; others miss work only when absolutely necessary. Turnover occurs when a person leaves the organization. If the individual who leaves is a good performer or if the organization has invested heavily in training the person, turnover can be costly.

**Individual Attitudes** Another set of individual-level outcomes influenced by managers consists of individual attitudes. (We discuss attitudes more fully in Chapter 4.) Levels of job satisfaction or dissatisfaction, organizational commitment, and organizational involvement all play an important role in organizational behavior.

**Stress** Stress, discussed more fully in Chapter 9, is another important individual-level outcome variable. Given its costs, both personal and organizational, it should not be surprising that stress is becoming an increasingly important topic for both researchers in organizational behavior and practicing managers.

## Group- and Team-Level Outcomes

Another set of outcomes exists at the group and team level. Some of these outcomes parallel the individual-level outcomes just discussed. For example, if an organization makes extensive use of work teams, team productivity and performance are important outcome variables. On the other hand, even if all the people in a group or team have the same or similar attitudes toward their jobs, the attitudes themselves are individual-level phenomena. Individuals, not groups, have attitudes.

But groups or teams can also have unique outcomes that individuals do not share. For example, as we will discuss in Chapter 11, groups develop norms that govern the behavior of individual group members. Groups also develop different levels of cohesiveness. Thus, managers need to assess both common and unique outcomes when considering the individual and group levels.

## Organization-Level Outcomes

Finally, a set of outcome variables exists at the organization level. As before, some of these outcomes parallel those at the individual and group levels, but others are unique. For example, we can measure and compare organizational productivity. We can also develop organization-level indicators of absenteeism and turnover. But profitability is generally assessed only at the organizational level.

Organizations are also commonly assessed in terms of financial performance: stock price, return on investment, growth rates, and so on. They are also evaluated in terms of their ability to survive and of the extent to which they satisfy important constituents such as investors, government regulators, employees, and unions.

Clearly, then, the manager must balance different outcomes across all three levels of analysis. In many cases, these outcomes appear to contradict one another. For example, paying workers high salaries can enhance satisfaction and reduce turnover, but it also may detract from bottom-line performance. Similarly, exerting strong pressure to increase individual performance may boost short-term profitability but increase turnover and job stress. Thus, the manager must look at the full array of outcomes and attempt to balance them in an optimal fashion. The manager's ability to do this is a major determinant of the organization's success.

# Synopsis

By its very nature, management requires an understanding of human behavior, to help managers better comprehend those at different levels in the organization, those at the same level, those in other organizations, and themselves.

The manager's job can be characterized in terms of four functions, three sets of roles, and four skills. The basic managerial functions are planning, organizing, leading, and controlling. The roles consist of three interpersonal roles, three informational roles, and four decision-making roles. The four basic skills necessary for effective management are technical, interpersonal, conceptual, and diagnostic skills.

Several organizational challenges confront managers. One major organizational challenge is workforce expansion and reduction. Another is the new workplace itself. Organization change also poses significant organizational challenges for managers. Information technology and new ways of organizing are two other important organizational challenges.

There are also several important environmental challenges to consider. Determining the most effective competitive strategy and matching people to that strategy is one important challenge. Today, global competition is one of the most critical environmental challenges. Ethics and social responsibility are significant as well. The manager must also emphasize product and service quality and manage technology successfully.

Managing for effectiveness involves balancing a variety of individual-level, group- and team-level, and organization-level outcome variables.

## Discussion Questions

1. Is it possible for managers to worry too much about the behavior of their subordinates? Why or why not?
2. The text identifies four basic managerial functions. Based on your own experiences or observations, provide examples of each function.
3. Which managerial skills do you think are among your strengths? Which are among your weaknesses? How might you improve the latter?
4. The text argues that we cannot understand organizations without understanding the behavior of the people within them. Do you agree or disagree with this assertion? Why?
5. Interview a local manager or business owner to find out his or her views on the importance of individual behavior to the success of the organization. Report your findings to the class.
6. What advice would you give managers to help them prepare better to cope with changes in workforce diversity?
7. How has information technology changed your role as a student? Have the changes been positive or negative?
8. Identify firms that use each of the three competitive strategies noted in the text.
9. Of the five environmental challenges noted in the text, which do you think is most important? Which is least important? Give reasons for your answers.
10. Are there any businesses that have not been affected by globalization? Explain.
11. What individual-, group-, or organization-level outcome variables of consequence can you identify beyond those noted in the text?

## Organizational Behavior Case for Discussion

### Work Hard, or Get a Life?

People everywhere seem to be working longer hours. Sometimes they do it to survive, sometimes because they want to, and sometimes because they see it as a means to an end. Consider, for example, Julie Herendeen, Richard Thibeault, and Josh McIntyre. Herendeen has an MBA from Harvard, and is considered to be one of the best and the brightest young managers at Netscape. Herendeen's work day starts at 6:30 A.M., when she checks her email from her home computer.

By 8:30, Julie is in her office cubicle. She immediately turns on her computer and discovers a new string of emails that have arrived since she last checked only two hours earlier. She eats fast-food breakfast at her computer while she answers these messages. Throughout the day, Herendeen is kept busy in a variety of meetings and conferences. Finally, around 5:00 in the evening, when many workers in other industries are headed home, Julie escapes the endless litany of meetings and conversations and finally makes it to her own desk again, where she sits and begins to work. At 8:30 that evening, she's still working. During the last three and a half hours, she has continued to respond to email and voicemail. She has also developed an outline of a sales presentation. Finally, at 9:00 she leaves her office. Herendeen says she loves her work and can't see doing anything else.

Richard Thibeault also works long hours. Thibeault manages an Au Bon Pain bakery café in Boston. But much of what he has to do doesn't seem like management at all. Like many other businesses, Au Bon Pain has cut back on its workforce and is holding store managers strictly accountable for keeping costs in line. Thus, Thibeault does a lot of work himself that he once had employees to do. For example, he is often at work at 3:00 A.M. to start baking rolls and pastries. During the day he also empties trash, fills in at the cash register when his employees take a lunch break, and cleans tables.

Since Au Bon Pain does little evening business, he can often get off around 4:00 or so in the afternoon during the week. He also works long hours on Saturday and Sunday as well. Thibeault recently calculated that he was working around 70 hours a week, and earning the equivalent of $7.83 an hour—scarcely more than the wages his part-time workers make. But he is under constant pressure from the home office to keep shaving costs while also boosting revenues. He doesn't know how much longer he can keep it up, though. His doctor is already telling him he needs to quit before he suffers serious health problems.

Finally, Josh McIntyre works at a small electronics factory in California. He has a law degree and started out as an attorney with a major law firm in a big city. But from the day he started he was miserable. While the pay was good, the pressure was unrelenting. He routinely worked 70 or more hours a week, and sometimes exceeded 100. McIntyre was doing very well, and received regular feedback that the partners were very pleased with his work and that big things were on the horizon.

One night, however, as he was walking to his car at 10:00, he suddenly realized that it was his birthday. No one had known it, and it had passed without fanfare. Indeed, he had not talked to anyone outside his law practice for weeks—had not watched television, had not exercised, had not read a novel. In short, all he was doing was working. The next day, he tendered his resignation and moved to a small town near his family home. McIntyre's brother helped him get a job assembling electrical components. He makes an hourly wage, but works only 40 hours a week.

McIntyre says that he is happier now than he's ever been in his life. He isn't making much money, but has plenty of personal time to do the things he enjoys in life. For example, he has learned to play the guitar and is taking up gardening. He still thinks about the law, however, and intends to get back into it soon. However, his plan is to start a small practice in a rural community where he can avoid the big-city pressures and stress that drove him away in the first place.

### Case Questions

1. How are management and organizational behavior interrelated in the three examples described in this case?
2. Which of the organizational and environmental challenges identified in the chapter are most clearly illustrated in these examples?
3. Which of these three individuals would you most and least like to be? Why?

References: Anne Field, "A Living or a Life?" *Fast Company*, January 2000-February 2000, pp. 256–267; *Hoover's Handbook of American Business 2000* (Austin, Texas: Hoover's Business Press, 2000), pp. 1020–1021; "For Richard Thibeault, Being a 'Manager' Is a Blue-Collar Life," *Wall Street Journal*, October 1, 1996, pp. A1, A12; Stratford Sherman, "A Day in the Life of a Netscape Exec," *Fortune*, May 13, 1996, pp. 124–130.

## Experiencing Organizational Behavior

### Managing in Today's Organization

**Purpose:** This exercise is intended to help you develop a deeper and more complete appreciation of the complexities and nuances of managing individual behavior in organizational settings.

**Format:** You will first develop a scenario regarding a behavior problem of your own choosing, along with a recommended course of action. You will then exchange scenarios with a classmate and compare recommendations.

**Procedure:** Select one of the organizational challenges (downsizing, workforce diversity, the new workforce, change, information technology, or new ways of organizing) or environmental challenges (competitive strategy, global competition, ethics and social responsibility, quality and productivity, or technology) discussed in this chapter. Working alone (perhaps as an outside-of-class assignment, if requested by your instructor), write a brief scenario (one page or less) describing a hypothetical organization facing that challenge. Your scenarios should provide a bit of background about the firm, the specific challenge it is facing, and some detail about why that particular challenge is relevant.

On a separate page, recommend a course of action that a manager might take to address that challenge. For example, if your challenge is to cope with a new form of technology or a need to enhance quality, your recommendation might be to form employee advisory groups to help implement the technology or to establish a new employee reward system to improve quality. Try hard to clearly and logically link the scenario to the recommendation, and provide enough detail that the appropriateness of your plan is readily apparent.

Next, exchange scenarios with one of your classmates. Without discussing it, read the classmate's scenario and develop your own recommendations to address it. After you have finished, verbally summarize your recommendations for your colleague and listen to his or her summary of recommendations for your scenario. Then exchange the written recommendations you prepared for your own scenarios and read them. Discuss similarities and differences between the two sets of recommendations. Explain the logic behind the recommendations you originally proposed and listen carefully to the logic your colleague used to develop his or her own recommendations.

### Follow-up Questions

1. Were the two sets of recommendations basically the same or basically different? Did the discussion alter your view of what should be done?
2. The contingency view, discussed in Chapter 1, would suggest that different courses of action might be equally effective. How likely is it that each of the two sets of recommendations you and your colleague developed might work?

## Building Organizational Behavior Skills

### Assessing Your Own Management Skills

The questions below are intended to provide insights into your confidence about your capabilities regarding the management skills discussed in this chapter. Answer each question by circling the scale value that best reflects your feelings.

1. I generally do well in quantitative courses like math, statistics, accounting, and finance.

| 5 | 4 | 3 | 2 | 1 |
|---|---|---|---|---|
| Strongly Agree | Agree | Neither Agree Nor Disagree | Disagree | Strongly Disagree |

2. I get along well with most people.

| 5 | 4 | 3 | 2 | 1 |
|---|---|---|---|---|
| Strongly Agree | Agree | Neither Agree Nor Disagree | Disagree | Strongly Disagree |

3. It is usually easy for me to see how material in one of my classes relates to material in other classes.

| 5 | 4 | 3 | 2 | 1 |
|---|---|---|---|---|
| Strongly Agree | Agree | Neither Agree Nor Disagree | Disagree | Strongly Disagree |

4. I can usually figure out why a problem occurred.

| 5 | 4 | 3 | 2 | 1 |
|---|---|---|---|---|
| Strongly Agree | Agree | Neither Agree Nor Disagree | Disagree | Strongly Disagree |

5. When I am asked to perform a task or to do some work, I usually know how to do it or else can figure it out pretty quickly.

| 5 | 4 | 3 | 2 | 1 |
|---|---|---|---|---|
| Strongly Agree | Agree | Neither Agree Nor Disagree | Disagree | Strongly Disagree |

6. I can usually understand why people behave as they do.

| 5 | 4 | 3 | 2 | 1 |
|---|---|---|---|---|
| Strongly Agree | Agree | Neither Agree Nor Disagree | Disagree | Strongly Disagree |

7. I enjoy classes that deal with theories and concepts.

| 5 | 4 | 3 | 2 | 1 |
|---|---|---|---|---|
| Strongly Agree | Agree | Neither Agree Nor Disagree | Disagree | Strongly Disagree |

8. I usually understand why things happen as they do.

| 5 | 4 | 3 | 2 | 1 |
|---|---|---|---|---|
| Strongly Agree | Agree | Neither Agree Nor Disagree | Disagree | Strongly Disagree |

9. I like classes that require me to "do things"—write papers, solve problems, research new areas, and so forth.

| 5 | 4 | 3 | 2 | 1 |
|---|---|---|---|---|
| Strongly Agree | Agree | Neither Agree Nor Disagree | Disagree | Strongly Disagree |

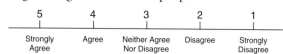

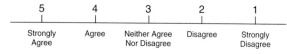

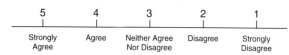

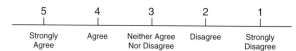

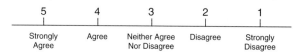

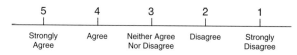

10. Whenever I work in a group, I can usually get others to accept my opinions and ideas.

| 5 | 4 | 3 | 2 | 1 |
|---|---|---|---|---|
| Strongly Agree | Agree | Neither Agree Nor Disagree | Disagree | Strongly Disagree |

11. I am much more interested in understanding the "big picture" than in dealing with narrow, focused issues.

| 5 | 4 | 3 | 2 | 1 |
|---|---|---|---|---|
| Strongly Agree | Agree | Neither Agree Nor Disagree | Disagree | Strongly Disagree |

12. When I know what I am supposed to do, I can usually figure out how to do it.

| 5 | 4 | 3 | 2 | 1 |
|---|---|---|---|---|
| Strongly Agree | Agree | Neither Agree Nor Disagree | Disagree | Strongly Disagree |

Instructions: Add up your point values for questions 1, 5, and 9; this reflects your assessment of your technical skills. The point total for questions 2, 6, and 10 reflects interpersonal skills; the point total for questions 3, 7, and 11 reflects conceptual skills; the point total for questions 4, 8, and 12 reflects diagnostic skills. Higher scores indicate stronger confidence in that realm of management. [Note: This brief instrument has not been scientifically validated and is to be used for classroom discussion only.]

## Developing OB Internet Skills

**Introduction:** People use the Internet for a wide array of purposes. For example, among the most popular things that people do on the Internet are emailing their friends, playing games, shopping at sites such as Amazon.com, checking out new movie and music sites, and getting the latest news, weather, and sports updates. Managers, similarly, often use the Internet to obtain information that they subsequently use to make decisions and run their organizations. This exercise will help you better understand how to do this.

**Internet Assignment:** This chapter identified a number of contemporary organizational and environmental challenges faced by managers today. For example, among those discussed are workforce diversity, information technology, new ways of organizing, globalization, social responsibility, quality, and productivity. Select one of these challenges that most interests you. Assume that you are a manager facing a specific problem or opportunity in the area you have selected; or perhaps you just want to learn more about the topic for your own general purposes. Search the Internet to locate several different web sites that seem most valuable and relevant for your particular topic.

**Follow-up:** Select the three sites that seem to be especially useful and relevant. Describe the strengths and weaknesses of each. Finally, respond to the following instructions and/or questions:

1. How confident would you be in making a critical decision based on the information you found on the Internet? Why?
2. Why might some topics have more Internet resources than others?
3. What other information sources might be important for learning more about your topic (in addition to the Internet)?

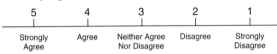

chapter 3

# Managing Global and Workforce Diversity

## Management Preview

The workforce in organizations today is becoming increasingly diverse. This development affects our lives as workers and poses numerous challenges for managers. In some organizations the increase is due to changing demographics among the general population of society, whereas in other situations the increasing diversity is caused by globalization of an organization's products, services, suppliers, customers, and employees. Regardless of the cause of the diversity in an organization, the result is that management must deal with the diversity and develop ways to manage it. In this chapter we explore how to manage these cross-cultural issues. We first examine the different types and sources of diversity affecting organizations today. We then trace the emergence of international management issues and describe the dimensions and the complexities of this organizational diversity. Next, we discuss the primary and secondary dimensions of diversity. We also examine cross-cultural factors that affect individual, interpersonal, and organizational issues. We conclude with some comments on managing multicultural and multinational organizations. First, though, we begin by describing the diversity programs in operation at AT&T. ■

AT&T has a long history of promoting diversity: It has focused on the inclusion of minorities and women since the 1970s. It has made hiring a diverse staff a priority and has boosted the diversity of its senior-level management significantly since 1984. Between 1984 and 1995, minorities went from 0.5 percent of senior management to 12 percent, and women went from 2 percent to 12 percent of senior management. Each year the company surveys employees about diversity issues and sets diversity objectives by department. In 1998, approximately one-half of those newly hired by AT&T were women and one-third were minorities.

In addition to hiring, AT&T has focused much attention on the training, development, and promotion of minorities through all ranks and types of jobs. The guiding philosophy at AT&T has been that it just made sense that its workforce reflect the increasingly diverse society in which the company does business. AT&T's record with suppliers has also been exemplary. Its supplier diversity program has been in place since 1968, with more than $10 million in minority purchases in the past thirty years. The diversity strategy reaches out into the community also, in corporate giving to women and minority cultural programs, artists, civic groups, and educational programs, and in that AT&T encourages its employees to volunteer in multicultural community development programs.

*"A diverse workforce enhances our creativity and understanding of customers."*
*— Mike Armstrong, chairman and CEO of AT&T**

Perhaps the most interesting aspect of AT&T's diversity focus is the employee groups, some of which have existed since the 1970s. Business Resource Groups (BRGs) are active for African-Americans; Asian-Pacific Americans; women; Latinos; Native Americans; gay, lesbian, bisexual, and transgendered people; and people with disabilities. These BRGs have developed specific services for AT&T customers. For example, the BRG for people with disabilities makes sure that any service offered by AT&T considers accessibility in its design. BRGs also help design internal programs for their members to help increase their skills and promote their visibility for job openings.

AT&T makes diversity a part of every aspect of its organization. Mike Armstrong, chairman and CEO, notes that "diversity encompasses succession planning, supplier diversity, and community relationships." Following the philosophy that it makes good sense to diversify the workforce at every level seems to have made good sense for the company also.[1] ■

Not every organization has had diversity programs in place for thirty years as does AT&T. And not all organizations have such a wide range of programs as does AT&T. However, more and more organizations are developing and expanding their internal and external programs in the areas of diversity. Those who do are finding that it makes good business sense to do so. Organizations such as Ernst and Young, the Anderson School at UCLA, Pitney Bowes, and Pfizer are using innovative ways to utilize an increasingly diverse workforce through various diversity initiatives, diversity roundtables, diversity seminars, and diversity marketing to reach new employees, suppliers, and customers that make a difference on the bottom line. It is essential that managers be aware of the different aspects of diversity, the wide range of diversity programs in use, and the impact of diversity on corporate performance. We start this chapter with a more detailed discussion of the meaning and nature of diversity in organizations.

## The Nature of Diversity in Organizations

You have no doubt heard the term "diversity" many times, but what does it mean in the workplace today? Usually when we speak of diversity, we think only of the gender, racial, and ethnic differences in the workforce. More broadly, the term refers to a mixture of items, objects, or people that are characterized by differences and similarities.[2] The similarities can be as important as the differences. After all, none of us are exactly alike. We may be similar but never the same. Thus, it is important to note that although two employees may have the same gender, ethnicity, and even university education, they are different employees who may act differently and react differently to various management styles. In the workplace, we refer to this variation with such terms as "cultural diversity," "workforce diversity," and "cultural variety." Managers have to deal simultaneously with similarities and differences among people in organizations.[3] They must deal with diversity within their own organizations and in the organizations they encounter all over the world. The opportunities and difficulties inherent in managing multicultural organizations will be a key management challenge in the twenty-first century.

The increasing diversity of the workforce is due to four trends. First, the tight job market makes it very important to find the best workers and then utilize them to do the best for the organization. Second, more companies are focusing their marketing efforts on the growing buying power in the minority markets. A diverse, or segmented, marketing effort requires a marketing team that represents the markets being targeted. Third, more companies are seeking to expand their markets around the world. It takes more diverse thinking to effectively reach global markets. Finally, companies that have sought to reach globally via expansion, acquisitions, and mergers inevitably go through a period of consolidation to reduce duplication of efforts around the world and to capitalize on the synergies of cross-border operations. Typically, consolidation means that employees from around the world are thrust together in newly streamlined units, resulting in more diverse groups. These four trends, then, are the drivers behind the increasing diversity in the workforce.[4]

## What Is Workforce Diversity?

**Workforce diversity** is the similarities and differences in such characteristics as age, gender, ethnic heritage, physical abilities and disabilities, race, and sexual orientation among the employees of organizations.

**Workforce diversity** is the similarities and differences in such characteristics as age, gender, ethnic heritage, physical abilities and disabilities, race, and sexual orientation among the employees of organizations. 3M defines its goals regarding workforce diversity as "valuing uniqueness, while respecting differences, maximizing individual potentials, and synergizing collective talents and experiences for the growth and success of 3M."[5] In a diverse workforce, managers are compelled to recognize and manage the similarities and differences that exist among the people in the organization.

**Stereotypes** tend to become rigid judgments about others that ignore the specific person and the current situation. Acceptance of stereotypes can lead to the dangerous process of prejudice toward others.

Employees' conceptions of work, expectations of rewards from the organization, and practices in relating to others are all influenced by diversity.[6] Managers of diverse work groups need to understand how the social environment affects employees' beliefs about work, and they must have the communication skills to develop confidence and self-esteem in members of diverse work groups. Many people tend to stereotype others in organizations. As described in Chapter 4, a **stereotype** is a generalization about a person or a group of persons based on certain characteristics or traits. Many managers fall into the trap of stereotyping workers as being like themselves and sharing the manager's orientation toward work, rewards, and relating to coworkers. However, if workers do not share those views, values, and beliefs, problems can arise. A second situation involving stereotyping occurs when managers stereotype workers according to some particular group such as age, gender, race, ethnic origin, or other characteristic. It is often easier for managers to group people based on easily identifiable characteristics and to treat these groups

These employees of Wal-Mart represent the company's drive to diversify its workforce from the sales floor to the executive suite. Wal-Mart believes it is more effective when people who represent their diverse customer base make decisions at all levels. This group includes two senior vice presidents, four vice presidents, and two corporate counsels.

as "different." Managers who stereotype workers based on assumptions about the characteristics of their group tend to ignore individual differences, which leads to rigid judgments about others that do not take into account the specific person and the current situation.[7]

**Prejudices** are judgments about others that reinforce beliefs about superiority and inferiority.

Stereotypes can lead to the even more dangerous process of prejudice toward others. **Prejudices** are judgments about others that reinforce beliefs about superiority and inferiority. They can lead to an exaggerated assessment of the worth of one group and a diminished assessment of the worth of others.[8] When people prejudge others, they make assumptions about the nature of the others that may or may not be true, and they manage accordingly. In other words, people build job descriptions, reward systems, performance appraisal systems, and management systems and policies that fit their stereotypes.

Management systems built on stereotypes and prejudices do not meet the needs of a diverse workforce. An incentive system may offer rewards that people do not value, job descriptions that do not fit the jobs and the people who do them, and performance evaluation systems that measure the wrong things. In addition, those who engage in prejudice and stereotyping fail to recognize employees' distinctive individual talents, which often leads these employees to lose self-esteem and possibly have lower levels of job satisfaction and performance. Stereotypes can also become self-fulfilling prophecies.[9] If we assume someone is incompetent and treat him or her that way, over time the employee may begin to share the same belief. This can lead to reduced productivity, lower creativity, and lower morale.

Of course, managers caught in this counterproductive cycle can change. As a first step they must recognize that diversity exists in organizations. Only then can they begin to manage it appropriately. Managers who do not recognize diversity may face an unhappy, disillusioned, and underutilized workforce.

## Who Will Be the Workforce of the Future?

Employment statistics can help us understand just how different the workforce of the future will be. Figure 3.1 compares the workforce composition of 1986 to projections for 2006. All workforce segments will increase as a percentage of the total workforce except the white male segment, which declines from 48.6 percent to 44.3 percent. This may not seem too dramatic, but it follows decades in which the white males have dominated the workforce, making up well over 50 percent of it. When one considers that the total U.S. workforce is expected to be over 150 million in 2006, a 4 percent drop represents a significant decline.[10]

We can also examine the nature of the growth in the workforce over the ten-year period from 1996 to 2006. Figure 3.2 shows the percentage of the growth attributable to each segment. Although the overall workforce growth is expected to be 11.1 percent, the growth rate for white males is expected to be only 6.8 percent. White females are expected to increase their percentage in the workforce by 12.2 percent, so that more than 62 percent of the women in the United States are expected to be working in 2006.

*"In 1996 forty-five percent of the labor force was age 40 or older. By 2006, more than one half of the labor force will be in this age category."*[11]

figure 3.1

**Workforce Composition: 1986–2006**

*In the period between 1986 and 2006, all workforce segments are expected to increase as a percentage of the total workforce except the white male segment, which declines from 48.6 percent to 44.3 percent.*

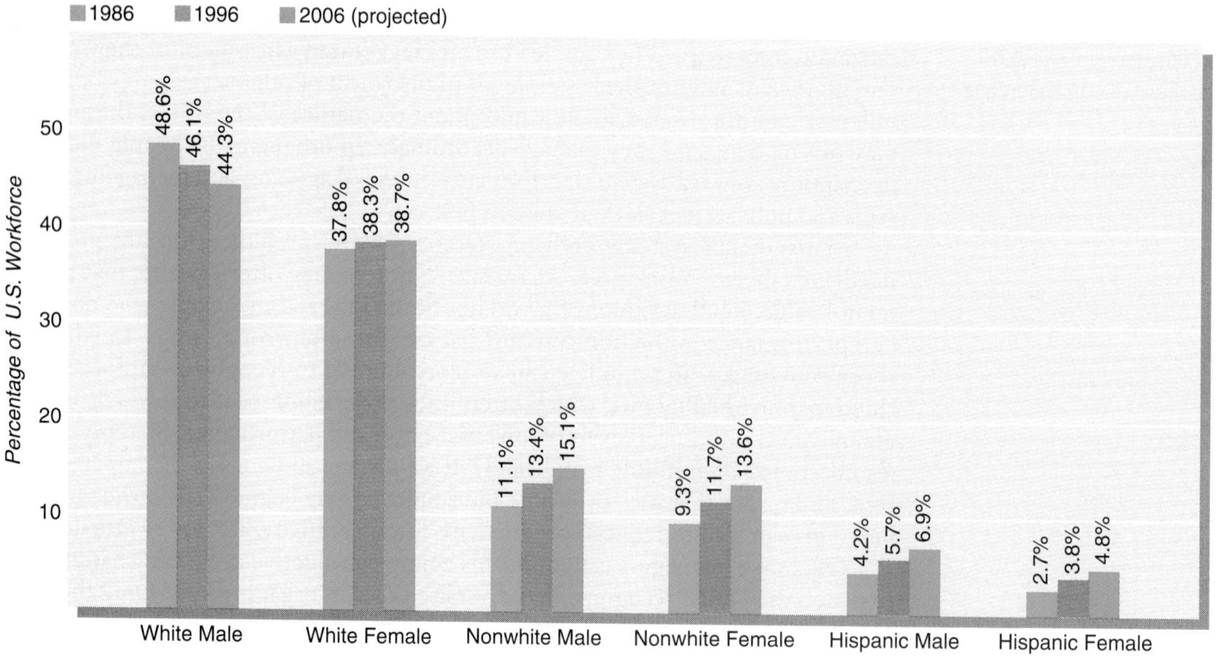


Reference: Bureau of Labor Statistics, *Monthly Labor Review*, November 1997.

figure 3.2

**Expected Percentage of Growth in Workforce: 1996–2006**

*There is no question that the composition of the workforce is changing in the United States. For the period from 1996 to 2006, the growth rate in all segments is higher for women than for men and higher for nonwhites than for whites.*

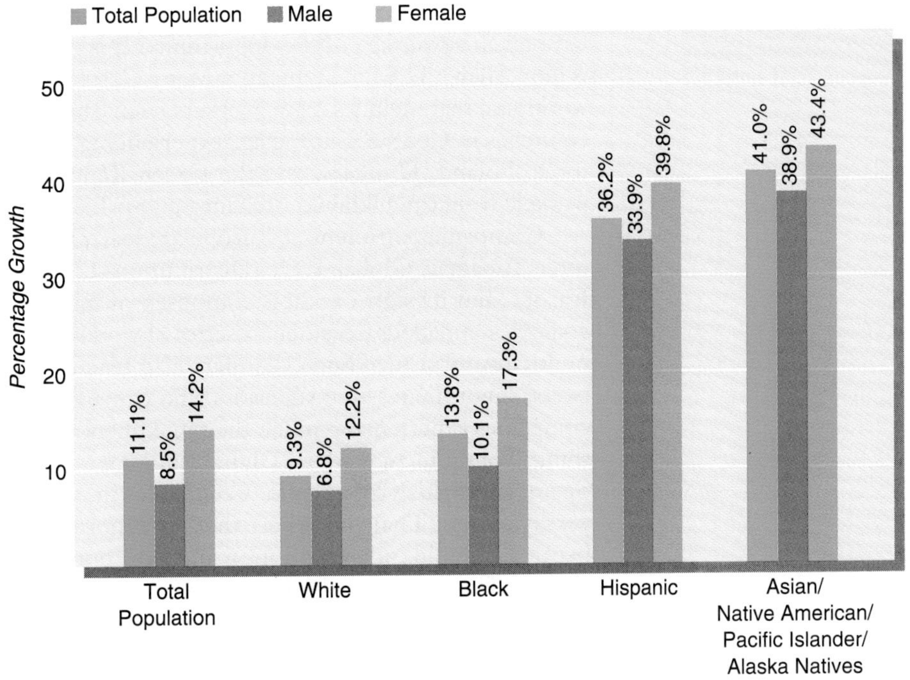


Reference: Bureau of Labor Statistics, *Monthly Labor Review,* November 1997.

Examining the age ranges of the workforce gives us another view of the changes. In earlier decades, young workers constituted the largest part of the workforce, but these young workers are aging. In fact, workers in the sixteen-to-twenty-four age group are expected to increase by only 5.76 million workers (1.7 percent) between 1996 and 2006. The number of workers in the forty-five-to-fifty-four age group is expected to increase by 9.4 million (2.6 percent), and the numbers of workers in the fifty-five-to-sixty-four age group is expected to increase by 9 million workers (3.6 percent).[12]

## Global Workforce Diversity

Similar statistics on workforce diversity are found in other countries. In Canada, for instance, minorities are the fastest-growing segment of the population and the workforce. In addition, women make up two-thirds of the growth in the Canadian workforce, increasing from 35 percent in the 1970s to 45 percent in 1991.[13] These changes have initiated a workforce revolution in offices and factories throughout Canada. Managers and employees are learning to adapt to changing demographics. A recent study found that 81 percent of the organizations surveyed by the Conference Board of Canada include diversity management programs for their employees.[14]

Increasing diversity in the workplace is even more dramatic in Europe, where employees have been crossing borders for many years. In fact, as of 1991, more than 2 million Europeans were working in another European country. When the European Union opened borders in 1992, this number increased significantly. It was expected that opening borders among the European community members primarily meant relaxing trade restrictions so goods and services could move among the member countries. In addition, however, workers were also free to move and have taken advantage of the opportunity. It is clear that diversity in the workforce is more than a U.S. phenomenon. Many German factories now have a very diverse workforce that includes many workers from Turkey. Several of the newly emerging countries in Central Europe are experiencing increasing diversity in their workforce. Poland, Hungary, and the Czech Republic are experiencing an influx of workers from the Ukraine, Afghanistan, Sri Lanka, China, and Somalia.[15]

Companies throughout Europe are learning to adjust to the changing workforce. Amadeus Global Travel Distribution serves the travel industry, primarily in Europe, but its staff of 650 is composed of individuals from thirty-two different countries. Amadeus developed a series of workshops to teach managers how to lead multicultural teams. Such seminars also teach them how to interact better with peers, subordinates, and superiors who come from a variety of countries.[16] Other companies experiencing much the same phenomenon in Europe and doing something about it include Mars, Digital Equipment, Hewlett-Packard Spain, Fujitsu in Spain, and British Petroleum. Companies in Asia are experiencing increasing diversity also. In Thailand, where there is a shortage of skilled and unskilled workers because of rapid industrialization and slow population growth, there is increasing demand for foreign workers to fill the gap, which creates problems integrating local with foreign workers.[17] Thus, the issues of workforce diversity are not prevalent only in the United States. The emergence of international management is discussed in the next major section of this chapter. But first, we describe why it is important to value diversity, rather than just tolerate it.

## The Value of Diversity

In the traditional view, the United States was seen as a "melting pot" of people from many different countries, cultures, and backgrounds. For centuries, it was assumed that people who were different or new to something should assimilate themselves into the existing situation. Although equal employment opportunity and accompanying affirmative action legislation have had significant effects on diversifying workplaces, they sometimes focused on bringing into the workplace people from culturally different groups and fully assimilating them into the existing organization. In organizations, however, integration proved to be difficult. People were slow to change and usually resistant to the change. Substantive career advancement opportunities rarely materialized for those who were "different."

The issue of workforce diversity has become increasingly important in the last few years as employees, managers, consultants, and the government finally realized that the composition of the workforce affects organizational productivity. Today, instead of a melting pot, the workplace in the United States is regarded as more of a tossed salad made up of a delightful mosaic of different flavors, colors, and textures. Rather than trying to assimilate those who are different into a single organizational culture, the current view is that organizations need to celebrate the differences and utilize the variety of talents, perspectives, and backgrounds of all employees.

**Valuing diversity** means putting an end to the assumption that everyone who is not a member of the dominant group must assimilate.

### Benefits of Valuing Diversity

**Valuing diversity** means putting an end to the assumption that everyone who is not a member of the dominant group must assimilate. This is not easily accomplished in most organizations. Truly valuing diversity is not merely giving lip service to an ideal, putting up with a necessary evil, promoting a level of tolerance for those who are different, or tapping into the latest fad. It is an opportunity to develop and utilize all of the human resources available to the organization for the benefit of the workers as well as the organization. Later in this chapter we discuss the benefits of creating a multicultural organization.

*"Diversifying our staff is not some side project. It is a core part of our business strategy."*
*— Jay Harris, publisher,* San Jose Mercury News[18]

Valuing diversity is not just the right thing to do for workers, it is the right thing to do for the organization, financially and economically. One of the most important benefits of diversity is the richness of ideas and perspectives that it makes available to the organization. Rather than relying on one homogeneous dominant group for new ideas and alternative solutions to increasingly complex problems, companies that value diversity have access to more perspectives of a problem. These fresh perspectives may lead to development of new products, opening of new markets, or improving service to existing customers.

Overall, the organization wins when it truly values diversity. A worker whom the organization values is more creative and productive. Valued workers in diverse organizations experience less interpersonal conflict because the employees understand each other. When employees of different cultural groups, backgrounds, and values understand each other, they have a greater sense of teamwork, stronger identification with the team, and deeper commitment to the organization and its goals.

**Assimilation** is the process through which members of a minority group are forced to learn the ways of the dominant group. In organizations, this means that when people of different types and backgrounds are hired, the organization attempts to mold them to fit the existing organizational culture.

### Assimilation

**Assimilation** is the process through which members of a minority group are forced to learn the ways of the majority group. In organizations this entails hiring people from diverse backgrounds and attempting to mold them to fit into the existing organizational culture. One way that companies attempt to make people fit in is by requiring that employees speak only one language. The "Working with Diversity" box describes some of the organizational problems that occur when an English-only policy is established. Most organizations develop systems such as performance evaluation and incentive programs that reinforce the values of the dominant group. (Chapter 18 discusses organizational culture as a means of reinforcing the organizational values and affecting the behavior of workers.) By universally applying the values of the majority group throughout the organization, assimilation tends to perpetuate false stereotypes and prejudices. Workers who are different are expected to meet the standards for dominant group members.[19] Sometimes those standards can pertain to dress, as shown in the following cartoon (on page 61).

Dominant groups tend to be self-perpetuating. Majority group members may avoid people who are "different" simply because they find communication difficult. Moreover, informal discussions over coffee and lunch and during after-hours socializing tend to be limited to people in the dominant group. What happens? Those who are not in the dominant group miss out on the informal communication opportunities in which office politics, company policy, and other issues are often discussed in great detail. Subsequently, employees not in the dominant group often do not understand the more formal communication and may not be included in necessary action taken in response. The dominant group likewise remains unaware of opinions from the "outside."

Similarly, since the dominant group makes decisions based on their values and beliefs, the minority group has little say in decisions regarding compensation, facility location, benefit plans, performance standards, and other work

WORKING WITH DIVERSITY

## *English-Only Rules in the Workplace*

Immigrants will make up 22 percent of the growth in the labor force in the United States through the year 2000. Along with their cultures, values, and beliefs they bring their native languages, which are usually not English. A growing issue is the extent to which a language other than English can be spoken at work.

Filipinos are the largest ethnic Asian group in the United States, and many Filipinos live in California. Some have been in the United States for many years, as has Adelaida Dimaranan, an assistant head nurse at Pomona Valley Hospital Medical Center. Aida and her fellow Filipino nurses often spoke their native language, Tagalog, while on break, on personal time, on the phone with family members, and occasionally and unintentionally on the job. After Aida had worked at the hospital for ten years, a new supervisor ruled that Aida could no longer speak Tagalog at work. Aida and her Filipino colleagues claimed that they were more comfortable speaking Tagalog among themselves, and sometimes Tagalog just came out. The supervisor objected to Aida's violation of the rule, demoted her, and transferred her to another department. Aida felt humiliated that she could no longer feel like a Filipino and sued the hospital. When mediation failed, the American Civil Liberties Union and the Asian Pacific American Legal Center filed suit for her, alleging a violation of Title VII of the Civil Rights Act of 1964, based on discrimination on the basis of race or national origin. In the legal case, a U.S. district judge ruled that the hospital's rule was not discriminatory but was an effort to improve patient care. But the hospital was also ordered to reinstate her to a comparable position, give her back pay, and remove any negative evaluations from her personnel file. Both sides intend to appeal.

In another case involving the Casa San Miguel convalescent home in Concord, California, Annie Mariano and eight other Filipinos were fired for violation of the English-only rule. These employees have also filed suit for discrimination. Management of Casa San Miguel claim to have imposed the regulation for the benefit of their elderly patients, most of whom speak only English.

Other situations are calling into question the legality and appropriateness of English-only rules in the workplace. Father Francis Barszczwewski of the Sacred Heart Church in Philadelphia announced in 1995 that all employees must cease speaking Polish during business hours. One worker, Jess Kania, a bilingual Polish-American, objected and was fired a few weeks later. Kania filed suit, claiming the policy constituted national-origin discrimination, and lost. In Chicago, Carlos Solero was fired three days after he refused to sign a work agreement that included a policy of English-only at the suburban manufacturing plant. Management said the intent of the English-only policy was to improve communication among workers at the plant. Solero and seven other Spanish speakers have filed lawsuits against the plant.

> *"We have nothing against speaking any other language as long as the customer's needs are being met."—Diana Rader, Human Resources Manager for Watlow Batavia, an Illinois firm sued by eight employees.**

Such cases are becoming more commonplace: ninety-one cases were filed in the United States in 1998. Court rulings have been mixed, upholding some such policies and overturning others. The key is the "business necessity" that is required for English-only policies to be justified. Safety issues, such as in an air traffic control tower or in specific situations in certain hazardous manufacturing locations, seem to be easiest to justify.

The issue is more than a legal one, however. Should employers require that employees speak English? If so, when and under what circumstances? Can employees gather and speak their native language among themselves? If they become highly animated with laughter and the supervisor thinks the laughter is at her or his expense, should this be allowed? Or is it only job-related speech that should be regulated? To what extent are employees' identities and characters stripped away by not being allowed to speak their native language?

References: Martha Irvine, "EEOC Sues Illinois Company Over 'English-Only' Policy," *Legal Intelligencer*, September 2, 1999, p. 4 (*quote on p. 4); Eric Matusewitch, "English-Only Rules Come Under Fire," *Legal Intelligencer*, December 30, 1998, p. 7; Carolyn Jung, "Filipino-Americans to Launch Civil Rights Groups," *Knight-Ridder/Tribune News Service*, November 11, 1994, p. 1112K6374; Benjamin Pimentel, "Controversy Moves into Courts: Many Tongues Lash the English-Only Rule," *San Francisco Chronicle*, March 18, 1994, p. A1; Norman Sklarewitz, "American Firms Lash Out at Foreign Tongues," *Business and Society Review*, Fall 1992, pp. 24–28; "Appeals of Discrimination Ruling Expected," *Modern Healthcare*, November 18, 1991, p. 26; Julie Solomon, "Firms Grapple with Language," *Wall Street Journal*, November 7, 1989, pp. B1, B10; Joe Schwartz, "Who's Ahead: Population Growth of Asian Ethnic Groups in the U.S." *American Demographics*, April 1988, pp. 16–17.

**"Wilkens, the next time we catch you coming to work in a suit and tie, I'm afraid we're going to have to let you go."**

Fitting into the corporate model is not exactly what it used to be with all of the Internet start-ups these days. In this situation, the "boss" expects the older gentleman in the suit and tie to conform to the more informal "dress code." But fitting in is not necessarily the best in every situation. Doing the right job in the right way is more important than wearing the right clothes and fitting in. The lessons of valuing diversity should have shown us that by now.

Reference: *Fast Company*, February–March 1999, p. 66. Richard Cline

issues that pertain directly to all workers. Workers who differ from the majority very quickly get the idea that to succeed in such a system, one must be like the dominant group in terms of values and beliefs, dress, and most other characteristics. Since success depends on assimilation, differences are driven underground.

Most organizations have a fairly predictable dominant group. Table 3.1 shows the results of interviews with members of several organizations who were asked to list the attributes reinforced by their organization's culture. Typically, white men in organizations view themselves as quite diverse. Others in the organizations view them as quite homogeneous, however, having attributes similar to those listed. Also typically, those who work in these dominant groups tend to be less aware of the problems that homogeneity can cause. Generally, those not in the dominant group feel the effects more keenly.

Not paying attention to cultural diversity can be very costly to the organization. In addition to blocking minority involvement in communication and decision making, there can also be tensions among workers, lower productivity, increased costs due to increasing absenteeism, increased employee turnover, increased equal employment opportunity and harassment suits, and lower morale among the workers.[20]

table 3.1

**Attributes Reinforced by the Culture in Typical Organizations**

| | |
|---|---|
| ■ Rational, linear thinker | ■ Age 35–49 |
| ■ Impersonal management style | ■ Competitive |
| ■ Married with children | ■ Protestant or Jewish |
| ■ Quantitative | ■ College graduate |
| ■ Adversarial | ■ Tall |
| ■ Careerist | ■ Heterosexual |
| ■ Individualistic | ■ Predictable |
| ■ Experience in competitive team sports | ■ Excellent physical condition |
| ■ In control | ■ Willing to relocate |
| ■ Military veteran | |

Reference: Marilyn Loden and Judy B. Rosener, *Workforce America! Managing Employee Diversity as a Vital Resource* (Homewood, Ill.: Business One Irwin, 1991), p. 43. Copyright © 1991 by Business One Irwin. Used with permission.

# The Emergence of International Management

A primary source of diversity in organizations is the increasing globalization of organizations and management. However, in many ways, international management is nothing new. Centuries ago, the Roman army was forced to develop a management system to deal with its widespread empire.[21] Likewise, the Olympic games, the Red Cross, and many similar organizations have international roots. From a business standpoint, however, international management is relatively new, at least to the United States.

## The Growth of International Business

In 1990, the volume of international trade in current dollars was almost thirty times greater than the amount in 1960, and the figures are projected to continue escalating. What has led to this dramatic increase? As Figure 3.3 shows, four major factors account for much of the momentum.

First, communication and transportation have advanced dramatically over the past few decades. Telephone service has improved, communication networks span the globe and can interact via satellite, and once-remote areas have become accessible. Telephone service in some developing countries is almost entirely by cellular phone technology rather than land-based wired telephone service. Fax machines and electronic mail allow managers to send documents around the world in seconds as opposed to the days it took just a few years ago. In short, it is simply easier to conduct international business today.

Second, businesses have expanded internationally to increase their markets. Companies in smaller countries, such as Nestlé in Switzerland, recognized long ago that their domestic markets were too small to sustain much growth and therefore moved into international activities. Many U.S. firms, on the other hand, had all the business they could handle until recently; hence, they are just beginning to consider international opportunities. As U.S. companies grow internationally, they have to confront many differences in the way various countries conduct business. Differences in laws, local customs, tariffs, and exchange rates are only a few of these. The issue of whether to give or take bribes and under-the-table payments is very important in some industries, as discussed in "The Business of Ethics" box. Companies in the tobacco industry have significantly increased their global efforts and are currently embroiled in a global controversy over whether it is ethical to heavily advertise tobacco products around the world.

Third, more and more firms are moving into the international realm to control costs, especially to reduce labor costs. Plans to cut costs this way do not always work out as planned, but many firms are successfully using inexpensive labor in Asia and Mexico.[22] In searching for lower labor costs, some companies have discovered well-trained workers and built more efficient plants that are closer to international markets.[23]

**figure 3.3 Forces That Have Increased International Business**

*Movement along the continuum from domestic to international business is due to four forces. Businesses subject to these forces are becoming more international.*

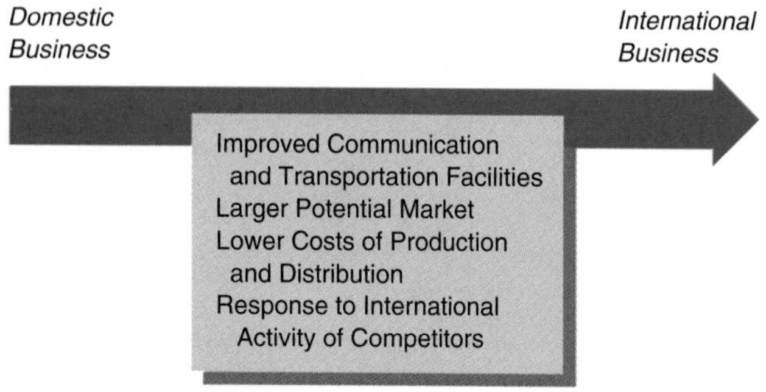

THE BUSINESS OF ETHICS

## *Competing Globally: With or Without Bribes?*

Using bribes to get things done is usually considered a necessary evil when doing business globally. In spite of the strict Foreign Corrupt Practices Act, passed in the United States in 1977, many U.S. companies are still finding ways to influence people in certain foreign countries, to locate the right person to make a contract decision, or to help win a contract bid. Some are paying fines for law violation, whereas others shrug it all off as part of doing business.

> *"It is time to get serious about bribery and corruption worldwide." — William M. Daley, U.S. Secretary of Commerce*

In 1999, Saybolt Inc. pled guilty to paying a $50,000 bribe to Panamanian government officials within the Panamanian Ministry of Commerce and Industries to obtain a lease from the government for a laboratory site adjacent to the Panama Canal in October 1995. In addition, David H. Mead, who was then president of Saybolt, was convicted of conspiracy, violation of the Foreign Corrupt Practices Act, and interstate travel to promote bribery.

In 1995, Lockheed Martin paid $24 million in fines (twice the profits) from a sale of three C-130H aircraft to the Egyptian government because the company made a $1.5 million payment to a government official who helped them get the contract. In the United States, that is illegal. In other countries it may also be illegal, technically, but government officials and the courts seem to look the other way. In 1996, Malaysia's trade minister, Rafidah Aziz, suggested that if other countries do not want to participate in bribery and other forms of corruption, they could take their business elsewhere. Although all Southeast Asian countries have laws against corruption and bribery, they tend to view corruption as a normal way of life and an accepted means of doing business.

New and ingenious ways of getting around the laws are becoming more popular. For example, foreign trips are often considered quite a nice benefit of doing business. Therefore, some U.S. firms are promising extensive and expensive training programs in the United States for managers and executives of firms in other countries who do business with them. When these foreign executives arrive in the United States, they spend some time in actual training, but they often travel around the country visiting other plants, Atlantic City and Las Vegas casinos, and Disney World.

Another way of contributing to the economy or government is to make large donations to schools, universities, and cultural institutions. For example, Boeing spent more than $100 million to train Chinese workers how to use its technology. IBM donated $25 million in hardware and software to twenty Chinese universities and funds scholarship programs as well. Are these types of contributions payments for action or buying goodwill? Although large companies can afford these types of donations, many small companies simply do not have the contacts or the money to make them work.

Many multinationals are creating joint ventures or utilizing consultants or agents in other countries to do most of the local work. Fees are paid into the joint venture or to the consultant. Where and how these fees are spent is often unknown to the U.S. firm. The venture or the consultant may be paying money in bribes that the U.S. company is unaware of. As long as the U.S. firms do not know how the money is spent, they probably will not be held liable in court. Payment for access to a decision maker may be called a "facilitation payment" and allowed. However, payment to an official to make a decision in the favor of the company may be called a bribe and not allowed.

Recently, thirty-four countries signed an agreement to criminalize bribery as recommended by the Organization for Economic Cooperation and Development (OECD) Convention on Combating Bribery. Yet, as of February 1999, only twelve of those countries had enacted laws that would actually implement the agreement: Bulgaria, Canada, Finland, Germany, Greece, Hungary, Iceland, Japan, Korea, Norway, the United Kingdom, and the United States. Major exporting countries, such as France, Italy, the Netherlands, and Belgium, are dragging their feet. Evidently, bribery as a way of doing business has strong ties with big business in those countries. Bribery is so entrenched in some countries that they continue to allow tax deductions for bribes paid to foreign government officials. Some have claimed the necessity for ending bribery is based on the contention that bribery is just not "right." Others have contended, however, that what is "right" is determined locally, not by some international decree.

References: William M. Daley, "Bribery: No Longer Business as Usual," *Financial Times*, February 15, 1999, p. 10 (quote on p. 10); "Saybolt Inc. Pleads Guilty and Is Fined $1.5 Million for Bribery of Panamanian Officials, Reports U.S. Attorney," *PR Newswire*, January 21, 1999; Vijay Joshi, "Malaysian Official Defends Bribes," *Arizona Republic*, April 26, 1996, p. E3; Dana Milbank and Marcus W. Brauchli, "How U.S. Concerns Compete in Countries Where Bribes Flourish," *Wall Street Journal*, September 29, 1995, pp. A1, A14.

Finally, many organizations have become international in response to competition. If an organization starts gaining strength in international markets, its competitors often must follow suit to avoid falling too far behind in sales and profitability. Exxon Mobil Corporation and Texaco realized they had to increase their international market share to keep pace with foreign competitors such as BP Amoco p.l.c. and Royal Dutch/Shell.

## Trends in International Business

The most striking trend in international business is obvious: growth. More and more businesses are entering the international marketplace, including many smaller firms. We read a great deal about the threat of foreign companies. For example, for many years successful Japanese automobile firms such as Toyota and Nissan produced higher-quality cars for lower prices than did U.S. firms. What we often overlook, however, is the success of U.S. firms abroad. Ford, for example, has long had a successful business in Europe and today employs less than half its total workforce on U.S. soil. And U.S. firms make dozens of products better than anyone else in the world.[24] General Motors Europe has had strong sales in Europe since 1985, rising to a 12.6 percent market share, the second best in Europe, behind Volkswagen.[25] In addition, many foreign firms (BMW and Mercedes) are now producing their products in the United States because of the lower wage rates, better tax rates, and improved quality.

Business transactions are also becoming increasingly blurred across national boundaries. Ford owns 25 percent of Mazda, General Motors and Toyota have a joint venture in California, Ford and Volkswagen have one in Argentina, and Honda and British Sterling have one worldwide. Indeed, some experts have started predicting that some multinational firms will soon start to lose their national identity altogether and become truly global corporations. Car makers are now becoming global, with mergers taking place all over the globe. Ford owns Jaguar, Daimler-Benz merged with Chrysler, BMW controls Rover, and everyone is looking at the Korean automakers.

International involvement has also increased across not-for-profit organizations. Universities offer study programs abroad, health-care and research programs span national boundaries, international postal systems are working more closely together, and athletic programs are increasingly being transplanted to different cultures.

Events in other parts of the world are having major effects on business. The unification of Germany and the movement of the formerly communist-controlled countries in Central Europe toward free-market economies are providing many new opportunities and challenges to business. In many ways, then, we are becoming a truly global economy. No longer will a firm be able to insulate itself from foreign competitors or opportunities. Thus, it is imperative that every manager develop and maintain at least a rudimentary understanding of the dynamics of international management.[26]

## Cross-Cultural Differences and Similarities

Since the primary concern of this discussion is human behavior in organizational settings, we focus on differences and similarities in behavior across cultures. Un-

These employees of a bank are practicing smiling at the Korean Air Service Academy in Seoul, Korea. The academy teaches proper greetings, Korean bowing, posture, and how to give polite refusals. The instructors report that it is often difficult to teach Koreans to smile because their culture has always valued a stern, serious person in business situations. But as Korean companies become more global, they are finding that customer service is often just as important as the quality of their products. Corporations that send their employees to the academy believe that improving customer relations is important to make their businesses more globally competitive.

fortunately, research in this area is still relatively new. Thus, many of the research findings we can draw on are preliminary at best.

**General Observations** In this section we describe a few general observations about similarities and differences across cultures. First, cultures and national boundaries do not necessarily coincide. Some areas of Switzerland are very much like Italy, other parts like France, and still other parts like Germany. Similarly, within the United States there are profound cultural differences among southern California, Texas, and the East Coast.[27]

Given this basic assumption, one review of the literature on international management reached five basic conclusions.[28] First, behavior in organizational settings indeed varies across cultures. Thus, employees in companies based in Japan, the United States, and Germany are likely to have different attitudes and patterns of behavior. The behavior patterns are likely to be widespread and pervasive within an organization.

Second, culture itself is one major cause of this variation. Culture is the set of shared values, often taken for granted, that help people in a group, organization, or society understand which actions are considered acceptable and which are considered unacceptable (we use this same definition in our discussion of organizational culture in Chapter 18). Thus, although the behavioral differences just noted may be caused in part by different standards of living, different geographical conditions, and so forth, culture itself is a major factor apart from other considerations.

Third, although behavior within organizational settings (e.g., motivation and attitudes) remains quite diverse across cultures, organizations and the way they are structured appear to be increasingly similar. Hence, managerial practices at a general level may be more and more alike, but the people who work within organizations still differ markedly.

Fourth, the same manager behaves differently in different cultural settings. A manager may adopt one set of behaviors when working in one culture but change those behaviors when moved to a different culture. For example, Japanese executives who come to work in the United States slowly begin to act more like U.S. managers and less like Japanese managers. This is often a source of concern for them when they are transferred back to Japan.[29]

Finally, cultural diversity can be an important source of synergy in enhancing organizational effectiveness. More and more organizations are coming to appreciate the virtues of cultural diversity, but they still know surprisingly little about how to manage it.[30] Organizations that adopt a multinational strategy can—with effort—become more than a sum of their parts. Operations in each culture can benefit from operations in other cultures through an enhanced understanding of how the world works.[31]

**Specific Cultural Issues** Geert Hofstede, a Dutch researcher, studied workers and managers in sixty countries and found that attitudes and behaviors differed significantly because of the values and beliefs in the various countries.[32] Table 3.2 shows how Hofstede's categories help us summarize differences for several countries.

**Individualism** is the extent to which people place primary value on themselves.

The two primary dimensions that Hofstede found are the individualism/collectivism continuum and power distance. **Individualism** exists to the extent that people in a culture define themselves by referring to themselves as singular per-

table 3.2

**Work-Related Differences in Ten Countries**

| Country | Individualism/ Collectivism | Power Distance | Uncertainty Avoidance | Masculinity | Long-Term Orientation |
|---|---|---|---|---|---|
| Canada | H | M | M | M | L |
| Germany | M | M | M | M | M |
| Israel | M | L | M | M | (no data) |
| Italy | H | M | M | H | (no data) |
| Japan | M | M | H | H | H |
| Mexico | H | H | H | M | (no data) |
| Pakistan | L | M | M | M | L |
| Sweden | H | M | L | L | M |
| United States | H | M | M | M | L |
| Venezuela | L | H | M | H | (no data) |

Note: H=high; M=moderate; L=low. These are only ten of the more than sixty countries that Hofstede and others have studied.

References: Adapted from Geert Hofstede and Michael Harris Bond, "The Confucius Connection: From Cultural Roots to Economic Growth," *Organizational Dynamics*, Spring 1988, pp. 5–21. Geert Hofstede, "Motivation, Leadership, and Organization: Do American Theories Apply Abroad?" *Organizational Dynamics*, Summer 1980, pp. 42–63.

sons rather than as part of one or more groups or organizations. At work, people from more individualistic cultures tend to be more concerned about themselves than about their work group, individual tasks are more important than relationships, and hiring and promotion are based on skills and rules. **Collectivism**, on the other hand, is characterized by tight social frameworks in which people tend to base their identities on the group or organization to which they belong. At work, this means that employee-employer links are more like family relationships, relationships are more important than individuals or tasks, and hiring and promotion are based on group membership. In the United States, a very individualistic culture, it is important to perform better than others and to stand out from the crowd. In Japan, a more collectivist culture, an individual tries to fit in with the group, strives for harmony, and prefers stability.

**Collectivism** is the extent to which they emphasize the good of the group or society.

**Power distance**, which can also be called **orientation to authority**, is the extent to which less powerful people accept the unequal distribution of power. In countries such as Mexico and Venezuela, for example, people prefer to be in a situation in which the authority is clearly understood and lines of authority are never bypassed. On the other hand, in countries such as Israel and Denmark, authority is not as highly respected and employees are quite comfortable circumventing lines of authority to accomplish something. People in the United States tend to be mixed, accepting authority in some situations but not in others.

**Power distance (orientation to authority)** is the extent to which less powerful persons accept the unequal distribution of power.

**Uncertainty avoidance**, which can also be called **preference for stability**, is the extent to which people feel threatened by unknown situations and prefer to be in clear and unambiguous situations. People in Japan and Mexico prefer stability to uncertainty, whereas uncertainty is normal and accepted in Sweden, Hong Kong, and the United Kingdom. **Masculinity**, which can also be called **assertiveness** or **materialism**, is the extent to which the dominant values in a society emphasize aggressiveness and the acquisition of money and things, as opposed to concern for people, relationships among people, and the overall quality of life. People in the United States are moderate on both the uncertainty avoidance and masculinity scales. Japan and Italy score high on the masculinity scale, while Sweden scores low.

**Uncertainty avoidance (preference for stability)** is the extent to which people prefer to be in clear and unambiguous situations.

**Masculinity (assertiveness** or **materialism)** is the extent to which the dominant values in a society emphasize aggressiveness and the acquisition of money and material goods, rather than concern for people, relationships among people, and the overall quality of life.

Hofstede's framework was later expanded to include **long-term** versus **short-term orientation**. Long-term values include focusing on the future, working on projects that have a distant payoff, persistence, and thrift. Short-term values are more oriented toward the past and the present and include respect for traditions and social obligations. Japan, Hong Kong, and China are highly long-term oriented. The Netherlands and Germany are moderately long-term oriented. The United States, Indonesia, West Africa, and Russia are more short-term oriented. Certain aspects of the culture of a specific culture can change over time. For example, the orientation toward making a profit in a free enterprise system versus working for the common good in a socialist or communist system may be changing in China, as discussed in the "Mastering Change" box.

People with a **short-term orientation** focus on the past or present; people with a **long-term orientation** focus on the future.

Hofstede's research is only one of several ways of categorizing differences across many different countries and cultures. His system is, however, widely accepted and used by many companies. The important issue is that people from diverse cultures value things differently from each other and that all employees need to take these differences into account as they work.

MASTERING CHANGE

## *China: Where Change Is Everywhere*

Although China celebrated the fiftieth anniversary of the Communist victory over the Nationalist army in October 1999, the real celebration should date back to 1978, when Deng Xiaoping began the introduction of market reforms that led to the prosperous private-enterprise economy of today. Prior to 1978 everything was owned, operated, planned, and controlled by the government. Perhaps most symbolic, in 1978 farmers were allowed to sell some of their own produce on the open market. The progress of free enterprise was still slow through the 1980s and into the 1990s. Stock exchanges were established in 1990 and 1992, but the state still controlled the economy and most businesses were closely linked to the government. Finally, in 1997, President Jiang Zemin officially endorsed private enterprise and initiated the sale of many state-owned enterprises (SOE) to the private sector. In 1999, private businesses were officially recognized by a change in the constitution and the laws governing business throughout the country. However, the Communist Party still controls many key industries, called strategic industries, such as telecommunications, power generation, and banking. There is even still some disagreement among the Communist Party Central Committee as to just how far the liberalization of private enterprise should go.

> *"A profitable state sector is a major political issue that concerns the fate of the socialist system." — Jiang Zemin, President, People's Republic of China*

For the most part the SOEs are inefficient, slow, overstaffed, and losing money. Government subsidies to SOEs were more than $18 million (U.S.) in 1998 and were increasing. The state embarked on a campaign of trying to make them profitable by laying off workers and introducing modern technology and management techniques. But as they laid off workers, the party realized that these workers needed jobs and turned to the private sector to save them from massive unemployment. As a result, President Jiang and Premier Zhu Rongji urged the continued development of the private sector. By 2004 it is expected that more than sixty percent of the economy will be in the private sector, with more than seventy five percent of the workforce to be employed in the private sector.

Following decades of having to almost hide their private businesses via a charade of collectivist-style ownership, private-business owners can now flaunt their independence as a virtue, in effect advertising the fact that their businesses are privately owned and operated. In many cases, such independence may indicate higher quality, good prices, excellent service, and the most advanced technology when compared with SOEs. Such advantages are due to the ability of private enterprises to quickly respond to market forces, to change products and processes quickly, to hire and fire employees, and to develop new technologies. They even pay taxes, which the local and state governments appreciate. Even more independence is experienced out in the provinces, where the shadow of the Communist Party is not as long as in Beijing. In the more progressive provinces, such as Zhejiang and Jiangsu, the economy of each area is dominated by private enterprises.

References: Dexter Roberts, Sheri Prasso, and Mark L. Clifford, "China's New Revolution," *Business Week*, September 27, 1999, pp. 72–78; "Chinese Leaders Try to Regain Reform Momentum," *Dow Jones Newswires*, September 21, 1999, http://interactive.wsj.com/archive/retrieve.cgi?id=DI-CO-19990921-005664.djml (quote on p. 2).

# Dimensions of Diversity

People do not have to be from different countries to have different values. Within a single country, be it the United States, Italy, or the former Yugoslav Republic of Macedonia, there are significant differences in values, beliefs, and the normally accepted ways of doing things. In the United States, race and gender were considered the primary dimensions of diversity during the past two decades. The earliest civil rights laws were aimed at correcting racial segregation. Other laws have dealt with discrimination on the basis of gender, age, and disability. However, diversity entails broader issues than these. In the largest sense, the diversity of the workforce refers to all of the ways that employees are similar and different. The importance of renewed interest in diversity is that it helps organizations reap the benefits of all the similarities and differences among workers. For the purposes of discussion, we have divided the many aspects of diversity into primary and secondary dimensions.

## Primary Dimensions of Diversity

The **primary dimensions of diversity** are factors that are either inborn or exert extraordinary influence on early socialization: age, ethnicity, gender, physical abilities, race, and sexual orientation.

The **primary dimensions of diversity** are those factors that are either inborn or exert extraordinary influence on early socialization. These include age, race and ethnicity, gender, physical and mental abilities, and sexual orientation.[33] These factors make up the essence of who we are as human beings. They define us to others, and because of how others react to them, these factors also define us to ourselves. These characteristics are enduring aspects of our human personality, and they sometimes present extremely complex problems to managers. In this section, we highlight a few issues surrounding the primary dimensions.

**Age** The age issue is multifaceted and very individualistic. As people age they become more diverse in more ways. As the United States and the world's economy and labor productivity continue to grow, the demand for labor is expected to grow at 2 percent annually. At the same time, fewer people are entering the workforce, and the workforce is growing older overall as the baby boomers move into the over-fifty age range. The median age of the workforce increased from 35.3 years in 1986 to 38.2 years in 1998 and is expected to be 40.6 years by 2006.[34] In addition, the labor force participation rates for workers over sixty-five is expected to increase from 16 to 20 percent.[35] This trend subsumes another—workforce participation rates for women over age fifty are increasing faster than for men over fifty; thus, women constitute more of the increase in older workers.

*"The labor force of older workers—identified as having the fastest rate of population growth and the greatest increases in labor force participation—is expected to grow by 7 million." — Howard Fullerton, Bureau of Labor Statistics*[36]

Several aspects of these data require managerial attention. First, benefit packages may need to be changed to appeal to older workers. For example, for workers with no children at home, family benefit packages may not be as attractive. Second, as the population ages, more people are living well into their eighties. A man who reaches age sixty-five is expected to live fourteen more years. A woman who reaches age sixty-five is expected to live another eighteen-and-a-half years. The over-eighty-five age group is the fastest-growing segment of the population.[37] Therefore, this age group's children, who may be over fifty and still active in the workforce, may need to become primary caregivers for their elderly parents. Primary caregivers for the elderly face increased stress, take more unscheduled days off, have more late arrivals and early departures, have above-average telephone use, and are absent more often.

Older workers may need additional and different training in new technologies and equipment to accommodate their special needs. For example, consider the functioning of the eye. As people get older, the amount of light that reaches the retina of the eye falls by about 50 percent because of the gradual yellowing of the lens. This changes perceptions of blue, green, and gray. The average sixty-year-old needs two-and-a-half times as much light to read comfortably as the average twenty-year-old.[38] Differences also exist in manual dexterity, hearing, perception, cognition, strength, and agility. Managers will need to adjust physical facilities, equipment, and training methods to expect maximum productivity from the entire workforce. In the past, little allowance was made for a worker who could not conform to the standard equipment and expectations of the workplace. In the future, the workplace will need to adjust to older workers.

**Race and Ethnicity** Racial and ethnic cultural differences may be more important than most managers initially realize, because critical differences exist across cultures in attitudes toward, beliefs about, and values surrounding work. The data show that people of different racial and ethnic backgrounds are increasing in number and in percentage of the workforce. Although much has been accomplished in recent years, racial and ethnic minorities still believe that a significant barrier exists that keeps them from the top executive positions in U.S. companies. One of the primary reasons for turnover or attrition among women and minorities is the "glass ceiling" barrier that exists in U.S. companies. The diversity director in one high-tech company estimates that the cost of recruiting and training one new worker to replace one who voluntarily leaves exceeds $112,000.[39] Another cost is lower morale and productivity among those who do not leave. Companies today simply cannot afford to ignore the impact of racial and ethnic differences in the workforce. The glass ceiling is still in place for minorities and women, in spite of the years of progress and the new emphasis on valuing diversity.

**Gender** Women were one of the first groups to be emphasized in the early attempts at providing equal employment opportunity and affirmative action. Many organizations have always included at least some women, of course; the issue now is that women hold positions other than secretary, nurse, teacher, and receptionist. Many companies have discovered that women hold many other types of jobs and are moving into more all the time. Apple found that over 40 percent of the sales force were women, who were generating more than $1.5 billion in sales.[40] Xerox noted that their workforce changed significantly. For example, during the 1980s the number of women increased from 29 to 32 percent of the workforce, the number of female managers doubled from 10 to 20 percent, the number of female professionals increased from 18 to 29 percent, and the number of females in the sales force almost doubled from 22 to 41 percent.[41] After recognizing this trend, Xerox increased its efforts to move more women into sales, professional, and managerial jobs, and developed programs to help all employees work together in its newly diverse workforce.

Until recently, most managers assumed that women should be treated the same as men and that they had the same reactions to issues. This is not always the case, however. Following a sales meeting, for example, men often go to the hotel bar for relaxation and an inevitable continuation of discussions. Women, however, often feel uncomfortable having social drinks with the men in the bar, and there-

Nancy Hopkins, a professor of molecular biology at the Massachusetts Institute of Technology, had never complained about the subtle slights against female professors—lower pay, smaller offices, and token committee assignments. However, when a course she designed was canceled in favor of a similar course to be developed by a male professor, she fought back. Rather than suing the university, Hopkins and other female professors confronted the administration and formed a task force to study the issues. Relying on data the task force generated from surveys and analyses of records, the administration admitted that discrimination had caused the women to receive less in salary, space, awards, and resources than their male counterparts and began to develop ways to correct the problems.

fore are often excluded from the continued discussions. Similar feelings arise when men leave a meeting to go to golf clubs, some of which prohibit women. Situations such as these may exclude women from valuable socialization processes necessary for groups to coordinate activities and accomplish goals and may have the unintended but systematic effect of excluding women from top management positions. Companies have found simple solutions to some of these situations by having sales meetings in conference centers and bringing refreshments into the meeting rooms after the meetings so all can participate in the follow-up sessions. Hosting dinners in the conference center can also help keep everyone involved after the formal meeting. The increasing number of women in the workforce means that employees with different attitudes, backgrounds, and capabilities need to be utilized, possibly in different ways than were the norm in many organizations.

During the 1970s and early 1980s, the women's movement enabled women to make great strides toward true equality in society in general and in the workplace specifically. Despite these advances, women's wages are still lower than men's, and most U.S. organizations have a glass ceiling that excludes many women from upper-level positions. Moreover, in the late 1980s and 1990s, there seems to have been a type of backlash on the part of some men against the progress made by women. This backlash takes many forms. It may become apparent when men are asked about their views of the women's movement. When men are "passed over" for opportunities to get promotions, to get into some graduate schools, and for other forms of advancement or opportunity, they often blame the women's movement as a force behind reverse discrimination. Some people blame all sorts of social ills on the women's movement, including increases in crime, divorce, and stress levels at work.[42]

In reality, extreme positions for or against the women's movement may not be constructive, and efforts to solve gender-based problems and inequities may be hindered by various groups calling names and pointing fingers. For managers, it is important to recognize that strong feelings exist on both sides, and that addressing tensions in the workplace over equality for all types of workers is paramount if managers and workers are to get their work done and reach organizational goals.

**Different Abilities** An often misunderstood group, one that is more diverse than any other, is people whose abilities are in some way limited compared with those of the general population. Disabilities may be of many different types. Some persons have missing or nonfunctioning limbs, some have sensory impairments, others have problems related to diseases such as multiple sclerosis, and others have mental limitations of various kinds. The rights of these people are protected under the Americans with Disabilities Act and the Rehabilitation Act. Employers cannot discriminate in any way regarding employment of persons with disabilities, and employers must make reasonable accommodations in the workplace to assist employees on the job. These workers are best referred to as "differently abled" or "physically or mentally challenged" to indicate respect for the abilities that make them unique and able to make valuable contributions to the organization.[43]

Physically or mentally challenged people are just like everyone else except for their one disability. They have to live, eat, sleep, and support themselves by working. They are often excellent employees in jobs appropriate for their skill types and levels. Reasonable accommodations to allow people to work may include such matters as equipment purchase or modification, restructuring of jobs, reassignment to other jobs, making facilities accessible, modifying work schedules, and modifying examination and training materials.[44] Each case needs to be considered individually and accommodations made for that specific case. One accommodation that is often important is the reaction of coworkers to hiring a physically or mentally challenged person. It may take some training and personal accommodation for the other members of the work group to adjust.

Many companies have attempted to appropriately accommodate differently challenged workers. Lotus Development has a hiring program that works in conjunction with Greater Boston Rehabilitation Services to hire differently abled workers in its assembly, packing, and shipping departments. Lotus provides a shuttle bus to the plant from the local train station and provides job coaches, special equipment, and new training programs to ensure the success of each worker. In addition, other Lotus employees participate in awareness programs to ease the entry of the new workers into the company. Eastman Kodak's warehouse in Oak Brook, Illinois, includes five employees who are both deaf and mute. The order-filling accuracy of these employees exceeds that of other employees and is over 99 percent. Eastman Kodak accommodated these employees by placing them in an area that had no forklifts or other heavy equipment and by adding special telephones that use a keyboard and screen for communication.[45]

**Sexual Orientation** Another dimension of diversity that may make some people uncomfortable but which is receiving increasing attention in organizations is sexual orientation. As in the population in general, it is estimated that 10 percent of the workforce is homosexual. Homosexuals work in all types of industries, including finance, insurance, science, engineering, and computers.[46] Although some homosexuals no longer try to hide their sexual preference, many still feel that they must keep it a secret. A California judge ordered a Shell Oil subsidiary to pay $5.3 million in damages to a worker who was fired because of his homosexuality.[47] On the other hand, companies such as Levi Strauss, Apple Computer, Digital Equipment Corporation, Boeing, Du Pont, and Xerox have lesbian and gay groups that operate openly, holding meetings, orientation sessions, and special gay pride weeks. As open as some companies have become, however, many still complain that a glass ceiling exists for homosexual managers ready to advance to executive positions. Companies must also decide whether to extend dependent health coverage to gay and lesbian partners, as Kodak and IBM did in 1996.[48] Regardless of the comfort level, tolerance, and openness among companies, managers of the future will have workers who may have a different sexual orientation than themselves.

## Secondary Dimensions of Diversity

**Secondary dimensions of diversity** include factors that are important to us as individuals and to some extent define us to others but are less permanent and can be adapted or changed: educational background, geographic location, income, marital status, military experience, parental status, religious beliefs, and work experience.

**Secondary dimensions of diversity** include factors that matter to us as individuals and to some extent define us to others but which are less permanent than primary dimensions and can be adapted or changed. These include educational background, geographic location, income, marital status, military experience, parental status, religious beliefs, and work experience. These factors may influence our lives as much as the primary dimensions. Many veterans of the Persian Gulf War, for example, were profoundly affected by the experience of serving in the military.

The impact of secondary dimensions may differ at various times in our lives. For example, moving to another part of the country or world may be traumatic for a parent with several children; a person with no close ties or dependents, on the other hand, may find it exciting. Family experiences may also influence a manager's degree of sympathy with the disruptions of work life that sometimes occur because of personal responsibilities.

Employees enter the workforce with unique experiences and backgrounds that affect their perspective of work rules, work expectations, and personal concerns. Although employees may have essentially the same work hours, job description, tenure with the company, and compensation, their reactions to the work situation may differ significantly because of differences in these primary and secondary dimensions of diversity.

# Managing the Multicultural Organization

Taking advantage of diversity in organizations poses difficult challenges, but it also presents new opportunities. Simply announcing that the organization values diversity is not enough. It requires that management develop a **multicultural organization** in which employees of mixed backgrounds, experiences, and cultures can contribute and achieve their fullest potential to benefit both themselves and the organization. Management must plan to manage diversity throughout the organization and work hard to implement the plan.

The **multicultural organization** has six characteristics: pluralism, full structural integration, full integration of informal networks, an absence of prejudice and discrimination, equal identification among employees with organizational goals for majority and minority groups, and low levels of intergroup conflict.

## Managerial Behavior Across Cultures

Some individual variations in people from different cultures shape the behavior of both managers and employees. Other differences are much more likely to influence managerial behavior.[49] In general, these differences relate to managerial beliefs about the role of authority and power in the organization. For example, managers in Indonesia, Italy, and Japan tend to believe that the purpose

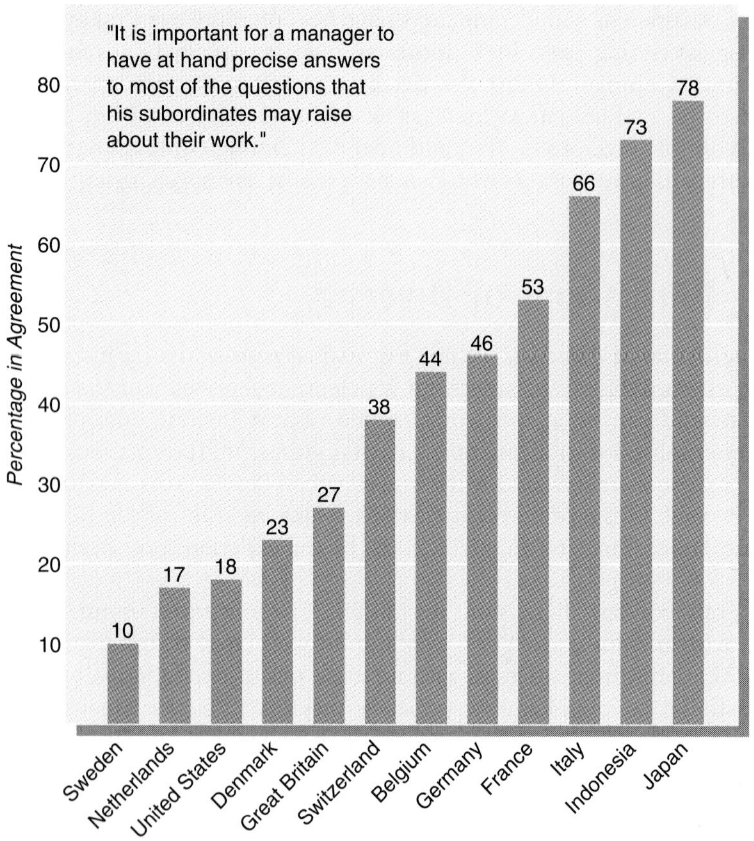


figure 3.4 **Differences Across Cultures in Managers' Beliefs About Answering Questions from Subordinates**

*Subordinates in various cultures have different beliefs regarding managers' ability to provide definite, precise answers to questions. Japan has the strongest expectations; Sweden has the weakest.*

Reference: Reprinted from *International Studies of Management and Organization*, vol. XIII, no. 1–2, Spring–Summer 1983, by permission of M. E. Sharpe, Inc., Armonk, N.Y. 10504.

of an organization structure is to let everyone know who his or her boss is (medium to high power distance). Managers in the United States, Germany, and Great Britain, in contrast, believe that organization structure is intended to coordinate group behavior and effort (low power distance). On another dimension, Italian and German managers believe it is acceptable to bypass one's boss to get things done, but among Swedish and British managers, bypassing one's superior is strongly prohibited.

Figure 3.4 illustrates findings on another interesting point. Managers in Japan strongly believe that a manager should be able to answer any question he or she is asked. Thus, they place a premium on expertise and experience. At the other extreme are Swedish managers, who have the least concern about knowing all the answers. They view themselves as problem solvers and facilitators who make no claim to omnipotence.

Some recent evidence suggests that managerial behavior is rapidly changing, at least among European managers. In general, these managers are becoming more career oriented, better educated, more willing to work cooperatively with labor, more willing to delegate, and more cosmopolitan.[50]

# Multicultural Organization as Competitive Advantage

Movement toward better management of a diverse workforce usually begins for one or more of three reasons. Some companies, such as Xerox, were obliged to develop better management of a workforce made more diverse by affirmative action. Other companies, such as Digital Equipment and Hewlett-Packard, grew very quickly to remain competitive and then realized that they had to work with multicultural constituencies. A third group of companies, which includes Avon Products, needed to have a diverse workforce to match the diversity in the marketplace.[51] Companies of all three types need to better manage their multicultural workforce to gain a competitive advantage in the marketplace. Business leaders, consultants, and academic scholars contend that having a multicultural organization can create competitive advantage in the six ways shown in Table 3.3: cost,

table 3.3

**Six Ways That Managing Diversity Can Create Competitive Advantage**

| Advantage | Contribution |
|---|---|
| Cost | Managing diversity well can trim the costs of integrating diverse workers. |
| Resource Acquisition | Companies that have the best reputation for managing diverse employees will have the best chance of hiring the best available diverse personnel. |
| Marketing | Increased insight and cultural sensitivity will improve the development and marketing of products and services for diverse segments of the population. |
| Creativity | Diversity of perspectives will improve levels of creativity throughout the organization. |
| Problem Solving | Problem solving and decision making will improve through groups with more diverse perspectives. |
| System Flexibility | Tolerance and valuing of diverse perspectives throughout the organization will make the organization more fluid, more flexible, and more responsive to environmental changes. |

Reference: Adapted from Taylor H. Cox and Stacy Blake, "Managing Cultural Diversity: Implications for Organizational Competitiveness," *Academy of Management Executive*, August 1991, p. 47. Used by permission of Academy of Management.

resource acquisition, marketing, creativity, problem solving, and system flexibility. Thus, a diverse workforce should be highly valued and managed well for reasons beyond the fact that doing so is socially responsible.[52]

Since the workforce is becoming more diverse, the companies that value and integrate diverse employees the fastest and the best will reap the most benefits. Lower personnel costs and improved quality of personnel are two obvious benefits for the company. In addition, access to diverse perspectives in problem solving, decision making, creativity, and product development and marketing activities is essential to creating a competitive advantage in the increasingly dynamic global marketplace.

## Creating the Multicultural Organization

A multicultural organization has six characteristics: pluralism, full structural integration, full integration of informal networks, an absence of prejudice and discrimination, equal identification with organizational goals for all groups, and low levels of intergroup conflict.[53] Developing the multicultural organization requires commitment from top management and a clear vision of the benefits of multiculturalism for the future of the organization. To achieve each of these characteristics requires specific activities, as shown in Table 3.4.

A **pluralistic organization** has diverse membership and takes steps to fully involve all people who differ from the dominant group.

A **pluralistic organization** is one that has mixed membership and takes steps to fully involve all people who differ from the dominant group. Creating pluralism requires training and orientation programs that increase awareness of cultural differences and build skills for working together. Programs that describe how people of different ages and genders differ in some respects but are similar in others can be included in programs for new and existing employees. Language and culture training can help employees in the majority group better understand those from

table 3.4

**Creating the Multicultural Organization: Above All—Top Management Support Throughout!**

| Characteristic | Tools |
|---|---|
| **Pluralism** | Training and orientation programs, ensuring minority group input, putting diversity into mission statements |
| **Full Structural Integration** | Education, training, affirmative action, performance appraisal and reward systems, benefits, work schedules |
| **Integration of Informal Networks** | Mentoring, social events, support groups |
| **Absence of Prejudice** | EEO seminars, focus groups, bias-reduction training programs, task forces |
| **Equal Identification with Goals** | Input of minority group into mission, goals, and strategies |
| **Minimal Intergroup Conflict** | Survey feedback, conflict reduction training |

Reference: Adapted from Taylor H. Cox, Jr., "The Multicultural Organization," *Academy of Management Executive,* August 1991, p. 41. Used by permission of Academy of Management.

different cultures. Companies such as Motorola and Pace Foods offer language training on company time and at company expense.

Organizations have several ways to ensure that minority groups have input. First, minorities should be included in regular meetings at all levels. For example, *USA Today*'s daily news meetings include members of varied racial, ethnic, education, and geographic groups.[54] Second, the organization must foster the development of minority advisory groups that meet regularly to discuss organizational issues and encourage top management to consult regularly with the groups. Organizations can also foster pluralism throughout the organization by explicitly stating in their mission statements and strategic policies that it is an integral part of the organization.

When an organization has minority-group members serving at all levels, performing all functions, and participating in all work groups, we say it has achieved full structural integration. This requires distributing education specialties and skill differences equally throughout the organization. Therefore, organizations must develop and support educational programs and skill building at all levels. They also must hire and promote minority-group members into positions at all levels and jobs that perform all organizational functions.

Performance measurement and reward systems, which are discussed in Chapter 8, also need to be changed to promote pluralism. Organizations need to determine how much managers incorporate multiculturalism into their work groups and whether they hire and promote with proper sensitivity to multicultural concerns. Desired changes need to be rewarded through formal incentives. Benefit plans and work schedules also need to be altered to accommodate differences in employee family situations, needs, and values.

Mentoring programs, special social events, and support groups for minorities can foster integration in informal networks. You might think such special groups and events would create more differences, but in practice they have the opposite effect. They give minority groups outlets to express their cultural identity and share part of themselves with dominant groups. Dominant group members can then better understand the cultural heritage and traditions of minority members.

Several means can be used to create a bias-free organization. Equal-opportunity seminars have been used to increase awareness among employees for quite a while. In addition, organizations can conduct in-house focus groups to examine attitudes and beliefs about cultural differences and organizational practices. They can run bias-reduction training programs, one- or two-day workshops designed to help employees identify and begin to modify negative attitudes toward people who are different. These programs usually include exercises and role plays that expose stereotypes about minority group members and help build the skills to eliminate these stereotypes. Another way to move toward a bias-free organization is to create task forces to monitor organizational policies and practices for evidence of unfairness. Such task forces need to be composed of employees from every level and those who perform the full range of organizational functions to ensure that top management is committed. All minorities should be represented to ensure that the full spectrum of views is considered.

Employees develop a sense of identity with the organization's mission, goals, and strategies as a result of all of the tools and techniques already discussed. When members of different groups participate fully in determining the organization's direction and deciding how to meet its goals, they better understand the organization and their place in it. Through training programs, mentoring programs, support groups, social events, and bias-free organization practices, employees who are different from the dominant group can become an integral part of the organization.

Intergroup conflict can be minimized in several ways. As discussed in Chapter 9, some forms of conflict can be healthy if they stimulate creativity in problem solving and decision making. However, conflict based on cultural differences that divides employees along cultural lines is usually considered unhealthy and detrimental to the multicultural organization. Survey feedback processes can be used to expose beliefs and attitudes toward others and to measure the success of the multicultural effort. Feedback to all relevant groups is important to ensure openness throughout the organization. Special training in conflict resolution has also been shown to help managers learn the skills of mediation and listening that are so important to managing conflict.

An integrated program involving activities of the sort described here can help the organization become truly multicultural. The transition is not easy or quick, but once multiculturalism is achieved, it can give to the organization advantages in the struggle to compete successfully.

# Synopsis

Workforce diversity is a function of the similarities and differences among employees in such characteristics as age, gender, ethnic heritage, physical or mental ability or disability, race, and sexual orientation. Managers of diverse work groups need to understand how their members' social conditioning affects their beliefs about work and must have the communication skills to develop confidence and self-esteem in their employees.

Stereotypes can lead to prejudice toward others; prejudice consists of judgments concerning the superiority or inferiority of others that can lead to exaggerating the worth of one group while disparaging the worth of others. Management systems built on stereotypes and prejudices are inappropriate for a diverse workforce.

Employment statistics show that the future workforce will be radically different from the workforce of today. The goal of valuing diversity is to utilize all of the differences among workers for the benefit of the workers and the organization.

International business has rapidly become an important part of almost every manager's life and is likely to become even more important in the future. Managers need to recognize that employees from different backgrounds are similar in some respects and different in others.

Diversity can be categorized as having primary and secondary dimensions. The primary dimensions of diversity are those that are either inborn or exert extraordinary influence on early socialization; dimensions of this type are age, ethnicity, gender, physical or mental abilities, race, and sexual orientation. Secondary dimensions of diversity include factors that are important to us as individuals and to some extent define us to others but which are less permanent and can be adapted or changed: educational background, geographic location, income, marital status, military experience, parental status, religious beliefs, and work experience.

A multicultural organization is one in which employees of different backgrounds, experiences, and cultures can contribute and achieve their fullest potential for the benefit of both themselves and the organization. Developing a multicultural organization is a significant step in managing a diverse workforce and may be crucial to sustaining a competitive advantage in the marketplace. A multicultural organization has six characteristics: pluralism, full structural integration, full integration of informal networks, an absence of prejudice and discrimination, equal identification with organizational goals among employees from both majority and minority groups, and low levels of intergroup conflict.

## Discussion Questions

1. Why do organizations need to be interested in managing diversity? Is it a legal or moral obligation or does it have some other purpose?
2. Summarize in your own words what the statistics tell us about the workforce of the future.
3. What are the two major differences between the primary and secondary dimensions of diversity? Which particular dimension seems to you to be the most difficult to deal with in organizations?
4. Identify ways in which the internationalization of business affects businesses in your community.
5. All things considered, do you think people from diverse cultures are more alike or more different? Explain the reasons for your answer.
6. What stereotypes exist about the motivational patterns of workers from other cultures?
7. What is the difference between assimilation of minority groups and valuing diversity in organizations?
8. Why does multiculturalism contribute to competitive advantage for an organization?
9. What are the characteristics of a multicultural organization?
10. Discuss three techniques that can contribute to the development of a multicultural organization.

## Organizational Behavior Case for Discussion

### Texaco Does It Wrong and Then Does It Right

November 1996: Texaco executives are caught on tape making racially biased remarks about an African-American who had filed a discrimination suit against the company and discussing how to destroy the evidence related to the case. Two weeks later, after the Reverend Jesse Jackson threatened a boycott of all Texaco products, Texaco agreed to settle the classaction discrimination suit for $176 million.

But the most important outcome is that Texaco made a commitment to turn around the discriminating culture of the organization. This is the story of that commitment.

The strategy for turning around the culture was a three-pronged one, with the oversight of a seven-member task force. Having a task force rather than a one-person overseer was significant in that it gave responsibility to people with different perspectives. Little things that might slip by one person were less likely to get overlooked with seven people watching. The strategy included (1) attracting a diverse workforce, (2) helping people reach their potential and achieve job satisfaction, and (3) setting up a "safety net" to help resolve disputes and grievances. The essence of the program is making diversity a competitive advantage and part of the company's overall business strategy. Texaco allocated $35 million to the task force to oversee all aspects of hiring, evaluation, pay, and promotion policies. The program has dozens of initiatives intended to create opportunities for minorities and women and includes an agreement for Texaco to report on its progress to the Equal Employment Opportunity Commission every year for five years.

One of the most controversial aspects of the program involves a bonus "pay for performance" plan tied to its diversity initiatives. Twenty percent of the annual cash bonuses for Texaco's top four hundred managers and executives are linked to increasing workplace diversity. In other words, in order to get 20 percent of their bonus, these top managers must demonstrate progress in the hiring and promotion of minorities and women and have high scores on a seven-point employee respect survey. Twenty percent can be a large amount for executives whose normal bonuses can be more than $100,000.

Some experts suggested that such a bonus system could be discriminatory and bad for the company if less qualified applicants were hired over more qualified applicants just to meet a quota. A Texaco human resource executive has claimed, however, that hiring and promotion goals are being met with no compromise of qualifications. Texaco's goals were to increase minority hiring from 23 percent to 29 percent and to increase the percentage of minorities in top jobs from 11 percent to 15 percent. Some have also argued that numerical quotas can often be achieved without corresponding changes in the mental attitude and treatment of minorities on the job. Texaco has faced that problem, however, and is committed to changing the thinking throughout the company. One initiative included a two-day training program that taught diversity not only as a racial or gender issue but as one that means accepting all types of international, cultural, educational, and individual differences among fellow employees. Texaco has also had to deal with the inevitable backlash from nonminorities, as well as the potential for separations and divisions within the company. Other features included a mentoring program, an ombudsman program, and a new alternative-dispute-resolution program.

Results? In the first year (1997), 36 percent of new hires were minorities, of which 49 percent were women; 20 percent of promotions were to minorities, of which 47 percent were women. At the end of 1998, Texaco agreed to pay $3.1 million to women managers who were paid less than men doing similar work. Texaco chairman and CEO Peter Bijur reported that in the first two years after the crisis (1997 and 1998), 59 percent of its new hires were women or from ethnic minorities and 49 percent of promotions were from these groups. In 1999, Texaco and Bijur received an award from A Better Chance, an African-American education group fronted by Oprah Winfrey, for making great strides in correcting the crisis and in recognition of Bijur's "outstanding commitment to diversity at Texaco." Bijur also recognizes that Texaco is not finished and promises continuing progress. In addition, Texaco has become symbolic of a situation that other companies want to avoid, and how to do so.

## Case Questions

1. What is Texaco doing to become a multicultural organization?
2. What is Texaco doing to convince its employees that it is serious?
3. Would you go to work for Texaco now? Why or why not?

References: Geoffrey Colvin, "The 50 Best Companies for Asians, Blacks, and Hispanics," *Fortune*, July 19, 1999, pp. 52–58; "Texaco Honored for Racial Policy," *Oil Daily*, June 23, 1999, Article A54975639, Item 9917400E; "Texaco to Pay Women $3.1 Million," *Oil Daily*, January 7, 1999, Article A53531519; Richard Kindleberger, "Texaco's Effort to Improve Climate for Minorities Has Mixed Results," *Knight-Ridder/Tribune Business News*, January 29, 1998, p. 129B1045; Ian Springsteel, "A Penny for Your Actions," *CFO, The Magazine for Senior Financial Executives*, August 1997, pp. 61–63.

# Experiencing Organizational Behavior

## Understanding Your Own Stereotypes and Attitudes Toward Others

**Purpose:** This exercise will help you better understand your own stereotypes and attitudes toward others.

**Format:** You will be asked to evaluate a situation and the assumptions you make in doing so. Then you will compare your results with those of the rest of the class.

**Procedure**

1. Read the situation described following to yourself, and decide who it is that is standing at your door and why you believe it to be that person. Make some notes as to your rationale for eliminating the other possibilities and selecting the one that you did. Answer the follow-up questions.
2. Working in small groups or with the class as a whole, discuss who might be standing at your door and why you believe it to be that person. Using the grid at the end of this exercise, record the responses of class members.
3. In class discussion, consider the stereotypes used to reach a decision and consider the following:
   a. How hard was it to let go of your original belief once you had formed it?
   b. What implications do first impressions of people have concerning how you treat them, what you expect of them, and your assessment of whether the acquaintance is likely to go beyond the initial stage?
   c. What are the implications of your responses to these questions concerning how you, as a manager, might treat a new employee? What will the impact be on that employee?
   d. What are the implications of your answers for yourself in terms of job hunting?

**Situation:** You have just checked into a hospital room for some minor surgery the next day. When you get to your room, you are told that the following people will be coming to speak with you within the next several hours.

1. The surgeon who will do the operation
2. A nurse
3. The secretary for the department of surgery
4. A representative of the company that supplies televisions to the hospital rooms
5. A technician who does laboratory tests
6. A hospital business manager
7. The dietitian

You have never met any of these people before and do not know what to expect.

About half an hour after your arrival, a woman who seems to be of Asian ancestry appears at your door dressed in a straight red wool skirt, a pink-and-white-striped polyester blouse with a bow at the neck, and red medium-high-heeled shoes that match the skirt. She is wearing gold earrings, a gold chain necklace, a gold wedding band, and a white hospital laboratory coat. She is carrying a clipboard.

### Follow-up Questions

1. Of the seven people listed, which of them is standing at your door? How did you reach this conclusion?
2. If the woman had not been wearing a white hospital laboratory coat, how might your perceptions of her have differed? Why?
3. If you find out that she is the surgeon who will be operating on you in the morning, and you thought initially that she was someone different, how confident do you now feel in her ability as a surgeon. Why?

| | Reasons | Number Who Made This Selection |
|---|---|---|
| Surgeon | | |
| Nurse | | |
| Secretary | | |
| Television Representative | | |
| Laboratory Technician | | |
| Business Manager | | |
| Dietitian | | |

Reference: Adapted from Janet W. Wohlberg and Scott Weighart, *OB in Action: Cases and Exercises*. Copyright © 1992 by Houghton Mifflin Company. Used by permission.

# Building Organizational Behavior Skills

## Cross-Cultural Awareness

The questions below are intended to provide insights into your awareness of other cultures. Please indicate the best answers to the questions listed below. There is no passing or failing answer. Use the following scale, recording it in the space before each question.

1 = definitely no 2 = not likely 3 = not sure
4 = likely 5 = definitely yes

_____ 1. I can effectively conduct business in a language other than my native language.

_____ 2. I can read and write a language other than my native language with great ease.

_____ 3. I understand the proper protocol for conducting a business card exchange in at least two countries other than my own.

_____ 4. I understand the role of the *keiretsu* in Japan or the *chaebol* in Korea.

_____ 5. I understand the differences in manager-subordinate relationships in two countries other than my own.

_____ 6. I understand the differences in negotiation styles in at least two countries other than my own.

_____ 7. I understand the proper protocols for gift giving in at least three countries.

_____ 8. I understand how a country's characteristic preference for individualism versus collectivism can influence business practices.

_____ 9. I understand the nature and importance of demographic diversity in at least three countries.

_____ 10. I understand my own country's laws regarding giving gifts or favors while on international assignments.

______ 11. I understand how cultural factors influence the sales, marketing, and distribution systems of different countries.

______ 12. I understand how differences in male-female relationships influence business practices in at least three countries.

______ 13. I have studied and understand the history of a country other than my native country.

______ 14. I can identify the countries of the European Community without looking them up.

______ 15. I know which gestures to avoid using overseas because of their obscene meanings.

______ 16. I understand how the communication style practiced in specific countries can influence business practices.

______ 17. I know in which countries I can use my first name with recent business acquaintances.

______ 18. I understand the culture and business trends in major countries in which my organization conducts business.

______ 19. I regularly receive and review news and information from and about overseas locations.

______ 20. I have access to and utilize a cultural informant before conducting business at an overseas location.

______ = Total Score

When you have finished, add up your score and compare it with those of others in your group. Discuss the areas of strengths and weaknesses of the group members. [Note: This brief instrument has not been scientifically validated and is to be used for classroom discussion purposes only.]

Reference: Neal R. Goodman, "Cross-Cultural Training for the Global Executive," in Richard W. Brislin and Tomoko Yoshida (eds.), *Improving Intercultural Interactions*, pp. 35–36, copyright © 1994 by Sage Publications, Inc. Reprinted by permission of Sage Publications, Inc.

## Developing OB Internet Skills

**Introduction:** The Internet is useful for many different types of activities in addition to emailing your friends. For managers it is perhaps most useful as a source of information. One way to use the Internet is to find out what information is available on a certain topic. For example, a manager could use the Internet to find out what other companies are doing related to workforce diversity. This exercise will let you practice finding and using some of that information.

**Internet Assignment:** This chapter described several ways that companies can become more multicultural, as well as different types of programs to increase the diversity of the workforce. Assume that the president of the company has charged you with the responsibility for finding out what other companies are doing to increase the hiring of qualified minorities and women. What types of programs are other companies finding successful? Search the Internet to look for answers to these questions.

**Follow-up:** Evaluate which sites provided the most useful information and answer the following questions:

1. Which sites did you find to have the most information? Did you use a library search engine to look for articles on the topic? Which ones were most useful? Why?
2. To what extent do you feel that you could rely on information from these sites to make critical decisions regarding workforce diversity?
3. Were any of the sites you found obviously biased toward one way of thinking or toward a particular group?

# Part 1 Integrative Running Case

## The AOL–Time Warner Deal

January 2000 brought with it global celebrations of the new millennium. It brought relief for some that the world had not been shut down by the Y2K bug, and disdain from others, who said the whole thing had been blown out of proportion to begin with. Some people saw it as a time of new beginnings; others saw it simply as the next page on their calendar. January 2000 also marked one of the most significant mergers in the history of business—the joining of America Online (AOL) and Time Warner into a new enterprise that some observers predicted would rewrite the rules of business for years to come.

AOL was born in the 1980s from the creative mind of Stephen Case. Case, in charge of new product development for Pizza Hut at the time, saw enormous potential in the emerging technologies that are today know collectively as the Internet. Case left Pizza Hut in 1983 and joined a fledgling online service for Atari computer users. After a few years of providing various specialty online services, this enterprise launched nationwide service in 1989 and changed its name to America Online in 1991. The firm went public, and Case was named CEO in 1992. AOL grew rapidly over the rest of the decade, attracting millions of subscribers and swallowing rival CompuServe and premier Internet portal Netscape along the way.

Time Warner, on the other hand, is an old-line company tracing its roots back almost a hundred years. Time, Inc. was founded in 1922 with the launch of its namesake magazine *Time*. Over decades Time also began publication of such periodicals as *Fortune*, *Sports Illustrated*, and *People*, and created the cable television network HBO. Warner Brothers was born alongside the Hollywood movie industry when it produced such classics as *Little Caesar* and *Casablanca*. Warner eventually grew to encompass a movie studio, television studios, cable television operations, and a publishing business headlined by such properties as *Superman* comics and *Mad* magazine. These two firms merged in 1989 to create Time Warner; this new media giant, led by CEO Gerald Levin, subsequently acquired TBS (consisting of CNN and other cable networks); launched numerous new magazines, including *Entertainment Weekly*; and started a new broadcast television network.

As the 1990s drew to a close, both AOL's Case and Time Warner's Levin realized that their firms had some major strategic weakness. AOL, for example, lacked two key competitive assets. For one thing, most of its services were carried by and delivered through telephone wire; many experts, though, were predicting that the future of this industry rests on so-called broadband technology such as cable television. And for another, AOL itself had precious little "content" to deliver—it simply connected information sources with users who wanted access to that information.

Time Warner, meanwhile, had both of the things AOL desperately needed. Time Warner Cable, for example, has over 13 million subscribers. And information content was the very thing Time Warner was based on—magazines, books, music, movies, and television programming. But the venerable media company itself, like so many of its old-line brethren, had failed to figure out for itself how to make the transformation to the e-world. At the time the merger was announced, Time Warner had already made a commitment of $500 million to develop a digital division, but most observers were unenthusiastic or downright skeptical about its ability to become a player.

The idea for a partnership was hatched in September 1999 at an international meeting of high-level CEOs in Paris; the players kept talking and met again two weeks later in Shanghai at a similar event. In October, Case called Levin directly and proposed a merger. Serious negotiations began in November. Two key AOL executives traveled to New York to meet with a senior vice president from Time Warner. The three managers locked themselves in a conference room and used poster-sized sheets of paper to sketch out how a combined firm might look. These sheets were then taken back to AOL headquarters for further examination. Finally, all the details were worked out, and then the only thing left was for the key players to mull things over and decide whether or not to proceed.

Levin made his decision during the millennium weekend while watching CNN's coverage of celebrations around the world. But because he and then Case still had to negotiate a few remaining details, a final accord wasn't reached until January 6, 2000. After the agreements were all signed, the deal was announced to a stunned business community on Monday, January 10. One observer went so far as to call it the most transformational event in his career. And indeed, the merger was so intriguing that many experts were simply at a loss to figure out what it truly means.

There were also literally thousands of unanswered questions. For example, while Case and Levin are, for the time being, at least coequals, a key player in the deal is Bob Pittman, an executive who worked for Time Warner for years before moving to AOL a few years ago. His responsibilities will include actually implementing the merger, a task that may well position him to eventually lead the new enterprise. Other questions relate to the organization design the new firm will adopt, the kind of culture that will emerge, and who will stay—and who will leave. Regardless of the answers to these questions, though, one thing is certain: it promises to be an interesting ride!

## Case Questions

1. How does the history of AOL and Time Warner help you to better understand the dynamics of this merger?
2. Identify how various management functions, roles, and skills are illustrated in this case.
3. Discuss how the various organizational and environment challenges are illustrated in this case.
4. In what ways might diversity have played a role in the merger?

References: "Happily Ever After?" *Time*, January 24, 2000, pp. 38–43; "Welcome to the 21st Century," *Business Week*, January 24, 2000, pp. 36–44; "You've Got Time Warner," *Wall Street Journal*, January 11, 2000, pp. B1, B12; "Deal Ignites Tech, Media Stocks," *USA Today*, January 11, 2000, pp. 1B, 2B.

chapter

# 4

# Foundations of Individual Behavior

## Management Preview

Think about human behavior as a jigsaw puzzle. Puzzles consist of various pieces that fit together in precise ways. And of course, no two puzzles are exactly alike. They have different numbers of pieces, the pieces are of different sizes and shapes, and they fit together in different ways. The same can be said of human behavior and its determinants. Each of us is a whole picture, like a fully assembled jigsaw puzzle, but the puzzle pieces that define us and the way those pieces fit together are unique. Thus, every person in an organization is fundamentally different from everyone else. To be successful, managers must recognize that these differences exist and attempt to understand them. In this chapter we explore some of the key characteristics that differentiate people from one another in organizations. We first investigate the psychological nature of individuals in organizations. We then look at elements of people's personalities that can influence behavior and consider individual attitudes and their role in organizations. In subsequent sections we examine perception and creativity. We close this chapter with an examination of various kinds of workplace behaviors that affect organizational performance. We begin, however, by describing how Levi Strauss & Co. has felt it necessary to enact painful changes in its relationship with its employees. ■

Levi Strauss & Co. and the ubiquitous denim blue jeans it sells around the world have been virtual icons for as long as baby-boomers can remember. The firm can trace its roots back to the mid-nineteenth century, when its namesake immigrated to the United States from Bavaria. Shortly after arriving in San Francisco during the California gold rush, Levi Strauss decided that it was a safer bet to produce equipment for other miners than it was to set out with his own pick and shovel. Work pants crafted from heavy canvas proved to be his most successful product, and the rest, as they say, is history.

Strauss began coloring the pants with blue pigments to hide dirt and grime and enlisted the aid of a friend to provide what would become the trademark rivets to key stress points. The firm grew slowly but surely for decades, always led by one of Strauss's direct descendants (the firm is led today by Robert D. Haas, Levi Strauss's great-great-grandnephew). But Levi's real growth started in the late 1950s, when its denim jeans became a virtual uniform for the youth of the United States. The momentum continued into the 1960s as denim took its place alongside incense, tie-dyed shirts, peace signs, and long hair as symbols of a rebellious youth. And as the baby-boomers of the 1950s and 1960s grew into adulthood, Levi's jeans became a fashion staple. Indeed, even the name Levi's became almost synonymous with blue jeans. During the 1970s through the 1990s, Levi's also expanded rapidly overseas and today sells its products in more than seventy countries.

Over a period of decades, Levi's also forged an innovative relationship with its employees. High levels of job security, an innovative reward structure, and an open and participative approach to management had created a loyal and dedicated workforce that helped keep the organization at the top of its industry. Indeed, when experts first began ranking "best places to work," Levi Strauss was always near the top of the list. Many employees spent their entire careers at Levi, seeing it almost like family and defending it against any and all critics.

*"You can stretch denim over a wide butt, but you can't stretch it over too many generations. The problem is, your parents wore Levi's, and kids want to wear something different." — Al Ries, Atlanta-based marketing consultant**

But as the decade of the nineties grew to a close, Levi Strauss seemed to hit a wall. And as a result, the firm found it necessary to reexamine every aspect of its business operations while simultaneously redefining its relationship with its workforce. The catalyst for change was a relatively sudden drop in market share. For example, in 1990 Levi held about one-third of the jeans market in the United States. But by the end of the decade, that figure had been cut in half. Especially disturbing was the fact that today's young consumers had particularly seemed to lose interest in Levi's products.

Faced with this alarming trend, company executives began an intense and detailed period of introspection to find out what was happening to the company. Their conclusion was that they had been so successful with their core baby-boomer consumers that they had essentially neglected younger consumers. As a result, top-end design brands like Tommy Hilfilger and Ralph Lauren and discounted store brands sold at Sears and J.C. Penney had seized significant market share from Levi. In addition, the firm's cost structure was out of line with that of other clothing manufacturers, who had already moved most of their production to lower-cost facilities in other countries. In contrast, Levi had tried to maintain most of its production inside the United States, even though labor costs in this country are higher than at many other locations.

Once they saw their problem, Levi managers took quick action along a number of fronts. Most painfully, in 1997 the firm announced that it was closing eleven U.S. factories and laying off a third of its North American workforce—its first layoff in history. In 1999, another twenty-two plants were shuttered and almost six thousand more workers released. Needless to say, these steps dramatically and unalterably changed the firm's relationship with its workforce. Its previously loyal workers quickly became disenchanted and embittered, and went from being the company's staunchest defenders to its biggest critics.

The company also acknowledged that it needed to alter the composition of its executive team to boost creativity and market knowledge. Too many company officials, executives said, had come up through the ranks and knew only one way of doing things—the old tried-and-true Levi's way. One of Levi's present goals is therefore to fill 30 percent of all new management jobs with outsiders. Experts agree that it will take the firm a while to get its act together again, but they also acknowledge that the changes seem to fit the situation as well as a pair of the firm's jeans fit after a long day at the office.[1] ■

The success previously enjoyed by Levi Strauss can be attributed to a number of things. Clearly, however, the loyalty and dedication of its workforce played a major role. The company and its workers had forged a mutually beneficial bond based on trust and security. But the recent steps taken by the company have altered that bond and are leading to a new definition of the relationship between Levi's and its workers. Just as its workers played a big role in the firm's past successes, so too will Levi's ability to successfully redefine its relationship with its employees be pivotal in the future. The key to how this might be done is an understanding of people in organizations and the various elements and characteristics that contribute to determining how and in what form they are willing to engage in behaviors that will benefit the organization.

# People in Organizations

As a starting point for understanding the behavior of people in organizations, in turn, we examine the basic nature of the individual-organization relationship. Understanding this relationship helps us appreciate the nature of individual differences. That is, these differences play a critical role in determining various important workplace behaviors of special relevance to managers.

## Psychological Contracts

Whenever we buy a car or sell a house, both buyer and seller sign a contract that specifies the terms of the agreement—who pays what to whom, when it is paid, and so forth. A psychological contract resembles a standard legal contract in some ways, but is less formal and well defined. Specifically, a **psychological contract** is a person's overall set of expectations regarding what he or she will contribute to the organization and what the organization will provide in return.[2] Unlike a business contract, a psychological contract is not written on paper, nor are all of its terms explicitly negotiated.

A **psychological contract** is a person's set of expectations regarding what he or she will contribute to the organization and what the organization, in return, will provide to the individual.

Figure 4.1 illustrates the essential nature of a psychological contract. The individual makes a variety of **contributions** to the organization—such things as effort, skills, ability, time, and loyalty. Jill Henderson, a branch manager for Merrill Lynch, uses her knowledge of financial markets and investment opportunities to help her clients make profitable investments. Her MBA in finance, coupled with hard work and motivation, has led her to become one of the firm's most promising young managers. The firm believed she had these attributes when it hired her, of course, and expected that she would do well.

An individual's **contributions** to an organization include such things as effort, skills, ability, time, and loyalty.

| Contributions from the Individual | Inducements from the Organization |
|---|---|
| ■ Effort | ■ Pay |
| ■ Ability | ■ Job Security |
| ■ Loyalty | ■ Benefits |
| ■ Skills | ■ Career Opportunities |
| ■ Time | ■ Status |
| ■ Competencies | ■ Promotion Opportunities |

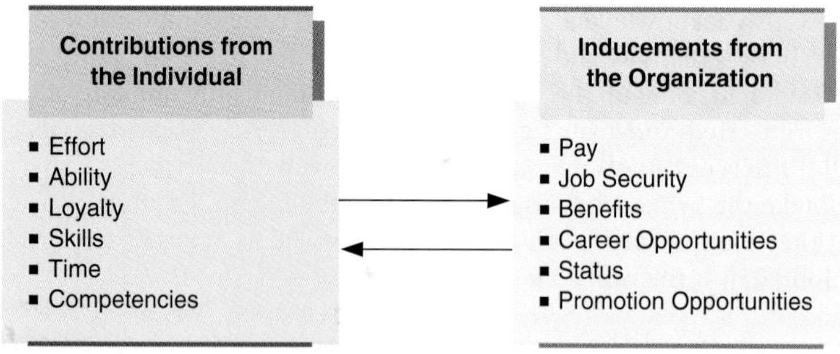

figure **4.1**   **The Psychological Contract**

*Psychological contracts govern the basic relationship between people and organizations. Individuals contribute such things as effort and loyalty. Organizations, in turn, offer such inducements as pay and job security.*

Organizations provide **inducements** to individuals in the form of tangible and intangible rewards.

In return for these contributions, the organization provides **inducements** to the individual. Some inducements, such as pay and career opportunities, are tangible rewards. Others, such as job security and status, are more intangible. Jill Henderson started at Merrill Lynch at a very competitive salary and has received an attractive wage increase each of the six years she has been with the firm. She has also been promoted twice and expects another promotion—perhaps to a larger office—in the near future.

In this instance, both Jill Henderson and Merrill Lynch apparently perceive that the psychological contract is fair and equitable. Both will be satisfied with the relationship and will do what they can to continue it. Henderson is likely to continue to work hard and effectively, and Merrill Lynch is likely to continue to increase her salary and give her promotions. In other situations, however, things might not work out as well. If either party sees an inequity in the contract, that party may initiate a change. The employee might ask for a pay raise or promotion, put forth less effort, or look for a better job elsewhere. The organization can also initiate change by training the worker to improve his or her skills, transferring the employee to another job, or firing the person.

All organizations face the basic challenge of managing psychological contracts. They want value from their employees, and they need to give employees the right inducements. For instance, underpaid employees may perform poorly or leave for better jobs elsewhere. Similarly, as illustrated in the cartoon, an employee may even occasionally start to steal organizational resources as a way to

Psychological contracts play an important role in the relationship between an organization and its employees. As long as both parties agree that the contributions provided by an employee and the inducements provided by the organization are balanced, both parties are satisfied and will likely maintain their relationship. But if a serious imbalance occurs, one or both parties may attempt to change the relationship. As illustrated here, for example, an employee who feels sufficiently dissatisfied may even resort to using company assets for his or her own personal gain.

Reference: DILBERT reprinted by permission of United Feature Syndicate, Inc.

balance the psychological contract. Overpaying employees who contribute little to the organization, though, incurs unnecessary costs.

Recent trends in downsizing and cutbacks have complicated the process of managing psychological contracts. For example, many organizations used to offer at least reasonable assurances of job permanence as a fundamental inducement to employees. Now, however, job permanence is less likely, so alternative inducements may be needed.[3] This is exactly the circumstance faced by Levi Strauss, as detailed earlier. Among the new forms of inducements some companies are providing are such things as additional training opportunities and a wide array of new benefits, such as recreational facilities, personal growth programs, and personal legal, career, and tax advice.[4]

*"Loyalty. Gratitude. Fortitude. They're dead, man. And who's the culprit? Maybe corporate America. After all, it was the big companies that in the late 1980s and early 1990s ended the traditional employment contract."* — *Nina Munk, business writer*[5]

Increased globalization of business also complicates the management of psychological contracts. For example, the array of inducements that employees deem to be of value varies across cultures. U.S. workers tend to value individual rewards and recognition, but Japanese workers are more likely to value group-based rewards and recognition. Workers in Mexico and Germany highly value leisure time and may thus prefer more time off from work, whereas workers in China place a lower premium on time off. A few years ago the Lionel Train Company, maker of toy electric trains, moved its operations to Mexico to capitalize on cheaper labor. The firm encountered problems, however, when it could not hire enough motivated employees to maintain quality standards and ended up making a costly move back to the United States.

A related problem faced by international businesses is the management of psychological contracts for expatriate managers. In some ways, this process is more like a formal contract than are other employment relationships. Managers selected for a foreign assignment, for instance, are usually given some estimate of the duration of the assignment and receive various adjustments in their compensation package—cost-of-living adjustments, education subsidies for children, personal travel expenses, and so forth. When the assignment is over, the manager must then be integrated back into the domestic organization. During the time of the assignment, however, the organization itself may have changed in many ways—new managers, new coworkers, new procedures, new business practices, and so forth. Thus, returning managers may very well come back to an organization that is quite different from the one they left and to a job quite different from what they expected.[6]

## The Person-Job Fit

**Person-job fit** is the extent to which the contributions made by the individual match the inducements offered by the organization.

One specific aspect of managing psychological contracts is managing the person-job fit. A good **person-job fit** is one in which the employee's contributions match the inducements the organization offers. In theory, each employee has a specific set of needs that he or she wants fulfilled and a set of job-related behaviors and abilities to contribute. If the organization can take perfect advantage of those behaviors and abilities and exactly fulfill the employee's needs, it will have achieved a perfect person-job fit.[7]

Understanding and managing the person-job fit is an important element in effective psychological contracts. For example, consider the case of Susan Latham, a professional animal handler. Latham has appeared in numerous commercials and in television and movie roles handling various animals. She is also a highly regarded animal trainer even when she is off-screen. It takes a person with special abilities indeed to work with snakes, rats, bullfrogs, dogs, cats, donkeys, and bears—all of which she has done. One reason she excels is because she is both very skilled in working with animals and also genuinely enjoys what she does. Thus, she has a very advanced level of person-job fit.

Of course, such a precise person-job fit is seldom achieved. For one thing, hiring procedures are imperfect. Managers can estimate employee skill levels when making hiring decisions and can improve them through training, but even simple performance dimensions are hard to measure objectively and validly. For another, both people and organizations change. An employee who finds a new job stimulating and exciting to begin with may find the same job boring and monotonous a few years later. An organization that adopts new technology needs new skills from its employees. Finally, each person is unique. Measuring skills and performance is difficult enough. Assessing attitudes and personality is far more complex. Each of these individual differences makes matching individuals with jobs a difficult and complex process.[8]

## Individual Differences

**Individual differences** are personal attributes that vary from one person to another.

As already noted, every individual is unique. **Individual differences** are personal attributes that vary from one person to another. Individual differences may be physical, psychological, and emotional. The individual differences that characterize a specific person make that person unique. As we see in the sections that follow, basic categories of individual differences include personality, attitudes, perception, and creativity. First, however, we need to note the importance of the situation in assessing the individual's behavior.

Are the specific differences that characterize a given person good or bad? Do they contribute to or detract from performance? The answer, of course, is that it depends on the circumstances. One person may be dissatisfied, withdrawn, and negative in one job setting but satisfied, outgoing, and positive in another. Working conditions, coworkers, and leadership are just a few of the factors that affect how a person performs and feels about a job. Thus, whenever managers attempt to assess or account for individual differences among their employees, they must also be sure to consider the situation in which behavior occurs.

Since managers need to establish effective psychological contracts with their employees and achieve optimal fits between people and jobs, they face a major challenge in attempting to understand both individual differences and contributions in relation to inducements and contexts. A good starting point in developing this understanding is to appreciate the role of personality in organizations.

# Personality and Organizations

The **personality** is the relatively stable set of psychological attributes that distinguish one person from another.

The **"big five" personality traits** are a set of fundamental traits that are especially relevant to organizations.

**Agreeableness** is the ability to get along with others.

**Conscientiousness** refers to the number of goals on which a person focuses.

**Personality** is the relatively stable set of psychological attributes that distinguish one person from another.[9] A longstanding debate among psychologists—often expressed as "nature versus nurture"—is the extent to which personality attributes are inherited from our parents (the "nature" argument) or shaped by our environment (the "nurture" argument). In reality, both biological and environmental factors play important roles in determining our personalities.[10] Although the details of this debate are beyond the scope of our discussion here, managers should strive to understand basic personality attributes and how they can affect people's behavior in organizational situations, not to mention employees' perceptions of and attitudes toward the organization.

## The "Big Five" Personality Traits

Psychologists have identified literally thousands of personality traits and dimensions that differentiate one person from another. But in recent years, researchers have identified five fundamental traits that are especially relevant to organizations. Because these five traits are so important and because they are currently receiving so much attention, they are now commonly called the **"big five" personality traits.**[11] Figure 4.2 illustrates these traits.

figure 4.2 **The "Big Five" Personality Framework**

*The "big five" personality framework is currently very popular among researchers and managers. These five dimensions represent fundamental personality traits presumed to be important in determining the behaviors of individuals in organizations. In general, experts agree that personality traits closer to the left end of each dimension are more positive in organizational settings, whereas traits closer to the right are less positive.*

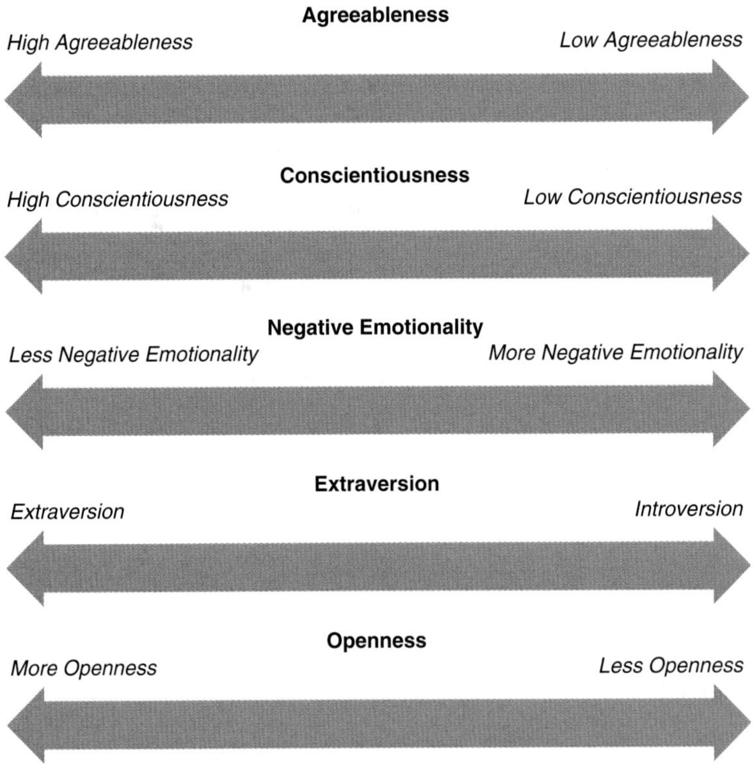


**Agreeableness** refers to a person's ability to get along with others. Agreeableness causes some people to be gentle, cooperative, forgiving, understanding, and good-natured in their dealings with others. But it results in others being irritable, short-tempered, uncooperative, and generally antagonistic toward other people. Researchers have not yet fully investigated the effects of agreeableness, but it seems likely that highly agreeable people are better at developing good working relationships with coworkers, subordinates, and higher-level managers, whereas less agreeable people are not likely to have particularly good working relationships. The same pattern might extend to relationships with customers, suppliers, and other key organizational constituents.

**Conscientiousness** refers to the number of goals on which a person focuses. People who focus on relatively few goals at one time are likely to be organized, systematic, careful, thorough, responsible, and self-disciplined; they tend to focus on a small number of goals at one time. Others, however, tend to pursue a wider array of goals, and, as a result, are more disorganized, careless, and irresponsible, as well as less thorough and less self-disciplined. Research has found that more conscientious people tend to be higher performers than less conscientious people in a variety of different jobs.[12] This pattern seems logical, of course, since conscientious people take their jobs seriously and approach their jobs in a highly responsible fashion.

**Negative emotionality** is characterized by moodiness and insecurity; those who have little negative emotionality are better able to withstand stress.

The third of the "big five" personality dimensions is **negative emotionality**. People with less negative emotionality are relatively poised, calm, resilient, and secure; people with more negative emotionality are more excitable, insecure, reactive, and subject to extreme mood swings. People with less negative emotionality might be expected to better handle job stress, pressure, and tension. Their stability might also lead them to be seen as being more reliable than their less stable counterparts.

**Extraversion** is the quality of being comfortable with relationships; the opposite extreme, introversion, is characterized by more social discomfort.

**Extraversion** reflects a person's comfort level with relationships. Extroverts are sociable, talkative, assertive, and open to establishing new relationships. Introverts are much less sociable, talkative, and assertive and more reluctant to begin new relationships. Research suggests that extroverts tend to be higher overall job performers than introverts, and that they are more likely to be attracted to jobs based on personal relationships, such as sales and marketing positions.

**Openness** is the capacity to entertain new ideas and to change as a result of new information.

Finally, **openness** reflects a person's rigidity of beliefs and range of interests. People with high levels of openness are willing to listen to new ideas and to change their own ideas, beliefs, and attitudes in response to new information. They also tend to have broad interests and to be curious, imaginative, and creative. On the other hand, people with low levels of openness tend to be less receptive to new ideas and less willing to change their minds. Further, they tend to have fewer and narrower interests and to be less curious and creative. People with more openness might be expected to be better performers because of their flexibility and the likelihood that they will be better accepted by others in the organization. Openness may also encompass a person's willingness to accept change; people with high levels of openness may be more receptive to change, whereas people with little openness may resist change.

The "big five" framework continues to attract the attention of both researchers and managers. The potential value of this framework is that it encompasses an integrated set of traits that appear to be valid predictors of certain behaviors in certain situations. Thus, managers who can both understand the framework and assess these traits in their employees are in a good position to understand how and why they behave as they do.[13] On the other hand, managers must be careful to not overestimate their ability to assess the "big five" traits in others. Even assessment using the most rigorous and valid measures is likely to be somewhat imprecise. Another limitation of the "big five" framework is that it is primarily based on research conducted in the United States. Thus, its generalizability to other cultures presents unanswered questions. Even within the United States a variety of other factors and traits are also likely to affect behavior in organizations.

## The Myers-Briggs Framework

Another interesting approach to understanding personalities in organizations is the Myers-Briggs framework. This framework, based on the classical work of Carl Jung, differentiates people in terms of four general dimensions: sensing, intuiting, judging, and perceiving. Higher and lower positions in each of the dimensions are used to classify people into one of sixteen different personality categories.[14]

**Locus of control** is the extent to which people believe their circumstances are a function of their own actions versus external factors beyond their control.

A person's **self-efficacy** is that person's beliefs about his or her capabilities to perform a task.

The Myers-Briggs Type Indicator (MBTI) is a popular questionnaire some organizations use to assess personality types. Indeed, it is among the most popular selection instruments used today, with as many as 2 million people taking it each year. Research suggests that the MBTI is a very useful method for determining communication styles and interaction preferences. In terms of personality attributes, however, questions exist about both the validity and the stability of the MBTI.

Locus of control, the extent to which people believe that their behavior has a real effect on what happens to them, is a very important personality trait. Kimberly Davis is an excellent example of someone with an internal locus of control—a strong belief that people are in control of their own lives. She is a general partner in IDG Ventures, a California-based venture capital firm. Davis scrutinizes about ten to fifteen proposals a week for her company to help fund; she actually funds only three or four per year. She bases her decisions in part on how likely she thinks it is that IDG's investment will help lead to success in the new ventures. Thus, Davis clearly thinks her decisions will shape the consequences of those decisions.

## Other Personality Traits at Work

Besides the "big five" and the characteristics assessed by the Myers-Briggs framework, several other personality traits influence behavior in organizations. Among the most important are locus of control, self-efficacy, authoritarianism, Machiavellianism, self-esteem, and risk propensity.

**Locus of control** is the extent to which people believe that their behavior has a real effect on what happens to them.[15] Some people, for example, believe that if they work hard they will succeed. They may also believe that people who fail do so because they lack ability or motivation. People who believe that individuals are in control of their lives are said to have an internal locus of control. Other people think that fate, chance, luck, or other people's behavior determines what happens to them. For example, an employee who fails to get a promotion may attribute that failure to a politically motivated boss or just bad luck, rather than to her or his own lack of skills or poor performance record. People who think that forces beyond their control dictate what happens to them are said to have an external locus of control.

**Self-efficacy** is a related but subtly different personality characteristic. A person's self-efficacy is that person's beliefs about his or her capabilities to perform a task.[16] People with high self-efficacy believe that they can perform well on a specific task, but people with low self-efficacy tend to doubt their ability to perform a specific task. Self-assessments of ability contribute to self-efficacy, but so does the individual's personality. Some people simply have more self-confidence than others. This belief in their ability to perform a task effectively results in their being more self-assured and better able to focus their attention on performance.[17]

**Authoritarianism** is the extent to which a person believes that power and status differences are appropriate within hierarchical social systems such as organizations.

Another important personality characteristic is **authoritarianism**, the extent to which a person believes that power and status differences are appropriate within hierarchical social systems such as organizations.[18] For example, people who are highly authoritarian may accept directives or orders from someone with more authority purely because the other person is "the boss." On the other hand, people who are not highly authoritarian, although they may still carry out reasonable directives from the boss, are more likely to question things, express disagreement with the boss, and even refuse to carry out orders if they are for some reason objectionable. A highly authoritarian manager may be relatively autocratic and demanding, and highly authoritarian subordinates are more likely to accept this behavior from their leader. On the other hand, a less authoritarian manager may allow subordinates a bigger role in making decisions, and less authoritarian subordinates respond positively to this behavior.[19] (This trait is also quite similar to the concept of power orientation discussed in Chapter 3.)

People who possess the personality trait of **Machiavellianism** behave to gain power and control the behavior of others.

**Machiavellianism** is another important personality trait. This concept is named after Niccolò Machiavelli, a sixteenth-century political philosopher and author. In his book *The Prince*, Machiavelli explained how the nobility could more easily gain and use power. The term "Machiavellianism" is now used to describe behavior directed at gaining power and controlling the behavior of others. Research suggests that degree of Machiavellianism varies from person to person. More Machiavellian individuals tend to be rational and nonemotional, may be willing to lie to attain their personal goals, put little emphasis on loyalty and friendship, and enjoy manipulating others' behavior. Less Machiavellian individuals are more emotional, less willing to lie to succeed, value loyalty and friendship highly, and get little personal pleasure from manipulating others.

**Self-esteem** is the extent to which a person believes he or she is a worthwhile and deserving individual.

**Self-esteem** is the extent to which a person believes that he or she is a worthwhile and deserving individual.[20] People with high self-esteem are more likely to seek higher-status jobs, be more confident in their ability to achieve higher levels of performance, and derive greater intrinsic satisfaction from their accomplishments. In contrast, people with less self-esteem may be more content to remain in lower-level jobs, be less confident of their ability, and focus more on extrinsic rewards.[21] Among the major personality dimensions, self-esteem is the one that has been most widely studied in other countries. Although more research is clearly needed, the published evidence suggests that self-esteem as a personality trait does indeed exist in a variety of countries and that its role in organizations is reasonably important across different cultures.[22]

**Risk propensity** is the degree to which a person is willing to take chances and make risky decisions.

**Risk propensity** is the degree to which a person is willing to take chances and make risky decisions. Managers with high risk propensity, for example, might experiment with new ideas and gamble on new products. They might also lead the organization in new and different directions. Such managers might be a catalyst for innovation, or on the other hand, might jeopardize the continued well-being of the organization if the risky decisions prove to be bad ones. Managers with low risk propensity might lead an organization to stagnation and excessive conservatism, or they might help the organization successfully weather turbulent and unpredictable times by maintaining stability and calm. Thus, the potential consequences of a manager's risk propensity depend heavily on the organization's environment. Interestingly, the recent booming economy and strong job market seem to have led to a general increase in the average individual's willingness to take risks.[23]

# Attitudes in Organizations

**Attitudes** are a person's complexes of beliefs and feelings about specific ideas, situations, or other people.

People's attitudes also affect their behavior in organizations. **Attitudes** are complexes of beliefs and feelings that people have about specific ideas, situations, or other people. Attitudes are important because they are the mechanism through which most people express their feelings. An employee's statement that he feels underpaid by the organization reflects his feelings about his pay. Similarly, when a manager says that she likes the new advertising campaign, she is expressing her feelings about the organization's marketing efforts.

## How Attitudes Are Formed

Attitudes are formed by a variety of forces, including our personal values, our experiences, and our personalities. For example, if we value honesty and integrity, we may form especially favorable attitudes toward a manager who we believe to be very honest and moral. Similarly, if we have had negative and unpleasant experiences with a particular coworker, we may form an unfavorable attitude toward her. Any of the "big five" or individual personality traits may also influence our attitudes. Understanding the basic structure of an attitude helps us see how attitudes are formed and can be changed.

**Attitude Structure** Attitudes are usually viewed as stable dispositions to behave toward objects in a certain way.[24] For any number of reasons, a person might decide that he or she does not like a particular political figure or a certain restaurant (a disposition). We would expect that person to express consistently negative opinions of the candidate or restaurant and to maintain the consistent, predictable intention of not voting for the political candidate or not eating at the restaurant. In this view, attitudes contain three components: affect, cognition, and intention.

**Affect** is a person's feelings toward something.

A person's **affect** is his or her feelings toward something. In many ways, affect is similar to emotion—it is something over which we have little or no conscious control.[25] For example, most people react to words such as "love," "hate," "sex," and "war" in a manner that reflects their feelings about what those words convey. Similarly, you may like one of your classes, dislike another, and be indifferent toward a third. If the class you dislike is an elective, you may not be particularly concerned. But if it is the first course in your chosen major, your affective reaction may cause you considerable anxiety.

**Cognitions** are the knowledge a person presumes to have about something.

**Cognition** is the knowledge a person presumes to have about something. You may believe you like a class because the textbook is excellent, the class meets at your favorite time, the instructor is outstanding, and the workload is light. This "knowledge" may be true, partially true, or totally false. For example, you may intend to vote for a particular candidate because you think you know where the candidate stands on several issues. In reality, depending on the candidate's honesty and your understanding of his or her statements, the candidate's thinking on the issues may be exactly the same as yours, partly the same, or totally different. Cognitions are based on perceptions of truth and reality, and, as we note later, perceptions agree with reality to varying degrees.

An **intention** is a component of an attitude that guides a person's behavior.

**Intention** guides a person's behavior. If you like your instructor, you may intend to take another class from him or her next semester. Intentions are not always translated into actual behavior, however. If the instructor's course next semester is scheduled for 8:00 A.M., you may decide that another instructor is just as good. Some attitudes, and their corresponding intentions, are much more central and significant to an individual than others. You may intend to do one thing (take a particular class) but later alter your intentions because of a more significant and central attitude (fondness for sleeping late).[26]

**Cognitive dissonance** is the anxiety a person experiences when he or she simultaneously possesses two sets of knowledge or perceptions that are contradictory or incongruent.

**Cognitive Dissonance** When two sets of cognitions or perceptions are contradictory or incongruent, a person experiences a level of conflict and anxiety called **cognitive dissonance**. Cognitive dissonance also occurs when people behave in a fashion that is inconsistent with their attitudes.[27] For example, a person may realize that smoking and overeating are dangerous yet continue to do both. Because the attitudes and behaviors are inconsistent with each other, the person probably will experience a certain amount of tension and discomfort and may try to reduce these feelings by changing the attitude, altering the behavior, or perceptually distorting the circumstances. For example, the dissonance associated with overeating might be resolved by continually deciding to go on a diet "next week."

Cognitive dissonance affects people in a variety of ways. We frequently encounter situations in which our attitudes conflict with each other or with our behaviors. Dissonance reduction is the way we deal with these feelings of discomfort and tension. In organizational settings, people contemplating leaving the organization may wonder why they continue to stay and work hard. As a result of this dissonance, they may conclude that the company is not so bad after all, that they have no immediate options elsewhere, or that they will leave "soon."

**Attitude Change** Attitudes are not as stable as personality attributes. For example, new information may change attitudes. A manager may have a negative attitude about a new colleague because of his lack of job-related experience. After working with the new person for a while, however, the manager may come to realize that he is actually very talented and subsequently develop a more positive attitude. Likewise, if the object of an attitude changes, a person's attitude toward that object may also change. Suppose, for example, that employees feel underpaid and, as a result, have negative attitudes toward the company's reward system. A big salary increase may cause these attitudes to become more positive. The "Mastering Change" box describes how recent changes at Delta affected employee attitudes in negative ways.

Attitudes can also change when the object of the attitude becomes less important or less relevant to the person. For example, suppose an employee has a negative attitude about her company's health insurance. When her spouse gets a new job with an organization that has outstanding insurance benefits, her attitude toward her own insurance may become more moderate simply because she no longer has to worry about it. Finally, as noted earlier, individuals may change their attitudes as a way to reduce cognitive dissonance.

Deeply rooted attitudes that have a long history are, of course, resistant to change. For example, over a period of years, a former airline executive named Frank Lorenzo developed a reputation in the industry of being antiunion and for cutting wages and benefits. As a result, employees throughout the industry came to dislike and distrust him. When he took over Eastern Air Lines, its employees had such a strong attitude of distrust toward him that they could never agree to cooperate with any of his programs or ideas. Some of them actually cheered months later when Eastern went bankrupt, even though it was costing them their own jobs!

MASTERING CHANGE

## *Attitude Problems Plague Delta*

Delta Airlines has long been one of the flagships of the U.S. air industry. Delta's image has been based on clean planes, plush amenities, and a distinctly warm and highly personalized service. Its employees have been treated exceptionally well, paid among the highest wages in the industry, and provided high-levels of job security. As a result, the firm has had a proud and stable workforce that, in turn, was pleased to deliver high-quality service to Delta passengers.

> "This has tested our people. There have been some morale problems. But so be it." — *Ronald Allen, CEO of Delta*

In response to competition from low-cost carriers like ValuJet and Southwest Airlines, executives at Delta launched a dramatic three-year cost-cutting program. One area that received major attention was the workforce as the firm shrunk by approximately eighty thousand employees. Many of these employees had twenty-five years or more experience with the firm. The airline then hired outside contractors to handle such things as airplane cleaning, maintenance and ground support, equipment, and baggage loading.

As a consequence of these steps, Delta's profit picture has improved immensely. At the same time, however, its image has been tarnished and many of the remaining employees feel resentful and bitter. For example, prior to cost cutting, Delta maintained one full-time mechanic at each gate. This mechanic was ready to immediately solve any routine problem that existed on an arriving aircraft. Now, however, the firm has one mechanic for every three or four gates. Thus, the individual mechanic must often move quickly between gates. As a result, some flights are delayed, some problems go uncorrected, and the mechanics complain about their workload.

To make matters worse, many of the new contract employees do not have the level of commitment to Delta as did their full-time predecessors. For example, during recent East Coast winter storms, many newly hired contract workers at Delta's primary hub, Atlanta, simply didn't show up for work. To make matters worse, the airline's reduced staff of baggage handlers was totally overwhelmed by their job. At one point, there were over five thousand bags sitting in Atlanta when they needed to be somewhere else. Meanwhile, inside the airport, long lines of angry passengers stood impatiently waiting for someone to help them. In the old days, experienced loyal Delta employees would have gone out of their way to make these passengers feel better. At the new Delta, part-time employees, with no understanding of the organization's heritage, stood in their place and often offered curt and/or incorrect suggestions to people.

Even in-flight service has been diminished. Delta has eliminated one flight attendant from virtually every aircraft it flies. For example, whereas the firm once used three flight attendants in coach on its Boeing 727s, the standard staffing is now two flight attendants, the Federal Aviation Administration (FAA) minimum. Similarly, in earlier times, cabin cleaning was performed by in-house crews who earned almost $8 an hour and who enjoyed full health benefits and travel privileges. Outside contractors now do the work, and many customers have started to complain about poor-quality cleaning, soiled carpets, and sticky tray tables.

Will Delta be able to overcome these problems? The firm's CEO acknowledges that the cost cutting has been anything but smooth. Moreover, he also acknowledges that the firm may have cut too deeply and eliminated people that it would have been better off having retained. Nevertheless, he says, the old days of high-cost benevolent operations are past. The firm has to remain cost focused and bottom-line oriented if it is to survive.

References: *Hoover's Handbook of American Business 2000* (Austin, Tex.: Hoover's Business Press, 2000), pp. 482–483; "Cost Cutting at Delta Raises the Stock Price but Lowers the Service," *Wall Street Journal*, June 20, 1996, pp. A1, A8 (quote on p. A8).

# Key Work-Related Attitudes

People in an organization form attitudes about many different things. Employees are likely to have attitudes about their salary, their promotion possibilities, their boss, employee benefits, the food in the company cafeteria, and the color of the company softball team uniforms. Of course, some of these attitudes are more important than others. Especially important attitudes are job satisfaction and organizational commitment.

**Job satisfaction** is the extent to which a person is gratified or fulfilled by his or her work.

Job Satisfaction **Job satisfaction** reflects the extent to which people find gratification or fulfillment in their work. Extensive research on job satisfaction shows that personal factors such as an individual's needs and aspirations determine this attitude, along with group and organizational factors such as relationships with coworkers and supervisors and working conditions, work policies, and compensation.[28]

A satisfied employee tends to be absent less often, to make positive contributions, and to stay with the organization.[29] In contrast, a dissatisfied employee may be absent more often, may experience stress that disrupts coworkers, and may be continually looking for another job. Contrary to what a lot of managers believe, however, high levels of job satisfaction do not necessarily lead to higher levels of productivity. One survey indicated that, also contrary to popular opinion, Japanese workers are less satisfied with their jobs than their counterparts in the United States.[30]

**Organizational commitment** is a person's identification with and attachment to an organization.

Organizational Commitment **Organizational commitment**, sometimes called job commitment, reflects an individual's identification with and attachment to the organization. A highly committed person will probably see herself as a true member of the firm (for example, referring to the organization in personal terms such as "we make high-quality products"), overlook minor sources of dissatisfaction, and see herself remaining a member of the organization. In contrast, a less committed person is more likely to see himself as an outsider (for example, referring to the organization in less personal terms like "they don't pay their employees very well"), to express more dissatisfaction about things, and to not see himself as a long-term member of the organization.[31]

Organizations can do few definitive things to promote satisfaction and commitment, but some specific guidelines are available. For one thing, if the organization treats its employees fairly and provides reasonable rewards and job security, its employees are more likely to be satisfied and committed. Allowing employees to have a say in how things are done can also promote these attitudes. Designing jobs so that they are stimulating can enhance both satisfaction and commitment. Research suggests that Japanese workers may be more committed to their organizations than are U.S. workers.[32] Other research suggests that some of the factors that may lead to commitment, including extrinsic rewards, role clarity, and participative management, are the same across different cultures.[33]

## Affect and Mood in Organizations

Researchers have recently started to renew their interest in the affective component of attitudes. Recall from our discussion above that the affect component of an attitude reflects our emotions. Managers once believed that emotion and feelings varied among people from day to day, but research now suggests that although some short-term fluctuation does indeed occur, there are also underlying stable predispositions toward fairly constant and predictable moods and emotional states.[34]

People who possess **positive affectivity** are upbeat and optimistic, have an overall sense of well-being, and see things in a positive light.

Some people, for example, tend to have a higher degree of **positive affectivity**. This means that they are relatively upbeat and optimistic, that they have an

People characterized by **negative affectivity** are generally downbeat and pessimistic, see things in a negative way, and seem to be in a bad mood.

overall sense of well-being, and that they usually see things in a positive light. Thus, they always seem to be in a good mood. People with more **negative affectivity** are just the opposite. They are generally downbeat and pessimistic, and they usually see things in a negative way. They seem to be in a bad mood most of the time.

*"[Mary Kay] is a company that understands that positive emotions can be good for the soul." — Gloria Mayfield Banks, senior sales director at Mary Kay Inc.*[35]

Of course, as noted above, short-term variations can occur among even the most extreme types. People with a lot of positive affectivity, for example, may still be in a bad mood if they have just been passed over for a promotion, gotten extremely negative performance feedback, or been laid off or fired, for instance. Similarly, those with negative affectivity may be in a good mood—at least for a short time—if they have just been promoted, received very positive performance feedback, or had other good things befall them. After the initial impact of these events wears off, however, those with positive affectivity generally return to their normal positive mood, whereas those with negative affectivity gravitate back to their normal bad mood.

# Perception in Organizations

**Perception** is the set of processes by which an individual becomes aware of and interprets information about the environment.

**Perception**—the set of processes by which an individual becomes aware of and interprets information about the environment—is another important element of workplace behavior. If everyone perceived everything the same way, things would be a lot simpler (and a lot less exciting!). Of course, just the opposite is true: people perceive the same things in very different ways.[36] Moreover, people often assume that reality is objective, that we all perceive the same things in the same way. To test this idea, we could ask students at the University of Florida and Florida State University to describe the most recent football game between their schools. We probably would hear two conflicting stories. These differences would arise primarily because of perception. The fans "saw" the same game but interpreted it in sharply contrasting ways.

Since perception plays a role in a variety of workplace behaviors, managers should understand basic perceptual processes. As implied in our definition, perception actually consists of several distinct processes. Moreover, in perceiving, we receive information in many guises, from spoken words to visual images of movements and forms. Through perceptual processes, the receiver assimilates the varied types of incoming information for the purpose of interpreting it.[37]

## Basic Perceptual Processes

Figure 4.3 shows two basic perceptual processes that are particularly relevant to managers—selective perception and stereotyping.

**Selective perception** is the process of screening out information that we are uncomfortable with or that contradicts our beliefs.

### Selective Perception

**Selective perception** is the process of screening out information that we are uncomfortable with or that contradicts our beliefs. For example, suppose a manager is exceptionally fond of a particular worker. The manager has a very positive attitude about the worker and thinks he is a top performer. One day the manager notices that the worker seems to be goofing off.

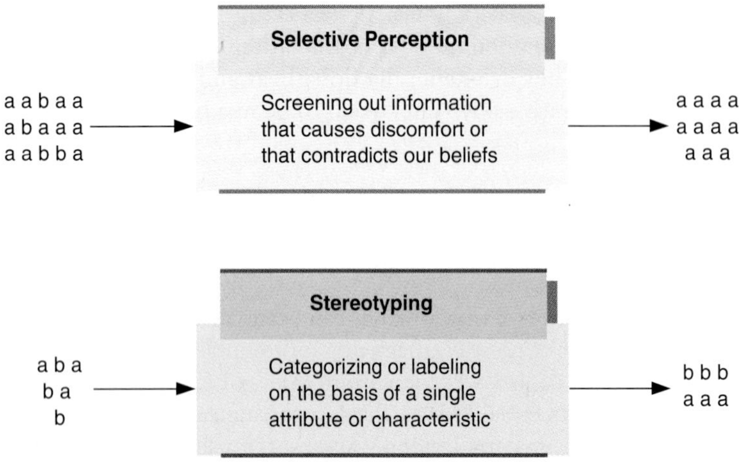


figure 4.3 **Basic Perceptual Processes**

*Perception determines how we become aware of information from our environment and how we interpret it. Selective perception and stereotyping are particularly important perceptual processes that affect behavior in organizations.*

Selective perception may cause the manager to quickly forget what he observed. Similarly, suppose a manager has formed a very negative image of a particular worker. She thinks this worker is a poor performer who never does a good job. When she happens to observe an example of high performance from the worker, she may quickly forget it. In one sense, selective perception is beneficial because it allows us to disregard minor bits of information. Of course, the benefit occurs only if our basic perception is accurate. If selective perception causes us to ignore important information, however, it can become quite detrimental.[38]

Stereotyping is the process of categorizing or labeling people on the basis of a single attribute.

Stereotyping **Stereotyping** is categorizing or labeling people on the basis of a single attribute. Certain forms of stereotyping can be useful and efficient. Suppose, for example, that a manager believes that communication skills are important for a particular job and that speech communication majors tend to have exceptionally good communication skills. As a result, whenever he interviews candidates for jobs, he pays especially close attention to speech communication majors. To the extent that communication skills truly predict job performance and that majoring in speech communication does indeed provide those skills, this form of stereotyping can be beneficial. Common attributes from which people often stereotype are race and sex. Of course, stereotypes along these lines are inaccurate and can be harmful. For example, suppose a human resource manager forms the stereotype that women can only perform certain tasks and that men are best suited for other tasks. To the extent that this affects the manager's hiring practices, he or she is (1) costing the organization valuable talent for both sets of jobs, (2) violating federal law, and (3) behaving unethically.

*"Based on repeated sightings by large numbers of people exchanging and confirming their impressions over time, stereotypes are no more than a mass exercise in inductive reasoning." — Dan Seligman, business writer[39]*

## Perception and Attribution

Attribution theory suggests that we attribute causes to behavior based on our observations of certain characteristics of that behavior.

Attribution theory has extended our understanding of how perception affects behavior in organizations.[40] **Attribution theory** suggests that we observe behavior and then attribute causes to it. That is, we attempt to explain why people behave as they do. The process of attribution is based on perceptions of reality, and these perceptions may vary widely among individuals. For example, as discussed in "The Business of Ethics" box, people will attribute different meaning to volunteer programs sponsored by companies based on their attributions of motive.

THE BUSINESS OF ETHICS

## *When Is a Volunteer* Really *a Volunteer?*

Few would argue that a business exerts a lot of influence of the people it employs. Not surprisingly, then, the latest trend in social responsibility is engendering a lot of debate because of the additional influence it may have over the employees of a business that jumps on the bandwagon. And just what is this bandwagon? Volunteerism—enticing people to use their time to help society.

For example, Shell Oil routinely pays employees to spend time helping with community service projects. A Shell attorney may devote a day to helping plant flowers in a park in a low-income neighborhood. Or a manager may tutor in a public school. Home Depot employees recently volunteered to renovate a women's shelter in Los Angeles. And LensCrafters recently pledged volunteers to give eye care to 1 million needy people by the year 2003.

But some observers question the appropriateness of company-sponsored volunteerism programs. For example, they point out that some employees may feel pressured to volunteer even if they don't want to. And even if employees agree with the concept, it may just be adding one more demand onto their already overloaded schedules. And there is certainly the possibility that some businesses may have more than altruism in mind and really just be seeking favorable publicity.

So how can these complications be minimized? While there are no clear answers, experts do offer a few suggestions. For one thing, strive to ensure that participation is *truly* voluntary. One indicator of this is to avoid keeping a record of who does and who does not get involved. For another, allow the volunteerism to be done during normal working hours and pay employees their normal wages, instead of doing the work on, say, the weekend or asking people to volunteer their own time. And yet another guideline is to keep the program quiet. Don't trumpet the volunteers and their activities in advertising campaigns. This will clearly force the manager to face the real motives behind the program and keep the focus on doing good, rather than on good public relations!

*"I don't want anyone thinking the company is doing this for any reason other than it's the right thing to do."* — Dave Brown, CEO of LensCrafters

*"There is a great deal of pressure to do whatever the boss asks, even if the boss does not intend it that way."* — Lewis Maltby, ACLU

References: "Good Works, Good Business," *USA Today*, April 25, 1997, pp. 1B, 2B (quote on p. 2B); "Volunteers May Feel More Like Draftees," *USA Today*, April 25, 1997, p. 1B (quote on p. 1B); Martha I. Finney, "Operations That Build Smiles, Confidence, Skills, and Community Goodwill," *HRMagazine*, April 1997, pp. 110–117.

Figure 4.4 illustrates the basic attribution theory framework. To start the process, we observe behavior, either our own or someone else's. We then evaluate that behavior in terms of its degrees of consensus, consistency, and distinctiveness. Consensus is the extent to which other people in the same situation behave in the same way. Consistency is the degree to which the same person behaves in the same way at different times. Distinctiveness is the extent to which the same person behaves in the same way in different situations. We form impressions or attributions as to the causes of behavior based on various combinations of consensus, consistency, and distinctiveness. We may believe the behavior is caused internally (by forces within the person) or externally (by forces in the person's environment).

For example, suppose you observe one of your subordinates being rowdy, disrupting others' work and generally making a nuisance of himself. If you can understand the causes of this behavior, you may be able to change it. If the employee is the only one engaging in the disruptive behavior (low consensus), if he behaves like

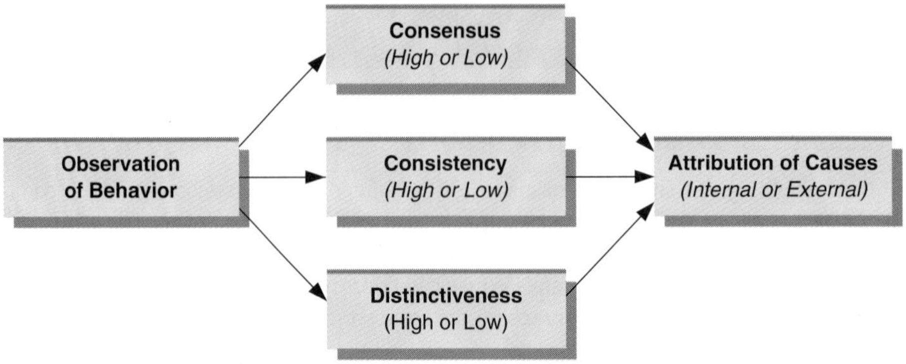


figure 4.4
**The Attribution Process**

*The attribution process involves observing behavior and then attributing causes to it. Observed behaviors are interpreted in terms of their consensus, their consistency, and their distinctiveness. The interpretations result in behavior being attributed to either internal or external causes.*

this several times each week (high consistency), and if you have seen him behave like this in other settings (low distinctiveness), a logical conclusion would be that internal factors are causing his behavior.

Suppose, however, that you observe a different pattern: everyone in the person's work group is rowdy (high consensus), and although the particular employee often is rowdy at work (high consistency), you have never seen him behave this way in other settings (high distinctiveness). This pattern indicates that something in the situation is causing the behavior—that is, that the causes of the behavior are external.

# Creativity in Organizations

Creativity is a person's ability to generate new ideas or to conceive of new perspectives on existing ideas.

Creativity is yet another important component of individual behavior in organizations. **Creativity** is the ability to generate new ideas or to conceive of new perspectives on existing ideas. What makes a person creative? How do people become creative? How does the creative process work? Although psychologists have not yet completely answered these questions, examining a few general patterns helps us understand the sources of individual creativity within organizations.[41]

## The Creative Individual

Numerous researchers have attempted to describe the common attributes of creative individuals. These attributes generally fall into three categories: background experiences, personal traits, and cognitive abilities.[42]

**Background Experiences and Creativity** Researchers have observed that many creative individuals were raised in environments that nurtured creativity. Mozart was raised in a family of musicians and began composing and performing music at age six. Pierre and Marie Curie, great scientists in their own right, raised a daughter, Irène, who won the Nobel Prize in chemistry. Thomas Edison's creativity was nurtured by his mother. However, people with very different background experiences have been creative. The African-American abolitionist and writer Frederick Douglass was born into slavery in Tuckahoe, Maryland, and had

Creativity, the ability to generate new ideas or to conceive of new perspectives on existing ideas, plays an especially strong role today in e-businesses. Phillip Van Rooyen, for example, is part of the web design team for Amazon.com. He and his co-workers spend their time thinking about how consumers use their web site, how their use might change in the future, and how to be prepared for those changes. At first, when Amazon.com sold only books, the task was fairly simple. But as the firm has branched out into music, videos, auctions, and other venues, the job has become more daunting. For example, Van Rooyen needs to continually think of how to better and more effectively link users and buyers from one area of Amazon.com to other areas.

very limited opportunities for education. Nonetheless, his powerful oratory and creative thinking helped lead to Lincoln's Emancipation Proclamation, which outlawed slavery in the United States.

**Personal Traits and Creativity** Certain personal traits have also been linked to creativity in individuals. The traits shared by most creative people are openness; an attraction to complexity; high levels of energy, independence, and autonomy; strong self-confidence; and a strong belief that one is, in fact, creative. Individuals who possess these traits are more likely to be creative than are those who do not.

**Cognitive Abilities and Creativity** Cognitive abilities are an individual's power to think intelligently and to analyze situations and data effectively. Intelligence may be a precondition for individual creativity—although most creative people are highly intelligent, not all intelligent people are necessarily creative. Creativity is also linked with the ability to think divergently and convergently. Divergent thinking allows people to see differences between situations, phenomena, or events. Convergent thinking allows people to see similarities between situations, phenomena, or events. Creative people are generally very skilled at both divergent and convergent thinking.

Interestingly, Japanese managers have recently questioned their own creative ability. The concern is that their emphasis on group harmony has perhaps stifled individual initiative and hampered the development of individual creativity. As a result, many Japanese firms, including Omron Corporation, Fuji Photo, and Shimizu Corporation, have launched employee training programs intended to boost the creativity of their employees.[43]

## The Creative Process

Although creative people often report that ideas seem to come to them "in a flash," individual creative activity actually tends to progress through a series of stages. Figure 4.5 summarizes the major stages of the creative process. Not all creative activity follows these four stages, but much of it does.

**Preparation**, usually the first stage in the creative process, includes education and formal training.

**Incubation** is the stage of less intense conscious concentration during which a creative person lets the knowledge and ideas acquired during preparation mature and develop.

### Preparation

The creative process normally begins with a period of **preparation**. Formal education and training are usually the most efficient ways to acquire a strong foundation of knowledge. To make a creative contribution to business management or business services, people must usually receive formal training and education in business. This is one reason for the strong demand for undergraduate- and master's-level business education. Formal business education can help a person get "up to speed" and begin making creative contributions quickly. Managers' experiences on the job after completing formal training can also contribute to the creative process. In an important sense, the education and training of creative people never really ends. It continues as long as they remain interested in the world and curious about how things work.

figure 4.5 **The Creative Process**

*The creative process generally follows the four steps illustrated here. Of course, there are exceptions, and the process is occasionally different. In most cases, however, these steps capture the essence of the creative process.*

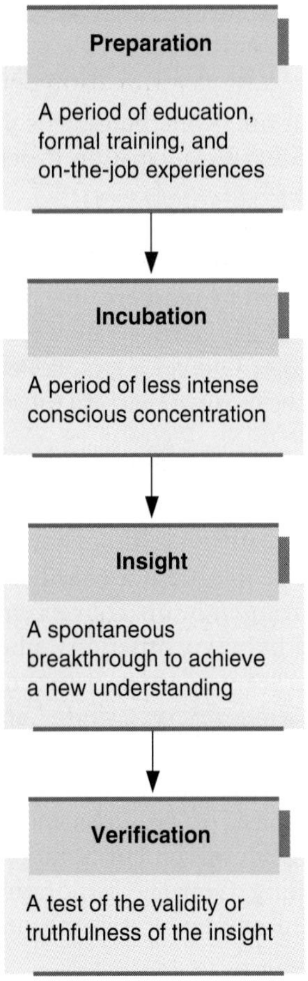


### Incubation

The second phase of the creative process is **incubation**—a period of less intense conscious concentration during which the knowledge and ideas acquired during preparation mature and develop. A curious aspect of incubation is that it is often helped along by pauses in concentrated rational thought. Some creative people rely on physical activity such as jogging or swimming to provide a "break" from thinking. Others read or listen to music. Sometimes sleep may even supply the needed pause. While out rowing one day, David Morse, a research scientist at Corning, hit on the answer to a difficult product improvement. Morse had a special interest in a new line of cookware called Visions. These glass pots and pans had many advantages over traditional cookware, but no one at Corning had succeeded in putting a nonstick surface on the glass. Looking for a solution to this problem, Morse put in many long days in the laboratory, but it was during his hours of rowing that the ideas and concepts that would enable him to devise a nonstick coating began to come together and mature. Morse may never have been able to solve this technical problem if he had not taken the time to let his ideas incubate.

**Insight** is the stage in the creative process when all the scattered thoughts and ideas that were maturing during incubation come together to produce a breakthrough.

**Insight** Usually occurring after preparation and incubation, **insight** is a breakthrough in which the creative person achieves a new understanding of some problem or situation. Insight represents a coming together of all the scattered thoughts and ideas that were maturing during incubation. It may occur suddenly or develop slowly over time. Insight can be triggered by some external event, such as a new experience or an encounter with new data that forces the individual to think about old issues and problems in new ways, or it can be a completely internal event in which patterns of thought finally coalesce in ways that generate new understanding.

One manager's key insight led to a complete restructuring of Citibank's back room operations. ("Back room operations" refers to the enormous avalanche of paperwork that a bank must process to serve its customers—listing checks and deposits, updating accounts, and preparing bank statements.) Historically, back room operations at Citibank had been managed as if they were part of the regular banking operation. When then–vice president John Reed arrived on the scene, he realized that these operations had more to do with manufacturing than with banking and could be managed as a paper-manufacturing process. On the basis of this insight, he hired former manufacturing managers from Ford and other automobile companies. By reconceptualizing the nature of back room operations, Reed substantially reduced costs for Citibank.

In **verification**, the final stage of the creative process, the validity or truthfulness of the insight is determined.

**Verification** Once an insight has occurred, **verification** determines the validity or truthfulness of the insight. For many creative ideas, verification includes scientific experiments to determine whether the insight actually leads to the results expected. In David Morse's case, the insight concerning how to apply a nonstick coating on glass pots was verified in several important experiments and practical trials. Without these experiments and trials, Morse's idea would have remained an interesting concept with little practical application. Verification may also include the development of a product or service prototype. A prototype is one product (or very few) built to see if the ideas behind them actually work. Product prototypes are rarely sold to the public but are very valuable in verifying the insights developed in the creative process. Once the new product or service is developed, verification in the marketplace is the ultimate test of the creative idea behind it.

## Enhancing Creativity in Organizations

Managers who wish to enhance and promote creativity in their organizations can do so in a variety of ways. One important method is to make creativity a part of the organization's culture, often through explicit goals. Firms that truly want to stress creativity, such as 3M and Rubbermaid, for example, state as goals that some percentage of future revenues is to be gained from new products. This clearly communicates that creativity and innovation are valued.

Another important part of enhancing creativity is to reward creative successes, while being careful to not punish creative failures. Many ideas that seem worthwhile on paper fail to pan out in reality. If the first person to come up with an idea that fails is fired or otherwise punished, others in the organization will become more cautious in their own work, and fewer creative ideas will emerge.

*"They say that genius is 99% perspiration and 1% inspiration. Most companies have that 99%. It's the 1% that's really hard, and that's why our clients are asking us to work with their people and not just their products."* — *Dennis Boyle, partner at Ideo, a respected creativity consulting firm*[44]

# Types of Workplace Behavior

**Workplace behavior** is a pattern of action by the members of an organization that directly or indirectly influences organizational effectiveness.

Now that we have looked closely at how individual differences can influence behavior in organizations, let's turn our attention to what we mean by workplace behavior. **Workplace behavior** is a pattern of action by the members of an organization that directly or indirectly influences the organization's effectiveness. One way to talk about workplace behavior is to describe its impact on performance and productivity, absenteeism and turnover, and organizational citizenship. Unfortunately, employees can exhibit dysfunctional behaviors as well. The "Working with Diversity" box highlights how one manager has been successful in channeling behaviors of workers that many other managers would probably shy away from into positive and beneficial outcomes for both individuals and the company.

## Performance Behaviors

**Performance behaviors** are all of the total set of work-related behaviors that the organization expects the individual to display.

**Performance behaviors** are the total set of work-related behaviors that the organization expects the individual to display. You might think of these as the "terms" of the psychological contract. For some jobs, performance behaviors can be narrowly defined and easily measured. For example, an assembly line worker who sits by a moving conveyor and attaches parts to a product as it passes by has relatively few performance behaviors. He or she is expected to remain at the workstation and correctly attach the parts. Performance can often be assessed quantitatively by counting the percentage of parts correctly attached.

For many other jobs, however, performance behaviors are more diverse and much more difficult to assess. For example, consider the case of a research-and-development scientist at Merck. The scientist works in a lab trying to find new scientific breakthroughs that have commercial potential. The scientist must apply knowledge learned in graduate school and experience gained from previous research. Intuition and creativity are also important. And the desired breakthrough may take months or even years to accomplish. Organizations rely on a number of different methods to evaluate performance. The key, of course, is to match the evaluation mechanism with the job being performed.

## Dysfunctional Behaviors

**Dysfunctional behaviors** are those that detract from organizational performance.

**Absenteeism** occurs when an individual does not show up for work.

Some work-related behaviors are dysfunctional in nature. **Dysfunctional behaviors** are those that detract from, rather than contribute to, organizational performance. Two of the more common ones are absenteeism and turnover. **Absenteeism** occurs when an employee does not show up for work. Some absenteeism has a legitimate cause, such as illness, jury duty, or death or illness in the

WORKING WITH DIVERSITY

## *Hiring High-Risk Employees Can Pay*

Most people associate gender, skin color, or other visible differences with the word "diversity." But in a small New England electronics firm it means something else altogether—troubled people worthy of a second chance. Microboard Processing, Inc., or MPI, is owned and managed by Craig Hoekenga. Mr. Hoekenga has a strong sense of social responsibility and believes that his best way of giving back to society is by offering second chances to high-risk employees.

*"Most employers want people with a good work ethic, social skills and an ability to produce the first day they come to work. Craig will take people who can't produce and will wait six or nine months for them to come through." — William R. Bellotti, Connecticut's deputy labor commissioner*

Almost one-third of MPI's employees might be classified as high-risk, and include former welfare recipients, people who have never held a steady job, convicted felons, and former drug addicts. And Hoekenga insists that at least 10 percent of each year's new hires be from a high-risk category. Although the firm also hires plenty of "conventional" employees, Hoekenga considers his high-risk workers to be the backbone of the company.

For example, Ruth Tinney recently applied for a job at MPI. She had not worked for several years, and had spent the last three years on welfare. Hoekenga gave her a two-week trial, and now she has a regular position as an assembly line worker. Not all new hires succeed, of course. About two or three out of every ten fail. For example, one former drug addict who had worked at the firm for over a year recently returned to drug abuse and went back to jail.

Hoekenga also points out that he has to give people a while to learn the ropes. Many, for example, have never held a steady job and do not understand the need for regular and prompt attendance. Therefore, MPI allows considerable latitude in absenteeism and tardiness during the first few weeks. The key is that they show improvement. The goal is to teach proper work habits during the first six months of employment. After that time, the firm takes a much harder line and cuts people less and less slack. But the ones who do make it feel an especially strong sense of loyalty and appreciation toward Hoekenga and his company and make enormous contributions to the firm's continuing profitability and growth.

References: "Loss of Health Benefits No Longer Threatens Disabled Job Seekers," *Wall Street Journal,* October 22, 1999, pp. A1, A8; "Making Risky Hires Into Valued Workers," *Wall Street Journal,* June 19, 1997, pp. B1, B2 (quote on page B2).

family. At other times, the employee may report a feigned legitimate cause that's actually just an excuse to stay home. When an employee is absent, legitimately or not, her or his work does not get done at all, or a substitute must be hired to do it. In either case, the quantity or quality of actual output is likely to suffer. Obviously, some absenteeism is expected, but organizations strive to minimize feigned absenteeism and reduce legitimate absences as much as possible.

Turnover occurs when people quit their jobs.

**Turnover** occurs when people quit their jobs. An organization usually incurs costs in replacing workers who have quit, and if turnover involves especially productive people, it is even more costly. Turnover seems to result from a number of factors, including aspects of the job, the organization, the individual, the labor market, and family influences. In general, a poor person-job fit is also a likely cause of turnover. People may also be prone to leave an organization if its inflexibility makes it difficult to manage family and other personal matters and may be more likely to stay if an organization provides sufficient flexibility to make it easier to balance work and nonwork considerations.

Other forms of dysfunctional behavior may be even more costly for an organization. Theft and sabotage, for example, result in direct financial costs for an organization. Sexual and racial harassment also cost an organization, both indirectly (by lowering morale, producing fear, and driving off valuable employees) and directly (through financial liability if the organization responds inappropriately). Workplace violence is also a growing concern in many organizations. Violence by disgruntled workers or former workers results in dozens of deaths and injuries each year.[45]

## Organizational Citizenship

**Organizational citizenship** is the extent to which a person's behavior makes a positive overall contribution to the organization.

Managers strive to minimize dysfunctional behaviors while trying to promote organizational citizenship. **Organizational citizenship** refers to the behavior of individuals who make a positive overall contribution to the organization.[46] Consider, for example, an employee who does work that is acceptable in terms of both quantity and quality. However, she refuses to work overtime, won't help newcomers learn the ropes, and is generally unwilling to make any contribution beyond the strict performance of her job. This person may be seen as a good performer, but she is not likely to be seen as a good organizational citizen.

Another employee may exhibit a comparable level of performance. In addition, however, he always works late when the boss asks him to, takes time to help newcomers learn their way around, and is perceived as being helpful and committed to the organization's success. He is likely to be seen as a better organizational citizen.

A complex mosaic of individual, social, and organizational variables determines organizational citizenship behaviors. For example, the personality, attitudes, and needs (discussed in Chapter 5) of the individual must be consistent with citizenship behaviors. Similarly, the social context, or work group, in which the individual works must facilitate and promote such behaviors (we discuss group dynamics in Chapter 11). And the organization itself, especially its culture, must be capable of promoting, recognizing, and rewarding these types of behaviors if they are to be maintained.[47] The study of organizational citizenship is still in its infancy, but preliminary research suggests that it may play a powerful role in organizational effectiveness.

# Synopsis

Understanding individuals in organizations is important for all managers. A basic framework for facilitating this understanding is the psychological contract—people's expectations regarding what they will contribute to the organization and what they will get in return. Organizations strive to achieve an optimal person-job fit, but this process is complicated by the existence of individual differences.

Personalities are the relatively stable sets of psychological and behavioral attributes that distinguish one person from another. The "big five" personality traits are agreeableness, conscientiousness, negative emotionality, extraversion, and openness. Other important personality traits include locus of control, self-efficacy, authoritarianism, Machiavellianism, self-esteem, and risk propensity.

Attitudes are based on emotion, knowledge, and intended behavior. Cognitive dissonance results from contradictory or incongruent attitudes, behaviors, or both. Job satisfaction or dissatisfaction and organizational commitment are important work-related attitudes. Employees' moods, assessed in terms of positive or negative affectivity, also affect attitudes in organizations.

Perception is the set of processes by which a person becomes aware of and interprets information about the environment. Basic perceptual processes include selective perception and stereotyping. Perception and attribution are also closely related.

Creativity is a person's ability to generate new ideas or to conceive of new perspectives on existing ideas. Background experiences, personal traits, and cognitive abilities affect an individual's creativity. The creative process usually involves four steps: preparation, incubation, insight, and verification.

Workplace behavior is a pattern of action by the members of an organization that directly or indirectly influences organizational effectiveness. Performance behaviors are the set of work-related behaviors the organization expects the individual to display to fulfill the psychological contract. Dysfunctional behaviors include absenteeism and turnover, as well as theft, sabotage, and violence. Organizational citizenship entails behaviors that make a positive overall contribution to the organization.

## Discussion Questions

1. What is a psychological contract? Why is it important? What psychological contracts do you currently have?
2. Sometimes people describe an individual as having "no personality." What is wrong with this statement? What does this statement actually mean?
3. Describe how the "big five" personality attributes might affect a manager's own behavior in dealing with subordinates.
4. What are the components of an individual's attitude?
5. Think of a person that you know who seems to have positive affectivity. Think of another who has more negative affectivity. How constant are they in their expressions of mood and attitude?
6. How does perception affect behavior?
7. What stereotypes do you form about people? Are they good or bad?
8. Describe a situation in which you came up with a new idea following the basic steps in the creative process described in the text.
9. Identify and describe several important workplace behaviors.
10. As a manager, how would you go about trying to make someone a better organizational citizen?

## Organizational Behavior Case for Discussion

### Personality and Perception at Sears and Montgomery Ward

Sears, Roebuck and Company and Montgomery Ward were founded just a few years apart (Sears in 1893 and Ward in 1872) and together controlled the retailing landscape in the United States for over half a century. For decades their growth and competitive strategies were mirror images of one another. For example, their department stores dominated downtown areas and were often located within a city block of each other. Reading their mail-order catalogs became a ubiquitous part of growing up. They even shared the same corporate headquarters location, downtown Chicago. But after decades of parallel strategies and growth, critical decisions at each firm coming at just about the same time put them on dramatically different paths, one to fortune and success and one to the brink of ruin.

These decisions came immediately after the end of World War II. Top executives at Sears looked carefully at demographic data and patterns and concluded that the citizens of the United States were on the verge of a massive exodus away from central downtown areas to the suburbs. These same executives, working closely as a team, decided to heavily invest in this trend by moving along with the families who were becoming "suburbanites." Thus, Sears began opening all of its new stores in suburban locations, for example. Further, these new stores were usually an anchor in an emerging new form of retailing—the enclosed shopping mall.

At Montgomery Ward, however, a different course was followed. Ward's CEO at the time was Sewell Avery, a strong-willed and domineering individual who seldom listened to others. Avery believed that the suburbs were a "fad." More significantly, he also subscribed to a distorted view of economic history appearing to suggest that a major depression had followed every significant war since the time of Napoleon. Since World War II had just ended, he reasoned, a major depression was certain to be on the horizon. And indeed, Sears was stretched so thin by its expansion that if a depression had occurred, the firm would have gone under.

But the Avery-anticipated depression never came, and Sears flourished. Between 1946, when its expansion started, and 1956, Sears's revenues more than doubled, and it grew to become the undisputed leader in the retailing industry. While the firm later encountered some setbacks in the 1980s and was overtaken by Wal-Mart, Sears has nonetheless remained a major force in the retailing industry and today remains profitable and financially healthy.

But Montgomery Ward never recovered from its CEO's decision to remain entrenched in the inner cities. Even worse, however, was Sewell Avery's steadfast commitment to his beliefs and his unwillingness to even consider that perhaps he was wrong. Amazingly, Montgomery Ward did not open a single new store between the years of 1941 and 1957. And during this entire era, Avery continued to cling to his beliefs that a depression was imminent, Sears would collapse, and Montgomery Ward would be able to buy its competitor at a fraction of its worth!

Ward's board finally gave up on Avery's vision in 1955 and forced him out. But by then it was too late. Sears and J.C. Penney had sewn up the best suburban locations and established themselves in the minds of suburbanites as "the" department stores. And Montgomery Ward was never really able to break back into the mix. The firm continued to stumble along, but reached its nadir in 1997, when it was finally forced to file for protection from its creditors under bankruptcy laws. Whether or not the venerable retailer will be able to figure out how to reinvent itself, of course, remains to be seen. But whatever the outcome, Montgomery Ward insiders can only think about what might have been if only Avery Sewell had seen the world differently and been willing to reconsider his decision a half a century earlier.

### Case Questions

1. Describe the role of personality in the histories of Sears and Montgomery Ward.
2. What role has perception played in the histories of Sears and Montgomery Ward?
3. Do you think that creativity played a role in the downfall of Montgomery Ward? If so, in what way?

References: *Hoover's Handbook of American Business 2000* (Austin, Texas: Hoover's Business Press, 2000), pp. 996–997, 1268–1269; "You Snooze, You Lose," *Newsweek*, July 21, 1997, p. 50.

## Experiencing Organizational Behavior

### Matching Personalities and Jobs

**Purpose:** This exercise will give you insights into the importance of personality in the workplace and into some of the difficulties associated with assessing personality traits.

**Format:** You will first try to determine which personality traits are most relevant to different jobs. You will then write a series of questions to help assess or measure those traits in prospective employees.

**Procedure:** First, read each of the job descriptions below.

### Sales Representative

This position involves calling on existing customers to ensure that they continue to be happy with your firm's products. The sales representative also works to get customers to buy more of your products and to attract new customers. A sales representative must be aggressive but not pushy.

### Office Manager

The office manager oversees the work of a staff of twenty secretaries, receptionists, and clerks. The manager hires them, trains them, evaluates their performance, and sets their pay. The manager also schedules working hours and, when necessary, disciplines or fires workers.

### Warehouse Worker

Warehouse workers unload trucks and carry shipments to shelves for storage. They also pull orders from customers from shelves and take products for packing. The job requires that workers follow orders precisely; there is little room for autonomy or interaction with others during work.

Working alone, think of a single personality trait that you think is especially important for a person to be able to effectively perform each of these three jobs. Next, write five questions that will help you assess how an applicant scores on that particular trait. These questions should be of the type that can be answered on five-point scales (i.e., strongly agree, agree, neither agree nor disagree, disagree, strongly disagree).

After completing your questions, exchange them with one of your classmates. Pretend you are a job applicant. Provide honest and truthful answers to your partner's questions. After you have both finished, discuss the traits each of you identified for each position and how well you think your classmate's questions actually measure those traits.

### Follow-up Questions

1. How easy is it to measure personality?
2. How important do you believe it is for organizations to consider personality in hiring decisions?
3. Do perceptions and attitudes affect how people answer personality questions?

## Building Organizational Behavior Skills

### Assessing Your Locus of Control

Read each pair of statements below and indicate whether you agree more with statement A or with statement B. There are no right or wrong answers. In some cases, you may agree somewhat with both statements; choose the one with which you agree more.

1. ___
   A. Making a lot of money is largely a matter of getting the right breaks.
   B. Promotions are earned through hard work and persistence.
2. ___
   A. There is usually a direct correlation between how hard I study and the grades I get.
   B. Many times the reactions of teachers seem haphazard to me.
3. ___
   A. The number of divorces suggests that more and more people are not trying to make their marriages work.
   B. Marriage is primarily a gamble.
4. ___
   A. It is silly to think you can really change another person's basic attitudes.
   B. When I am right, I can generally convince others.
5. ___
   A. Getting promoted is really a matter of being a little luckier than the next person.
   B. In our society, a person's future earning power is dependent upon her or his ability.
6. ___
   A. If one knows how to deal with people, they are really quite easily led.
   B. I have little influence over the way other people behave.
7. ___
   A. The grades I make are the result of my own efforts; luck has little or nothing to do with it.
   B. Sometimes I feel that I have little to do with the grades I get.

8. ____
   A. People like me can change the course of world affairs if we make ourselves heard.
   B. It is only wishful thinking to believe that one can readily influence what happens in our society at large.

9. ____
   A. A great deal that happens to me probably is a matter of chance.
   B. I am the master of my life.

10. ____
   A. Getting along with people is a skill that must be practiced.
   B. It is almost impossible to figure out how to please some people.

Give yourself 1 point each if you chose the following answers: 1B, 2A, 3A, 4B, 5B, 6A, 7A, 8A, 9B, 10A.

Sum your scores and interpret them as follows:

8–10 = high internal locus of control
6–7 = moderate internal locus of control
5 = mixed internal/external locus of control
3–4 = moderate external locus of control
1–2 = high external locus of control

(Note: This is an abbreviated version of a longer instrument. The scores obtained here are only an approximation of what your score might be on the complete instrument.)

Reference: Adapted from J. B. Rotter, "External Control and Internal Control," *Psychology Today*, June 1971, p. 42. Reprinted with permission from *Psychology Today* magazine. Copyright © 1971 (Sussex Publishers, Inc.).

## Developing OB Internet Skills

**Introduction:** Many organizations today, especially larger ones, conduct regular or periodic surveys intended to measure the job satisfaction and/or overall morale of their employees. Increasingly, more and more smaller to medium-size companies are also starting to do this. This exercise will help you see what role the Internet might be able to play in conducting such surveys.

**Internet Assignment:** Assume that you are the human resource manager of a medium-size but rapidly growing company. Your boss, the CEO, has just pointed out to you that turnover and complaints among the firm's employees appear to be increasing. He further suggested that he thinks that declining morale might be at least part of the problem. He has instructed you to develop and administer an attitude survey to see if this is indeed the case.

To carry out this assignment, first conduct an Internet search to see what you can learn about attitude surveys. Focus specifically on the availability of Internet-based surveys that are available for sale and consulting businesses that offer to provide attitude surveys for a fee.

**Follow-up:** Select the five most promising sites that you can identify and then describe the strengths and weaknesses of each. Finally, respond to the following instructions and/or questions:

1. What benefits can the Internet provide to managers interested in surveying their employees' attitudes?
2. What risks or concerns might you suggest to a manager interested in using the Internet to help determine how to measure attitudes?
3. Would you buy an Internet attitude measurement service or product based on its web site alone? Why or why not?

chapter

5

# Need-Based Perspectives on Motivation

**Management Preview** Given the complex array of individual differences discussed in Chapter 4, it should be obvious that people work for a wide variety of different reasons. Some people want money, some want challenge, and some want power. What each unique person in an organization wants from work plays an instrumental role in determining that person's motivation to work. As we see in this chapter, motivation is vital to all organizations. Indeed, the difference between highly effective organizations and less effective ones often lies in the motivations of their members. Thus, managers need to understand the nature of individual motivation, especially as it applies to work situations. This is the first of two chapters dealing with employee motivation. Here we examine need-based perspectives on motivation. (Some researchers call these "content perspectives.") In Chapter 6, we explore process-based perspectives on motivation. First, however, we discuss how organizations are increasingly recognizing that they may need to provide an array of rewards for their employees in order to meet different sets of needs. ■

Organizations often attempt to reward employees for their exceptional performance or for their loyalty when they remain with the firm for many years. These rewards have traditionally been in the form of cash payments, such as bonuses, or symbolic gifts like service pins or watches. Moreover, it has traditionally been the case that these rewards were given in a "one-size-fits-all" approach—that is, everyone who qualified for a reward got the same one that others got.

But managers are increasingly recognizing that different employees have different needs. As a result, the things that motivate one person, or that are recognized as being a reward, may differ significantly from the things that motivate another person, or that are seen by that individual as being a reward. Thus, organizations have started to search for newer and more creative ways to reward their top-performing and dedicated employees, and the trend would suggest that even more creative ideas are on the horizon.

Some of these new rewards are intrinsic to the job itself. For example, many companies are increasingly giving their top performers more say as to when and where they work. They are also giving them more frequent performance reviews (to provide faster promotion opportunities), larger pay raises, and incentives such as stock options. In addition, many companies continue to use traditional incentives such as dinners, cruises, and even preferred parking privileges to employees who meet certain targets or performance goals. Furthermore, although incentive programs have long been used for employees in sales positions, more and more organizations are now expanding the programs to include almost any employee who can help the firm meet its goals.

*"Leading companies are saying, if you produce here, you can pick your hours, your career track, and, in some ways, even the people you work with." — David Ulrich, compensation consultant**

But from another perspective, organizations are also looking toward even more creative extrinsic rewards and incentives as well. Some of the packages that have become popular include fly fishing trips to ranches in the western United States, kayaking trips to the mountains, white-water rafting trips, cooking classes at gourmet schools, and race-car driving schools. For example, Fighter Pilots USA is an Illinois-based entertainment company that offers customers a flight with an instructor in a fighter-trainer, complete with a simulated dogfight! Some major corporations have started offering the Fighter Pilots program as a reward for their best employees. For example, Lucent Technologies offers Fighter Pilots prizes to its best performers. And Ford Motor Company offers the prizes to its best and most loyal auto dealers. Fighter Pilots has seen its program become so popular that there are often waiting lists of companies wanting to send their most valued employees for a chance to be an ace!

These incentive programs not only are used to reward performance but are also a way of retaining valued employees. Typically, employees are not eligible to participate in these programs until they have been with an organization for a given period of time, providing some incentive for remaining for at least that long. In addition, organizations are becoming rather competitive and secretive about these new incentive plans. The logic is that, although competitors may offer more money, unless they also offer Caribbean cruises or weekend trips to a resort, an employee might view the total compensation package as less attractive and so be less tempted to change jobs.[1] ■

Managers in firms like those described above are on the alert for every possible vehicle for rewarding their most valued employees. But in order for a reward to have the intended effect, of course, it must be of value to the individual who receives it. For example, if an employee receives a nice plaque or certificate for outstanding performance, he will most likely feel very appreciated and will display the plaque or certificate prominently on his office wall. But if the employee already has so many plaques and framed certificates of appreciation and accomplishment that she has run out of wall space for hanging them, one more plaque or certificate might not mean very much. Thus, managers need to understand the different needs that motivate people to behave in various ways in order to most effectively capitalize on that motivation and provide truly meaningful rewards and recognition to their employees.

# The Nature of Motivation

**Motivation** is the set of forces that leads people to behave in particular ways.

**Motivation** is the set of forces that causes people to engage in one behavior rather than some alternative behavior.[2] Students who stay up all night to ensure that their term papers are the best they can be, salespersons who work on Saturdays to get ahead, and doctors who make follow-up phone calls to patients to check on their conditions are all motivated people. Of course, students who avoid the term paper by spending the day at the beach, salespersons who go home early to escape a tedious sales call, and doctors who skip follow-up calls to have more time for golf are also motivated, but their goals are different. From the manager's viewpoint, the objective is to motivate people to behave in ways that are in the organization's best interest.[3]

## The Importance of Motivation

Managers strive to motivate people in the organization to perform at high levels. This means getting them to work hard, to come to work regularly, and to make positive contributions to the organization's mission. But job performance depends

Motivation is the set of forces that causes people to engage in one behavior rather than some alternative behavior. A few years ago Lance Armstrong, a premier bicyclist, was diagnosed with advanced testicular cancer. Since the cancer had spread to his brain, lungs, and abdomen, doctors gave him less than a 50 percent chance of survival. He no doubt considered several options: fight the cancer and forget about bicycling, give up and wait to die, or try to live his life to the fullest in his remaining time. Armstrong chose to both fight the cancer and to again be recognized as among the world's great cyclists. His dreams culminated when he won the sport's premier event, the Tour de France, in 1999. Indeed, he became only the second American and the very first cancer survivor to ever win the race. And motivation played pivotal roles in both his choices and how he pursued them.

on ability and environment as well as motivation. This relationship can be stated as follows:

$$P = M + A + E$$

where $P$ = performance, $M$ = motivation, $A$ = ability, and $E$ = environment. To reach high levels of performance; an employee must want to do the job (motivation); must be able to do the job (ability); and must have the materials, resources, and equipment to do the job (environment). A deficiency in any one of these areas hurts performance. A manager should thus strive to ensure that all three conditions are met.[4]

Motivation is the most difficult factor to manage. If an employee lacks the ability to perform, he can be sent to training programs to learn new job skills. If the person cannot learn them, he can be transferred to a simpler job and replaced with a more skilled worker. If an employee lacks materials, resources, or equipment, the manager can take steps to provide them. For example, if a worker cannot complete a project without sales forecast data from marketing, the manager can contact marketing and request that information. But if motivation is deficient, the manager faces the more complex situation of determining what will motivate the employee to work harder.

## The Motivational Framework

A **need** is anything an individual requires or wants.

We can start to understand motivation by looking at need deficiencies and goal-directed behaviors. Figure 5.1 shows the basic motivational framework we use to organize our discussion.[5] A **need**—something an individual requires or wants—is the starting point. Motivated behavior usually begins when a person has one or more important needs. Although a need that is already satisfied may also motivate behavior (for example, the need to maintain a standard of living one has already achieved), unmet needs usually result in more intense feelings and behavioral changes. For example, if a person has yet to attain the standard of living she desires, this unmet need may stimulate her to action.

A need deficiency usually triggers a search for ways to satisfy it. Consider a person who feels her salary and position are deficient because she wants more income and because they do not reflect the importance to the organization of the work she does. She may feel she has three options: to simply ask for a raise and a promotion, to work harder in the hope of earning a raise and a promotion, and to look for a new job with a higher salary and a more prestigious title.

Next comes a choice of goal-directed behaviors. Although a person might pursue more than one option at a time (such as working harder while also looking for another job), most effort is likely to be directed at one option. In the next phase, the person actually carries out the behavior chosen to satisfy the need. She will probably begin putting in longer hours, working harder, and so forth. She will next experience either rewards or pun-

**figure 5.1 The Motivational Framework**

*This framework provides a useful way to see how motivational processes occur. When people experience a need deficiency, they seek ways to satisfy it, which results in a choice of goal-directed behaviors. After performing the behavior, the individual experiences rewards or punishments that affect the original need deficiency.*

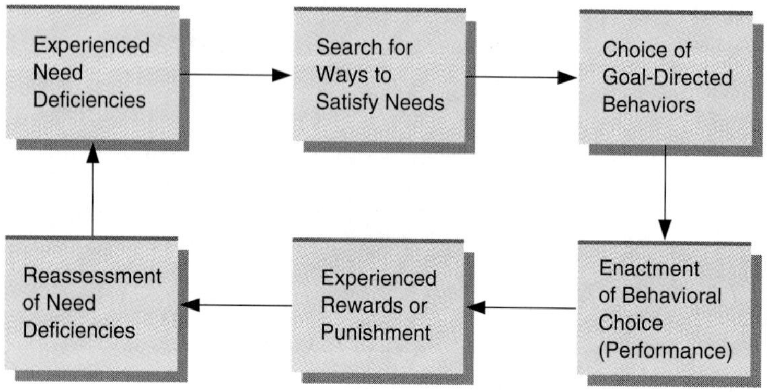

Goal-directed behaviors play a key role in the motivation process. Further, the intensity of such behaviors is largely determined by needs and need deficiencies. For example, virtually everyone will agree that they "need" higher grades, more money, an easier lifestyle, and a nicer car. But when faced with the realities of what it may take to fulfill those needs, they may decide that the needs are not really as important as they initially thought. As illustrated here, for instance, the effort required to become a top-level performer may be more than many people are willing to commit to.



ishment as a result of this choice. She may perceive her situation to be punishing if she ends up earning no additional recognition and not getting a promotion or pay raise. Alternatively, she may be rewarded by getting the raise and promotion because of her higher performance. The cartoon also highlights how goal-directed behaviors can change as a result of alternative choices for spending one's time!

Finally, the person assesses the extent to which the outcome achieved fully addresses the original need deficiency. Suppose the person wanted a 10 percent raise and a promotion to vice president. If she got both, she should be satisfied. On the other hand, if she got only a 7 percent raise and a promotion to assistant vice president, she will have to decide whether to keep trying, to accept what she got, or to choose one of the other options considered earlier. (Sometimes, of course, a need may go unsatisfied altogether despite the person's efforts.)

## Needs and Motives in Organizations

**Primary needs** are the basic physical requirements necessary to sustain life.

**Secondary needs** are requirements learned from the environment and culture in which the person lives.

As just noted, a need is simply something a person requires or wants. Not surprisingly, most people have many different needs. These needs can be grouped into two categories: primary and secondary needs. **Primary needs** are things that people require to sustain themselves, such as food, water, and shelter. Needs of this type are instinctive and physiologically based. **Secondary needs**, on the other hand, are requirements based more in psychology and are learned from the environment and culture in which the person lives. Examples include the needs for achievement, autonomy, power, order, affiliation, and understanding. The "Mastering Change" box examines how differing needs arise in differing personal situations.

Secondary needs often arise in organizational settings, so it is especially important to consider them when examining motivated behavior. For example, if people are to be satisfied with their psychological contracts with their organization, the inducements offered by the organization must be consistent with their own unique needs. A nice office and job security may not be sufficient if the employee is primarily seeking income and promotion opportunities.

People's needs also change with time. When you graduate and accept a new job, you may be very satisfied with your compensation. But if you do not receive a raise for several years, you will eventually become quite dissatisfied. Thus, efforts designed to motivate employees to behave in a certain way may lose their effectiveness as employees satisfy one set of needs and begin to identify another set. Some firms are experimenting with flexible reward systems as a way to satisfy an array of different needs.

A **motive** is a factor that determines a person's choice of one course of behavior from among several possibilities.

A **motive** is a person's reason for choosing one behavior from among several choices. Motives are derived from needs in that most behaviors are undertaken to satisfy one or more needs. For example, an individual may decide to have lunch to satisfy a need for food. He might choose to go to McDonald's because it is fast and convenient, Taco Bell because he's in the mood for Mexican food, or another spot simply because it's on the way to an afternoon business appointment. The reasons for each choice, then, reflect his motive.

Needs, motives, and behavior are interrelated in a fairly simple and straightforward manner. A need serves as a stimulus for action. Motives are the channels

MASTERING CHANGE

## *Motivating Temporary Workers*

One of the most significant changes sweeping American industry today is the dramatic increase in the number of temporary workers in many organizations. Interestingly, however, little is known about how the motivational profiles of temporary workers compare with those of permanent workers in an organization. Permanent workers apparently have a reasonably strong need for security, and they attempt to fill this need, at least in part, by seeking and then keeping a permanent job.

Temporary workers, on the other hand, appear to have a different motivational foundation. It is true that some temporary workers want a permanent job and only take temporary positions as a short-term measure, but some workers intentionally choose temporary employment over more stable, permanent jobs.

Some workers attracted to temporary jobs think the additional flexibility of such positions outweighs the loss of job security. Some temporary employment agencies give workers considerable discretion over when they make themselves available to work. Of course, people who aren't available enough may lose their standing with the agency. But as long as a person can work reasonably often, he or she might very comfortably work three or four days a week and thus have more leisure time.

Some workers are also attracted to temporary work because it offers them variety. When people work permanently for a single employer, their job context may change very slowly or not at all. They go to the same place and do much the same work every day. But temporary workers get a wider variety of job experiences. They may spend three weeks in one company, two months in another, one day in another, and six months in another. In each organization the individual may be doing very different kinds of work.

*"Managing the flexible workforce is much more of a general business issue than it was just a few years ago." — Bruce Steinberg, spokesperson for the National Association of Temporary and Staffing Services*

Finally, temporary employment gives people a chance to balance personal requirements with work. For example, a single parent may need to work to support the family but want some time off to spend with the children. Again, temporary employment may offer greater flexibility than a permanent full-time job.

References: "When Is a Temp Not a Temp?" *Business Week,* December 7, 1998, pp. 90–92; Douglas Powell, "Stretching Your Workforce Options," *HRMagazine,* July 1998, pp. 83–89; "Temporary Workers Getting Short Shrift," *USA Today,* April 11, 1997, pp. 1B, 2B (quote on p. 2B); Lucy A. Newton, "Stiff Competition for Talented Temps," *HRMagazine,* May 1996, pp. 91–94.

through which the individual thinks the need can best be satisfied, and thus reflect the person's behavioral choices. Finally, the manifestation of motives is actual behavior. For example, suppose an employee wants to advance her career to gain income and prestige (needs). She decides to work harder and do higher-quality work to impress her boss (motives). Thus, she works later each evening, comes into the office on Saturday, and pays more attention to detail as she strives for perfection (behaviors).

Motives can vary considerably in their degree of conscious deliberation and complexity. A simple decision about where to have lunch, for example, can be made quickly and without much thought. On the other hand, a major decision that affects the person's career or family may take much longer and involve many other considerations. The "Mastering Change" box describes how the needs and motives of some temporary workers may differ markedly from those of full-time, permanent workers.

# Historical Perspectives on Motivation

Historical views on motivation, although not always accurate, are of interest for several reasons. For one thing, they provide a foundation for contemporary thinking about motivation. For another, because they generally were based on common sense and intuition, an appreciation of their strengths and weaknesses can help managers gain useful insights into employee motivation in the workplace.

## Early Views of Motivation

We introduced the personality trait of Machiavellianism in Chapter 4. Recall that this trait centers on the need for power. To the extent that individuals actually want power, this need provides motivation and could therefore be considered one of the first approaches to understanding motivated behavior. But hedonism was a more far-reaching concept that shaped early thinking about motivation.

The concept of hedonism—the idea that people seek pleasure and comfort and try to avoid pain and discomfort—dominated early thinking on human motivation.[6] Although this seems reasonable as far as it goes, there are many kinds of behavior that it cannot explain. For example, why do recreational athletes exert themselves willingly and regularly, whereas a hedonist would prefer to relax? Why do people occasionally risk their lives for others in times of crisis? Why do volunteers work tirelessly to collect money for charitable causes? And why do some employees work extra hard, when a hedonist would prefer to loaf? As experts recognized that hedonism is an extremely limited—and often incorrect—view of human behavior, other perspectives emerged.

## The Scientific Management Approach

**Scientific management** assumed that employees are motivated by money.

As we noted in Chapter 1, Frederick W. Taylor, the chief advocate of **scientific management**, assumed that employees are economically motivated and work to earn as much money as they can.[7] Taylor once used the case of a Bethlehem Steel worker named Schmidt to illustrate the importance of money in motivation. Schmidt's job was to move heavy pieces of iron from one pile to another. He appeared to be doing an adequate job and regularly met the standard of 12.5 tons per day. Taylor, however, believed that Schmidt was strong enough to do much more. To test his ideas, Taylor designed a piece-rate pay system that would award

Schmidt a fixed sum of money for each ton of iron he loaded. Then he had the following conversation with Schmidt and observed his work:

> Taylor: "Schmidt, are you a high-priced man?"
>
> Schmidt: "Well, I don't know what you mean." [Several minutes of conversation ensue.]
>
> Taylor: "Well, if you are a high-priced man, you will do exactly as this [supervisor] tells you tomorrow, from morning until night. When he tells you to pick up [a piece of iron] and walk, you pick it up and walk, and when he tells you to sit down and rest, you sit down and rest. You do that right straight through the day. And what's more, no back talk. Do you understand that?"

The next day Schmidt started to work, and all day long, and at regular intervals was told by the supervisor who stood over him with a watch, "Now pick up a pig and walk. Now sit down and rest. Now walk, now rest. . . ." He worked when he was told to work, and rested when he was told to rest, and at half-past five in the afternoon, had loaded 47.5 tons on the car. And he practically never failed to work at this pace and do the task that was set him during the three years Taylor was at Bethlehem.[8]

Evidence suggests that Taylor may have fabricated the conversation just related; Schmidt himself may have been an invention.[9] If so, Taylor's willingness to lie shows just how strongly he believed in his economic view of human motivation and in the need to spread the doctrine. But researchers soon recognized that scientific management's assumptions about motivation could not always explain complex human behavior. The next perspective on motivation to emerge was the human relations approach.

## The Human Relations Approach

The **human relations approach** to motivation suggested that favorable employee attitudes result in motivation to work hard.

The **human relations approach**, which we also discussed in Chapter 1, arose from the Hawthorne studies.[10] Douglas McGregor's popular Theory X and Theory Y, for example, exemplified this view of employee motivation. The human relations perspective suggested that people are motivated by things other than money; in particular, employees are motivated by and respond to their social environment at work. Favorable employee attitudes, such as job satisfaction, were presumed to result in improved employee performance. In Chapter 6, we explore this relationship in more detail. At this point it is sufficient to say, as we did in Chapter 1, that the human relations approach left many questions about human behavior unanswered. However, one of the primary theorists associated with this movement, Abraham Maslow, helped develop an important need theory of motivation.

# Need Theories of Motivation

**Need theories of motivation** assume that need deficiencies cause behavior.

Need theories represent the starting point for most contemporary thought on motivation,[11] although these theories too attracted critics.[12] The basic premise of **need theories**, consistent with our motivation framework introduced earlier, is that humans are motivated primarily by deficiencies in one or more important needs or need categories. Need theorists have attempted to identify and categorize the needs that are most important to people. As indicated earlier, some observers call these "content theories," because they deal with the content, or substance, of what motivates behavior. The best-known need theories are the hierarchy of needs and the ERG theory.

## The Hierarchy of Needs

The hierarchy of needs, developed by psychologist Abraham Maslow in the 1940s, is the best-known need theory.[13] Influenced by the human relations school, Maslow argued that human beings are "wanting" animals: they have innate desires to satisfy a given set of needs. Furthermore, Maslow believed that these needs are arranged in a hierarchy of importance, with the most basic needs at the foundation of the hierarchy.

Maslow's **hierarchy of needs theory** assumes that human needs are arranged in a hierarchy of importance.

Figure 5.2 shows Maslow's **hierarchy of needs**. The three sets of needs at the bottom of the hierarchy are called deficiency needs, because they must be satisfied for the individual to be fundamentally comfortable. The top two sets of needs are termed growth needs, because they focus on personal growth and development.

The most basic needs in the hierarchy are *physiological needs*. They include the needs for food, sex, and air. Next in the hierarchy are *security needs:* things that offer safety and security, such as adequate housing and clothing and freedom from worry and anxiety. *Belongingness needs*, the third level in the hierarchy, are primarily social. Examples include the need for love and affection and the need to be accepted by peers. The fourth level, *esteem needs*, actually encompasses two slightly different kinds of needs: the need for a positive self-image and self-respect and the need to be respected by others. At the top of the hierarchy are *self-actualization needs*. These involve realizing our full potential and becoming all that we can be.

*"It's nice to have a job that pays halfway decent, if you've got to do it." — Joe Sizemore, hourly wage earner at a factory in Blacksburg, Virginia*[14]

Maslow believed that each need level must be satisfied before the level above it becomes important. Thus, once physiological needs have been satisfied, their importance diminishes, and security needs emerge as the primary sources of motivation.

figure **5.2**

**The Hierarchy of Needs**

*Maslow's hierarchy of needs consists of five basic categories of needs. This figure illustrates both general and organizational examples of each type of need. Of course, each individual has a wide variety of specific needs within each category.*

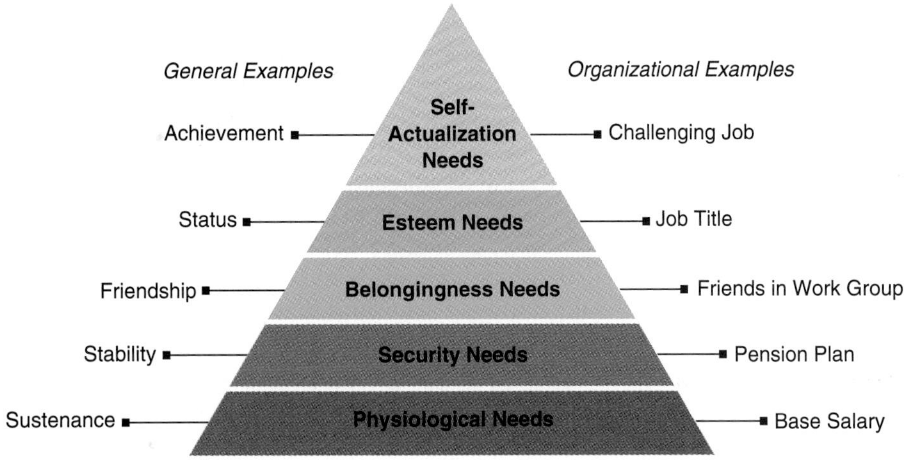


Reference: Adapted from Abraham H. Maslow, "A Theory of Human Motivation," *Psychological Review*, Vol. 50, 1943, pp. 374–396.

According to Maslow's hierarchy of needs, previously satisfied needs can again become motivational under certain circumstances. Consider this Seattle woman, for example. She may very well have left her nice apartment with little or no thought of security and then decided to stop at her neighborhood Starbucks for a cup of coffee and maybe a muffin on her way to work. Meanwhile, protestors working to make a statement against the World Trade Organization meeting in Seattle at the time began attacking various symbols of globalization—including Starbucks. As the glass around her was shattering and objects were being thrown into the store she forgot all about her coffee and focused again on her security needs, which included getting safely out of harm's way.

This escalation up the hierarchy continues until the self-actualization needs become the primary motivators. Suppose, for example, that Jennifer Wallace earns all the money she needs and is very satisfied with her standard of living. Additional income may have little or no motivational impact on her behavior. Instead, Jennifer will strive to satisfy other needs, such as a desire for higher self-esteem.

However, if a previously satisfied lower-level set of needs becomes deficient again, the individual returns to that level. For example, suppose that Jennifer Wallace is unexpectedly fired. At first, she may not be worried because she has savings and confidence that she can find another good job. As her savings dwindle, however, she will become increasingly motivated to seek new income. Initially, she may seek a job that both pays well and that satisfies her esteem needs. But as her financial situation grows increasingly grim, she may lower her expectations regarding esteem and instead focus almost exclusively on simply finding a job with a reliable paycheck.

In most businesses, physiological needs are probably the easiest to evaluate and to meet. Adequate wages, toilet facilities, ventilation, and comfortable temperatures and working conditions are measures taken to satisfy this most basic level of needs. Security needs in organizations can be satisfied by such things as job continuity (no layoffs), a grievance system (to protect against arbitrary supervisory actions), and an adequate insurance and retirement system (to guard against financial loss from illness and to ensure retirement income).

Most employees' belongingness needs are satisfied by family ties and group relationships both inside and outside the organization. In the workplace, people usually develop friendships that provide a basis for social interaction and can play a major role in satisfying social needs. Managers can help satisfy these needs by fostering a sense of group identity and interaction among employees. At the same time, managers can be sensitive to the probable effects on employees (such as low performance and absenteeism) of family problems or lack of acceptance by coworkers. Esteem needs in the workplace are met at least partially by job titles, choice offices, merit pay increases, awards, and other forms of recognition. Of course, to be sources of long-term motivation, tangible rewards such as these must be distributed equitably and be based on performance.

Self-actualization needs are perhaps the hardest to understand and the most difficult to satisfy. For example, it is difficult to assess how many people completely meet their full potential. In most cases, people who are doing well on Maslow's hierarchy will have satisfied their esteem needs and will be moving toward self-actualization. Working toward self-actualization may be the ultimate motivation for most people, rather than actually achieving it.

Research shows that the need hierarchy does not generalize very well to other countries. For example, in Greece and Japan, security needs may motivate employees more than self-actualization needs. Likewise, belongingness needs are especially important in Sweden, Norway, and Denmark. Research has also found differences in the relative importance of different needs in Canada, India, Mexico, Peru, Puerto Rico, Thailand, and Turkey.[15] The "World View" box (on page 124) further reinforces the notion that needs vary across cultures.

Maslow's needs hierarchy makes a certain amount of intuitive sense. And because it was the first motivation theory to be popularized, it is also one of the best known among practicing managers. Yet research has revealed a number of deficiencies in the theory. For example, five levels of needs are not always present, the actual hierarchy of needs does not always conform to Maslow's model, and need structures are more unstable and variable than the theory would lead us to believe.[16] And sometimes managers are overly clumsy or superficial in their attempts to use a theory such as this one. Thus, the theory's primary contribution seems to lie in providing a general framework for categorizing needs.[17]

## ERG Theory

The **ERG theory** describes existence, relatedness, and growth needs.

The ERG theory, developed by Yale psychologist Clayton Alderfer, is another important need theory of motivation.[18] In many respects, **ERG theory** extends and refines Maslow's needs hierarchy concept, although there are several important differences between the two. The *E*, *R*, and *G* stand for three basic need categories: existence, relatedness, and growth. *Existence needs*—those necessary for basic human survival—roughly correspond to the physiological and security needs of Maslow's hierarchy. *Relatedness needs*, involving the need to relate to others, are similar to Maslow's belongingness and esteem needs. Finally, *growth needs* are analogous to Maslow's needs for self-esteem and self-actualization.

In contrast to Maslow's approach, ERG theory suggests that more than one kind of need—for example, relatedness and growth needs—may motivate a person at the same time. A more important difference from Maslow's hierarchy is that ERG theory includes a satisfaction-progression component and a frustration-regression component (see Figure 5.3 on page 125). The satisfaction-progression concept suggests that after satisfying one category of needs, a person progresses to the next level. On this point, the need hierarchy and ERG theory agree. The need hierarchy, however, assumes the individual remains at the next level until the needs at that level are satisfied. In contrast, the frustration-regression component of ERG theory suggests that a person who is frustrated in trying to satisfy a higher level of needs eventually will regress to the preceding level.[19]

Suppose, for instance, that Nick Hernandez has satisfied his basic needs at the relatedness level and now is trying to satisfy his growth needs. That is, he has

WORLD VIEW

## *Different Culture, Different Needs*

Changing the work-related needs, motives, and values of one person in an organization is a daunting challenge. Consider, then, the difficulties inherent in trying to change the needs, motives, and values of an entire population. This is exactly the task being confronted by businesses in Saudi Arabia. For decades, Saudi Arabia relied heavily on so-called guest workers to perform most of its menial and service-oriented jobs. People from Pakistan, Egypt, and the Philippines, for example, found it easy to enter Saudi Arabia and to find steady work performing jobs that locals found unattractive. Companies in Saudi Arabia routinely hired these guest workers for less attractive jobs and paid them relatively low wages. Most guest workers found jobs as restaurant workers, security guards, custodians and maintenance people, and package couriers.

*"If I'm supposed to be here at 8 and I come in at 9, why can't I stay until 3:30 instead of 2:30?" — Khalid Al Sharif, Saudi worker fired for repeatedly coming to work late*

Recently, however, the government of Saudi Arabia has had to change its liberal guest worker policy. For one thing, a huge baby boom of Saudis is now reaching employment age, and there aren't enough jobs to go around. For another, the government, a large employer itself, is in the midst of downsizing and has fewer jobs to offer citizens. So officials are now taking a much harder stance on guest workers—few new guest workers are being admitted. As current workers' visas expire, they are not renewed, and those workers are forced to leave the country. A new law bans foreign workers from owning cars. In some cities in Saudi Arabia, a retail store can be closed down automatically if someone other than a Saudi national is working behind the counter. And the government has ordered all companies to increase the native workforce 5 percent each year.

A problem, however, arises from the prevailing work ethic of Saudi workers. Because most have grown up in a privileged setting and have had autonomy over where and when they worked, they find it difficult to adjust to more regimented and routine work situations. For example, a typical Saudi trying to cope with a new job situation has difficulty understanding why he can't come to work at 9:00 instead of 8:00 and make up the time by simply working an hour longer in the evening. Progress is being made in some companies, but others still face major challenges. For example, McDonald's is having trouble attracting enough qualified Saudis to hold management positions in its restaurants. Most Saudis consider restaurant work demeaning, regardless of the actual position held.

And even though many workers are trying, they still have a difficult time adjusting to a traditional work environment. For example, when beginning higher-level business dealings in Saudi Arabia, it is typical to spend a considerable time exchanging information and asking questions about one another's families. The young Saudis now working in lower-level positions still adhere to this practice in some cases and may trade as much as a dozen or more pleasantries with one another before getting down to business. They are also prone to showing unfailing hospitality to visitors. This approach is desirable in some situations, but in others it can be quite dysfunctional. For example, some Saudi workers have been known to walk off their job at a busy airline counter to have tea with a friend who has strolled up—Saudis consider it rude to not be sociable with visitors, regardless of the circumstance!

References: Ricky W. Griffin and Michael W. Pustay, *International Business—A Managerial Perspective,* 2nd ed., Chapter 14, pp. 510–541 (Reading, Mass.: Addison-Wesley, 1999); "McDonald's Problems in Kitchen Don't Dim the Lure of Franchises," *Wall Street Journal,* June 3, 1998, pp. A1, A6; "Certain Work Is Foreign to Saudis, But That's Changing," *Wall Street Journal,* September 12, 1996, pp. A1, A4 (quote on p. A1).

many friends and social relationships and is now trying to learn new skills and advance in his career. For a variety of reasons, such as organizational constraints (i.e., few challenging jobs, a glass ceiling, etc.) and the absence of opportunities to advance, he is unable to satisfy those needs. No matter how hard he tries, he

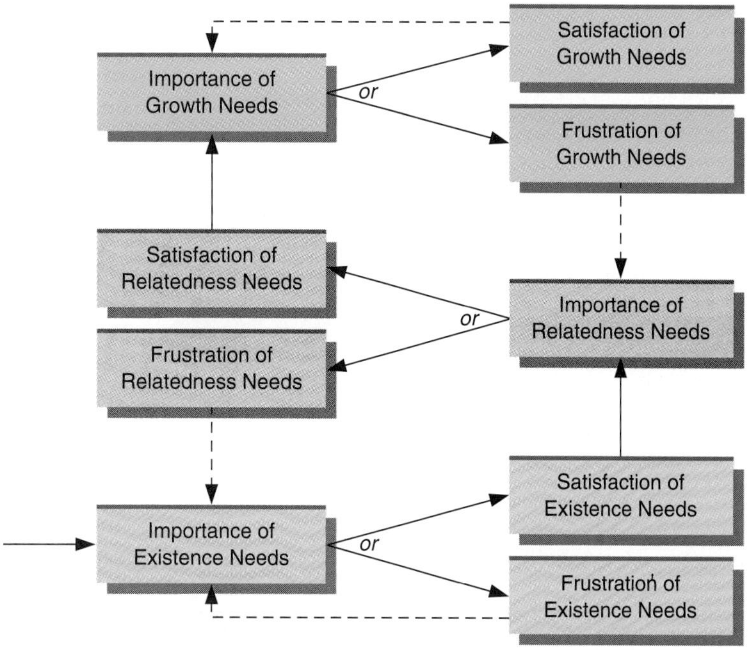


figure 5.3

**The ERG Theory**

*The ERG theory includes an important process missing from other need hierarchies—the frustration-regression component, which suggests that if a person becomes frustrated attempting to satisfy one level of needs, he or she may regress to a need level that was previously satisfied. Only if a need level is satisfied does the person progress to a higher level.*

seems stuck in his current position. According to ERG theory, frustration of his growth needs will cause Nick's relatedness needs to once again become dominant as motivators. As a result, he will put renewed interest into making friends and developing social relationships.

# The Dual-Structure Theory

Another important foundational theory of motivation is the dual-structure theory, which is in many ways similar to the need theories just discussed. This theory was originally called the two-factor theory, but the more contemporary name used here is more descriptive. This theory has played a major role in managerial thinking about motivation.

## Development of the Theory

The **dual-structure theory** identifies motivation factors, which affect satisfaction, and hygiene factors, which determine dissatisfaction.

Frederick Herzberg and his associates developed the **dual-structure theory** in the late 1950s and early 1960s.[20] Herzberg began by interviewing approximately two hundred accountants and engineers in Pittsburgh. He asked them to recall times when they felt especially satisfied and motivated by their jobs and times when they felt particularly dissatisfied and unmotivated. He then asked them to describe what caused the good and bad feelings. The responses to the questions were recorded by the interviewers and later subjected to content analysis. (In a content analysis, the words, phrases, and sentences used by respondents are analyzed and categorized according to their meanings.)

To his surprise, Herzberg found that entirely different sets of factors were associated with the two kinds of feelings about work. For example, a person who

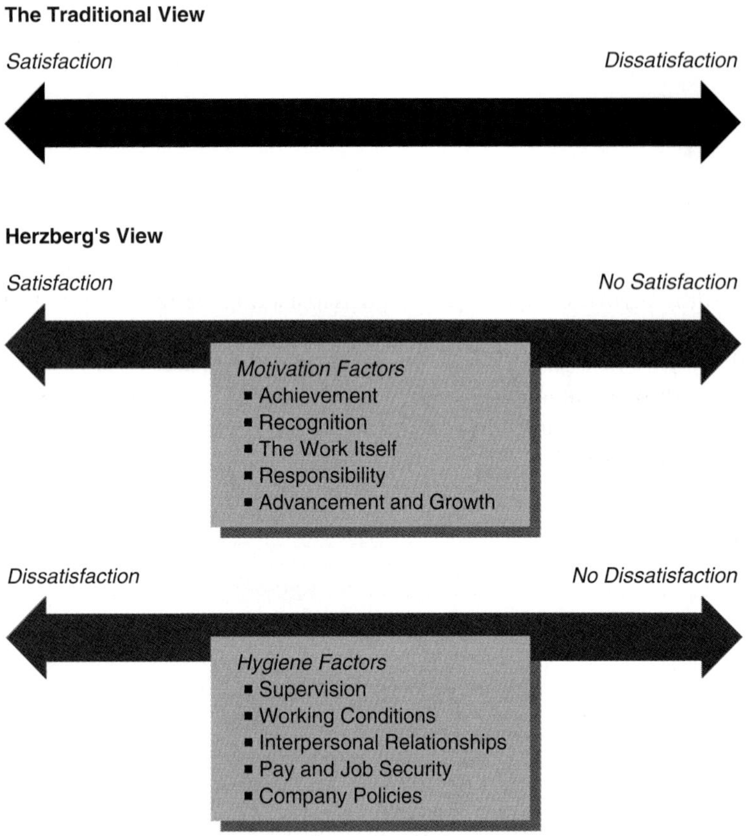


figure 5.4 **The Dual-Structure Theory of Motivation**

*The traditional view of satisfaction suggested that satisfaction and dissatisfaction were opposite ends of a single dimension. Herzberg's dual-structure theory found evidence of a more complex view. In this theory, motivation factors affect one dimension, ranging from satisfaction to no satisfaction. Other workplace characteristics, called "hygiene factors," are assumed to affect another dimension, ranging from dissatisfaction to no dissatisfaction.*

indicated "low pay" as a cause of dissatisfaction would not necessarily identify "high pay" as a cause of satisfaction and motivation. Instead, people associated entirely different causes, such as recognition or achievement, with satisfaction and motivation.

The findings led Herzberg to conclude that prevailing thinking about satisfaction and motivation was incorrect. As Figure 5.4 shows, job satisfaction was being viewed as a single-structure construct, ranging from satisfaction to dissatisfaction. If this were the case, Herzberg reasoned, a single set of factors should influence movement back and forth along the continuum. But because his research had identified differential influences from two different sets of factors, Herzberg argued that two different dimensions must be involved. Thus, he saw motivation as a dual-structured phenomenon.

Figure 5.4 also illustrates the dual-structure concept that there is one dimension ranging from satisfaction to no satisfaction and another ranging from dissatisfaction to no dissatisfaction. The two dimensions must presumably be associated with the two sets of factors identified in the initial interviews. Thus, this theory proposed, employees might be either satisfied or not satisfied and, at the same time, dissatisfied or not dissatisfied.[21]

**Motivation factors** are intrinsic to the work itself and include factors such as achievement and recognition.

**Hygiene factors** are extrinsic to the work itself and include factors such as pay and job security.

In addition, Figure 5.4 lists the primary factors identified in Herzberg's interviews. **Motivation factors**, such as achievement and recognition, were often cited by people as primary causes of satisfaction and motivation. While these factors apparently could cause satisfaction and motivation when present in a job; when they were absent, the result was feelings of no satisfaction rather than dissatisfaction. The other set of factors, **hygiene factors**, came out in response to the question about dissatisfaction and lack of motivation. The respondents suggested that pay, job security, supervisors, and working conditions, if seen as inadequate, could lead to feelings of dissatisfaction. When these factors were considered acceptable, however, the person still was not necessarily satisfied; rather, he or she was simply not dissatisfied.[22]

*"Offering flexible work hours, generous stock options, and an anything-goes dress code isn't enough, it turns out, if the office is dingy, dull or developer-conceived rather than custom-made."* — *Kevin Helliker,* Wall Street Journal *reporter*[23]

To use the dual-structure theory in the workplace, Herzberg recommended a two-stage process. First, the manager should try to eliminate situations that cause dissatisfaction, which Herzberg assumed to be the more basic of the two dimensions. For example, suppose that Susan Kowalski wants to use the dual-structure theory to enhance motivation in the group of seven technicians she supervises. Her first goal would be to achieve a state of no dissatisfaction by addressing hygiene factors. Suppose, for example, that she discovers that their pay is a bit below market rates and that a couple of them are worried about job security. Her response would be to secure a pay raise for them and to allay their concerns about job security.

According to the theory, once a state of no dissatisfaction exists, trying to further improve motivation through the hygiene factors is a waste of time. At that point, the motivation factors enter the picture. Thus, when she is sure that she has adequately dealt with hygiene issues, she should try to increase opportunities for achievement, recognition, responsibility, advancement, and growth. As a result, she is helping her subordinates feel satisfied and motivated.

Unlike many other theorists, Herzberg described explicitly how managers could apply his theory. In particular, he developed and described a technique called "job enrichment" for structuring employee tasks.[24] (We discuss job enrichment in Chapter 7.) Herzberg tailored this technique to his key motivation factors. This unusual attention to application may explain the widespread popularity of the dual-structure theory among practicing managers.

## Evaluation of the Theory

Because it gained popularity so quickly, the dual-structure theory has been scientifically scrutinized more than most other theories in organizational behavior.[25] The results have been contradictory, to say the least. The initial study by Herzberg and his associates supported the basic premises of the theory, as did a few follow-up studies.[26] In general, studies that use the same methodology as Herzberg did (content analysis of recalled incidents) tend to support the theory.[27] However, this methodology has itself been criticized. Studies that use other methods to measure satisfaction and dissatisfaction frequently find results quite different from Herzberg's.[28] If the theory is "method bound," as it appears to be, its validity is questionable.

Several other criticisms have been directed against the theory. Critics say the original sample of accountants and engineers may not represent the general working population. Furthermore, they maintain that the theory fails to account for individual differences. Also, subsequent research has found that a factor such as pay may affect satisfaction in one sample and dissatisfaction in another, and that the effect of a given factor depends on the individual's age and organizational level. In addition, the theory does not define the relationship between satisfaction and motivation.[29]

Research has also suggested that the dual-structure framework varies across cultures. Only limited studies have been conducted, but findings suggest that employees in New Zealand and Panama assess the impact of motivation and hygiene factors differently than U.S. workers.[30]

It is not surprising, then, that the dual-structure theory is no longer held in high esteem by organizational behavior researchers.[31] Indeed, the field has since adopted far more complex and valid conceptualizations of motivation, most of which we discuss in Chapter 6. But because of its initial popularity and its specific guidance for application, the dual-structure theory merits a special place in the history of motivation research.

# Other Important Needs

Each theory discussed so far describes interrelated sets of important individual needs. Several other key needs have been identified; these needs are not allied with any single integrated theoretical perspective. The three most frequently mentioned are the needs for achievement, affiliation, and power.[32]

## The Need for Achievement

The **need for achievement** is the desire to accomplish a task or goal more effectively than in the past.

The **need for achievement** is most frequently associated with the work of David McClelland.[33] This need arises from an individual's desire to accomplish a goal or task more effectively than in the past. Need for achievement has been studied at both the individual and societal levels. At the individual level, the primary aim of research has been to pinpoint characteristics of those who have a high need for achievement, the outcomes associated with a high need for achievement, and methods for increasing the need for achievement.

*"There's a self-imposed pressure, when you get into an environment like HP's [Hewlett-Packard] and you're surrounded by overachievers. You want to be successful and you want the company to be successful." — Craig Byquist, HP manufacturing engineering manager*[34]

**Characteristics of High-Need Achievers** Individuals who have a high need for achievement tend to set moderately difficult goals and to make moderately risky decisions. For example, when people playing ring toss are allowed to stand anywhere they want to, players with a low need for achievement tend to stand either so close to the target that there is no challenge or so far away that they have little chance of hitting the mark. High-need achievers stand at a distance that offers challenge but also allows frequent success. Suppose, for example, that Mark Cohen, a regional manager for a national retailer, sets a sales increase goal for his stores of either 1 percent or 50 percent. The first goal is probably too easy, and the second is probably impossible to reach. But a midrange goal of, say, 15 percent might present a reasonable challenge and be within reach. This goal might more accurately reflect a high need for achievement.

High-need achievers also want immediate, specific feedback on their performance. They want to know how well they did something as quickly after finishing it as possible. For this reason, high-need achievers frequently take jobs in sales, where they get almost immediate feedback from customers, and avoid jobs in areas such as research and development, where tangible progress is slower and feedback comes at longer intervals. If Mark Cohen asks his managers for their sales performance only on a periodic basis, he might not have a high need for achievement. But if he is constantly calling each store manager in his territory to ask about their sales increases, this indicates a high need for achievement on his part.

Preoccupation with work is another characteristic of high-need achievers. They think about it on their way to work, during lunch, and at home. They find it difficult to put their work aside, and they become frustrated when they must stop working on a partly completed project. If Cohen seldom thinks about his business in the evening, he may not be a high-need achiever.

Finally, high-need achievers tend to assume personal responsibility for getting things done. They often volunteer for extra duties and find it difficult to delegate part of a job to someone else. Accordingly, they get a feeling of accomplishment when they have done more work than their peers without the assistance of others. Suppose Mark Cohen visits a store one day and finds that the merchandise is poorly displayed, that the floor is dirty, and that sales clerks don't seem motivated to help customers. If he has a low need for achievement, he might point the problems out to the store managers and then leave. But if his need for achievement is high, he may very well stay in the store for a while, personally supervising the changes that need to be made.

**Consequences of Achievement** Although high-need achievers tend to be successful, they often do not achieve top management posts. The most common explanation is that high need for achievement helps people advance quickly through the ranks, but that the traits associated with the need often conflict with the requirements of high-level management positions. Because of the amount of work they are expected to do, top executives must be able to delegate tasks to others; they seldom receive immediate feedback; and they often must make decisions that are either more or less risky than a high-need achiever would be comfortable with.[35] The "Working with Diversity" box (on page 130) describes another perspective on the potential consequences of achievement. Specifically, some women managers are finding that they can most effectively meet their need for achievement by leaving corporate jobs and starting their own new businesses.

High-need achievers tend to do well as individual entrepreneurs with little or no group reinforcement. Steven Jobs, the cofounder of both Apple Computer and NeXT Computer, and Bill Gates, founder and CEO of Microsoft, are both recognized as high-need achievers. Another noted high-need achiever is Lawrence Bossidy, CEO of Honeywell. During his tenure with the firm, he has increased its stock price by nearly 400 percent, but he continues to push himself and his top management team toward ever greater sales and profits.[36]

**Achievement and Economic Development** McClelland also conducted research on the need for achievement at the societal level. He believed that a nation's level of economic prosperity correlates with its citizens' need for achievement.[37] The higher the percentage of a country's population that has a high need for achievement, the stronger and more prosperous the nation's economy; conversely, the lower the percentage, the weaker the economy. The reason for this correlation is that high-need achievers tend toward entrepreneurial success. Hence, one would expect a country with many high-need achievers to have a high level of business activity and economic stimulation.

## The Need for Affiliation

The **need for affiliation** is the need for human companionship.

Individuals also experience the **need for affiliation**—the need for human companionship.[38] Researchers recognize several ways that people with a high need for affiliation differ from those with a lower need. Individuals with a high need tend to want reassurance and approval from others and usually are genuinely concerned about others' feelings. They are likely to act and think as they believe others want them to, especially those with whom they strongly identify and those whose friend-

WORKING WITH DIVERSITY

## *Seeking New Opportunities . . .*

White males still dominate the executive suites of many old-line businesses—oil, steel, and automobile manufacturing, for example. A primary reason for this is that when these companies were founded a hundred or more years ago, few women or minorities had employment opportunities. It was a "man's world," so to speak, and the Carnegies, Rockefellers, Fords, and Vanderbilts who launched the heavy manufacturing industries that until recently dominated the U.S. economy wanted to keep it that way. The organizational cultures and practices that grew from their views thus served as barriers to women and minorities. And even though all this may have changed over the last several years, relatively few women and minorities have had the chance to break into the top managerial ranks of companies like Mobil, Bethlehem Steel, and General Motors.

But newer high-tech industries such as computer manufacturing, software development, and information technology don't have this long legacy of male dominance. Not surprisingly, then, women and minorities are finding it much easier to excel in these areas than in old-line manufacturing companies. Indeed, high-tech hotbeds like Silicon Valley in California and Austin, Texas, are just as open and receptive to women and minority executives and entrepreneurs as they are to white males.

For example, Christina Jones cofounded Trilogy Development Group in Austin, then left and started another company called pcOrder.com, Inc. The first business was a software development company, and the second helps computer and software companies market their products over the Internet. Over half of her sixty employees are women.

*"High-achieving women are leaving corporations to start their own businesses, mainly because they feel it gives them more control of their lives." — Sharon Hadary, executive director of the National Foundation for Women Business Owners*

In California, success stories are even more abundant. Mary Ann Byrnes, for example, has started a successful company that uses submarine recognition technology in a business that can disconnect stolen cellular telephones. Lounette Dyer owns a growing company that helps marketers refine and get more information from their customer databases. And Maureen Lawrence's business is at the forefront of developing the next generation of data networking equipment. Clearly, then, diversity and high-tech seem to go hand in hand.

References: Nelson D. Schwartz, "Secrets of Fortune's Fastest-Growing Companies," *Fortune,* September 6, 1999, pp. 72–86; "Women Increase Standing As Business Owners," *USA Today,* June 29, 1999, p. 1B; "The Best Entrepreneurs," *Business Week,* January 12, 1998, pp. 70–73; "More Women Quit Lucrative Jobs to Start Their Own Businesses," *Wall Street Journal,* November 11, 1996, pp. A1, A8 (quote on p. A1).

ship they desire. As we might expect, people with a strong need for affiliation most often work in jobs with a lot of interpersonal contact, such as sales and teaching positions.

For example, suppose that Watanka Jackson is seeking a job as a geologist or petroleum field engineer, a job that will take her into remote areas for long periods of time with little interaction with coworkers. Aside from her academic training, one reason for the nature of her job search might be that she has a low need for affiliation. In contrast, a classmate of hers, William Pfeffer, may be seeking a job in the corporate headquarters of a petroleum company. His preferences might be dictated, at least in part, by a preference for being around other people in the workplace; he has a higher need for affiliation.

The need for affiliation is a powerful force that affects motivation in a variety of ways. And as the world becomes more and more diverse, the need for affiliation is being pursued in increasingly varied ways. For example, some American parents who adopt children from abroad recognize that while their adopted children are being raised as Americans those children nevertheless need to maintain ties and develop relationships with others from their own country. Colorado Heritage Camps, set in Estes Park, Colorado, has emerged to help meet this need. It caters to children from Korea, Vietnam, India, Latin America, and the Philippines who have been adopted by and are being raised by American parents.

## The Need for Power

The **need for power** is the desire to control the resources in one's environment.

A third major individual need is the **need for power**—the desire to control one's environment, including financial, material, informational, and human resources.[39] People vary greatly along this dimension. Some individuals spend much time and energy seeking power; others avoid power if at all possible. Some experts think that H. Ross Perot's periodic quests for the U.S. presidency are fueled by a high need for power.

People with a high need for power can be successful managers if three conditions are met. First, they must seek power for the betterment of the organization rather than for their own interests. Second, they must have a fairly low need for affiliation, because fulfilling a personal need for power may well alienate others in the workplace. Third, they need plenty of self-control to curb their desire for power when it threatens to interfere with effective organizational or interpersonal relationships.[40]

# Integrating the Need-Based Perspectives

This chapter has examined several views of individual motives and needs. Despite their differences, the theories intersect at several points.[41] Both the need hierarchy and the ERG theory, for instance, determined a hierarchy of needs, whereas the dual-structure theory proposed two discrete continuums for two need categories. The individual needs identified by each of the three theories are actually strikingly similar. Figure 5.5 illustrates the major likenesses among them.

The hygiene factors described by the dual-structure theory correspond closely to the lower three levels of the need hierarchy. In particular, pay and working con-

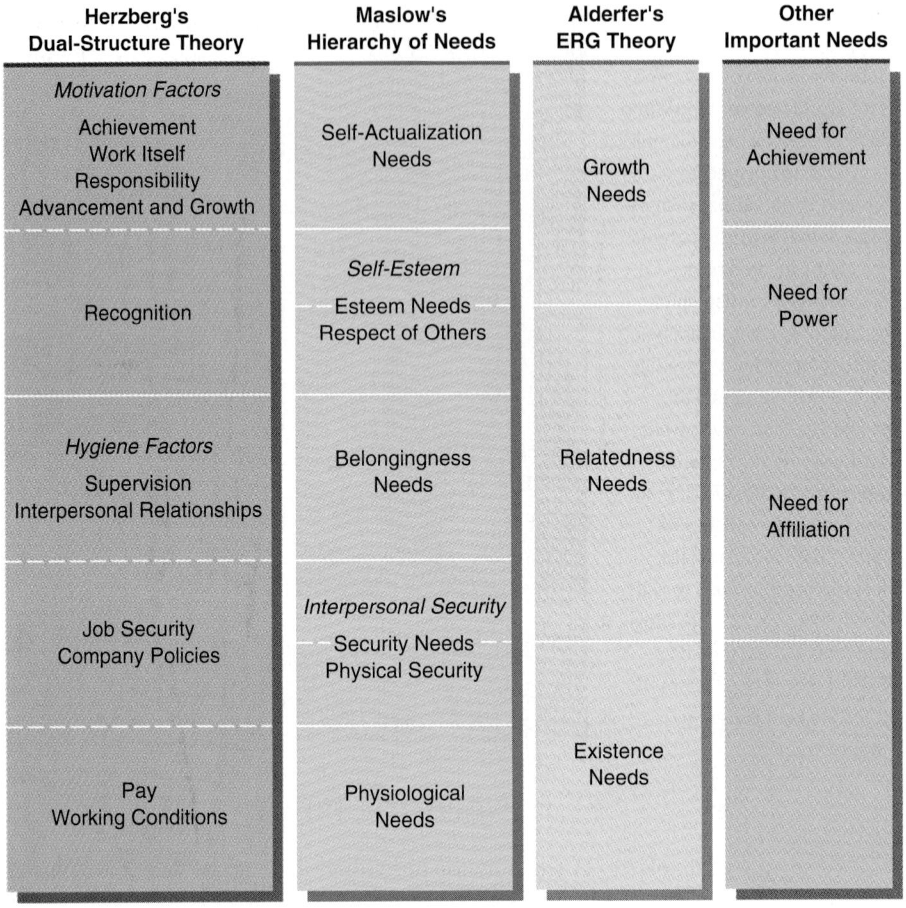


figure 5.5

**Parallels Among the Need-Based Perspectives on Motivation**

*Each of the need theories of motivation reflects its own unique concepts and ideas, but there are also many commonalties and parallels among them. For example, as shown here, certain hygiene factors from the dual-structure theory, such as supervision and interpersonal relations, correspond closely with Maslow's belongingness needs, the ERG theory's relatedness needs, and the need for affiliation.*

ditions correspond to physiological needs; job security and company policies correspond to security needs; and supervision and interpersonal relations correspond to belongingness needs. Meanwhile, the dual-structure motivation factors parallel the top two levels of the need hierarchy. Recognition, for example, is comparable to esteem; achievement, the work itself, responsibility, and advancement and growth might all be categorized as part of the self-actualization process.

There are also clear similarities between Maslow's need hierarchy and the ERG theory. The existence needs in the ERG theory correspond to the physiological and physical security needs in the hierarchy perspective. The relatedness needs overlap with the interpersonal security needs, the belongingness needs, and the need for respect from others in the need hierarchy. Finally, the growth needs correspond to Maslow's self-esteem and self-actualization needs.

The independent individual needs we discussed can also be correlated with the need theories. The need for affiliation clearly is analogous to relatedness needs in the ERG theory, belongingness needs in the need hierarchy, and interpersonal relations in the dual-structure theory. The need for power overlaps with the ERG theory's relatedness and growth needs; the need for achievement parallels ERG's growth needs and the need hierarchy's self-actualization needs.

Unfortunately, despite the many conceptual similarities among the need theories that have emerged over the years, the theories share an inherent weakness.[42] They do an adequate job of describing the factors that motivate behavior, but they tell us very little about the actual processes of motivation.[43] Even if two people are obviously motivated by interpersonal needs, they may pursue quite different paths to satisfy those needs. In Chapter 6, we describe other theories that try to solve that part of the motivation puzzle.

## Synopsis

Motivation is the set of forces that cause people to behave as they do. Motivation starts with a need. People search for ways to satisfy their needs and then behave accordingly. Their behavior results in rewards or punishment. To varying degrees, an outcome may satisfy the original need.

A need is anything an individual requires or wants. Primary needs are things that people require to sustain themselves, such as food, water, and shelter. Secondary needs are more psychological in character and are learned from the environment and culture in which the person lives. A motive is a person's reason for choosing one certain behavior from among several choices.

The earliest view of motivation was based on the concept of hedonism, the idea that people seek pleasure and comfort and try to avoid pain and discomfort. Scientific management extended this view, asserting that money is the primary human motivator in the workplace. The human relations view suggested that social factors are primary motivators.

According to Abraham Maslow, human needs are arranged in a hierarchy of importance, from physiological to security to belongingness to esteem and, finally, to self-actualization. The ERG theory is a refinement of Maslow's original hierarchy that includes a frustration-regression component.

In Herzberg's dual-structure theory, satisfaction and dissatisfaction are two distinct dimensions instead of opposite ends of the same dimension. Motivation factors are presumed to affect satisfaction and hygiene factors to affect dissatisfaction. Herzberg's theory is well known among managers but has several deficiencies.

Other important individual needs include the needs for achievement, affiliation, and power. These needs are part of Murray's theory but have been more widely studied in isolation.

## Discussion Questions

1. Is it possible for someone to be unmotivated, or is all behavior motivated?
2. In what meaningful ways might the motivational process vary in different cultures?
3. Is it useful to characterize motivation in terms of a deficiency? Why or why not? Is it possible to characterize motivation in terms of excess? If so, how?
4. When has your level of performance been directly affected by your motivation? By your ability? By the environment?
5. What similarities exist between the views of human motivation of scientific management theorists and those of human relations theorists? How do they differ?
6. Identify examples from your own experience that support, and others that refute, Maslow's hierarchy of needs theory.
7. Do you think the hierarchy of needs theory or the ERG model has the greatest value? Explain.
8. Do you agree or disagree with the basic assumptions of Herzberg's dual-structure theory? Why?
9. Which of the need theories discussed in the chapter has the most practical value for managers? Which one has the least practical value?
10. How do you evaluate yourself in terms of your needs for achievement, affiliation, and power?
11. Do you agree or disagree that the need for achievement can be learned? Do you think it might be easier to learn it as a young child or as an adult?

# Organizational Behavior Case for Discussion

## Motivating Knowledge Workers

Some observers stereotype people from California as being somehow different from those in the rest of the world. This stereotype is totally inaccurate in most ways, but it is true that at least one segment of the population of California is distinctive. That segment is the people who work in the so-called Silicon Valley area, in the high-tech companies that push the frontiers of technological and information breakthroughs.

Consider the typical day of one such worker, Collette Michaud. After a recent twelve-hour day at work, Michaud treated herself to a 9:00 P.M. workout—and then went back to work. This is her normal routine, six days a week, for months at a time. Michaud works as a project manager for Lucas Arts Entertainment, overseeing the creation of CD-ROM computer games. All told, her typical work week is around 100 hours. Like most of her high-tech comrades in the Silicon Valley, she doesn't punch a time clock. She simply works when she wants to, which appears to be most of the time.

What could conceivably motivate a person to live this sort of a lifestyle? A number of unique opportunities converge in Silicon Valley to provide a useful motivational framework for people with certain inclinations. One common motivator for people in this industry seems to be money. Today, over a third of all high-tech companies give stock options to employees, compared to less than a twentieth of all other companies. Thus, more than in any other industry, the potential exists to make a lot of money in a relatively short time. And even if a person doesn't get rich, the basic compensation package is very attractive. For example, software and semiconductor workers in the Silicon Valley average more than $70,000 a year, compared with about $27,000 a year for the average U.S. worker.

Another important motivator for people in this industry may be pure love of what they do. Although the money is no doubt important, these employees acknowledge that they would not work as hard as they do solely for money. Indeed, many equate high-tech work with that of a musician—they derive so much intrinsic pleasure from the work that the job itself is the primary attraction.

A third motivator in the industry seems to be the chance for high visibility. These employees have a much higher chance than others of becoming well known to customers. For example, when Lucas Arts releases the CD-ROM game that Collette Michaud is supervising, tens of thousands of consumers will be buying the game and playing it on their computers. And her name will be featured prominently in the credits, in much the way that a movie producer's name is shown in theaters.

Peer pressure and acceptance are also important motivators. Everyone in the industry works a lot of hours, so that sort of work schedule has become the norm for the entire industry. When people go to work, they know that they are going to work long hours; it is simply accepted, and they do it because everyone else does. Those who don't may be ridiculed and scorned by their peers.

Finally, these jobs offer autonomy. Indeed, many current management fads, such as empowerment, were really born in the Silicon Valley. Companies such as Hewlett-Packard and Apple Computer have basically thrown away most of the command-and-control orientation of traditional organizations. Employees don't punch a time clock, they don't have to maintain a certain prescribed schedule, and they don't have to adhere to corporate dress codes. Instead, they can come and go as they like; they can bring their pets to work; they can work out of their home. In short, they have considerable autonomy to work where, when, and how they choose. To many workers today, this flexibility is very attractive.

### Case Questions

1. How does Maslow's theory of motivation explain the behavior of Silicon Valley workers?
2. How does Herzberg's dual-structure theory explain it?
3. Do the needs for achievement, affiliation, and power play a role in motivating these workers?

References: "Show Us the Money," *Newsweek*, April 19, 1999, pp. 43–45; "Net Elite: 'It's Not About Money,'" *USA Today*, February 22, 1999, pp. B1, B2; Mary Ann Von Glinow, *The New Professionals* (Cambridge, Mass.: Ballinger, 1998); "Sleep and a Social Life Take a Back Seat," *USA Today*, April 3, 1996, pp. 1A, 2A.

# Experiencing Organizational Behavior

## Relating Your Needs to the Theories of Motivation

**Purpose:** This exercise asks you to apply the theories discussed in the chapter to your own needs and motives.

**Format:** First, you will develop a list of things you want from life. Then you will categorize them according to one of the theories in the chapter. Next, you will discuss your results with a small group of classmates.

**Procedure:** Prepare a list of approximately fifteen things you want from life. These can be very specific (such as a new car) or very general (such as a feeling of accomplishment in school). Try to include some things you want right now and other things you want later in life. Next, choose the one motivational theory discussed in this chapter that best fits your set of needs. Classify each item from your "wish list" in terms of the need or needs it might satisfy.

Your instructor will then divide the class into groups of three. Spend a few minutes in the group discussing each person's list and its classification according to needs.

After the small-group discussions, your instructor will reconvene the entire class. Discussion should center on the extent to which each theory can serve as a useful framework for classifying individual needs. Students who found that their needs could be neatly categorized and those who found little correlation between their needs and the theories are especially encouraged to share their results.

## Follow-up Questions

1. As a result of this exercise, do you now have more or less trust in need theories as viable management tools?
2. Could a manager use some form of this exercise in an organizational setting to enhance employee motivation?

# Building Organizational Behavior Skills

## Assessing Your Own Needs

**Introduction:** Needs are one factor that influences motivation. The following assessment surveys your judgments about your personal needs that might be partially shaping your motivation.

**Instructions:** Judge how descriptively accurate each of the following statements is about you. You may find making a decision difficult in some cases, but you should force a choice. Record your answers next to each statement according to the following scale:

| | |
|---|---|
| Very Descriptive of Me | = 5 |
| Fairly Descriptive of Me | = 4 |
| Somewhat Descriptive of Me | = 3 |
| Not Very Descriptive of Me | = 2 |
| Not Descriptive of Me at All | = 1 |

____ 1. I aspire to accomplish difficult tasks, maintain high standards, and am willing to work toward distant goals.

____ 2. I enjoy being with friends and people in general and accept people readily.

____ 3. I am easily annoyed and am sometimes willing to hurt people to get my way.

____ 4. I try to break away from restraints or restrictions of any kind.

____ 5. I want to be the center of attention and enjoy having an audience.

____ 6. I speak freely and tend to act on the "spur of the moment."

____ 7. I assist others whenever possible, giving sympathy and comfort to those in need.

____ 8. I believe in the saying that "there is a place for everything and everything should be in its place." I dislike clutter.

____ 9. I express my opinions forcefully, enjoy the role of leader, and try to control my environment as much as I can.

____10. I want to understand many areas of knowledge and value synthesizing ideas and generalization.

**Interpretation:** This set of needs was developed by H. A. Murray, a psychologist, in 1938, and operationalized by another psychologist, J. W. Atkinson. These needs correspond one-to-one to the items on the assessment questionnaire. Known as Murray's Manifest Needs because they are visible through behavior, they are:

1. Achievement
2. Affiliation
3. Aggression
4. Autonomy
5. Exhibition
6. Impulsivity
7. Nurturance
8. Order
9. Power
10. Understanding

Although little research has evaluated Murray's theory, the different needs have been researched. People seem to have a different profile of needs underlying their motivations at different ages. The more any one or more are descriptive of you, the more you see yourself as having that particular need active in your motivational makeup. For more information, see H. A. Murray, *Explorations in Personality* (New York: Oxford University Press, 1938); and J. W. Atkinson, *An Introduction to Motivation* (Princeton, N.J.: Van Nostrand, 1964).

## Developing OB Internet Skills

**Introduction:** As emphasized throughout this chapter, people have a wide array of needs, and organizations may attempt to help meet these needs with numerous kinds of rewards. This exercise will help you better understand the kinds of rewards and other incentives that might be available for use by an organization.

**Internet Assignment:** Using a search engine, locate web sites on the Internet for words and phrases such as: *incentives*, *rewards*, *bonuses*, and *employee incentives*. From among the sites you find, pick out a small number (i.e., 3–5) that appear to be for firms that are trying to sell or otherwise promote rewards and incentives that they will supply. You might also search for information on the Incentive Federation, which represents incentive providers.

**Follow-up:** Using the web site information you have found, make a list of the five most unusual or unique incentives that you identified. Finally, respond to the following instructions and questions:

1. Relate each incentive to one or more employee needs.
2. Evaluate the likely effectiveness of each incentive.
3. What are the relative strengths and weaknesses of each of the incentives?
4. Did learning about any of these incentives trigger ideas for other incentives that you had not thought of before?

chapter

# 6

# Process-Based Perspectives on Motivation

## Management Preview

In Chapter 5 we introduced the concept of employee motivation in organizations and discussed several need-based perspectives. The general distinction between those basic approaches and the more advanced theories discussed in this chapter rests on the difference between *content* and *process*. The need-based theories reflect a content perspective in that they attempt to describe what factor or factors motivate behavior—they try to list specific things that motivate behavior. The more sophisticated process-based perspectives introduced in this chapter focus on how motivated behavior occurs—they explain how people go about satisfying their needs. Process-based perspectives also describe how people choose among behavioral alternatives. We begin this chapter by discussing the equity theory of motivation, and then we describe the expectancy theory. Next, we discuss learning and reinforcement, organizational behavior modification, and attribution theory. First, though, let's examine how motivation has played a key role at a new e-company named TixToGo.

What would it take to get someone to work for free? Or, more realistically of course, what would it take to get someone to work for no income today but with the potential for a big payoff in the future? That's the question a Silicon Valley start-up company recently asked. And, perhaps surprisingly, the answers it found were that the right people would actually be quite enthusiastic about this prospect—so long as the potential rewards were substantial and the probability of getting them within reason.

The company in question is TixToGo, specializing in selling events or activities such as tours and programs for other vendors. The firm was actually a fledgling

Internet site when its founder approached Lu Cordova, head of a consulting company and acting director of another Internet start-up firm, with an offer to become CEO. He wanted her to run the firm while he devoted more time to looking for new funding. The only problem was that TixToGo only had $12,000 in the bank and, with four other full-time employees, had no money to pay Cordova! Although she was intrigued with the firm's prospects, she had no interest in working for free. So she devised her own compensation plan centered around the promise that she would be given an attractive salary retroactive to her start date, payable in cash and/or equity, if the firm was successful in obtaining new funding.

*"Taking the job was like putting money on a horse. I could lose, or I could win big."*
*— Janet Jordan, director of administration for TixToGo**

But just because she was willing to buy into this plan didn't mean that anyone else would. The skeptics were quickly proven wrong, however, when Cordova was able to attract six full-time employees, two part-timers, and eight outside consultants and contractors—all on deferred pay. Moreover, each individual was given the option of taking the deferred pay in cash or stock. Calling it deferred pay, though, could be a bit optimistic. Why? Because if TixToGo never obtains the funding being sought, none of the employees, including Cordova, will ever be paid a cent.

So why would someone accept this deal? One major reason is the potential payoff if the company succeeds in locating new funding. Most of the new employees have chosen their future compensation in stock. The number of shares of stock an individual will receive, in turn, will be determined by dividing the dollar amount of the person's salary by the per-share valuation used in determining the venture capitalists' stake ($11 per share). As a result, an individual could end up with several thousand shares of stock. If the firm then subsequently goes public, a truly big payoff would be in the offing.

The outside consultants and contractors all bought into the same deal. Each took part of their fees in cash, generally just enough to cover their costs, and the rest in stock based on the same per-share valuation estimate offered to employees. For example, one contractor put together a television commercial for TixToGo. Its normal fee would have been $250,000. In this instance, though, it took $70,000 in cash and $20,000 in stock. As with employees, if the stock price takes off, each contractor stands to make a bundle.

This point, in turn, leads to the other piece of this puzzle: how realistic is it for employees and contractors to expect a big payday in the future? Given the recent spate of successful high-technology public offerings and the initial interest shown by investors, TixToGo does appear to have a promising future. One investor, for instance, wrote Cordova a check for $50,000 on the basis of its compensation system alone—without even seeing a business plan. TixToGo also seems to be attracting the attention of several other potential big-time investment groups, so the prospects for success seem to be quite promising indeed.[1] ■

Lu Cordova and her colleagues at TixToGo obviously have a certain way of looking at things. Specifically, each has shown a clear willingness to assume some personal risks in anticipation of possible future rewards. Both their willingness to do this and the framework at TixToGo that attracted their attention, in turn, demonstrate how motivational processes work in organizations. Specifically, various complex theories and frameworks that describe or address motivational processes can shed new light on how and why employees behave as they do and help managers structure rewards and other work-related outcomes so as to enhance employee motivation and performance.[2] We begin our discussion of these theories and frameworks with equity theory.

# The Equity Theory of Motivation

**Equity theory** focuses on people's desire to be treated with what they perceive as equity and to avoid perceived inequity.

**Equity** is the belief that we are being treated fairly in relation to others; **inequity** is the belief that we are being treated unfairly in relation to others.

The **equity theory** of motivation is based on the relatively simple premise that people in organizations want to be treated fairly.[3] The theory defines **equity** as the belief that we are being treated fairly in relation to others and **inequity** as the belief that we are being treated unfairly compared with others. Equity theory is just one of several theoretical formulations derived from social comparison processes.[4] Social comparisons involve evaluating our own situation in terms of others' situations. In this chapter, we focus mainly on equity theory because it is the most highly developed of the social comparison approaches and the one that applies most directly to the work motivation of people in organizations.

## Forming Equity Perceptions

People in organizations form perceptions of the equity of their treatment through a four-step process. First, they evaluate how they are being treated by the firm. Second, they form a perception of how a "comparison-other" is being treated. The comparison-other might be a person in the same work group, someone in another part of the organization, or even a composite of several people scattered throughout the organization.[5] Third, they compare their own circumstances with those of the comparison-other, and this comparison is the basis for a perception of either equity or inequity. Fourth, depending on the strength of this feeling, the person may choose to pursue one or more of the alternatives discussed in the next section.

Equity theory describes the equity comparison process in terms of an input-to-outcome ratio. Inputs are an individual's contributions to the organization—such factors as education, experience, effort, and loyalty. Outcomes are what the person receives in return—pay, recognition, social relationships, intrinsic rewards, and similar things. Thus, this part of the equity process is essentially a personal assessment of one's psychological contract. A person's assessments of inputs and outcomes for both self and others are based partly on objective data (for example, the person's own salary) and partly on perceptions (such as the comparison-other's level of recognition). The equity comparison thus takes the following form:

$$\frac{\text{Outcomes (self)}}{\text{Inputs (self)}} \quad \text{compared with} \quad \frac{\text{Outcomes (other)}}{\text{Inputs (other)}}$$

If the two sides of this psychological equation are in balance, the person experiences a feeling of equity; if the two sides do not balance, a feeling of inequity results. We should stress, however, that a perception of equity does not require that the perceived outcomes and inputs be equal, but only that their ratios be the same. A person may believe that his comparison-other deserves to make more money because she works harder, thus making her higher ratio of outcome to input acceptable.

WORKING WITH DIVERSITY

## *Too* Family Friendly?

Family-friendly benefits and benefit packages are all the rage today. Indeed, companies sometimes seem to bend over backward to accommodate the needs of workers with families. Extra insurance and on-site childcare are two such benefits that are increasingly common today. In addition, some organizations also provide extra flexibility to their workers with small children. For example, Xerox subsidizes childcare for its workers who earn less than $50,000 a year. And many firms allow workers with children to come in later, take longer lunches, and/or leave work earlier.

*"Some bosses say: 'You don't have a family at home so you can stay late on this project.' Or: 'You don't have anybody.' The spectrum of insensitivity is quite wide." — Joseph Gibbons, human resources consultant*

In general, no one can really argue with the merits of such programs. For example, they make it easier for parents—especially single ones—to work outside of the home. Moreover, it allows those same workers to better manage the balance between their work and their personal responsibilities at home. But sometimes an organization may go so far to help employees who have children that it ends up penalizing those who don't. For example, whereas working parents may get additional benefits—such as subsidized childcare—employees who don't need that benefit generally don't get something in its place. Thus, they are getting less from the organization, they argue, than are employees with children. Further, most analysts agree that childless employees partially subsidize the cost of health care of workers with children. This stems from the fact that health insurance premiums are based on the degree to which a given labor force incurs medical expenses. Employees with children, in turn, are likely to have higher medical costs, thus raising the premiums for everyone.

But critics argue that inequities can sometimes go even further. For example, when managers need to get people to work late on projects, there may be a tendency for them to look first to single employees without families. They may also be more likely to give employees with families special consideration when it comes to scheduling business travel. Although most childless employees are comfortable with acknowledging that their colleagues with children may need extra consideration, they also sometimes chafe under the feeling that the organization may be taking advantage of them. That is, although giving parents extra benefits when there are no costs to childless employees may be acceptable, directly or indirectly adding the costs of those benefits to childless employees may create resentment. Thus, managers must carefully assess the benefits they are providing to working parents and balance those against the costs being passed on to childless employees.

References: "Holiday on Ice: Stuck at the Office," *USA Today*, November 18, 1998, p. B5; "Employees Without Kids Say They Have Lives, Too," *USA Today*, November 12, 1997, pp. 1B, 2A (quote on p. 2A); "Domestic Partner Benefits on Rise," *USA Today*, October 14, 1997, p. 8B.

Only if the other person's outcomes seem disproportionate to her inputs does the comparison provoke a perception of inequity. The "Working with Diversity" box highlights some equity concerns that are arising in some organizations about family-friendly benefit options.

## Responses to Equity and Inequity

Figure 6.1 summarizes the results of an equity comparison. The perception of equity generally motivates the person to maintain the status quo. She continues to provide the same level of input to the organization as long as her outcomes do not change and the inputs and outcomes of the comparison-other do not change. A

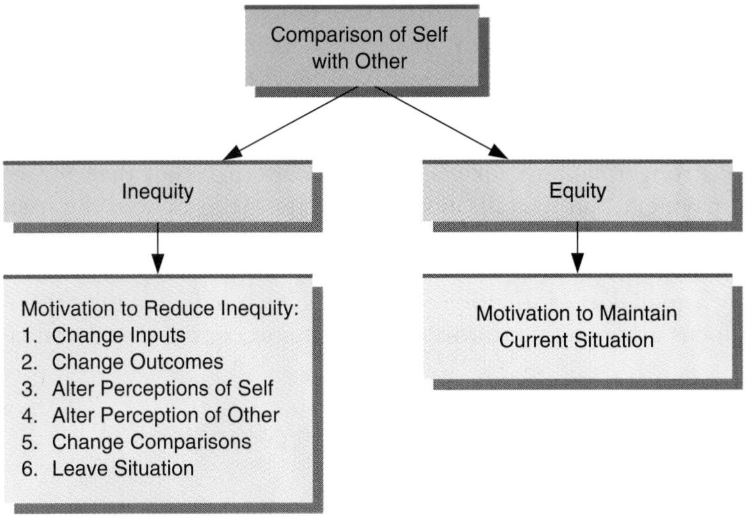


**figure 6.1 Responses to Perceptions of Equity and Inequity**

*People form equity perceptions by comparing their situation with that of someone else. If they experience equity, they are motivated to maintain the current situation. If they experience inequity, they are motivated to use one or more of the strategies shown here to reduce the inequity.*

person who perceives inequity, however, is motivated to reduce it, and the greater the inequity, the stronger the level of motivation.

People use one of six common methods to reduce inequity.[6] First, we may change our own inputs. Thus, we may put more or less effort into the job, depending on which way the inequity lies, as a way to alter our ratio. If we believe we are being underpaid, for example, we may decide not to work as hard.

Second, we may change our own outcomes. We might, for example, demand a pay raise, seek additional avenues for growth and development, or even resort to stealing as a way to "get more" from the organization. Or we might alter our perceptions of the value of our current outcomes, say by deciding that our present level of job security is greater and more valuable than we originally thought.

A third, more complex response is to alter our perceptions of ourselves and our behavior. After perceiving an inequity, for example, we may change our original self-assessment and thus decide that we are really contributing less but receiving more than we originally believed. For example, we might decide that we are not really working as many hours as we first thought—that some of the time spent in the office is really just socializing.

Fourth, we may alter our perception of the other's inputs or outcomes. After all, much of our assessment of other people is based on perceptions, and perceptions can be changed. For example, if we feel underrewarded, we may decide that our comparison-other is working more hours than we originally believed—say by coming in on weekends and taking work home at night.

Fifth, we may change the object of comparison. We may conclude, for instance, that the current comparison-other is the boss's personal favorite, is unusually lucky, or has special skills and abilities. A different person would thus provide a more valid basis for comparison. Indeed, we might change comparison-others fairly often.

Finally, as a last resort, we may simply leave the situation. That is, we might decide that the only way to feel better about things is to be in a different situation altogether. Transferring to another department or seeking a new job may be the only way to reduce inequity.

## Evaluation and Implications

Most research on equity theory has been narrowly focused, dealing with only one ratio, between pay (hourly and piece-rate) and the quality or quantity of worker output given overpayment and underpayment.[7] Findings support the predictions of equity theory quite consistently, especially when the worker feels underpaid.

When people being paid on a piece-rate basis experience inequity, they tend to reduce their inputs by decreasing quality and to increase their outcomes by producing more units of work. When a person paid by the hour experiences inequity, the theory predicts an increase in quality and quantity if the person feels overpaid and a decrease in quality and quantity if the person feels underpaid. Research provides stronger support for responses to underpayment than for responses to overpayment, but overall, most studies appear to uphold the basic premises of the theory.[8] One interesting new twist on equity theory suggests that some people are more sensitive than others to perceptions of inequity. That is, some people pay a good deal of attention to their relative standing in the organization. Others focus more on their own situation without considering the situations of others.[9]

*"It's really the high-performer we should be rewarding with time off, instead of seniority." — Bruce Tulgan, human resources consultant*[10]

The equity theory of motivation suggests that people compare themselves with others in terms of their inputs to their organization relative to their outcomes. But in these days of high-flying Internet start-ups and a booming economy, equity perceptions may be about as stable as a house of cards. Take Jonathan Bates, for example. When he first went to work at Excite@Home, lucrative stock options quickly made him a multimillionaire. And it seemed that everyone he knew drove a BMW and had a Rolex. But when the firm's stock plunged, Bates' income dropped substantially, and he suddenly found himself struggling to keep up. Like many of his contemporaries, though, Bates is optimistic that he will again be able to reap the benefits of his talents.

Social comparisons clearly are a powerful factor in the workplace.[11] For managers, the most important implication of equity theory concerns organizational rewards and reward systems. Because "formal" organizational rewards (pay, task assignments, and so forth) are more easily observable than "informal" rewards (intrinsic satisfaction, feelings of accomplishment, and so forth), they are often central to a person's perceptions of equity.

Equity theory offers managers three messages. First, everyone in the organization needs to understand the basis for rewards. If people are to be rewarded more for high-quality work than for quantity of work, for instance, that fact needs to be clearly communicated to everyone. Second, people tend to take a multifaceted view of their rewards; they perceive and experience a variety of rewards, some tangible and others intangible. Finally, people base their actions on their perceptions of reality. If two people make exactly the same salary but each thinks the other makes more, each bases his or her experience of equity on the perception, not the reality. Hence, even if a manager believes two employees are being fairly rewarded, the employees themselves may not necessarily agree if their perceptions differ from the manager's.

# The Expectancy Theory of Motivation

Expectancy theory is a more encompassing model of motivation than equity theory. Over the years since its original formulation, the theory's scope and complexity have continued to grow.

## The Basic Expectancy Model

**Expectancy theory** suggests that people are motivated by how much they want something and the likelihood they perceive of getting it.

The basic expectancy theory model emerged from the work of Edward Tolman and Kurt Lewin.[12] Victor Vroom, however, is generally credited with first applying the theory to motivation in the workplace.[13] The theory attempts to determine how individuals choose among alternative behaviors. The basic premise of **expectancy theory** is that motivation depends on how much we want something and how likely we think we are to get it. The cartoon clearly illustrates how this can work in businesses today!

A simple example further illustrates this premise. Suppose a recent college graduate is looking for her first managerial job. While scanning the want ads, she sees that Exxon is seeking a new executive vice president to oversee its foreign operations. The starting salary is $600,000. The student would love the job, but she does not bother to apply because she recognizes that she has no chance of getting it. Reading on, she sees a position that involves scraping bubble gum from underneath desks in college classrooms. The starting pay is $5.85 an hour, and no experience is necessary. Again, she is unlikely to apply—even though she thinks she could get the job, she does not want it.

Then she comes across an advertisement for a management training position with a large company. No experience is necessary, the primary requirement is a college degree, and the starting salary is $35,000. She will probably apply for this position because (1) she wants it, and (2) she thinks she has a reasonable chance of getting it. (Of course, this simple example understates the true complexity of most choices. Job-seeking students may have strong geographic preferences, have other job opportunities, and also be considering graduate school. Most decisions, in fact, are quite complex.)

People work for a variety of different reasons, and with a goal of achieving a variety of different rewards and outcomes. Moreover, they are generally motivated by the likelihood that the rewards and outcomes they want are actually attainable as a result of their efforts. For example, in the situation illustrated here, the recruiter tries dangling several different incentives in front of the recruit, but each is met with disdain. Until, of course, just the right incentive is mentioned! When this happens, the recruit goes from being totally blasé to being fired up and ready to work.

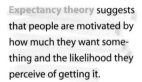

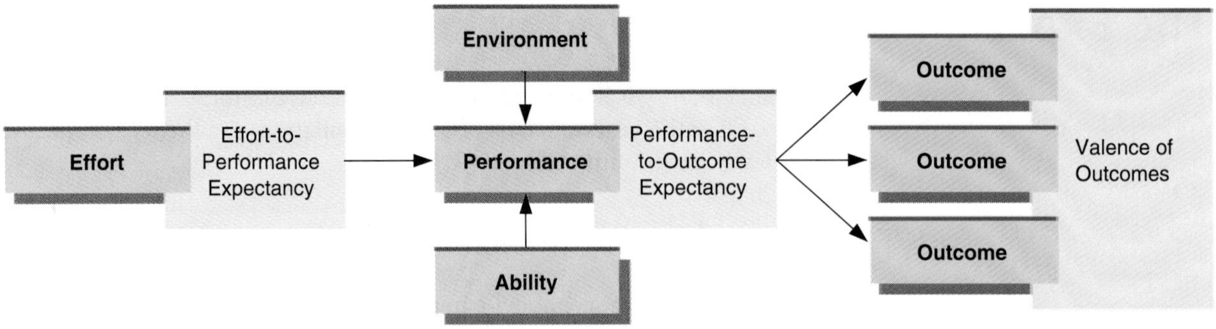


figure 6.2 **The Expectancy Theory of Motivation**

*The expectancy theory is the most complex model of employee motivation in organizations. As shown here, the key components of expectancy theory are effort-to-performance expectancy, performance-to-outcome expectancy, and outcomes, each of which has an associated valence. These components interact with effort, the environment, and ability to determine an individual's performance.*

Figure 6.2 summarizes the basic expectancy model. The model's general components are effort (the result of motivated behavior), performance, and outcomes, consistent with our discussion in Chapter 5. Expectancy theory emphasizes the linkages among these elements, which are described in terms of expectancies and valences.

**Effort-to-performance expectancy** is a person's perception of the probability that effort will lead to performance.

Effort-to-Performance Expectancy **Effort-to-performance expectancy** is a person's perception of the probability that effort will lead to successful performance. If we believe our effort will lead to higher performance, this expectancy is very strong, perhaps approaching a probability of 1.0, where 1.0 equals absolute certainty that the outcome will occur. If we believe our performance will be the same no matter how much effort we make, our expectancy is very low—perhaps as low as 0, meaning that there is no probability that the outcome will occur. A person who thinks there is a moderate relationship between effort and subsequent performance—the normal circumstance—has an expectancy somewhere between 1.0 and 0. At TixToGo, employees apparently believe that they have a high effort-to-performance expectancy, partially explaining their willingness to work with no guaranteed income.

**Performance-to-outcome expectancy** is the individual's perception of the probability that performance will lead to certain outcomes.

Performance-to-Outcome Expectancy **Performance-to-outcome expectancy** is a person's perception of the probability that performance will lead to certain other outcomes. If a person thinks a high performer is certain to get a pay raise, this expectancy is close to 1.0. At the other extreme, a person who believes raises are entirely independent of performance has an expectancy close to 0. Finally, if a person thinks performance has some bearing on the prospects for a pay raise, his or her expectancy is somewhere between 1.0 and 0. In a work setting, several performance-to-outcome expectancies are relevant because, as Figure 6.2 shows, several outcomes might logically result from performance. Each outcome then has its own expectancy. Again, employees at TixToGo have a high performance-to-outcome expectancy.

An **outcome** is anything that results from performing a particular behavior.

**Valence** is the degree of attractiveness or unattractiveness a particular outcome has for a person.

Outcomes and Valences An **outcome** is anything that might potentially result from performance. High-level performance conceivably might produce such outcomes as a pay raise, a promotion, recognition from the boss, fatigue, stress, or less time to rest, among others. The **valence** of an outcome is the relative attractiveness or unattractiveness—the value—of that outcome to the person. Pay raises,

The expectancy theory of motivation suggests that people are motivated to pursue outcomes that they value and they believe they have a reasonable probability of attaining. These Angolan men are sifting through alluvial pits in search of diamonds. Their employer is motivated because the gems from this area are among the world's finest and command staggering prices, and because Angola has become a very fertile source of new diamond fields. The workers themselves toil because there are few good jobs available for them elsewhere and because they are paid a bonus for each diamond they find. And occasionally, workers also are able to pocket a diamond undetected by their supervisor and sell it on the black market for a handsome price.

promotions, and recognition might all have positive valences, whereas fatigue, stress, and less time to rest might all have negative valences. At TixToGo, employees apparently all share a positive valence for a financial windfall as a reasonably likely outcome.

People vary in the strength of their outcome valences. Work-related stress may be a significant negative factor for one person but only a slight annoyance to another. Similarly, a pay increase may have a strong positive valence for someone desperately in need of money, a slight positive valence for someone interested mostly in getting a promotion—or, for someone in an unfavorable tax position, even a negative valence! The "Mastering Change" box discusses how many workers today have different goals for their lives, further complicating the job of the manager trying to motivate her or his workforce.

The basic expectancy framework suggests that three conditions must be met before motivated behavior occurs. First, the effort-to-performance expectancy must be well above zero. That is, the worker must reasonably expect that exerting effort will produce high levels of performance. Second, the performance-to-outcome expectancies must be well above zero. Thus, the person must believe that performance will realistically result in valued outcomes. Third, the sum of all the valences for the potential outcomes relevant to the person must be positive. One or more valences may be negative so long as the positives outweigh the negatives. For example, stress and fatigue may have moderately negative valences, but if pay, promotion, and recognition have very high positive valences, the overall valence of the set of outcomes associated with performance will still be positive.

Conceptually, the valences of all relevant outcomes and the corresponding pattern of expectancies are assumed to interact in an almost mathematical fashion to determine a person's level of motivation. Most people do assess likelihoods of and preferences for various consequences of behavior, but they seldom approach them in such a calculating manner.

*"Even if I were to get a better job offer somewhere else, I would have to think twice about giving up the kind of benefits that my company offers." — Katherine Lechler, graphics designer for* CMP *trade magazine*[14]

MASTERING CHANGE

## *Pursuing Different Dreams*

In the past, most people aspiring to a business career had a clear vision of how to measure success: get a job with a big company; work long, hard hours; and hope to move up the corporate ladder. The "corner office" or the "executive suite" were the basic career goals for most of these individuals. And if their dreams didn't come true, they still had a reliable paycheck and job security.

But a growing number of managers now entering the workforce appear to have a different set of dreams. Although many business school graduates still want the status, security, and allure of a big corporate job, others want something very different. For example, one recent study found that only 1 percent of the one thousand adults surveyed listed a job as a corporate manager as their first choice for a career. Similarly, the percentage of the graduates of Stanford's MBA program who took a job with a big company declined from 70 percent to 50 percent during a recent five-year period.

So what do the people who spurn a corporate career choose instead? Some start their own businesses. Others look for a small start-up they can buy. Still others go into consulting. And among those who do opt for a corporate career, quite a few say, at least in private, that they only want to earn enough money to have some financial security. Then they, too, plan to pursue their dreams in a different arena.

*"If your aspiration is to be a bureaucratic in-fighter, you may be well suited for a large organization. But you've got to* **swallow more than I care to.** *On some level, you can't be who you really are during the workday."* — *Daniel Grossman, talented manager who chose to start his own business*

But why are some people so turned off by big companies? Most offer one or more of the following reasons: (1) some big companies reward the best politicians, not the best performers; (2) in a big company you may get pigeon-holed or stuck in a dead-end job; (3) it takes too long to get responsibility and authority; (4) big companies impose too many constraints on when and where you work; and (5) top managers at big companies are too cautious and discourage risk and innovation. Of course, these generalizations represent the perceptions of only some people, and even if they are true, they don't apply to all companies or to all settings. But they do explain why some people are seeking different career options and why the entrepreneurial spirit is stronger today than ever before.

References: "It's Your Choice," *Fast Company,* January–February 2000, pp. 184–199; "Where the Next Generation Wants to Work," *Fortune*, October 11, 1999, p. 322; "The Search for the Young and Gifted," *Business Week,* October 4, 1999, pp. 108–116; Kenneth Labich, "Kissing Off Corporate America," *Fortune,* February 20, 1995, pp. 44–51 (quote on p. 44).

## The Porter-Lawler Model

The original presentation of expectancy theory placed it in the mainstream of contemporary motivation theory. Since then, the model has been refined and extended many times. Most modifications have focused on identifying and measuring outcomes and expectancies. An exception is the variation of expectancy theory developed by Porter and Lawler. These researchers used expectancy theory to develop a novel view of the relationship between employee satisfaction and performance.[15] Although the conventional wisdom was that satisfaction leads to performance, Porter and Lawler argued the reverse: if rewards are adequate, high levels of performance may lead to satisfaction.

The Porter-Lawler model appears in Figure 6.3. Some of its features are quite different from the original version of expectancy theory. For example, the extended model includes abilities, traits, and role perceptions. At the beginning of the moti-

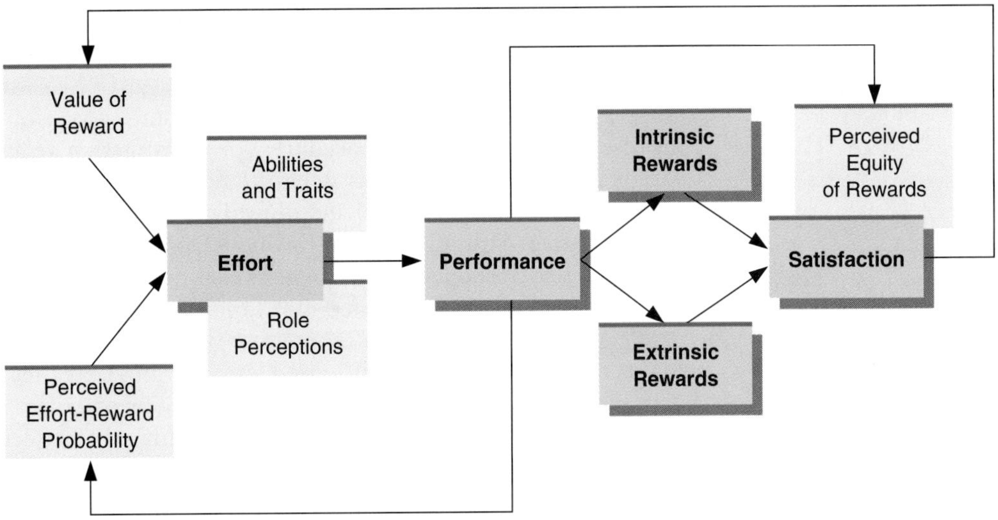


figure 6.3 **The Porter-Lawler Model**

*The Porter and Lawler expectancy model provides interesting insights into the relationships between satisfaction and performance. As illustrated here, this model predicts that satisfaction is determined by the perceived equity of intrinsic and extrinsic rewards for performance. That is, rather than satisfaction causing performance, which many people might predict, this model argues that it is actually performance that eventually leads to satisfaction.*

Reference: Figure from Porter, Lyman W., and Edward E. Lawler, *Managerial Attitudes and Performance*. Copyright © 1968. Reproduced by permission of the publisher, McGraw-Hill, Inc.

vational cycle, effort is a function of the value of the potential reward for the employee (its valence) and the perceived effort-reward probability (an expectancy). Effort then combines with abilities, traits, and role perceptions to determine actual performance.

Performance results in two kinds of rewards. Intrinsic rewards are intangible—a feeling of accomplishment, a sense of achievement, and so forth. Extrinsic rewards are tangible outcomes such as pay and promotion. The individual judges the value of his or her performance to the organization and uses social comparison processes (as in equity theory) to form an impression of the equity of the rewards received. If the rewards are regarded as equitable, the employee feels satisfied. In subsequent cycles, satisfaction with rewards influences the value of the rewards anticipated, and actual performance following effort influences future perceived effort-reward probabilities.

## Evaluation and Implications

Expectancy theory has been tested by many different researchers in a variety of settings and using a variety of methods.[16] As noted earlier, the complexity of the theory has been both a blessing and a curse.[17] Nowhere is this double-edged quality more apparent than in the research undertaken to evaluate the theory. Several studies have supported various parts of the theory. For example, both kinds of expectancy and valence have been found to be associated with effort and performance in the workplace.[18] Research has also confirmed expectancy theory's claims that people will not engage in motivated behavior unless they (1) value the expected rewards, (2) believe their efforts will lead to performance, and (3) believe their performance will result in the desired rewards.[19]

However, expectancy theory is so complicated that researchers have found it quite difficult to test.[20] In particular, the measures of various parts of the model may lack validity, and the procedures for investigating relationships among the variables have often been less scientific than researchers would like. Moreover, people are seldom as rational and objective in choosing behaviors as expectancy theory implies. Still, the logic of the model, combined with the consistent, albeit modest, research support for it, suggests that the theory has much to offer.[21]

Research has also suggested that expectancy theory is more likely to explain motivation in the United States than in other countries. People from the United States tend to be very goal oriented and to think that they can influence their own success. Thus, under the right combinations of expectancies, valences, and outcomes, they will be highly motivated. But different patterns may exist in other countries. For example, many people from Moslem countries think that God determines the outcome of every behavior, so the concept of expectancy is not applicable.[22]

Because expectancy theory is so complex, it is difficult to apply directly in the workplace. A manager would need to figure out what rewards each employee wants and how valuable those rewards are to each person, measure the various expectancies, and finally adjust the relationships to create motivation. Nevertheless, expectancy theory offers several important guidelines for the practicing manager. Some of the more fundamental guidelines include:

1. Determine the primary outcomes each employee wants.
2. Decide what levels and kinds of performance are needed to meet organizational goals.
3. Make sure the desired levels of performance are possible.
4. Link desired outcomes and desired performance.
5. Analyze the situation for conflicting expectancies.
6. Make sure the rewards are large enough.
7. Make sure the overall system is equitable for everyone.[23]

# Learning and Motivation

**Learning** is a relatively permanent change in behavior or behavioral potential resulting from direct or indirect experience.

Learning is another key component in employee motivation. In any organization, employees quickly learn which behaviors are rewarded and which are ignored or punished. Thus, learning plays a critical role in maintaining motivated behavior. **Learning** is a relatively permanent change in behavior or behavioral potential that results from direct or indirect experience.[24] For example, we can learn to use a new software application program by practicing and experimenting with its various functions and options.

## How Learning Occurs

**Classical conditioning** is a simple form of learning that links a conditioned response with an unconditioned stimulus.

**The Traditional View: Classical Conditioning** The most influential historical approach to learning is classical conditioning, developed by Ivan Pavlov in his famous experiments with dogs.[25] **Classical conditioning** is a simple form of learning in which a conditioned response is linked with an unconditioned stimulus. In organizations, however, only simple behaviors and responses can be learned in this manner. For example, suppose an employee receives very bad news one day from his boss. It's possible that the employee could come to associate, say, the color of the boss's suit that day with bad news. Thus, the next time the boss wears that same suit to the office, the employee may experience dread and foreboding.

But this form of learning is obviously simplistic and not directly relevant to motivation. Learning theorists soon recognized that although classical conditioning offered some interesting insights into the learning process, it was inadequate as an explanation of human learning. For one thing, classical conditioning relies on simple cause-and-effect relationships between one stimulus and one response; it cannot deal with the more complex forms of learned behavior that typify human beings. For another, classical conditioning ignores the concept of choice; it assumes that behavior is reflexive, or involuntary. Therefore, this perspective cannot explain situations in which people consciously and rationally choose one course of action among many. Because of these shortcomings of classical conditioning, theorists eventually moved on to other approaches that seemed more useful in explaining the processes associated with complex learning.

**The Contemporary View: Learning as a Cognitive Process** Although it is not tied to a single theory or model, contemporary learning theory generally views learning as a cognitive process; that is, it assumes that people are conscious, active participants in how they learn.[26] Figure 6.4 illustrates some underpinnings of the cognitive view of learning.[27]

First, the cognitive view suggests that people draw on their experiences and use past learning as a basis for their present behavior. These experiences represent knowledge, or cognitions. For example, an employee faced with a choice of job assignments will use previous experiences in deciding which one to accept. Second, people make choices about their behavior. The employee recognizes that she has two alternatives and chooses one. Third, people recognize the consequences of their choices. Thus, when the employee finds the job assignment rewarding and fulfilling, she will recognize that the choice was a good one and will understand why. Finally, people evaluate those consequences and add them to prior learning, which affects future choices. Faced with the same job choices next year, the employee will probably be motivated to choose the same one.[28] As implied earlier, several perspectives on learning take a cognitive view. Perhaps foremost among them is reinforcement theory. Although reinforcement theory per se is not really new, it has been applied to organizational settings only in the last few years.

**Reinforcement theory** is based on the idea that behavior is a function of its consequences.

figure 6.4 **Learning as a Cognitive Process**

*Contemporary thinking suggests that individual learning is a cognitive process. Specifically, the idea is that prior learning influences our behavioral choices. The perceived consequences of the choices we make regarding behavior become in turn a part of our learning and affect future behavioral choices.*

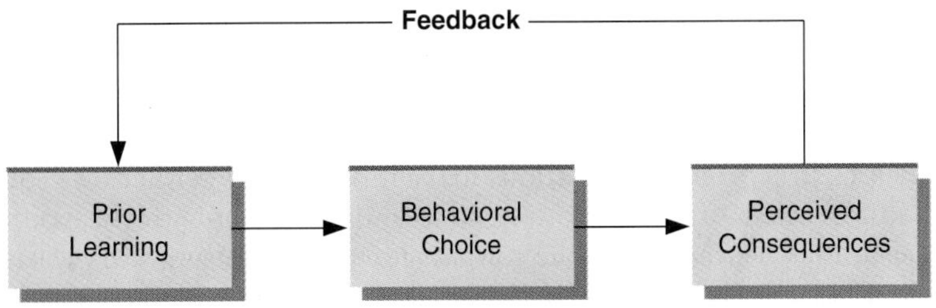


## Reinforcement Theory and Learning

Reinforcement theory (also called "operant conditioning") is generally associated with the work of B. F. Skinner.[29] In its simplest form, **reinforcement theory** suggests that behavior is a function of its consequences.[30] Behavior that results in pleasant consequences is more likely to be repeated (the employee will be motivated to repeat the current behavior), and behavior that results in unpleasant consequences is less likely to be repeated (the employee will be motivated to engage in different behaviors). Reinforcement theory also suggests that in any given situation, people explore a variety of possible behaviors. Future behavioral choices are affected by the consequences of earlier behaviors. Cognitions, as already noted, also play an important role. Thus, rather than assuming the mechanical stimulus-response linkage suggested by the traditional classical view of learning, contemporary theorists believe that people consciously explore different behaviors and systematically choose those that result in the most desirable outcomes.

Suppose a new employee at Monsanto in St. Louis wants to learn the best way to get along with his boss. At first, the employee is very friendly and informal, but the boss responds by acting aloof and, at times, annoyed. Because the boss does not react positively, the employee is unlikely to continue this behavior. In fact, the employee starts acting more formal and professional and finds the boss much more receptive to this posture. The employee will probably continue this new set of behaviors because it results in positive consequences.

**Reinforcement** is the consequences of behavior.

**Positive reinforcement** is a reward or other desirable consequence that a person receives after exhibiting behavior.

**Avoidance**, or **negative reinforcement**, is the opportunity to avoid or escape from an unpleasant circumstance after exhibiting behavior.

**Extinction** decreases the frequency of behavior by eliminating a reward or desirable consequence that follows that behavior.

### Types of Reinforcement in Organizations

The consequences of behavior are called **reinforcement**. Managers can use various kinds of reinforcement to affect employee behavior. The four basic forms of reinforcement—positive reinforcement, avoidance, extinction, and punishment—are summarized in Figure 6.5.

**Positive reinforcement** is a reward or other desirable consequence that follows behavior. Providing positive reinforcement after a particular behavior motivates employees to maintain or increase the frequency of that behavior.[31] A compliment from the boss after completing a difficult job and a salary increase following a period of high performance are examples of positive reinforcement. This type of reinforcement is in use at Corning's ceramics factory in Virginia, where workers receive bonuses for pulling blemished materials from assembly lines before they go into more expensive stages of production.[32]

**Avoidance**, also known as **negative reinforcement**, is another means of increasing the frequency of desirable behavior. Rather than receiving a reward following a desirable behavior, the person is given the opportunity to avoid an unpleasant consequence. For example, suppose that a boss habitually criticizes employees who dress casually. To avoid criticism, an employee may routinely dress to suit the supervisor's tastes. The employee is motivated to engage in desirable behavior (at least from the supervisor's viewpoint) to avoid an unpleasant, or aversive, consequence.

**Extinction** decreases the frequency of behavior, especially behavior that was previously rewarded. If rewards are withdrawn for behaviors that were previously reinforced, the behaviors will probably become less frequent and eventually die out. For example, a manager with a small staff may encourage frequent visits from subordinates as a way to keep in touch with what is going on. Positive reinforcement might include cordial conversation, attention to subordinates' concerns, and encouragement to come in again soon. As the staff grows, however, the manager may find that such unstructured conversations make it difficult to get her own job done. She then might brush off casual conversation and reward only to-the-point "business" conversations. Withdrawing the rewards for casual chatting will probably extinguish that behavior. We should also note that if managers, inadvertently

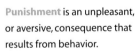

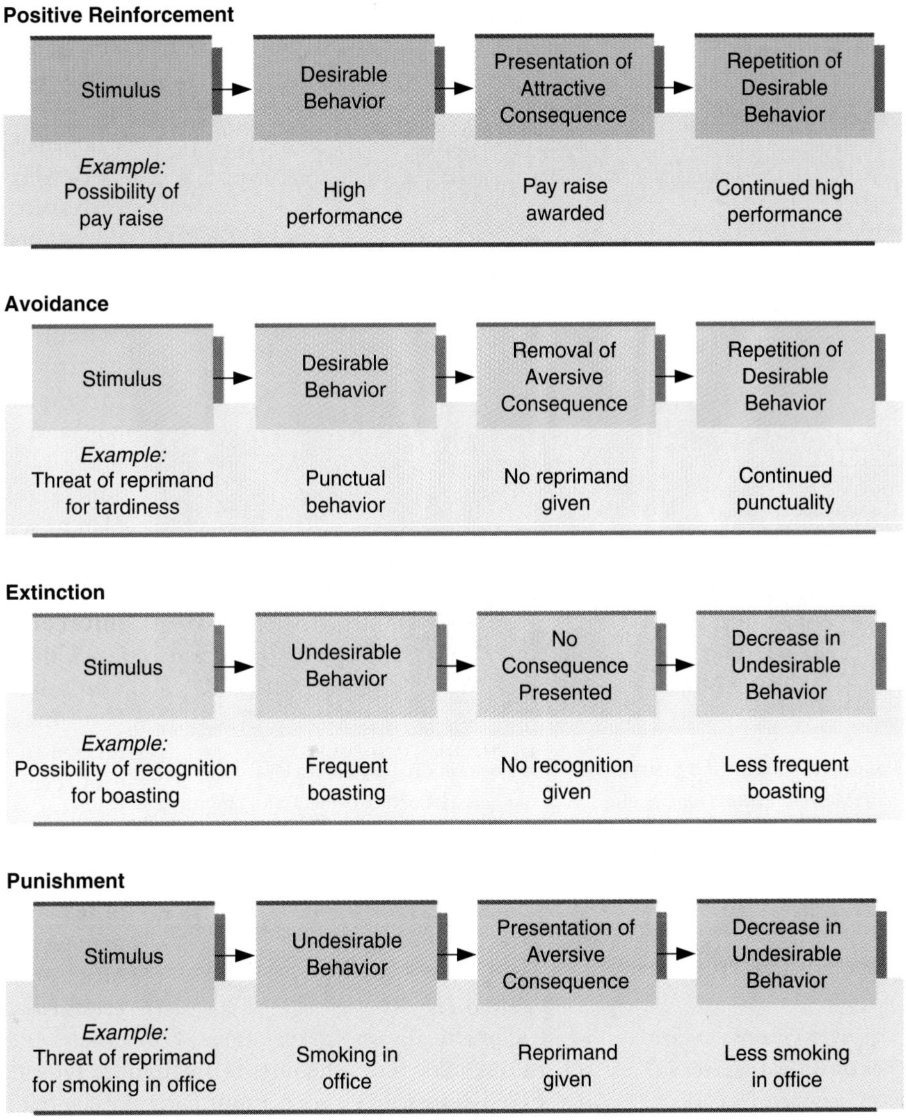


figure **6.5**

**Kinds of Reinforcement**

*There are four basic kinds of reinforcement managers can use to motivate employee behavior. The first two, positive reinforcement and avoidance, can be used to motivate employees to continue to engage in desirable behaviors (such as working hard). The other two, extinction and punishment, might be used to motivate employees to change undesirable behaviors (such a goofing off).*

or otherwise, cease to reward valuable behaviors such as good performance and punctuality, those behaviors too may become extinct.[33]

**Punishment** is an unpleasant, or aversive, consequence that results from behavior.

Punishment, like extinction, also tends to decrease the frequency of undesirable behaviors. **Punishment** is an unpleasant, or aversive, consequence of a behavior.[34] Examples of punishment are verbal or written reprimands, pay cuts, loss of privileges, layoffs, and termination. Many experts question the value of punishment and believe that managers use it too often and use it inappropriately. In some situations, however, punishment may be an appropriate tool for altering behavior. Many instances of life's unpleasantness teach us what to do by means of punishment. Falling off a bike, drinking too much, or going out in the rain without an umbrella all lead to punishing consequences (getting bruised, suffering a hangover, and getting wet), and we often learn to change our behavior as a

Positive reinforcement is a reward that follows behavior. To help build a loyal customer base, Midwest Express Airlines offers its passengers a lot of nice extras. During morning hours, Midwest has free coffee and newspapers at its gates. On afternoon flights, passengers get fresh warm chocolate chip cookies, like these being offered by the firm's CEO, Timothy Hoeksema. Evening flights include dinners of steak and shrimp. By offering better rewards than its competitors, Midwest continues to grow significantly faster than industry averages.

result. Furthermore, certain types of undesirable behavior may have far-reaching negative effects if they go unpunished. For instance, an employee who sexually harasses a coworker, a clerk who steals money from the petty cash account, and an executive who engages in illegal stock transactions all deserve punishment.

**Schedules of Reinforcement in Organizations** Should the manager try to reward every instance of desirable behavior and punish every instance of undesirable behavior? Or is it better to apply reinforcement according to some plan or schedule? As you might expect, it depends on the situation. Table 6.1 summarizes five basic **schedules of reinforcement** that managers can use.[35]

**Continuous reinforcement** rewards behavior every time it occurs. Continuous reinforcement is very effective in motivating desirable behaviors, especially in the early stages of learning. When reinforcement is withdrawn, however, extinction sets in very quickly. But continuous reinforcement poses serious difficulties, because the manager must monitor every behavior of an employee and provide effective reinforcement. This approach, then, is of little practical value to managers. Offering partial reinforcement according to one of the other four schedules is much more typical.

**Fixed-interval reinforcement** is reinforcement provided on a predetermined, constant schedule. The Friday-afternoon paycheck is a good example of a fixed-interval reinforcement. Unfortunately, in many situations the fixed-interval schedule does not necessarily maintain high performance levels. If employees know the boss will drop by to check on them every day at 1:00 P.M., they may be motivated to work hard at that time, hoping to gain praise and recognition or to avoid the boss's wrath. At other times of the day, the employees probably will not work as hard because they have learned that reinforcement is unlikely except during the daily visit.

**Variable-interval reinforcement** also uses time as the basis for applying reinforcement, but it varies the interval between reinforcements. This schedule is inappropriate for paying wages, but it can work well for other types of positive reinforcement, such as praise and recognition, and for avoidance. Consider again the group of employees just described. Suppose that instead of coming by at exactly 1:00 P.M. every day, the boss visits at a different time each day: 9:30 A.M. on Monday, 2:00 P.M. on Tuesday, 11:00 A.M. on Wednesday, and so on. The following week, the times change. Because the employees do not know just when to expect the boss, they may be motivated to work hard for a longer period—until her

**Schedules of reinforcement** indicate when or how often managers should reinforce certain behaviors.

With **continuous reinforcement**, behavior is rewarded every time it occurs.

**Fixed-interval reinforcement** provides reinforcement on a fixed time schedule.

**Variable-interval reinforcement** varies the amount of time between reinforcements.

table 6.1
**Schedules of Reinforcement**

| Schedule of Reinforcement | Nature of Reinforcement |
|---|---|
| Continuous | Behavior is reinforced every time it occurs. |
| Fixed-Interval | Behavior is reinforced according to some predetermined, constant schedule based on time. |
| Variable-Interval | Behavior is reinforced after periods of time, but the time span varies from one time to the next. |
| Fixed-Ratio | Behavior is reinforced according to the number of behaviors exhibited, with the number of behaviors needed to gain reinforcement held constant. |
| Variable-Ratio | Behavior is reinforced according to the number of behaviors exhibited, but the number of behaviors needed to gain reinforcement varies from one time to the next. |

visit. Afterward, though, they may drop back to lower levels because they have learned that she will not be back until the next day.

**Fixed-ratio reinforcement** provides reinforcement after a fixed number of behaviors.

The fixed- and variable-ratio schedules gear reinforcement to the number of desirable or undesirable behaviors rather than to blocks of time. With **fixed-ratio reinforcement**, the number of behaviors needed to obtain reinforcement is constant. Assume, for instance, that a work group enters its cumulative performance totals into the firm's computer network every hour. The manager of the group uses the network to monitor its activities. He might adopt a practice of dropping by to praise the group every time it reaches a performance level of five hundred units. Thus, if the group does this three times on Monday, he stops by each time; if it reaches the mark only once on Tuesday, he stops by only once. The fixed-ratio schedule can be fairly effective in maintaining desirable behavior. Employees may acquire a sense of what it takes to be reinforced and be motivated to maintain their performance.

**Variable-ratio reinforcement** varies the number of behaviors between reinforcements.

With **variable-ratio reinforcement**, the number of behaviors required for reinforcement varies over time. An employee performing under a variable-ratio schedule is motivated to work hard because each successful behavior increases the probability that the next one will result in reinforcement. With this schedule, the exact number of behaviors needed to obtain reinforcement is not crucial; what is important is that the intervals between reinforcement not be so long that the worker gets discouraged and stops trying. The supervisor in the fixed-ratio example could reinforce his work group after it reaches performance levels of 325, 525, 450, 600, and so on. A variable-ratio schedule can be quite effective, but it is difficult and cumbersome to use when formal organizational rewards, such as pay increases and promotions, are the reinforcers. A fixed-interval system is the best way to administer these rewards.

## Related Aspects of Learning

Several additional aspects of learning also pertain to motivated behavior in organizations. Among them are reinforcement generalization, reinforcement discrimination, and social learning.

**Reinforcement generalization** is the process through which a person extends recognition of similar or identical behavior-reinforcement relationships to different settings.

Reinforcement Generalization **Reinforcement generalization** is the process through which a person extends recognition of similar or identical behavior-reinforcement relationships to different settings.[36] People learn what behaviors are likely to produce reinforcement, and, when they encounter a similar behavior opportunity in different surroundings, they may expect the same response to elicit a similar consequence. For example, Mike Holmgren recently left the head coaching position for the Green Bay Packers for a similar job with the Seattle Seahawks. Because the job is essentially the same (coaching) and the organization is the same (professional football team), he will almost certainly believe that he can employ the same methods and techniques that were a success for him at Green Bay in his new position. Or consider a plant manager for General Electric who has a history of effective troubleshooting. Over the years he has been assigned to several plants, each with a serious operating problem. After successfully dealing with the difficulties, he has always received an extended vacation, a bonus, and a boost in his base salary. He has learned the basic contingencies, or requirements, of reinforcement for his job: working hard and solving the plant's problems results in several positive reinforcers. When the manager gets his next assignment, he will probably generalize from his past experiences. Even though he will be in a different plant with different problems and employees, he will know what is expected of him and understand what it takes to be rewarded.

**Reinforcement discrimination** is the process of recognizing differences between behavior and reinforcement in different settings.

Reinforcement Discrimination **Reinforcement discrimination** is the ability to recognize differences in behavior-reinforcement relationships in different situations.[37] It is the capacity to recognize that behaviors that were reinforced a certain way in one situation may be reinforced differently in a new situation. For example, a successful college coach taking a job coaching a professional team should understand that while the games may be similar, the players and their relationship with the team are very different. Indeed, a few years ago John Calipari left the job of head basketball coach at the University of Massachusetts for the same job with the NBA's New Jersey Nets. He was subsequently fired, in large part because he was unable to duplicate the successes at the professional level that he had enjoyed at the collegiate level. Had he recognized the differences from the beginning, he might very well have enjoyed greater success.

*"People will say this isn't college basketball, but you reach back to past experiences when you're in a new position." — John Calipari, on his transition from college to NBA coach*[38]

Similarly, suppose the troubleshooting plant manager is assigned to a plant that is running smoothly. His routine response to new situations has always been to identify and solve problems, but he now must discriminate between his new situation and his earlier ones. In this situation he may recognize that he needs a different set of behaviors, or responses, to meet performance expectations and receive positive reinforcement.

**Social learning** occurs when people observe the behaviors of others, recognize their consequences, and alter their own behavior as a result.

Social Learning in Organizations In recent years, managers have begun to recognize the power of social learning.[39] **Social learning** occurs when people observe the behaviors of others, recognize their consequences, and alter their own behavior as a result.[40] A person can learn to do a new job by observing others or by watching videotapes. Or an employee may learn to avoid being late by seeing the boss chew out fellow workers. Social learning theory, then, suggests that individual behavior is determined by a person's cognitions and social environment.[41] More specifically, people are presumed to learn behaviors and attitudes at least partly in response to what others expect of them.

Several conditions must be met to produce an appropriate environment for social learning. First, the behavior being observed and imitated must be relatively simple. Although we can learn by watching someone else how to push three or four buttons to set specifications on a machine or to turn on a computer, we probably cannot learn a complicated sequence of operations for the machine or how to run software on a computer without also practicing the various steps ourselves. Second, social learning usually involves observed and imitated behavior that is concrete, not intellectual. We can learn by watching others how to respond to the different behaviors of a particular manager or how to assemble a few component parts into a final assembled product. But we probably cannot learn through simple observation how to write computer software, how to write complicated text, how to conceptualize, or how to think abstractly. Finally, for social learning to occur we must possess the physical ability to imitate the behavior observed. Most of us, even if we watch televised baseball games or tennis matches every weekend, cannot hit a curveball like Ken Griffey Jr., or execute a backhand like Venus Williams.

Social learning influences motivation in a variety of ways.[42] Indeed, many of the behaviors we exhibit in our daily work lives are learned from others. Suppose a new employee joins an existing work group. She already has some basis for knowing how to behave, from her education and previous experience. However, the group provides a set of very specific cues she can use to tailor her behavior to fit her new situation. The group may indicate how the organization expects its members to dress, how people are "supposed" to feel about the boss, and so forth. Hence, the employee learns how to behave in the new situation partly in response to what she already knows and partly in response to what others suggest and demonstrate.

# Organizational Behavior Modification

Learning theory alone has important implications for managers, but organizational behavior modification has even more practical applications. Organizational behavior modification is an important application of reinforcement theory some managers use to enhance motivation and performance.

## Behavior Modification in Organizations

**Organizational behavior modification**, or **OB mod**, is the application of reinforcement theory to people in organizational settings.

**Organizational behavior modification**, or **OB mod**, is the application of reinforcement theory to people in organizational settings.[43] Reinforcement theory says that we can increase the frequency of desirable behaviors by linking those behaviors with positive consequences and decrease undesirable behaviors by linking them with negative consequences. OB mod characteristically uses positive reinforcement to encourage desirable behaviors in employees. Figure 6.6 illustrates the basic steps in OB mod.

The first step is to identify performance-related behavioral events—that is, desirable and undesirable behaviors. A manager of an electronics store might decide

figure 6.6

**Steps in Organizational Behavior Modification**

*Organizational behavior modification involves using reinforcement theory to motivate employee behavior. By employing the steps shown here, managers can often isolate behaviors they value and then link specific rewards to those behaviors. As a result, employees will be more likely to engage in those behaviors in the future.*

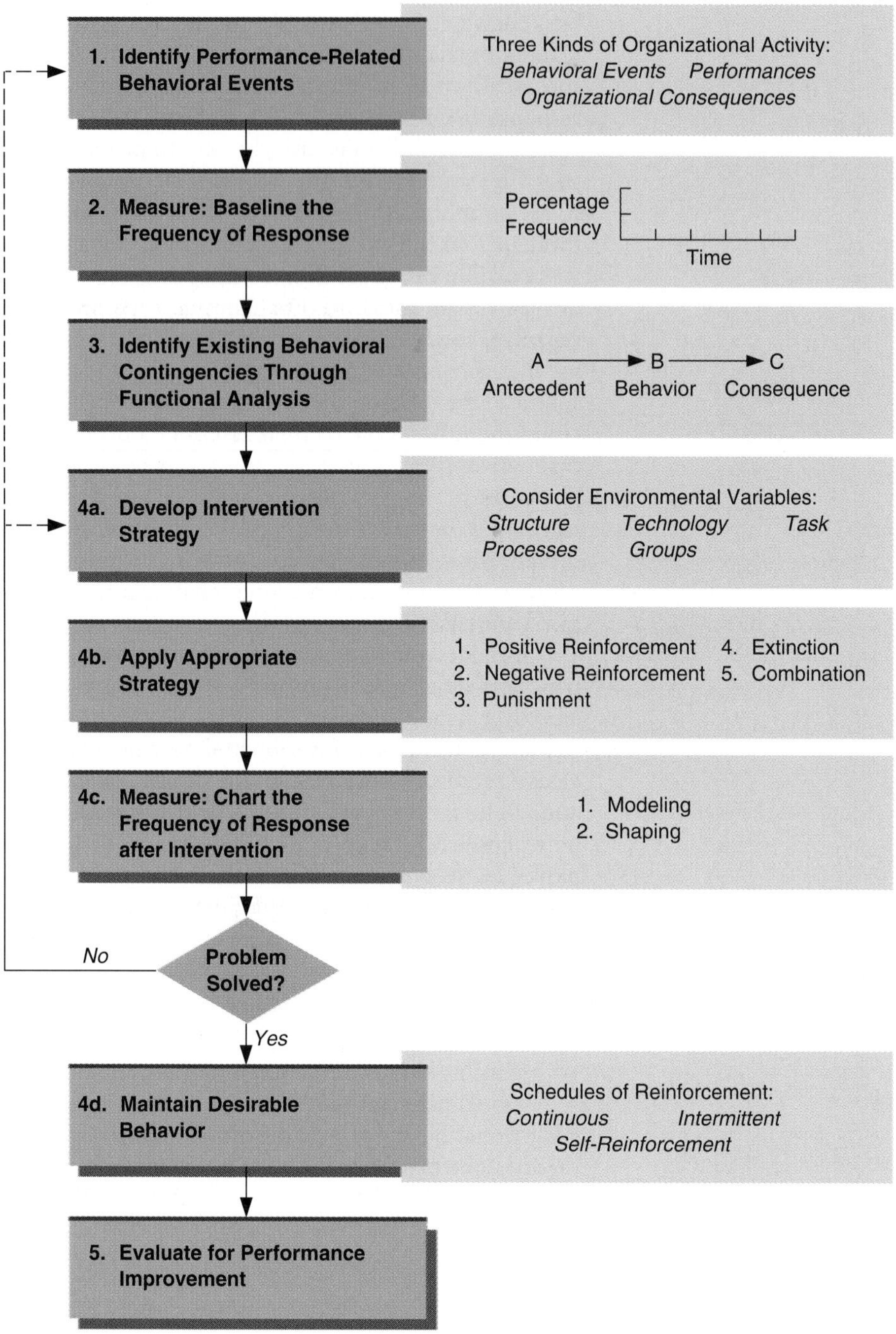


Reference: Reprinted, by permission of the publisher, from *Personnel,* July–August 1974. 

that the most important behavior for salespeople working on commission is to greet customers warmly and show them the exact merchandise they came in to see. Note in Figure 6.6 that three kinds of organizational activity are associated with this behavior: the behavioral event itself, the performance that results, and the organizational consequences that befall the individual.

Next, the manager measures baseline performance—the existing level of performance for each individual. This usually is stated in terms of a percentage frequency across different time intervals. For example, the electronics store manager may observe that a particular salesperson presently is greeting around 40 percent of the customers each day as desired. Performance management techniques, described in Chapter 8, are used for this purpose.

The third step is to identify the existing behavioral contingencies, or consequences, of performance; that is, what happens now to employees who perform at various levels? If an employee works hard, does he or she get a reward or just get tired? The electronics store manager may observe that when customers are greeted warmly and assisted competently, they buy something 40 percent of the time, whereas customers who are not properly greeted and assisted make a purchase only 20 percent of the time.

At this point, the manager develops and applies an appropriate intervention strategy. In other words, some element of the performance-reward linkage—structure, process, technology, groups, or the task—is changed to make high-level performance more rewarding. Various kinds of positive reinforcement are used to guide employee behavior in desired directions. The electronics store manager might offer a sales commission plan whereby salespeople earn a percentage of the dollar amount taken in by each sale. The manager might also compliment salespeople who give appropriate greetings and ignore those who do not. The reinforcement helps shape the behavior of salespeople. In addition, an individual salesperson who does not get reinforced may imitate the behavior of more successful salespersons.[44] In general, this step relies on the reward system in the organization, as discussed previously.

After the intervention step, the manager again measures performance to determine whether the desired effect has been achieved. If not, the manager must redesign the intervention strategy or repeat the entire process. For instance, if the salespeople in the electronics store are still not greeting customers properly, the manager may need to look for other forms of positive reinforcement—perhaps a higher commission.

If performance has increased, the manager must try to maintain the desirable behavior through some schedule of positive reinforcement. For example, higher commissions might be granted for every other sale, for sales over a certain dollar amount, and so forth. (As we saw earlier, a reinforcement schedule defines the interval at which reinforcement is given.)

Finally, the manager looks for improvements in individual employees' behavior. Here the emphasis is on offering significant longer-term rewards, such as promotions and salary adjustments, to sustain ongoing efforts to improve performance.[45]

## The Effectiveness of OB Mod

Since the OB mod approach is relatively simple, it has been used by many types of organizations, with varying levels of success.[46] A program at Emery Air Freight prompted much of the initial enthusiasm for OB mod, and other success stories have caught the attention of practicing managers.[47] B.F. Goodrich increased productivity over 300 percent, and Weyerhaeuser increased productivity by at least 8 percent in three different work groups.[48] These results suggest that OB mod is a valuable method for improving employee motivation in many situations.

*Turner Brothers Trucking Inc. uses "behavioral observation of one another by workers, productivity bonuses that include a safety component, and measurement of learning from defensive driving courses by third-party road observations" as part of its OB mod program. — Garry M. Ritzky, human resources director for Turner Brothers Trucking, Inc.*[49]

OB mod also has certain drawbacks. For one thing, not all applications have worked. A program at Standard Oil of Ohio was discontinued because it failed to meet its objectives; another program at Michigan Bell was only modestly successful. Further, managers frequently have only limited means for providing meaningful reinforcement for their employees. Further, much of the research testing of OB mod has gone on in laboratories and thus is hard to generalize to the real world. And even if OB mod works for a while, the impact of the positive reinforcement may wane once the novelty has worn off, and employees may come to view it as a routine part of the compensation system.[50]

## The Ethics of OB Mod

Although OB mod has considerable potential for enhancing motivated behavior in organizations, its critics raise ethical issues about its use. The primary ethical argument is that use of OB mod compromises individual freedom of choice. Managers may tend to select reinforcement contingencies that produce advantages for the organization, with little or no regard for what is best for the individual employee. Thus, workers may be rewarded for working hard, producing high-quality products, and so forth. Behaviors that promote their own personal growth and development or that reduce their level of personal stress may go unrewarded.

An element of manipulation is also involved in OB mod. Indeed, its very purpose is to shape the behaviors of others. Thus, rather than giving employees an array of behaviors to choose from, managers may continually funnel employee efforts through an increasingly narrow array of behavioral options such that they eventually have little choice but to select the limited set behaviors approved of by managers.

These ethical issues are, of course, real concerns that should not be ignored. At the same time, many other methods and approaches used by managers have the same goal of shaping behavior. Thus, OB mod is not really unique in its potential for misuse or misrepresentation. The keys are for managers to recognize and not abuse their ability to alter subordinate behavior and for employees to maintain control of their own work environment to the point that they are fully cognizant of the behavioral choices they are making.

# Attribution and Motivation

**Attribution theory** suggests that employees observe their own behavior, determine whether it is a response to external or internal factors, and shape their future motivated behavior accordingly.

In Chapter 4, we discussed the role of attribution in perception. **Attribution theory** also has motivational implications.[51] According to the attributional view of employee motivation, a person observes his or her behavior through the processes of self-perception. On the basis of these perceptions, the individual decides whether his or her behavior is a response primarily to external or to internal factors. A person who believes he is extrinsically motivated will seek extrinsic rewards, such as pay or status symbols, as future incentives. One who feels she is intrinsically motivated will look more for intrinsic incentives in the future.

Although little work has been done on attribution theory's applications to motivation, there have been some intriguing findings. For example, Deci reasoned that paying an intrinsically motivated person on an incentive basis (that is, providing extrinsic rewards) would make him or her more extrinsically motivated and less intrinsically motivated. Deci's research has indicated that if people are paid to do something they already like to do (that is, that they are intrinsically motivated to do), their level of "liking" diminishes. Furthermore, if the pay is later withheld, their level of effort diminishes. Thus, attributional processes appear to play a meaningful role in employee motivation in the workplace.[52]

## Synopsis

The equity theory of motivation assumes that people want to be treated fairly. It hypothesizes that people compare their own input-to-outcome ratio in the organization to the ratio of a comparison-other. If they feel their treatment has been inequitable, they take steps to reduce the inequity.

Expectancy theory, a somewhat more complicated model, follows from the assumption that people are motivated to work toward a goal if they want it and think they have a reasonable chance of achieving it. Effort-to-performance expectancy is the belief that effort will lead to performance. Performance-to-outcome expectancy is the belief that performance will lead to certain outcomes. Valence is the desirability to the individual of the various possible outcomes of performance. The Porter-Lawler version of expectancy theory provides useful insights into the relationship between satisfaction and performance. This model suggests that performance may lead to a variety of intrinsic and extrinsic rewards. When perceived as equitable, these rewards lead to satisfaction.

Learning also plays a role in employee motivation. Various kinds of reinforcement provided according to different schedules can increase or decrease motivated behavior. People can also generalize and discriminate among different behavior-reinforcement situations and are affected by social learning processes.

Organizational behavior modification is a strategy for using learning and reinforcement principles to enhance employee motivation and performance. This strategy relies heavily on the effective measurement of performance and the provision of rewards to employees after they perform at a high level.

Attribution processes also affect motivation. Attribution theory suggests that employees perceive their behavior as stemming from either external or internal causes and are motivated by rewards that correspond to the causes of their behavior.

## Discussion Questions

1. Besides distinctions between need-based and process-based perspectives, are there any basic differences between the motivation theories discussed in Chapters 5 and 6?
2. Have you ever experienced inequity in a job or a class? How did it affect you?
3. Which is likely to be a more serious problem, perceptions of being underrewarded or perceptions of being overrewarded?
4. What are some managerial implications of equity theory beyond those discussed in the chapter?

5. Do you think expectancy theory is too complex for direct use in organizational settings? Why or why not?
6. Do the relationships between performance and satisfaction suggested by Porter and Lawler seem valid? Cite examples that both support and refute the model.
7. Have you ever experienced classical conditioning? If so, what were the circumstances?
8. Think of occasions on which you experienced each of the four types of reinforcement.
9. Identify the five types of reinforcement that you receive most often. On what schedule do you receive each of them?
10. What is your opinion about the ethics of OB mod?
11. Cite personal examples of attributional processes and motivation.

# Organizational Behavior Case for Discussion

## Motivation at Mirage

People who frequent gambling casinos usually do so because they find the activity of wagering to be a pleasurable one. These people often forget, however, that gambling itself is a big business, a business that must be effectively managed if its owners are to remain in operation. Just as any business relies on people to carry out its work, casinos need employees to manage and work in hotel operations, entertainment venues, gift shops, parking operations, and the gaming areas themselves. Moreover, they rely on managers to oversee their marketing, financial, and human resource functions. While people may debate the morality of legalized gambling, there is no question as to its profitability.

One of the most successful businesses in the gambling industry today is Mirage Resorts, Inc. Stephen Wynn was the primary owner and chief executive officer of Mirage Resorts before selling it to MGM Grand in early 2000. The company is best known for its elaborate Mirage and Treasure Island resort properties in Las Vegas. The Mirage resort, for example, has 3,030 hotel rooms, a 95,000-square-foot casino, and features such attractions as Siegfried & Roy's Royal White Tigers and a dolphin exhibit. The Treasure Island resort includes full-size replicas of a British frigate and a pirate ship that engages in live sea battles.

The company also owns the Golden Nugget casinos in Las Vegas and Laughlin and has a 50 percent stake in the Casino Iguazu in Argentina. In addition, Mirage has new projects under development for other areas in Nevada as well as New Jersey and Mississippi. Most industry observers credited the success of Mirage to Wynn himself and the innovative management practices he pioneered. Wynn, for example, has all the characteristics of a charismatic and inspirational leader. He is interesting and well informed, and can inspire others to follow his lead.

Another integral part of Mirage's success was Wynn's approach to dealing with his employees. For example, he once observed, "I have found that you can never go wrong indulging your employees." Thus, throughout his company he regularly looked for ways to recognize superior performance. One routine part of this management system was what Wynn called his "Gotcha" awards. These awards could be handed out at the discretion of a first-line supervisor to any employee observed doing his or her job in an exceptionally competent manner. The most common Gotcha awards were an extra day off with pay or a gift certificate good for merchandise at one of Mirage's gift shops or restaurants.

Employees and supervisors of the year at each Mirage casino were also treated to Hawaiian vacations and a banquet that cost the company about $400,000. In addition, while it is common in entertainment operations like hotels to give employees free food, most competitors use leftovers from the guest buffet as a source of food for employees. Under Wynn's leadership Mirage workers, however, enjoyed fresh and free meals in gleaming new cafeterias.

Another management innovation pioneered by Wynn was what he called planned insubordination.

Essentially, managers at Mirage Resorts were required to explain why any given task needed to be accomplished. If subordinates found the explanation to be unconvincing, they were not required to perform the task. This caused managers to carefully consider the reasons behind their decisions before announcing them and helped subordinates more fully understand how the business was being managed.

And what were the effects of these benevolent human resource strategies? For one thing, Mirage's turnover rate of 12 percent has been less than half the industry average. Moreover, despite the fact that almost half of Mirage's workers belong to unions, no grievances were filed against the firm for more than four years. Because the company was seen as such an attractive place to work, Mirage could attract good employees and pay them at or even sometimes below market rates.

### Case Questions

1. What motivational theories and techniques were being used by Wynn?
2. How well do you think Wynn's management style would work in other settings?
3. If you were one of Mirage's competitors, how would you deal with the fact that its casinos seem to be the preferred places to work in Las Vegas today?

References: *Hoover's Handbook of American Business 2000* (Austin, Tex.: Hoover's Business Press, 2000), pp. 982–983; "Picasso Among the High Rollers," *Forbes*, May 19, 1997, pp. 44–46; Kenneth Labich, "Gambling's Kings," *Fortune*, July 22, 1996, pp. 80–88.

## Experiencing Organizational Behavior

### Understanding the Dynamics of Expectancy Theory

**Purpose:** This exercise will help you recognize both the potential value and the complexity of expectancy theory.

**Format:** Working alone, you will be asked to identify the various aspects of expectancy theory that are pertinent to your class. You will then share your thoughts and results with some of your classmates.

**Procedure:** Considering your class as a workplace and your effort in the class as a surrogate for a job, do the following:

1. Identify six or seven things that might happen as a result of good performance in your class (for example, a good grade or a recommendation from your instructor). Your list must include at least one undesirable outcome (for example, a loss of free time).
2. Using a value of 10 for "extremely desirable," −10 for "extremely undesirable," and 0 for "complete neutrality," assign a valence to each outcome. In other words, the valence you assign to each outcome should be somewhere between 10 and −10, inclusive.
3. Assume you are a high performer. On that basis, estimate the probability of each potential outcome. Express this probability as a percentage.
4. Multiply each valence by its associated probability, and add the results. This total is your overall valence for high performance.
5. Assess the probability that if you exert effort, you will be a high performer. Express that probability as a percentage.
6. Multiply this probability by the overall valence for high performance calculated in step 4. This score reflects your motivational force—that is, your motivation to exert strong effort.

Now form groups of three or four. Compare your scores on motivational force. Discuss why some scores differ widely. Also, note whether any group members had similar force scores but different combinations of factors leading to those scores.

### Follow-up Questions

1. What does this exercise tell you about the strengths and limitations of expectancy theory?
2. Would this exercise be useful for a manager to run with a group of subordinates? Why or why not?

## Building Organizational Behavior Skills

### Assessing Your Equity Sensitivity

The questions that follow are intended to help you better understand your equity sensitivity. Answer each question on the scales by circling the number that best reflects your personal feelings.

1. I think it is important for everyone to be treated fairly.

| 5 | 4 | 3 | 2 | 1 |
|---|---|---|---|---|
| Strongly Agree | Agree | Neither Agree Nor Disagree | Disagree | Strongly Disagree |

2. I pay a lot of attention to how I am treated, in comparison to how others are treated.

| 5 | 4 | 3 | 2 | 1 |
|---|---|---|---|---|
| Strongly Agree | Agree | Neither Agree Nor Disagree | Disagree | Strongly Disagree |

3. I get really angry if I think I'm being treated unfairly.

| 5 | 4 | 3 | 2 | 1 |
|---|---|---|---|---|
| Strongly Agree | Agree | Neither Agree Nor Disagree | Disagree | Strongly Disagree |

4. It makes me uncomfortable if I think someone else is not being treated fairly.

| 5 | 4 | 3 | 2 | 1 |
|---|---|---|---|---|
| Strongly Agree | Agree | Neither Agree Nor Disagree | Disagree | Strongly Disagree |

5. If I thought I was being treated unfairly, I would be very motivated to change things.

| 5 | 4 | 3 | 2 | 1 |
|---|---|---|---|---|
| Strongly Agree | Agree | Neither Agree Nor Disagree | Disagree | Strongly Disagree |

6. It doesn't really bother me if someone else gets a better deal than me.

| 5 | 4 | 3 | 2 | 1 |
|---|---|---|---|---|
| Strongly Agree | Agree | Neither Agree Nor Disagree | Disagree | Strongly Disagree |

7. It is impossible for everyone to be treated fairly all the time.

| 5 | 4 | 3 | 2 | 1 |
|---|---|---|---|---|
| Strongly Agree | Agree | Neither Agree Nor Disagree | Disagree | Strongly Disagree |

8. When I'm a manager, I'll make sure that all of my employees are treated fairly.

| 5 | 4 | 3 | 2 | 1 |
|---|---|---|---|---|
| Strongly Agree | Agree | Neither Agree Nor Disagree | Disagree | Strongly Disagree |

9. I would quit my job if I thought I was being treated unfairly.

| 5 | 4 | 3 | 2 | 1 |
|---|---|---|---|---|
| Strongly Agree | Agree | Neither Agree Nor Disagree | Disagree | Strongly Disagree |

10. Short-term inequities are okay, because things all even out in the long run.

| 5 | 4 | 3 | 2 | 1 |
|---|---|---|---|---|
| Strongly Agree | Agree | Neither Agree Nor Disagree | Disagree | Strongly Disagree |

Instructions: Add up your total points (note that some items have a "reversed" numbering arrangement). If you scored 35 or above, you are highly sensitive to equity and fairness; 15 or less, you have very little sensitivity to equity and fairness; between 35 and 15, you have moderate equity sensitivity.

## Developing OB Internet Skills

**Introduction:** A role-playing exercise is one in which you try to put yourself in someone else's position and then try to imagine how that individual might perceive or react to a situation. For this exercise, assume that you work in each of the following jobs and earn the salaries noted:

- Newspaper reporter with 5 years' experience making $30,000 a year
- Plant manager with 20 years' experience making $50,000

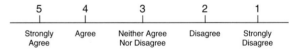

- Sales representative for a medical equipment firm with 10 years' experience making $200,000 a year
- Retail store manager with 1 year of experience making $20,000 a year

**Internet Assignment:** Use the Internet to locate salary data for others in similar jobs and with corresponding experience. As a result of what you learn, assess whether you are likely to feel equity or inequity; if the feeling is most likely to be inequity, decide which form you are likely to experience (that is, overrewarded or underrewarded).

**Follow-up:** For any instances in which you are likely to experience inequity, decide how you might react.

Finally, respond to the following instructions and questions:

1. How easy or difficult was it to locate data on the Internet for this exercise?
2. Given the growth of the Internet, do you think more people will start using it for comparisons such as this one, or will people still rely mostly on "real" coworkers?
3. Aside from the raw data, what additional information would you really need in this situation before meaningful levels of equity and/or inequity could be formulated?

chapter 7

# Job Design, Employee Participation, and Alternative Work Arrangements

**Management Preview** Managers determine what jobs will be performed in their organizations and how those jobs will be performed. But managers must also determine how to motivate people and how to optimize their performance. The long-term key to success in business is to create jobs that optimize the organization's requirements for productivity and efficiency while simultaneously motivating and satisfying the employees who perform those jobs. As people and organizations change, and as we continue to learn more about management, managers need to occasionally review the existing jobs in their organization and make whatever changes are necessary to improve them. This chapter is the first of two that address the strategies managers use to optimize the performance of their employees. We begin with a discussion of job design, starting with a look at historical approaches to job design. Then we discuss an important contemporary perspective on jobs, the job characteristics theory. Next, we describe how social information affects job design and review the importance of employee participation and empowerment. Finally, we discuss alternative work arrangements that can be used to enhance motivation and performance. First, though, we look at some relatively common but very unappealing jobs so we can better appreciate how great these challenges can be! ■

The business press has hit upon what seems to be an interesting trend in work. Business magazines and newspapers are regularly publishing articles about the dynamic nature of work in the United States and about how many jobs are being changed. Indeed, because of the publicity given the shift toward service-sector and professional jobs, many people assume that the number of unpleasant and undesirable jobs has declined. In fact, nothing could be further from the truth. It is true that millions of Americans work in gleaming air-conditioned facilities, but many others work in dirty, grimy, and unsafe settings. Consider, for example, the jobs in a chicken-processing facility.

Much like a manufacturing assembly line, a chicken-processing facility is organized around a moving conveyor system. Workers call it "the chain." In reality, it's a steel cable with large clips that carries dead chickens down what might be called a "disassembly line." Standing along this line are dozens of workers who do, in fact, take the animals apart as they pass. Even the titles of the jobs are unsavory. Among the first set of jobs along the chain is the "skinner." These people use sharp instruments to cut and pull the skin off the dead chicken. Toward the middle of the line are the "gut pullers." These workers reach inside the chicken carcasses and remove the intestines and other organs. At the end of the line are the "gizzard cutters," who tackle the more difficult organs attached to the inside of the chicken's carcass. These organs have to be individually cut and removed for disposal.

The work is obviously distasteful, and the pace of the work is unrelenting: On a good day the chain moves an average of ninety chickens a minute for nine hours. And the workers are essentially held captive by the moving chain. For example, no one can vacate a post to use the bathroom or for other reasons without the permission of the supervisor. In some plants, taking an unauthorized bathroom break can result in suspension without pay. But the noise in a typical chicken-processing plant is so loud that the supervisor can't hear someone calling for relief unless the person happens to be standing close by.

*"The rule is, you can't go to the bathroom more than three times a day, unless you got a doctor's permit." — Supervisor in a chicken-processing plant explaining the rules to a new worker**

Far from becoming automated and professionalized, jobs such as these are actually becoming increasingly common. Fueled by Americans' growing appetites for lean, easy-to-cook meat, the number of poultry workers has almost doubled since 1980, and today they constitute a work force of around a quarter of a million people. Indeed, the chicken-processing industry has become a major component of the state economies of Georgia, North Carolina, Mississippi, Arkansas, and Alabama.

Besides being unpleasant and dirty, many jobs in a chicken-processing plant are dangerous and unhealthy. Some workers, for example, have to fight the live birds when they are first hung on the chains. These workers are routinely scratched and pecked by the chickens. And the air inside a typical chicken-processing plant is difficult to breathe. Workers are usually supplied with paper masks, but most don't use them because they are hot and confining. And the work space itself is so tight that the workers often cut themselves—and sometimes their coworkers—with the knives, scissors, and other instruments they use to perform their jobs. Indeed, poultry processing ranks third among industries in the United States for cumulative trauma injuries such as carpal tunnel syndrome. The inevitable chicken feathers, feces, and blood also contribute to the hazardous and unpleasant work environment.[1] ■

Not all jobs in a chicken-processing plant are as unpleasant as those described above. And certainly many workers in these plants are grateful just to have a job. But the very fact that these jobs are so plentiful underscores a basic problem that confronts many businesses today. That problem is the balancing of organizational pressures for efficiency against individual dignity and work-life quality. In the discussion that follows we will explore many of these problems and issues in more detail. First, however, we will introduce a general framework that can guide managers as they attempt to put into practice the various need- and process-based theories of motivation.

# Motivation and Employee Performance

Chapters 5 and 6 described a variety of need- and process-based perspectives on motivation. We noted in those discussions, however, that no single theory or model completely explains motivation—each covers only some of the factors that actually result in motivated behavior. Moreover, even if one theory were applicable in a particular situation, a manager might still need to translate that theory into operational terms. Thus, while using the actual theories as tools, managers need to understand various operational procedures, systems, and methods for enhancing motivation and performance.

Figure 7.1 illustrates a basic framework for relating various theories of motivation to potential and actual motivation and to operational methods for translating this potential and actual motivation into performance. The left side of the figure illustrates that motivated behavior can be induced by need-based or process-based circumstances. That is, people may be motivated to satisfy various specific needs (as described by the various need-based theories in Chapter 5), or through various processes, such as perceptions of inequity, expectancy relationships, and reinforcement contingencies (as described by the various process-based theories in Chapter 6).

These need- and process-based concepts result in the situation illustrated in the center of the figure—a certain potential exists for motivated behavior directed at enhanced performance. For example, suppose that an employee wants more social relationships—that is, he wants to satisfy belongingness, relatedness, or affiliation needs. This means that there is potential for the employee to want to perform at a higher level if he thinks that higher performance will satisfy those social needs. Likewise, if high performance in the past was followed by strong positive reinforcement, there is again a potential for motivation directed at enhanced performance.

But managers may need to take certain steps to translate the potential for motivation directed at enhanced performance into real motivation and real enhanced performance. In some cases, these steps may be tied to the specific need or process

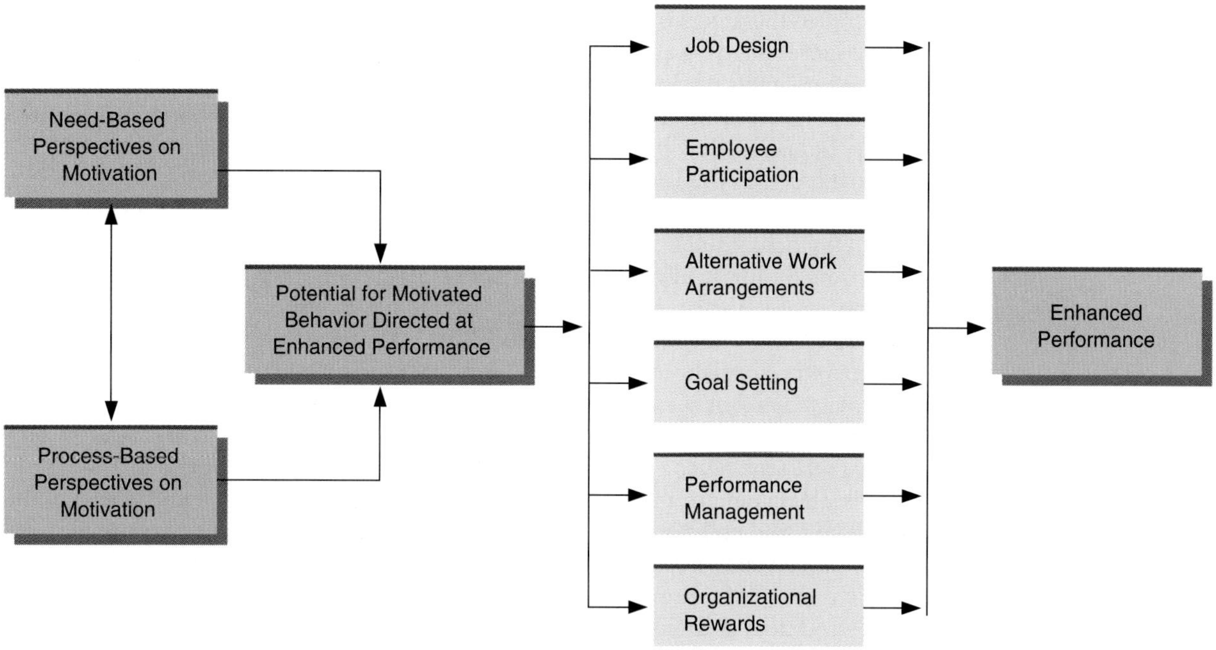


figure 7.1 **Enhancing Performance in Organizations**

*Managers can use a variety of methods to enhance performance in organizations. The need- and process-based perspectives on motivation explain some of the factors involved in increasing the potential for motivated behavior directed at enhanced performance. Managers can then use such means as goal setting, job design, alternative work arrangements, performance management, rewards, and organizational behavior modification to help translate this potential into actual enhanced performance.*

that has created the existing potential. For example, providing more opportunities for social interaction contingent on improved performance might capitalize on an employee's social needs. More typically, however, a manager needs to go further to help translate potential into real performance.

The right side of Figure 7.1 names some of the more common methods used to enhance performance. This chapter covers the first three—job design, employee participation and empowerment, and alternative work arrangements. The other three, goal setting, performance management, and organizational rewards, are discussed in Chapter 8.

# The Evolution of Job Design

**Job design** is how organizations define and structure jobs.

Job design is an important method managers can use to enhance employee performance.[2] **Job design** is how organizations define and structure jobs. As we will see, properly designed jobs can have a positive impact on the motivation, performance, and job satisfaction of those who perform them. On the other hand, poorly designed jobs can impair motivation, performance, and job satisfaction.

Until the nineteenth century, many families grew the things they needed, especially food. General craft jobs arose as people ceased or reduced their own food production, used their labor to produce other goods such as clothing and furniture, and traded these goods for food and other necessities. Over time, people's work became increasingly specialized as they followed this general pattern. For example, the general craft of clothing production splintered into specialized craft jobs such as weaving, tailoring, and sewing. This evolution toward specialization accelerated as the Industrial Revolution swept Europe in the 1700s and 1800s, followed by the United States in the later 1800s.

The trend toward specialization eventually became a subject of formal study. The two most influential students of specialization were Adam Smith and Charles Babbage. Smith, an eighteenth-century Scottish economist, originated the phrase "division of labor" in his classic book *An Inquiry into the Nature and Causes of the Wealth of Nations*, published in 1776.[3] The book tells the story of a group of pin makers who specialized their jobs to produce many more pins per person in a day than each could have made by working alone.

In Smith's time, pin making, like most other production work, was still an individual job. One person would perform all of the tasks required: drawing out a strip of wire, clipping it to the proper length, sharpening one end, attaching a head to the other end, and polishing the finished pin. With specialization, one person did nothing but draw out wire, another did the clipping, and so on. Smith attributed the dramatic increases in output to factors such as increased dexterity owing to practice, decreased time changing from one production operation to another, and the development of specialized equipment and machinery. The basic principles described in *The Wealth of Nations* provided the foundation for the assembly line.

Charles Babbage wrote *On the Economy of Machinery and Manufactures* in 1832.[4] Extending Smith's work, Babbage cited several additional advantages of job specialization: relatively little time was needed to learn specialized jobs, waste decreased, workers needed to make fewer tool and equipment changes, and workers' skills improved through the frequent repetition of tasks.

As the Industrial Revolution spread to the United States from Europe, job specialization proliferated throughout industry. It began in the mid-1880s and reached its peak with the development of scientific management in the early 1900s.

## Job Specialization

**Job specialization**, as advocated by scientific management, can help improve efficiency, but it can also promote monotony and boredom.

Frederick W. Taylor, the chief proponent of **job specialization**, argued that jobs should be scientifically studied, broken down into small component tasks, and then standardized across all workers doing the jobs.[5] (Recall our discussion of scientific management in Chapter 1.) Taylor's view was consistent with the premises of division of labor as discussed by Smith and Babbage. In practice, job specialization generally brought most, if not all, of the advantages its advocates claimed. Specialization paved the way for large-scale assembly lines and was at least partly responsible for the dramatic gains in output U.S. industry achieved for several decades after the turn of the century.

On the surface, job specialization appears to be a rational and efficient way to structure jobs. The jobs in chicken-processing plants detailed in the opening case for this chapter, for instance, are highly specialized and result in high levels of productivity. In practice, however, performing those jobs can cause problems, foremost among them the extreme monotony of highly specialized tasks. Consider the job of assembling toasters. A person who does the entire assembly may find the job complex and challenging, albeit inefficient. If the job is specialized so that the worker simply inserts a heating coil into the toaster as it passes along on an assem-

Job specialization is still a cornerstone in many sectors of the economy such as the automobile industry. But even when businesses rely on assembly lines, they nevertheless work to make them more efficient. Volkswagen, for example, built this new assembly plant in Brazil. While production relies heavily on moving conveyors, the plant is a showcase of innovation. For example, the assembly line itself is wide enough for workers to stand and work on the car as it moves, making it unnecessary for them to shuffle along and keep up with a moving belt.

bly line, the process may be efficient, but it is unlikely to interest or challenge the worker. A worker numbed by boredom and monotony may be less motivated to work hard and more inclined to do poor-quality work or to complain about the job. Moreover, related work pressure, as illustrated in more detail in the "Talking Technology" box, can also result in more accidents. For these reasons, managers began to search for job design alternatives to specialization.

*"Automation . . . has created work that is faster than ever before, subject to Orwellian control and electronic surveillance, and reduced to limited tasks that are numbingly repetitive, potentially crippling, and stripped of any meaningful skills or the chance to develop them." — Tony Horwitz,* Wall Street Journal *reporter*[6]

One of the primary catalysts for this search was a famous 1952 study of jobs in the automobile industry. The purpose of this study was to assess how satisfied automobile workers were with various aspects of their jobs.[7] The workers indicated that they were reasonably satisfied with their pay, working conditions, and the quality of their supervision. However, they expressed extreme dissatisfaction with the actual work they did. The plants were very noisy, and the moving assembly line dictated a rigid, grueling pace. Jobs were highly specialized and standardized.

The workers complained about six facets of their jobs: mechanical pacing by an assembly line, repetitiveness, low skill requirements, involvement with only a portion of the total production cycle, limited social interaction with others in the workplace, and lack of control over the tools and techniques used in the job. These sources of dissatisfaction were a consequence of the job design prescriptions of scientific management. Thus, managers began to recognize that although job specialization might lead to efficiency, if carried too far, it would have a number of negative consequences.[8]

TALKING TECHNOLOGY

## *Using Technology to Promote Worker Safety*

Forest-products businesses have never been known for their safe, pleasant, and comfortable work environments. Paper mills, sawmills, and plywood factories, for example, are characterized by deafening noise, huge razor-toothed blades, shredders and grinders, long chutes loaded with rumbling tons of lumber, and giant vats full of boiling water and caustic chemicals. The products they make are heavy, awkward in size, and often full of painful splinters, and the machinery used to make them requires frequent maintenance and close contact with sharp edges and dangerous moving parts.

Georgia-Pacific Corporation is one of the world's largest forest-products businesses. Throughout much of its history, the firm had an unenviable safety record even for what experts see as a highly dangerous and hazardous industry. For example, between 1986 and 1990, the firm averaged nine serious injuries per year per 100 employees, and 26 workers lost their lives on the job. Several factors contributed to these statistics. For example, top management continually reinforced the importance of keeping production lines moving at all costs. As a result, workers would often attempt to perform routine maintenance or repair broken equipment parts without shutting down the line. And if they didn't have a pair of safety gloves handy, they would carry around heavy—and sharp—saw blades with their bare hands rather than "waste" an extra few minutes to take appropriate safety precautions.

But all this started to change about ten years ago when a new top-management team came in. These managers were appalled at the firm's poor safety record and vowed to make it a source of pride rather than a source of embarrassment. The starting point was altering the firm's basic culture so as to reinforce safe rather than risky practices and behaviors. And Georgia-Pacific implemented an array of new rules and regulations that explicitly promote safe work and punish those responsible for unnecessarily hazardous or dangerous actions.

*"Once, you weren't considered a real Georgia-Pacific mill guy unless you were* ***missing a few fingers.*** *Now, after a corporate makeover, safety comes first." — A. D. "Pete" Correll, CEO of Georgia-Pacific*

So far, the results have been impressive. Accident rates dropped consistently every year in the 1990s, for example, and very few workers lose their lives anymore. At one of the firm's most hazardous plants, injuries run about 0.7 per 100 workers annually. The Occupational Safety and Health Administration (OSHA) indicates that this is about one-third the injury rate at the average bank! And the company has realized that being more cautious and following safer work procedures has actually boosted its productivity, rather than lowering it. This increase in output relates to the fact that stopping a production line to correct a problem usually takes only a few minutes, whereas stopping it because of an accident or injury might shut down production for hours—or even days.

References: *Hoover's Handbook of American Business 2000* (Austin: Hoover's Business Press, 2000), pp. 664–666; Anne Fisher, "Danger Zone," *Fortune*, September 8, 1997, pp. 165–167 (quote on p. 165).

# Early Alternatives to Job Specialization

In response to the automobile plant study, other reported problems with job specialization, and a general desire to explore ways to create less monotonous jobs, managers began to seek alternative ways to design jobs. In the United States, managers formulated two alternative approaches: job rotation and job enlargement.

**Job rotation** is systematically moving workers from one job to another in an attempt to minimize monotony and boredom.

### Job Rotation

**Job rotation** involves systematically shifting workers from one job to another to sustain their motivation and interest. Figure 7.2 contrasts job rotation and job specialization. Under specialization, each task is broken down into

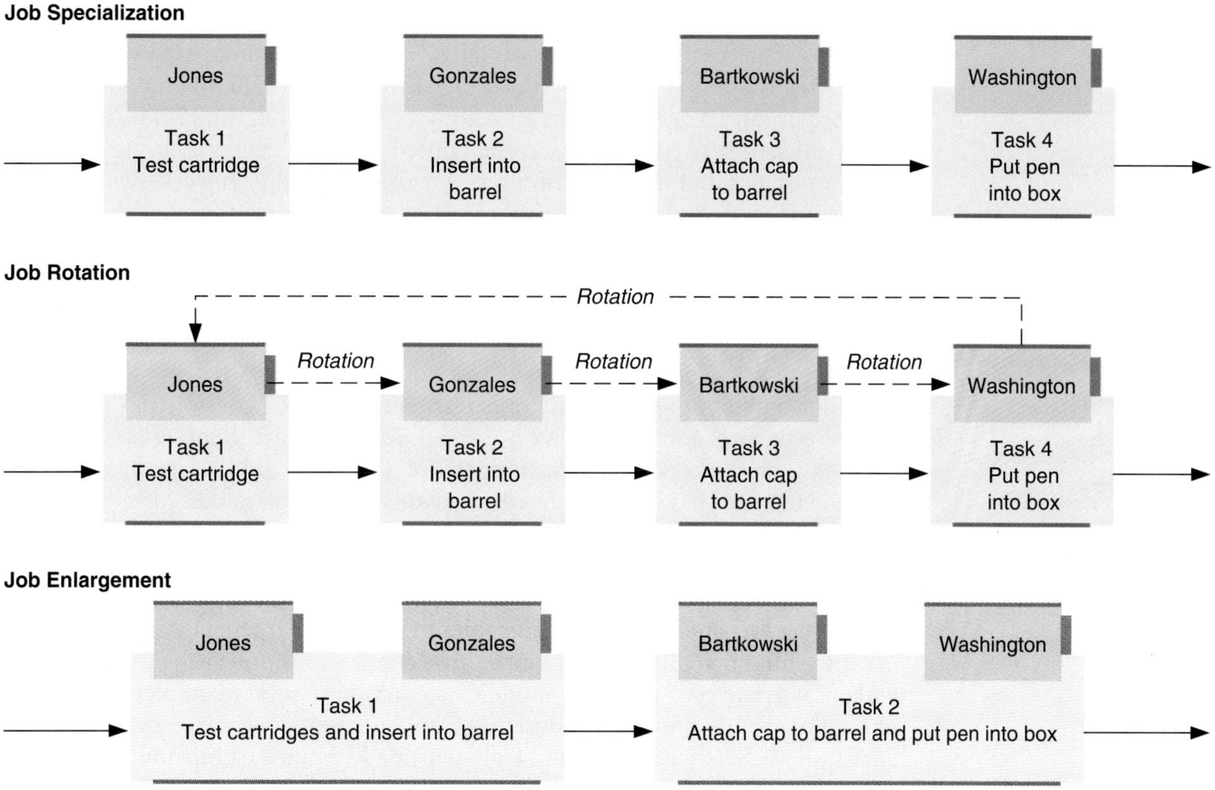


figure **7.2** **Job Specialization, Rotation, and Enlargement**

*Job specialization involves breaking down a job into small component tasks. As illustrated here, each worker then performs one of these tasks. In job rotation, the tasks remain the same, but workers rotate among them. Job enlargement combines small tasks into somewhat larger ones; an individual worker is assigned to each of the new enlarged jobs.*

small parts. For example, assembling pens might involve four discrete steps: testing the ink cartridge, inserting the cartridge into the barrel of the pen, screwing the cap onto the barrel, and inserting the assembled pen into a box. One worker performs each of these four tasks.

When job rotation is introduced, the tasks themselves stay the same. However, as Figure 7.2 shows, the workers who perform them are systematically rotated across the various tasks. Jones, for example, starts out with job 1 (testing ink cartridges). On a regular basis—perhaps weekly or monthly—she is systematically rotated to job 2, to job 3, to job 4, and back to job 1. Gonzalez, who starts out on job 2 (inserting cartridges into barrels), rotates ahead of Jones to jobs 3, 4, 1, and back to 2.

Numerous firms have used job rotation, including American Cyanamid, Baker International, Ford, and Prudential Insurance. Job rotation did not entirely live up to expectations, however.[9] The problem again was narrowly defined, routine jobs. If a rotation cycle takes workers through the same old jobs, the workers simply experience several routine and boring jobs instead of just one. Although a worker may begin each job shift with a bit of renewed interest, the effect usually is short-lived.

Rotation may also decrease efficiency. For example, it clearly sacrifices the proficiency and expertise that grow from specialization. At the same time, job rotation is an effective training technique because a worker rotated through a variety of related jobs acquires a larger set of job skills. Thus, there is increased flexibility in transferring workers to new jobs. Many U.S. firms now use job rotation for training or other purposes, but few rely on it to motivate workers. Pilgrim's Pride, one of the largest chicken-processing firms in the United States, is currently using job rotation, for instance, but not for motivation. As noted in the opening case, workers in a chicken-processing plant are subject to cumulative trauma injuries such as carpal tunnel syndrome. Managers at Pilgrim's believe that rotating workers across different jobs can reduce these injuries.[10]

**Job enlargement** involves giving workers more tasks to perform.

Job Enlargement **Job enlargement**, or horizontal job loading, is expanding a worker's job to include tasks previously performed by other workers. This process is also illustrated in Figure 7.2. Before enlargement, workers perform a single, specialized task; afterward, they have a "larger" job to do. After enlargement, Jones and the other workers each do a "bigger" job than they did previously. Since assembling the pens has been redefined as two tasks rather than four. Jones and Gonzalez do the first task, while Bartkowski and Washington do the other. The logic behind this change is that the increased number of tasks in each job reduces monotony and boredom.

Maytag was one of the first companies to use job enlargement.[11] In the assembly of washing machine water pumps, for example, jobs done sequentially by six workers at a conveyor belt were modified so that each worker completed an entire pump alone. Other organizations that implemented job enlargement included AT&T, the U.S. Civil Service, and Colonial Life Insurance Company.

Unfortunately, job enlargement also failed to have the desired effects. Generally, if the entire production sequence consisted of simple, easy-to-master tasks, merely doing more of them did not significantly change the worker's job. If the task of putting two bolts on a piece of machinery was "enlarged" to putting on three bolts and connecting two wires, for example, the monotony of the original job essentially remained.

## Job Enrichment

**Job enrichment** entails giving workers more tasks to perform and more control over how to perform them.

Job rotation and job enlargement seemed promising but eventually disappointed managers seeking to counter the ill effects of extreme specialization. They failed partly because they were intuitive, narrow approaches rather than fully developed, theory-driven methods. Consequently, a new, more complex approach to task design—job enrichment—was developed. **Job enrichment** is based on the dual-structure theory of motivation, as discussed in Chapter 5. That theory contended that employees could be motivated by positive job-related experiences such as feelings of achievement, responsibility, and recognition. To create this kind of motivation, job enrichment relies on vertical job loading—not only adding more tasks to a job, as in horizontal loading, but giving the employee more control over those tasks.[12]

AT&T, Texas Instruments, IBM, and General Foods have all used job enrichment. For example, AT&T used job enrichment in a group of eight typists who were responsible for preparing service orders. Managers believed turnover in the group was too high and performance too low. Analysis revealed several deficiencies in the work. The typists worked in relative isolation, and any service representative could ask them to type work orders. As a result, they had little client contact or responsibility, and they received scant feedback on their job performance. The job enrichment program focused on creating a typing team. Each member of the team was paired with a service representative, and the tasks were restructured: ten discrete steps were replaced with three more complex ones. In addition, the typists began to get specific feedback on performance, and their job titles were changed to reflect their greater responsibility and status. As a result of these changes, the number of orders delivered on time increased from 27 to 90 percent, accuracy improved, and turnover dropped significantly.[13]

Texas Instruments used job enrichment to improve janitorial jobs. The company gave janitors more control over their schedules and let them sequence their own cleaning jobs and purchase their own supplies. The outcome? Turnover dropped, cleanliness improved, and the company reported estimated cost savings of approximately $103,000.[14]

At the same time, we should note that many job enrichment programs have failed. Some companies have found job enrichment to be cost-ineffective, and others believe that it simply did not produce the expected results.[15] Several programs at Prudential Insurance, for example, were abandoned because managers believed they were benefiting neither employees nor the firm. Some of the criticism is associated with the dual-structure theory of motivation, on which job enrichment is based. In Chapter 5, we reviewed the major objections: the theory confuses employee satisfaction with motivation, is fraught with methodological flaws, ignores situational factors, and is not convincingly supported by research.[16]

Because of these and other problems, job enrichment recently has fallen into disfavor among managers. Yet some valuable aspects of the concept can be salvaged. The efforts of managers and academic theorists ultimately have led to more complex and sophisticated viewpoints. Many of these advances are evident in the job characteristics approach, which we consider next.

# The Job Characteristics Approach

The **job characteristics approach** focuses on the motivational attributes of jobs.

The **job characteristics approach** focuses on the specific motivational properties of jobs. The most current view is the job characteristics theory. The theory also suggests that social information affects job design properties.

## The Job Characteristics Theory

The **job characteristics theory** identifies three critical psychological states: experienced meaningfulness of the work, experienced responsibility for work outcomes, and knowledge of results.

The **job characteristics theory**, diagrammed in Figure 7.3, was developed by Hackman and Oldham.[17] At the core of the theory is the idea of critical psychological states. These states are presumed to determine the extent to which characteristics of the job enhance employee responses to the task. The three critical psychological states are:

1. *Experienced meaningfulness of the work*—the degree to which the individual experiences the job as generally meaningful, valuable, and worthwhile.
2. *Experienced responsibility for work outcomes*—the degree to which individuals feel personally accountable and responsible for the results of their work.
3. *Knowledge of results*—the degree to which individuals continuously understand how effectively they are performing the job.[18]

If employees experience these states at a sufficiently high level, they are likely to feel good about themselves and to respond favorably to their jobs. Hackman and figure **7.3**

**The Job Characteristics Theory**

*The job characteristics theory is an important contemporary model of how to design jobs. By using five core job characteristics, managers can enhance three critical psychological states. These states, in turn, can improve a variety of personal and work outcomes. Individual differences also affect how the job characteristics affect people.*

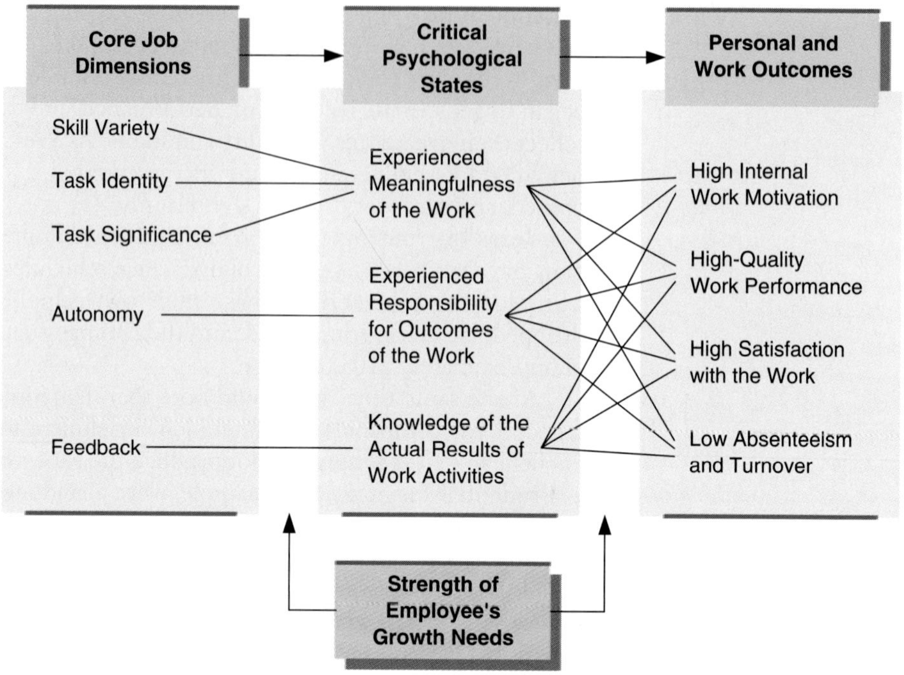


Reference: J. R. Hackman and G. R. Oldham, "Motivation Through the Design of Work: Test of a Theory," *Organizational Behavior and Human Performance,* vol. 16, 1976, pp. 250–279. Copyright 1976 by Academic Press. Used by permission of the publisher and the author.

Oldham suggest that the three critical psychological states are triggered by five characteristics of the job, or core job dimensions:

1. *Skill variety*—the degree to which the job requires a variety of activities that involve different skills and talents.
2. *Task identity*—the degree to which the job requires completion of a "whole" and an identifiable piece of work; that is, the extent to which a job has a beginning and an end with a tangible outcome.
3. *Task significance*—the degree to which the job affects the lives or work of other people, both in the immediate organization and in the external environment.
4. *Autonomy*—the degree to which the job allows the individual substantial freedom, independence, and discretion to schedule the work and determine the procedures for carrying it out.
5. *Feedback*—the degree to which the job activities give the individual direct and clear information about the effectiveness of his or her performance.

Figure 7.3 shows that these five job characteristics, operating through the critical psychological states, affect a variety of personal and work outcomes: high internal work motivation (that is, intrinsic motivation), high-quality work performance, high satisfaction with the work, and low absenteeism and turnover. The figure also suggests that individual differences play a role in job design. People with strong needs for personal growth and development will be especially motivated by the five core job characteristics. On the other hand, people with weaker needs for personal growth and development are less likely to be motivated by the core job characteristics.

Figure 7.4 expands the basic job characteristics theory by incorporating general guidelines to help managers implement it.[19] Managers can use such means as

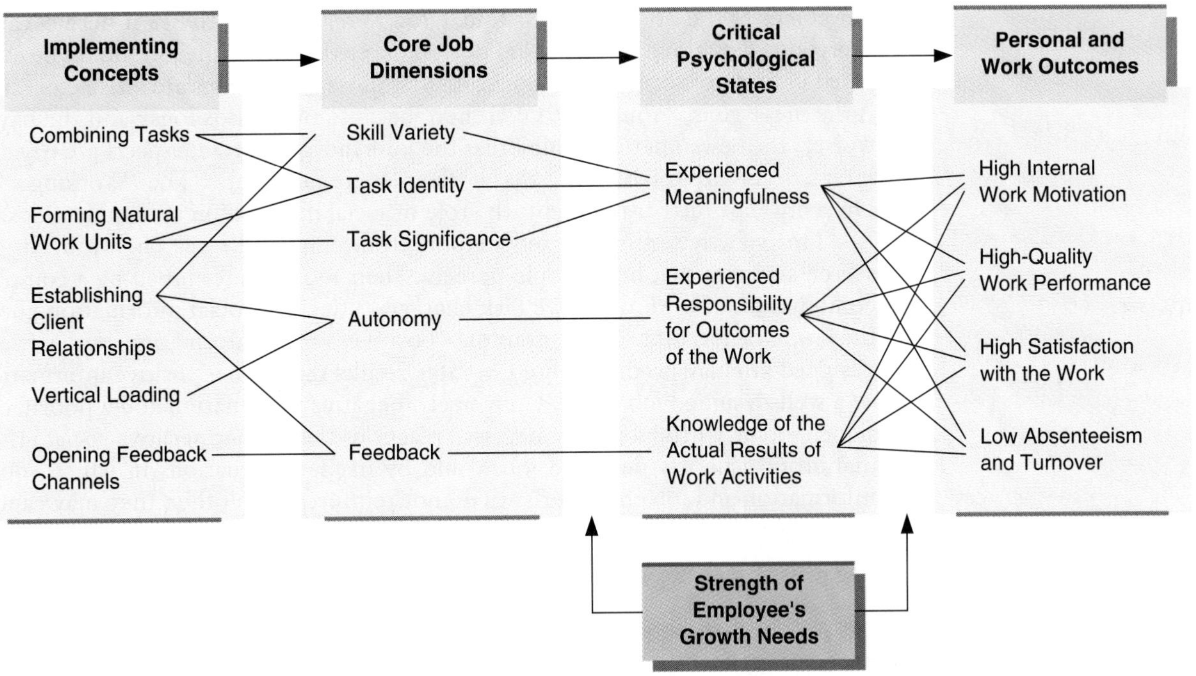


figure 7.4 **Implementing the Job Characteristics Theory**

*Managers should use a set of implementation guidelines if they want to apply the job characteristics theory in their organization. This figure shows some of these guidelines. For example, managers can combine tasks, form natural work units, establish client relationships, vertically load jobs, and open feedback channels.*

Reference: J. R. Hackman, G. R. Oldham, R. Janson, and K. Purdy, "A New Stage for Job Enrichment." Copyright © 1975 by the Regents of the University of California. Reprinted from *California Management Review,* vol. 17, no. 4. By permission of The Regents.

forming natural work units (that is, grouping similar tasks together), combining existing tasks into more complex ones, establishing direct relationships between workers and clients, increasing worker autonomy through vertical job loading, and opening feedback channels. Theoretically, such actions should enhance the motivational properties of each task. Using these guidelines, sometimes in adapted form, several firms have successfully implemented job design changes, including 3M, Volvo, AT&T, Xerox, Texas Instruments, and Motorola.[20]

Much research has been devoted to this approach to job design.[21] This research has generally supported the theory, although performance has seldom been found to correlate with job characteristics.[22] Several apparent weaknesses in the theory have also come to light. First, the measures used to test the theory are not always as valid and reliable as they should be.[23] Further, the role of individual differences frequently has not been supported by research. Finally, guidelines for implementation are not specific, and managers usually tailor them to their own specific circumstances.[24] Still, the theory remains a popular perspective on studying and changing jobs.[25]

## Social Information and Job Design

Research has also suggested that social information in the workplace may influence how individuals perceive and react to job characteristics.[26] For example, if a newcomer to the organization is told, "You're really going to like it here because everybody gets along so well," that person may assume that the job should be evaluated in terms of social interactions and that those interactions are satisfactory. But if the message is, "You won't like it here because the boss is lousy and the pay is worse," the newcomer may think that the job's most important aspects are pay and interactions with the boss and that both areas are deficient.[27] The "Working with Diversity" box further highlights the role of social information in organizations.

This view has gotten mixed support from empirical research.[28] Indeed, research suggests that how people perceive their jobs is determined by a complex combination of both objective task characteristics and social information about those characteristics.[29] For example, positive social information and a well-designed job may produce more favorable results than either positive information or a well-designed job alone. Conversely, negative information and a poorly designed job may produce more negative reactions than either negative social information or a poorly designed job would by itself. In situations in which social information and job characteristics do not reinforce each other, they may cancel each other out. For example, negative social information may diminish the positive

WORKING WITH DIVERSITY

## *Managing Diversity at Marriott*

Diversity is a fact of life in organizations today. And although there are many benefits of diversity, the potential for conflict increases also significantly. Different backgrounds, perspectives, customs, and values combine to make it ever more likely that people will disagree and see things in different ways. And this is especially true when it comes to their jobs.

For example, take the Marriott Marquis Hotel in New York's Time Square. The hotel employs 1,700 people from seventy countries and who speak forty-seven languages. One major reason for the hotel's diversity is its labor pool—the area is populated by a diverse set of immigrants, and it is often these residents who apply for jobs. But the hotel managers also strongly believe the diverse work force is an asset, in part because it fits the multicultural clientele who frequent the hotel.

But managing the diversity at Marriott can be a challenge. For example, consider the case of Jessica Brown, an African-American quality-assurance manager responsible for housekeeping. Ms. Brown says that when she rewards other African-Americans, some of her Latina/Latino employees criticize her for playing favorites. But when she rewards the Latinas/Latinos, some African-Americans accuse her of ignoring them.

*"All you can really do is hope [the resentment] goes away eventually. And it usually does."* — *Cynthia Keating, Marriott manager*

Balancing religious preferences is also complicated. One manager, Victor Aragona, recently sought out a room attendant to fix an overflowing bathtub. The attendant, meanwhile, was found prostrate on a towel in the housekeeper's closet, bowing to Mecca and saying his daily Islamic prayers. Rather than disturb him, Aragona fixed the bathtub himself.

To help cope with these challenges, Marriott offers frequent training programs in multiculturalism and conflict management. These courses are required for all managers, and are also open to most nonmanagers as well. Even so, the hotel still finds it necessary to offer periodic and regular refresher courses to help people work together with a minimum of conflict.

References: *Hoover's Handbook of American Business 2000* (Austin: Hoover's Business Press, 2000), pp. 910–911; "In a Factory Schedule, Where Does Religion Fit In?" *Wall Street Journal,* March 4, 1999, pp. B1, B12; Roy Johnson, "The 50 Best Companies for Blacks and Hispanics," *Fortune,* August 3, 1998, pp. 94–106; "How One Hotel Manages Staff Diversity," *Wall Street Journal,* November 20, 1996, pp. B1, B11 (quote on p. B11).

effects of a well-designed job, whereas positive information may at least partly offset the negative consequences of a poorly designed job.[30]

# Participation, Empowerment, and Motivation

**Participation** entails giving employees a voice in making decisions about their own work.

**Empowerment** is the process of enabling workers to set their own work goals, make decisions, and solve problems within their sphere of responsibility and authority.

Participative management and empowerment are two more important methods managers can use to enhance employee motivation. In a sense, participation and empowerment are extensions of job design, because each fundamentally alters how employees in an organization perform their jobs. **Participation** occurs when employees have a voice in decisions about their own work. (One important model that helps managers determine the optimal level of employee participation, the Vroom-decision tree approach, is discussed in Chapter 13.) **Empowerment** is the process of enabling workers to set their own work goals, make decisions, and solve problems within their spheres of responsibility and authority. Thus, empowerment is a somewhat broader concept that promotes participation in a wide variety of areas, including but not limited to work itself, work context, and work environment.[31]

## Early Perspectives on Participation and Empowerment

The human relations movement in vogue from the 1930s through the 1950s (see Chapter 1) assumed that employees who are happy and satisfied will work harder.

Participation and empowerment are often implemented through the use of work teams. Consider, for example, this rescue squad. Its members must work together as a team and must have the autonomy to make critical decisions on their own in order to perform effectively. Rescue squads often practice various drills and exercises to polish their skills and improve their teamwork. Occasionally, they even compete against other teams at forums such as this—the annual International Extrication Competition.

This view stimulated management interest in having workers participate in a variety of organizational activities. Managers hoped that if employees had a chance to participate in decision making concerning their work environment, they would be satisfied, and this satisfaction would supposedly result in improved performance. But managers tended to see employee participation merely as a way to increase satisfaction, not as a source of potentially valuable input. Eventually, managers began to recognize that employee input was useful in itself, apart from its presumed effect on satisfaction. In other words, they came to see employees as valued human resources who can contribute to organizational effectiveness.[32]

The role of participation and empowerment in motivation can be expressed in terms of both the need-based perspectives discussed in Chapter 5 and the expectancy theory discussed in Chapter 6. Employees who participate in decision making may be more committed to executing decisions properly. Furthermore, successfully making a decision, executing it, and then seeing the positive consequences can help satisfy one's need for achievement, provide recognition and responsibility, and enhance self-esteem. Simply being asked to participate in organizational decision making may also enhance an employee's self-esteem. In addition, participation should help clarify expectancies; that is, by participating in decision making, employees may better understand the linkage between their performance and the rewards they want most.

## Areas of Participation

At one level, employees can participate in addressing questions and making decisions about their own jobs. Instead of just telling them how to do their jobs, for example, managers can ask employees to make their own decisions about how to do them. Drawing from their own expertise and experience with their tasks, workers might be able to improve their own productivity. In many situations, they might also be well qualified to make decisions about what materials to use, what tools to use, and so forth.

It might also help to let workers make decisions about administrative matters, such as work schedules. If jobs are relatively independent of one another, employees might decide when to change shifts, take breaks, go to lunch, and so forth. A work group or team might also be able to schedule vacations and days off for all of its members. Furthermore, employees are getting increasing opportunities to participate in broader issues of product quality. Participation of this type has become a hallmark of successful Japanese and other international firms, and many U.S. companies have followed suit.[33]

*"I give people license to be themselves and motivate others in that way. We give people the opportunity to be mavericks. You don't have to fit into a constraining mold at work." — Herb Kelleher, CEO of Southwest Airlines*[34]

## Techniques and Issues in Empowerment

In recent years many organizations have actively sought ways to extend participation beyond the traditional areas. Simple techniques such as suggestion boxes and question-and-answer meetings allow a certain degree of participation, for example.

The basic motive has been to better capitalize on the assets and capabilities inherent in all employees. Thus, many managers today prefer the term "empowerment" to "participation" because it implies a more comprehensive involvement.

One method some firms use to empower their workers is the use of work teams. This method grew out of early attempts to use what Japanese firms call "quality circles." A quality circle is a group of volunteer employees who voluntarily meet regularly to identify and propose solutions to problems related to quality. This use of quality circles quickly grew to encompass a wider array of work groups, now generally called "work teams." These teams are collections of employees empowered to plan, organize, direct, and control their own work. Their supervisor, rather than being a traditional "boss," plays more the role of a coach. We discuss work teams more fully in Chapter 12.

The other method some organizations use to facilitate empowerment is to change their overall method of organizing. The basic pattern is for an organization to eliminate layers from its hierarchy, thereby becoming much more decentralized. Power, responsibility, and authority are delegated as far down the organization as possible, so control of work is squarely in the hands of those who actually do it. Chapter 17 addresses these trends in more detail.

Regardless of the specific technique used, however, empowerment only enhances organizational effectiveness if certain conditions exist. First, the organization must be sincere in its efforts to spread power and autonomy to lower levels of the organization. Token efforts to promote participation in just a few areas are unlikely to succeed. This point is clearly illustrated in the cartoon. Second, the organization must be committed to maintaining participation and empowerment. Workers will be resentful if they are given more control, only to later have it reduced or taken away altogether. Third, the organization must be systematic and patient in its efforts to empower workers. Turning over too much control too quickly can spell disaster. Finally, the organization must be prepared to increase its commitment to training. Employees being given more freedom concerning how

Participation and empowerment can play powerful roles in motivating employees. But in order for these benefits to have any hope of fruition, managers must ensure that their efforts to involve employees in decision making are sincere and genuine. For example, if employees sense that their manager is asking for their opinion only for symbolic purposes and has already made a decision, things can backfire in unfortunate ways. In the instance shown here, the manager is asking for opinions but is obviously not going to listen to what anyone has to say—and the employees know it!

Reference: DILBERT reprinted by permission of United Feature Syndicate, Inc.

they work are likely to need additional training to help them exercise that freedom most effectively.

# Alternative Work Arrangements

Beyond the actual design of jobs and the use of participation and empowerment, many organizations today are experimenting with a variety of alternative work arrangements. These arrangements are generally intended to enhance employee motivation and performance by giving them more flexibility about how and when they work. Among the more popular alternative work arrangements are variable work schedules, flexible work schedules, job sharing, and telecommuting.[35]

## Variable Work Schedules

There are many exceptions, of course, but the traditional work schedule in the United States has long been days that start at 8:00 or 9:00 in the morning and end at 5:00 in the evening, five days a week (and of course, managers often work many additional hours outside of these times). Although the exact starting and ending times vary, most companies in other countries have also used a well-defined work schedule. But such a schedule makes it difficult to attend to routine personal business—going to the bank, seeing a doctor or dentist for a checkup, having a parent-teacher conference, getting an automobile serviced, and so forth. Employees locked into this work schedule may find it necessary to take a sick or vacation day to handle these activities. On a more psychological level, some people may feel so powerless and constrained by their job schedules that they grow resentful and frustrated.

In a **compressed work week** employees work a full forty-hour week in fewer than the traditional five days.

To help counter these problems, one alternative some businesses use is a compressed work schedule.[36] An employee following a **compressed work week** schedule works a full forty-hour week in fewer than the traditional five days. Most typically, this schedule involves working ten hours a day for four days, leaving an extra day off. Another alternative is for employees to work slightly less than ten hours a day but to complete the forty hours by lunchtime on Friday. And a few firms have tried having employees work twelve hours a day for three days, followed by four days off. Firms that have used these forms of compressed work weeks include John Hancock, Atlantic Richfield, and R.J. Reynolds. One problem with this schedule is that if everyone in the organization is off at the same time, the firm may have no one on duty to handle problems or deal with outsiders on the off day. On the other hand, if the company staggers days off across the work force, people who don't get the more desirable days off (Monday and Friday, for most people) may be jealous or resentful. Another problem is that when employees put in too much time in a single day, they tend to get tired and perform at a lower level later in the day.

A popular schedule some organizations are beginning to use is called a "nine-eighty" schedule. Under this arrangement, an employee works a traditional schedule one week and a compressed schedule the next, getting every other Friday off. That is, they work eighty hours (the equivalent of two weeks of full-time work) in nine days. By alternating the regular and compressed schedules across half of its work force, the organization is fully staffed at all times and still gives employees two additional full days off each month. Shell Oil and Amoco Chemicals are two of the firms that currently use this schedule.

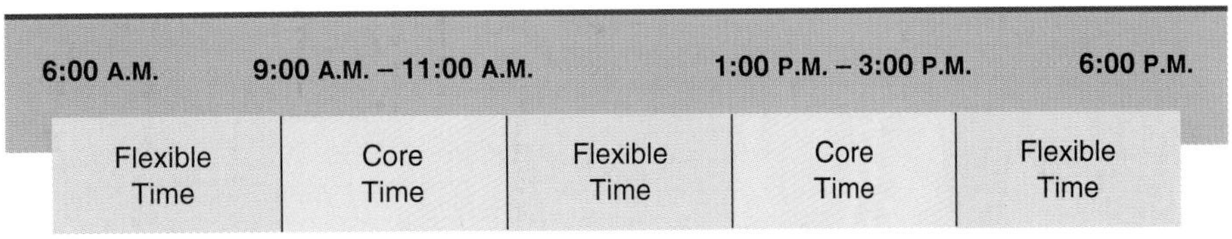


figure 7.5
**Flexible Work Schedules**

*Flexible work schedules are an important new work arrangement used in some organizations today. All employees must be at work during "core time." In the hypothetical example shown here, core time is from 9 to 11 A.M. and 1 to 3 P.M. The other time, then, is flexible—employees can come and go as they please during this time, as long as the total time spent at work meets organizational expectations.*

## Flexible Work Schedules

Another promising alternative work arrangement is **flexible work schedules**, sometimes called **flextime**. The compressed work schedules discussed earlier give employees time off during "normal" working hours, but they must still follow a regular and defined schedule on the days they do work. Flextime, however, usually gives employees less say over what days they work but more personal control over when they work on those days.

**Flexible work schedules**, or **flextime**, give employees more personal control over the hours they work each day.

Figure 7.5 illustrates how flextime works. The workday is broken down into two categories: flexible time and core time. All employees must be at their workstations during core time, but they can choose their own schedules during flexible time. Thus, one employee may choose to start work early in the morning and leave in midafternoon, another to start in the late morning and work until late afternoon, and a third to start early in the morning, take a long lunch break, and work until late afternoon.

The major advantage of this approach, as already noted, is that workers get to tailor their workday to fit their personal needs. A person who needs to visit the dentist in the late afternoon can just start work early. A person who stays out late one night can start work late the next day. And the person who needs to run some errands during lunch can take a longer midday break. On the other hand, flextime is more difficult to manage, because others in the organization may not be sure when a person will be available for meetings other than during the core time. Expenses such as utilities will also be higher, since the organization must remain open for a longer period each day.

Some organizations have experimented with a plan in which workers set their own hours, but then must follow that schedule each day. Others allow workers to modify their own schedule each day. Organizations that have used the flexible work schedule method for arranging work include Control Data Corporation, du Pont, Metropolitan Life, Texaco, and some offices in the U.S. government.

## Job Sharing

In **job sharing**, two or more part-time employees share one full-time job.

Yet another potentially useful alternative work arrangement is job sharing. In **job sharing**, two part-time employees share one full-time job. Job sharing may be desirable for people who want to work only part-time or when job markets are tight. For its part, the organization can accommodate the preferences of a broader range of employees and may benefit from the talents of more people. Perhaps the simplest job-sharing arrangement to visualize is that of a receptionist. To share this job, one worker would staff the receptionist's desk from, say, 8:00 A.M. to noon each day, the office might close from noon to 1:00 P.M., and a second worker would staff the desk from 1:00 in the afternoon until 5:00. To the casual observer or visitor to the office, the fact that two people serve in one job is essentially irrelevant. The

Job sharing is an alternative work arrangement in which two part-time employees share one full-time job. For example, Sandra Cavanah, on the left, and Kathleen Layendecker, on the right, share the position of vice president at Snowball.com, an Internet company. Each talented woman wanted to pursue a career in a high-tech firm, but each also wanted to protect some time for her children. While the job sharing arrangement requires careful coordination between the two of them, both Cavanah and Layendecker believe that the arrangement is proving to be very beneficial for themselves, their children, and Snowball.com. Moreover, their boss, originally skeptical that a high-level position like vice president could actually be shared, has changed his view and now agrees that everyone has benefited from the arrangement.

responsibilities of the job in the morning and the afternoon are not likely to be interdependent. Thus, the position can easily be broken down into two or perhaps even more components.

Organizations sometimes offer job sharing as a way to entice more workers to the organization. If a particular kind of job is difficult to fill, a job-sharing arrangement might make it more attractive to more people. There are also cost benefits to the organization. Since the employees may only be working part-time, the organization does not have to give them the same benefits that full-time employees receive. The organization can also tap into a wider array of skills when it provides job-sharing arrangements. The firm gets the advantage of the two sets of skills from one job.

Some workers like job sharing because it gives them flexibility and freedom. Certain workers, for example, may only want part-time work. Stepping into a shared job may also give them a chance to work in an organization that otherwise only wants to hire full-time employees. When the job sharer isn't working, she or he may attend school, take care of the family, or simply enjoy leisure time.

Job sharing does not work for every organization, and it isn't attractive to all workers, but it has produced enough success stories to suggest that it will be around for a long time. Among the organizations that are particularly committed to job-sharing programs are the Bank of Montreal, United Airlines, and the National School Board Association. Each of these organizations, and dozens more like them, reports that job sharing has become a critically important part of its human resource system. Although job sharing has not been scientifically evaluated, it appears to be a useful alternative to traditional work scheduling.

## Telecommuting

**Telecommuting** is a work arrangement in which employees spend part of their time working off-site.

A relatively new approach to alternative work arrangements is **telecommuting**—allowing employees to spend part of their time working off-site, usually at home. By using email, computer networks, and other technology, many employees can maintain close contact with their organization and do as much work at home as they could in their office. The increased power and sophistication of modern communication technology is making telecommuting easier and easier.

*"Working at home for me has been wonderful. I know my mom is O.K., and this allows me to focus on doing my job better." — Shelley Comes, quality consultant for Hewlett-Packard*[37]

On the negative side, although many employees thrive under this arrangement, others do not. Some grow to feel isolated and miss the social interaction of the workplace. And some people simply lack the self-control and discipline to walk from the breakfast table to their desk and start working. "The Business of Ethics" box discusses another type of problem that concerns some organizations—the safety and health of their employees who are working at home. Managers may also

### THE BUSINESS OF ETHICS

### *Safety Starts at Home*

It's an interesting convergence of legal and social trends. Influenced primarily by the Occupational Safety and Health Act of 1970, many organizations today are paying close attention to hazards and unsafe conditions in the workplace. At the same time, though, more and more people are moving into telecommuter roles in which they do a portion of their work at home. So, since many employees are working at home, what kinds of obligations does an organization have to ensure that people who are working at home enjoy the same protections there as they do in the office or factory? What happens, for example, if an employee falls down stairs while going to a home office in the basement of a home? Or what happens if a worker develops carpal tunnel syndrome because of a poorly configured workstation at home?

Many legal experts contend that the same protections that apply at work also apply to people who are working in their homes. As a result, most companies that allow telecommuting are paying more attention to home office safety for their workers. For example, AT&T provides its telecommuters with equipment, tips on how to avoid injuries, and, if the employee wants, a free home office safety inspection. Merrill Lynch requires inspections of home offices and mandates that telecommuters go through a two-week training program.

*"In order to be a telecommuter, you have to have approved lights, desk, chair, computer pads, you name it." — Bobbie Collins, manager at Merrill Lynch*

But not everyone thinks these practices are to their advantage. Some workers, for example, see home inspections by their employers as an invasion of their privacy. And some employers complain that the extra costs of monitoring safety in workers' homes would be so high that they are considering banning or cutting back on telecommuting opportunities for their workers. Who knows where all this will lead? Only time—and the courts, no doubt—will tell.

References: "Work à la Modem," *Business Week,* October 4, 1999, pp. 170–176; Jonathan Segal, "Home Sweet Office?" *HRMagazine,* April 1998, pp. 119–129; "Working at Home Raises Job Site Safety Issues," *USA Today,* January 29, 1998, p. 1B (quote on p. 1B).

encounter coordination difficulties in scheduling meetings and other activities that require face-to-face contact. Still, given the boom in communication technology and the pressures for flexibility, many more organizations will no doubt be using telecommuting in the years to come.

But on the plus side, many employees like telecommuting because it gives them added flexibility. By spending one or two days a week at home, for instance, they have the same kind of flexibility to manage personal activities as is afforded by flextime or compressed schedules. Some employees also feel that they get more work done by staying at home, because they are less likely to be interrupted. Organizations may benefit for several reasons as well: (1) they can reduce absenteeism and turnover, since employees need to take less "formal" time off, and (2) they can save on facilities such as parking space, because fewer people are at work on any given day.

## Synopsis

Managers seek to enhance employee performance by capitalizing on the potential for motivated behavior intended to improve performance. Methods often used to translate motivation into performance involve job design, participation and empowerment, alternative work arrangements, performance management, goal setting, and rewards.

Job design is how organizations define and structure jobs. Historically, there was a general trend toward increasingly specialized jobs, but more recently the movement has consistently been away from extreme specialization. Two early alternatives to specialization were job rotation and job enlargement. Job enrichment approaches stimulated considerable interest in job design.

The job characteristics theory grew from early work on job enrichment. One basic premise of this theory is that jobs can be described in terms of a specific set of motivational characteristics. Another is that managers should work to enhance the presence of those motivational characteristics in jobs, but should also take individual differences into account. Today the emerging opinion is that employees' job perceptions and attitudes are jointly determined by objective task properties and social information.

Participative management and empowerment can help improve employee motivation in many business settings. New management practices, such as the use of various kinds of work teams and of flatter, more decentralized methods of organizing, are each intended to empower employees throughout the organization. Organizations that want to empower their employees need to understand a variety of issues as they go about promoting participation.

Alternative work arrangements are commonly used today to enhance motivated job performance. Among the more popular alternative arrangements are compressed work weeks, flexible work schedules, job sharing, and telecommuting.

## Discussion Questions

1. What are the primary advantages and disadvantages of job specialization? Were they the same in the early days of mass production?
2. Under what circumstances might job enlargement be especially effective? Especially ineffective? How about job rotation?
3. Do any trends today suggest a return to job specialization?
4. What are the strengths and weaknesses of job enrichment? When might it be useful?
5. Do you agree or disagree that individual differences affect how people respond to their jobs? Explain.
6. What are the primary similarities and differences between job enrichment and the approach proposed by job characteristics theory?

7. Can you recall any instances in which social information affected how you perceived or felt about something?
8. What are the motivational consequences of participative management from the frame of reference of expectancy and equity theories?
9. What motivational problems might result from an organization's attempt to set up work teams?
10. Which form of alternative work schedule might you prefer?
11. How do you think you would like telecommuting?

# Organizational Behavior Case for Discussion

## Employee Participation at Chaparral Steel

Although few people may have heard of Chaparral Steel, the company enjoys a stellar reputation as one of the most effective firms in the steel industry. Chaparral was founded in 1973 in a small town south of Dallas and today enjoys annual sales of almost $500 million. In earlier times, most steel companies were large, bureaucratic operations like U.S. Steel (now USX) and Bethlehem Steel. However, increased competition from low-cost foreign steel firms—especially those in Japan and Korea—has caused major problems for these manufacturers with their high overhead costs and inflexible modes of operation.

These competitive pressures, in turn, have also led to the formation of so-called minimills like Chaparral. These minimills are consciously designed to be much smaller and more flexible than the traditional steel giants. Because of their size, technology, and flexibility, these firms are able to maintain much lower production costs and to respond more quickly to customer requests. Today, Chaparral is recognized as one of the best of this new breed of steel companies. For example, whereas most mills produce one ton of steel with an average of 3 to 5 hours of labor, Chaparral produces a ton with less than 1.2 hours of labor. Chaparral has also successfully avoided all efforts to unionize its employees.

Since its inception, Chaparral has been led by Gordon Forward. Forward knew that if Chaparral was going to succeed with what was then a new strategic orientation in the industry, it would also need to be managed in new and different ways. One of the first things he decided to do as a part of his new approach was to systematically avoid the traditional barriers that tend to be created between management and labor, especially in older industries like steel. For example, he mandated that there would be no reserved parking spaces in the parking lot nor separate dining area inside the plant for managers. Everyone dresses casually at the work site, and people throughout the firm are on a first-name basis with one another. Workers take their lunch and coffee breaks whenever they choose, and the coffee is even provided free for everyone!

Forward also insisted that all employees be paid on a salary basis—no time clocks or time sheets for anyone, from the president down to the custodians. Workers are organized into teams, and each team selects its own "leader." The teams also interview and select new members, as needed, and are responsible for planning their own work, setting their own work schedules, and even allocating vacation days among themselves. And teams are also responsible for implementing any disciplinary actions that need to be taken toward a member. Finally, no one has a specific and narrowly defined job that must be routinely performed on a continuous and monotonous basis. That is, each team has an array of tasks and functions for which it is responsible; the teams themselves are encouraged to ensure that everyone on the team knows how to perform all of its assigned tasks and functions and to regularly rotate people across them.

Forward clearly believes in trusting everyone in the organization. For example, when the firm recently needed a new rolling mill lathe, it budgeted $1 million for its purchase, then put the purchase decision in the hands of an operating machinist. This machinist, in turn, investigated various options, visited other mills in Japan and Europe, and then recommended an alternative piece of machinery costing less than half of the budgeted amount. Forward also helped pioneer an innovative concept called "open-book management"—any employee at Chaparral can see any document, record, or other piece of information at any time and for any reason.

Chaparral also recognizes the importance of investing in and rewarding people. Continuous education is an integral part of the firm's culture, with a variety of different classes being offered all the time. For example, one recent slate of classes included metallurgy, electronics, finance, and English. The classes are intended to be of value to both individual workers and to the organization as a whole. The classes are scheduled on-site and in the evening. Some include community college credit (there are tuition charges for these classes, although the company pays for half the costs), while others are noncredit only (there are no charges for these classes). Forward has a goal that at any given time at least 85 percent of Chaparral's employees will be enrolled in at least one class.

Everyone also participates in the good—and bad—times at Chaparral. For example, all workers have a guaranteed base salary that is basically adequate, but which, by itself, is below the standard market rate. In addition, however, each employee gets a pay-for-performance bonus based on his or her individual achievements. Finally, there are also company-wide bonuses paid to everyone on a quarterly basis. These bonuses are tied to overall company performance. The typical bonuses increase an employee's total compensation to a level well above the standard market rate. Thus, hard work and dedication on everyone's part means that everyone can benefit.

### Case Questions

1. Describe how managers at Chaparral Steel appear to be implementing various need- and process-based theories of motivation.
2. Discuss the apparent role and nature of job design at Chaparral.
3. Describe how Chaparral uses participation and empowerment to motivate its workers.

References: Ricky W. Griffin and Ronald J. Ebert, *Business Essentials*, 2nd ed. (Englewood Cliffs, N.J.: Prentice-Hall, 1998), p. 119; John Case, "HR Learns How to Open the Books," *HRMagazine*, May 1998, pp. 70–76; John Case, "Opening the Books," *Harvard Business Review*, March–April 1997, pp. 118–129; Brian Dumaine, "Chaparral Steel: Unleash Workers and Cut Costs," *Fortune*, May 18, 1992, p. 88.

## Experiencing Organizational Behavior

### Learning About Job Design

**Purpose:** This exercise will help you assess the processes involved in designing jobs to make them more motivating.

**Format:** Working in small groups, you will diagnose the motivating potential of an existing job, compare its motivating potential to that of other jobs, suggest ways to redesign the job, and then assess the effects of your redesign suggestions on other aspects of the workplace.

**Procedure:** Your instructor will divide the class into groups of three or four people each. In assessing the characteristics of jobs, use a scale value of 1 ("very little") to 7 ("very high").

1. Using the scale values, assign scores on each core job dimension used in the job characteristics theory (see page 173) to the following jobs: secretary, professor, food server, auto mechanic, lawyer, short-order cook, department store clerk, construction worker, and newspaper reporter.
2. Researchers often assess the motivational properties of jobs by calculating their motivating potential score (MPS). The usual formula for MPS is:

$$(\text{Variety} + \text{Identity} + \text{Significance})/3 \\ \times \text{Autonomy} \times \text{Feedback}$$

   Use this formula to calculate the MPS for each job in step 1.
3. Your instructor will now assign your group one of the jobs from the list. Discuss how you might reasonably go about enriching the job.
4. Calculate the new MPS score for the redesigned job, and check its new position in the rank ordering.
5. Discuss the feasibility of your redesign suggestions. In particular, look at how your recommended changes might necessitate changes in other jobs, in the reward system, and in the selection criteria used to hire people for the job.
6. Briefly discuss your observations with the rest of the class.

### Follow-up Questions

1. How might the social-information-processing model explain some of your own perceptions in this exercise?
2. Are some jobs simply impossible to redesign?

# Building Organizational Behavior Skills

## The Job Characteristics Inventory

The questionnaire below was developed to measure the central concepts of the job characteristics theory. Answer the questions in relation to the job you currently hold or the job you most recently held.

### Characteristics from Hackman and Oldham's Job Diagnostic Survey

Reference: J. R. Hackman and G. R. Oldham, *Work Redesign* (adapted from pages 275–294). © 1980 by Addison-Wesley Publishing Co., Inc. Reprinted by permission of Addison-Wesley Longman, Inc.

### Skill Variety

1. How much *variety* is there in your job? That is, to what extent does the job require you to do many different things at work, using a variety of your skills and talents?

| 1 | 2 | 3 | 4 | 5 | 6 | 7 |
|---|---|---|---|---|---|---|
| Very little; the job requires me to do the same routine things over and over again. | | | Moderate variety | | | Very much; the job requires me to do many different things, using a number of different skills and talents. |

2. The job requires me to use a number of complex or high-level skills.

*How accurate is the statement in describing your job?*

| 1 | 2 | 3 | 4 | 5 | 6 | 7 |
|---|---|---|---|---|---|---|
| Very inaccurate | Mostly inaccurate | Slightly inaccurate | Uncertain | Slightly accurate | Mostly accurate | Very accurate |

3. The job is quite simple and repetitive.*

*How accurate is the statement in describing your job?*

| 1 | 2 | 3 | 4 | 5 | 6 | 7 |
|---|---|---|---|---|---|---|
| Very inaccurate | Mostly inaccurate | Slightly inaccurate | Uncertain | Slightly accurate | Mostly accurate | Very accurate |

### Task Identity

1. To what extent does your job involve doing a *"whole" and identifiable piece of work*? That is, is the job a complete piece of work that has an obvious beginning and end? Or is it only a small *part* of the overall piece of work, which is finished by other people or by automatic machines?

| 1 | 2 | 3 | 4 | 5 | 6 | 7 |
|---|---|---|---|---|---|---|
| My job is only a tiny part of the overall piece of work; the results of my activities cannot be seen in the final product or service. | | | My job is a moderate-sized "chunk" of the overall piece of work; my own contribution can be seen in the final outcome. | | | My job involves doing the whole piece of work, from start to finish; the results of my activities are easily seen in the final product or service. |

2. The job provides me a chance to completely finish the pieces of work I begin.

*How accurate is the statement in describing your job?*

| 1 | 2 | 3 | 4 | 5 | 6 | 7 |
|---|---|---|---|---|---|---|
| Very inaccurate | Mostly inaccurate | Slightly inaccurate | Uncertain | Slightly accurate | Mostly accurate | Very accurate |

3. The job is arranged so that I do *not* have the chance to do an entire piece of work from beginning to end.*

*How accurate is the statement in describing your job?*

| 1 | 2 | 3 | 4 | 5 | 6 | 7 |
|---|---|---|---|---|---|---|
| Very inaccurate | Mostly inaccurate | Slightly inaccurate | Uncertain | Slightly accurate | Mostly accurate | Very accurate |

### Task Significance

1. In general, how significant or important is your job? That is, are the results of your work likely to significantly affect the lives or well-being of other people?

| 1 | 2 | 3 | 4 | 5 | 6 | 7 |
|---|---|---|---|---|---|---|
| Not very significant; the outcomes of my work are *not* likely to have important effects on other people. | | | Moderately significant | | | Highly significant; the outcomes of my work can affect other people in very important ways. |

2. This job is one where a lot of people can be affected by how well the work gets done.

*How accurate is the statement in describing your job?*

| 1 | 2 | 3 | 4 | 5 | 6 | 7 |
|---|---|---|---|---|---|---|
| Very inaccurate | Mostly inaccurate | Slightly inaccurate | Uncertain | Slightly accurate | Mostly accurate | Very accurate |

3. The job itself is *not* very significant or important in the broader scheme of things.*

*How accurate is the statement in describing your job?*

| 1 | 2 | 3 | 4 | 5 | 6 | 7 |
|---|---|---|---|---|---|---|
| Very inaccurate | Mostly inaccurate | Slightly inaccurate | Uncertain | Slightly accurate | Mostly accurate | Very accurate |

### Autonomy

1. How much *autonomy* is there in your job? That is, to what extent does your job permit you to decide *on your own* how to go about doing your work?

| 1 | 2 | 3 | 4 | 5 | 6 | 7 |
|---|---|---|---|---|---|---|
| Very little; the job gives me almost no personal "say" about how and when the work is done. | | | Moderate autonomy; many things are standardized and not under my control, but I can make some decisions about the work. | | | Very much; the job gives me almost complete responsibility for deciding how and when the work is done. |

2. The job gives me considerable opportunity for independence and freedom in how I do the work.

*How accurate is the statement in describing your job?*

| 1 | 2 | 3 | 4 | 5 | 6 | 7 |
|---|---|---|---|---|---|---|
| Very inaccurate | Mostly inaccurate | Slightly inaccurate | Uncertain | Slightly accurate | Mostly accurate | Very accurate |

3. The job denies me any chance to use my personal initiative or judgment in carrying out the work.*

*How accurate is the statement in describing your job?*

| 1 | 2 | 3 | 4 | 5 | 6 | 7 |
|---|---|---|---|---|---|---|
| Very inaccurate | Mostly inaccurate | Slightly inaccurate | Uncertain | Slightly accurate | Mostly accurate | Very accurate |

### Feedback

1. To what extent does *doing the job itself* provide you with information about your work performance? That is, does the actual *work itself* provide clues about how well you are doing—aside from any "feedback" coworkers or supervisors may provide?

| 1 | 2 | 3 | 4 | 5 | 6 | 7 |
|---|---|---|---|---|---|---|
| Very little; the job itself is set up so I could work forever without finding out how well I am doing. | | | Moderately; sometimes doing the job provides "feedback" to me; sometimes it does not. | | | Very much; the job is set up so that I get almost constant "feedback" as I work about how well I am doing. |

2. Just doing the work required by the job provides many chances for me to figure out how well I am doing.

*How accurate is the statement in describing your job?*

| 1 | 2 | 3 | 4 | 5 | 6 | 7 |
|---|---|---|---|---|---|---|
| Very inaccurate | Mostly inaccurate | Slightly inaccurate | Uncertain | Slightly accurate | Mostly accurate | Very accurate |

3. The job itself provides very few clues about whether or not I am performing well.*

*How accurate is the statement in describing your job?*

| 1 | 2 | 3 | 4 | 5 | 6 | 7 |
|---|---|---|---|---|---|---|
| Very inaccurate | Mostly inaccurate | Slightly inaccurate | Uncertain | Slightly accurate | Mostly accurate | Very accurate |

*Scoring:* Responses to the three items for each core characteristic are averaged to yield an overall score for that characteristic.

Items marked with a "*" should be scored as follows: 1 = 7; 2 = 6; 3 = 5; 6 = 2; 7 = 1

$$\textbf{Motivating potential score} \times \left(\frac{\textbf{Skill variety} \times \textbf{Task identity} \times \textbf{Task significance}}{3}\right) \times \textbf{Autonomy} \times \textbf{Feedback}$$

## Developing OB Internet Skills

**Introduction:** The Internet is increasingly being used by individuals who are looking for a job. Start by imagining three different kinds of jobs that you might have an interest in (e.g., nurse, accountant, artist, pilot). Try to make the jobs as relevant as possible to your own true interests and aspirations.

**Internet Assignment:** Use the Internet to search for job or career opportunities in each of the three areas you identified. Select the one job in each set that provides the most information prospective employees might find useful.

**Follow-up:** How easy or difficult was this task? Did it make you more or less interested in using the Internet to look for a job? Finally, respond to the following questions:

1. Would it be possible to use the job characteristics model as a framework for comparing and contrasting jobs? That is, can you make informed assessments as to the extent to which the jobs you found have higher or lower levels of variety, autonomy, and the other characteristics?
2. Can you assess the degree to which you would have opportunities to participate in various ways in the jobs you found?
3. Can you determine the extent to which the jobs provide flexibility with respect to alternative work arrangements?

chapter

# 8

# Goal Setting, Performance Management, and Rewards

## Management Preview

This chapter continues our discussion of how managers can use various strategies and techniques to enhance employee motivation and performance. Essentially, this chapter follows a logical progression of discrete activities that, taken together, provide an integrated, systematic approach to motivating employee performance. That sequence involves setting goals, evaluating performance, and providing rewards. We begin by examining the role and importance of goal setting in employee motivation. Next we introduce performance management and measurement. Then we discuss in more detail how a good performance management system contributes to total quality management. We subsequently turn to reward systems and their role in motivation. We conclude by identifying important types of rewards and exploring perspectives on managing reward systems. First, however, we will describe a relatively new approach to performance management based on accelerated performance reviews. ■

Most organizations have traditionally conducted performance appraisals for everyone on a routine schedule of once a year, either on the anniversary of their hiring date or during one common period when everyone is evaluated. This schedule has especially been applied to new employees, who were told when they started working when their first review would be. Part of the logic underlying this system was that newcomers were considered to be on probation until their first review. In addition, organizations felt that new employees might need an extended period of time to learn the ropes and to have a reasonable time in which to establish their capabilities.

From the standpoint of the newcomers themselves, they often saw value in having ample time to learn their jobs before being evaluated. On the other hand, they also knew that increased compensation and promotions are usually tied to performance appraisals, so there would be little or no opportunity for them to seek a pay raise or to be given greater job responsibilities until that first review had been completed. Thus, the standard review cycle had both pluses and minuses for new employees.

*"More businesses are promising certain job candidates accelerated performance reviews—typically after six months, rather than the normal 12."* — *Joann Lublin,* Wall Street Journal *reporter**

In recent years, though, this cycle has gradually been altered in some firms. This change has come about in large part because of the tight labor market in certain areas, especially in the rapidly growing field of high technology. Because the highly skilled workers needed by high-tech firms are well aware of their value to prospective employers, some of the more enterprising and self-assured ones have started requesting—or in some cases demanding—promises of earlier reviews so as to have an opportunity to ratchet up their salaries more quickly. In addition, the practice of early reviews has also started spreading outside the high-tech environment to include such areas as banking, accounting, and insurance.

Firms in these areas are finding that by offering earlier reviews they have a better chance of landing the very top prospects. Moreover, a guaranteed review after six months is rapidly become almost an expectation in the eyes of some of the most promising recruits. One recent survey of executive search firms found that over 27 percent of new management positions currently being filled come with the assurance of an initial six-month review. But one thing that is often overlooked in this trend is that the recruit still has to ask. If not, the company is likely to stick with its normal one-year cycle.

So, can it get any faster? Absolutely. For example, consider the case of software programmer David Parvin, a recent college graduate being courted by Cougar Mountain Software, a Boise, Idaho, company. Parvin learned that Cougar Mountain was providing reviews of its new hires after thirty days. But Parvin wanted an even-faster evaluation, so he demanded a two-week review! Sure enough, during his first two weeks on the job he so impressed his bosses that they gave him a 7.1 percent pay raise. During his first eighteen months on the job he continued to request frequent reviews, earning a total of six raises and one major promotion.

Although such a review cycle may seem extreme, one reason it has worked is that Cougar Mountain has a history of rapid reviews. Indeed, about 10 percent of its new hires get a raise after thirty days, and almost all get a raise within three months. The firm's managers also believe that this practice helps Cougar Mountain retain its most valuable employees. In an industry with extremely high turnover, Cougar Mountain's turnover among all employees is only around 10 percent, and among its very best employees it is an incredible 1 percent.

Of course, this approach can also create some problems. In addition to the extra administrative time and expense needed to manage an organic performance appraisal and salary adjustment system, there are also potential morale problems with other employees. To address this concern, some companies require those who will be getting rapid reviews to keep their arrangement a secret so as to not create problems with other employees. But word is still likely to get out, especially if there are more than just a few new employees who are getting this special attention.

As for the future, there seems to be a difference of opinion as to whether or not this practice will continue. Some experts, for example, predict that as soon as the tight labor market begins to loosen (for example, when firms stop adding new jobs), firms will quickly move to drop the rapid review process. Others, however, believe that just the opposite will occur, and that firms may well come to value the flexibility that this system affords and want to apply it to everyone. That is, so long as they review and reward their more highly valued workers on an accelerated schedule, they may also be able to slow the process for less valued workers. Thus, a well-established worker with a history of being judged as adequate may get evaluated even less frequently—and get fewer raises—than is the case today.[1] ■

For years management experts have advocated the importance of linking performance to rewards. That is, organizations should attempt to provide more significant rewards to their higher-performing employees than to their lower-performing ones. But until recently, even when firms adopted this model, they assessed performance and allocated rewards only on an annual basis. However, as illustrated in the chapter opening case, this practice is being changed in a number of different ways today. At an even more fundamental level is the role of goals. As you will see when we discuss goal setting, goals provide context and direction for assessing performance and allocating rewards.[2]

# Goal Setting and Motivation

A **goal** is a desirable objective.

Goal setting is a very useful method of enhancing employee performance. From a motivational perspective, a **goal** is a desirable objective. Goals are used for two purposes in most organizations. First, they provide a useful framework for managing motivation. Managers and employees can set goals for themselves and then work toward them. Thus, if the organization's goal is to increase sales by 10 percent, a manager can use individual goals to help attain an overall goal. Second, goals are an effective control device; control is monitoring by management of how well the organization is performing. Comparing people's short-term performances with their goals can be an effective way to monitor the organization's long-run performance.

Our **self-efficacy** is the extent to which we believe we can accomplish our goals even if we failed to do so in the past.

Social learning theory perhaps best describes the role and importance of goal setting in organizations.[3] This perspective suggests that feelings of pride or shame about performance are a function of the extent to which people achieve their goals. A person who achieves a goal will be proud of having done so, whereas a person who fails to achieve a goal will feel personal disappointment, and perhaps even shame. People's degree of pride or disappointment is affected by their **self-efficacy**, the extent to which they feel that they can still meet their goals even if they failed to do so in the past.

## The Goal-Setting Theory

Social learning theory provides insights into why and how goals can motivate behavior. It also helps us understand how different people cope with failure to reach

Goals, or desirable objectives, play two important roles in organizations: they provide a framework for managing motivation and they are effective control devices. For example, Stephen Kahn has one overarching goal for Delia's Inc.: to be the dominant marketer to teenage consumers. Delia's currently focuses on teenage girls, a group of 28 million consumers that spends $60 billion annually. His goal of dominating this market segment keeps his employees tightly focused on searching for more and more ways to appeal to these consumers. Kahn motivates his employees by tying part of their compensation to their contributions toward the firm's goal. In addition, he regularly compares Delia's performance against his own short-term objectives and against the performance of key competitors.

their goals. It is the research of Edwin Locke and his associates that most decisively showed the utility of goal-setting theory in a motivational context.[4]

Locke's goal-setting theory of motivation assumes that behavior is a result of conscious goals and intentions. Therefore, by setting goals for people in the organization, a manager should be able to influence their behavior. Given this premise, the challenge is to develop a thorough understanding of the processes by which people set goals and then work to reach them. In the original version of goal-setting theory, two specific goal characteristics—goal difficulty and goal specificity—were expected to shape performance. The "Talking Technology" box describes how Pier 1 Imports, a large national retailer, uses technology to communicate information about goals and performance and to boost motivation in ways that are consistent with the goal-setting theory.

**Goal difficulty** is the extent to which a goal is challenging and requires effort.

### Goal Difficulty

**Goal difficulty** is the extent to which a goal is challenging and requires effort. If people work to achieve goals, it is reasonable to assume they will work harder to achieve more difficult goals. But a goal must not be so difficult that it is unattainable. If a new manager asks her sales force to increase sales by 300 percent, the group may become disillusioned. A more realistic but still difficult goal—perhaps a 50 percent increase—would be a better incentive. A substantial body of research supports the importance of goal difficulty.[5] In one study, managers at Weyerhaeuser set difficult goals for truck drivers hauling loads of timber from cutting sites to wood yards. Over a nine-month period, the drivers increased the quantity of wood they delivered by an amount that would have required $250,000 worth of new trucks at the previous per-truck average load.[6]

Reinforcement fosters motivation toward difficult goals. A person who is rewarded for achieving a difficult goal will be more inclined to strive toward the next difficult goal than will someone who received no reward for reaching the first goal.

**Goal specificity** is the clarity and precision of a goal.

### Goal Specificity

**Goal specificity** is the clarity and precision of the goal. A goal of "increasing productivity" is not very specific; a goal of "increasing productivity by 3 percent in the next six months" is quite specific. Some goals, such as those involving costs, output, profitability, and growth, are readily specified. Other goals, such as improving employee job satisfaction and morale, company image and reputation, ethics, and socially responsible behavior, are much harder to state in specific terms.

TALKING TECHNOLOGY

## Goals Drive Performance at Pier 1

The name of the game in retailing is sales. Virtually all measures of retailing performance revolve around sales figures—sales increases, seasonal sales fluctuations, sales compared to inventory, and so forth. One especially common performance measure is the increase in daily sales in a particular store relative to the store's sales one year before. Pier 1 Imports is using information technology to help make this performance measure, as well as others, an even more critical part of each Pier 1 store's daily business.

*"Do you realize that the Green Hills store is doing just $700 a day more than us? Someday we could pass them." — Eva Goldyn, Pier 1 store manager*

In the past, daily sales reports could only be calculated at the end of the day, so employees didn't know how well they were doing until it was too late to do anything about it. But now, sales figures are tabulated at each Pier 1 store on a continuous basis and displayed on a computer monitor in the employee lounge area. And Pier 1 employees are encouraged to check on the store's performance regularly. This has allowed the firm to do an even better job of boosting sales by establishing daily improvement goals. For example, a store manager might inform employees about last year's sales figures for a given day and then set a goal of surpassing that sales level by a specific percentage.

In larger metropolitan areas, where Pier 1 has multiple stores, the same technology is being used to pit one store against the others. Each store knows not only how well it's doing, but also how the other stores in the area are doing. This information allows them to compete with their own sales performance from the previous year, and with other regional stores. In order to ensure that Pier 1 employees do indeed work to meet their goals, their incentive system ties employee bonuses to sales performance. Thus, the goals help direct employee attention while also providing a clear avenue for employees to boost their income. And none of it would be possible without Pier 1's elaborate sales information system powered by local and network computer systems.

References: *Hoover's Handbook of American Business 2000* (Austin, Texas: Hoover's Business Press, 2000), pp. 1140–1141; "Pressure at Pier 1: Beating Sales Numbers of Year Earlier Is a Storewide Obsession," *Wall Street Journal*, December 7, 1995, pp. B1, B2 (quote on page B1).

Like difficulty, specificity has been shown to be consistently related to performance.[7] The study of timber truck drivers mentioned earlier also examined goal specificity. The initial loads the truck drivers were carrying were found to be 60 percent of the maximum weight each truck could haul. The managers set a new goal for drivers of 94 percent, which the drivers were soon able to reach. Thus, the goal was quite specific as well as difficult.

Locke's theory attracted much widespread interest and research support from both researchers and managers, so Locke, together with Gary Latham, eventually proposed an expanded model of the goal-setting process. The expanded model, shown in Figure 8.1, attempts to capture more fully the complexities of goal setting in organizations.

Goal acceptance is the extent to which a person accepts a goal as his or her own.

Goal commitment is the extent to which a person is personally interested in reaching a goal.

The expanded theory argues that goal-directed effort is a function of four goal attributes: difficulty and specificity, which we have already discussed, and acceptance and commitment. **Goal acceptance** is the extent to which a person accepts a goal as his or her own. **Goal commitment** is the extent to which he or she is personally interested in reaching the goal. The manager who vows to take whatever steps are necessary to cut costs by 10 percent has made a commitment to achieve the goal. Factors that can foster goal acceptance and commitment include participating in the goal-setting process, making goals challenging but realistic, and believing that goal achievement will lead to valued rewards.[8]

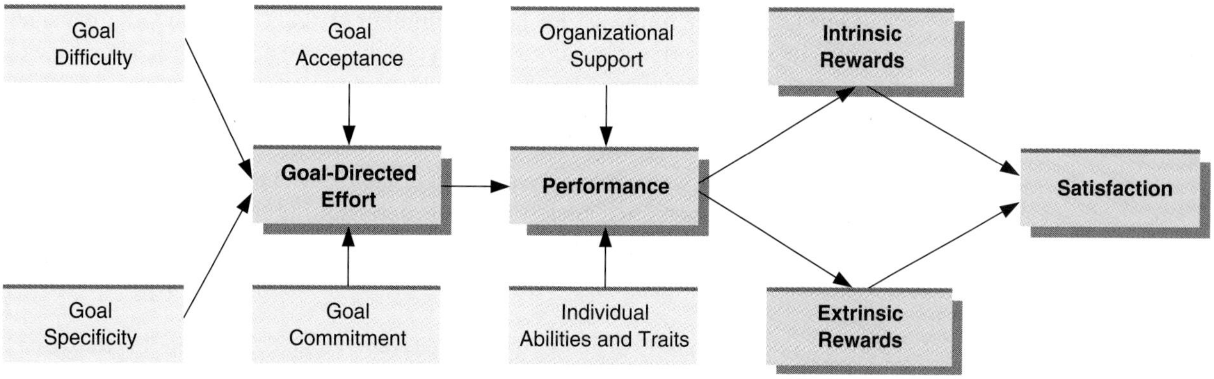


figure 8.1 **The Goal-Setting Theory of Motivation**

*The goal-setting theory of motivation provides an important means of enhancing the motivation of employees. As illustrated here, appropriate goal difficulty, specificity, acceptance, and commitment contribute to goal-directed effort. This effort, in turn, has a direct impact on performance.*

Reference: Goal-Setting Motivational Technique That Works by Gary P. Latham, et al. Reprinted from *Organizational Dynamics*, Autumn, 1979. © 1979 with permission from Elsevier Science, Inc.

The interaction of goal-directed effort, organizational support, and individual abilities and traits determines actual performance. Organizational support is whatever the organization does to help or hinder performance. Positive support might mean making enough personnel and raw materials available to meet the goal; negative support might mean failing to fix damaged equipment. Individual abilities and traits are the skills and other personal characteristics necessary to do a job. As a result of performance, a person receives various intrinsic and extrinsic rewards, which in turn influence satisfaction. Note that the latter stages of this model are quite similar to those of the Porter-Lawler expectancy model discussed earlier.

## Broader Perspectives on Goal Setting

**Management by objectives (MBO)** is a collaborative goal-setting process through which organizational goals cascade down throughout the organization.

Some organizations undertake goal setting from the somewhat broader perspective of **management by objectives**, or **MBO**.[9] MBO is essentially a collaborative goal-setting process through which organizational goals systematically cascade down through the organization. Our discussion describes a generic approach, but many organizations adapt MBO to suit their own purposes.

A successful MBO program starts with top managers establishing overall goals for the organization.[10] After these goals are set, managers and employees throughout the organization collaborate to set subsidiary goals. First, the overall goals are communicated to everyone. Then each manager meets with each subordinate. During these meetings, the manager explains the unit goals to the subordinate, and the two determine together how the subordinate can contribute to the goals most effectively. The manager acts as a counselor and helps ensure that the subordinate develops goals that are verifiable. For example, a goal of "cutting costs by 5 percent" is verifiable, whereas a goal of "doing my best" is not. Finally, manager and subordinate ensure that the subordinate has the resources needed to reach his or her goals. The entire process spirals downward as each subordinate meets with his or her own subordinates to develop their goals. Thus, as we noted earlier, the initial goals set at the top cascade down through the entire organization.

During the time frame set for goal attainment (usually one year), the manager periodically meets with each subordinate to check progress. It may be necessary to modify goals in light of new information, to provide additional resources, or to take some other action. At the end of the specified time period, managers hold a final evaluation meeting with each subordinate. At this meeting, manager and subordinate assess how well goals were met and discuss why. This meeting often serves as the annual performance review as well, determining salary adjustments and other rewards based on reaching goals. This meeting may also serve as the initial goal-setting meeting for the next year's cycle.

*"Big, hairy, audacious goals . . . are a powerful way to stimulate progress—change, improvement, innovation, renewal—while simultaneously preserving your core values and purpose." — Jim Collins, management consultant*[11]

## Evaluation and Implications

Goal-setting theory has been widely tested in a variety of settings. Research has demonstrated fairly consistently that goal difficulty and specificity are closely associated with performance. Other elements of the theory, such as acceptance and commitment, have been studied less frequently. A few studies have shown the importance of acceptance and commitment, but little is currently known about how people accept and become committed to goals. Goal-setting theory may also focus too much attention on the short run at the expense of long-term considerations. Despite these questions, however, goal setting is clearly an important way for managers to convert motivation into actual improved performance.

From the broader perspective, MBO is also a very successful technique. Alcoa, Tenneco, Black & Decker, General Foods, and Du Pont, for example, have used it extensively. MBO's popularity stems in part from its many strengths. For one thing, MBO clearly has the potential to motivate employees because it helps implement goal-setting theory on a systematic basis throughout the organization. It also clarifies the basis for rewards, and it can spur communication. Performance appraisals are easier and more clear-cut under MBO. Further, managers can use the system for control purposes.

However, using MBO also presents pitfalls. Sometimes top managers do not really participate; that is, the goals really start in the middle of the organization and may not reflect the real goals of top management. If employees believe this to be true, they may become cynical, interpreting the lack of participation by top management as a sign that the goals are not important and that their own involvement is therefore a waste of time. MBO also has a tendency to overemphasize quantitative goals to enhance verifiability. Another potential liability is that an MBO system requires a great deal of paperwork and record keeping, since every goal must be documented. Finally, some managers do not really let subordinates participate in goal setting but, instead, merely assign goals and order subordinates to accept them.

On balance, MBO is often an effective and useful system for managing goal setting and enhancing performance in organizations. Research suggests that it can actually do many of the things its advocates claim, but that it must also be handled carefully. In particular, most organizations need to tailor it to their own unique circumstances. Properly used, MBO can also be an effective approach to managing an organization's reward system. It requires, however, individual, one-on-one interactions between each supervisor and each employee, and these one-on-one interactions can often be difficult because of the time they take and the likelihood that at least some of them will involve critical assessments of unacceptable performance.

# Performance Management in Organizations

As described above, most goals are oriented toward some element of performance. Managers can do a variety of things to enhance employee motivation and performance, including redesigning jobs, allowing greater participation, creating alternative work arrangements, and setting goals. They may also fail to do things that might have improved motivation and performance, and they may inadvertently even do things that reduce motivation and performance. Thus, it is clearly important that performance be approached as something that can and should be managed.

**Performance measurement**, or **performance appraisal** is the process by which someone (1) evaluates an employee's work behaviors by measurement and comparison with previously established standards, (2) documents the results, and (3) communicates the results to the employee.

## The Nature of Performance Management

The core of performance management is the actual measurement of the performance of an individual or group. **Performance measurement**, or **performance appraisal**, is the process by which someone (1) evaluates an employee's work behaviors by measurement and comparison with previously established standards, (2) documents the results, and (3) communicates the results to the employee.[12] A performance management system (PMS) comprises the processes and activities involved in performance appraisals, as shown in Figure 8.2.

figure **8.2** **The Performance Management System**

*An organization's performance management system plays an important role in determining its overall level of effectiveness. This is especially true when the organization is attempting to employ total quality management. Key elements of a performance management system, as shown here, include the timing and frequency of evaluations, the choice of who does the evaluation, the choice of measurement procedures, the storage and distribution of performance information, and the recording methods. These elements are used by managers and employees in most organizations.*

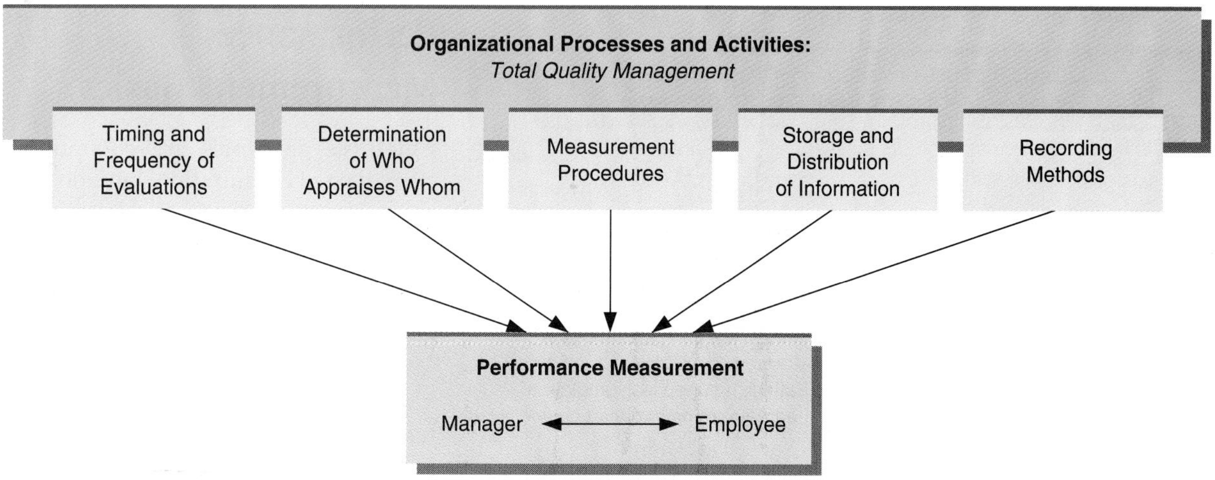

Simple performance appraisal involves a manager and an employee, whereas the PMS incorporates the total quality management context along with the organizational policies, procedures, and resources that support the activity being appraised. The timing and frequency of evaluations, choice of who appraises whom, measurement procedures, storage and distribution of information, and methods of recording the evaluations are all aspects of the PMS.

## Purposes of Performance Measurement

Performance measurement may serve many purposes. The ability to provide valuable feedback is one critical purpose. Feedback, in turn, tells the employee where she or he stands in the eyes of the organization. Appraisal results, of course, are also used to decide and justify reward allocations. Performance evaluations may be used as a starting point for discussions of training, development, and improvement. Finally, the data produced by the performance appraisal system can be used to forecast future human resource needs, to plan management succession, and to guide other human resource activities, such as recruiting, training, and development programs.

Job performance feedback is the primary use of appraisal information. Performance appraisal information can indicate that an employee is ready for promotion or that he or she needs additional training to gain experience in another area of company operations. It may also show that a person does not have the skills for a certain job and that another person should be recruited to fill that particular role. Other purposes of performance appraisal can be grouped into two broad categories, judgment and development, as shown in Figure 8.3.

Performance appraisals with a judgmental orientation focus on past performance and are concerned mainly with measuring and comparing performance and with the uses of the information generated.[13] Appraisals with a developmental orientation focus on the future and use information from evaluations to improve performance. If improved future performance is the intent of the appraisal process, the manager may focus on goals or targets for the employee, on eliminating obstacles or problems that hinder performance, and on future training needs.

**figure 8.3 Purposes of Performance Measurement**

*Performance measurement plays a variety of roles in most organizations. This figure illustrates that these roles can help managers judge an employee's past performance and help managers and employees improve future performance.*

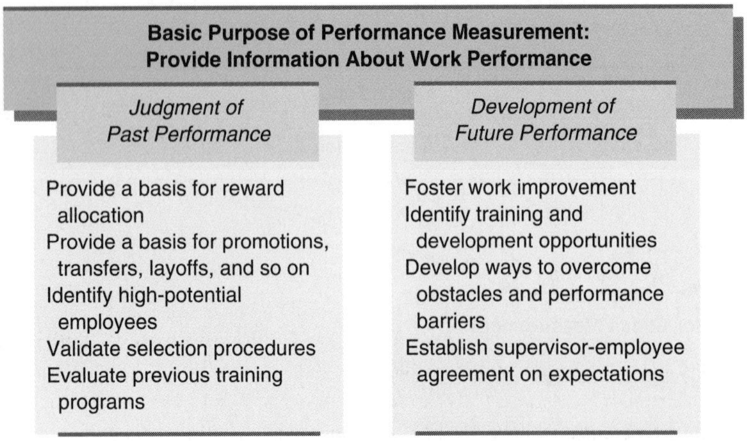
Basic Purpose of Performance Measurement:
Provide Information About Work Performance
Judgment of
Past Performance
Provide a basis for reward allocation
Provide a basis for promotions, transfers, layoffs, and so on
Identify high-potential employees
Validate selection procedures
Evaluate previous training programs
Development of
Future Performance
Foster work improvement
Identify training and development opportunities
Develop ways to overcome obstacles and performance barriers
Establish supervisor-employee agreement on expectations

## Performance Measurement Basics

Employee appraisals are common in every type of organization, but how they are performed may vary. Many issues must be considered in determining how to conduct an appraisal. Two of the most important issues are who does the appraisals and how often they are done.[14]

**The Appraiser** In most appraisal systems, the employee's primary evaluator is the supervisor. This stems from the obvious fact that the supervisor is presumably in the best position to be aware of the employee's day-to-day performance. Further, it is the supervisor who has traditionally provided performance feedback to employees and determined performance-based rewards and sanctions. Problems often arise, however, if the supervisor has incomplete or distorted information about the employee's performance. For example, the supervisor may have little firsthand knowledge of the performance of an employee who works alone outside the company premises, such as a salesperson who makes solo calls on clients or a maintenance person who handles equipment problems in the field. Similar problems may arise when the supervisor has a limited understanding of the technical knowledge involved in an employee's job.

*"We were miles apart on his performance. I thought it was adequate at best, he thought it was outstanding." — James Sauter, CEO of a newspaper publishing company*[15]

One solution to these problems is a multiple-rater system that incorporates the ratings of several people familiar with the employee's performance.[16] One possible alternative, for example, is to use the employee as an evaluator. Although they may not actually do so, most employees are capable of evaluating themselves in an unbiased manner.

**360-degree feedback** is a performance management system in which people receive performance feedback from those on all sides of them in the organization—their boss, their colleagues and peers, and their own subordinates.

One of the more interesting approaches being used in many companies today is something called **360-degree feedback**—a performance management system in which people receive performance feedback from those on all sides of them in the organization—their boss, their colleagues and peers, and their own subordinates. Thus, the feedback comes from all around them, 360 degrees. This form of performance evaluation can be very beneficial to managers because it typically gives them a much wider range of performance-related feedback than a traditional evaluation. That is, rather than focusing narrowly on objective performance, such as sales increases or productivity gains, 360-degree feedback often focuses on such things as interpersonal relations and style. For example, one person may learn that she stands too close to other people when she talks, another that he has a bad temper. These are the kinds of things a supervisor might not even be aware of, much less report as part of performance appraisal. Subordinates or peers are much more willing to provide this sort of feedback.

Of course, to benefit from 360-degree feedback, a manager must have a thick skin. The manager is likely to hear some personal comments on sensitive topics, which may be threatening. Thus, a 360-degree feedback system must be carefully managed so that its focus remains on constructive rather than destructive criticism. Because of its potential advantages and in spite of its potential shortcomings, many companies today are using this approach to performance feedback. AT&T, Nestlé, Pitney Bowes, and Chase Manhattan Bank are just a few of the major companies today using 360-degree feedback to help managers improve a wide variety of performance-related behaviors.[17]

**Frequency of the Appraisal** Another important issue is the frequency of appraisals. Regardless of the employee's level of performance, the type of task, or the employee's need for information on performance, the organization usually conducts performance appraisals on a regular basis, typically once a year. Annual performance appraisals are convenient for administrative purposes such as record keeping and predictability. Some organizations also conduct appraisals semiannually.[18] Several systems for monitoring employee performance on an "as-needed" basis have been proposed as an alternative to the traditional annual system.

Managers in international settings must ensure that they incorporate cultural phenomena in their performance appraisal strategies. For example, in highly individualistic cultures such as the United States, appraising performance at the individual level is both common and accepted. But in collectivistic cultures such as Japan, performance appraisals almost always need to be focused more on group performance and feedback. And in countries where people put a lot of faith in destiny, fate, or some form of divine control, employees may not be receptive to performance feedback at all, believing that their actions are irrelevant to the results that follow them.

# Performance Measurement and Total Quality Management

**Total quality management (TQM)** is a form of management that focuses on the customer, an environment of trust and openness, working in teams, breaking down internal organizational barriers, team leadership and coaching, shared power, and continuous improvement; use of this approach often involves fundamental changes in the organization's culture.

An area in which performance management is especially important to many organizations today is total quality management. **Total quality management (TQM)** is a form of management that focuses on the customer, an environment of trust and openness, working in teams, breaking down internal organizational barriers, team leadership and coaching, shared power, and continuous improvement. Adopting TQM usually means fundamentally changing the organization's culture. In general, experts agree that to practice TQM, performance management is imperative.[19] Indeed, all of the winners of the Malcolm Baldrige National Quality Award have incorporated elements of TQM into their performance management systems. One of the basic tenets of TQM is continuous improvement.

## Continuous Improvement

Some managers have traditionally approached performance as something to be maintained. That is, they assume that motivation, environment, and ability result in a constant level of performance. A logical extension of this assumption would be that performance will only increase when motivation, the environment, or ability improves. In this view, performance increases in a stair-step fashion—plateaus of flat performance are followed by sharp increases. The left part of Figure 8.4 illustrates this view.

The **continuous improvement** perspective suggests that performance should constantly be enhanced.

The premise of **continuous improvement**, in contrast, is that under a TQM program performance can—and should—be increased constantly. The right part of Figure 8.4 illustrates this viewpoint. The founder of the TQM philosophy, W. Edwards Deming, called for the elimination of numerical productivity and work-standard-type goals, because they focused management's attention on short-run targets and away from satisfying the customer. Instead, he proposed that the goals for employees, teams, and the organization as a whole be continuous improvement in quality and customer service, decreased cycle time, skill upgrading, reduced machine setup time, and increased machine run time. Although originally developed for traditional manufacturing settings, the concept of continuous improvement has been applied to a wide array of organizations.

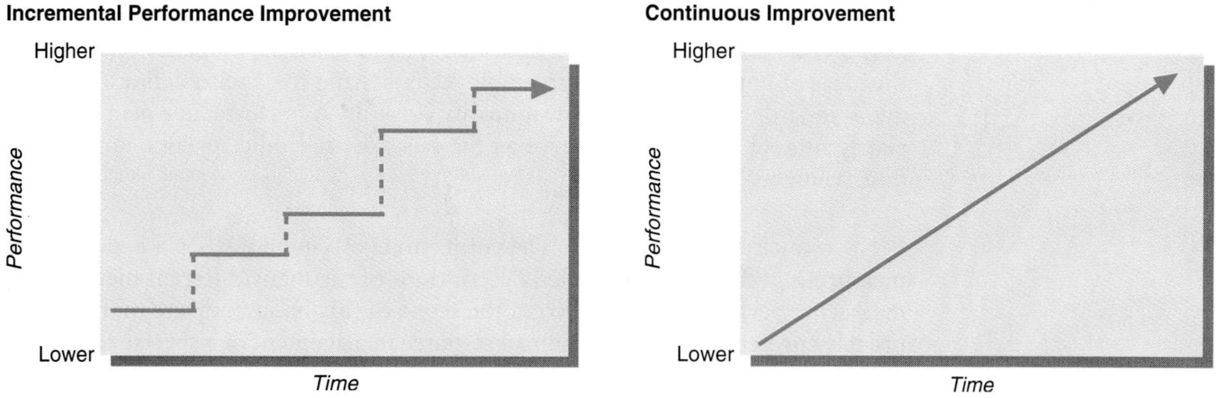


**figure 8.4 Incremental Versus Continuous Improvement**

*Traditional approaches to improving performance, as illustrated on the left of this figure, focused on incremental improvement. That is, managers assumed that motivation, environment, and ability resulted in a constant level of performance. Only by changing one or more of these elements could performance be improved. The concept of continuous improvement, illustrated on the right part of the figure, assumes that performance can be elevated on a constant basis.*

The performance management systems organizations use vary greatly in their methods and in their effectiveness. Some work, some don't, and some are constantly being changed in a search for improvements.[20] Four factors are crucial in incorporating the principles of TQM into a performance management system and achieving continuous improvement: commitment to objectives, job analysis, a performance plan, and performance measurement.

**Commitment to Objectives** A successful performance management system is based on a strong commitment from the entire organization, especially top management, to improve quality. This commitment is made manifest in the objectives of the system. Top managers must know what they want the PMS to accomplish and communicate their objectives to those responsible for developing and managing the system. When objectives are clear and organizational commitment to quality improvement is strong, supervisors are confident that the time and effort they devote to performance management are worthwhile, which increases their interest in using the performance reviews to change behaviors and improve performance. Clearly stated objectives also allow managers to monitor the program, evaluate it periodically, and make any necessary adjustments.

**Job analysis** is the process of systematically gathering information about specific jobs to use in developing a performance measurement system, to write job or position descriptions, and to develop equitable pay systems.

A **performance plan** is an understanding between an employee and a manager concerning what and how a job is to be done such that both parties know what is expected and how success is defined and measured.

**Job Analysis** The second factor of an effective PMS is a sound job analysis system that provides comprehensive and accurate descriptions of all jobs in the organization. **Job analysis** is the process of systematically gathering information about specific jobs to use in developing a PMS, in writing job or position descriptions, and in developing equitable pay systems. To evaluate an employee's job performance fairly, the job must be precisely and clearly defined.

**Performance Plan** Closely tied to the job analysis is the performance plan. A **performance plan** is an understanding between an employee and manager of what and how the job is to be done such that both parties know what is expected and how success is defined and measured. In TQM terms, a performance plan defines the areas of improvement that an employee is striving for. It also defines the goals and standards for improvement in quality or skills. A performance plan can help clarify mutual expectations, serve as the basis for periodic reviews, and reduce disagreements.

Performance Measurement The cornerstone of a good PMS is the method for measuring performance. Detailed descriptions of the many different methods for measuring performance are beyond the scope of this book; they are more appropriately covered in a course in human resource management or a specialized course in performance appraisal. However, we can present a few general comments about how to measure performance.

The measurement method provides the information managers use to make decisions about salary adjustment, promotion, transfer, training, and discipline. The courts and Equal Employment Opportunity guidelines have mandated that performance measurements be based on job-related criteria rather than on some other factor, such as friendship, age, sex, religion, or national origin. In addition, to provide useful information for the decision maker, performance appraisals must be valid, reliable, and free of bias. They must not produce ratings that are consistently too lenient or too severe or that all cluster in the middle. They must also be free of perceptual and timing errors.[21]

Some of the most popular methods for evaluating individual performance are graphic rating scales, checklists, essays or diaries, behaviorally anchored rating scales, forced-choice systems, and MBO. These systems are easy to use and familiar to most managers. However, two major problems are common to all individual methods: a tendency to rate most individuals at about the same level, and inability to discriminate among variable levels of performance.[22]

Comparative methods evaluate two or more employees by comparing them with each other on various performance dimensions. The most popular comparative methods are ranking, forced distribution, paired comparisons, and the use of multiple raters in making comparisons. Comparative methods, however, are more difficult than the individual methods to use, are unfamiliar to many managers, and may require sophisticated development procedures and a computerized analytical system to extract usable information.

## The Learning Organization

A recent refinement of the TQM approach is the so-called learning organization. Organizations that adopt this approach work to integrate continuous improvement with continuous employee learning and development. Specifically, a **learning organization** is one that works to facilitate the lifelong learning and personal development of all of its employees while continually transforming itself to respond to changing demands and needs.[23]

A **learning organization** is one that works to facilitate the lifelong learning and personal development of all of its employees while continually transforming itself to respond to changing demands and needs.

Managers might approach the concept of a learning organization from a variety of perspectives, but improved TQM, continuous improvement, and performance measurement are frequent goals. The idea is that the most consistent and logical strategy for achieving continuous improvement is to constantly upgrade employee talent, skill, and knowledge. For example, if each employee in an organi-

A learning organization facilitates the lifelong learning and personal development of all its employees while continuously transforming itself to respond to changing demands and needs. A good case-in-point is Viant, Inc., a consulting firm that specializes in helping companies build and maintain web-based businesses. All Viant employees are encouraged to avail themselves of the myriad learning opportunities the firm provides for them. Viant's goal, according to its CEO, is a simple one: find good people, then make sure they are constantly broadening their skills.

zation learns one new thing each day and can translate that knowledge into work-related practice, continuous improvement logically follows. Indeed, organizations that wholeheartedly embrace this approach believe that only by constant employee learning can continuous improvement really occur.

In recent years many different organizations have implemented this approach. For example, the Shell Oil Company recently purchased an executive conference center north of its headquarters in Houston. The center boasts state-of-the-art classrooms and instructional technology, lodging facilities, a restaurant, and recreational amenities such as a golf course, swimming pool, and tennis courts. Line managers at the firm rotate through the Shell Learning Center, as the facility has been renamed, and serve as teaching faculty. Such teaching assignments last anywhere from a few days to several months. At the same time, all Shell employees routinely attend training programs, seminars, and related activities to learn the latest information they need to contribute more effectively to the firm. Recent seminar topics cover a broad range: time management, the implications of the Americans with Disabilities Act, balancing work and family demands, and international trade theory, among others.

# Individual Rewards in Organizations

The **reward system** consists of all organizational components, including people, processes, rules and procedures, and decision-making activities, involved in allocating compensation and benefits to employees in exchange for their contributions to the organization.

As noted earlier, one of the primary purposes of performance management is to provide a basis for rewarding employees. We now turn our attention to rewards and their impact on employee motivation and performance. The **reward system** consists of all organizational components—including people, processes, rules and procedures, and decision-making activities—involved in allocating compensation and benefits to employees in exchange for their contributions to the organization.[24] As we examine organizational reward systems, it is important to keep in mind their role in psychological contracts (as discussed in Chapter 4) and employee motivation (as discussed in Chapters 5 and 6). Rewards constitute many of the inducements that organizations provide to employees as their part of the psychological contract, for example. Rewards also satisfy some of the needs employees attempt to meet through their choice of work-related behaviors.

## Roles, Purposes, and Meanings of Rewards

The purpose of the reward system in most organizations is to attract, retain, and motivate qualified employees. The organization's compensation structure must be equitable and consistent to ensure equality of treatment and compliance with the law. Compensation should also be a fair reward for the individual's contributions to the organization, although in most cases these contributions are difficult, if not impossible, to measure objectively. Given this limitation, managers should be as fair and as equitable as possible. Finally, the system must be competitive in the external labor market for the organization to attract and retain competent workers in appropriate fields.

Beyond these broad considerations, an organization must develop its philosophy of compensation based on its own conditions and needs, and this philosophy must be defined and built into the actual reward system. For example, Wal-Mart has a policy that none of its employees will be paid the minimum wage. Even though it may pay some people only slightly more than this minimum, the firm nevertheless wants to communicate to everyone that it places a higher value on their contributions than just having to pay them the lowest wage possible.

The organization needs to decide what types of behaviors or performance it wants to encourage with a reward system, because what is rewarded tends to recur. Possible behaviors include performance, longevity, attendance, loyalty, contributions to the "bottom line," responsibility, and conformity. Performance measurement, as described earlier, assesses these behaviors, but the choice of which behaviors to reward is a function of the compensation system. A reward system must also take into account volatile economic issues such as inflation, market conditions, technology, labor union activities, and so forth.

The **surface value** of a reward to an employee is its objective meaning or worth.

The **symbolic value** of a reward to an employee is its subjective and personal meaning or worth.

It is also important for the organization to recognize that organizational rewards have many meanings for employees. Intrinsic and extrinsic rewards carry both surface and symbolic value. The **surface value** of a reward to an employee is its objective meaning or worth. A salary increase of 5 percent, for example, means that an individual has 5 percent more spending power than before, whereas a promotion, on the surface, means new duties and responsibilities. But managers must recognize that rewards also carry **symbolic value**. Consider what frequently happens when a professional sports team signs a top college prospect for a huge bonus and salary. The new player often feels enormous pressure to live up to the salary, whereas veteran players may grumble that their pay should be increased to keep the salary structure in balance.

Thus, rewards convey to people not only how much they are valued by the organization but their importance relative to others. Consider again a 5 percent salary increase. If the recipient later finds out that everyone else got 3 percent or less, she will feel vitally important to the organization, someone whose contributions are recognized and valued. On the other hand, if everyone else got at least 8 percent, the person will probably believe the organization places little value on her contributions. In short, then, managers need to tune in to the many meanings rewards can convey—not only the surface messages but the symbolic messages.

## Types of Rewards

Most organizations use several different types of rewards. The most common are base pay (wages or salary), incentive systems, benefits, perquisites, and

An individual's **compensation package** is the total array of money (wages, salary, commission), incentives, benefits, perquisites, and awards provided by the organization.

awards. These rewards are combined to create an individual's **compensation package**.

Base Pay For most people, the most important reward for work is the pay they receive. Obviously, money is important because of the things it can buy, but as we just noted, it can also symbolize an employee's worth. Pay is very important to an organization for a variety of reasons. For one thing, an effectively planned and managed pay system can improve motivation and performance. For another, employee compensation is a major cost of doing business—as much as 50 to 60 percent in many organizations—so a poorly designed system can be an expensive proposition. Finally, since pay is considered a major source of employee dissatisfaction, a poorly designed system can result in problems in other areas, such as turnover and low morale.

**Incentive systems** are plans in which employees can earn additional compensation in return for certain types of performance.

Incentive Systems **Incentive systems** are plans in which employees can earn additional compensation in return for certain types of performance. Examples of incentive programs include:

1. *Piecework programs,* which tie a worker's earnings to the number of units produced.
2. *Gain-sharing programs,* which grant additional earnings to employees or work groups for cost-reduction ideas.[25]
3. *Bonus systems,* which provide managers with lump-sum payments from a special pool based on the financial performance of the organization or a unit.
4. *Long-term compensation,* which gives managers additional income based on stock price performance, earnings per share, or return on equity.
5. *Merit pay plans,* which base pay raises on the employee's performance.
6. *Profit-sharing plans,* which distribute a portion of the firm's profits to all employees at a predetermined rate.
7. *Employee stock option plans,* which set aside stock in the company for employees to purchase at a reduced rate.

Plans oriented mainly toward individual employees may cause increased competition for the rewards and some possibly disruptive behaviors, such as sabotaging a coworker's performance, sacrificing quality for quantity, or fighting over customers. A group incentive plan, on the other hand, requires that employees trust one another and work together. Of course, incentive systems have advantages and disadvantages.

*"Performance-based pay used to be limited to executives, managers, and sales forces. Now it's at the factory floor."* — *Marc Wallace, consultant*[26]

Long-term compensation for executives is particularly controversial because of the large sums of money involved and the basis for the payments. Executive compensation is one of the more controversial subjects that U.S. businesses have had to face in recent years. News reports and the popular press seem to take great joy in telling stories about how this or that executive has just received a huge windfall from his or her organization. Clearly, successful top managers deserve significant rewards. The job of a senior executive, especially a CEO, is grueling, stressful, and takes talent and decades of hard work to reach. Only a small handful of managers ever attain a top position in a major corporation. The question is whether some companies are overrewarding such managers for their contributions to the organization.[27]

To understand the ethical context of this decision, consider the following statistics. From 1990 to 1995, the pay for the average worker in the United States increased by 16 percent—from $22,976 in 1990 to $26,652 in 1995. During the same period, worker layoffs increased by 39 percent—from 316,047 to 439,882. Corporate profits, meanwhile, increased at a rate of 75 percent from 1990 to 1995, with the 1990 level being $176 billion and the 1995 level $308 billion. But CEO pay increased an amazing 92 percent during the same period, the average growing from $1.95 million in 1990 to $3.75 million in 1995. Keep in mind, of course, that these numbers are only averages. The high-end salaries of some executives are truly staggering. For example, in 1998, Jack Welch, the CEO of General Electric, received $8 million in salary and bonuses plus another $12.5 million in long-term compensation, giving him total pay for the year in excess of $20.5 million.

When a firm is growing rapidly and its profits are also growing rapidly, relatively few objections can be raised to paying the CEO well. However, objections arise when an organization is laying off workers, its financial performance is perhaps less than might be expected, and the CEO is still earning a huge amount of money. It is these situations that dictate that a board of directors take a close look at the appropriateness of its actions.

**Benefits** are an important form of indirect compensation.

### Benefits

Another major component of the compensation package is the employee benefits plan. **Benefits** are often called "indirect compensation." Typical benefits provided by businesses include the following:

1. *Payment for time not worked*, both on and off the job. On-the-job free time includes lunch, rest, coffee breaks, and wash-up or get-ready time. Off-the-job time not worked includes vacation, sick leave, holidays, and personal days.

Most businesses provide a variety of different benefits for their employees. In today's era of low unemployment and worker shortages in many economic sectors, companies are searching more and more for creative benefits to retain their valued employees. Among the more innovative benefits offered by some companies these days are sports facilities, like basketball courts, putting greens, beach volleyball, and horseshoe pits, and personal expression programs, like sculpting classes, poetry lessons, and writing workshops. Some companies are providing employees with amenities such as nap rooms or, in the case of Gould Evans Goodman, a Kansas City architectural firm, a nap tent—literally, a tent containing a sleeping bag, pillow, alarm clock, and soothing music.

2. *Social Security contributions.* The employer contributes half the money paid into the system established under the Federal Insurance Contributions Act (FICA). The employee pays the other half.
3. *Unemployment compensation.* People who have lost their jobs or are temporarily laid off get a percentage of their wages from the state.
4. *Disability and workers' compensation benefits.* Employers contribute funds to help workers who cannot work due to occupational injury or ailment.
5. *Life and health insurance programs.* Most organizations offer insurance at a cost far below what individuals would pay to buy insurance by themselves.
6. *Pension plans.* Most organizations offer plans to provide supplementary income to employees after they retire.

A company's Social Security, unemployment, and workers' compensation contributions are set by law. But how much to contribute for other kinds of benefits is up to each company. Some organizations contribute more to the cost of these benefits than others. Some companies pay the entire cost; others pay a percentage of the cost of certain benefits, such as health insurance, and bear the entire cost of others. Offering benefits beyond wages became a standard component of compensation during World War II as a way to increase employee compensation when wage controls were in effect. Since then, competition for employees and employee demands (expressed, for instance, in union bargaining) has caused companies to increase these benefits. In many organizations today, benefits now account for 30 to 40 percent of payroll. The "Mastering Change" box also illustrates how many companies today are offering workers more flexibility in terms of the benefits that they can choose to take.

The burden of providing employee benefits is growing heavier for firms in the United States than it is for organizations in other countries, especially among unionized firms. For example, consider the problem that General Motors faces. Workers at GM's brake factory in Dayton, Ohio, earn an average of $27 an hour in wages. They also earn another $16 an hour in benefits, including full health-care coverage with no deductibles, full pension benefits after thirty years of service, life and disability insurance, and legal services. Thus, GM's total labor costs at the factory average $43 an hour. A German rival, Robert Bosch GmbH, meanwhile, has a nonunionized brake plant in South Carolina. It pays its workers an average of $18 an hour in wages, and its hourly benefit cost is around $5. Bosch's benefits include medical coverage with a $2,000 deductible, 401(k) retirement plans with employee participation, and life and disability coverage. Bosch's total hourly labor costs, therefore, are only $23. Toyota, Nissan, and Honda buy most of their brakes for their U.S. factories from Bosch, whereas General Motors must use its own factory to supply brakes. Thus, foreign competitors realize considerable cost advantages over GM in the brakes they use, and this pattern runs across a variety of other component parts as well.[28]

**Perquisites** are special privileges awarded to selected members of an organization, usually top managers.

Perquisites **Perquisites** are special privileges awarded to selected members of an organization, usually top managers. For years, the top executives of many businesses were allowed privileges such as unlimited use of the company airplane, motor home, vacation home, and executive dining room. In Japan, a popular perquisite is a paid membership in an exclusive golf club; a common perquisite in England is first-class travel. In the United States, the Internal Revenue Service has recently ruled that some "perks" constitute a form of income and thus can be taxed. The IRS decision has substantially changed the nature of these benefits, but

MASTERING CHANGE

## *New Forms of Employee Benefits*

Whereas most benefits packages once all looked about the same, in today's competitive business climate, flexible benefits programs are all the rage. By flexible, experts mean that companies are giving employees more choices about their benefits and providing benefits that themselves add flexibility to the daily lives of employees.

> *"[Climbing the rock wall] is* ***a relaxing way to separate myself from everything that's going on in the office."*** *— Tom Richardson, Clif Bar marketing coordinator*

For example, take the case of Katherine Lechler, a young graphics designer for a trade publication. Her employer provides high-quality on-site childcare for her two children. She pays about 20 percent less than she would for commercial childcare, has lunch with them each day, and knows that she can be at their side at a moment's notice. For its part, the company gets a higher percentage of Ms. Lechler's work time and makes it more difficult for her to look for a job with some other company that might not provide the same benefits.

Another increasingly popular benefit is on-site counseling of various types. ATS, for instance, a large telecommunications firm, provides psychological counseling for its employees. People use the service to work through personal and family problems, career issues, or just about anything else in which a trained psychologist can be of help. Again, the firm benefits as well. The part-time psychologist costs about a fifth of what ATS saves on hiring new people—the turnover is a third of its industry average.

Similarly, Marriott International provides employees a twenty-four-hour toll-free hotline staffed by social workers. Employees can call for advice on everything from setting up a family budget to dealing with a child's problems at school to selecting the best automobile insurance policy. Marriott spends about $1 million annually to operate the service, but estimates that it saves $4 million in reduced absenteeism and lower turnover.

Small businesses are getting in on the act as well. Russell, Karsh, & Hagen, an eleven-person public relations firm in Denver, allows its employees to donate public relations work—on company time—to their favorite charity. While this might not be a benefit per se, it nevertheless helps employees see that the firm is interested in supporting those things valued by employees.

Another small public relations firm in New Jersey, Daly Gray, allows staffers to tack on a couple of extra vacation days whenever they travel on company business. The president even donates some of his own frequent-flyer miles to make it easier for his employees to travel. And again, both the firm and its employees benefit.

Indeed, these and other kinds of benefits continue to grow in popularity. One recent survey, for example, found that human resource managers expect part-time work options, telecommuting, and flexible work hours to all grow significantly by the year 2001. In addition, the same survey found rapid and continuing growth in other benefit options as well, including long-term-care insurance, group financial planning, prepaid legal services, group auto insurance, and group homeowners insurance. And one firm—Clif Bar—even provides a rock-climbing wall for its employees!

References: "Climbing Walls on Company Time," *Wall Street Journal*, December 1, 1998, p. B1 (quote on p. B1); "Perks That Work," *Time*, November 9, 1998, pp. 165–168.

they have not entirely disappeared, nor are they likely to. Today, however, many perks tend to be more job related. For example, popular perks today include a car and driver (so the executive can work while being transported to and from work) and cellular telephones (so the executive can conduct business anywhere). More than anything else, perquisites seem to add to the status of their recipients and thus may increase job satisfaction and reduce turnover.[29]

Organizations often seek to recognize, reward, and motivate their best employees by giving them various awards. One long-standing tradition, for example, is to provide awards to long-term employees at key anniversary dates to reward their loyalty and dedication and to recognize the value of seniority. But in order for such programs to be effective, the awards and prizes themselves must have value to the employee being recognized. For example, as illustrated here, although some employees might see extra time with their boss as a reward, others clearly see things in a different way!

Reference: DILBERT reprinted by permission of United Feature Syndicate, Inc.

**Awards** In many companies, employees receive awards for everything from seniority to perfect attendance, from zero defects (quality work) to cost reduction suggestions. Award programs can be costly in the time required to run them and in money if cash awards are given. But award systems can improve performance under the right conditions. In one medium-sized manufacturing company, careless work habits were pushing up the costs of scrap and rework (the cost of scrapping defective parts or reworking them to meet standards). Management instituted a zero-defects program to recognize employees who did perfect or near-perfect work. The first month, two workers in shipping caused only one defect in over two thousand parts handled. Division management called a meeting in the lunchroom and recognized each worker with a plaque and a ribbon. The next month, the same two workers had two defects and there was no award. The following month, the two workers had zero defects, and once again top management called a meeting to give out plaques and ribbons. Elsewhere in the plant, defects, scrap, and rework decreased dramatically as workers evidently sought recognition for quality work. What worked in this particular plant may or may not work in others. And of course, as illustrated in the cartoon above, managers and workers can sometimes have very different perceptions as to the value of different awards!

# Managing Reward Systems

Much of our discussion on reward systems has focused on general issues. As Table 8.1 shows, however, the organization must address other issues in developing organizational reward systems. The organization must consider its ability to pay employees at certain levels, economic and labor market conditions, and the impact of the pay system on organizational financial performance. In addition, the organization must consider the relationship between

table 8.1

**Issues to Consider in Developing Reward Systems**

| Issue | Important Examples |
|---|---|
| Pay Secrecy | • Open, closed, partial<br>• Link with performance appraisal<br>• Equity perceptions |
| Employee Participation | • By human resource department<br>• By joint employee/management committee |
| Flexible System | • Cafeteria-style benefits<br>• Annual lump sum or monthly bonus<br>• Salary versus benefits |
| Ability to Pay | • Organization's financial performance<br>• Expected future earnings |
| Economic and Labor Market Factors | • Inflation rate<br>• Industry pay standards<br>• Unemployment rate |
| Impact on Organizational Performance | • Increase in costs<br>• Impact on performance |
| Expatriate Compensation | • Cost of living differentials<br>• Managing related equity issues |

performance and rewards, as well as the issues of reward system flexibility, employee participation in the reward system, pay secrecy, and expatriate compensation.

## Linking Performance and Rewards

For managers to take full advantage of the symbolic value of pay, employees must perceive that their rewards are linked to their performance. For example, if everyone in an organization starts working for the same hourly rate and then receives a predetermined wage increase every six months or year, there is clearly no relationship between performance and rewards. Instead, the organization is indicating that all entry-level employees are worth the same amount, and pay increases are tied solely to the time an employee works in the organization. This holds true whether the employee is a top, average, or mediocre worker. The only requirement is that the employee work well enough to avoid being fired.

At the other extreme, an organization might attempt to tie all compensation to actual performance. Thus, each new employee might start at a different wage, as determined by his or her experience, education, skills, and other job-related factors. After joining the organization, the individual then receives rewards based on actual performance. One employee, for example, might start at $8 an hour because she has ten years of experience and a good performance record at her previous employer's. Another might start the same job at a rate of $6.50 an hour because he has only four years' experience and an adequate but not outstanding performance record. Assuming the first employee performs up to expectations, she might also get several pay increases, bonuses, and awards throughout the year, whereas the second employee might get only one or two small increases and no other rewards. Of course organizations must ensure that pay differences are based strictly on performance (including seniority), not on factors that do not relate to performance (such as gender, ethnicity, etc.).

In reality, most organizations attempt to develop a reward strategy somewhere between these two extremes. Because it is really quite difficult to differentiate all employees, most firms use some basic compensation level for everyone. For example, they might start everyone performing a specific job at the same rate, regardless of experience. They might also work to provide reasonable incentives and other inducements for high performers, while making sure they don't ignore the average employees. The key fact for managers to remember is simply that if they expect rewards to motivate performance, employees must see a clear, direct link between their own job-related behaviors and the attainment of those rewards.[30] The "World View" box illustrates an interesting case of how Japanese companies are looking more favorably on incentive-based reward systems.

WORLD VIEW

## *Japan Shifts to Merit Pay*

When looking for a job last spring, Tokyo's Kyosuke Okumura, 21, wanted an employer who would promote him based on how well—not on how long—he did his job.

As a result, he was largely forced to consider American companies.

But that is slowly changing as more Japanese companies, in an effort to cut costs and increase productivity, switch to performance- from seniority-based pay schemes.

Toyota Motor is among the latest. Earlier this month, it announced a shift to a full merit system for the last 20,000 of its 70,000 white-collar workers.

Fujitsu, Sony, Matsushita Electric Industrial and Kao recently have announced or implemented similar changes.

Tokyo human resources consultant Shunsuke Takahashi estimates that one-fifth of Japan's companies now have some form of performance-based pay and another 30% are considering it.

"The change is being driven by sheer desperation. It will gather momentum as it gets accepted more and more," says Merrill Lynch's Mahendra Negi in Tokyo.

In 1992, Honda Motor was one of the first to abandon Japan's Confucian system of seniority by age. But the trend has picked up in recent years as Japan's economy struggles to come out of a decade-long slump.

As companies restructure, labor costs are an obvious target.

Merit-based pay enables companies to reward workers who produce more, thus lowering labor costs as a percentage of revenue.

Workers have little room to complain. Japan's unemployment rate in May was 4.6%, down from a record 4.7% in April. Many companies are cutting jobs.

Yet the companies face obstacles, including the possibility of:

*"The change is being driven by sheer desperation. It will gather momentum as it gets accepted more and more."*
*— Mahendra Negi, Merrill Lynch*

- *Lower morale.* The change to a merit system will hit older workers, the most expensive employees, especially hard.

  It may also result in a loss of "face" for older workers who will be more likely to find themselves with younger bosses.
- *Poor execution.* To rate individual performance, job expectations need to be clear. That is not the case in Japan where group evaluations have been more common, says Hiroshi Menjo of the McKenna Group consultants.
- *Worker unease.* Japanese workers have been trained to cooperate with each other, not to compete. Even high-performers may be uneasy with the notion that coworkers make less, says Yukio Noguchi, economics professor at Tokyo University.

Because the change affects decades of tradition, he expects companies to make it slowly. "This is a needed step, but it will be gradual," he says.

Reference: "Japan Shifts to Merit Pay: Move Will Reward Performance, Not Seniority," *USA Today*, July 23, 1999, p. 5B (quote on page 5B). 

## Flexible Reward Systems

A **flexible reward system** allows employees to choose the combination of benefits that best suits their needs.

Flexible, or cafeteria-style, reward systems are a recent and increasingly popular variation on the standard compensation system. A **flexible reward** system allows employees to choose the combination of benefits that best suits their needs. For example, a younger worker just starting out might prefer to have especially strong health-care coverage with few deductibles. A worker with a few years of experience might prefer to have child-care benefits. A midcareer employee with more financial security might prefer more time off with pay. And older workers might prefer to have rewards concentrated into their retirement plan.

Some organizations are starting to apply the flexible approach to pay. For example, employees sometimes have the option of taking an annual salary increase in one lump sum rather than in monthly increments. General Electric recently implemented such a system for some of its managers. UNUMProvident Corporation, a large insurance firm, allows all of its employees the option of drawing a full third of their annual compensation in the month of January. This makes it easier for them to handle such major expenses as purchasing a new automobile, buying a home, or covering college education expenses for children. Obviously, the administrative costs of providing this level of flexibility are greater, but many employees value this flexibility and may develop strong loyalty and attachment to an employer who offers this kind of compensation package.

## Participative Pay Systems

In keeping with the current trend toward worker involvement in organizational decision making, employee participation in the pay process is also increasing. A participative pay system may involve the employee in the system's design, administration, or both. A pay system can be designed by staff members of the organization's human resources department, a committee of managers in the organization, an outside consultant, the employees, or a combination of these sources. Organizations that have used a joint management-employee task force to design the compensation system have generally succeeded in designing and implementing a plan that managers could use and that employees believed in. Employee participation in administering the pay system is a natural extension of having employees participate in its design. Examples of companies that have involved employees in the administration of the pay system include Romac Industries, where employees vote on the pay of other employees; Graphic Controls, where each manager's pay is determined by a group of peers; and the Friedman-Jacobs Company, where employees set their own wages based on their perceptions of their performance.

## Pay Secrecy

When a company has a policy of open salary information, the exact salary amounts for employees are public knowledge. State governments, for instance, make public the salaries of everyone on their payrolls. A policy of complete secrecy means that no information is available to employees regarding other employees' salaries, average or percentage raises, or salary ranges. The National Labor Relations Board recently upheld an earlier ruling that an employer starting or enforcing a rule that forbids "employees to discuss their salaries" constitutes interference, restraint, and

As the globalization of business continues, more and more firms will need to address issues related to compensating and rewarding expatriates. For example, consider Nancy and Jim Cox. After Jim accepted an assignment in Hong Kong to open *USA Today*'s first Asian Bureau, the company first had to determine an appropriate compensation upgrade to offset the higher costs of living there. The company also had to create a special insurance program for the Cox family because its own managed care program had no provisions for offshore health care. Other parts of the package provided to Cox and his family included two round-trips back home per year and an extra supplement to cover long distance telephone calls. Nancy Cox, meanwhile, left a high-ranking job and had to spend six months searching for a new job in Hong Kong. Increasingly, therefore, companies that send managers on foreign assignment also will need to provide some form of accommodation for trailing spouses.

coercion of protected employee rights under the National Labor Relations Act. Although a few organizations have completely public or completely secret systems, most are somewhere in the middle.

## Expatriate Compensation

Expatriate compensation is yet another important issue in managing reward systems. Consider, for example, a manager living and working in Houston currently making $100,000 a year. That income allows the manager to live in a certain kind of home, drive a certain kind of car, have access to certain levels of medical care, and live a certain kind of lifestyle. Now suppose the manager is asked to accept a transfer to Tokyo, Geneva, or London, cities where the cost of living is considerably higher than in Houston. The same salary cannot begin to support a comparable lifestyle in those cities. Consequently, the employer is almost certain to redesign the manager's compensation package such that the employee's lifestyle in the new location will be comparable to that in the old.

Now consider a different scenario. Suppose the same manager is asked to accept a transfer to an underdeveloped nation. The cost of living in this nation might be quite low by U.S. standards. But there may also be relatively few choices in housing, poorer schools and medical care, a harsh climate, greater personal danger, or similar unattractive characteristics. The firm will probably have to pay the manager some level of additional compensation to offset the decrement in quality of lifestyle. Thus, developing rewards for expatriates is a complicated process.

Figure 8.5 illustrates the approach to expatriate compensation used by one major multinational corporation. The left side of the figure shows how a U.S. employee uses her or his salary—part of it goes for taxes, part is saved, and the rest is consumed. When a person is asked to move abroad, a human resource manager works with the employee to develop an equitable balance sheet for the new compensation package. As shown on the right side of the figure, the individual's compensation package will potentially consist of six components. First, the individual will receive income to cover what his or her taxes and Social Security

figure 8.5

**The Expatriate Compensation Balance Sheet**

*Organizations that ask employees to accept assignments in foreign locations must usually adjust their compensation levels to account for differences in cost of living and similar factors. Amoco uses the system shown here. The employee's domestic base salary is first broken down into the three categories shown on the left. Then adjustments are made by adding compensation to the categories on the right until an appropriate, equitable level of compensation is achieved.*

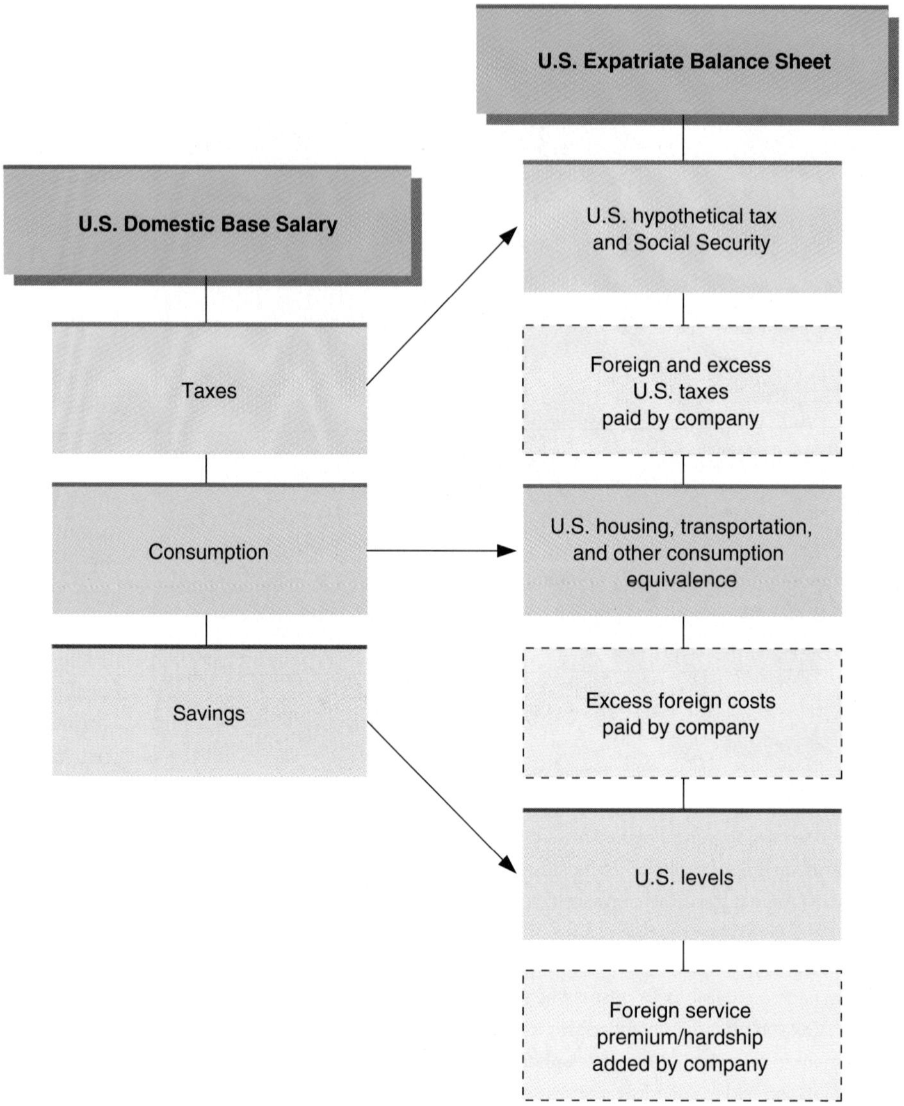


payments in the United States will be. The individual may also have to pay foreign taxes and additional U.S. taxes as a result of the move, so the company covers this as well.

Next, the firm also pays an amount adequate to the employee's current consumption levels in the United States. If the cost of living is greater in the foreign location than at home, the firm pays the excess foreign costs. The employee also receives income for saving comparable to what he or she is currently saving. Finally, if the employee faces a hardship because of the assignment, an additional foreign service premium or hardship allowance is added by the firm. Not surprisingly, then, expatriate compensation packages can be very expensive for an organization and must be carefully developed and managed.[31]

# Synopsis

A goal is a desirable objective. The goal-setting theory of motivation suggests that appropriate goal difficulty, specificity, acceptance, and commitment will result in higher levels of motivated performance. Management by objectives, or MBO, extends goal setting throughout an organization by cascading goals down from the top of the firm to the bottom.

Performance measurement is the process by which work behaviors are measured and compared with established standards and the results recorded and communicated. Its purposes are to evaluate employees' work performance and to provide information for organizational uses such as compensation, personnel planning, and employee training and development. Two primary issues in performance appraisal are who does the appraisals and how often they are done. Performance can be appraised through individual assessment methods (graphic rating scales, checklists, essays, behaviorally anchored rating scales, forced choice, and management by objectives); comparative techniques (ranking, forced distribution, and paired comparison); and new approaches that use multiple raters and comparative methods.

To practice total quality management (TQM), performance measurement is imperative. Continuous improvement, the foundation of total quality management, requires effective performance management. The essential elements for success of TQM are commitment to objectives, job analysis, performance plans, and measurement of performance. Learning organizations attempt to promote continuous improvement through a strategy of constant employee learning, training, and development.

The purpose of the reward system is to attract, retain, and motivate qualified employees and to maintain a pay structure that is internally equitable and externally competitive. Rewards have both surface and symbolic value. Rewards take the form of money, benefits, perquisites, awards, and incentives. Factors such as motivational impact, cost, and fit with the organizational system must be considered when designing or analyzing a reward system.

The effective management of a reward system requires that performance be linked with rewards. Managing rewards entails dealing with issues such as flexible reward systems, employee participation in the pay system, the secrecy of pay systems, and expatriate rewards.

# Discussion Questions

1. Critique the goal-setting theory of motivation.
2. Develop a framework whereby an instructor could use goal setting in running a class such as this one.
3. Why are employees not simply left alone to do their jobs, instead of having their performance measured and evaluated all the time?
4. In what ways is your performance as a student evaluated?
5. How can you apply total quality management to your job as an independent student?
6. Can performance on some jobs simply not be measured? Why or why not?
7. What conditions make it easier for an organization to achieve continuous improvement? What conditions make it more difficult?
8. As a student in this class, what "rewards" do you receive in exchange for your time and effort? What are the rewards for the professor who teaches this class? How do your contributions and rewards differ from those of some other student in the class?
9. Do you expect to obtain the rewards you discussed in question 8 on the basis of your intelligence, your hard work, the number of hours you spend in the library, your height, your good looks, your work experience, or some other personal factor?
10. What rewards are easiest for managers to control? What rewards are more difficult to control?
11. Often institutions in federal and state governments give the same percentage pay raise to all their employees. What do you think is the effect of this type of pay raise on employee motivation?

# Organizational Behavior Case for Discussion

## Rewarding the Hourly Worker

Hourly workers—people who are paid a set dollar amount for each hour or fraction of an hour they work—have long been the backbone of the U.S. economy. But times are changing, and with them so also is the lot of the hourly worker. Like most employment conditions, organizations can take a wider variety of approaches to managing compensation for hourly workers. And nowhere are these differences more apparent than the contrasting conditions for hourly workers at General Motors and Wal-Mart.

General Motors is an old, traditional industrial company that up until recently was the nation's largest employer. And for decades, its hourly workers have been protected by strong labor unions like the United Auto Workers (UAW). These unions, in turn, have forged contracts and working conditions that almost seem archaic in today's economy. Consider, for example, the employment conditions of Tim Philbrick, a forty-two-year-old plant worker and union member at the firm's Fairfax plant near Kansas City who has worked for GM for twenty-three years.

Mr. Philbrick makes almost $20 an hour in base pay. With a little overtime, his annual earnings top $60,000. But even then, he is far from the highest-paid factory worker at GM. Skilled-trade workers like electricians and toolmakers make $2 to $2.50 an hour more, and with greater overtime opportunities often make $100,000 or more per year. Mr. Philbrick also gets a no-deductible health insurance policy that allows him to see any doctor he wants. He also gets four weeks of vacation per year, plus two weeks at Christmas and at least another week in July when the plant is closed. In addition, he gets two paid twenty-three-minute breaks and a paid thirty-minute lunch break per day. He also has the option of retiring after thirty years with full benefits.

GM estimates that, with benefits, its average worker makes more than $43 an hour. Perhaps not surprisingly, then, the firm is always looking for opportunities to reduce its work force through attrition and cutbacks, with the goal of replacing production capacity with lower-cost labor abroad. The UAW, on the other hand, of course, is staunchly opposed to further workforce reductions and cutbacks. And long-standing work rules strictly dictate who gets overtime, who can be laid off and who can't, and myriad other employment conditions for Mr. Philbrick and his peers.

But the situation at GM is quite different—in a lot of ways—from conditions at Wal-Mart. Along many different dimensions Wal-Mart is slowly but surely supplanting General Motors as the quintessential U.S. corporation. For example, it is growing rapidly, is becoming more and more ingrained in the American lifestyle, and now employs more people than GM did in its heyday. But the hourly worker at Wal-Mart has a much different experience than the hourly worker at GM.

For example, consider Ms. Nancy Handley, a twenty-seven-year-old Wal-Mart employee who oversees the men's department at a big store in St. Louis. Jobs like Ms. Handley's are paid between $9 and $11 an hour, or about $20,000 a year. About $100 a month is deducted from her paycheck to help cover the costs of benefits. Her health insurance has a $250 deductible; she then pays 20 percent of her health-care costs so long as she uses a set of approved physicians. Her prescriptions cost between $5 and $10 each. She also has dental coverage; after her $50 deductible, she pays 20 percent of these costs as well. During her typical workday, Ms. Handley gets two fifteen-minute breaks and an hour for lunch, but she has to punch out at the time clock and doesn't get paid during these times.

But Ms. Handley doesn't feel mistreated by Wal-Mart. Far from it, she says she is appropriately compensated for what she does. She has received three merit raises in the last seven years, for example, and has considerable job security. Moreover, if she decides to try for advancement, Wal-Mart seems to offer considerable potential. For example, several thousand hourly workers a year are promoted to the ranks of management. While the length of their work week increases, so too does their pay. And Ms. Handley is clearly not unique in her views—Wal-Mart employees routinely reject any and all overtures from labor unions and are among the most loyal and committed in the United States today.

### Case Questions

1. Compare and contrast hourly working conditions at General Motors and Wal-Mart.

2. Describe the most likely role that the hourly compensation at these two companies plays in motivating their employees.
3. Discuss how goal setting might be used for each of the two jobs profiled in this case.

References: *Hoover's Handbook of American Business 2000* (Austin: Hoover's Business Press, 2000), pp. 654–655, 1514–1515; "'I'm Proud of What I've Made Myself Into—What I've Created,'" *Wall Street Journal*, August 28, 1997, pp. B1, B5; "'That's Why I Like My Job . . . I Have an Impact on Quality,'" *Wall Street Journal*, August 28, 1997, pp. B1, B8.

## Experiencing Organizational Behavior

### Using Compensation to Motivate Workers

**Purpose:** The purpose of this exercise is to illustrate how compensation can be used to motivate employees.

**Format:** You will be asked to review eight managers and make salary adjustments for each.

**Procedure:** Listed below are your notes on the performance of eight managers who work for you. You (either individually or as a group, depending on your instructor's choice) have to recommend salary increases for eight managers who have just completed their first year with the company and are now to be considered for their first annual raise. Keep in mind that you may be setting precedents and that you need to keep salary costs down. However, there are no formal company restrictions on the kind or raises you can give. Indicate the sizes of the raise that you would like to give each manager by writing a percentage next to each name.

**Variations:** The instructor might alter the situation in one of several ways. One way is to assume that all of the eight managers entered the company at the same salary, say $30,000, which gives a total salary expense of $240,000. If upper management has allowed a salary raise pool of 10 percent of the current salary expenses, then you as the manager have $24,000 to give out as raises. In this variation, students can deal with actual dollar amounts rather than just percentages for the raises. Another interesting variation is to assume that all of the managers entered the company at different salaries, averaging $30,000. (The instructor can create many interesting possibilities for how these salaries might vary.) Then, the students can suggest salaries for the different managers.

_____ % Abraham McGowan. Abe is not, as far as you can tell, a good performer. You have checked your view with others and they do not feel that he is effective either. However, you happen to know he has one of the toughest work groups to manage. His subordinates have low skill levels, and the work is dirty and hard. If you lose him, you are not sure whom you could find to replace him.

_____ % Benjy Berger. Benjy is single and seems to live the life of a carefree bachelor. In general, you feel that his job performance is not up to par, and some of his "goofs" are well known to his fellow employees.

_____ % Clyde Clod. You consider Clyde to be one of your best subordinates. However, it is obvious that other people do not consider him to be an effective manager. Clyde has married a rich wife, and as far as you know he does not need additional money.

_____ %David Doodle. You happen to know from your personal relationship with "Doodles" that he badly needs more money because of certain personal problems he is having. As far as you are concerned, he also happens to be one of the best of your subordinates. For some reason, your enthusiasm is not shared by your other subordinates, and you have heard them make joking remarks about his performance.

_____ % Ellie Ellesberg. Ellie has been very successful so far in the tasks she has undertaken. You are particularly impressed by this since she has a hard job. She needs money more than many of the other people, and you are sure that they respect her because of her good performance.

_____ % Fred Foster. Fred has turned out to be a very pleasant surprise to you. He has done an excellent job and it is generally accepted among the others that he is one of the best people. This surprises you because he is generally frivolous and does not seem to care very much about money and promotion.

_____ % Greta Goslow. Your opinion is that Greta is just not cutting the mustard. Surprisingly enough, however, when you check to see how others feel about her, you discover that her work is very highly regarded. You also know that she badly needs a raise. She was just recently widowed and is finding it extremely difficult to support her household and her young family of four.

_____ % Harry Hummer. You know Harry personally, and he just seems to squander his money continually. He has a fairly easy job assignment, and your view is that he does not do it particularly well. You are, therefore, quite surprised to find that several of the other new managers think that he is the best of the new group.

After you have made the assignments for the eight people, you will have a chance to discuss them either in groups or in the larger class.

### Follow-up Questions

1. Is there a clear difference between the highest and lowest performer? Why or why not?
2. Did you notice differences in the types of information that you had available to make the raise decisions? How did you use the different sources of information?
3. In what ways did your assignment of raises reflect different views of motivation?

Reference: Edward E. Lawler III, "Motivation Through Compensation," adapted by D. T. Hall, in *Instructor's Manual for Experiences in Management and Organizational Behavior* (New York: John Wiley & Sons, 1975). Reprinted by permission of the author.

## Building Organizational Behavior Skills

### Diagnosing Poor Performance and Enhancing Motivation

**Introduction:** Formal performance appraisal and feedback are part of assuring proper performance in an organization. The following assessment is designed to help you understand how to detect poor performance and overcome it.

**Procedure:** Please respond to the following statements by writing a number from the following rating scale in the left-hand column. Your answers should reflect your attitudes and behaviors as they are *now*.

| | |
|---|---|
| Strongly agree | = 6 |
| Agree | = 5 |
| Slightly agree | = 4 |
| Slightly disagree | = 3 |
| Disagree | = 2 |
| Strongly disagree | = 1 |

When another person needs to be motivated,

_____ 1. I always approach a performance problem by first establishing whether it is caused by a lack of motivation or ability.

_____ 2. I always establish a clear standard of expected performance.

_____ 3. I always offer to provide training and information, without offering to do the task myself.

_____ 4. I am honest and straightforward in providing feedback on performance and assessing advancement opportunities.

_____ 5. I use a variety of rewards to reinforce exceptional performance.

_____ 6. When discipline is required, I identify the problem, describe its consequences, and explain how it should be corrected.

_____ 7. I design task assignments to make them interesting and challenging.

_____ 8. I determine what rewards are valued by the person and strive to make those available.

_____ 9. I make sure that the person feels fairly and equitably treated.

_____ 10. I make sure that the person gets timely feedback from those affected by task performance.

_____ 11. I carefully diagnose the causes of poor performance before taking any remedial or disciplinary actions.

_____ 12. I always help the person establish performance goals that are challenging, specific, and time-bound.

____13. Only as a last resort do I attempt to reassign or release a poorly performing individual.

____14. Whenever possible I make sure that valued rewards are linked to high performance.

____15. I consistently discipline when effort is below expectations and capabilities.

____16. I try to combine or rotate assignments so that the person can use a variety of skills.

____17. I try to arrange for the person to work with others in a team, for the mutual support of all.

____18. I make sure that the person is using realistic standards for measuring fairness.

____19. I provide immediate compliments and other forms of recognition for meaningful accomplishments.

____20. I always determine if the person has the necessary resources and support to succeed in the task.

Reference: David A. Whetten and Kim S. Cameron, *Developing Management Skills*, 2nd edition, pp. 336–337. 

## Developing OB Internet Skills

**Introduction:** As noted in the chapter, many businesses today use incentives to encourage and reward higher levels of performance. This exercise will give you more understanding of how incentives work.

**Internet Assignment:** Assume that you are a human resource manager with a moderate-sized service organization. The firm has just been taken over by a major corporation, and you have received notification that you will be responsible for moving from the firm's current compensation model, which rewards people on the basis of seniority, to an incentive system tying rewards to performance. Search the Internet for resources that might assist you in planning and managing this change.

**Follow-up:** Describe the kinds of information you were able to locate and characterize its likely value to you. Finally, respond to the following questions:

1. What additional information would you need, besides what was available on the Internet, to actually make the plan as described here?
2. Regardless of the type and value of information you were able to locate, do you think more information will be available on the Internet in the future?
3. The exercise indicates that you work for a service company. Would the processes and outcome have been different if you worked for a manufacturer instead? Why or why not?

chapter

# 9

# Managing Stress and the Work-Life Balance

## Management Preview

Many people today work long hours, face constant deadlines, and are subject to pressure to produce more and more. Organizations and the people who run them are under constant pressure to increase income while keeping costs in check. To do things faster and better—but with fewer people—is the goal of many companies today. An unfortunate effect of this trend is to put too much pressure on people—operating employees, other managers, and oneself. The results can indeed be increased performance, higher profits, and faster growth. But stress, burnout, turnover, aggression, and other unpleasant side effects can also occur. In this chapter, we examine how and why stress occurs in organizations and how to better understand and control it. First, we explore the nature of stress. Then we look at such important individual differences as Type A and Type B personality profiles and their role in stress. Next, we discuss a number of causes of stress and consider the potential consequences of stress. We then highlight several things people and organizations can do to manage stress at work. We conclude by discussing an important factor related to stress—linkages between work and the nonwork parts of people's lives. But before we begin, let's examine how work is increasingly encroaching on traditional leisure periods like weekends. ■

Looking forward to a relaxing weekend? Think again.

If you're like most employees, you'll be working. Overwhelming job demands have many putting in extra hours during their time off.

Employees are working from home because of more available technology, but they're also making weekend appearances at work.

Many say they're no longer surprised to be greeting coworkers in the office on a Sunday afternoon.

"There's almost always a handful of people in on Saturdays," says Bob Carr, an investment broker with A.G. Edwards & Sons in Champaign, Ill. "For me, it's catch-up time. I can catch up on things I don't have time to do."

He's not the only one playing catch-up. A 1997 survey by Steelcase found 73% of those in offices of 100 or more do some weekend work. And 60% sacrifice some part of their weekend once a month or more.

Job cutbacks in the early 1990s have left many feeling leisure time is an unaffordable luxury. Others say they are working on their free time because they're bombarded by meetings, email messages and phone calls during the week. Some say weekends are the only time they can focus on getting important projects done.

"We think we have all these great tools to save our time," says Paula Ancona, author of *SuccessAbilities*, a guide to career success. "Instead it just extends our week. We're never out of touch anymore."

*"There's almost always a handful of people in on Saturdays. For me, it's catch-up time. I can catch up on things I don't have time to do." — Bob Carr, investment broker with A.G. Edwards & Sons**

Iris Goldfein, with the professional services firm Coopers & Lybrand, often works at home in Chicago on the weekend. "Because of the lack of distractions, you definitely get more done," Goldfein says.

Some attribute the trend to "face time." Workers anxious about job security feel they have to put in extra effort or risk being seen as expendable.

The extra hours, which don't always bring extra pay, can leave employees feeling burned out and resentful. Instead of easing the workload, technology is making it harder for employees to escape the office.

"We're going in the wrong direction," says Barbara Brandt, at Shorter Work-Time Group, a nonprofit organization based in Somerville, Mass. "We need to have shorter hours and flexible time."

But some say there's a silver lining. Employees may be giving up more of their free time because they feel passionate about the work they do.

"If people are working in jobs they don't like, they're more stressed," says Ellen Galinsky, president of Families and Work Institute. "If it's a job they love, they may feel more energized."[1] ■

Reference: "Workplace Demands Taking Up More Weekends" *USA Today*, April, 24, 1998, p. 1B. Copyright 1998, *USA Today*. Reprinted with permission.

Expanding work hours seem to be becoming increasingly widespread. Although some people work on the weekends to help reduce stress during other periods of the week, others no doubt see the weekend work itself as stressful. Moreover, when people work on the weekend, their relationships with their family and friends are also affected. To better understand how these processes affect different individuals, we first describe the nature of stress itself.

# The Nature of Stress

Many people think of stress as a simple problem. In reality, however, stress is complex and often misunderstood.[2] To learn how job stress truly works, we must first define it and then describe the process through which it develops.

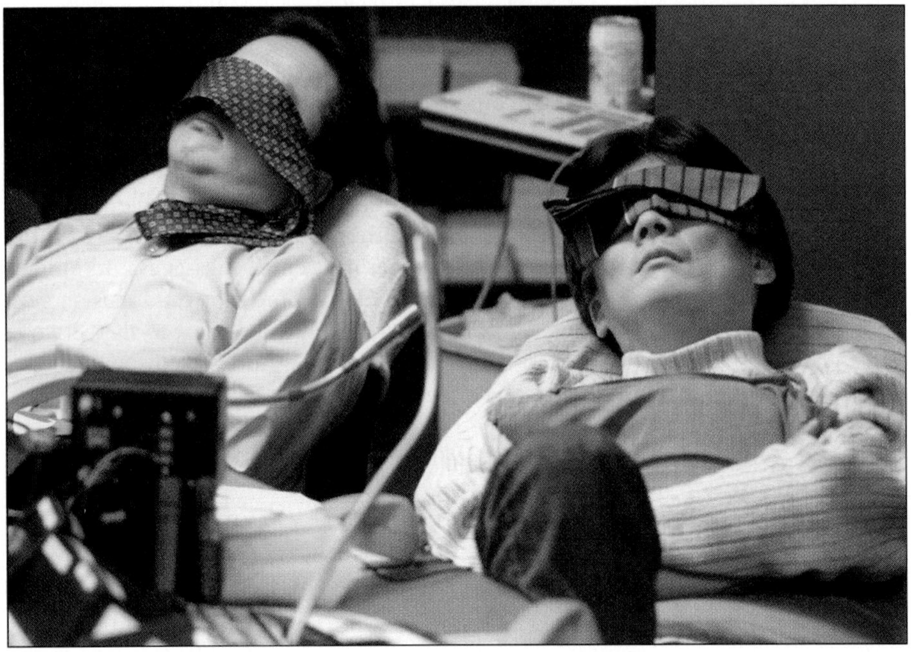

Stress is how people respond to stimuli that place excessive psychological or physical demands on them. Individuals who work on securities trading floors, for example, are subject to intense and constant pressure to simultaneously make numerous trades for multiple buyers and sellers, and to execute each transaction at just the right time. At the end of the workday, they often feel psychologically and physically exhausted. Indeed, these Japanese foreign-currency traders are clearly exhausted already, and they are only taking a break from their work!

## Stress Defined

**Stress** is a person's adaptive response to a stimulus that places excessive psychological or physical demands on that person.

Stress has been defined in many ways, but most definitions say that stress is caused by a stimulus, that the stimulus can be either physical or psychological, and that the individual responds to the stimulus in some way.[3] Here, then, we define **stress** as a person's adaptive response to a stimulus that places excessive psychological or physical demands on him or her.

Given the underlying complexities of this definition, we need to examine its components carefully. First is the notion of adaptation. As we discuss presently, people may adapt to stressful circumstances in any of several ways. Second is the role of the stimulus. This stimulus, generally called a *stressor*, is anything that induces stress. Third, stressors can be either psychological or physical. Finally, the demands the stressor places on the individual must be excessive for stress to result. Of course, what is excessive for one person may be perfectly tolerable for another. The point is simply that a person must perceive the demands as excessive or stress will not result.

## The Stress Process

Much of what we know about stress today can be traced to the pioneering work of Dr. Hans Selye.[4] Among Selye's most important contributions were his identification of the general adaptation syndrome and the concepts of eustress and distress.

The **general adaptation syndrome (GAS)** identifies three stages of response to a stressor: alarm, resistance, and exhaustion.

### General Adaptation Syndrome

Figure 9.1 graphically shows the **general adaptation syndrome (GAS)**. According to this model, each of us has a normal level of resistance to stressful events. Some of us can tolerate a great deal of stress and others much less, but we all have a threshold at which stress starts to affect us.

The GAS begins when a person first encounters a stressor. The first stage is called alarm. At this point, the person may feel some degree of panic and begin to

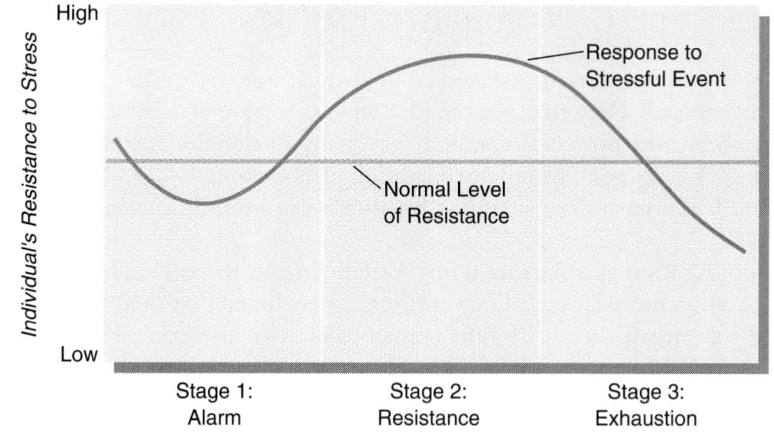


figure 9.1 **The General Adaptation Syndrome**

*The general adaptation syndrome, or GAS, perspective describes three stages of the stress process. The initial stage is called alarm. As illustrated here, a person's resistance often dips slightly below the normal level during this stage. Next comes actual resistance to the stressor, usually leading to an increase above the person's normal level of resistance. Finally, in stage 3, exhaustion may set in, and the person's resistance declines sharply below normal levels.*

wonder how to cope. The individual may also have to resolve a fight-or-flight question: Can I deal with this, or should I run away? For example, suppose a manager is assigned to write a lengthy report overnight. Her first reaction may be "How will I ever get this done by tomorrow?"

If the stressor is too extreme, the person may simply be unable to cope with it. In most cases, however, the individual gathers his or her strength (physical or emotional) and begins to resist the negative effects of the stressor. The manager with the long report to write may calm down, call home to tell her kids that she's working late, roll up her sleeves, order out for dinner, and get to work. Thus, at stage 2 of the GAS, the person is resisting the effects of the stressor.

Often, the resistance phase ends the GAS. If the manager completes the report earlier than she expected, she may drop it in her briefcase, smile to herself, and head home tired but happy. On the other hand, prolonged exposure to a stressor without resolution may bring on stage 3 of the GAS: exhaustion. At this stage, the person literally gives up and can no longer fight the stressor. For example, the manager may fall asleep at her desk at 3 A.M. and fail to finish the report.

**Eustress** is the pleasurable stress that accompanies positive events.

**Distress** is the unpleasant stress that accompanies negative events.

**Eustress and Distress** Selye also pointed out that the sources of stress need not be bad.[5] For example, receiving a bonus and then having to decide what to do with the money can be stressful. So can getting a promotion, gaining recognition, getting married, and similar "good" things. Selye called this type of stress **eustress**. As we will see later, eustress can lead to a number of positive outcomes for the individual.

Of course, there is also negative stress. Called **distress**, this is what most people think of when they hear the word "stress." Excessive pressure, unreasonable demands on our time, and bad news all fall into this category. As the term suggests, this form of stress generally results in negative consequences for the individual.

For purposes of simplicity, we will continue to use the simple term "stress" throughout this chapter. But as you read and study the chapter, remember that stress can be either good or bad. It can motivate and stimulate us, or it can lead to any number of dangerous side effects.

# Individual Differences and Stress

We have already alluded to the fact that stress can affect different people in different ways. Given our earlier discussion of individual differences back in Chapter 4, of course, this should come as no surprise.[6] The most fully developed individual difference relating specifically to stress is the distinction between Type A and Type B personality profiles.

## Type A and Type B Personality Profiles

Type A and Type B profiles were first observed by two cardiologists, Meyer Friedman and Ray Rosenman.[7] They first got the idea when a worker repairing the upholstery on their waiting-room chairs noted that many of the chairs were worn only on the front. This suggested to the two cardiologists that many heart patients were anxious and had a hard time sitting still—they were literally sitting on the edge of their seats!

Using this observation as a starting point, Friedman and Rosenman began to study the phenomenon more closely. They eventually concluded that their patients were exhibiting one of two very different types of behavior patterns. Their research also led them to conclude that the differences were personality based. They labeled these two behavior patterns Type A and Type B.

**Type A** people are extremely competitive, highly committed to work, and have a strong sense of time urgency.

**Type B** people are less competitive, less committed to work, and have a weaker sense of time urgency.

The extreme **Type A** individual is extremely competitive, very devoted to work, and has a strong sense of time urgency. Moreover, this person is likely to be aggressive, impatient, and highly work oriented. He or she has a lot of drive and motivation and wants to accomplish as much as possible in as short a time as possible. The manager highlighted in the cartoon is almost certainly a Type A individual!

The extreme **Type B** person, in contrast, is less competitive, is less devoted to work, and has a weaker sense of time urgency. This person feels less conflict with either people or time and has a more balanced, relaxed approach to life. She or he has more confidence and is able to work at a constant pace.

A common-sense expectation might be that Type A people are more successful than Type B people. In reality, however, this is not necessarily true—the Type B person is not necessarily any more or less successful than the Type A. There are several possible explanations for this. For example, Type A people may alienate others because of their drive and may miss out on important learning opportuni-

Roy Delgado
"SURE, SURE ... I'M HAVING A GREAT VACATION .."

Among other things, Type A individuals are very devoted to work and have a lot of drive and motivation. This manager, for example, is clearly mixing business with pleasure! To the extent that he is choosing to keep in contact with his office while on vacation, he may see this as simply a part of his work. On the other hand, of course, people may suffer a variety of difficulties if they never disengage from work. Indeed, although Type A individuals may achieve fast short-term career success, they may also be more susceptible to burnout later in life.

Reference: Roy Delgado & Associates.

ties in their quest to get ahead. Type Bs, on the other hand, may have better interpersonal reputations and may learn a wider array of skills.

*"I've literally lost my ability to relax."* — *George Bell, president of ExciteAtHome, an Internet firm*[8]

Friedman and Rosenman pointed out that people are not purely Type A or Type B; instead, people tend toward one or the other type. For example, an individual might exhibit marked Type A characteristics much of the time but still be able to relax once in a while and even occasionally forget about time.

Friedman and Rosenman's initial research on the Type A and Type B profile differences yielded some alarming findings. In particular, they suggested that Type As were much more likely to get coronary heart disease than were Type Bs.[9] However, follow-up research by other scientists has suggested that the relationship between Type A behavior and the risk of coronary heart disease is not all that straightforward.[10]

Although the reasons are unclear, recent findings suggest that Type As are much more complex than originally believed. For example, in addition to the characteristics already noted, they are likely to be depressed and hostile. Any one of these characteristics or a combination of them can lead to heart problems. Moreover, different approaches to measuring Type A tendencies have yielded different results.

Finally, in one study that found Type As to actually be less susceptible to heart problems than Type Bs, the researchers offered an explanation consistent with earlier thinking: because Type As are compulsive, they seek treatment earlier and are more likely to follow their doctors' orders![11]

## Hardiness and Optimism

**Hardiness** is a person's ability to cope with stress.

**Optimism** is the extent to which a person sees life in relatively positive or negative terms.

Two other important individual differences related to stress are hardiness and optimism. Research suggests that some people have what are termed hardier personalities than others.[12] **Hardiness** is a person's ability to cope with stress. People with hardy personalities have an internal locus of control, are strongly committed to the activities in their lives, and view change as an opportunity for advancement and growth. Such people are seen as relatively unlikely to suffer illness if they experience high levels of pressure and stress. On the other hand, people with low hardiness may have more difficulties in coping with pressure and stress.

Another potentially important individual difference is optimism. **Optimism** is the extent to which a person sees life in positive or negative terms. A popular metaphor used to convey this idea is the glass half filled with water. A person with a lot of optimism will tend to see it as half full, whereas a person with less optimism (a pessimist) will often see it as half empty. Optimism is also related to positive and negative affectivity, as discussed earlier in Chapter 4. In general, optimistic people tend to handle stress better. They will be able to see the positive characteristics of the situation and recognize that things may eventually improve. In contrast, less optimistic people may focus more on the negative characteristics of the situation and expect things to get worse, not better.

Cultural differences also are important in determining how stress affects people. For example, research by Cary Cooper suggests that American executives may experience less stress than executives in many other countries, including Japan and Brazil. The major causes of stress also differ across countries. In Germany, for example, major causes of stress are time pressure and deadlines. In South Africa, long work hours more frequently lead to stress. And in Sweden, the major cause of stress is the encroachment of work on people's private lives.[13]

Other research suggests that women are perhaps more prone to experience the psychological effects of stress, whereas men may report more physical effects.[14] Finally, some studies suggest that people who see themselves as complex individuals are better able to handle stress than people who view themselves as relatively simple.[15] We should add, however, that the study of individual differences in stress is still in its infancy. It would therefore be premature to draw rigid conclusions about how different types of people handle stress.

# Common Causes of Stress

**Organizational stressors** are factors in the workplace that can cause stress.

Many things can cause stress.[16] Figure 9.2 shows two broad categories: organizational stressors and life stressors. It also shows three categories of stress consequences: individual consequences, organizational consequences, and burnout.

**figure 9.2 Causes and Consequences of Stress**

*The causes and consequences of stress are related in complex ways. As shown here, most common causes of stress can be classified as either organizational stressors or life stressors. Similarly, common consequences include individual and organizational consequences, as well as burnout.*

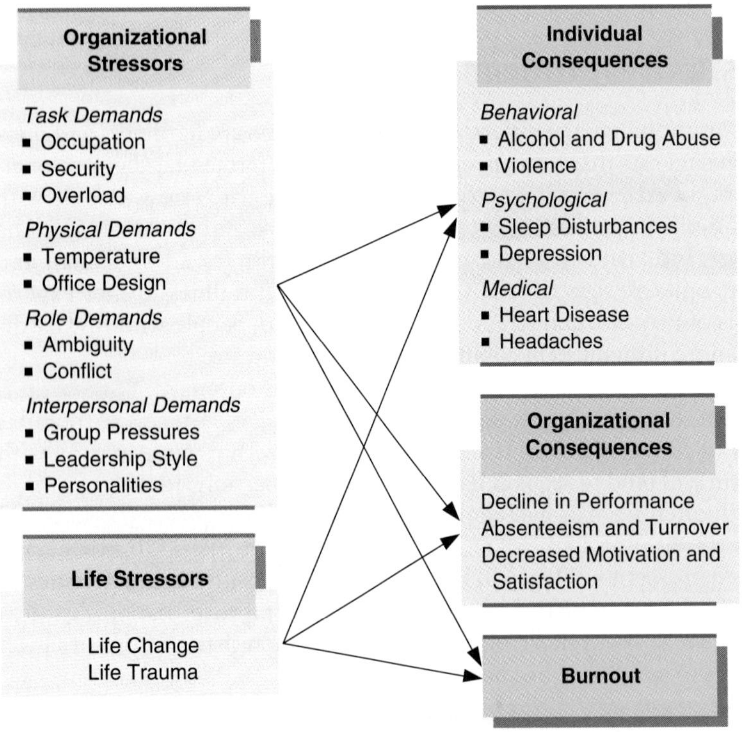


Reference: Adapted from James C. Quick and Jonathan D. Quick, *Organizational Stress and Preventive Management* (McGraw-Hill, 1984), pp. 19, 44, and 76.

## Organizational Stressors

**Organizational stressors** are various factors in the workplace that can cause stress. Four general sets of organizational stressors are task demands, physical demands, role demands, and interpersonal demands.[17]

### Task Demands

**Task demands** are stressors associated with the specific job a person performs. Some occupations are by nature more stressful than others. The jobs of surgeons, air-traffic controllers, and professional football coaches are more stressful than those of general practitioners, airplane baggage loaders, and football team equipment managers. Table 9.1 lists a representative sample of stressful jobs from among a total set of 250 jobs studied. As you can see, the job of U.S. president was found to be the most stressful, followed by the jobs of firefighter and senior executive. Toward the middle of the distribution are jobs such as mechanical engineer, chiropractor, technical writer, and bank officer. The jobs of broadcast technician, bookkeeper, and actuary were among the least stressful jobs in this study.

table 9.1

**The Most Stressful Jobs**

*How selected occupations ranked in an evaluation of 250 jobs**

| Rank | Occupation | Stress Score | Rank | Occupation | Stress Score |
|---|---|---|---|---|---|
| 1 | U.S. president | 176.6 | 103 | Market-research analyst | 42.1 |
| 2 | Firefighter | 110.9 | 104 | Personnel recruiter | 41.8 |
| 3 | Senior executive | 108.6 | 113 | Hospital administrator | 39.6 |
| 6 | Surgeon | 99.5 | 119 | Economist | 38.7 |
| 10 | Air-traffic controller | 83.1 | 122 | Mechanical engineer | 38.3 |
| 12 | Public-relations executive | 78.5 | 124 | Chiropractor | 37.9 |
| 16 | Advertising account executive | 74.6 | 132 | Technical writer | 36.5 |
| 17 | Real-estate agent | 73.1 | 144 | Bank officer | 35.4 |
| 20 | Stockbroker | 71.7 | 149 | Retail salesperson | 34.9 |
| 22 | Pilot | 68.7 | 150 | Tax examiner/collector | 34.8 |
| 25 | Architect | 66.9 | 154 | Aerospace engineer | 34.6 |
| 31 | Lawyer | 64.3 | 166 | Industrial designer | 32.1 |
| 33 | Physician (general practitioner) | 64.0 | 173 | Accountant | 31.1 |
| 35 | Insurance agent | 63.3 | 193 | Purchasing agent | 28.9 |
| 42 | Advertising salesperson | 59.9 | 194 | Insurance underwriter | 28.5 |
| 47 | Auto salesperson | 56.3 | 212 | Computer programmer | 26.5 |
| 50 | College professor | 54.2 | 216 | Financial planner | 26.3 |
| 60 | School principal | 51.7 | 229 | Broadcast technician | 24.2 |
| 67 | Psychologist | 50.0 | 241 | Bookkeeper | 21.5 |
| 81 | Executive-search consultant | 47.3 | 245 | Actuary | 20.2 |

*Among the criteria used in the rankings: overtime, quotas, deadlines, competitiveness, physical demands, environmental conditions, hazards encountered, initiative required, stamina required, win-lose situations, and working in the public eye.

Reference: The Most Stressful Jobs, February 26, 1996. Reprinted by permission of *Wall Street Journal*, © 1996 Dow Jones & Company, Inc. All rights reserved worldwide.

**Task demands** are stressors associated with the specific job a person performs.

Beyond specific task-related pressures, other aspects of a job may pose physical threats to a person's health. Unhealthy conditions exist in occupations such as coal mining and toxic waste handling. Security is another task demand that can cause stress. Someone in a relatively secure job is not likely to worry unduly about losing that position. Threats to job security can increase stress dramatically. For example, stress generally increases throughout an organization during a period of layoffs or immediately after a merger with another firm. This has been observed at a number of organizations, including AT&T, Safeway, and Digital Equipment.[18]

A final task demand stressor is overload. Overload occurs when a person simply has more work than he or she can handle. The overload can be either quantitative (the person has too many tasks to perform or too little time to perform

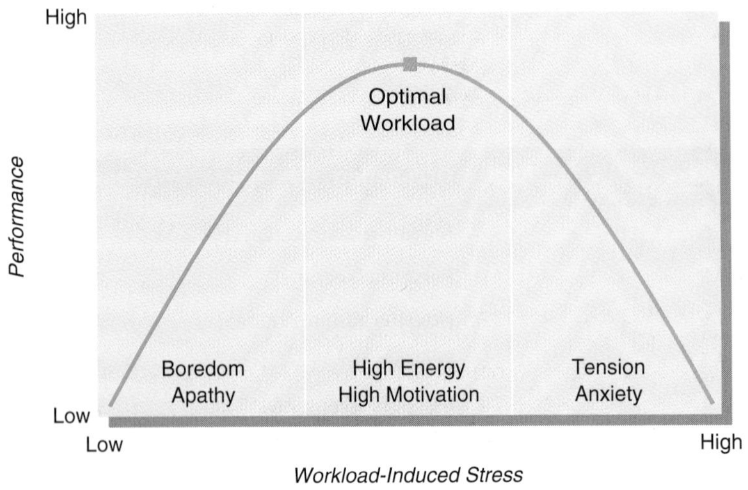


figure 9.3 **Workload, Stress, and Performance**

*Too much stress is clearly undesirable, but too little stress can also lead to unexpected problems. For example, too little stress may result in boredom and apathy and be accompanied by low performance. And although too much stress can cause tension, anxiety, and low performance, for most people there is an optimal level of stress that results in high energy, motivation, and performance.*

them) or qualitative (the person may believe he or she lacks the ability to do the job). We should note that the opposite of overload may also be undesirable. As Figure 9.3 shows, low task demands can result in boredom and apathy just as overload can cause tension and anxiety. Thus, a moderate degree of workload-related stress is optimal, because it leads to high levels of energy and motivation.

**Physical demands** are stressors associated with the job's physical setting, such as the adequacy of temperature and lighting and the physical requirements the job makes on the employee.

Physical Demands The **physical demands** of a job are its physical requirements on the worker; these demands are a function of the physical characteristics of the setting and the physical tasks the job involves. One important element is temperature. Working outdoors in extreme temperatures can result in stress, as can working in an improperly heated or cooled office. Strenuous labor such as loading heavy cargo or lifting packages can lead to similar results. Office design also can be a problem. A poorly designed office can make it difficult for people to have privacy or promote too much or too little social interaction. Too much interaction may distract a person from his or her task, whereas too little may lead to boredom or loneliness. Likewise, poor lighting, inadequate work surfaces, and similar deficiencies can create stress.[19] And shift work can cause disruptions for people because of the way it affects their sleep and leisure-time activities.

*"It's hard to have a life when your hours are always changing." — Unidentified shift worker*[20]

**Role demands** are stressors associated with the role a person is expected to play.

A **role** is a set of expected behaviors associated with a particular position in a group or organization.

**Role ambiguity** arises when a role is unclear.

Role Demands **Role demands** also can be stressful to people in organizations. A **role** is a set of expected behaviors associated with a particular position in a group or organization. As such, it has both formal (i.e., job-related and explicit) and informal (i.e., social and implicit) requirements. People in an organization or work group expect a person in a particular role to act in certain ways. They transmit these expectations both formally and informally. Individuals perceive role expectations with varying degrees of accuracy and then attempt to enact that role. However, "errors" can creep into this process, resulting in stress-inducing problems called role ambiguity, role conflict, and role overload.[21]

**Role ambiguity** arises when a role is unclear. If your instructor tells you to write a term paper but refuses to provide more information, you will probably experience ambiguity. You do not know what the topic is, how long the paper should be, what format to use, or when the paper is due. In work settings, role ambiguity can stem from poor job descriptions, vague instructions from a supervisor, or unclear cues from coworkers. The result is likely to be a subordinate who does not know what to do. Role ambiguity can thus be a significant source of stress.

Role demands can be very powerful in most organizational settings. Take, for example, the pressures faced by Ila Borders. Borders is a starting pitcher for the Madison, Wisconsin Black Wolf, a professional minor league baseball team. She is also the first woman ever to play pro baseball in a men's league. As a baseball player, she has to contend with the pressures associated with competitive professional sports. As a woman, she has to contend with scrutiny from both the public and the media beyond that focused on her teammates. In the off-season, she works as a substitute teacher, and so must remain current in her academic field as well.

**Role conflict** occurs when the messages and cues from others about the role are clear but contradictory or mutually exclusive.[22] One common form is *interrole conflict*—conflict between roles. For example, if a person's boss says that to get ahead one must work overtime and on weekends, and the same person's spouse says that more time is needed at home with the family, conflict may result.[23] *Intrarole conflict* may occur when the person gets conflicting demands from different sources within the context of the same role. A manager's boss may tell her that she needs to put more pressure on subordinates to follow new work rules. At the same time, her subordinates may indicate that they expect her to get the rules changed. Thus, the cues are in conflict, and the manager may be unsure about which course to follow.

*Intrasender conflict* occurs when a single source sends clear but contradictory messages. This might occur if the boss says one morning that there can be no more overtime for the next month but after lunch tells someone to work late that same evening. *Person-role conflict* results from a discrepancy between the role requirements and the individual's personal values, attitudes, and needs. If a person is told to do something unethical or illegal, or if the work is distasteful (for example, firing a close friend), person-role conflict is likely. Role conflict of all varieties is of particular concern to managers. Research has shown that conflict may occur in a variety of situations and lead to a variety of adverse consequences, including stress, poor performance, and rapid turnover.[24]

**Role conflict** occurs when the messages and cues constituting a role are clear but contradictory or mutually exclusive.

**Role overload** occurs when expectations for the role exceed the individual's capabilities.

A final consequence of a weak role structure is **role overload**, which occurs when expectations for the role exceed the individual's capabilities. When a manager gives an employee several major assignments at once while increasing the person's regular workload, the employee will probably experience role overload. Role overload may also result when an individual takes on too many roles at one time. For example, a person trying to work extra hard at his job, run for election to the school board, serve on a committee in church, coach Little League baseball, maintain an active exercise program, and be a contributing member to his family will probably encounter role overload. "The Business of Ethics" box discusses several examples of how role demands can cause stress.

**Interpersonal demands** are stressors associated with group pressures, leadership, and personality conflicts.

### Interpersonal Demands

A final set of organizational stressors consists of three **interpersonal demands**: group pressures, leadership, and interpersonal conflict.

THE BUSINESS OF ETHICS

## *Growing Work Demands*

Once upon a time, around the middle of the twentieth century, experts forecasted a utopian society in which leisure time was abundant and people had little hard work to do. When was this supposed to happen? Just about now. But in reality, of course, almost the opposite has happened. Many people report that they work longer hours than ever before, worry about job security, and feel an array of workplace pressures ranging from stress to tension to anxiety.

*"You could feel the tension. It wasn't anything to see somebody cry over stress. When a job gets you to that point, it's not worth it." — Teresa Williford, former customer service representative at BellSouth*

These circumstances have been brought about by a variety of factors. For one thing, in this age of doing more with less, managers are sometimes simply pressuring their employees to work harder and longer hours. Similarly, because people can no longer expect to work for one employer for their entire careers, they may focus more attention on the possibilities of layoffs or outright job loss. And the proliferation of dual-career couples, single parents, and other demographic changes make it harder for people to find time to attend to normal activities like banking, exercise, and so forth. In 1973, the median number of hours of work per week in the United States was 40.6, and the median number of hours of leisure was 26.2. By 1997, however, the median number of hours of work per week had increased to 50.8, and median number of hours of leisure had declined to 19.5 hours per week.

So what are the effects of these trends? For one thing, employers may be getting more work out of their employees. But on the other hand, some experts suggest that stress and stress-related problems cost U.S. companies over $200 billion annually. These costs include such things as higher health-care costs, turnover, unscheduled absenteeism, and declining morale. And, in particular, more workers are filing stress-related claims under worker's compensation programs. These claims have increased in number from 911 in 1981 to 4,997 in 1996.

How are companies responding to all this? Increasingly, more and more companies and their managers are recognizing both the organizational and the human costs of excess stress. As a result, many are now actively seeking ways to lower stress by reducing job demands and/or by offering stress reduction benefits. For example, Public Service Electric & Gas, a New Jersey firm, offers yoga and stress management classes to its employees. Rourke, MS&L, a Boston-based public relations firm, gives its employees $75 a quarter that can be spent on exercise classes, massages, and similar stress reduction activities. Indeed, these kinds of programs are proliferating rapidly. At the same time, though, stress is still a major problem in many companies and to many workers.

References: "The American Way of Work (Move!) May Be Easing Up," *Wall Street Journal*, January 19, 2000, p. B1; *The Wall Street Journal Almanac 1999* (New York: Ballantine Books, 1999), p. 231; "The New Paternalism," *Forbes*, November 2, 1998, pp. 68–70; "Workplace Hazard Gets Attention," *USA Today*, May 5, 1998, pp. 1B, 2B (quote on p. 1B).

Group pressures may include pressure to restrict output, pressure to conform to the group's norms, and so forth. For instance, as we have noted before, it is quite common for a work group to arrive at an informal agreement about how much each member will produce. Individuals who produce much more or much less than this level may be pressured by the group to get back in line. An individual who feels a strong need to vary from the group's expectations (perhaps to get a pay raise or promotion) will experience a great deal of stress, especially if acceptance by the group is also important to him or her.

Leadership style also may cause stress. Suppose an employee needs a great deal of social support from his leader. The leader, however, is quite brusque and shows no concern or compassion for him. This employee will probably feel stressed. Similarly, assume an employee feels a strong need to participate in decision making and to be active in all aspects of management. Her boss is very autocratic and refuses to consult subordinates about anything. Once again stress is likely to result.[25]

Finally, conflicting personalities and behaviors may cause stress. Conflict can occur when two or more people must work together even though their personalities, attitudes, and behaviors differ. For example, a person with an internal locus of control—that is, who always wants to control how things turn out—might get frustrated working with a person with an external locus of control who likes to wait and just let things happen. Likewise, a smoker and a nonsmoker who are assigned adjacent offices obviously will experience stress.[26]

A **life change** is any meaningful change in a person's personal or work situation; too many life changes can lead to health problems.

## Life Stressors

Stress in organizational settings also can be influenced by events that take place outside the organization. Life stressors generally are categorized in terms of life change and life trauma.[27]

Life stressors can interact with organizational stressors to create serious problems for people. Michael Norlen used to practice law. However, he also suffers from depression. When the pressures of practicing law grew too great for Norlen to handle, he would stop answering telephone calls, forget to pay bills, ignore court dates, and sleep as much as sixteen hours a day. Not surprisingly, both his law practice and his family suffered along with him. Finally, a friend offered him a job delivering newspapers. He works from 1:30 A.M. to 6 A.M. everyday, but the work has little pressure or stress. He reports that he actually enjoys the job, and that the reduced work pressure makes it easier for him to handle the life stress that he continues to battle.

**Life Change** Thomas Holmes and Richard Rahe first developed and popularized the notion of life change as a source of stress.[28] A **life change** is any meaningful change in a person's personal or work situation. Holmes and Rahe reasoned that major changes in a person's life can lead to stress and eventually to disease. Table 9.2 summarizes their findings on major life change events. Note that several of these events relate directly (fired from work, retirement) or indirectly (change in residence) to work.

Each event's point value supposedly reflects the event's impact on the individual. At one extreme, a spouse's death, assumed to be the most traumatic event considered, is assigned a point value of 100. At the other extreme, minor violations of the law rank only 11 points. The points themselves represent life change units, or LCUs. Note also that the list includes positive events (marriage and vacations) as well as negative ones (divorce and trouble with the boss).

Holmes and Rahe argued that a person can handle a certain threshold of LCUs, but beyond that level problems can set in. In particular, they suggest that people who encounter more than 150 LCUs in a given year will experience a decline in their health the following year. A score of between 150 and 300 LCUs supposedly carries a 50 percent chance of major illness, whereas

table 9.2

**Life Changes and Life Change Units**

| Rank | Life Event | Mean Value | Rank | Life Event | Mean Value |
|---|---|---|---|---|---|
| 1 | Death of spouse | 100 | 23 | Son or daughter leaving home | 29 |
| 2 | Divorce | 73 | 24 | Trouble with in-laws | 29 |
| 3 | Marital separation | 65 | 25 | Outstanding personal achievement | 28 |
| 4 | Jail term | 63 | 26 | Spouse beginning or ending work | 26 |
| 5 | Death of close family member | 63 | 27 | Beginning or ending school | 26 |
| 6 | Personal injury or illness | 53 | 28 | Change in living conditions | 25 |
| 7 | Marriage | 50 | 29 | Revision of personal habits | 24 |
| 8 | Fired at work | 47 | 30 | Trouble with boss | 23 |
| 9 | Marital reconciliation | 45 | 31 | Change in work hours or conditions | 20 |
| 10 | Retirement | 45 | 32 | Change in residence | 20 |
| 11 | Change in health of family member | 44 | 33 | Change in schools | 20 |
| 12 | Pregnancy | 40 | 34 | Change in recreation | 19 |
| 13 | Sex difficulties | 39 | 35 | Change in church activities | 19 |
| 14 | Gain of new family member | 39 | 36 | Change in social activities | 18 |
| 15 | Business readjustment | 39 | 37 | Mortgage or loan less than $10,000* | 17 |
| 16 | Change in financial state | 38 | 38 | Change in sleeping habits | 16 |
| 17 | Death of close family friend | 37 | 39 | Change in the number of family get-togethers | 15 |
| 18 | Change to different line of work | 36 | 40 | Change in eating habits | 15 |
| 19 | Change in number of arguments with spouse | 35 | 41 | Vacation | 13 |
| 20 | Mortgage over $10,000* | 31 | 42 | Christmas | 12 |
| 21 | Foreclosure of mortgage or loan | 30 | 43 | Minor violations of the law | 11 |
| 22 | Change in responsibilities of work | 29 | | | |

The amount of life stress that a person has experienced in a given period of time, say one year, is measured by the total number of life change units (LCUs). These units result from the addition of the values (shown in the right-hand column) associated with events that the person has experienced during the target time period.

*With inflation, the value of a mortgage that produces stress may be nearer to $100,000; however, no research confirms this figure.

Reference: From Thomas H. Holmes and Richard H. Rahe, "The Social Adjustment Rating Scale." Reprinted from *Journal of Psychosomatic Research,* Vol. 11, 1967. Reprinted with permission from Elsevier Science, Inc.

the chance of major illness is said to increase to 70 percent if the number of LCUs exceeds 300. These ideas offer some insight into the potential impact of stress and underscore our limitations in coping with stressful events. However, research on Holmes and Rahe's proposals has provided only mixed support.

A **life trauma** is any upheaval in an individual's life that alters his or her attitudes, emotions, or behaviors.

**Life Trauma** Life trauma is similar to life change, but it has a narrower, more direct, and shorter-term focus. A **life trauma** is any upheaval in an individual's life that alters his or her attitudes, emotions, or behaviors. To illustrate, according to the life change view, a divorce adds to a person's potential for health problems in the following year. At the same time, the person will obviously also experience emotional turmoil during the actual divorce process. This turmoil is a form of life trauma and will clearly cause stress, much of which may spill over into the workplace.[29]

Major life traumas that may cause stress include marital problems, family difficulties, and health problems initially unrelated to stress. For example, suppose a person learns she has developed arthritis that will limit her favorite activity, skiing. Her dismay over the news may translate into stress at work. Similarly, a worker going through a family breakup will almost certainly go through difficult periods, some of which will affect his or her job performance.

# Consequences of Stress

Stress can have a number of consequences. As we already noted, if the stress is positive, the result may be more energy, enthusiasm, and motivation. Of more concern, of course, are the negative consequences of stress. Referring back to Figure 9.2, we see that stress can produce individual consequences, organizational consequences, and burnout.[30]

We should first note that many of the factors listed are obviously interrelated. For example, alcohol abuse is shown as an individual consequence, but it also affects the organization the person works for. An employee who drinks on the job may perform poorly and create a hazard for others. If the category for a consequence seems somewhat arbitrary, be aware that each consequence is categorized according to the area of its primary influence.

## Individual Consequences

The individual consequences of stress, then, are the outcomes that mainly affect the individual. The organization also may suffer, either directly or indirectly, but it is the individual who pays the real price. Stress may produce behavioral, psychological, and medical consequences.

**Behavioral Consequences** The behavioral consequences of stress may harm the person under stress or others. One such behavior is smoking. Research has clearly documented that people who smoke tend to smoke more when they experience stress. There is also evidence that alcohol and drug abuse are linked to stress, although this relationship is less well documented.[31] Other possible behavioral consequences are accident proneness, violence, and appetite disorders.

**Psychological Consequences** The psychological consequences of stress relate to a person's mental health and well-being. When people experience too much stress at work, they may become depressed or find themselves sleeping too much or not enough. Stress may also lead to family problems and sexual difficulties.[32]

**Medical Consequences** The medical consequences of stress affect a person's physical well-being. Heart disease and stroke, among other illnesses, have been linked to stress. Other common medical problems resulting from too much stress include headaches, backaches, ulcers and related stomach and intestinal disorders, and skin conditions such as acne and hives.[33]

## Organizational Consequences

Clearly, any of the individual consequences just discussed can also affect the organization. Other results of stress have even more direct consequences for organizations. These include decline in performance, withdrawal, and negative changes in attitudes.

*"Today [companies] are looking at the economic cost of things like dual-career couples, single parents, and stress." — Bradley Googins, director of Boston College's Center for Corporate Community Relations*[34]

**Performance** One clear organizational consequence of too much stress is a decline in performance. For operating workers, such a decline can translate into poor-quality work or a drop in productivity. For managers, it can mean faulty decision making or disruptions in working relationships as people become irritable and hard to get along with.

**Withdrawal** Withdrawal behaviors also can result from stress. For the organization, the two most significant forms of withdrawal behavior are absenteeism and quitting. People who are having a hard time coping with stress in their jobs are more likely to call in sick or consider leaving the organization for good. Stress can also produce other, more subtle forms of withdrawal. A manager may start missing deadlines or taking longer lunch breaks. An employee may withdraw psychologically by ceasing to care about the organization and the job.[35] As noted above, employee violence is a potential individual consequence of stress. This also has obvious organizational implications as well, especially if the violence is directed at an employee or at the organization in general.[36]

**Attitudes** Another direct organizational consequence of employee stress relates to attitudes. As we just noted, job satisfaction, morale, and organizational commitment can all suffer, along with motivation to perform at high levels. As a result, people may be more prone to complain about unimportant things, do only enough work to get by, and so forth.

## Burnout

**Burnout** is a general feeling of exhaustion that develops when an individual simultaneously experiences too much pressure and has too few sources of satisfaction.

Burnout, another consequence of stress, has clear implications for both people and organizations. **Burnout** is a general feeling of exhaustion that develops when a person simultaneously experiences too much pressure and has too few sources of satisfaction.[37]

Burnout generally develops in the following way.[38] First, people with high aspirations and strong motivation to get things done are prime candidates for burnout under certain conditions. They are especially vulnerable when the organization suppresses or limits their initiative while constantly demanding that they serve the organization's own ends.

table 9.3

**Managers' Perceptions of Stress in the Workplace**

| Percentage of senior and middle managers agreeing with each of the following: | 1994 | 1982 |
|---|---|---|
| Burnout is a serious problem. | 68% | 40% |
| Managers are working too many hours. | 65 | 39 |
| More and more, managers are physically exhausted by the end of the workday. | 64 | 38 |
| Managers often take too much work home with them. | 60 | 47 |
| Emotional exhaustion is common among managers. | 58 | —* |
| Depression is more common among managers than it used to be. | 45 | —* |
| Managers have adequate support staff to accomplish their goals. | 32 | —* |
| Managers are more isolated than they used to be. | 21 | —* |
| Managers have high job security. | 5 | 26 |

*These questions were not included in the earlier study.

Reference: Opinion Research Corp., p. R4, February 26, 1996. Reprinted by permission of *Wall Street Journal* © 1996 Dow Jones & Company, Inc. All rights reserved worldwide.

In such a situation, the individual is likely to put too much of himself or herself into the job. In other words, the person may well keep trying to meet his or her own agenda while simultaneously trying to fulfill the organization's expectations. The most likely effects of this situation are prolonged stress, fatigue, frustration, and helplessness under the burden of overwhelming demands. The person literally exhausts his or her aspirations and motivation, much as a candle burns itself out. Loss of self-confidence and psychological withdrawal follow. Ultimately, burnout results. At this point, the individual may start dreading going to work in the morning, may put in longer hours but accomplish less than before, and may generally display mental and physical exhaustion.

Table 9.3 summarizes some interesting data about managers' perceptions of burnout and related problems. For example, in 1982 about 40 percent of a sample of senior and middle managers felt that burnout was a serious problem. But in 1994, 68 percent indicated that it was a serious problem. The data illustrate several other interesting—and sobering—findings.

# Managing Stress in the Workplace

Given that stress is widespread and so potentially disruptive in organizations, it follows that people and organizations should be concerned about how to manage it more effectively. And in fact they are. Many strategies have been developed to help manage stress in the workplace. Some are for individuals, and others are geared toward organizations.[39]

## Individual Coping Strategies

Many strategies for helping individuals manage stress have been proposed. Figure 9.4 lists five of the more popular.

**Exercise** Exercise is one method of managing stress. People who exercise regularly are less likely to have heart attacks than inactive people. More directly, research has suggested that people who exercise regularly feel less tension and stress, are more self-confident, and show greater optimism. People who do not exercise regularly feel more stress, are more likely to be depressed, and experience other negative consequences.

**Relaxation** A related method of managing stress is relaxation. We noted at the beginning of the chapter that coping with stress requires adaptation. Proper relaxation is an effective way to adapt. Relaxation can take many forms. One way to relax is to take regular vacations. A recent study found that people's attitudes toward a variety of workplace characteristics improved significantly following a vacation.[40] People can also relax while on the job. For example, it has been recommended that people take regular rest breaks during their normal workday.[41] A popular way of resting is to sit quietly with closed eyes for ten minutes every afternoon. (Of course, it might be necessary to have an alarm clock handy!)

**Time Management** Time management is often recommended for managing stress. The idea is that many daily pressures can be eased or eliminated if a person does a better job of managing time. One popular approach to time management is to make a list every morning of the things to be done that day. Then you group the items on the list into three categories: critical activities that must be performed, important activities that should be performed, and optional or trivial things that can be delegated or postponed. Then, of course, you do the things on the list in their order of importance. This strategy helps people get more of the important things done every day. It also encourages delegation of less important activities to

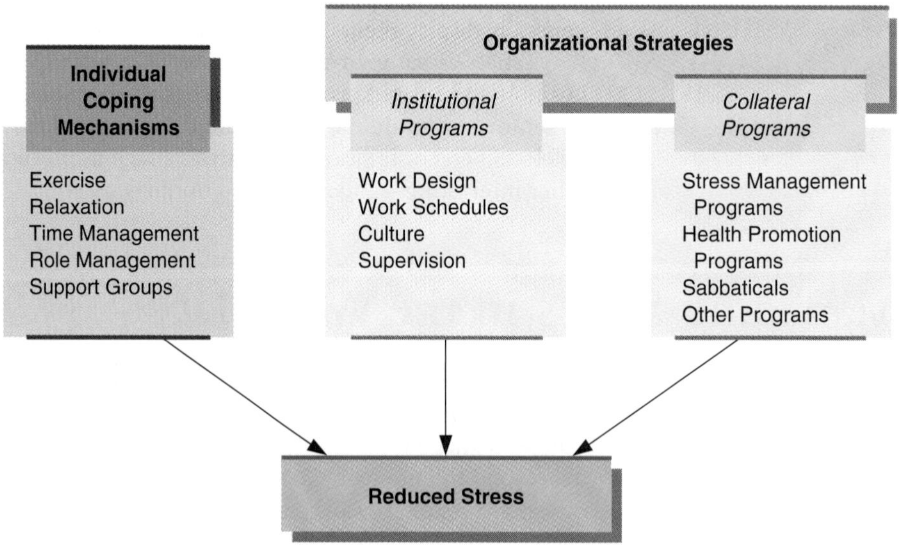


**figure 9.4**
**Individual and Organizational Coping Strategies**

*Just as individual and organizational factors can cause stress, there are individual and organizational strategies for coping with stress. This figure shows the individual coping mechanisms most experts recommend and several institutional and collateral organizational programs.*

TALKING TECHNOLOGY

## *Cell Phones Create Stress*

One of the most ubiquitous devices in organizations today is the cellular telephone. Only a few years ago, cell phones were a rarity. Now, however, walking through any large airport or business center, the observer sees dozens of people sitting in chairs, leaning against the wall, or strolling around as they conduct business on their cell phones.

*"The cell phone is **the entry point**. The falling cost of technology makes it increasingly accessible to everyone."*
*— Mohammed Yunus, banking executive*

The advent of cell phones has given many managers an opportunity to become considerably more productive. It's easier for them to make telephone calls on the road, to stay in touch with clients and customers, and to maintain contact with their offices. At the same time, cell phones pose certain problems for many busy executives. Specifically, because these executives are always available for contact, they have less "down time" and less opportunity to "disconnect" from their work.

In the past, for example, managers had free time when they were traveling to and from work or when they were away from their offices at lunch. Now, many are readily accessible during these times because of their cell phones. Thus, what might have once been a nice one-hour break for lunch in the middle of the day may be a continuation of work as the individual makes and receives telephone calls while at the corner deli.

The astute manager who wants to regain some control over this aspect of his or her work life really has more control than might be expected. Simply put, all the manager has to do is turn the cell phone off. Obviously, if the individual is expecting an urgent telephone call, taking the cellular phone to lunch might not be a bad idea. But if nothing pressing is on the horizon, perhaps the manager should simply leave the phone behind and have a few minutes of rest from the ongoing demands of the executive's life.

References: "It Takes a Cell Phone," *Wall Street Journal,* June 25, 1999, pp. B1, B6 (quote on p. B6); "Technology Overload," *Wall Street Journal,* June 21, 1999, pp. R1–R26; "Stress Busters for Busy Execs," *Fortune,* July 8, 1996, p. 37; "Breaking Point," *Newsweek,* March 6, 1995, pp. 56–61.

others. The "Talking Technology" box illustrates how managers can better manage their time by using their cellular telephones more selectively.

**Role Management** Somewhat related to time management is the idea of role management, in which the individual actively works to avoid overload, ambiguity, and conflict. For example, if you do not know what is expected of you, you should not sit and worry about it. Instead, ask for clarification from your boss. Another role management strategy is to learn to say no. As simple as saying no might sound, a lot of people create problems for themselves by always saying yes. Besides working in their regular jobs, they agree to serve on committees, volunteer for extra duties, and accept extra assignments. Sometimes, of course, we have no choice but to accept an extra obligation (if our boss tells us to complete a new project, we will probably have to do it). In many cases, however, saying no is an option.[42]

**Support Groups** A final method for managing stress is to develop and maintain support groups. A support group is simply a group of family members or friends with whom a person can spend time. Going out after work with a couple of coworkers to a basketball game, for example, can help relieve the stress that builds up during the day. Supportive family and friends can help people deal with normal stress on an ongoing basis. Support groups can be particularly useful during times of crisis. For example, suppose an employee has just learned that she did not get the promotion she has been working toward for months. It may help her tremendously if she has good friends to lean on, be it to talk to or to yell at.[43]

## Organizational Coping Strategies

Organizations are also increasingly realizing that they should be involved in managing their employees' stress. There are two different rationales for this view. One is that because the organization is at least partly responsible for creating the stress, it should help relieve it. The other is that workers experiencing lower levels of harmful stress will function more effectively. Two basic organizational strategies for helping employees manage stress are institutional programs and collateral programs.

*"Employers are being held increasingly liable for job stress. From a financial perspective, employers are finding they have to do something." — Paul Rosch, president of the American Institute of Stress*[44]

**Institutional Programs** Institutional programs for managing stress are undertaken through established organizational mechanisms.[45] For example, properly designed jobs (discussed in Chapter 7) and work schedules (also discussed in Chapter 7) can help ease stress. Shift work, in particular, can cause major problems for employees because they constantly have to adjust their sleep and relaxation patterns. Thus, the design of work and work schedules should be a focus of organizational efforts to reduce stress.[46]

Individuals and organizations can adopt a variety of coping strategies to better deal with stress. At Autodesk, a computer-aided-design software firm, employees must work long, stressful hours to help the firm remain competitive. In return, the firm offers such stress-reduction benefits as Yoga classes, like this one, and six-week paid sabbaticals every four years. Other increasingly popular strategies for stress reduction include on-site childcare, college-planning assistance, take-home meals, and personal concierge services. While any and all of these may have other benefits as well, each can help people better cope with the daily pressures they face at work and at home.

The organization's culture (covered in Chapter 18) also can be used to help manage stress. In some organizations, for example, there is a strong norm against taking time off or going on vacation. In the long run, such norms can cause major stress. Thus, the organization should strive to foster a culture that reinforces a healthy mix of work and nonwork activities.

Finally, supervision can play an important institutional role in managing stress. A supervisor can be a major source of overload. If made aware of their potential for assigning stressful amounts of work, supervisors can do a better job of keeping workloads reasonable.

**Collateral Programs** In addition to institutional efforts aimed at reducing stress, many organizations are turning to collateral programs. A collateral stress program is an organizational program specifically created to help employees deal with stress. Organizations have adopted stress management programs, health promotion programs, and other kinds of programs for this purpose. More and more companies are developing their own programs or adopting existing programs of this type.[47] For example, Lockheed Martin offers screening programs for its employees to detect signs of hypertension. The "Mastering Change" box discusses examples of various so-called wellness programs.

MASTERING CHANGE

## *Promoting Wellness in the Workplace*

In the early 1990s, a popular benefit many companies attempted to develop was a "wellness program." Companies invested in on-site gyms and weight-loss classes, believing that a healthier work force would help them cut their medical costs, help employees reduce stress, and boost productivity. Unfortunately, the people generally attracted to these programs were the very ones who didn't really need them—individuals who were already fit and who already exercised regularly on their own. The sedentary and out-of-shape workers were no more interested in exercising on company property than they were in exercising at home. Consequently, many of the anticipated benefits of wellness programs failed to materialize.

> *"If I see my doctor for 5 or 10 minutes a couple of times a year, there's **not a lot of opportunity** to work with me. The worksite has the person captive 8 to 10 hours a day."*
> *— Stephanie Pronk, health-promotion expert and consultant*

Now some of the same organizations are refocusing their efforts on trying to improve overall wellness in the workplace. For example, at Champion International Corporation, the firm renegotiated its insurance coverage so that employees could obtain cholesterol screenings, pap smears, and similar tests at no cost. Johnson & Johnson provides $500 discounts on insurance coverage to all employees who agree to have their blood pressure, cholesterol, and body fat checked once a year. And Quaker Oats Company gives employees up to $140 in credit in the company's flexible benefit program if they make a healthy lifestyle pledge. For example, pledging to exercise aerobically three times a week is worth a $20 credit. Drinking in moderation and refraining from smoking are worth $50 each.

Tenneco, one of the pioneers in workplace wellness programs and stress management efforts, still maintains its facilities and programs today, but it has changed its focus a bit. Rather than simply providing the exercise facility for employees, the firm now goes to great lengths to educate all employees on healthier lifestyle options. For example, its company newspaper regularly includes articles on how to quit smoking, how to control weight, how to manage pressure, and similar issues.

References: "Healthy Profits," *Time,* November 1, 1999, p. 110W (quote on p. 110W); personal interview with John Marlin, former Tenneco executive, June 1999; "'Wellness Plans' Try to Target the Not-So-Well," *Wall Street Journal,* June 20, 1996, pp. B1, B2; Lee Smith, "Stamina: Who Has It, Why You Need It, How You Get It," *Fortune,* November 28, 1994, pp. 127–139.

Many firms today also have employee fitness programs. These programs attack stress indirectly by encouraging employees to exercise, which is presumed to reduce stress. On the negative side, this kind of effort costs considerably more than stress management programs, because the firm must invest in physical facilities. Still, more and more companies are exploring this option.[48] Both Tenneco and L.L. Bean, for example, have state-of-the-art fitness centers for their employees.

Finally, organizations try to help employees cope with stress through other kinds of programs. For example, existing career development programs are used for this purpose. General Electric is renowned for its excellent career development program. Other companies use programs promoting everything from humor to massage to yoga as antidotes for stress.[49] Of course, little or no research supports some of the claims made by advocates of these programs. Thus, managers must take steps to ensure that any organizational effort to help employees cope with stress is at least reasonably effective.

# Work-Life Linkages

At numerous points in this chapter we have alluded to relationships between a person's work and life. In this final brief section we will make these relationships a bit more explicit.

## Fundamental Work-Life Relationships

Work-life relationships can be characterized in any number of ways.[50] Consider, for example, the basic dimensions of the part of a person's life tied specifically to work. Common dimensions would include such things as an individual's current job (including working hours, job satisfaction, and so forth), his or her career goals (the person's aspirations, career trajectory, and so forth), interpersonal relations at work (with the supervisor, subordinates, coworkers, and others), and job security.

Part of each person's life is also distinctly separate from work. These dimensions might include the person's spouse or life companion, dependents (such as children or elderly parents), personal life interests (hobbies, leisure time interests, religious affiliations, community involvement), and friendship networks.

*"I'd like to participate more in school or camp stuff, but I can't manage my schedule in a way to allow that. I'm letting go of everything for myself, except for exercise on weekends. And I've given up any attempt to manage our finances." — Jeffrey Welch, staff worker in a large New York bank*[51]

**Work-life relationships** are interrelationships between a person's work life and personal life.

**Work-life relationships**, then, include any relationships between dimensions of the person's work life and the person's personal life. For example, a person with numerous dependents (a nonworking spouse or domestic partner, dependent children, dependent parents, etc.) may prefer a job with a relatively high salary, fewer overtime demands, and less travel. On the other hand, a person with no dependents may be less interested in salary, more receptive to overtime, and enjoy job-related travel.

Stress will occur when there is a basic inconsistency or incompatibility between a person's work and life dimensions. For example, if a person is the sole care provider for a dependent elderly parent but has a job that requires considerable travel and evening work, stress is likely to result.

## Balancing Work-Life Linkages

Balancing work-life linkages is, of course, no easy thing to do. Demands from both sides can be extreme, and people may need to be prepared to make tradeoffs. The important thing is to recognize the potential tradeoffs in advance so that they can be carefully weighed and a comfortable decision made. Some of the strategies for doing this were discussed earlier. For example, working for a company that offers flexible work schedules may be an attractive option.[52]

Individuals must also recognize the importance of long-term versus short-term perspectives in balancing their work and personal lives. For example, people may have to respond a bit more to work than to life demands in the early years of their careers. In midcareer, they may be able to achieve a more comfortable balance. And in later career stages, they may be able to put life dimensions first, by refusing to relocate, by working shorter hours, and so forth.

People also have to decide for themselves what they value and what tradeoffs they are willing to make. For instance, consider the dilemma faced by a dual-career couple when one partner is being transferred to another city. One option is for one of the partners to subordinate her or his career for the other partner, at least temporarily. For example, the partner being transferred can turn it down, risking a potential career setback or the loss of the job. Or the other partner may resign from his or her current position and seek another one in the new location. The couple might also decide to live apart, with one moving and the other staying. The partners might also come to realize that their respective careers are more important to them than their relationship and decide to go their separate ways.

# Synopsis

Stress is a person's adaptive response to a stimulus that places excessive psychological or physical demands on that person. According to the general adaptation syndrome (GAS) perspective, the three stages of response to stress are alarm, resistance, and exhaustion. Two important forms of stress are eustress and distress.

Type A personalities are more competitive and time driven than Type B personalities. Initial evidence suggested that Type As are more susceptible to coronary heart disease, but recent findings provide less support for this idea. Hardiness, optimism, cultural context, and gender may also affect stress.

Stress can be caused by many factors. Major organizational stressors are task demands, physical demands, role demands, and interpersonal demands. Life stressors include life change and life trauma.

Stress has many consequences. Individual consequences can include behavioral, psychological, and medical problems. On the organizational level, stress can affect performance and attitudes or cause withdrawal. Burnout is another possibility.

Primary individual mechanisms for managing stress are exercise, relaxation, time management, role management, and support groups. Organizations use both institutional and collateral programs to control stress.

People have numerous dimensions to their work and personal lives. When these dimensions are interrelated, individuals must decide for themselves which are more important and how to balance them.

## Discussion Questions

1. Describe one or two recent times when stress had both good and bad consequences for you.
2. Describe a time when you successfully avoided stage 3 of the GAS and another time when you got to stage 3.
3. Do you consider yourself a Type A or a Type B person? Why?
4. Can a person who is a Type A change? If so, how?
5. What are the major stressors for a student?
6. Is an organizational stressor or a life stressor likely to be more powerful?
7. What consequences are students most likely to suffer as a result of too much stress?
8. Do you agree that a certain degree of stress is necessary to induce high energy and motivation?
9. What can be done to prevent burnout? If someone you know is suffering burnout, how would you advise that person to recover from it?
10. Do you practice any of the stress reduction methods discussed in the text? Which ones? Do you use others not mentioned in the text?
11. Has the work-life balance been an issue in your life?

## Organizational Behavior Case for Discussion

### Over the Edge

Almost everyone experiences stress in one form or another. The effects of stress may include such things as anxiety and high blood pressure. Occasionally, however, people are under so much stress that they are pushed over the edge. They reach a breaking point and take action that results in destruction and occasionally death. Consider the case of James Daniel Simpson, a quiet and reserved young man whom no one ever expected to cause trouble.

Throughout his high school years in El Paso, Simpson was quiet and reserved. He caused no problems but made few friends. Classmates and neighbors recall him as being polite and dependable. They also note that he didn't talk much and usually kept to himself. After graduating in 1985, he enrolled at the University of Texas at El Paso, but he did not graduate. Simpson subsequently worked in a variety of jobs until moving to Corpus Christi in 1992.

Soon after arriving there, Simpson went to work for the Walter Rossler Company. The firm performed consulting work for area refinery industries, specializing in ultrasonic inspections. Rossler paid $1,900 for Simpson to enroll in some training courses at a local college. Like other employees who took advantage of Rossler's training incentive, Simpson signed an agreement to repay the money if he left the company for any reason within three years of the date of the agreement. The agreement itself was dated November 3, 1993.

By all accounts, Simpson was an average worker—he was adequate but did not distinguish himself in any way. He occasionally came to work late, but his overall performance was satisfactory. The only major complaint that Simpson himself voiced was his objection to the company's policy requiring employees to come and go through the back door. He resented this policy because a few managers and secretaries were "exempt" and were allowed to use the front door.

In September 1994, Simpson quit his job at Rossler and began to look for other work. After repeated attempts to recover the money Rossler had spent for Simpson's training, the company filed a lawsuit against him on November 1, 1994. The suit was eventually settled out of court, with Simpson agreeing to repay $700 of the total amount. Rossler also provided unsatisfactory references for Simpson as he continued to search for a new job.

Over the next six months, Simpson's savings dwindled, and his prospects for work disappeared. In February 1995, he bought two guns from a Corpus Christi gun dealer. One gun was a Ruger 9mm semiautomatic pistol (an expensive handgun costing around $500); the other was an inexpensive .32-caliber handgun. Shortly thereafter, he ran out of money and pawned his television, one of his last assets.

On the afternoon of Monday, April 3, 1995, Simpson drove to a local park and fired several shots into the air. After leaving the park at around 4:30 P.M., he drove to the offices of the Walter Rossler Company and parked in front of the building. His former coworkers at Rossler had often chided him for using an antitheft alarm in his old, beat-up Subaru. On this day, however, he did not bother to set the alarm.

He walked directly to the building and entered through the front door. Once inside, he systematically walked through the facility, shooting and killing five people. He appeared to be seeking out specific targets. The five individuals killed were Walter Charles Rossler (company president), Joann Rossler (corporate secretary), Patty Gilmore (secretary), Richard Lee Tomlinson (vice president for operations), and Derek Harrison (sales representative).

As he approached each one, Simpson first cursed them and then shot them. Along the way, he bypassed at least two employees without so much as a second glance. He also spared Lisa Rossler, daughter of the owners, and her infant son. Simpson then walked out through the back door of the building and into a small shed. Once inside, he killed himself with a single shot to the head.

### Case Questions

1. Describe how stress may have played a role in this tragedy.
2. What individual and organizational sources of stress can be identified in this case?
3. Do you think that any of the individual or organizational strategies described in the chapter for dealing with stress could have kept this situation from occurring?

References: Joel H. Neuman and Robert A. Baron, "Workplace Violence and Workplace Aggression: Evidence Concerning Specific Forms, Potential Causes, and Preferred Targets," *Journal of Management*, 1998, vol. 24, no. 3, pp. 391–419; "Employers on Guard for Violence," *Wall Street Journal*, April 5, 1995, p. 3A; "Dialing the Stress-Meter Down," *Newsweek*, March 6, 1995, p. 62.

## Experiencing Organizational Behavior

### Learning How Stress Affects You

**Purpose:** This exercise is intended to help you develop a better understanding of how stress affects you.

**Format:** Following is a set of questions about your job. If you work, respond to the questions in terms of your job. If you do not work, respond to the questions in terms of your role as a student.

**Procedure:** This quiz will help you recognize your level of stress on the job. Take the test, figure your score, and then see if your stress level is normal, beginning to be a problem, or dangerous. Answer the following statements by putting a number in front of each:

1—seldom true
2—sometimes true
3—mostly true

____ 1. Even over minor problems, I lose my temper and do embarrassing things, like yell or kick a garbage can.

____ 2. I hear every piece of information or question as criticism of my work.

____ 3. If someone criticizes my work, I take it as a personal attack.

____ 4. My emotions seem flat whether I'm told good news or bad news about my performance.

____ 5. Sunday nights are the worst time of the week.

____ 6. To avoid going to work, I'd even call in sick when I'm feeling fine.

____ 7. I feel powerless to lighten my work load or schedule, even though I've always got far too much to do.

____ 8. I respond irritably to any request from coworkers.

____ 9. On the job and off, I get highly emotional over minor accidents, such as typos or spilt coffee.

____ 10. I tell people about sports or hobbies that I'd like to do but say I never have time because of the hours I spend at work.

____ 11. I work overtime consistently, yet never feel caught up.

____ 12. My health is running down; I often have headaches, backaches, stomachaches.

____13. If I even eat lunch, I do it at my desk while working.

____14. I see time as my enemy.

____15. I can't tell the difference between work and play; it all feels like one more thing to be done.

____16. Everything I do feels like a drain on my energy.

____17. I feel like I want to pull the covers over my head and hide.

____18. I seem off center, distracted—I do things like walk into mirrored pillars in department stores and excuse myself.

____19. I blame my family—because of them, I have to stay in this job and location.

____20. I have ruined my relationship with coworkers whom I feel I compete against.

Scoring: Add up the points you wrote beside the questions. Interpret your score as follows:

20–29: You have normal amounts of stress.

30–49: Stress is becoming a problem. You should try to identify its source and manage it.

50–60: Stress is at dangerous levels. Seek help or it could result in worse symptoms, such as alcoholism or illness.

### Follow-up Questions

1. How valid do you think your score is?
2. Is it possible to anticipate stress ahead of time and plan ways to help manage it?

Reference: "Stress on the job? Ask yourself," *USA Today*, June 16, 1987. 

## Building Organizational Behavior Skills

### Are You Type A or Type B?

This test will help you develop insights into your own tendencies toward Type A or Type B behavior patterns. Answer the questions honestly and accurately about either your job or your school, whichever requires the most time each week. Then calculate your score according to the instructions that follow the questions. Discuss your results with a classmate. Critique each other's answers and see if you can help each other develop a strategy for reducing Type A tendencies.

Choose from the following responses to answer the questions below:

a. Almost always true
b. Usually true
c. Seldom true
d. Never true

____ 1. I do not like to wait for other people to complete their work before I can proceed with mine.

____ 2. I hate to wait in most lines.

____ 3. People tell me that I tend to get irritated too easily.

____ 4. Whenever possible I try to make activities competitive.

____ 5. I have a tendency to rush into work that needs to be done before knowing the procedure I will use to complete the job.

____ 6. Even when I go on vacation, I usually take some work along.

____ 7. When I make a mistake, it is usually because I have rushed into the job before completely planning it through.

____ 8. I feel guilty about taking time off from work.

____ 9. People tell me I have a bad temper when it comes to competitive situations.

____10. I tend to lose my temper when I am under a lot of pressure at work.

____11. Whenever possible, I will attempt to complete two or more tasks at once.

____12. I tend to race against the clock.

____13. I have no patience with lateness.

____14. I catch myself rushing when there is no need.

Score your responses according to the following key:

- *An intense sense of time urgency* is a tendency to race against the clock, even when there is little reason to. The person feels a need to hurry for hurry's sake alone, and this tendency has appropriately been called hurry sickness. Time urgency is measured by items 1, 2, 8, 12, 13, and 14. Every a or b answer to these six questions scores one point.
- *Inappropriate aggression and hostility* reveals itself in a person who is excessively competitive and who cannot do anything for fun. This inappropriately aggressive behavior easily evolves into frequent displays of hostility, usually at the slightest provocation or frustration. Competitiveness and hostility is measured by items 3, 4, 9, and 10. Every a or b answer scores one point.
- *Polyphasic behavior* refers to the tendency to undertake two or more tasks simultaneously at inappropriate times. It usually results in wasted time because of an inability to complete the tasks. This behavior is measured by items 6 and 11. Every a or b answer scores one point.
- *Goal directedness without proper planning* refers to the tendency of an individual to rush into work without really knowing how to accomplish the desired result. This usually results in incomplete work or work with many errors, which in turn leads to wasted time, energy, and money. Lack of planning is measured by items 5 and 7. Every a or b response scores one point.

TOTAL SCORE = _____

If your score is 5 or greater, you may possess some basic components of the Type A personality.

Reference: From D. A. Girdano, G. S. Everly, Jr., and E. E. Dusek, *Controlling Stress and Tension: A Holistic Approach*, 3/e.  Reprinted/adapted by permission of Allyn & Bacon.

## Developing OB Internet Skills

**Introduction:** More and more companies today are experimenting with various practices intended to make them more "family-friendly." For example, offering on-site childcare and flexible work schedule options presumably makes it easier for employees with children to balance the demands of the job with the demands of parenting. This exercise will help you learn more about family-friendly business practices.

**Internet Exercise:** Assume that your boss, the CEO, has just read an article extolling the virtues and benefits of being a family-friendly organization and has suggested that your business should look into this. Although you know that the CEO's motives are superficial, at best, you also see this as a real opportunity to improve the quality of life for your firm's employees and truly make your business more family-friendly. Search the Internet to research family-friendly business practices.

**Follow-up:** Identify ten different practices that might come under the heading of being family-friendly. Finally, respond to the following instructions and questions:

1. Develop arguments for and against implementing each of the ten practices you have identified.
2. Rank-order the ten practices in terms of your own personal preferences for them.
3. Do you think each of these practices will become more or less popular in the future? Why?

# Part II Integrative Running Case

## The People Behind the AOL–Time Warner Deal

As described at the end of Part I, the merger between America Online (AOL) and Time Warner attracted worldwide attention and was hailed by some as a major defining moment for the twenty-first century. To better understand the reasons underlying the merger and why it all seemed to make so much sense but still came as a major surprise, it is necessary to take a closer look at the two key players, AOL CEO Stephen Case and Time Warner CEO Gerald Levin. Indeed, from the beginning of their dialogue, everyone involved knew that the beliefs and goals of these two key individuals alone would either make or break the deal.

Shortly after finishing his college education at Williams College in 1980, Stephen Case applied for a position at Time, Inc.'s cable television network, HBO. Even at that relatively early date, Case believed that his future was in the telecommunications industry. As it turns out, he was also a visionary who foresaw the blending of information, entertainment, media, and computers into interconnected networks that would fundamentally alter how people work and interact with one another. And he knew he wanted to be part of creating and implementing that vision.

When he didn't get the job at HBO, Case went to work for Procter & Gamble before moving to Pizza Hut to head that firm's new product development group. Then he left Pizza Hut and helped launch AOL. His insights into the then-emerging Internet environment and his conceptual skills about merging technology and information in ways both attractive and beneficial to customers played key roles in the success enjoyed by AOL. It really came as no surprise to those who know him when Case was named CEO of the firm the same year it went public, 1992.

Case is generally known among his friends and family as an introvert. He talks little, for example, and often prefers to spend time alone with his thoughts. But he also firmly believes that he can make a difference in everything he undertakes. For instance, he has always been willing to take risks, both in terms of his own career and in his business ventures. His own confidence is apparent to those who know him, and he always seems self-assured about every action and decision he makes. But at the same time, he is remarkably ego-free. He is always willing to give credit to others, to share the spotlight, and to downplay his own role in matters.

Many people who don't really know him incorrectly stereotype Case as some sort of a computer geek. They assume that since he heads up a major high-tech business like AOL, he must obviously spend a lot of time working with that technology. In truth, however, he is much more of a conceptualizer than a technician. For example, he typically knows how he wants a media interface to work or to look but usually has no real technical insights into how to create or design that interface. Thus, his role is most often to describe the broad concepts of how he wants something to work, but he leaves it to others to actually figure out how to make it work.

During the early years of the business, Case, like most other entrepreneurs, worked long hours, and seven-day work weeks were the norm, not the exception. But through this difficult start-up period he always managed to maintain an effective balance in his life, spending time with his family and maintaining a healthy lifestyle. He credits a network of close personal friends as being instrumental during this time; he also set up a small gym in his office so he could maintain an exercise program and work off the stresses and strains of his work.

But perhaps most central to Case's personal success has been the complex set of factors that have served as a continual source of motivation for him. For one thing, he has maintained an unwavering commitment to his own personal view of the information age. For another, his own personal gain is actually secondary. He certainly expects to be compensated for his efforts and to share financially in the success of his business. But as one observer noted, he is less interested in owning the world than in changing it. Among the indicators of his beliefs is the passionate enthusiasm he has for **helping.org**, an AOP portal that links volunteers and donors with nonprofit groups. Another is his support for My Government, AOL's public-affairs site, which helps citizens become more involved. Case has also established a $150 million foundation, headed up by his wife, Jean, and has given another $30 million directly to his own favorite causes, including churches and schools.

Interestingly, even though they would seem to be far more different than alike, Levin actually has several things in common with Case. For example, Levin has also long been fascinated by technology, but, like Case, he excels on the conceptual side and generally leaves the implementation details to others. Levin is also somewhat introverted, has passion for his work, exudes confidence to others, and has an inner toughness and resilience that have helped him get to the top. He has also managed to keep his ego in check and has a strong commitment to the social mission of business as well.

But both Case and Levin have also been the targets of critics over the years. For example, many experts have written both AOL and Case off several times in the past, usually pointing to various operating problems at AOL (nicknaming the firm "America on Hold" at one point because the firm had more subscribers than it could efficiently handle). Some also laughed at Case when he was predicting a bright future for AOL at the same time as it seemed to be adrift from the rest of the telecommunications giants. Perhaps because Levin has been around longer, he has received even more barbs. For example, some of his harshest critics call him a Machiavellian opportunist solely interested in acquiring more power for himself.

Perhaps it is because Case and Levin have so many things in common that they seem so amenable to sharing power at the new AOL–Time Warner. For example, even though AOL is the acquiring firm, Case made it clear from day one that he wanted Levin to head up the new enterprise for at least the foreseeable future. Indeed, the way most people see things, Case is not likely to ever be CEO of the new firm, instead maintaining for himself the freedom and flexibility to focus on new ideas and to conceptualize new and better ways of doing things.

But if it may be easy for Case and Levin to work together, and if the issues of merging AOL and Time Warner can be boiled down to a few catch phrases, the operational details of putting the two companies together are indeed staggering in their complexity. Time Warner has 70,000 employees, while AOL has slightly over 12,000. But although Case and Levin seem comfortable with how they will share power at the top, given that AOL is the acquirer, its senior managers may expect more control and a faster path to the top for themselves. There are also key issues associated with executive compensation, an area where Case and Levin do (apparently) have divergent views. For example, Case's base salary prior to the merger was less than \$300,000 a year, while Levin's was \$5 million (of course, both also received lucrative stock options as well).

Myriad decisions are also necessary at the more operational levels of the new firm. For example, AOL has a companywide flexible work scheduling program, whereas Time Warner has maintained more rigid and traditional forms of work scheduling. AOL has also been highly participative throughout its ranks, whereas Time Warner was decentralized in some areas but nevertheless kept decision-making authority on many key issues centralized at the top. And whereas AOL generally focused both performance measurement and rewards at the team level, Time Warner again more traditionally focused both performance measurement and rewards at the individual level. Thus, although many experts believe that AOL–Time Warner may indeed be a corporate marriage made in heaven, others think the devil will be in the details.

## Case Questions

1. How do the foundations of individual behavior play a role in helping to understand Stephen Case and Gerald Levin?
2. How would you characterize the needs and processes that apparently motivate Case and Levin?
3. How are issues of work arrangements, performance management and rewards, and stress illustrated in this case?
4. Beyond the examples specifically noted or implied in the case, describe other areas in which individual behavior, motivation, job design, participation, work arrangements, goal setting, performance management, rewards, stress, and work-life linkages both affect and are affected by the merger of AOL and Time Warner.

References: Marc Gunther, "These Guys Want it All," *Fortune*, February 7, 2000, pp. 70–78; "Morning After," *Forbes*, February 7, 2000, pp. 54–56; "Happily Ever After?" *Time*, January 24, 2000, pp. 38–43; "A Two-Man Network," *Time*, January 24, 2000, pp. 46–50; "Welcome to the 21st Century," *Business Week*, January 24, 2000, pp. 36–44.

chapter

# 10

# Communication in Organizations

## Management Preview

Communication is something that most of us take for granted. We have been doing it so long that we really pay little attention to the process. Especially in organizations, we focus more on doing our jobs and less on how we communicate about those jobs. But today, as methods of communication are changing so rapidly, we need to pay more attention to the process that effectively links what we do to others in the organization. In this chapter, we focus on the important processes of interpersonal communication and information processing. First, we discuss the importance of communication in organizations and some important aspects of international communication in organizations. Next, we describe the methods of organizational communication and examine the basic communication process. Then we examine the potential effects of computerized information processing and telecommunications. Next, we explore the development of communication networks in organizations. Finally, we discuss several common problems of organizational communication and methods of managing communication. First, though, we begin by describing how telecommunications are changing the way many people work at Automotive Careers of Texas and Nationwide Insurance. ■

Telecommunications are changing the daily business activities around the world. Cellular phones, portable laptop computers, fax machines, personal organizers, voicemail, email, and telecommuting are taking workers out of the traditional office and putting them in cars, at home, and in clients' offices, hotels, and temporary cubicles far from headquarters. With all of these new ways of communicating with coworkers, bosses, employees, suppliers, and customers, it is no wonder that the way we work is changing. Workers still must do their jobs, often better and faster than ever before; they just do not do them in the office all the time. At Automotive Careers of Texas, all business is conducted via electronic methods. Employees have no office to go to every day, or any day, for that matter. The company's seven staff members live in different cities around the state as they do employment searches for client companies via fax, email, voicemail, and telephone. In fact, they may never see the employees they recruit; they only communicate with them electronically.

*"With all the electronic devices available today offices have become passé, so to speak." — Bob Marco, senior associate general manager, Automotive Careers of Texas**

Telecommuters usually have all of the newest electronic equipment and rarely go to the office. At Nationwide Insurance, most telecommuters go to the office once a week to pick up things that cannot be sent electronically. But otherwise they are not that much different from other workers. They all communicate via email, voicemail, and fax anyway, whether they are full-time telecommuters or not. Many companies that allow, or encourage, employees to telecommute require periodic face-to-face meetings or "checking in" to make sure that things are going well from both perspectives (employer and employee). Checking in periodically keeps the person in touch with the rest of the office, combats the sense of isolation that some telecommuters have reported, and keeps the linkage and rapport among employees alive, tangible, and effective. The increasing use of telecommuters should have positive impacts on the ability of companies to stay in closer touch with customers and suppliers, thereby speeding up product and service delivery and total responsiveness. Benefits to the employee include more flexible time to spend with family, less commute time, and more time with customers and people important to the organization.[1] ■

The use of electronic communication technology greatly changed our communication during the past decade. Our lives, too, are now different simply because we are more mobile and can communicate in so many forms with anyone so fast. We do not even have to go to the office anymore. Not going to the office was an indication of laziness and marginal performers less than a generation ago. Regardless of the technology involved, however, the basics of interpersonal communication remain important. Communication is important in all phases of organizational behavior, but it is especially crucial in decision making, performance appraisal, motivation, and ensuring that the organization functions effectively. We begin our discussion of the role communication plays in organizational behavior by presenting the most basic elements of communication.

# The Nature of Communication in Organizations

**Communication** is the social process in which two or more parties exchange information and share meaning.

**Communication** is the social process in which two or more parties exchange information and share meaning.[2] Communication has been studied from many perspectives. In this section, we provide an overview of the complex and dynamic communication process and discuss some important issues relating to international communication in organizations.

## The Purposes of Communication in Organizations

Communication among individuals and groups is vital in all organizations. Some of the purposes of organizational communication are shown in Figure 10.1. The primary purpose is to achieve coordinated action.[3] Just as the human nervous system responds to stimuli and coordinates responses by sending messages to the various parts of the body, communication coordinates the actions of the parts of an organization. Without communication, an organization would be merely a collection of

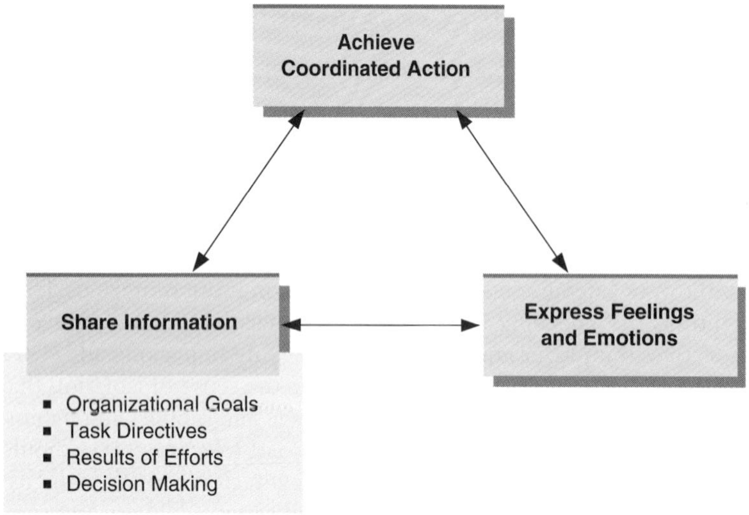


figure 10.1 **Three Purposes of Organizational Communication**

*Achieving coordinated action is the prime purpose of communication in organizations. Sharing information properly and expressing emotions help achieve coordinated action.*

individual workers doing separate tasks. Organizational action would lack coordination and be oriented toward individual rather than organizational goals.

A second purpose of communication is information sharing. The most important information relates to organizational goals, which give members a sense of purpose and direction. Another information-sharing function of communication is to give specific task directions to individuals. Whereas information on organizational goals gives employees a sense of how their activities fit into the overall picture, task communication tells them what their job duties are and are not. Employees must also receive information on the results of their efforts, as in performance appraisals.

Communication is essential to the decision-making process as well, as we discuss in Chapter 15. Information, and thus information sharing, are needed to define problems, generate and evaluate alternatives, implement decisions, and control and evaluate results.

Finally, communication expresses feelings and emotions. Organizational communication is far from a collection of facts and figures. People in organizations, like people anywhere else, often need to communicate emotions such as happiness, anger, displeasure, confidence, and fear.

In these days of portable phones, cellular phones, email, and other types of instant communication, nothing can replace the standard office phone. In this photo, U.S. Secretary of State Madeleine Albright and Palestinian leader Yasir Arafat share a phone call from U.S. President Bill Clinton regarding the latest developments in the peace talks between the Palestinians and the Israelis. These two were very excited about the progress made that day. The telephone call allowed these two to share their enthusiasm with the President and discuss the prospects for the agreement much more directly and intimately than would have been possible using email or other written forms. An agreement was signed the next day.

## Communication Across Cultures

Communication is an aspect of interpersonal relations that obviously is affected by the international environment, partly because of language issues and partly because of coordination issues.

**Language** Differences in languages are compounded by the fact that the same word can mean different things in different cultures. For example, as Table 10.1 indicates, "Coca-Cola" means "bite the head of a dead tadpole" in the first Chinese characters that were used in advertising. Finally the company found other Chinese characters. The table lists other interesting examples of minor communication failures across cultures.

table 10.1
**Examples of International Communication Problems**

| Source of Problem | Examples |
|---|---|
| Language | One firm, trying to find a name for a new soap powder, tested the chosen name in fifty languages. In English, it meant "dainty." Translations into other languages meant "song" (Gaelic), "aloof" (Flemish), "horse" (African), "hazy" or "dimwitted" (Persian), and "crazy" (Korean). The name was obscene in several Slavic languages. |
| | The Chevy Nova was *no va* in Spanish, which means "doesn't go." |
| | *Coca-Cola* in Chinese meant "bite the head of a dead tadpole." |
| | Idioms cannot be translated literally: "to murder the King's English" becomes "to speak French like a Spanish cow" in French. |
| Nonverbal Signs | Shaking your head up and down in Greece means "no," and swinging it from side to side means "yes." |
| | In most European countries, it is considered impolite not to have both hands on the table. |
| | The American sign for "OK" is rude in Spain and vulgar in Brazil. |
| Colors | Green: Popular in Moslem countries<br>Suggests disease in jungle-covered countries<br>Suggests cosmetics in France, Sweden, and the Netherlands |
| | Red: Blasphemous in African countries<br>Stands for wealth and masculinity in Great Britain |
| Product | Campbell Soup was unsuccessful in Britain until the firm added water to its condensed soup so the cans would be the same size as the cans of soup the British were used to purchasing. |
| | Long-life packaging, which is commonly used for milk in Europe, allows milk to be stored for months at room temperature if it is unopened. Americans are still wary of it. |
| | Coca-Cola had to alter the taste of its soft drink in China when the Chinese described it as "tasting like medicine." |

References: Adapted from David A. Ricks, *Blunders in International Business* (Cambridge, Mass.: Blackwell Publishers, 1993); David A. Ricks, *Big Business Blunders: Mistakes in Multinational Marketing* (Homewood, Ill.: Dow Jones–Irwin, 1983); Nancy Bragganti and Elizabeth Devine, *The Traveler's Guide to European Customs and Manners* (St. Paul, Minn.: Meadowbrook Books, 1984); and several *Wall Street Journal* articles.

Note in the table that elements of nonverbal communication also vary across cultures. Colors and body language can convey quite a different message in one culture than in another. For example, the American sign for "OK" (making a loop with thumb and first finger) is considered rude in Spain and vulgar in Brazil. Managers should be forewarned that they can take nothing for granted in dealing with people from other cultures. They must take the time to become as fully acquainted as possible with the verbal and nonverbal languages of that culture. The "World View" box describes some of the issues involved in the worldwide use of English for business communication.

WORLD VIEW

## *A World Language of Business?*

What does it take to communicate in business around the world? Does the person who engages in business in many different countries have to know how to speak and read the language of every country? Maybe you think that English is a "world language." Language is simply the symbols we use to share meaning. As companies are becoming more global, the people who represent them around the world are finding a different system of symbols, or language, to share the meanings and are experiencing great difficulty in some places and relative ease in others. They are finding that language often means more than just word-for-word translations.

> *"The English language is now represented in every continent and in the islands of three major oceans." — David Crystal, British linguist and world authority on English*

For example, U.S. business people who go to Sweden find it easy to do business there because Swedes are strongly influenced by the U.S. culture, have good English-speaking skills, and are familiar with the U.S. management style. There are, however, subtle differences in consensus building and group dynamics. On the other hand, U.S. business people often experience difficulties in Great Britain, where the language is English, but the meanings are sometimes quite different. In addition to the actual meanings of words being different, the cultures affect the way words are interpreted. Business in Great Britain is conducted within a framework of rituals and customs that reflect an attitude that is quite different from the U.S. way of doing business. For example, the use of formal titles and forms of address are very important to the British, whereas in the U.S. titles are usually forgotten and people are commonly addressed by their first names. To address a British person to whom you have just been introduced by his or her first name is considered rude. His or her title, such as "Lord" or "Lady," or at least Mr. or Mrs., should always be used until the relationship becomes much more informal.

Using multiple languages to conduct business is quite common in Europe, where the population is accustomed to crossing borders and dealing with people from different countries. Many European business people speak their own language plus one or two others, usually English, German, or French. But what about English? English is spoken by about 1.5 billion people (about one-fourth of the world population) around the world and is used as the primary foreign language in more than 100 countries. Interestingly, another one-fourth of the world population speaks Chinese, but Chinese is not considered to have the worldwide status of English. The rise of English as a potential candidate for a world language can be traced to the early worldwide colonization by Great Britain and the emergence of global industries that are based in English. Some of these English-centric industries are telecommunication, computer technology and software, medicine, entertainment, and the media. Although English is growing in use and English language schools are increasing around the world, the global traveler must still know something of the language and the culture of the countries to be visited. Most experts recommend the global business person to at least know basic greetings and a few conversational phrases in the language of the country to be visited and pay close attention to the seemingly little formalities that go along with the actual words.

References: Cynthia L. Kemper, "Sacre Bleu! English as a Global Lingua Franca? Why English Is Rapidly Achieving Worldwide Status," *Communication World,* June–July 1999, pp. 41–44, (quote on p. 43); Mirjaliisa Charles, "Europe: Oral Business Communication," *Business Communication Quarterly,* September 1998, pp. 85–94; James Calvert Scott, "Dear???: Understanding British Forms of Address," *Business Communication Quarterly,* September 1998, pp. 50–61; Valerie Frazee, "Building Relationships in Sweden," *Workforce,* October 1997, pp. S19–20.

**Coordination** International communication is closely related to issues of coordination. For example, an American manager who wants to talk with his or her counterpart in Hong Kong or Singapore must contend not only with language differences but also with a time difference of many hours. When the American manager needs to talk on the telephone, the Hong Kong executive may be home asleep. Organizations are finding increasingly innovative methods for coordinating their activities in scattered parts of the globe. Merrill Lynch, for example, has developed its own satellite-based telephone network to monitor and participate in the worldwide money and financial markets.[4]

# Methods of Communication

The three primary methods of communicating in organizations are written, oral, and nonverbal. Often the methods are combined. Considerations that affect the choice of method include the audience (whether it is physically present), the nature of the message (its urgency or secrecy), and the costs of transmission. Figure 10.2 shows various forms each method can take.

## Written Communication

Typically organizations produce a great deal of written communication of many kinds. A letter is a formal means of communicating with an individual, generally someone outside the organization. Probably the most common form of written communication in organizations is the office memorandum, or memo. Memos usually are addressed to a person or group inside the organization.[5] They tend to deal with a single topic and are more impersonal (as they often are destined to more than one person) but less formal than letters. Most email is similar to the traditional memo, although even less formal.

Other common forms of written communication include reports, manuals, and forms. Reports generally summarize the progress or results of a project and often provide information to be used in decision making. Manuals have various functions in organizations. Instruction manuals tell employees how to operate machines; policy and procedures manuals inform them of organizational rules; operations manuals describe how to perform tasks and respond to work-related problems. Forms are standardized documents on which to report information. As such, they

**figure 10.2 Methods of Communication in Organizations**

*The three methods of communication in organizations are related to each other. Each one supplements the other, although each can also stand alone.*

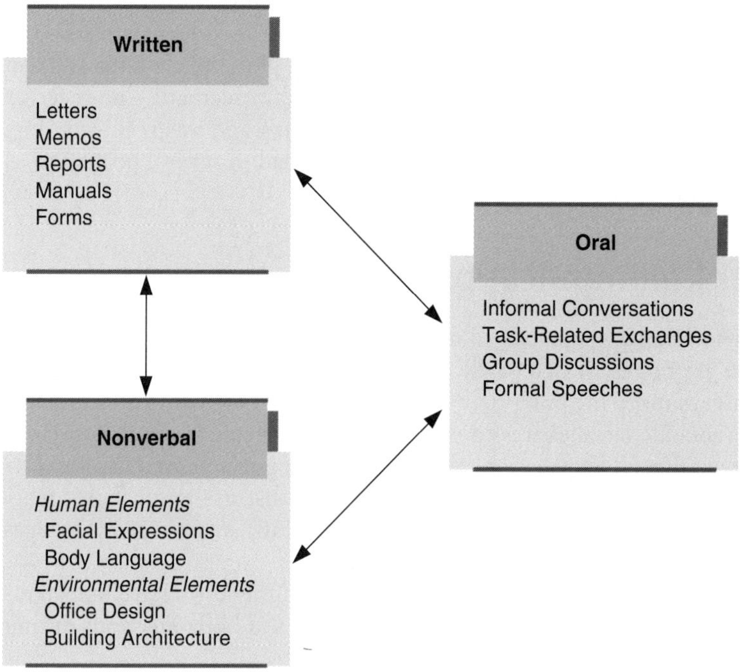

represent attempts to make communication more efficient and information more accessible. A performance appraisal form is an example.

## Oral Communication

The most prevalent form of organizational communication is oral. Oral communication takes place everywhere—in informal conversations, in the process of doing work, in meetings of groups and task forces, and in formal speeches and presentations. Recent studies identified oral communication skills as the number one criterion for hiring new college graduates.[6] Business school leaders have been urged by industry to develop better communication skills in their graduates.[7] Even in Europe, employers are complaining that the number one problem with current graduates is the lack of oral communication skills, citing cultural factors and changes in the educational process as primary causes.[8]

The oral form of communication is particularly powerful because it includes not only speakers' words but also their changes in tone, pitch, speed, and volume. As listeners, people use all of these cues to understand oral messages. Try this example with a friend or work colleague. Say the following sentence several times, each time placing the emphasis on a different word. "The boss gave Joe a raise." See how the meaning changes depending on the emphasis! Moreover, receivers interpret oral messages in the context of previous communications and, perhaps, the reactions of other receivers. (Try saying another sentence before saying the phrase about the boss—such as "Joe is so lazy" or "Joe is such a good worker.") Quite often top management of the organization sets the tone for oral communication throughout the organization.

The popular voicemail has all the characteristics of traditional verbal communication except there is no feedback. The sender just leaves the message on the machine with no feedback or confirmation that the message was, or will be, received. With no confirmation, the sender does know for sure that the message will be received as the sender intended it. Therefore, it may be wise for the receiver of a voicemail to quickly put a message on the sender's voicemail that the original message was received. But then the "great voicemail phone tag" is at its worst! Also the receiver then has an excuse in the event that something goes wrong later and can always say that a return message was left on the sender's voicemail! The receiver can also pass the blame by saying that no such voice message was received. The lack of confirmation, or two-way communication, can lead to several problems, as will be discussed in later sections of this chapter.

## Nonverbal Communication

Nonverbal communication includes all the elements associated with human communication that are not expressed orally or in writing. Sometimes nonverbal communication conveys more meaning than words do. Human elements of nonverbal communication include facial expressions and physical movements, both conscious and unconscious. Facial expressions have been categorized as (1) interest-excitement, (2) enjoyment-joy, (3) surprise-startle, (4) distress-anguish, (5) fear-terror, (6) shame-humiliation, (7) contempt-disgust, and (8) anger-rage.[9] The eyes are the most expressive component of the face.

Physical movements and "body language" are also highly expressive human elements. Body language includes both actual movement and body positions during

Communication is all about sending meaning from one person to another and need not always require words. One of the reasons for the omnipresent cubicles in corporate life is to facilitate communication among coworkers. A new, nonverbal method of communication is now available to help fellow cubicle dwellers let each other know whether or not they are open to interruption and communication. Protoblocs, shown in this picture, are foam-rubber blocks in three shapes and colors, each with special meaning, much like traffic lights. The red cube means "Stop! Do not interrupt under any circumstances!" The green pyramid means the opposite, or that the cubicle occupant is open to interruptions and communication from others. The yellow ball means "Interrupt with caution." Putting the appropriate symbol up on the cubicle wall, in effect, communicates to others whether or not the occupant is ready to communicate. Organizations such as the World Bank, AOL, and Freddie Mac have experimented with this system.

communication. The handshake is a common form of body language. Other examples include making eye contact, which expresses a willingness to communicate; sitting on the edge of a chair, which may indicate nervousness or anxiety; and sitting back with arms folded, which may convey an unwillingness to continue the discussion. Table 10.1 lists examples of nonverbal sources of communication problems in other countries.

Environmental elements such as buildings, office space, and furniture can also convey messages. A spacious office, expensive draperies, plush carpeting, and elegant furniture can combine to remind employees or visitors that they are in the office of the president and CEO of the firm. On the other hand, the small metal desk set in the middle of the shop floor accurately communicates the organizational rank of a first-line supervisor. Thus, office arrangements convey status, power, and prestige and create an atmosphere for doing business. The physical setting can also be instrumental in the development of communication networks, because a centrally located person can more easily control the flow of task-related information.[10]

# The Communication Process

Communication is a social process in which two or more parties exchange information and share meaning. The process is social because it involves two or more people. It is a two-way process and takes place over time rather than instantaneously. The communication process illustrated in Figure 10.3 shows a loop between the source and the receiver.[11] Note the importance of the

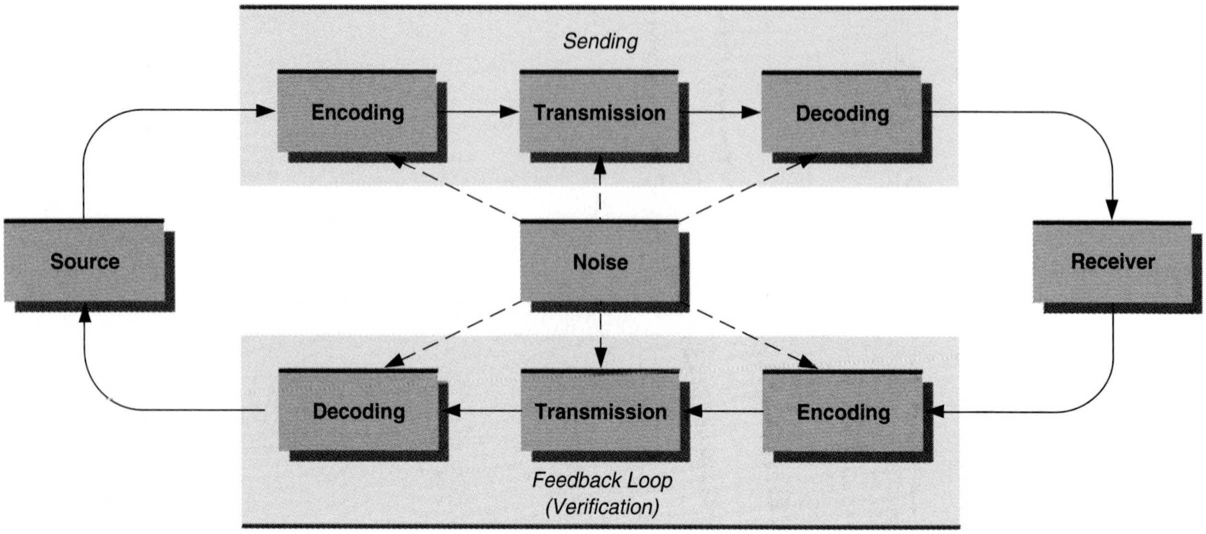


figure 10.3 **The Communication Process**

*The communication process is a loop that connects the sender and the receiver and operates in both directions. Communication is not complete until the original sender knows that the receiver understands the message.*

feedback portion of the loop; upon receiving the message, the receiver responds with a message to the source to verify the communication. Each element of the basic communication process is important. If one part is faulty, the message may not be communicated as it was intended. A simple organizational example might be when a manager attempts to give direction to an employee regarding the order in which to do two tasks. (We refer to this example again in later discussions.) The manager wants to send a message and have the employee understand precisely the meaning the manager intends. Each part of the communication process is described below.

## Source

The **source** is the individual, group, or organization interested in communicating something to another party.

The **source** is the individual, group, or organization interested in communicating something to another party. In group or organizational communication, an individual may send the message on behalf of the organization. The source is responsible for preparing the message, encoding it, and entering it into the transmission medium. In some cases, the receiver chooses the source of information, as when a decision maker seeks information from trusted and knowledgeable individuals.[12] The source in organizational communication is often the manager giving directions to employees.

## Encoding

**Encoding** is the process by which the message is translated from an idea or thought into transmittable symbols.

**Encoding** is the process by which the message is translated from an idea or thought into symbols that can be transmitted. The symbols may be words, numbers, pictures, sounds, or physical gestures and movements. In a simple example, the manager may use words in English as the symbols, usually spoken or written.

In this cartoon, mother and daughter are both speaking English, yet they do not seem to be communicating very well. The meaning of one key word makes such a difference in how each responds. The meaning of that key word really depends on the particular perspective of the sender or the receiver.

Reference: SALLY FORTH reprinted with special permission of King Feature Syndicate.

The source must encode the message in symbols that the receiver can decode properly; that is, the source and the receiver must attach the same meaning to the symbols. When we use the symbols of a common language, we assume those symbols have the same meaning to everyone who uses them. Yet the inherent ambiguity of symbol systems can lead to decoding errors. In verbal communication, for example, some words have different meanings for different people. Parents and children often use the same word, but the differences in their position and age may lead them to interpret words quite differently, as shown in the cartoon. If the manager only speaks Spanish and the employee only speaks German, the message is unlikely to be understood. The meanings of words used by the sender may differ depending on the nonverbal cues, such as facial expression, that the sender transmits along with them.

*"From the point of view of the speakers, language is a symbolic system that they use to communicate." — Michael Agar, author of* Language Shock—Understanding the Culture of Conversation[13]

**Transmission** is the process through which the symbols that represent the message are sent to the receiver.

The **medium** is the channel, or path, through which the message is transmitted.

## Transmission

**Transmission** is the process through which the symbols that carry the message are sent to the receiver. The **medium** is the channel, or path, of transmission. The medium for face-to-face conversation is sound waves. The same conversation conducted over the telephone involves not only sound waves but electrical impulses and the line that connects the two phones. To tell the employee in what order to do tasks, the manager could tell the employee face to face or use the telephone, a memo, email, or voicemail.

Communications media range from interpersonal media, such as talking or touching, to mass media, such as newspapers, magazines, or television broadcasts. Different media have different capacities for carrying information. For example, a face-to-face conversation generally has more carrying capacity than a letter, because it allows the transmission of more than just words.[14] In addition, the medium can help determine the effect the message has on the receiver. Calling a prospective client on the telephone to make a business proposal is a more personal approach than sending a letter and is likely to elicit a different response. It is important that a sender choose the medium that is most likely to correspond to the type of message that needs to be sent and understood.[15]

## Decoding

**Decoding** is the process by which the receiver of the message interprets its meaning.

**Decoding** is the process by which the receiver of the message interprets its meaning. The receiver uses knowledge and experience to interpret the symbols of the message; in some situations, he or she may consult an authority such as a dictionary or a code book. Up to this point the receiver has been relatively inactive, but the receiver becomes more active in the decoding phase. The meaning the receiver attaches to the symbols may be the same as or different from the meaning intended by the source. If the meanings differ, of course, communication breaks down, and misunderstanding is likely. In our example, if the employee does not understand the language or a particular word, then the employee will not have the same meaning as the sender (manager) and may do the tasks in the wrong order or not do them at all.

## Receiver

The **receiver** is the individual, group, or organization that perceives the encoded symbols; the receiver may or may not decode them and try to understand the intended message.

The **receiver** of the message may be an individual, a group, an organization, or an individual acting as the representative of a group. The receiver decides whether to decode the message, whether to make an effort to understand it, and whether to respond. Moreover, the intended receiver may not get the message at all, whereas an unintended receiver may, depending on the medium and symbols used by the source and the attention level of potential receivers. An employee may share the same language (know the symbols) used by the manager but may not want to get the sender's meaning.

The key skill for proper reception of the message is good listening. The receiver may not concentrate on the sender, the message, or the medium such that the message is lost. Listening is an active process that requires as much concentration and effort from the receiver as sending the message does for the sender. The "Building Organizational Behavior Skills" exercise at the end of this chapter gives you an opportunity to assess your personal listening skills.

The expression of emotions by the sender and receiver enters into the communication process at several points. First, the emotions may be part of the message, entering into the encoding process. For example, if the manager's directions are encoded with a sense of emotional urgency—for example, if they are given with a high-pitched or loud voice—the employee may move quickly to follow directions. However, if the message is urgent but the manager's tone of voice is low and does not send urgent signals, employees may not engage in quick action. Second, as the message is decoded, the receiver may let his or her emotions perceive a message different from what the sender intended. Third, emotion-filled feedback from the intended receiver can cause the sender to modify her or his subsequent message.[16]

## Feedback

**Feedback** is the process in which the receiver returns a message to the sender that indicates receipt of the message.

**Feedback** is the receiver's response to the message. Feedback verifies the message by telling the source whether the receiver received and understood the message. The feedback may be as simple as a phone call from the prospective client expressing interest in the business proposal or as complex as a written brief on a complicated point of law sent from an attorney to a judge. In our example, the employee can respond to the manager's directions by a verbal or written response indicating that he or she does or does not understand the message. Feedback could also be nonverbal, as when, in our example, the employee does not do either task. With typical voicemail, the feedback loop is missing, which can lead to many communication problems.

**Noise** is any disturbance in the communication process that interferes with or distorts communication.

## Noise

**Channel noise** is a disturbance in communication that is primarily a function of the medium.

**Noise** is any disturbance in the communication process that interferes with or distorts communication. Noise can be introduced at virtually any point in the communication process. The principal type, called **channel noise**, is associated with

Just as the man in this picture, you sometimes seem to be the only person in the world who is not talking on a cell phone. In addition to facilitating communication between the two people on the phone, cell phones are increasing the noise in the environment as more than 75 million cell phones are in use in the U.S. The ringers are often loud and annoying, and most cell phone users talk too loudly. Communication is easier, faster, and more convenient with cell phones. And excessive noise can be reduced by using the vibration system rather than the audible ringer, keeping calls as short as possible, and not using cell phones in theaters, concerts, plays, lectures, churches, and especially while driving.

the medium.[17] Radio static and "ghost" images on television are examples of channel noise. When noise interferes in the encoding and decoding processes, poor encoding and decoding can result. Emotions that interfere with an intended communication may also be considered a type of noise. An employee may not hear the directions given by the manager owing to noisy machinery on the shop floor or competing input from other people.

Effective communication occurs when information or meaning has been shared by at least two people. Therefore, communication must include the response from the receiver back to the sender. The sender cannot know if the message has been conveyed as intended if there is no feedback from the receiver, as when we leave voicemail. Both parties are responsible for the effectiveness of the communication. The evolution of new technology in recent years presents novel problems in ensuring that communications work as sender and receiver expect them to.

# Electronic Information Processing and Telecommunications

Changes in the workplace are occurring at an astonishing rate. Many innovations are based on new technologies—computerized information processing systems, new types of telecommunication systems, the Internet, emerging intranets, and various combinations of these technologies. Experts have estimated that performance of new information technology (at the same cost) doubles every eighteen months.[18] Managers can now send and receive memos and other documents to one person or a group scattered around the world from their computers using the Internet, and they can do so in their cars or via their notebook computers and cellular phones on the commuter train. Soon they may be doing the same thing on their wristwatches. Employees are now telecommuting from home rather than going to the office every day. The "Mastering Change" box describes one such telecommuter, Jill Fallick, of Morningstar Inc. Whole new industries are developing around information storage, transmission, and retrieval that were not even dreamed of a few years ago.

*"The number of e-mail messages sent on an average day in the U.S. was 3.5 billion in 1999 and is expected to total 8 billion by 2002." — Research by International Data Corporation[19]*

The "office of the future" is here, as was discussed in the opening case. It just may not be in a typical office building. Every office now has a facsimile (fax) machine, a copier, and personal computers, many of them linked into a single integrated system and to numerous databases and electronic mail systems. Car companies advertise that their cars and trucks have equipment for your cellular telephone, computer, and fax machine. The electronic office links managers, clerical employees, professional workers, sales personnel, and often suppliers and customers in a worldwide communication network that uses a combination of computerized data storage, retrieval, and transmission systems. All of this new technology is changing how communication occurs in organizations. A survey of

MASTERING CHANGE

## *Telecommuting at Morningstar Inc.*

Jill Fallick is a product manager for Morningstar Inc., a Chicago-based investment research firm that is a leading provider of investment information, research, and analysis. Its extensive line of Internet, software, and print products provides unbiased data and commentary on mutual funds, U.S. and international equities, closed-end funds, and variable annuities. Established in 1984, Morningstar continues to be the industry's most trusted source on key investment issues of the day. Its reputation is based on the quality of the information that its staff provides to investors.

Rather than lose Jill when her husband was transferred to California, Morningstar asked her to stay with the company and telecommute. Isolated and alone in the extra bedroom of her new home in California, Jill struggled with how to contribute from so far away. Her initial projects did not succeed as well as everyone hoped, but she liked the company, her manager, and the type of work she did, so she kept working. Finally she discovered that the relationships she had built up over the years when she was actually in the office were her strong point. She found that she could be a coach to various project managers on such things as budgeting, market research, and new-product development from her office in California.

Jill is surrounded by electronic equipment. In addition to her own computer, printer, three phone lines, and a cable modem, the company paid for a fax machine and copier to facilitate her work. It took a lot of trust from Jill, as well as from the people back in Chicago, to make Jill's telecommuting successful.

*"The main differences are that when you're telecommuting you're **far more productive** than you can ever hope to be in the office." — Laura Lallos, a former telecommuter with Morningstar Inc.*

Another Morningstar employee, Laura Lallos, returned to Chicago after telecommuting for eighteen months from Oregon. Benefits for Laura included not having to waste time commuting to work and not having to go to endless meetings. However, she also noted that she did lose touch with the daily activities and the people at the company while she was in Oregon. But Jill Fallick is still thankful for the opportunity to telecommute. Her work has really been enhanced now that she can do all of her research on the Internet and complete her new projects all from her home.

References: Robert Barker, "Work à la Modem," *Business Week,* October 4, 1999, pp. 170–176; "Morningstar Names Tim Armour President," *Business Wire* (online), June 10, 1999.

one hundred companies (see Figure 10.4) shows that 17 percent of communication is done through computers.[20]

In fact, the computer-integrated organization is becoming commonplace. Ingersol Milling Machine of Rockford, Illinois, boasts a totally computer-integrated operation in which all major functions—sales, marketing, finance, distribution, and manufacturing—exchange operating information quickly and continuously via computers. For example, product designers can send specifications directly to machines on the factory floor, and accounting personnel receive online information about sales, purchases, and prices instantaneously. The computer system parallels and greatly speeds up the entire process.[21]

Computers are facilitating the increase in telecommuting across the United States and reducing the number of trips to the office to get work done. IBM provided many of their employees with notebook computers and told them to not come to the office but to use the computers to do the work out in the field and send it in electronically.[22] Other companies, such as Motorola and AT&T, have encouraged such telecommuting by employees. Employees report increased productivity,

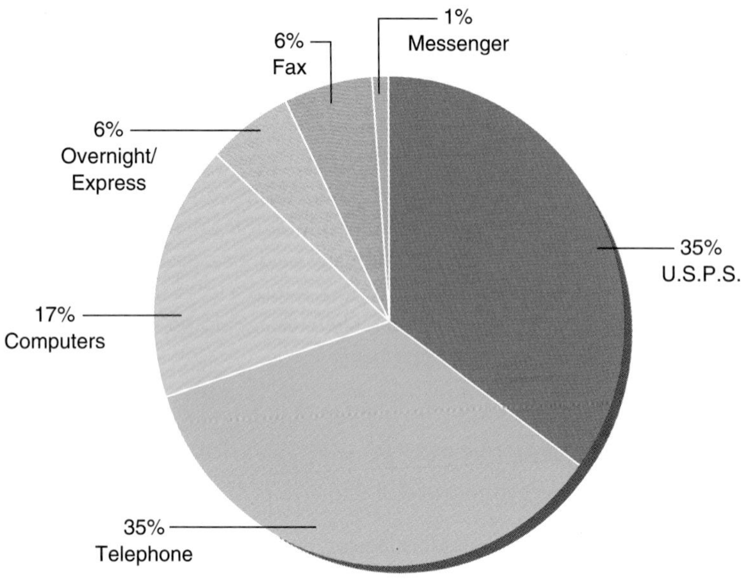


figure 10.4 **Most Frequently Used Methods of Communicating**

*Although the postal service and the telephone remain the most frequently used methods of communication, the use of computers for communication had risen to 17 percent in 1996. This is almost three times the use of fax machines, and with the increasing use of email and the Internet, it is probably still increasing.*

Reference: Reprinted from Barbara Ettone, "Communications Breakdown," *Management Review*, June 1996, p. 10. American Management Association International. Reprinted by permission of American Management Association International, New York. All rights reserved.

less fatigue caused by commuting, reduced commuting expenses, and increased personal freedom. In addition, telecommuting may reduce air pollution and overcrowding. Some employees have reported, however, that they miss the social interaction of the office. Some managers have also expressed concerns about the quantity and quality of the work telecommuting employees do when away from the office.

Research conducted among office workers using a new electronic office system indicated that attitudes toward the system were generally favorable. The users reported improvements in "communications, information access, preparation of written material, and worker collaboration."[23] On the other hand, reduction of face-to-face meetings may depersonalize the office. Some observers are also concerned that companies are installing electronic systems with little consideration for the social structures of the office. As departments adopt computerized information systems, the activities of work groups throughout the organization are likely to become more interdependent, which may alter power relationships among the groups. Most employees quickly learn the system of power, politics, authority, and responsibility in the office. A radical change in work and personal relationships caused by new office technology may disrupt normal ways of accomplishing tasks, thereby reducing productivity. Other potential problems include information overload, loss of records in a "paperless" office, and the dehumanizing effects of electronic equipment. In effect, new information processing and transmission technologies mean new media, symbols, message transmission methods, and networks for organizational communication.[24]

The real increases in organizational productivity due to information technology may come from the ability to communicate in new and different ways rather than from simply speeding up existing communication patterns. For example, to remain competitive in a very challenging global marketplace, companies will need to be able to generate, disseminate, and implement new ideas more effectively.[25] In effect, organizations will become "knowledge-based" learning organizations that are continually generating new ideas to improve themselves. This can only occur when expert knowledge is communicated and available throughout the organization.

One of these new ways of communicating is idea sharing, or knowledge sharing, by sharing information on what practices work best. A computer-based system is necessary to store, organize, and then make available to others the best practices from throughout the company.[26] For example, the large pharmaceutical company,

Eli Lilly, has developed a company-wide intranet for all sixteen thousand employees. This system makes available internal email, corporate policies, and directories and enables information sharing throughout the organization.[27] Electronic information technology is, therefore, speeding up existing communication and developing new types of organizational communication processes with potential new benefits and problems for managers.

# Communication Networks

Communication links individuals and groups in a social system. Initially, task-related communication links develop in an organization so that employees can get the information they need to do their jobs and coordinate their work with that of others in the system. Over a long period, these communication relationships become a sophisticated social system composed of both small-group communication networks and a larger organizational network. These networks structure both the flow and the content of communication and support the organizational structure.[28] The pattern and content of communication also support the culture, beliefs, and value systems that enable the organization to operate.

## Small-Group Networks

To examine interpersonal communication in a small group, we can observe the patterns that emerge as the work of the group proceeds and information flows from some people in the group to others.[29] Four such patterns are shown in Figure 10.5. The lines identify the communication links most frequently used in the groups.

In a **wheel network**, information flows between the person at the end of each spoke and the person in the middle.

In a **chain network**, each member communicates with the person above and below, except for the individuals on each end, who communicate with only one person.

In a **circle network**, each member communicates with the people on both sides but with no one else.

In an **all-channel network**, all members communicate with all other members.

A **wheel network** is a pattern in which information flows between the person at the end of each spoke and the person in the middle. Those on the ends of the spokes do not directly communicate with each other. The wheel network is a feature of the typical work group, where the primary communication occurs between the members and the group manager. In a **chain network**, each member communicates with the person above and below, except for the individuals on each end, who communicate with only one person. The chain network is typical of communication in a vertical hierarchy, in which most communication travels up and down the chain of command. Each person in a circle network communicates with the people on both sides but not with anyone else. The **circle network** often is found in task forces and committees. Finally, in an **all-channel network**, all the members communicate with all the other members. The all-channel network often is found in informal groups that have no formal structure, leader, or task to accomplish.

Communication may be more easily distorted by noise when much is being communicated or when the communication must travel a great distance.[30] Improvements in electronic communication technology, such as computerized mail systems and intranets, are reducing this effect. A relatively central position gives a person an opportunity to communicate with all of the other members, so a member in a relatively central position can control the information flow and may become a leader of the group. This leadership position is separate and distinct from the formal group structure, although a central person in a group may also emerge as a formal group leader over a long period.

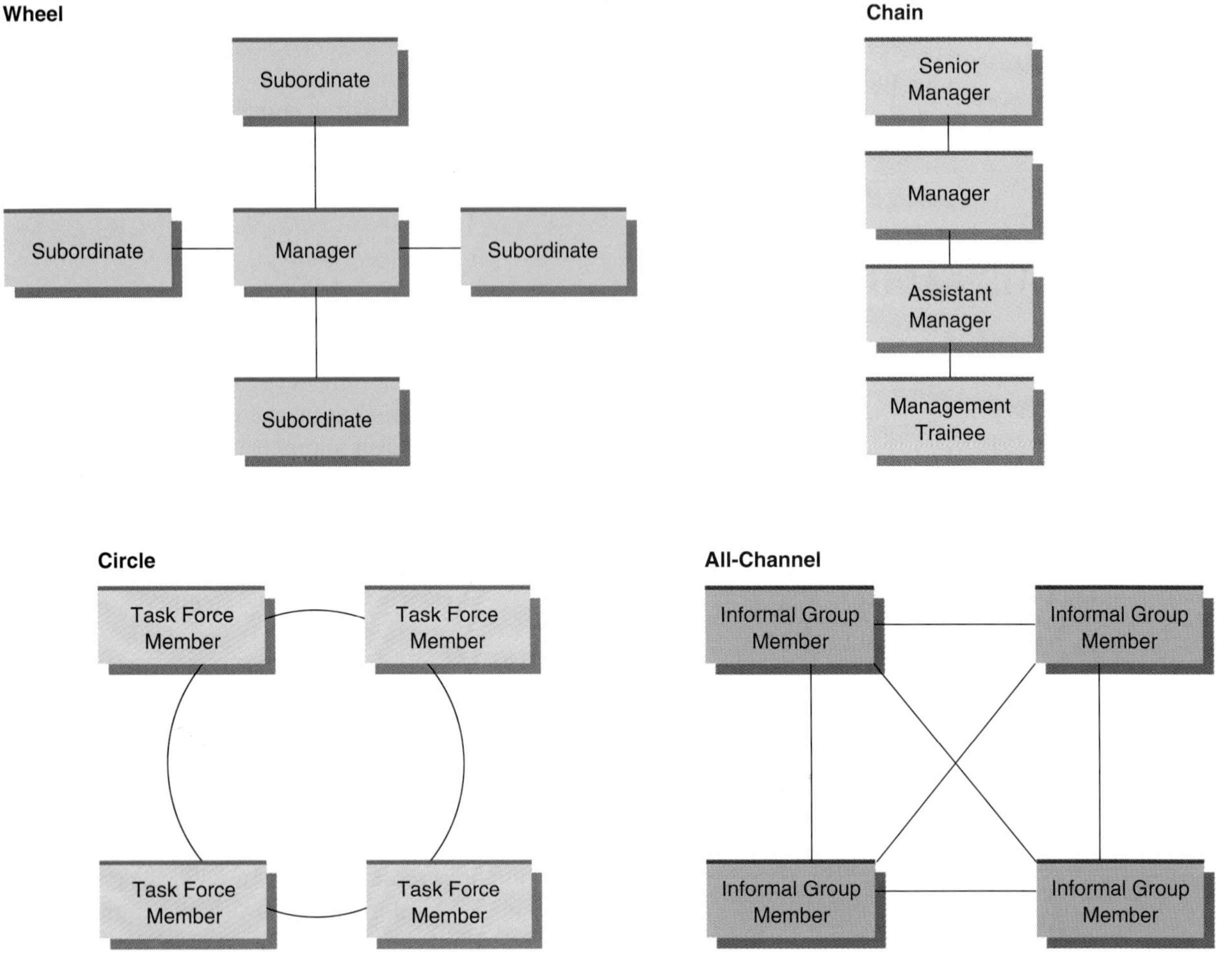


**figure 10.5 Small-Group Communication Networks**

*These four types of communication networks are the most common in organizations. The lines represent the most frequently used communication links in small groups.*

**Communication networks** form spontaneously and naturally as the interactions among workers continue over time.

**Communication networks** form spontaneously and naturally as interactions among workers continue. They are rarely permanent, since they change as the tasks, interactions, and memberships change. The patterns and characteristics of small-group communication networks are determined by the factors summarized in Table 10.2. The task is crucial in determining the pattern of the network. If the group's primary task is decision making, an all-channel network may develop to provide the information needed to evaluate all possible alternatives. If, however, the group's task mainly involves the sequential execution of individual tasks, a chain or wheel network is more likely, because communication among members may not be important to the completion of the tasks.

The environment (the type of room in which the group works or meets, the seating arrangement, the placement of chairs and tables, the geographical disper-

table 10.2

**Factors Influencing the Development of Small-Group Networks**

| Factor | Example |
|---|---|
| Task | Decision making<br>Sequential production |
| Environment | Type of room, placement of chairs and tables, dispersion of members |
| Personal Characteristics | Expertise, openness, speaking ability, degree of familiarity among group members |
| Group Performance Factors | Composition, size, norms, cohesiveness |

sion, and other aspects of the group's setting) can affect the frequency and types of interactions among members. For example, if most members work on the same floor of an office building, the members who work three floors down may be considered outsiders and develop weaker communication ties to the group. They may even form a separate communication network.

Personal factors also influence the development of the communication network. These include technical expertise, openness, speaking ability, and the degree to which members are acquainted with one another. For example, in a group concerned mainly with highly technical problems, the person with the most expertise may dominate the communication flow during a meeting.

The group performance factors that influence the communication network include composition, size, norms, and cohesiveness. For example, group norms in one organization may encourage open communication across different levels and functional units, whereas the norms in another organization may discourage such lateral and diagonal communication. These performance factors are discussed in Chapter 11.

Because the outcome of the group's efforts depends on the coordinated action of its members, the communication network strongly influences group effectiveness. Thus, to develop effective working relationships in the organization, managers need to make a special effort to manage the flow of information and the development of communication networks. Managers can, for example, arrange offices and work spaces to foster communication among certain employees. Managers may also attempt to involve members who typically contribute little during discussions by asking them direct questions such as "What do you think, Tom?" or "Maria, please tell us how this problem is handled in your district." Methods such as the nominal group technique, discussed in Chapter 15, can also encourage participation.

One other factor that is becoming increasingly important in the development of communication networks is the advent of electronic groups, fostered by electronic distribution lists, chat rooms, discussion boards, and other computer networking systems. This form of communication results in a network of people who may have little or no face-to-face communication but still may be considered a group communication network. For example, your professor is probably a member of an electronic group of other professors who share an interest in the topic of this course. Through the electronic group, they keep up with new ideas in the field.

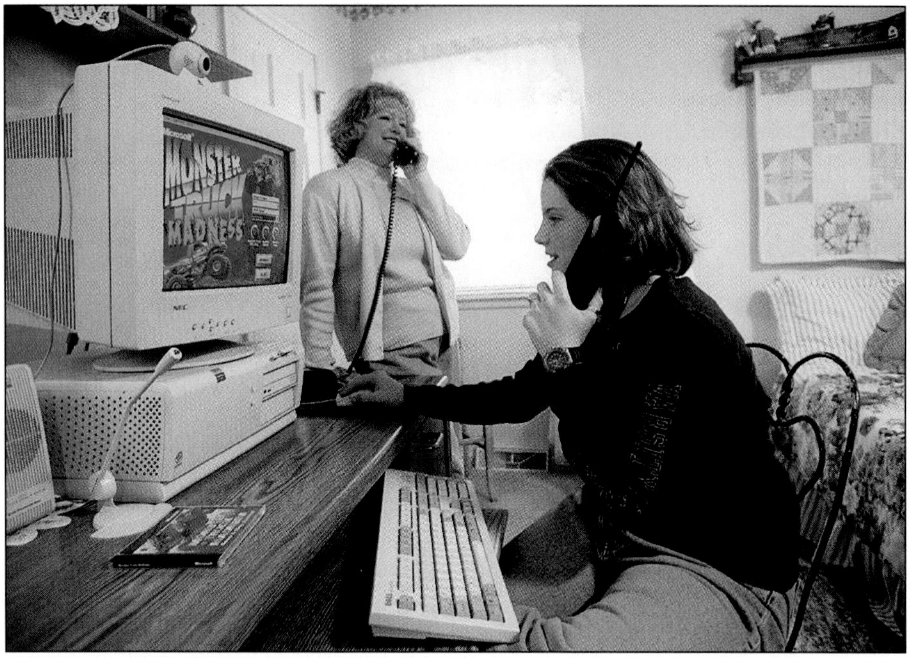


This family is participating in an experiment that networks virtually every communication system in the house. The ION system integrates their home PC, both telephones, and a small video camera so they can play video games against and talk with opponents around the world, participate in a video conference with coworkers anywhere in the world, and stay linked with family and friends. ION stands for "integrated on-demand network" and is being offered by Sprint in partnership with Cisco. With this new technology, communication networks may now be available at home as well as at work.

## Organizational Communication Networks

An organization chart shows reporting relationships from the line worker up to the CEO of the firm. The lines of an organization chart may also represent channels of communication through which information flows, yet communication may also follow paths that cross traditional reporting lines. Information moves not only from the top down—from CEO to group members—but upward from group members to the CEO. In fact, a good flow of information to the CEO is an important determinant of the organization's success.[31]

Several companies have realized that the key to their continuing success was improved internal communication. General Motors was known for its extremely formal, top-down communication system. In the mid-1980s, however, the formality of its system came under fire from many sources: labor leaders, employees, managers, and even Ross Perot, who became a major shareholder in GM after he sold his company, Electronic Data Systems, to GM in 1984 for $250 million. GM's response was to embark on a massive communication improvement program that included sending employees to public-speaking workshops, improving the more than 350 publications it sends out, providing videotapes of management meetings to employees, and using satellite links between headquarters and field operations to establish two-way conversations around the world.[32]

Downward communication generally provides directions, whereas upward communication provides feedback to top management. Communication that flows horizontally or crosses traditional reporting lines usually is related to task performance. For example, a design engineer, a manufacturing engineer, and a quality engineer may communicate about the details of a particular product design, thus making it easy to manufacture and inspect. Horizontal communication often travels faster than vertical communication because it need not follow organizational protocols and procedures.

Organizational communication networks may diverge from reporting relationships as employees seek better information with which to do their jobs. Employees

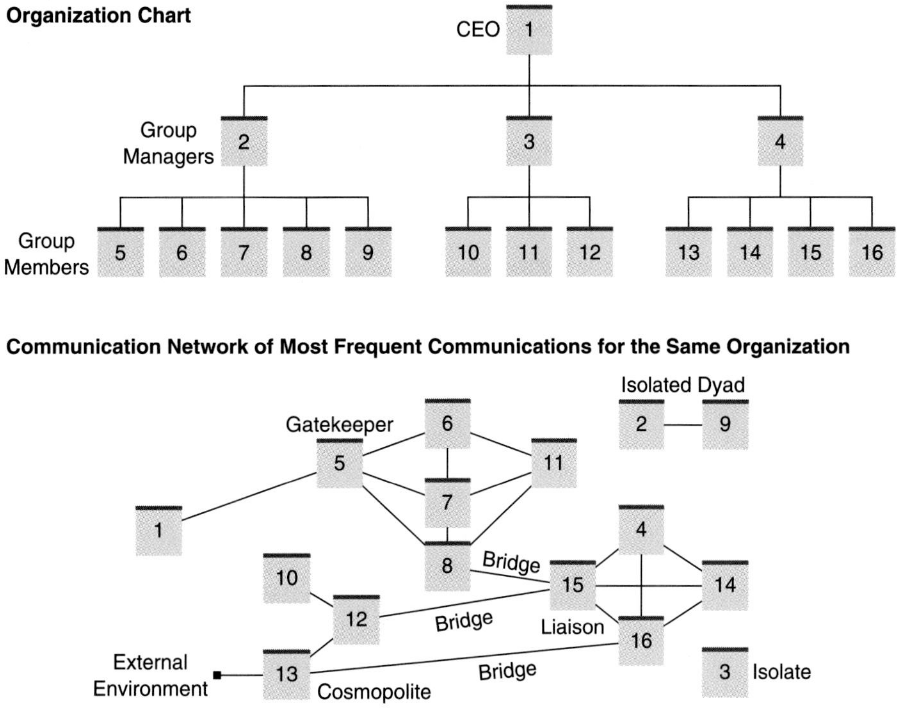


**figure 10.6**

**Comparison of an Organization Chart and the Organization's Communication Network**

*A simple organization chart compared with actual communication patterns. Note how the actual communication patterns are quite different from the reporting relationships shown in the organization chart.*

often find that the easiest way to get their jobs done or to obtain the necessary information is to go directly to employees in other departments rather than through the formal channels shown on the organization chart. Figure 10.6 shows a simple organization chart and the organization's real communication network. The communication network links the individuals who most frequently communicate with one another; the firm's CEO, for example, communicates most often with employee 5. (This does not mean that individuals not linked in the communication network never communicate, but only that their communications are relatively infrequent.) Perhaps the CEO and the employee interact frequently outside of work, in church, or service organizations such as Kiwanis, or at sporting events. Such interactions may lead to close friendships that carry over into business relationships. The figure also shows that the group managers do not have important roles in the communication network, contrary to commonsense expectations.

The gatekeeper has a strategic position in the network that allows him or her to control information moving in either direction through a channel.

The liaison serves as a bridge between groups, tying groups together and facilitating the communication flow needed to integrate group activities.

The cosmopolite links the organization to the external environment and may also be an opinion leader in the group.

The isolate and the isolated dyad tend to work alone and to interact and communicate little with others.

The roles that people play in organizational communication networks can be analyzed in terms of their contribution to the functioning of the network.[33] The most important roles are labeled in the bottom portion of Figure 10.6. A **gatekeeper** (employee 5) has a strategic position in the network that allows him or her to control information moving in either direction through a channel. A **liaison** (employee 15) serves as a bridge between groups, tying groups together and facilitating the communication flow needed to integrate group activities. Employee 13 performs the interesting function of **cosmopolite**, who links the organization to the external environment by, for instance, attending conventions and trade shows, keeping up with outside technological innovations, and having more frequent contact with sources outside the organization. This person may also be an opinion leader in the group. Finally, the **isolate** (employee 3) and the **isolated dyad** (employees 2 and 9) tend to work alone and to interact and communicate little with others.

Each of these roles and functions plays an important part in the overall functioning of the communication network and in the organization as a whole. Understanding these roles can help both managers and group members facilitate communication. For instance, the manager who wants to be sure that the CEO receives certain information is well advised to go through the gatekeeper. If the employee who has the technical knowledge necessary for a particular project is an isolate, the manager can take special steps to integrate the employee into the communication network for the duration of the project.

Recent research has indicated some possible negative impacts of communication networks. Employee turnover has been shown to occur in clusters related to employee communication networks.[34] That is, employees who communicate regularly in a network may share feelings about the organization and thus influence one another's intentions to stay or quit. Communication networks therefore may have both positive and negative consequences.

As we discuss in Chapters 16 and 17, a primary function of organizational structure is to coordinate the activities of many people doing specialized tasks. Communication networks in organizations provide this much-needed integration.[35] In fact, in some ways, communication patterns influence organizational structure.[36] Some companies are finding that the need for better communication forces them to create smaller divisions. The fewer managerial levels and improved team spirit of these divisions tend to enhance communication flows.[37] Ford Motor Company is attempting to increase communication through the use of its computerized internal communication network, or intranet, as described in the "Talking Technology" box.

TALKING TECHNOLOGY

## *Ford Uses the Intranet to Link Employees*

Ford has been a leader in the use of information-sharing technologies via an intranet since the early 1990s, when the company linked engineering and design centers in the United States, Europe, and Asia in the development of the new Taurus automobile, introduced in 1996. Later in the decade, Ford went even further by developing intranet links in almost all other areas of the company as well. Ford and various suppliers have developed net caching systems so that all employees can link to the Internet and through the intranet to increase total employee productivity. One system will enable employees to link to the company's human resource system, that includes an employee expense tracking system.

Another system lets employees do all of their travel expense reporting via the company intranet. Those employees who travel for business can utilize the new system for submitting and tracking business expenses online—in multiple languages, currencies, and country reporting. Filing of expenses and getting reimbursed are done much more quickly, and the information is available to managers for approval, analysis, and control. As global companies like Ford increase worldwide employee travel, intranet-based expense systems can play an important role in keeping track of travel expenses. Capturing and analyzing expense reports enables the company to better track and allocate expenses to projects and provides the information necessary to bargain and negotiate with travel-related vendors—for example, data on hotels, airlines, rental car companies, airport parking, and value-added taxes. Even credit card expense data can be imported for proper allocation, recording, and payment. Ford is using its intranet linkages to provide more ways to link employees to each other and to company systems, all in the effort to increase individual and corporate productivity.

References: "Captura Software Announces Pilot Program at Ford Motor Company: Web-Enabling Traditional Paper-Based Expenses Management Practices," *Business Wire,* September 29, 1999; "Authoria and AG Consulting Partner to Deliver HR and Benefits Solutions," *Business Wire,* September 27, 1999; "Ford Selects the Network Appliance NetCache Solution for Global, Enterprise Web Infrastructure," *Business Wire,* July 19, 1999.

# Managing Communication

Communication **fidelity** is the degree of correspondence between the message intended by the source and the message understood by the receiver.

As simple as the process of communication may seem, messages are not always understood. The degree of correspondence between the message intended by the source and the message understood by the receiver is called communication **fidelity**.[38] Fidelity can be diminished anywhere in the communication process, from the source to the feedback. Moreover, organizations may have characteristics that impede the flow of information. Table 10.3 summarizes the most common types of breakdowns and barriers in organizational communication.

## Improving the Communication Process

To improve organizational communication one must understand potential problems. Using the basic communication process, we can identify several ways to overcome typical problems.

**Source** The source may intentionally withhold or filter information on the assumption that the receiver does not need it to understand the communication. Withholding information, however, may render the message meaningless or cause an erroneous interpretation. For example, during a performance appraisal interview, a manager may not tell the employee all of the sources of information being used to make the evaluation, thinking that the employee does not need to know them. If the employee knew, however, he or she might be able to explain certain behaviors or otherwise alter the manager's perspective of the evaluation and thereby make it more accurate. Filtering may be more likely to occur in electronic communication such as email or voicemail since they carry an implied importance for brevity and conciseness. Selective filtering may cause a breakdown in communication that cannot be repaired, even with good follow-up communication.[39]

To avoid filtering, the communicator needs to understand why it occurs. Filtering can result from lack of understanding of the receiver's position, from the sender's need to protect his or her own power by limiting the receiver's access to information, or from doubts about what the receiver might do with the information. The sender's primary concern, however, should be the message. In essence, the sender must determine exactly what message he or she wants the receiver to understand, send the receiver enough information to understand the message but not enough to create an overload, and trust the receiver to use the information properly.

table 10.3 **Communication Problems in Organizations**

| Root of the Problem | Type of Problem |
|---|---|
| Source | Filtering |
| Encoding and Decoding | Lack of common experience<br>Semantics; jargon<br>Medium problems |
| Receiver | Selective attention<br>Value judgments<br>Lack of source credibility<br>Overload |
| Feedback | Omission |
| Organizational Factors | Noise<br>Status differences<br>Time pressures<br>Overload<br>Communication structure |

**Encoding and Decoding** Encoding and decoding problems occur as the message is translated into or from the symbols used in transmission. Such problems can relate to the meaning of the symbols or to the transmission itself. As Table 10.3 shows, encoding and decoding problems include lack of common experience between source and receiver, problems related to semantics and the use of jargon, and difficulties with the medium.

Clearly, the source and the receiver must share a common experience with the symbols that express the message if they are to encode and decode them in exactly the same way. People who speak different languages or come from different cultural backgrounds may experience problems of this sort. But even people who speak the same language can misunderstand each other.

Semantics is the study of language forms.

**Semantics** is the study of language forms, and semantic problems occur when people attribute different meanings to the same words or language forms. For example, when discussing a problem employee, the division head may tell her assistant, "We need to get rid of this problem." The division head may have meant that the employee should be scheduled for more training or transferred to another division. However, the assistant may interpret the statement differently and fire the problem employee.

Jargon is the specialized or technical language of a trade, profession, or social group.

The specialized or technical language of a trade, field, profession, or social group is called **jargon**. Jargon may be a hybrid of standard language and the specialized language of a group. For example, experts in the computer field use terms such as "gigs," "megs," "RAM," and "bandwidth" that have no meaning to those unfamiliar with computers. The use of jargon makes communication within a close group of colleagues more efficient and meaningful, but outside the group it has the opposite effect. Sometimes a source person comfortable with jargon uses it unknowingly in an attempt to communicate with receivers who do not understand it, thus causing a communication breakdown. In other cases, the source may use jargon intentionally to obscure meaning or to show outsiders that he or she belongs to the group that uses the language.

The use of jargon is acceptable if the receiver is familiar with it. Otherwise, it should be avoided. Repeating a jargon-containing message in clearer terms should help the receiver understand it. In general, the source and the receiver should clarify the set of symbols to be used before they communicate. Also, the receiver can ask questions frequently and, if necessary, ask the source to repeat all or part of the message.

The source must send the message through a medium appropriate to the message itself and to the intended receiver. For example, a commercial run on an AM radio station will not have its intended effect if the people in the desired market segment listen only to FM radio.

**Receiver** Several communication problems originate in the receiver, including problems with selective attention, value judgments, source credibility, and overload. Selective attention exists when the receiver attends only to selected parts of a message—a frequent occurrence with oral communication. For example, in a college class, some students may hear only part of the professor's lecture as their minds wander to other topics. To focus receivers' attention on the message, senders often engage in attention-getting behaviors such as varying the volume, repeating the message, and offering rewards.

Value judgments are influenced by the degree to which a message reinforces or challenges the receiver's basic personal beliefs. If a message reinforces the receiver's beliefs, he or she may pay close attention and believe it completely, without examination. On the other hand, if the message challenges those beliefs, the receiver may entirely discount it. Thus, if a firm's sales manager predicts that the demand for new baby care products will increase substantially over the next two years, he may ignore reports that the birthrate is declining.

The receiver may also judge the credibility of the source of the message. If the source is perceived to be an expert in the field, the listener may pay close attention to the message and believe it. Conversely, if the receiver has little respect for the source, he or she may disregard the message. The receiver considers both the message and the source in making value judgments and determining credibility. An expert in nuclear physics may be viewed as a credible source if the issue is building a nuclear power plant, yet the same person's evaluation of the birthrate may be disregarded, perhaps correctly. This is one reason that trial lawyers ask expert witnesses about their education and experience at the beginning of testimony: to establish credibility.

A receiver experiencing communication overload is receiving more information than she or he can process. In organizations, this can happen very easily; a receiver can be bombarded with computer-generated reports and messages from superiors, peers, and sources outside the organization. It is not unusual for middle managers or telecommuters to receive one hundred email messages per day. Unable to take in all the messages, decode them, understand them, and act on them, the receiver may use selective attention and value judgments to focus on the messages that seem most important. Although this type of selective attention is necessary for survival in an information-glutted environment, it may mean that vital information is lost or overlooked.

Verification is the feedback portion of communication in which the receiver sends a message to the source indicating receipt of the message and the degree to which he or she understood the message.

Feedback The purpose of feedback is **verification**, in which the receiver sends a message to the source indicating receipt of the message and the degree to which it was understood. Lack of feedback can cause at least two problems. First, the source may need to send another message that depends on the response to the first; if the source receives no feedback, the source may not send the second message or may be forced to send the original message again. Second, the receiver may act on the unverified message; if the receiver misunderstood the message, the resulting act may be inappropriate.

Because feedback is so important, the source must actively seek it and the receiver must supply it. Often it is appropriate for the receiver to repeat the original message as an introduction to the response, although the medium or symbols used may be different. Nonverbal cues can provide instantaneous feedback. These include body language and facial expressions, such as anger and disbelief.[40]

The source needs to be concerned with the message, the symbols, the medium, and the feedback from the receiver. Of course, the receiver is concerned with these things too, but from a different point of view. In general, the receiver needs to be source oriented just as the source needs to be receiver oriented. Table 10.4 gives specific suggestions for improving the communication process.

## Improving Organizational Factors in Communication

Organizational factors that can create communication breakdowns or barriers include noise, status differences, time pressures, and overload. As previously stated, disturbances anywhere in the organization can distort or interrupt meaningful communication. Thus, the noise created by a rumored takeover can disrupt the orderly flow of task-related information. Status differences between source and receiver can cause some of the communication problems just discussed. For example, a firm's chief executive officer may pay little attention to communications from employees far lower on the organization chart, and employees may pay little attention to communications from the CEO. Both are instances of selective attention table 10.4 **Improving the Communication Process**

| Focus | Source | | Receiver | |
|---|---|---|---|---|
| | Question | Corrective Action | Question | Corrective Action |
| Message | What idea or thought are you trying to get across? | Give more information. Give less information. Give entire message. | What idea or thought does the sender want you to understand? | Listen carefully to the entire message, not just to part of it. |
| Symbols | Does the receiver use the same symbols, words, jargon? | Say it another way. Employ repetition. Use receiver's language or jargon. Before sending, clarify symbols to be used. | What symbols are being used—for example, foreign language, technical jargon? | Clarify symbols before communication begins. Ask questions. Ask sender to repeat message. |
| Medium | Is this a channel that the receiver monitors regularly? Sometimes? Never? | Use multiple media. Change medium. Increase volume (loudness). | What medium or media is the sender using? | Monitor several media. |
| Feedback | What is the receiver's reaction to your message? | Pay attention to the feedback, especially nonverbal cues. Ask questions. | Did you correctly interpret the message? | Repeat message. |

prompted by the organization's status system. Time pressures and communication overloads are also detrimental to communication. When the receiver is not allowed enough time to understand incoming messages, or when there are too many messages, he or she may misunderstand or ignore some of them. Effective organizational communication provides the right information to the right person at the right time and in the right form.

The **grapevine** is an informal system of communication that coexists with the formal system.

**Reduce Noise** Noise is a primary barrier to effective organizational communication. A common form of noise is the rumor **grapevine**, an informal system of communication that coexists with the formal system.[41] The grapevine usually transmits information faster than official channels do. Because the accuracy of this information often is quite low, however, the grapevine can distort organizational communication. Management can reduce the effects of the distortion by using the grapevine as an additional channel for disseminating of information and by constantly monitoring it for accuracy.

**Foster Informal Communication** Thomas J. Peters and Robert H. Waterman described communication in well-run companies as "a vast network of informal, open communications."[42] Informal communication fosters mutual trust, which minimizes the effects of status differences. Open communication can also contribute to better understanding between diverse groups in an organization. Monsanto Company created fifteen-member teams in its Agricultural Group, the primary objective being increasing communication and awareness among various diverse groups. Its Chemical Group set up diversity pairs of one supervisor and one worker to increase communication and awareness. In both cases, Monsanto found that increasing communication between people who were different paid handsome benefits for the organization.[43] Open communication also allows information to be communicated when it is needed rather than when the formal information system allows it to emerge. Peters and Waterman further describe communication in effective companies as chaotic and intense, supported by the reward structure and the physical arrangement of the facilities. This means that the performance appraisal and reward system, offices, meeting rooms, and work areas are designed to encourage frequent, unscheduled, and unstructured communication throughout the organization.

**Develop a Balanced Information System** Many large organizations have developed elaborate formal information systems to cope with the potential problems of information overload and time pressures. In many cases, however, the systems have created problems rather than solving them. Often they produce more information than managers and decision makers can comprehend and use in their jobs. They also often use only formal communication channels and ignore various informal lines of communication. Furthermore, the systems frequently provide whatever information the computer is set up to provide—information that may not apply to the most pressing problem at hand. The result of all these drawbacks is loss of communication effectiveness.

Organizations need to balance information load and information-processing capabilities.[44] In other words, they must take care not to generate more information than people can handle. It is useless to produce sophisticated statistical reports that managers have no time to read. Furthermore, the new technologies that are making more information available to managers and decision makers must be unified to produce usable information.[45] Information production, storage, and processing capabilities must be compatible with one another and, equally important, with the needs of the organization.

Some companies—for example, General Electric, McDonnell Douglas, Anheuser-Busch, and McDonald's—have formalized an upward communication system that uses a corporate "ombudsman" position.[46] A highly placed executive who is available outside the formal chain of command to hear employees' complaints usually holds this position. The system provides an opportunity for disgruntled employees to complain without fear of losing their jobs and may help some companies achieve a balanced communication system.

# Synopsis

Communication is the process by which two parties exchange information and share meaning. It plays a role in every organizational activity. The purposes of communication in organizations are to achieve coordinated action, to share information, and to express feelings and emotions.

People in organizations communicate through written, oral, and nonverbal means. Written communications include letters, memos, email, reports, and the like. Oral communication is the type most commonly used. Personal elements, such as facial expressions and body language, and environmental elements, such as office design, are forms of nonverbal communication.

Communication among individuals, groups, or organizations is a process in which a source sends a message and a receiver responds. The source encodes a message into symbols and transmits it through a medium to the receiver, who decodes the symbols. The receiver then responds with feedback, an attempt to verify the meaning of the original message. Noise—anything that distorts or interrupts communication—may interfere in virtually any stage of the process.

The fully integrated communication-information office system—the electronic office—links personnel in a communication network through a combination of computers and electronic transmission systems. The full range of effects of such systems has yet to be fully realized.

Communication networks are systems of information exchange within organizations. Patterns of communication emerge as information flows from person to person in a group. Typical small-group communication networks include the wheel, chain, circle, and all-channel networks.

The organizational communication network, which constitutes the real communication links in an organization, usually differs from the arrangement on an organization chart. Roles in organizational communication networks include those of gatekeeper, liaison, cosmopolite, and isolate.

Managing communication in organizations involves understanding the numerous problems that can interfere with effective communication. Problems may arise from the communication process itself and from organizational factors such as status differences.

## Discussion Questions

1. How is communication in organizations an individual process as well as an organizational process?
2. Discuss the three primary purposes of organizational communication.
3. Describe a situation in which you tried to carry on a conversation when no one was listening. Were any messages sent during the "conversation"?
4. A college classroom is a forum for a typical attempt at communication as the professor tries to communicate the subject to the students. Describe classroom communication in terms of the basic communication process outlined in the chapter.
5. Is there a communication network (other than professor-to-student) in the class in which you are using this book? If so, identify the specific roles that people play in the network. If not, why has no network developed? What would be the benefits of having a communication network in this class?
6. Why might educators typically focus most communication training on the written and oral methods and pay little attention to the nonverbal methods? Do you think that more training emphasis should be placed on nonverbal communication? Why or why not?
7. Is the typical classroom means of transferring information from professor to student an effective form of communication? Where does it break down? What are the communication problems in the college classroom?
8. Whose responsibility is it to solve classroom communication problems: the students', the professor's, or the administration's?
9. Have you ever worked in an organization in which communication was a problem? If so, what were some causes of the problem?
10. What methods were used, or should have been used, to improve communication in the situation you described in question 9?
11. Would the use of advanced computer information processing or telecommunications have helped solve the communications problem you described in question 9?
12. What types of communication problems will new telecommunications methods probably be able to solve? Why?
13. What types of communications would NOT be appropriate to send by email? Or by voicemail?
14. Which steps in the communication process are usually left out, or at least, poorly done when email and voicemail are used for communication?

# Organizational Behavior Case for Discussion

## Is Big Brother Reading Your Email?

As millions of workers gain access to the Internet at work, highly volatile employee issues about appropriate use of company resources and privacy are becoming increasingly salient these days. United Parcel Service of America Inc. caught one employee using a company computer to run a personal business. Lockheed Martin Corp. dismissed an employee for causing a flood of personal emails that choked the company mail system. What are some of the questionable ways that employees could use the company computer, email system, and the Internet? Is it okay for employees to engage in Internet stock trading to make a quick profit? Is it permissible to use the Internet to look for another job? Most companies encourage employees to be involved in civic issues, so why not use the company email system to promote your favorite political candidate or issue?

Corporate policy on the subject is highly encouraged by corporate lawyers. For example, Boeing Co. has a policy that allows employees to use corporate faxes, Internet access, and the email system for personal reasons as long as it does not cause embarrassment to the company and is of appropriate duration and frequency. Some activities, such as chain letters, obscenity, and political and religious messages are strictly prohibited. Ameritech Corp., for example, expressly forbids the use of computers and other company equipment for any use other than business purposes. Other companies may be more, or less, restrictive, but make it clear that the company may have access to virtually any document or activity generated on company computers and related systems. Twenty-seven percent of large U.S. firms were checking employee email in 1999, a significant increase from just two years earlier. Some experts claim that this is no different than employee use of any company resource for personal use. On the other hand, some employee rights groups are challenging such unimpeded access to employee files by employers.

Corporations now have the capability to monitor every use of company computers. A new product by Telemate.Net can monitor a company's network and print out a report that identifies every Internet use and can report by frequency, by department, and other categories. Some of its clients in 1999 were Arthur Andersen and Co., Maytag Corp., Philip Morris Cos., and Sears, Roebuck and Co. It can also report by individual employee and show game playing, job hunting, pornographic sites, and shopping. At Wolverton & Associates, a civil engineering company in Georgia, the information technology manager found that 4 percent of the company's total bandwidth was being used by employees downloading music from broadcast.com. And that was only the third-most-visited site by employees. Surveillance technology is certain to become even more sophisticated as companies become more intent on keeping employees doing real work on their computers. So, big brother is watching!

### Case Questions

1. Have you ever used company computers to do things that are not job related? Did you feel guilty about that? Did you even consider that it might be against company policy?
2. What are the implications of this for you as an employee whose job involves extensive use of company computers to do your job? How can you protect yourself from being accused by the company of misusing company property for personal reasons?
3. What are the issues for a first line manager who may have to monitor computer use by her or his employees?

References: Michael J. McCarthy, "Managers & Managing: Bosses and Workers Face Internet Dilemma—Highly Sophisticated Software Creates Combustible Issue Between Managers and Staff," *Wall Street Journal Europe*, October 26, 1999, p. 4; Michael J. McCarthy, "Managers & Managing: Bosses and Workers Face Internet Dilemma—Internet Empowerment Comes with Unexpected Twists on Uncharted Ethical Road," *Wall Street Journal Europe*, October 26, 1999, p. 4; Michael J. McCarthy, "Now the Boss Knows Where You're Clicking," *Wall Street Journal*, October 21, 1999, p. B1; Michael J. McCarthy, "Virtual Morality: A New Workplace Quandary," *Wall Street Journal*, October 21, 1999, p. Bl.

# Experiencing Organizational Behavior

## The Importance of Feedback in Oral Communication

**Purpose:** This exercise demonstrates the importance of feedback in oral communication.

**Format:** You will be an observer or play the role of either a manager or an assistant manager trying to tell a coworker where a package of important materials is to be picked up. The observer's role is to make sure the other two participants follow the rules and to observe and record any interesting occurrences.

**Procedure:** The instructor will divide the class into groups of three. (Any extra members can be roving observers.) The three people in each group will take the roles of manager, assistant manager, and observer. In the second trial, the manager and the assistant manager will switch roles.

*Trial 1:* The manager and the assistant manager should turn their backs to each other so that neither can see the other. Here is the situation: The manager is in another city that he or she is not familiar with but that the assistant manager knows quite well. The manager needs to find the office of a supplier to pick up drawings of a critical component of the company's main product. The supplier will be closing for the day in a few minutes; the drawings must be picked up before closing time. The manager has called the assistant manager to get directions to the office. However, the connection is faulty; the manager can hear the assistant manager, but the assistant manager can hear only enough to know the manager is on the line. The manager has redialed once, but there was no improvement in the connection. Now there is no time to lose. The manager has decided to get the directions from the assistant without asking questions.

Just before the exercise begins, the instructor will give the assistant manager a detailed map of the city that shows the locations of the supplier's office and the manager. The map will include a number of turns, stops, stoplights, intersections, and shopping centers between these locations. The assistant manager can study it for no longer than a minute or two. When the instructor gives the direction to start, the assistant manager describes to the manager how to get from his or her present location to the supplier's office. As the assistant manager gives the directions, the manager draws the map on a piece of paper.

The observer makes sure that no questions are asked, records the beginning and ending times, and notes how the assistant manager tries to communicate particularly difficult points (including points about which the manager obviously wants to ask questions) and any other noteworthy occurrences.

After all pairs have finished, each observer "grades" the quality of the manager's map by comparing it with the original and counting the number of obvious mistakes. The instructor will ask a few managers who believe they have drawn good maps to tell the rest of the class how to get to the supplier's office.

*Trial 2:* In trial 2, the manager and the assistant manager switch roles, and a second map is passed out to the new assistant managers. The situation is the same as in the first trial, except that the telephones are working properly and the manager can ask questions of the assistant manager. The observer's role is the same as in trial 1—recording the beginning and ending times, the methods of communication, and other noteworthy occurrences.

After all pairs have finished, the observers grade the maps, just as in the first trial. The instructor then selects a few managers to tell the rest of the class how to get to the supplier's office. The subsequent class discussion should center on the experiences of the class members and the follow-up questions.

### Follow-up Questions:

1. Which trial resulted in more accurate maps? Why?
2. Which trial took longer? Why?
3. How did you feel when a question needed to be asked but could not be asked in trial 1? Was your confidence in the final result affected differently in the two trials?

# Building Organizational Behavior Skills

## Diagnosing Your Listening Skills

**Introduction:** Good listening skills are essential for effective communication and are often overlooked when communication is analyzed. This self-assessment questionnaire examines your ability to listen effectively.

**Instructions:** Go through the following statements, checking "Yes" or "No" next to each one. Mark each question as truthfully as you can in light of your behavior in the last few meetings or gatherings you attended.

**Yes No**

___ ___ 1. I frequently attempt to listen to several conversations at the same time.

___ ___ 2. I like people to give me only the facts and then let me make my own interpretation.

___ ___ 3. I sometimes pretend to pay attention to people.

___ ___ 4. I consider myself a good judge of nonverbal communications.

___ ___ 5. I usually know what another person is going to say before he or she says it.

___ ___ 6. I usually end conversations that don't interest me by diverting my attention from the speaker.

___ ___ 7. I frequently nod, frown, or in some other way let the speaker know how I feel about what he or she is saying.

___ ___ 8. I usually respond immediately when someone has finished talking.

___ ___ 9. I evaluate what is being said while it is being said.

___ ___ 10. I usually formulate a response while the other person is still talking.

___ ___ 11. The speaker's "delivery" style frequently keeps me from listening to content.

___ ___ 12. I usually ask people to clarify what they have said rather than guess at the meaning.

___ ___ 13. I make a concerted effort to understand other people's point of view.

___ ___ 14. I frequently hear what I expect to hear rather than what is said.

___ ___ 15. Most people feel that I have understood their point of view when we disagree.

### Scoring

The correct answers according to communication theory are as follows:

**No** for statements 1, 2, 3, 5, 6, 7, 8, 9, 10, 11, 14.
**Yes** for statements 4, 12, 13, 15.

If you missed only one or two responses, you strongly approve of your own listening habits, and you are on the right track to becoming an effective listener in your role as manager. If you missed three or four responses, you have uncovered some doubts about your listening effectiveness, and your knowledge of how to listen has some gaps. If you missed five or more responses, you probably are not satisfied with the way you listen, and your friends and coworkers may not feel you are a good listener either. Work on improving your active listening skills.

Reference: Ethel C. Glenn and Elliott A. Pond, "Listening Self-Inventory," from *Supervisory Management*, January 1989, pp. 12–15. 

# Developing OB Internet Skills

**Introduction:** Taking the first international assignment can be a daunting task. Everybody has to have that first international experience. The difficulty of the work assignment is compounded by the difficulties caused by the assignment being in a foreign country.

**Internet Assignment:** Assume that you have just been told that your skills are needed in your company's subsidiary division in Saudi Arabia. This division is responsible for all sales and service of your company's products in the Middle East region. Your knowledge of the product, its use, and potential problems are your specialty. This is your first experience with servicing the product on-site in a foreign country, and you are eager to take on this assignment. However, you know very little about the languages, customs, and business practice in any of the countries of the Middle East.

Your manager suggests that you use the Internet to begin to explore the region, its languages, customs, and business practices. First, conduct an Internet search to see what you can learn about this region of the world that might be helpful. Focus on languages, customs, and business practices.

**Follow-up:** Choose the three or four most helpful sites that you found. Be sure to note the strengths and weakness of each. Finally, respond to the following questions:

1. What characteristics do the most beneficial sites have in common?
2. Who were the authors and sources of the most beneficial sites? Why would those authors (or sponsors) go to the trouble of creating such a site?
3. In addition to using the sites you found, what additional resources will you need to be successful in this assignment?

chapter

# 11

# Group Dynamics

## Management Preview

Almost every person can identify several groups to which she or he belongs. Some groups are based in friendships and personal relationships, whereas others are more formally established and may be part of a larger organization. All organizations have numerous groups that do some part of the organization's work. The performance and productivity of an organization is the total of the output and productivity of all of the individuals and groups that exist within it. Large companies around the world are restructuring their organizations around work groups and teams to increase productivity and innovation and improve customer service.

This chapter is the first of a two-chapter sequence on groups and teams in organizations—groups such as the traditional work groups that most people belong to in their work organizations, pit crews at stock-car races, the Zebra teams that reenergized the black-and-white photo-processing unit at Eastman Kodak, a football team, an engineering work group, or a group of nurses working the night shift at a local hospital. Here we cover the basics of group dynamics—the reasons for group formation, the types of groups in organizations, group performance factors, and the potential for conflict in groups. In Chapter 12, we consider how organizations are using teams today.

We begin this chapter by defining "group" and summarizing the importance of groups in organizations. We then describe different types of groups and discuss the stages in which they evolve from newly formed groups into mature, high-performing units. Next, we identify four key factors that affect group performance. We then move to a discussion of how groups interact with other groups in organizations, and of conflict between groups in organizations. Finally, we summarize the important elements in managing groups in organizations. But first, we start with a description of what made the New York Yankees the best sports franchise of the twentieth century. ■

The New York Yankees were the best sports franchise of the twentieth century. There's no doubt. They won twenty-five World Championships in the twentieth century—that's one every four years, on average. No other sports franchise even came close. Early and midcentury they won by sheer force—by having All-Stars at many positions and by hitting more home runs than anyone else did. The club that finished the century did it by far different means: they were truly a cohesive unit of forty players, managers, trainers, and coaches devoted to each other. It seemed as if at every important moment someone different would come through with the key performance that won the game.

*"But if you happen to click as a group, your teamwork and commitment may even be strengthened." — Joe Torre, manager, New York Yankees**

To end the century the Yankees won three of the last four World Series Championships in devastating and unprecedented fashion with 12 straight World Series victories. In 1998 they won 125 games while losing only 50. In 1999 they won 109 games. Yet in neither year did they have any player voted to start in one of the eight fielding positions in the All-Star Game. Several players were picked later to play in both All-Star Games, but not even their best players were considered to be the best at their position. During the 1999 season the club was beset by personal troubles: a player and the manager with cancer, and the deaths of former players and two players' fathers. But through it all the members of the club supported each other; everyone picking each other up and doing their part to win. The strong feelings the players had for each other made this club extraordinarily successful.[1] ■

Making a collection of people perform at the highest levels is a complex process—whether a sports team, a work group, or a school committee. Figure 11.1 presents a three-phase model of group dynamics. In the first phase, the reasons for forming the group determine what type of group it will be. A four-step process of group development occurs during the second stage; the precise nature of these steps depends on four primary group performance factors. In the final phase, a mature, productive, adaptive group has evolved. As the model shows, mature groups interact with other groups, meet goals, and sometimes have conflicts with other groups. This model serves as the framework for our discussion of groups in this chapter.

## Overview of Groups and Group Dynamics

Work groups consist of people who are trying to make a living for themselves and their families. The work group is often the primary source of social identity for employees, and the nature of the group can affect their performance at work as well as their relationships outside the organization.[2]

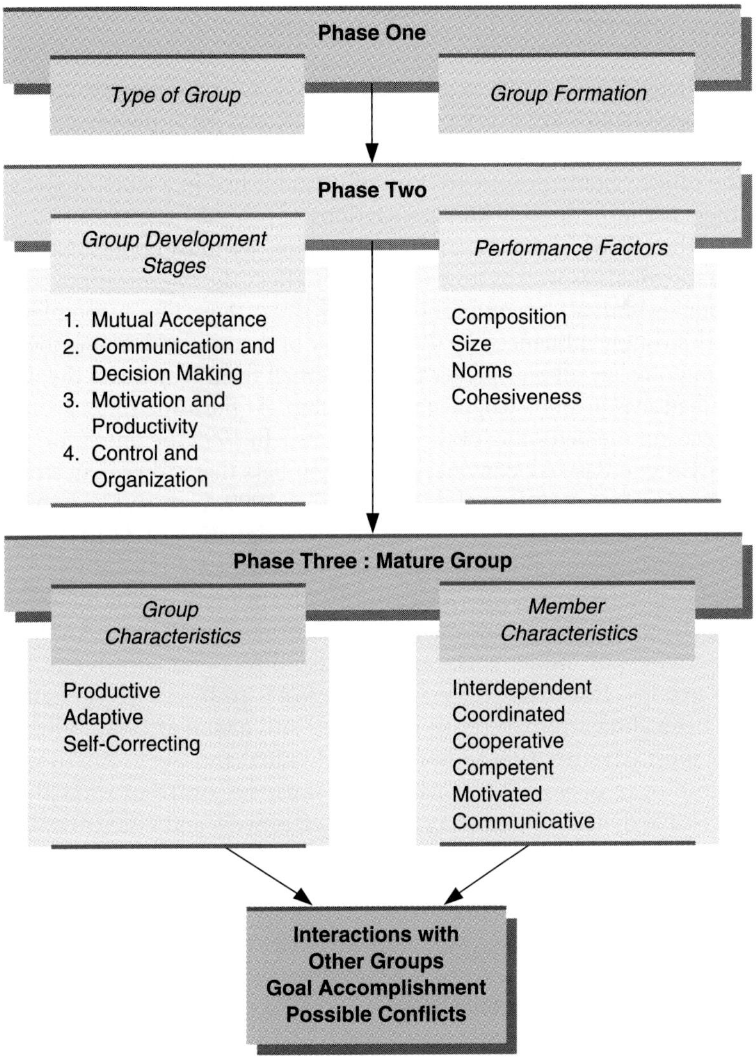


figure 11.1 **A General Model of Group Dynamics**

*This model serves as the framework for this chapter. In phase one, the reasons for group formation determine what type of group it will be. In the second phase, groups evolve through four stages under the influence of four performance factors. Finally, a mature group emerges that interacts with other groups and can pursue organizational goals; conflicts with other groups sometimes occur.*

A group in an organization often takes on a life of its own that transcends the individual members.

## "Group" Defined

Definitions of "group" are as abundant as studies of groups. Groups can be defined in terms of perceptions, motivation, organization, interdependencies, and interactions.[3] A simple and comprehensive definition has been offered by Marvin Shaw: A **group** is two or more persons who interact with one another such that each person influences and is influenced by each other person.[4] The concept of interaction is essential to this definition. Two people who are physically near each other are not a group unless they interact and have some influence on each other. Coworkers may work side by side on related tasks, but if they do not interact they are not a group. The presence of others may influence the performance of a group: an audience may stimulate the performance of actors, or an evaluator may inhibit the employee's behavior.[5] However, neither the audience nor the evaluator can be considered part of a group unless interaction occurs.

Although groups often have goals, our definition does not state that group members must share a goal or motivation. This omission implies that members of a group may identify little or not at all with the group's goal. People can be a part of a group and enjoy the benefits of group membership without wanting to pursue any group goal. Members may satisfy needs just by being members, without pursuing anything. Of course, the quality of the interactions and the group's performance may be affected by members' lack of interest in the group goal.

A **group** is two or more people who interact with one another such that each person influences and is influenced by each other person.

Our definition of "group" also suggests a limit on group size. A collection of people so large that its members cannot interact with and influence one another does not meet this definition. And in reality, the dynamics of large assemblies of people usually differ significantly from those of small groups. Our focus in this chapter is on small groups in which the members interact with and influence one another.

## The Importance of Studying Groups

We must study the behavior of people in group settings if we are to understand organizational behavior. Groups are everywhere in our society. Most people belong to several groups—family, bowling team, church group, fraternity or sorority, or work group at the office.[6] Some groups are formally established in a work or social organization; others are more loosely knit associations of people.

To understand the behavior of people in organizations, we must understand the forces that affect individuals as well as how individuals affect the organization. The behavior of individuals both affects and is affected by the group. The accomplishments of groups are strongly influenced by the behavior of their individual members. For example, adding one key all-star player to a basketball team may make the difference between a bad season and a league championship. At the same time, groups have profound effects on the behaviors of their members.[7] In 1999 the union for the umpires for Major League Baseball convinced their members that rather than strike they should all resign. So, most of them did in September 1999. Unfortunately, Major League Baseball called their bluff and accepted the resignation of 22 of them.[8] Thus, the behavior of many individuals was affected by factors within the group.

From a managerial perspective, the work group is the primary means by which managers coordinate individuals' behavior to achieve organizational goals. Managers direct the activities of individuals, but they also direct and coordinate interactions within groups. For example, managers' efforts to boost salespersons' performance has been shown to have both individual and group effects.[9] Therefore, the manager must pay attention to both the individual and the group in trying to improve employee performance. Managers must be aware of individual needs and interpersonal dynamics to manage groups effectively and efficiently, because the behavior of individuals is key to the group's success or failure.

## Group Formation

Groups are formed to satisfy both organizational and individual needs. They form in organizations because managers expect people working together in groups will be better able to complete and coordinate organizational tasks. Organizations of all types are forming teams to improve some aspect of the work, such as productivity or quality. Electromation created several worker-management teams to discuss absenteeism, pay scales, attendance bonuses, no-smoking policies, and communication.

Individuals join groups to satisfy a need. An employee may join a work group to get or keep a job. Individuals may form an informal group or join an existing one for many reasons: attraction to people in the group, to its activities (such as playing bridge, running marathons, or gardening), or to its goals. Some people join groups just for companionship, or to be identified as members of the group. In any case, people join groups for personal need satisfaction. In other words, they expect that they will get something in return for their membership in the group.

Understanding why groups form is important in studying individual behavior in group situations. Suppose some people join a bridge group primarily for social contact. If a more competitive player substitutes for a regular player one evening, she or he joins the group (temporarily) with the goal of playing rigorous, competitive bridge. The substitute may be annoyed when the game slows down or stops altogether because the other players are absorbed in a discussion. The regular members, on the other hand, may be irritated when the substitute interrupts the

This group of four formerly homeless men The Hermitage Artists, living and working together in what used to be a run-down apartment house and studio in Troy, New York. Together Michael Lavery, Jim Kennedy, Andy Stutter, and Paul Cunningham take discarded wood and create works of art in the form of picture frames, statues, boxes, elaborate desks, and other beautiful forms. The business is thriving because they live and work together in the apartments and studio they have renovated. Their togetherness enables them to help each other with personal and work problems.

discussion or criticizes his or her partner for faulty technique. To resolve the resulting conflict, one must understand the different reasons why each person joined the group. The inconsistencies in behavior arise because each member is trying to satisfy a different need. To settle the dispute, the regulars and the substitute may have to be more tolerant of each other's behavior, at least for the rest of the evening. Even if that occurs, however, the substitute player may not be invited back the next time a regular member cannot attend.

Thus, understanding why people join groups sheds light on apparent inconsistencies in behavior and the tensions likely to result from them. Managers are better equipped to manage certain kinds of conflict that arise in groups in organizations when they understand why groups form.

# Types of Groups

Our first task in understanding group processes is to develop a typology of groups that provides insight into their dynamics. Groups may be loosely categorized according to their degrees of formalization (formal or informal) and permanence (relatively permanent or relatively temporary). Table 11.1 shows this classification scheme.

A formal group is formed by an organization to do its work.

A command group is a relatively permanent, formal group with functional reporting relationships and is usually included in the organization chart.

## Formal Groups

**Formal groups** are established by the organization to do its work. Formal groups include command (or functional) groups, task groups, and affinity groups. A **command group** is relatively permanent and is characterized by functional reporting

table 11.1
**Classification Scheme for Types of Groups**

| | Relatively Permanent | Relatively Temporary | |
|---|---|---|---|
| Formal | **Command Groups**<br>Quality-assurance department<br>Cost-accounting group | **Task Groups**<br>Search committee for a new school superintendent<br>Task force on new-product quality | **Affinity Groups**<br>New product development group |
| Informal | **Friendship Groups**<br>Friends who do many activities together (attend the theater, play games, travel) | **Interest Groups**<br>Bowling group<br>Women's network | |

A **task group** is a relatively temporary, formal group established to do a specific task.

**Affinity groups** are collections of employees from the same level in the organization who meet on a regular basis to share information, capture emerging opportunities, and solve problems.

relationships, such as a group manager and those who report to the manager. Command groups are usually included in the organization chart. A **task group** is created to perform a specific task, such as solving a particular quality problem, and is relatively temporary. **Affinity groups** are relatively permanent collections of employees from the same level in the organization who meet on a regular basis to share information, capture emerging opportunities, and solve problems.[10]

In business organizations, most employees work in command groups, as typically specified on an official organization chart. The size, shape, and organization of a company's command groups can vary considerably. Typical command groups in organizations include the quality-assurance department, the industrial engineering department, the cost-accounting department, and the personnel department. Other types of command groups include work teams organized as in the Japanese style of management, in which subsections of manufacturing and assembly processes are each assigned to a team of workers. The team members decide among themselves who will do each task.

Teams are becoming widespread in automobile manufacturing. General Motors organized its highly automated assembly lines into work teams of between five and twenty workers.[11] Although participative teams are becoming more popular, command groups, whether entire departments or sophisticated work teams, are the dominant type of work group in organizations. Federal Express organized its clerical workers into teams that manage themselves.[12]

Task, or special-project, groups are usually temporary and are often established to solve a particular problem. The group usually dissolves once it solves the problem or makes recommendations. People typically remain members of their command groups, or functional departments, while simultaneously serving in a task group and continuing to carry out the normal duties of their jobs. The members' command group duties may be temporarily reduced if the task group requires a great deal of time and effort. Task groups exist in all types of organizations around the world. For example, the Pope established a special task force of cardinals to study the financial condition of the Vatican and develop new ways to raise money.[13]

Affinity groups are a special type of formal group: they are set up by the organization, yet they are not really part of the formal organization structure. They are not really command groups because they are not part of the organizational hierarchy, yet they are not task groups because they stay in existence longer than any one task. Affinity groups are groups of employees who share roles, responsibilities, duties, and interests, and which represent horizontal slices of the normal organizational hierarchy. Because the members share important characteristics, such as roles, duties, and levels, they are said to have an affinity for one another. The members of affinity groups usually have very similar job titles and similar duties but are in different divisions or departments in the organization.

*"Through affinity groups, business leaders can tap into the latent knowledge, skills and abilities of the organization as it operates naturally." — Dominic J. Monetta, president of Resource Alternatives, Inc.*[14]

Affinity groups meet regularly, and members have assigned roles, such as recorder, reporter, facilitator, and meeting organizer. Members follow simple rules, such as communicating openly and honestly, listening actively, respecting confidentiality, honoring time agreements, being prepared, staying focused, being individually accountable, and being supportive of each other and the group. The greatest benefits of affinity groups are that they cross existing boundaries of the organization and facilitate better communication among diverse departments and division across the organization.

## Informal Groups

An **informal group** is established by its members.

A **friendship group** is relatively permanent and informal and draws its benefits from the social relationships among its members.

An **interest group** is relatively temporary and informal and is organized around a common activity or interest of its members.

Whereas formal groups are established by an organization, **informal groups** are formed by their members and consist of friendship groups, which are relatively permanent, and interest groups, which may be shorter lived. **Friendship groups** arise out of the cordial relationships among members and the enjoyment they get from being together. **Interest groups** are organized around a common activity or interest, although friendships may develop among members.

Good examples of interest groups are the networks of working women that developed during the 1980s. Many of these groups began as informal social gatherings of women who wanted to meet with other women working in male-dominated organizations, but they soon developed into interest groups whose benefits went far beyond their initial social purposes. The networks became information systems for counseling, job placement, and management training. Some networks were eventually established as formal, permanent associations; some remained informal groups based more on social relationships than on any specific interest; others were dissolved. These groups may be partly responsible for the dramatic increase in the percentage of women in managerial and administrative jobs.[15]

# Stages of Group Development

Groups are not static—they typically develop through a four-stage process: (1) mutual acceptance, (2) communication and decision making, (3) motivation and productivity, and (4) control and organization.[16] The stages and the activities that typify them are shown in Figure 11.2. We treat the stages as separate and distinct. It is difficult to pinpoint exactly when a group moves from one stage to another, however, because the activities in the phases tend to overlap.

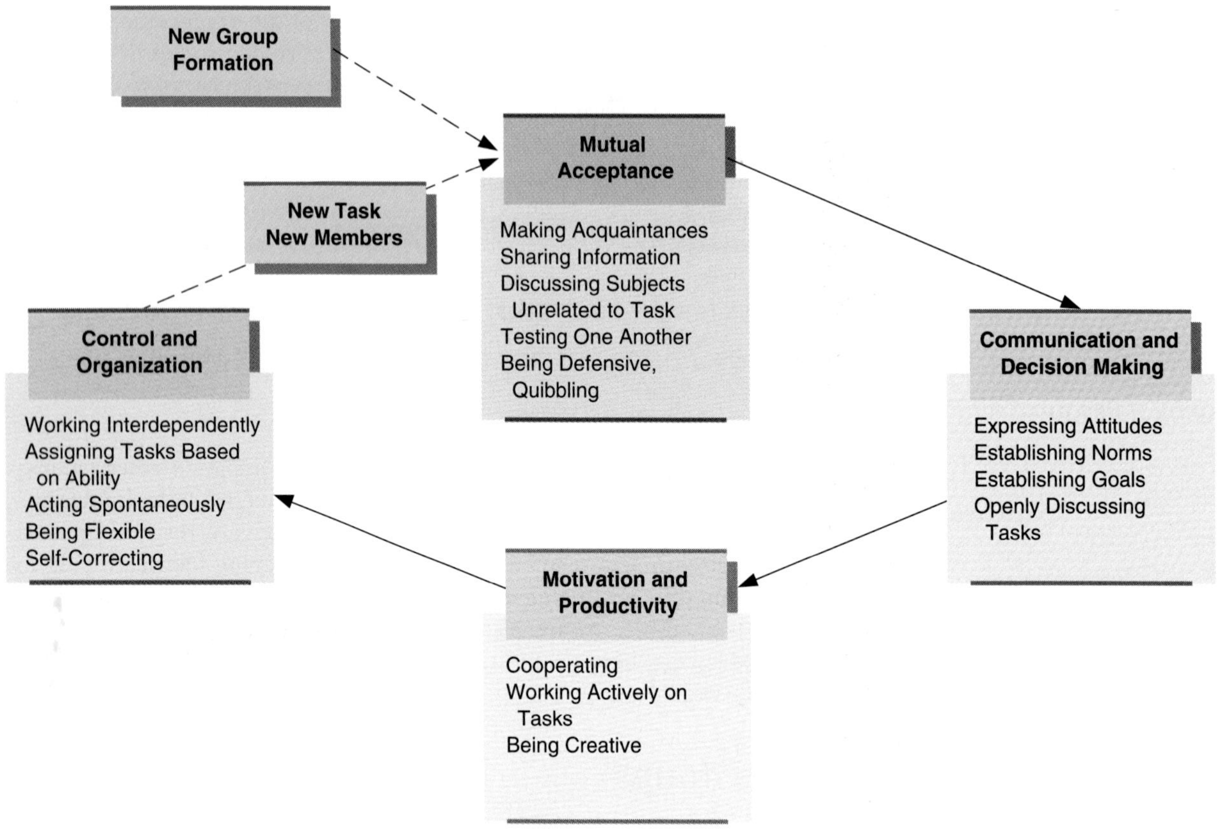


figure 11.2 **Stages of Group Development**

*This figure shows the stages of evolution from a newly formed group to a mature group. Note that as new members are added or an existing group gets a new task, the group needs to go through the stages again.*

## Mutual Acceptance

The **mutual acceptance** stage of group development is characterized by members sharing information about themselves and getting to know each other.

In the **mutual acceptance** stage of group development, the group forms and members get to know one another by sharing information about themselves. They often test one another's opinions by discussing subjects that have little to do with the group, such as the weather, sports, or recent events within the organization. Some aspects of the group's task, such as its formal objectives, may also be discussed at this stage. However, such discussion probably will not be very productive because the members are unfamiliar with one another and do not know how to evaluate one another's comments. If the members do happen to know one another already, this stage may be brief, but it is unlikely to be skipped altogether because this is a new group with a new purpose. Besides, there are likely to be a few members whom the others do not know well or at all.[17]

*"The first prerequisite of effective teamwork is trust." — John Mackey, CEO of Whole Foods*[18]

As the members get to know one another, discussion may turn to more sensitive issues, such as the organization's politics or recent controversial decisions. At this stage, members may have little arguments and feud a bit as they explore one

These people are members of the Acorn Community in Mineral, Virginia, which has a variety of small businesses, including a craft tinnery and subscription-based agriculture. They formed their community in 1993, so they could live and work consistently with their values, and they choose to do business only in things that fit with their principles of nonviolence, ecological soundness, and equal participation in the commune's governance. Their strong orientation to their principles has probably helped them work their way through all of the phases of group development. The community now has 20 people living and working together on 70 acres.

another's views on various issues and learn about each other's reactions, knowledge, and expertise. From the discussion, members come to understand how similar their beliefs and values are and the extent to which they can trust one another. Members may discuss their expectations about the group's activities in terms of their previous group and organizational experience.[19] Eventually, the conversation turns to the business of the group. When this discussion becomes serious, the group is moving to the next stage of development, communication and decision making.

## Communication and Decision Making

The group progresses to the **communication and decision-making** stage once group members have begun to accept one another. In this stage, members discuss their feelings and opinions more openly; they may show more tolerance for opposing viewpoints and explore different ideas to bring about a reasonable solution or decision. The membership usually begins to develop norms of behavior during this stage. Members discuss and eventually agree on the group's goals. Then they are assigned roles and tasks to accomplish the goals.

In the communication and decision-making stage of group development, members discuss their feelings more openly and agree on group goals and individual roles in the group.

In the motivation and productivity stage of group development, members cooperate, help each other, and work toward accomplishing tasks.

In the control and organization stage of group development, the group is mature; members work together and are flexible, adaptive, and self-correcting.

## Motivation and Productivity

In the next stage, **motivation and productivity**, the emphasis shifts away from personal concerns and viewpoints to activities that will benefit the group. Members perform their assigned tasks, cooperate with each other, and help others accomplish their goals. The members are highly motivated and may carry out their tasks creatively. In this stage, the group is accomplishing its work and moving toward the final stage of development.

## Control and Organization

In the final stage, **control and organization**, the group works effectively toward accomplishing its goals. Tasks are assigned by mutual agreement and according to ability. In a mature group, the members' activities are relatively spontaneous and flexible, rather than subject to rigid structural restraints. Mature groups evaluate their activities and potential outcomes and take corrective actions if necessary. The characteristics of flexibility, spontaneity, and self-correction are very important if the group is to remain productive over an extended period.

Not all groups go through all four stages. Some groups disband before reaching the final stage. Others fail to complete a stage before moving on to the next one.[20] Rather than spend the time necessary to get to know one another and build trust, for example, a group may cut short the first stage of development because of pressure from its leader, from deadlines, or from an outside threat (such as the boss). If members are forced into activities typical of a later stage while the work of an earlier stage remains incomplete, they are likely to become frustrated: the group may not develop completely and may be less productive than it could be.[21] Group productivity depends on successful development at each stage. A group that evolves fully through the four stages of development usually becomes a mature, effective group.[22] Its members are interdependent, coordinated, cooperative, competent at their jobs, motivated to do them, self-correcting, and in active communication with one another.[23] The process does not take a long time if the group makes a good, solid effort and pays attention to the processes. The cartoon presents an extreme view of development process.

Finally, as working conditions and relationships change, either through a change in membership or when a task is completed and a new task is begun, groups may need to reexperience one or more of the stages of development to maintain the cohesiveness and productivity characteristic of a well-developed group. The San Francisco Forty-Niners, for example, returned from the NFL strike of 1987 to an uncomfortable and apprehension-filled period. Their coach, Bill Walsh, conducted rigorous practices but also allowed time for players to get together to air their feelings. Slowly, team unity returned, and players began joking and socializing again as they prepared for the rest of the 1987 season.[24] Their redevelopment as a mature group resulted in Super Bowl victories in 1989 and 1990.

Although these stages are not separate and distinct in all groups, many groups make fairly predictable transitions in activities at about the midpoint of the period available to complete a task.[25] A group may begin with its own distinctive approach to the problem and maintain it until about halfway through the allotted time. The midpoint transition is often accompanied by a burst of concentrated activity, reexamination of assumptions, dropping old patterns of activity, adopting new perspectives on the work, and making dramatic progress. Following these midpoint

**"My new approach to effective team development will take a bit longer. In my plan, we raise them from birth."**

Although it is essential that groups go through all four stages of development in order to become a mature, productive group, it really is not necessary to grow them from birth. Groups, if given good direction and coaching, can go through all four steps in a relatively short period of time.

Reference: © Randy Glasbergen

activities, the new patterns of activity may be maintained until close to the end of the period allotted for the activity. Another transition may occur just before the deadline. At this transition, groups often go into the completion stage, launching a final burst of activity to finish the job.

# Group Performance Factors

The performance of any group is affected by several factors other than its reasons for forming and the stages of its development. In a high-performing group, a group synergy often develops in which the group's performance is more than the sum of the individual contributions of its members. Several additional factors may account for this accelerated performance.[26] The four basic **group performance factors** are composition, size, norms, and cohesiveness.

**Group performance factors**—composition, size, norms, and cohesiveness—affect the success of the group in fulfilling its goals.

**Group composition** is the degree of similarity or difference among group members on factors important to the group's work.

## Composition

The composition of a group plays an important role in determining group productivity.[27] **Group composition** is most often described in terms of the homogeneity or heterogeneity of the members. A group is *homogeneous* if the members are similar in one or several ways that are critical to the work of the group, such as age, work experience, education, technical specialty, or cultural background. In *heterogeneous* groups, the members differ in one or more ways that are critical to the work of the group. Homogeneous groups often are created in organizations when people are assigned to command groups based on a similar technical specialty. Although the people who work in such command groups may differ in some ways, such as age or work experience, they are homogeneous in terms of a critical work performance variable: technical specialty.

This group of people in Minneapolis is part of Retirees Offering Community Service, a group formed by The Prudential Insurance Company of America. Howard L. Agee, a former marketing executive with Prudential, started the program because he still wanted to contribute even though he had retired from the company. Retired volunteers meet monthly to organize projects, such as food distribution and reading fairs. The homogeneity of the group probably contributes to their success.

Much research has explored the relationship between a group's composition and its productivity. The group's heterogeneity in terms of age and tenure with the group has been shown to be related to turnover: groups with members of different ages and experiences with the group tend to experience frequent changes in membership.[28] The "Working with Diversity" box describes how the NASCAR pit crew for star driver Jeff Gordon is a diverse group. Table 11.2 summarizes task variables that make a homogeneous or heterogeneous group more effective. A homogeneous group is likely to be more productive when the group task is simple, cooperation is necessary, the group tasks are sequential, or quick

WORKING WITH DIVERSITY

## The Rainbow Warriors

Ray Evernham is commonly known as the premier crew chief in the National Association for Stock Car Auto Racing (NASCAR) racing. He was named Crew Chief of the Year in 1994, and his car and driver, Jeff Gordon, have been winning the annual racing championship and setting earnings records every year since. One of the reasons is the crew put together, trained, and managed by Evernham.

From the start, Evernham set out to make the crew different from others. He named them the Rainbow Warriors, gave them uniforms striped in bright rainbow colors, and trained them differently than most crews are trained. But he started out by hiring people who had never been involved in stock car racing and who were very different types of people. His belief was that when you start with different people, you get different outcomes. With people who were not familiar with stock car racing, the crew developed several new and innovative ways of doing things that make that split-second difference that gives driver Gordon an edge. In addition, Evernham trained and even rehearsed the crew differently to prepare for race day. Where most racing teams put the car first, with speed and reliability, Evernham feels that the crew is just as important as the car. If they can be one second faster than the competition in the pit, the difference for Gordon can be 300 feet on the track. It is hard to argue with his success. Unfortunately, Evernham resigned in late 1999, apparently to try his organizational skills for someone else's team. It will be interesting to watch to see how Gordon's car performs with a new crew chief.

*"When you have a team with different kinds of people, you get a chance to do things differently." — Ray Evernham, NASCAR crew chief*

References: Ed Hinton, "Gordon's Gamble," *Sports Illustrated,* October 11, 1999, p. 32; Ed Hinton, "Breaking Up: Jeff Gordon's Crew Chief Is Moving On to Greener Pastures," *Sports Illustrated,* October 4, 1999. p. 112; Chuck Salter, "Life in the Fast Lane" *Fast Company,* October 1998, pp. 172–178 (quote on p. 176).

action is required. A heterogeneous group is more likely to be productive when the task is complex, requires a collective effort (that is, each member does a different task and the sum of these efforts constitutes the group output), demands creativity, and when speed is less important than thorough deliberations. For example, a group asked to generate ideas for marketing a new product probably needs to be heterogeneous to develop as many different ideas as possible.

The link between group composition and type of task is explained by the interactions typical of homogeneous and heterogeneous groups. A homogeneous group tends to have less conflict, fewer differences of opinion, smoother communication, and more interactions. When a task requires cooperation and speed, a homogeneous group is therefore more desirable. If, however, the task requires complex analysis of information and creativity to arrive at the best possible solution, a heterogeneous group may be more appropriate because it generates a wide range of viewpoints. More discussion and more conflict are likely, both of which can enhance the group's decision making.

table 11.2 **Task Variables and Group Composition**

| A homogeneous group is more useful for: | A heterogeneous group is more useful for: |
|---|---|
| Simple tasks | Complex tasks |
| Sequential tasks | Collective tasks |
| Tasks that require cooperation | Tasks that require creativity |
| Tasks that must be done quickly | Tasks that need not be done quickly |

Reference: Based on discussion in Bernard M. Bass and Edward C. Ryterband, *Organizational Psychology,* 2nd ed. (Allyn & Bacon, 1979). Reprinted by permission.

Group composition becomes especially important as organizations become increasingly diverse. Cultures differ in the importance they place on group membership and in how they view authority, uncertainty, and other important factors. Increasing attention is being focused on how to deal with groups made up of people from different cultures.[29] In general, a manager in charge of a culturally diverse group can expect several things. First, members will probably distrust each other. Stereotyping also will present a problem, and communication problems will almost certainly arise. Thus, the manager needs to recognize that such groups will seldom function smoothly, at least at first. Managers may therefore need to spend more time helping a culturally diverse group through the rough spots as it matures, and they should allow a longer-than-normal time before expecting it to carry out its assigned task.

Many organizations are creating joint ventures and other types of alliances with organizations from other countries. Joint ventures have become common in the automobile and electronics industries, for example. However, managers from the United States tend to exhibit individualistic behaviors in a group setting, whereas managers from more collectivistic countries, such as the People's Republic of China, tend to exhibit more group-oriented behaviors.[30] Thus, when these two different types of managers work together in a joint venture, the managers must be trained to be cautious and understanding in their interactions and in the types of behaviors they exhibit. As we discussed in Chapter 3, all employees need training in how to work with people from different cultures.

## Size

**Group size** is the number of members of the group; group size affects the number of resources available to perform the task.

A group can have as few as two members or as many members as can interact and influence one another. **Group size** can have an important effect on performance. A group with many members has more resources available and may be able to complete a large number of relatively independent tasks. In groups established to generate ideas, those with more members tend to produce more ideas, although the rate of increase in the number of ideas diminishes rapidly as the group grows.[31] Beyond a certain point, the greater complexity of interactions and communication may make it more difficult for a large group to achieve agreement.

Interactions and communication are much more likely to be formalized in larger groups. Large groups tend to set agendas for meetings and to follow a protocol or parliamentary procedure to control discussion. As a result, some time that otherwise might be available to work on tasks is taken up in administrative duties such as organizing and structuring the interactions and communications within the group. Also, the large size may inhibit participation of some people and increase absenteeism; some people may stop trying to make a meaningful contribution and may even stop coming to group meetings if repeated attempts to contribute or participate are thwarted by the sheer number of similar efforts by other members.[32] Furthermore, large groups present more opportunities for interpersonal attraction, leading to more social interactions and fewer task interactions. **Social loafing** is the tendency of some members of groups not to put forth as much effort in a group situation as they would working alone.[33] Social loafing often results from the assumption by some members that if they do not work hard, other members will pick up the slack. How much of a problem this becomes depends on the nature of the task, the characteristics of the people involved, and the ability of the group leadership to be aware of the potential problem and do something about it.

**Social loafing** is the tendency of some members of groups to put forth less effort in a group than they would when working alone.

The most effective size of a group, therefore, is determined by the group members' ability to interact and influence each other effectively. The need for interaction is affected by the maturity of the group, the tasks of the group, the maturity of individual members, and the ability of the group leader or manager to manage the communication, potential conflicts, and task activities. In some situations, the most effective group size is three or four; other groups can function effectively with fifteen or more members.

## Norms

A **norm** is a standard against which the appropriateness of a behavior is judged.

A **norm** is a standard against which the appropriateness of a behavior is judged.[34] Thus, norms determine the behavior expected in a certain situation. Group norms usually are established during the second stage of group development (communication and decision making) and carried forward into the maturity stage.[35] By providing a basis for predicting others' behaviors, norms enable people to behave in a manner consistent with and acceptable to the group. Without norms, the activities in a group would be chaotic.

*"On great teams, players know their own roles and everyone else's role, too. The more you know about how a teammate plays his position, the better you'll play your own position." — Steve Bzomowski, former assistant basketball coach at Harvard University and president, Never Too Late Basketball Camps, Inc.*[36]

Norms result from the combination of members' personality characteristics, the situation, the task, and the historical traditions of the group. Lack of conformity to group norms may result in verbal abuse, physical threats, ostracism, or ejection from the group. Group norms are enforced, however, only for actions that are important to group members.[37] For example, if the office norm is for employees to wear suits to convey a professional image to clients, a staff member who wears blue jeans and a sweatshirt violates the group norm and will hear about it quickly. But if the norm is that dress is unimportant because little contact with clients occurs in the office, the fact that someone wears blue jeans may not even be noticed.

Norms serve four purposes:

1. Norms help the group survive. Groups tend to reject deviant behavior that does not help meet group goals or contribute to the survival of the group if it is threatened. Accordingly, a successful group that is not under threat may be more tolerant of deviant behavior.

2. Norms simplify and make more predictable the behaviors expected of group members. Because they are familiar with norms, members do not have to analyze each behavior and decide on a response. Members can anticipate the actions of others on the basis of group norms, usually resulting in increased productivity and goal attainment.

3. Norms help the group avoid embarrassing situations. Group members often want to avoid damaging other members' self-images and are likely to avoid certain subjects that might hurt a member's feelings.

4. Norms express the central values of the group and identify the group to others. Certain clothes, mannerisms, or behaviors in particular situations may be a rallying point for members and may signify to others the nature of the group.[38]

Norms usually regulate the behavior of group members rather than their thoughts or feelings.[39] Members thus may believe one thing but do another to maintain membership in a group. For example, during the so-called Iran-Contra Affair of 1985–1987, there were several meetings in which President Ronald Reagan and aides such as Lt. Col. Oliver North, National Security Advisor Robert McFarlane, and Central Intelligence Agency director William Casey discussed the sale of arms to Iran in exchange for American hostages.[40] Secretary of State George P. Schultz and Secretary of Defense Caspar W. Weinberger were known to be against the sale of arms to Iran even indirectly, through Israel. The president and others strongly favored such arms sales and were eager to achieve the release of American hostages held in Iran. Thus, Schultz and Weinberger did not attend meetings in which further arms sales were authorized.[41] Although it is not clear whether the members excluded them or they excluded themselves by not attending, group norms clearly affected the meetings and outcomes. From the group's perspective, the norm was to go along with the group and approve the arms transfer. Anyone who continued to argue against the transfer would not be in the group. Thus, Schultz and Weinberger knew that they were in the minority and were making it uncomfortable for the president. If they wanted to maintain their valued membership in the president's cabinet as heads of two of the most powerful agencies of the executive branch, they knew they should not continue to cause trouble. Thus, group norms regarding how presidential advisors should act may have led them to decide not to attend.

**Group cohesiveness** is the extent to which a group is committed to staying together.

**figure 11.3 Factors That Affect Group Cohesiveness and Consequences of Group Cohesiveness**

*The factors that increase and decrease cohesiveness and the consequences of high and low cohesiveness indicate that, although it is often preferable to have a highly cohesive group, in some situations the effects of a highly cohesive group can be negative for the organization.*

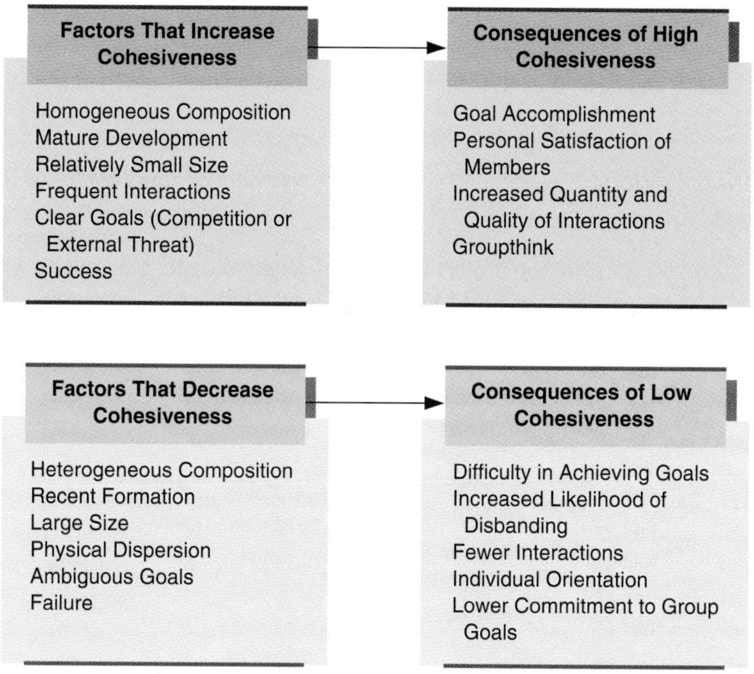


## Cohesiveness

**Group cohesiveness** is the extent to which a group is committed to remaining together; it results from "all forces acting on the members to remain in the group."[42] The forces that create cohesiveness are attraction to the group, resistance to leaving the group, and the motivation to remain a member of the group.[43] As shown in Figure 11.3, group cohesiveness is related to many aspects of group dynamics that we have already discussed—maturity, homogeneity, manageable size, and frequency of interactions.

The figure also shows that group cohesiveness can be increased by competition or by the presence of an external threat.[44] Either factor can focus members' attention on a clearly defined goal and increase their willingness to work together. The threats by the Major League Baseball owners to use replacement umpires had the immediate effect of unifying the umpires against the owners. The umpires became more cohesive and vowed more strongly than ever to stick together when they resigned. However, when the owners accepted the resignation of 22 umpires, the umpires tried to rescind their letters of resignation. The owners did not let them and the courts upheld their right to do so.[45] Similarly, in the Iran-Contra affair, the inner group (Casey, North, McFarlane, and Vice Admiral John M. Poindexter) became cohesive due to the need for secrecy and the threat of exposure by Congress and the media.[46]

Finally, successfully reaching goals often increases the cohesiveness of a group because people are proud to be identified with a winner and to be thought of as competent and successful. This may be one reason behind the popular phrase "Success breeds success." The "Talking Technology" box describes how Intel manages to keep its culture of innovation moving by creating groups that are successful. A group that is successful may become more cohesive and hence possibly even more successful. Of course, other factors can get in the way of continued success, such as personal differences, egos, and the lure of more individual success in other activities.

Research on group performance factors has focused on the relationship between cohesiveness and group productivity. Highly cohesive groups appear to be more effective at achieving their goals than groups that are low in cohesiveness, especially in research and development groups in U.S. companies.[47] However, highly cohesive groups will not necessarily be more productive in an organizational sense than groups with low cohesiveness. As Figure 11.4 illustrates, when a group's goals are compatible with the organizational goals, a cohesive group prob-

TALKING TECHNOLOGY

## *Intel's Culture of Innovation*

Intel Corporation became famous for its innovations, not so much in microprocessors as in how it brought them to market. Its former CEO Andy Grove described Intel as a three-legged stool consisting of: engineering, manufacturing, and marketing. As Intel continues to grow and change, it has moved from providing high-performance microprocessors for desktop PCs to making microprocessors for server infrastructures to making chip sets and communications chips. But innovation was, and still is, its strength.

*"A small initial success can go a long way toward building team confidence." — Albert Yu, senior vice president of Intel's Microprocessor Products Group*

At Intel, Albert Yu has two jobs. The first one is to visualize the next generation of Intel microprocessors. The second is to foster an attitude at Intel that continues the company's time-honored traditions of giving no quarter, raising the bar, and maintaining Intel's only-the-paranoid-survive team spirit. Yu recommends that innovative teams should be composed of members from different parts of the organization. He feels that innovative teams need to have people with expertise in accounting, architecture, engineering, manufacturing and other diverse disciplines, as well as a mixture of personalities. Some members should be wild, others conservative; some should be idealists, others pragmatists.

Yu also recommends giving the new team a small, but real, project to help them get to know how each other works and to find out who belongs on the team. Then, before the project is completed, begin to move people to more advanced projects. Once a project is completed, people want to move on to more challenges, not sit around and watch the completed project. Creating new project teams before the old ones are finished will keep people energized.

References: Eric Nee, "The Geek Elite: They Reprogrammed American Life—and Digitized the Globe," *Fortune,* November 8, 1999, pp. 220–224; David Kirkpatrick "Andy Grove: The PC Industry Won't Be the PC Industry," *Fortune,* May 24, 1999, p. 160; Pat Dillon, "Failure Is Just Part of the Culture of Innovation. Accept It and Become Stronger," *Fast Company,* December 1998, pp. 132–136 (quote on p. 136).

figure 11.4

**Group Cohesiveness, Goals, and Productivity**

*This figure shows that the best combination is for the group to be cohesive and for the group's goals to be congruent with the organization's goals. The lowest potential group performance also occurs with highly cohesive groups, when the group's goals are not consistent with the organization's goals.*

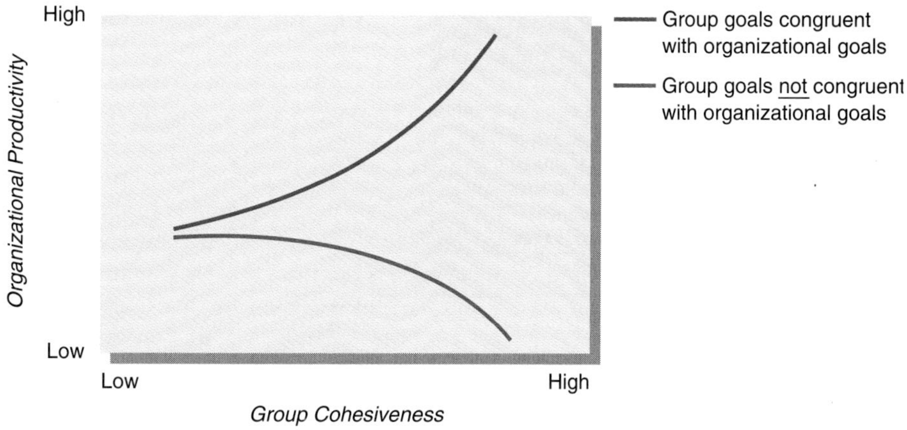


ably will be more productive than one that is not cohesive. In other words, if a highly cohesive group has the goal of contributing to the good of the organization, it is very likely to be productive in organizational terms. But if such a group decides on a goal that has little to do with the business of the organization, it will probably achieve its own goal even at the expense of any organizational goal. In a study of group characteristics and productivity, group cohesiveness was the only factor that was consistently related to high performance for research and development engineers and technicians.[48]

Groupthink occurs when a group's overriding concern is a unanimous decision rather than critical analysis of alternatives.

Cohesiveness may also be a primary factor in the development of certain problems for some decision-making groups. An example is **groupthink**, which occurs when a group's overriding concern is a unanimous decision rather than critical analysis of alternatives.[49] (In Chapter 15 we go into more detail in describing groupthink.) These problems, together with the evidence regarding group cohesiveness and productivity, mean that a manager must carefully weigh the pros and cons of fostering highly cohesive groups.

# Intergroup Dynamics

A group's contribution to an organization depends on its interactions with other groups as well as on its own productivity. Many organizations are increasing their use of cross-functional teams to address more complex and increasingly important organizational issues. The result has been heightened emphasis on the teams' interactions with other groups. Groups that actively interact with other groups by asking questions, initiating joint programs, and sharing their team's achievements are usually the most productive.

Interactions are the key to understanding intergroup dynamics. The orientation of the groups toward their goals takes place under a highly complex set of conditions that determine the relationship among the groups. The most important of these factors are presented in the model of intergroup dynamics in Figure 11.5. The model emphasizes three primary factors that influence intergroup interactions: group characteristics, organizational setting, and task and situational bases of interaction.

First, we must understand the key characteristics of the interacting groups. Each group brings to the interaction its own unique features. As individuals become a part of a group, they tend to identify so strongly with the group that their

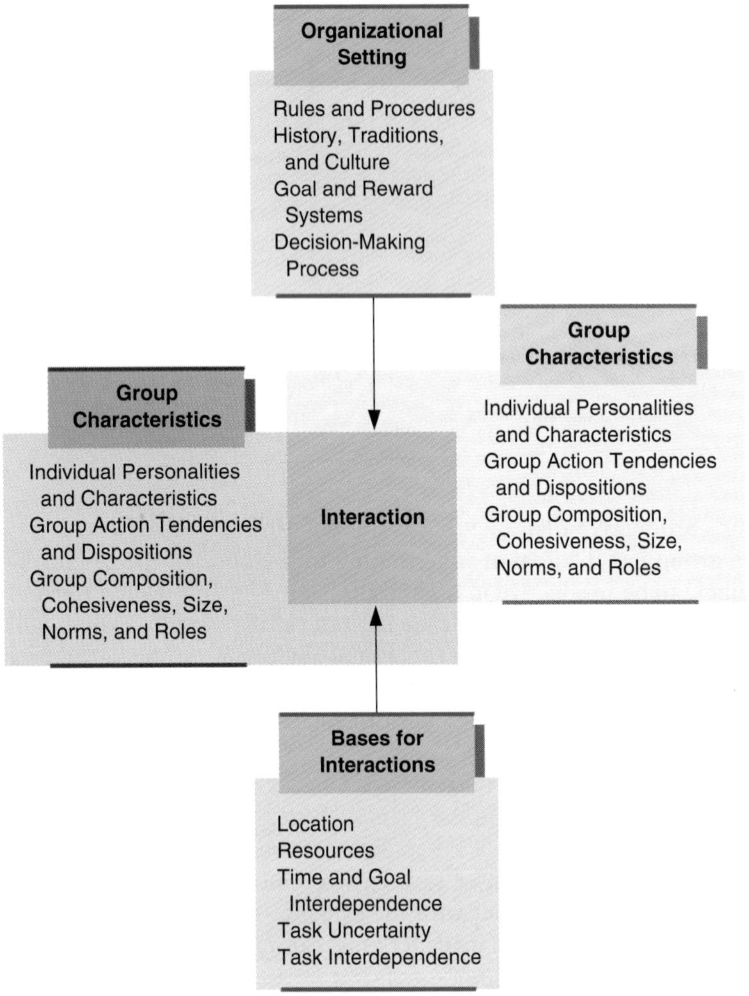


figure 11.5 **Factors That Influence Intergroup Interactions**

*The nature of the interactions between groups depends on the characteristics of the groups involved, the organizational setting, and the task and situational setting for the interaction.*

views of other groups become biased, and harmonious relationships with other groups may be difficult to achieve.[50] Furthermore, the individuals in the group contribute to the group processes, which influences the group's norms, size, composition, and cohesiveness; all of these factors affect the interactions with other groups. Thus, understanding the individuals in the group and the key characteristics of the group can help managers monitor intergroup interactions.

Second, the organizational setting in which the groups interact can have a powerful influence on intergroup interactions. The organization's structure, rules and procedures, decision-making processes, and goals and reward systems all affect interactions. For example, organizations in which frequent interactions occur and strong ties among groups exist usually are characterized as low-conflict organizations.[51] Third, the task and situational bases of interactions focus attention on the working relationships among the interacting groups and on the reasons for the interactions. As Figure 11.5 shows, five factors affect intergroup interactions: location, resources, time and goal interdependence, task uncertainty, and task interdependence. These factors both create the interactions and determine their characteristics, such as the frequency of interaction, the volume of information exchange among groups, and the type of coordination the groups need to interact and function. For example, if two groups depend heavily on each other to perform a task about which much uncertainty exists, they need a great deal of information from each other to define and perform the task.

# Conflict in Groups and Organizations

**Conflict** is disagreement among parties. It has both positive and negative characteristics.

Conflict often occurs when groups interact in organizations. In its simplest form, **conflict** is disagreement among parties. When people, groups, or organizations disagree over significant issues, conflict is often the result. Often political behavior or battles over limited resources generate conflict between groups. In particular, it frequently occurs when a person or a group believes its attempts to achieve its goal are being blocked by another person or group. For example, conflict may arise over financial resources, the number of authorized positions in work groups, or the number of laptop computers to be purchased for departments. Conflict may also result from anticipating trouble. For example, a person may behave antagonistically toward another person whom he or she expects to pose obstacles to goal achievement.[52]

Although conflict often is considered harmful, and thus something to avoid, it can also have some benefits. A total absence of conflict can lead to apathy and lethargy. A moderate degree of focused conflict, on the other hand, can stimulate new ideas, promote healthy competition, and energize behavior. In some organizations, especially profit-oriented ones, many managers believe that conflict is dysfunctional. On the other hand, managers in not-for-profit organizations view conflict as beneficial and conducive to higher-quality decision making.[53]

## The Nature of Conflict

Figure 11.6 illustrates the relationship between competition and conflict. Competition occurs when groups strive for the same goal, have little or no antagonism toward one another, and behave according to rules and procedures. In conflict, on the other hand, one group's goals jeopardize the other's, there is open antagonism among the groups, and few rules and procedures regulate behavior. When this happens, the goals become extremely important, the antagonism increases, rules and procedures are violated, and conflict occurs.[54] We have more to say about competition later in this section.

## Reactions to Conflict

The most common reactions to conflict are avoidance, accommodation, competition, collaboration, and compromise.[55] Whenever conflict occurs between groups or organizations, it is really the people who are in conflict. In many cases, however, people are acting as representatives of the groups to which they belong. In effect, they work together, representing their group as they strive to do their part in helping the group achieve its goals. Thus, whether the conflict is between people acting as individuals or people acting as representatives of groups, the five types of interactions can be analyzed in terms of relationships among the goals of the people or the groups they represent.

**Goal compatibility** is the extent to which the goals of more than one person or group can be achieved at the same time.

Reactions to conflict can be differentiated along two dimensions: how important each party's goals are to that party, and how compatible the goals are, as shown in Figure 11.7. The importance of reaching a goal may range from very high to very low. The degree of **goal compatibility** is the extent to which the

figure 11.6
**Competition-Conflict Relationship**

*Although competition and conflict are similar, they differ. Competition can lead to conflict when goals are threatened, open antagonism occurs, and rules are no longer observed.*

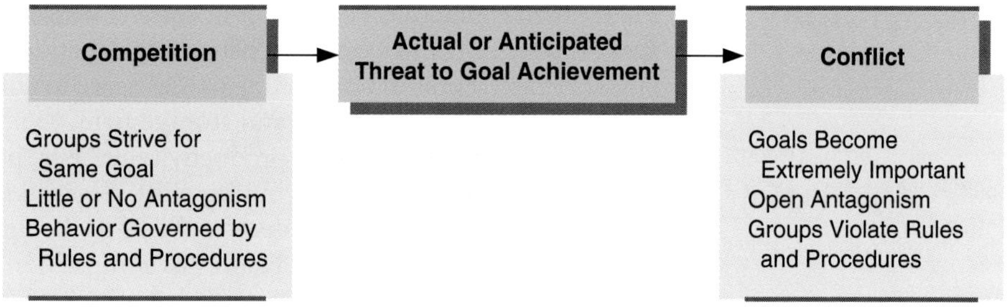

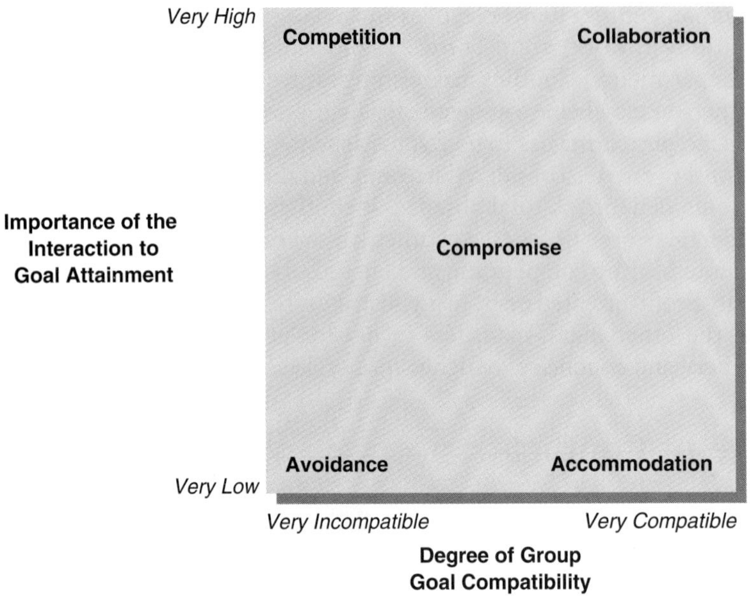


figure 11.7 **Five Types of Reactions to Conflict**

*The five types of reactions to conflict stem from the relative importance of interaction to goal attainment and the degree of goal compatibility.*

Reference: Adapted from Kenneth Thomas, "Conflict and Conflict Management," in Marvin Dunnette (ed.), *Handbook of Industrial and Organizational Psychology* (Chicago: Rand McNally, 1976), pp. 889–935. Reprinted by permission.

goals can be achieved simultaneously. In other words, the goals are compatible if one party can meet its goals without preventing the other from meeting its goals. The goals are incompatible if one party's meeting its goals prevents the other party from meeting its goals. The goals of different groups may be very compatible, completely incompatible, or somewhere in between.

Avoidance **Avoidance** occurs when an interaction is relatively unimportant to either party's goals and the goals are incompatible, as in the bottom left corner of Figure 11.7. Because the parties to the conflict are not striving toward compatible goals and the issues in question seem unimportant, the parties simply try to avoid interacting with one another. For example, one state agency may simply ignore another agency's requests for information. The requesting agency can then practice its own form of avoidance by not following up on the requests.

**Avoidance** occurs when the interacting parties' goals are incompatible and the interaction between groups is relatively unimportant to the attainment of the goals.

**Accommodation** occurs when the parties' goals are compatible and the interaction between groups is relatively unimportant to the goals' attainment.

**Competition** occurs when the goals are incompatible and the interactions between groups are important to meeting goals.

Accommodation **Accommodation** occurs when the goals are compatible but the interactions are not considered important to overall goal attainment, as in the bottom right corner of Figure 11.7. Interactions of this type may involve discussions of how the parties can accomplish their interdependent tasks with the least expenditure of time and effort. This type of interaction tends to be very friendly.[56] For example, during a college's course scheduling period, potential conflict exists between the marketing and economic departments. Both departments offer morning classes. Which department is allocated the 9:00 A.M. time slot and which one the 10:00 A.M. time slot is not that important to either group. Their overall goal is that the classes are scheduled so that students will be able to take courses.

Competition **Competition** occurs when the goals are incompatible and the interactions are important to each party's meeting its goals, as in the top left corner of Figure 11.7. If all parties are striving for a goal but only one can reach the goal, the parties will be in competition. As we noted earlier, if a competitive situation gets out of control, as when overt antagonism occurs and there are no rules or procedures to follow, then competition can result in conflict. Thus, competition may lead to conflict. Sometimes conflict can also change to competition if the parties agree to rules to guide the interaction and conflicting parties agree to not be hostile toward each other.

In one freight warehouse and storage firm, the first, second, and third shifts each sought to win the weekly productivity prize by posting the highest productivity record. Workers on the winning shift received recognition in the company newspaper. Because the issue was important to each group and the interests of the groups were incompatible, the result was competition.

The competition among the shifts encouraged each shift to produce more per week, which increased the company's output and eventually improved its overall welfare (and thus the welfare of each group). Both the company and the groups benefited from the competition because it fostered innovative and creative work methods, which further boosted productivity. After about three months, however, the competition got out of control. The competition among the groups led to poorer overall performance as the groups started to sabotage other shifts and inflate records. The competition became too important, open antagonism resulted, rules were ignored, and the competition changed to open conflict, resulting in actual decreases in work performance.[57]

**Collaboration** occurs when the interaction between groups is very important to goal attainment and the goals are compatible.

Collaboration **Collaboration** occurs when the interaction between groups is very important to goal attainment and the goals are compatible, as in the top right corner of Figure 11.7. In the class scheduling situation mentioned earlier, conflict may arise over which courses to teach in the first semester and which ones in the second. Both departments would like to offer specific courses in the fall. However, by discussing the issue and refocusing their overall goals to match students' needs, the marketing and economics departments can collaborate on developing a proper sequence of courses. At first glance, this may seem to be simple interaction in which the parties participate jointly in activities to accomplish goals after agreeing on the goals and their importance. In many situations, however, it is no easy matter to agree on goals, their importance, and especially the means for achieving them. In a collaborative interaction, goals may differ but be compatible. Parties to a conflict may initially have difficulty working out the ways in which all can achieve their goals. However, because the interactions are important to goal attainment, the parties are willing to continue to work together to achieve the goals. Collaborative relationships can lead to new and innovative ideas and solutions to differences among the parties.[58]

**Compromise** occurs when the interaction is moderately important to meeting goals and the goals are neither completely compatible nor completely incompatible.

Compromise **Compromise** occurs when the interactions are moderately important to goal attainment and the goals are neither completely compatible nor completely incompatible. In a compromise situation, parties interact with others striving to achieve goals, but they may not aggressively pursue goal attainment in either a competitive or collaborative manner because the interactions are not that important to goal attainment. On the other hand, the parties may neither avoid one another nor be accommodating because the interactions are somewhat important. Often each party gives up something, but because the interactions are only moderately important, they do not regret what they have given up.

Contract negotiations between union and management are usually examples of compromise. Each side brings numerous issues of varying importance to the bargaining table. The two sides give and take on the issues through rounds of offers and counteroffers. The complexity of such negotiations is increasing as negotiations spread to multiple plants in different countries. Agreements between management and labor in a plant in the United States may be unacceptable to both parties in Canada.[59] Weeks of negotiations ending in numerous compromises usually result in a contract agreement between the union and management.

In summary, when groups are in conflict, they may react in several different ways. If the goals of the parties are very compatible, the parties may engage in mutually supportive interactions—that is, collaboration or accommodation. If the goals are very incompatible, each may attempt to foster its own success at the expense of the other's, engaging in competition or avoidance.

# Managing Conflict

One must know when to resolve conflict and when to stimulate it if one is to avoid its potentially disruptive effects. When a potentially harmful conflict situation exists, a manager needs to engage in **conflict resolution**. As Figure 11.8 shows, conflict needs to be resolved when it causes major disruptions in the organization and absorbs time and effort that could be used more productively. Conflict should also be resolved when its focus is on the group's internal goals rather than on organizational goals.

**Conflict resolution** occurs when a manager resolves a conflict that has become harmful or serious.

*"I've learned that confrontation doesn't have to be frightening or violent; you can confront people in a determined respectful way.... Deal with it."* — *Joe Torre, manager, New York Yankees*[60]

We describe the principal conflict-handling strategies later in this section. First, remember that sometimes a manager should be concerned about the absence of conflict. An absence of conflict may indicate that the organization is stagnant and that employees are content with the status quo. It may also suggest that work groups are not motivated to challenge traditional and well-accepted ideas.[61] **Conflict stimulation** is the creation and constructive use of conflict by a manager.[62] Its purpose is to bring about situations in which differences of opinion are exposed for examination by all. For example, if competing organizations are making significant changes in products, markets, or technologies, it may be time for a manager to stimulate innovation and creativity by challenging the status quo. Conflict may give employees the motivation and opportunity to reveal differences of opinion that they previously kept to themselves. When all parties to the conflict are interested enough in an issue to challenge other groups, they often expose their hidden doubts or opinions. This, in turn, allows the parties to get to the heart of the matter and often to develop unique solutions to the problem. Indeed, the interactions may lead the groups to recognize that a problem in fact exists. Conflict, then, can be a catalyst for creativity and change in an organization.

**Conflict stimulation** is the creation and constructive use of conflict by a manager.

Several methods can be used to stimulate conflict under controlled conditions.[63] These include altering the physical location of groups to stimulate more interactions, forcing more resource sharing, and implementing other changes in relationships among groups. In addition, training programs can be used to increase

## figure 11.8

**Conflict Management Alternatives**

*Conflict management may involve resolution or stimulation of conflict, depending on the situation.*

| Conflict Management | |
| --- | --- |
| **Use Resolution under These Conditions** | **Use Stimulation under These Conditions** |
| Conflict has become disruptive. Too much time and effort are spent on conflict rather than on productive efforts. Conflict focuses on internal goals of the group rather than on organizational goals. | Work groups are stagnant and comfortable with the status quo. Consensus among groups is too easily reached. Groups are not creative or motivated to challenge traditional ideas. Change within the organization is needed to remain competitive. |

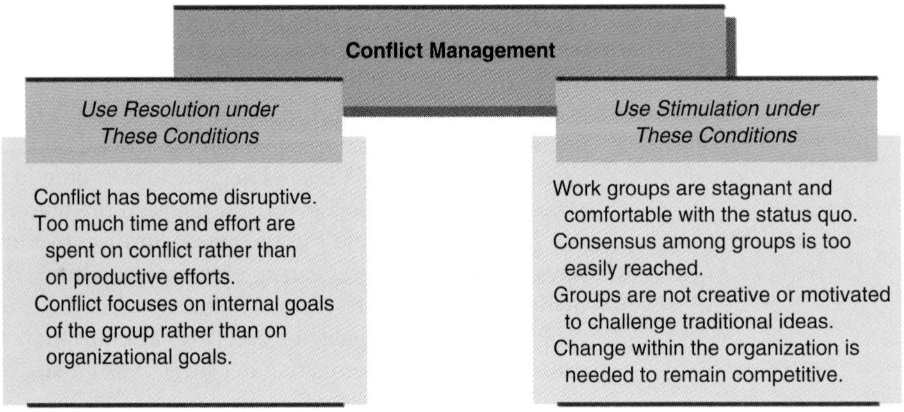

employee awareness of potential problems in group decision making and group interactions. Adopting the role of "devil's advocate" in discussion sessions is another way to stimulate conflict among groups. In this role, a manager challenges the prevailing consensus to ensure that all alternatives have been critically appraised and analyzed. Although this role is often unpopular, it is a good way to stimulate constructive conflict.

Of course, too much conflict is also a concern. If conflict becomes excessive or destructive, the manager needs to adopt a strategy to reduce or resolve it. Managers should first attempt to determine the source of the conflict. If the source of destructive conflict is a particular person or two, it might be appropriate to alter the membership of one or both groups. If the conflict is due to differences in goals, perceptions of the difficulty of goal attainment, or the importance of the goals to the conflicting parties, then the manager can attempt to move the conflicting parties into one of the five types of reactions to conflict, depending on the nature of the conflicting parties.

To foster collaboration, it might be appropriate to try to help people see that their goals are really not as different as they seem to be. The manager can help groups view their goals as part of a superordinate goal to which the goals of both conflicting parties can contribute. A **superordinate goal** is a goal of the overall organization and is more important to the well-being of the organization and its members than the more specific goals of the conflicting parties. If the goals are not really that important and are very incompatible, the manager may need to develop ways to help the conflicting parties avoid each other. Similarly, accommodation, competition, or compromise might be appropriate for the conflicting parties.

A **superordinate goal** is an organizational goal that is more important to the well-being of the organization and its members than the more specific goals of interacting parties.

# Managing Group and Intergroup Dynamics in Organizations

Managing groups in organizations is difficult. Managers must know what types of groups—command or task, formal or informal—exist in the organization. If a certain command group is very large, there will probably be several informal subgroups to be managed. A manager might want to take advantage of existing informal groups, "formalizing" some of them into command or task groups based on a subset of the tasks to be performed. Other informal groups may need to be broken up to make task assignment easier. In assigning tasks to people and subgroups, the manager must also consider individual motivations for joining groups and the composition of groups.

Quite often, a manager can help make sure a group develops into a productive unit by nurturing its activities in each stage of development. Helpful steps include encouraging open communication and trust among the members, stimulating discussion of important issues and providing task-relevant information at appropriate times, and helping analyze external factors such as competition and external threats and opportunities. Managers might also encourage the development of norms and roles within the group to help its development.

In managing a group, managers must consider both the goals of individual members and the goals of the group as a whole. Developing a reward structure that lets people reach their own goals by working toward those of the group can result in a very productive group. A manager may also be able to improve group cohesiveness, for example, by trying to stimulate competition, by provoking an

These employees of the Housing Development and Preservation department in New York City are participating in a laughing therapy seminar presented by Dr. Madan Kataria of India. Kataria recommends that people should laugh at least fifteen minutes a day to drive away the ills of stress, depression, and other ailments. As managers struggle with developing good group dynamics and managing group relationships, they should remember that people need to enjoy themselves in their work groups. Having a happy, healthy work group can make the development processes smoother, more enjoyable, and productive.

external threat to the group, by establishing a goal-setting system, or by employing participative approaches.

Managers must carefully choose strategies for dealing with interactions among groups after thorough examination and analysis of the groups, their goals, their unique characteristics, and the organizational setting in which the interactions occur. Managers can use a variety of strategies to increase the efficiency of intergroup interactions. One common mechanism is to encourage groups to focus on a superordinate goal, as mentioned earlier. In other situations, management might want to use a **linking role**, a position for a person or group that coordinates the activities of two or more organizational groups. This may add a layer of management, but in very important situations it may be worthwhile. Finally, management may need to change reporting relationships, decision-making priorities, and rules and procedures to properly manage group interactions.

A **linking role** is a position for a person or group that serves to coordinate the activities of two or more organizational groups.

In summary, managers must be aware of the implications—organizational and social—of their attempts to manage people in groups. Groups affect how their members behave, and it is member behavior that adds up to total group performance. Groups are so prevalent in our society that managers must strive to understand them better.

## Synopsis

A group is two or more people who interact so as to influence one another. It is important to study groups because groups are everywhere in our society, because they can profoundly affect individual behavior, and because the behavior of individuals in a group is key to the group's success or failure. The work group is the primary means by which managers coordinate individual behavior to achieve organizational goals. Individuals form or join groups because they expect to satisfy personal needs.

Groups may be differentiated on the bases of relative permanence and degree of formality. The three types of formal groups are command, task, and affinity groups. Friendship and interest groups are the two types of informal groups. Command groups are relatively permanent work groups established by the organization and usually are specified on an organization chart. Task groups, although also established by the organization, are relatively temporary and exist only until the specific task is accomplished. Affinity groups are formed by the organization, are composed of employees at the same level and doing similar jobs, and come together regularly to share information and discuss organizational issues. In friendship groups, the affiliation among members arises from close social relationships and the enjoyment that comes from being together. The common bond in interest groups is the activity in which the members engage.

Groups develop in four stages: mutual acceptance, communication and decision making, motivation and productivity, and control and organization. Although the stages are sequential, they may overlap. A group that does not fully develop within each stage will not fully mature as a group, resulting in lower group performance.

Four additional factors affect group performance: composition, size, norms, and cohesiveness. The homogeneity of the people in the group affects the interactions that occur and the productivity of the group. The effect of increasing the size of the group depends on the nature of the group's tasks and the people in the group. Norms help people function and relate to one another in predictable and efficient ways. Norms serve four purposes: they facilitate group survival, simplify and make more predictable the behaviors of group members, help the group avoid embarrassing situations, and express the central values of the group and identify the group to others.

To comprehend intergroup dynamics we must understand the key characteristics of groups: that each group is unique, that the specific organizational setting influences the group, and that the group's task and setting have an effect on group behavior. The five bases of intergroup interactions determine the characteristics of the interactions between groups, including their frequency, how much information is exchanged, and what type of interaction occurs.

Interactions among work groups involve some of the most complex relationships in organizations. They are based on five factors: location, resources, time and goal interdependence, task uncertainty, and task interdependence. Being physically near one another naturally increases groups' opportunities for interactions. If groups use the same or similar resources, or if one group can affect the availability of the resources needed by another group, the potential for frequent interactions increases. The nature of the tasks groups perform, including time and goal orientation, the uncertainties of group tasks, and group interdependencies, influences how groups interact.

Conflict is disagreement between parties; it is a common cause of stress in organizations. Five types of reactions to conflict are avoidance, accommodation, competition, collaboration, and compromise. The types of interactions are determined by the compatibility of goals and the importance of the interaction to group goal attainment. Managers should recognize that conflict can be beneficial as well as harmful.

Managers must be aware of the many factors that affect group performance and understand the individual as well as the group issues.

## Discussion Questions

1. Why is it useful for a manager to understand group behavior? Why is it useful for an employee?
2. Our definition of a group is somewhat broad. Would you classify each of the following collections of people as a group? Explain why.
   a. Seventy thousand people at a football game
   b. Students taking this course
   c. People in an elevator
   d. People on an escalator
   e. Employees of IBM
   f. Employees of your local college bookstore
3. List four groups to which you belong. Identify each as formal or informal.
4. Explain why each group you listed in question 3 formed. Why did you join each group? Why might others have decided to join each group?

5. In which stage of development is each of the four groups listed in question 3? Did any group move too quickly through any of the stages? Explain.
6. Analyze the composition of two of the groups to which you belong. How are they similar in composition? How do they differ?
7. Are any of the groups to which you belong too large or too small to get their work done? If so, what can the leader or the members do to alleviate the problem?
8. List two norms each for two of the groups to which you belong. How are these norms enforced?
9. Discuss the following statement: "Group cohesiveness is the good, warm feeling we get from working in groups and is something that all group leaders should strive to develop in the groups they lead."
10. Consider one of the groups to which you belong and describe the interactions that group has with another group.
11. Do you agree or disagree with the assertion that conflict can be both good and bad? Cite examples of both cases.

# Organizational Behavior Case for Discussion

## Procter & Gamble Seeks to Innovate

Procter & Gamble (P&G) is the typical great American company. It had $37 billion in revenues in 1998, more than four times more than its closest competitors in its primary industries. P&G has more than 300 brands (Tide, Crisco, Crest, and Charmin) in 140 countries and more than 110,000 employees. With that many brands and virtually worldwide coverage, its methods required pervasive adherence to precedent and doing things the P&G way. The company had been successful because everything was done by the same formula. But P&G started missing its growth projections. From 1994 to 1999, it lost about 10 percent of its global market share. In 1998, it expected to grow by 8 percent but actually grew by only 3 percent. In effect, P&G had stopped growing and was losing market share to rival Colgate-Palmolive.

In January 1999, P&G elevated Durk Jager, a twenty-nine-year P&G veteran, with three years as chief operating officer, to the position of chief executive officer. Jager's mission: to make changes and get the company back on the growth track. Jager blamed P&G's fall on the company's lack of new products and promptly promised a return to 8 percent growth by 2005. In his first year, Jager was called "Crazy Man Durk," among other things, but he made no excuses that he was there to break things, such as structure, culture, and comfort levels. Jager believes P&G's core business must be innovation, and that to innovate it must get away from its normal methods of operation. He has therefore reorganized the company structure from geographically based to product-based units and has cut 15,000 jobs. It used to take P&G five years to get a new product to market, compared to less than half that for its competitors. No one would take the risks for fear of jeopardizing their precious volume and market share numbers. In addition to a cumbersome structure, Jager knew he had to change the culture of the company to an innovative, risk-taking one.

To begin to shake things up in the cosmetics product development department, P&G sent twenty-two chemical engineers, biologists, and project leaders to a Virtual Thinking Expedition run by Rolf Smith from Colorado. The department knew they had to learn how to think and work together differently. Rolf's Virtual Thinking Expedition, which he has led for groups from other leading companies, seemed like the fastest way to do that. In an expedition similar to an Outward Bound exercise the group spent five days in the mountains of Virginia being forced to rethink the way they think. One activity included an all-day hike and climb in Virginia's Great Falls Park. The climb was arduous, requiring the group members to trust each other and take risks with each other in order to make it to the top and survive. Part of the climb was a sheer rock face requiring helmets and harnesses. Some made it, and some fell (they were saved by the group's safety ropes), but they all came back working together. The lessons relating climbing to thinking were obvious. But not so obvious were the lessons the group learned about working together. The rope linking the climbers together can be a metaphor for the invisible rope that keeps a high-performing innovative group together. The rope tension has to be kept at just the right level or the climbers will fall, just as emotional tensions must be at the right level or the group members' ability to think, create, and innovate will fall apart. Tensions became high during some of the sessions, and members really let others know how they felt about each other, both good and not so good. The key is that members had to go through these difficult experiences in order to learn how to work together as a group.

### Case Questions

1. What group performance factors might have been affected by this group's experiences?
2. How might the group's development process have been affected by these experiences?
3. How can this type of learning and development be created for other groups without going on a five-day hiking and mountain climbing experience?

References: "Procter & Gamble: Jager's Gamble," *Economist*, October 30, 1999, p. 75; Katrina Brooker, "Can Procter & Gamble Change Its Culture, Protect Its Market Share, and Find the Next Tide?" *Fortune*, April 26, 1999, pp. 146–152; Anna Muoio, "Idea Summit," *Fast Company*, January/February 1999, pp. 151–164.

## Experiencing Organizational Behavior

### Benefits of a Group

**Purpose:** This exercise demonstrates the benefits a group can bring to a task.

**Format:** You will be asked to do the same task both individually and as part of a group.

**Procedure:** You will need a pen or pencil and an 8 1/2" by 11" sheet of paper. Working alone, do the following:

#### Part 1

1. Write the letters of the alphabet in a vertical column down the left side of the paper: A–Z.
2. Your instructor will randomly select a sentence from any written document and read out loud the first twenty-six letters in that sentence. Write these letters in a vertical column immediately to the right of the alphabet column. Everyone should have an identical set of twenty-six two-letter combinations.
3. Working alone, think of a famous person whose initials correspond to each pair of letters, and write the name next to the letters—for example, "MT Mark Twain." You will have ten minutes. Only one name per set is allowed. One point is awarded for each legitimate name, so the maximum score is twenty-six points.
4. After time expires, exchange your paper with another member of the class and score each other's work. Disputes about the legitimacy of names will be settled by the instructor. Keep your score for use later in the exercise.

#### Part 2

Your instructor will divide the class into groups of five to ten people. All groups should have approximately the same number of members. Each group now follows the procedure given in part 1. Again write the letters of the alphabet down the left side of the sheet of paper, this time in reverse order: Z–A. Your instructor will dictate a new set of letters for the second column. The time limit and scoring procedure are the same. The only difference is that the groups will generate the names.

#### Part 3

Each team identifies the group member who came up with the most names. The instructor places these "best" students into one group. Then all groups repeat part 2, but this time the letters from the reading will be in the first column and the alphabet letters will be in the second column.

#### Part 4

Each team calculates the average individual score of its members on part 1 and compares it with the team score from parts 2 and 3, kept separately. Your instructor will put the average individual score and team scores from each part of each group on the board.

## Follow-up Questions

1. Are there differences in the average individual scores and the team scores? What are the reasons for the diffference, if any?
2. Although the team scores in this exercise usually are higher than the average individual scores, under what conditions might individual averages exceed group scores?

Reference: John E. Jones and J. William Pfeiffer (eds.), adapted from *The Handbook for Group Facilitators*, pp. 19–20. 

# Building Organizational Behavior Skills

## Group Cohesiveness

**Introduction:** You are probably a member of many different groups: study groups for school, work groups, friendship groups within a social club such as a fraternity or sorority, and interest groups. You probably have some feel for how tightly knit or cohesive each of those groups is. This exercise will help you diagnose the cohesiveness of one of those groups.

**Instructions:** First, pick one of the small groups to which you belong for analysis. Be sure that it is a small group, say between three and eight people. Next, rate on the following scale of 1 (poorly) to 5 (very well) how well you feel the group works together.

How well does this group work together?

| 1 | 2 | 3 | 4 | 5 |
|---|---|---|---|---|
| Poorly | Not Very Well | About Average | Pretty Well | Very Well |

Now answer the following six questions about the group. Put a check in the blank next to the answer that best describes how you feel about each question.

1. How many of the people in your group are friendly toward each other?
   ____ (5) All of them
   ____ (4) Most of them
   ____ (3) Some of them
   ____ (2) A few of them
   ____ (1) None of them
2. How much trust is there among members of your group?
   ____ (1) Distrust
   ____ (2) Little trust
   ____ (3) Average trust
   ____ (4) Considerable trust
   ____ (5) A great deal of trust
3. How much loyalty and sense of belonging is there among group members?
   ____ (1) No group loyalty of sense of belonging
   ____ (2) A little loyalty and sense of belonging
   ____ (3) An average sense of belonging
   ____ (4) An above-average sense of belonging
   ____ (5) A strong sense of belonging
4. Do you feel that you are really a valuable part of your group?
   ____ (5) I am really a part of my group.
   ____ (4) I am included in most ways.
   ____ (3) I am included in some ways, but not others.
   ____ (2) I am included in a few ways, but not many.
   ____ (1) I do not feel I really belong.
5. How friendly are your fellow group members toward each other?
   ___ (1) Not friendly
   ___ (2) Somewhat friendly
   ___ (3) Friendly to an average degree
   ___ (4) Friendlier than average
   ___ (5) Very friendly
6. If you had a chance to work with a different group of people doing the same task, how would you feel about moving to another group?
   ____ (1) I would want very much to move.
   ____ (2) I would rather move than stay where I am.
   ____ (3) It would make no difference to me.
   ____ (4) I would rather stay where I am than move.
   ____ (5) I would want very much to stay where I am.

Now add up the numbers you chose for all six questions and divide by 6. Total from all six questions = _____ / 6 = _____. This is the group cohesiveness score for your group.

Compare this number with the one you checked on the scale at the beginning of this exercise about how well you feel this group works together. Are they about the same, or are they quite different? If they are about the same, then you have a pretty good feel for the group and how it works. If they are quite different, then you probably need to analyze what aspects of the group functioning you misunderstood. (This is only part of a much longer instrument; it has not been scientifically validated in this form and is to be used for class discussion purposes only.)

Reference: The six questions were taken from the Groupthink Assessment Inventory by John R. Montanari and Gregory Moorhead, "Development of the Groupthink Assessment Inventory," *Educational and Psychological Measurement*, 1989, vol. 39, pp. 209–219. Reprinted by permission of Gregory Moorhead.

## Developing OB Internet Skills

**Introduction:** The focus of this chapter has been on intergroup conflict in organizations However, there are many different types of conflict, such as interpersonal conflict, political conflict, international conflict, military conflict, religious conflict, marital conflict, and others. Choose two different types of conflict to research on the Internet. You may use the ones mentioned here or some other type of conflict.

**Internet Assignment:** Use the Internet to research the two types of conflict that you have chosen. You may have to be creative in your search to find information on some of them.

**Follow-up:** How much information were you able to find on the types of conflict you chose? What different types of literature were you able to find on each? Finally, respond to the following questions about your findings:

1. How difficult was it to find out information on these topics?
2. Was the approach to conflict in the areas you researched quite different or similar to the conflict approach described in the text?
3. Why do you think the differences and similarities you found exist?

chapter 12

# Using Teams in Organizations

## Management Preview

Teams are an integral part of the management process in many organizations today. But the notion of teams as a way of organizing work is not new. Neither is it an American or Japanese innovation. One of the earliest uses and analyses of teams was the work of the Tavistock Institute in the late 1940s in the United Kingdom (discussed in more detail in Chapter 17).[1] Major companies such as Hewlett-Packard, Xerox, Procter & Gamble, General Motors, and General Mills have been using teams as a primary means of accomplishing tasks for many years.[2] The popular business press, such as *Fortune, Business Week, Forbes,* and the *Wall Street Journal,* regularly report on the use of teams in businesses around the world. The use of teams is not a fad of the month or some new way to manipulate workers into producing more at their own expense to enrich owners. Managers and experts agree that teams can be the way to organize and manage successfully in the twenty-first century.

This chapter presents a summary of many of the current issues involving teams in organizations. First, we define what "team" means and differentiate teams from normal work groups. We then discuss the rationale for using teams, including both the benefits and the costs. Next, we describe six types of teams in use in organizations today. Then we present the steps involved in implementing teams. Finally, we take a brief look at two essential issues that must be addressed. But first, we look at how an Australian company, Lend Lease Corporation, uses teams. ■

What kind of company with 4,500 employees and worldwide operations does not have an organization chart or a personnel, or human resource, department, yet claims it is passionate about its people and that its people love to work for the company? Lend Lease Corporation, headquartered in Sydney, Australia, is a financial services and property management and investment company that has made a profit for twenty-five consecutive years. In 1998–1999, Lend

Lease posted a net profit of U.S. $273.60, a significant increase over the previous year. Rather than a human resource department, it established the Lend Lease Foundation as a separate unit dedicated to its people. Each year each employee gets about $1,000 to spend on such things as gym memberships, yoga, reimbursement for family travel, home office setup, and computer training.

*"It was amazing.... None of them thought they could contribute to creating a global strategy, but they came together and unlocked enormous potential."* — *Stuart Hornery, chairman, Lend Lease Corp.**

Lend Lease also set up Springboard, an activity in which 250 employees work together in teams of 50 that meet for five days off-site to solve real business problems. These teams become the foundation for networking and long-lasting relationships within the company. One special team called Retailing the Globe was challenged to develop ways to raise their retail shopping center business from $40 million per year to $150 million. The Retailing the Globe team came back with a complete global strategic plan to take the business to $250 million per year.[3] ■

The Lend Lease Corporation certainly has a successful way of utilizing people and teams. It is quite successful in the insurance, financial services, and property management and investment business. The company's commitment to utilizing teams and investing in and taking care of its people is based on its trust that people do make the difference. This chapter describes some of the techniques for making the best use of teams in organizations.

# Differentiating Teams from Groups

Teams have been used, written about, and studied under many names and organizational programs: self-directed teams, self-managing teams, autonomous work groups, participative management, and many others. Groups and teams are not the same thing, although the two words are often used interchangeably in popular usage. A brief look at a dictionary shows that "group" usually refers to an assemblage of people or objects gathered together, whereas "team" usually refers to people or animals organized to work together.[4] Thus, a "team" places more emphasis on concerted action than a "group." In common, everyday usage, however, "committee," "group," "team," and "task force" are often used interchangeably.

In organizations, teams and groups are quite different. As we noted in Chapter 11, a group is two or more persons who interact with one another such that each person influences and is influenced by each other person. We specifically noted that individuals interacting and influencing each other need not have a common goal. The collection of people who happen to report to the same supervisor or manager in an organization can be called a "work group." Group members may be satisfying their own needs in the group and have little concern for a common objective. This is where a team and a group differ. In a team, all team members are committed to a common goal.

We could therefore say that a team is a group with a common goal. But teams differ from groups in other ways, too, and most experts are a bit more specific in

A **team** is a small number of people with complementary skills who are committed to a common purpose, common performance goals, and approach for which they hold themselves mutually accountable.

defining teams. A more elaborate definition is this: "A **team** is a small number of people with complementary skills who are committed to a common purpose, performance goals, and approach for which they hold themselves mutually accountable."[5] Several facets of this definition need further explanation. A team includes few people, much like the small group described in Chapter 11, because the interaction and influence processes needed for the team to function can only occur when the number of members is small. When many people are involved, they have difficulty interacting and influencing each other, utilizing their complementary skills, meeting goals, and holding themselves accountable. Regardless of the name, by our definition, mature, fully developed teams are self-directing, self-managing, and autonomous. If they are not, then someone from outside the group must be giving directions, so the group cannot be considered a true team.

*"Down with bosses! Up with teams! is the new battle cry of the world's leading organizations." — Charles C. Manz and Henry P. Sims Jr., leading authorities on the emergence of teams in organizations.*[6]

Teams include people with a mix of skills appropriate to the tasks to be done. Three types of skills are usually required in a team. First, the team needs to have members with the technical or functional skills to do the jobs. Some types of engineering, scientific, technological, legal, or business skills may be necessary. Second, some team members need to have problem-solving and decision-making skills to help the team identify problems, determine priorities, evaluate alternatives, analyze tradeoffs, and make decisions about the direction of the team. Third, members need interpersonal skills to manage communication flow, resolve conflict, direct questions and discussion, provide support, and recognize the interests of all members of the team. Not all members will have all of the required skills, especially when the team first convenes; different members will have different skills. However, as the team grows, develops, and matures, team members will come to have more of the necessary skills.

Having a common purpose and common performance goals sets the tone and direction of the team. A team comes together to take action to pursue a goal, unlike a work group, in which members report to the same supervisor or work in the same department. The purpose becomes the focus of the team, which makes all decisions and takes all actions in pursuit of the goal. Teams often spend days or weeks establishing the reason for their existence, which builds strong identification and fosters commitment to it. Usually, the defining purpose comes first, followed by development of specific performance goals. For example, a team of local citizens, teachers, and parents may come together for the purpose of making the local schools the best in the state. Then the team establishes specific performance goals to serve as guides for decision making, to maintain the focus on action, to differentiate this team from other groups who may want to improve schools, and to challenge people to commit themselves to the team. One further note on the importance of purpose and performance goals for teams: Katzenbach and Smith studied more than thirty teams and found that demanding, high-performance goals often challenge members to create a real team, as opposed to a group, because when goals are truly demanding, members must pull together, find resources within themselves, develop and use the appropriate skills, and take a common approach to reach the goals.[7]

Agreeing on a common approach is especially important for teams, because it is often the approach that differentiates one team from others. The team's approach usually covers how work will be done, social norms regarding dress, attendance at meetings, tardiness, norms of fairness and ethical behavior, and what will and will not be included in the team activities.

Finally, the definition states that teams hold themselves mutually accountable for results, rather than merely meeting a manager's demands for results, as in the traditional approach. If the members translate accountability to an external manager into internal, or mutual, accountability, the group moves toward acting like a team. Mutual accountability is essentially a promise that members make to each other to do everything possible to achieve their goals, and it requires the commitment and trust of all members. It is the promise of each member to hold himself or herself accountable for the team's goals that earns each individual the right to express her or his views and expect them to get a fair and constructive hearing. With this promise, members maintain and strengthen the trust necessary for the team to succeed. The clearly stated high-performance goals and the common approach serve as the standards to which the team holds itself. Because teams are mutually accountable for meeting performance goals, three other differences between groups and teams become important: job categories, authority, and reward systems. The differences for traditional work groups and work teams are shown in Table 12.1.

## Job Categories

The work of conventional groups is usually described in terms of highly specialized jobs that require minimal training and moderate effort. Tens or even hundreds of people may have similar job descriptions and see little relationship between their effort and the end result or finished product. In teams, on the other hand, members have many different skills that fit into one or two broad job categories. Neither workers nor management worries about who does what job as long as the team puts out the finished product or service and meets its performance goals.

## Authority

As shown in Table 12.1, in conventional work groups, the supervisor directly controls the daily activities of workers. In teams, the team discusses what activities need to be done and determines for itself who has the necessary skills and will do each task. The team makes the decisions rather than the supervisor. If a

table 12.1

**Differences Between Teams and Traditional Work Groups**

| Issue | Conventional Work Groups | Teams |
|---|---|---|
| Job Categories | Many narrow categories | One or two broad categories |
| Authority | Supervisor directly controls daily activities | Team controls daily activities |
| Reward System | Depends on the type of job, individual performance, and seniority | Based on team performance and individual breadth of skills |

Reference: Adapted from Jack D. Osburn, Linda Moran, and Ed Musselwhite, with Craig Perrin, *Self-Directed Work Teams: The New American Challenge* (Homewood, Ill.: Business One Irwin, 1990), p. 11.

David Steward is the CEO and chairman of World Wide Technology (WWT), a company that provides state-of-the-art electronic business solutions. It has developed partnerships with Lucent Technologies, Sun Microsystems, Oracle, and Cisco Systems, to name just a few. In 1993, WWT was $2 million in debt with little hope for survival. Steward turned the company around by creating a more team-oriented approach. He opened the books to the rest of management and engaged them in turning the company around. Together the management team set new goals and directions for the company and worked to achieve them as a team. The new team-oriented approach succeeded. WWT had $135 million in revenues in 1999 and was ranked number 11 on the *Black Enterprise Industrial/Service 100* list.

"supervisor" remains on the team, the role usually changes to that of coach, facilitator, or one who helps the teams make decisions, rather than the traditional role of decision maker and controller.

## Reward Systems

How employees are rewarded is vital to the long-term success of an organization. The traditional reward and compensation systems suitable for individual motivation (discussed in Chapter 8) are simply not appropriate in a team-based organization. In conventional settings, employees are usually rewarded on the basis of their individual performance, their seniority, or their job classification. In a team-based situation, team members are rewarded for mastering a range of skills needed to meet team performance goals, and rewards are sometimes based on team performance. Such a pay system tends to promote the flexibility that teams need to be responsive to changing environmental factors. Three types of reward systems are common in a team environment: skill-based pay, gain-sharing systems, and team bonus plans.

**Skill-Based Pay** Skill-based pay systems require team members to acquire a set of the core skills needed for their particular team, plus additional special skills, depending on career tracks or team needs. Some programs require all members to acquire the core skills before any member receives additional pay. Usually employees can increase their base compensation by some fixed amount, say $0.30 per hour for each additional skill acquired, up to some fixed maximum. Companies using skill-based pay systems include Eastman Chemical Company, Colgate-Palmolive Company, and Pfizer.[8]

**Gain-Sharing Systems** Gain-sharing systems usually reward all team members from all teams based on the performance of the organization, division, or plant. Such a system requires a baseline performance that must be exceeded for team members to receive some share of the gain over the baseline measure. Westinghouse gives equal one-time, lump-sum bonuses to everyone in the plant based on improvements in productivity, cost, and quality.[9] Employee reaction is usually positive, because when employees work harder to help the company, they share in the profits they helped generate. On the other hand, when business conditions or other factors outside of their control make it impossible to generate improvements over the preset baseline, employees may feel disappointed and even disillusioned with the process.

Team Bonus Plans Team bonus plans are similar to gain-sharing plans except that the unit of performance and pay is the team rather than a plant, a division, or the entire organization. Each team must have specific performance targets or baseline measures that the team considers realistic for the plan to be effective. Companies using team bonus plans include Milwaukee Insurance Company, Colgate-Palmolive, and Harris Corporation.[10]

Changes in an organizational compensation system can be traumatic and threatening to most employees. However, matching the reward system to the way that work is organized and accomplished can have very positive benefits. The three types of team-based reward systems presented can be used in isolation for simplicity, or in some combination to address different types of issues for each organization.

# Why Teams? Benefits and Costs of Teams in Organizations

With the popularity of teams increasing so rapidly around the world, it is possible that some organizations are starting to use teams simply because everyone else is doing it, which is obviously the wrong reason. The reason to create teams is because teams make sense for that organization. The best reason to start teams in any organization is the positive benefits that can result from a team-based environment: enhanced performance, employee benefits, reduced costs, and organizational enhancements. Four categories of benefits and some examples are shown in Table 12.2.

## Enhanced Performance

Enhanced performance can come in many forms, including improved productivity, quality, and customer service. Working in teams enables workers to avoid wasted effort, reduce errors, and react better to customers, resulting in more output for each unit of employee imput.

*"I learned a long time ago that a team will always defeat an individual." —John Chambers, CEO of Cisco Systems, Inc.*[11]

Such enhancements result from pooling of individual efforts in new ways and from striving to continuously improve for the benefit of the team. For example, a General Electric plant in North Carolina experienced a 20 percent increase in productivity after team implementation.[12] K Shoes reported a 19 percent increase in productivity and significant reductions in rejects in the manufacturing process.[13]

table 12.2

**Benefits of Teams in Organizations**

| Type of Benefit | Specific Benefit | Organizational Examples |
|---|---|---|
| **Enhanced Performance** | • Increased productivity<br>• Improved quality<br>• Improved customer service | Ampex: On-time customer delivery rose 98%.<br>K Shoes: Rejects per million dropped from 5,000 to 250.<br>Eastman: Productivity rose 70%. |
| **Employee Benefits** | • Quality of work life<br>• Lower stress | Milwaukee Mutual: Employee assistance program usage dropped to 40% below industry average. |
| **Reduced Costs** | • Lower turnover, absenteeism<br>• Fewer injuries | Kodak: Reduced turnover to one-half the industry average.<br>Texas Instruments: Reduced costs more than 50%.<br>Westinghouse: Costs down 60%. |
| **Organizational Enhancements** | • Increased innovation, flexibility | IDS Mutual Fund Operations: Improved flexibility to handle fluctuations in market activity.<br>Hewlett-Packard: Innovative order-processing system. |

References: Adapted from Richard S. Wellins, William C. Byham, and George R. Dixon, *Inside Teams* (San Francisco: Jossey-Bass, 1994); Charles C. Manz and Henry P. Sims Jr., *Business Without Bosses* (New York: Wiley, 1993).

## Employee Benefits

Employees tend to benefit as much as organizations in a team environment. Much attention has focused on the differences between the baby-boom generation and the "postboomers" in attitudes toward work, its importance to their lives, and what they want from it. In general, younger workers tend to be less satisfied with their work and the organization, to have lower respect for authority and supervision, and to want more than a paycheck every week. Teams can provide the sense of self-control, human dignity, identification with the work, and sense of self-worth and self-fulfillment that current workers seem to strive for. Rather than relying on the traditional, hierarchical, manager-based system, teams give employees freedom to grow and gain respect and dignity by managing themselves, making decisions about their work, and really making a difference in the world around them.[14] As a result employees have a better work life, face less stress at work, and make less use of employee assistance programs.

## Reduced Costs

As empowered teams reduce scrap, make fewer errors, file fewer worker compensation claims, and reduce absenteeism and turnover, organizations based on teams are showing significant cost reductions. Team members feel that they have a stake in the

Chuck Sapp is a member of the North Carolina Rescue Team that assists in the rescue of people during and following natural disasters, such as floods. This team practices suturing chicken legs (supervised by medical doctors) while they wait to be called into action. In emergency rescue operations, teams are necessary to success. No individual or disconnected group of people could possibly do this work. Excellent teamwork is the only way to rescue people from rooftops and save lives.

outcomes, want to make contributions because they are valued, and are committed to their team and do not want to let it down. Wilson Sporting Goods reported saving $10 million per year for five years thanks to its teams. Colgate-Palmolive reported that technician turnover was extremely low—more than 90 percent of technicians were retained after five years—once it moved to a team-based approach.[15]

## Organizational Enhancements

Other improvements in organizations that result from moving from a hierarchically based, directive culture to a team-based culture include increased innovation, creativity, and flexibility. Use of teams can eliminate redundant layers of bureaucracy and flatten the hierarchy in large organizations. Employees feel closer and more in touch with top management. Employees who feel their efforts are important are more likely to make significant contributions. In addition, the team environment constantly challenges teams to innovate and solve problems creatively. If the "same old way" does not work, empowered teams are free to throw it out and develop a new way. With increasing global competition, organizations must constantly adapt to keep abreast of changes. Teams provide the flexibility to react quickly. The "World View" box describes how some companies are staying flexible with global teams. One of Motorola's earliest teams challenged a long-standing top-management policy regarding supplier inspections in order to reduce the cycle times and improve delivery of crucial parts.[16] After several attempts, management finally allowed the team to change the system and reaped the expected benefits.

WORLD VIEW

## *Global SWAT Teams*

Dell hires mostly foreign managers and uses expatriate managers in its offices around the world. However, it also uses a group of specialized executives to move around the globe assisting local managers set up new operations or solve problems. For example, Buddy Griffin heads a team that spends six months to a year in various locations around the world setting up factory operations. Mr. Griffin started out in manufacturing at the Austin, Texas, plant and went on to design plant facilities in Ireland, Malaysia, China, and Brazil.

Microsoft is another company that uses teams that operate globally. These teams move around the world and communicate via email on all types of different projects.

Many companies believe that it is essential for the next generation of managers to have international management experience. Working with cross-border teams and assignments teaches individuals how to deal with, and be a leader in, different cultures. Other companies with this philosophy are Bestfoods, Merck, Pfizer, American Express, and General Electric, all companies on *Fortune* magazine's list of the World's Most Admired Companies.

*"In our domestic operations and our global business, flexibility is a must."—Andy Esparza, vice president for global staffing at Dell*

References: Jeremy Kahn, "The World's Most Admired Companies," *Fortune,* October 11, 1999, pp. 267–282 (quote on p. 272); Eryn Brown, "America's Most Admired Companies," *Fortune,* March 1, 1999, pp. 68–73.

## Costs of Teams

The costs of teams are usually expressed in terms of the difficulty of changing to a team-based organization. Managers have expressed frustration and confusion about their new roles as coaches and facilitators, especially if they developed their managerial skills under the old traditional hierarchical management philosophy. Some managers have felt as if they were working themselves out of a job as they turned over more and more of their old directing duties to the team.[17]

Employees may also feel like losers during the change to a team culture. Some traditional staff groups, such as technical advisory staffs, may feel that their jobs are in jeopardy as teams do more and more of the technical work formerly done by technicians. New roles and pay scales may need to be developed for the technical staff in these situations. Often, technical people have been assigned to a team or a small group of teams and become members who fully participate in team activities.

Another cost associated with teams is the slowness of the process of full team development. As discussed elsewhere in this chapter, it takes a long time for teams to go through the full development cycle and become mature, efficient, and effective. The cartoon shows how a company can go overboard with teams. If top management is impatient with the slow progress, teams may be disbanded, returning the organization to its original hierarchical form with significant losses for employees, managers, and the organization.

Probably the most dangerous cost is premature abandonment of the change to a team-based organization. If top management gets impatient with the team change process and cuts it short, never allowing teams to fully develop and realize benefits, all the hard work of employees, middle managers, and supervisors is lost. Employee confidence in management in general and in the decision makers in par-

It does not look as if these people are going to move fast enough to solve their problem. It can take a long time for a collection of people to fully develop into a mature, cohesive, self-correcting, mutually accountable, high-performing team. But these folks are going to take even longer.

Reference: © Randy Glasbergen

**"Let's form a committee to create a task force to develop a team to determine the fastest way to deal with the problem."**

ticular may suffer for a long time. The losses in productivity and efficiency will be very difficult to recoup. Management must therefore be fully committed before initiating a change to a team-based organization.

# Types of Teams

Many different types of teams exist in organizations today. Some evolved naturally in organizations that permit various types of participative and empowering management programs. Others have been formally created at the suggestion of enlightened management. One easy way to classify teams is by what they do; for example, some teams make or do things, some teams recommend things, and some teams run things. The most common type of teams are quality circles, work teams, and problem-solving teams; management teams are also quite common.

## Quality Circles

**Quality circles** are small groups of employees from the same work area who regularly meet to discuss and recommend solutions to workplace problems.

**Quality circles** (QCs) are small groups of employees from the same work area who meet regularly (usually weekly or monthly) to discuss and recommend solutions to workplace problems.[18] QCs were the first type of team created in U.S. organizations, becoming most popular during the 1980s in response to growing Japanese competition. QCs had some success in reducing rework and cutting defects on the shop floors of many manufacturing plants. Some attempts have been made to use QCs in offices and service operations, too. They exist alongside the traditional management structure and are relatively permanent. The role of QCs is to investigate a variety of quality problems that might come up in the workplace. They do not replace the work group or make decisions about how the work is done. Interest in QCs has dropped somewhat, although a 1994 survey indicated that 65 percent of companies still have them.[19] QCs are teams that make recommendations.

## Work Teams

**Work teams** include all the people working in an area, are relatively permanent, and do the daily work, making decisions regarding how the work of the team is done.

**Work teams** tend to be permanent, like QCs, but they are the teams that do the daily work, rather than auxiliary committees.[20] A team of nurses, orderlies, and various technicians responsible for all patients on a floor or wing in a hospital is a work team. Rather than investigate a specific problem, evaluate alternatives, and recommend a solution or change, a work team does the actual daily work of the unit. The difference between a traditional work group of nurses and the patient care team is that the latter has the authority to decide how the work is done, in what order, and by whom; the entire team is responsible for all patient care. When the team decides how the work is to be organized or done, it becomes a self-managing team, to which accrue all of the benefits described in this chapter. Work teams are teams that make or do things.

## Problem-Solving Teams

**Problem-solving teams** are temporary teams established to attack specific problems in the workplace.

**Problem-solving teams** are temporary teams established to attack specific problems in the workplace. Teams can use any number of methods to solve the problem, as discussed in Chapter 15. After solving the problem, the team is usually disbanded, allowing members to return to their normal work. A 1994 survey found that 91 percent of U.S. companies utilize problem-solving teams regularly.[21] High-performing problem-solving teams are often cross-functional, meaning that team members come from many different functional areas. Crisis teams are problem-solving teams created only for the duration of an organizational crisis and are usually composed of people from many different areas. Problem-solving teams are teams that make recommendations for others to implement.

## Management Teams

**Management teams** consist of managers from various areas; they coordinate work teams.

**Management teams** consist of managers from various areas and coordinate work teams. They are relatively permanent because their work does not end with the completion of a particular project or the resolution of a problem. Management teams must concentrate on the teams that have the most impact on overall corporate performance. The primary job of management teams is to coach and counsel other teams to be self-managing by making decisions within the team. The second most important task of management teams is to coordinate work between work teams that are interdependent in some manner. Digital Equipment Corporation recently announced it was abandoning its team matrix structure because the matrix of teams was not well organized and coordinated. Team members at all levels reported spending hours and hours in meetings trying to coordinate among teams, leaving too little time to get the real work done.[22]

*"I couldn't do this job if I didn't have them." — **Jack Welch, CEO of General Electric on the importance of his top-management team.**[23]*

Top-management teams may have special types of problems. First, the work of the top-management team may not be conducive to teamwork. Vice presidents or heads of divisions may be in charge of different sets of operations that are not related and do not need to be coordinated. Jack Welch, CEO of General Electric, is known for his take-charge attitude, but he attributes much of his success to his top-management team.

Forcing that type of top management group to be a team may be inappropriate. Second, top managers often have reached high levels in the organization because they have certain characteristics or abilities to get things done. For successful managers to alter their style, to pool resources, and to sacrifice their independence and individuality can be very difficult.[24]

## Product Development Teams

**Product development teams** are combinations of work teams and problem-solving teams that create new designs for products or services that will satisfy customer needs.

**Product development teams** are combinations of work teams and problem-solving teams that create new designs for products or services that will satisfy customer needs. They are similar to problem-solving teams because when the product is fully developed and in production, the team may be disbanded. As global competition and electronic information storage, processing, and retrieving capabilities increase, companies in almost every industry are struggling to cut product development times. The primary organizational means of accomplishing this important task is the "blue-ribbon" cross-functional team. Boeing's development of the 777 commercial airplane and the platform teams of Chrysler are typical examples.

The rush to market with new designs can lead to numerous problems for product development teams. The primary problems of poor communication and coordination of typical product development processes in organizations can be rectified by creating self-managing cross-functional product development teams.[25]

## Virtual Teams

**Virtual teams** work together by computer and other electronic communication utilities; members move in and out of meetings and the team itself as the situation dictates.

**Virtual teams** are teams that may never actually meet together in the same room—their activities take place on the computer via teleconferencing and other electronic information systems. Engineers in the United States can connect audibly and visually directly with counterparts all around the globe, sharing files via Internet, electronic mail, and other communication utilities; all participants can look at the same drawing, print, or specification, so decisions are made much faster.

IBM manager Joanna Dapkevich works at home part of the time, yet she still manages to stay in touch with her team by telephone and other electronic media. IBM is convinced that employees can be more productive if they are better able to integrate their work with the rest of their lives, which includes balancing the demands of family. Since Dapkevich's new work arrangement began, her team of customer service reps has dramatically increased their customer satisfaction ratings.

With electronic communication systems team members can move in or out of a team or a team discussion as the issues warrant.

# Implementing Teams in Organizations

Implementing teams in organizations is not easy; it takes a lot of hard work, time, training, and patience. Changing from a traditional organizational structure to a team-based structure is much like other organizational changes (which we discuss in Chapter 19). It is really a complete cultural change for the organization. Typically, the organization is hierarchically designed in order to provide clear direction and control. Yet, many organizations need to be able to react quickly to a dynamic environment. Team procedures artificially imposed on existing processes are a recipe for disaster. In this section we present several essential elements peculiar to an organizational change to a team-based situation.

## Planning the Change

The change to a team-based organization requires a lot of analysis and planning before it is implemented; the decision cannot be made overnight and quickly implemented. It is such a drastic departure from the traditional hierarchy and authority-and-control orientation that significant planning, preparation, and training are prerequisites. The planning actually takes place in two phases, the first leading to the decision about whether to move to a team-based approach and the second while preparing for implementation.

**Making the Decision** Prior to making the decision, top management needs to establish the leadership for the change, develop a steering committee, conduct a feasibility study, and then make the go/no-go decision, as shown in Table 12.3. Top management must be sure that the team culture is consistent with its strategy, as we discuss in Chapter 18. Quite often the leadership for the change is the chief executive officer, the chief operating officer, or another prominent person in top management. Regardless of the position, the person leading the change needs to (1) have a strong belief that employees want to be responsible for their work, (2) be able to demonstrate the team philosophy, (3) articulate a coherent vision of the team environment, and (4) have the creativity and authority to overcome obstacles as they surface.[26]

The leader of the change needs to put together a steering committee to help explore the organization's readiness for the team environment and lead it through the planning and preparation for the change. The steering committee can be of any workable size, from two to ten people who are influential and know the work and the organization. Members may include plant or division managers, union representatives, human resource department representatives, and operational-level employees. The work of the steering committee includes visits to sites that might be candidates for utilizing work teams, visits to currently successful work teams, data gathering

table 12.3 **The First Four Steps of Planning to Change to Teams**

| | |
|---|---|
| Step 1: | Establish leadership |
| Step 2: | Develop a steering committee |
| Step 3: | Conduct a feasibility study |
| Step 4: | Make the go/no-go decision |

Reference: Jack D. Orsburn, Linda Moran, and Ed Musselwhite, with Craig Perrin, *Self-Directed Work Teams: The New American Challenge* (Homewood, Ill.: Business One Irwin, 1990), pp. 35–49.

and analysis, low-key discussions, and deliberating and deciding whether to use a consultant during the change process.

A feasibility study is a necessity before making the decision to use teams. The steering committee needs to know if the work processes are conducive to team use; if the employees are willing and able to work in a team environment; if the managers in the unit to be converted are willing to learn and apply the hands-off managerial style necessary to make teams work; if the organization's structure and culture are ready to accommodate a team-based organization; if the market for the unit's products or services is growing or at least stable enough to absorb the increased productive capacity that teams will be putting out; and if the community will support the transition teams. Without answers to these questions, management is merely guessing and hoping that teams will work and may be destined for many surprises that could doom the effort.

After establishing the leadership, setting up the steering committee, and conducting a feasibility study, the go/no-go decision can be made. The committee and top management will need to jointly decide to go ahead if conditions are right. On the other hand, if the feasibility study indicates that questions exist as to whether the organizational unit is ready, the committee can decide to postpone implementation while changes are made in personnel, organizational structure, organizational policies, or market conditions. The committee could also decide to implement training and acculturation for employees and managers in the unit in preparation for later implementation.

**Preparing for Implementation** Once the decision is made to change to a team-based organization, much needs to be done before implementation can begin. Preparation consists of the following five steps: clarifying the mission, selecting the site for the first work teams, preparing the design team, planning the transfer of authority, and drafting the preliminary plan.

The mission statement is simply an expression of purpose that summarizes the long-range benefits the company hopes to gain by moving to a team environment. It must be consistent with the organization's strategy as it establishes a common set of assumptions for executives, middle managers, support staff, and the teams. In addition, it sets the parameters or boundaries within which the change will take place. It may identify which divisions or plants will be involved or what levels will be converted to teams. The mission statement attempts to stimulate and focus the energy of those people who need to be involved in the change. The mission can focus on continuous improvement, employee involvement, increasing performance, competition, customer satisfaction, and contributions to society. The steering committee should involve many people from many different areas to foster fuller involvement in the change.

Once the mission is established, the steering committee needs to decide where teams will be implemented first. Selection of the first site is crucial because it sets the tone for the success of the total program. The best initial site would be one that includes workers from multiple job categories, one where improving performance or reaching the targets set in the mission is feasible, and one where workers accept the idea of using teams. Also valuable are a tradition or history of success and a staff that is receptive to training, especially training in interpersonal skills. One manufacturing company based its choice of sites for initial teams not on criteria such as these but on the desire to reward the managers of successful divisions or to "fix" areas performing poorly. Team implementation in that company was very slow and not very successful.[27] Initial sites must also have a local "champion" of the team concept.

Once the initial sites have been identified, the steering committee needs to set up the team who will design the other teams. The design team is a select group of employees, supervisors, and managers who will work out the staffing and operational details to make the teams perform well. The design team selects the initial team members, prepares members and managers for teams, changes work processes for use with the team design, and plans the transition from the current state to the new self-managed teams. The design team usually spends the first three months learning from the steering committee, visiting sites where teams are being used successfully, and spending a significant amount of time in classroom training. Considering the composition of the teams is one of the most important decisions the design team has to make. The "Talking Technology" box describes one important factor to be considered.

Planning the transfer of authority from management to teams is the most important phase of planning the implementation. It is also the most distinctive and difficult part of moving to a team-based organization. It is difficult because it is so

**TALKING TECHNOLOGY**

## *Working with Geeks—Novell's Secrets*

Silicon Valley and all the new electronically driven companies survive, profit, or die on the backs of the technology gurus that develop the sophisticated systems, hardware, and software upon which these firms are based. Eric Schmidt, CEO of Novell, Inc. managed to turn around the struggling company in less than two years, partly because of his ability to manage these technical wizards. He uses the term "geek" (and can because he is one, with a Ph.D. in computer science) to describe this group of technologists that rule the cyberworld. Some of Schmidt's keys to success in this world are to have your own geeks, get to know your geeks, learn what your geeks are looking for, and create new ways to promote your geeks.

*"One of the main characteristics of geeks is that they are very truthful. They are taught to think logically." — Eric Schmidt, CEO of Novell, Inc.*

Some of Schmidt's most interesting ideas involve working with geeks in teams. He suggests, first of all, that putting geeks together on teams with other geeks creates productive peer pressure. Geeks care a great deal about how other geeks and the professional community perceive them. They are good at judging the quality of technical work. Some are quite arrogant, but Schmidt claims that having them work in teams together is the best way to control them—by letting them control each other.

Schmidt's second team-based suggestion is that too many geeks spoil the soup. By this he means that teams should be kept small. Too many geeks on the development team increases the time it will take to complete the project. He claims that smaller teams work faster to complete the job. He strongly urges breaking large projects down into smaller, more manageable projects and making each subteam responsible for shipping their small part of the project to the other teams on a timely basis. This keeps the project on time and makes the teams responsible to each other.

Schmidt's turnaround of Novell is based on the original idea of networking that made the company successful several years earlier. That time, leadership at the top let the company get distracted. Microsoft's NT software came along and won market share. This time, however, Schmidt expects to utilize his geeks to keep Novell's networking software hot on the market.

References: Russ Mitchell, "How to Manage Geeks," *Fast Company,* June 1999, pp. 175–180 (quote on p. 176). "Novell: Eric Schmidt Turns Company Around," Economist, April 3, 1999, p. 54; Russ Mitchell, "I Survived Microsoft: Novell's Geeky New CEO Aims to Prosper in Bill's World," *U.S. News & World Report,* June 15, 1998, pp. 38–42.

different from the traditional, hierarchical organization management system. It is a gradual process, one that takes from two to five years in most situations. Teams must learn new skills and make new decisions related to their work, all of which takes time. It is, essentially, a cultural change for the organization.

The last stage of planning the implementation is to write the tentative plan for the initial work teams. The draft plan combines the work of the steering and design committees and becomes the primary working document that guides the continuing work of the design teams and the first work teams. The draft plan (1) recommends a process for selecting the people who will be on the first teams; (2) describes roles and responsibilities for all the people who will be affected (team members, team leaders, facilitators, support teams, managers, and top management); (3) explains what training the several groups will need; (4) identifies specifically which work processes will be involved; (5) describes what other organizational systems will be affected; and (6) lays out a preliminary master schedule for the next two to three years. Once the steering committee and top management approve the preliminary plan, the organization is ready to start the implementation.

## Phases of Implementation

Implementation of self-managing work teams is a long and difficult process, often taking two to five years. During this period, the teams go through a number of phases (Figure 12.1); these phases are not, however, readily apparent at the time the team is going through them.

**Phase 1: Start-Up** In phase 1, team members are selected and prepared to work in teams so that the teams have the best possible chance of success. Much of the initial training is informational or "awareness" training that sends the message that top management is firmly committed to teams and that teams are not experimental. The steering committee usually starts the training at the top, and the training and information are passed down the chain to the team members. Training covers the rationale for moving to a team-based organization, how teams were selected, how they work, the roles and responsibilities of teams, compensation, and job security. In general, training covers the technical skills necessary to do the work of the team, the administrative skills necessary for the team to function within the organization, and the interpersonal skills necessary to work with people in the team and throughout the organization. Sometimes the interpersonal skills are important. Perhaps most important is establishing the idea that teams are not "unmanaged" but "differently managed." The difference is that the new teams manage themselves. Team boundaries are also identified, and the preliminary plan is adjusted to fit the particular team situations. Employees typically feel that much is changing during the first few months, enthusiasm runs high, and the anticipation of employees is quite positive. Performance by teams increases at start-up because of this initial enthusiasm for the change.

**Phase 2: Reality and Unrest** After perhaps six to nine months, team members and managers report frustration and confusion about the ambiguities of the new situation. For employees, unfamiliar tasks, more responsibility, and worry about job security replace hope for the opportunities presented by the new approach. All of the training and preparation, as important as it is, is never enough to prepare for the storm and backlash. Cummins Engine Company held numerous "prediction

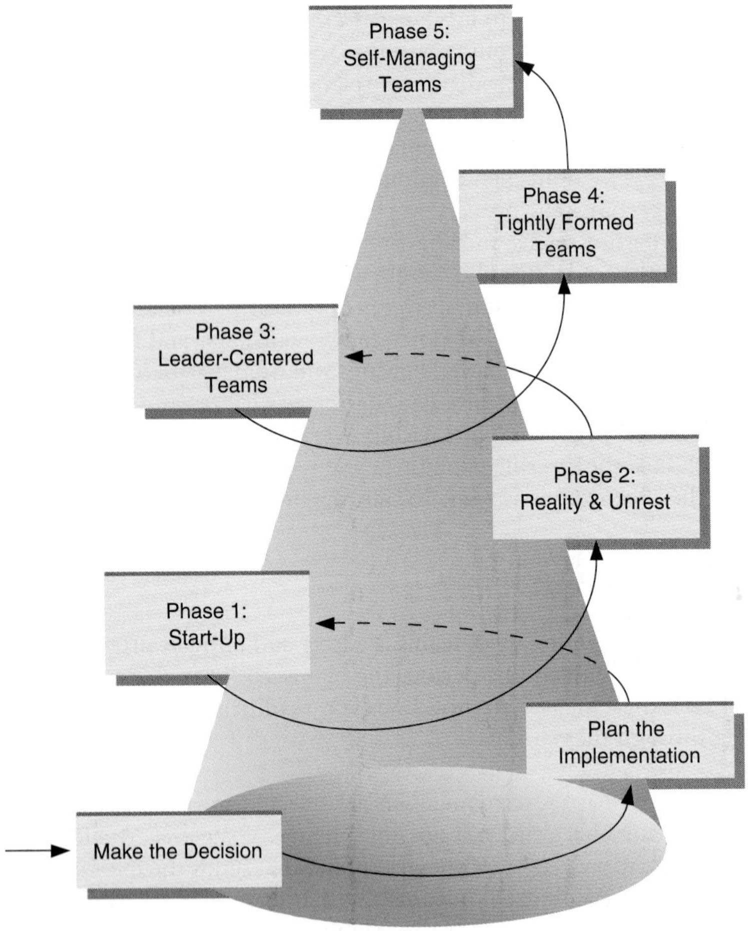


figure 12.1 **Phases of Team Implementation**

*Implementation of teams in organizations is a long and arduous process. After the decision is made to initiate teams, the steering committee develops the plans for the design team, which plans the entire process. The goal is for teams to become self-managing. The time it takes for each stage varies with the organization.*

workshops" in an effort to prepare employees and managers for the difficulties that lay ahead, all to no avail. Their employees reported the same problems that employees of other companies did. The best advice is to perform phase 1 very well and then make managers very visible, continue to work to clarify the roles and responsibilities of everyone involved, and reinforce the positive behaviors that do occur.[28]

Some managers make the mistake of staying completely away from the newly formed teams, thinking that the whole idea is to let teams manage themselves. In reality, managers need to be very visible to provide encouragement, to monitor team performance, to act as intermediaries between teams, to help teams acquire needed resources, to foster the right type of communication, and sometimes to protect teams from those who want to see them fail. Managers, too, feel the unrest and confusion. The change they supported results in more work for them. In addition, there is the real threat, at least initially, that work will not get done, projects may not get finished, or orders will not get shipped on time, and that they will be blamed for the problems.[29] Managers also report they still have to intervene and solve problems for the teams because the teams do not know what they are doing.

**Phase 3: Leader-Centered Teams** As the discomfort and frustrations of the previous phase peak, teams usually long for a system that resembles the old manager-centered organizational structure (see Figure 12.1). However, members are learning about self-direction and leadership from within the team and usually start to focus on a single leader in the team. In addition, the team begins to think of itself as a unit as members learn to manage themselves. Managers begin to get a sense of the positive possibilities of organizing in teams and begin to slowly withdraw from the daily operation of the unit to begin focusing on standards, regulations, systems, and resources for the team.[30] This phase is not a setback to team development, although it may seem like one, because development of and reliance on one internal leader is a move away from focusing on the old hierarchy and traditional lines of authority.

The design and steering committees need to be sure that two things happen during this phase.[31] First, they need to encourage the rise of strong internal team leaders. The new leaders can either be company appointed or team appointed. Top management sometimes prefers the additional control they get from appointing the team leaders, assuming that production will continue through the team transition. On the other hand, if the company-appointed leaders are the former managers, team members have trouble believing that anything has changed. Team-appointed leaders can be a problem if the leaders are not trained properly and oriented toward team goals.

*"The most important thing that a captain can do is to see the ship from the eyes of the crew." — D. Michael Abrashoff, U.S. Navy*[32]

If the team-appointed leader is ineffective, the team usually recognizes the problem and makes the adjustments necessary to get the team back on track. Another possibility for team leadership is a rotating system in which the position changes every quarter, month, week, or even day. A rotating system fosters professional growth of all members of the team and reinforces the strength of the team's self-management.

The second important issue for this phase is to help each team develop its own sense of identity. Visits to observe mature teams in action can be a good step for newly formed teams. Recognizing teams and individuals for good performance is always powerful, especially when the teams choose the recipients. Continued training in problem-solving steps, tools, and techniques is imperative. Managers need to push as many problem-solving opportunities as possible down to the team level. Finally, as team identity develops, teams develop social activities and display T-shirts, team names, logos, and other items that show off their identity. All of these are a sure sign that the team is moving into phase 4.

**Phase 4: Tightly Formed Teams** The fourth phase of team implementation is when teams become tightly formed to the point that their internal focus can become detrimental to other teams and the organization as a whole. Such teams are usually extremely confident of their ability to do everything. They are solving problems, managing their schedule and resources, and resolving internal conflicts. However, communication with external teams begins to diminish, the team covers up for underperforming members, and interteam rivalries can turn sour, leading to unhealthy competition.

To avoid the dangers of the intense team loyalty and isolation inherent to phase 4, managers need to make sure that teams continue to do the things that enabled them to prosper thus far. First, teams need to keep the communication channels with other teams open through councils of rotating team representatives who meet regularly to discuss what works and what does not; teams who communicate and cooperate with other teams should be rewarded. At the Digital Equipment plant in Connecticut, team representatives meet weekly to share successes and failures so that all can avoid problems and improve the ways their teams operate.[33] Second, management needs to provide performance feedback through computer terminals in the work area that give up-to-date information on performance, or via regular feedback meetings. At TRW plants, management introduced peer performance appraisal at this stage of the team implementation process. They found that in phase 4, teams were ready to take on this administrative task but needed significant training in how to perform and communicate appraisals. Third, teams need to follow the previously developed plan to transfer authority and responsibility to the teams and to be sure that all team members have followed the plan to get training

Members of the MediHealth Outsourcing management team surround the company's co-founders, Ron and Paula Lawlor, showing their affection for their CEO (Ron) and president (Paula). The Lawlors work hard to recruit, hire, motivate, and retain talented, hard-working people as part of the team at MediHealth. The company is a medical records outsourcing firm based in King of Prussia, Pennsylvania. Team members have ultimate flexibility to get their work done, set their own hours, and even take time off for family activities, as long as they meet their goals. Managers are given the total financial information for the entire company and then run their divisions with maximum autonomy, as if it were their own business. Everybody gets a bonus when the company meets its targets, and even when the overall company does not reach its financial targets, individuals receive a bonus if they meet their goals. Teamwork is working at MediHealth.

in all of the skills necessary to do the work of the team. By the end of phase 4, the team should be ready to take responsibility for managing itself.

**Phase 5: Self-Managing Teams** Phase 5 is the end result of the months or years of planning and implementation. Mature teams are meeting or exceeding their performance goals. Team members are taking responsibility for team-related leadership functions. Managers and supervisors have withdrawn from the daily operations and are planning and providing counseling for teams. Probably most important, mature teams are flexible; taking on new ideas for improvement, making changes as needed to membership, roles, and tasks, and doing whatever it takes to meet the strategic objectives of the organization. Although the teams are mature and functioning quite well, several things need to be done to keep them on track. First and foremost, individuals and teams need to continue training in job skills and team and interpersonal skills. Second, support systems need to be constantly improved to facilitate team development and productivity. Third, teams always need to improve their internal customer and supplier relationships within the organization. Partnerships among teams throughout the organization can help the internal teams continue to meet the needs of external customers.

# Essential Team Issues

This chapter has described the many benefits of teams and the process of changing to a team-based organization. Teams can be utilized in small and large organizations, on the shop floor and in offices, and in countries around the world. Teams must be initiated for performance-based business reasons, and proper planning and implementation strategies must be used. In this section we discuss two essential issues that cannot be overlooked as organizations move to team-based setup: team performance and start at the top.

## Team Performance

Organizations typically expect too much too soon when they implement teams. In fact, things often get worse before they get better.[34] Figure 12.2 shows how, shortly after implementation, team performance often declines and then rebounds to rise to the original levels and above. Management at Investors Diversified Services, the financial services giant in Minneapolis, Minnesota, expected planning for team start-up to take three or four months.

*"Every project we take on starts with a question: How can we do what's never been done before?"* — ***Stuart Hornery, chairman, Lend Lease Corp.***[35]

The actual planning took eight and a half months.[36] It often takes a year or more before performance levels return to at least their before-team levels. If teams are implemented without proper planning, their performance may never return to prior levels. The long lead time for improving performance can be discouraging to managers who reacted to the fad for teams and expected immediate returns.

The phases of implementation discussed in the previous sections correspond to key points on the team performance curve. At the start-up, performance is at its normal levels, although sometimes the anticipation of, and enthusiasm for, teams cause a slight increase in performance. In phase 2, reality and unrest, teams are often confused and frustrated with the training and lack of direction from top management, to the point that actual performance may decline. In phase 3, leader-centered teams become more comfortable with the team idea and refocus on the work of the team. They once again have established leadership, although it is with an internal leader rather than an external manager or supervisor. Thus, their performance usually returns to at least their former levels. In phase 4, teams are beginning to experience the real potential of teamwork and are producing above their prior levels. Finally, in phase 5, self-managing teams are mature, flexible, and usually setting new records for performance.

**figure 12.2 Performance and Implementation of Teams**

*The team performance curve shows that performance initially drops as reality sets in and team members experience frustration and unrest. However, performance soon increases and rises to record levels as the teams mature and become self-managing.*

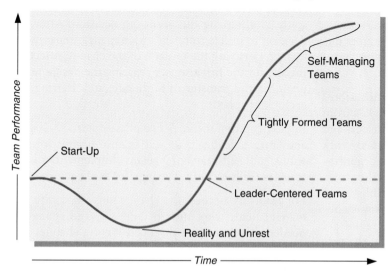

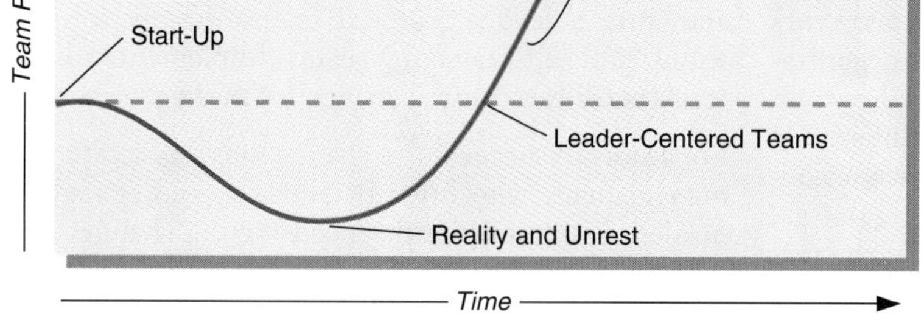


Reference: Translated and reprinted by permission of Harvard Business School Press. From *The Wisdom of Teams: Creating the High Performance Organization* by Jon R. Katzenbach and Douglas K. Smith (Boston, MA). Copyright © 1993 by McKinley & Company, Inc., all rights reserved.

Organizations changing to a team-based arrangement need to recognize the time and effort involved in making such a change. Hopes for immediate, positive results can lead to disappointment. The most rapid increases in performance occur between the leader-centered phase and the team-centered phase because teams have managed to get past the difficult, low-performance stages, have had a lot of training, and are ready to utilize their independence and freedom to make decisions about their own work. Team members are deeply committed to each other and to the success of the team. In phase 5, management needs to make sure that teams are focused on the strategic goals of the organization.

## Start at the Top

The question of where to start in team implementation is really no issue at all. Change starts at the top in every successful team implementation. Top management has three important roles to play. First, top management must decide to go to a team-based organization for sound business performance–related reasons. A major cultural change cannot be made because it is the fad, because the boss went to a seminar on teams, or because a quick fix is needed. Second, top management is instrumental in communicating the reasons for the change to the rest of the organization. Third, top management has to support the change effort during the difficult periods. As discussed previously, performance usually goes down in the early phases of team implementation. Top-management support may involve verbal encouragement of team members, but organizational support systems for the teams are also needed. Examples of support systems for teams include more efficient inventory and scheduling systems, better hiring and selection systems, improved information systems, and appropriate compensation systems.

## Synopsis

Groups and teams are not the same. A team is a small number of people with complementary skills who are committed to a common purpose, common performance goals, and a common approach for which they hold themselves mutually accountable. Teams differ from traditional work groups in their job categories, authority, and reward systems.

Teams are used because they make sense for a specific organization. Organizational benefits include enhanced performance, employee benefits, and reduced costs, among others.

Many different types of teams exist in organizations. Quality circles are small groups of employees from the same work area who meet regularly to discuss and recommend solutions to work place problems. Work teams perform the daily operations of the organization and make decisions about how to do the work. Problem-solving teams are temporarily established to solve a particular problem. Management teams consist of managers from various areas; these teams are relatively permanent and coach and counsel the new teams. Product development teams are teams assigned the task of developing a new product or service for the organization. Members of virtual teams usually meet via teleconferencing, may never actually sit in the same room together, and often have a fluid membership.

Planning the change entails all the activities leading to the decision to utilize teams and then preparing the organization for the initiation of teams. Essential steps include establishing leadership for the change, creating a steering committee, conducting a feasibility study, and making the go/no-go decision. After the decision to utilize teams has been made, preparations include clarifying the mission of the change, selecting the site for the first teams, preparing the design team, planning the transfer of authority, and drafting the preliminary plan.

Implementation includes five phases: start-up, reality and unrest, leader-centered teams, tightly formed teams, and self-managing teams. Implementation of teams is really a cultural change for the organization.

For teams to succeed, the change must start with top management, who must decide why the change is needed, communicate the need for the change, and support the change. Management must not expect too much too soon because team performance tends to decrease before it returns to prior levels and then increases to record levels.

# Discussion Questions

1. Why is it important to make a distinction between "group" and "team"? What kinds of behaviors might be different in these assemblages?
2. How are other organizational characteristics different for a team-based organization?
3. Some say that changing to a team-based arrangement "just makes sense" for organizations. What are the four primary reasons why this might be so?
4. If employees are happy working in the traditional boss-hierarchical organization, why should a manager even consider changing to a team-based organization?
5. How are the six types of teams related to each other?
6. Explain the circumstances under which a cross-functional team is useful in organizations.
7. Which type of team is the most common in organizations? Why?
8. Why is planning the change important in the implementation process?
9. What can happen if your organization prematurely starts building a team-based organization by clarifying the mission and then selecting the site for the first work teams?
10. What are two of the most important issues facing team-based organizations?

# Organizational Behavior Case for Discussion

## Team-Based System at Consolidated Diesel

Consolidated Diesel Co. was formed in 1980 as a joint venture between the Cummins Engine Company and the J.I. Case Company. Its only plant, in Whitakers, North Carolina, has been a social experiment since its very beginning. Based on a sociotechnical approach to work, the company's guiding principle is that when people have a say in determining how they work, they are both more satisfied and more productive. All employees are on work teams, plus they are divided into fifteen teams that regularly meet with management to discuss the company.

Management policies stem from Consolidated Diesel's inherent belief in the people who work there and are centered in four key areas. First, the company plays fairly—from bonuses to which shift employees work. Second, there is extensive cross-training, because workers understand what other workers are going through only if they have done the other person's job. Respect for each other comes from that kind of cross-training. Third, the company listens to the employees and involves them in making decisions and solving problems. When Consolidated Diesel had to add capacity because of customer demand in 1998, it let the teams design the new work schedules. Using the schedule the teams developed, the plant put out more engines, and no one had to work on Saturdays. Finally, the teams are involved in things that are important—they solve important workplace problems and even hire and fire their own members, when necessary.

The company also believes in the power of information. Everything is shared with every employee, whether it is good news or bad. General Manager Jim Lyons meets with all employees in small groups, takes all questions, and answers them on the spot if he has the information. If he does not, he follows up with the information on the company newsletter and a closed-circuit TV network. In addition, Lyons and other managers spend one to two hours every day walking around the company offices and manufacturing areas talking to the people. Lyons says most people call him by his first name. The company has high standards for themselves and for their suppliers. They annually give out awards when suppliers are doing a great job.

And the results of this social experiment? FANTASTIC! By every measure the performance is at the top. Productivity? One engine every 72 seconds. Revenue? 1998 revenue was $250 million. Turnover? Less than 2 percent and no layoffs . . . ever. Number of supervisors? One for every 100 employees when the industry average is normally 1 for 25. Injury rate? One-fifth of the national average. Consolidated Diesel clearly creates the trust and the teams that enable people to make the difference.

## Case Questions

1. Would you like to work in a plant like Consolidated Diesel? Why or why not?
2. Are there other factors that the success of this plant could be attributed to, other than the team-based system it employs?
3. If this team-based system is so successful, why don't other similar plants adopt these methods?

References: Curtis Sittenfeld, "Power to the People," *Fast Company*, July/August 1999, pp. 178–189; "Timely Choices—Kronos System Successes," *Management Accounting*, June 1997, p. S14; "Usui International Corp. (1995 Supplier of the Year Award)," *Diesel Progress Engines & Drives*, March 1996, p. 35.

# Experiencing Organizational Behavior

## Using Teams

**Introduction:** The use of groups and teams is becoming more common in organizations throughout the world. The following assessment surveys your beliefs about the effective use of teams in work organizations.

**Instructions:** You will agree with some of the statements and disagree with others. In some cases, you may find making a decision difficult, but you should force a choice. Record your answers next to each statement according to the following scale:

4 = Agree Strongly
3 = Agree Somewhat
2 = Disagree Somewhat
1 = Disagree Strongly

____ 1. Each individual in a work team should have a clear assignment so that individual accountability can be maintained.

____ 2. For a team to function effectively, the team must be given complete authority over all aspects of the task.

____ 3. One way to get teams to work is to simply assemble a group of people, tell them in general what needs to be done, and let them work out the details.

____ 4. Once a team "gets going," management can turn its attention to other matters.

____ 5. To ensure that a team develops into a cohesive working unit, managers should be especially careful not to intervene in any way during the initial start-up period.

____ 6. Training is not critical to a team because the team will develop any needed skills on its own.

____ 7. It's easy to provide teams with the support they need because they are basically self-motivating.

____ 8. Teams need little or no structure to function effectively.

____ 9. Teams should set their own direction, with managers determining the means to the selected end.

____ 10. Teams can be used in any organization.

For interpretation, see the Interpretation Guide in the *Instructor's Resource Manual.*

Reference: Adapted from J. Richard Hackman (ed.), *Groups That Work (and Those That Don't)*, pp. 493–504. Copyright © 1990. Reprinted by permission of Jossey-Bass Inc., a subsidiary of John Wiley & Sons, Inc.

# Building Organizational Behavior Skills

## Using Teams

**Purpose:** This exercise will help you understand some of the benefits of teamwork.

**Format:** Your instructor will divide the group into teams of four to six people. (These could be previously formed teams or new teams.) Teams should arrange their desks or chairs so that they can interact and communicate well with each other.

**Procedure:** Consider that your team is an engineering design team assigned to work out this difficult problem, which is the key to getting a major purchase contract from a large influential buyer. The task seems simple, but working out such tasks (at different levels of complexity) can be very important to organizations.

1. It is important for your team to work together to develop your solution.
2. Look at the following figure. Your task is to create a single square by making only **two** straight-line cuts and then reassembling the pieces so that all material is used in the final product.

The Figure:

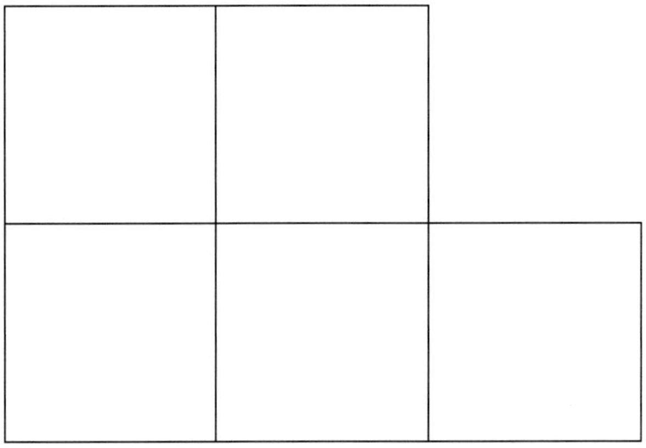

3. It might be easier to trace the design onto stiff paper or cardboard to facilitate working with the pieces.
4. Your instructor has access to the correct answer key from the *Instructor's Resource Manual.*

### Follow-up Questions

1. How did the other members of your team help or hinder your ability to solve the problem?
2. Did your team have a leader throughout the exercise? If so, can you identify why that person emerged as the leader?
3. What type of training would have helped your team solve the problem better or faster?

Reference: From John W. Newstrom and Edward E. Scannell, *Games Trainers Play: Experiential Learning Exercises,* p. 259. Copyright © 1980. Reproduced by permission of The McGraw-Hill Companies.

## Developing OB Internet Skills

**Introduction:** There are many resources available on the Internet for those who want to know more about how to develop teams in organizations. The available resources include books, tapes, videos, training programs, and consulting firms that specialize in helping organizations develop more teamwork.

**Internet Assignment:** Use the Internet to find some of these available resources. Try to find links to at least three different types of resources that could be used. Go as far as you can to find out what types of help each resource is likely to provide.

**Follow-up:** How much information were you able to find? Were you able to find out how much each of these different types of resources might cost? Finally, answer the following questions:

1. If you were doing this search for your company which of these resources would you be most likely to recommend to your boss, and why?
2. Which of the Internet sites that you found were the most helpful, and why?
3. Would you recommend this method of searching for help to others?

chapter 13

# Leadership Models and Concepts

## Management Preview

The mystique of leadership makes it one of the most widely debated, studied, and sought-after commodities of organizational life. Managers talk about the characteristics that make an effective leader, and organizational scientists have extensively studied leadership and myriad related phenomena. We begin this chapter, the first of two devoted to leadership, with a discussion of the meaning of leadership, including its definition and distinctions between leadership and management. We then turn to historical views of leadership, focusing on the trait and behavioral approaches. Next, we examine three leadership theories that have formed the basis for most leadership research: the LPC theory developed by Fiedler, the path-goal theory, and Vroom's decision tree approach to leadership. We conclude by describing two other contemporary models of leadership. In our next chapter we explore other elements of leadership, focusing more specifically on influence processes in organizations. To begin, however, we discuss the leadership challenges facing Carly Fiorina as she takes the reins at Hewlett-Packard Co. ■

Hewlett-Packard in many ways helped define California's storied Silicon Valley. Founded in 1938 in a garage by Bill Hewlett and David Packard, HP became one of the most admired corporations in the world. Hewlett and Packard combined technical and business genius to create an informal, egalitarian culture where brilliant engineers could shine. Their approach to business became so entrenched at the firm that its very culture took on a persona insiders called the "HP way."

Hewlett and Packard stepped aside in 1978 and turned the reins of the company over to John Young, a career engineer at the firm. Young oversaw the company's rise as a major player in the computer industry. But as the 1990s began, Young became convinced that HP's various units were growing too independent of one another and started creating a new organizational structure intended to centralize decision making, reduce unit autonomy, and improve coordination. Lew Platt, another HP insider, took over in 1992 and accelerated the centralization of control at the company. Unfortunately, however, no one in HP's senior management realized that the new structure was actually creating bureaucratic inertia.

But as the 1990s were drawing to a close, HP's performance began to slip. The high-technology industry and its various marketplaces, almost overnight, it seems, became so tightly interwoven with the Internet that the pace of doing business changed dramatically. HP's rigid hierarchy, meanwhile, resulted in such slow decision making and sluggish operations that the firm began to fall behind its competitors at an alarming rate. The firm's board of directors, fortunately, quickly realized that something drastic needed to be done. And they also realized that the job had to start with something no insider could be expected to do—shaking off the revered "HP way" and remaking the firm from its very core.

*"What Hewlett-Packard needs today is decisive leadership." — Unidentified HP executive**

Enter Carly Fiorina. Ms. Fiorina was already clearly establishing herself as one of the most savvy business leaders in the world. She had spent most of her career with AT&T. Her rise up the corporate ladder, observers agreed, came because of her dual capabilities as a decisive and business-focused leader and the personal connections she was able to establish with those around her. She had come onto center stage by taking over Lucent Technologies, a former subsidiary of AT&T, and in very short order totally transforming it from a stodgy manufacturing-driven maker of telephone equipment into a major force in the Internet economy.

HP's search committee for a new leader looked at three hundred serious candidates and then narrowed their choice to four. They then identified four essential capabilities they believed HP's next leader must possess: (1) conceptual and communication skills, (2) operations savvy, (3) the power to create a sense of urgency, and (4) the ability to embed an Internet mindset throughout the firm. They concluded that Fiorina was the best of the lot.

Before she accepted the job, Fiorina made sure she knew what was involved. And she quickly learned that she would face several major challenges, starting with the need to shake up the HP culture and reinstill into everyone the entrepreneurial spirit that had once personified the firm. But she also knew that HP had a rock-solid technological base and a stable of respected and market-leading products. The firm also has a cadre of exceptionally gifted senior managers, most of whom clearly understood the need to bring in an outsider and who were eager to accept a new direction and vision for the firm. And to a person, they seemed to believe that Carly Fiorina is just what the firm needs to move ahead.[1] ■

Hewlett-Packard is a firm that realized it needed a new kind of leader. Carly Fiorina, meanwhile, had established a strong reputation as an outstanding leader. The firm and Ms. Fiorina decided that she might be just the person to help get HP back on track. In some organizational settings, leaders make the difference between enormous success and overwhelming failure. But in others, leaders may appear to have no significant effect on the organization whatsoever. And although some leaders are effective in one organization but not in others, some succeed no matter where they are. Yet despite hundreds of studies on leadership, researchers have found no simple way to account for these inconsistencies. Why, then, should we study leadership? First, leadership is of great practical importance to organizations. Second, researchers have isolated and verified some key variables that influence leadership effectiveness.[2]

# The Nature of Leadership

Because "leadership" is a term that is often used in everyday conversation, you might assume that it has a common meaning. In fact, just the opposite is true—like other key organizational behavior terms, such as "personality" and "motivation," "leadership" is used in a variety of ways. Thus, we first clarify its meaning as used in this book.

## The Meaning of Leadership

**Leadership** is both a process and a property. As a process, leadership involves the use of noncoercive influence. As a property, leadership is the set of characteristics attributed to someone who is perceived to use influence successfully.

We will define **leadership** in terms of both process and property.[3] As a process, leadership is the use of noncoercive influence to direct and coordinate the activities of group members to meet a goal. As a property, leadership is the set of characteristics attributed to those who are perceived to use such influence successfully.[4] From an organizational viewpoint, leadership is vital because it has such a powerful influence on individual and group behavior. Moreover, because the goal toward which the group directs its efforts is often the desired goal of the leader, it may or may not mesh with organizational goals.[5]

Leadership involves neither force nor coercion. A manager who relies solely on force and formal authority to direct the behavior of subordinates is not exercising leadership.[6] Thus, as described more fully below, a manager or supervisor may or may not also be a leader. It is also important to note that a leader may possess the characteristics attributed to him or her; on the other hand, the leader may merely be perceived as possessing them.

Leadership is both a complex and a compelling concept. Whether the setting is a business, a government, or an educational institution, most people would agree that having a good leader is desirable. But what determines a good leader? In some cultures, like Toro, in the western region of Uganda, people believe that leaders are born. That's why their young king, seven-year-old Oyo Nyimba Kabamba Iguru Rukidi IV, has sovereignty over a million people. They clearly believe that he is their leader. And as is usually the case in monarchies, this belief is based on birthright and ancestry. In other settings, leaders are selected on the basis of ability, power, or other attributes.

## Leadership Versus Management

From these definitions, it should be clear that leadership and management are related, but they are not the same. A person can be a manager, a leader, both, or neither.[7] Some of the basic distinctions between the two are summarized in Table 13.1. On the left side of the table are four elements that differentiate leadership from management. The two columns show how each element differs when considered from a management and a leadership point of view. For example, when executing plans, managers focus on monitoring results, comparing them with goals, and correcting deviations. In contrast, the leader focuses on energizing people to overcome bureaucratic hurdles to help reach goals. Thus, when Carly Fiorina monitors the performance of her employees, she is playing the role of manager. But when she inspires them to work harder at achieving their goals, she is playing the role of leader.

To further underscore the differences, consider the various roles that might typify managers and leaders in a hospital setting. The chief of staff of a large hospital is clearly a manager by virtue of the position itself. At the same time, this individual may not be respected or trusted by others and may have to rely solely on the authority vested in the position to get people to do things. But an emergency room nurse with no formal authority may be quite effective at taking charge of a chaotic situation and directing others in how to deal with specific patient

table 13.1

**Distinctions Between Management and Leadership**

| Activity | Management | Leadership |
|---|---|---|
| Creating an Agenda | **Planning and budgeting.** Establishing detailed steps and timetables for achieving needed results; allocating the resources necessary to make those needed results happen | **Establishing direction.** Developing a vision of the future, often the distant future, and strategies for producing the changes needed to achieve that vision |
| Developing a Human Network for Achieving the Agenda | **Organizing and staffing.** Establishing some structure for accomplishing plan requirements, staffing that structure with individuals, delegating responsibility and authority for carrying out the plan, providing policies and procedures to help guide people, and creating methods or systems to monitor implementation | **Aligning people.** Communicating the direction by words and deeds to all those whose cooperation may be needed to influence the creation of teams and coalitions that understand the vision and strategies and accept their validity |
| Executing Plans | **Controlling and problem solving.** Monitoring results vs. plan in some detail, identifying deviations, and then planning and organizing to solve these problems | **Motivating and inspiring.** Energizing people to overcome major political, bureaucratic, and resource barriers to change by satisfying very basic, but often unfulfilled, human needs |
| Outcomes | Produces a degree of predictability and order and has the potential to consistently produce major results expected by various stakeholders (e.g., for customers, always being on time; for stockholders, being on budget) | Produces change, often to a dramatic degree, and has the potential to produce extremely useful change (e.g., new products that customers want, new approaches to labor relations that help make a firm more competitive) |

Reference: From *A Force for Change: How Leadership Differs from Management*, by John P. Kotter, 1990. Reprinted with permission of The Free Press, a Division of Simon & Schuster Inc.

problems. Others in the emergency room may respond because they trust the nurse's judgment and have confidence in the nurse's decision-making skills.

The head of pediatrics, supervising a staff of twenty other doctors, nurses, and attendants, may also enjoy their complete respect, confidence, and trust. They readily take her advice and follow directives without question, and often go far beyond what is necessary to help carry out the unit's mission. Thus, being a manager does not ensure that a person is also a leader—any given manager may or may not also be a leader. Similarly, a leadership position can also be formal, as when someone appointed to head a group has leadership qualities, or informal, as when a leader emerges from the ranks of the group according to a consensus of the members. The chief of staff described above is a manager but not a leader. The emergency room nurse is a leader but not a manager. And the head of pediatrics is both.

*Managers "know how to write business plans, while leaders get companies—and people—to change." — Carol Bartz, CEO of Autodesk Inc.*[8]

Organizations need both management and leadership if they are to be effective. "The Business of Ethics" box underscores the high premium that businesses put on effective leadership. Indeed, as the box suggests, some organizations might place such a high value on their leaders so as to call into question the rewards they

THE BUSINESS OF ETHICS

## *When Is a Golden Parachute Really a Golden Egg?*

Imagine getting forced out of your job, and receiving over $90 million in severance pay! That's just what happened when Michael Ovitz was asked to leave his job as president of the Walt Disney Company. But while this "going away package" was in a class by itself, attractive exit packages have become the norm, rather than the exception today.

For example, John Ameriman recently retired as CEO at Mattel. But while retirement to some might mean rocking on the porch, Ameriman still receives over $1 million in annual salary as an adviser to the new CEO. Phillip Rooney left WMX Technologies but will receive severance pay of $12.5 million paid out over five years. And Joel Alvord retired as chair of Shawmut after it was acquired by Fleet Financial, and was rewarded with a $15.5 million in exit pay.

Such arrangements are often called "golden parachutes." The idea is that to attract high-profile executives with proven track records a firm may have to guarantee them some package of benefits if they are either terminated, asked to retire prematurely, or lose their job as a result of a merger. And most experts agree that some form of such compensation is generally appropriate and fair. For example, Michael Ovitz gave up controlling interest in another major business in order to take the job at Disney.

*"People are being allowed to dictate terms that give huge rewards under all [situations], including abject failure." — Graef Crystal, compensation consultant*

At the same time, critics believe that these parachutes may have gotten out of hand. For example, its one thing to promise a reasonable exit package to cover the executive until she or he finds a new job. But its altogether different to provide multiyear, multimillion-dollar packages. Even worse, critics contend, is giving such packages to managers who did a poor job and who are leaving simply so the company can get someone better for the job.

References: "Do You Need an Expert on Widgets to Head a Widget Company?" *Wall Street Journal,* January 21, 1998, pp. A1, A10. "Where Parting Is Such a Sweet Deal," *Business Week,* March 31, 1997, pp. 42–45 (quote on p. 43).

are providing to them. Regardless, however, leadership is necessary to create and direct change and to help the organization get through tough times. Management is necessary to achieve coordination and systematic results and to handle administrative activities during times of stability and predictability. Management in conjunction with leadership can help achieve planned orderly change, and leadership in conjunction with management can keep the organization properly aligned with its environment. In addition, managers and leaders also play a major role in setting the moral climate of the organization and in determining the role of ethics in its culture.

# Early Approaches to Leadership

Although leaders and leadership have profoundly influenced the course of human events, careful scientific study began only about a century ago. Early study focused on the traits, or personal characteristics, of leaders.[9] Later research shifted to examine actual leader behaviors.

The trait approach to leadership assumes that leaders have a set of relatively stable and enduring traits that sets them apart from others. When the U.S. women's soccer team burst into international prominence, Mia Hamm was the team's acknowledged leader. Hamm has achieved numerous personal and team milestones during her career; she is the greatest scorer in international soccer history and her team won the World Cup in 1999. Among the traits that are ascribed to Hamm are talent, energy, self-confidence, motivation, and drive. And it is this set of traits that is most frequently mentioned in concert with her leadership abilities.

## Trait Approaches to Leadership

Lincoln, Napoleon, Joan of Arc, Hitler, and Gandhi are names that most of us know quite well. Early researchers believed that notable leaders such as these had some unique set of qualities or traits that distinguished them from their peers. Moreover, these traits were presumed to be relatively stable and enduring. Following this **trait approach**, these researchers focused on identifying leadership traits, developing methods for measuring them, and using the methods to select leaders.[10]

Hundreds of studies guided by this research agenda were conducted during the first several decades of this century. The earliest writers believed that important leadership traits included in-telligence, dominance, self-confidence, energy, activity, and task-relevant knowledge. The results of subsequent studies gave rise to a long list of additional traits. Unfortunately, the list quickly became so long as to lose any semblance of practical value. In addition, the results of many studies were inconsistent.

For example, one early argument was that effective leaders such as Lincoln

The **trait approach** to leadership attempted to identify stable and enduring character traits that differentiated effective leaders from nonleaders.

tended to be taller than ineffective leaders. But critics were quick to point out that Hitler and Napoleon, both effective leaders in their own way, were not tall. Some writers have even tried to relate leadership to such traits as body shape, astrological sign, or handwriting patterns. The trait approach also had a significant theoretical problem in that it could neither specify nor prove how presumed leadership traits are connected to leadership per se. For these and other reasons, the trait approach was all but abandoned several decades ago.

In recent years, however, the trait approach has received renewed interest. For example, some researchers have sought to reintroduce a limited set of traits back into the leadership literature. These traits include drive, motivation, honesty and integrity, self-confidence, cognitive ability, knowledge of the business, and charisma (which is discussed in Chapter 14).[11] Some people even believe that biological factors may play a role in leadership as well. Although it is too early to know whether these traits have validity from a leadership perspective, it does appear that a serious and scientific assessment of appropriate traits may further our understanding of the leadership phenomenon.

Similarly, other work has also started examining the role of gender and other diversity factors in leadership. For example, do women and men tend to lead differently? Some early research suggests that there are indeed fundamental differences in leadership as practiced by women and men.[12] Given that most leadership theories and research studies have focused on male leaders, developing a better understanding of how females lead is clearly an important next step. Similarly, are there differences in the leadership styles exhibited by individuals of different ethnicity? Or between younger and older leaders? Again, few answers exist for these questions, but researchers are beginning to address them.

The role of national culture may also be important. There may be important leadership differences in different cultures.[13] U.S. business leaders often talk today about growth, profits, strategy, and competition. But Japanese leaders are more prone to stress group cohesiveness and identity. And Kim Sang Phi, chair of South Korea's Samsung group, is fond of talking about management theory, morality, and etiquette.[14] The "World View" box describes the leadership style of a great Japanese business leader. Thus, as with gender, ethnicity, and age, researchers need to focus attention on cultural differences in terms of leadership traits, roles, and behaviors.[15]

## Behavioral Approaches to Leadership

The **behavioral approach** to leadership tried to identify behaviors that differentiated effective leaders from nonleaders.

In the late 1940s, most researchers began to shift away from the trait approach to leadership and to look at leadership as an observable process or activity. The goal of this so-called **behavioral approach** was to determine what behaviors are associated with effective leadership.[16] The researchers assumed that the behaviors of effective leaders differed somehow from the behaviors of less effective leaders and that the behaviors of effective leaders would be the same across all situations. The behavioral approach to the study of leadership included the Michigan studies, the Ohio State studies, and the leadership grid.

*"Well, it wasn't too many years ago that the dictatorial approach, the command-and-control management style, was accepted. Today, it's more about working through people, being more of a leader and empowering other executives on the team to carry out the mission. — Thomas Neff, leadership expert*[17]

WORLD VIEW

## *Japan's Greatest Leader*

While not exactly a household name, Konosuke Matsushita may have been the greatest business leader in the history of Japan. Many consumers today know Matsushita as the company that makes such well-known brand-name products as Panasonic, Quasar, JVC, and Technics. And Matsushita is the world's largest consumer products maker.

Matsushita got his start in 1917. At the time he worked for Osaka Light, an electric utility. But he quit his job when his boss refused to listen to his ideas about a new type of electric socket. He subsequently invested 200 yen (about $50)—his entire life savings—to start a small electric business. His first workers contributed their time for free because he could not afford to pay them. After a shaky start, his company began to introduce one or two new products a month. His first "indulgence" was to pay his workers and to start hiring new employees.

In 1922, he got his big break. At the time, bicycle lights were powered either by candles or by large, bulky batteries. Matsushita developed a new battery that was smaller, lighter, and that lasted much longer than conventional ones. With this new product, Matsushita Electric took off. But the cornerstone of Matsushita's business remained the loyal and dedicated employees who believed in his ability and integrity.

> *"Cut production by half, starting now, but don't dismiss any employees. We'll reduce output not by laying off workers, but by having them work half-days. We will continue to pay the same wages they are getting now, but we will eliminate all holidays. We'll ask all the workers to do their best to try to sell the stock backlog."* — *Konosuke Matsushita*

Even during the great depression of 1929, Matsushita refused to lay off workers. And when the world economy recovered, his firm again took off on its path to multinational status. Even though Matsushita died in 1989, the firm that bears his name remains firmly entrenched atop its industry. And its concerns for its workers has remained a central and enduring part of the firm's corporate culture.

References: *Hoover's Handbook of World Business 2000* (Austin, Hoover's Business Press, 2000), pp. 336–337; John P. Kotter, "Matsushita: The World's Greatest Entrepreneur?" *Fortune,* March 31, 1997, pp. 105–111; John P. Kotter, *Matsushita Leadership* (New York: Free Press, 1997).

The **Michigan leadership studies** defined job-centered and employee-centered leadership as opposite ends of a single leadership continuum.

**Job-centered leader behavior** involves paying close attention to the work of subordinates, explaining work procedures, and demonstrating a strong interest in performance.

**Employee-centered leader behavior** involves attempting to build effective work groups with high performance goals.

### The Michigan Studies

The **Michigan leadership studies** were a program of research conducted at the University of Michigan.[18] The goal of this work was to determine the pattern of leadership behaviors that results in effective group performance. From interviews with supervisors and subordinates of high- and low-productivity groups in several organizations, the researchers collected and analyzed descriptions of supervisory behavior to determine how effective supervisors differed from ineffective ones. Two basic forms of leader behavior were identified—job centered and employee centered—as shown in the top portion of Figure 13.1.

The leader who exhibits **job-centered leader behavior** pays close attention to the work of subordinates, explains work procedures, and is mainly interested in performance. The leader's primary concern is efficient completion of the task. The leader who engages in **employee-centered leader behavior** attempts to build effective work groups with high performance goals. The leader's main concern is with high performance, but that goal is to be accomplished by paying attention to the human aspects of the group. These two styles of leader behavior were presumed to be at opposite ends of a single continuum. Thus, Likert and his associates suggested that any given leader could exhibit either job-centered or

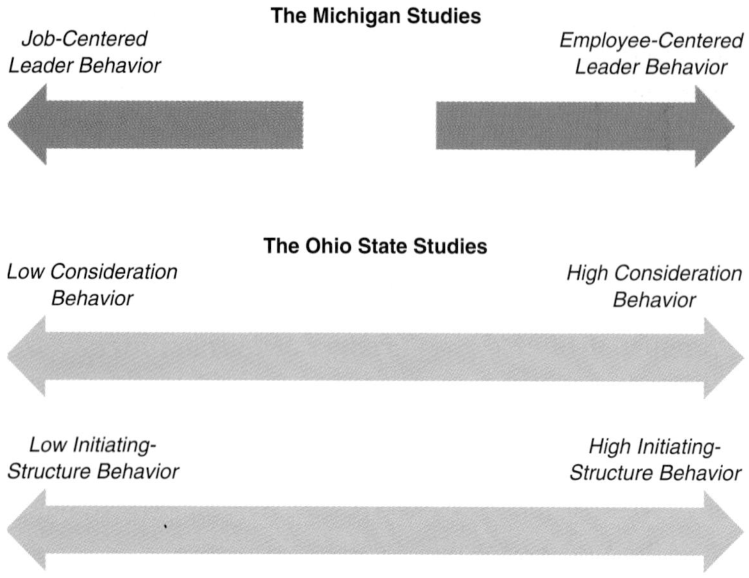


**figure 13.1 Early Behavioral Approaches to Leadership**

*Two of the first behavioral approaches to leadership were the Michigan and Ohio State studies. The results of the Michigan studies suggested that there are two fundamental types of leader behavior, job-centered and employee-centered, which were presumed to be at opposite ends of a single continuum. The Ohio State studies also found two similar kinds of leadership behavior, "consideration" and "initiating-structure," but this research suggested that these two types of behavior were actually independent dimensions.*

employee-centered leader behavior, but not both at the same time. Moreover, they suggested that employee-centered leader behavior was more likely to result in effective group performance than was job-centered leader behavior.

**The Ohio State Studies** The **Ohio State leadership studies** were conducted about the same time as the Michigan studies (in the late 1940s and early 1950s).[19] During this program of research, behavioral scientists at Ohio State University developed a questionnaire, which they administered in both military and industrial settings, to assess subordinates' perceptions of their leaders' behavior. The Ohio State studies identified several forms of leader behavior but tended to focus on the two most significant ones: consideration and initiating-structure.

When engaging in **consideration behavior**, the leader is concerned with the subordinates' feelings and respects subordinates' ideas. The leader-subordinate relationship is characterized by mutual trust, respect, and two-way communication. The cartoon illustrates this form of behavior. When using **initiating-structure behavior**, on the other hand, the leader clearly defines the leader-subordinate roles so that subordinates know what is expected of them. The leader also establishes channels of communication and determines the methods for accomplishing the group's task.

The **Ohio State leadership studies** defined leader consideration and initiating-structure behaviors as independent dimensions of leadership.

**Consideration behavior** involves being concerned with subordinates' feelings and respecting subordinates' ideas.

**Initiating-structure behavior** involves clearly defining the leader-subordinate roles so that subordinates know what is expected of them.

Unlike the employee-centered and job-centered leader behaviors, consideration and initiating structure were not thought to be on the same continuum. Instead, as shown in the bottom portion of Figure 13.1, they were seen as independent dimensions of the leader's behavioral repertoire. As a result, a leader could exhibit high initiating-structure behavior and low consideration or low initiating-structure behavior and high consideration. A leader could also exhibit high or low levels of each behavior simultaneously. For example, a leader may clearly define subordinates' roles and expectations but exhibit little concern for their feelings. Alternatively, she or he may be concerned about subordinates' feelings but fail to define roles and expectations clearly. But the leader might also demonstrate concern for performance expectations and employee welfare simultaneously.

The Ohio State researchers also investigated the stability of leader behaviors over time. They found that a given individual's leadership pattern appeared to change little as long as the situation remained fairly constant.[20] Another topic they looked at was the combinations of leader behaviors that were related to effectiveness. At first, they believed that leaders who exhibit high levels of both behaviors would be most effective. An early study at International Harvester (now Navistar Corporation), however, found that employees of supervisors who ranked high on initiating structure were higher performers but also expressed lower levels of satis-

Leader behaviors have long played a fundamental role in various leadership models and theories. Moreover, certain behaviors are especially common in different approaches to leadership. One such behavior, variously termed employee-centered behavior, consideration behavior, or concern for people, obviously relates to how leaders treat their subordinates. But as Charlie Brown will no doubt learn from Lucy, the effectiveness of consideration behavior by the leader may be substantially diminished when others have to ask for it!

Reference: PEANUTS Reprinted by permission of United Feature Syndicate, Inc.

faction. Conversely, employees of supervisors who ranked high on consideration had lower performance ratings but also had fewer absences from work.[21] Later research showed that these conclusions were misleading because the studies did not consider all the important variables. In other words, the situational context limits the extent to which consistent and uniform relationships exist between leader behaviors and subordinate responses. As a result, there are no simple explanations of what constitutes effective leader behavior because leader effectiveness varies from one situation to another.

The **Leadership Grid** evaluates leadership behavior along two dimensions, concern for production and concern for people, and suggests that effective leadership styles include high levels of both behaviors.

**The Leadership Grid** The **Leadership Grid** was developed as a framework for portraying types of leadership behavior and their various potential combinations.[22] Created primarily as a consulting tool to apply the Ohio State findings, the grid consists of two dimensions. The first dimension is concern for production. A manager's concern for production is rated on a nine-point scale, where 9 represents high concern and 1 indicates low concern. A manager who has high concern for production is task oriented and focuses on getting results or accomplishing the mission. The second dimension is concern for people, also rated on a nine-point scale, with 9 for high and 1 for low. As might be expected, a manager who has a high concern for people avoids conflict and strives for friendly relations with subordinates.

These two dimensions are combined and integrated to form a nine-by-nine grid. The grid thus identifies an array of possible leader behavior combinations. The developers of the grid suggest that the 9, 9 combination of leadership behaviors is the most effective leadership style; that is, a manager who has a high concern for people and production simultaneously will be the most effective leader. This recommendation, although based on the grid developers' experiences as consultants to firms like Gulf Oil (now a part of Chevron) and Exxon and on anecdotal evidence from managers who have used the grid, has been shown to be less than optimal in many situations.[23]

The Michigan, Ohio State, and grid behavioral models attracted considerable attention from managers and behavioral scientists. Unfortunately, later research on each model revealed significant weaknesses. For example, the models were not always supported by research and were even found to be ineffective in some settings.[24] The behavioral approaches were valuable in that they identified several fundamental leader behaviors that are still used in most leadership theories today. Moreover, they moved leadership research away from the narrow trait theory. The Michigan and Ohio State studies were exploratory in nature, and they have given researchers several fundamental insights into basic leadership processes. However, in trying to precisely specify a set of leader behaviors effective in all situations, as attempted by the Leadership Grid, the studies overlooked the enormous complexities of individual behavior in organizational settings.

In the end, the most basic shortcoming of these studies was that they failed to meet their primary goal—to identify universal leader-behavior and follower-response patterns and relationships. Managers and behavioral scientists thus realized that still different approaches were needed to accommodate the complexities of leadership. Consequently, they began to focus on contingency theories to better explain leadership and its consequences. These theories assume that appropriate leader behavior will vary across settings. Their focus is on better understanding how different situations call for different forms of leadership. The three major contingency theories are discussed next, beginning with the LPC theory.

*"One of the assets I bring to Saturn is my experience with different kinds of relationships." — Cynthia Trudell, newly appointed president of Saturn Motors*[25]

# The LPC Theory of Leadership

The **LPC theory of leadership** suggests that a leader's effectiveness depends on the situation.

Fred Fiedler developed the **LPC theory of leadership**. The LPC theory attempts to explain and reconcile both the leader's personality and the complexities of the situation.[26] (This theory was originally called the contingency theory of leadership. However, because this label has come to have generic connotations, new labels are being used to avoid confusion. "LPC" stands for "least-preferred coworker," a concept we explain later in this section.) The LPC theory contends that a leader's effectiveness depends on the situation and, as a result, some leaders may be effective in one situation or organization but not in another. The theory also explains why this discrepancy may occur and identifies leader-situation matches that should result in effective performance.

## Task Versus Relationship Motivation

Fiedler and his associates maintain that leadership effectiveness depends on the match between the leader's personality and the situation. Fiedler devised special terms to describe a leader's basic personality traits in relation to leadership: "task motivation" versus "relationship motivation." He also conceptualized the situational context in terms of its favorableness for the leader, ranging from highly favorable to highly unfavorable.

In some respects, the ideas of task and relationship motivation resemble the basic concepts identified in the behavioral approaches. Task motivation closely parallels job-centered and initiating-structure leader behavior, and relationship motivation is similar to employee-centered and consideration leader behavior. A major difference, however, is that Fiedler viewed task versus relationship motivation as being grounded in personality in a way that is basically constant for any given leader.

The **least-preferred coworker (LPC) scale** presumes to measure a leader's motivation.

The degree of task or relationship motivation in a given leader is measured by the **least-preferred coworker (LPC) scale**.[27] The LPC scale instructions ask respondents (i.e., leaders) to think of all the persons with whom they have worked and to then select their least-preferred coworker. Respondents then describe this coworker by marking a series of sixteen scales anchored at each end by a positive or negative quality or attribute.[28] For example, three of the items Fiedler uses in the sales are:

| | | | | | | | | | |
|---|---|---|---|---|---|---|---|---|---|
| Pleasant | 8 | 7 | 6 | 5 | 4 | 3 | 2 | 1 | Unpleasant |
| Inefficient | 1 | 2 | 3 | 4 | 5 | 6 | 7 | 8 | Efficient |
| Unfriendly | 1 | 2 | 3 | 4 | 5 | 6 | 7 | 8 | Friendly |

The higher numbers on the scales are associated with a positive evaluation of the least-preferred coworker. (Note that the higher scale numbers are associated with the more favorable term and that some items reverse both the terms and the scale values. The latter feature forces the respondent to read the scales more carefully and to provide more valid answers.) Respondents who describe their least-preferred coworker in relatively positive terms receive a high LPC score, whereas those who use relatively negative terms receive a low LPC score.

Fiedler assumed that these descriptions actually say more about the leader than about the least-preferred coworker. He believed, for example, that everyone's least preferred coworker is likely to be equally "unpleasant" and that differences in descriptions actually reflect differences in personality traits among the leaders responding to LPC scale. Fiedler contended that high-LPC leaders are basically more concerned with interpersonal relations, whereas low-LPC leaders are more concerned with task-relevant problems. Not surprisingly, controversy has always surrounded the LPC scale. Researchers have offered several interpretations of the LPC score, arguing that it may be an index of behavior, personality, or some other unknown factor.[29] Indeed, the LPC measure—and its interpretation—have long been among the most debated aspects of this theory.

## Situational Favorableness

Fiedler also identified three factors that determine the favorableness of the situation. In order of importance (from most to least important), these factors are leader-member relations, task structure, and leader position power.

*Leader-member relations* refers to the personal relationship that exists between subordinates and their leader. This relationship is based on the extent to which subordinates trust, respect, and have confidence in their leader, and vice versa. A high degree of mutual trust, respect, and confidence obviously indicates good leader-member relations, and a low degree indicates poor leader-member relations.

*Task structure* is the second most important determinant of situational favorableness. A structured task is routine, simple, easily understood, and unambiguous. The LPC theory presumes that structured tasks are more favorable because the leader need not be closely involved in defining activities and can devote time to other matters. On the other hand, an unstructured task is one that is nonroutine, ambiguous, and complex. Fiedler argues that an unstructured task is more unfavorable because the leader must play a major role in guiding and directing the activities of subordinates.

Finally, *leader position power* is the power inherent in the leader's role itself. If the leader has considerable power to assign work, reward and punish employees, and recommend them for promotion, position power is high and favorable. If, however, the leader must have job assignments approved by someone else, does not control rewards and punishment, and has no voice in promotions, position power is low and unfavorable; that is, many decisions are beyond the leader's control.

**Leader Motivation and Situational Favorableness** Fiedler and his associates conducted numerous studies examining the relationships among leader motivation, situational favorableness, and group performance. Table 13.2 summarizes the results of these studies.

To begin interpreting the results, let's first examine the situational favorableness dimensions shown in the table. The various combinations of these three dimensions result in eight different situations, as arrayed across the first three lines of the table. These situations in turn define a continuum ranging from very favorable to very unfavorable situations from the leaders' perspective. Favorableness is noted in the fourth line of the table. For example, good relations, a structured task, and either high or low position power result in a very favorable situation for the leader. But poor relations, an unstructured task, and either high or low position power create very unfavorable conditions for the leader.

The table also identifies the leadership approach that is supposed to achieve high group performance in each of the eight situations. These linkages are shown in the bottom line of the table. A task-oriented leader is appropriate for very favorable as well as very unfavorable situations. For example, the LPC theory predicts that if leader-member relations are poor, the task is unstructured, and leader position power is low, a task-oriented leader will be effective. It also predicts that a task-oriented leader will be effective if leader-member relations are good, the task is structured, and leader position power is high. Finally, for situations of intermediate favorability, the theory suggests that a person-oriented leader will be most likely to get high group performance.

**Leader-Situation Match** What happens if a person-oriented leader faces a very favorable or very unfavorable situation or a task-oriented leader faces a situation of intermediate favorability? Fiedler refers to these leader-situation combinations as "mismatches." Recall that a basic premise of his theory is that leadership behavior is a personality trait. Thus, the mismatched leader cannot adapt to the situation and achieve effectiveness. Fiedler contends that when a leader's style and the situation do not match, the only available course of action is to change the situation through "job engineering."[30]

For example, Fiedler suggests that if a person-oriented leader ends up in a situation that is very unfavorable, the manager should attempt to improve matters by

**table 13.2**
**The LPC Theory of Leadership**

| Leader-Member Relations | Good | | | | Poor | | | |
|---|---|---|---|---|---|---|---|---|
| Task Structure | Structured | | Unstructured | | Structured | | Unstructured | |
| Position Power | High | Low | High | Low | High | Low | High | Low |
| Situational Favorableness | Very favorable | | | Moderately favorable | | | Very unfavorable | |
| Recommended Leader Behavior | ↓ Task-oriented behavior | | | ↓ Person-oriented behavior | | | ↓ Task-oriented behavior | |

spending more time with subordinates to improve leader-member relations and by laying down rules and procedures to provide more task structure. Fiedler and his associates have also developed a widely used training program for supervisors on how to assess situational favorability and change the situation to achieve a better match.[31] Weyerhaeuser and Boeing are among the firms that have experimented with Fiedler's training program.

## Evaluation and Implications

The validity of Fiedler's LPC theory has been heatedly debated because of the inconsistency of the research results. Apparent shortcomings of the theory are that the LPC measure lacks validity, that the theory is not always supported by research, and that Fiedler's assumptions about the inflexibility of leader behavior are unrealistic.[32] The theory itself, however, does represent an important contribution because it returned the field to a study of the situation and explicitly considered the organizational context and its role in effective leadership.

# The Path-Goal Theory of Leadership

Another important contingency approach to leadership is the path-goal theory. Developed jointly by Martin Evans and Robert House, the path-goal theory focuses on the situation and leader behaviors rather than on fixed traits of the leader.[33] The path-goal theory thus allows for the possibility of adapting leadership to the situation.

## Basic Premises

The path-goal theory has its roots in the expectancy theory of motivation discussed in Chapter 6. Recall that expectancy theory says that a person's attitudes and behaviors can be predicted from the degree to which the person believes job performance will lead to various outcomes (expectancy) and the value of those outcomes (valences) to the individual. The **path-goal theory of leadership** argues that subordinates are motivated by their leader to the extent that the behaviors of that leader influence their expectancies. In other words, the leader affects subordinates' performance by clarifying the behaviors (paths) that will lead to desired rewards (goals). Ideally, of course, getting a reward in an organization depends on effective performance. Path-goal theory also suggests that a leader may behave in different ways in different situations.

The **path-goal theory of leadership** suggests that effective leaders clarify the paths (behaviors) that will lead to desired rewards (goals).

### Leader Behaviors

As Figure 13.2 shows, path-goal theory identifies four kinds of leader behavior: directive, supportive, participative, and achievement oriented. With *directive leadership*, the leader lets subordinates know what is expected of them, gives specific guidance as to how to accomplish tasks, schedules work to be done, and maintains definitive standards of performance for subordinates. A leader exhibiting *supportive leadership* is friendly and shows concern for subordinates' status, well-being, and needs. With *participative leadership*, the leader consults with subordinates about issues and takes their suggestions into account before making a decision. Finally, *achievement-oriented leadership* involves setting challenging goals, expecting subordinates to perform at their highest level, and

figure 13.2

**The Path-Goal Theory of Leadership**

*The path-goal theory of leadership specifies four kinds of leader behavior: directive, supportive, participative, and achievement-oriented. Leaders are advised to vary their behaviors in response to such situational factors as personal characteristics of subordinates and environmental characteristics.*

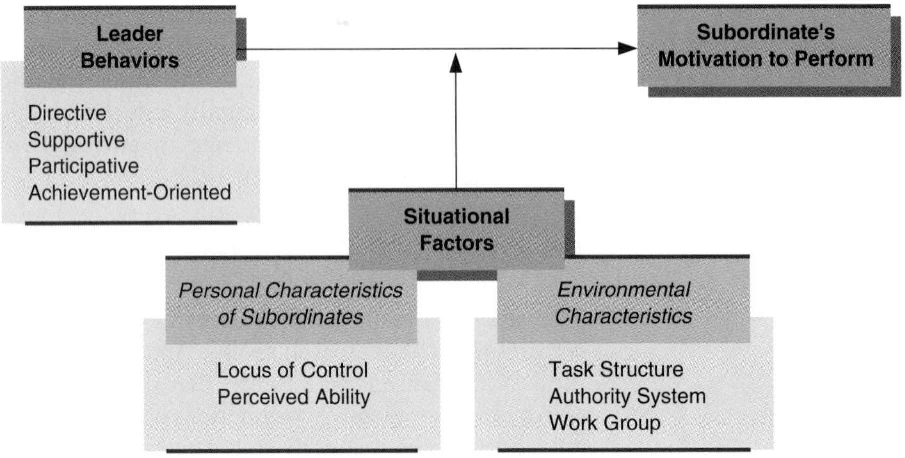


showing strong confidence that subordinates will put forth effort and accomplish the goals.[34] Unlike Fiedler's contingency theory, path-goal theory assumes that leaders can change their behavior and exhibit any or all of these leadership styles. The theory also predicts that the appropriate combination of leadership styles depends on situational factors.

**Situational Factors** The path-goal theory proposes two types of situational factors that influence how leader behavior relates to subordinate satisfaction: the personal characteristics of the subordinates and the characteristics of the environment (see Figure 13.2).

The path-goal theory of leadership encompasses four kinds of leader behavior. Carol Williams, founder, owner, and leader of Carol H. Williams Advertising, uses each of these behaviors on a regular basis. For example, she occasionally uses directive behavior to set performance expectations and provide guidance. Williams also demonstrates supportive behavior through her care and interest in her employees. She frequently uses participative leadership as well. In this scene, for example, she is meeting with a team of her employees as they discuss how to proceed with a new project. Finally, she is also very achievement-oriented in that she sets challenging goals and provides constant encouragement for everyone to work toward those goals.

Two important personal characteristics of subordinates are locus of control and perceived ability. Locus of control, discussed in Chapter 4, refers to the extent to which individuals believe that what happens to them results from their own behavior or from external causes. Research indicates that individuals who attribute outcomes to their own behavior may be more satisfied with a participative leader (since they feel their own efforts can make a difference), whereas individuals who attribute outcomes to external causes may respond more favorably to a directive leader (since they think their own actions are of little consequence).[35] Perceived ability pertains to how people view their ability with respect to the task. Employees who rate their own ability relatively high are less likely to feel a need for directive leadership (since they think they know how to do the job), whereas those who perceive their own ability to be relatively low may prefer directive leadership (since they think they need someone to show them how to do the job).

Important environmental characteristics are task structure, the formal authority system, and the primary work group. The path-goal theory proposes that leader behavior will motivate subordinates if it helps them cope with environmental uncertainty created by those characteristics. In some cases, however, certain forms of leadership will be redundant, decreasing subordinate satisfaction. For example, when task structure is high, directive leadership is less necessary and therefore less effective; similarly, if the work group gives the individual plenty of social support, a supportive leader will not be especially attractive. Thus, the extent to which leader behavior matches the people and the environment in the situation is presumed to influence subordinates' motivation to perform.

For another example, consider the success of Barbara Samson, founder of Intermedia, a Florida telephone company. To get her idea from the drawing board into the business world, Samson had to use directive leadership to organize her employees. But she also had to use supportive leadership to help them get through the tough times during the early days of start-up. When she met with investors, she had to demonstrate achievement-oriented leadership to convey her goals and strategies. And as her business has grown, she increasingly uses participative leadership to spread decision-making authority throughout the firm.[36]

### Evaluation and Implications

The path-goal theory was designed to provide a general framework for understanding how leader behavior and situational factors influence subordinate attitudes and behaviors. But the intention of the path-goal theorists was to stimulate research on the theory's major propositions, not to offer definitive answers. Researchers hoped that a more fully developed formal theory of leadership would emerge from continued study. Further work actually has supported the theory's major predictions, but it has not validated the entire model.[37] Moreover, many of the theory's predictions remain overly general and have not been fully refined and tested.

## Vroom's Decision Tree Approach to Leadership

**Vroom's decision tree approach** to leadership attempts to prescribe how much participation subordinates should be allowed in making decisions.

The third major contemporary approach to leadership is **Vroom's decision tree approach.** The earliest version of this model was proposed by Victor Vroom and Philip Yetton and later revised and expanded by Vroom and Arthur Jago.[38] Most recently, Vroom has developed yet another refinement of the original model.[39]

Like the path-goal theory, this approach attempts to prescribe a leadership style appropriate to a given situation. It also assumes that the same leader may display different leadership styles. But Vroom's approach concerns itself with only a single aspect of leader behavior: subordinate participation in decision making.

## Basic Premises

Vroom's decision tree approach assumes that the degree to which subordinates should be encouraged to participate in decision making depends on the characteristics of the situation. In other words, no one decision-making process is best for all situations. After evaluating a variety of problem attributes (characteristics of the problem or decision), the leader determines an appropriate decision style that specifies the amount of subordinate participation.

*"Wellington would spend hours every day meeting with his officers on strategy. He pulled the strings, but he didn't even carry a weapon." — Ralph Hayles, expert in military leadership*[40]

Vroom's current formulation suggests that managers use one of two different decision trees.[41] One tree (the time-driven model) is to be used when the leader's primary concern is making an effective decision as quickly as possible. The other tree (the development-driven model) is to be used when the leader is mainly concerned with developing the decision-making capabilities of others. After deciding

Vroom's Decision Tree approach to leadership suggests that leaders should vary the degree of participation they provide to subordinates in making decisions. Gordon Bethune, CEO of Continental Airlines, is a strong proponent of this idea. One of the hallmarks of his remarkable turnaround at Continental is what he calls "Working Together." The idea is that workers on the firing lines know more about how to do their jobs than do managers back at headquarters, and that all employees of the firm should be striving toward the same goals. Thus, whenever possible he looks for ways to put decision making responsibility in the hands of the right people. At the same time, though, Bethune also knows that not all decisions can be delegated and makes sure that decisions best made by senior managers stay at that level.

which tree to use, the leader then assesses the problem in terms of seven situational factors. These situational factors, in order of consideration, are decision significance, the importance of commitment by followers, the leader's expertise, the likelihood of commitment by followers, group support, group expertise, and team competence. Each factor is assessed as being "high" or "low" (although not every factor will be present in every situation). For instance, the first factor is decision significance. If the decision is extremely important and may have a major impact on the organization (i.e., choosing a location for a new plant), its significance is high. But if the decision is routine and its consequences not terribly important (i.e., selecting a color for the firm's softball team uniforms), its significance is low. This assessment guides the manager through the paths of the decision tree to a recommended course of action.

The two decision trees are shown in Figures 13.3 and 13.4. The problem attributes (situational factors) are arranged along the top of the decision tree. To use the model, the decision maker starts at the left side of the diagram and assesses the first problem attribute (decision significance). The answer determines the path to the second node on the decision tree, where the next attribute (importance of commitment) is assessed. This process continues until a terminal node is reached. In this way, the manager identifies an effective decision-making style for the situation.

The various decision styles reflected at the ends of the tree branches represent different levels of subordinate participation that the manager should attempt to adopt in a given situation. The five styles are defined as follows:

*Decide:* The manager makes the decision alone and then announces or "sells" it to the group.

*Delegate:* The manager allows the group to define for itself the exact nature and parameters of the problem and to then develop a solution.

*Consult (group):* The manager presents the problem to group members at a meeting, gets their suggestions, and then makes the decision.

*Consult (individually):* The manager presents the program to group members individually, obtains their suggestions, and then makes the decision.

*Facilitate:* The manager presents the problem to the group at a meeting, defines the problem and its boundaries, and then facilitates group member discussion as they make the decision.

Vroom's decision tree approach represents a very focused but quite complex perspective on leadership. To compensate for this difficulty, Vroom has developed expert software to help managers assess a situation accurately and quickly and to then make an appropriate decision regarding employee participation.[42] Many firms, including Halliburton Company, Litton Industries, and Borland International, have provided their managers with training in how to use the various versions of this model.

## Evaluation and Implications

Because Vroom's current approach is relatively new, it has not been fully scientifically tested. The original model and its subsequent refinement, however, attracted a great deal of attention and generally was supported by research.[43] For example, there is some support for the idea that individuals who make decisions consistent

| | Decision Significance | Importance of Commitment | Leader Expertise | Likelihood of Commitment | Group Support | Group Expertise | Team Competence | |
|---|---|---|---|---|---|---|---|---|
| PROBLEM STATEMENT | H | H | H | H | - | - | - | Decide |
| | | | | L | H | H | H | Delegate |
| | | | | | | | L | Consult (Group) |
| | | | | | | L | - | |
| | | | | | L | - | - | |
| | | | L | H | H | H | H | Facilitate |
| | | | | | | | L | Consult (Individually) |
| | | | | | | L | - | |
| | | | | | L | - | - | |
| | | | | L | H | H | H | Facilitate |
| | | | | | | | L | Consult (Group) |
| | | | | | | L | - | |
| | | | | | L | - | - | |
| | | L | H | - | - | - | - | Decide |
| | | | L | - | H | H | H | Facilitate |
| | | | | | | | L | Consult (Individually) |
| | | | | | | L | - | |
| | | | | | L | - | - | |
| | L | H | - | H | - | - | - | Decide |
| | | | | L | - | - | H | Delegate |
| | | | | | | | L | Facilitate |
| | | L | - | - | - | - | - | Decide |

figure 13.3 **Vroom's Time-Driven Decision Tree**

*This matrix is recommended for situations where time is of the highest importance in making a decision. The matrix operates like a funnel. You start at the left with a specific decision problem in mind. The column headings denote situational factors that may or may not be present in that problem. You progress by selecting High or Low (H or L) for each relevant situational factor. Proceed down from the funnel, judging only those situational factors for which a judgment is called for, until you reach the recommended process.*

Reference: Victor H. Vroom's Time-Driven Model from *A Model of Leadership Style*, copyright Vroom, 1998.

with the predictions of the model are more effective than those who make decisions inconsistent with it. The model therefore appears to be a tool that managers can apply with some confidence in deciding how much subordinates should participate in the decision-making process.

| | Decision Significance | Importance of Commitment | Leader Expertise | Likelihood of Commitment | Group Support | Group Expertise | Team Competence | |
|---|---|---|---|---|---|---|---|---|
| PROBLEM STATEMENT | H | H | - | H | H | H | H | Decide |
| | | | | | | | L | Facilitate |
| | | | | | | L | - | Consult (Group) |
| | | | | | L | - | - | |
| | | | | L | H | H | H | Delegate |
| | | | | | | | L | Facilitate |
| | | | | | | L | - | |
| | | | | | L | - | - | Consult (Group) |
| | | L | - | - | H | H | H | Delegate |
| | | | | | | | L | Facilitate |
| | | | | | | L | - | Consult (Group) |
| | | | | | L | - | - | |
| | L | H | - | H | - | - | - | Decide |
| | | | | L | - | - | - | Delegate |
| | | L | - | - | - | - | - | Decide |

figure 13.4 **Vroom's Development-Driven Decision Tree**

*This matrix is to be used when the leader is more interested in developing employees than in making the decision as quickly as possible. Just as with the time-driven tree shown in Figure 13.3, the leader assesses up to seven situational factors. These factors, in turn, funnel the leader to a recommended process for making the decision.*

Reference: Victor H. Vroom's Development-Driven Model from *A Model of Leadership Style*, copyright Vroom, 1998.

# Other Contemporary Approaches to Leadership

Because leadership is such an important area, managers and researchers continue to study it. As a result, new ideas, theories, and perspectives are continuously being developed. Two of the better known are the leader-member exchange model and the Hersey and Blanchard theory.

The **leader-member exchange (LMX) model** of leadership stresses the fact that leaders develop unique working relationships with each of their subordinates.

## The Leader-Member Exchange Model

The **leader-member exchange (LMX) model** of leadership, conceived by George Graen and Fred Dansereau, stresses the importance of variable relationships between supervisors and each of their subordinates.[44] Each superior-subordinate pair is referred to as a "vertical dyad." The model differs from earlier approaches

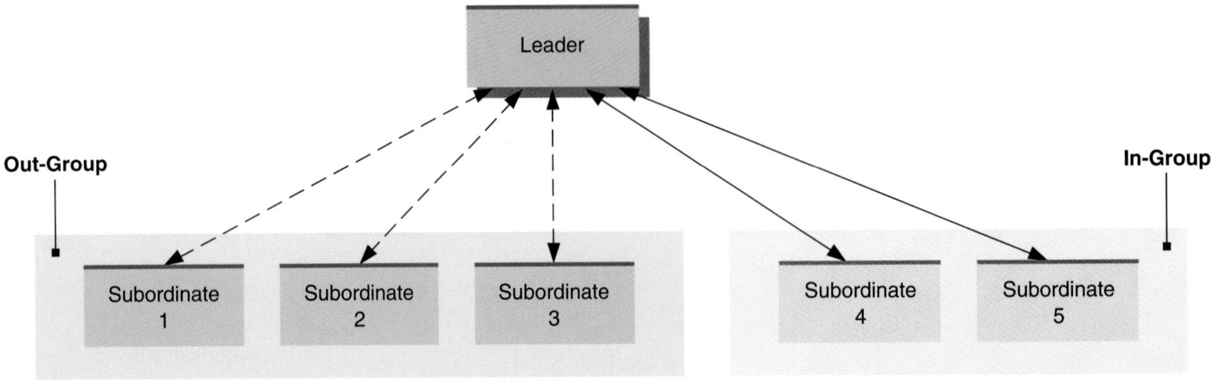


figure 13.5

**The Leader-Member Exchange (LMX) Model**

*The LMX model suggests that leaders form unique independent relationships with each of their subordinates. As illustrated here, a key factor in the nature of this relationship is whether the individual subordinate is in the leader's out-group or in-group.*

in that it focuses on the differential relationship leaders often establish with different subordinates. Figure 13.5 shows the basic concepts of the leader-member exchange theory.

The model suggests that supervisors establish a special relationship with a small number of trusted subordinates referred to as the in-group. The in-group usually receives special duties requiring responsibility and autonomy; they may also receive special privileges. Subordinates who are not a part of this group are called the out-group, and they receive less of the supervisor's time and attention. Note in the figure that the leader has a dyadic, or one-to-one, relationship with each of the five subordinates.

Early in his or her interaction with a given subordinate, the supervisor initiates either an in-group or out-group relationship. It is not clear how a leader selects members of the in-group, but the decision may be based on personal compatibility and subordinates' competence. Research has confirmed the existence of in-groups and out-groups. In addition, studies generally have found that in-group members have a higher level of performance and satisfaction than out-group members.[45]

## The Hersey and Blanchard Model

The **Hersey and Blanchard model** of leadership identifies different combinations of leadership presumed to work best with different levels of organizational maturity on the part of followers.

Another popular perspective among practicing managers is the Hersey and Blanchard model. Like the Leadership Grid discussed earlier, this model was developed as a consulting tool. The **Hersey and Blanchard model** is based on the notion that appropriate leader behavior depends on the readiness of the leader's followers.[46] In this instance, maturity (or readiness) refers to the subordinate's degree of motivation, competence, experience, and interest in accepting responsibility. Figure 13.6 shows the basic model.

The figure suggests that as the maturity of followers improves, the leader's basic style should also change. When subordinate maturity is low, for example, the leader should rely on a "telling" style by providing direction and defining roles.

figure 13.6

**The Hersey and Blanchard Theory of Leadership**

*The Hersey and Blanchard theory suggests that leader behaviors should vary in response to the maturity of followers. This figure shows the nature of this variation. The curved line suggests that relationship leader behavior should start low, gradually increase, but then decrease again as follower maturity increases. But task behavior, shown by the straight line, should start high when followers lack maturity and then continuously diminish as they gain maturity.*

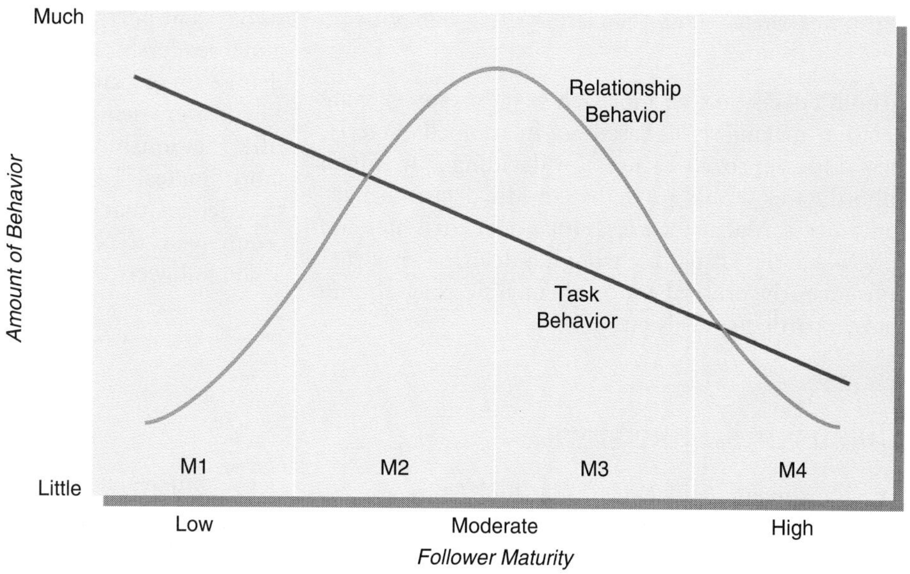


Reference: The Situational Leadership Model is the registered trademark of the Center for Leadership Studies, Escondido, CA. Excerpt from P. Hersey, *Management Organizational Behavior Utilizing Human Resources,* 3le, 1977, p. 165.

When low to moderate maturity exists, the leader should use a "selling" style by offering direction and role definition accompanied by explanation and information. In a case of moderate to high follower maturity, the leader should use a "participating" style, allowing them to share in decision making. Finally, when follower maturity is high, the leader is advised to use a "delegating" style by allowing followers to work independently, with little or no overseeing.

# Synopsis

Leadership is both a process and a property. Leadership as a process is the use of noncoercive influence to direct and coordinate the activities of group members to meet goals. As a property, leadership is the set of characteristics attributed to those who are perceived to use such influence successfully. Leadership and management are related but distinct phenomena.

Early leadership research attempted primarily to identify important traits and behaviors of leaders. The Michigan and Ohio State studies each identified two kinds of leader behavior, one focusing on job factors, the other on people factors. The Michigan studies viewed these behaviors as points on a single continuum, whereas the Ohio State studies suggested that they were separate dimensions. The Leadership Grid suggests that the most effective leaders are those who have a high concern for both people and production.

Newer contingency theories of leadership attempt to identify appropriate leadership styles on the basis of the situation. Fiedler's least-preferred coworker (LPC) theory stated that leadership effectiveness depends on a match between the leader's style (viewed as a trait of the leader) and the favorableness of the situation. Situation favorableness, in turn, is determined by task structure, leader-member relations, and leader position power. Leader behavior is presumed to reflect a constant personality trait and therefore cannot easily be changed.

The path-goal theory focuses on appropriate leader behavior for various situations. The path-goal theory suggests that directive, supportive, participative, or achievement-oriented leader behavior may be appropriate, depending on the personal characteristics of subordinates and the characteristics of the environment. Unlike the LPC theory, this view presumes that leaders can alter their behavior to best fit the situation.

Vroom's decision tree approach suggests appropriate decision-making styles based on situation characteristics. This approach focuses on deciding how much subordinates should participate in the decision-making process. Managers assess situational attributes and follow a series of paths through a decision tree that subsequently prescribes for them how they should make a particular decision.

Two recent perspectives that are not rooted in traditional leadership theories are the leader-member exchange theory and the Hersey and Blanchard model. The leader-member exchange model focuses on specific relationships between a leader and individual subordinates. The Hersey and Blanchard model acknowledges that leader behavior toward a particular group needs to change as a function of the "maturity" of the followers.

## Discussion Questions

1. How would you define leadership? Compare and contrast your definition with the one given in this chapter.
2. Cite examples of managers who are not leaders and leaders who are not managers. What makes them one and not the other? Also, cite examples of both formal and informal leaders.
3. What traits do you think characterize successful leaders? Do you think the trait approach has validity?
4. What other forms of leader behavior besides those cited in the chapter can you identify?
5. Critique Fiedler's LPC theory. Are other elements of the situation important? Do you think Fiedler's assertion about the inflexibility of leader behavior makes sense? Why or why not?
6. Do you agree or disagree with Fiedler's assertion that leadership motivation is basically a personality trait? Why?
7. Compare and contrast the LPC and path-goal theories of leadership. What are the strengths and weaknesses of each?
8. Of the three major leadership theories—the LPC theory, the path-goal theory, and Vroom's decision tree approach—which is the most comprehensive? Which is the narrowest? Which has the most practical value?
9. How realistic do you think it is for managers to attempt to use Vroom's decision tree approach as prescribed? Explain.
10. Which of the two contemporary theories of leadership do you believe holds the most promise? Why?
11. Could either of the two contemporary perspectives be integrated with any of the three major theories of leadership? If so, how?

## Organizational Behavior Case for Discussion

### Leading for Change at Ford

In many ways Jacques Nasser may be the quintessential business leader for the twenty-first century. He was born in Lebanon but grew up in Australia and joined Ford's Australian operation more than thirty years ago as a financial analyst. As Nasser worked his way up the company's hierarchy, he subsequently held increasingly important jobs, first in Latin America and then in Europe. He moved to the United States after being promoted to the key position of president of Ford's Automotive Operations. Finally, in 1999, he became Ford's CEO.

Almost from the day he arrived in Detroit Nasser began to shake things up. For decades the firm had been a stable, hierarchical company that efficiently made cars and, in recent years at least, earned solid profits. But Nasser had a new vision for Ford, one that will, in his opinion, take the company to the very forefront of its industry and transform it into a nimble, flexible organization better attuned to the international automobile industry he sees emerging.

And indeed, the forefront of the industry is exactly where Nasser has set his sights, even though he downplays that goal publicly. After all, General Motors has held the crown as the world's largest automobile company for decades. But while GM's global market share has slowly declined to around 16 percent, Ford's has surged to about 13 percent—clearly putting Ford within striking distance. To help achieve his ambitions, Nasser has also brought in dozens of senior managers from outside the staid Ford ranks. For instance, he hired Michael Lombardi away from British Petroleum, where he managed that firm's branded service station operation, and put him in charge of Ford's dealer mechanics program. He also hired the former number two BMW executive, Wolfgang Reitzle. And to jump start Ford's growth, he bought Sweden's Volvo AB.

Nasser has also made several major changes in Ford's organization structure. Most significantly, he decided to group newly acquired Volvo with Jaguar and Aston Martin, English properties Ford had acquired years earlier, with its own Lincoln division, creating a new unit called the Premier Automotive Group. This new unit will be headed up by the aforementioned Wolfgang Reitzle and headquartered in Europe. Nasser also overhauled the structure of Ford's new-car design operation and mandated that all senior executives move into the same building so as to promote interaction and stimulate new ways of thinking.

Nasser's own approach to running Ford is also a bit unique. He is seldom in his office, instead visiting Ford facilities around the world. Indeed, he keeps a calendar marked with national holidays from around the world so as to better coordinate his travel schedule. For example, he recently took advantage of the Thanksgiving lull in the United States to visit Australia. Nasser also communicates with Ford employees regularly. For instance, every week he writes a chatty email updating employees on what's going on, sending it to more than 89,000 employee mailboxes around the world. He is also stressing the importance of motivation and hard work. For example, he has tied executive compensation to stock performance for the first time since Ford went public in the 1950s. And a recurring message he takes to all Ford employees—who own about 20 percent of the firm's stock—is how their own individual contributions add to shareholder value.

Finally, Nasser also works hard to ensure that the company stays firmly on track in its quest for growth and improved performance. For example, he recently set a goal of reducing total costs by $1 billion, with Ford of Europe specifically assigned a cost-reduction target of half of that total. Because the firm's efforts were so successful, the goal was raised not once but twice, with total reductions eventually reaching $3 billion. Nasser is also committed to cutting the time Ford needs to launch new products. Not all that long ago, U.S. automakers needed five years to take a new product from the idea stage to showroom floors. The standard has been cut to three years, but Nasser wants future development cycles to be two years—or less.

Will Ford find its way to the top under Nasser's leadership, or will the company trip up somewhere on down the line? While no one can predict the future with certainty, most experts do agree that the international automobile industry is in a continuing state of flux. For example, Daimler-Benz acquired Chrysler and renamed itself DaimlerChrysler. And within months the new company toyed briefly with the idea of acquiring Nissan. Meanwhile, General Motors has a long-standing strategic alliance with Toyota, and was reported to have looked into buying BMW. Clearly, then, managers in the automobile industry face a real obstacle course as they navigate their firms toward the future.

## Case Questions

1. Describe as many different kinds of leader behavior as you can from this case.
2. Relate each of the theories and models of leadership in this chapter to Jacques Nasser.
3. Would you want to work for Nasser? Why or why not?

References: Sue Zesiger, "Ford's Hip Transplant," *Fortune*, May 10, 1999, pp. 82–92; "Making Bold Strokes, Fine Points, Nasser Puts His Mark on Ford," *Wall Street Journal*, April 7, 1999, pp. A1, A8; "Driving Change: An Interview with Ford Motor Company's Jacques Nasser," *Harvard Business Review*, March–April 1999, pp. 76–88; "Ford's Heir-Apparent Is a Maverick Outsider," *Wall Street Journal*, February 13, 1998, pp. B1, B6.

# Experiencing Organizational Behavior

## Understanding Successful and Unsuccessful Leadership

**Purpose:** This exercise will help you better understand the behaviors of successful and unsuccessful leaders.

**Format:** You will be asked to identify contemporary examples of successful and unsuccessful leaders and then to describe how these leaders differ.

**Procedure:**

1. Working alone, each student should list the names of ten people he or she thinks of as leaders in public life. Note that the names should not necessarily be confined to "good" leaders, but instead should also identify "strong" leaders.
2. Next, students should form small groups and compare their lists. This comparison should focus on common and unique names, as well as the kinds of individuals listed (i.e., male or female, contemporary or historical, business or nonbusiness, etc.).
3. From all the lists, choose two leaders whom most people would consider very successful and two who would be deemed unsuccessful.
4. Identify similarities and differences between the two successful leaders and between the two unsuccessful leaders.
5. Relate the successes and failures to at least one theory or perspective discussed in the chapter.
6. Select one group member to report your findings to the rest of the class.

### Follow-up Questions

1. What role does luck play in leadership?
2. Are there factors about the leaders you researched that might have predicted their success or failure before they achieved leadership roles?
3. What are some criteria of successful leadership?

# Building Organizational Behavior Skills

## Applying Vroom's Decision Tree Approach

This skillbuilder will help you better understand your own leadership style regarding employee participation in decision making. Mentally play the role described in the following scenario, then make the comparisons suggested at the end of the exercise.

You are the southwestern United States branch manager of an international manufacturing and sales organization. The firm's management team is looking for ways to increase efficiency. As one part of this effort, the company recently installed an integrated computer network linking sales representatives, customer service employees, and other sales support staff. Sales were supposed to increase and sales expenses to drop as a result.

However, exactly the opposite has occurred: sales have dropped a bit, and expenses are up. You have personally inspected the new system and believe the hardware is fine. However, you believe the software linking the various computers is less than ideal.

The subordinates you have quizzed about the system, on the other hand, think the entire system is fine. They attribute the problems to a number of factors, including inadequate training in how to use the system, a lack of incentive for using it, and generally poor morale. Whatever the reasons given, each worker queried had strong feelings about the issue.

Your boss has just called you and expressed concern about the problems. He has indicated that he has confidence in your ability to solve the problem and will leave it in your hands. However, he wants a report on how you plan to proceed within one week.

First, think of how much participation you would normally be inclined to allow your subordinates in making this decision. Next, apply Vroom's decision tree approach to the problem and see what it suggests regarding the optimal level of participation. Compare your normal approach to the recommended solution.

## Developing OB Internet Skills

**Introduction:** Leadership traits are a deceptively appealing approach to describing leadership. This exercise will give you more insights into both the value and the complexities inherent in trying to take a trait approach to understanding leadership.

**Internet Assignment:** Use multiple search engines to locate several Internet sites that deal with leadership. Narrow the list to those that focus specifically on the nature and meaning of leadership—what qualities leaders possess, how to develop those qualities, and so forth. Next, identify at least six traits that Internet sites purport to relate to leadership. Now do follow-up searches using those traits as key terms. Visit those sites and see how many of them implicitly or explicitly attempt to relate the trait to leadership in some way or another.

**Follow-up:** Does the information you located on the Internet make you more or less confident that leadership and traits are related than you were before? Finally, respond to the following questions:

1. What qualities or traits do you ascribe to effective leaders?
2. Do you believe leaders are born or made? How does this belief map onto the trait approach to leadership?
3. What advice would you offer to someone who is a firm believer in the trait approach?
4. What advice would you offer to someone who believes that traits are totally unrelated to leadership?

chapter

# 14

# Leadership and Influence Processes

## Management Preview

As we learned in Chapter 13, leadership is a powerful, complex, and amorphous concept. This chapter explores many of the skills and personal resources that affect leaders and leadership. We first revisit the role of influence in leadership. We then introduce and discuss two contemporary influence-based perspectives on leadership, transformational leadership and charismatic leadership. Next, we discuss various substitutes for leadership that may exist in organizations. We then describe power and political behavior in organizations, influence-based phenomena that often involve leadership. Finally, we introduce and explore impression management, a related but distinct concept. First, though, we discuss how a new leadership team at McDonald's is working to improve the venerable burger maker's fortunes. ■

Suppose you were handed the reins to one of the largest and most entrenched restaurant businesses in the world. Further suppose that you knew major changes were needed but that you would face considerable resistance as you tried to actually enact a meaningful transformation of the business. This is the exact challenge facing Jack Greenberg when he was recently appointed CEO of McDonald's.

Although McDonald's "golden arches" have become a ubiquitous part of the landscape, the hamburger giant has been stumbling in recent years. For example, McDonald's menu items rank among the worst-tasting of any restaurant chain in consumer surveys. The firm hasn't had a major new product success since Chicken McNuggets in 1983. One misstep after another caused the company's stock price to plummet. Finally, in 1998, the firm's board of directors had had enough and forced the CEO to resign. Their choice to replace him was Jack Greenberg, McDonald's chief financial officer.

*"This was a company coming to a crisis. Greenberg's done a fantastic job bringing a new sense of urgency and getting rid of their corporate arrogance." — Chris Davis, financial advisor controlling 9 million shares of McDonald's stock**

From the very beginning, Greenberg knew that major changes were needed. But he also knew that the dominant corporate culture and insular group of senior executives who had spent their entire careers with the firm would be major obstacles to his vision for change. Accordingly, one of his first major initiatives was to reduce corporate staff by 23 percent. These cuts included several top managers, some of whom were eased into early retirement and others who were simply informed that their employment contracts would be subject to review at renewal time. Most read the handwriting on the wall and left for other jobs.

Greenberg then replaced some of these top managers with strong external candidates. For example, he lured a top Pizza Hut executive to take the position of president of McDonald's USA. Others were recruited from such disparate backgrounds as Taco Bell and General Electric. Greenberg argued that these moves would bring in fresh new perspectives and ideas. Not stated, but clearly understood, was also the fact that the new management team would be loyal to Greenberg, making it easier for him to further implement change.

Greenberg also rearranged the decision-making hierarchy. In the past, all key decisions were made at headquarters, and local franchisees had virtually no flexibility for modifying their menus or offering product discounts. But under Greenberg's new system, both of these things are different. Franchisees and corporate managers stationed in the field now have considerable autonomy to offer discounts and run special local promotions. And new menu items are being developed on a regional or even local basis, rather than having them developed at headquarters and then forced on all franchisees.

One of the most sweeping changes has been a $500 million investment in new food preparation technology. Instead of storing precooked foods in taste-sapping bins, computers now project customer traffic, and food is prepared closer to when it will actually be ordered and consumed. Special orders are also much easier to accommodate than before.

So how have things worked out? While it's far too early to know for sure, things do seem to be swinging in a positive direction. Several regional products, for example, have become quite popular. And investors like what they see, driving the stock price up and generally applauding these various new initiatives. While he might still face some unforeseen obstacles in the future, for now, at least, Greenberg seems to be putting the sauce back in the burger.[1] ■

Jack Greenberg is dealing with one of the most significant challenges any leader can face—the need to transform an organization from one thing into something different. In order to have any chance for success, Greenberg has had to rely on power and political processes to facilitate key changes in the executive ranks of McDonald's. He felt that these changes were necessary, however, if he was to have any meaningful chance to influence the organization. And influence, as we will see, is the foundation of effective leadership.

# Leadership as Influence

Recall that in Chapter 13 we defined leadership (from a process perspective) as the use of noncoercive influence to direct and coordinate the activities of group members to meet goals. We then described a number of leadership

Influence is a fundamental cornerstone of leadership. Influence, in turn, is the ability to affect the perceptions, attitudes, or behaviors of others. The Dalai Lama clearly meets this test of leadership, given the widespread influence he has had over others. His words, his writings, and his behaviors are meticulously scrutinized by his followers, and they are quick to follow even his most subtle directions or suggestions. Corporate and government leaders can also have significant influence as well. This influence plays a major role in their successes or failures as they work to carry out their responsibilities as leaders in their own unique organizational contexts.

models and theories based variously on leadership traits, behaviors, and contingencies. Unfortunately, most of these models and theories essentially ignore the influence component of leadership. That is, they tend to focus on the characteristics of the leader (traits, behaviors, or both) and the responses from followers (satisfaction, performance, or both, for instance) with little regard for how the leader actually exercises influence in an effort to bring about the desired responses from followers.

But influence should actually be seen as the cornerstone of the process. Regardless of the leader's traits or behaviors, leadership only matters if influence actually occurs. That is, a person's effectiveness in affecting the behavior of others through influence is the ultimate determinant of whether she or he is really a leader. No one can truly be a leader without the ability to influence others. And if someone does have the ability to influence others, he or she clearly has the potential to become a leader.[2]

**Influence** is the ability to affect the perceptions, attitudes, or behaviors of others.

**Influence** can be defined as the ability to affect the perceptions, attitudes, or behaviors of others.[3] If a person can make another person recognize that her working conditions are more hazardous than she currently believes them to be (change in perceptions), influence has occurred. Likewise, if an individual can convince someone else that the organization is a much better place to work than he currently believes it to be (change in attitude), influence has occurred. And if someone can get others to work harder or to file a grievance against their boss (change in behavior), influence has occurred.[4] Note, too, that influence can be used in ways that are beneficial or harmful.[5] Someone can be influenced to help clean up a city park on the weekend as part of a community service program, for example, or be influenced to use or sell drugs. Jack Greenberg is using his influence to change a corporation.

*"In a network, all you have is influence. That's all you've got. . . . In a hierarchy the CEO is always CEO, but in networks leadership is always shifting." — Jessica Lipnack, communications consultant*[6]

# Influence-Based Approaches to Leadership

Influence has become a more significant component of some leadership models and concepts in recent years. The two contemporary approaches to leadership discussed in this section, for example, are each tied directly or indirectly to influence. These approaches are transformational leadership and charismatic leadership.

## Transformational Leadership

Transformational leadership, a relative newcomer to the leadership literature, focuses on the basic distinction between leading for change and leading for stability.[7] According to this viewpoint, much of what a leader does occurs in the course of normal, routine work-related transactions—assigning work, evaluating performance, making decisions, and so forth. Occasionally, however, the leader has to initiate and manage major change, such as managing a merger, creating a work group, or defining the organization's culture. The first set of issues involves transactional leadership, whereas the second entails transformational leadership.[8]

Recall from Chapter 13 the distinction between management and leadership. Transactional leadership is essentially the same as management in that it involves routine, regimented activities. Closer to the general notion of leadership, however, is **transformational leadership,** the set of abilities that allows the leader to recognize the need for change, to create a vision to guide that change, and to execute the change effectively. Only a leader with tremendous influence can hope to perform these functions successfully. Some experts believe that change is such a vital organizational function that even successful firms need to change regularly to avoid complacency and stagnation; accordingly, leadership for change is also important.[9] The "World View" box recounts the achievements of one very successful transformational leader.

**Transformational leadership** is the set of abilities that allows the leader to recognize the need for change, to create a vision to guide that change, and to execute that change effectively.

Some leaders can adopt either transformational or transactional perspectives, depending on their circumstances. Others are able to do one or the other but not both. The first CEO of Compaq Computer, Ron Canion, was clearly an excellent transactional leader. He built the firm from a single new idea and managed it efficiently and profitably for several years. But the environment changed to the point that Compaq needed to change as well, and Canion was apparently unable to recognize the need for change, to lead the firm through those changes, or both. His replacement, Eckhard Pfeiffer, apparently excelled at transformational leadership as he led the firm through several very successful new initiatives and transformations. But when this work was done and Compaq needed to refocus on efficient and effective operations best directed by a transactional leader, Pfeiffer faltered and he too was replaced with Michael D. Capellas. The new CEO at McDonald's, Jack Greenberg, meanwhile, seems to have both sets of skills. For example, he was a very transactional leader when he led the firm's financial management function but is now leading a major new transformation strategy.

## Charismatic Leadership

Perspectives based on charismatic leadership, like the trait theories discussed in Chapter 13, assume that charisma is an individual characteristic of the leader.

WORLD VIEW

## *The Sky's the Limit*

When most people think of airplane manufacturers, they think of Boeing and Airbus. But one of the most successful airplane manufacturers today is a relatively unknown Canadian firm called Bombardier Aerospace. And much of the credit for Bombardier's success is due to its outgoing CEO, Laurent Beaudoin. When Beaudoin took over the firm in 1967, Bombardier was earning about $10 million a year selling snowmobiles. But as Beaudoin took the final steps toward retirement, he transformed the company into a transportation powerhouse with annual sales of $8.3 billion, a world market leader in executive jets, commercial aircraft, and subway cars.

What has been Beaudoin's secret? Observers think there have been two keys to his success. One talent frequently displayed by Beaudoin is his almost uncanny ability to buy distressed firms at rock-bottom prices and to turn them into powerhouses. For example, he led Bombardier into the airplane market by buying the money-losing Canadair from the Canadian government. He added Learjet Corporation when its ailing parent, Integrated Resources, filed for bankruptcy. Together these two acquisitions have allowed Bombardier to overtake Gulfstream Aerospace in the executive jet market and to establish a dominant position in the newly emerging market for regional jets for such commercial carriers as Continental and American. Indeed, one senior executive at Bombardier projects that by 2004 the firm should be able to double sales and profits from 1999 levels without making any new acquisitions.

But Beaudoin attributes most of his success to his ability to distinguish between routine day-to-day administrative activities and fundamental leadership processes associated with change and transformation. Indeed, he equates the leadership function to that of a conductor of an orchestra. Just as the conductor doesn't make any music but instead coordinates and inspires the talents of musicians, a leader should guide and direct, but stay out of the way so that talented people can follow their instincts and do their jobs the way they think best. Moreover, according to Beaudoin, the leader should let administrators take care of basic business matters while she or he seeks to better understand the right vision for the firm. And so as Beaudoin steps down and turns the reins over to his hand-groomed successor, Robert Brown, investors seem to be reassured by the fact that Beaudoin has spent most of his time with Brown talking about leadership, conducting, and vision. This, they say, is a good thing.

*"I see myself as the conductor of an orchestra. I don't play all the instruments, but I can tell you when they're playing in tune." — Laurent Beaudoin, retired Bombardier Aerospace CEO*

References: "Bombardier's Master Builder," *Forbes,* April 19, 1999, pp. 162–166; *Hoover's Handbook of World Business 2000* (Austin: Hoover's Business Press, 2000), pp. 132–133.

**Charisma** is a form of interpersonal attraction that inspires support and acceptance from others.

**Charismatic leadership** is a type of influence based on the leader's personal charisma.

**Charisma** is a form of interpersonal attraction that inspires support and acceptance. **Charismatic leadership** is accordingly a type of influence based on the leader's personal charisma. All else being equal, then, someone with charisma is more likely to be able to influence others than someone without charisma. For example, a highly charismatic supervisor will be more successful in influencing subordinate behavior than a supervisor who lacks charisma. Thus, influence is again a fundamental element of this perspective.[10]

*"What I learned as a leader is that you don't [mess with] people under hostile circumstances. You tell them the truth." — Robert Swan, explorer and acknowledged charismatic leader[11]*

Charismatic leadership is a type of influence based on the leader's personal charisma. Jeff Bezos, founder and CEO of Amazon.com, clearly relies on this form of influence as he leads his company. He has a clear vision of where he wants his firm to go; he is ethical in his conduct; and he is a happy and pleasant person to be around. Amazon.com employees almost invariably express true affection and admiration for him. It's also pretty typical that when Bezos visits a group of employees they will start asking him for his autograph, as this group has done.

Robert House first proposed a theory of charismatic leadership based on research findings from a variety of social science disciplines.[12] His theory suggests that charismatic leaders are likely to have a lot of self-confidence, firm confidence in their beliefs and ideals, and a strong need to influence people. They also tend to communicate high expectations about follower performance and express confidence in followers. Herb Kelleher, CEO of Southwest Airlines, is an excellent example of a charismatic leader. Kelleher, or "Uncle Herbie" as he is known inside the company, possesses a unique combination of executive skill, honesty, and playfulness. These qualities have attracted a group of followers at Southwest who are willing to follow his lead without question and to dedicate themselves to carrying out his decisions and policies with unceasing passion.[13]

Figure 14.1 portrays the three elements of charismatic leadership in organizations that most experts acknowledge today.[14] First, the leader needs to be able to envision the future, to set high expectations, and to model behaviors consistent with meeting those expectations. Next, the charismatic leader must be able to

figure 14.1

**The Charismatic Leader**

*The charismatic leader is characterized by three fundamental attributes. As illustrated here, these are behaviors resulting in envisioning, energizing, and enabling. Charismatic leaders can be a powerful force in any organizational setting.*

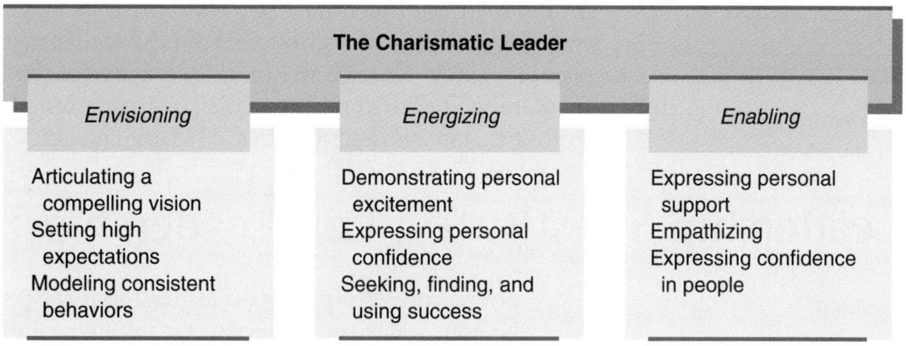


Reference: David A. Nadler and Michael L. Tushman, "Beyond the Charismatic Leader: Leadership and Organizational Change," *California Management Review*, Winter 1990, pp. 70–97.

WORKING WITH DIVERSITY

## *Leading with Charisma!*

Talk about challenges! First, as part of the Latino culture, Mexican men are generally unenthusiastic about following the lead of a woman. Second, low-wage employees are often reluctant to make waves because they know they can be easily replaced. So why is it that one of the most respected (or feared, depending on your point of view) labor organizers today is Yanira Merino, an immigrant from El Salvador, who specializes in organizing low-wage employees in industries, such as food processing, that are staffed largely by immigrant workers?

*"You know the risks we are taking. If we are caught, we could lose our jobs. But we want to make a change. We want to go for it." — Yanira Merino, union organizer*

Part of the answer is Merino's charisma. She speaks eloquently and with passion. She also takes risks, and others are willing to follow her lead. And finally, she fights for downtrodden workers in places where they have traditionally been treated with little respect and given few opportunities for advancement. For example, the first plant she organized was a tuna-processing factory in California. The plant had a divisive bonus policy that pitted one worker against another, and the supervisors routinely told ethnic jokes and made sexually harassing comments.

From there Merino moved on to a poultry factory in North Carolina. Again, workers were treated with little respect, and working conditions were abysmal. And again, Merino's organizing efforts paid off, and the workers are now represented by a union. From North Carolina, Merino has moved back to southern California and is working to organize immigrant manufacturing workers. Who knows, admirers say, she may end up being the next Mother Jones.

References: "Shattering the AFL-CIO's Glass Ceiling," *Business Week,* November 13, 1995, p. 46; "Can Unions Organize Low-Paid Workers? Watch This Woman," *Wall Street Journal,* October 23, 1995, pp. A1, A10 (quote on p. A1).

energize others by demonstrating personal excitement, personal confidence, and patterns of success. Finally, the charismatic leader enables others by supporting them, empathizing with them, and expressing confidence in them.[15]

Charismatic leadership ideas are quite popular among managers today and are the subject of numerous books and articles.[16] Unfortunately, few studies have specifically attempted to test the meaning and impact of charismatic leadership. Lingering ethical concerns about charismatic leadership also trouble some people. These concerns stem from the fact that some charismatic leaders inspire such blind faith in their followers that the followers may engage in inappropriate, unethical, or even illegal behaviors, just because the leader instructed them to do so.[17] For example, David Koresh, the infamous leader of the Branch Davidians in Waco, Texas, relied heavily on his personal charisma to influence his followers. A more positive example is described in the "Working with Diversity" box.

# Leadership Substitutes: Can Leadership Be Irrelevant?

Another interesting twist on leadership is the premise that it may sometimes be unnecessary or irrelevant. An implicit assumption made by each leadership and influence perspective described thus far is that the leader and the follower can be differentiated. That is, one person, the leader, is trying to influence

Leadership substitutes allow people to perform effectively without the direction or supervision of a leader. The Container Store has become one of the "Best Companies to Work for in America" by implicitly using this approach in running its stores. Each employee has virtually unlimited discretion in how to respond to customer requests and meet customer needs. The firm hires only the best and most motivated sales people; it instructs them in all phases of how the company operates; and it informs them about all aspects of the business. Then, it turns them loose and lets them do their jobs in the best way they choose.

or control another, the follower. But the concept of leadership substitutes points out that in some situations leadership may not be necessary.

## The Nature of Leadership Substitutes

**Leadership substitutes** are individual, task, and organizational characteristics that tend to outweigh the leader's ability to affect subordinates' satisfaction and performance.

**Leadership substitutes** are individual, task, and organizational characteristics that tend to outweigh the leader's ability to affect subordinates' satisfaction and performance.[18] In other words, if certain factors are present, the employee will perform his or her job capably without the direction of the leader. Unlike traditional theories, which assume that hierarchical leadership is always important, the premise of the leadership substitutes perspective is that leader behaviors are irrelevant in many situations.

## Workplace Substitutes

Ability, experience, training, knowledge, need for independence, professional orientation, and indifference to organizational rewards are individual characteristics that may neutralize leader behaviors. For example, an employee who has the skills and abilities to perform her job and a high need for independence may not need—and may even resent—a leader who tries to provide direction and structure.

A task characterized by routine, a high degree of structure, frequent feedback, and intrinsic satisfaction may also render leader behavior irrelevant. Thus, if the task gives the subordinate enough intrinsic satisfaction, she or he may not need support from a leader.

Explicit plans and goals, rules and procedures, cohesive work groups, a rigid reward structure, and physical distance between supervisor and subordinate are organizational characteristics that may substitute for leadership. For example, if job goals are explicit and there are many rules and procedures for task performance, a leader providing directions may not be necessary. Preliminary research has provided support for the concept of leadership substitutes, but additional research is needed to identify other potential substitutes and their impact on leadership effectiveness.[19]

### Superleadership

**Superleadership** occurs when a leader gradually and purposefully turns over power, responsibility, and control to a self-managing work group.

A relatively new addition to the literature on leadership substitutes is the notion of superleadership. **Superleadership** occurs when a leader gradually turns over power, responsibility, and control to a self-managing work group. As we discussed more fully in Chapter 12, many firms today are making widespread use of work teams who function without a formal manager. A big challenge faced by these firms is what to do with the existing group leader. Although some managers cannot handle this change and leave, a superleader can alter his or her own personal style and become more of a coach or facilitator than a supervisor.[20]

*"Leaders are lonely, because they must think and dream about their work—all day, every day, day after day." — Lorraine Monroe, principal of Harlem's Frederick Douglas School, considered one of New York's greatest educational success stories*[21]

## Power in Organizations

Influence is also closely related to the concept of power. Power is one of the most significant forces that exists in organizations. Moreover, it can be an extremely important ingredient in organizational success—or organizational failure. In this section we first describe the nature of power. We then examine the types and uses of power.

### The Nature of Power

**Power** is the potential ability of a person or group to exercise control over another person or group.

Power has been defined in dozens of different ways; no one definition is generally accepted. Drawing from the more common meanings of the term, we define **power** as the potential ability of a person or group to exercise control over another person or group.[22] Power is distinguished from influence due to the element of control; the more powerful control the less powerful. Thus, power might be thought of as an extreme form of influence.[23]

One obvious aspect of our definition is that it expresses power in terms of potential; that is, we may be able to control others but may choose not to exercise that control. Nevertheless, simply having the potential may be enough to influence others in some settings. We should also note that power may reside in individuals (such as managers and informal leaders); in formal groups (such as departments and committees); and in informal groups (such as a clique of influential people). Finally, we should note the direct link between power and influence. If a person can convince another person to change his or her opinion on some issue, to engage in or refrain from some behavior, or to view circumstances in a certain way, that person has exercised influence—and used power.

Considerable differences of opinion exist about how thoroughly power pervades organizations. Some people argue that virtually all interpersonal relations are influenced by power, whereas others believe that exercise of power is confined only to certain situations. Whatever the case, power is undoubtedly a pervasive part of organizational life. It affects decisions ranging from the choice of strategies to the color of the new office carpeting. It makes or breaks careers. And it enhances or limits organizational effectiveness.

## Types of Power

Within the broad framework of our definition, there obviously are many types of power. These types usually are described in terms of bases of power and position power versus personal power.

### Bases of Power

The most widely used and recognized analysis of the bases of power is the framework developed by John R. P. French and Bertram Raven.[24] French and Raven identified five general bases of power in organizational settings: legitimate, reward, coercive, expert, and referent power.

**Legitimate power** is power that is granted by virtue of one's position in the organization.

**Legitimate power**, essentially the same thing as authority, is granted by virtue of one's position in an organization. Managers have legitimate power over their subordinates. The organization specifies that it is legitimate for the designated individual to direct the activities of others. The bounds of this legitimacy are defined partly by the formal nature of the position involved and partly by informal norms and traditions. For example, it was once commonplace for managers to expect their secretaries not only to perform work-related activities such as typing and filing but to also run personal errands such as picking up laundry and buying gifts. In highly centralized mechanistic and bureaucratic organizations such as the military, the legitimate power inherent in each position is closely specified, widely known, and strictly followed. In more organic organizations, such as research and development labs and software firms, the lines of legitimate power are often blurry. Employees may work for more than one boss at the same time, and leaders and followers may be on a nearly equal footing.

**Reward power** is the extent to which a person controls rewards that another person values.

**Reward power** is the extent to which a person controls rewards that are valued by another. The most obvious examples of organizational rewards are pay, promotions, and work assignments. If a manager has almost total control over the pay his subordinates receive, can make recommendations about promotions, and has considerable discretion to make job assignments, he or she has a high level of reward power. Reward power can extend beyond material rewards. As we noted in our discussions of motivation theory in Chapters 5 and 6, people work for a variety of reasons in addition to pay. For instance, some people may be motivated primarily by a desire for recognition and acceptance. To the extent that a manager's praise and acknowledgment satisfy those needs, that manager has even more reward power.

**Coercive power** is the extent to which a person has the ability to punish or physically or psychologically harm someone else.

**Coercive power** exists when someone has the ability to punish or physically or psychologically harm another person. For example, some managers berate subordinates in front of everyone, belittling their efforts and generally making their lives miserable. Certain forms of coercion may be subtle. In some organizations, a particular division may be notorious as a resting place for people who have no future with the company. Threatening to transfer someone to a dead-end branch or some other undesirable location is thus a form of coercion. Clearly, the more negative the sanctions a person can bring to bear on others, the stronger is her or his coercive power. At the same time, the use of coercive power carries a considerable cost in employee resentment and hostility.

*"Colleagues know immediately when the boss is upset. His blue eyes flash with anger, and he intimidates subordinates with long silences. Indeed, in an era when team-building and employee empowerment are in vogue, Piëch prefers fear as a motivator." — David Woodruff and Keith Naughton, business writers, referring to new Volkswagen CEO Ferdinand Piëch[25]*

**Expert power** is the extent to which a person controls information that is valuable to someone else.

Control over expertise or, more precisely, over information is another source of power. For example, to the extent that an inventory manager has information that a sales representative needs, the inventory manager has **expert power** over the sales representative. The more important the information and the fewer the alternative sources for getting it, the greater the power. Expert power can reside in many niches in an organization; it transcends positions and jobs. Although legitimate, reward, and coercive power may not always correspond exactly to formal authority, they often do. Expert power, on the other hand, may be associated much less with formal authority. Upper-level managers usually decide on the organization's strategic agenda, but individuals at lower levels in the organization may have the expertise those managers need to do the tasks. A research scientist may have crucial information about a technical breakthrough of great importance to the organization and its strategic decisions. Or an assistant may take on so many of the boss's routine and mundane activities that the manager loses track of such details and comes to depend on the assistant to keep things running smoothly. In other situations, lower-level participants are given power as a way to take advantage of their expertise.

**Referent power** is power through identification. If José is highly respected by Adam, José has referent power over Adam. Like expert power, referent power does not always correlate with formal organizational authority. In some ways, referent power is similar to the concept of charisma in that it often involves trust, similarity, acceptance, affection, willingness to follow, and emotional involvement. Referent power

There are many different types of power in an organization. For example, consider Carlos Ghosn, CEO of Nissan. For much of the 1990s, Nissan consistently lost money and market share. After Renault bought the company, it put Ghosn in charge of fixing its problems. Thus, he has the legitimate power to mandate change and expect results. He can also use his reward power to distribute rewards to those who meet his expectations and coercive power to punish those who don't. Because Ghosn is a respected senior executive in the industry, he also has expert power among his followers. And because he is well-liked and admired, he also enjoys a measure of referent power as well.

**Referent power** exists when one person wants to be like or imitates someone else.

usually surfaces as imitation. For example, suppose a new department manager is the youngest person in the organization to have reached that rank. Further, it is widely believed that she is being groomed for the highest levels of the company. Other people in the department may begin to imitate her, thinking that they too may be able to advance. They may begin dressing like her, working the same hours, and trying to pick up as many work-related pointers from her as possible.

**Position Versus Personal Power** The French and Raven framework is only one approach to examining the origins of organizational power. Another approach categorizes power in organizations in terms of position or personal power.

**Position power** resides in the position, regardless of who is filling that position.

**Position power** is power that resides in the position, regardless of who holds it. Thus, legitimate, reward, and some aspects of coercive and expert power can all contribute to position power. Position power is thus similar to authority. In creating a position, the organization simultaneously establishes a sphere of power for the person filling that position. He or she will generally have the power to direct the activities of subordinates in performing their jobs, to control some of their potential rewards, and to have a say in their punishment and discipline. There are, however, limits to a manager's position power. A manager cannot order or control activities that fall outside his or her sphere of power—for instance, directing a subordinate to commit crimes, to perform personal services, or to take on tasks that clearly are not part of the subordinate's job.

**Personal power** resides in the person, regardless of the position being filled.

**Personal power** is power that resides with an individual, regardless of his or her position in the organization. Thus, the primary bases of personal power are referent and some traces of expert, coercive, and reward power. Charisma may also contribute to personal power. Someone usually exercises personal power through rational persuasion or by playing on followers' identification with him or her. An individual with personal power often can inspire greater loyalty and dedication in followers than someone who has only position power. The stronger influence stems from the fact that the followers are acting more from choice than from necessity (as dictated, for example, by their organizational responsibilities) and thus will respond more readily to requests and appeals. Of course, the influence of a leader who relies only on personal power is limited, because followers may freely decide not to accept his or her directives or orders.

The distinctions between formal and informal leaders are also related to position and personal power. A formal leader will have, at minimum, position power. And an informal leader will similarly have some degree of personal power. Just as a person may be both a formal and an informal leader, he or she can have both position and personal power simultaneously. Indeed, such a combination usually has the greatest potential influence on the actions of others.[26] Figure 14.2 illustrates how personal and position power may interact to determine how much overall power a person has in a particular situation. An individual with both personal and position power will have the strongest

**figure 14.2 Position Power and Personal Power**

*Position power resides in a job, whereas personal power resides in an individual. When these two types of power are broken down into high and low levels and related to one another, the two-by-two matrix shown here is the result. For example, the upper right cell suggests that a leader with high levels of both position and personal power will have the highest overall level of power. Other combinations result in differing levels of overall power.*

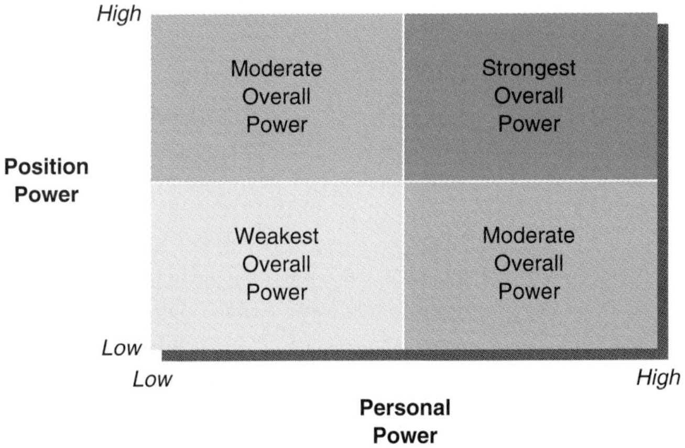

overall power. Likewise, an individual with neither personal nor position power will have the weakest overall power. Finally, when either personal or position power is high but the other is low, the individual will have a moderate level of overall power.

## The Uses of Power in Organizations

Power can be used in many ways in an organization. But because of the potential for its misuse and the concerns that it may engender, it is important that managers fully understand the dynamics of using power. Gary Yukl has presented a useful perspective for understanding how power may be wielded.[27] His perspective includes two closely related components. The first relates power bases, requests from individuals possessing power, and probable outcomes in the form of prescriptions for the manager. Table 14.1 indicates the three outcomes that may result when a

table **14.1**

**Uses and Outcomes of Power**

| Source of Leader Influence | Type of Outcome | | |
|---|---|---|---|
| | **Commitment** | **Compliance** | **Resistance** |
| **Referent Power** | *Likely* | *Possible* | *Possible* |
| | If request is believed to be important to leader | If request is perceived to be unimportant to leader | If request is for something that will bring harm to leader |
| **Expert Power** | *Likely* | *Possible* | *Possible* |
| | If request is persuasive and subordinates share leader's task goals | If request is persuasive but subordinates are apathetic about leader's task goals | If leader is arrogant and insulting, or subordinates oppose task goals |
| **Legitimate Power** | *Possible* | *Likely* | *Possible* |
| | If request is polite and very appropriate | If request or order is seen as legitimate | If arrogant demands are made or request does not appear proper |
| **Reward Power** | *Possible* | *Likely* | *Possible* |
| | If used in a subtle, very personal way | If used in a mechanical, impersonal way | If used in a manipulative, arrogant way |
| **Coercive Power** | *Very Unlikely* | *Possible* | *Likely* |
| | | If used in a helpful, nonpunitive way | If used in a hostile or manipulative way |

Reference: Table adapted by Gary A. Yukl from information in John R. P. French Jr., and Bertram Raven, "The Bases of Social Power," in Dorwin P. Cartwright (ed.), *Studies in Social Power* (Ann Arbor: Institute for Social Research, University of Michigan, 1959), pp. 150–167. Data used by permission of the Institute for Social Research.

leader tries to exert power.[28] These outcomes depend on the leader's base of power, how that base is operationalized, and the subordinate's individual characteristics (for example, personality traits or past interactions with the leader).

*Commitment* will probably result from an attempt to exercise power if the subordinate accepts and identifies with the leader. Such an employee will be highly motivated by requests that seem important to the leader. For example, a leader might explain that a new piece of software will greatly benefit the organization if it is developed soon. A committed subordinate will work just as hard as the leader to complete the project, even if that means working overtime. Sam Walton once asked all Wal-Mart employees to start greeting customers with a smile and an offer to help. Because Wal-Mart employees generally were motivated by and loyal to Walton, most of them accepted his request.

*Compliance* means the subordinate is willing to carry out the leader's wishes as long as doing so will not require extra effort. That is, the person will respond to normal, reasonable requests that are perceived to clearly be within the normal boundaries of the job. But the person will not be inclined to do anything extra or to go beyond the normal expectations for the job. Thus, the subordinate may work at a reasonable pace but refuse to work overtime, insisting that the job will still be there tomorrow. Many ordinary requests from a boss meet with compliant responses from subordinates.

*Resistance* occurs when the subordinate rejects or fights the leader's wishes. For example, suppose an unpopular leader asks employees to volunteer for a company-sponsored community activity project. The employees may reject this request, largely because of their feelings about the leader. A resistant subordinate may even deliberately neglect the project to ensure that it is not done as the leader wants. When Frank Lorenzo ran Continental Airlines, some employees occasionally disobeyed his mandates as a form of protest against his leadership of the firm.

Table 14.2 suggests ways for leaders to use various kinds of power most effectively. By effective use of power we mean using power in the way that is most likely to engender commitment or at the least compliance and that is least likely to engender resistance. For example, to suggest a somewhat mechanistic approach, managers may enhance their referent power by choosing subordinates with backgrounds similar to their own. They might, for instance, build a referent power base by hiring several subordinates who went to the same college they did. A more subtle way to exercise referent power is through role modeling: the leader behaves as she or he wants subordinates to behave. As noted earlier, since subordinates relate to and identify with the leader with referent power, they may subsequently attempt to emulate that person's behavior.[29]

In using expert power, managers can subtly make others aware of their education, experience, and accomplishments. To maintain credibility, a leader should not pretend to know things that he or she really does not know. A leader whose pretensions are exposed will rapidly lose expert power. A confident and decisive leader demonstrates a firm grasp of situations and takes charge when circumstances dictate. Managers should also keep themselves informed about developments related to tasks that are valuable to the organization and relevant to their expertise.

A leader who recognizes employee concerns works to understand the underlying nature of these issues and takes appropriate steps to reassure subordinates. For example, if employees feel threatened by rumors that they will lose office space after an impending move, the leader might ask them about this concern and then find out just how much office space there will be and tell the subordinates. Finally, to avoid threatening the self-esteem of subordinates, a leader should be careful not

**table 14.2**
**Guidelines for Using Power**

| Basis of Power | Guidelines for Use |
|---|---|
| **Referent Power** | Treat subordinates fairly<br>Defend subordinates' interests<br>Be sensitive to subordinates' needs, feelings<br>Select subordinates similar to oneself<br>Engage in role modeling |
| **Expert Power** | Promote image of expertise<br>Maintain credibility<br>Act confident and decisive<br>Keep informed<br>Recognize employee concerns<br>Avoid threatening subordinates' self-esteem |
| **Legitimate Power** | Be cordial and polite<br>Be confident<br>Be clear and follow up to verify understanding<br>Make sure request is appropriate<br>Explain reasons for request<br>Follow proper channels<br>Exercise power regularly<br>Enforce compliance<br>Be sensitive to subordinates' concerns |
| **Reward Power** | Verify compliance<br>Make feasible, reasonable requests<br>Make only ethical, proper requests<br>Offer rewards desired by subordinates<br>Offer only credible rewards |
| **Coercive Power** | Inform subordinates of rules and penalties<br>Warn before punishing<br>Administer punishment consistently and uniformly<br>Understand the situation before acting<br>Maintain credibility<br>Fit punishment to the infraction<br>Punish in private |

Reference: Reprinted from Gary A. Yukl, *Leadership in Organization,* 2nd ed., © 1989, pp. 44–49, Prentice-Hall, Inc., Englewood Cliffs, N.J.

to flaunt expertise or behave like a "know-it-all." The fallacy of doing so is clearly illustrated in the cartoon!

In general, a leader exercises legitimate power by formally requesting that subordinates do something. The leader should be especially careful to make requests diplomatically if the subordinate is sensitive about his or her relationship with the leader. This might be the case, for example, if the subordinate is older or more experienced than the leader. But although the request should be polite, it should be made confidently. The leader is in charge and needs to convey his or her command of the situation. The request should also be clear. Thus, the leader may need to follow up to ascertain that the subordinate has understood the request properly. To ensure that a request is seen as appropriate and legitimate to the situation, the leader may need to explain the reasons for it. Often subordinates do not understand the rationale behind a request and consequently are unenthusiastic about it. It is important, too, to follow proper channels when dealing with subordinates.

Leaders are expected to use their expert power to inform, guide, and direct the actions of others. When their expertise is relevant and important, and when it is provided in a supportive fashion with employee development in mind, others value and appreciate both the leader and the information. But when the information is actually trivial or is presented in a condescending or demeaning manner, people may be offended and resist what the leader is trying to accomplish. In this illustration, the boss's clumsy attempt to provide information results in Dilbert expressing sarcasm and disrespect.

Reference: DILBERT reprinted by permission of United Feature Syndicate, Inc.

Suppose a manager has asked a subordinate to spend his day finishing an important report. Later, while the manager is out of the office, her boss comes by and asks the subordinate to drop that project and work on something else. The subordinate will then be in the awkward position of having to choose which of two higher-ranking individuals to obey. Exercising authority regularly will reinforce its presence and legitimacy in the eyes of subordinates. Compliance with legitimate power should be the norm, because if employees resist a request, the leader's power base may diminish. Finally, the leader exerting legitimate power should attempt to be responsive to subordinates' problems and concerns in the same ways we outlined for using expert power.

Reward power is, in some respects, the easiest base of power to use. Verifying compliance simply means that leaders should find out whether subordinates have carried out their requests before giving rewards; otherwise, subordinates may not recognize a performance-reward linkage. The request that is to be rewarded must be both reasonable and feasible, because even the promise of a reward will not motivate a subordinate who thinks a request should not or cannot be carried out.

The same can be said for a request that seems improper or unethical. Among other things, the follower may see a reward linked to an improper or unethical request, such as a bribe or other shady offering. Finally, if the leader promises a reward that subordinates know she or he cannot actually deliver, or if they have little use for a reward the manager can deliver, they will not be motivated to carry out the request. Further, they may grow skeptical of the leader's ability to deliver rewards that are worth something to them.

Coercion is certainly the most difficult form of power to exercise. Because coercive power is likely to cause resentment and to erode referent power, it should be used infrequently, if at all. Compliance is about all one can expect from using coercive power, and that only if the power is used in a helpful, nonpunitive way—that is, if the sanction is mild and fits the situation and if the subordinate learns from it. In most cases, resistance is the most likely outcome, especially if coercive power is used in a hostile or manipulative way.

The first guideline for using coercive power—that subordinates should be fully informed about rules and the penalties for violating them—will prevent accidental violations of a rule, which pose an unpalatable dilemma for a leader. Overlooking an infraction on the grounds that the perpetrator was ignorant may undermine the rule or the leader's legitimate power, but carrying out the punishment probably will create resentment. One approach is to provide reasonable warning before inflicting punishment, responding to the first violation of a rule with a warning about the consequences of another violation. Of course, a serious infraction such as a theft or violence warrants immediate and severe punishment.

The disciplinary action needs to be administered consistently and uniformly, because doing so shows that punishment is both impartial and clearly linked to the infraction. Leaders should obtain complete information about what has happened before they punish, because punishing the wrong person or administering uncalled-for punishment can stir great resentment among subordinates. Credibility must be maintained, because a leader who continually makes threats but fails to carry them out loses both respect and power. Similarly, if the leader uses threats that subordinates know are beyond his or her ability to impose, the attempted use of power will be fruitless. Obviously, too, the severity of the punishment generally should match the seriousness of the infraction. Finally, punishing someone in front of others adds humiliation to the penalty, which reflects poorly on the leader and makes those who must watch and listen uncomfortable as well.

# Politics and Political Behavior

**Organizational politics** is activities carried out by people to acquire, enhance, and use power and other resources to obtain their desired outcomes.

A concept closely related to power in organizational settings is politics, or political behavior. We can define **organizational politics** as activities people perform to acquire, enhance, and use power and other resources to obtain their preferred outcomes in a situation in which there is uncertainty or disagreement.[30] Thus, political behavior is the general means by which people attempt to obtain and use power. Put simply, the goal of such behavior is to get one's own way about things.[31]

## The Pervasiveness of Political Behavior

A classic survey provides some interesting insights into how managers perceive political behavior in their organizations.[32] Roughly one-third of the 428 managers who responded to this survey believed political behavior influenced salary decisions in their organizations, while 28 percent felt it affected hiring decisions. Moreover, three-quarters of them also believed political behavior is more prevalent at higher levels of the organization than at lower levels. More than half believed that politics is unfair, unhealthy, and irrational but also acknowledged that successful executives must be good politicians and that it is necessary to behave politically to get ahead. The survey results suggest that managers see political behavior as an undesirable but unavoidable facet of organizational life.[33]

Politics often is viewed as synonymous with dirty tricks or backstabbing and therefore as something distasteful and best left to others. But the results of the survey just described demonstrate that political behavior in organizations, like power,

## figure 14.3

**A Model of Ethical Political Behavior**

*Political behavior can serve both ethical and unethical purposes. This model helps illustrate circumstances in which political behavior is most and least likely to have ethical consequences. By following the paths through the model, a leader concerned about the ethics of an impending behavior can gain insights into whether ethical considerations are really a central part of the behavior.*

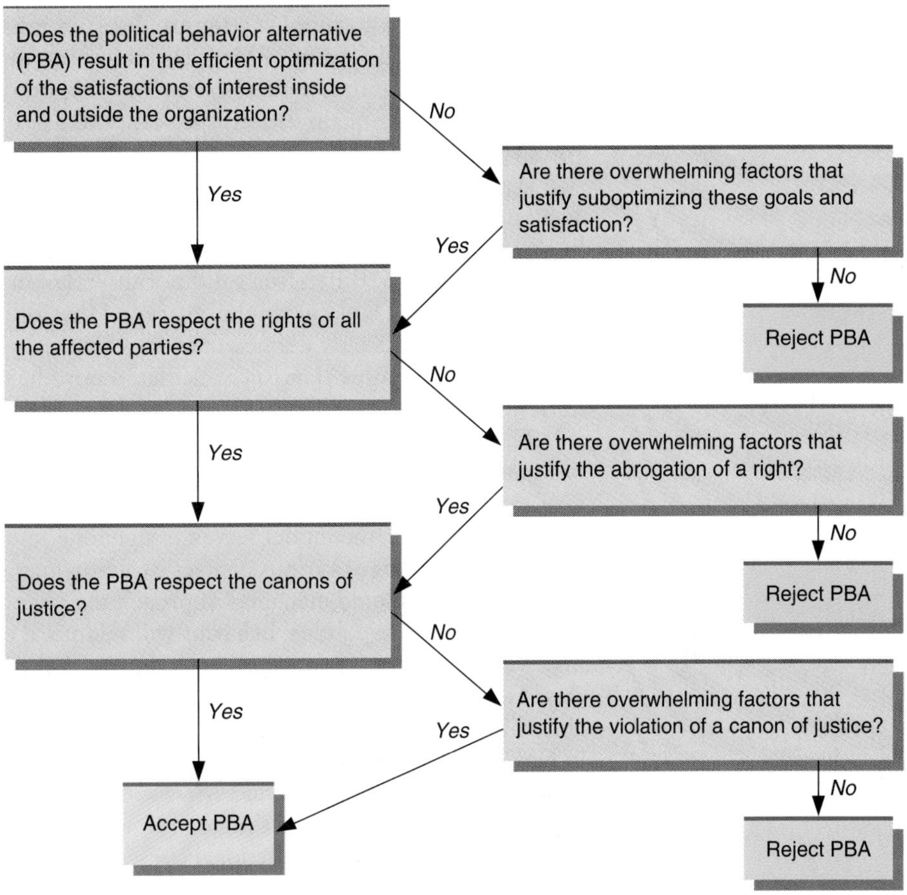


Reference: Gerald F. Cavanaugh, Dennis J. Moberg, and Manuel Velasques, "The Ethics of Organizational Politics." *Academy of Management Review*, July 1981, p. 368. Used with permission.

is pervasive. Thus, rather than ignoring or trying to eliminate political behavior, managers might more fruitfully consider when and how organizational politics can be used constructively.

Figure 14.3 presents an interesting model of the ethics of organizational politics.[34] In the model, a political behavior alternative (PBA) is a given course of action, largely political in character, in a particular situation. The model considers political behavior ethical and appropriate under two conditions: (1) if it respects the rights of all affected parties, and (2) if it adheres to the canons of justice (that is, to a commonsense judgment of what is fair and equitable). Even if the political behavior does not meet these tests, it may be ethical and appropriate under certain circumstances. For example, politics may provide the only possible basis for deciding which employees to let go during a recessionary period of cutbacks. In all cases in which nonpolitical alternatives exist, however, the model recommends rejecting political behavior that abrogates rights or justice.

To illustrate how the model works, consider Susan Jackson and Bill Thompson, both assistant professors of English. University regulations stipulate that only one of the assistant professors may be tenured; the other must be let go. Both Susan and Bill submit their credentials for review. By most objective criteria, such as number of publications and teaching evaluations, the two faculty members' qualifications are roughly the same. Because he fears termination, Bill begins an active political campaign to support a tenure decision favoring him. He continually reminds the tenured faculty of his intangible contributions, such as his friendship with influential campus administrators. Susan, on the other hand, decides to say nothing and let her qualifications speak for themselves. The department ultimately votes to give Bill tenure and let Susan go.

Was Bill's behavior ethical? Assuming that his comments about himself were accurate and that he said nothing to disparage Susan, his behavior did not affect her rights; that is, she had an equal opportunity to advance her own cause but chose not to do so. Bill's efforts did not directly hurt Susan but only helped himself. On the other hand, it might be argued that Bill's actions violated the canons of justice because clearly defined data on which to base the decision were available. Thus, one could argue that Bill's calculated introduction of additional information into the decision was unjust.

This model has not been tested empirically. Indeed, its very nature may make it impossible to test. Further, as the preceding demonstrates, it often is difficult to give an unequivocal yes or no answer to the questions, even under the simplest circumstances. Thus, the model serves as a general framework for understanding the ethical implications of various courses of action managers might take.

How, then, should managers approach the phenomenon of political behavior? Trying to eliminate political behavior will seldom, if ever, work. In fact, such action may well increase political behavior because of the uncertainty and ambiguity it creates. At the other extreme, universal and freewheeling use of political behavior probably will lead to conflict, feuds, and turmoil.[35] In most cases, a position somewhere in between is best: The manager does not attempt to eliminate political activity, recognizing its inevitability, and may try to use it effectively, perhaps following the ethical model just described. At the same time, the manager can take certain steps to minimize the potential dysfunctional consequences of abusive political behavior.

## Managing Political Behavior

Managing organizational politics is not easy. The very nature of political behavior makes it tricky to approach in a rational and systematic way. Success will require a basic understanding of three factors: the reasons for political behavior, common techniques for using political behavior, and strategies for limiting the effects of political behavior.

### Reasons for Political Behavior

Political behavior occurs in organizations for five basic reasons: ambiguous goals, scarce resources, technology and environment, nonprogrammed decisions, and organizational change (see Figure 14.4).[36]

Most organizational goals are inherently ambiguous. Organizations frequently espouse goals such as "increasing our presence in certain new markets" or "increasing our market share." The ambiguity of such goals provides an opportunity for political behavior, because people can view a wide range of behaviors as helping meet the goal. In reality, of course, many of these behaviors may actually be designed for the personal gain of the individuals involved. For example, a top manager might argue that the corporation should pursue its goal of entry into a new market by buying out another firm instead of forming a new division. The manager may appear to have the good of the corporation in mind—but what if he owns some of the target firm's stock and stands to make money on a merger or acquisition?

Whenever resources are scarce, some people will not get everything they think they deserve or need. Thus, they are likely to engage in political behavior as a

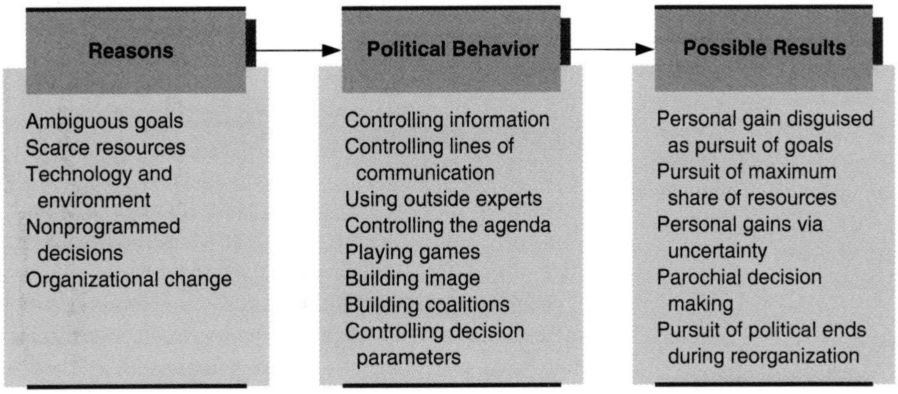

Reasons
Ambiguous goals
Scarce resources
Technology and environment
Nonprogrammed decisions
Organizational change
Political Behavior
Controlling information
Controlling lines of communication
Using outside experts
Controlling the agenda
Playing games
Building image
Building coalitions
Controlling decision parameters
Possible Results
Personal gain disguised as pursuit of goals
Pursuit of maximum share of resources
Personal gains via uncertainty
Parochial decision making
Pursuit of political ends during reorganization


figure 14.4

**Use of Political Behavior: Reasons, Techniques, and Possible Consequences**

*People choose to engage in political behavior for many reasons. Depending on the reasons and circumstances, a person interested in using political behavior can employ a variety of techniques, which will produce a number of intended—and possibly unintended—consequences.*

means of inflating their share of the resources. In this way, a manager seeking a larger budget might present accurate but misleading or incomplete statistics to inflate the perceived importance of her department. Because no organization has unlimited resources, incentives for this kind of political behavior are always present.[37]

Technology and environment may influence the overall design of the organization and its activities. The influence stems from the uncertainties associated with nonroutine technologies and dynamic, complex environments. These uncertainties favor the use of political behavior, because in a dynamic and complex environment, it is imperative that an organization respond to change. An organization's response generally involves a wide range of activities, from purposeful activities to uncertainty to a purely political response. In the last case, a manager might use an environmental shift as an argument for restructuring his or her department to increase his or her own power base.

Political behavior is also likely to arise whenever many nonprogrammed decisions need to be made. Nonprogrammed-decision situations involve ambiguous circumstances that allow ample opportunity for political maneuvering. The two faculty members competing for one tenured position is an example. The nature of the decision allowed political behavior, and, in fact, from Bill's point of view, the nonprogrammed decision demanded political action.

As we discuss in Chapter 19, changes in organizations occur regularly and can take many forms. Each such change introduces some uncertainty and ambiguity into the organizational system, at least until it has been completely institutionalized. The period during which this is occurring usually affords much opportunity for political activity. For instance, a manager worried about the consequences of a reorganization may resort to politics to protect the scope of his or her authority.

**The Techniques of Political Behavior** Several techniques are used in practicing political behavior. Unfortunately, because these techniques have not been systematically studied, our understanding of them is based primarily on informal observation and inference.[38] To further complicate this problem, the participants themselves may not even be aware that they are using particular techniques. Figure 14.4 also summarizes the most frequently used techniques.[39]

One technique of political behavior is to control as much information as possible. The more critical the information and the fewer the people who have access to it, the larger the power base and influence of those who do. For example, suppose a top manager has a report compiled as a basis for future strategic plans. Rather than distributing the complete report to peers and subordinates, he shares only parts of it with the few managers who must have the information. Because no one but the manager has the complete picture, he has power and is engaging in politics to control decisions and activities according to his own ends.

Similarly, some people create or exploit situations to control lines of communication, particularly access to others in the organization. Secretaries frequently control access to their bosses. A secretary may put visitors in contact with the boss, send them away, delay the contact by ensuring that phone calls are not returned promptly, and so forth. People in these positions often find that they can use this type of political behavior quite effectively.

Using outside experts, such as consultants or advisers, can be an effective political technique. The manager who hires a consultant may select one whose views match her own. Because the consultant realizes that the manager was responsible for selecting him, he feels a certain obligation to her. Although the consultant truly attempts to be objective and unbiased, he may unconsciously recommend courses of action favored by the manager. Given the consultant's presumed expertise and neutrality, others in the organization accept his recommendations without challenge. By using an outside expert, the manager has ultimately gotten what she wants.

Controlling the agenda is another common political technique. Suppose a manager wants to prevent a committee from approving a certain proposal. The manager first tries to keep the decision off the agenda entirely, claiming that it is not yet ready for consideration, or attempts to have it placed last on the agenda. As other issues are decided, he sides with the same set of managers on each decision, building up a certain assumption that they are a team. When the controversial item comes up, he can defeat it through a combination of collective fatigue, the desire to get the meeting over with, and the support of his carefully cultivated allies. This technique, then, involves group polarization. A less sophisticated tactic is to prolong discussion of prior agenda items so that the group never reaches the controversial one. Or the manager may raise so many technical issues and new questions about the proposal that the committee decides to table it. In any of these cases, the manager will have used political behavior for his or her own ends.

Game playing is a complex technique that may take many forms. When playing games, managers simply work within the rules of the organization to increase the probability that their preferred outcomes will come about. Suppose a manager is in a position to cast the deciding vote on an upcoming issue. She does not want to alienate either side by voting on it. One game she might play is to arrange to be called out of town on a crucial business trip when the vote is to take place. Assuming that no one questions the need for the trip, she will successfully maintain her position of neutrality and avoid angering either opposing camp.[40]

Another game would involve using any of the techniques of political behavior in a purely manipulative or deceitful way. For example, a manager who will soon be making recommendations about promotions tells each subordinate, in "strictest confidence," that he or she is a leading candidate and needs only to increase his or her performance to have the inside track. Here the manager is using his control over information to play games with his subordinates. A recent power struggle at W.R. Grace further illustrates manipulative practices. One senior executive fired the CEO's son and then allegedly attempted to convince the board of directors to oust the CEO and to give him the job. The CEO, in response, fired his rival and then publicly announced that the individual had been forced out because he had sexually harassed Grace employees.[41]

The technique of building coalitions has as its general goal convincing others that everyone should work together to accomplish certain things. A manager who believes she does not control enough votes to pass an upcoming agenda item may visit with other managers before the meeting to urge them to side with her. If her preferences are in the best interests of the organization, this may be a laudable strategy for her to follow. But if she herself is the principal beneficiary, the technique is not desirable from the organization's perspective.

At its extreme, coalition building, which is frequently used in political bodies, may take the form of blatant reciprocity. In return for Roberta Kline's vote on an issue that concerns him, José Montemayor agrees to vote for a measure that does not affect his group at all but is crucial to Kline's group. Depending on the circumstances, this practice may benefit or hurt the organization as a whole.

The technique of controlling decision parameters can be used only in certain situations and requires much subtlety. Instead of trying to control the actual decision, the manager backs up one step and tries to control the criteria and tests on which the decision is based. This allows the manager to take a less active role in the actual decision but still achieve his or her preferred outcome. For example, suppose a district manager wants a proposed new factory to be constructed on a site in his region. If he tries to influence the decision directly, his arguments will be seen as biased and self-serving. Instead, he may take a very active role in defining the criteria on which the decision will be based, such as target population, access to rail transportation, tax rates, distance from other facilities, and the like. If he is a skillful negotiator, he may be able to influence the decision parameters such that his desired location subsequently appears to be the ideal site as determined by the criteria he has helped shape. Hence, he gets just what he wants without playing a prominent role in the actual decision.

**Limiting the Effects of Political Behavior** Although it is virtually impossible to eliminate political activity in organizations, managers can limit its dysfunctional consequences. The techniques for checking political activity target both the reasons it occurs in the first place and the specific techniques that people use for political gain.

Opening communication is one very effective technique for restraining the impact of political behavior. For instance, with open communication, the basis for allocating scarce resources will be known to everyone. This knowledge, in turn, will tend to reduce the propensity to engage in political behavior to acquire those resources, because people already know how decisions will be made. Open communication also limits the ability of any single person to control information or lines of communication.

A related technique is to reduce uncertainty. Several of the reasons political behavior occurs—ambiguous goals, nonroutine technology, an unstable environment, and organizational change—and most of the political techniques themselves are associated with high levels of uncertainty. Political behavior can be limited if the manager can reduce uncertainty. Consider an organization about to transfer a major division from Florida to Michigan. Many people will resist the idea of moving north and may resort to political behavior to forestall their own transfer. However, the manager in charge of the move could announce who will stay and who will go at the same time that news of the change spreads throughout the company, thereby curtailing political behavior related to the move.

The adage "forewarned is forearmed" sums up the final technique for controlling political activity. Simply being aware of the causes and techniques of political behavior can help a manager check their effects. Suppose a manager anticipates that several impending organizational changes will increase the level of political activity. As a result of this awareness, the manager quickly infers that a particular subordinate is lobbying for the use of a certain consultant only because the subordinate thinks the consultant's recommendations will be in line with his own. Attempts to control the agenda, engage in game playing, build a certain image, and control decision parameters often are transparently obvious to the knowledgeable observer. Recognizing such behaviors for what they are, an astute manager may be able to take appropriate steps to limit their impact.

# Impression Management in Organizations

**Impression management** is a direct and intentional effort by someone to enhance his or her own image in the eyes of others.

Impression management is a subtle form of political behavior that deserves special mention. **Impression management** is a direct, intentional effort by someone to enhance his or her image in the eyes of others. The "Mastering Change" box discusses one interesting new trend that involves impression management. People engage in impression management for a variety of reasons. For one thing, they may do so to further their own careers. By making themselves look good,

MASTERING CHANGE

## *The Casual Look*

One of the most obvious changes in corporate America in recent years has been the clear shift toward casual attire. Gone are the dark suits, the power ties, and wing-tipped shoes; gone are the severe blazers, high-necked collars, and black pumps. In their place are khaki pants and skirts, open-collared shirts, and walking shoes. Although some bastions of the more formal era still exist (Wall Street, for example, and many larger banks), more and more firms are relaxing dress codes and letting people wear whatever they want to work. Whatever they want, that is, up to a point . . .

Perhaps surprisingly, what constitutes casual attire leaves some people in a quandary. And this is especially true among individuals who are particularly concerned about the impressions they make on others. For example, when a person works at a place with casual dress policies, to not join in would be a real problem. Just imagine wearing an Armani suit when everyone else is wearing Dockers! But a person keenly focused on impressions might take extra precautions to avoid dressing down too much. Such a person, for instance, might be more prone to only wear khaki pants that have been starched and pressed and shirts with a fancy designer logo.

In some ways the issues of casual dress are even more complex for women. After all, men only have to take off their wool trousers and replace them with cotton slacks, take off their necktie, and they've made the transformation. But women have many more decisions to make—pants versus skirts, skirts versus dresses, more jewelry versus less jewelry, and so on and so on.

*"Dressing casual is easy. But dressing casual and still looking like a professional—that takes some real skill." — Anonymous Tenneco executive*

Compounding the problem even further is the belief held by some that people today simply don't understand as much how to dress as people did in earlier times. For example, understanding the proper length for pants (dress or casual), matching colors, and caring for shoes are simple skills that fewer salespeople have today. And because salespeople don't have the skills as frequently as before, less information is being passed on to customers. Of course, for the person truly motivated to advance on the basis of impression management, these complications make it in some ways easier than before to stand out in a crowd. But then there are the other people who embrace casual attire for the sheer pleasure of not having to wear a tie or walk on heels.

References: "A Dressing-Down on Dressing Up," *Wall Street Journal,* July 20, 1999, pp. B1, B4; W. Mark Fruin, *Knowledge Works* (New York: Oxford University Press, 1997); Thomas A. Stewart, "Get with the New Power Game," *Fortune,* January 13, 1997, pp. 58–62.

they think they are more likely to receive rewards, attractive job assignments, and promotions. They may also engage in impression management to boost their own self-esteem. When people have a solid image in an organization, others make them aware of it through their compliments, respect, and so forth. Another reason people use impression management is to acquire more power and hence more control.

People attempt to manage how others perceive them through a variety of mechanisms. Appearance is one of the first things people think of. Hence, a person motivated by impression management will pay close attention to choice of attire, selection of language, and the use of manners and body posture. People interested in impression management are also likely to jockey to be associated only with successful projects. By being assigned to high-profile projects led by highly successful managers, a person can begin to link his or her own name with such projects in the minds of others.

Sometimes people too strongly motivated by impression management become obsessed by it and resort to dishonest or unethical means. For example, some people have been known to take credit for others' work in an effort to make themselves look better. People have also been known to exaggerate or even falsify their personal accomplishments in an effort to enhance their image.[42]

## Synopsis

Influence can be defined as the ability to affect the perceptions, attitudes, or behaviors of others. Influence is a cornerstone of leadership. Whereas the basic leadership models discussed in Chapter 13 acknowledge influence, they do not directly include it as part of the leadership process.

In recent years, new leadership approaches have attempted to more directly consider the use of influence. Transformational leadership, one such approach, is the set of abilities that allow a leader to recognize the need for change, to create a vision to guide that change, and to execute the change effectively. Another influence-based approach to leadership considers charismatic leadership. Charisma, the basis of this approach, is a form of interpersonal attraction that inspires support and acceptance.

Leadership substitutes are individual, task, and organizational characteristics that tend to outweigh a leader's ability to affect subordinates' satisfaction and performance. Superleadership, a special type of leadership substitute, occurs when a leader gradually and purposefully turns over power, responsibility, and control to a self-managing work group.

Power is the potential ability of a person or group to exercise control over another person or group. The five bases of power are legitimate power (granted by virtue of one's position in the organization); reward power (control of rewards valued by others); coercive power (the ability to punish or harm); expert power (control over information that is valuable to the organization); and referent power (power through personal identification). Position power is tied to a position regardless of the individual who holds it. Personal power is power that resides in a person regardless of position. Attempts to use power can result in commitment, compliance, or resistance.

Organizational politics is activities people perform to acquire, enhance, and use power and other resources to obtain their preferred outcomes in a situation in which uncertainty or disagreement exists. Research indicates that most managers do not advocate use of political behavior but acknowledge that it is a necessity of organizational life. Because managers cannot eliminate political activity in the organization, they must learn to cope with it. Understanding how to manage political behavior requires understanding why it occurs, what techniques it employs, and strategies for limiting its effects.

Impression management is a direct, intentional effort by someone to enhance his or her image in the eyes of others. People engage in impression management for a variety of reasons and use a variety of methods to influence how others see them.

# Discussion Questions

1. Can a person without influence be a leader? Does having influence automatically make someone a leader?
2. Do all organizations need transformational leaders? Do all organizations need transactional leaders? Why are some leaders able to play both roles, whereas others can perform only one?
3. Who are some of the more charismatic leaders today?
4. What might happen if two people, each with significant, equal power, attempt to influence each other?
5. Cite examples based on a professor-student relationship to illustrate each of the five bases of organizational power.
6. Is there a logical sequence in the use of power bases that a manager might follow? For instance, should the use of legitimate power usually precede the use of reward power, or vice versa?
7. Cite examples in which you have been committed, compliant, and resistant as a result of efforts to influence you. Think of times when your attempts to influence others led to commitment, compliance, and resistance.
8. Do you agree or disagree with the assertion that political behavior is inevitable in organizational settings?
9. The term "politics" is generally associated with governmental bodies. Why do you think it has also come to be associated with the behavior in organizations described in the chapter?
10. Recall examples of how you have either used or observed others using the techniques of political behavior identified in the chapter. What other techniques can you suggest?
11. Have you ever engaged in impression management? Some people might think that, as long as it doesn't get out of hand, impression management is fine; others may think it is misleading and always inappropriate. What do you think?

# Organizational Behavior Case for Discussion

## Leading for Change at adidas

For years adidas ruled the market for athletic sportswear. But bumbling management allowed Nike to swoop in and take control. Under new leadership, however, adidas is beginning to bounce back and shows signs of making the sneaker wars a real battle. Adidas was founded in 1948 by Adi Dassler, a brilliant Bavarian shoe designer. In the 1956 Olympics, virtually every athlete who competed wore adidas shoes. And no less a player than Kareem Abdul-Jabbar wore adidas shoes when he dominated the National Basketball Association.

But internal problems seriously weakened the firm. First, Adi's brother Rudolf left and started in his own firm, Puma. Adi's son Horst also split from the family and started another competing manufacturer. Horst later returned to the fold and took over the firm's management in 1985. Neglect and the onslaught of Nike and Reebok had taken their toll. When Horst died in 1987, adidas's market share had fallen from a high of 70 percent to just 2 percent. And no one in the family was prepared to step in and take over.

Horst's sisters sold the company to a French financier named Bernard Tapie in 1989 for a paltry $320 million. Tapie professed to have big plans for the firm and promised to bring in $100 million in new investment to get adidas back on its feet. Unfortunately, Tapie became so involved in politics that he, too, paid the company little attention. He subsequently became embroiled in a soccer-fixing scandal while serving as France's urban affairs minister, was sentenced to prison, declared bankruptcy, and turned adidas over to his creditors.

The creditors, in turn, turned to Robert Louis-Dreyfuss, another French financier, and asked him to take over control of adidas. Louis-Dreyfuss had no experience in the shoe or sportswear businesses but did have a sterling reputation as a turnaround artist. As soon as he moved into the president's office, he was astonished to be asked to personally approve a sales representative's expense account for $300. He knew at that moment that his challenges centered around bureaucracy and old-fashioned business practices.

Over the course of the next few weeks, Louis-Dreyfuss replaced the entire top management team at adidas, all of whom were German. He brought in new executives from other countries and designated English as the firm's official language. He also renegotiated all of the firm's manufacturing contracts to get costs in line with those of Nike and Reebok. And as he got costs under control, he turned to marketing.

Louis-Dreyfuss doubled the firm's marketing budget and instructed managers in that department to get busy with new, innovative, and aggressive ideas for taking back market share previously lost to competitors. These managers, in turn, enlisted the endorsements of sports stars like Steffi Graf and Kobe Bryant. Their biggest coup, however, was getting the New York Yankees to strike a deal that all of their players would wear adidas shoes.

Adidas still faces an uphill battle. But Louis-Dreyfuss has shown remarkable acumen for managing in a highly competitive industry. Among his more recent victories have been signing up the several major national soccer teams and acquiring Salomon, a major ski equipment manufacturer. After this acquisition, the firm's legal corporate name was changed to adidas-Salomon. Louis-Dreyfuss believes that the firm will continue its renaissance and will one day soon take what he sees as its rightful place alongside Nike—and ahead of Reebok and other competitors—atop the athletic apparel industry.

### Case Questions

1. What leadership theory or concept best explains Louis-Dreyfuss's success at adidas?
2. What can other leaders learn from Louis-Dreyfuss?
3. What roles do you think that power and politics may have played at adidas?

References: *Hoover's Handbook of World Business 2000* (Austin: Hoover's Business Press, 2000), pp. 68–69; "Adidas Is Dropping the Other Shoes," *International Herald Tribune*, March 20, 1998, pp. 15, 19; "An Adrenalin Rush at Adidas," *Business Week*, September 29, 1997, p. 136; Charles P. Wallace, "Adidas—Back in the Game," *Fortune*, August 18, 1997, pp. 176–182.

## Experiencing Organizational Behavior

### Learning About Ethics and Power

**Purpose:** This exercise will help you appreciate some of the ambiguities involved in assessing the ethics of power and political behavior in organizations.

**Format:** First, you will identify examples of more and less ethical uses of power and political behavior. Then you will discuss, compare, and contrast your examples with those generated by some of your classmates.

**Procedure:**

1. Identify and write down three examples of situations in which you think it would be ethical to use power and political behavior. For example, you might think it is ethical to use them to save the job of a coworker whom you think is a very good—but misunderstood—employee.
2. Identify and write down three examples of situations in which you think it would be unethical to use power and political behavior. For instance, you might think it is unethical to use power and political behavior to gain a job for which you are really not qualified.
3. Form small groups of three or four members each. Each member of the group should read his or her examples of ethical and unethical uses of power and political behavior.
4. Discuss the extent to which the group members agree on the ethics for each situation.
5. See if your group members can think of different situations in which the ethical context changes. For example, if everyone agrees that a given situation is ethical, see if the group can think of slightly different circumstances in which, in essentially the same situation, using power and political behavior would become more unethical.

### Follow-up Questions

1. How realistic was this exercise? What did you learn from it?
2. Could you assess real-life situations relating to the ethics of political activity using this same process?

# Building Organizational Behavior Skills

## Are You a Charismatic Leader?

**Introduction:** Charismatic leaders articulate a vision, show concern for group members, communicate high expectations, and create high-performing organizations. This assessment exercise measures your charismatic potential.

**Instructions:** The following statements refer to the possible ways in which you might behave toward others when you are in a leadership role. Please read each statement carefully and decide to what extent it applies to you. Then put a check on the appropriate number.

| | |
|---|---|
| To a very great extent | = 5 |
| To a considerable extent | = 4 |
| To a moderate extent | = 3 |
| To a slight extent | = 2 |
| To little or no extent | = 1 |

1. I pay close attention to what others say when they are talking. 1 2 3 4 5
2. I communicate clearly. 1 2 3 4 5
3. I am trustworthy. 1 2 3 4 5
4. I care about other people. 1 2 3 4 5
5. I do not put excessive energy into avoiding failure. 1 2 3 4 5
6. I make the work of others more meaningful. 1 2 3 4 5
7. I seem to focus on the key issues in a situation. 1 2 3 4 5
8. I get across my meaning effectively, often in unusual ways. 1 2 3 4 5
9. I can be relied on to follow through on commitments. 1 2 3 4 5
10. I have a great deal of self-respect. 1 2 3 4 5
11. I enjoy taking carefully calculated risks. 1 2 3 4 5
12. I help others feel more competent in what they do. 1 2 3 4 5
13. I have a clear set of priorities. 1 2 3 4 5
14. I am in touch with how others feel. 1 2 3 4 5
15. I rarely change once I have taken a clear position. 1 2 3 4 5
16. I focus on strengths, of myself and of others. 1 2 3 4 5
17. I seem most alive when deeply involved in some project. 1 2 3 4 5
18. I show others that they are all part of the same group. 1 2 3 4 5
19. I get others to focus on the issues I see as important. 1 2 3 4 5
20. I communicate feelings as well as ideas. 1 2 3 4 5
21. I let others know where I stand. 1 2 3 4 5
22. I seem to know just how I "fit" into a group. 1 2 3 4 5
23. I learn from mistakes and do not treat errors as disasters, but as learning. 1 2 3 4 5
24. I am fun to be around. 1 2 3 4 5

For interpretation, see the Interpretation Guide in the *Instructor's Resource Manual.*

The questionnaire measures six facets of charismatic leadership. Your score can range from 4 to 20 for each section. Each question is stated as a measure of the extent to which you engage in the behavior—or elicit the feelings. The higher your score, the more you demonstrate charismatic leader behaviors.

**Index 1: Management of Attention** (1, 7, 13, 19). Your score: ____. You pay especially close attention to people with whom you are communicating. You are also "focused in" on the key issues under discussion and help others to see clearly these key points. You have clear ideas about the relative importance or priorities of different issues under discussion.

**Index 2: Management of Meaning** (2, 8, 14, 20). Your score: ____. This set of items centers on your communication skills, specifically your ability to get the meaning of a message across, even if this means devising some quite innovative approach.

**Index 3: Management of Trust** (3, 9, 15, 21).
Your score: ____. The key factor is your perceived trustworthiness as shown by your willingness to follow through on promises, avoid "flip-flop" shifts in position, and willingness to take clear positions.

**Index 4: Management of Self** (4, 10, 16, 22).
Your score: ____. This index concerns your general attitudes toward yourself and others—that is, your overall concern for others and their feelings, as well as for "taking care of" feelings about yourself in a positive sense (e.g., self-regard).

**Index 5: Management of Risk** (5, 11, 17, 23).
Your score: ____. Effective charismatic leaders are deeply involved in what they do and do not spend excessive amounts of time or energy on plans to "protect" themselves against failure. These leaders are willing to take risks, not on a hit-or-miss basis, but after careful estimation of the odds of success or failure.

**Index 6: Management of Feelings** (6, 12, 18, 24).
Your score: ____. Charismatic leaders seem to consistently generate a set of positive feelings in others. Others feel that their work becomes more meaningful and that they are the "masters" of their own behavior—that is, they feel competent. They feel a sense of community, a "we-ness" with their colleagues and coworkers.

Reference: Marshall Sashkin and William C. Morris, *Experiential Exercises in Management Book*, p. 132. 

## Developing OB Internet Skills

**Introduction:** One form of influence described in this chapter is impression management. This exercise will help you see the relationships that might exist between impression management and the Internet.

**Internet Assignment:** Many individuals today have their own web pages. Some are career oriented—here I am, here's what I can do, and so forth. Others are more a reflection of the individual's employer and the work the person does for that employer. For example, the partners in a law firm might each have their own page outlining their particular legal qualifications, expertise, and so forth. Still others appear to be making more of a personal statement about the individual, such as lists of favorite music, sports teams, artists, and so forth. Using whatever means you prefer (search engines, referrals, hot links, directories), obtain addresses for and visit five different individual web sites.

**Follow-up:** Carefully review each of the five web sites you have visited. Write a brief statement for each, describing the kind of impression that the individual is apparently wanting to make about her or himself—professional, talented, cool, or whatever. Next, exchange web site addresses with a classmate, visit those sites, and repeat the exercise. Finally, respond to the following questions:

1. How similar or dissimilar were the descriptions written by you and your classmate?
2. How interested do you think each individual really is in portraying an image or impression of him- or herself?
3. Do you have a web page? If so, to what extent is image or impression important to you? If you don't have a web page, what role might impression management play if you were to decide to create one?

chapter 15

# Decision Making and Negotiation

## Management Preview

Making decisions is the most basic of all management activities. Some decisions involve major events that have a dramatic impact on a firm's future growth, profits, and even survival. Others, such as choosing the colors of the firm's new letterhead or deciding when to reorder office supplies, are much less significant. But all decisions are important on some level, so managers need to understand how decisions are made.

This chapter explores decision making in detail. We start by examining the nature of decision making. Next, we describe several different approaches to understanding the decision-making process. We then identify and discuss two related behavioral aspects of decision making. Next, we discuss several important issues in group decision making. We conclude by presenting a powerful approach to negotiation. But first we describe some decisions recently made at Coca-Cola. ■

Doug Ivester became CEO of Coca-Cola in 1997 following the death of the immensely popular Roberto Goizueta, who had run the company for sixteen years. So it is only natural that critics and shareholders would take dead aim on Ivester when earnings began to slide a little. But they may have a right to following several decision-making situations that Ivester faced recently.

In 1998 Coca-Cola agreed to buy the non-U.S. soft-drink brands of Cadbury Schweppes. Since Coca-Cola holds almost 50 percent of the soft-drink business in many European countries where Cadbury Schweppes was also strong, the deal faced close scrutiny from European regulators. Ivester attempted to structure the deal to avoid the watchful eyes of regulators in a move that, at first, appeared clever. Regulators caught on, however, and Ivester had to restructure the deal, dropping most European countries and the price. Next, Coca-Cola agreed to buy Groupe Pernod Ricard's Orangina brand. Regulators quickly jumped to slow that deal down and accused Coca-Cola of being arrogant. The company was taking risks in an area (Europe) that already provided 26 percent of its worldwide revenue.

Then, while Ivester was in France on business, he was notified that some Belgian school children had gotten sick after drinking Coke. The firm's technical experts quickly found the minor problem and corrected it. Ivester dismissed the problem and flew home without so much as an apology or show of concern to the Belgians. Meanwhile, Coke was banned in Belgium. Then, fungicide on the bottom of cans shipped from France showed up. Ivester dismissed that as also minor and declared there was nothing wrong with Coke. At about the same time, four current and former employees filed a racial discrimination suit against the company. Again, Ivester declared that the company had done nothing wrong.

*"Doug believes everything should go through a logical sequence. He's fixed on where he wants the company to be." — James Chestnut, chief financial officer, Coca-Cola**

Meanwhile earnings were flat, and investors were not happy. Considering all the important and highly visible decisions made by Ivester within his first two years as CEO, he may be lucky to still be in office. He was known as a deeply rational thinker, with long-term strategic plans and contingency plans for every move. He staunchly defends his actions as being in the long-term best interests of the company, its shareholders, and customers.

In December 1999, Mr. Ivester unexpectedly resigned as CEO. Douglas N. Daft, a Coca-Cola veteran who had most recently headed Coca-Cola's Asian operations, replaced Ivester. Many observers expected Mr. Daft to simply be a "caretaker" while a more permanent replacement was found. However, he has made numerous decisions that show he is far more than a temporary CEO. First he cut 6,000 jobs; this is nearly 20 percent of the company's payroll. Second, Daft reassigned hundreds of headquarters staff to operating positions around the world, effectively decentralizing management. In many ways Daft is reversing the decisions of Ivester and returning to the ways of Goizueta, the CEO before Ivester, by bringing back several of Goizueta's staff and reducing pressure on bottlers around the world to conform to standards and meet the targets set by Coca-Cola headquarters in Atlanta. Local managers will have more leeway to run local ad campaigns, introduce new brands, and set prices that are appropriate for their area and culture.[1] ■

The person at the top, Doug Ivester at Coca-Cola, is paid to make the tough decisions. He might have been criticized no matter what decisions he had made in those situations. They were not simple or easy decisions to make. Ivester claims to be focused on the goal of what is good for the company in the long term and makes his decisions accordingly. This chapter describes many different perspectives of decision making.

# The Nature of Decision Making

**Decision making** is the process of choosing from among several alternatives.

**Decision making** is choosing one alternative from among several. Consider football, for example. The quarterback can run any of perhaps a hundred plays. With the goal of scoring a touchdown always in mind, he chooses the play that seems to promise the best outcome. His choice is based on his

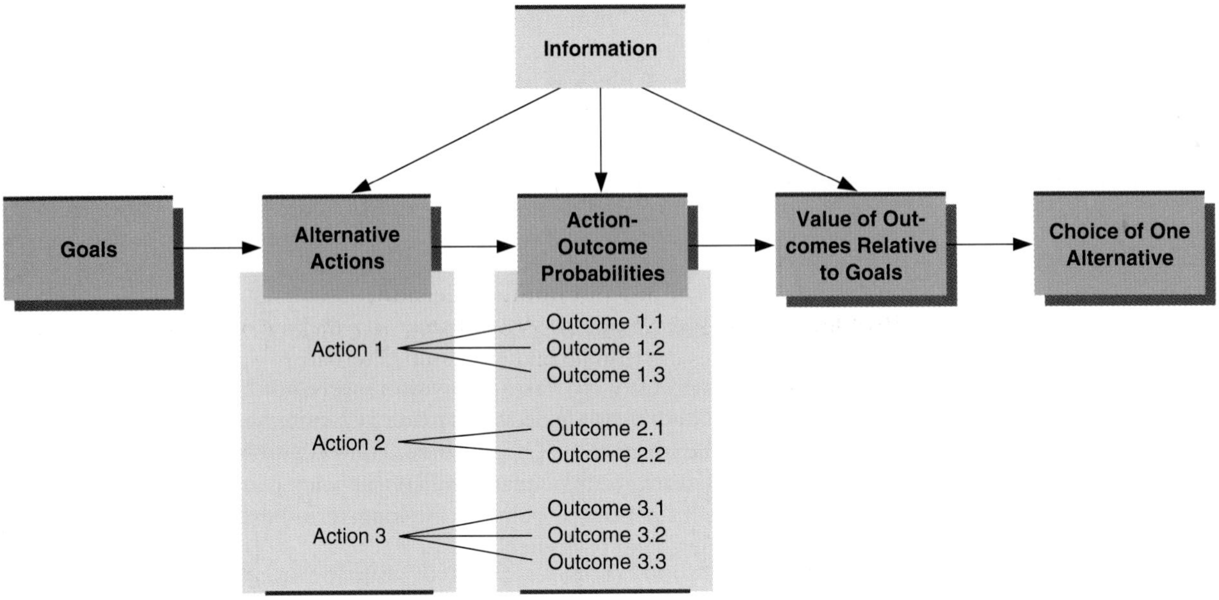


figure 15.1 **Elements of Decision Making**

*A decision maker has a goal, evaluates the outcomes of alternative courses of action in terms of the goal, and selects one alternative to be implemented.*

understanding of the game situation, the likelihood of various outcomes, and his preference for each outcome.

Figure 15.1 shows the basic elements of decision making. A decision maker's actions are guided by a goal. Each of several alternative courses of action is linked with various outcomes. Information is available on the alternatives, on the likelihood that each outcome will occur, and on the value of each outcome relative to the goal. The decision maker chooses one alternative on the basis of his or her evaluation of the information.

Decisions made in organizations can be classified according to frequency and to information conditions. In a decision-making context, frequency is how often a particular decision recurs, and information conditions describe how much information is available about the likelihood of various outcomes.

## Types of Decisions

A **programmed decision** is a decision that recurs often enough for a decision rule to be developed.

A **decision rule** is a statement that tells a decision maker which alternative to choose based on the characteristics of the decision situation.

The frequency of recurrence determines whether a decision is programmed or nonprogrammed. A **programmed decision** recurs often enough for a decision rule to be developed. A **decision rule** tells decision makers which alternative to choose once they have information about the decision situation. The appropriate decision rule is used whenever the same situation is encountered. Programmed decisions usually are highly structured; that is, the goals are clear and well known, the decision-making procedure is already established, and the sources and channels of information are clearly defined.[2]

Airlines use established procedures when an airplane breaks down and cannot be used on a particular flight. Passengers may not view the issue as a programmed decision, because they experience this situation relatively infrequently. But the airlines know that equipment problems that render a plane unfit for service arise regularly. Each airline has its own set of clear procedures to use in the event of equipment problems. A given flight may be delayed, canceled, or continued on a different plane, depending on the nature of the problem and other circumstances (such as the number of passengers booked, the next scheduled flight for the same destination, and so forth).

A **nonprogrammed decision** is a decision that recurs infrequently and for which there is no previously established decision rule.

**Problem solving** is a form of decision making in which the issue is unique and alternatives must be developed and evaluated without the aid of a programmed decision rule.

When a problem or decision situation has not been encountered before, however, a decision maker cannot rely on previously established decision rules. Such a decision is called a **nonprogrammed decision**, and it requires problem solving. **Problem solving** is a special form of decision making in which the issue is unique—it requires developing and evaluating alternatives without the aid of a decision rule. Nonprogrammed decisions are poorly structured because information is ambiguous, there is no clear procedure for making the decision, and the goals are often vague.[3]

*"Solve it, solve it quickly, solve it right or wrong. If you solved it wrong, it would come back and slap you in the face, and then you could solve it right." — Thomas J. Watson Jr., CEO, and son of the founder, of IBM[4]*

Table 15.1 summarizes the characteristics of programmed and nonprogrammed decisions. Note that programmed decisions are more common at the lower levels of the organization, whereas a primary responsibility of top management is to make the difficult, nonprogrammed decisions that determine the organization's long-term effectiveness. By definition, the strategic decisions for which top management is responsible are poorly structured and nonroutine and have far-reaching consequences.[5] Programmed decisions, then, can be made according to previously tested rules and procedures. Nonprogrammed decisions generally require that the decision maker exercise judgment and creativity.[6] In other words, all problems require a decision, but not all decisions require problem solving.

table 15.1
**Characteristics of Programmed and Nonprogrammed Decisions**

| Characteristics | Programmed Decisions | Nonprogrammed Decisions |
|---|---|---|
| Type of Decision | Well structured | Poorly structured |
| Frequency | Repetitive and routine | New and unusual |
| Goals | Clear, specific | Vague |
| Information | Readily available | Not available, unclear channels |
| Consequences | Minor | Major |
| Organizational Level | Lower levels | Upper levels |
| Time for Solution | Short | Relatively long |
| Basis for Solution | Decision rules, set procedures | Judgment and creativity |

## Information Required for Decision Making

Decisions are made to bring about desired outcomes, but the information available about those outcomes varies. The range of available information can be considered as a continuum whose endpoints represent complete certainty when all alternative outcomes are known, and complete uncertainty when alternative outcomes are unknown. At points between the two extremes, risk is involved; the decision maker has some information about the possible outcomes and may be able to estimate the probability of their occurrence.

Under the condition of certainty, the manager knows the outcomes of each alternative.

Different information conditions present different challenges to the decision maker.[7] For example, suppose the marketing manager of PlayStation is trying to determine whether to launch an expensive promotional effort for a new video game (see Figure 15.2). For simplicity, assume there are only two alternatives: to promote the game or not to promote it. Under a condition of **certainty**, the manager knows the outcomes of each alternative. If the new game is promoted heavily, the company will realize a $10 million profit. Without promotion, the company will realize only a $2 million profit. Here the decision is simple: promote the game.

figure 15.2

**Alternative Outcomes Under Different Information Conditions**

*The three decision-making conditions of certainty, risk, and uncertainty for the decision about whether to promote a new video game to the market.*

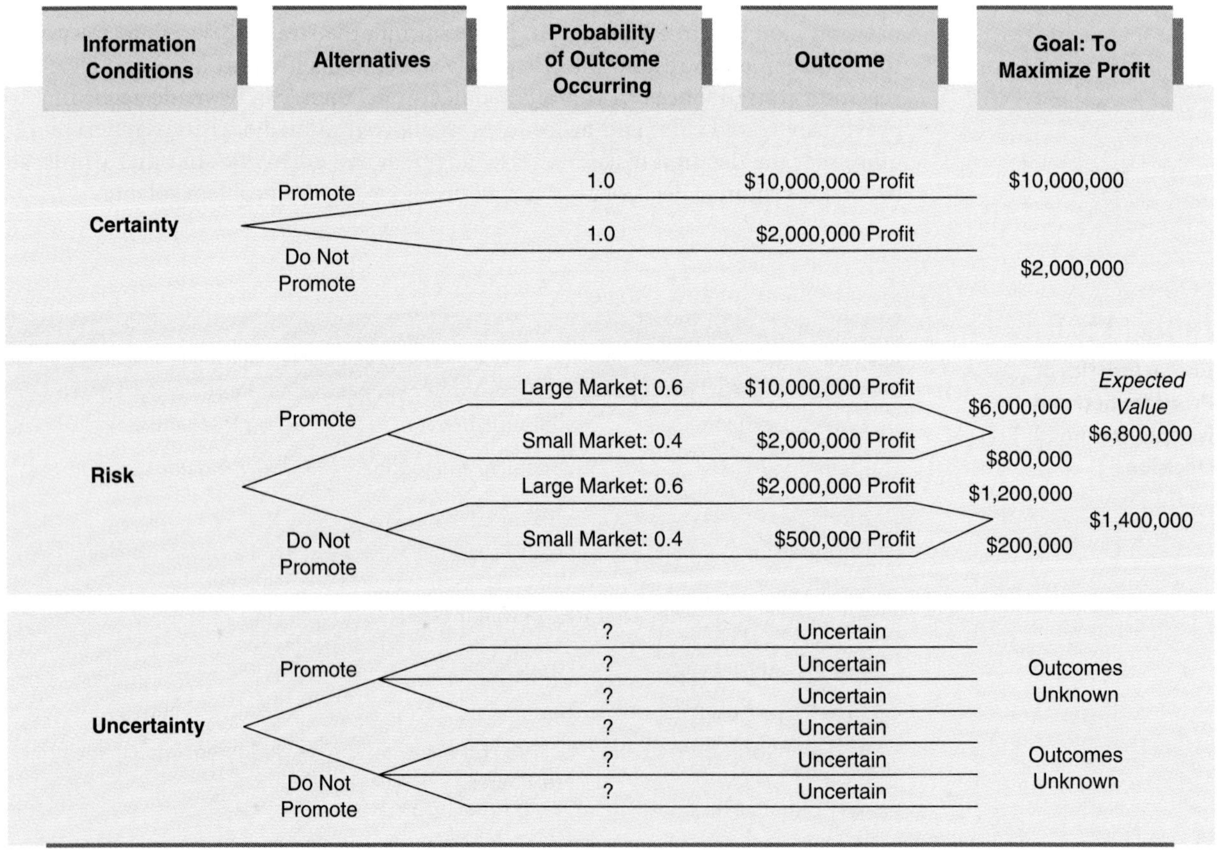

(Note: These figures are created for the purposes of this example and are not actual profit figures for any company.)

Under the condition of risk, the decision maker cannot know with certainty what the outcome of a given action will be but has enough information to estimate the probabilities of various outcomes.

Under a condition of **risk**, the decision maker cannot know with certainty what the outcome of a given action will be but has enough information to estimate the probabilities of various outcomes. Thus, working from information gathered by the market research department, the marketing manager in our example can estimate the likelihood of each outcome in a risk situation. In this case, the alternatives are defined by the size of the market. The probability for a large video game market is 0.6, and the probability for a small market is 0.4. The manager can calculate the expected value of the promotional effort based on these probabilities and the expected profits associated with each. To find the expected value of an alternative, the manager multiplies each outcome's value by the probability of its occurrence. The sum of these calculations for all possible outcomes represents that alternative's expected value. In this case, the expected value of alternative 1—to promote the new game—is as follows:

$$0.6 \times \$10{,}000{,}000 = \$6{,}000{,}000$$

$$+\ 0.4 \times \$\ 2{,}000{,}000 = \$\ \ 800{,}000$$

$$\text{Expected value of alternative 1} = \$6{,}800{,}000$$

The expected value of alternative 2—not to promote the new game—is $1,400,000 (see Figure 15.2). The marketing manager should choose the first alternative, because its expected value is higher. The manager should recognize, however, that although the numbers look convincing, they are based on incomplete information and are only estimates of probability.

Under the condition of uncertainty the decision maker lacks enough information to estimate the probability of possible outcomes.

The decision maker who lacks enough information to estimate the probability of outcomes (or perhaps even to identify the outcomes at all) faces a condition of **uncertainty**.[8] In the PlayStation example, this might be the case if sales of video games had recently collapsed and it was not clear whether the precipitous drop was temporary or permanent or when information to clarify the situation would be available. Under such circumstances, the decision maker may wait for more information to reduce uncertainty or rely on judgment, experience, and intuition to make the decision.

Decision making, however, is not always so easy to classify in terms of certainty, uncertainty, and risk. Some individuals are more likely to take risks than others are, as was discussed in Chapter 4. In addition, in some parts of the world it may be more common to take risks than in others, as was discussed in Chapter 3. The "Mastering Change" box illustrates how one Japanese entrepreneur was successful in going against the risk-taking norms of his culture.

# The Decision-Making Process

Q3

Several approaches to decision making offer insights into the process by which managers arrive at their decisions. The rational approach is appealing because of its logic and economy. Yet these very qualities raise questions about this approach, because actual decision making often is not a wholly rational process. The behavioral approach, meanwhile, attempts to account for the limits on rationality in decision making. The practical approach combines features of the rational and behavioral approaches. Finally, the personal approach focuses on the decision-making processes individuals use in difficult situations.

MASTERING CHANGE

## *Risk Taking in Japan*

The foundations of Japan's postwar recovery and prosperity were top-down industrial policy, which told banks where money was needed and which projects were to be funded, and the mutual loyalty between employer and worker. Individuals did not take risks and were rarely funded to start new businesses. Entrepreneurship was unheard of. That is, until the 1990s and the economic downturn created many executives who needed continuing business education and an MBA. Enter Yoshito Hori.

*"Now we're entering a* **new cycle,** *where it's easier for entrepreneurs to be born." — Yoichi Morishita, president of Matsushita Electric Industrial Co.*

Yoshito Hori was early in a promising career for Sumitomo Corporation, the huge international trading company. Mr. Hori's career, following graduation from a prestigious university, was developing nicely as he helped oversee power plant ventures in Southeast Asia for Sumitomo. His performance was excellent, and the company paid for his two-year MBA program at Harvard Business School. Hearing his classmates dream of starting their own companies, he took courses in business start-ups and returned to Sumitomo with a dream of starting a business school for part-time business professionals in Japan. After his proposal was turned down by Sumitomo executives, in 1992 Hori started offering business classes on the weekends, under the name Globis Business School. After a few months he borrowed money from family and quit his job at Sumitomo, much against the warnings of company executives. And he took on two partners. With some luck and skill he landed a few contracts for continuing education with large companies, including Sumitomo.

As happens to many start-ups, cash was running short in the summer of 1993, but banks would not lend money to three young single guys with no collateral. Pooling every cent they could find, they ran a big ad and were swamped with new students in the fall. By 1994, business and profits had tripled to $1.2 million, and Hori started branching out. Globis moved into teaching more courses, publishing books, and running a venture capital fund for new start-ups, Globis Capital. In March 1999, Hori met another young entrepreneur, Eugene Matthews, which led to Alan Patricof and the formation of Apax Globis Partners & Co., which raised $100 million to finance management buyouts for Japanese executives. The new fund is expected to capitalize on significant change in the Japanese economy that is likely to result in large conglomerates spinning off subsidiaries to current management and investors. Hori's adventure in risk taking at just the right time went against Japanese business culture. But he has made it pay off.

References: Andy Thompson, "Patricof Aiming to Break Down Barriers in Japan," *European Venture Capital Journal,* August 1, 1999, p. ITEM99201016; Bill Spindle, "Corporate Truant Has Lesson in Risk-Taking for Hidebound Japan," *Wall Street Journal,* July 21, 1999, pp. A1, A6 (quote on p. A1); Jennifer Jury, "Apax Globis Japan Joint Venture Seeks $100 Million," *European Venture Capital Journal,* May 1, 1999, p. SECD99134014.

# The Rational Approach

The **rational decision-making approach** is a systematic, step-by-step process for making decisions.

The **rational decision-making approach** assumes that managers follow a systematic, step-by-step process. It further assumes the organization is economically based and managed by decision makers who are entirely objective and have complete information.[9] Figure 15.3 identifies the steps of the process, starting with stating a goal and running logically through the process until the best decision is made, implemented, and controlled.

**State the Situational Goal** The rational decision-making process begins with the statement of a situational goal—that is, a goal for a particular situation. The

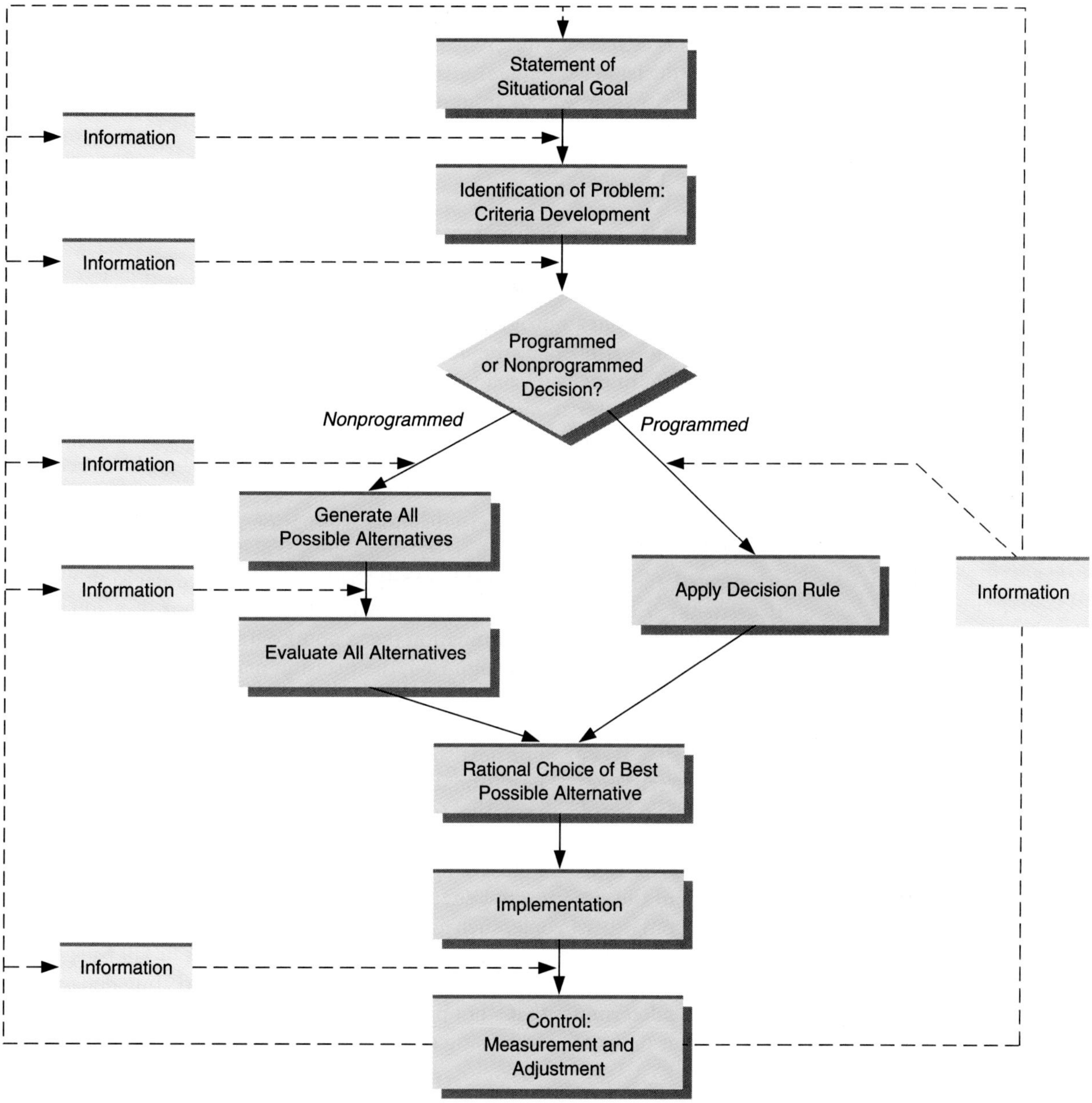


figure 15.3 **The Rational Decision-Making Process**

*The rational model follows a systematic, step-by-step approach from goals to implementation, measurement, and control.*

goal of a marketing department, for example, may be to obtain a certain market share by the end of the year. (Some models of decision making do not start with a goal. We include it because it is the standard used to determine whether there is a decision to be made.)

Identify the Problem The purpose of problem identification is to gather information that bears on the goal. If there is a discrepancy between the goal and the actual state, action may be needed. In the marketing example, the group may gather information about the company's actual market share and compare it with the desired market share. A difference between the two represents a problem that necessitates a decision. Reliable information is very important in this step. Inaccurate information can lead to an unnecessary decision or no decision when one is required.

*"The formulation of a problem is often more essential than its solution." — **Rolf Smith, president of Virtual Thinking Expedition Company, quoting Albert Einstein**[10]*

**Determining Decision Type** Next, the decision makers must determine if the problem represents a programmed or a nonprogrammed decision. If a programmed decision is needed, the appropriate decision rule is invoked, and the process moves on to the choice among alternatives. A programmed marketing decision may be called for if analysis reveals that competitors are outspending the company on print advertising. Because creating print advertising and buying space for it are well-established functions of the marketing group, the problem requires only a programmed decision.

Although it may seem simple to diagnose a situation as programmed, apply a decision rule, and arrive at a solution, mistakes can still occur. Choosing the wrong decision rule or assuming the problem calls for a programmed decision when a nonprogrammed decision actually is required can result in poor decisions. The same caution applies to the determination that a nonprogrammed decision is called for. If the situation is wrongly diagnosed, the decision maker wastes time and resources seeking a new solution to an old problem, or "reinventing the wheel."

**Generate Alternatives** The next step in making a nonprogrammed decision is to generate alternatives. The rational process assumes that decision makers will generate all the possible alternative solutions to the problem. However, this assumption is unrealistic, because even simple business problems can have scores of possible solutions. Decision makers may rely on education and experience as well as knowledge of the situation to generate alternatives. In addition, they may seek information from other people, such as peers, subordinates, and supervisors. Decision makers may analyze the symptoms of the problem for clues or fall back on intuition or judgment to develop alternative solutions.[11] If the marketing department in our example determines that a nonprogrammed decision is required, it will need to generate alternatives for increasing market share.

**Evaluate Alternatives** Evaluation involves assessing all possible alternatives in terms of predetermined decision criteria. The ultimate decision criterion is "Will this alternative bring us nearer to the goal?" In each case, the decision maker must examine each alternative for evidence that it will reduce the discrepancy between the desired state and the actual state. The evaluation process usually includes: (1) describing the anticipated outcomes (benefits) of each alternative, (2) evaluating the anticipated costs of each alternative, and (3) estimating the uncertainties and risks associated with each alternative.[12] In most decision situations, the decision maker does not have perfect information regarding the outcomes of all alternatives. At one extreme, as shown earlier in Figure 15.2, outcomes may be known with certainty; at the other, the decision maker has no information whatsoever, so the outcomes are entirely uncertain. But risk is the most common situation.

This executive is having trouble choosing one alternative from the available choices, but he may be acknowledging that there are more choices than just yes or no. His "maybe" may indicate that there are some contingencies that need to be planned for.



Choose an Alternative The choice of an alternative is usually the most crucial step in the decision-making process. Choosing consists of selecting the alternative with the highest possible payoff, based on the benefits, costs, risks, and uncertainties of all alternatives. In the PlayStation promotion example, the decision maker evaluated the two alternatives by calculating their expected values. Following the rational approach, the manager would choose the alternative with the largest expected value.

Even with the rational approach, however, difficulties can arise in choosing an alternative. First, when two or more alternatives have equal payoffs, the decision maker must obtain more information or use some other criterion to make the choice. Second, when no single alternative will accomplish the objective, some combination of two or three alternatives may have to be implemented. Finally, if no alternative or combination of alternatives will solve the problem, the decision maker must obtain more information, generate more alternatives, or change the goals.[13] The executive in the cartoon seems to have more than two alternatives.

Contingency plans are alternative actions to take if the primary course of action is unexpectedly disrupted or rendered inappropriate.

An important part of the choice phase is the consideration of **contingency plans**—alternative actions that can be taken if the primary course of action is unexpectedly disrupted or rendered inappropriate.[14] Planning for contingencies is part of the transition between choosing the preferred alternative and implementing it. In developing contingency plans, the decision maker usually asks such questions as "What if something unexpected happens during the implementation of this alternative?" or "If the economy goes into a recession, will the choice of this alternative ruin the company?" or "How can we alter this plan if the economy suddenly rebounds and begins to grow?"

Implement the Plan Implementation puts the decision into action. It builds on the commitment and motivation of those who participated in the decision-making process (and may actually bolster individual commitment and motivation). To succeed, implementation requires the proper use of resources and good management skills. Following the decision to promote the new PlayStation game heavily, for example, the marketing manager must implement the decision by assigning the project to a work group or task force. The success of this team depends on the leadership, the reward structure, the communications system, and group dynamics. Sometimes the decision maker begins to doubt a choice already made. This doubt is called *post decision dissonance* or more generally, **cognitive dissonance**.[15] To reduce the tension created by the dissonance, the decision maker may seek to rationalize the decision further with new information.

**Cognitive dissonance** is the anxiety a person experiences when two sets of knowledge or perceptions are contradictory or incongruent.

**Control: Measure and Adjust** In the final stage of the rational decision-making process, the outcomes of the decision are measured and compared with the desired goal. If a discrepancy remains, the decision maker may restart the decision-making process by setting a new goal (or reiterating the existing one). The decision maker, unsatisfied with the previous decision, may modify the subsequent decision-making process to avoid another mistake. Changes can be made in any part of the process, as Figure 15.3 illustrates by the arrows leading from the control step to each of the other steps. Decision making therefore is a dynamic, self-correcting, and ongoing process in organizations.

Suppose a marketing department implements a new print advertising campaign. After implementation, it constantly monitors market research data and compares its new market share to the desired market share. If the advertising has the desired effect, no changes will be made in the promotion campaign. If, however, the data indicate no change in the market share, additional decisions and implementation of a contingency plan may be necessary. For example, when Nissan introduced its luxury car line Infiniti, it relied on a Zen-like series of ads that featured images of rocks, plants, and water—but no images of the car. At the same time, Toyota was featuring pictures of its new luxury car line, Lexus, which quickly established itself in the market. When Infiniti managers realized their mistake, they quickly pulled the old ads and started running new ones centered around images of their car.[16]

**Strengths and Weaknesses of the Rational Approach** The rational approach has several strengths. It forces the decision maker to consider a decision in a logical, sequential manner, and the in-depth analysis of alternatives enables the decision maker to choose on the basis of information rather than emotion or social pressure. But the rigid assumptions of this approach often are unrealistic.[17] The amount of information available to managers usually is limited by either time or cost constraints, and most decision makers have limited ability to process information about the alternatives. In addition, not all alternatives lend themselves to quantification in terms that will allow for easy comparison. Finally, because they cannot predict the future, it is unlikely that decision makers will know all possible outcomes of each alternative.[18]

## The Behavioral Approach

Whereas the rational approach assumes that managers operate logically and rationally, the behavioral approach acknowledges the role and importance of human behavior in the decision-making process. In particular, a crucial assumption of the behavioral approach is that decision makers operate with bounded rationality rather than with the perfect rationality assumed by the rational approach. **Bounded rationality** is the idea that although individuals seek the best solution to a problem, the demands of processing all the information bearing on the problem, generating all possible solutions, and choosing the single best solution are beyond the capabilities of most decision makers. Thus, they accept less-than-ideal solutions based on a process that is neither exhaustive nor entirely rational. For example, one recent study found that under time pressure, groups usually eliminate all but the two most favorable alternatives and then process the remaining two in great detail.[19] Thus, decision makers operating with bounded rationality limit the inputs to the decision-making process and base decisions on judgment and personal biases as well as logic.[20]

**Bounded rationality** is the idea that decision makers cannot deal with information about all the aspects and alternatives pertaining to a problem and therefore choose to tackle some meaningful subset of it.

The **behavioral approach** is characterized by (1) the use of procedures and rules of thumb, (2) suboptimizing, and (3) satisficing. Uncertainty in decision making can initially be reduced by relying on procedures and rules of thumb. If, for example, increasing print advertising has increased a company's market share in the past, that linkage may be used by company employees as a rule of thumb in decision making. When the previous month's market share drops below a certain level, the company might increase its print advertising expenditures by 25 percent during the following month.

The **behavioral approach** uses rules of thumb, suboptimizing, and satisficing in making decisions.

**Suboptimizing** is knowingly accepting less than the best possible outcome. Frequently it is not feasible to make the ideal decision in a real-world situation given organizational constraints. The decision maker often must suboptimize to avoid unintended negative effects on other departments, product lines, or decisions.[21] An automobile manufacturer, for example, can cut costs dramatically and increase efficiency if it schedules the production of one model at a time. Thus, the production group's optimal decision is single-model scheduling. But the marketing group, seeking to optimize its sales goals by offering a wide variety of models, may demand the opposite production schedule: short runs of entirely different models. The groups in the middle, design and scheduling, may suboptimize the benefits the production and marketing groups seek by planning long runs of slightly different models. This is the practice of the large auto manufacturers such as General Motors and Ford, which make several body styles in numerous models on the same production line.

**Suboptimizing** is knowingly accepting less than the best possible outcome to avoid unintended negative effects on other aspects of the organization.

The final feature of the behavioral approach is **satisficing**: examining alternatives only until a solution that meets minimal requirements is found and then ceasing to look for a better one.[22] The search for alternatives usually is a sequential process guided by procedures and rules of thumb based on previous experiences with similar problems. The search often ends when the first minimally acceptable choice is encountered. The resulting choice may narrow the discrepancy between the desired and the actual states, but it is not likely to be the optimal solution. As the process is repeated, incremental improvements slowly reduce the discrepancy between the actual and desired states.

**Satisficing** is examining alternatives only until a solution that meets minimal requirements is found.

## The Practical Approach

Because of the unrealistic demands of the rational approach and the limited, short-run orientation of the behavioral approach, neither is entirely satisfactory. However, the worthwhile features of each can be combined into a practical approach to decision making, shown in Figure 15.4. The steps in this process are the same as in the rational approach; however, the conditions recognized by the behavioral

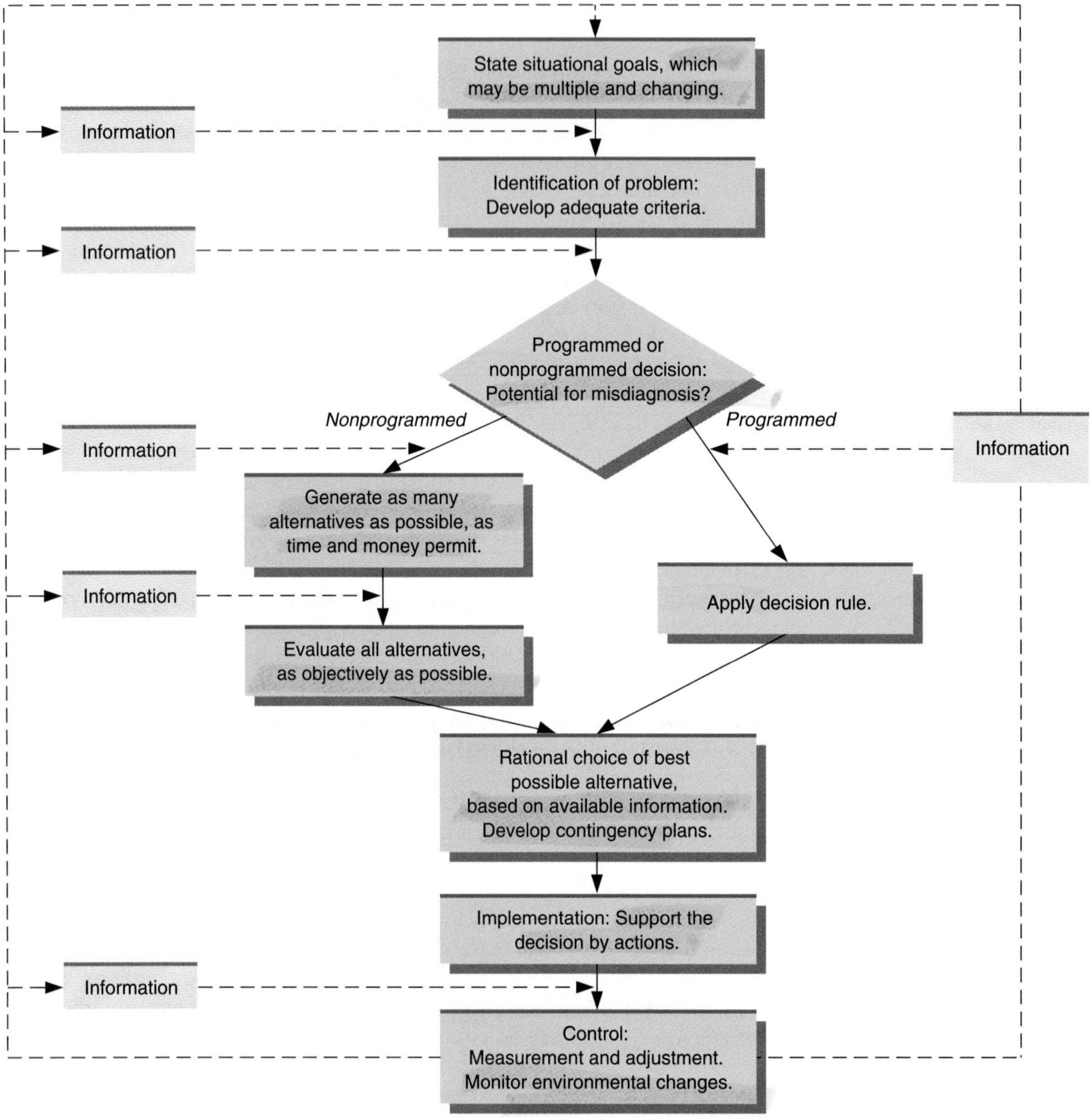


figure 15.4

**Practical Approach to Decision Making with Behavioral Guidelines**

*The practical model applies some of the conditions recognized by the behavioral approach to the rational approach to decision making. Although similar to the rational model, the practical approach recognizes personal limitations at each point (or step) in the process.*

The **practical approach** to decision making combines the steps of the rational approach with the conditions in the behavioral approach to create a more realistic process for making decisions in organizations.

approach are added to provide a more realistic process. For example, the **practical approach** suggests that rather than generating all alternatives, the decision maker should try to go beyond rules of thumb and satisficing limitations and generate as many alternatives as time, money, and other practicalities of the situation allow. In this synthesis of the two approaches, the rational approach provides an analytical framework for making decisions, whereas the behavioral approach provides a moderating influence.

In practice, decision makers use some hybrid of the rational, behavioral, and practical approaches to make the tough day-to-day decisions in running organizations. Some decision makers use a methodical process of gathering all available information, developing and evaluating alternatives, and seeking advice from knowledgeable people before making a decision. Others fly from one decision to another, making seemingly hasty decisions and barking out orders to subordinates. The second group would seem to not use much information or a rational approach to making decisions. Recent research, however, has shown that managers who make decisions very quickly probably are using just as much, or more, information and generating and evaluating as many alternatives as slower, more methodical decision makers.[23]

## The Personal Approach

Although the models just described have provided significant insight into decision making, they do not fully explain the processes people engage in when they are nervous, worried, and agitated over making a decision that has major implications for them, their organization, or their families. In short, they still do not reflect the conditions under which many decisions are made. One attempt to provide a more realistic view of individual decision making is the model presented by Irving Janis and Leon Mann.[24] The Janis-Mann process, called the **conflict model**, is based on research in social psychology and individual decision processes and is a very personal approach to decision making. Although the model may appear complex, if you examine it one step at a time and follow the example in this section, you should easily understand how it works. The model has five basic characteristics:

The **conflict model** is a very personal approach to decision making because it deals with the personal conflicts that people experience in particularly difficult decision situations.

1. It deals only with important life decisions—marriage, schooling, career, and major organizational decisions—that commit the individual or the organization to a certain course of action following the decision.

2. It recognizes that procrastination and rationalization are mechanisms by which people avoid making difficult decisions and coping with the associated stress.

3. It explicitly acknowledges that some decisions probably will be wrong and that the fear of making an unsound decision can be a deterrent to making any decision at all.

4. It provides for **self-reactions**—comparisons of alternatives with internalized moral standards. Internalized moral standards guide decision making as much as economic and social outcomes do. A proposed course of action may offer many economic and social rewards, but if it violates the decision maker's moral convictions, it is unlikely to be chosen.

**Self-reactions** are comparisons of alternatives with internalized moral standards.

5. It recognizes that at times the decision maker is ambivalent about alternative courses of action; in such circumstances, it is very difficult to make a wholehearted commitment to a single choice. Major life decisions seldom allow compromise, however; usually they are either-or decisions that require commitment to one course of action.

The Janis-Mann conflict model of decision making is shown in Figure 15.5. A concrete example will help explain each step. Our hypothetical individual is Richard,

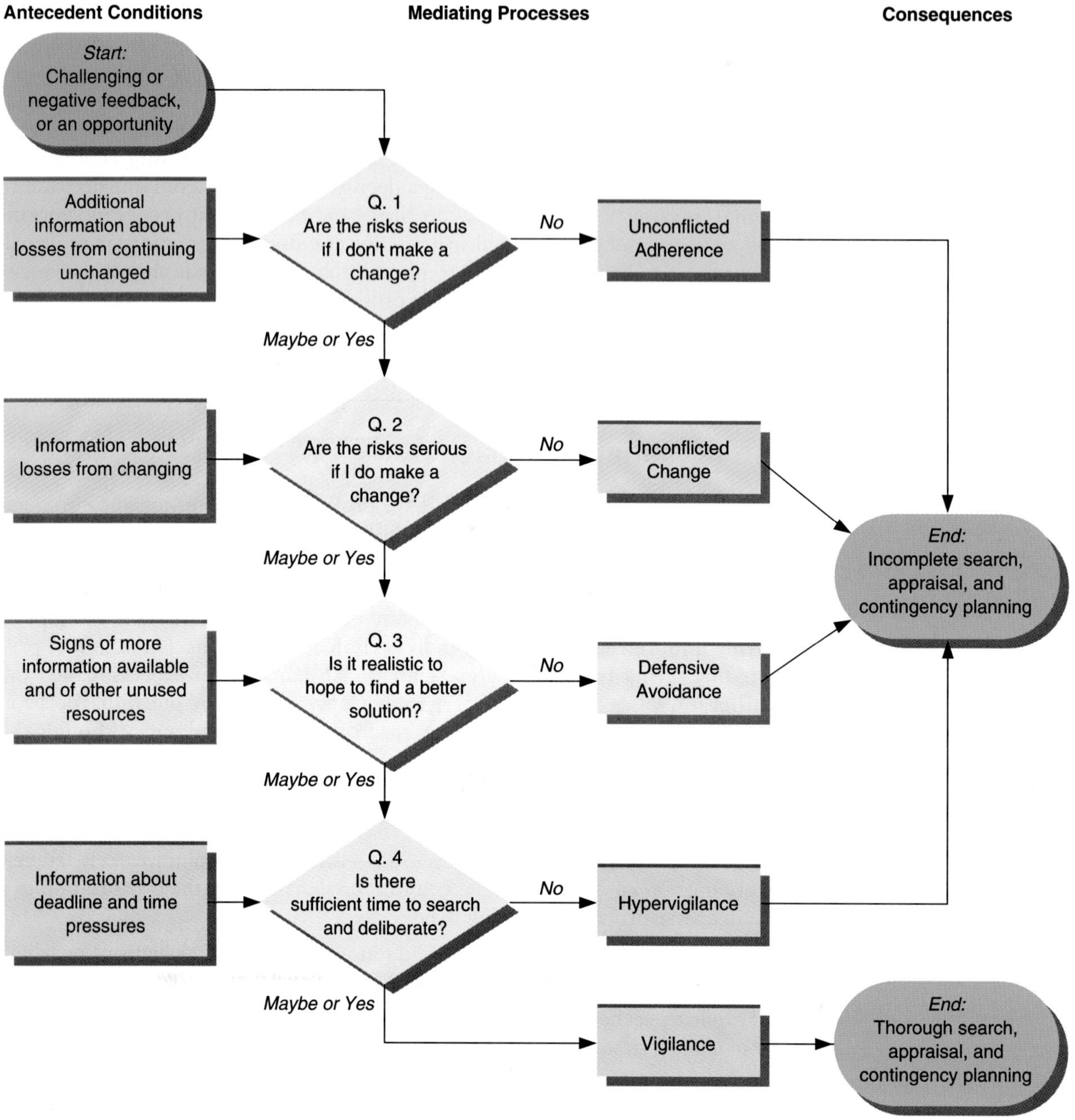


figure 15.5 **Janis-Mann Conflict Model of Decision Making**

*A decision maker answering yes to all four questions will engage in vigilant information processing.*

Reference: Adapted with the permission of The Free Press, a division of Simon & Schuster from *Decision Making: A Psychological Analysis of Conflict, Choice, and Commitment,* by Irving L. Janis and Leon Mann. Copyright © 1977 by The Free Press.

a thirty-year-old engineer with a working wife and two young children. Richard has been employed at a large manufacturing company for eight years. He keeps abreast of his career situation through visits with peers at work and in other companies, through feedback from his manager and others regarding his work and future with the firm, through the alumni magazine from his university, and from other sources.

Dan Meyers seems to be very happy now that he has finally changed jobs. He remained loyal in his former job for 15 years. As a loyal employee he may have thought that the risks were not serious if he did not change, so he remained in unconflicted adherence to the job. But over time, that stance began to change as he became increasingly dissatisfied. When the long hours, being on call seven days a week, equipment constantly breaking, and frozen salary finally got to him, he found a better job that pays him $15,000 more per year.

At work one morning, Richard learns that he has been passed over for a promotion for the second time in a year. He investigates the information, which can be considered negative feedback, and confirms it. As a result, he seeks out other information regarding his career at the company, the prospect of changing employers, and the possibility of going back to graduate school to get an MBA. At the same time, he asks himself, "Are the risks serious if I do not make a change?" If the answer is no, Richard will continue his present activities. In the model's terms, this option is called **unconflicted adherence**. If instead the answer is yes or maybe, Richard will move to the next question in the model.

The second step asks, "Are the risks serious if I do make a change?" If Richard goes on to this step, he will gather information about potential losses from making a change. He may, for example, find out whether he would lose health insurance and pension benefits if he changed jobs or went back to graduate school. If he believes that changing presents no serious risks, Richard will make the change, called an **unconflicted change**. Otherwise, Richard will move on to the next step.

But suppose Richard has determined that the risks are serious whether or not he makes a change. He believes he must make a change because he will not be promoted further in his present company, yet serious risks are also associated with making a change—perhaps loss of benefits, uncertain promotion opportunities in another company, and lost income from going to graduate school for two years. In the third step, Richard wonders, "Is it realistic to hope to find a better solution?" He continues to look for information that can help him make the decision. If the answer to this third question is no, Richard may give up the hope of finding anything better and opt for what Janis and Mann call **defensive avoidance**; that is, he will make no change and avoid any further contact with the issue. A positive response, however, will move Richard onward to the next step.

Here the decision maker, who now recognizes the serious risks involved yet expects to find a solution, asks, "Is there sufficient time to search and deliberate?" Richard now asks himself how quickly he needs to make a change. If he believes he has little time to deliberate, perhaps because of his age, he will experience what Janis and Mann call **hypervigilance**. In this state, he may suffer severe psychological stress and engage in frantic, superficial pursuit of some satisficing strategy. (This might also be called "panic"!) If, on the other hand, Richard believes he has two to

**Unconflicted adherence** entails continuing with current activities if doing so does not entail serious risks.

**Unconflicted change** involves making changes in present activities if doing so presents no serious risks.

**Defensive avoidance** entails making no changes in present activities and avoiding any further contact with associated issues because there appears to be no hope of finding a better solution.

**Hypervigilance** is frantic, superficial pursuit of some satisficing strategy.

**Vigilant information processing** involves thoroughly investigating all possible alternatives, weighing their costs and benefits before making a decision, and developing contingency plans.

three years to consider various alternatives, he will undertake **vigilant information processing**, in which he will thoroughly investigate all possible alternatives, weigh their costs and benefits before making a choice, and develop contingency plans.

Negative answers to the questions in the conflict model lead to responses of unconflicted adherence, unconflicted change, defensive avoidance, and hypervigilance. All are coping strategies that result in incomplete search, appraisal, and contingency planning. A decision maker who gives the same answer to all the questions will always engage in the same coping strategy. However, if the answers change as the situation changes, the individual's coping strategies may change as well. The decision maker who answers yes to each of the four questions is led to vigilant information processing, a process similar to that outlined in the rational decision-making model. The decision maker objectively analyzes the problem and all alternatives, thoroughly searches for information, carefully evaluates the consequences of all alternatives, and diligently plans for implementation and contingencies.

# Related Behavioral Aspects of Decision Making

The behavioral, practical, and personal approaches each have behavioral components, but the manager must consider two additional behavioral aspects of decision making. These are ethics and escalation of commitment.

## Ethics and Decision Making

**Ethics** are an individual's personal beliefs about what is right and wrong or good and bad.

As we noted in Chapter 2, **ethics** are a person's beliefs about what constitutes right and wrong behavior. Ethical behavior is that which conforms to generally accepted social norms; unethical behavior does not conform to generally accepted social norms. Some decisions made by managers may have little or nothing to do with their own personal ethics, but many other decisions are influenced by the manager's ethics. For example, decisions involving such disparate issues as hiring and firing employees, dealing with customers and suppliers, setting wages and assigning tasks, and maintaining one's expense account are all subject to ethical influences.

In general, ethical dilemmas for managers may center on direct personal gain, indirect personal gain, or simple personal preferences. Consider, for example, a top executive contemplating a decision about a potential takeover. His or her stock option package may result in enormous personal gain if the decision goes one way, even though stockholders may benefit more if the decision goes the other way. An indirect personal gain may result when a decision does not directly add value to a manager's personal worth but does enhance her or his career. Or the manager may face a choice about relocating a company facility where one of the options is closest to his or her residence.

*"Every day everybody in the company has to make decisions about what they're going to put first and what they're going to put second."* — *Clayton Christensen, Harvard Business School*[25]

Managers should carefully and deliberately consider the ethical context of every one of their decisions. The goal, of course, is for the manager to make the decision that is in the best interest of the firm, as opposed to the best interest of the manager. This requires personal honesty and integrity. Managers also find it helpful to discuss potential ethical dilemmas with colleagues. Others can often provide an objective view of a situation that may help a manager avoid unintentionally making an unethical decision.

## Escalation of Commitment

**Escalation of commitment** is the tendency to persist in an ineffective course of action when evidence reveals that the project cannot succeed.

Sometimes people continue to try to implement a decision despite clear and convincing evidence that substantial problems exist. **Escalation of commitment** is the tendency to persist in an ineffective course of action when evidence indicates that the project is doomed to failure. A good example is the decision by the government of British Columbia to hold EXPO '86 in Vancouver. Originally, the organizers expected the project to break even financially, so the province would not have to increase taxes to pay for it. As work progressed, it became clear that expenses were far greater than had been projected. But organizers considered it too late to call off the event, despite the huge losses that obviously would occur. Eventually, the province conducted a $300 million lottery to try to cover the costs.[26] Similar examples abound in stock market investments, in political and military situations, and in organizations developing any type of new project. The Iridium project, discussed in the "World View" box, may be another example of escalation of commitment.

WORLD VIEW

### *Continued Investment in Iridium?*

You may have heard of the Iridium project, a system in which a mobile phone can be used from anywhere in the world through a collection of sixty-six satellites encircling the earth. Iridium is a separate company backed by Motorola and others, and Motorola was involved in making the satellites and the handsets. The idea is great: to be able to make a phone call from anywhere on the planet at any time. For those people who need instant, worldwide connections from remote places in the world, it is an idea whose time had come, finally.

But along the way the project hit a few snags. First, launching and positioning the satellites was not easy. Governments around the globe had to give their approval. The satellites alone cost more than $5 billion to build and launch. The handsets are about the size of a brick with an antenna and cost $3,000, in addition to the $4 to $7 per minute usage charge. In March of 1999, Iridium announced that first-quarter revenue estimates would be low, and the stock price dropped from $72 to around $20 a share.

Motorola announced its intention to remain involved and that new, smaller handsets were on the way as the company filed for reorganization under the bankruptcy laws. By the fall of 1999, Iridium still had only 10,000 subscribers, well short of the 40,000 demanded by the banks who hold $800 million in loans. But competition is on the way as others are learning from the Iridium experience and will be entering the market. Iridium is truly an advancement in communications technology. But is it worth the investment? Should investors continue to support it, or is it just throwing good money after bad?

*"Iridium will prove that the stock's drop was a classic overreaction of the market."* —*John Coates, analyst for Salomon Smith Barney*

References: Alan Cane, "Teledesic Reviews Plan After Fall of Iridium," *Financial Times*, October 13, 1999, p. 33; Christopher Price, "$5bn Venture Was 'Wrong Product at Wrong Time,'" *Financial Times*, October 8, 1999, p. 39; Henry Goldblatt, "Just a *Few* Customers Shy of a Business Plan," *Fortune*, March 29, 1999, p. 40 (quote on p. 40).

Barry Staw has suggested several possible reasons for escalation of commitment.[27] Some projects require much front-end investment and offer little return until the end, so the investor must stay in all the way to get any payoff. These "all or nothing" projects require unflagging commitment. Furthermore, investors' or project leaders' egos often become so involved with the project that their identities are totally wrapped up in it.[28] Failure or cancellation seems to threaten their reason for existence. They therefore continue to push the project as potentially successful despite strong evidence to the contrary. Other times, the social structure, group norms, and group cohesiveness support a project so strongly that cancellation is impossible. Organizational inertia also may force an organization to maintain a failing project. Thus, escalation of commitment is a phenomenon that has a strong foundation.

How can an individual or organization recognize that a project needs to be stopped before it results in throwing good money after bad? Several suggestions have been made; some are easy to put to use, and others are more difficult. Having good information about a project is always a first step in preventing the escalation problem. Usually it is possible to schedule regular sessions to discuss the project, its progress, the assumptions on which it originally was based, the current validity of these assumptions, and any problems with the project. An objective review is necessary to maintain control.

Some organizations have begun to make separate teams responsible for the development and implementation of a project to reduce ego involvement. Often the people who initiate a project are those who know the most about it, however, and their expertise can be valuable in the implementation process. Staw suggests that a general strategy for avoiding the escalation problem is to try to create an "experimenting organization" in which every program and project is reviewed regularly and managers are evaluated on their contribution to the total organization rather than to specific projects.[29]

# Group Decision Making

People in organizations work in a variety of groups—formal and informal, permanent and temporary. Most of these groups make decisions that affect the welfare of the organization and the people in it. Here we discuss several issues surrounding how groups make decisions: group polarization, groupthink, and group problem solving.

## Group Polarization

Members' attitudes and opinions with respect to an issue or a solution may change during group discussion. Some studies of this tendency have showed the change to be a fairly consistent movement toward a more risky solution, called "risky shift."[30] Other studies and analyses have revealed that the group-induced shift is not always toward more risk; the group is just as likely to move toward a more conservative view.[31] Generally, **group polarization** occurs when the average of the group members' postdiscussion attitudes tends to be more extreme than average prediscussion attitudes.[32]

**Group polarization** is the tendency for a group's average postdiscussion attitudes to be more extreme than its average prediscussion attitudes.

Several features of group discussion contribute to polarization.[33] When individuals discover in group discussion that others share their opinions, they may feel more strongly about their opinions, resulting in a more extreme view. Persuasive arguments also can encourage polarization. If members who strongly support a particular position are able to express themselves cogently in the discussion, less avid supporters of the position may become convinced that it is correct. In addition, members may believe that because the group is deciding, they are not individually responsible for the decision or its outcomes. This diffusion of responsibility may enable them to accept and support a decision more radical than those they would make as individuals.

Polarization can profoundly affect group decision making. If group members are known to lean toward a particular decision before a discussion, it may be expected that their postdecision position will be even more extreme. Understanding this phenomenon may be useful for one who seeks to affect their decision.

## Groupthink

**Groupthink** is a mode of thinking that occurs when members of a group are deeply involved in a cohesive in-group, and desire for unanimity offsets their motivation to appraise alternative courses of action.

As discussed in Chapters 11 and 12, highly cohesive groups and teams often are very successful at meeting their goals, although they sometimes have serious difficulties as well. One problem that can occur is groupthink. **Groupthink**, according to Irving L. Janis, is "a mode of thinking that people engage in when they are deeply involved in a cohesive in-group, when the members' strivings for unanimity override their motivation to realistically appraise alternative courses of action."[34] When groupthink occurs, then, the group unknowingly makes unanimity rather than the best decision its goal. Individual members may perceive that raising objections is not appropriate. Groupthink can occur in many decision-making situations in organizations. The current trend toward increasing use of teams in organizations may increase instances of groupthink because of the susceptibility of self-managing teams to this type of thought.[35]

### Symptoms of Groupthink

The three primary conditions that foster the development of groupthink are cohesiveness, the leader's promotion of his or her preferred solution, and insulation of the group from experts' opinions. Based on analysis of the disaster associated with the explosion of the space shuttle Challenger in 1986, the original idea of groupthink symptoms was enhanced to include the effects of increased time pressure and the role of the leader in not stimulating critical thinking in developing the symptoms of groupthink.[36] Figure 15.6 outlines the revised groupthink process.

A group in which groupthink has taken hold exhibits eight well-defined symptoms:

1. An *illusion of invulnerability*, shared by most or all members, that creates excessive optimism and encourages extreme risk taking.
2. *Collective efforts to rationalize or discount warnings* that might lead members to reconsider assumptions before recommitting themselves to past policy decisions.
3. An *unquestioned belief in the group's inherent morality*, inclining members to ignore the ethical and moral consequences of their decisions.
4. *Stereotyped views of "enemy" leaders* as too evil to warrant genuine attempts to negotiate or as too weak or stupid to counter whatever risky attempts are made to defeat their purposes.
5. *Direct pressure on a member* who expresses strong arguments against any of the group's stereotypes, illusions, or commitments, making clear that such dissent is contrary to what is expected of loyal members.

figure 15.6

**The Groupthink Process**

*Groupthink can occur when a highly cohesive group with a directive leader is under time pressure; it can result in a defective decision process and low probability of successful outcomes.*

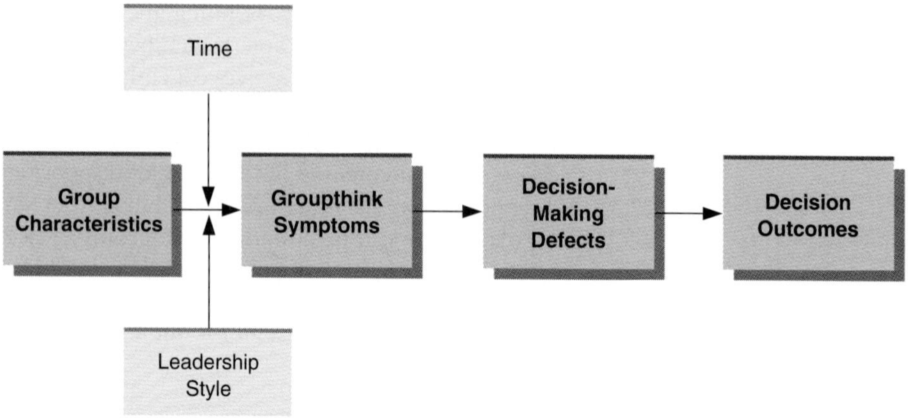


Reference: Gregory Moorhead, Richard Ference, and Chris P. Neck, "Group Decision Fiascoes Continue: Space Shuttle *Challenger* and a Revised Groupthink Framework," *Human Relations,* 1991, vol. 44, pp. 539–550.

6. *Self-censorship of deviations* from the apparent group consensus, reflecting each member's inclination to minimize the importance of his or her doubts and counterarguments.

7. A *shared illusion of unanimity,* resulting partly from self-censorship of deviations, augmented by the false assumption that silence means consent.

8. The *emergence of self-appointed "mindguards,"* members who protect the group from adverse information that might shatter their shared complacency about the effectiveness and morality of their decisions.[37]

Janis contends that the group involved in the Watergate cover-up—Richard Nixon, H. R. Haldeman, John Ehrlichman, and John Dean—may have been a victim of groupthink. Evidence of most of the groupthink symptoms can be found in the unedited transcripts of the group's deliberations.[38]

**Decision-Making Defects and Decision Quality** When groupthink dominates group deliberations, the likelihood that decision-making defects will occur increases. The group is less likely to survey a full range of alternatives and may focus on only a few (often one or two). In discussing a preferred alternative, the group may fail to examine it for nonobvious risks and drawbacks. The group may not reexamine previously rejected alternatives for nonobvious gains or some means of reducing apparent costs even when they receive new information. The group may reject expert opinions that run counter to its own views and may choose to consider only information that supports its preferred solution. The decision to launch the space shuttle *Challenger* in January 1986 may have been a product of groupthink, because due to the increased time pressure to make a decision and the leaders' style, negative information was ignored by the group that made the decision.[39] Finally, the group may not consider any potential setbacks or countermoves by competing groups and therefore may fail to develop contingency plans. It should be noted that Janis contends that these six defects may arise from other common problems as well: fatigue, prejudice, inaccurate information, information overload, and ignorance.[40]

Defects in decision making do not always lead to bad outcomes or defeats. Even if its own decision-making processes are flawed, one side can win a battle be-

**table 15.2**
**Prescriptions for Preventing Groupthink**

**A. Leader prescriptions**
1. Assign everyone the role of critical evaluator.
2. Be impartial; do not state preferences.
3. Assign the devil's advocate role to at least one group member.
4. Use outside experts to challenge the group.
5. Be open to dissenting points of view.

**B. Organizational prescriptions**
1. Set up several independent groups to study the same issue.
2. Train managers and group leaders in groupthink prevention techniques.

**C. Individual prescriptions**
1. Be a critical thinker.
2. Discuss group deliberations with a trusted outsider; report back to the group.

**D. Process prescriptions**
1. Periodically break the group into subgroups to discuss the issues.
2. Take time to study external factors.
3. Hold second-chance meetings to rethink issues before making a commitment.

cause of the poor decisions made by the other side's leaders. Nevertheless, decisions produced by defective processes are less likely to succeed.

Although the arguments for the existence of groupthink are convincing, the hypothesis has not been subjected to rigorous empirical examination. Research supports parts of the model but leaves some questions unanswered.[41]

**Prevention of Groupthink** Several suggestions have been offered to help managers reduce the probability of groupthink in group decision making.[42] Summarized in Table 15.2, these prescriptions fall into four categories depending on whether they apply to the leader, the organization, the individual, or the process. All are designed to facilitate the critical evaluation of alternatives and discourage the single-minded pursuit of unanimity.

## Participation

A major issue in group decision making is the degree to which employees should participate in the process. Early management theories, such as those of the scientific management school, advocated a clear separation between the duties of managers and workers: Management was to make the decisions, and employees were to implement them.[43] Other approaches have urged that employees be allowed to participate in decisions to increase their ego involvement, motivation, and satisfaction.[44] Numerous research studies have shown that whereas employees who seek responsibility and challenge on the job may find participation in the decision-making process both motivating and enriching, other employees may regard such participation as a waste of time and a management imposition.[45]

Whether employee participation in decision making is appropriate depends on the situation. In tasks that require an estimation, a prediction, or a judgment of accuracy—usually referred to as judgmental tasks—groups typically are superior to individuals, simply because more people contribute to the decision-making process.[46] However, one especially capable individual may make a better judgment than a group.

In problem-solving tasks, groups generally produce more and better solutions than do individuals. But groups take far longer than individuals to develop solutions and make decisions. An individual or very small group may be able to accomplish some things much faster than a large, unwieldy group or organization. In addition, individual decision making avoids the special problems of group decision making, such as groupthink or group polarization. If the problem to be solved is fairly straightforward, it may be more appropriate to have a single capable individual concentrate on solving it. On the other hand, complex problems are more appropriate for groups. Such problems can often be divided into parts and the parts assigned to individuals or small groups who bring their results back to the group for discussion and decision making.

*"When good people are given good information, they typically make good decisions."*
*— Jim Lyons, general manager, Consolidated Diesel Co.*[47]

An additional advantage to group decision making is that it often creates greater interest in the task.[48] Heightened interest may increase the time and effort given to the task, resulting in more ideas, a more thorough search for solutions, better evaluation of alternatives, and improved decision quality.

The Vroom decision tree approach to leadership (discussed in Chapter 13) is one popular way of determining the appropriate degree of subordinate participation.[49] The model includes decision styles that vary from "decide" (the leader alone makes the decision) to "delegate" (the group makes the decision, with each member having an equal say). The choice of style rests on seven considerations that concern the characteristics of the situation and the subordinates.

Participation in decision making is also related to organizational structure. For example, decentralization involves delegating some decision-making authority throughout the organizational hierarchy. The more decentralized the organization, the more its employees tend to participate in decision making. Whether one views participation in decision making as pertaining to leadership, organization structure, or motivation, it remains an important aspect of organizations that continues to occupy managers and organizational scholars.[50]

## Group Problem Solving

A typical interacting group may have difficulty with any of several steps in the decision-making process. One common problem arises in the generation-of-alternatives phase: the search may be arbitrarily ended before all plausible alternatives have been identified. Several types of group interactions can have this effect. If members immediately express their reactions to the alternatives as they are first proposed, potential contributors may begin to censor their ideas to avoid embarrassing criticism from the group. Less confident group members, intimidated by members who have more experience, higher status, or more power, also may censor their ideas for fear of embarrassment or punishment. In addition, the group leader may limit idea generation by enforcing requirements concerning time, appropriateness, cost, feasibility, and the like.

To improve the generation of alternatives, managers may employ any of three techniques to stimulate the group's problem-solving capabilities: brainstorming, the nominal group technique, or the Delphi technique.

When Toyota discovered that the average age of its U.S. buyers was 46, it set a goal of targeting a generation of customers who are ten years younger. In order to create a stable of new cars that appeal to younger buyers, Toyota put together the genesis team—a diverse group of young people from around the company—to solve the problem. The genesis team was given a budget of $30 million to spend on the development and promotion of three cars that would appeal to younger buyers. So far, the company has launched the new subcompact ECHO, a new sporty two-door Celica, and the new racy convertible MR2 Spyder. The sales have exceeded expectations and the median age of buyers has dropped to 33 for the Celica and 38 for the ECHO, compared to 43 for the Tercel it replaced. The genesis group had its headquarters in a building separate from the company headquarters in Torrance, California and had free rein to make a different kind of Toyota. It looks as if it has worked.

**Brainstorming** is a technique used in the idea-generation phase of decision making that assists in development of numerous alternative courses of action.

With the **nominal group technique**, group members follow a generate-discussion-vote cycle until they reach an appropriate decision.

### Brainstorming

**Brainstorming**, a technique made popular in the 1950s, is most often used in the idea-generation phase of decision making and is intended to solve problems that are new to the organization and have major consequences. In brainstorming, the group convenes specifically to generate alternatives. The members present ideas and clarify them with brief explanations. Each idea is recorded in full view of all members, usually on a flip chart. To avoid self-censoring, no attempts to evaluate the ideas are allowed. Group members are encouraged to offer any ideas that occur to them, even those that seem too risky or impossible to implement. (The absence of such ideas, in fact, is evidence that group members are engaging in self-censorship.) In a subsequent session, after the ideas have been recorded and distributed to members for review, the alternatives are evaluated.

The intent of brainstorming is to produce totally new ideas and solutions by stimulating the creativity of group members and encouraging them to build on the contributions of others. Brainstorming does not provide the resolution to the problem, an evaluation scheme, or the decision itself. Instead, it should produce a list of alternatives that is more innovative and comprehensive than one developed by the typical interacting group.

### The Nominal Group Technique

The **nominal group technique** is another means of improving group decision making. Whereas brainstorming is used primarily to generate alternatives, this technique may be used in other phases of decision making, such as identification of the problem and of appropriate criteria for evaluating alternatives. To use this technique, a group of individuals convenes to address an issue. The issue is described to the group, and each individual writes a list of ideas; no discussion among the members is permitted. Following the five-to-ten-minute idea-generation period, individual members take turns reporting their ideas, one at a time, to the group. The ideas are recorded on a flip chart, and members are encouraged to add to the list by building on the ideas of others. After all ideas have been presented, the members may discuss them and continue to build on them or proceed to the next phase. This part of the process can also be carried out without a face-to-face meeting or by mail, telephone, or computer. A meeting, however, helps members develop a group feeling and puts interpersonal pressure on the members to do their best in developing their lists.[51]

After the discussion, members privately vote on or rank the ideas or report their preferences in some other agreed-upon way. Reporting is private to reduce any feelings of intimidation. After voting, the group may discuss the results and continue to generate and discuss ideas. The generation-discussion-vote cycle can continue until an appropriate decision is reached.

The nominal group technique has two principal advantages. It helps overcome the negative effects of power and status differences among group members, and it can be used to explore problems to generate alternatives, or to evaluate them. Its primary disadvantage lies in its structured nature, which may limit creativity.

The **Delphi technique** is a method of systematically gathering judgments of experts for use in developing forecasts.

**The Delphi Technique** The **Delphi technique** was originally developed by Rand Corporation as a method to systematically gather the judgments of experts for use in developing forecasts. It is designed for groups that do not meet face to face. For instance, the product development manager of a major toy manufacturer might use the Delphi technique to probe the views of industry experts to forecast developments in the dynamic toy market.

The manager who wants the input of a group is the central figure in the process. After recruiting participants, the manager develops a questionnaire for them to complete. The questionnaire is relatively simple in that it contains straightforward questions that deal with the issue, trends in the area, new technological developments, and other factors the manager is interested in. The manager summarizes the responses and reports back to the experts with another questionnaire. This cycle may be repeated as many times as necessary to generate the information the manager needs.

The Delphi technique is useful when experts are physically dispersed, anonymity is desired, or the participants are known to have trouble communicating with one another because of extreme differences of opinion.[52] This method also avoids the intimidation problems that may exist in decision-making groups. On the other hand, the technique eliminates the often fruitful results of direct interaction among group members.

# Negotiation

**Negotiation** is the process in which two or more parties (people or groups) reach agreement even though they have different preferences.

One special way that decisions are made in organizations is through negotiation. **Negotiation** is the process in which two or more parties (people or groups) reach agreement even though they have different preferences. In its simplest form the parties involved may be two individuals who are trying to decide who will pay for lunch. A little more complexity is involved when two people, such as an employee and manager, sit down to decide on personal performance goals for the next year against which the employee's performance will be measured. Even more complex are the negotiations that take place between labor unions and management of a company, or between two companies as they negotiate the terms of a joint venture. The key issues are that at least two parties are involved, their preferences are different, and they need to reach agreement.

## Four Approaches to Negotiation

The study of negotiation has grown steadily since the 1960s. Four primary approaches to negotiation have dominated this study: individual differences, situational characteristics, game theory, and cognitive approaches. Each of these is briefly described in the following sections.

**Individual Differences** Early psychological approaches concentrated on the personality traits of the negotiators.[53] Traits investigated have included demographic characteristics and personality variables. Demographic characteristics have included age, gender, and race, among others. Personality variables have included risk taking, locus of control, tolerance for ambiguity, self-esteem, authoritarianism, and Machiavellianism. The assumption of this type of research was that the key to successful negotiation was selecting the right person to do the negotiation, one who had the appropriate demographic characteristics or personality. This assumption seemed to make sense because negotiation is such a personal and interactive process. However, the research rarely showed the positive results expected because situational variables negated the effects of the individual differences.[54]

**Situational Characteristics** Situational characteristics are the context within which negotiation takes place. They include such things as the types of communication between negotiators, the potential outcomes of the negotiation, the relative power of the parties (both positional and personal), the time frame available for negotiation, the number of people representing each side, and the presence of other parties. Some of this research has contributed to our understanding of the negotiation process. However, the shortcomings of the situational approach are similar to those of the individual characteristics approach. Many situational characteristics are external to the negotiators and beyond their control. Often the negotiators cannot change their relative power positions or the setting within which the negotiation occurs. So,

This picture shows the celebration that followed the announcement of the trade agreement signed by the United States and China in November 1999. These negotiations took place over 13 years and often stalemated over various issues. Charlene Barshefsky was the United States trade representative that finally was able to bring about the final deal. China will open its markets to United States companies in exchange for the United States backing of China's attempt to join the World Trade Organization. As a member of the WTO, China will have more favorable access to worldwide markets. The protracted negotiations included detailed arrangements for the lowering of industrial and agricultural tariffs.

although we have learned a lot from research on the situational issues, we still need to learn much more about the process.

**Game Theory** Game theory was developed by economists using mathematical models to predict the outcome of negotiation situations. It requires that every alternative and outcome be analyzed with probabilities and numerical outcomes reflecting the preferences for each outcome. In addition, the order in which different parties can make choices and every possible move are predicted, along with associated preferences for outcomes. The outcomes of this approach are exactly what negotiators want: a predictive model of how negotiation should be conducted. One major drawback is that it requires the ability to describe all possible options and outcomes for every possible move in every situation before the negotiation starts. This is often very tedious, if possible at all. Another problem is that it assumes that negotiators are rational at all times. Other research in negotiation has shown that negotiators often do not act rationally. Therefore, this approach, while elegant in its prescriptions, is usually unworkable in a real negotiation situation.

**Cognitive Approaches** The fourth approach is the cognitive approach, which recognizes that negotiators often depart from perfect rationality during negotiation; it tries to predict how and when negotiators will make these departures. Howard Raiffa's decision analytic approach focuses on providing advice to negotiators actively involved in negotiation.[55] Bazerman and Neale have added to Raiffa's work by specifying eight ways in which negotiators systematically deviate from rationality.[56] The types of deviations they describe include escalation of commitment to a previously selected course of action, overreliance on readily available information, assuming that the negotiations produce fixed-sum outcomes, and anchoring negotiation in irrelevant information. These cognitive approaches have advanced the study of negotiation a long way beyond the early individual and situational approaches. Negotiators can use them to attempt to predict in advance how the negotiation might take place.

figure 15.7 **The PRAM Model of Negotiation**

*The PRAM model shows the four steps in setting up negotiation so that both parties win.*

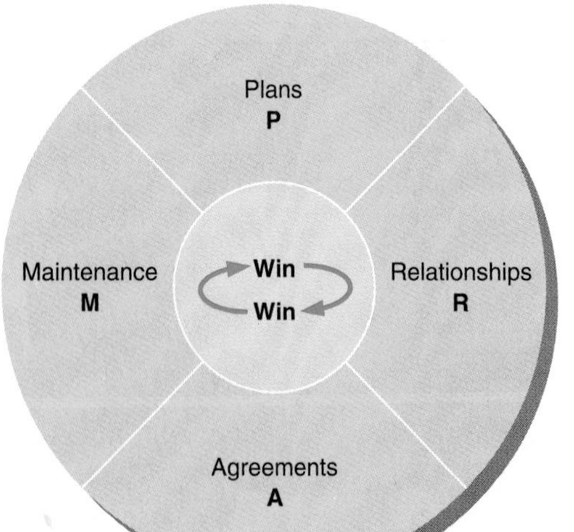


Reference: Reprinted with the permission of Pocket Books, a division of Simon & Schuster, from *The Win-Win Negotiator: How to Negotiate Favorable Agreements That Last,* by Ross R. Reck, Ph.D., and Brian G. Long, Ph.D. Copyright © 1985, 1987 by Brian G. Long and Ross R. Reck.

## Win-Win Negotiation

In addition to the approaches to negotiation described above, a group of approaches proposed by consultants and advisors is meant to give negotiators a specific model to use in carrying out difficult negotiations. One of the best of these is the "Win-Win Negotiator" developed by Ross Reck and his associates.[57] The Win-Win approach (see Figure 15.7) does not treat negotiation as a game in which there are winners and losers. Instead, it approaches negotiation as an opportunity for both sides to be winners, to get what they want out of the agreement. The focus is on both parties reaching agreement such that both are committed to fulfilling their end of the agreement and to returning for more agreements in the future. In other words, both parties want to have their needs satisfied. In addition, this approach does not advocate either a "tough guy" or a "nice guy" approach to negotiation, both of which are popular in the literature. It assumes that both parties work together to find ways to satisfy both parties at the same time.

The PRAM model guides the negotiator through the four steps of planning for agreement, building relationships, reaching agreements, and maintaining relationships.

The Win-Win approach is a four-step approach illustrated in the **PRAM model** shown in Figure 15.7. The PRAM four-step approach proposes that proper planning, building relationships, getting agreements, and maintaining the relationships are the key steps to successful negotiation.

*Planning* requires that each negotiator set his or her own goals, anticipate the goals of the other, determine areas of probable agreement, and develop strategies for reconciling areas of probable disagreement.

Developing Win-Win *relationships* requires that negotiators plan activities that allow positive personal relationship to develop, cultivate a sense of mutual trust, and allow relationships to fully develop before discussing business in earnest. The development of trust between the parties is probably the single most important key to success in negotiation.

Forming Win-Win *agreements* requires that each party confirm the other party's goals, verify areas of agreement, propose and consider positive solutions to reconcile areas of disagreement, and jointly resolve any remaining differences. The key in reaching agreement is to realize that both parties share many of the goals. The number of areas of disagreement is usually small.

Finally, Win-Win *maintenance* entails providing meaningful feedback based on performance, each of the parties holding up their end of the agreement, keeping in contact, and reaffirming trust between the parties. The assumption is that both parties want to keep the relationship going so that future mutually beneficial transactions can occur. Both parties must uphold their ends of the agreement and do what they said they would do. Finally, keeping in touch is as easy as a telephone call or lunch visit.

In summary, the PRAM model provides simple advice for conducting negotiations. The four steps are easy to remember and carry out as long as games played by other parties do not distract the negotiator. The focus is on planning, agreeing on goals, trust, and keeping commitments.

# Synopsis

Decision making is the process of choosing one alternative from several. The basic elements of decision making include choosing a goal, considering alternative courses of action, assessing potential outcomes of the alternatives, each with its own value relative to the goal, and choosing one alternative based on evaluation of the outcomes. Information is available regarding the alternatives, outcomes, and values.

Programmed decisions are well structured, recurring decisions made according to set decision rules. Nonprogrammed decisions involve nonroutine, poorly structured situations with unclear sources of information; these decisions cannot be made according to existing decision rules. Decision making may also be classified according to the information available. The classifications—certainty, risk, and uncertainty—reflect the amount of information available regarding the outcomes of alternatives.

The rational approach views decision making as a completely rational process in which goals are established, a problem is identified, alternatives are generated and evaluated, a choice is made and implemented, and control is exercised. The use of procedures and rules of thumb, suboptimizing, and satisficing characterize the behavioral model. The rational and behavioral views can be combined into a practical model. The Janis-Mann conflict model recognizes the personal anxiety individuals face when they must make important decisions.

Two related behavioral aspects of decision making are escalation of commitment and ethics. Escalation of commitment to an ineffective course of action occurs in many decision situations. Psychological, social, ego, and organizational factors may cause it. Ethics also play an important role in many managerial decisions.

Group decision making involves problems as well as benefits. One possible problem is group polarization, the shift of members' attitudes and opinions to a more extreme position following group discussion. Another difficulty is groupthink, a mode of thinking in which the urge toward unanimity overrides the critical appraisal of alternatives. Yet another concern involves employee participation in decision making. The appropriate degree of participation depends on the characteristics of the situation.

Negotiation is the process through which two or more parties (people or groups) reach agreement even though they have different preferences. Research on negotiation has examined individual differences, situational characteristics, game theory, and cognitive approaches. The Win-Win approach provides a simple four-step model to successful negotiation: planning, relationships, agreement, and maintenance.

## Discussion Questions

1. Some have argued that people, not organizations, make decisions and that the study of "organizational" decision making is therefore pointless. Do you agree with this argument? Why or why not?
2. What information did you use in deciding to enter the school you now attend?
3. When your alarm goes off each morning, you have a decision to make: whether to get up and go to school or work, or to stay in bed and sleep longer. Is this a programmed or nonprogrammed decision? Why?
4. Describe at least three points in the decision-making process at which information plays an important role.
5. How does the role of information in the rational model of decision making differ from the role of information in the behavioral model?
6. Why does it make sense to discuss several different models of decision making?
7. Can you think of a time when you satisficed when making a decision? Have you ever suboptimized?
8. Describe a situation in which you experienced escalation of commitment to an ineffective course of action. What did you do about it? Do you wish you had handled it differently? Why or why not?
9. How are group polarization and groupthink similar? How do they differ?
10. Describe a situation in which you negotiated an agreement, maybe buying a car or a house. How did the negotiation process compare to the PRAM approach? How did it differ? Were you satisfied with the result of the negotiation?

## Organizational Behavior Case for Discussion

### Encouraging Dissent at AT&T

AT&T wants to be your full provider of communications services . . . again! Remember the breakup that created the "Baby Bells" in 1984, when AT&T was forced to create the smaller, regional telephone systems to handle all local telephone service? AT&T kept the profitable long-distance business.

Times have changed. The Baby Bells are recombining, long-distance service is highly competitive and less profitable, and cable television companies have wired lots of homes. By the end of 1997, AT&T was described as sluggish, incompetent, boring, and no longer the steady, high-performing stock it had once been.

The turnaround began when Mike Armstrong was hired as CEO in November 1997. Armstrong made lots of changes to improve morale, provide direction, and spend money in order to refocus the core business of the company. He changed the pay and performance system so that those who perform are the only ones to get annual bonuses, and morale improved. He sold off some divisions and invested more than $70 million in other divisions that brought the company closer to being a full-service provider of communications. Armstrong wants the company to be a significant player in the cable television business and use that service line to provide local and long-distance telephone service, plus own a nationwide wireless phone system that is easy to use for everyone with a cellular phone. All the while AT&T's stock price has continued to improve, so shareholders are happy.

It is not only *what* decisions Mike Armstrong has made, it is *how* the decisions have been made that has been important. Many times when a new CEO comes into a company in trouble, the first order of business is to clean house of all or most of the existing managers and replace them with executives who agree with the new CEO's philosophy. Armstrong did just the opposite. He left the existing executives in place, although a couple have left on their own to take top positions in other companies. He evidently did not want to be surrounded by managers who agreed with everything he wanted to do. In fact, he encouraged his managers to disagree with him and each other. No plan or project was off-limits to discussion or criticism. Management meetings were full of debate and conflict among participants.

The discussion regarding the purchase of TCI Cable was subject to intense debate since the move into cable television was such a distinct departure from AT&T's primary business—at the time, at least. Armstrong encouraged managers to push their own ideas and argue for them in meetings. Arguments had to be well reasoned and backed up, but no legitimate point of view was dismissed. Sitting back and smiling in agreement was not the way to behave in those meetings. Managers who eventually "lost" in those discussions were not fired or demoted. In fact, Armstrong would take great pains to talk to those individuals and keep them on board and working for the company. The result is a company that is on target and moving in a new direction.

### Case Questions

1. What kinds of decision-making problems did Armstrong avoid by encouraging discussion and conflict in management meetings?
2. What other methods could he have used to avoid similar problems?
3. What are some other benefits of this type of participation in decision making?

References: Andrew Kupfer, "Mike Armstrong's AT&T: Will the Pieces Come Together?" *Fortune*, April 26, 1999, pp. 82–89; Rebecca Blumenstein, "Naughty or Nice: A New CEO's Choice: Keep the Old Team or Bring Your Own: AT&T's Mike Armstrong Is No 'Chainsaw Al'; at Least, He Isn't Yet: Hiring Thorough Acquisitions," *Wall Street Journal*, December 23, 1998, p. A1; Fred Vogelstein, "The Man with the Right Connections: C. Michael Armstrong Is Revving Up AT&T," *U.S. News & World Report*, August 10, 1998, p. 43; Henry Goldblatt, "AT&T Finally Has an Operator," *Fortune*, February 16, 1998, pp. 79–82.

## Experiencing Organizational Behavior

### Programmed and Nonprogrammed Decisions

**Purpose:** This exercise will allow you to take part in making a hypothetical decision and help you understand the difference between programmed and nonprogrammed decisions.

**Format:** You will be asked to perform a task both individually and as a member of a group.

**Procedure:** Following is a list of typical organizational decisions. Your task is to determine whether they are programmed or nonprogrammed. Number your paper, and write *P* for programmed or *N* for nonprogrammed next to each number.

Your instructor will divide the class into groups of four to seven. All groups should have approximately the same number of members. Your task as a group is to make the determinations outlined above. In arriving at your decisions, do not use techniques such as voting or negotiating ("Okay, I'll give in on this one if you'll give in on that one.") The group should discuss the difference between programmed and nonprogrammed decisions and each decision situation until all members at least partly agree with the decision.

### Decision List

1. Hiring a specialist for the research staff in a highly technical field
2. Assigning workers to daily tasks
3. Determining the size of dividend to be paid to shareholders in the ninth consecutive year of strong earnings growth
4. Deciding whether to officially excuse an employee's absence for medical reasons
5. Selecting the location for another branch of a 150-branch bank in a large city
6. Approving the appointment of a new law school graduate to the corporate legal staff
7. Making annual assignments of graduate assistants to faculty
8. Approving an employee's request to attend a local seminar in his or her special area of expertise
9. Selecting the appropriate outlets for print advertisements for a new college textbook
10. Determining the location for a new fast-food restaurant in a small but growing town on the major interstate highway between two very large metropolitan areas

### Follow-up Questions

1. To what extent did group members disagree about which decisions were programmed and which were nonprogrammed?
2. What primary factors did the group discuss in making each decision?
3. Were there any differences between the members' individual lists and the group lists? If so, discuss the reasons for the differences.

## Building Organizational Behavior Skills

### Rational Versus Practical Approaches to Decision Making

Managers need to recognize and understand the different models that they use to make decisions. They also need to understand the extent to which they are predisposed to be relatively autocratic or relatively participative in making decisions. To develop your skills in these areas, perform the following activity.

First, assume you are the manager of a firm that is rapidly growing. Recent sales figures strongly suggest the need for a new plant to produce more of your firm's products. Key issues include where the plant might be built and how large it might be (for example, a small, less expensive plant to meet current needs that could be expanded in the future versus a large and more expensive plant that might have excess capacity today but meet long-term needs better).

Using the rational approach diagrammed in Figure 15.3, trace the process the manager might use to make the decision. Note the kinds of information that might be required and the extent to which other people might need to be involved in making the decision at each point.

Next, go back and look at various steps in the process where behavioral processes might intervene and affect the overall process. Will bounded rationality come into play? How about satisficing?

Finally, use the practical approach shown in Figure 15.4 and trace through the process again. Again note where other input may be needed. Try to identify places in the process where the rational and practical approaches are likely to result in the same outcome and places where differences are most likely to occur.

## Developing OB Internet Skills

**Introduction:** Individual or corporate decisions are not often written about in the popular media unless the result has catastrophic consequences. In this chapter we have described several political, military, and otherwise public decisions and their consequences. But other decisions certainly have been made that could be analyzed if they were described in a public way. You may have been affected by some, maybe by the decision to cancel a flight you were booked on, or the decision to close a retail store at which you worked.

**Internet Assignment:** Use the Internet to find information on a decision that may not be widely known, but which could be analyzed. Decisions that companies make affect the lives of many people, as in the decision to close a plant, or change advertising campaigns, or invest in new research. These decisions may be hard to find at first. However, by thinking about products or services you use, companies you buy from, stores you shop in, or trips you have taken, you should be able to come up with a decision that some company or organization made that affected you and is written about in newspapers or magazines. Look up as many articles as you can about that company or organization and the particular decision. Find out as much as possible about that decision and the results of it.

**Follow-up:** How easy or difficult was it to find information on the decision you chose? How much information was available on the Internet? Did you find out enough information to really understand how and why the decision was made? Finally, respond to the following questions:

1. Do you agree with the decision?
2. Was it clear from the information who was responsible for making the decision?
3. How would you have made this decision differently?

# Part III Integrative Running Case

## Influence Processes at Work in the AOL–Time Warner Deal

The America Online–Time Warner merger in January 2000 discussed in the cases at the end of Parts I and II presented the background of the companies and the people who run them. Clearly, this was a merger of unequaled proportions between two very different companies. The two leaders, Stephen Case of AOL and Gerald Levin of Time Warner, were strikingly similar, as was described in the Part II case. Both were introverted, not prone to demand all of the attention for themselves, confident in their decision making, passionate about their work, and committed to the mission of the company. Their routes to power were quite different, however, as Case left several jobs because of his impatience with the pace of action and change, whereas Levin stuck it out for twenty-eight years with the same company, working his way through the bureaucracy, surviving the political infighting of the merger between Time, Inc. and Warner Communications in 1989, and then integrating the powerful Ted Turner following the purchase of Turner Broadcasting in 1995. Plus, Levin is from a different generation than Case, being twenty years his senior.

Initially, at least, the talk has been congenial. Both men talk about the combination being a merger of equals and about sharing power. Levin won the battle to be chief executive officer before it even began by making it clear to Case that he (Levin) would be CEO and would not work for Case. But Case was named chairman of the board, seemingly a position that the CEO would answer to. Position titles are one thing, but when tough decisions must be made regarding layoffs, combining departments and divisions, products and services, and territories, the person with the power will have the final say. Turf wars are likely to develop between divisions, products and services, clients and customers, and old friends and new friends that can only be settled by going to the next higher level of authority in the hierarchy for resolution.

Important decisions have to be made about the various products and services the new company will offer. For example, how will AOL integrate its broadband strategy with Time Warner's cable systems and Roadrunner, the high-speed connection company, without disrupting its current alliances with Bell Atlantic, GTE, and DIRECTV? The new company will also have to integrate Time Warner's Book-of-the-Month Club and Columbia House record club online without encouraging the wrath of AOL's big money deals with Amazon.com, Barnesandnoble.com, and Blockbuster.

The new management team will consist of five executives: Stephen Case, chairman; Gerald Levin, CEO; Robert Pittman and Richard Parsons, co-COOs, and Ted Turner, former vice chair of Time Warner, whose new title and duties were not immediately announced. The balance in this group leans toward Time Warner, since Levin, Parsons, and Turner come directly from Time Warner. Decisions and recommendations for the merger will have to be approved by this group

In taking the chairman position rather than the CEO position, Case retained his special team of advisors, known as "Steve's Senior Staff" at AOL, as direct reports in the new company: AOL vice chairman Kenneth J. Novack, public relations consultant Kenneth Larer, senior vice president George Vradenberg III (the firm's public policy coordinator), and chief technology officer William Raduchel. This group met every Monday for lunch to discuss the most pressing issues facing the company and was largely responsible for the merger in the first place. In reporting directly to Case, these four will not be subject to decisions made by CEO Levin and thus be safe from layoffs. The by-laws proposed for the new company state very clearly that those four executives can be appointed and removed only by the action or approval of the chairman of the board. This also would seem to indicate that Case would continue to oversee the broad sweep and direction of the new company to include technology policy, venture-type investments, philanthropy, future innovation, and global public policy. The arrangement would also seem to make these four people immune from decisions made by Levin, and they will not have to jockey for power in the new hierarchy.

Although it seems unusual for the chairman to carve out these four areas to report to him, it means that all of the operating divisions and administrative divisions will report to Levin. That could mean that Levin might have more say-so in operating decisions and some of the difficult merging of functions and operations in the new company. Case seems to be glad to be rid of the day-to-day operational decisions. The real question will be how he reacts when some of the operating decisions go against some of his AOL buddies. Case's power will be most felt in the boardroom, however, where he will be chairman. The new board will be comprised of sixteen members, eight picked by each company. But those who have watched and worked with Levin warn that he is a master of organizational politics. Even in the worst of crises it is difficult to imagine that twelve board members (75 percent) would agree to unseat either the chairman or the CEO.

Another factor to be considered is the location of the headquarters of the two companies. Both locations seemed appropriate for their respective companies—Time Warner in the traditional center of power, New York City, and AOL in the entrepreneurial, high-tech northern Virginia area. In the short run, each would like to stay in their former headquarters, as both facilities will remain operational. The chairman, Case, will need to be in New York City, where the corporate headquarters will be, rather than in his beloved Virginia. On the other hand, most of the daily operations of AOL will remain in Dulles, where the CEO and heads of operations will need to be. Case's roles as policy maker and deal maker would seem to demand his presence in New York. His other role of technology chief would seem to require his presence in Virginia, where the programmers and systems analysts are. The AOL headquarters in Virginia will not be easy to move. AOL employs more than 3,500 workers in the Dulles area and Prince William County, with plans to significantly increase those numbers in the near future as new buildings on AOL's 154-acre campus come online. If the past is a predictor, AOL has often let newly acquired companies stay put. Netscape, for example, has stayed in its original location in Silicon Valley. How much time will each one spend on the other's turf? What is the impact of being on-site to exercise power? Can political moves be effective when the CEO is not on-site?

Two men will share the chief operating officer title and position as co-COOs: Robert Pittman and Richard Parsons. Pittman has experience in both the media side and the Internet side, having been an executive at Time Warner before moving over to be the president and COO at AOL in 1996. Parsons, formerly the president of Time Warner, is noted for his diplomatic skills, which could come in handy in a political dogfight. Pittman is clearly expected to be the heir apparent; but so was Jaime Dimon at the merged Citigroup and he was forced out after a few months, as discussed in Chapter 17. One analyst noted that Pittman may be the key to the whole deal and warned that if Pittman goes into Time Warner as a missionary goes to convert the heathens in movies, publishing, and cable that the Internet is the way to heaven, he may have a difficult time. If, on the other hand, he shows respect for the Time Warner ways and shows genuine interest in learning about its businesses and working together to find new and exciting opportunities, the possibilities may be staggering.

## Case Questions

1. How will communication be one of the most important aspects of how this merger will work?
2. How will the former positions and style of the two leaders interact to make or break this merger?
3. Describe how power will play a role in the continuing efforts to merge these two giants.
4. How will the future of this merger depend on who best manages the organizational politics of the situation?

References: Marc Gunther, "These Guys Want It All," *Fortune*, February 7, 2000, pp. 71–78; Mitchell Lee Marks, "Egos Can Make—and Unmake—Mergers," *Asian Wall Street Journal*, January 27, 2000, p. 10; Carol Hymowitz, "In the Lead: AOL's Bosses, an Unusual Pair, Share Vision—Partners' Joint Control Could Lead to Creation of Management Model," *Asian Wall Street Journal*, January 25, 2000, p. 8; Daniel Okrent, "Happily Ever After?" *Time*, January 24, 2000, pp. 39–43; Joshua Cooper Ramo, "A Two-Man Network," *Time*, January 24, 2000, pp. 46–50; Richard Siklos, Catherine Yang, Andy Reinhardt, Peter Burrows, and Rob Hof, "Welcome to the 21st Century," *Business Week*, January 24, 2000, pp. 36–44; Peter Behr and Greg Schneider, "And If AOL Moves HQ from No Va?: A Vast Influence on the Area May Fade After the Merger with Time Warner, *Washington Post*, January 17, 2000, p. F16; Martin Peers and Nikhil Deogun, "AOL's Case to Retain Link to Key Aides After Merger," *Wall Street Journal*, Brussels, January 17, 2000, p. 7; Matt Murray, Nikhil Deogun, and Nick Wingfield, "A Marriage Meant to Be: AOL, Time Warner Merger Is Facing Questions, Doubts," *Arizona Republic*, January 16, 2000, p. D1; David S. Hilzenrath and Ariana Eunjung Cha, "AOL's Case Moves to Ensure His Power," *Washington Post*, January 15, 2000, p. E01.

chapter

16

# Dimensions of Organization Structure

## Management Preview

It seems as if organizations are always "restructuring." They rearrange the organization chart and make people report to different managers. What they are really doing is trying to find the best way to set up the structure of the organization. This is the first in a two-chapter sequence in which we explore how the structure of an organization can be a major factor in how successfully the organization achieves its goals. In this chapter, we present the basics of organization structure, its building blocks, and the classical ways of designing organization structures. Chapter 17 integrates the basic elements of structure, taking into consideration other factors such as the environment and technology, and presents several perspectives on organization design.

In this chapter, we begin with an overview of organizations and organization structure, defining both terms and placing organization structure in the context of organizational goals and strategy. Second, we discuss the two major perspectives of organizing, the structural configuration view and the operational view. We then discuss the often confusing concepts of responsibility and authority and present an alternative view of authority. Finally, we explain several of the classic views of how organizations should be structured. But first we describe how Sony is changing its organization structure. ■

Masaru Ibuka and Akio Morita founded Tokyo Telecommunications Engineering Corporation in 1946. They developed the first transistor radio in 1955 and changed the name of the company to Sony in 1958. Since that time, the firm has developed revolutionary products such as the Trinitron color television, the Walkman, the compact disc player, the Betacam, the Handycam, the PlayStation, and the MiniDisc system—making Sony the world's leading manufacturer of audio, video, electronic communications, and information technology. Sony employs more than 170,000 people worldwide and had consolidated sales of more than $56 million in 1999. Although it has become a huge multinational enterprise, Sony still follows its founding principle of invention based on innovative technology, and tries to maintain its original small-company spirit.

*"Our top management felt that to prepare the company for the digital network era of the 21st century, it was important to have the most appropriate organization structure in place." — Yoshihide Nakamura, deputy president, Sony Core Technology and Network Company**

And in 1999, Sony restructured its entire operations into four divisional companies: the Home Network Company, the Personal IT Network Company, the Core Technology and Network Company, and Sony Computer Entertainment, Inc. (its only product is the Sony PlayStation). The four smaller divisions are intended to help management and employees maintain that small-company spirit. In addition to reorganizing, Sony plans to consolidate its seventy factories into fifty-five and to reduce its workforce by 10 percent. In addition, two-thirds of the total staff at the central research labs will be reassigned to one of the four new divisions. Spending on research and development is not expected to change much with the reorganization, but it should let the four autonomous units be more flexible.[1] ■

Top management at Sony believes that to be successful in the new digital age, they had to change the organization structure of the company in order to compete. This is not unusual in business and industry these days as many of them struggle to remain competitive in a rapidly changing world. This chapter introduces many of the key concepts of organization structure and sets the stage for understanding the many aspects of developing the appropriate organization design, discussed in Chapter 17.

# The Nature of Organization Structure

In other chapters we discuss key elements of the individual and the factors that tie the individual and the organization together. In a given organization, these factors must fit together within a common framework: the organization's structure.

## Organization Defined

An **organization** is a group of people working together to attain common goals.

An **organization** is a group of people working together to achieve common goals.[2] Top management determines the direction of the organization by defining its purpose, establishing goals to meet that purpose, and formulating strategies to achieve the goals.[3] The definition of purpose gives the organization reason to exist; in effect, it answers the question "What business are we in?"

**Organizational goals** are objectives that management seeks to achieve in pursuing the firm's purpose.

Establishing goals converts the defined purpose into specific, measurable performance targets. **Organizational goals** are objectives that management seeks to achieve in pursuing the purpose of the firm. Goals motivate people to work together. Although each individual's goals are important to the organization, it is the organization's overall goals that are most important. Goals keep the organization on track by focusing the attention and actions of the members. They also give the organization a forward-looking orientation. They do not address past success or failure; rather, they force members to think about and plan for the future.

*"We needed to give people a beacon that they could follow when they were having a tough time with prioritization, leadership, where to go, what hills to take." — Steven A. Ballmer, the new CEO of Microsoft, describing why the software giant was reorganizing.*[4]

**Organization structure** is the system of task, reporting, and authority relationships within which the organization does its work.

Finally, strategies are specific action plans that enable the organization to achieve its goals and thus its purpose. Pursuing a strategy involves developing an organization structure and the processes to do the organization's work.

All organizations have many different tasks to be done and employees with different sets of skills. The West Los Angeles Animal Hospital has several veterinarians, technicians, office staff, and other helpers who work together in a coordinated fashion to serve their clients. Shannon, a one-year-old Labrador retriever, is receiving acupuncture with a needle warmed with slow-burning herbs to help relieve her upset stomach. Her doctor, Dr. William Farber, often uses holistic methods and acupuncture to treat his patients. Although Dr. Farber works for the West Los Angeles Animal Hospital, he can use whatever methods he chooses to make the animals feel better as long as he stays within the rules of the hospital and contributes to the goals of the organization.

## Organization Structure

**Organization structure** is the system of task, reporting, and authority relationships within which the work of the organization is done. Thus, structure defines the form and function of the organization's activities. Structure also defines how the parts of an organization fit together, as is evident from an organization chart.

The purpose of an organization's structure is to order and coordinate the actions of employees to achieve organizational goals. The premise of organized effort is that people can accomplish more by working together than they can separately. The work must be coordinated properly, however, if the potential gains of collective effort are to be realized. Consider what might happen if the thousands of employees at Compaq Computers worked without any kind of structure. Each person might try to build a computer that he or she thought would sell. No two computers would be alike, and each would take months or years to build. The costs of making the computers would be so high that no one would be able to afford them. To produce computers that are both competitive in the marketplace and profitable for the com-

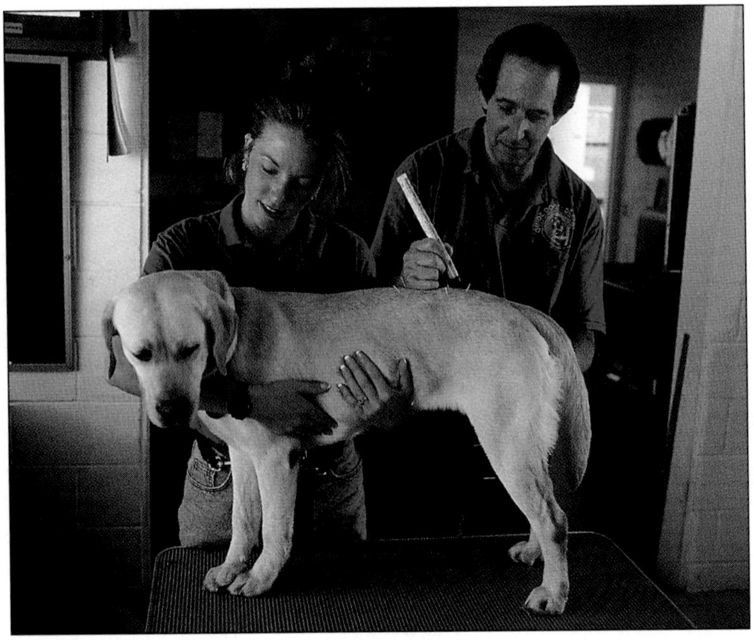

MASTERING CHANGE

## *Athletics Is Big Business*

Everyone knows that professional athletics is big business, with all the trappings of any medium-sized corporation. But have you looked at the athletic department at your local major university lately? The top fifty university athletic departments resemble most corporations. Their core business is usually football, and they have many subsidiary businesses, such as other men's and women's sports. They have numerous sources of revenue, including the sale of merchandise, television income, and sponsorship income from companies such as Nike. They are probably even structured much like a corporation, with functional departments such as finance, marketing, public relations, and human resources (also known as recruiting). The University of Texas athletic department generated $36.1 million in revenue from football alone out of its total revenue of $45.4 million in 1998–1999. University of Texas athletic director (aka CEO) DeLoss Dodds noted that if the athletic department were really a normal business, it probably would eliminate all other sports and exploit its core competency—football.

> *"In my business, we put our paychecks in the mouths of 18 to 22 year olds we can't fire." — Mack Brown, head football coach (and COO) at the University of Texas*

Although football has always been the kingpin on campus, the total budgets have not always been of the current magnitude. The crisis at the University of Texas came in 1992, when seven female athletes filed a lawsuit against the university, claiming it was not in compliance with Title IX, the clause in the Education Amendments Act of 1972 that requires athletic programs to offer equality for women in participation, scholarship allocation, recruitment spending, and coaching resources. Title IX essentially required that most athletic departments double their budget and virtually every activity. Rather than fight the lawsuit, Texas chose to elevate the role of all women's sports on campus. However, to support women's athletics, the university had to dramatically increase the revenue generated by all campus sports. Thus, football had to increase its revenue generation, creating even greater pressure to win. Winning brings in more money to support the rest of the department. In order to generate more revenue, Texas had to increase the emphasis on marketing and merchandising at every level, as well as double its recruiting, student maintenance, training, tutoring, and advising activities.

Currently, women's sports get 43 percent of the athletic department budget, compared with 37 percent when the suit was filed, and represent 43.7 percent of the athletes on campus. So, rather than decrease men's activities, facing the crisis, the University of Texas has increased revenue producing sports in order to be able to compete. And Texas does compete well in most sports. It has one of the most successful athletic programs in the country.

References: Roy S. Johnson, "How One College Program Runs the Business: Inside Longhorn Inc." *Fortune,* December 20, 1999, pp. 160–174 (quote on p. 170); Erik Spanberg, "Nike Likes Texas' Return to Football Prominence," *Business Journal-Portland,* November 19, 1999, p. 17.

pany, Compaq must have a structure in which its employees and managers work together in a coordinated manner. All organizations have some type of structure, even the university athletic departments, as discussed in the "Mastering Change" box.

The task of coordinating the activities of thousands of workers to produce computers that do the work expected of them and that are guaranteed and easy to maintain may seem monumental. Yet whether the goal is to mass produce computers or to make soap, the requirements of organization structure are similar. First, the structure must identify the various tasks or processes necessary for the organization to reach its goals. This dividing of tasks into smaller parts is often called "division of labor." Even small organizations (those with fewer than one hundred employees) use division of labor.[5] Second, the structure must combine and coordinate the divided tasks to achieve a desired level of output. The more interdependent the divided tasks, the more coordination is required.[6] Every organization structure addresses these two fundamental requirements.[7] The various ways of approaching these requirements are what make one organization structure different from another.

Organization structure can be analyzed in three ways. First, we can examine its configuration—that is, its size and shape—as depicted on an organization chart. Second, we can analyze its operational aspects or characteristics, such as separation of specialized tasks, rules and procedures, and decision making. Finally, we can examine responsibility and authority within the organization. In this chapter, we describe organization structure from all three points of view.

# Structural Configuration

An **organization chart** is a diagram showing all people, positions, reporting relationships, and lines of formal communication in the organization.

The structure of an organization is most often described in terms of its organization chart. See Figure 16.1 for an example. A complete **organization chart** shows all people, positions, reporting relationships, and lines of formal com-

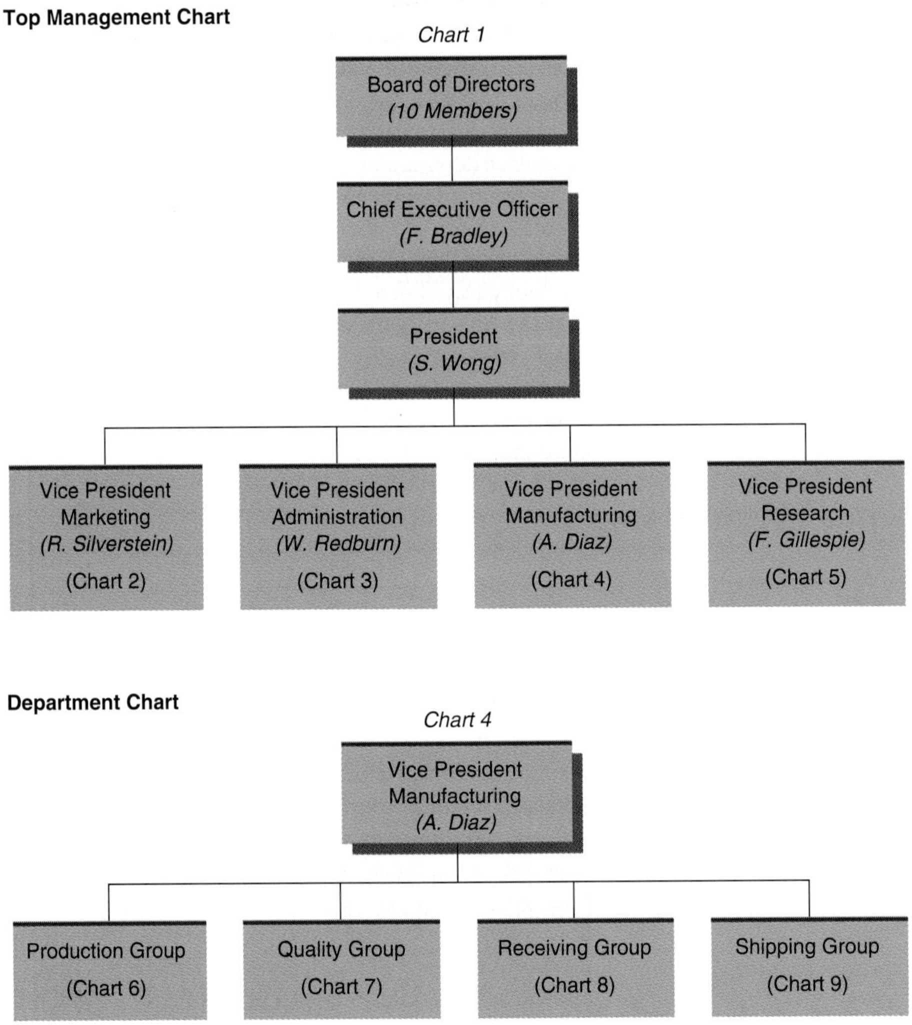


**figure 16.1**

**Examples of Organization Charts**

*These two charts show the similarities between a top-management chart and a department chart. In each, managers have four other managers or work groups reporting to them.*

munication in the organization. (However, as we discussed in Chapter 10, communication is not limited to these formal channels.) For large organizations, several charts may be necessary to show all positions. For example, one chart may show top management, including the board of directors, the chief executive officer, the president, all vice presidents, and important headquarters staff units. Subsequent charts may show the structure of each department and staff unit. Figure 16.1 depicts two organization charts for a large firm; top management is shown in the upper portion of the figure and the manufacturing department in the lower portion. Notice that the structures of the different manufacturing groups are given in separate charts.

The **configuration** of an organization is its shape, which reflects the division of labor and the means of coordinating the divided tasks.

An organization chart depicts reporting relationships and work group memberships and shows how positions and small work groups are combined into departments, which together make up the **configuration**, or shape, of the organization. The configuration of organizations can be analyzed in terms of how the two basic requirements of structure—division of labor and coordination of the divided tasks—are fulfilled.

## Division of Labor

The **division of labor** is the way the organization's work is divided into different jobs to be done by different people.

**Division of labor** is the extent to which the organization's work is separated into different jobs to be done by different people. Division of labor is one of the seven primary characteristics of structuring described by Max Weber,[8] but the concept can be traced back to the eighteenth-century economist Adam Smith. As we noted in Chapter 7, Smith used a study of pin making to promote the idea of dividing production work to increase productivity.[9] Division of labor grew more popular as large organizations became more prevalent in a manufacturing society. This has continued, and most research indicates that large organizations usually have more division of labor than smaller ones.[10]

Division of labor has been found to have both advantages and disadvantages (see Table 16.1). Modern managers and organization theorists are still struggling with the primary disadvantage: division of labor often results in repetitive, boring jobs that undercut worker satisfaction, involvement, and commitment.[11] In addition, extreme division of labor may be incompatible with new, integrated computerized manufacturing technologies that require teams of highly skilled workers.[12]

However, division of labor need not result in boredom. Visualized in terms of a small organization such as a basketball team, it can be quite dynamic. A basketball team consists of five players, each of whom plays a different role on the team.

table 16.1

**Advantages and Disadvantages of Division of Labor**

| Advantages | Disadvantages |
|---|---|
| Efficient use of labor | Routine, repetitive jobs |
| Reduced training costs | Reduced job satisfaction |
| Increased standardization and uniformity of output | Decreased worker involvement and commitment |
| Increased expertise from repetition of tasks | Increased worker alienation |
| | Possible incompatibility with computerized manufacturing technologies |

In professional basketball the five positions typically are center, power forward, small forward, shooting guard, and point guard. The tasks of the players in each position are quite different, so players of different sizes and skills are on the floor at any one time. The teams that win championships, such as the San Antonio Spurs and the Chicago Bulls, use division of labor by having players specialize in doing specified tasks, and doing them impeccably. Similarly, organizations must have specialists who are highly trained and know their specific jobs very well.

## Coordinating the Divided Tasks

Three basic mechanisms are used to help coordinate the divided tasks: departmentalization, span of control, and administrative hierarchy. These mechanisms focus on grouping tasks in some meaningful manner, creating work groups of manageable size, and establishing a system of reporting relationships among supervisors and managers. When companies reorganize, they are usually changing the ways in which the division of labor is coordinated. To some people affected by a reorganization it may seem that things are still just as disorganized as they were before, as illustrated in the cartoon. But there really is a purpose for such reorganization efforts. Top management expects that the work will be better coordinated under the new system.

**Departmentalization** is the manner in which divided tasks are combined and allocated to work groups.

### Departmentalization

**Departmentalization** is the manner in which divided tasks are combined and allocated to work groups. It is a consequence of the division of labor. Because employees engaged in specialized activities can lose sight of overall organizational goals, their work must be coordinated to ensure that it contributes to the welfare of the organization.

It seems that organizations are always reorganizing from one type of disorganization to another. Reorganizing too often may leave employees confused about whom they report to and who reports to them. Usually, however, companies reorganize so that the activities of the people who really do the work will be better coordinated.

Reference: © Randy Glasbergen.

**"Our reorganization is finally completed. Our old disorganized system has been replaced by our new disorganized system."**

There are many possible ways to group, or departmentalize, tasks. The five groupings most often used are business function, process, product or service, customer, and geography. The first two, function and process, derive from the internal operations of the organization; the others are based on external factors. Most organizations tend to use a combination of methods, and departmentalization often changes as organizations evolve.[13]

Departmentalization by business function is based on traditional business functions such as marketing, manufacturing, and human resource administration (see Figure 16.2). In this configuration employees most frequently associate with those engaged in the same function, which helps in communication and cooperation. In a functional group, employees who do similar work can learn from one another by sharing ideas about opportunities and problems they encounter on the job. Unfortunately, functional groups lack an automatic mechanism for coordinating the flow of work through the organization.[14] In other words, employees in a functional structure tend to associate little with those in other parts of the organization. The result can be a narrow focus that limits the coordination of work among functional groups, as when the engineering department fails to provide marketing with product information because it is too busy testing materials to think about sales.

Departmentalization by process is similar to functional departmentalization, except that the focus is much more on specific jobs grouped according to activity. Thus, as Figure 16.2 illustrates, the firm's manufacturing jobs are divided into certain well-defined manufacturing processes: drilling, milling, heat treatment, painting, and assembly. Hospitals often use process departmentalization, grouping the professional employees, such as therapists, according to the types of treatment they provide.

Process groupings encourage specialization and expertise among employees, who tend to concentrate on a single operation and share information with departmental colleagues. A process orientation may develop into an internal career path

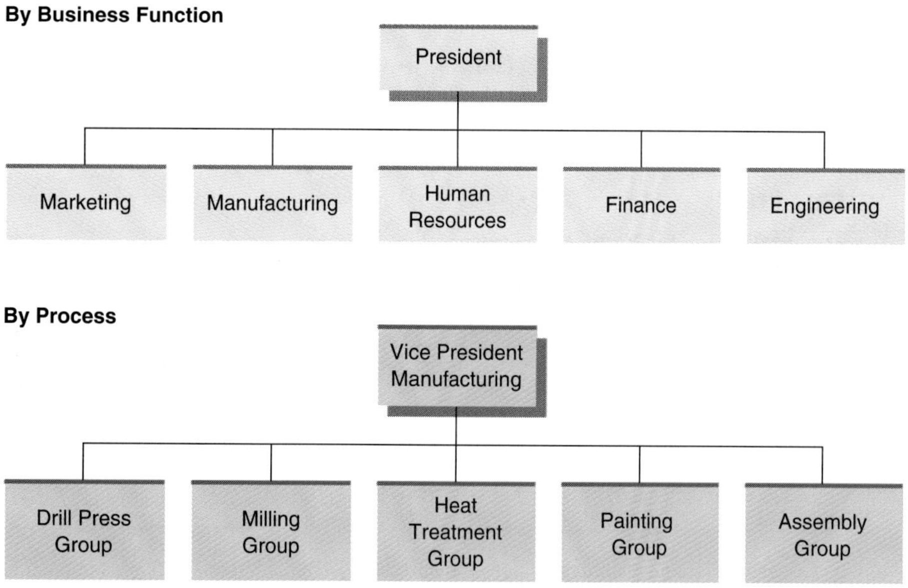


figure 16.2

**Departmentalization by Business Function and by Process**

*These two charts compare departmentalization by business function and by process. "Functions" are the basic business functions, whereas "processes" are the specific categories of jobs that people do.*

and managerial hierarchy within the department. For example, a specialist might become the "lead" person for that specialty—that is, the lead welder or lead press operator. As in functional grouping, however, narrowness of focus can be a problem. Employees in a process group may become so absorbed in the requirements and execution of their operations that they disregard broader considerations, such as overall product flow.[15]

Departmentalization by product or service occurs when employees who work on a particular product or service are members of the same department regardless of their business function or the process in which they are engaged. In the late 1980s, IBM reorganized its operations into five autonomous business units: personal computers, medium-size office systems, mainframes, communications equipment, and components.[16] Although it worked for a while, the company took quite a downturn in the early 1990s.

Facing the Internet age at the beginning of the new century, IBM added several new divisions: a global computer services group to provide computing services, an Internet division to develop, manufacture, and distribute products for the new Internet age, and the Pervasive Computing Division to develop strategies centered on devices, software, and services that make the Internet accessible anywhere, anytime. These new divisions continued IBM's departmentalization by product or service.

Colgate-Palmolive changed its organization structure by eliminating the typical functional divisions, such as basic research, processing, and packaging. Instead, employees were organized into teams based on products, such as pet food, household products, and oral hygiene products. This configuration is shown in Figure 16.3. Since the reorganization, new-product development has increased significantly and cost savings are estimated to be about $40 million.[17]

Departmentalization according to product or service obviously enhances interaction and communication among employees who produce the same product or service and may reduce coordination problems. In this type of configuration, there may be less process specialization but more specialization in the peculiarities of the specific product or service. IBM expected that the new alignment would allow all employees, from designers to manufacturing workers to marketing experts, to become specialists in a particular product line. The disadvantage is that employees may become so interested in their particular product or service that they miss technological improvements or innovations developed in other departments.

figure **16.3**

**Departmentalization by Product or Service**
**a) Colgate-Palmolive's Old Functional Departmentalization**
**b) Colgate-Palmolive's New Product Departmentalization**

*Colgate-Palmolive changed its departmentalization scheme and increased its new product development with cost savings estimated at $40 million.*

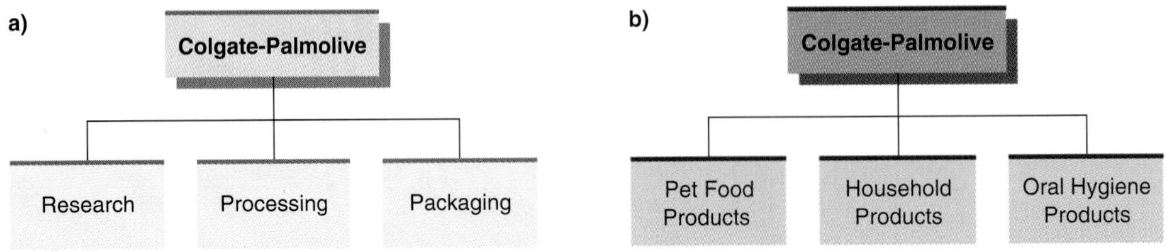

figure 16.4

**Departmentalization by Customer and by Geographic Region**

*Departmentalization by customer or by geographic region is often used in marketing or sales departments in order to focus on specific needs or locations of customers.*

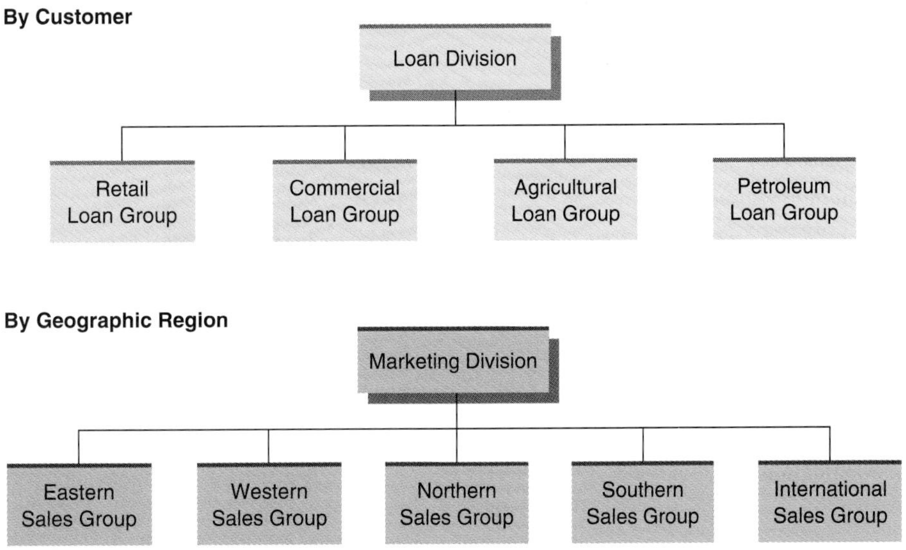


Departmentalization by customer is often called "departmentalization by market." Many lending institutions in Texas, for example, have separate departments for retail, commercial, agriculture, and petroleum loans, as shown in Figure 16.4. When significant groups of customers differ substantially from one another, organizing along customer lines may be the most effective way to provide the best product or service possible. This is why hospital nurses often are grouped by the type of illness they handle; the various maladies demand different treatment and specialized knowledge.[18]

With customer departmentalization there is usually less process specialization because employees must remain flexible to do whatever is necessary to enhance the relationship with customers. This configuration offers the best coordination of the work flow to the customer; however, it may isolate employees from others in their special areas of expertise. For example, if each of a company's three metallurgical specialists is assigned to a different market-based group, these individuals are unlikely to have many opportunities to discuss the latest technological advances in metallurgy.

Departmentalization by geography means that groups are organized according to a region of the country or world. Sales or marketing groups often are arranged by geographic region. As Figure 16.4 illustrates, the marketing effort of a large multinational corporation can be divided according to major geographical divisions. Using a geographically based configuration may result in significant cost savings and better market coverage. On the other hand, it may isolate work groups from activities in the organization's home office or in the technological community because the focus of the work group is solely on affairs within the region. Such a regional focus may foster loyalty to the work group that exceeds commitment to the larger organization. In addition, work-related communication and coordination among groups may be somewhat inefficient.

Many large organizations use a mixed departmentalization scheme. Such organizations may have separate operating divisions based on products, but within each division, departments may be based on business function, process, customers, or geographic region (see Figure 16.5). Which methods work best depends on the

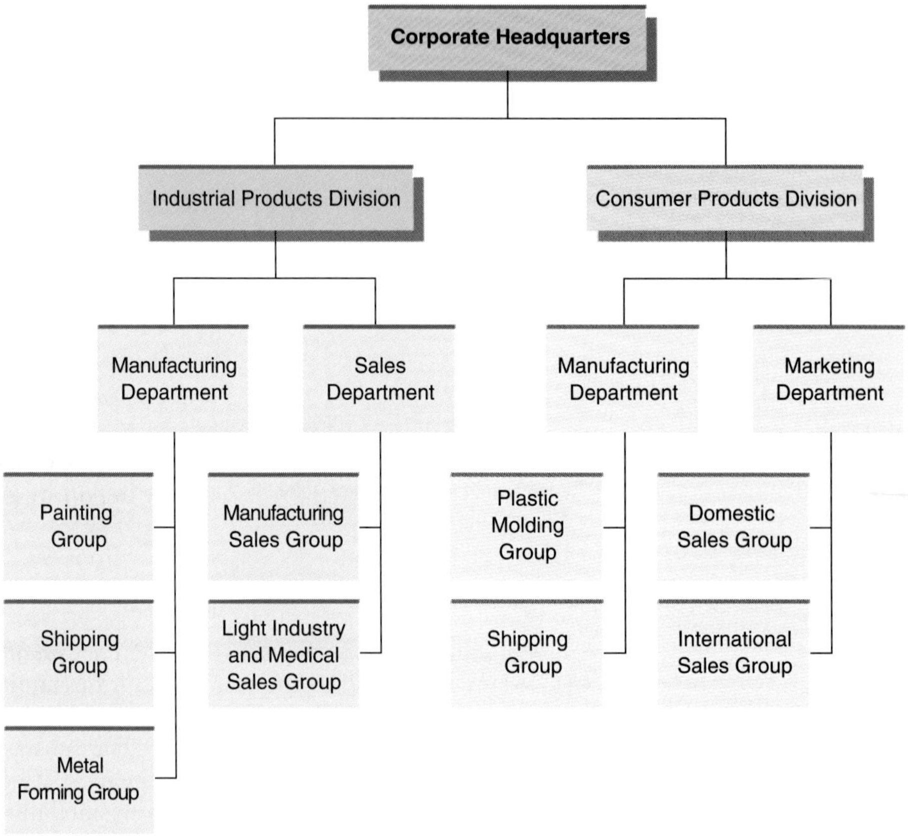


figure 16.5

**Mixed Departmentalization**

*A mixed departmentalization scheme is often used in very large organizations with more complex structures. Headquarters is organized based on products. Industrial products and consumer products are departmentalized on the basis of function. The manufacturing departments are based on process. Sales is based on customer. Marketing is based on geographical regions.*

organization's activities, communication needs, and coordination requirements. Another type of mixed structure often occurs in joint ventures, which are becoming increasingly popular.

The span of control is the number of people who report to a manager.

Span of Control The second dimension of organizational configuration, **span of control**, is the number of people reporting to a manager; thus, it defines the size of the organization's work groups. Span of control is also called "span of management." A manager who has a small span of control can maintain close control over workers and stay in contact with daily operations. If the span of control is large, close control is not possible. Figure 16.6 shows examples of small and large spans of control. Supervisors in the upper portion of the figure have a span of control of sixteen, whereas in the lower portion, supervisors have a span of control of eight.

A number of formulas and rules have been offered for determining the optimal span of control in an organization,[19] but research on the topic has not conclusively identified a foolproof method.[20] Henry Mintzberg concluded that the optimal unit size, or span of control, depends on five conditions:

1. The coordination requirements within the unit, including factors such as the degree of job specialization
2. The similarity of the tasks in the unit
3. The type of information available or needed by unit members
4. Differences in the members' need for autonomy
5. The extent to which members need direct access to the supervisor[21]

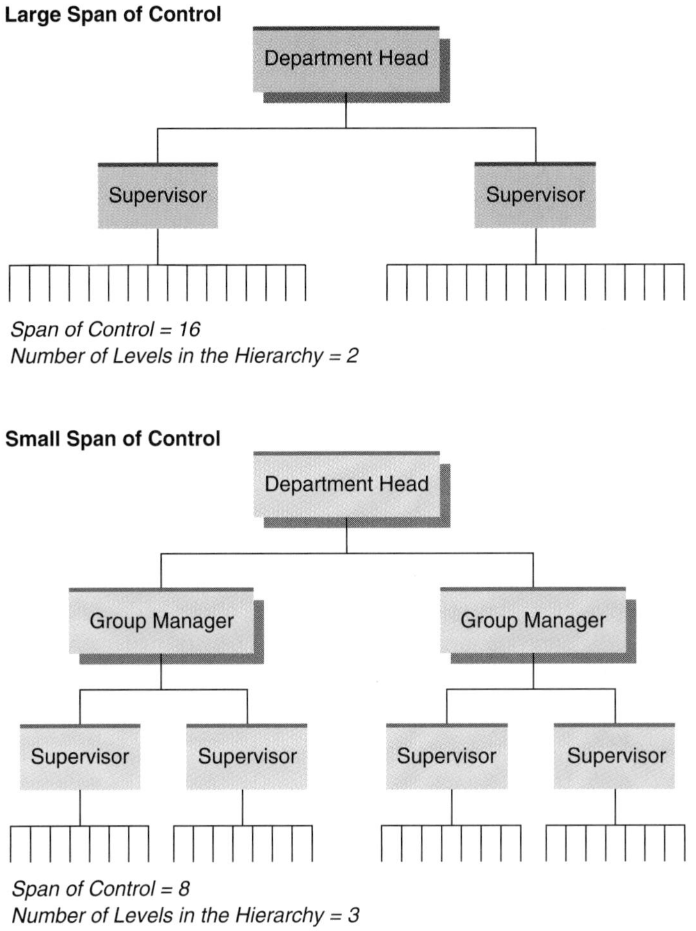


figure 16.6

**Span of Control and Levels in the Administrative Hierarchy**

*These charts show how span of control and the number of levels in the administrative hierarchy are inversely related. The thirty-two first-level employees are in two groups of sixteen in the top chart and in four groups of eight in the bottom chart. Either may be appropriate, depending on the work situation.*

For example, a span of control of sixteen (as shown in Figure 16.6) might be appropriate for a supervisor in a typical manufacturing plant where experienced workers do repetitive production tasks. On the other hand, a span of control of eight or fewer (as shown in Figure 16.6) might be appropriate in a job shop or custom-manufacturing facility in which workers do many different things and the tasks and problems that arise are new and unusual.[22]

Administrative Hierarchy The **administrative hierarchy** is the system of reporting relationships in the organization, from the first level up through the president or CEO. It results from the need for supervisors and managers to coordinate the activities of employees. The size of the administrative hierarchy is inversely related to the span of control: organizations with a small span of control have many managers in the hierarchy; those with a large span of control have a smaller administrative hierarchy. Companies often rearrange their administrative hierarchies to achieve more efficient operations. Gateway 2005 rearranged its management and moved the company's headquarters, as discussed in the "Talking Technology" box.

Using Figure 16.6 again, we can examine the effects of small and large spans of control on the number of hierarchical levels. The smaller span of control for the supervisors in the lower portion of the figure requires that there be four supervisors rather than two. Correspondingly, another management layer is needed to keep the department head's span of control at two. Thus, when the span of control is small, the workers are under tighter supervision, and there are more administrative levels. When the span of control is large, as in the upper portion of the figure, production workers are not closely supervised, and there are fewer administrative levels. Because it measures the number of management personnel, or administrators, in the organization, the administrative hierarchy is sometimes called the "administrative component," "administrative intensity," or "administrative ratio."

The **administrative hierarchy** is the system of reporting relationships in the organization, from the lowest to the highest managerial levels.

The size of the administrative hierarchy also relates to the overall size of the organization. As an organization's size increases, so do its complexity and the requirements for coordination, necessitating proportionately more people to manage the business. However, this conclusion defines the administrative component as including the entire administrative hierarchy—that is, all of the support staff

TALKING TECHNOLOGY

## *Gateway Reinvents Itself*

Gateway 2000 is now Gateway 2005. Always a maverick in the high-tech world of personal computers, Chairman Theodore W. Waitt spent 1998 changing everything about the unusual company except the boxes he ships computers in—they remain black-and-white spotted like a Holstein cow. But in a period in which all other computer makers are experiencing declining sales and earnings, Gateway is still doing well—partially because it now does so much more than just sell, make, and ship personal computers. No one knows when the changes will stop, not even Waitt, who claims the company has been completely reinvented almost every year since he started it in North Sioux City, South Dakota.

*"Every year for the past 14 years, we've been a new company."*
*—Theodore W. Waitt, founder Gateway 2005*

So what's new? Waitt started by reinventing his management team. He could not get new top managers to join him in South Dakota, so he moved the company to a fashionable area near San Diego, California, and hired ten of his top fourteen managers in 1998. Waitt has stepped down as CEO, promoting associate Jeffrey Weitzen as CEO, although Waitt is still chairman. Weitzen joined Gateway in January 1998 and was influential in developing the change strategy for the company. Gateway now plans to do so much more that just sell you a PC box. It has reorganized to develop more ways to stay close to its buyers. Gateway wants to help you trade in your obsolete PC every two years, to be your Internet shopping service, and to provide your Internet service, your peripherals, and the technology to help you integrate your television, personal computers, shopping, games, and personal business. The company estimates that in a few years, PCs will still provide lots of revenues, but other goods and services will provide most of its earnings. A new management team and organization structure were necessary to make that possible.

References: David Kirkpatrick, "New Home. New CEO. Gateway Is Moo and Improved," *Fortune*, December 20, 1999, pp. 44–46; "Weitzen to Become Gateway's New CEO; Waitt Still Chairman," *Wall Street Journal*, December 9, 1999, p. B16; William J. Holstein and Susan Gregory Thomas, "Gateway Gets Citified," *U.S. News & World Report*, May 3, 1999, p. 42; Elizabeth Corcoran, "Gateway 2005," *Forbes*, March 8, 1999, p. 52.

groups, such as personnel and financial services, legal staff, and others. Defined in this way, the administrative component in a large company may seem huge compared with the number of production workers. On the other hand, research that separates the support staff and clerical functions from the management hierarchy has found that the ratio of managers to total employees actually decreases with increases in the organization's size. Other, more recent research has shown that the size of the administrative hierarchy and the overall size of the organization are not related in a straightforward manner, especially during periods of growth and decline.[23]

*"There used to be eleven layers between me and the lowest-level employees; now there are five." — William Stavropoulos, CEO of Dow Chemical, describing Dow's new organization structure.[24]*

The popular movement of downsizing has been partially a reaction to the complexity that comes with increasing organization size. Much of the literature on organizational downsizing has proposed that it results in lower overhead costs, less bureaucracy, faster decision making, smoother communications, and increases in productivity.[25]

These expectations are due to the effort to reduce the administrative hierarchy by cutting out layers of middle managers. Unfortunately, many downsizing efforts have resulted in poorer communication, reduced productivity, and lower employee morale because the downsizing is done indiscriminately, without regard for the jobs that people actually do, the coordination needs of the organization, and the additional training that may be necessary for the survivors.[26]

# Structure and Operations

Some important aspects of organization structure do not appear on the organization chart and thus are quite different from the configurational aspects discussed in the previous section. In this section, we examine the structural policies that affect operations and prescribe or restrict how employees behave in their organizational activities.[27] The two primary aspects of these policies are centralization of decision making and formalization of rules and procedures.

## Centralization

**Centralization** is a structural policy in which decision-making authority is concentrated at the top of the organizational hierarchy.

The first structural policy that affects operations is **centralization**, wherein decision-making authority is concentrated at the top of the organizational hierarchy. At the opposite end of the continuum is decentralization, in which decisions are made throughout the hierarchy.[28] Increasingly, centralization is being discussed in terms of participation in decision making.[29] In decentralized organizations, lower-level employees participate in making decisions. The changes that Jack Smith made in 1993 and 1996 at General Motors were intended to decentralize decision making throughout the company. Smith dismantled the old divisional structure, created a single unit called North American Operations, and abolished a tangle of management committees that slowed down decision making. Managers are now encouraged to make decisions on new designs and pricing that used to take weeks to circulate through the committee structure on their way to the top.[30]

*"Decisions weren't getting made because of structural impediments." — Ben Rosen, chairman of the board of Compaq, describing the reasons for Compaq's 1999 change in management.*[31]

Decision making in organizations is more complex than the simple centralized-decentralized classification indicates. In Chapter 15, we discussed organizational decision making in more depth. One of the major distinctions we made there was that some decisions are relatively routine and require only the application of a decision rule. These decisions are programmed decisions, whereas those that are not routine are nonprogrammed. The decision rules for programmed decisions are formalized for the organization. This difference between programmed and nonprogrammed decisions tends to cloud the distinction between centralization and decentralization. For even if decision making is decentralized, the decisions themselves may be programmed and tightly circumscribed.

If there is little employee participation in decision making, then decision making is centralized, regardless of the nature of the decisions being made. At the other extreme, if individuals or groups participate extensively in making nonprogrammed decisions, the structure can be described as truly decentralized. If

At Abercrombie & Fitch, the CEO Michael Jeffries makes the decisions on just about everything having to do with the company from the themes for its stores to hiring employees. Everything is highly choreographed by Jeffries from company headquarters in Columbus, Ohio, from the casual feeling in the stores to the coordination of which shoes employees are allowed to wear with each type of pants. For example, black shoes are never to be worn because Abercrombie feels they don't represent the desired college campus image. Jeffries even designs the store displays and web sites—even how each store smells! He believes that if he loses control for even a short time, sales suffer, as happened in the area of women's sweaters in 1999.

individuals or groups participate extensively in decision making but mainly in programmed decisions, the structure is called "formalized decentralization." Formalized decentralization is a common way to provide decision-making involvement for employees at many different levels in the organization while maintaining control and predictability.

Participative management has been described as a total management system in which people are involved in the daily decision making and management of the organization. As part of an organization's culture, participative management can contribute significantly to the long-term success of an organization.[32] It has been described as effective and, in fact, morally necessary in organizations. Thus, for many people, participation in decision making has become more than a simple aspect of organization structure. Caution is required, however, because if middle managers are to make effective decisions, as participative management requires, they must have sufficient information.[33] Honda Motor Co. originally chose a product departmentalization strategy when it introduced the Acura.[34] Honda of America, however, later changed its structure by decentralizing and using more participation with great success.[35]

## Formalization

**Formalization** is the degree to which rules and procedures shape the jobs and activities of employees.

**Formalization** is the degree to which rules and procedures shape employees' jobs and activities. The purpose of formalization is to predict and control how employees behave on the job.[36] Rules and procedures can be both explicit and implicit. Explicit rules are set down in job descriptions, policy and procedures manuals, or office memos. (In one large company that continually issues directives attempting to limit employee activities, workers refer to them as "Gestapo" memos because they require employees to follow harsh rules.) Implicit rules may develop as employees become accustomed to doing things in a certain way over a period of time.[37] Though unwritten, these established ways of getting things done become standard operating procedures with the same effect on employee behavior as written rules.

We can assess formalization in organizations by looking at the proportion of jobs that are governed by rules and procedures and the extent to which those rules permit variation. More formalized organizations have a higher proportion of rule-bound jobs and less tolerance for rule violations.[38] Increasing formalization may affect the design of jobs throughout the organization,[39] as well as employee motivation[40] and work group interactions.[41] The specific effects of formalization on employees are still unclear, however.[42]

Organizations tend to add more rules and procedures as the need for control of operations increases. Some organizations have become so formalized that they have rules for how to make new rules! One large state university created such rules in the form of a three-page document entitled "Procedures for Rule Adoption" that was added to the four-inch-thick Policy and Procedures Manual. The new policy first defines terms such as "university," "board," and "rule" and lists ten exceptions that describe when this policy on rule adoptions does not apply. It then presents a nine-step process for adopting a new rule within the university.

Other organizations are trying to become less formalized by reducing the number of rules and procedures employees must follow. In this way, Chevron cut the number of its rules and procedures from over four hundred to eighteen. Highly detailed procedures for hiring were eliminated in favor of letting managers make hiring decisions based on common sense.[43]

Another approach to organizational formalization attempts to describe how, when, and why good managers should bend or break a rule.[44] Although rules exist in some form in almost every organization, how strictly they are enforced varies significantly from one organization to another and even within a single organization. Some managers argue that "a rule is a rule" and that all rules must be enforced to control employee behaviors and prevent chaos in the organization. Other managers act as if "all rules are made to be broken" and see rules as stumbling blocks on the way to effective action. Neither point of view is better for the organization; rather, a more balanced approach is recommended.

The test of a good manager in a formalized organization may be how well he or she uses appropriate judgment in making exceptions to rules. A balanced approach to making exceptions to rules should do two things. First, it should recognize that individuals are unique and that the organization can benefit from making exceptions that capitalize on exceptional capabilities. For example, suppose an engineering design department with a rule mandating equal access to tools and equipment acquires a limited amount of specialized equipment, such as personal computers. The department manager decides to make an exception to the equal-access rule by assigning the computers to the designers the manager believes will use them the most and with the best results instead of making them available for use by all. Second, a balanced approach should recognize the commonalties among employees. Managers should make exceptions to rules only when there is a true and meaningful difference between individuals rather than base exceptions on features such as race, sex, appearance, or social factors.

# Responsibility and Authority

Responsibility and authority are related to both configurational and operational aspects of organization structure. For example, the organization chart shows who reports to whom at all levels in the organization. From the operational perspective, the degree of centralization defines the locus of decision-making authority in the organization. However, often there is some confusion about what responsibility and authority really mean for managers and how the two terms relate to each other.

## Responsibility

**Responsibility** is an obligation to do something with the expectation of achieving some act or output.

**Responsibility** is an obligation to do something with the expectation that some act or output will result. For example, a manager may expect an employee to write and present a proposal for a new program by a certain date; thus, the employee is responsible for preparing the proposal.

Responsibility ultimately derives from the ownership of the organization. The owners hire or appoint a group, often a board of directors, to be responsible for managing the organization, making the decisions, and reaching the goals set by the owners. A downward chain of responsibility is then established. The board hires a president to be responsible for running the organization. The president hires more people and holds them responsible for accomplishing designated tasks that enable the president to produce the results expected by the board and the owners.

*"I think it's a mistake to designate a No. 2 to run the business. I like a CEO who does that job himself." — Warren Buffett, commenting on the lack of a No. 2 person at Coca-Cola.*[45]

The chain extends throughout the organization because each manager has an obligation to fulfill: to appropriately employ organizational resources (people, money, and equipment) to meet the owners' expectations. Although managers seemingly pass responsibility on to others to achieve results, each manager is still held responsible for the outputs of those to whom he or she delegates tasks.

A manager responsible for a work group assigns tasks to members of the group. Each group member is then responsible for doing his or her task. Yet the manager remains responsible for each task and for the work of the group as a whole. This means that managers can take on the responsibility of others but cannot shed their own responsibility onto those below them in the hierarchy.

## Authority

**Authority** is power that has been legitimized within a particular social context.

**Authority** is power that has been legitimized within a specific social context.[46] (Power is discussed in Chapter 14.) Only when power is part of an official organizational role does it become authority. Authority includes the legitimate right to use resources to accomplish expected outcomes. As we discussed in the previous section, the authority to make decisions may be restricted to the top levels of the organization or dispersed throughout the organization.

Like responsibility, authority originates in the ownership of the organization. The owners establish a group of directors who are responsible for managing the organization's affairs. The directors, in turn, authorize people in the organization to make decisions and to use organizational resources. Thus, they delegate authority, or power in a social context, to others.

Authority is linked to responsibility because a manager responsible for accomplishing certain results must have the authority to use resources to achieve those results.[47] The relationship between responsibility and authority must be one of parity; that is, the authority over resources must be sufficient to enable the manager to meet the output expectations of others.

This picture shows Felipe Pérez Roque, the 34-year-old protégé of Fidel Castro, leader of the communist government in Cuba. Castro, who has been in power more than 40 years, still controls most governmental affairs in Cuba, but he is gradually beginning the transition so that the government can survive when he is no longer around. Roque, although quite young and still relatively unknown, has been involved behind the scenes for more than a decade, leading the students' union, heading various construction projects, moving into the Palace of the Revolution as Castro's private secretary, and serving as his country's foreign minister. As foreign minister, Roque has been delegated the job of leading the battle against the United States embargo, once the primary job of Castro, himself.

But authority and responsibility differ in significant ways. Responsibility cannot be delegated down to others (as discussed in the previous section), but authority can. One complaint often heard from employees is that they have too much responsibility but not enough authority to get the job done. This indicates a lack of parity between responsibility and authority. Managers usually are quite willing to hold individuals responsible for specific tasks but are reluctant to delegate enough authority to do the job. In effect, managers try to rid themselves of responsibility for results (which they cannot do), yet they rarely like to give away their cherished authority over resources.

**Delegation** is the transfer to others of authority to make decisions and use organizational resources.

**Delegation** is the transfer of authority to make decisions and use organizational resources to others. Delegation of authority to make decisions to lower-level managers is common in organizations today. The important thing is to give lower-level managers authority to carry out the decisions they make. Managers typically have difficulty in delegating successfully. In the "Building Organizational Behavior Skills" exercise at the end of this chapter you will have a chance to practice delegation.

The Iran-Contra affair of 1987–88 is a good example of the difference between authority and responsibility. Some believe the Reagan administration confused delegation of authority with abdication of responsibility.[48] President Reagan delegated a great deal of authority to subordinates but did not require that they keep him informed, and they made no effort to do so. Hence, delegation of authority by the administration was appropriate and necessary, but failing to require progress reports to keep informed and in control of operations resulted in the administration trying to avoid responsibility. Although the president did hold his subordinates responsible for their actions, he ultimately—and rightfully—retained full responsibility.

## An Alternative View of Authority

So far we have described authority as a "top-down" function in organizations; that is, authority originates at the top and is delegated downward, as the managers at the top consider appropriate. In author Chester Barnard's alternative perspective, authority is seen as originating in the individual, who can choose whether or not to follow a directive from above. The choice of whether to comply with a directive is based on the degree to which the individual understands it, feels able to carry it out, and believes it to be in the best interests of the organization and consistent with personal values.[49] This perspective has been called the **acceptance theory of authority** because it means that the manager's authority depends on the subordinate's acceptance of the manager's right to give the directive and to expect compliance.

The **acceptance theory of authority** says that the authority of a manager depends on the subordinate's acceptance of the manager's right to give directives and to expect compliance with them.

For example, assume that you are a marketing analyst, and your company has a painting crew in the maintenance department. For some reason your manager has told you to repaint your own office over the weekend. You probably would question your manager's authority to make you do this work. In fact, you would probably refuse to do it. If you received a similar request to work over the weekend to finish a report, you would be more likely to accept it and carry it out. Thus, by either accepting or rejecting the directives of a supervisor, workers can limit supervisory authority.[50] In most organizational situations, employees accept a manager's right to expect compliance on normal, reasonable directives because of the manager's legitimate position in the organizational hierarchy or in the social context of the organization. They may choose to disobey a directive and must accept the consequences if they do not accept the manager's right.

# Classic Views of Structure

The earliest views of organization structure combined the elements of organization configuration and operation into recommendations on how organizations should be structured. These views have often been called "classical organization theory" and include Max Weber's idea of the ideal bureaucracy, the classic organizing principles of Henri Fayol, and the human organization view of Rensis Likert. Although all three are universal approaches, their concerns and structural prescriptions differ significantly.

## Ideal Bureaucracy

Weber's **ideal bureaucracy** is characterized by a hierarchy of authority and a system of rules and procedures designed to create an optimally effective system for large organizations.

Weber's **ideal bureaucracy**, presented in Chapter 1, was an organizational system characterized by a hierarchy of authority and a system of rules and procedures that, if followed, would create a maximally effective system for large organizations. Weber, writing at a time when organizations were inherently inefficient, claimed that the bureaucratic form of administration is superior to other forms of management with respect to stability, control, and predictability of outcomes.[51]

Weber's ideal bureaucracy had seven essential characteristics and utilized several of the building blocks discussed in this chapter, including the division of labor, hierarchy of authority, and rules and procedures. Weber intended these characteristics to ensure order and predictability in relationships among people and jobs in the bureaucracy. But it is easy to see how the same features can lead to sluggishness, inefficiency, and red tape. The administrative system can easily break down if any of the characteristics are carried to an extreme or are violated. For example, if endless arrays of rules and procedures bog down employees who must find the precise rule to follow every time they do something, responses to routine client or customer requests may slow to a crawl. Moreover, subsequent writers have said that Weber's view of authority is too rigid and have suggested that the bureaucratic organization may impede creativity and innovation and result in a lack of compassion for the individual in the organization.[52] In other words, the impersonality that is supposed to foster objectivity in a bureaucracy may result in serious difficulties for both employees and the organization. However, some organizations retain some characteristics of a bureaucratic structure while remaining innovative and productive.

*"The challenge is to find ways to constantly refresh the components of bureaucracy so that it remains the healthy kind rather than the destructive kind." — Roger R. Klene, President and COO of Mott Corporation*[53]

Paul Adler has recently countered the currently popular movements of "bureaucracy busting" by noting that large-scale, complex organizations still need some of the basic characteristics that Weber described—hierarchical structure, formalized procedures, and staff expertise—in order to avoid chaos and ensure efficiency, conformance quality, and timeliness. Adler further proposes a second type of bureaucracy that essentially serves an enabling function in organizations.[54] The need for bureaucracy is not past. Bureaucracy, or at least some of its elements, is still critical for designing effective organizations.

## The Classic Principles of Organizing

Henri Fayol, a French engineer and chief executive officer of a mining company, presented a second classic view of the organization structure at the turn of the century. Drawing on his experience as a manager, Fayol was the first to classify the essential elements of management—now usually called **management functions**—as planning, organizing, command, coordination, and control.[55] In addition, he presented fourteen principles of organizing that he considered an indispensable code for managers (see Table 16.2).

The **management functions** set forth by Henri Fayol include planning, organizing, command, coordination, and control.

Fayol's principles have proved extraordinarily influential; they have served as the basis for the development of generally accepted means of organizing. For example, Fayol's "unity of command" principle means that employees should receive directions from only one person, and "unity of direction" means that tasks with the same objective should have a common supervisor. Combining these two principles with division of labor, authority, and responsibility results in a system of tasks and reporting and authority relationships that is the very essence of organizing. Fayol's principles thus provide the framework for the organization chart and the coordination of work.

The classic principles have been criticized on several counts. First, they ignore factors such as individual motivation, leadership, and informal groups—the human element in organizations. This line of criticism asserts that the classic principles result in a mechanical organization into which people must fit, regardless of their interests, abilities, or motivations. The principles have also been criticized for their lack of operational specificity in that Fayol described the principles as universal truths but did not specify the means of applying many of them. Finally, Fayol's principles have been discounted because they were not supported by scientific evidence; Fayol presented them as universal principles, backed by no evidence other than his experience.[56]

table 16.2

**Fayol's Classic Principles of Organizing**

| Principle | Fayol's Comments |
|---|---|
| 1. Division of work | Individuals and managers work on the same part or task. |
| 2. Authority and responsibility | Authority—right to give orders; power to exact obedience; goes with responsibility for reward and punishment. |
| 3. Discipline | Obedience, application, energy, behavior. Agreement between firm and individual. |
| 4. Unity of command | Employee receives orders from one superior. |
| 5. Unity of direction | One head and one plan for activities with the same objective. |
| 6. Subordination of individual interest to general interest | Objectives of the organization come before objectives of the individual. |
| 7. Remuneration of personnel | Pay should be fair to the organization and the individual; discussed various forms. |
| 8. Centralization | Proportion of discretion held by the manager compared to that allowed to subordinates. |
| 9. Scalar chain | Line of authority from lowest to top. |
| 10. Order | A place for everyone and everyone in his or her place. |
| 11. Equity | Combination of kindness and justice; equality of treatment. |
| 12. Stability of tenure of personnel | Stability of managerial personnel; time to get used to work. |
| 13. Initiative | Power of thinking out and executing a plan. |
| 14. Esprit de corps | Harmony and union among personnel is strength. |

Reference: From *General and Industrial Management*, by Henri Fayol. Copyright © Lake Publishing 1984, Belmont, CA 94002. Used with permission.

## Human Organization

Rensis Likert's **human organization** approach is based on supportive relationships, participation, and overlapping work groups.

Rensis Likert called his approach to organization structure the **human organization**.[57] Because Likert, like others, had criticized Fayol's classic principles for overlooking human factors, it is not surprising that his approach centered on the principles of supportive relationships, employee participation, and overlapping work groups.

The term "supportive relationships" suggests that in all organizational activities, individuals should be treated in such a way that they experience feelings of support, self-worth, and importance. By "employee participation" Likert meant that the work group needs to be involved in decisions that affect it, thereby enhancing the employee's sense of supportiveness and self-worth. The principle of "overlapping work groups" means that work groups are linked, with managers serving as the "linking pins." Each manager (except the highest ranking) is a member of two groups: a work group that he or she supervises and a management group composed of the manager's peers and their supervisor. Coordination and communication grow stronger when the managers perform the linking function by sharing problems, decisions, and information both upward and downward in the groups to which they belong. The human organization concept rests on the assumption that people work best in highly cohesive groups oriented toward organizational goals. Management's function is to make sure the work groups are linked for effective coordination and communication.

Likert described four systems of organizing, which he called management systems, whose characteristics are summarized in Table 16.3. System 1, the exploitive authoritative system, can be characterized as the classic bureaucracy. System 4, the

table 16.3 **Characteristics of Likert's Four Management Systems**

| Characteristic | System 1: Exploitive Authoritative | System 2: Benevolent Authoritative | System 3: Consultative | System 4: Participative Group |
|---|---|---|---|---|
| **Leadership** | | | | |
| • Trust in subordinates | None | None | Substantial | Complete |
| • Subordinates' ideas | Seldom used | Sometimes used | Usually used | Always used |
| **Motivational Forces** | | | | |
| • Motives tapped | Security, status | Economic, ego | Substantial | Complete |
| • Level of satisfaction | Overall dissatisfaction | Some moderate satisfaction | Moderate satisfaction | High satisfaction |
| **Communication** | | | | |
| • Amount | Very little | Little | Moderate | Much |
| • Direction | Downward | Mostly downward | Down, up | Down, up, lateral |
| **Interaction-Influence** | | | | |
| • Amount | None | None | Substantial | Complete |
| • Cooperative teamwork | None | Virtually none | Moderate | Substantial |
| **Decision Making** | | | | |
| • Locus | Top | Policy decided at top | Broad policy decided at top | All levels |
| • Subordinates involved | Not at all | Sometimes consulted | Usually consulted | Fully involved |
| **Goal Setting** | | | | |
| • Manner | Orders | Orders with comments | Set after discussion | Group participation |
| • Acceptance | Covertly resisted | Frequently resisted | Sometimes resisted | Fully accepted |
| **Control Processes** | | | | |
| • Level | Top | None | Some below top | All levels |
| • Information | Incomplete, inaccurate | Often incomplete, inaccurate | Moderately complete, accurate | Complete, accurate |
| **Performance** | | | | |
| • Goals and Training | Mediocre | Fair to good | Good | Excellent |

Reference: Adapted from Rensis Likert, *New Patterns of Management* (New York: McGraw-Hill, 1961), pp. 223–233; and Rensis Likert, *The Human Organization* (New York: McGraw-Hill, 1967), pp. 197, 198, 201, 203, 210, and 211.

participative group, is the organization design Likert favored. System 2, the benevolent authoritative system, and system 3, the consultative system, are less extreme than either system 1 or system 4.

Likert described all four systems in terms of eight organizational variables: leadership processes, motivational forces, communication processes, interaction-influence processes, decision-making processes, goal-setting processes, control processes, and performance goals and training. Likert believed that work groups should be able to overlap horizontally as well as vertically where necessary to accomplish tasks. This feature is directly contrary to the classic principle that advocates unity of command. In addition, rather than the hierarchical chain of command, Likert favored the linking-pin concept of overlapping work groups for making decisions and resolving conflicts.

Research support for Likert's human organization emanates primarily from Likert and his associates' work at the Institute for Social Research at the University of Michigan. Although their research has upheld the basic propositions of the approach, it is not entirely convincing. One review of the evidence suggested that although research has shown characteristics of System 4 to be associated with positive worker attitudes and, in some cases, increased productivity, it is not clear that the characteristics of the human organization "caused" the positive results.[58] It may have been that positive attitudes and high productivity allowed the organization structure to be participative and provided the atmosphere for the development of supportive relationships. Likert's design has also been criticized for focusing almost exclusively on individuals and groups and not dealing extensively with structural issues. Overall, the most compelling support for this approach is at the individual and work-group levels. In some ways, Likert's System 4 is much like the team-based organization popular today.

Thus, the classic views of organization embody the key elements of organization structure. Each view, however, combined these key elements in different ways and with other management elements. These three classic views are typical of how the early writers attempted to prescribe a universal approach to organization structure that would be best in all situations. In the next chapter we describe other views of organization structure that may be effective, depending on the organizational situation.

## Synopsis

The structure of an organization is the system of task, reporting, and authority relationships within which the organization does its work. The purpose of organization structure is to order and coordinate the actions of employees to achieve organizational goals. Every organization structure addresses two fundamental issues: dividing available labor according to the tasks to be performed and combining and coordinating divided tasks to ensure that tasks are accomplished.

An organization chart shows reporting relationships, work group memberships, departments, and formal lines of communication. In a broader sense, an organization chart shows the configuration, or shape, of the organization. Configuration has four dimensions: division of labor, departmentalization, span of control, and administrative hierarchy. Division of labor is the separation of work into different jobs to be done by different people. Departmentalization is the manner in which the divided tasks are combined and allocated to work groups for coordination. Tasks can be combined into departments on the basis of business function, process, product, customer, and geographic region. Span of control is the number of people reporting to a manager; it also defines the size of work groups and is inversely related to the number of hierarchical levels in the organization. The administrative hierarchy is the system of reporting relationships in the organization.

Structural policies prescribe how employees should behave in their organizational activities. Such policies include formalization of rules and procedures and centralization of decision making. Formalization is the degree to which rules and procedures shape employees' jobs and activities. The purpose of formalization is to predict and control how employees behave on the job. Explicit rules are set down in job descriptions, policy and procedures manuals, and office memos. Implicit rules develop over time as employees become accustomed to doing things in certain ways.

Centralization concentrates decision-making authority at the top of the organizational hierarchy; under decentralization, decisions are made throughout the hierarchy.

Responsibility is an obligation to do something with the expectation of achieving some output. Authority is power that has been legitimized within a specific social context. Authority includes the legitimate right to use resources to accomplish expected outcomes. The relationship between responsibility and authority needs to be one of parity; that is, employees must have enough authority over resources to meet the expectations of others.

Weber's ideal bureaucracy, Fayol's classic principles of organizing, and Likert's human organization cover many of the key features of organization structure. Weber's bureaucratic form of administration was intended to ensure stability, control, and predictable outcomes. Rules and procedures, division of labor, a hierarchy of authority, technical competence, separation of ownership, rights and property differentiation, and documentation characterize the ideal bureaucracy.

Fayol's classic principles included departmentalization, unity of command, and unity of direction; they came to be generally accepted as means of organizing. Taken together, the fourteen principles provided the basis for the modern organization chart and for coordinating work.

Likert's human organization was based on the principles of supportive relationships, employee participation, and overlapping work groups. Likert described the human organization in terms of eight variables based on the assumption that people work best in highly supportive and cohesive work groups oriented toward organization goals.

## Discussion Questions

1. Define "organization structure" and explain its role in the process of managing the organization.
2. What is the purpose of organization structure? What would an organization be like without a structure?
3. In what ways are aspects of the organization structure analogous to the structural parts of the human body?
4. How is labor divided in your college or university? In what other ways could your college or university be departmentalized?
5. What types of organizations could benefit from a small span of control? What types might benefit from a large span of control?
6. Discuss how increasing formalization might affect the role conflict and role ambiguity of employees. How might the impact of formalization differ for research scientists, machine operators, and bank tellers?
7. How might centralization or decentralization affect the job characteristics specified in job design?
8. When a group makes a decision, how is responsibility for the decision apportioned among the members?
9. Why do employees typically want more authority and less responsibility?
10. Consider the job you now hold or one that you held in the past. Did your boss have the authority to direct your work? Why did he or she have this authority?
11. Describe at least four features of organization structure that were important parts of the classic view of organizing.

# Organizational Behavior Case for Discussion

## Disney Reorganizes to Rebound

In 1999, the Walt Disney Co. experienced a decline in key performance indicators that had many investors concerned about the future financial health of the company. The stock price was down 37 percent because, operating income was down 17 percent, net income was down 26 percent, and earnings per share were down 27 percent. All of this occurred after thirteen years of success following the company's financial crisis in the mid-1980s. Most of the attention this time focused on CEO Michael Eisner, who is credited with Disney's earlier turnaround and the successes of the past thirteen years. Eisner claims that the declining numbers do not indicate any sort of major problem, but he is a very "hands-on" CEO. He is autocratic and likes to get his hands into all parts of the organization. This autocratic style may have been necessary to accomplish the earlier turnaround, but the result was a corporate structure that is hierarchical, very centralized, and slow. Top management, sometimes Eisner himself, has to approve decisions on everything.

However, some argue that the company is now too large for Eisner to continue to be so involved. In the 1980s, Disney was little more than a couple of theme parks and a maker of family movies. Now there are games, toys, retail stores, cruise ships, magazine publishing, professional sports teams (the Anaheim Mighty Ducks hockey team and the Anaheim Angels baseball team), television networks, more movies, more theme parks, and an Internet operation with which Eisner plans to rival Yahoo and America Online. As a former Disney insider put it, "This isn't Mickey's house anymore. It's a multibillion-dollar company."

Eisner finally made some changes in operations and organization structure to reposition the company. However, Disney's merger of Capital Cities/ABC, the entertainment giant, was slow to realize the expected gains. But Robert Iger, who came with the Capital Cities/ABC acquisition, was credited with making the merger work. The plan was to take advantage of the Disney content with ABC's distribution system through both cable and broadcast. All of the distribution, which included ABC broadcasting and its television stations, ESPN, the Disney Channel, ABC Radio, Lifetime, A&E, the History Channel, and E! Entertainment, have grown slowly at around 3 percent, and the expected synergies have not been realized. In addition, all of the toy, game, and video merchandising is now worldwide. The question for Eisner was how to run all of these diverse and global operations.

In the entertainment area, Eisner merged the Touchstone Television group with ABC. Observers are watching closely because ABC has always been a very decentralized operation whereas Disney and Touchstone have been highly centralized. Only time will tell how they will work out their differences. Disney and ABC also combined all of their Internet businesses into one unit that included Infoseek, Go Network, ABCNews.com, ESPN.com, Disney.com, Family.com, and others.

International operations also underwent significant changes. All of Disney's international operations grew in a haphazard manner as the different business areas—films, television, retail stores, cable, and theme parks—developed at different times and reported back to their business headquarters in the United States. Now each business reports to regional executives in charge of key continental operations and regional headquarters. First, there is Robert Iger, President of Walt Disney International, whose role was to bring coordinated leadership to all international operations. For example, Etienne de Villiers was president and managing director of Walt Disney International—Europe, the Middle East, and Africa and reported directly to Mr. Iger. Under de Villiers were country/region managing directors. Claus Gydesen was managing director for Germany, Austria, and Switzerland, and was based in Munich. Philippe Laco was managing director for France, Belgium, the Netherlands, and Luxembourg and was based in Paris. Umberto Virri was managing director for Italy and Greece and was based in Milan. Laszlo Hubay Cebrian was managing director for Spain and Portugal. Stuart Warrener was managing director for Central and Eastern Europe, the Middle East, and Africa. And Mats Caneman was managing director for the Nordic Region. De Villiers acted as the managing director for the United Kingdom. Each managing director facilitated coordination among all of the Disney business units at the country/region level. They focused on each unique market, yet provided an integrated view of Disney's consumers, customers, and partners. Reporting relationships were quite different. For example, the CEO of Euro Disney outside of Paris reported jointly to de Villiers and to Paul Pressler, who was head of Walt Disney Attractions. The expectation is to create an integrated regional strategy.

A similar structure was created for Latin America. Reporting to Iger was Diego Lerner, president and managing director of Walt Disney International—Latin America. The four regional groupings were: (1) the Argentina office—Argentina, Uruguay, and Paraguay; (2) the Andean region—Chile, Peru, Ecuador, Colombia, and Venezuela; (3) the Mexico group—Mexico, Panama, Central America, and the Caribbean; and (4) Brazil. The regional headquarters was in Brazil and included regional heads of finance, global licensing, business planning, human resources, business operations, broadcasting, publishing, marketing, and brand development. The strategy was to provide one Disney for the consumer, to be more efficient in running existing businesses, and to generate new business opportunities.

Changes such as these were not intended to delegate authority and decision making away from top management and Michael Eisner. Instead they were intended to shorten the distance between Eisner and the rest of operations. Michael Eisner made all of these changes in order to streamline operations and cut expenses.

In early 2000, Robert Iger was promoted to be President and Chief Operating Officer, in effect the number 2 position to Eisner. The new Executive Management Committee included Eisner, Iger, chief of corporate operations Stanford M. Litvack, vice chairman Roy Disney, chief financial officer Thomas Staggs, chief strategic officer Peter Murphy, and all Disney division heads.

### Case Questions

1. How would you characterize the changes that Eisner is making in the organization structure of Walt Disney Co.?
2. Do you think that his new structure will work for Disney over the next ten or twenty years?
3. Give examples of the different aspects of structure that Eisner has changed and which ones he has not changed?

References: Jill Goldsmith, "Mouse House Eager for Iger," *Variety;* January 31, 2000, p. 3, Bernard Weinraub, "Disney Names New President in Reshuffling, *New York Times*, January 25, 2000, p. C1; "Disney Appoints International Team for Latin America," *Business Wire*, November 9, 1999; "Disney Appoints International Team for Europe," *Business Wire*, October 27, 1999; Marc Gunther, "Eisner's Mouse Trap," *Fortune*, September 6, 1999, pp. 106–118; Geraldine Fabrikant, "Hey There! Hi There! It's a New Michael Eisner," *New York Times*, August 18, 1999, p. C1; Bruce Orwall, "Disney Considers Job Cuts in Its Global Film Business," *Wall Street Journal Europe*, June 28, 1999, p. 16.

## Experiencing Organizational Behavior

### Understanding Organization Structure

**Purpose:** This exercise will help you understand the configurational and operational aspects of organization structure.

**Format:** You will interview at least five employees in different parts of either the college or university you attend or a small- to medium-sized organization and analyze its structure. (You may want to coordinate this exercise with the exercise in Chapter 17.)

**Procedure:** If you use a local organization, your first task is to find one with fifty to five hundred employees. The organization should have more than two hierarchical levels, but it should not be too complex to understand in a short period of study. You may want to check with your professor before contacting the company. Your initial contact should be with the highest-ranking manager, if possible. Be sure that top management is aware of your project and gives their approval.

If you use your local college or university, you could talk to professors, secretaries, and other administrative staff in the admissions office, student services department, athletic department, library, or many other areas. Be sure to represent a variety of jobs and levels in your interviews.

Using the material in this chapter, interview employees to obtain the following information on the structure of the organization.

1. The type of departmentalization (business function, process, product, customer, geographic region)

2. The typical span of control at each level of the organization
3. The number of levels in the hierarchy
4. The administrative ratio (ratio of managers to total employees and ratio of managers to production employees)
5. The degree of formalization (to what extent are rules and procedures written down in job descriptions, policy and procedures manuals, and memos?)
6. The degree of decentralization (to what extent are employees at all levels involved in making decisions?)

Interview three to five employees of the organization at different levels and in different departments. One should hold a top-level position. Be sure to ask the questions in a way that is clear to the respondents; they may not be familiar with the terminology used in this chapter.

Students should produce a report with a paragraph on each configurational and operational aspect of structure listed in this exercise as well as an organization chart of the company, a discussion of differences in responses from the employees interviewed and any unusual structural features (for example, a situation in which employees report to more than one person or to no one). You may want to send a copy of your report to the company's top management.

### Follow-up Questions

1. Which aspects of structure were the hardest to obtain information about? Why?
2. If there were differences in the responses of the employees you interviewed, how do you account for them?
3. If you were president of the organization you analyzed, would you structure it in the same way? Why or why not? If not, how would you structure it differently?

## Building Organizational Behavior Skills

### Making Delegation Work

Tasks and decisions must be delegated to others if what remains of middle management is to survive. With all of the recent downsizing, those who are left must do more with less time and fewer resources. In addition, the essence of total quality management is allowing others—teams and individuals—to make decisions about their work. On the other hand, many managers and supervisors complain that they do not know how to delegate effectively. The following twelve points should improve your delegation.

If you hold any type of managerial assignment or job at work or in a student club or association, you could delegate some job or task to another person. Try the following simple steps.

1. Choose a specific task and time frame. Know exactly what task is to be delegated and by when.
2. Specify in writing exactly why you are delegating this task.
3. Put down in writing exactly what you expect to be done and how it will be measured.
4. Be sure that the person or team is competent to do the task, or at least knows how to acquire the competence if they do not have it initially.
5. Be certain that those who must do the tasks really want to take on more responsibility.
6. Measure or oversee the work without being conspicuous and bothersome to those doing the task.
7. Predict how much it will cost to correct mistakes that might be made.
8. Make sure that YOUR boss knows that you are delegating this task and approves.
9. Be sure that you will be able to provide the appropriate rewards to the person or team who takes on this additional responsibility if they succeed.
10. Be ready with another task to delegate when the person or team succeeds with this one.
11. Be sure to delegate both responsibility for the task and the authority to utilize the appropriate resources to get the job done.

References: Selwyn W. Becker, "TQM Does Work: Ten Reasons Why Misguided Attempts Fail," *Management Review*, May 1993, pp. 30–33; Janet Houser Carter, "Minimizing the Risks from Delegation," *Supervisory Management*, February 1993, pp. 1–2; John Lawrie, "Turning Around Attitudes About Delegation," *Supervisory Management*, December 1990, pp. 1–2.

# Developing OB Internet Skills

**Introduction:** Drawing an organizational chart seems like such an easy thing to do, but surprisingly some organizations do not have an up-to-date chart for their current organization structure. Some large, publicly traded organizations have some type of chart that at least shows the way their top level is structured. This exercise should help you learn more about organization structure.

**Internet Assignment:** Use any search engines that are available to you to look up the organization chart of several organizations. You may have to go to documents that are reported to the Securities and Exchange Commission in order to find them. Pick four companies for which you can find good and recent organization charts and that are in different industries. See if you can describe the configurational and operational aspects of structure described in this chapter.

**Follow-up:** How difficult was it to find the organization charts of actual companies? How extensive were the organization charts that you found? Were they up-to-date? Finally, respond to the following questions:

1. How many levels did the companies show on the charts? Did the companies vary a great deal, or were they pretty similar?
2. Did the companies vary in terms of the span of control? How much?
3. Were you able to see to what extent each organization is decentralized or how formalized its rules are? Why or why not?

chapter

# 17

# Organization Design

## Management Preview

Why is it that when some companies' products mature, the economy changes, or low-cost foreign competition enters the market, some companies die but others adjust and become stronger than ever? One key reason is organization design. Within the organization, design coordinates the efforts of the people, work groups, and departments. Designing a system of task, reporting, and authority relationships that leads to the efficient accomplishment of organizational goals is a challenge managers must be prepared to face. In Chapter 16, we discussed the tools with which managers design a system that enables the organization to be effective. In this chapter, we integrate these basic elements of structure, take into consideration other factors such as the environment and technology, and present several perspectives on organization design. We begin this chapter by discussing organization designs based on the contingency approach. In this discussion we describe how an organization's size, technology, and environment combine with its strategy to determine various aspects of organization design. Next, we examine several organization designs: mechanistic and organic designs, the sociotechnical systems perspective, the Mintzberg framework for classifying organization structures, matrix designs, and virtual organizations. We conclude with an examination of contemporary organization design issues. But first, we describe the reorganization at Compaq Computer Corporation.

Compaq Computer Corporation was named Company of the Year in 1997 by *Forbes* magazine. It was a real star performer with a great future ahead of it in the new information age. It acquired Tandem Computers in late 1997 and Digital Equipment Corporation in early 1998. Compaq expected that these acquisitions would move it into higher-margin, up-market businesses and into the important telecom sector. By late 1998, however, the company was in trouble with declining sales, lower profits and earnings, and the loss of eleven top executives since mid-1997. Finally, the board stepped in, forcing the resignation of CEO Eckhard Pfeiffer in April 1999. The board created a three-person team to run the company as it searched for a new president and CEO. Michael Capellas was chosen by the summer of 1999, and a new day was dawning for Compaq.

*"The core PC business was coming under attack, the market was shifting just as the integration was draining management attention." — Michael Capellas, CEO, Compaq**

First, the company completely reorganized into three organizational groups, each reporting directly to Capellas: Enterprise Solutions and Services, Personal Computers, and Consumer Electronics. These divisions reflect Compaq's new, more focused strategy and should be the integrative force to bring together the units acquired earlier. The company admits its problems were self-inflicted, its operations were inefficient, and its customers and distributors were unhappy. As Compaq tried to integrate the new acquisitions, it seemed to have forgotten its core business: selling personal computers to users. Compaq had been using a matrix-type structure that put more emphasis on geography than on business functions. The new organization is more focused on products and customers, with each division having clear profit-and-loss responsibility. Although the problems are not over for Compaq, it seems to have streamlined its operations and given everyone clear marching orders. It will be interesting to see if the structural changes enable the company to regain its top position.[1] ■

Compaq Computer Corporation is not alone when it turns to a reorganization to solve performance problems; many companies do it. The primary issue is how to determine which organizational form is right for a given organization. In this chapter we describe several approaches to organization design.

# Contingency Approaches to Organization Design

In the **universal approach** to organization design, prescriptions or propositions are designed to work in any circumstances.

Under the **contingency approach** to organization design, the desired outcomes for the organization can be achieved in several ways.

Organization designs vary from rigid bureaucracies to flexible matrix systems. Most theories of organization design take either a universal or a contingency approach. A **universal approach** is one whose prescriptions or propositions are designed to work in any situation. Thus, a universal design prescribes the "one best way" to structure the jobs, authority, and reporting relationships of the organization, regardless of factors such as the organization's external environment, the industry, and the type of work to be done. The classical approaches discussed in Chapter 16 are all universal approaches. A **contingency approach**, on the other hand, suggests that organizational efficiency can be achieved in several ways. In a contingency design, specific conditions such as the environment, technology, and the organization's work force determine the structure. Figure 17.1 shows the distinction between the universal and contingency approaches. This distinction is similar to the one between universal and contingency approaches to motivation (Chapters 5 and 6), job design (Chapter 7), and leadership (Chapters 13 and 14). Although no one particular

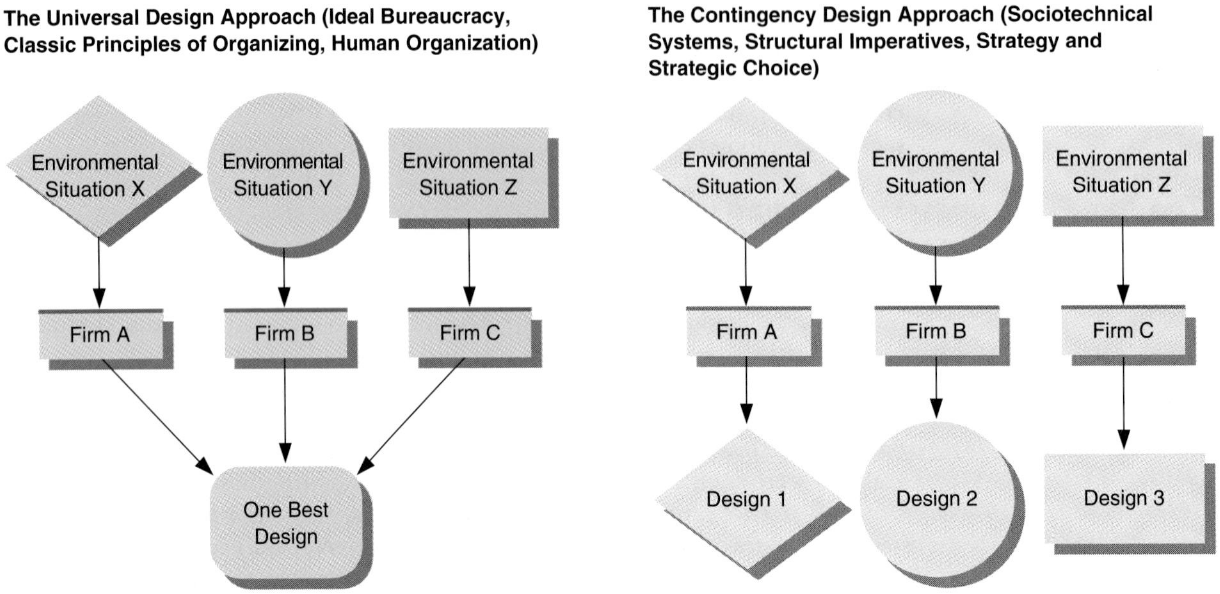


figure 17.1

**Universal and Contingency Approaches to Organization Design**

*The universal approach looks for the single best way to design an organization regardless of situational issues. The contingency approach designs the organization to fit the situation.*

form of organization is generally accepted, the contingency approach most closely represents current thinking.

Weber, Fayol, and Likert (see Chapter 16) each proposed an organization design that is independent of the nature of the organization and its environment. Although each of these approaches contributed to our understanding of the organizing process and the practice of management, none has proved to be universally applicable. In this chapter we turn to several contingency designs, which attempt to specify the conditions, or contingency factors, under which they are likely to be most effective. The contingency factors include such things as the strategy of the organization, its technology, the environment, the organization's size, and the social system within which the organization operates.

*"Sony started as a small venture company with a strong orientation towards international markets in the early postwar years. Over the past decades, Sony has turned into a huge multinational enterprise. A reorganization has become inevitable."*

*— Mario Tokoro, president, Sony Computer Science Laboratories, corporate executive vice president, and director, Information & Network Technologies Laboratory, Sony Corporation*[2]

The contingency approach has been criticized as unrealistic, in that managers are expected to observe a change in one of the contingency factors and to make a rational structural alteration. On the other hand, Donaldson has argued that it is reasonable to expect organizations to respond to lower organizational performance, which may result from a lack of response to some significant change in one or several contingency factors.[3]

# Strategy, Structural Imperatives, and Strategic Choice

The decision about how to design the organization structure is based on numerous factors. In this section, we present several views of the determinants of organization structure and integrate them into a single approach. We begin with the strategic view.

## Strategy

Strategy is the plans and actions necessary to achieve organizational goals.

A **strategy** is the plans and actions necessary to achieve organizational goals.[4] Kellogg, for example, has attempted to be the leader in the ready-to-eat cereal industry by pursuing a strategy that combines product differentiation and market segmentation. Over the years, Kellogg has successfully introduced new cereals made from different grains in different shapes, sizes, colors, and flavors in its effort to provide any type of cereal the consumer might want.[5]

After studying the history of seventy companies, Alfred Chandler drew certain conclusions about the relationship between an organization's structure and its business strategy.[6] Chandler observed that a growth strategy to expand into a new product line is usually matched with some type of decentralization, a decentralized structure being necessary to deal with the problems of the new product line.

Chandler's "structure follows strategy" concept seems to appeal to common sense. Management must decide what the organization is to do and what its goals are before deciding how to design the organization structure, which is how the organization will meet those goals. This perspective assumes a purposeful approach to designing the structure of the organization.

Jerry Yang, co-founder of Yahoo!, is shown here after signing an historic alliance agreement with Ford Motor Company CEO Jacques Nasser. Ford changed its strategy from being the huge metal-bending auto manufacturer to a dynamic, web-based consumer-marketing firm. This remarkable transformation required that Ford completely change its organization structure in order to utilize computerized information processing and telecommunications in every aspect of its business, from Internet-based customer contact before and after the sale to complete integration of its supplier system. Early on Nasser brought in new executives from outside the auto industry and teamed them with younger Ford executives, and, as older executives retired, transformed the management team into a younger, more computer-savvy group ready to execute the new strategy.

## Structural Imperatives

The structural-imperatives approach to organization design probably has been the most discussed and researched

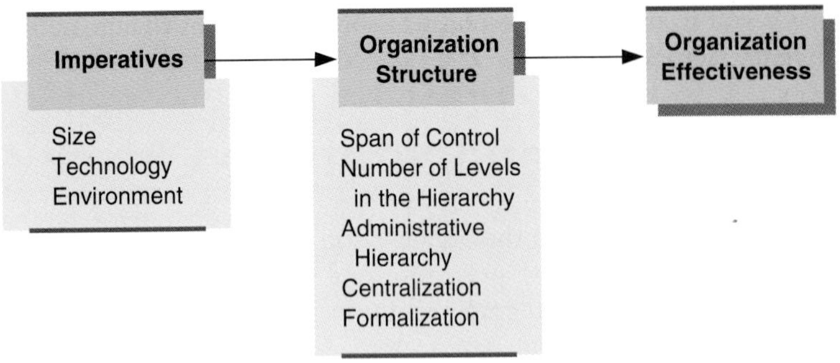


figure 17.2 **The Structural Imperatives Approach**

*Organizational size, environment, and technology determine how an organization should be structured to be effective.*

contingency perspective of the last thirty years. This perspective was not formulated by a single theorist or researcher, and it has not evolved from a systematic and cohesive research effort; rather, it gradually emerged from a vast number of studies that sought to address the question "What are the compelling factors that determine how the organization must be structured to be effective?" As Figure 17.2 shows, the three factors that have been identified as **structural imperatives** are size, technology, and environment.

**Structural imperatives**—size, technology, and environment—are the three primary determinants of organization structure.

Size The size of an organization can be gauged in many ways. Usually it is measured in terms of total number of employees, value of the organization's assets, total sales in the previous year (or number of clients served), or physical capacity. The method of measurement is very important, although the different measures usually are correlated.[7]

Generally, larger organizations have a more complex structure than smaller ones. Peter Blau and his associates concluded that large size is associated with greater specialization of labor, a larger span of control, more hierarchical levels, and greater formalization.[8] These multiple effects are shown in Figure 17.3. Increasing size leads to more specialization of labor within a work unit, which increases the amount of differentiation among work units and the number of levels in the hierarchy, resulting in a need for more intergroup formalization. With greater specialization within the unit, there is less need for coordination within groups; thus, the span of control can be larger. Larger spans of control mean fewer first-line managers, but the need for more intergroup coordination may require more second- and third-line managers and staff personnel to coordinate

figure 17.3

**Impact of Large Size on Organization Structure**

*As organizations grow larger, their structures usually change in predictable ways. Larger organizations tend to have more complex structures, larger spans of control, and more rules and procedures.*

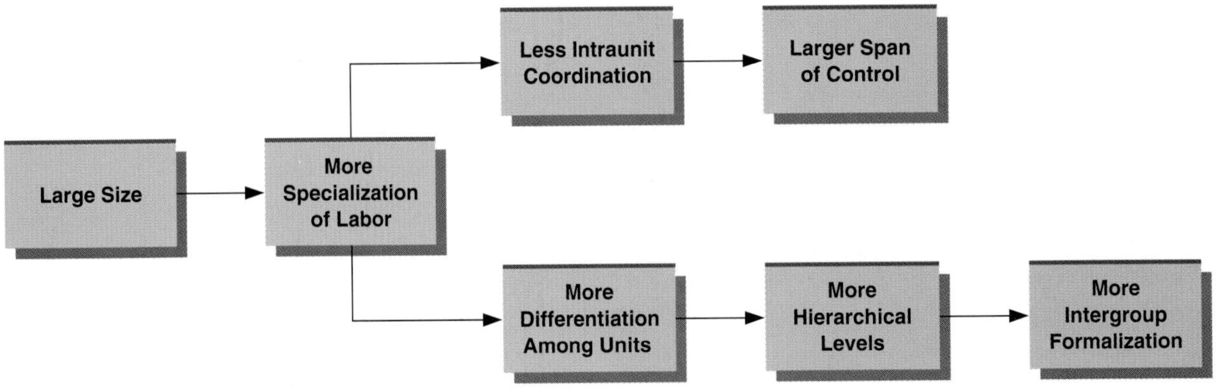

them. Large organizations may therefore be more efficient because of their large spans of control and reduced administrative overhead; however, the greater differentiation among units makes the system more complex. Studies by researchers associated with the University of Aston in Birmingham, England, and others have shown similar results.[9]

Economies of scale are another advantage of large organizations. In a large operation, fixed costs—for example, plant and equipment—can be spread over more units of output, thereby reducing the cost per unit. In addition, some administrative activities, such as purchasing, clerical work, and marketing, can be accomplished for a large number of units at the same cost as for a small number. Their cost can then be spread over the larger number of units, again reducing unit cost.

Companies such as AT&T Technologies, General Electric's Aircraft Engines products group, and S.C. Johnson & Son have gone against the conventional wisdom that larger is always better in manufacturing plants. They cite as their main reasons the smaller investment required for smaller plants, the reduced need to produce a variety of products, and the desire to decrease organizational complexity (that is, reduce the number of hierarchical levels and shorten lines of communication). In a number of instances, smaller plants have resulted in increased team spirit, improved productivity, and higher profits.[10]

Other studies have found that the relationship between size and structural complexity is less clear than the Blau results indicated. These studies suggest that size must be examined in relation to the technology of the organization.[11]

**Organizational downsizing** is a popular trend aimed at reducing the size of corporate staff and middle management to reduce costs.

Traditionally, as organizations have grown, several layers of advisory staff have been added to help coordinate the complexities inherent in any large organization. In contrast, a current trend is to cut staff throughout the organization. Known as **organizational downsizing**, this popular trend is aimed primarily at reducing the size of corporate staff and middle management to reduce costs. Results of downsizing have been mixed, with some observers noting that indiscriminate across-the-board cuts may leave the organization weak in certain key areas. Companies such NYNEX, Eastman Kodak, Digital Equipment Corporation, and RJR Nabisco have made cutbacks with disastrous results. NYNEX Corporation, the telephone company, had to hire back hundreds of employees who had taken an early retirement program to try to build back its reputation for customer service. In addition, the New York Public Service Commission ordered NYNEX to rebate $50 million to 5 million customers because it had fallen behind in responding to problems owing to its staff reductions. Eastman Kodak is paying more for contract workers who are doing the work that laid-off workers used to do. In addition, Kodak is rehiring some of those laid off at increased salaries and incurring the costs of recruiting and rehiring. There are always some unintended consequences of downsizing, as shown in the cartoon.

In sales, cutting costs can be disastrous. Digital Equipment Company eliminated hundreds of sales and marketing staff because it reported losing $3 million per day! Customers then reported never seeing a DEC representative for months and began to use other computer equipment suppliers, such as IBM and Hewlett-Packard. In fact, some of the laid-off salespeople were hired by the competitors and immediately pulled former DEC customers with them. Following a merger, RJR Nabisco decided to merge sales forces for its foods group, which handles Grey Poupon Mustard and Milkbone dog biscuits, with the Planters Lifesavers Company, which makes gums, candies, and nuts. Problems arose when the lack of compatibility in product types and in outlets began to surface. Sales representatives had trouble covering the much broader array of products and selling to twice as many

There are often unintended consequences of downsizing. Often those employees who survive the downsizing usually are required to pick up the work of those who have left. This poor guy got a promotion and a new title, but he now has more jobs to do.

Reference: © Randy Glasbergen.

GLASBERGEN
"I downsized our staff so effectively, they promoted me to Executive Vice President. They also made me custodian, receptionist and parking garage attendant."

outlets. As a result, customers were not called on promptly, and sales suffered significantly. Initially, profit margins did improve, but the next year operating earnings fell to 25 percent of their former levels.[12]

However, positive results often include quicker decision making because fewer layers of management must approve every decision. One review of research on organizational downsizing found that it had both psychological and sociological impacts. This study suggested that in a downsizing environment, size affects organization design in very complex ways.[13]

**Organizational technology** refers to the mechanical and intellectual processes that transform inputs into outputs.

Technology **Technology** consists of the mechanical and intellectual processes that transform raw materials into products and services for customers. For example, the primary technology employed by major oil companies transforms crude oil (input) into gasoline, motor oil, heating oil, and other petroleum-based products (outputs). Prudential Insurance uses actuarial tables and information-processing technologies to produce its insurance services. Of course, most organizations use multiple technologies. Oil companies use research and information-processing technologies in their laboratories, where new petroleum products and processes are generated.

Although there is general agreement that technology is important, the means by which this technology has been evaluated and measured have varied widely. Five approaches to examining the technology of the organization are shown in Table 17.1. For convenience, we have classified these approaches according to the names of their proponents.

In an early study of the relationship between technology and organization structure, Joan Woodward categorized manufacturing technologies by their complexity: unit or small-batch, large-batch or mass production, and continuous process.[14] Tom Burns and George Stalker proposed that the rate of change in technology determines the best method of structuring the organization.[15] Charles Perrow developed a technological continuum, with routine technologies at one end and nonroutine technologies at the other, and claimed that all organizations could be classified on his routine-to-nonroutine continuum.[16] Thompson claimed that all organizations could be classified into one of three technological categories: long-linked, mediating, and intensive.[17] Finally, a group of English researchers at the University of Aston developed three categories of technology based on the type

table 17.1

**Summary of Approaches to Technology**

| Approach | Classification of Technology | Example |
|---|---|---|
| **Woodward** (1958 and 1965) (cit. no. 14) | Unit or small-batch | Customized parts made one at a time |
| | Large-batch or mass production | Automobile assembly line |
| | Continuous process | Chemical plant, petroleum refinery |
| **Burns and Stalker** (1961) (cit. no. 15) | Rate of technological change | Slow: large manufacturing; rapid: computer industry |
| **Perrow** (1967) (cit. no. 16) | Routine | Standardized products (Procter & Gamble, General Foods) |
| | Nonroutine | New technology products or processes (computers, telecommunications) |
| **Thompson** (1967) (cit. no. 17) | Long-linked | Assembly line |
| | Mediating | Bank |
| | Intensive | General hospital |
| **Aston studies: Hickson, Pugh, and Pheysey** (1969) (cit. no. 18) | Work flow integration; operations, materials, and knowledge technologies | Technology differs in various parts of the organization |

of work flow involved: operations, material, and knowledge.[18] These perspectives on technology are somewhat similar in that all (except the Aston typology) address the adaptability of the technological system to change. Large-batch or mass production, routine, and long-linked technologies are not very adaptable to change. At the opposite end of the continuum, continuous-process, nonroutine, and intensive technologies are readily adaptable to change.

One major contribution of the study of organizational technology is the recognition that organizations have more than one important "technology" that enables them to accomplish their tasks. Instead of examining technology in isolation, the Aston group recognized that size and technology are related in determining organization structure.[19] They found that in smaller organizations, technology had more direct effects on the structure. In large organizations, however, they found, like Blau, that structure depended less on the operations technology and more on size considerations, such as the number of employees. In large organizations, each department or division may have a different technology that determines how that department or division should be structured. In short, in small organizations the structure depended primarily on the technology, whereas in large organizations the need to coordinate complicated activities was the most important factor. Thus, both organizational size and technology are important considerations in organization design.

Global technology variations come in two forms: variations in available technology and variations in attitudes toward technology. The technology available affects how organizations can do business. Many underdeveloped countries, for example, lack electric power sources, telephones, and trucking equipment, not to mention computers and robots. A manager working in such a country must be prepared to deal with many frustrations. Some Brazilian officials convinced a U.S. company to build a high-tech plant in their country. Midway through construction, however, the government of Brazil decided it would not allow the company to import some accurate measuring instruments it needed to produce its products. The new plant was abandoned before it opened.[20]

Attitudes toward technology also vary across cultures. Surprisingly, Japan only began to support basic research in the 1980's. For many years, the Japanese government encouraged its companies to take basic research findings discovered elsewhere (often in the United States) and figure out how to apply them to consumer products (applied research). In the mid-1980s, however, the government changed its stance and started to encourage basic research as well.[21] Most Western nations have a generally favorable attitude toward technology, whereas until the 1990's China and other Asian countries (with the exception of Japan) did not.

The **organizational environment** is everything outside an organization and includes all elements—people, other organizations, economic factors, objects, and events—that lie outside the boundaries of the organization.

The **general environment** includes the broad set of dimensions and factors within which the organization operates, including political-legal, sociocultural, technological, economic, and international factors.

The **task environment** includes specific organizations, groups, and individuals that influence the organization.

### Environment

The **organizational environment** includes all of the elements—people, other organizations, economic factors, objects, and events—that lie outside the boundaries of the organization. The environment is composed of two layers: the general environment and the task environment. The **general environment** includes all of a broad set of dimensions and factors within which the organization operates, including political-legal, social, cultural, technological, economic, and international factors. The **task environment** includes specific organizations, groups, and individuals that influence the organization. People in the task environment include customers, donors, regulators, inspectors, and shareholders. Among the organizations in the task environment are competitors, legislatures, and regulatory agencies. Economic factors in the task environment might include interest rates, international trade factors, and the unemployment rate in a particular area. Objects in the task environment include such things as buildings, vehicles, and trees. Events that may affect organizations include weather, elections, or war.

It is necessary to determine the boundaries of the organization to understand where the environment begins. These boundaries may be somewhat elusive, or at least changeable, and thus difficult to define. But for the most part we can say that certain people, groups, or buildings are either in the organization or in the environment. For example, a college student shopping for a personal computer is part of the environment of Apple, Compaq, IBM, and other computer manufacturers. However, if the student works for one of these computer manufacturers, he or she is not part of that company's environment but is within the boundaries of the organization.

This definition of organizational environment emphasizes the expanse of the environment within which the organization operates. It may give managers the false impression that the environment is outside their control and interest. But because the environment completely encloses the organization, managers must be constantly concerned about it. Most managers these days are aware that the environment is changing rapidly. The difficulty for most is to determine how those changes affect the company.

*"The company has changed and the world has changed, but Michael hasn't changed. Now he's got to change." — former Disney executive speaking about Michael Eisner, chairman of Walt Disney*[22]

The manager, then, faces an enormous, only vaguely specified environment that somehow affects the organization. Managing the organization within such an environment may seem an overwhelming task. The alternatives for the manager are to (1) ignore the environment because of its complexity and focus on managing the internal operations of the company; (2) exert maximum energy in gathering information on every part of the environment and in trying to react to every environmental factor; and (3) pay attention to specific aspects of the task environment, responding only to those that most clearly affect the organization.

To ignore environmental factors entirely and focus on internal operations leaves the company in danger of missing major environmental shifts, such as changes in customer preferences, technological breakthroughs, and new regulations. To expend large amounts of energy, time, and money exploring every facet of the environment may take more out of the organization than it may return.

The third alternative—to carefully analyze segments of the environment that most affect the organization and to respond accordingly—is the most prudent course. The issue, then, is to determine which parts of the environment should receive the manager's attention. In the remainder of this section, we examine two perspectives on the organizational environment: the analysis of environmental components and environmental uncertainty.

Forces in the environment have different effects on different companies. Hospital Corporation of America, for example, is very much influenced by government regulations and medical and scientific developments. Quite different environmental forces, on the other hand, affect McDonald's: consumer demand, disposable income, cost of meat and bread, and gasoline prices. Thus, the task environment, the specific set of environmental forces that influence the operations of an organization, varies among organizations.

The environmental characteristic that brings together all of these different environmental influences and appears to have the most effect on the structure of the organization is uncertainty. **Environmental uncertainty** exists when managers have little information about environmental events and their impact on the organization.[23] Uncertainty has been described as resulting from complexity and dynamism in the environment. **Environmental complexity** is the number of environmental components that impinge on organizational decision making. **Environmental dynamism** is the degree to which these components change.[24] With these two dimensions, we can determine the degree of environmental uncertainty, as illustrated in Figure 17.4.

**Environmental uncertainty** exists when managers have little information about environmental events and their impact on the organization.

**Environmental complexity** is the number of environmental components that impinge on organizational decision making.

**Environmental dynamism** is the degree to which environmental components that impinge on organizational decision making change.

In cell 1, a low-uncertainty environment, there are few important components, and they change infrequently. A company in the cardboard container industry might have a highly certain environment when demand is steady, manufacturing processes are stable, and government regulations have remained largely unchanged.

In contrast, in cell 4, many important components are involved in decision making, and they change often. Thus, cell 4 represents a high-uncertainty environment. The banking environment is now highly uncertain. With deregulation and the advent of interstate operations, banks today must compete with insurance companies, brokerage firms, real estate firms, and even department stores. The toy industry also is in a highly uncertain environment. As they develop new toys, toy companies must stay in tune with movies, television shows, cartoons, and with public sentiment as well. Between 1983 and 1988, Saturday morning cartoons were little more than animated stories about children's toys. Recently, however, due to

| Rate of Environmental Change | Simple | Complex |
|---|---|---|
| *Static* | **Cell 1: Low Perceived Uncertainty**<br>1. Small number of factors and components in the environment<br>2. Factors and components are somewhat similar to one another<br>3. Factors and components remain basically the same<br>*Example: cardboard container industry* | **Cell 2: Moderately Low Perceived Uncertainty**<br>1. Large number of factors and components in the environment<br>2. Factors and components are not similar to one another<br>3. Factors and components remain basically the same<br>*Example: state universities* |
| *Dynamic* | **Cell 3: Moderately High Perceived Uncertainty**<br>1. Small number of factors and components in the environment<br>2. Factors and components are somewhat similar to one another<br>3. Factors and components of the environment continually change<br>*Example: fashion industry* | **Cell 4: High Perceived Uncertainty**<br>1. Large number of factors and components in the environment<br>2. Factors and components are not similar to one another<br>3. Factors and components of environment continually change<br>*Example: banking industry* |

**Environmental Complexity**

figure **17.4**

**Classification of Environmental Uncertainty**

*This four-cell matrix describes all four levels of environmental dynamism and complexity and shows how they combine to create low or high environmental uncertainty.*

Reference: Reprinted from "Characteristics of Organizational Environments and Perceived Uncertainty," by Robert B. Duncan, published in *Administrative Science Quarterly,* vol. 17, no. 3 (Sept. 1972), p. 320, by permission of *Administrative Science Quarterly.* 

disappointing sales of many toys presented in cartoons designed to promote them, most toy companies have left the toy-based cartoon business. Many toys are now sold that are based on movies.[25]

Environmental characteristics and uncertainty have been important factors in explaining organization structure, strategy, and performance. For example, the characteristics of the environment affect how managers perceive the environment, which in turn affects how they adapt the structure of the organization to meet environmental demands.[26] The environment has also been shown to affect the degree to which a firm's strategy enhances its performance.[27] That is, a certain strategy will enhance organizational performance to the extent that it is appropriate for the environment in which the organization operates. Finally, the environment is directly related to organizational performance.[28] The environment and the organization's response to it are crucial to success.

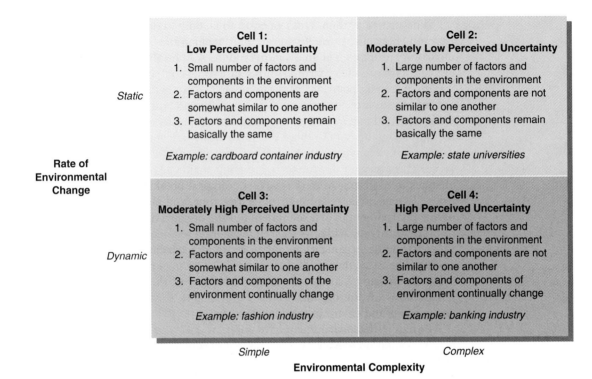

An organization attempts to continue as a viable entity in a dynamic environment. The environment completely encloses the organization, and managers must be constantly concerned about it. The organization as a whole, as well as departments and divisions within it, is created to deal with different challenges, problems, and uncertainties. James Thompson suggested that organizations design a structure to protect the dominant technology of the organization, smooth out any problems, and keep down coordination costs.[29] Thus, organization structures are designed to coordinate relevant technologies and protect them from outside disturbances. Structural components such as inventory, warehousing, and shipping help buffer the technology used to transform inputs into outputs. For instance, demand for products usually is cyclical or seasonal and is subject to many disturbances, but the warehouse inventory helps the manufacturing system function as if the environment accepted output at a steady rate, maximizing technological efficiency and helping the organization respond to fluctuating demands of the market.

Organizations with international operations must contend with additional levels of complexity and dynamism, both within and across cultures. Many cultures have relatively stable environments. For example, the economies of Sweden, and the United States are fairly stable. Although competitive forces within them vary, they generally remain strong, free-market economies. In contrast, the environments of other countries are much more dynamic. For example, France's policies on socialism versus private enterprise tend to change dramatically with each election. At present, far-reaching changes in the economic and management philosophies of most Western European countries make their environments far more dynamic than that of the United States.

Environments also vary widely in terms of their complexity. The Japanese culture, which is fairly stable, is also quite complex. Japanese managers are subject to an array of cultural norms and values that are far more encompassing and resistant to change than those U.S. managers face. India too has an extremely complex environment, which continues to be influenced by its old caste system.

## Strategic Choice

The previous two sections describe how structure is affected by the strategy of the organization and by the structural imperatives of size, technology, and environment. These approaches may seem to contradict each other, considering that both approaches attempt to specify the determinants of structure. This apparent clash has been resolved by refining the strategy concept to include the role of the top management decision maker in determining the organization's structure.[30] In effect, this view inserts the manager as the decision maker who evaluates the imperatives and the organization strategy and then designs the organization structure. The role of top management in determining the structure of the organization is significant. As discussed in the opening case, newly appointed CEOs often change the structure. "The Business of Ethics" box describes another case in which the top management made many structural decisions.

The importance of the role of top management can be understood by comparing Figure 17.5 with Figure 17.2. Figure 17.5 shows structural imperatives as contextual factors within which the organization must operate and that affect the purposes and goals of the organization. The manager's choices for organization structure are affected by the organization's strategy (purposes and goals), the imperatives (contextual factors), and the manager's personal value system and experience.[31] Organizational effectiveness depends on the fit among the size, the technology, the environment, the strategies, and the structure. The Thermos Company noted new environmental conditions, reinvented their approach, and came up with an innovative new product, an electric cooking grill.[32]

THE BUSINESS OF ETHICS

## *How Many Heads Does It Take to Run Citigroup?*

*"I have a theory of relatives too, I don't hire them." — What Jack Warner, Hollywood producer, was supposed to have said to Albert Einstein*

Citicorp and Travelers Group agreed to merge in the spring of 1998. Those two companies are in the same general industry, providing financial services, but are in different parts of it, so analysts expected the merger to fit together pretty well. But no matter how things seem at first, mergers can be very difficult to pull off. At the time, it was announced that the chairman of Citicorp, John S. Reed, and the chairman of Travelers, Sanford Weill, would run the new company as co-CEOs for a while, but it was generally expected that Reed would soon leave and that Weill would stay on as CEO. But as difficulties of the merger became more evident, Weill would not let Reed go, so the co-CEO arrangement lasted. Not only were there two CEOs, the crucial job of merging the corporate financial services businesses of the two firms was the job of a three-person team: Jamie Dimon from Travelers, Derych Maughan from the old Salomon Brothers of Citicorp, and Victor Menezes from Citicorp. So Citigroup had three people in one position reporting to two people in one position. Confusing! After eight months, the three-headed monster was split up. Maughan was moved to a different spot on the organization chart, and Dimon was fired (more on that later), leaving Menezes to pair with somebody else, Michael Carpenter from Travelers.

The Dimon situation is interesting. Dimon had been Weill's favored assistant since his hiring in 1982. They had worked together a long time and usually confided in each other on major decisions. But Dimon ran into trouble when he failed to promote Weill's daughter, Jessica Weill Bibliowicz, into a top job at Smith Barney, owned by Citicorp. She subsequently left the company to take a job as president of a financial advisory firm. Weill supposedly blamed Dimon for the departure of his daughter. When it was time to appoint Dimon as head of the newly formed Salomon Smith Barney (after another merger), Weill created another co-CEO arrangement appointing both Dimon and Maughan. Furthermore, following the Citicorp and Travelers merger to Citigroup, Weill and Reed decided that they alone would be the insiders on the board of the new company. Dimon, who had helped build Travelers, was snubbed again. In addition, when Sandy Weill suggested that his son, Marc, should get a new position in the merged group, guess who said no? Dimon! So when the three-headed group assigned to put together the corporate business did not get the job done on time, it was not a surprise who would lose out. By October 1998, Dimon was gone.

In August 1999, the company announced a separation of duties: Weill would be doing more operational duties, whereas Reed would focus on advanced opportunities, the Internet, human resources, and legal issues. Some analysts believed this to be a sign that Weill had, in effect, won the CEO position. But by October 1999, Weill and Reed were still both co-CEOs, and the company had brought in another person, Robert Rubin, former U.S. secretary of the treasury, to be chairman of the executive committee of the board, not chairman and not co-CEO.

References: "Three's Company," *Economist*, October 30, 1999, p. 80; "Citigroup: So Much for 50-50," *Business Week*, August 16, 1999, p. 80; Carol J. Loomis, "Citigroup: Scenes from a Merger," *Fortune*, January 11, 1999, pp. 76–88 (quote on p. 80).

Another perspective on the link between strategy and structure is that the relationship may be reciprocal; that is, the structure may be set up to implement the strategy, but the structure may then affect the process of decision making, influencing such matters as the centralization or decentralization of decision making and the formalization of rules and procedures.[33] Thus, strategy determines structure, which in turn affects strategic decision making. A more complex view, suggested by Herman Boschken, is that strategy is a determinant of structure and

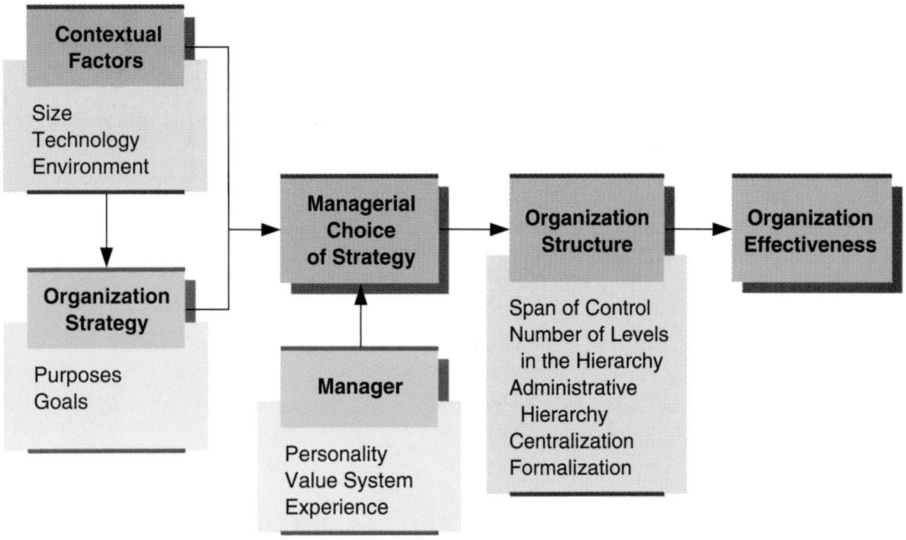


figure 17.5
**The Strategic Choice Approach to Organization Design**

*The integration of the structural imperative approach to organization design with the strategic choice approach takes into account the role of the manager, whose perspective on contextual factors and the organization, along with personal preferences, values, and experience, help determine the structure of the organization.*

long-term performance but only when the subunits doing the planning have the ability to do the planning well.[34]

The relationship between strategic choice and structure is actually more complicated than the concept that "structure follows strategy" conveys. However, this relationship has received less research attention than the idea of structural imperatives. And, of course, some might view strategy simply as another imperative, along with size, technology, and environment. But the strategic-choice view goes beyond the imperative perspective because it is a product of both the analyses of the imperatives and the organization's strategy.

# Organizational Designs

The previous section described several factors that determine how organizations are structured. In this section we present several different organizational designs that have been created to adapt organizations to the many contingency factors they face. We discuss mechanistic and organic structures, the sociotechnical system perspective, Mintzberg's designs, matrix designs, and virtual organizations.

## Mechanistic and Organic Designs

A **mechanistic structure** is primarily hierarchical; interactions and communications typically are vertical, instructions come from the boss, knowledge is concentrated at the top, and loyalty and obedience are required to sustain membership.

As we discussed in the previous section, most theorists believe that organizations need to be able to adapt to changes in the technology. For example, if the rate of change in technology is slow, the most effective design is bureaucratic or, to use Burns and Stalker's term, "mechanistic." As summarized in Table 17.2, a **mechanistic structure** is primarily hierarchical in nature, interactions and communications are mostly vertical, instructions come from the boss, knowledge is concentrated at the top, and continued membership requires loyalty and obedience.

table 17.2
**Mechanistic and Organic Organization Designs**

| Characteristic | Mechanistic | Organic |
|---|---|---|
| Structure | Hierarchical | Network based on interests |
| Interactions, Communication | Primarily vertical | Lateral throughout |
| Work Directions, Instructions | From supervisor | Through advice, information |
| Knowledge, Information | Concentrated at top | Throughout |
| Membership, Relationship with Organization | Requires loyalty, obedience | Commitment to task, progress, expansion |

*"Informality gives you speed." — Jack Welch, CEO of GE*[35]

An **organic structure** is set up like a network; interactions and communications are horizontal, knowledge resides wherever it is most useful to the organization, and membership requires a commitment to the organization's tasks.

But if the technology is changing rapidly, the organization needs a structure that allows more flexibility and faster decision making so that it can react quickly to change. This design is called "organic." An **organic structure** resembles a network—interactions and communications are more lateral, knowledge resides wherever it is most useful to the organization, and membership requires a commitment to the tasks of the organization. An organic organization is generally expected to be faster at reacting to changes in the environment.

## Sociotechnical Systems Designs

A **system** is an interrelated set of elements that function as a whole.

An **open system** is a system that interacts with its environment.

The **sociotechnical systems approach** to organization design views the organization as an open system structured to integrate the technical and social subsystems into a single management system.

A **technical (task) subsystem** is the means by which inputs are transformed into outputs.

The foundation of the sociotechnical systems approach to organizing is systems theory, discussed in Chapter 1. There we defined a **system** as an interrelated set of elements that function as a whole. A system may have numerous subsystems, each of which, like the overall system, includes inputs, transformation processes, outputs, and feedback. We also defined an **open system** as one that interacts with its environment. A complex system is made up of numerous subsystems in which the outputs of some are the inputs to others. The **sociotechnical systems approach** views the organization as an open system structured to integrate the two important subsystems: the technical (task) subsystem and the social subsystem.

The **technical (task) subsystem** is the means by which inputs are transformed into outputs. The transformation processes may take many forms. In a steel foundry, it would entail the way steel is formed, cut, drilled, chemically treated, and painted. In an insurance company or financial institution, it would be the way information is processed. Often, significant scientific and engineering expertise is applied to these transformation processes to get the highest productivity at the lowest cost. For example, Fireplace Manufacturers of Santa Ana, California, a manufacturer of prefabricated metal fireplaces, implemented "just in time" (JIT) manufacturing and inventory systems to improve the productivity of its plant.[36] Under this system, component parts arrive "just in time" to be used in the manufacturing process, reducing the costs of storing them in a warehouse until they are needed. In effect, JIT redesigns the transformation process, from the introduction of raw materials to the shipping of the finished product. In three years, Fireplace Manufacturers' inventory costs dropped from $1.1 million to $750,000, while sales doubled over the same period. The transformation process usually is regarded as technologically and economically driven; that is, whatever process is most productive and costs the least is generally the most desirable.

A **social subsystem** includes the interpersonal relationships that develop among people in organizations.

The **social subsystem** includes the interpersonal relationships that develop among people in organizations. Employees learn one another's work habits, strengths, weaknesses, and preferences while developing a sense of mutual trust. The social relationships may be manifested in personal friendships and interest groups. Communication, about both work and employees' common interests, may be enhanced by friendship or hampered by antagonistic relationships. The Hawthorne studies (discussed in Chapter 1) were the first serious studies of the social subsystems in organizations.[37]

The sociotechnical systems approach was developed by members of the Tavistock Institute of England as an outgrowth of a study of coal mining. The study concerned new mining techniques that were introduced to increase productivity but failed because they entailed splitting up well-established work groups.[38] The Tavistock researchers concluded that the social subsystem had been sacrificed to the technical subsystem. Thus, improvements in the technical subsystem were not realized because of problems in the social subsystem. More recently, Lifeline Systems, a manufacturer of electronic medical equipment that implemented just-in-time systems, recognized the potential problems of employee acceptance and emphasized the role of management in getting employees to go along with the changes.[39]

**Autonomous work groups** are used to integrate an organization's technical and social subsystems for the benefit of the larger system.

The Tavistock group proposed that an organization's technical and social subsystems could be integrated through autonomous work groups. The aim of **autonomous work groups** is to make technical and social subsystems work together for the benefit of the larger system. These groups are developed using concepts of task design, particularly job enrichment, and ideas about group interaction, supervision, and other characteristics of organization design. To structure the task, authority, and reporting relationships around work groups, organizations should delegate to the groups themselves decisions regarding job assignments, training, inspection, rewards, and punishments. Management is responsible for coordinating the groups according to the demands of the work and task environment. Autonomous work groups often evolve into self-managing teams, as was discussed in Chapter 12.

Organizations in turbulent environments tend to rely less on hierarchy and more on the coordination of work among autonomous work groups. Sociotechnical systems theory asserts that the role of management is twofold: to monitor the environmental factors that impinge on the internal operations of the organization and to coordinate the social and technical subsystems. Although the sociotechnical systems approach has not been thoroughly tested, it has been tried with some success in the General Foods plant in Topeka, Kansas; the Saab-Scania project in Sweden; and the Volvo plant in Kalmar, Sweden.[40] The development of the sociotechnical systems approach is significant in its departure from the universal approaches to organization design and in its emphasis on jointly harnessing the technical and human subsystems. The popular movements in management today include many of the principles of the sociotechnical systems design approach. The development of cross-functional teams to generate and design new products and services is a good example (see Chapter 12).

## Mintzberg's Designs

In this section we describe the concrete organization designs proposed by Henry Mintzberg. The universe of possible designs is large, but fortunately we can divide designs into a few basic forms. Mintzberg proposed that the purpose of organizational design was to coordinate activities, and he suggested a range of coordinating mechanisms that are found in operating organizations.[41] In Mintzberg's view, organization structure reflects how tasks are divided and then coordinated. He described five major ways in which tasks are coordinated: by mutual adjustment, by direct supervision, and by standardization of worker (or input) skills, work processes, or outputs (see Figure 17.6). These five methods can exist side by side within an organization.

*Coordination by mutual adjustment* (1 in Figure 17.6) simply means that workers use informal communication to coordinate with one another, whereas *coordination by direct supervision* (2 in Figure 17.6) means that a manager or supervisor coordinates the actions of workers. As noted, *standardization* may be used as a coordination mechanism in three different ways: (1) we can standardize the *input skills* (3 in Figure 17.6)—that is, the worker skills that are inputs to the work process; (2) we can standardize the *work processes* themselves (4 in Figure 17.6)—that is, the methods workers use to transform inputs into outputs; and (3) we can standardize the *outputs* (5 in Figure 17.6)—that is, the products or services or the performance levels expected of workers. Standardization usually is developed by staff analysts and enforced by management such that skills, processes, and output meet predetermined standards.

Mintzberg further suggested that the five coordinating mechanisms roughly correspond to stages of organizational development and complexity. In the very

figure **17.6**

**Mintzberg's Five Coordinating Mechanisms**

*Mintzberg described five methods of coordinating the actions of organizational participants. The dashed lines in each diagram show the five different means of coordination: (1) mutual adjustment, (2) direct supervision, and standardization of (3) input skills, (4) work processes, and (5) outputs.*

Reference: Henry Mintzberg, *The Structuring of Organizations: A Synthesis of the Research.* © 1979, p. 4. Reprinted by permission of Prentice Hall, Inc., Englewood Cliffs, N.J.

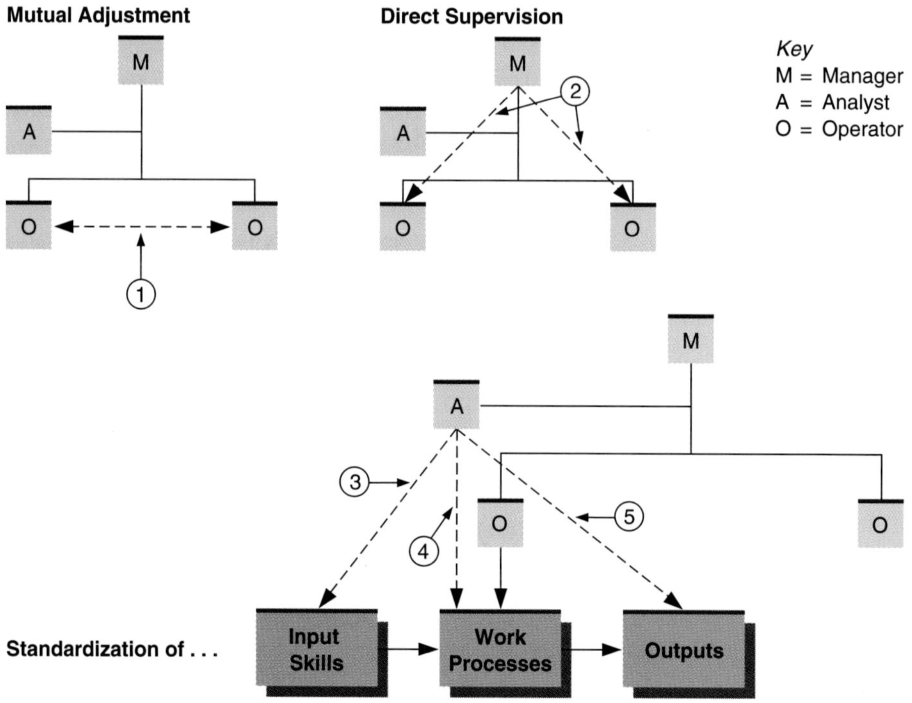

small organization, individuals working together communicate informally, achieving coordination by mutual adjustment. As more people join the organization, coordination needs become more complex, and direct supervision is added. For example, two or three people working in a small fast-food business can coordinate the work simply by talking to each other about the incoming orders for hamburgers, fries, and drinks. However, direct supervision becomes necessary in a larger restaurant with more complex cooking and warming equipment and several shifts of workers.

In large organizations, standardization is added to mutual adjustment and direct supervision to coordinate the work. The type of standardization depends on the nature of the work situation—that is, the organization's technology and environment. Standardization of work processes may achieve the necessary coordination when the organization's tasks are fairly routine. Thus, the larger fast-food outlet may standardize the making of hamburger patties: the meat is weighed, put into a hamburger press, and compressed into a patty. McDonald's is well known for this type of standardized process.

In other complex situations, standardization of the output may allow employees to do the work in any appropriate manner as long as the output meets specifications. Thus, the cook may not care how the hamburger is pressed, only that the right amount of meat is used and that the patty is the correct diameter and thickness. In other words, the worker may use any process as long as the output is a standard burger.

A third possibility is to coordinate work by standardizing worker skills. This approach is most often adopted in situations in which processes and outputs are difficult to standardize. In a hospital, for example, each patient must be treated as a special situation; the hospital process and output therefore cannot be standardized. Similar diagnostic and treatment procedures may be used with more than one patient, but the hospital relies on the skills of the physicians and nurses, which are standardized through their professional training, to coordinate the work. Organizations may have to depend on workers' mutual adjustment to coordinate their own actions in the most complex work situations or where the most important elements of coordination are the workers' professional training and communication skills. In effect, mutual adjustment can be an appropriate coordinating mechanism in both the simplest and the most complex situations. Analysis of the success of McDonald's shows that some part of its success is due to the degree of standardization. (See the "Mastering Change" box.)

Mintzberg pointed out that the five methods of coordination can be combined with the basic components of structure to develop five structural forms: the simple structure, the machine bureaucracy, the professional bureaucracy, the divisionalized form, and the adhocracy. Mintzberg called these structures pure or ideal types of designs.

The **simple structure**, typical of relatively small or new organizations, has little specialization or formalization; power and decision making are concentrated in the chief executive.

**Simple Structure** The **simple structure** characterizes relatively small, usually young organizations in a simple, dynamic environment. The organization has little specialization and formalization, and its overall structure is organic. Power and decision making are concentrated in the chief executive, often the owner-manager, and the flow of authority is from the top down. The primary coordinating mechanism is direct supervision. The organization must adapt quickly to survive because of its dynamic and often hostile environment. Most small businesses—a car dealership, a locally owned retail clothing store, or a candy manufacturer with only regional distribution—have a simple structure.

MASTERING CHANGE

## *McDonald's Makes Some Fast Changes*

The competition among fast-food companies is becoming fierce, and the changes are happening fast. But can the reasons for McDonald's success be maintained while it changes? Aside from his unique idea of friendly fast food, the premier contribution of founder Ray Kroc was his almost fanatical emphasis on standardization—of products, training, procedures, decor, and pricing. He wanted to guarantee that customers could get the exact eating experience in New York as in California. His obsession with conformity was the primary reason for the success of McDonald's. The menu was virtually the same everywhere. The meat patties were exactly the same weight and thickness. Even the procedures for making shakes were the same. Clearly Kroc followed Mintzberg's standardization by skills, work processes, and outputs. However, that standardization may have been part of the reason for the company's problems in later years. Warmed-over burgers were no longer in as much demand as they once were. In 1997, profits were sagging and the stock price was way down.

Enter new chief executive officer, Jack M. Greenberg in 1998, and the turnaround began. Greenberg's first moves included bringing in outsiders to fill key management slots, allowing franchise managers to make price discounting decisions, and retrofitting restaurants with new "Made for You" systems that allow the burgers to not be made until they are ordered, thus avoiding the warming bins that destroy the taste. Other changes are being made outside the traditional burger stores. McDonald's is investing in and franchising Mexican grills and pizza restaurants. Chipotle Mexican Grill and Donatos Pizza are featuring fresh ingredients along with their not-so-American tastes. The Mexican burritos take about one minute to make from the order, while the pizzas take almost six minutes. Now that the saturation point may be near for standardized burgers, McDonald's may have found a way to keep the profits coming.

> *"The food is spicy and fresh, every restaurant is designed differently, and there is no kids menu." — Steve Ells, founder and CEO of Chipotle Mexican Grill*

References: Meryl Davids, "Ray Kroc (1902–1984)," *Journal of Business Strategy*, September 1999, p. ITEM99270016; ; C. J. Rewick, "Big Mac's Attack: A Ground-Level Look at McDonald's Non-Burger Strategy," *Crain's Chicago Business*, May 17, 1999, p. 3; David Leonhardt, "Mickey D Wakes Up and Smells the Cilantro," *Business Week*, February 22, 1999, p. 88 (quote on p. 88); David Leonhardt and Ann Therese Palmer, "Getting Off Their McButts," *Business Week*, February 22, 1999, pp. 84–88; "Big McTurnaround," *Restaurants & Institutions*, February 1, 1999, p. 20.

In a **machine bureaucracy**, which typifies large, well-established organizations, work is highly specialized and formalized, and decision making is usually concentrated at the top.

**Machine Bureaucracy** The **machine bureaucracy** is typical of large, well-established companies in simple, stable environments. Work is highly specialized and formalized, and decision making is usually concentrated at the top. Standardization of work processes is the primary coordinating mechanism. This highly bureaucratic structure does not have to adapt quickly to changes because the environment is both simple and stable. Examples include large mass-production firms, such as Container Corporation of America; some automobile companies; and providers of services to mass markets, such as insurance companies.

A **professional bureaucracy** is characterized by horizontal specialization by professional area of expertise, little formalization, and decentralized decision making.

**Professional Bureaucracy** Usually found in a complex and stable environment, the **professional bureaucracy** relies on standardization of skills as the primary means of coordination. There is much horizontal specialization by professional areas of expertise but little formalization. Decision making is decentralized and takes place where the expertise is. The only means of coordination available to the organization is standardization of skills—the professionally trained employees.

East Coast Petroleum Corp. was founded by Loretta T. DeGrazia in 1985 and has grown to the point that it employs up to 20 employees (in season) and sells more than 4 million gallons of heating oil to over 2400 customers each year. DeGrazia has now regained control following problems in 1995 when a manager almost ran the company into the ground. She is back in control, using a simple structure, dealing with suppliers and customers, and getting the company back on its feet. The company's small size allows it to respond faster to unique customer needs.

Although it lacks centralization, the professional bureaucracy stabilizes and controls its tasks with rules and procedures developed in the relevant profession. Hospitals, universities, and consulting firms are examples.

The **divisionalized form**, typical of old, very large organizations, is divided according to the different markets served; horizontal and vertical specialization exists between divisions and headquarters, decision making is divided between headquarters and divisions, and outputs are standardized.

**Divisionalized Form** The **divisionalized form** is characteristic of old, very large firms operating in a relatively simple, stable environment with several diverse markets. It resembles the machine bureaucracy except that it is divided according to the various markets it serves. There is some horizontal and vertical specialization between the divisions (each defined by a market) and headquarters. Decision making is clearly split between headquarters and the divisions, and the primary means of coordination is standardization of outputs. The mechanism of control required by headquarters encourages the development of machine bureaucracies in the divisions.

The classic example of the divisionalized form is General Motors, which, in a reorganization in the 1920s, adopted a design that created divisions for each major car model.[42] Although the divisions have been reorganized and the cars changed several times, the concept of the divisionalized organization is still very evident at GM.[43] General Electric uses a two-tiered divisionalized structure, dividing its numerous businesses into strategic business units, which are further divided into sectors.[44]

In an **adhocracy**, typically found in young organizations in highly technical fields, decision making is spread throughout the organization, power resides with the experts, horizontal and vertical specialization exists, and there is little formalization.

**Adhocracy** The **adhocracy** is typically found in young organizations engaged in highly technical fields, where the environment is complex and dynamic. Decision making is spread throughout the organization, and power is in the hands of experts. There is horizontal and vertical specialization but little formalization, resulting in a very organic structure. Coordination is by mutual adjustment through frequent personal communication and liaison. Specialists are not grouped together in functional units but are deployed into specialized market-oriented project teams.

The typical adhocracy is usually established to foster innovation, something to which the other four types of structures are not particularly well suited. Numerous U.S. organizations—Johnson & Johnson, Procter & Gamble, Monsanto, and 3M, for example—are known for their innovation and constant stream of new products.[45] These organizations are either structured totally as adhocracies or have large divisions set up as adhocracies. Johnson & Johnson established a new-products division over thirty years ago to encourage continued innovation, creativity, and risk taking. The division continues to succeed; Johnson & Johnson in the United States has introduced more than two hundred new products in the past several years. Most of the new start-up ".com" companies are probably structured as adhocracies.

Mintzberg believed that fit among parts is the most important consideration in designing an organization. Not only must there be a fit among the structure, the structural imperatives (technology, size, and environment), and organizational strategy, but the components of structure (rules and procedures, decision making, specialization) must fit together and be appropriate for the situation. Mintzberg suggested that an organization will not function effectively when these characteristics are not put together properly.[46]

## Matrix Organization Design

One other organizational form deserves attention here: the matrix organization design. Matrix design is consistent with the contingency approach, because it is useful only in certain situations. One of the earliest implementations of the matrix design was at TRW Systems Group in 1959.[47] Following TRW's lead, other firms in aerospace and high-technology fields created similar matrix structures.

The **matrix design** combines two different designs to gain the benefits of each; typically combined are a product or project departmentalization scheme and a functional structure.

The **matrix design** attempts to combine two different designs to gain the benefits of each. The most common matrix form superimposes product or project departmentalization on a functional structure (see Figure 17.7). Each department and project has a manager; each employee, however, is a member of both a functional department and a project team. The dual role means that the employee has two supervisors, the department manager and the project leader.

A matrix structure is appropriate when three conditions exist:

1. There is external pressure for a dual focus, meaning that factors in the environment require the organization to focus its efforts equally on responding to multiple external factors and on internal operations.
2. There is pressure for a high information-processing capacity.
3. There is pressure for shared resources.[48]

In the aerospace industry in the early 1960s, all these conditions were present. Private companies had a dual focus: their customers, primarily the federal government, and the complex engineering and technical fields in which they were engaged. Moreover, the environments of these companies were changing very rapidly. Technological sophistication and competition were increasing, resulting in growing environmental uncertainty and an added need for information processing. The final condition stemmed from the pressure on the companies to excel in a very competitive environment despite limited resources. The compa-

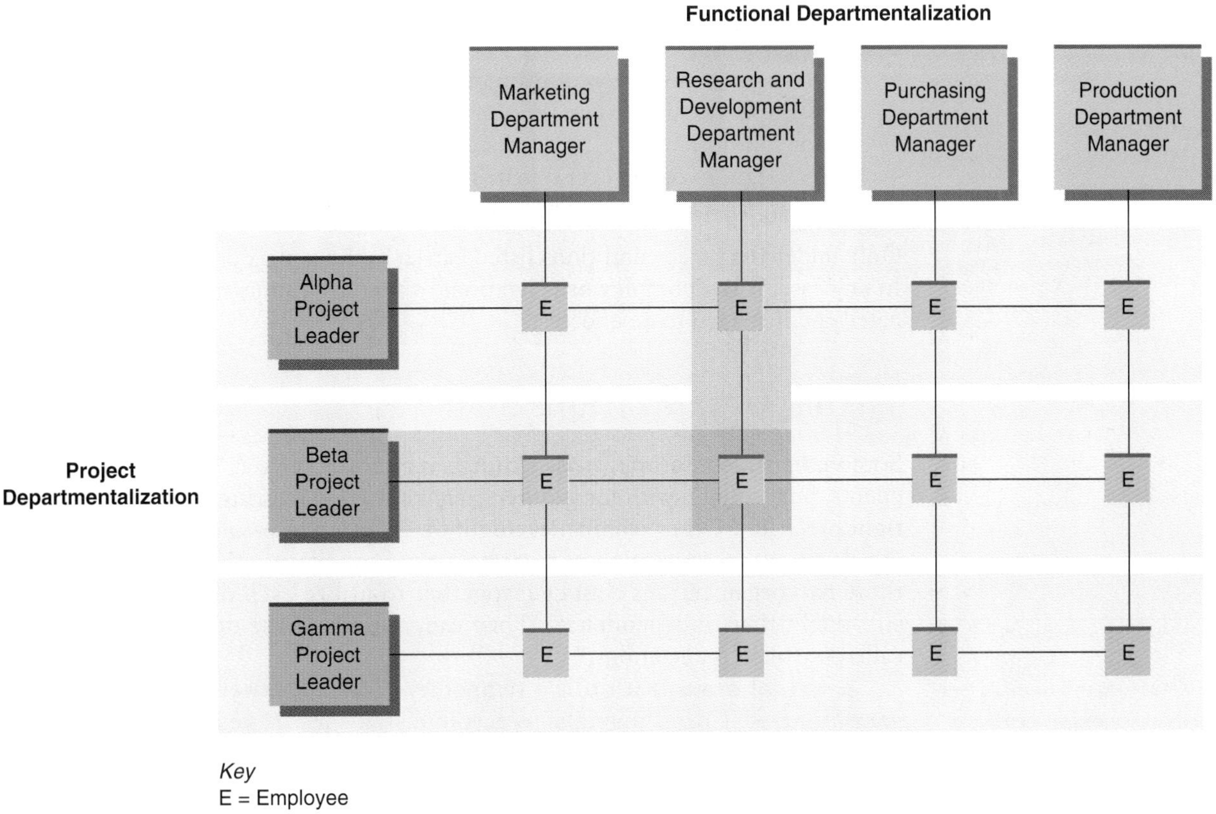


figure 17.7
**A Matrix Organization Design**

*A matrix organization design superimposes two different types of departmentalization onto each other—for example, a functional structure and a project structure.*

nies concluded that it was inefficient to assign their highly professional—and highly compensated—scientific and engineering personnel to just one project at a time.

Built into the matrix structure is the capacity for flexible and coordinated responses to internal and external pressures. Members can be reassigned from one project to another as demands for their skills change. They may work for a month on one project, be assigned to the functional home department for two weeks, and then be reassigned to another project for the next six months. The matrix form improves project coordination by assigning project responsibility to a single leader rather than dividing it among several functional department heads. Furthermore, it improves communication because employees can talk about the project with members of both the project team and the functional unit to which they belong. In this way, solutions to project problems may emerge from either group. Many different types of organizations have used the matrix form of organization, notably large-project manufacturing firms, banks, and hospitals.[49]

The matrix organizational form thus provides several benefits for the organization. It is not, however, trouble-free. Typical problems include the following:

1. The dual reporting system may cause role conflict among employees.
2. Power struggles may occur over who has authority on which issues.
3. Matrix organization often is misinterpreted to mean that a group must make all decisions; as a result, group decision-making techniques may be used when they are not appropriate.
4. If the design involves several matrices, each laid on top of another, there may be no way to trace accountability and authority.[50]

Only under the three conditions listed earlier is the matrix design likely to work. In any case, it is a complex organizational system that must be carefully coordinated and managed to be effective.

## Virtual Organizations

Some companies do one or two things very well, such as sell to government clients, but struggle with most others, such as manufacturing products with very tight precision. Other companies might be great at close-tolerance manufacturing, but lousy at reaching out to certain types of clients. Wouldn't it be nice if those two organizations could get together to utilize each other's strengths but still retain their independence? They can, and many are doing so in what are called "virtual organizations."

A **virtual organization** is a temporary alliance between two or more organizations that band together to undertake a specific venture.

A **virtual organization** is a temporary alliance between two or more organizations that band together to accomplish a specific venture. Each partner contributes to the partnership what it does best. The opportunity is usually something that needs a quick response to maximize the market opportunity. A slow response will probably result in losses. Therefore, a virtual organization allows different organizations to bring their best capabilities together without worrying about learning how to do something that they have never done before. Thus, the reaction time is faster, mistakes are fewer, and profits are quicker. Sharing of information among partners is usually facilitated by electronic technology such as computers, faxes, and electronic mail systems, thereby avoiding the expenses of renting new office space for the venture or costly travel time between companies.

There are no restrictions on how large or small organizations or projects need to be to take advantage of this type of alliance. In fact, some very small organizations are working together quite well. In Phoenix, Arizona, a public relations firm, a graphic design firm, and an advertising firm are working together on projects that have multiple requirements beyond those offered by any single firm. Rather than turn down the business or try to hire additional staff to do the extra work, the three firms work together to better serve client needs. The clients like the arrangement because they get high-quality work and do not have to shop around for someone to do little pieces of work. The networking companies feel that the result is better creativity, more teamwork, more efficient use of resources, and better service for their clients.

More typically, however, large companies create virtual organizations. Corning is involved in nineteen partnerships on many different types of projects, and they are pleased with most of their ventures and plan to do more. Intel worked with two Japanese organizations to manufacture flash memory chips for computers. One of the Japanese companies was not able to complete its part of the project, leaving Intel with a major product-delivery problem. Intel's chairman at the time, Andrew Grove, was not too happy about that venture and may not participate in others.[51]

The virtual organization is not just another management fad. It has become one answer to the rapid changes brought about by changing technology and global competition. Management scholars have mixed opinions on the effectiveness of such arrangements. Although it may seem odd, this approach can produce substantial benefits in some situations.

# Contemporary Organization Design

The current proliferation of design theories and alternative forms of organization gives practicing managers a dizzying array of choices. The task of the manager or organization designer is to examine the firm and its situation and to design a form of organization that meets its needs. A partial list of contemporary alternatives includes such approaches as downsizing, rightsizing, reengineering the organization, team-based organizations, and the virtual organization. These approaches often make use of total quality management, employee empowerment, employee involvement and participation, reduction in force, process innovation, and networks of alliances. Practicing managers must deal with the new terminology, the temptation to treat such new approaches as fads, and their own organizational situation before making major organization design shifts. In this section we describe two currently popular approaches—reengineering and rethinking the organization—as well as global organization structure and design issues. We conclude with a summary of the dominant themes in contemporary organization design.

## Reengineering the Organization

**Reengineering** is the radical redesign of organizational processes to achieve major gains in cost, time, and provision of services.

**Reengineering** is the radical redesign of organizational processes to achieve major gains in cost, time, and provision of services. It forces the organization to start from scratch to redesign itself around its most important processes rather than beginning with its current form and making incremental changes. It assumes that if a company had no existing structure, departments, jobs, rules, or established ways of doing things, reengineering would design the organization as it should be for future success. The process starts with determining what the customers actually want from the organization and then developing a strategy to provide it. Once the strategy is in place, strong leadership from top management can create a core team of people to design an organizational system to achieve the strategy.[52] Reengineering is a process of redesigning the organization that does not necessarily result in any particular organizational form.

## Rethinking the Organization

**Rethinking** the organization means looking at organization design in totally different ways, perhaps even abandoning the classic view of organization as a pyramid.

Also currently popular is the concept of rethinking the organization. **Rethinking** the organization is also a process for restructuring that throws out traditional assumptions that organizations should be structured with boxes and horizontal and vertical lines. Robert Tomasko makes some suggestions for new organizational forms for the future.[53] He suggests that the traditional pyramid shape of organizations may be inappropriate for current business practices. Traditional structures, he contends, may have too many levels of management arranged in a hierarchy to be efficient and to respond to dynamic changes in the environment.

*"Every year for the past 14 years, we've been a new company." — Ted Waitt, founder and chairman of the board, Gateway 2005*[54]

Rethinking organizations might entail thinking of the organization structure as a dome rather than a pyramid, the dome being top management, which acts as an umbrella, covering and protecting those underneath but leaving them alone to do their work. Internal units underneath the dome would have the flexibility to interact with each other and with environmental forces. Companies such as Microsoft Corporation and Royal Dutch Petroleum have some of the characteristics of this dome approach to organization design. American Express Financial Advisors restructured from a vertical organization into a horizontal organization as a result of their rethinking everything about the ways they needed to meet customers' needs.[55]

Kellogg is rethinking how it develops new products. CEO Carlos Gutierrez believes that diversity and the creativity of people drive innovation, so he created cross-functional teams in which market researchers, food technologists, and engineers work together to come up with new snack and breakfast foods and other new products. One of the new products, Raisin Bran Crunch, caught on quite well and had more than one-percent market share in 1999. New packaging and manufacturing innovations are also encouraged. One idea was to package a carton of milk and a spoon with individual-sized portions of cereal for those who like to eat on the run. Researchers are encouraged to spend up to 15 percent of their time on their own ideas. The new systems are expected to greatly increase the number and quality of new ideas that are successful in the market.

## Global Organization Structure and Design Issues

Managers working in an international environment must consider not only similarities and differences among firms in different cultures but the structural features of multinational organizations.

**Between-Culture Issues** "Between-culture issues" are variations in the structure and design of companies operating in different cultures. As might be expected, such companies have both differences and similarities. For example, one study compared the structures of fifty-five U.S. and fifty-one Japanese manufacturing plants. Results suggested that the Japanese plants had less specialization, more "formal" centralization (but less "real" centralization), and taller hierarchies than their U.S. counterparts. The Japanese structures were also less affected by their technology than the U.S. plants.[56]

Many cultures still take a traditional view of organization structure not unlike the approaches used in this country during the days of classical organization theory. For example, Tom Peters, a leading U.S. management consultant and coauthor of *In Search of Excellence*, spent some time lecturing to managers in China. They were not interested in his ideas about decentralization and worker participation, however. Instead, the most frequently asked question concerned how a manager determined the optimal span of control.[57]

In contrast, many European companies are increasingly patterning themselves after successful U.S. firms, stemming in part from corporate raiders in Europe emulating their U.S. counterparts and partly from the managerial work force becoming better educated. Together, these two factors have caused many European firms to become less centralized and to adopt divisional structures by moving from functional to product departmentalization.[58]

### Multinational Organization

More and more firms have entered the international arena and have found it necessary to adapt their designs to better cope with different cultures.[59] For example, after a company has achieved a moderate level of international activity, it often establishes an international division, usually at the same organizational level as other major functional divisions. Levi-Strauss uses this organization design. One division, Levi-Strauss International, is responsible for the company's business activities in Europe, Canada, Latin America, and Asia.

For an organization that has become more deeply involved in international activities, a logical form of organization design is the international matrix. This type of matrix arrays product managers across the top. Project teams headed by foreign market managers cut across the product departments. A company with three basic product lines, for example, might establish three product departments (of course, it would include domestic advertising, finance, and operations departments as well). Foreign market managers can be designated for, say, Canada, Japan, Europe, Latin America, and Australia. Each foreign market manager is then responsible for all three of the company's products in his or her market.[60]

Finally, at the most advanced level of multinational activity, a firm might become an international conglomerate. Nestlé and Unilever N.V. fit this type. Each has an international headquarters (Nestlé in Vevey, Switzerland, and Unilever in Rotterdam, the Netherlands) that coordinates the activities of businesses scattered around the globe. Nestlé has factories in fifty countries and markets its products in virtually every country in the world. Over 96 percent of its business is done outside of Switzerland, and only about 7,000 of its 160,000 employees reside in its home country.

## Dominant Themes of Contemporary Designs

The four dominant themes of current design strategies are (1) the effects of technological and environmental change, (2) the importance of people, (3) the necessity of staying in touch with the customer, and (4) the global organization. Technology and the environment are changing so fast and in so many unpredictable ways that no organization structure will be appropriate for long. The changes in electronic information processing, transmission, and retrieval alone are so vast that employee relationships, information distribution, and task coordination need to be reviewed almost daily.[61] The emphasis on productivity through people that was energized by Thomas Peters and Robert Waterman Jr. in the 1980s continues in almost every aspect of contemporary organization design.[62] In addition, Peters and Austin further emphasized the importance of staying in touch with customers at the initial stage in organization design.[63]

These popular contemporary approaches and the four dominant factors argue for a contingency design perspective. Unfortunately, there is no "one best way." Managers must consider the impact of multiple factors—sociotechnical systems, strategy, the structural imperatives, changing information technology, people, global considerations, and a concern for end users—on their particular organization and design the organization structure accordingly.

## Synopsis

Universal approaches to organization design attempt to specify the one best way to structure organizations for effectiveness. Contingency approaches, on the other hand, propose that the best way to design organization structure depends on a variety of factors. Important contingency approaches to organization design center on the organizational strategy, the determinants of structure, and strategic choice.

Initially, strategy was seen as the determinant of structure: the structure of the organization was designed to implement its purpose, goals, and strategies. Taking managerial choice into account in determining organization structure is a modification of this view. The manager designs the structure to accomplish organizational goals, guided by an analysis of the contextual factors, the strategies of the organization, and personal preferences.

The structural imperatives are size, technology, and environment. In general, large organizations have more complex structures and usually more than one technology. The structures of small organizations, on the other hand, may be dominated by one core operations technology. The structure of the organization is also established to fit with the environmental demands and buffer the core operating technology from environmental changes and uncertainties.

Organization designs can take many forms. A mechanistic structure relies on the administrative hierarchy for communication and directing activities. An organic design is structured like a network; communications and interactions are horizontal and diagonal across groups and teams throughout the organization.

In the sociotechnical systems view, the organization is an open system structured to integrate two important subsystems: the technical (task) subsystem and the social subsystem. According to this approach, organizations should structure the task, authority, and reporting relationships around the work group, delegating to the group decisions on job assignments, training, inspection, rewards, and punishments. The task of management is to monitor the environment and coordinate the structures, rules, and procedures.

Mintzberg's ideal types of organization design were derived from a framework of coordinating mechanisms. The five types are simple structure, machine bureaucracy, professional bureaucracy, divisionalized form, and adhocracy. Most organizations have some characteristics of each type, but one is likely to predominate. Mintzberg believed that the most important consideration in designing an organization is the fit among parts of the organization.

The matrix design combines two types of structure (usually functional and project departmentalization) to gain the benefits of each. It usually results in a multiple command and authority system. Benefits of the matrix form include increased flexibility, cooperation, and communication and better use of skilled personnel. Typical problems are associated with the dual reporting system and the complex management system needed to coordinate work.

Virtual organizations are temporary alliances between several organizations that agree to work together on a specific venture. Reaction time to business opportunities can be very fast with these types of alliances. In effect, organizations create a network of other organizations to enable them to respond to changes in the environment.

Contemporary organization design is contingency oriented. Currently popular design strategies are reengineering the organization and rethinking the organization. Four factors influencing design decisions are the changing technological environment, concern for people as valued resources, the need to keep in touch with customers, and global impacts on organizations.

# Discussion Questions

1. What are the differences between universal approaches and contingency approaches to organization design?
2. Define "organizational environment" and "organizational technology." In what ways do these concepts overlap?
3. Identify and describe some of the environmental and technological factors that affect your college or university. Give specific examples of how they affect you as a student.
4. How does organization design usually differ for large and small organizations?
5. What might be the advantages and disadvantages of structuring the faculty members at your college or university as an autonomous work group?
6. What do you think are the purposes, goals, and strategies of your college or university? How are they reflected in its structure?
7. Which of Mintzberg's pure forms is best illustrated by a major national political party (Democratic or Republican)? A religious organization? A football team? The U.S. Olympic Committee?
8. In a matrix organization, would you rather be a project leader, a functional department head, or a highly trained technical specialist? Why?
9. Discuss what you think the important design considerations will be for organization designers in the year 2020.
10. How would your college or university be different if you rethought or reengineered how it is designed?

# Organizational Behavior Case for Discussion

## Microsoft Reorganizes and Reorganizes

Microsoft was not in trouble when it decided to reorganize in 1999, either time. In 1998, revenues rose by 30 percent to more than $3 billion, average income per employee was $257,000, and market capitalization was more than $400 billion. Those are hardly the types of numbers that spur massive reorganization among most companies. But, of course, Microsoft is not like most other companies. So, why did Microsoft reorganize?

In late 1998, Bill Gates named Steve Ballmer as the first president of Microsoft in seven years. After his appointment Ballmer walked the halls, talking with employees from every level in every division. Most importantly, he listened to employees describe what they thought needed to be done. He got lots of stories and complaints about the company's being slow to react to market changes, stubborn resistance to new ways of thinking, and not listening to what customers want. One story described a proposal to add a small, but unique feature to a piece of software. Writing the software code would take only thirty minutes, but it took ten meetings and three months to get management approval. Other managers described their frustration with the structure and wanted more authority and autonomy and less micromanagement. In addition, talented people were leaving so fast that people were talking about the brain drain at Microsoft. Gates and Ballmer had been involved in almost every decision, thereby subverting the decision-making authority of managers at every level. At the same time, competition was increasing from every direction: from Novell, Sun

Microsystems, Netscape, and hundreds of small firms whose only mission is to beat Microsoft. Customers wanted specific features in their software that Microsoft either did not provide or was too slow in providing. That left a lot of room for the competition to serve the needs of the customers and make more sales.

Ballmer's reaction was to reinvent the company from its structure to its culture in what he called "Vision 2," announced in March 1999. First, he and Gates agreed that the old ways of doing things were too slow. The old structure had two primary divisions: one for applications and one for operating systems. The new idea was to make the company more responsive to the changing marketplace. This strategy was not a reversal of Microsoft's old philosophy of putting a PC on every desk and in every home but was rather an extension of it. Gates and Ballmer envisioned increasing use of a variety of computing devices anytime and anywhere, and Microsoft wants to be the software provider for integrative computing. The company created eight operating divisions, six of which are based on customers rather than on technology: business and enterprises, business productivity, software developers, consumers and commerce, home and retail, consumer windows, sales and support, and research. More than just rearrange the pieces, Microsoft has made these divisions autonomous. The heads of each division are free to run their divisions as they wish, as long as they meet revenue and profit goals. The new division heads were quite excited as they reacted to being head of their own small businesses, with control over product development as well as a sales force for the first time. Gates and Ballmer have both had to consciously avoid falling into the old roles of making decisions for everybody. It is strictly hands off of the operating divisions.

At first, there were a few problems as to which division each set of products should be assigned. For example, the Windows CE product (for the handheld, palm-sized personal companions) was originally assigned to the same group that was developing new versions of Windows 98 for consumer PCs. However, when Bob Muglia, head of the business productivity group, had great difficulty getting and integrating information from his palm-sized companion and his company email using the Exchange program, he realized that those products needed to be able to work together. So, the Windows CE product was put into his business productivity group.

Other than minor adjustments, the reorganization has gone quite well—that is, until December 1999, when Microsoft recombined the divisions that were consumer oriented into one division headed by Robert Belluzzo, a new executive with long experience at Hewlett-Packard and Silicon Graphics. The new division will put together all products that affect consumer product makers, cable televisions, and the home and retail group, which has responsibility for PC games and hardware and retail sales. The company now has four major groups: Consumer Products, Platforms, Business Productivity, and Developers. From the original two divisions based on technology, to six consumer-based divisions, to four broader consumer-based divisions all in one year is a lot for people to feel comfortable with. To cap off the reorganization, Gates stepped down as CEO leaving the chief executive job to Ballmer. Gates names himself "chief software architect" as he plans to lead the company into the new Internet future. The hard work really begins as employees at all levels learn how to work together to reach the performance and profit targets.

## Case Questions

1. Describe the various configurational and operational aspects of structure that were changed by Microsoft in 1999.
2. What do you think were the contingency factors, or the imperatives, that forced the company to change?
3. Do you think that Microsoft should consider using a matrix design? Why or why not?

References: David Kirkpatrick, "The New Face of Microsoft," *Fortune*, Febuary 7, 2000, pp. 87–96; David Bank, "Microsoft Reshuffles Its Executive Team," *Wall Street Journal*, December 6, 1999, p. B8; David Bank, "Telecommunications (A Special Report): The Business—Window in the Future: Bob Muglia Is the Man in Charge of Preparing Microsoft for the Wireless Battles," *Wall Street Journal*, September 20, 1999, p. R20; Michael Moeller, Steve Hamm, and Timothy J. Mullaney, "Remaking Microsoft," *Business Week*, May 17, 1999, pp. 106–114; Eric Nee, "Microsoft Gets Ready to Play a New Game," *Fortune*, April 26, 1999, pp. 107–112.

# Experiencing Organizational Behavior

## Studying a Real Organization

**Purpose:** This exercise will help you understand the factors that determine the design of organizations.

**Format:** You will interview at least five employees in different parts of the college or university that you attend or employees of a small- to medium-sized organization and analyze the reasons for its design. (You may want to coordinate this exercise with the "Experiencing Organizational Behavior" exercise in Chapter 16.)

**Procedure:** If you use a local organization, your first task is to find one with between fifty and five hundred employees. (It should not be part of your college or university.) If you did the exercise for Chapter 16, you can use the same company for this exercise. The organization should have more than two hierarchical levels, but it should not be too complex to understand with a short period of study. You may want to check with your professor before contacting the company. Your initial contact should be with the highest-ranking manager you can reach. Make sure that top management is aware of your project and gives its approval.

If you use your local college or university, you could talk to professors, secretaries, and other administrative staff in the admissions office, student services department, athletic department, library, and many others. Be sure to include employees from a variety of jobs and levels in your interviews.

Using the material in this chapter, you will interview employees to obtain the following information on the structure of the organization:

1. What is the organization in business to do? What are its goals and its strategies for achieving them?
2. How large is the company? What is the total number of employees? How many work full time? How many work part time?
3. What are the most important components of the organization's environment?
4. Is the number of important environmental components large or small?
5. How quickly or slowly do these components change?
6. Would you characterize the organization's environment as certain, uncertain, or somewhere in between? If in between, describe approximately how certain or uncertain.
7. What is the organization's dominant technology; that is, how does it transform inputs into outputs?
8. How rigid is the company in its application of rules and procedures? Is it flexible enough to respond to environmental changes?
9. How involved are employees in the daily decision making related to their jobs?
10. What methods are used to ensure control over the actions of employees?

Interview at least five employees of the college or company at different levels and in different departments. One should hold a top-level position. Be sure to ask the questions in a way the employees will understand; they may not be familiar with some of the terminology used in this chapter.

The result of the exercise should be a report describing the technology, environment, and structure of the company. You should discuss the extent to which the structure is appropriate for the organization's strategy, size, technology, and environment. If it does not seem appropriate, you should explain the reasons. If you also used this company for the exercise in Chapter 16, you can comment further on the organization chart and its appropriateness for the company. You may want to send a copy of your report to the cooperating company.

### Follow-up Questions

1. Which aspects of strategy, size, environment, and technology were the most difficult to obtain information about? Why?
2. If there were differences in the responses of the employees you interviewed, how do you account for them?
3. If you were the president of the organization you analyzed, would you structure it in the same way? Why or why not? If not, how would you structure it differently?
4. How did your answers to questions 2 and 3 differ from those in the exercise in Chapter 16?

# Building Organizational Behavior Skills

## Diagnosing Organization Structure

**Introduction:** You are probably involved with many different organizations—the place you work, a social or service club, a church, the college or university you attend. This assessment will help you diagnose the structure of one of those organizations. You could use this assessment on the organization that you analyzed in the preceding "Experiencing Organizational Behavior" exercise.

**Instructions:** First, pick one of the organizations you belong to or know a lot about. Then read each statement below and determine the degree to which you agree or disagree with that statement about your organization using the following scale.

| 5 | 4 | 3 | 2 | 1 |
|---|---|---|---|---|
| Strongly Agree | Agree | Don't Know | Disagree | Strongly Disagree |

Then place the number of the response that best represents your organization in the space before each statement.

____ 1. If people believe that they have the right approach to carrying out their job, they can usually go ahead without checking with their superior.

____ 2. People in this organization don't always have to wait for orders from their superiors on important matters.

____ 3. People in this organization share ideas with their superior.

____ 4. Different individuals play important roles in making decisions.

____ 5. People in this organization are likely to express their feelings openly on important matters.

____ 6. People in this organization are encouraged to speak their minds on important matters, even if it means disagreeing with their superior.

____ 7. Talking to other people about the problems someone might have in making decisions is an important part of the decision-making process.

____ 8. Developing employees' talents and abilities is a major concern of this organization.

____ 9. People are encouraged to make suggestions before decisions are made.

____10. In this organization, most people can have their point of view heard.

____11. Superiors often seek advice from subordinates before making decisions.

____12. Subordinates play an active role in running this organization.

____13. For many decisions, the rules and regulations are developed as we go along.

____14. It is not always necessary to go through channels in dealing with important matters.

____15. Employees do not consistently follow the same rules and regulations.

____16. There are few rules and regulations for handling any kind of problem that may arise in making most decisions.

____17. People from different departments are often put together in task forces to solve important problems.

____18. For special problems, we usually set up a temporary task force until we meet our objectives.

____19. Jobs in this organization are not clearly defined.

____20. In this organization, adapting to changes in the environment is important.

____ = Total Score

When you have finished, add up the numbers to get a total score. Your instructor can help you interpret your scores by referring to the *Instructor's Resource Manual.*

Reference: From Ricky W. Griffin, *Management*, 5/e, which is adapted from Robert T. Keller, *Type of Management System.* Griffin copyright © 1996 by Houghton Mifflin Company. Keller copyright © 1988. Used by permission of Houghton Mifflin Company and Robert T. Keller.

## Developing OB Internet Skills

**Introduction:** The way an organization is structured depends on many different factors and is really only meaningful within its particular situation, as this chapter has described. This exercise will help you understand the relationships among these factors.

**Internet Assignment:** Using the same information and web sites you used for the Internet assignment in Chapter 16, see if you can categorize each of those organization structures in terms of the types of structures discussed in this chapter. Then, see if you can find more information about the environment, technology, size, strategy, and managerial factors for each of the four companies you used in that exercise. You may have to use additional web sites or search engines to find out more about the companies.

**Follow-up:** Review each of the web sites you have used in the Internet assignments for this chapter and Chapter 16. Write a brief analysis of the different types of information found in each. Finally, respond to the following questions:

1. To what extent did the organization structure of each organization seem to fit with the other information you found on each organization?
2. Do you think that the official web sites of companies should include all of the information you found? Why or why not?
3. Were the web sites easy to use to find the information you needed?

chapter

18

# Organization Culture

**Management Preview** Many organizations attribute their success to a strong and firmly entrenched culture. Companies such as Sony, Boeing, Nike, Hewlett-Packard, and many others are successful because they each have a culture that is unique and appropriate just for them. But culture is an often elusive concept that can be easily misunderstood. In this chapter we describe the organization cultures of several different organizations and show how organizations can develop their own. We begin this chapter by exploring the nature and historical foundations of organization culture. Next, we describe the process of creating the culture. We then examine two basic approaches to describing the characteristics of organization culture and discuss three important issues in organization culture. Finally, we show how organization culture can be managed to enhance the organization's effectiveness. But first, we describe an unusual corporate culture at Siebel Systems. ■

Siebel Systems, maker of corporate software for managing sales, customer service, and marketing efforts, was identified by *Fortune* magazine in 1999 as number 1 on their list of the one hundred fastest-growing U.S. companies. Founded in 1993, Siebel Systems' revenue growth in 1999 was 218 percent, its revenues were over $300 million, and its market share was approaching 51 percent. In two years, its stock price had increased 580 percent from its initial public offering in 1996.

Located in the heart of Silicon Valley, which is noted for its relaxed dress codes and informality, Siebel Systems has exactly the opposite culture. From the very beginning, Tom Siebel and cofounder Pat House consciously established a highly professional corporate culture. Siebel Systems is a rule-driven, high-performance company in which jackets and ties are mandatory, employees are not allowed to eat at their desks, office doors must remain open at all times, walls are covered with customer logos, and conference rooms, such as the Kellogg Room, are named after customer companies. Siebel believes that the customer room names and elaborate displays of customer logos drive home the company's customer focus to employees and can be impressive to customers as well.

*"I care what my customers say, my employees say, my shareholders say." — Tom Siebel, chairman and CEO of Siebel Systems**

The company was started by the two former Oracle sales and marketing managers who were determined to develop a software product that would fully automate the marketing, sales force, and customer service database for companies. After discovering what sales force managers wanted in such a product, they formed Siebel Systems and hired software developers. Their first product hit the market in 1995 and took off. Siebel developed alliances with Charles Schwab that led to large sales to Schwab offices. A second alliance with Andersen Consulting led to widespread use by Andersen clients.

Tom Siebel has been portrayed as an egomaniac running a culture of fear and arrogance. Competitors whom he has beaten out for customers claim that the high-performance demands to make the customer happy at all costs create unhappy employees and high turnover. Siebel, however, points out that the company has a very low turnover. Salespeople make at least $200,000 per year, and the stock purchase plan for employees has made many rich. The company philosophy is to have a total organizational focus to do whatever it takes to ensure that the customer is satisfied.[1] ■

Siebel Systems developed a culture that reflected its founders and was just right for their company. The founders had the vision and set the expectations for the company from the very start. What about existing companies? All companies have some sort of culture. But it is not easy to create this kind of successful culture for every organization.

# The Nature of Organization Culture

In the early 1980s, organization culture became a central concern in the study of organizational behavior. Hundreds of researchers began to work in this area. Numerous books were published, important academic journals dedicated entire issues to the discussion of culture, and almost overnight, organizational behavior textbooks that omitted culture as a topic of study became obsolete.

Interest in organization culture was not limited to academic researchers. Businesses expressed a far more intense interest in culture than in other aspects of organizational behavior. *Business Week*, *Fortune*, and other business periodicals published articles that touted culture as the key to an organization's success and suggested that managers who could manage through their organization's culture almost certainly would rise to the top.[2]

Although the enthusiasm of the early 1980s has waned somewhat, the study of organization culture remains important. The assumption is that organizations with a strong culture perform at higher levels than those without a strong culture.[3] For example, studies have shown that organizations with strong cultures that are strategically appropriate, and that have norms that permit the organization to change, actually do perform well.[4] Other studies have shown that different functional units may require different types of cultures.[5] The research on the impact of culture on organizational performance is mixed, however, depending on how the research is done and what variables are measured.

Many researchers have begun to weave the important aspects of organization culture into their research on more traditional topics. Now there are fewer headline stories in the popular business press about culture and culture management, but organization culture has become a common topic for managers interested in improving organizational performance, as the opening case about Siebel Systems illustrates. The enormous amount of research on culture completed in the last twenty years has fundamentally shifted the way both academics and managers look at organizations. Some of the concepts developed in the analysis of organization culture have become basic parts of the business vocabulary, and the analysis of organization culture is one of the most important specialties in the field of organizational behavior.

## What Is Organization Culture?

A surprising aspect of the recent rise in interest in organization culture is that the concept, unlike virtually every other concept in the field, has no single widely accepted definition. Indeed, it often appears that authors feel compelled to develop their own definitions, which range from very broad to highly specific. For example, Deal and Kennedy define a firm's culture as "the way we do things around here."[6] This very broad definition presumably could include the way a firm manufactures its products, pays its bills, treats its employees, and performs any other organizational operation. More specific definitions include those of Schein ("the pattern of basic assumptions that a given group has invented, discovered, or developed in learning to cope with its problems of external adaptation and internal integration"[7]) and Peters and Waterman ("a dominant and coherent set of shared values conveyed by such symbolic means as stories, myths, legends, slogans, anecdotes, and fairy tales"[8]). Table 18.1 lists these and other important definitions of organization culture.

Despite the apparent diversity of these definitions, a few common attributes emerge. First, all the definitions refer to some set of values held by individuals in a firm. These values define what is good or acceptable behavior and what is bad or unacceptable behavior. In some organizations, for example, it is unacceptable to blame customers when problems arise. Here the value "the customer is always right" tells managers what actions are acceptable (not blaming the customer) and what actions are not acceptable (blaming the customer). In other organizations, the dominant values might support blaming customers for problems, penalizing employees who make mistakes, or treating employees as the firm's most valuable assets. In each case, values help members of an organization understand how they should act.

A second attribute common to many of the definitions in Table 18.1 is that the values that make up an organization's culture are often taken for granted; that is, they are basic assumptions made by the firm's employees, rather than being written in a book or made explicit in a training program. It may be as difficult for an organization to articulate these basic assumptions as it is for people to express their

table 18.1

**Definitions of Organization Culture**

| Definition | Source |
|---|---|
| "A belief system shared by an organization's members" | J. C. Spender, "Myths, Recipes and Knowledge-Bases in Organizational Analysis" (Unpublished manuscript, Graduate School of Management, University of California at Los Angeles, 1983), p. 2. |
| "Strong, widely shared core values" | C. O'Reilly, "Corporations, Cults, and Organizational Culture: Lessons from Silicon Valley Firms" (Paper presented at the Annual Meeting of the Academy of Management, Dallas, Texas, 1983), p. 1. |
| "The way we do things around here" | T. E. Deal and A. A. Kennedy, *Corporate Cultures: The Rites and Rituals of Corporate Life* (Reading, Mass.: Addison-Wesley, 1982), p. 4. |
| "The collective programming of the mind" | G. Hofstede, *Culture's Consequences: International Differences in Work-Related Values* (Beverly Hills, Calif.: Sage, 1980), p. 25. |
| "Collective understandings" | J. Van Maanen and S. R. Barley, "Cultural Organization: Fragments of a Theory" (Paper presented at the Annual Meeting of the Academy of Management, Dallas, Texas, 1983), p. 7. |
| "A set of shared, enduring beliefs communicated through a variety of symbolic media, creating meaning in people's work lives" | J. M. Kouzes, D. F. Caldwell, and B. Z. Posner, "Organizational Culture: How It Is Created, Maintained, and Changed" (Presentation at OD Network National Conference, Los Angeles, October 9, 1983). |
| "A set of symbols, ceremonies, and myths that communicates the underlying values and beliefs of that organization to its employees" | W. G. Ouchi, *Theory Z: How American Business Can Meet the Japanese Challenge* (Reading, Mass.: Addison-Wesley, 1981), p. 41. |
| "A dominant and coherent set of shared values conveyed by such symbolic means as stories, myths, legends, slogans, anecdotes, and fairy tales" | T. J. Peters and R. H. Waterman Jr., *In Search of Excellence: Lessons from America's Best-Run Companies* (New York: Harper & Row, 1982), p. 103. |
| "The pattern of basic assumptions that a given group has invented, discovered, or developed in learning to cope with its problems of external adaptation and internal integration" | E. H. Schein, "The Role of the Founder in Creating Organizational Culture," *Organizational Dynamics,* Summer 1985, p. 14. |

personal beliefs and values. Several authors have argued that organization culture is a powerful influence on individuals in firms precisely because it is not explicit but becomes an implicit part of employees' values and beliefs.[9]

Some organizations have been able to articulate the key values in their cultures. Some have even written down these values and made them part of formal

The E*Trade employees shown here are taking a cooking class together to learn about teamwork. This is an example of how CEO Christos Cotsakos shares his belief in the phrase "a lust of being different." He is trying to create a culture of being different. He also had employees race Formula One race cars at speeds of up to 150 mph in order for them to learn about speed. Cotsakos believes in having employees experience culture rather than just hear about it.

training procedures. E*Trade Group, Inc., the online stock and mutual fund trading company, uses unique ways of creating the company culture. Chief Executive Officer Christos M. Cotsakos is building a culture that is edgy, a bit bizarre, and sometimes brilliant that he sums up in five words, "A lust for being different." He tells new recruits that the company has to be on the offensive and predatory, like infantrymen in a war. He once asked his newly hired vice president of international business development to stand on a chair and reveal something about himself to 40 strangers in the company.[10]

Even when firms can articulate and describe the basic values that make up their cultures, however, the values most strongly affect actions when people in the organization take them for granted. An organization's culture is not likely to powerfully influence behavior when employees must constantly refer to a handbook to remember what the culture is. When the culture becomes part of them—when they can ignore what is written in the book because they already have embraced the values it describes—the culture can have an important impact on their actions.

*"I began to realize that my own values were no longer in alignment with those of the organization." — Richard Barrett, partner in Barrett and Associates*[11]

The final attribute shared by many of the definitions in Table 18.1 is an emphasis on the symbolic means through which the values in an organization's culture are communicated. Although, as we noted, companies sometimes could directly describe these values, their meaning is perhaps best communicated to employees through the use of stories, examples, and even what some authors call "myths" or "fairy tales." Stories typically reflect the important implications of values in a firm's culture. Often they develop a life of their own. As they are told and retold, shaped and reshaped, their relationship to what actually occurred becomes less important than the powerful impact the stories have on the way that people

MASTERING CHANGE

## *Telling Stories at Nike*

People are telling lots of stories at Nike these days. The stories are about Nike and told by Nike employees. The stories tell of CEO Phil Knight, who used to sell shoes out of the trunk of his car, Knight's former track coach and co-founder Bill Bowerman, the late distance runner Steve Prefontaine, and others who have shaped the company. In fact, there are a lot of people telling stories about how the company was founded and about people getting things done. For example, Steve Prefontaine was constantly trying to get better equipment for distance runners. Bill Bowerman decided his track team needed better running shoes and poured rubber into the family waffle iron, thus creating the first waffle-soled running shoes and revolutionizing the running shoe industry.

*"But we have a little bit more than a history. We have a heritage, something that's* ***still relevant*** *today. If we connect people to that, chances are that they won't view Nike as just another place to work." — Dave Pearson, a training manager and storyteller for Nike*

Nike believes the best way to ensure the company's future is to make sure that all employees know about the company's past. All employees go through a two-day orientation program that starts with stories about the past and how Nike's founders forged ways to do things differently. A "Heritage Wall" at company headquarters in Beaverton, Oregon, includes pictures from the company's early days and memorabilia such as the first waffle sole made by Bowerman. Nike has a team of technical representatives called "Ekins" (Nike spelled backward) who go through a nine-day training session and whose job it is to spread the word about Nike and its heritage to employees at Footlocker, Athlete's Foot, and other large retailers.

Nike believes that the stories employees hear about the past and how the company was formed and developed have a great deal to do with shaping the future. The stories are not about marketing plans or intricate financial analysis, but about people doing extraordinary things that made a difference in what the company is today. The stories about Prefontaine and Bowerman reinforce the founding principle that the company has always been about improving an athlete's performance.

References: Eric Ransdell, "The Nike Story? Just Tell It!" *Fast Company,* January–February 2000, pp. 44–46 (quote on p. 46); Claude Solnik, "Co-Founder of Nike Dies Christmas Eve," *Footwear News,* January 3, 2000, p. 2; Rosemary Feitelberg, "Bowerman's Legacy Runs On," *WWD,* December 30, 1999, p. 8.

behave every day. The "Mastering Change" box describes how Nike is communicating its culture to its employees and others.

Some organization stories have become famous. At E*Trade CEO Cotsakos has done many things that have become famous around the company because he does not follow the rule for the typical investment company. To make people move faster he organized a day of racing in Formula One cars at speeds of around 150 miles per hour. To create a looser atmosphere around the office he has employees carry around rubber chickens or wear propeller beanies. To bond the employees together he organized gourmet-cooking classes.[12] The stories of these incidents and others are told to new employees and are spread throughout the company affecting the behavior of many more people than those who actually took part in each event.

**Organization culture** is the set of values that helps the organization's employees understand which actions are considered acceptable and which are unacceptable.

We can use the three common attributes of definitions of culture just discussed to develop a definition with which most authors probably could agree: **organization culture** is the set of shared values, often taken for granted, that help people in an organization understand which actions are considered acceptable and which are considered unacceptable. Often these values are communicated through stories and other symbolic means.

## Historical Foundations

Although research on organization culture exploded onto the scene in the early 1980s, the antecedents of this research can be traced to the origins of social science. Understanding the contributions of other social science disciplines is particularly important in the case of organization culture, for many of the dilemmas and debates that continue in this area reflect differences in historical research traditions.

**Anthropological Contributions** Anthropology is the study of human cultures.[13] Of all the social science disciplines, anthropology is most closely related to the study of culture and cultural phenomena. Anthropologists seek to understand how the values and beliefs that make up a society's culture affect the structure and functioning of that society. Many anthropologists believe that to understand the relationship between culture and society, it is necessary to look at a culture from the viewpoint of the people who practice it—from the "native's point of view."[14] To reach this level of understanding, anthropologists immerse themselves in the values, symbols, and stories that people in a society use to bring order and meaning to their lives. Anthropologists usually produce book-length descriptions of the values, attitudes, and beliefs that underlie the behaviors of people in one or two cultures.[15]

Whether the culture is that of a large, modern corporation or a primitive tribe in New Guinea or the Philippines, the questions asked are the same: How do people in this culture know what kinds of behavior are acceptable and what kinds are unacceptable? How is this knowledge understood? How is this knowledge communicated to new members? Through intense efforts at accurate description, the values and beliefs that underlie actions in an organization become clear. However, these values can be fully understood only in the context of the organization in which they developed. In other words, a description of the values and beliefs of one organization is not transferable to those of other organizations; each culture is unique.

**Sociological Contributions** Sociology is the study of people in social systems, such as organizations and societies. Sociologists have long been interested in the causes and consequences of culture. In studying culture, sociologists have most often focused on informal social structure. Émile Durkheim, an important early sociologist, argued that the study of myth and ritual is an essential complement to the study of structure and rational behavior in societies.[16] By studying rituals, Durkheim argued, we can understand the most basic values and beliefs of a group of people.

Many sociological methods and theories have been used in the analysis of organization cultures. Sociologists use systematic interviews, questionnaires, and other quantitative research methods rather than the intensive study and analysis of anthropologists. Practitioners using the sociological approach generally produce a fairly simple typology of cultural attributes and then show how the cultures of a relatively large number of firms can be analyzed with this typology.[17] The major pieces of research on organization culture that later spawned widespread business interest—including Ouchi's *Theory Z*, Deal and Kennedy's *Corporate Cultures*, and Peters and Waterman's *In Search of Excellence*[18]—used sociological methods. Later in this chapter, we review some of this work in more detail.

**Social Psychology Contributions** Social psychology is a branch of psychology that includes the study of groups and the influence of social factors on individuals. Although most research on organization culture has used anthropological or sociological methods and approaches, some has borrowed heavily from social psychology. Social psychological theory, with its emphasis on the creation and manipulation of symbols, lends itself naturally to the analysis of organization culture.

For example, research in social psychology suggests that people tend to use stories or information about a single event more than they use multiple observations to make judgments.[19] Thus, if your neighbor had trouble with a certain brand of automobile, you will probably conclude that the brand is bad even though the car company can generate reams of statistical data to prove that the situation with your neighbor's car was a rarity.

The impact of stories on decision making suggests an important reason why organization culture has such a powerful influence on the people in an organization. Unlike other organizational phenomena, culture is best communicated through stories and examples, and these become the basis that individuals in the organization use to make judgments. If a story says that blaming customers is a bad thing to do, then blaming customers is a bad thing to do. This value is communicated much more effectively through the cultural story than through some statistical analysis of customer satisfaction.[20]

**Economics Contributions** The influence of economics on the study of organization culture is substantial enough to warrant attention, although it has been less significant than the influence of anthropology and sociology. Economic analysis treats organization culture as one of a variety of tools that managers can use to create some economic advantage to the organization.

The economics approach attempts to link the cultural attributes of firms with their performance, rather than simply describing the cultures of companies as the sociological and anthropological perspectives do. In *Theory Z*, for example, Ouchi does not just say that Type Z companies differ from other kinds of companies—he asserts that Type Z firms outperform other firms.[21] When Peters and Waterman say they are in search of excellence, they define excellence, in part, as consistently high financial performance.[22] These authors are using cultural explanations of financial success.

Researchers disagree about the extent to which culture affects organization performance. Several authors have investigated the conditions under which organization culture is linked with superior financial performance.[23] This research suggests that under some relatively narrow conditions, a link between culture and performance may exist. However, the fact that a firm has a culture does not mean it will perform well; indeed, a variety of cultural traits can actually hurt performance. For example, a firm could have a culture that includes values like "customers are too ignorant to be of much help," "employees cannot be trusted," "innovation is not important," and "quality is too expensive." The firm would have a strong culture, but the culture might impair its performance. The relationship between culture and performance depends, to some extent at least, on the values expressed in the organization's culture.

## Culture Versus Climate

In the past twenty years, since the concept of organizational culture has become popular, managers have often asked about the similarities and differences between organizational culture and organizational climate. Some people, managers and researchers alike, have argued that they are really the same thing, although their research bases are different, as we explain below.

The two concepts are similar in that both are concerned with the overall work atmosphere of an organization. In addition, they both deal with the social context in organizations, and both are assumed to affect the behaviors of people who work in organizations.[24]

**Organization climate** usually refers to current situations in an organization and the linkages among work groups, employees, and work performance.

The two concepts differ in several significant ways, however. Much of the study of climate was based in psychology, whereas the study of organizational culture was based in anthropology and sociology. **Organization climate** usually refers to current situations in an organization and the linkages among work groups, employees, and work performance. Climate, therefore, is usually more easily manipulated by management to directly affect the behavior of employees. Organization culture, on the other hand, usually refers to the historical context within which a situation occurs and the impact of this context on the behaviors of employees. Organization culture is generally considered much more difficult to alter in short-run situations because it has been defined over the course of years of history and tradition.

The two concepts also differ in their emphases. Organizational culture is often described as the means through which people in the organization learn and communicate what is acceptable and unacceptable in an organization—its values and norms.[25] Most descriptions of organization climate do not deal with values and norms. So descriptions of climate are concerned with the current atmosphere in an organization, whereas organizational culture is based on the history and traditions of the organization and emphasizes values and norms about employee behavior.

# Creating the Organization Culture

To the entrepreneur who starts a business, creating the culture of the company may seem secondary to the basic processes of creating a product or service and selling it to customers or clients. However, as the company grows and becomes successful, it usually develops a culture that distinguishes it from other companies and that is one of the reasons for its success. In other words, a company succeeds as a result of what the company does, its strategy, and how it does it, its culture. The culture is linked to the strategic values, whether one is starting up a new company or trying to change the culture of an existing company.[26] The process of creating an organization culture is really a process of linking its strategic values with its cultural values, much as the structure of the organization is linked to its strategy, as we described in Chapter 17. The process is shown in Table 18.2.

table 18.2 **Creating Organizational Culture**

| |
|---|
| Step1—Formulate Strategic Values |
| Step 2—Develop Cultural Values |
| Step 3—Create Vision |
| Step 4—Initiate Implementation Strategies |
| Step 5—Reinforce Cultural Behaviors |

## Establish Values

**Strategic values** are the basic beliefs about an organization's environment that shape its strategy.

The first two steps in the process involve establishing values. First, management must determine the strategic values of the organization. **Strategic values** are the basic beliefs about an organization's environment that shape its strategy. They are developed following an environmental scanning process and strategic analysis that evaluate economic, demographic, public policy, technological, and social trends to identify needs in the marketplace that the organization can meet. Strategic values, in effect, link the organization with its environment. Dell Computer believed that customers would buy computers from a catalogue if the price were right, rather than going to computer stores as the conventional wisdom dictated they would. The $6.8 billion business resulted.[27]

**Cultural values** are the values that employees need to have and act on for the organization to act on the strategic values.

The second set of required values is the cultural values of the organization. **Cultural values** are the values employees need to have and to act on for the organization to carry out its strategic values. They should be grounded in the organization's beliefs about how and why the organization can succeed. Organizations that attempt to develop cultural values that are not linked to their strategic values may end up with an empty set of values that have little relationship to their business. In other words, employees need to value work behaviors that are consistent with and support the organization's strategic values: low-cost production, customer service, or technological innovation.

*"So my biggest concern is that somehow, through maladroitness, through inattention, through misunderstanding, we lose the esprit de corps, the culture, the spirit. If we ever do lose that, we will have lost our most valuable competitive asset."*
*— Herb Kelleher, CEO of Southwest Airlines*[28]

## Create Vision

After developing its strategic and cultural values, the organization must establish a vision of its direction. This "vision" is a picture of what the organization will be like at some point in the future. It portrays how the strategic and cultural values will combine to create the future. For example, an insurance company might establish a vision of "protecting the lifestyles of 2 million families by the year 2005." In effect, it synthesizes both the strategic and cultural values as it communicates a performance target to employees. The conventional wisdom has been that the vision statement is written first, but experience suggests that the strategic and cultural values must be established first for the vision to be meaningful.

## Initiate Implementation Strategies

The next step, initiating implementation strategies, builds on the values and initiates the action to accomplish the vision. The strategies cover many factors, from developing the organization design to recruiting and training employees who share the values and will carry them out. Consider a bank that has the traditional orientation of handling customer loans, deposits, and savings. If the bank changes, placing more emphasis on customer service, it may have to recruit a different type of employee, one who is capable of building relationships. The bank will also have to

Pamela Barefoot, shown here in the center with two of her employees at Blue Crab Bay Company, believes in communicating in order to grow the company. Blue Crab Bay Company grew from sales of $5,000 to $600,000 in its first five years, primarily because Barefoot was constantly communicating personally with her employees. Through all of the personal communication, Barefoot was telling and showing employees her vision for the company and developing the culture of the company. The basic management skills of communication, accountability, and trust are crucial to developing the kind of culture she wants the company to have as it continues to grow.

commit to serious, long-term training of its current employees to teach them the new service-oriented culture. The strategic and cultural values are the stimulus for the implementation practices.

### Reinforce Cultural Behaviors

The final step is to reinforce the behaviors of employees as they act out the cultural values and implement the organization's strategies. Reinforcement can take many forms. First, the formal reward system in the organization must reward desired behaviors in ways that employees value. Second, stories must be told throughout the organization about employees who engaged in behaviors that epitomize the cultural values. Third, the organization must engage in ceremonies and rituals that emphasize employees doing the things that are critical to carrying out the organization's vision. In effect, the organization must "make a big deal out of employees doing the right things." For example, if parties are held only for retirement or to give out longevity and service pins, the employees get the message that retirement and length of service are the only things that matter. On the other hand, holding a ceremony for a group of employees who provided exceptional customer service reinforces desirable employee behaviors. Reinforcement practices are the final link between the strategic and cultural values and the creation of the organizational culture.

## Approaches to Describing Organization Culture

The models discussed in this section provide valuable insights into the dimensions along which organization cultures vary. No single framework for describing the values in organization cultures has emerged; however, several frameworks have been suggested. Although these frameworks were developed in the 1980s, their ideas about organizational culture are still influential today. Some of the "excellent" companies that they described are less excellent now, but the concepts are in use in companies all over the world. Managers should evaluate the various parts of the frameworks described and use the parts that fit the strategic and cultural values for their own organization.

## The Ouchi Framework

The Type Z firm is committed to retaining employees; evaluates workers' performance based on both qualitative and quantitative information; emphasizes broad career paths; exercises control through informal, implicit mechanisms; requires that decision making occur in groups and be based on full information sharing and consensus; expects individuals to take responsibility for decisions; and emphasizes concern for people.

One of the first researchers to focus explicitly on analyzing the cultures of a limited group of firms was William G. Ouchi. Ouchi analyzed the organization cultures of three groups of firms, which he characterized as (1) typical U.S. firms, (2) typical Japanese firms, and (3) **Type Z** U.S. firms.[29]

Through his analysis, Ouchi developed a list of seven points on which these three types of firms can be compared. He argued that the cultures of typical Japanese firms and U.S. Type Z firms are very different from those of typical U.S. firms, and that these differences explain the success of many Japanese firms and U.S. Type Z firms and the difficulties faced by typical U.S. firms. The seven points of comparison developed by Ouchi are presented in Table 18.3.

### Commitment to Employees

According to Ouchi, typical Japanese and Type Z U.S. firms share the cultural value of trying to keep employees. Thus, both types of firms lay off employees only as a last resort. In Japan, the value of "keeping employees on" often takes the form of lifetime employment, although some Japanese companies following the economic troubles of the past few years are challenging this value. A person who begins working at some Japanese firms has had a virtual guarantee that he or she will never be fired. In U.S. Type Z companies, this cultural value is manifested in a commitment to what Ouchi called "long-term employment." Under the Japanese system of lifetime employment, employees usually cannot be fired. Under the U.S. system, workers and managers can be fired, but only if they are not performing acceptably.

table 18.3

**The Ouchi Framework**

| Cultural Value | Expression in Japanese Companies | Expression in Type Z U.S. Companies | Expression in Typical U.S. Companies |
|---|---|---|---|
| Commitment to Employees | Lifetime employment | Long-term employment | Short-term employment |
| Evaluation | Slow and qualitative | Slow and qualitative | Fast and quantitative |
| Careers | Very broad | Moderately broad | Narrow |
| Control | Implicit and informal | Implicit and informal | Explicit and formal |
| Decision Making | Group and consensus | Group and consensus | Individual |
| Responsibility | Group | Individual | Individual |
| Concern for People | Holistic | Holistic | Narrow |

Ouchi suggested that typical U.S. firms do not have the same cultural commitment to employees as Japanese firms and U.S. Type Z firms. In reality, U.S. workers and managers often spend their entire careers in a relatively small number of companies. Still, there is a cultural expectation that if there is a serious downturn in a firm's fortunes, change of ownership, or a merger, workers and managers will be let go. For example, when Wells Fargo Bank bought First Interstate Bank in Arizona, it expected to lay off about 400 employees in Arizona and 5,000 in the corporation as a whole. However, eight months after the purchase, Wells Fargo had eliminated over 1,000 employees in Arizona alone and a total of 10,800. Wells Fargo has a reputation as a vicious cutter following a takeover and seems to be living up to it.[30]

**Evaluation** Ouchi observed that in Japanese and Type Z U.S. companies, appropriate evaluation of workers and managers is thought to take a very long time—up to ten years—and requires the use of qualitative as well as quantitative information about performance. For this reason, promotion in these firms is relatively slow, and promotion decisions are made only after interviews with many people who have had contact with the person being evaluated. In typical U.S. firms, on the other hand, the cultural value suggests that evaluation can and should be done rapidly and should emphasize quantitative measures of performance. This value tends to encourage short-term thinking among workers and managers.

**Careers** Ouchi next observed that the careers most valued in Japanese and Type Z U.S. firms span multiple functions. In Japan, this value has led to very broad career paths, which may lead to employees gaining experience in six or seven distinct business functions. The career paths in Type Z U.S. firms are somewhat narrower.

However, the career path valued in typical U.S. firms is considerably narrower. Ouchi's research indicated that most U.S. managers perform only one or two different business functions in their careers. This narrow career path reflects, according to Ouchi, the value of specialization that is part of so many U.S. firms.

**Control** All organizations must exert some level of control to achieve coordinated action. Thus, it is not surprising that firms in the United States and Japan have developed cultural values related to organizational control and how to manage it. Most Japanese and Type Z U.S. firms assume that control is exercised through informal, implicit mechanisms. One of the most powerful of these mechanisms is the organization's culture. In contrast, typical U.S. firms expect guidance to come through explicit directions in the form of job descriptions, delineation of authority, and various rules and procedures, rather than from informal and implicit cultural values.

From a functional perspective, organization culture could be viewed as primarily a means of social control based on shared norms and values.[31] Control comes from knowing that someone who matters is paying close attention to what we do and will tell us if our actions are appropriate or not. In organizations, control can come from formal sources, such as the organization structure or your supervisor, or from social sources, such as the organization's culture. In Ouchi's view, control is based in formal organizational mechanisms in typical U.S. firms, whereas control is more social in nature, and derived from the organization culture's shared norms and values, in Japanese and Type Z U.S. firms.

**Decision Making** Japanese and Type Z U.S. firms have a strong cultural expectation that decision making occurs in groups and is based on principles of full information sharing and consensus. In most typical U.S. firms, individual decision making is considered appropriate.

**Responsibility** Closely linked to the issue of group versus individual decision making are ideas about responsibility. Here, however, the parallels between Japanese firms and Type Z U.S. firms break down. Ouchi showed that in Japan, strong cultural norms support collective responsibility; that is, the group as a whole, rather than a single person, is held responsible for decisions made by the group. In both Type Z U.S. firms and typical U.S. firms, individuals expect to take responsibility for decisions.

Linking individual responsibility with individual decision making, as typical U.S. firms do, is logically consistent. Similarly, group decision making and group responsibility, the situation in Japanese firms, seem to go together. But how do Type Z U.S. firms combine the cultural values of group decision making and individual responsibility?

Ouchi suggested that the answer to this question depends on a cultural view we have already discussed: slow, qualitative evaluation. The first time a manager uses a group to make a decision, it is not possible to tell whether the outcomes associated with that decision resulted from the manager's influence or the quality of the group. However, if a manager works with many groups over time, and if these groups consistently do well for the organization, it is likely that the manager is skilled at getting the most out of the groups. This manager can be held responsible for the outcomes of group decision-making processes. Similarly, managers who consistently fail to work effectively with the groups assigned to them can be held responsible for the lack of results from the group decision-making process.

**Concern for People** The last cultural value examined by Ouchi deals with a concern for people. Not surprisingly, in Japanese firms and Type Z firms, the cultural value that dominates is a holistic concern for workers and managers. Holistic concern extends beyond concern for a person simply as a worker or manager to concern about that person's home life, hobbies, personal beliefs, hopes, fears, and aspirations. In typical U.S. firms, the concern for people is a narrow one that focuses on the workplace. A culture that emphasizes a strong concern for people, rather than one that emphasizes a work or task orientation, can decrease worker turnover.[32]

**Theory Z and Performance** Ouchi argued that the cultures of Japanese and Type Z firms help them outperform typical U.S. firms. Toyota imported the management style and culture that succeeded in Japan into its manufacturing facilities in North America. Toyota's success has often been attributed to the ability of Japanese and Type Z firms to systematically invest in their employees and operations over long periods, resulting in steady and significant improvements in long-term performance.

## The Peters and Waterman Approach

Tom Peters and Robert Waterman, in their bestseller *In Search of Excellence*, focused even more explicitly than Ouchi on the relationship between organization

**table 18.4**

**The Peters and Waterman Framework**

| Attributes of an Excellent Firm | |
|---|---|
| 1. Bias for action | 5. Hands-on management |
| 2. Stay close to the customer | 6. Stick to the knitting |
| 3. Autonomy and entrepreneurship | 7. Simple form, lean staff |
| 4. Productivity through people | 8. Simultaneously loose and tight organization |

culture and performance. Peters and Waterman chose a sample of highly successful U.S. firms and sought to describe the management practices that led to their success.[33] Their analysis rapidly turned to the cultural values that led to successful management practices. These "excellent" values are listed in Table 18.4.

**Bias for Action** According to Peters and Waterman, successful firms have a bias for action. Managers in these firms are expected to make decisions even if all the facts are not in. Peters and Waterman argued that for many important decisions, all the facts will never be in. Delaying decision making in these situations is the same as never making a decision. Meanwhile, other firms probably will have captured whatever business initiative existed. On average, according to these authors, organizations with cultural values that include a bias for action outperform firms without such values.

**Stay Close to the Customer** Peters and Waterman believe that firms whose organization cultures value customers over everything else outperform firms without this value. The customer is a source of information about current products, a source of ideas about future products, and the ultimate source of a firm's current and future financial performance. Focusing on the customer, meeting the customer's needs, and pampering the customer when necessary all lead to superior performance. After losing money for years, Scandinavian Airlines focused its culture on customer service and finally started making money in 1989, when many other airlines were experiencing financial difficulties.[34]

*"The only thing that matters to me is that we are using information technology to make our customers happy." — Tom Siebel, chairman and CEO of Siebel Systems[35]*

**Autonomy and Entrepreneurship** Peters and Waterman maintained that successful firms fight the lack of innovation and the bureaucracy usually associated with large size. They do this by breaking the company into smaller, more manageable pieces and then encouraging independent, innovative activities within smaller business segments. Stories often exist in these organizations about the junior engineer who takes a risk and influences major product decisions, or of the junior manager, dissatisfied with the slow pace of a product's development, who implements a new and highly successful marketing plan.

**Productivity Through People** Like Ouchi, Peters and Waterman believe successful firms recognize that their most important assets are their people—both workers and managers—and that the organization's purpose is to let its people flourish. It is a basic value of the organization culture—a belief that treating people with respect and dignity is not only appropriate but essential to success.

**Hands-on Management** Peters and Waterman noted that the firms they studied insisted that senior managers stay in touch with the firms' essential business. It is an expectation, reflecting a deeply embedded cultural norm, that managers should manage not from behind the closed doors of their offices but by "wandering around" the plant, the design facility, the research and development department, and so on.

**Stick to the Knitting** Another cultural value characteristic of excellent firms is their reluctance to engage in business outside their areas of expertise. These firms reject the concept of diversification, the practice of buying and operating businesses in unrelated industries. This notion is currently referred to as relying on the company's "core competencies," or what the company does best.

**Simple Form, Lean Staff** According to Peters and Waterman, successful firms tend to have few administrative layers and relatively small corporate staff groups. In excellently managed companies, importance is measured not only by the number of people who report to a manager but also by the manager's impact on the organization's performance. The cultural values in these firms tell managers that their staffs' performance rather than their size is important.

**Simultaneously Loose and Tight Organization** The final attribute of organization culture identified by Peters and Waterman appears contradictory. How can a firm be simultaneously loosely and tightly organized? The resolution of this apparent paradox is found in the firms' values. The firms are tightly organized because all their members understand and believe in the firms' values. This common cultural bond is a strong glue that holds the firms together. At the same time, however, the firms are loosely organized because they tend to have less administrative overhead, fewer staff members, and fewer rules and regulations. The result is increased innovation and risk taking and faster response times.

The loose structure is possible only because of the common values held by people in the firm. When employees must make decisions, they can evaluate their options in terms of the organization's underlying values—whether the options are consistent with a bias for action, service to the customer, and so on. By referring to commonly held values, employees can make their own decisions about what actions to take. In this sense, the tight structure of common cultural values makes possible the loose structure of fewer administrative controls.

# Emerging Issues in Organization Culture

As the implementation of organization culture continues, it inevitably changes and develops new perspectives. Many new ideas about productive environments build on earlier views such as those of Ouchi, Peters and Waterman, and others. Typical of these approaches are the total quality management movement, worker participation, and team-based management, which were discussed in earlier chapters. Three other movements are briefly discussed in this section: innovation, empowerment, and procedural justice.

These people are owners of the new electronic robot pet dogs, named Aibo, created by Sony to illustrate the use of their new operating system that controls the flow of real-time digital data streams like video. The new operating system is the latest innovation that Sony hopes will propel it to be the leader in the network society based on their technology, software, and content. Sony expects that innovation will be the key to battling its traditional rivals in the electronics industry as well as taking on Microsoft on the software side.

## Innovation

**Innovation** is the process of creating and doing new things that are introduced into the marketplace as products, processes, or services.

**Innovation** is the process of creating and doing new things that are introduced into the marketplace as products, processes, or services. Innovation involves every aspect of the organization, from research through development, manufacturing, and marketing. One of the organization's biggest challenges is to bring innovative technology to the needs of the marketplace in the most cost-effective manner possible.[36] Note that innovation does not only involve the technology to create new products. True organizational innovation is pervasive throughout the organization. According to *Fortune* magazine, the most admired organizations are those that are the most innovative.[37] Those companies are innovative in every way—staffing, strategy, research, and business processes.

Many risks are associated with being an innovative company. The most basic is the risk that decisions about new technology or innovation will backfire. As research proceeds and engineers and scientists continue to develop new ideas or solutions to problems, there is always the possibility that the innovation will fail to perform as expected. For this reason, organizations commit considerable resources to testing innovations.[38] A second risk is the possibility that a competitor will make decisions enabling it to get an innovation to the market first. The marketplace has become a breeding ground for continuous innovation. Motorola, for example, is striving to build a company in which customer needs shape new-product development without crippling the firm's technological leadership in its basic products.

*"I could sit here and beat estimates by a penny a share the rest of my life, and two years from now be annihilated by the freight train that's the Internet. . . . Or I can step up to the gallows today to be hanged, but do so proactively." — David Dunkel, CEO of Romac International*[39]

**Radical innovation** is a major breakthrough that changes or creates whole industries.

**Systems innovation** creates a new functionality by assembling parts in new ways.

**Incremental innovation** continues the technical improvement and extends the applications of radical and systems innovations.

**Types of Innovation** Innovation can be either radical, systems, or incremental. A **radical innovation** is a major breakthrough that changes or creates whole industries. Examples include xerography (which was invented by Chester Carlson in 1935 and became the hallmark of Xerox Corporation), steam engines, and the internal combustion engine (which paved the way for today's automobile industry). **Systems innovation** creates a new functionality by assembling parts in new ways. For example, the gasoline engine began as a radical innovation and became a systems innovation when it was combined with bicycle and carriage technology to create automobiles. **Incremental innovation** continues the technical improvement and extends the applications of radical and systems innovations. There are many more incremental innovations than there are radical and systems innovations. In fact, several incremental innovations are often necessary to make radical and systems innovations work properly. Incremental innovations force organizations to continuously improve their products and keep abreast or ahead of the competition.

**New Ventures** New ventures based on innovations require entrepreneurship and good management to work. The profile of the entrepreneur typically includes a need for achievement, a desire to assume responsibility, a willingness to take risks, and a focus on concrete results. Entrepreneurship can occur inside or outside large organizations. Outside entrepreneurship requires all of the complex aspects of the innovation process. Inside entrepreneurship occurs within a system that usually discourages chaotic activity.

**Intrapreneurship** is entrepreneurial activity that takes place within the context of a large corporation.

Large organizations typically do not accept entrepreneurial types of activities. Thus, for a large organization to be innovative and develop new ventures, it must actively encourage entrepreneurial activity within the organization. This form of activity, often called **intrapreneurship**, usually is most effective when it is a part of everyday life in the organization and occurs throughout the organization rather than in the research and development department alone.

**Corporate Research** The most common means of developing innovation in the traditional organization is through corporate research, or research and development. Corporate research is usually set up to support existing businesses, provide incremental innovations in the organization's businesses, and explore potential new technology bases. It often takes place in a laboratory, either on the site of the main corporate facility or some distance away from normal operations.

Corporate researchers are responsible for keeping the company's products and processes technologically advanced. Product life cycles vary a great deal, depending on how fast products become obsolete and whether substitutes for the product are developed. Obviously, if a product becomes obsolete or some other product can be substituted for it, the profits from its sales will decrease. The job of corporate research is to prevent this from happening by keeping the company's products current.

The corporate culture can be instrumental in fostering an environment in which creativity and innovation occur. Sony and Hewlett-Packard are examples of two companies that are trying to change their organization cultures to be more innovative.

## Empowerment

One of the most popular buzzwords in management today is "empowerment." Almost every new approach to quality, meeting the competition, getting more out of

**Empowerment** is the process of enabling workers to set their own work goals, make decisions, and solve problems within their sphere of responsibility and authority.

employees, productivity enhancement, and corporate turnarounds deals with employee empowerment. As we discussed in Chapter 7, **empowerment** is the process of enabling workers to set their own goals, make decisions, and solve problems within their spheres of responsibility and authority. Fads are often dismissed as meaningless and without substance because they are misused and overused, and the concept of empowerment, too, can be taken too lightly.

Empowerment is simple and complex at the same time. It is simple in that it tells managers to quit bossing people around so much and to let them do their jobs. It is complex in that managers and employees typically are not trained to do that. A significant amount of time, training, and practice may be needed to truly empower employees. In Chapter 7, we discussed some techniques for utilizing empowerment and conditions in which empowerment can be effective in organizations.

Empowerment can be much more than a motivational technique, however. In some organizations it is the cornerstone of organizational culture. At E*Trade CEO Cotsakos believes that people should be empowered and then encouraged to take responsibility and solve their own problems. When the chief information officer and the chief financial officer got into what seemed to be an unresolvable spat, they turned to Cotsakos for resolution. He insisted that they work it out between them for the good of the company. He sent them each a bouquet of roses bearing the message, "We're a team. Let's work it out." and made them think the other sent them. They worked it out and developed a better understanding of each other's role in the company.[40]

Empowerment can be viewed as liberating employees, but sometimes "empowerment" entails little more than delegating a task to an employee and then watching over the employee too closely. Employees may feel that this type of participation is superficial and that they are not really making meaningful decisions. The concept of liberating employees suggests that they should be free to do what they think is best without fear that the boss is standing by to veto or change the work done by the employee.[41]

## Procedural Justice

**Procedural justice** is the extent to which the dynamics of an organization's decision-making processes are judged to be fair by those most affected by them.

Another movement in management that may be viewed as a cultural issue is procedural justice. **Procedural justice** is the extent to which the dynamics of an organization's decision-making processes are judged to be fair by those most affected by them. Especially in the United States, employees are demanding more say in determining work rules and matters pertaining to health and safety on the job and the provision of certain benefits for all employees. Furthermore, each generation of new employees may feel more entitled to having certain kinds of influence in the organization, especially on matters pertaining to their work. Employees who expect to have more input into decision making may or may not comply with decisions or directives from top management that they have little or no part in.

The lack of procedural justice may lead to less compliant attitudes on the part of lower-level managers. This has been shown to come into play in strategic decision making in multinational organizations. The exercise of procedural justice can be an effective way to engender compliance from subsidiary managers in large multinationals.[42] The extent to which this movement continues may depend on the overall cultural shifts in society and the extent to which the employee empowerment becomes entrenched in organizations and management practice.

# Managing Organizational Culture

The work of Ouchi, Peters and Waterman, and many others demonstrates two important facts. First, organizational cultures differ among firms; second, these different organizational cultures can affect a firm's performance. Based on these observations, managers have become more concerned about how to best manage the cultures of their organizations. The three elements of managing organizational culture are (1) taking advantage of existing culture, (2) teaching organizational culture, and (3) changing organizational culture.

## Taking Advantage of the Existing Culture

Most managers are not in a position to create an organizational culture; rather, they work in organizations that already have cultural values. For these managers, the central issue in managing culture is how best to use the cultural system that already exists. It may be easier and faster to alter employee behaviors within the existing culture than it is to change the history, traditions, and values that already exist.[43]

*"The benefit of having a strong culture is it's binding." — John S. Reed, co-CEO of Citigroup[44]*

To take advantage of an existing cultural system, managers must first be fully aware of the culture's values and what behaviors or actions those values support. Becoming fully aware of an organization's values usually is not easy, however; it involves more than reading a pamphlet about what the company believes in. Managers must develop a deep understanding of how organizational values operate in the firm—an understanding that usually comes only through experience.

This picture illustrates how Merck, the number one drug maker, develops its top managers by sending them around the world to get close to customers and their cultures. Merck is well known as a truly global company with its worldwide research labs and marketing expertise. Merck executives are among the most international in the world, coming from Sweden, Norway, New Zealand, Egypt, and the United States, yet each one is expected to learn the Merck culture by working extensively in the United States before going to other countries. Merck makes cultural fit a primary criterion in its promotion from within policy.

This understanding, once achieved, can be used to evaluate the performances of others in the firm. Articulating organizational values can be useful in managing others' behaviors. For example, suppose a subordinate in a firm with a strong cultural value of "sticking to its knitting" develops a business strategy that involves moving into a new industry. Rather than attempting to argue that this business strategy is economically flawed or conceptually weak, the manager who understands the corporate culture can point to the company's organizational value: "In this firm, we believe in sticking to our knitting."

Senior managers who understand their organization's culture can communicate that understanding to lower-level individuals. Over time, as these lower-level managers begin to understand and accept the firm's culture, they require less direct supervision. Their understanding of corporate values guides their decision making.

## Teaching the Organizational Culture: Socialization

**Socialization** is the process through which individuals become social beings.

**Organizational socialization** is the process through which employees learn about the firm's culture and pass their knowledge and understanding on to others.

**Socialization** is the process through which individuals become social beings.[45] As studied by psychologists, it is the process through which children learn to be adults in a society—how they learn what is acceptable and polite behavior and what is not, how they learn to communicate, how they learn to interact with others, and so on. In complex societies, the socialization process takes many years.

**Organizational socialization** is the process through which employees learn about their firm's culture and pass their knowledge and understanding on to others. Employees are socialized into organizations, just as people are socialized into societies; that is, they come to know over time what is acceptable in the organization and what is not, how to communicate their feelings, and how to interact with others. They learn both through observation and through efforts by managers to communicate this information to them. The cartoon shows a dramatic example of a manager telling an employee how he should think about the company. Research into the process of socialization indicates that for many employees, socialization programs do not necessarily change their values but make them more aware of the differences between personal and organization values and help them develop ways to cope with the differences.[46]

A variety of organizational mechanisms can affect the socialization of workers in organizations. Probably the most important are the examples that new employees see in the behavior of experienced people. Through observing examples, new employees develop a repertoire of stories they can use to guide their actions. When a decision needs to be made, new employees can ask, "What would my boss do in this situation?" This is not to suggest that formal training, corporate pamphlets, and corporate statements about organization culture are unimportant in the socialization process. However, these factors tend to support the socialization process based on people's close observations of the actions of others.

In some organizations, the culture described in pamphlets and presented in formal training sessions conflicts with the values of the organization as they are expressed in the actions of its people. For example, a firm may say that employees are its most important asset but treat employees badly. In this setting, new employees quickly learn that the rhetoric of the pamphlets and formal training sessions has little to do with the real organization culture. Employees who are socialized into this system usually come to accept the actual cultural values rather than those formally espoused.

GLASBERGEN
"I want the public to think of us as 'The Company With A Heart'. But I want *you* to think of us as the company that will chew you up, spit you out and smear you into the carpet if you screw up."


This boss is trying to socialize the employee by telling him how he should think about the company. But he is not doing this employee a favor by trying to differentiate between outsiders' perception of the company and the internal culture of the company. In most situations, outsiders feel the internal culture of the company as much as employees do. If the company is a "chew you up" culture inside, that attitude will usually carry over into how employees treat customers, suppliers, and other people outside the company.

Reference: © 1996 Randy Glasbergen.

## Changing the Organizational Culture

Much of our discussion to this point has assumed that an organization's culture enhances its performance. When this is the case, learning what an organization's cultural values are and using those values to help socialize new workers and managers is very important, for such actions help the organization succeed. However, as Ouchi's and Peters and Waterman's research indicates, not all firms have cultural values that are consistent with high performance. Ouchi found that Japanese firms and U.S. Type Z firms have performance-enhancing values. Peters and Waterman identified performance-enhancing values associated with successful companies. By implication, some firms not included in Peters and Waterman's study must have had performance-reducing values. What should a manager who works in a company with performance-reducing values do?

The answer to this question is, of course, that top managers in such firms should try to change their organization's culture. However, this is a difficult thing to do.[47] Organizational culture resists change for all the reasons it is a powerful influence on behavior—it embodies the firm's basic values, it is often taken for granted, and it is typically communicated most effectively through stories or other symbols. When managers attempt to change organizational culture, they are attempting to change people's basic assumptions about what is and is not appropriate behavior in the organization. Changing from a traditional organization to a team-based organization (discussed in Chapter 12) is one example of an organizational culture change. Another is Boeing's decision in 1999 to change from a family culture to a performance culture, as discussed in "The Business of Ethics" box.

Despite these difficulties, some organizations have changed their cultures from performance-reducing to performance-enhancing.[48] This change process

THE BUSINESS OF ETHICS

## *Boeing Crushes Its Paternalistic Culture*

Boeing has always taken care of its people. Its culture has always been known as one that was warm and fuzzy—a "feel good" family type of culture. Long-time employees were referred to as "heritage" employees, people felt as if the company really cared about their welfare, and most major promotions were made from within. But by 1998, the financial numbers were not looking too good. In 1997, two assembly lines were shut down because of production problems, competition from European Airbus Industrie was taking away customers, margins and earnings were dropping, and the stock price was exceedingly low. Most Wall Street analysts assumed that popular CEO Phil Condit was on the way out and that President Harry Stonecipher, formerly chairman of the acquired McDonnell Douglas, would step up. Condit was seen as the feel-good insider, and Stonecipher would be brought in to get tough and make the appropriate cuts.

*"In a family culture, you never throw out a bad performer."*
*— Harry Stonecipher, president, Boeing Company*

But Condit retained his job by developing a turnaround strategy with his top staff in a three-day planning retreat. The plan aimed at specific production problems and included a controversial strategy to develop a performance-oriented culture to replace the existing paternalistic one. The company laid off 38,000 people in 1999 and was planning to lay off another 10,000 in 2000. Several top executives and upper managers were fired. The new emphasis on dramatic increases in production efficiency, higher-quality work to reduce rework, streamlining every operation, and outsourcing was a major change. The focus was on performance at every level, with a target of a 10 percent reduction in production time per plane. Early results showed promise: profits rose 172 percent internationally in the second quarter of 1999.

Most of these changes were initiated in early 1999 as the company was preparing for intense labor negotiations with the International Association of Machinists, Boeing's dominant labor union for production workers, whose contract expired in September 1999. Everyone remembered the sixty-nine-day strike of 1995 and was afraid that another strike would be disastrous, since Boeing needed to produce a record 620 planes in 1999 to meet the demand stirred up by marketing and sales. Finally, in September 1999, Condit stepped into the negotiations and offered a contract that included an 11 percent wage increase over three years, a signing bonus that averaged more than $4,000 per employee, and improved job security provisions. The contract was perceived as "cushy" in order to ensure there would be no strike. The surprise was that none of the provisions were tied to productivity increases, as had been expected.

References: Bellamy Pailthorp, "Safe Landing for Boeing," *U.S. News & World Report*, September 13, 1999, p. 43; Janet Rae-Dupree, "Can Boeing Get Lean Enough?" *Business Week*, August 30, 1999, p. 182; Aaron Bernstein, "Boeing's Unions Are Worried About Job Security—The CEO's," *Business Week*, July 5, 1999, p. 30; Kenneth Labich, "Boeing Finally Hatches a Plan," *Fortune*, March 1, 1999, pp. 101–106 (quote on p. 102).

will be described in more detail in Chapter 19. The earlier section on creating organizational culture describes the importance of linking the strategic values and the cultural values in creating a new organizational culture. We briefly discuss other important elements of the cultural change process in the following sections.

**Managing Symbols** Research suggests that organization culture is understood and communicated through the use of stories and other symbolic media. If this is correct, managers interested in changing cultures should attempt to substitute stories and myths that support new cultural values for those that support old ones. They can do so by creating situations that give rise to new stories.

Suppose an organization traditionally has held the value "employee opinions are not important." When management meets in this company, the ideas and opinions of lower-level people—when discussed at all—are normally rejected as foolish and irrelevant. The stories that support this cultural value tell about managers who tried to make a constructive point only to have that point lost in personal attacks from superiors.

An upper-level manager interested in creating a new story, one that shows lower-level managers that their ideas are valuable, might ask a subordinate to prepare to lead a discussion in a meeting and follow through by asking the subordinate to take the lead when the topic arises. The subordinate's success in the meeting will become a new story, one that may displace some of the many stories suggesting that the opinions of lower-level managers do not matter.

**The Difficulty of Change** Changing a firm's culture is a long and difficult process. A primary problem is that upper-level managers, no matter how dedicated they are to implementing some new cultural value, may sometimes inadvertently revert to old patterns of behavior. This happens, for example, when a manager dedicated to implementing the value that lower-level employees' ideas are important vehemently attacks a subordinate's ideas.

This mistake generates a story that supports old values and beliefs. After such an incident, lower-level managers may believe that the boss says he wants their input and ideas, but nothing could be further from the truth. No matter what the boss says or how consistent his behavior is, some credibility has been lost, and cultural change has been made more difficult.

**The Stability of Change** The process of changing a firm's culture starts with a need for change and moves through a transition period in which efforts are made to adopt new values and beliefs. In the long run, a firm that successfully changes its culture will find that the new values and beliefs are just as stable and influential as the old ones. Value systems tend to be self-reinforcing. Once they are in place, changing them requires an enormous effort. Thus, if a firm can change its culture from performance-reducing to performance-enhancing, the new values are likely to remain in place for a long time.

## Synopsis

Organizational culture has become one of the most discussed subjects in the field of organizational behavior. It burst on the scene in the 1980s with books by Ouchi, Peters and Waterman, and others. Interest has not been restricted to academics, however. Practicing managers are also interested in organizational culture, especially as it relates to performance.

There is little agreement about how to define organizational culture. A comparison of several important definitions suggests that most have three things in common: they define culture in terms of the values that individuals in organizations use to prescribe appropriate behavior; they assume that these values are usually taken for granted; and they emphasize the stories and other symbolic means through which the values are typically communicated.

Current research on organizational culture reflects various research traditions. The most important contributions have come from anthropology and sociology. Anthropologists have tended to focus on the organizational cultures of one or two firms and have used detailed descriptions to help outsiders understand organizational culture from the "natives' point of view." Sociologists typically have used survey methods to study the organizational cultures of larger numbers of firms. Two other influences on current work in organizational culture are social psychology, which emphasizes the manipulation of symbols in organizations, and economics. The economics approach sees culture both as a tool used to manage and as a determinant of performance.

Creating organizational culture is a five-step process. It starts with formulating strategic and cultural values for the organization. Next, a vision for the organization is created, followed by institution of implementation strategies. The final step is reinforcing the cultural behaviors of employees.

Although no single framework for describing organization culture has emerged, several have been suggested. The most popular efforts in this area have been Ouchi's comparison of U.S. and Japanese firms and Peters and Waterman's description of successful firms in the United States. Ouchi and Peters and Waterman suggested several important dimensions, along which organizational values vary, including treatment of employees, definitions of appropriate means for decision making, and assignment of responsibility for the results of decision making.

Emerging issues in the area of organizational culture include innovation, employee empowerment, and procedural justice. Innovation is the process of creating and doing new things that are introduced into the marketplace as products, processes, or services. The organizational culture can either help or hinder innovation. Employee empowerment, in addition to being similar to employee participation as a motivation technique, is now viewed by some as a type of organizational culture. Empowerment occurs when employees make decisions, set their own work goals, and solve problems in their own area of responsibility. Procedural justice is the extent to which the dynamics of an organization's decision-making processes are judged to be fair by those most affected by them.

Managing the organizational culture requires attention to three factors. First, managers can take advantage of cultural values that already exist and use their knowledge to help subordinates understand them. Second, employees need to be properly socialized, or trained, in the cultural values of the organization, either through formal training or by experiencing and observing the actions of higher-level managers. Third, managers can change the culture of the organization through managing the symbols, addressing the extreme difficulties of such a change, and relying on the durability of the new organization culture once the change has been implemented.

## Discussion Questions

1. A sociologist or anthropologist might suggest that the culture in U.S. firms simply reflects the dominant culture of the society as a whole. Therefore, to change the organization culture of a company, one must first deal with the inherent values and beliefs of the society. How would you respond to this claim?
2. Psychology has been defined as the study of individual behavior. Organizational psychology is the study of individual behavior in organizations. Many of the theories described in the early chapters of this book are based in organizational psychology. Why was this field not identified as a contributor to the study of organization culture along with anthropology, sociology, social psychology, and economics?
3. Describe the culture of an organization with which you are familiar. It might be one in which you currently work, one in which you have worked, or one in which a friend or family member works. What values, beliefs, stories, and symbols are significant to employees of the organization?
4. Discuss the similarities and differences between the organizational culture approaches of Ouchi and Peters and Waterman.
5. Describe how organizations use symbols and stories to communicate values and beliefs. Give

some examples of how symbols and stories have been used in organizations with which you are familiar.

6. What is the role of leadership (discussed in Chapters 13 and 14) in developing, maintaining, and changing organizational culture?

7. Review the characteristics of organization structure described in earlier chapters and compare them with the elements of culture described by Ouchi and Peters and Waterman. Describe the similarities and differences, and explain how some characteristics of one may be related to characteristics of the other.

8. Discuss the role of organization rewards in developing, maintaining, and changing the organization culture.

9. How are empowerment and procedural justice similar to each other? How do they differ?

10. Describe how the culture of an organization can affect innovation.

# Organizational Behavior Case for Discussion

## Defining the "Astra USA" Way

Astra USA was a United States subsidiary of the Swedish Astra AB, one of the world's largest pharmaceutical companies, and was headed by Swedish-born Lars Bildman, a twenty-two-year veteran of Astra. Since disaster struck in 1996, Bildman has been fired, the unit has been sold to British pharmaceutical giant AstraZeneca, and lawsuits are everywhere . . . all because of the organizational culture. Here's what happened.

In 1995, Astra USA had sales of $5.3 billion with good growth in revenues of $323 million, 1,500 employees, and nice headquarters in Massachusetts. Its products include Xylocaine, a local anesthetic, and Rhinocort, an allergy medication.

Astra USA was in the news in the spring of 1996, when it faced numerous charges of sexual harassment. *Business Week* reported more than a dozen cases of women who claimed unwelcome sexual advances or expectations of sexual favors from middle managers and executives, including those in top management. As disturbing as these revelations were regarding the treatment of women within the company, it is also interesting to understand how this type of culture was created and maintained throughout the organization.

The cultural training started at the hiring process. Attractiveness was one of the female hiring criteria. If hiring managers could not visualize having drinks and partying with a potential employee, she probably would not be hired. Once hired to the high-paying sales positions, recruits were put through a rigorous nine-week training program at a hotel near company headquarters, where trainees learned "the Astra Way," which included courses in sales instruction, anatomy and physiology, and memorization of sales presentations. Rules regarding dress and dinner etiquette were communicated and strictly enforced. The program has been described as militaristic, demanding, and domineering. In addition, the trainees were told about the importance of working hard and playing hard, especially when it comes to socializing with customers. On open-bar nights at the hotel, managers would join the students, paying special attention to the females. Evidently, the managers' expectations were made quite clear to the female students and reinforced at sales meetings three times a year.

Employees who complained about the unwanted attention, both males and females, were not promoted or were fired for "poor performance." Some formal complaints were filed against the company but settled out of court, the complainants promising silence. Offended employees feared for their jobs both with Astra and with other companies in the industry. They feared that if other companies heard they had been troublemakers, they might not be hired anywhere. Male managers throughout the company were intimidated into altering their behavior toward certain employees favored by top management. Others seemed to go along with top management and began acting the same way. The attitude permeated the company. The cultural training had been effective.

Three top managers, including Mr. Bildman, were fired or suspended.

Then the lawsuits started. In an Equal Employment Opportunity Commission lawsuit filed in 1998, the charges were that the highest managers in the company engaged in a continuous pattern of sexual harassment of female sales representatives by making sexually offensive comments, engaging in unwanted touching, and requiring female sales representatives to socialize with them as a condition of employment. Also filed in 1998 was a suit against Bildman alleging that he engaged in sexual harassment and tolerated sexual harassment by others and adding charges of fraud, breach of fiduciary duty, and waste of corporate assets. Bildman denied the allegations and filed a countersuit claiming that the company breached their contract with him and charging that the company tried to discredit him and destroy his reputation.

Meanwhile, the company is trying to pick up the pieces and get on with business. In addition to being sold to the British-based company, Astra has new leadership at the top and has been attempting to drastically change its culture. It has developed and implemented sexual harassment training programs, new initiatives by the human resource department, and a work-family task force designed to help employees balance their work and family lives. One major focus has been to redefine "the Astra Way" that was at the heart of the earlier problems. The company also developed programs aimed at moving women and minorities into more senior positions. Managers and employees agree that the culture of harassment must be changed and that significant cultural change will not arrive overnight.

### Case Questions

1. What is the difference between a top manager "fooling around" inappropriately and creating a culture of harassment?
2. How did the culture of Astra contribute to the costly lawsuits at Astra?
3. What types of programs should the company be using to change the culture of Astra?

References: Mark Maremont, "A Case Puts a Value on Touching and Fondling," *Wall Street Journal*, May 25, 1999, p. B1; Betsy Morris, "Addicted to Sex," *Fortune*, May 10, 1999, pp. 66–80; Diane E. Lewis, "Sex-Harassment Lawsuits Push Astra Officials to Change Firm's Culture," *Knight-Ridder/Tribune Business News*, December 4, 1996, p. 1204B0944, *Boston Globe;* Mark Maremont, "Aftershocks Are Rumbling Through Astra," *Business Week*, May 20, 1996, p. 35; Mark Maremont, "Abuse of Power," *Business Week*, May 13, 1996, pp. 86–98; "The Cult of Astra," *Business Week*, May 13, 1996, p. 166.

## Experiencing Organizational Behavior

### Culture of the Classroom

**Purpose:** This exercise will help you appreciate the fascination as well as the difficulty of examining culture in organizations.

**Format:** The class will divide into groups of four to six. Each group will analyze the organization culture of a college class. Students in most classes that use this book will have taken many courses at the college they attend and therefore should have several classes in common.

**Procedure:** The class is divided into groups of four to six on the basis of classes the students have had in common.

1. Each group should first decide which class it will analyze. Each person in the group must have attended the class.
2. Each group should list the cultural factors to be discussed. Items to be covered should include:
   a. Stories about the professor
   b. Stories about the exams
   c. Stories about the grading
   d. Stories about other students
   e. The use of symbols that indicate the students' values
   f. The use of symbols that indicate the instructor's values
   g. Other characteristics of the class as suggested by the frameworks of Ouchi and Peters and Waterman.
3. Students should carefully analyze the stories and symbols to discover their underlying meanings. They should seek stories from other members of the group to ensure that all aspects of the class cul-

ture are covered. Students should take notes as these items are discussed.

4. After twenty to thirty minutes of work in groups, the instructor will reconvene the entire class and ask each group to share its analysis with the rest of the class.

### Follow-up Questions

1. What was the most difficult part of this exercise? Did other groups experience the same difficulty?
2. How did your group overcome this difficulty? How did other groups overcome it?
3. Do you believe your group's analysis accurately describes the culture of the class you selected? Could other students who analyzed the culture of the same class come up with a very different result? How could that happen?
4. If the instructor wanted to try to change the culture in the class you analyzed, what steps would you recommend that he or she take?

## Building Organizational Behavior Skills

### An Empowering Culture: What It Is and What It Is Not

What does it mean to empower people? Below is a brief definition, along with three behaviors that masquerade as empowerment, often with devastating results. See how well you can distinguish among them by choosing the one that best describes the supervisory behavior. Answers appear in the *Instructor's Resource Manual.* The quiz and answers were prepared by Donna Deeprose of Deeprose Consulting in New York.

**Empower:** to enable an employee to set work goals, make decisions, and solve problems.

**Exploit:** to take advantage of an employee to meet an unspoken goal of one's own.

**Abandon:** to delegate, but provide no support.

**Delude:** to give the appearance of empowering, but to withhold the freedom the employee needs to be successful.

1. A supervisor gives an employee authority to handle a project. When the employee complains about difficulties, the supervisor responds, "Don't worry, I'll handle it from now on."

   Behavior: ______________________

2. Same situation as (1), except that when the employee comes to the supervisor for help, the supervisor's response is, "This is your project. You take care of it."

   Behavior: ______________________

3. Same as (1) and (2), except that the supervisor discusses the problem with the employee and guides the employee into determining an appropriate next move.

   Behavior: ______________________

4. An employee has asked for additional responsibilities. The supervisor delegates to the employee total responsibility for a time-consuming report. The supervisor leaves at 5 P.M. each day, while the employee works late to complete the report.

   Behavior: ______________________

5. A supervisor keeps up with the company's changing mission, objectives, and plans, and keeps employees informed of how well all these changes influence the work unit.

   Behavior: ______________________

## Developing OB Internet Skills

**Introduction:** This chapter has presented several different perspectives and a variety of examples of the concept of organizational culture. This exercise will give you a chance to learn more about culture in real organizations.

**Internet Assignment:** As you near graduation you may become interested in interviewing for a job you can take after graduation. Pick several companies that you think you might want to work for. Rank-order the companies in the order in which you would choose to work for them (at least at this point). Then, starting from the top, look up articles on the management of each company, searching specifically for articles that describe something about the culture of the company. Not all companies have articles written about them that describe their culture, so it may take several tries to find articles that do. Remember, an article that has a description of an organization's culture may not always use the word "culture." So read carefully.

**Follow-up:** Describe the kinds of information you were able to locate. How much valuable information on culture did the articles provide? Finally, respond to the following questions:

1. What other information is needed to better understand the culture of these companies?
2. Should there be more information about companies' management style and culture available on the Internet?
3. Which types of companies have the best management information on the Internet?

chapter

# 19

# Organization Change and Development

## Management Preview

Companies constantly face pressures to change. Significant decreases in revenues and profits, forecasts of changing economic conditions, consumer purchasing patterns, technological and scientific factors, and competition, both foreign and domestic, can force top management to evaluate their organization and consider significant changes.

This chapter presents several perspectives on change in organizations. First, we examine the forces for change and discuss several approaches to planned organization change. Then, we consider organization development processes and the resistance to change that usually occurs. The chapter briefly covers several international and cross-cultural factors that affect organization change processes. Finally, we discuss how to manage organization change and development efforts in organizations. First, however, we describe how Dick Brown is changing Electronic Data Systems Corporation. ■

Electronic Data Systems Corporation (EDS), founded in 1962 by Ross Perot, effectively invented the computer service business. Under Perot, EDS grew and prospered until Perot sold it to General Motors in 1984. Perot stayed on two years before leaving to start his new company, Perot Systems. EDS continued to grow in revenues, at 8 percent per year, and in total personnel—to more than 130,000 employees in forty-seven countries. But its revenue growth was substantially less than the growth for the industry. Profits began to stagnate in 1994. In 1996, GM spun off EDS to its shareholders. Operating profit dropped from 21 percent in 1995 to 16 percent in 1998. Earnings per share fell, and revenue per employee was 55 percent below that of rival IBM's Global Services unit. Sales were below expectations, probably because nearly one-third of the sales force had not made a sale in more than two years. By late 1998, EDS's stock price had dropped 50 percent since 1996. It was clear to shareholders and board members that EDS was in trouble. Immediate changes were needed. Board member James Baker, former U.S. secretary of state, led the search for an outsider who would shake the place up. The board hired Dick Brown to turn the company around.

Brown, with twenty-eight years in the telecommunications industry, came from Cable & Wireless in Great Britain, where he had taken major steps in turning that company around. When Brown came to EDS, he found a company that was, in effect, wallowing in its own success, had no clear direction from the top, had lost its performance culture, and had become bloated with employees. Early on, he cut 5,000 jobs, including many executives, in what employees now call "Brown-sizing." He introduced a "forced ranking" for comparing employees on the basis of their performance and tied pay to the rankings. Brown answers his own telephone calls and sends regular emails to every employee to update them on what is going on. These group emails were initially a problem because this high-tech computer services provider had no companywide messaging system!

*"We've got to execute, execute, execute. That means measuring ourselves better, raising the performance bar, adding people in key spots, and winning with the army we've got." — Dick Brown, chairman and CEO of EDS**

In order to be sure that clients would get the best expertise the company had to solve their problems, Brown reorganized the divisions from what had been "pools of expertise" into focused business units. He created four global lines of business (E.solutions, Business Process Management, Information Solutions, and A.T. Kearney Consulting) to combine business and technical strengths to sell and deliver services. Six global industry teams (Products & Retailing; Financial Services & Travel and Transportation; Communications, Entertainment & Media; Health Care; Energy & Chemicals; and Government) were created to contribute industry insight and relationships to meet client needs.

To further symbolize to employees and clients alike that this was not the old EDS anymore, the corporate logo was changed from a square to a circle, possibly to resemble the dot that will be driving the company's future in e-business systems. For a variety of reasons, EDS is no longer the square company it was, thanks to Dick Brown.[1] ■

Dick Brown made a lot of changes at EDS that he thought were necessary to turn around a company that was in trouble. In this case, declining financial performance was the trigger for the board and shareholders to seek to make changes. Internally, the forces for change were probably a combination of several factors that caused the share price to drop, which got the attention of shareholders and the board.

# Forces for Change

An organization is subject to pressures for change from far too many sources to discuss them all here. Moreover, it is difficult to predict what type of pressures for change will be most significant in the next decade because the complexity of events and the rapidity of change are increasing. However, it is possible—and important—to discuss the broad categories of pressures that probably will have major effects on organizations. The four areas in which the pressures for change appear most powerful involve people, technology, infor-

This picture of the warehouse of Kbkids.com just before Christmas illustrates the crunch that occurred at the joint venture between the toy retail chain K*B Toys and BrainPlay. They had more than 237,000 hits per day before the Christmas toy season ever hit. The web site opened in the summer with a great selection of toys, games, and Pokemon figures, but the unexpected demand overwhelmed the web site and the warehouse. Other online toy retailers experienced the same problem. Executives of the company claim that starting a web-based retail operation is just like starting a store-based retailer, just ten times faster.

mation processing and communication, and competition. Table 19.1 gives examples of each of these categories.

## People

Approximately 56 million people were born between 1945 and 1960. These baby boomers differ significantly from previous generations with respect to education, expectations, and value systems.[2] As this group has aged, the median age of the U.S. population has gradually increased, passing thirty-two for the first time in 1988[3] and further increasing to 35.6 in 1999.[4] The special characteristics of baby boomers show up in distinct purchasing patterns that affect product and service innovation, technological change, and marketing and promotional activities.[5] Employment practices, compensation systems, promotion and managerial succession systems, and the entire concept of human resource management are also affected.

Other population-related pressures for change involve the generations that sandwich the baby boomers: the increasing numbers of senior citizens and those born after 1960. The parents of the baby boomers are living longer, healthier lives than previous generations, and today they expect to live the "good life" that they missed when they were raising their children. The impact of the large number of senior citizens is already evident in part-time employment practices, in the marketing of everything from hamburgers to packaged tours of Asia, and in service areas such as health care, recreation, and financial services. The post-1960 generation of workers who are entering the job market differ from the baby boomers.

The increasing diversity of the work force in coming years will mean significant changes for organizations. This increasing diversity was discussed in some detail in Chapter 3. In addition, employees will be faced with a different work environment in the twenty-first century. The most descriptive word for this new

**table 19.1**
**Pressures for Organization Change**

| Category | Examples | Type of Pressure for Change |
|---|---|---|
| **People** | Generation X<br>Baby boomers<br>Senior citizens<br>Work-force diversity | Demands for different training, benefits, workplace arrangements, and compensation systems |
| **Technology** | Manufacturing in space<br>Internet<br>Artificial Intelligence | More education and training for workers at all levels, more new products, products move faster to market |
| **Information Processing and Communication** | Computer, satellite communications<br>Videoconferencing | Faster reaction times, immediate responses to questions, new products, different office arrangements, telecommuting |
| **Competition** | Worldwide markets<br>International trade agreements<br>Emerging nations | Global competition, more competing products with more features and options, lower costs, higher quality |

work environment is "change." Employees must be prepared for constant change. Change is occurring in organizations' cultures, structures, work relationships, customer relationships, and in the actual jobs that people do. People will have to be completely adaptable to new situations while maintaining productivity under the existing system.[6]

## Technology

Not only is technology changing, the rate of technological change is increasing. In 1970, for example, all engineering students owned slide rules and used them in almost every class. By 1976, slide rules had given way to portable electronic calculators. In the mid-1980s, some universities began issuing microcomputers to entering students or assuming those students already owned them. In 1993, the Scholastic Aptitude Test (SAT), which many college-bound students take to get into college, allowed calculators to be used during the test! And students cannot make it through the university without owning or at least having ready access to a personal computer. The dormitory rooms at many universities are wired for direct computer access for email, class assignments, and access to the Internet. Technological development is increasing so rapidly in almost every field that it is quite difficult to predict which products will dominate ten years from now. As described in the "Talking Technology" box, companies such as DuPont are completely changing their core product strategy based on their predictions of the future.

Interestingly, organization change is self-perpetuating. With the advances in information technology, organizations generate more information, and it circulates more quickly. Consequently, employees can respond more quickly to problems, so the organization can respond more quickly to demands from other organizations, customers, and competitors.[7]

New technology will affect organizations in ways we cannot yet predict. Artificial intelligence—computers and software programs that think and learn in

TALKING TECHNOLOGY

## DuPont Changes from Oil to Corn

DuPont is undergoing a radical shift in the basic technology it employs to make the majority of its products: from its old reliance on petrochemicals to a new emphasis on corn and biotechnology. This is the second such major shift in the company's almost two-hundred-year history. Near the end of the nineteenth century, DuPont switched from making gunpowder to chemicals. The chemical focus has been on various uses and processes related to petroleum. For example, for more than sixty years, DuPont has made a lot of money from nylon and other petroleum products it developed, such as Dacron, Teflon, and Nomex. The crux of DuPont's present shift is the change from a chemical company to a science company. To go along with the change in emphasis, the company has dropped its old slogan of "Better Things for a Better Life" and created a new slogan, "The Miracles of Science." Basically, the company has reduced its investments in petrochemicals and increased its investments in the areas of biology, agronomy, genetics, and catalysis. For example, in 1981, when oil resources were tight, DuPont bought Conoco in order to assure a consistent supply of petroleum for its plants. In 1999, it sold Conoco and invested $7.7 billion in the purchase of 80 percent of Pioneer Hi-Bred International, an agricultural seed company.

*"I told him, 'You're going to make mistakes. Just don't make any that are unfixable.'" — Edgar Woolard, former CEO of DuPont*

The architect of this shift is Chad Holliday, chairman and CEO. In addition to changing DuPont's core strategy, Holliday is trying to change the way everybody in the company does their jobs. He is stirring up culture changes as well as process improvement at every level. He recognizes that the biotechnology-based business is much faster to change than was the petrochemical-based business. Therefore, he is emphasizing speed and more speed in everything the company does. In 1998, Holliday reorganized DuPont's eighty-one businesses into three categories: the foundation group (polyester and nylon), the differentiated group (Corian, Kevlar, and Lycra), and the life science group (agricultural and pharmaceutical). He clearly sent the message that the company would be reducing its capital investment in the chemical business. He also embraced such popular techniques as the statistical process control system called Six Sigma, which has been used so successfully at Motorola, General Electric, and other companies. More than $25 million has been spent on training in Six Sigma, from which Holliday expects to generate a productivity increase of 4 percent by 2001. Many expected DuPont to sell off the chemical divisions. But the company chose instead to use the cash these divisions generated to invest in agricultural and biotech businesses. Then in 1999, Holliday reorganized again, replacing the three categories with eight smaller business units, such as specialty fibers, pigments and chemicals, and performance coatings.

Holliday is also chief cheerleader and trainer for the Six Sigma training program. He sends out a biweekly email to all employees on some aspect of management or operations. He feels that this is one of his chief ways to make sure that everyone gets the message and gets on board with the new strategy. So far, the stock price has not been reacting too well to the strategic change. Many experts agree with the shift but are not too happy with the poor execution of the changes. Holliday remains steadfast in his commitment to the new strategy and the potential for the new products currently in development with the various research groups.

References: "DuPont Adopts New Direction in China," *Xinhua News Agency,* September 7, 1999, p. 1008250h0104; Alex Taylor III, "Why DuPont Is Trading Oil for Corn," *Fortune,* April 26, 1999, pp. 154n–160 (quote on p. 157); Jay Palmer, "New DuPont: For Rapid Growth, an Old-Line Company Looks to Drugs, Biotechnology," *Barron's,* May 11, 1998, p. 31.

much the same way as humans do—is already assisting in geological exploration.[8] Several companies are developing systems to manufacture chemicals and exotic electronic components in space. The Internet and the World Wide Web are changing the way companies and individuals communicate, market, buy, and distribute faster than organizations can respond. Thus, as organizations respond more quickly to changes, change occurs more rapidly, which in turn necessitates more rapid responses.

## Information Processing and Communication

Advances in information processing and communication have paralleled each other. A new generation of computers, which will mark another major increase in processing power, is being designed. Satellite systems for data transmission are already in use. Today people can carry telephones in their briefcases along with their portable computers and pocket-size televisions.

In the future, people may not need offices as they work with computers and communicate through new data transmission devices. Work stations, both in and outside of offices, will be more electronic than paper and pencil. For years, the capability existed to generate, manipulate, store, and transmit more data than managers could use, but the benefits were not fully realized. Now the time has come to utilize all of that information-processing potential, and companies are making the most of it. Typically, companies received orders by mail in the 1970s, by 800 number in the 1980s, by fax machine in the late 1980s and early 1990s, and by electronic data exchange in the mid-1990s. Orders used to take a week; now they are instantaneous, and companies must be able to respond immediately, all because of changes in information processing and communication.[9]

## Competition

Although competition is not a new force for change, competition today has some significant new twists. First, most markets are international because of decreasing transportation and communication costs and the increasing export orientation of business. The adoption of trade agreements such as the North American Free Trade Agreement (NAFTA) and the World Trade Organization (WTO) has changed the way business operates. In the future, competition from industrialized countries such as Japan and Germany will take a back seat to competition from the booming industries of developing nations. The Internet is creating new competitors overnight and in ways that could not have been imagined five years ago.

*"There are always challengers. We've seen them before. They are good for us. They make us work harder." — John Chambers, Cisco CEO*[10]

Developing nations may soon offer different, newer, cheaper, or higher-quality products while enjoying the benefits of low labor costs, abundant supplies of raw materials, expertise in certain areas of production, and financial protection from their governments that may not be available in older industrialized states. Nokia, a Finnish company, is locked in a battle with Motorola and Ericcson for the worldwide cellular phone market. In order to meet the global competitive challenges Nokia changed its approach to marketing by holding global strategy sessions and training managers to think globally yet act locally by developing a good understanding of local cultures. They had to adjust to the fact that mass marketing differs widely among the U.S., Europe, and Asia.[11] Organizations that are not ready for these new sources of competition may not last long in the new century.

# Processes for Planned Organization Change

External forces may impose change on an organization. Ideally, however, the organization will not only respond to change but anticipate it, prepare for it through planning, and incorporate it in the organization strategy. Organization change can be viewed from a static point of view, such as that of Lewin (see below), or from a dynamic perspective.

## Lewin's Process Model

Planned organization change requires a systematic process of movement from one condition to another. Kurt Lewin suggested that efforts to bring about planned change in organizations should approach change as a multistage process.[12] His model of planned change is made up of three steps—unfreezing, change, and refreezing—as shown in Figure 19.1.

**Unfreezing** is the process by which people become aware of the need for change.

**Unfreezing** is the process by which people become aware of the need for change. If people are satisfied with current practices and procedures, they may have little or no interest in making changes. The key factor in unfreezing is making employees understand the importance of a change and how their jobs will be affected by it. The employees who will be most affected by the change must be made aware of why it is needed, which in effect makes them dissatisfied enough with current operations to be motivated to change.

Change itself is the movement from the old way of doing things to a new way. Change may entail installing new equipment, restructuring the organization, implementing a new performance appraisal system—anything that alters existing relationships or activities.

**Refreezing** is the process of making new behaviors relatively permanent and resistant to further change.

**Refreezing** makes new behaviors relatively permanent and resistant to further change. Examples of refreezing techniques include repeating newly learned skills in a training session and role playing to teach how the new skill can be used in a real-life work situation. Refreezing is necessary because without it, the old ways of doing things might soon reassert themselves while the new ways are forgotten. For example, many employees who attend special training sessions apply themselves diligently and resolve to change things in their organizations. But when they return to the workplace, they find it easier to conform to the old ways than to make waves. There usually are few, if any, rewards for trying to change the organizational status

figure 19.1

**Lewin's Process of Organization Change**

*In Lewin's three-step model, change is a systematic process of transition from an old way of doing things to a new way. Inclusion of an "unfreezing" stage indicates the importance of preparing for the change. The refreezing stage reflects the importance of following up on the change to make it permanent.*

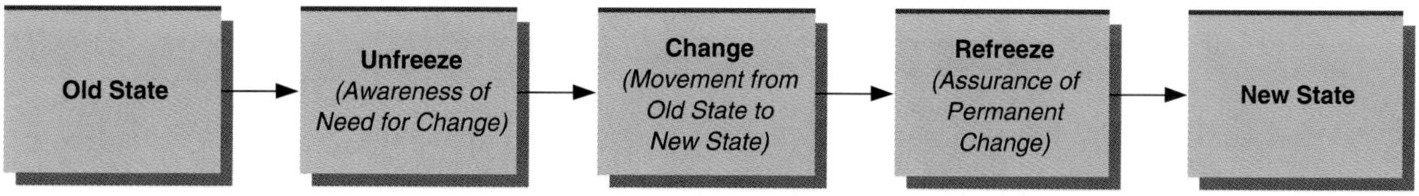

quo. In fact, the personal sanctions against doing so may be difficult to tolerate. Learning theory and reinforcement theory (see Chapter 6) can play important roles in the refreezing phase.

## The Continuous Change Process Model

Perhaps because Lewin's model is very simple and straightforward, virtually all models of organization change use his approach. However, it does not deal with several important issues. A more complex, and more helpful, approach is illustrated in Figure 19.2. This approach treats planned change from the perspective of top management and indicates that change is continuous. Although we discuss each step as if it were separate and distinct from the others, it is important to note that, as change becomes continuous in organizations, different steps are probably occurring simultaneously throughout the organization. The model incorporates Lewin's concept into the implementation phase.

In this approach, top management perceives that certain forces or trends call for change, and the issue is subjected to the organization's usual problem-solving and decision-making processes (see Chapter 15). Usually, top management defines its goals in terms of what the organization or certain processes or outputs will be like after the change. Alternatives for change are generated and evaluated, and an acceptable one is selected.

A **change agent** is a person responsible for managing a change effort.

Early in the process, the organization may seek the assistance of a **change agent**—a person who will be responsible for managing the change effort. The change agent may also help management recognize and define the problem or the need for the change and may be involved in generating and evaluating potential plans of action. The change agent may be a member of the organization, an out-

figure **19.2**

**Continuous Change Process Model of Organization Change**

*The continuous change process model incorporates the forces for change, a problem-solving process, a change agent, and transition management. It takes a top-management perspective and highlights the fact that in organizations today, change is a continuous process.*

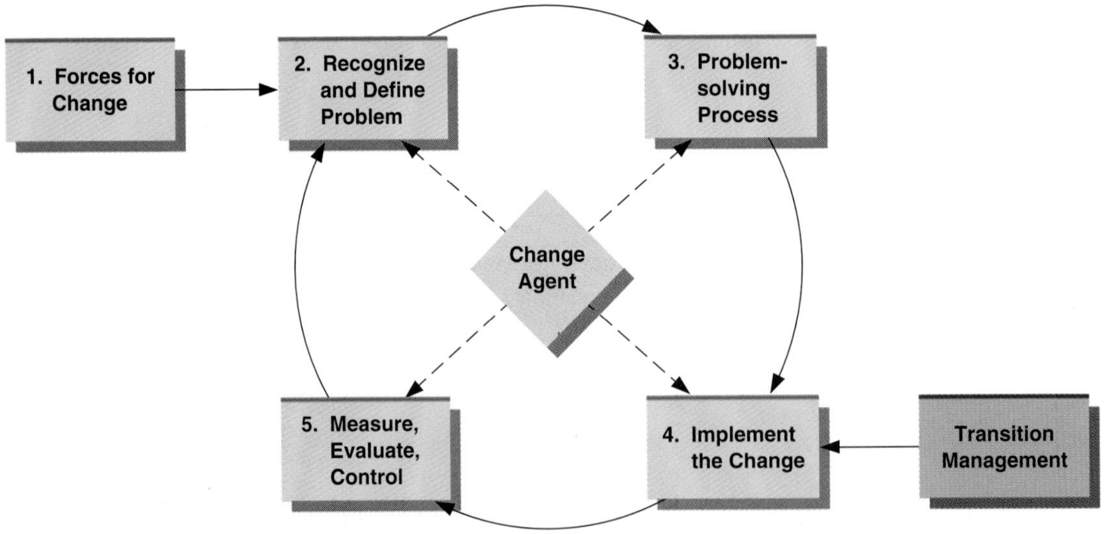

Eileen Gittins, Adeeb Shana'a, and Amit Desai combined their two software companies, Personify and Anubis Solutions, which had been competitors, in order to capitalize on opportunities for both. Blending the two companies' personnel and cultures was more important to closing the deal than the financial details. Gittins spent a lot of time at the Anubis offices to get the feel of the other company. The two companies took all of their employees on a boat ride where employees could dance and get to know each other socially. The change was easy after that. The two companies spent extra time and effort up front, which really smoothed the transition that was necessary to make the merger work.

sider such as a consultant, or even someone from headquarters whom employees view as an outsider. An internal change agent is likely to know the organization's people, tasks, and political situations, which may be helpful in interpreting data and understanding the system; but an insider may also be too close to the situation to view it objectively. (In addition, a regular employee would have to be removed from his or her regular duties to concentrate on the transition.) An outsider, then, is often received better by all parties because of his or her assumed impartiality. Under the direction and management of the change agent, the organization implements the change through Lewin's unfreeze, change, and refreeze process.

The final step is measurement, evaluation, and control. The change agent and the top management group assess the degree to which the change is having the desired effect; that is, they measure progress toward the goals of the change and make appropriate changes if necessary. The more closely the change agent is involved in the change process, the less distinct the steps become. The change agent becomes a "collaborator" or "helper" to the organization as she or he is immersed in defining and solving the problem with members of the organization. When this happens, the change agent may be working with many individuals, groups, and departments within the organization on different phases of the change process. When the change process is moving along from one stage to another it may not be readily observable because of the total involvement of the change agent in every phase of the project. Throughout the process, however, the change agent brings in new ideas and viewpoints that help members look at old problems in new ways. Change often arises from the conflict that results when the change agent challenges the organization's assumptions and generally accepted patterns of operation.

*"One of the foremost things we need is a change agent—and Dick Brown fits the bill." — James Baker III, former U.S. secretary of state and EDS board member[13]*

Through the measurement, evaluation, and control phase, top management determines the effectiveness of the change process by evaluating various indicators of organizational productivity and effectiveness or employee morale. It is hoped that the organization will be better after the change than before. However, the uncertainties and rapid change in all sectors of the environment make constant organization change a certainty for most organizations.

**Transition management** is the process of systematically planning, organizing, and implementing change.

**Transition management** is the process of systematically planning, organizing, and implementing change, from the disassembly of the current state to the realization of a fully functional future state within an organization.[14] Once change begins, the organization is in neither the old state nor the new state, yet business must go on. Transition management ensures that business continues while the change is occurring, and thus it must begin before the change occurs. The members of the regular management team must take on the role of transition managers and coordinate organizational activities with the change agent. An interim management structure or interim positions may be created to ensure continuity and control of the business during the transition. Communication about the changes to all involved, from employees to customers and suppliers, plays a key role in transition management.[15]

# Organization Development

On one level, organization development is simply the way organizations change and evolve. Organization change can involve personnel, technology, competition, and other areas. Employee learning and formal training, transfers, promotions, terminations, and retirements are all examples of personnel-related changes. Thus, in the broadest sense, organization development means organization change.[16] However, the term as used here means something more specific. Over the past thirty years, organization development has emerged as a distinct field of study and practice. Experts now substantially agree as to what constitutes organizational development in general, although arguments about details continue.[17] Our definition of organization development is an attempt to describe a very complex process in a simple manner. It is also an attempt to capture the best points of several definitions offered by writers in the field.

## Organization Development Defined

**Organization development** is the process of planned change and improvement of the organization through application of knowledge of the behavioral sciences.

**Organization development** is the process of planned change and improvement of organizations through the application of knowledge of the behavioral sciences. Three points in this definition make it simple to remember and use. First, organization development involves attempts to plan organization changes, which excludes spontaneous, haphazard initiatives. Second, the specific intention of organization development is to improve organizations. This point excludes changes that merely imitate those of another organization, are forced on the organization by external pressures, or are undertaken merely for the sake of changing. Third, the planned improvement must be based on knowledge of the behavioral sciences, such as organizational behavior, psychology, sociology, cultural anthropology, and related fields of study, rather than on financial or technological considerations. Under our definition, the replacement of manual personnel records with a computerized system would not be considered an instance of organization development. Although such a change has behavioral effects, it is a technology-driven reform rather than a behavioral one. Likewise, alterations in record keeping necessary to support new government-mandated reporting requirements are not a part of organization development, because the change is obligatory and the result of an external force. The three most basic types of techniques are systemwide, task and technological, and group and individual.

## Systemwide Organization Development

**Structural change** is a systemwide organization development involving a major restructuring of the organization or instituting programs such as quality of work life.

The most comprehensive type of organization change involves a major reorientation or reorganization—usually referred to as a **structural change** or a systemwide rearrangement of task division and authority and reporting relationships. A structural change affects performance appraisal and rewards, decision making, and communication and information-processing systems. As we discussed in Chapter 17, reengineering and rethinking the organizations are two contemporary approaches to systemwide structural change. Reengineering can be a difficult process, but it has great potential for organizational improvement. It requires that managers challenge long-held assumptions about everything they do and set outrageous goals and expect they will be met.

*"One of the wonderful things about business: You have to work hard to forget what you know. If I like the business model I have now, I am not going to like it in five years." — Larry Bossidy, former CEO of AlliedSignal (before its merger with Honeywell)*[18]

An organization may change the way it divides tasks into jobs, groups jobs into departments and divisions, and arranges authority and reporting relationships among positions. It may move from functional departmentalization to a system based on products or geography, for example, or from a conventional linear design to a matrix or a team-based design. Other changes may include dividing large groups into smaller ones or merging small groups into larger ones. In addition, the degree to which rules and procedures are written down and enforced, as well as the locus of decision-making authority, may be altered. Supervisors may become "coaches" or "facilitators" in a team-based organization. The organization will have transformed both the configurational and the operational aspects of its structure if all these changes are made.

No systemwide structural change is simple.[19] A company president cannot just issue a memo notifying company personnel that on a certain date they will report to a different supervisor and be responsible for new tasks and expect everything to change overnight. Employees have months, years, and sometimes decades of experience in dealing with people and tasks in certain ways. When these patterns are disrupted, employees need time to learn the new tasks and to settle into the new relationships. Moreover, they may resist the change for a number of reasons; we discuss resistance to change later in this chapter. Therefore, organizations must manage the change process. The "World View" box describes how Jacques Nasser, CEO of Ford, is managing the organization-wide change process at Ford.

**Quality of work life** is the extent to which workers can satisfy important personal needs through their experiences in the organization.

Another systemwide change is the introduction of quality-of-work-life programs. J. Lloyd Suttle defined **quality of work life** as the "degree to which members of a work organization are able to satisfy important personal needs through their experiences in the organization."[20] Quality-of-work-life programs focus strongly on providing a work environment conducive to satisfying individual needs. The emphasis on improving life at work developed during the 1970s, a period of increasing inflation and deepening recession. The development was rather surprising, because an expanding economy and substantially increased resources are

WORLD VIEW

## *Ford Tries to Create a World View*

Ford Motor Company has long been known for the independence of its different divisions. Ford Europe was free to run its operations as it felt was best for the European markets. The same went for Ford Australia and Ford in the United States. The company was really a bunch of big fiefdoms, independently managed for their own best interests. This fiefdom mentality was an outgrowth of the history of the company as it developed following its founding in 1905 by Henry Ford, one of the first true internationalists in industry. During the company's first twenty years, Ford would send a son or other top executive off to run assembly plants in other countries, making the same car that was made in the United States. For the next thirty years, Ford's foreign operations got swept up in nationalistic movements that were developing around the world, and each operation developed its own identity, models, productions systems, and even accounting systems. Following the nationalistic period, a movement toward regionalism developed as regional associations formed, such as NAFTA and the Common Market in Europe (now the European Union). The regional model brought the identifiable groups down to four—one each in the United States, Europe, South America, and Asia-Pacific.

*"You can't reinvent a company like Ford overnight; we have too much tradition. But there is no question that we have to change our fundamental approach to work—we have to change our DNA. And teaching does that better than any other way I know." — Jacques Nasser, CEO of Ford Motor Company*

CEO Jacques Nasser, who has worked in almost all of those regional companies, is now preaching a new message. Nasser is convinced that the wave of the future is for one global company to replace the fiefdoms. More than just operationally, he has set out to change the fiefdom mentality in Ford around the world. He is convinced that a truly globally integrated organization will better respond and satisfy consumer wants in the twenty-first century, which will in turn impact financial returns and the capital markets. Nasser points out that in the fiefdom mentality people are focused on what will make their division profitable, often even at the expense of the total company. His goal is to get everyone to think about, and then act on, what is best for the company as a whole. He sees his job as changing the mindset of virtually everyone in the company.

Nasser's campaign is a multifaceted program of small group discussions, exercises in community service, and 360-degree feedback that teaches Ford is a global organization with a single strategic focus on consumers and shareholder value. He believes the change must get to every individual manager, designer, engineer, and plant worker. The three major components are the Capstone, Business Leadership Institute, and Executive Partnering programs. The Capstone program involves Nasser and his senior leadership team as teachers with twenty-four senior executives as participants. A five-day workshop of teaching, discussions, and team-building exercises is followed by the assignment of diverse six-person teams to significant improvement projects. Each team has six months to tackle and solve the problem. Senior executives have taught the Business Leadership Institute to all 55,000 salaried managers. Participants spend three days in teaching and discussion followed by one-hundred-day projects and community service. Each team makes a video that contrasts the old Ford with the new Ford. In the Executive Partnering program, young managers with leadership potential are assigned to shadow seven executives over eight weeks. The young managers are exposed to everything the executives encounter during that time. In addition, at least three young managers are assigned to work together to solve an immediate business problem during their partnering experience.

Through all of these teaching/learning experiences, managers are taught to focus on the company as a worldwide enterprise. Their focus is on what is good for consumers and long-term shareholder value. Nasser is convinced that his teaching philosophy is already having multiple impacts.

References: "Ford Enters New Era of E-Communication: New Web Sites Connect Dealers, Consumer, Suppliers," *PR Newswire,* January 24, 2000, p. 7433; Suzy Wetlaufer, "Driving Change," *Harvard Business Review,* March–April 1999, pp. 77–85 (quote on p. 77); "Ford's Passing Fancy," *Business Week,* March 15, 1999, p. 42.

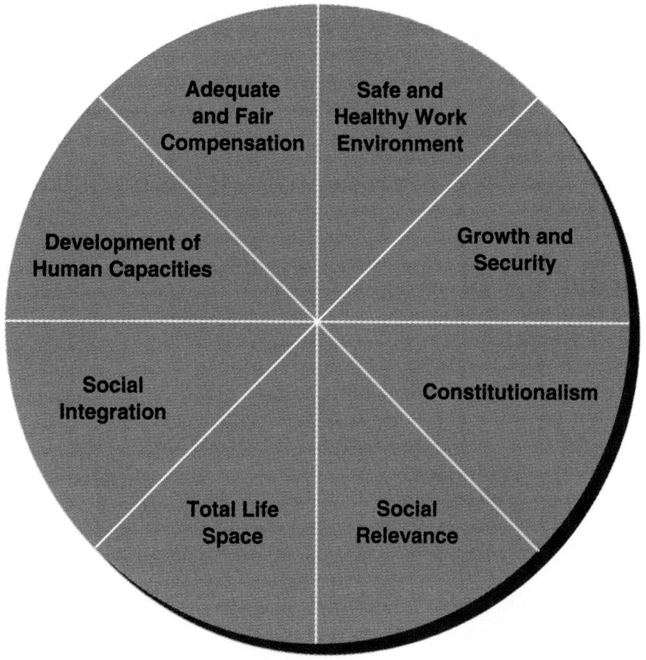


figure 19.3

**Walton's Categorization of Quality-of-Work-Life Programs**

*Quality-of-work-life programs can be categorized into eight types. The expected benefits of these programs are increased employee morale, productivity, and organizational effectiveness.*

Reference: Adapted from Richard E. Walton, "Quality of Work Life: What Is It?" *Sloan Management Review*, Fall 1973, pp. 11–21, by permission of the publisher. 

the conditions that usually induce top management to begin people-oriented programs. Top management viewed improving life at work as a means of improving productivity.

Any movement with broad and ambiguous goals tends to spawn diverse programs, each claiming to be based on the movement's goals, and quality of work life is no exception. These programs vary substantially, although most espouse a goal of "humanizing the workplace." Richard Walton divided them into the eight categories shown in Figure 19.3.[21] Obviously, many types of programs can be accommodated by the categories, from changing the pay system to establishing an employee bill of rights that guarantees workers the rights to privacy, free speech, due process, and fair and equitable treatment.

Total quality management, which was discussed in several earlier chapters, can also be viewed as a systemwide organization development program. In fact, some might consider total quality management as a broad program that includes structural change as well as quality of work life. It differs from quality of work life in that it emphasizes satisfying customer needs by making quality-oriented changes rather than focusing on satisfying employee needs at work. Often, however, the employee programs are very similar.

The benefits gained from quality-of-work-life programs differ substantially, but generally they are of three types. A more positive attitude toward the work and the organization, or increased job satisfaction, is perhaps the most direct benefit.[22] Another is increased productivity, although it is often difficult to measure and separate the effects of the quality-of-work-life program from the effects of other organizational factors. A third benefit is increased effectiveness of the organization as measured by its profitability, goal accomplishment, shareholder wealth, or resource exchange. The third gain follows directly from the first two: If employees have more positive attitudes about the organization and their productivity increases, everything else being equal, the organization should be more effective.

## Task and Technological Change

Another way to bring about systemwide organization development is through changes in the tasks involved in doing the work, the technology, or both. The direct alteration of jobs usually is called task redesign. Changing how inputs are

Neil Wilkin, an engineer at the National Institute of Standards and Technology, is checking a lathe's performance. The testing machine produces data that can be transmitted via high-speed network to the maintenance department from anywhere in the world. The maintenance department can then make adjustments and corrections to the machine tool. The implications for the way the machine tool manufacturing, inspection, and maintenance work is done are enormous. It will change the way that inspection and maintenance work is done, which means that the jobs of testers and maintenance technicians will have to be redesigned. While the change in the machine is a technological change, the resulting job and organizational changes will require organization development in order to properly integrate the technological changes.

transformed into outputs is called "technological change" and also usually results in task changes. Strictly speaking, changing the technology is typically not part of organization development, whereas task redesign usually is.

The structural changes discussed in the preceding section are explicitly systemwide in scope. Those we examine in this section are more narrowly focused and may not seem to have the same far-reaching consequences. It is important to remember, however, that their impact is felt throughout the organization. The discussion of task design in Chapter 7 focused on job definition and motivation and gave little attention to implementing changes in jobs. Here we discuss task redesign as a mode of organization change.

Several approaches to introducing job changes in organizations have been proposed. One is by a coauthor of this book, Ricky W. Griffin. Griffin's approach is an integrative framework of nine steps that reflect the complexities of the interfaces between individual jobs and the total organization.[23] The process, shown in Table 19.2, includes the steps usually associated with change, such as recognizing the need for a change, selecting the appropriate intervention, and evaluating the change. But Griffin's approach inserts four additional steps into the standard sequence: diagnosis of the overall work system and context, including examination of the jobs, work force, technology, organization design, leadership, and group dynamics; evaluating the costs and benefits of the change; formulating a redesign strategy; and implementing supplemental changes.

Diagnosis includes analysis of the total work environment within which the jobs exist. It is important to evaluate the organization structure, especially the work rules and decision-making authority within a department, when job changes are being considered.[24] For example, if jobs are to be redesigned to give employees more freedom in choosing work methods or scheduling work activities, diagnosis of the present system must determine whether the rules will allow that to happen. Diagnosis must also include evaluation of the work group and teams and intragroup dynamics (discussed in Chapters 11 and 12). Furthermore, it must determine whether workers have or can easily obtain the new skills to perform the redesigned task.

It is extremely important to recognize the full range of potential costs and benefits associated with a job redesign effort. Some are direct and quantifiable; others

| | |
|---|---|
| Step 1: | Recognition of a need for a change |
| Step 2: | Selection of task redesign as a potential intervention |
| Step 3: | Diagnosis of the work system and context |
| | a. Diagnosis of existing jobs |
| | b. Diagnosis of existing work force |
| | c. Diagnosis of technology |
| | d. Diagnosis of organization design |
| | e. Diagnosis of leader behavior |
| | f. Diagnosis of group and social processes |
| Step 4: | Cost-benefit analysis of proposed changes |
| Step 5: | Go/no-go decision |
| Step 6: | Formulation of the strategy for redesign |
| Step 7: | Implementation of the task changes |
| Step 8: | Implementation of any supplemental changes |
| Step 9: | Evaluation of the task redesign effort |

Reference: Ricky W. Griffin, *Task Design: An Integrative Framework* (Glenview, Ill.: Scott, Foresman, 1982), p. 208. Used by permission.

table 19.2 **Integrated Framework for Implementation of Task Redesign in Organizations**

are indirect and not quantifiable. Redesign may involve unexpected costs or benefits; although these cannot be predicted with certainty, they can be weighed as possibilities. Factors such as short-term role ambiguity, role conflict, and role overload can be major stumbling blocks to a job redesign effort.

Implementing a redesign scheme takes careful planning, and developing a strategy for the intervention is the final planning step. Strategy formulation is a four-part process. First, the organization must decide who will design the changes. Depending on the circumstances, the planning team may consist of only upper-level management or may include line workers and supervisors. Next, the team undertakes the actual design of the changes based on job design theory and the needs, goals, and circumstances of the organization. Third, the team decides the timing of the implementation, which may require a formal transition period during which equipment is purchased and installed, job training takes place, new physical layouts are arranged, and the bugs in the new system are worked out. Fourth, strategy planners must consider whether the job changes require adjustments and supplemental changes in other organizational components, such as reporting relationships and the compensation system.

## Group and Individual Change

Groups and individuals can be involved in organization change in a vast number of ways. Retraining a single employee can be considered an organization change if the training affects the way the employee does his or her job. Familiarizing managers with the Leadership grid or the Vroom decision tree (Chapter 13) is an attempt at change. In the first case, the goal is to balance management concerns for production and people; in the second, the goal is to increase the participation of rank-and-file employees in the organization's decision making. In this section, we present an overview of four popular types of people-oriented change techniques: training, management development programs, team building, and survey feedback.

**Training** Training generally is designed to improve employees' job skills. Employees may be trained to run certain machines, taught new mathematical skills, or acquainted with personal growth and development methods. Stress management programs are becoming popular for helping employees, particularly executives, understand organizational stress and develop ways to cope with it.[25] Training may also be used in conjunction with other, more comprehensive organization changes. For instance, if an organization is implementing a management-by-objectives program, training in establishing goals and reviewing goal-oriented performance is probably needed. One important type of training that is becoming increasingly common is training people to work in other countries. Companies such as

Motorola give extensive training programs to employees at all levels before they start an international assignment. Training includes intensive language courses, cultural courses, and courses for the family.

Among the many training methods, the most common are lecture, discussion, a lecture-discussion combination, experiential methods, case studies, and films or videotapes. Training can take place in a standard classroom, either on company property or in a hotel, at a resort, or at a conference center. On-the-job training provides a different type of experience in which the trainee learns from an experienced worker. Most training programs use a combination of methods determined by the topic, the trainees, the trainer, and the organization.

A major problem of training programs is transferring employee learning to the workplace. Often an employee learns a new skill or a manager learns a new management technique but upon returning to the normal work situation finds it easier to go back to the old way of doing things. As we discussed earlier, the process of refreezing is a vital part of the change process, and some way must be found to make the accomplishments of the training program permanent.

**Management Development Programs** Management development programs, like employee training programs, attempt to foster certain skills, abilities, and perspectives. Often, when a highly qualified technical person is promoted to manager of a work group, he or she lacks training in how to manage or deal with people. In such cases, management development programs can be important to organizations, both for the new manager and for his or her subordinates.

Typically, management development programs use the lecture-discussion method to some extent but rely most heavily on participative methods, such as case studies and role playing. Participative and experiential methods allow the manager to experience the problems of being a manager as well as the feelings of frustration, doubt, and success that are part of the job. The subject matter of this type of training program is problematic, however, in that management skills, including communication, problem diagnosis, problem solving, and performance appraisal, are not as easy to identify or to transfer from a classroom to the workplace as the skills required to run a machine. In addition, rapid changes in the external environment can make certain managerial skills obsolete in a very short time. As a result, some companies are approaching the development of their management team as an ongoing, career-long process and require their managers to attend refresher courses periodically.

One training approach involves managers in an intense exercise that stimulates the daily operation of a real company. Such simulations emphasize problem-solving behavior rather than competitive tactics and usually involve extensive debriefing, in which a manager's style is openly discussed and criticized by trained observers as the first step to improvement. IBM and AT&T have commissioned experts to create a simulation specifically for their managers. Although the cost of custom simulations is high, it is reportedly repaid in benefits from individual development.[26]

As corporate America invests hundreds of millions of dollars in management development, certain guiding principles are evolving: (1) Management development is a multifaceted, complex, and long-term process to which there is no quick or simple approach; (2) organizations should carefully and systematically identify their unique developmental needs and evaluate their programs accordingly; (3) management development objectives must be compatible with organizational objectives; and (4) the utility and value of management development remain more an article of faith than a proven fact.[27]

**Team Building** When interaction among group members is critical to group success and effectiveness, team development, or team building, may be useful. Team building emphasizes members' working together in a spirit of cooperation and generally has one or more of the following goals:

1. To set team goals and priorities
2. To analyze or allocate the way work is performed
3. To examine how a group is working—that is, to examine processes such as norms, decision making, and communications
4. To examine relationships among the people doing the work[28]

Total quality management efforts usually focus on teams, and the principles of team building must be applied to make them work. Team participation is especially important in the data-gathering and evaluation phases of team development. In data gathering, the members share information on the functioning of the group. The opinions of the group thus form the foundation of the development process. In the evaluation phase, members are the source of information about the effectiveness of the development effort.[29]

Like total quality management and many other management techniques, team building should not be thought of as a one-time experience, perhaps something undertaken on a retreat from the workplace; rather, it is a continuing process. It may take weeks, months, or years for a group to learn to pull together and function as a team. Team development can be a way to train the group to solve its own problems in the future. Research on the effectiveness of team building as an organization development tool so far is mixed and inconclusive. For more details on developing teams in organizations, please refer to Chapter 12.

**Survey Feedback** Survey feedback techniques can form the basis for a change process. In this process, data are gathered, analyzed, summarized, and returned to those who generated them to identify, discuss, and solve problems. A survey feedback process is often set in motion either by the organization's top management or by a consultant to management. By providing information about employees' beliefs and attitudes, a survey can help management diagnose and solve an organization's problems. A consultant or change agent usually coordinates the process and is responsible for data gathering, analysis, and summary. The three-stage process is shown in Figure 19.4.[30]

The use of survey feedback techniques in an organization development process differs from their use in traditional attitude surveys. In an organization development process, data are (1) returned to employee groups at all levels in the organization and (2) used by all employees working together in their normal work groups to

figure 19.4

**The Survey Feedback Process**

*The survey feedback process has three distinct stages, which must be fully completed for the process to be most effective. As an organization development process, its purpose is to fully involve all employees in data analysis, problem identification, and development of solutions.*

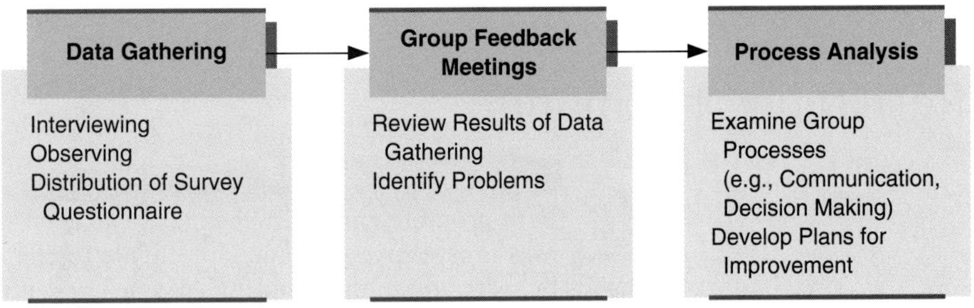

identify and solve problems. In traditional attitude surveys, top management reviews the data and may or may not initiate a new program to solve problems the survey has identified.

In the data-gathering stage, the change agent interviews selected personnel from appropriate levels to determine the key issues to be examined. Information from these interviews is used to develop a survey questionnaire, which is distributed to a large sample of employees. The questionnaire may be a standardized instrument, an instrument developed specifically for the organization, or a combination of the two. The questionnaire data are analyzed and aggregated by group or department to ensure that respondents remain anonymous.[31] Then the change agent prepares a summary of the results for the group feedback sessions. From this point on, the consultant is involved in the process as a resource person and expert.

The feedback meetings generally involve only two or three levels of management. Meetings are usually held serially, first with a meeting of the top management group, followed by meetings of employees throughout the organization. The group manager rather than the change agent typically leads sessions to transfer "ownership" of the data from the change agent to the work group. The feedback consists primarily of profiles of the group's attitudes toward the organization, the work, the leadership, and other topics on the questionnaire. During the feedback sessions, participants discuss reasons for the scores and the problems that the data reveal.

In the process analysis stage, the group examines the process of making decisions, communicating, and accomplishing work, usually with the help of the consultant. Unfortunately, groups often overlook this stage as they become absorbed in the survey data and the problems revealed during the feedback sessions. Occasionally, group managers simply fail to hold feedback and process analysis sessions. Change agents should ensure that managers hold these sessions and that they are rewarded for doing so. The process analysis stage is important because its purpose is to develop action plans to make improvements. Several sessions may be required to discuss the process issues fully and settle on a strategy for improvements. Groups often find it useful to document the plans as they are discussed and to appoint a member to follow up on implementation. Generally, the follow-up assesses whether communication and communication processes have actually been improved. A follow-up survey can be administered several months to a year later to assess how much these processes have changed since they were first reported.

The survey feedback method is probably one of the most widely used organization change and development interventions. If any of its stages are compromised or omitted, however, the technique becomes less useful. A primary responsibility of the consultant or change agent, then, is to ensure that the method is fully and faithfully carried through.

# Resistance to Change

Change is inevitable; so is resistance to change. Paradoxically, organizations both promote and resist change. As an agent for change, the organization asks prospective customers or clients to change their current purchasing habits by switching to the company's product or service, asks current customers to change by increasing their purchases, and asks suppliers to reduce the costs of raw materials. The organization resists change in that its structure and control systems protect the daily tasks of producing a product or service from uncertainties in the environment. The organization must have some elements of permanence to avoid mirroring the instability of the environment. Yet it must also react to external shifts with internal change to maintain currency and relevance in the marketplace.

*"There has to be a crisis to push us to take a risk. But often we lack a sense of urgency. And in a company as big as ours, urgency can be a difficult thing to feel." — Jeff Leppla, Procter & Gamble employee*[32]

A commonly held view is that all resistance to change needs to be overcome, but that is not always the case. Resistance to change can be used for the benefit of the organization and need not be eliminated entirely. By revealing a legitimate concern that a proposed change may harm the organization or that other alternatives might be better, resistance may alert the organization to reexamine the change.[33] For example, an organization may be considering acquiring a company in a completely different industry. Resistance to such a proposal may cause the organization to examine the advantages and disadvantages of the move more carefully. Without resistance, the decision might be made before the pros and cons have been sufficiently explored.

Resistance may come from the organization, the individual, or both. Determining the ultimate source is often difficult, however, because organizations are composed of individuals. Table 19.3 summarizes various types of organizational and individual sources of resistance.

table 19.3

**Organizational and Individual Sources of Resistance**

| Organizational Sources | Examples |
|---|---|
| Overdetermination | Employment system, job descriptions, evaluation, and reward system |
| Narrow Focus of Change | Structure changed with no concern given to other issues, e.g., jobs, people |
| Group Inertia | Group norms |
| Threatened Expertise | People move out of area of expertise |
| Threatened Power | Decentralized decision making |
| Resource Allocation | Increased use of part-time help |

| Individual Sources | Examples |
|---|---|
| Habit | Altered tasks |
| Security | Altered tasks or reporting relationships |
| Economic Factors | Changed pay and benefits |
| Fear of the Unknown | New job, new boss |
| Lack of Awareness | Isolated groups not heeding notices |
| Social Factors | Group norms |

## Organizational Sources of Resistance

Daniel Katz and Robert Kahn have identified six major organizational sources of resistance: overdetermination, narrow focus of change, group inertia, threatened expertise, threatened power, and changes in resource allocation.[34] Of course, not every organization or every change situation displays all six sources.

**Overdetermination** Organizations have several systems designed to maintain stability. For example, consider how organizations control employees' performance. Job candidates must have certain specific skills so that they can do the job the organization needs them to do. New employees are given a job description, and the supervisor trains, coaches, and counsels the employee in job tasks. The new employee usually serves some type of probationary period that culminates in a performance review; thereafter, the employee's performance is regularly evaluated. Finally, rewards, punishment, and discipline are administered depending on the level of performance. Such a system is said to be characterized by **overdetermination**, or **structural inertia**,[35] in that one could probably have the same effect on employee performance with fewer procedures and safeguards. In other words, the structure of the organization produces resistance to change because it was designed to maintain stability.

**Overdetermination**, or **structural inertia**, occurs because numerous organizational systems are in place to ensure that employees and systems behave as expected to maintain stability.

**Narrow Focus of Change** Many efforts to create change in organizations adopt too narrow a focus. Any effort to force change in the tasks of individuals or groups must take into account the interdependencies among organizational elements such as people, structure, tasks, and the information system. For example, some attempts at redesigning jobs fail because the organization structure within which jobs must function is inappropriate for the redesigned jobs.[36]

**Group Inertia** When an employee attempts to change his or her work behavior, the group may resist by refusing to change other behaviors that are necessary complements to the individual's changed behavior. In other words, group norms may act as a brake on individual attempts at behavior change.

**Threatened Expertise** A change in the organization may threaten the specialized expertise that individuals and groups have developed over the years. A job redesign or a structural change may transfer responsibility for a specialized task from the current expert to someone else, threatening the specialist's expertise and building his or her resistance to the change.

**Threatened Power** Any redistribution of decision-making authority, such as with reengineering or team-based management, may threaten an individual's power relationships with others. If an organization is decentralizing its decision making, managers who wielded their decision-making powers in return for special favors from others may resist the change because they do not want to lose their power base.

**Resource Allocation** Groups that are satisfied with current resource allocation methods may resist any change they believe will threaten future allocations. Resources in this context can mean anything from monetary rewards and equipment to additional seasonal help to more computer time.

These six sources explain most types of organization-based resistance to change. All are based on people and social relationships. Many of these sources of resistance can be traced to groups or individuals being afraid of losing something—resources, power, or comfort in a routine.

## Individual Sources of Resistance

Individual sources of resistance to change are rooted in basic human characteristics such as needs and perceptions. Researchers have identified six reasons for individual resistance to change: habit, security, economic factors, fear of the unknown, lack of awareness, and social factors (see Table 19.3).[37]

**Habit** It is easier to do a job the same way every day if the steps in the job are repeated over and over. Learning an entirely new set of steps makes the job more difficult. For the same amount of return (pay), most people prefer to do easier rather than harder work.

**Security** Some employees like the comfort and security of doing things the same old way. They gain a feeling of constancy and safety from knowing that some things stay the same despite all the change going on around them. People who believe their security is threatened by a change are likely to resist the change.

**Economic Factors** Change may threaten employees' steady paychecks. Workers may fear that change will make their jobs obsolete or reduce their opportunities for future pay increases.

**Fear of the Unknown** Some people fear anything unfamiliar. Changes in reporting relationships and job duties create anxiety for such employees. Employees become familiar with their bosses and their jobs and develop relationships with others within the organization, such as contact people for various situations. These relationships and contacts help facilitate their work. Any disruption of familiar patterns may create fear because it can cause delays and foster the belief that nothing is getting accomplished. The cartoon shows how people sometimes act brave, but when alone, they worry about what the changes might bring.

**Lack of Awareness** Because of perceptual limitations, such as lack of attention or selective attention, a person may not recognize a change in a rule or procedure and thus may not alter his or her behavior. People may pay attention only to things that support their point of view. As an example, employees in an isolated regional

This little guy brags to his coworkers that he is not worried about the reorganization when he really *is* worried about it. In any organization change, most people worry about how the changes will affect their job and their future. Most people learn how to survive in the job and the work environment and fear the unknowns that changes might bring.

sales office may not notice—or may ignore—directives from headquarters regarding a change in reporting procedures for expense accounts. They may therefore continue the current practice as long as possible.

Social Factors People may resist change for fear of what others will think. As we mentioned before, the group can be a powerful motivator of behavior. Employees may believe change will hurt their image, result in ostracism from the group, or simply make them "different." For example, an employee who agrees to conform to work rules established by management may be ridiculed by others who openly disobey the rules.

# Managing Successful Organization Change and Development

In conclusion, we offer seven keys to managing change in organizations. They relate directly to the problems identified earlier and to our view of the organization as a comprehensive social system. Each can influence the elements of the social system and may help the organization avoid some of the major problems in managing the change. Table 19.4 lists the points and their potential impacts.

## Consider International Issues

One factor to consider is how international environments dictate organization change. As we already noted, the environment is a significant factor in bringing about organization change. Given the additional environmental complexities multi-

table 19.4

**Keys to Managing Successful Organization Change and Development**

| Key | Impact |
| --- | --- |
| Consider international issues. | Keep in touch with the latest global developments and how change is handled in different cultures. |
| Take a holistic view of the organization. | Helps anticipate the effects of change on the social system and culture. |
| Start small. | Works out details and shows the benefits of the change to those who might resist. |
| Secure top management support. | Gets dominant coalition on the side of change: safeguards structural change; heads off problems of power and control. |
| Encourage participation by those affected by the change. | Minimizes transition problems of control, resistance, and task redefinition. |
| Foster open communication. | Minimizes transition problems of resistance and information and control systems. |
| Reward those who contribute to change. | Minimizes transition problems of resistance and control systems. |

national organizations face, it follows that organization change may be even more critical to them than to purely domestic organizations.

A second point to remember is that acceptance of change varies widely around the globe. Change is a normal and accepted part of organization life in some cultures. In other cultures, change causes many more problems. Managers should remember that techniques for managing change that have worked routinely back home may not work at all and may even trigger negative responses if used indiscriminately in other cultures.[38]

## Take a Holistic View

Managers must take a holistic view of the organization and the change project. A limited view can endanger the change effort because the subsystems of the organization are interdependent. A holistic view encompasses the culture and dominant coalition as well as the people, tasks, structure, and information subsystems.

## Start Small

Peter Senge claims that every truly successful, systemwide change in large organizations starts small.[39] He recommends that change start with one team, usually an executive team. One team can evaluate the change, make appropriate adjustments along the way, and most importantly, show that the new system works and gets desired results. If the change makes sense, it begins to spread to other teams, groups, divisions, and system wide. Senge described how at Shell and Ford, significant changes started small, with one or two parallel teams, and then spread as others saw the benefits of the change. When others see the benefits, they automatically drop their inherent resistance and join in. They can voluntarily join and be committed to the success of the change effort.

*"Just as nothing in nature starts big, so the way to start creating a change is with a pilot group—a growth seed." — Peter Senge, author and expert on organization change*[40]

## Secure Top Management Support

The support of top management is essential to the success of any change effort. As the organization's probable dominant coalition, it is a powerful element of the social system, and its support is necessary to deal with control and power problems. For example, a manager who plans a change in the ways tasks are assigned and responsibility is delegated in his or her department must notify top management and gain its support. Complications may arise if disgruntled employees complain to high-level managers who have not been notified of the change or do not support it. The employees' complaints may jeopardize the manager's plan—and perhaps her or his job.

## Encourage Participation

Problems related to resistance, control, and power can be overcome by broad participation in planning the change. Allowing people a voice in designing the change may give them a sense of power and control over their own destinies, which may help to win their support during implementation.

## Foster Open Communication

Open communication is an important factor in managing resistance to change and overcoming information and control problems during transitions. Employees typically recognize the uncertainties and ambiguities that arise during a transition and seek information on the change and their place in the new system. In the absence of information, the gap may be filled with inappropriate or false information, which may endanger the change process. Rumors tend to spread through the grapevine faster than accurate information can be disseminated through official channels. A manager should always be sensitive to the effects of uncertainty on employees, especially in a period of change; any news, even bad news, seems better than no news.

## Reward Contributors

Although this last point is simple, it can easily be neglected. Employees who contribute to the change in any way need to be rewarded. Too often, the only people acknowledged after a change effort are those who tried to stop it. Those who quickly grasp new work assignments, work harder to cover what otherwise might not get done in the transition, or help others adjust to changes deserve special credit—perhaps a mention in a news release or the internal company newspaper, special consideration in a performance appraisal, a merit raise, or a promotion. From a behavioral perspective, individuals need to benefit in some way if they are to willingly help change something that eliminates the old, comfortable way of doing the job.

In the current dynamic environment, managers must anticipate the need for change and satisfy it with more responsive and competitive organization systems. These seven keys to managing organization change may also serve as general guidelines for managing organizational behavior, because organizations must change or face elimination.

# Synopsis

Change may be forced on an organization, or an organization may change in response to the environment or an internal need. Forces for change are interdependent and influence organizations in many ways. Currently, the areas in which the pressures for change seem most powerful involve people, technology, information and communication, competition, and social trends.

Planned organization change involves anticipating change and preparing for it. Lewin described organization change in terms of unfreezing, the change itself, and refreezing. In the continuous change process model, top management recognizes forces encouraging change, engages in a problem-solving process to design the change, and implements and evaluates the change.

Organization development is the process of planned change and improvement of organizations through the application of knowledge of the behavioral sciences. It is based on a systematic change process and focuses on managing the culture of the organization. The most comprehensive change involves altering the structure of the organization through a reorganization of departments, reporting relationships, or authority systems.

Quality-of-work-life programs focus on providing a work environment in which employees can satisfy individual needs. Task and technological changes alter the way the organization accomplishes its primary tasks. Along with the steps usually associated with change, task redesign entails diagnosis, cost-benefit analysis, formulation of a redesign strategy, and implementation of supplemental changes.

Frequently used group and individual approaches to organization change are training and management development programs, team building, and survey feedback techniques. Training programs are usually designed to improve employees' job skills, to help employees adapt to other organization changes (such as a management-by-objectives program), or to develop employees' awareness and understanding of problems such as workplace safety or stress. Management development programs attempt to foster in current or future managers the skills, abilities, and perspectives important to good management. Team-building programs are designed to help a work team or group develop into a mature, functioning team by helping it define its goals or priorities, analyze its tasks and the way they are performed, and examine relationships among the people doing the work. As used in the organization development process, survey feedback techniques involve gathering data, analyzing and summarizing them, and returning them to employees and groups for discussion and to identify and solve problems.

Resistance to change may arise from several individual and organizational sources. Resistance may indicate a legitimate concern that the change is not good for the organization and may warrant a reexamination of plans.

To manage change in organizations, international issues must be considered and managers should take a holistic view of the organization and start small. Top management support is needed, and those most affected must participate. Open communication is important, and those who contribute to the change effort should be rewarded.

## Discussion Questions

1. Is most organization change forced on the organization by external factors or fostered from within? Explain.
2. What broad category of pressures for organization change other than the four discussed in the chapter can you think of? Briefly describe it.
3. Which sources of resistance to change present the most problems for an internal change agent? For an external change agent?
4. Which stage of the Lewin model of change do you think is most often overlooked? Why?
5. What are the advantages and disadvantages of having an internal change agent rather than an external change agent?
6. How does organization development differ from organization change?
7. How and why would organization development differ if the elements of the social system were not interdependent?
8. Do quality-of-work-life programs rely more on individual or organizational aspects of organizational behavior? Why?
9. Describe how the job of your professor could be redesigned. Include a discussion of other subsystems that would need to be changed as a result.
10. Which of the seven keys for successfully managing an organizational change effort seem to be the most difficult to manage? Why?

## Organizational Behavior Case for Discussion

### Nissan Goes Against the Grain

Nissan Motor was in trouble. By the end of 1998 Nissan was running annual losses of over $200 million, and its debt was $19.4 billion, forcing the company to spend over $1 billion in interest payments alone. Nissan had a poor brand image, no models that really energized buyers, and no distinctive competence such as styling was to Mazda and engine technology was to Honda. Nissan sold only 621,528 cars and trucks in 1998 (compared with over 830,000 in 1985). Its market share had dropped to 3.5 percent. Analysts criticized its stodgy management and dysfunctional culture, which showed no visible signs of improvement—that is, until Nissan took a $5 billion cash infusion from Renault in exchange for 36.8 percent of the company.

Rather than attempt to fully integrate the two companies, Renault intends to maintain their separation, calling their relationship an alliance, not a merger. Renault sees the alliance as a way to break out of Europe and utilize Nissan's marketing and distribution in the United States and Asia. Renault sent Carlos Ghosn (rhymes with "bone") to Tokyo to be Nissan's chief operating officer, with a full license to make the changes necessary to turn the company around. Ghosn is Brazilian-born and French-educated, speaks five languages (is learning Japanese), and is typical of the global executives who are taking over many companies, such as Jacques Nasser of Ford. Ghosn has held major jobs on four continents, including running the Michelin tire operation in South Carolina and engineering a major turnaround of Renault. Ghosn is a no-nonsense type of manager. He took seventeen Renault managers with him to Tokyo, including a chief financial officer and the head of product development.

The revival plan was developed by nine cross-functional, cross-cultural teams. Each team was charged with making proposals to grow the business and reduce costs, with no sacred cows, no taboos, no constraints, and no cultural cop-outs from the United States, Europe, or Japan. The final plan, announced in October 1999, called for the closing of five Japanese plants, reducing the number of employees by 21,000 globally by 2002, changing supplier relationships, unwinding cross-shareholdings to reduce debt, and funneling the cost savings into product development. A major emphasis will be on turning the multiregional alliance into a multicultural global car company. The plan includes a commitment to reduce debt by at least 50 percent and increase operating profit to 4.5 percent of sales by 2002.

Ghosn's plan faced tough opposition, not only throughout the company, but from Japan as well. The plan included several features that went against the prevailing culture of Japanese society. For example, the massive layoffs violated the long-held tradition of lifetime employment in Japan. Ghosn's plan to close plants sent shock waves through several Japanese towns. Such plant closures were unheard of and created quite a backlash of outrage targeted at Mr. Ghosn. Another aspect of the plan involved major human resource innovations that are not common in Japan. For example, Ghosn wanted promotions based on performance rather than on seniority or personal loyalties. In addition, he wanted to develop a stock option plan for several hundred key employees. Neither approach was received favorably by the Japanese workers' unions. In another unusual practice, Ghosn has even hired auto executives from other Japanese auto companies.

Ghosn's plan to sell Nissan's share holdings in affiliated companies that were also suppliers was not received well either because it is strictly against Japanese corporate practice. Ghosn figured he could cut $95 million if he reduced the number of banks Nissan dealt with from four hundred to ten. He made it clear to suppliers that the number of suppliers would be cut in half and that all suppliers had to cut costs by 20 percent if they expected to continue to supply Nissan. Needless to say, the hundreds of suppliers in the industry were not happy as they scrambled to find ways to cut costs. Inside Nissan, the reaction to Ghosn's plan to centralize all purchasing was equally poorly received.

Probably the most interesting affront to Japanese culture occurred in the executive offices of Nissan. Ghosn was brought in as chief operating officer of Nissan, reporting to the chief executive officer and chairman, Yoshikazu Hanawa. Hanawa was the one who made it known that Nissan would be interested in some sort of alliance and an infusion of cash. Hanawa let Ghosn have the driver's seat in all matters related to turning the company around. Hanawa stayed around to work with the government and other external duties. During the announcement of the turnaround plan, Hanawa deferred all questions to (his subordinate) Mr. Ghosn. Mr. Ghosn has offered to resign if Nissan does not make a profit by the end of the fiscal year 2000. Many people will be watching.

## Case Questions

1. Describe the change process that Ghosn used to turn this company around.
2. How many cultural customs of Japan did Mr. Ghosn violate? Was it necessary for him to do that?
3. If you had been a senior manager at Nissan prior to the changes, what would have been your reaction to the foreigner coming and making so many changes that violate the normal way of doing things in your country and company?

References: Alexandra Harney, "Asia-Pacific: Job Cuts Shock Nissan Town," *Financial Times*, January 25, 2000, p. 10; "Nissan's Ghosn Calls Cultural Clashes 'A Luxury for the Rich,'" *PR Newswire*, January 18, 2000, p. 4309; Alex Taylor III, "The Man Who Vows to Change Japan Inc.," *Fortune*, December 20, 1999, pp. 189–198; Michael Zielenziger, "Nissan Says New Strategy Will Be a Standout," *Knight-Ridder/Tribune Business News*, November 18, 1999, p. IKRB9932205D; "Remaking Nissan," *Business Week*, November 15, 1999, p. 38.

# Experiencing Organizational Behavior

## Planning a Change at the University

**Purpose:** This exercise will help you understand the complexities of change in organizations.

**Format:** Your task is to plan the implementation of a major change in an organization.

**Procedure:**

### Part 1

The class will divide into five groups of approximately equal size. Your instructor will assign each group one of the following changes:

1. A change from the semester system to the quarter system (or the opposite, depending on the school's current system).
2. A requirement that all work—homework, examinations, term papers, problem sets—be done on computer, and submitted via computers.
3. A requirement that all students live on campus.
4. A requirement that all students have reading, writing, and speaking fluency in at least three languages, including English and Japanese, to graduate.
5. A requirement that all students room with someone in the same major.

First, decide what individuals and groups must be involved in the change process. Then decide how the change will be implemented using Lewin's process of organization change (Figure 19.1) as a framework. Consider how to deal with resistance to change, using Tables 19.3 and 19.4 as guides. Decide whether a change agent (internal or external) should be used. Develop a realistic timetable for full implementation of the change. Is transition management appropriate?

### Part 2

Using the same groups as in Part 1, your next task is to describe the techniques you would use to implement the change described in Part 1. You may use structural changes, task and technology methods, group and individual programs, or any combination of these. You may need to go to the library to gather more information on some techniques.

You should also discuss how you will utilize the seven keys to successful change management discussed at the end of the chapter.

Your instructor may make this exercise an in-class project, but it is also a good semester-ending project for groups to work on outside class. Either way, the exercise is most beneficial when the groups report their implementation programs to the entire class. Each group should report on which change techniques are to be used, why they were selected, how they will be implemented, and how problems will be avoided.

## Follow-up Questions

### Part 1

1. How similar were the implementation steps for each change?
2. Were the plans for managing resistance to change realistic?
3. Do you think any of the changes could be successfully implemented at your school? Why or why not?

### Part 2

1. Did various groups use the same technique in different ways or to accomplish different goals?
2. If you did outside research on organization development techniques for your project, did you find any techniques that seemed more applicable than those in this chapter? If so, describe one of them.

# Building Organizational Behavior Skills

## Support for Change

**Introduction:** The questions following are designed to help people understand the level of support or opposition to change within an organization. Scores on this scale should be used for classroom discussion only.

**Instructions:** Think of an organization that you have worked for in the past or an organization to which you currently belong, and consider the situation when a change was imposed at some point in the recent past. Then circle the number that best represents your feeling about each statement or question.

1. **Values and Vision**

   *(Do people throughout the organization share values or vision?)*

   1 2 3 4 5 6 7
   Low High

2. **History of Change**

   *(Does the organization have a good track record in handling change?)*

   1 2 3 4 5 6 7
   Low High

3. **Cooperation and Trust**

   *(Do they seem high throughout the organization?)*

   1 2 3 4 5 6 7
   Low High

4. **Culture**

   *(Is it one that supports risk taking and change?)*

   1 2 3 4 5 6 7
   Low High

5. **Resilience**

   *(Can people handle more?)*

   1 2 3 4 5 6 7
   Low High

6. **Rewards**

   *(Will this change be seen as beneficial?)*

   1 2 3 4 5 6 7
   Low High

7. **Respect and Face**

   *(Will people be able to maintain dignity and self-respect?)*

   1 2 3 4 5 6 7
   Low High

8. **Status Quo**

   *(Will this change be seen as mild?)*

   1 2 3 4 5 6 7
   Low High

A Guide to Scoring and explanation is available in the *Instructor's Resource Manual.*

Reference: From Rick Maurer, *Beyond the Wall of Resistance*, 1996 (Austin: Bard Press), pp. 104–105. Used by permission of Bard Press.

## Developing OB Internet Skills

**Introduction:** Many organizations utilize organizationwide surveys to assess the needs and concerns of their employees. On the basis of the results of such surveys, many organizations make significant organizational changes. This exercise will help you understand more about organizational surveys.

**Internet Assignment:** Your organization has a new CEO who has been brought in to make changes. Her first priority is to survey all employees to find out what employees think about the company, what they want from the company, and what their needs and concerns are. You have been assigned to find several organizational surveys that could be used by your company. Search the Internet for resources that might assist you in finding several different surveys and other related resources.

**Follow-up:** Describe the kinds of information you were able to locate and characterize its likely value to you. Finally, respond to the following questions:

1. What additional information would you need, besides what was available on the Internet, to actually use one of the surveys you found?
2. How would the type of survey you use be different if you were a large multinational company versus a small manufacturing company with employees at only one location?

# Part IV Integrative Running Case

## The AOL Time Warner Deal—From Two Organizations to One

As described in the cases at the ends of Parts I, II, and III, the merger between America Online and Time Warner attracted worldwide attention and provided many different angles from which it could be analyzed. Stephen Case said that the mission of AOL was "to build a global medium as central to people's lives as the telephone or television . . . and even more valuable." And that was *before* the merger. So why was anyone surprised? Take a look at the activities included in this merger: cable, television, radio, the Internet, communication, retailing, financial services, health care, education, travel, and all sorts of publishing. How will this new company arrange the tasks and reporting relationships so that all of those tasks get done? The reporting relationships were among the most interesting. In most situations, the CEO works at the pleasure of the board, in effect reporting only to the board. In some cases, the CEO also holds the title/position of chairman of the board. The issue of who holds these positions is often a major problem when two companies merge. Analysts can usually tell which company really is the more powerful by watching these position dynamics. Usually, the larger company is the acquirer and the smaller company is the acquired. The CEO of the acquired company usually ends up in the more subordinate position to the acquiring company's CEO. In this merger, however, it was difficult to determine which company was larger. AOL's stock was worth more (nearly 2.5 times as much as Time Warner's in December 1999), but Time Warner had far more employees and total annual revenues. The final deal was that Time Warner stockholders would receive 1.5 AOL shares for each Time Warner share held. Most people now consider that AOL held the upper hand as the acquirer and Time Warner was the acquired.

In this situation, the two heads of the former organizations, Stephen Case of AOL and Gerald Levin of Time Warner, had no intention of reporting to each other. In fact, as talks progressed, Levin made it clear that he would be CEO and would not report to Case. Case, as CEO of the acquiring company, reportedly offered the CEO position to Levin as an enticement to seal the deal and opted to be chairman of the board of the new company. Both men were well protected in the deal as neither could be removed from their offices or their duties changed unless 75 percent of the board voted to do so. No one believed that Case could stay hands-off and run the board meetings while Levin ran the company.

Reporting to Case were four senior executives from AOL: vice chairman Kenneth J. Novack, public relations consultant Kenneth Larer, senior vice president George Vradenberg III (the firm's public policy coordinator), and chief technology officer William Raduchel. These people and their expertise seemed to indicate that Case would continue to oversee the broad sweep and direction of the new company to include technology policy, venture-type investments, philanthropy, future innovation, and global public policy. This special team of advisors was known as "Steve's Senior Staff" at AOL before the merger and was largely responsible for the merger in the first place. These four were not subject to decisions made by CEO Levin and were safe from layoffs because the by-laws proposed for the new company stated very clearly that those four executives could only be removed by the action or approval of the chairman of the board.

As CEO, Levin was in charge of operations for the merged company. Reporting to him were two chief operating officers, or co-COOs, Robert Pittman and Richard Parsons. Pittman had been the president of AOL; Parsons had been president and COO of Time Warner. Pittman had been called the most indispensable executive on the team and the heir apparent, possibly because of his experience as an executive at Time Warner. Also included in the five-person management team was Ted Turner, former vice chair of Time Warner, whose new title and duties were not immediately announced. Most experts expected this five-person team to last three to six months. Clearly, there were overlaps in many functional departments between the two firms. In other areas, however, the businesses of the two companies were very different. Conceptually, some analysts noted that Time Warner had the content that customers want, and AOL had the pipes for delivery of that information. Some of those activities were difficult to integrate and combine across companies. The task for the co-COOs was to combine those tasks that could be and develop ways to coordinate the other tasks across the new company.

AOL was the typical young and fast-growing Internet company. Decisions were made and ideas were implemented quickly. The popular view of such Internet companies was that most employees were computer geeks and nerds. Some implementations may have been too fast, taking place before the rest of the company was ready. For example, when AOL changed to a flat-rate fee per month for its subscribers, the demand was so high that it took months for the company to develop the capacity to serve all of the new customers. You may recall the popular saying at that time that AOL really stood for "America On Hold." The pace was fast and often loud. One former AOL executive left the company because he got tired of all the yelling at meetings. AOL was a relatively lean operation with little extravagant spending; they had a part-time lease on one corporate jet. Employees at AOL typically wore open-collar shirts, indicating a very relaxed working atmosphere.

Time Warner, on the other hand, was much older, more hierarchical with a clear chain of command, and more resistant to change. Time Warner had been comprised of six separately operating divisions, from the music group to the publishing house, each with strong leaders. Operational decisions were left for the six division heads, who were not criticized as long as their divisions were making high profits. Mr. Levin had been with Time for twenty-eight years, having worked his way up through the hierarchy and surviving the mergers with Warner Communications in 1989 and Turner Broadcasting in 1995. Spending was not lavish, but "necessary expenses" certainly were defined differently; Time Warner owned four corporate jets. Most employees wore traditional business dress, as might be expected in New York City.

Time Warner had tried unsuccessfully to create its own Internet operations, spending hundreds of millions of dollars for several years. The merger with AOL gave it the number one delivery vehicle. On the other hand, AOL will be hard-pressed to keep its innovativeness and responsiveness to its client base as it gets larger and swallows the Time Warner operations. The real test of the deal will be in how the combined company creates new delivery mechanisms and new content in ways that are not even imaginable now. Internally, that can only come about if the roles and responsibilities are clarified throughout the new company and everybody gets to work, rather than talking about the merger. Other companies are developing systems to do what the combined AOL and Time Warner do now. If the combination turns out to be too unwieldy, the potential synergies may never be realized.

## Case Questions

1. Try to draw the organization chart for the top three levels for the new company. Include the names and titles for as many as you can.
2. Describe the cultural differences between these two companies. How do you think the new culture will evolve?
3. What are some of the external threats to the success of the new company?
4. What types of change mechanisms would you use to help facilitate the changes that will be needed for this new company to thrive?

References: Marc Gunther, "These Guys Want It All," *Fortune*, February 7, 2000, pp. 71–78; Mitchell Lee Marks, "Egos Can Make—and Unmake—Mergers," *Asian Wall Street Journal*, January 27, 2000, p. 10; Carol Hymowitz, "In the Lead: AOL's Bosses, An Unusual Pair, Share Vision—Partners' Joint Control Could Lead to Creation of Management Model," *Asian Wall Street Journal*, January 25, 2000, p. 8; Daniel Okrent, "Happily Ever After?" *Time*, January 24, 2000, pp. 39–43; Joshua Cooper Ramo, "A Two-Man Network," *Time*, January 24, 2000, pp. 46–50; Richard Siklos, Catherine Yang, Andy Reinhardt, Peter Burrows, and Rob Hof, "Welcome to the 21st Century," *Business Week*, January 24, 2000, pp. 36–44; Sarah Schafer, "Clash of Corporate Cultures Can Weaken Merger's Potential," *Boston Sunday Globe*, January 23, 2000, p. H5; Martin Peers and Nikhil Deogun, "Technology Journal: AOL's Case to Retain Link to Key Aides After Merger," *Wall Street Journal Europe*, January 17, 2000, p. 7; David Hilzenrath and Ariana Eunjung Cha, "AOL's Case moves to Ensure his Power," *Washington Post*, January 15, 2000, p. E01.

# Appendix A

# Research Methods in Organizational Behavior

We have referred to theories and research findings as a basis for our discussion throughout this book. In this appendix, we further examine how theories and research findings about organizational behavior are developed. First, we highlight the role of theory and research. We then identify the purposes of research and describe the steps in the research process, types of research designs, and methods of gathering data. We conclude with a brief discussion of some related issues.

## The Role of Theory and Research

Some managers—and many students—fail to see the need for research. They seem confused by what appears to be an endless litany of theories and by sets of contradictory research findings. They often ask, "Why bother?"

Indeed, few absolute truths have emerged from studies of organizational behavior. Management in general and organizational behavior in particular, however, are in many ways fields of study still in their infancy. Thus, it stands to reason that researchers in these fields have few theories that always work. In addition, their research cannot always be generalized to settings other than those in which the research was originally conducted.

Still, theory and research play valuable roles.[1] Theories help investigators organize what they do know. They provide a framework that managers can use to diagnose problems and implement changes. They also serve as road signs that help managers solve many problems involving people. Research also plays an important role. Each study conducted and published adds a little more to the storehouse of knowledge available to practicing managers. Questions are posed and answers developed. Over time, researchers can become increasingly confident of findings as they are applied across different settings.[2]

## Purposes of Research

**Scientific research** is the systematic investigation of hypothesized propositions about the relationships among natural phenomena.

As much as possible, researchers try to approach problems and questions of organizational behavior scientifically. **Scientific research** is the systematic investigation of hypothesized propositions about the relationships among

**Basic research** is concerned with discovering new knowledge rather than solving specific problems.

**Applied research** is conducted to solve particular problems or answer specific questions.

natural phenomena. The aims of science are to describe, explain, and predict phenomena.[3] Research can be classified as basic or applied. **Basic research** is concerned with discovering new knowledge rather than solving particular problems. The knowledge made available through basic research may not have much direct application to organizations, at least when it is first discovered.[4] Research scientists and university professors are the people who most often conduct basic research in organizational behavior.

**Applied research**, on the other hand, is conducted to solve particular problems or answer specific questions. The findings of applied research are, by definition, immediately applicable to managers. Consultants, university professors, and managers themselves conduct much of the applied research performed in organizations.

## The Scientific Research Process

To result in valid findings, research should be conducted according to the scientific process shown in Figure AA.1. The starting point is a question or problem.[5] For example, a manager wants to design a new reward system to enhance employee motivation but is unsure about what types of rewards to offer or how to tie them to performance. This manager's questions therefore are "What kinds of rewards will motivate my employees?" and "How should those rewards be tied to performance?"

The next step is to review existing literature to determine what is already known about the phenomenon. Something has probably been written about most problems or questions today's managers face. Thus, the goal of the literature review is to avoid "reinventing the wheel" by finding out what others have already learned. Basic research generally is available in journals such as the *Academy of Management Journal*, *Academy of Management Review*, *Administrative Science Quarterly*, *Journal of Applied Psychology*, *Organizational Behavior and Human Decision Processes*, *Journal of Management*, and *Organization Science*. Applied research findings are more likely to be found in such sources as the *Harvard Business Review*, *Academy of Management Executive*, *Organizational Dynamics*, *HRMagazine*, and *Personnel Psychology*.

Based on the original question and the review of the literature, researchers formulate hypotheses—predictions of what they expect to find. The hypothesis is an important guide for the researcher's design of the study because it provides a very clear and precise statement of what the researcher wants to test. That means that study can be specifically designed to test the hypothesis.

figure AA.1 **The Research Process**

*The scientific research process follows a logical and rational sequence of activities. Using this process enables researchers to place greater confidence in their findings. Of course, in some instances compromises may be necessary in order to study some phenomena in certain settings. For example, studying potentially controversial subjects like power, politics, or ethics may be difficult if the process is followed rigidly.*

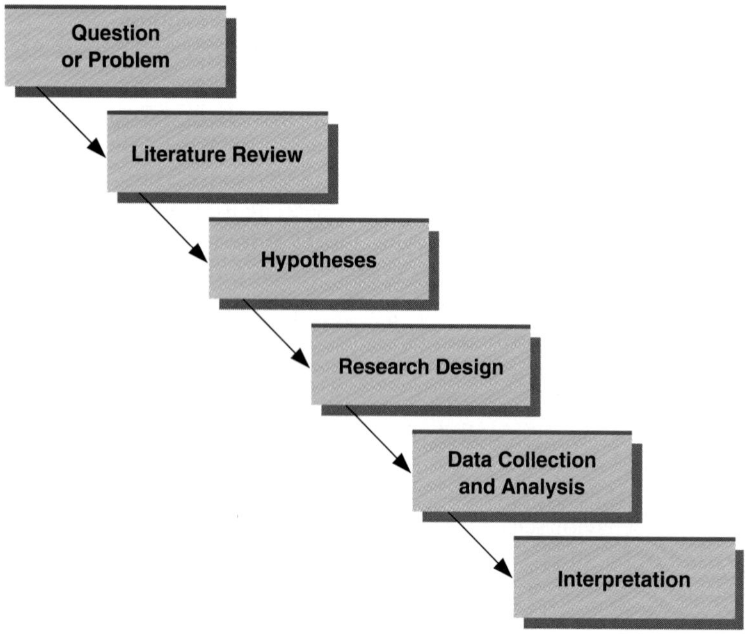

The research design is the plan for doing the research. (We discuss the more common research designs later.) As part of the research design, the researcher must determine how variables will be measured. Thus, if satisfaction is one factor being considered, the researcher must decide how to measure it.

After data have been collected, they must be analyzed. (We also discuss common methods for gathering data later.) Depending on the study design and hypotheses, data analysis may be relatively simple and straightforward or may require elaborate statistical procedures. Methods for analyzing data are beyond the scope of this discussion.

Finally, the results of the study are interpreted; that is, the researcher figures out what they mean. They may provide support for the hypothesis, fail to support the hypothesis, or suggest a relationship other than that proposed in the hypothesis. An important part of the interpretation process is recognizing the limitations imposed on the findings by weaknesses in the research design.

Many researchers go a step further and try to publish their findings. Several potential sources for publication are the journals mentioned in the discussion of literature review. Publication is important because it helps educate other researchers and managers and also provides additional information for future literature reviews.[6]

# Types of Research Designs

A **research design** is the set of procedures used to test the predicted relationships among natural phenomena.

A **research design** is the set of procedures used to test the predicted relationships among natural phenomena. The design addresses such issues as how the relevant variables are to be defined, measured, and related to one another. Managers and researchers can draw on a variety of research designs, each with its own strengths and weaknesses. Four general types of research designs often are used in the study of organizational behavior (see Table AA.1); each type has several variations.[7]

## Case Study

A **case study** is an in-depth analysis of one setting.

A **case study** is an in-depth analysis of a single setting. This design frequently is used when little is known about the phenomena being studied and the researcher wants to look at relevant concepts intensively and thoroughly. A variety of methods are used to gather information, including interviews, questionnaires, and personal observation.[8]

The case study research design offers several advantages. First, it allows the researcher to probe one situation in detail, yielding a wealth of descriptive and explanatory information. The case study also facilitates the discovery of unexpected relationships. Because the researcher observes virtually everything that happens

table AA.1
**Types of Research Designs**

| Type | Dominant Characteristic |
|---|---|
| **Case Study** | Useful for thorough exploration of unknown phenomena |
| **Field Survey** | Provides easily quantifiable data |
| **Laboratory Experiment** | Allows researcher high control of variables |
| **Field Experiment** | Takes place in realistic setting |

in a given situation, she or he may learn about issues beyond those originally chosen for study.

The case study design also has several disadvantages. The data it provides cannot be readily generalized to other situations because the information is so closely tied to the situation studied. In addition, case study information may be biased by the researcher's closeness to the situation. Case study research also tends to be very time consuming.

Nevertheless, the case study can be an effective and useful research design as long as the researcher understands its limitations and takes them into account when formulating conclusions.

## Field Survey

A **field survey** typically relies on a questionnaire distributed to a sample of people selected from a larger population.

A **field survey** usually relies on a questionnaire distributed to a sample of people chosen from a larger population.

If a manager is conducting the study, the sample often is drawn from a group or department within her or his organization. If a researcher is conducting the study, the sample typically is negotiated with a host organization interested in the questions being addressed. The questionnaire generally is mailed or delivered by hand to participants at home or at work and may be returned by mail or picked up by the researcher. The respondents answer the questions and return the questionnaire as directed. The researcher analyzes the responses and tries to make inferences about the larger population from the representative sample.[9] Field surveys can focus on a variety of topics relevant to organizational behavior, including employees' attitudes toward other people (such as leaders and coworkers), attitudes toward their jobs (such as satisfaction with the job and commitment to the organization), and perceptions of organizational characteristics (such as the challenge inherent in the job and the degree of decentralization in the organization).[10]

Field surveys provide information about a much larger segment of the population than do case studies. They also provide an abundance of data in easily quantifiable form, which facilitates statistical analysis and the compilation of normative data for comparative purposes.

Field surveys also have several disadvantages. First, survey information may reveal only superficial feelings and reactions to situations rather than deeply held feelings, attitudes, or emotions. Second, the design and development of field surveys require a great deal of expertise and can be very time consuming. Furthermore, relationships among variables tend to be accentuated in responses to questionnaires because of what is called common method variance. This means that people may tend to answer all the questions in the same way, creating a misleading impression. A final, very important point is that field surveys give the researcher little or no control. The researcher may lack control over who completes the questionnaire, when it is filled out, the mental or physical state of the respondent, and many other important conditions. Thus, the typical field survey has many inherent sources of potential error.[11]

Nonetheless, surveys can be a very useful means of gathering large quantities of data and assessing general patterns of relationships among variables.

## Laboratory Experiment

The **laboratory experiment** gives the researcher the most control. By creating an artificial setting similar to a real work situation, the researcher can control almost

A **laboratory experiment** involves creating an artificial setting similar to a real work situation to allow control over almost every possible factor in that setting.

every possible factor in that setting. He or she can then manipulate the variables in the study and examine their effects on other variables.[12]

As an example of how laboratory experiments work, consider the relationship between how goals are developed for subordinates and the subordinates' subsequent level of satisfaction. To explore this relationship, the researcher structures a situation in which some subjects (usually students but occasionally people hired or recruited from the community) are assigned goals while others determine their own goals. Both groups then work on a hypothetical task relevant to the goals, and afterward all subjects fill out a questionnaire designed to measure satisfaction. Differences in satisfaction between the two groups could be attributed to the method used for goal setting.

Laboratory experiments prevent some of the problems of other types of research. Advantages include a high degree of control over variables and precise measurement of variables. A major disadvantage is the lack of realism; rarely does the laboratory setting exactly duplicate the real-life situation. A related problem is the difficulty in generalizing the findings to organizational settings. Finally, some organizational situations, such as plant closings or employee firings, cannot be realistically simulated in a laboratory.

## Field Experiment

A **field experiment** is similar to a laboratory experiment but is conducted in a real organization.

A **field experiment** is similar to a laboratory experiment except that it is conducted in a real organization. In a field experiment, the researcher attempts to control certain variables and to manipulate others to assess the effects of the manipulated variables on outcome variables. For example, a manager interested in the effects of flexible working hours on absenteeism and turnover might design a field experiment in which one plant adopts a flexible work schedule program and another plant, as similar as possible to the first, serves as a control site. Attendance and turnover are monitored at both plants. If attendance increases and turnover decreases in the experimental plant and there are no changes at the control site, the manager probably will conclude that the flexible work schedule program was successful.

The field experiment has certain advantages over the laboratory experiment. The organizational setting provides greater realism, making generalization to other organizational situations more valid. Disadvantages include the lack of control over other events that might occur in the organizational setting (such as additional changes the firm introduces); contamination of the results if the various groups discover their respective roles in the experiment and behave differently because of that knowledge; greater expense; and the risk that the experimental manipulations will contribute to problems within the company.

# Methods of Gathering Data

The method of gathering data is a critical concern of the research design. Data-gathering methods may be grouped into four categories: questionnaires, interviews, observation, and nonreactive measures.[13]

## Questionnaires

A *questionnaire* is a collection of written questions about the respondents' attitudes, opinions, perceptions, demographic characteristics, or some combination of these factors. Usually the respondent fills out the questionnaire and returns it to the researcher. To facilitate scoring, the researcher typically uses questions with a variety of answers, each of which has an associated score. Some questionnaires have a few open-ended questions that allow respondents to elaborate on their answers. Designing a questionnaire that will provide the information the researcher desires is a very complex task and one that has received considerable attention. Some researchers have recently begun using computer networks to distribute questionnaires and collect responses.

### Interviews

An *interview* resembles a questionnaire, but the questions are presented to the respondent orally by an interviewer. The respondent usually is allowed to answer questions spontaneously rather than being asked to choose among alternatives defined by the researcher. Interviews generally take much more time to administer than questionnaires, and they are more difficult to score. The benefit of interviews is the opportunity for the respondent to speak at length on a topic, thereby providing a richness and depth of information not normally yielded by questionnaires.

### Observation

*Observation*, in its simplest form, is watching events and recording what is observed. Researchers use several types of observation. In structured observation, the observer is trained to look for and record certain activities or types of events. In participant observation, the trained observer actually participates in the organizational events as a member of the work team and records impressions and observations in a diary or daily log. In hidden observation, the trained observer is not visible to the subjects. A hidden camera or a specially designed observation room may be used.

### Nonreactive Measures

When a situation is changed because of data gathering, we say the activity has caused a reaction in the situation. *Nonreactive measures*, also called "unobtrusive measures," have been developed for gathering data without disturbing the situation being studied. When questionnaires, interviews, and obtrusive observations may cause problems in the research situation, the use of nonreactive measures may be an appropriate substitute. Nonreactive measures include examination of physical traces, use of archives, and simple observation. At some universities, for example, sidewalks are not laid down around a new building until it has been in use for some time. Rather than ask students and faculty about their traffic patterns or try to anticipate them, the designers observe the building in use, see where the grass is most heavily worn, and put sidewalks there.

## Related Issues in Research

Three other issues are of particular interest to researchers: causality, reliability and validity, and ethical concerns.[14]

## Causality

Scientific research attempts to describe, explain, and predict phenomena. In many cases, the purpose of the research is to reveal causality; that is, researchers attempt to describe, explain, and predict the cause of a certain event. In everyday life, people commonly observe a series of events and infer causality about the relationship among them. For example, you might observe that a good friend is skipping one of her classes regularly. You also know that she is failing that class. You might infer that she is failing the class because of her poor attendance. But the causal relationship may be just the reverse: your friend may have had a good attendance record until her poor performance on the first test destroyed her motivation and led her to stop attending class. Given the complexities associated with human behavior in organizational settings, the issues of causality, causal inference, and causal relations are of considerable interest to managers and researchers alike.

In the behavioral sciences, causality is difficult to determine because of the interrelationships among variables in a social system. Causality cannot always be empirically proven, but it may be possible to infer causality in certain circumstances. In general, two conditions must be met for causality to be attributed to an observed relationship among variables. The first is temporal order: if $x$ causes $y$, then $x$ must occur before $y$. Many studies, especially field surveys, describe the degree of association among variables with highly sophisticated mathematical techniques, but inferring a causal relationship is difficult because the variables are measured at the same point in time. On the basis of such evidence, we cannot say whether one variable or event caused the other, whether they were both caused by another variable, or whether they are totally independent of each other.

The second condition is the elimination of spuriousness. If we want to infer that $x$ caused $y$, we must eliminate all other possible causes of $y$. Often a seemingly causal relationship between two variables is due to their joint association with a third variable, $z$. To be able to say the relationship between $x$ and $y$ is causal, we must rule out $z$ as a possible cause of $y$. In the behavioral sciences, so many variables may influence one another that tracing causal relationships is like walking in an endless maze. Yet despite the difficulties of the task, we must continue trying to describe, explain, and predict social phenomena in organizational settings if we are to advance our understanding of organizational behavior.[15]

## Reliability and Validity

The **reliability** of a measure is the extent to which it is consistent over time.

The **reliability** of a measure is the extent to which it is consistent over time. Suppose that a researcher measures a group's job satisfaction today with a questionnaire and then measures the same thing in two months. Assuming that nothing has changed, individual responses should be very similar. If they are, the measure can be assessed as having a high level of reliability. Likewise, if question 2 and question 10 ask about the same thing, responses to these questions should be consistent. If measures lack reliability, little confidence can be placed in the results they provide.

**Validity** is the extent to which a measure actually reflects what it was intended to measure.

**Validity** describes the extent to which research measures what it was intended to measure. Suppose that a researcher is interested in employees' satisfaction with their jobs. To determine this, he asks them a series of questions about their pay, supervisors, and working conditions. He then averages their answers and uses the average to represent job satisfaction. We might argue that this is not a valid measure.

Pay, supervision, and working conditions, for example, may be unrelated to the job itself. Thus, the researcher has obtained data that do not mean what he thinks they mean—they are not valid. The researcher, then, must use measures that are valid as well as reliable.[16]

## Ethical Concerns

Last, but certainly not least, the researcher must contend with ethical concerns. Two concerns are particularly important.[17] First, the researcher must provide adequate protection for participants in the study and not violate their privacy without their permission. For example, suppose that a researcher is studying the behavior of a group of operating employees. A good way to increase people's willingness to participate is to promise that their identities will not be revealed. Having made such a guarantee, the researcher is obligated to keep it.

Likewise, participation should be voluntary. All prospective subjects should have the right to not participate or to withdraw their participation after the study has begun. The researchers should explain all procedures in advance to participants and should not subject them to any experimental conditions that could harm them either physically or psychologically. Many government agencies, universities, and professional associations have developed guidelines for researchers to use to guarantee protection of human subjects.

The other issue involves how the researcher reports the results. In particular, it is important that research procedures and methods be reported faithfully and candidly. This enables readers to assess for themselves the validity of the results reported. It also allows others to do a better job of replicating (repeating) the study, perhaps with a different sample, to learn more about how its findings generalize.

# Appendix B

# Career Dynamics

Now that baby boomers are moving up the corporate ladder into middle management, a problem has become apparent: some people of the following generation, often called the "busters," do not like working for some of the boomers. This group of workers born after 1965 has also been called "Generation X." In fact some members of Generation X are leaving the corporate world for small businesses, often starting their own.[1] Career paths are not what they used to be.

As companies downsize, reengineer, and rethink the corporation, there are fewer jobs in the middle and at the top, and thus fewer opportunities to climb the ladder. Many of the boomers have either been downsized into redeployment groups and eventually laid off, or they have become disillusioned with their middle-level management positions. Some finally discover that they are in the wrong occupation. Many have quit, for a variety of personal and professional reasons. For example, many parents are reducing the hours on the job and taking pay cuts to spend more time with their families. Mark Jefferson, an architect in Phoenix, reduced his hours to coach his seven-year-old son's baseball team. In a recent survey by Robert Half International, 76 percent of those surveyed would give up rapid career advancement for more family or personal time.[2] Many of Generation X are unhappy, unsuccessful, or both because they are in the wrong occupation or profession. This means that nearly 30 million people are unhappy in their jobs. The impact on organizational productivity is immense.

A new type of worker is becoming common in many companies: the high-tech nomad. These are people who do freelance work as consultants or contract workers on a project-by-project basis for companies around the world. A job may last a week or six months. The hourly rate is high, but the worker gives up the job security and benefits that typically come from a permanent position with an established company. These types of jobs are on the increase because of the massive downsizing by many companies.[3] Globally, the situation is different. Joblessness is increasing worldwide. Almost one-third of the Earth's 2.8 billion workers are unemployed or underemployed.[4] An underemployed worker is one who is doing a job for which she or he is overqualified. A combination of factors is causing this global jobs problem. In industrialized countries, most companies are struggling to become more efficient to remain competitive globally. In the developing and transitional-economy countries, the struggle is to modernize the means of production and train workers to do the jobs.

Clearly, on a global basis, people may just be happy to have a job. But even those who have jobs seem to be dissatisfied with them and looking for something more. If these problems are to be solved, both individuals and organizations need to know more about jobs, careers, career choices, and career management.

Why are so many people dissatisfied with their jobs and careers? How can organizations help employees pursue the careers that offer the greatest benefit to both employees and the organization? Why do so many people change not only their jobs but also the type of work they do several times during their work lives? How can organizations ensure that when employees leave the company, either by quitting or by retiring, highly qualified people will quickly and efficiently replace them? The issues reflected in these questions have led organizations to invest large amounts of money, time, and effort in developing career management programs. In addition, researchers have begun to systematically study careers.

In this appendix, we examine individual and organizational perspectives on careers. We describe several aspects of career choices. Then we explore the career stages and conclude by discussing organizational career planning.

# Individual and Organizational Perspectives on Careers

A **career** is a perceived sequence of attitudes and behaviors associated with work-related experiences and activities over the person's life span.

People often use the word "career" to refer to the professional occupations of others and not to their own work or job. Indeed, many people do not even expect to have careers—they expect to have jobs.[5] A **career** is a "perceived sequence of attitudes and behaviors associated with work-related experiences and activities over the span of the person's life."[6] Whereas a job is what a person does to bring home a paycheck, a career is a more satisfying and productive activity.[7] Thus, a career involves a long-term series of jobs and work experiences.

People's careers may reflect their personal interests. As people evaluate job opportunities, those with a career perspective usually are concerned with factors such as those listed in Table AB.1. Note how these matters reflect a long-term perspective: People are concerned about the future of technological change, economic conditions, and personal advancement. Many see opportunities for advancement

table AB.1
**Individual Career Issues**

| Career Issues | Examples |
|---|---|
| **Opportunity for Advancement Slowing** | More people entering popular careers |
| **Technical Obsolescence Accelerating** | Rapidly changing automation, computerization |
| **Rate of Economic Growth Declining** | Economy not expanding, fewer jobs created |
| **New Entrants into the Labor Market Receiving More Favorable Treatment** | Higher starting salaries and prerequisites for new hires |
| **Companies Reorganizing** | Downsizing, reducing layers of middle management |
| **Aging** | Career options narrow, fewer opportunities |

Reference: Adapted from C. Hymowitz, "Stable Cycles of Executive Careers Shattered by Upheaval in Business," *Wall Street Journal*, May 26, 1987, p. 31. Reprinted by permission of *Wall Street Journal*, slowing as more people enter popular career fields. They see the rate of technical obsolescence accelerating with the advent of new and better computers and automated manufacturing processes. People trying to establish their careers may worry when the rate of economic growth is declining. They also see that new entrants are treated better than people already in the labor market—getting higher starting salaries, better opportunities, and the like. Furthermore, companies are reorganizing and downsizing, which is increasing uncertainty and decreasing opportunities for advancement. Finally, aging is a concern; as people get older, their career options frequently narrow and their opportunities shrink.[8]

Organizations have a different perspective on careers.[9] They want to ensure that managerial succession is orderly and efficient so that when managers need to be replaced because of promotion, retirement, accident or illness, termination, or resignation, highly qualified people can replace them quickly and easily. Organizations also want their employees to pursue careers in which they are interested and for which they have been properly trained. If employees are unhappy with their career choices and opportunities, they may not perform well or may choose to leave the organization. Thus, to achieve high levels of performance and lower levels of turnover, organizations have an investment in ensuring that people and careers match.

Clearly, although their perspectives are not identical, employees and organizations can both benefit from working together to improve career management. Career choices, however, remain in the hands of individuals.

# Career Choices

Career choices arise more than once during a lifetime, because both people and career opportunities change. People need not be "locked in" to a particular career choice. Knowing that they can change careers can help individuals avoid becoming poor performers in their jobs as a result of career frustration.

Career choices are not something to take lightly, however; they are important in their own right, and they form the basis for future career decisions. As Figure AB.1 indicates, making a career choice involves six steps. First, the person must become aware that a career choice is needed. This awareness may arise in a variety of ways. A recent high school graduate may recognize the need to make a choice after being urged to find a job or declare a college major. A person already pursuing a career may consider choosing a new one after receiving a negative performance evaluation, being turned down for a big promotion, or being fired or laid off.

Second, the worker must obtain information about himself or herself and about available career options. Personal interests, skills, abilities, and desires can be identified by self-reflection as well as by formal and informal consultations with others. In addition, information about the demands and rewards of various careers is available from numerous sources, including career counselors, placement officers, friends, and family.

The third step in the career choice process involves evaluating the information and looking for matches between the person's wants and needs and the characteristics of potential careers. This can be frustrating and confusing as the person finds that every job has advantages as well as disadvantages. Although the help of a competent advisor or counselor is valuable, the next step—the career decision—rests with the individual. In the fourth step, the individual must make a commitment to

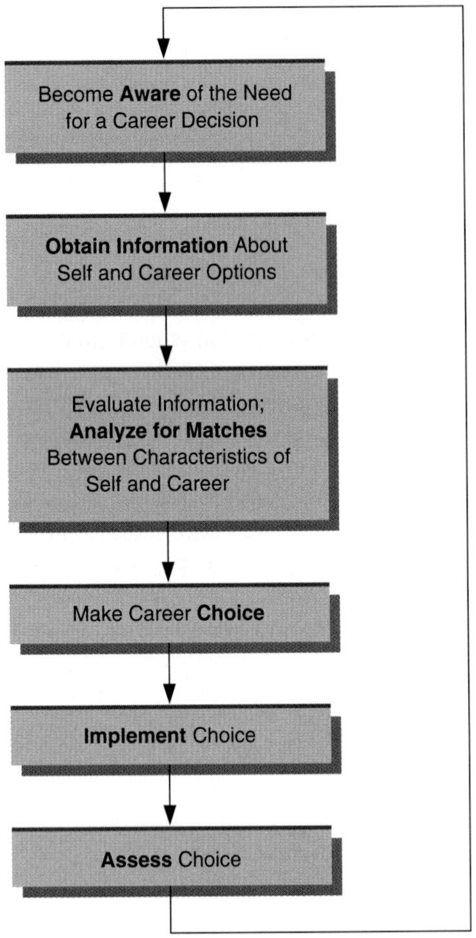


figure AB.1 **A Simplified Model of Individual Career Choice**

*People are never "locked in" to a particular job, occupation, or organization. Periodically, they make career choices just as they make other decisions. Good information is the key to making important life and work career decisions.*

a career or a set of highly similar careers. Commitment means making the decision and initiating the next step, implementation.

Implementing the decision involves actively pursuing the career; preparing through training, education, or internships; obtaining a position; and finally, working. After a time, the individual must assess the choice. As long as the result of the assessment is satisfactory, the individual continues to pursue the career. If the conclusion is unsatisfactory, the individual becomes aware of the need for another career choice and the process begins again.

In making career decisions, people are subjected to a number of pressures. As indicated in Figure AB.2, these pressures may be personal, social, or work related. An individual's personality and goals may be better suited to some careers than to others, and lack of agreement between the types of careers that suit the person's personality and those appropriate to his or her personal goals can create internal conflicts. Social factors that create career pressure include urging from family or friends to quit a job or to take one job rather than another. Some people are now evaluating the balance between certain life and social issues and the time devoted to work. In a recent survey, two-thirds of Americans indicated they would trade more personal and leisure time for lower pay. Many of the respondents said they were not willing to give up their personal lives for the benefit of a company that could lay them off at any time.[10] Religious dictates also impose powerful career-related pressures on some people.

Work factors can also create career-related pressures. A person's current position in an organization may open certain career options, but other options may simply be unavailable to one in that position. This is true of some state government jobs; if one wants to run for political office, one must resign from any other government job first. In addition to formal requirements, informal expectations are associated with most jobs. Certain job and career-related behaviors may be expected from a person in a particular position, which usually puts pressure on the job holder to do the things expected. For example, coworkers may expect a colleague to seek managerial jobs to advance in the organization, whereas the person may enjoy the current job and not wish to move into management.

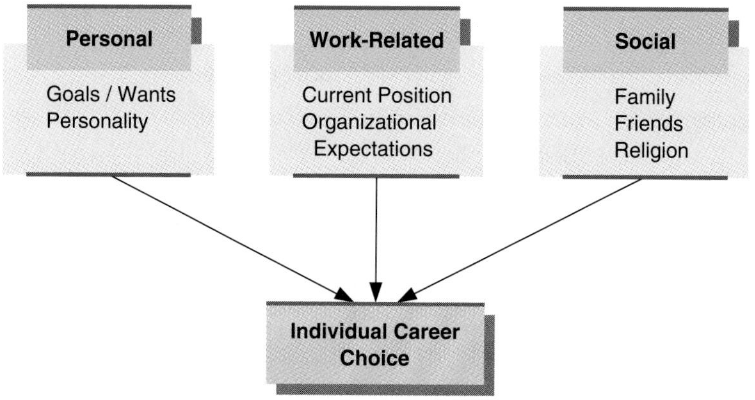


figure AB.2 **Pressures on Individual Career Choice**

*Many different pressures force people to make choices regarding their careers. These pressures may have conflicting influences on career decisions.*

## Choice of Occupation

One major career decision is choice of occupation. An **occupation**, or occupational field, is a group of jobs that are similar in terms of the type of tasks and training involved. Occupations can usually be pursued in many different organizations, whereas jobs are organization-specific. The United States Bureau of the Census identifies hundreds of occupations, including accountant, auctioneer, baker, carpenter, cashier, dancer, embalmer, farmer, furrier, huckster, loom fixer, railroad conductor, receptionist, stock handler, waiter, weaver, and weigher.[11] Of course, these occupations are not equally appealing to people. Rankings of the desirability of occupations have been generally stable. For instance, professions dominate the upper end of such evaluations. The occupation of physician is nearly always among those ranked as having the highest prestige, as are college and university professor, judge, and lawyer. The lowest-prestige occupations are more mixed. Bellhops, bootblacks, cleaners and janitorial workers, teamsters, and ushers are among those consistently rated low in prestige.

An **occupation** is a group of jobs that are similar with respect to the type of tasks and training involved.

Theories that explain how people choose among the many occupations available to them emphasize either content or process.[12] Content theories deal with factors that influence career decisions, such as prestige, pay, and working conditions. Process theories, on the other hand, deal with how people make these decisions.

Content theories focus on six major factors that influence the occupations people choose:

1. The values and attitudes of the individual's family, especially parents[13]
2. Interests and needs[14]
3. Skills and abilities[15]
4. Education
5. General economic conditions
6. Political and social conditions

Process theories suggest that people make occupational choices in stages over time, seeking to match their needs and occupational demands. According to this approach, although people begin considering occupations when they are very young, their thinking evolves and becomes more specific over time.[16]

One process model of occupational choice has been proposed by J. L. Holland. According to Holland, there are six basic personality types—realistic, investigative, artistic, social, enterprising, and conventional—each of which is characterized by a set of preferences, interests, and values. Occupations can also be grouped: working with things, working with observations and data, working with people, working in very ordered ways, exercising power, and using self-expression.[17] As people evaluate occupations over time, they attempt to match their occupational activities to their personality types. Table AB.2 shows Holland's proposed match between personality types and various occupational activities.

**table AB.2**

**Holland Typology of Personality and Sample Occupations**

| | |
|---|---|
| **Realistic** | |
| Personal characteristics | Shy, genuine, materialistic, persistent, stable |
| Sample occupations | Mechanical engineer, drill press operator, aircraft mechanic, dry cleaner, waitress |
| **Investigative** | |
| Personal characteristics | Analytical, cautious, curious, independent, introverted |
| Sample occupations | Economist, physicist, actuary, surgeon, electrical engineer |
| **Artistic** | |
| Personal characteristics | Disorderly, emotional, idealistic, imaginative, impulsive |
| Sample occupations | Journalist, drama teacher, advertising manager, interior decorator, architect |
| **Social** | |
| Personal characteristics | Cooperative, generous, helpful, sociable, understanding |
| Sample occupations | Interviewer, history teacher, counselor, social worker, clergy |
| **Enterprising** | |
| Personal characteristics | Adventurous, ambitious, energetic, domineering, self-confident |
| Sample occupations | Purchasing agent, real estate salesperson, market analyst, attorney, personnel manager |
| **Conventional** | |
| Personal characteristics | Efficient, obedient, practical, calm, conscientious |
| Sample occupations | File clerk, CPA, typist, keypunch operator, teller |

Reference: Table from *Career Management*, by Jeffrey H. Greenhaus, copyright © 1987 by The Dryden Press. Reprinted by permission of the publisher. Adapted from J. L. Holland, *Making Vocational Choices: A Theory of Careers*. Prentice Hall, Englewood Cliffs, N.J.: 1973. Used with permission of the author.

Another process model is similar to the expectancy model of motivation introduced in Chapter 6. This framework assumes that people base their occupational choices on their probability of success.[18] Thus, in an expectancy approach, a person uses information on the anticipated outcomes of being employed in a given occupation and the probability of obtaining those outcomes to assess the attractiveness of the occupation.

This process may be used in comparing two occupations. For example, some people face a new occupational choice after several years in their chosen field. From an expectation point of view, the person may attempt to compare the costs and benefits of remaining in his or her current field against the advantages and disadvantages of a new occupation. The costs may include loss of such benefits as seniority, pension, and earning power if extensive retraining is involved. But the employee may gain benefits such as higher long-term earnings, a different lifestyle, and daily activities that seem inherently more enjoyable.

The choice of occupation is more difficult now than it has ever been. Rather than being based in organizations and positions, new careers will be a series of tasks accomplished, skills mastered, and projects completed.[19] Managerial careers will also be vastly different in the twenty-first century. A group of human resource managers and executive recruiters agreed that managerial careers of this century will be based on a knowledge-based technical specialty, cross-functional and international experience, competence in collaborative leadership, self-management skills, and personal traits such as flexibility, integrity, and trustworthiness.[20]

## Choice of Organization

People must choose not only an occupation but an organization in which to pursue that occupation. This is an important choice—being an engineer for a municipal government, for instance, may be far different from being an engineer for a private aerospace corporation. Indeed, some organizational differences—such as profit or not for profit, large or small, private or governmental, and military or nonmilitary—may greatly influence the individual's ability to reach his or her goals and have a satisfying career.

Research suggests that in choosing an organization, individuals generally seek companies that can provide some minimally acceptable level of economic return—a sort of "base pay." Beyond that, the most frequently desired features of the organization involve the chance it gives employees to engage in interesting, challenging, or novel activities.[21] The type and size of the organization, its reputation, and its geographic location do not seem as important to people making career choices as the level of economic return and the nature of the activities they will be doing.[22]

## Changes in Midcareer

As people change, grow older, and mature, they may need to reevaluate their careers and make new choices. Someone who dropped out of school early in life, for example, may decide that that choice restricted career options too much and may return to school to open up new career opportunities. Life experiences may broaden a person's skills so that new career options become available. One increasingly popular career change option is to take one or more part-time jobs. Some research suggests that the part-time option may benefit the employee as well as the organization.[23] Another increasingly popular choice is to become a "permanent" temporary, or contract, worker. Companies are finding that this option can benefit both the organization and the temporary worker.[24]

Sometimes people find that as they have changed, their definition of career success has changed. Although these people may not need to move from one occupation to another, some adaptation may be in order. Career adaptation may involve retraining to perform better on the job or to move to another job within the same career field. Adaptation may also mean changing organizations while pursuing the same general occupation. Adaptation may be caused by organizational changes such as mergers, acquisition, downsizing, and layoffs. Often, employees choose to make major changes during periods of organizational change because of perceived shifts in the work environment, the economy, or technology. Andy Grove, former chairman and CEO of Intel Corporation, pointed out that the Internet and the hundreds of mergers and acquisitions are causing virtually everyone to reevaluate their career options and become more adaptable in their perspectives of their career.[25]

# Career Stages

Career stages are the periods in which the person's work life is characterized by specific needs, concerns, tasks, and activities.

The gradual changes that occur over time in careers are called **career stages**, which are periods in which the individual's work life is characterized by distinctive needs, concerns, tasks, and activities. Career stages are changing as the organizational, technological, and economic environments change. Even the definition of career success is changing. Where once career success was measured by how high in the organization a person reached or how much money he or she earned, in the future career success will be measured in psychological terms. Psychological success is "the feeling of pride and personal accomplishment that comes from achieving one's most important goals in life, be they achievement, family happiness, inner peace, or something else."[26]

And while it was once the norm to stay with one organization for one's entire career, that no longer is the case. In fact, in the future, people are likely to change occupations as well as organizations several times during their lives. Figure AB.3 shows how career stages may progress as people move from one occupation and organization to another over their entire careers. Within each major stage are five substages: entry (exploration), trial (socialization), establishment, mastery, and exit (withdrawal).

## Entry

The entry stage (exploration stage) is characterized by self-examination, role tryouts, and occupational exploration.

The **entry stage** is also known as the **exploration stage**. Exploration may be the more accurate label for the early part of the stage, in which self-examination, role tryouts, and occupational exploration occur. This is the stage during which education and training are most commonly pursued. During the latter part of the stage, the person begins work by trying out jobs associated with the career. This trial period may involve many different jobs as the individual explores a variety of organizations, occupations, and careers. Performance during this stage is represented in Figure AB.3 as a dashed line to indicate unpredictability.[27]

## Trial

During the trial stage (socialization stage), individuals more specifically explore jobs, and performance begins to improve.

The **trial**, or **socialization**, stage usually begins with a period (shown in the figure by a dashed line) during which the individual continues to explore jobs, but much more narrowly than before. Then, as he or she focuses on a specific job, performance begins to improve. The person is in the early phases of becoming established in the career. The sequence of getting established has been found to consist of three phases: "getting in" (entry), "breaking in" (trial period), and "settling in" (establishment).[28]

During the socialization stage, people begin to form attachments and make commitments, both to others (new friends and coworkers) and to the organizations they work for. Employees begin to learn the organization's goals, norms, values, and preferred ways of doing things; in other words, they learn the culture of the organization (see Chapter 18). In particular, they learn an appropriate set of role behaviors and develop work skills and abilities particular to their jobs and organi-

figure AB.3

**A Model of Career Stages**

*Career stages differ for different people. Some people have few major career changes; some people have many. At each major career change, however, a person may go through a five-step progression: entry, trial, establishment, mastery, and exit. This figure indicates there may be several segments in a person's career, each one going through the five stages. The dashed lines and question marks indicate/signify the uncertainties people face.*

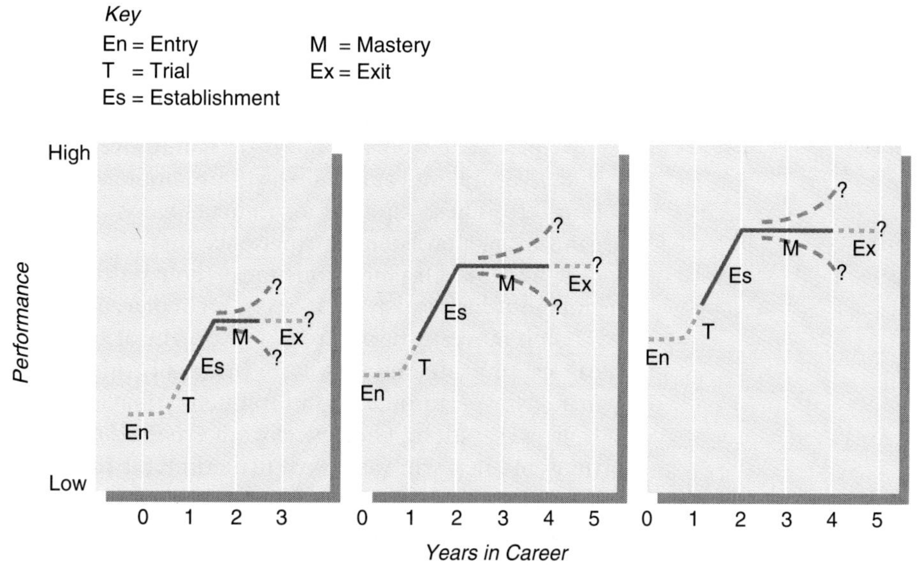


Reference: Adapted from Douglas T. Hall, "Protean Careers of the 21st Century," *Academy of Management Executive,* November 1996, p. 9. Used with permission of the author.

zations. They begin to demonstrate that, at least to some degree, they are learning to accept the values and norms of the organization.[29]

During the socialization period, people must make many adjustments. They must learn to accept the fact that the organization and its people may be quite different from what they had anticipated. When they discover, for example, that other people do not appreciate their ideas, they must learn to deal with resistance to change. Employees must also be prepared to face dilemmas that involve making on-the-job decisions. Dilemmas may pit loyalties to the job, to good performance, to the boss, and to the organization against one another. Career dilemmas may also involve ethical considerations.[30]

An organization can take action to ensure that this stage is successful.[31] It can provide a relaxed orientation program for new personnel. It can see to it that the first job is challenging and that relevant training is provided. It can ensure that timely and reliable feedback is provided to people in this early stage of their careers. Finally, it can place new personnel in groups with high standards to encourage modeling of acceptable norms.

## Establishment

In the **establishment stage (settling-down stage)**, the individual gets more recognition for improved performance.

**Job hopping** occurs when an individual makes fewer adjustments within the organization and moves to different organizations to advance his or her career.

The **establishment stage**, also known as the **settling-down stage**, evolves as the person is recognized for the improved performance that comes with development and growth. The individual is learning his or her career and performing well in it. Soon he or she becomes less dependent on others.

As in the other stages, adjustments are often necessary. Some individuals, of course, are less likely than others to make adjustments and learn. Those who are unsuccessful may change careers or adapt in another way—by job hopping. **Job hopping** occurs when people make fewer adjustments within organizations and instead move to different organizations to advance their careers. It has gained acceptance and increased in recent years as more organizations have used outsiders to replace key managers to improve organization performance.[32] Workers are cautioned to not "job-hop" too fast, but to make sure the new job fits their skills and goal aspirations.[33]

Vertical and horizontal, or lateral, movement also occurs frequently in this stage. Vertical movement involves promotions, whereas lateral movement involves transfers. These kinds of movements teach people about various jobs in the organization, a broadening experience that can benefit both the individuals and the organization. Organizations meet their staffing needs through such movement, and individuals satisfy their needs for achievement and recognition.

Job moves, whether to a new organization or within the same organization, can cause problems, however. Invariably, higher-level jobs bring increased demands for performance, and frequently managers moving into these jobs receive little preparation. They usually are expected to step right into top executive positions and perform well, with little time for socialization into a new system. Furthermore, moves often necessitate relocation to other parts of the country, placing stress on not only the job holder but on his or her family.

Organizations can take steps to manage promotions and transfers to reduce problems. Longer-term, careful career planning may reduce the need to relocate, since much of the broadening may be accomplished at one location. The timing and spacing of moves can be coordinated with, or at least adjusted to, the individual's family situation. More important, better training can be provided to enable the individual to make the move more readily and with substantially less stress.

## Mastery

In the **mastery stage**, individuals develop a stronger attachment to their organizations and lose some career flexibility, and performance may vary.

In the **mastery stage**, individuals develop a stronger attachment to their organizations and, hence, lose some career flexibility. Performance varies considerably in this stage. It may continue to grow, level off, or decline. If performance continues to grow, this stage progresses as a direct extension of the establishment stage. If performance levels or drops, career changes may result.

If leveling off occurs, the individual is said to have reached a "plateau" in her or his career. Responses to plateauing can be effective or ineffective for the individual and the organization. Those who respond effectively to plateaus have been termed "solid citizens"; they have little chance for further advancement but continue to make valuable contributions to the organization. Those whose responses are ineffective are referred to as "deadwood;" they too have little chance for promotion, but they contribute little to the organization.[34]

Solid citizens become interested in establishing and guiding the next generation of organization members. As a result, they frequently begin to act as mentors for younger people in the organization (we discuss mentoring later). As mentors, they show younger members the ins and outs of organization politics and help them learn the values and norms of the organization. These individuals also begin to reexamine their goals in life and rethink their long-term career plans. In some cases, this leads to new values (or the reemergence of older ones) that cause the individuals to quit their jobs or pass up chances for promotions.[35] In other cases, individuals achieve new insights and begin to move upward again; such individuals are known as "late bloomers."[36]

Individuals who have become deadwood are more difficult to deal with. Their knowledge, loyalty, and understanding of plateauing, however, represent value to the organization and could make them salvageable. Perhaps rewards other than advancement can keep these persons productive. Their jobs may be redesigned (see Chapters 7 and 17) to facilitate performance, or they may be reassigned within the organization. And, of course, career counseling programs (discussed later in this appendix) could help them reach a better understanding of their situations and opportunities.[37]

If performance declines, the individual may be experiencing some type of midlife crisis, which is associated with such matters as awareness of physical aging and the nearness of death, reduced career performance, the recognition that life goals may not be met, and changes in family and work relationships. Individuals handle midlife crises differently. Some develop new patterns for coping with the pressures of careers. They may change careers or modify the way they are handling their current careers. Others have a more difficult time and may need professional assistance.

Changing jobs during the mastery stage has become fairly common. Many such moves prove highly beneficial to the person. Several "executive dropouts," for example, have become successful entrepreneurs, such as James L. Patterson, who left IBM to cofound Quantum Corporation.[38] Of course, not all job changes at this stage lead to success. Some job changers find, much to their dismay, that the grass is not greener in the new job, and they experience just as much frustration and disappointment as they did in the old job.[39]

## Exit

In the **exit (withdrawal) stage**, the general pattern is one of decreasing performance as individuals prepare to move on or retire.

The final stage—**exit**, or **withdrawal**—frequently involves the end of this major career stage as individuals move to another occupation, organization, or both. For older workers, it may be the end of full-time employment as they face retirement and other options. The general pattern is one of decreasing performance as people recognize their loss of interest or productivity and begin to search for alternatives. Again, individual adaptation may be positive—beginning a new career, helping others, or learning to accept retirement—or it may be negative—becoming indifferent, giving up, or developing abnormally strong dependence on family and friends. As shown in Figure AB.3, a new and different career stage may begin with new exploration and training and a new period of performance and growth. People may go through two, three, or more of these major career stages during their working lives.

Although legislation may restrict an organization's power to force retirement at age sixty-five, many individuals nevertheless quit full-time employment at about that age, and many organizations encourage even earlier retirement for many of their members. Problems may arise for people who are not prepared for the changes retirement brings. A person who is not ready to retire or feels forced to do so may have an especially difficult time adapting to those changes. To help employees adjust, many organizations are initiating preretirement programs that include information on health, housing, financial planning, legal issues, time management, and social programs for maintaining involvement in the community.

Hall and Hall have argued that the use of the career growth cycle can help organizations manage careers, especially at this crucial stage.[40] The career growth cycle suggests that the organization should provide employees with challenging job goals, support, feedback, and proper counseling to foster career growth for employees. Initially, the organization ensures that jobs offer challenging goals and supports employees' efforts to achieve those goals. If feedback is positive, the employees experience psychological success, which enhances their self-esteem and leads to greater involvement. Less positive feedback, however, which people often receive in the withdrawal stage has the opposite effect. In this instance, the organization provides counseling to help the individual adapt to the changing circumstances.

## Mentoring

**Mentoring** occurs when an older, more experienced person helps a younger employee grow and advance by providing advice, support, and encouragement.

Mentoring programs can be an excellent way for an organization to help manage the career stages of its employees. **Mentoring** is an arrangement in which more experienced workers help less experienced workers grow and advance by providing advice, support, and encouragement. Despite some criticisms of formal mentoring programs, many organizations have implemented them, and many others rely on more traditional informal networks. These companies believe that creating a bond between a senior and a junior employee helps both and benefits the company as well. From the protégé, the mentor often learns about the feelings and attitudes of a younger generation, and he or she may learn about new research and techniques as well. The mentoring process can breathe new life into the career of a person who may be nearing the withdrawal stage.[41] The younger colleague can pick up practical skills from the mentor and gain insights into the organization culture and philosophy that otherwise might take years to discover. A strong, secure bond between the two can lead one or both to do more innovative, important work than they might do on their own.[42]

For the company, this kind of bond can pay off in a number of ways. As the baby-boom generation ages and the Generation X workers burst onto the scene, businesses have to try harder to find and keep good employees. An employee who feels secure in the company because of a good mentoring relationship is less likely to think about looking for another job. Mentors can be especially important for employees who might have trouble fitting into the organization. To move up in a company dominated by an "old-boy" network, for instance, women and minority employees often need contacts of their own in the company's higher ranks. Similarly, multinational corporations may find mentors useful in helping managers from other countries fit into the culture of the corporation. Mentors can also help executives of merged companies adjust to the philosophies and expectations of their new employees.[43]

To get the most out of mentoring programs, experts say, companies must do more than just put two people together and hope for the best.[44] They need to determine what the goals of the program are: to teach specific skills, help new people get along with other employees, or introduce employees to corporate philosophies. Clarifying these goals should help the organization decide who will make the best mentors. Middle managers may be best at helping new people develop specific skills, whereas senior managers may be more effective at passing on the company's vision. In any case, a key element in any mentoring program is matching the two individuals, for the protégé needs to believe that he or she is gaining a friend rather than another boss.

Research into the career stages of people in organizations continues. A recent phenomenon among managers is the occurrence of gaps in career development. These may occur because of changing lifestyles, taking time off for childbearing and child rearing, and for a variety of other reasons. A recent study, however, showed that such career gaps seem to have more negative effects on the careers of men than on those of women.[45]

# Organizational Career Planning

In **career planning**, individuals evaluate their abilities and interests, consider alternative career opportunities, establish career goals, and plan practical development activities.

Career planning, the process of planning one's life work, involves evaluating abilities and interests, considering alternative career opportunities, establishing career goals, and planning practical development activities.[46] Organizations have a vested interest in the careers of their members, and career planning and development programs help them enhance employees' job performance and thus the overall effectiveness of the organization.

## Purposes of Career Planning

Organizational career planning programs can help companies identify qualified personnel and future managers, improve job satisfaction and other attitudes, increase the involvement of key employees, and improve the vital match between individual and organizational wants and needs.[47] The purpose of career planning, then, is to ensure that such enhanced individual and organizational performance occurs.

**Career pathing** is the identification of a certain sequence of jobs in a career that represents a progression through the organization.

Organizational career planning is a complex process involving many conflicting concerns, some of which are listed in Figure AB.4. Reliable and valid personnel decision techniques must be used to ensure that career planning achieves its purposes. Careers should offer employees broad enough experience to develop their skills. The organization must ensure that women and minorities are hired, especially in managerial positions, and that they are compensated fairly. These concerns also involve issues such as nepotism, dual careers, and age discrimination. Career planning may also involve establishing a functional stress management program (see Chapter 9).

figure AB.4 **Organizational Career-Planning Concerns**

*Organizations, like individuals, must address many different issues in their career-planning efforts, which makes career planning a difficult and complex process.*

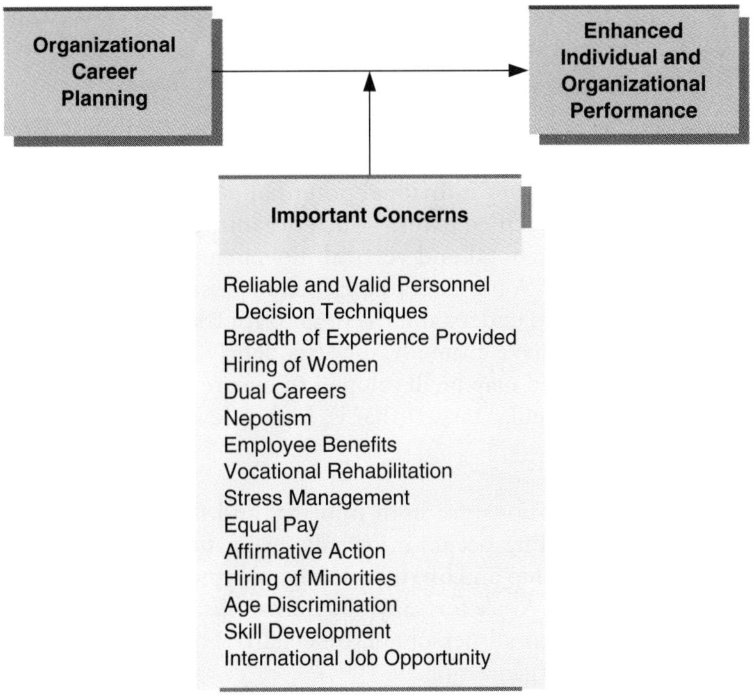


## Types of Career Programs

Research suggests that organizational career planning programs fit into seven general categories: career pathing, career counseling, human resource planning, career information systems, management development, training, and special programs.[48]

### Career Pathing

**Career pathing** is identifying career tracks, or sequences of jobs, that represent a coherent progression vertically and laterally through the organization. Figure AB.5 illustrates two such paths for college graduates, one for an engineering or technical career and one for a sales or marketing career. Some organizations figure AB.5

**Two Examples of Possible Career Paths**

*These two career paths are for illustration only and do not necessarily map out a specific career for any one individual. In the future, either of these paths could represent just one major career stage, leading into another, totally different stage in a few years.*

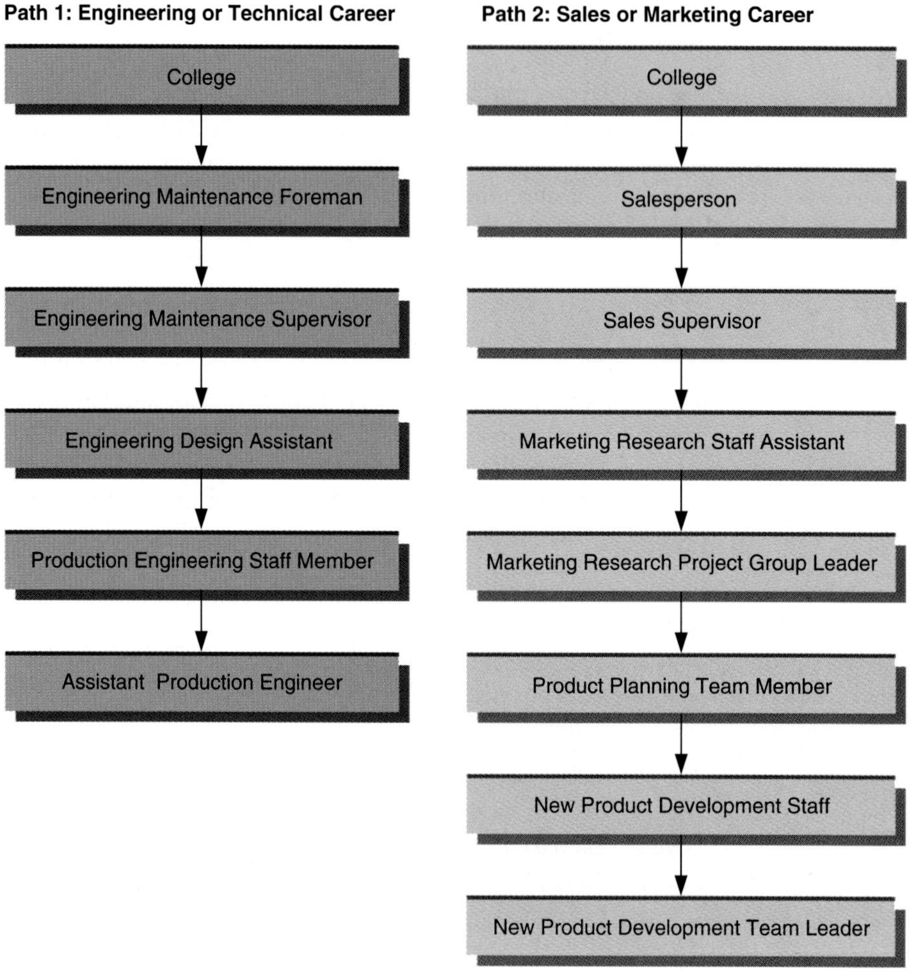


clearly specify paths such as these, whereas others allow far more flexibility. Most organizations do not adhere too strictly to specific career paths, because doing so might limit the full utilization of individual potential, and there are always many exceptions to particular specified paths.[49] Such organizations give employees opportunities for both horizontal and vertical movement to develop their skills and breadth of experience. Some career paths include assignments overseas to help prospective top managers understand the organization's international operations. Career paths usually have a time frame (frequently five to ten years), may be updated periodically, and may be developed to ensure that the work experiences are relevant to a particular target (that is, higher-level) position in the organization.

**Career Counseling** Organizations use both informal and formal approaches to career counseling.[50] Counseling occurs informally as part of the day-to-day supervisor-subordinate relationship and often during employment interviews and performance evaluations as well. More formally, the human resources department often offers career counseling to all personnel, especially those who are being moved up, down, or out of the organization.[51]

**Human resource planning** involves forecasting the organization's human resource needs, developing replacement charts (charts showing a planned succession of personnel) for all levels of the organization, and preparing inventories of the skills and abilities individuals need to move within the organization.

**Human Resource Planning** **Human resource planning** involves forecasting the organization's human resource needs, developing replacement charts (charts showing a planned succession of personnel) for all levels of the organization, and preparing inventories of the skills and abilities individuals need to move within the organization. Human resource planning and development systems can be quite complex and involve both individual and organizational activities. Basically, however, such systems involve developing plans, matching organizations and individuals, assessing needs, and implementing the plans. It is the specific applications that lead to the complexity of the system.

**Career Information Systems** When internal job markets are combined with formal career counseling, the result is a career information system. Internal job markets exist when the organization first announces job openings to organization members. News about openings may appear on bulletin boards, in newsletters, and in memoranda. A career information center keeps up-to-date information about such openings, as well as information about employees who are seeking other jobs or careers within the organization. Career information systems, then, can serve not only to develop the organization's resources but also to provide information that may increase employees' motivation to perform.

**Management Development** Management development programs vary considerably. They may consist simply of policies that hold managers directly responsible for the development of their successors, or they may outline elaborate formal educational programs. Management development is receiving increasing attention in all types of organizations. On average, managers are participating in from twenty to forty hours per year of education and development activities dealing with topics such as time management, problem solving and decision making, strategic planning, and leadership.[52] Developmental programs in smaller organizations (those with fewer than one thousand employees) tend to focus on management and supervisory skills, communication, and behavioral skills. In larger organizations, development activities typically concentrate on executive development, new management techniques, and computer literacy.[53] Management development is discussed in more detail in Chapter 19.

**Training** More specialized efforts to improve skills usually are termed "training." These activities include on-the-job training, formalized job rotation programs, in-house training sessions to develop specific technical job skills, programs on legal and political changes that affect specific jobs, tuition reimbursement programs, and student intern programs. The emphasis is usually on specific job skills, immediate performance being of greater concern than long-term career development. Of course, continued improvement in job performance carries implications of evolving career opportunities.

**Special Programs** Training and development programs may be designed for and offered to special groups within the organization. Examples include preretirement programs and programs designed to help organization members cope with midlife career crises. Many organizations now offer outplacement counseling—programs designed to help employees who are leaving the organization, either voluntarily or involuntarily.[54] Outplacement programs help people preserve their dignity and sense of self-worth when they are fired, and they can reduce negative feelings toward the organization. Other special programs have been developed for women, minorities, and differently abled personnel to help them solve their special career problems.[55] Some organizations also have special programs to help personnel move from technical to managerial positions. Still other organizations have begun programs to deal with smokers, because it has become clear that they pose health risks not only to themselves but also to others.[56]

## Career Management

**Career management** is the process of implementing organizational career planning.

**Career management** is the implementation of organizational career planning. As Table AB.3 shows, top management support is needed to establish a climate that fosters career development. All human resource activities within the organization must be coordinated, and human resource managers from various areas should be involved at least as consultants. The career-planning programs must be open to all members of the organization, so they must be flexible to accommodate individual differences. Realistic feedback should be provided to participants, with the focus on psychological success rather than simply advancement. Implementation of new programs should begin with small pilot programs that emphasize periodic assessment of both employee skills and the program itself.[57]

It is extremely important that supervisors be involved and that they be trained carefully lest they neglect or mishandle their roles and negate the positive effects of career-planning programs. The roles of supervisors include communicating information about careers; counseling to help subordinates identify their skills and understand their options; evaluating subordinates' performance, strengths, and weaknesses; coaching or teaching skills and behaviors to those who need support; advising about the realities of the organization; serving as mentors or role models for subordinates; brokering, or bringing together subordinates and those who might have positions better suited to them; and informing subordinates about opportunities.[58]

## Results of Career Planning

Organizational career planning has many important results.[59] Employees develop a more realistic sense of what is expected of them on the job and what their future with the organization will entail. Planning clarifies supervisory roles in career

table AB.3

**Key Ingredients for Career Management**

| | |
|---|---|
| ■ Top management support | ■ Equal access and open enrollment |
| ■ Coordination with other human resource activities | ■ Focus on psychological success rather than advancement |
| ■ Involvement of supervisors | ■ Flexibility for individual needs |
| ■ Use of human resource managers as consultants | ■ Climate setting for career development |
| ■ Periodic skill assessment | ■ Small pilot programs |
| ■ Realistic feedback about career progress | ■ Periodic program assessment |

Reference: From *Managing Careers in Organizations*, by Daniel C. Feldman. Copyright © 1988 by Scott, Foresman and Company. Used by permission of the author.

counseling, increases personal career-planning ability through knowledge and education, and uses human resource systems more effectively. All of these effects strengthen career commitment as individuals develop plans to take charge of their careers. Ultimately, then, the organization can better use the talent of its members, reduce turnover, and improve individual and corporate performance.

These benefits are not, however, guaranteed. If the existence of an organizational career-planning program raises individuals' expectations unrealistically, dysfunctional consequences may result. Anxiety may increase, supervisors may spend too much time counseling their subordinates, and human resource systems may become overloaded. These effects lead to frustration, disappointment, and reduced commitment. In the end, talent is inadequately used, turnover increases, and individual and organizational performance suffers. The key to keeping employee expectations realistic is for all supervisors and managers to be trained to provide only factual information about jobs and employees' true prospects. Clearly, organizations must use career-planning programs carefully to ensure positive results.

# Endnotes

## Chapter 1

*Quoted in Charles Fishman, "Sanity Inc.," *Fast Company*, January 1999, p. 89.

**1.** Charles Fishman, "Sanity Inc.," *Fast Company*, January 1999, pp. 84–96; Shelly Branch, "The 100 Best Companies to Work for in America," *Fortune*, January 11, 1999, pp. 118–144.

**2.** For a classic discussion of the meaning of organizational behavior, see Larry Cummings, "Toward Organizational Behavior," *Academy of Management Review*, January 1978, pp. 90–98. For recent updates, see the annual series *Research in Organizational Behavior* (Greenwich, Conn.: JAI Press). See also Jerald Greenberg (ed.), *Organizational Behavior—The State of the Science* (Hillsdale, N.J.: Lawrence Erlbaum Associates, 1994); and Cary L. Cooper and Denise M. Rousseau (eds.), *Trends in Organizational Behavior VI* (New York: John Wiley & Sons, 1999).

**3.** Daniel A. Wren, *The Evolution of Management Thought*, 4th ed. (New York: Wiley, 1994), Chapters 1 and 2. See also Stephen J. Carroll and Dennis A. Gillen, "Are the Classical Management Functions Useful in Describing Managerial Work?" *Academy of Management Review*, January 1987, pp. 38–51; and Daniel A. Wren, "Management History: Issues and Ideas for Teaching and Research," *Journal of Management*, Summer 1987, pp. 339–350.

**4.** Quoted in "Why Business History?" *Audacity*, Fall 1992, p. 15.

**5.** "Builders & Titans of the 20th Century," *Time*, December 7, 1998, pp. 70–217.

**6.** Alfred Kieser, "Why Organization Theory Needs Historical Analyses—And How This Should Be Performed," *Organization Science*, November 1994, pp. 608–617.

**7.** Frederick W. Taylor, *Principles of Scientific Management* (New York: Harper, 1911).

**8.** Quoted in Alan Farnham, "The Man Who Changed Work Forever," *Forbes*, July 21, 1997, p. 114.

**9.** See "The Line Starts Here," *Wall Street Journal*, January 11, 1999, pp. R25–R28.

**10.** For critical analyses, see Charles D. Wrege and Amedeo G. Perroni, "Taylor's Pig-Tale: A Historical Analysis of Frederick W. Taylor's Pig-Iron Experiment," *Academy of Management Journal*, March 1974, pp. 6–27; and Charles D. Wrege and Ann Marie Stoka, "Cooke Creates a Classic: The Story Behind Taylor's Principles of Scientific Management," *Academy of Management Review*, October 1978, pp. 736–749. For a more favorable review, see Edwin A. Locke, "The Ideas of Frederick W. Taylor: An Evaluation," *Academy of Management Review*, January 1982, pp. 14–24. See Oliver E. Allen, "'This Great Mental Revolution,'" *Audacity*, Summer 1996, pp. 52–61, for a recent discussion of the practical value of Taylor's work.

**11.** Max Weber, *Theory of Social and Economic Organization*, trans. A. M. Henderson and T. Parsons (London: Oxford University Press, 1921).

**12.** Raymond A. Katzell and James T. Austin, "From Then to Now: The Development of Industrial-Organizational Psychology in the United States," *Journal of Applied Psychology*, 1992, vol. 77, no. 6, pp. 803–835.

**13.** Hugo Münsterberg, *Psychology and Industrial Efficiency* (Boston: Houghton Mifflin, 1913); and Wren, *Evolution of Management Thought*. See also Frank J. Landy, "Hugo Münsterberg: Victim or Visionary?" *Journal of Applied Psychology*, 1992, vol. 77, no. 6, pp. 787–802; and Frank J. Landy, "Early Influences on the Development of Industrial and Organizational Psychology," *Journal of Applied Psychology*, 1997, vol. 82, no. 4, pp. 467–477.

**14.** Elton Mayo, *The Human Problems of Industrial Civilization* (New York: Macmillan, 1933); Fritz J. Roethlisberger and William J. Dickson, *Management and the Worker* (Cambridge, Mass.: Harvard University Press, 1939).

**15.** Alex Carey, "The Hawthorne Studies: A Radical Criticism," *American Sociological Review*, June 1967, pp. 403–416; Lyle Yorks and David A. Whitsett, "Hawthorne, Topeka, and the Issue of Science Versus Advocacy in Organizational Behavior," *Academy of Management Review*, January 1985, pp. 21–30.

**16.** Douglas McGregor, *The Human Side of Enterprise* (New York: McGraw-Hill, 1960); Abraham Maslow, "A Theory of Human Motivation," *Psychological Review*, July 1943, pp. 370–396. See also Paul R. Lawrence, "Historical Development of Organizational Behavior," in Jay W. Lorsch (ed.), *Handbook of Organizational Behavior* (Englewood Cliffs, N.J.: Prentice-Hall, 1987), pp. 1–9.

**17.** Quoted in Kenneth Labich, "Gambling's Kings," *Fortune*, July 22, 1996, pp. 80–88.

**18.** See "Conversation with Lyman W. Porter," *Organizational Dynamics*, Winter 1990, pp. 69–79.

**19.** Jeffrey Pfeffer and John F. Veiga, "Putting People First for Organizational Success," *Academy of Management Executive*, May 1999, pp. 37–48.

**20.** Joseph W. McGuire, "Retreat to the Academy," *Business Horizons*, July–August 1982, pp. 31–37; Kenneth Thomas and Walter G. Tymon, "Necessary Properties of Relevant Research: Lessons from Recent Criticisms of the Organizational Sciences," *Academy of Management Review*, July 1982, pp. 345–353. See also Jeffrey Pfeffer, "The Theory-Practice Gap: Myth or Reality?" *Academy of Management Executive*, February 1987, pp. 31–32.

**21.** Fremont Kast and James Rosenzweig, "General Systems Theory: Applications for Organization and

Management," *Academy of Management Journal*, December 1972, pp. 447–465.
22. See Michael Goold and Andrew Campbell, "Desperately Seeking Synergy," *Harvard Business Review*, September–October 1998, pp. 131–143.
23. See Fremont Kast and James Rozenzweig (eds.), *Contingency Views of Organization and Management* (Chicago: SRA, 1973), for a classic overview and introduction.
24. Ram Charan and Geoffrey Colvin, "Why CEOs Fail," *Fortune*, June 21, 1999, pp. 68–78.
25. James Terborg, "Interactional Psychology and Research on Human Behavior in Organizations," *Academy of Management Review*, October 1981, pp. 569–576; Benjamin Schneider, "Interactional Psychology and Organizational Behavior," in Larry Cummings and Barry Staw (eds.), *Research in Organizational Behavior* (Greenwich, Conn.: JAI Press, 1983), vol. 5, pp. 1–32; Danile B. Turban and Thomas L. Keon, "Organizational Attractiveness: An Interactionist Perspective," *Journal of Applied Psychology*, 1993, vol. 78, no. 2, pp. 184–193.
26. See Milton Hakel, "The Past, Present, and Future of OB Applications by Consulting Academicians," in Jerald Greenberg (ed.), *Organizational Behavior—The State of the Science* (Hillsdale, N.J.: Lawrence Erlbaum Associates, 1994), pp. 275–288.
27. Martha Finney, "Books That Changed Careers," *HRMagazine*, June 1997, p. 141.
28. Nanette Fondas, "Feminization Unveiled: Management Qualities in Contemporary Writings," *Academy of Management Review*, January 1997, pp. 257–282. See also Anne Fisher, "What Women Can Learn from Machiavelli," *Fortune*, April 14, 1997, p. 162.

## Chapter 2

*Quoted in Sheila M. Puffer (interviewer), "Continental Airlines' CEO Gordon Bethune on Teams and New Product Development," *Academy of Management Executive*, August 1999, vol. 13, no. 3, p. 32.
1. Robert Levering and Milton Moskowitz, "The 100 Best Companies to Work For," *Fortune*, January 10, 2000, pp. 82–110; Sheila M. Puffer (interviewer), "Continental Airlines' CEO Gordon Bethune on Teams and New Product Development," *Academy of Management Executive*, August 1999, vol. 13, no. 3, pp. 28–35; *Hoover's Handbook of American Business 1999* (Austin: Hoover's Business Press, 1998), pp. 426–427.
2. Henry Mintzberg, "Rounding Out the Manager's Job," *Sloan Management Review*, Fall 1994, pp. 11–26.
3. Brian Dumaine, "The New Non-Manager Managers," *Fortune*, February 22, 1993, pp. 80–84.
4. Mauro F. Guillen, "The Age of Eclecticism: Current Organizational Trends and the Evolution of Managerial Models," *Sloan Management Review*, Fall 1994, pp. 75–86.
5. Quoted in Ram Charan and Geoffrey Colvin, "Why CEOs Fail," *Fortune*, June 21, 1999, pp. 68–78 (quote on p. 74).
6. John P. Kotter, "What Effective General Managers Really Do," *Harvard Business Review*, March–April 1999, pp. 145–159. See also David H. Freedman, "Is Management Still a Science?" *Harvard Business Review*, November–December 1992, pp. 26–38.
7. Henry Mintzberg, "The Manager's Job: Folklore and Fact," *Harvard Business Review*, July–August 1975, pp. 49–61.
8. Robert L. Katz, "The Skills of an Effective Administrator," *Harvard Business Review*, September–October 1987, pp. 90–102.
9. Associated Press news reports published as "Justin to Close Two Boot Factories," *Bryan-College Station Eagle*, August 15, 1999, p. E1; "Kellogg Workers to Lose Jobs," ibid., p. C4.
10. Quoted in "Kellogg Workers to Lose Jobs," p. C4.
11. Patricia L. Nemetz and Sandra L. Christensen, "The Challenge of Cultural Diversity: Harnessing a Diversity of Views to Understand Multiculturalism," *Academy of Management Review*, April 1996, pp. 434–462; Frances J. Milliken and Luis L. Martins, "Searching for Common Threads: Understanding the Multiple Effects of Diversity in Organizational Groups," *Academy of Management Review*, 1996, vol. 21, no. 2, pp. 402–433.
12. Geoffrey Colvin, "The 50 Best Companies for Asians, Blacks, and Hispanics," *Fortune*, July 19, 1999, pp. 52–57.
13. Quoted in Chuck Salter, "Insanity Inc.," *Fast Company*, January 1999, pp. 100–108 (quote on p. 102).
14. Craig L. Pearce and Charles P. Osmond, "Metaphors for Change: The ALPS Model of Change Management," *Organizational Dynamics*, Winter 1996, pp. 23–35.
15. "Leaders of Corporate Change," *Fortune*, December 14, 1992, pp. 102–114.
16. Brian Dumaine, "Times Are Good? Create a Crisis," *Fortune*, June 28, 1993, pp. 123–130.
17. Peter F. Drucker, "The Information Executives Truly Need," *Harvard Business Review*, January–February 1995, pp. 54–62.
18. Rick Tetzeli and Mary Cronin, "Getting Your Company's Internet Strategy Right," *Fortune*, March 18, 1996, pp. 72–78.
19. "The E-Gang," *Forbes*, July 26, 1999, pp. 145–157.
20. Rahul Jacob, "The Struggle to Create an Organization for the 21st Century," *Fortune*, April 3, 1995, pp. 90–99; Susan Sonnesyn Brooks, "Managing a Horizontal Revolution," *HRMagazine*, June 1995, pp. 52–57.
21. Michael Porter, *Competitive Strategy* (New York: Free Press, 1980).
22. Jeffrey Pfeffer, "Producing Sustainable Competitive Advantage Through the Effective Management of People," *Academy of Management Executive*, February 1995, pp. 55–69; Carl Long and Mary Vickers-Koch, "Using Core Capabilities to Create Competitive Advantage," *Organizational Dynamics*, Summer 1995, pp. 39–55.
23. For an overview, see Ricky W. Griffin and Michael W. Pustay, *International Business—A Managerial*

*Perspective*, 2nd ed. (Reading, Mass.: Addison-Wesley, 1999).
**24.** Quoted in "Driving Change: An Interview with Ford Motor Company's Jacques Nasser," *Harvard Business Review*, March–April 1999, pp. 76–88 (quote on p. 80).
**25.** Thomas M. Garrett and Richard J. Klonoski, *Business Ethics*, 3rd ed. (Englewood Cliffs, N.J.: Prentice-Hall, 1992).
**26.** Jerry W. Anderson Jr., "Social Responsibility and the Corporation," *Business Horizons*, July–August 1986, pp. 22–27.
**27.** David M. Messick and Max H. Bazerman, "Ethical Leadership and the Psychology of Decision Making," *Sloan Management Review*, Winter 1996, pp. 9–22.
**28.** Ross Johnson and William O. Winchell, *Management and Quality* (Milwaukee: American Society for Quality Control, 1989).
**29.** "Quality," *Business Week*, November 30, 1992, pp. 66–75.
**30.** Joel Dreyfuss, "Victories in the Quality Crusade," *Fortune*, October 10, 1988, pp. 80–88.
**31.** Patricia Sellers, "Companies That Serve You Best," *Fortune*, May 31, 1993, pp. 74–88.
**32.** "Service Productivity Is Rising Fast—And So Is the Fear of Lost Jobs," *Wall Street Journal*, June 8, 1995, pp. A1, A10.

## Chapter 3

*Quoted in "AT&T: Diversity, A Business Imperative," *Fortune*, June 21, 1999, p. S25.
**1.** John W. Ellis IV, "AT&T Links Diversity to Specific Unit Goals," *Advertising Age*, February 17, 1997, pp. S14–15; "AT&T: Diversity, A Business Imperative," *Fortune*, June 21, 1999, p. S25.
**2.** R. Roosevelt Thomas Jr., "Redefining Diversity," *HRFOCUS*, April 1996, pp. 6–7.
**3.** Ibid.
**4.** "Diversity Today: Developing and Retaining the Best Corporate Talent," *Fortune*, June 21, 1999, pp. S2–S4.
**5.** Michael L. Wheeler, "Diversity: Making the Business Case," *Business Week*, December 9, 1996; special advertising section.
**6.** Elaine Carter, Elaine Kepner, Malcolm Shaw, and William Brooks Woodson, "The Effective Management of Diversity," *S.A.M. Advanced Management Journal*, Autumn 1982, pp. 49–53.
**7.** Marilyn Loden and Judy B. Rosener, *Workforce America! Managing Employee Diversity as a Vital Resource* (Homewood, Ill.: Business One Irwin, 1991), pp. 58–62.
**8.** Ibid., p. 60.
**9.** Ibid., pp. 68–70.
**10.** Howard N. Fullerton Jr., "Labor Force 2006: Slowing Down and Changing Composition," *Monthly Labor Review*, November 1997, pp. 23–38.
**11.** Ibid., p. 37.
**12.** Ibid., p. 25.
**13.** Michael Crawford, "The New Office Etiquette," *Canadian Business*, May 1993, pp. 22–31.
**14.** Harish C. Jain and Anil Verma, "Managing Workforce Diversity for Competitiveness: The Canadian Experience" *International Journal of Manpower*, April–May 1996, pp. 14–30.
**15.** "Plenty of Muck, Not Much Money," *Economist*, May 8, 1999, p. 52.
**16.** Barry Louis Rubin, "Europeans Value Diversity," *HRMagazine*, January 1991, pp. 38–41, 78.
**17.** Ron Corben, "Thailand Faces a Shrinking Work Force," *Journal of Commerce and Commercial*, December 26, 1996, p. 5a.
**18.** "Lone Knights: Knight Ridder Is a Rare Beacon Among Newspapers," *Fortune*, July 19, 1999, p. 68.
**19.** Wheeler, "Diversity: Making the Business Case."
**20.** Lennie Copeland, "Making the Most of Cultural Differences at the Workplace," *Personnel*, June 1988, pp. 52–60.
**21.** M. J. Gent, "Theory X in Antiquity, or the Bureaucratization of the Roman Army," *Business Horizons*, January–February 1984, pp. 53–54.
**22.** Henry W. Lane and Joseph J. DiStefano, *International Management Behavior* (Ontario: Nelson 1988).
**23.** Brian O'Reilly, "Your New Global Workforce," *Fortune*, December 14, 1992, pp. 58–66.
**24.** Christopher Knowlton, "What America Makes Best," *Fortune*, March 28, 1988, pp. 40–54.
**25.** Alex Taylor III, "Why GM Leads the Pack in Europe," *Fortune*, May 17, 1993, pp. 83–86.
**26.** Richard M. Steers and Edwin L. Miller, "Management in the 1990s: The International Challenge," *Academy of Management Executive*, February 1988, pp. 21–22.
**27.** Simcha Ronen and Oded Shenkar, "Clustering Countries on Attitudinal Dimension: A Review and Synthesis," *Academy of Management Review*, July 1985, pp. 435–454.
**28.** Nancy J. Adler, Robert Doktor, and Gordon Redding, "From the Atlantic to the Pacific Century," *Journal of Management*, Summer 1986, pp. 295–318.
**29.** Brian O'Reilly, "Japan's Uneasy U.S. Managers," *Fortune*, April 25, 1988, pp. 245–264.
**30.** "Learning to Accept Cultural Diversity," *Wall Street Journal*, September 12, 1990, pp. B1, B9.
**31.** Tamotsu Yamaguchi, "The Challenge of Internationalization," *Academy of Management Executive*, February 1988, pp. 33–36.
**32.** Geert Hofstede, *Culture's Consequences: International Differences in Work-Related Values* (Beverly Hills: Sage Publications, 1980).
**33.** Loden and Rosener, *Workforce America!* p. 19.
**34.** Fullerton, "Labor Force 2006," p. 30.
**35.** Sar A. Levitan, "Older Workers in Today's Economy," presentation at the Textbook Author's Conference, Washington, D.C., October 21, 1992.
**36.** Fullerton, "Labor Force 2006," p. 33.
**37.** Beverly Hynes-Grace, "To Thrive, Not Merely Survive," presentation at the Textbook Author's Conference, Washington, D.C., October 21, 1992.
**38.** Ibid.
**39.** Wheeler, "Diversity: Making the Business Case."

**40.** Copeland, "Making the Most of Cultural Differences at the Workplace," pp. 52–60.
**41.** Charlene Marmer Soloman, "The Corporate Response to Workforce Diversity," *Personnel Journal,* August 1989, pp. 42–54.
**42.** Susan Faludi, *BACKLASH: The Undeclared War Against American Women* (New York: Doubleday, 1991).
**43.** Loden and Rosener, *Workforce America!* pp. 85–86.
**44.** Richard L. Drach, "Making Reasonable Accommodations Under the ADA," *Employment Relations Today,* Summer 1992, pp. 167–175.
**45.** Toby B. Gooley, "Ready, Willing, and Able!" *Traffic Management,* October 1993, pp. 63–67.
**46.** Thomas A. Stewart, "Gay in Corporate America," *Fortune,* December 16, 1991, pp. 42–56.
**47.** Ibid., p. 45.
**48.** Wheeler, "Diversity: Making the Business Case."
**49.** André Laurent, "The Cultural Diversity of Western Conceptions of Management," *International Studies of Management and Organization,* Spring–Summer 1983, pp. 75–96.
**50.** See Brian O'Reilly, "Your New Global Workforce," *Fortune,* December 14, 1992, pp. 58–66; Richard I. Kirkland Jr., "Europe's New Managers," *Fortune,* September 29, 1986, pp. 56–60.
**51.** Bill Leonard, "Ways to Make Diversity Programs Work," *HRMagazine,* April 1991, pp. 37–39, 98.
**52.** Taylor H. Cox and Stacy Blake, "Managing Cultural Diversity: Implications for Organizational Competitiveness," *Academy of Management Executive,* August 1991, pp. 45–56.
**53.** Taylor H. Cox, "The Multicultural Organizational," *Academy of Management Executive,* May 1991, pp. 34–47.
**54.** Ibid., p. 42.

## Chapter 4

*Quoted in "Company Cuts Jobs, Closes Plants As Sales Shrink, Popularity Fades," *USA Today,* February 23, 1999, p. 2B.
**1.** "Its Share Shrinking, Levi Strauss Lays Off 6,395," *Wall Street Journal,* November 4, 1997, pp. B1, B8; "Levi's Is Hiking Up Its Pants," *Business Week,* December 1, 1997, pp. 70–75; "Company Cuts Jobs, Closes Plants As Sales Shrink, Popularity Fades," *USA Today,* February 23, 1999, pp. 1B, 2B.
**2.** Denise M. Rousseau and Judi McLean Parks, "The Contracts of Individuals and Organizations," in Larry L. Cummings and Barry M. Staw (eds.), *Research in Organizational Behavior*; vol. 15 (Greenwich, Conn.: JAI Press, 1993), pp. 1–43.
**3.** Denise M. Rousseau, "Changing the Deal While Keeping the People," *Academy of Management Executive,* February 1996, pp. 50–58.
**4.** For example, see "Climbing Walls on Company Time," *Wall Street Journal,* December 1, 1998, pp. B1, B14.
**5.** Quoted in Nina Munk, "The New Organization Man," *Fortune,* March 16, 1998, p. 68.
**6.** Richard A. Guzzo, Katherine A. Noonan, and Efrat Elron, "Expatriate Managers and the Psychological Contract," *Journal of Applied Psychology,* vol. 79, no. 4, pp. 617–626.
**7.** Jennifer A. Chatman, "Improving Interactional Organizational Research: A Model of Person-Organization Fit," *Academy of Management Review,* July 1989, pp. 333–349; Charles A. O'Reilly III, Jennifer Chatman, and David F. Calwell, "People and Organizational Culture: A Profile Comparison Approach to Assessing Person-Organization Fit," *Academy of Management Journal,* September 1991, pp. 487–516.
**8.** Amy L. Kristof, "Person-Organization Fit: An Integrative Review of Its Conceptualizations, Measurement, and Implications," *Personnel Psychology,* Spring 1996, pp. 1–49.
**9.** Lawrence Pervin, "Personality," in Mark Rosenzweig and Lyman Porter (eds.), *Annual Review of Psychology* (Palo Alto, Calif.: Annual Reviews, 1985), vol. 36, pp. 83–114; S. R. Maddi, *Personality Theories: A Comparative Analysis,* 4th ed. (Homewood, Ill.: Dorsey, 1980).
**10.** Jennifer George, "The Role of Personality in Organizational Life: Issues and Evidence," *Journal of Management,* 1992, vol. 18, pp. 185–213.
**11.** L. R. Goldberg, "An Alternative 'Description of Personality': The Big Five Factor Structure," *Journal of Personality and Social Psychology,* 1990, vol. 59, pp. 1216–1229; M. R. Barrick and M. K. Mount, "The Big Five Personality Dimensions and Job Performance," *Personnel Psychology,* 1991, Summer, pp. 1–26.
**12.** Barrick and Mount, "The Big Five Personality Dimensions and Job Performance."
**13.** Michael K. Mount, Murray R. Barrick, and J. Perkins Strauss, "Validity of Observer Ratings of the Big Five Personality Factors," *Journal of Applied Psychology,* 1994, vol. 79, no. 2, pp. 272–280; See also Scott E. Seibert, J. Michael Crant, and Maria L. Kraimer, "Proactive Personality and Career Success," *Journal of Applied Psychology,* 1999, vol. 84, no. 3, pp. 416–427; and Margaret A. McManus and Mary L. Kelly, "Personality Measures and Biodata: Evidence Regarding Their Incremental Predictive Value in the Life Insurance Industry," *Personnel Psychology,* 1999, Summer, pp. 137–158.
**14.** A. L. Hammer, *Introduction to Types and Careers* (Palo Alto, Calif.: Consulting Psychologists Press, 1993).
**15.** J. B. Rotter, "Generalized Expectancies for Internal vs. External Control of Reinforcement," *Psychological Monographs,* 1966, vol. 80, pp. 1–28; Bert De Brabander and Christopher Boone, "Sex Differences in Perceived Locus of Control," *Journal of Social Psychology,* 1990, vol. 130, pp. 271–276.
**16.** Marilyn E. Gist and Terence R. Mitchell, "Self-Efficacy: A Theoretical Analysis of Its Determinants and Malleability," *Academy of Management Review,* April 1992, pp. 183–211.
**17.** Cynthia Lee and Phillip Bobko, "Self-Efficacy Beliefs: Comparison of Five Measures," *Journal of Applied Psychology,* 1994, vol. 79, no. 3, pp. 364–369; Peg Thoms, Keirsten S. Moore, and Kimberly S. Scott, "The

Relationship Between Self-Efficacy for Participating in Self-Managed Work Groups and the Big Five Personality Dimensions," *Journal of Organizational Behavior,* 1996, vol. 17, pp. 349–362.
**18.** T. W. Adorno, E. Frenkel-Brunswick, D. J. Levinson, and R. N. Sanford, *The Authoritarian Personality* (New York: Harper & Row, 1950).
**19.** "Who Becomes an Authoritarian?" *Psychology Today,* March 1989, pp. 66–70.
**20.** Jon L. Pierce, Donald G. Gardner, and Larry L. Cummings, "Organization-Based Self-Esteem: Construct Definition, Measurement, and Validation," *Academy of Management Journal,* September 1989, pp. 622–648.
**21.** Roy J. Blitzer, Colleen Petersen, and Linda Rogers, "How to Build Self-Esteem," *Training and Development,* February 1993, pp. 58–65.
**22.** Michael Harris Bond and Peter B. Smith, "Cross-Cultural Social and Organizational Psychology," in Janet Spence (ed.), *Annual Review of Psychology,* vol. 47 (Palo Alto, Calif.: Annual Reviews, 1996), pp. 205–235.
**23.** "How Life on the Edge Became Mainstream in Today's America," *Wall Street Journal,* August 3, 1999, pp. A1, A10.
**24.** Charles E. Kimble, *Social Psychology: Studying Human Interaction* (Dubuque, Iowa: William C. Brown, 1990); Frank E. Saal and Patrick A. Knight, *Industrial/Organizational Psychology* (Belmont, Calif.: Brooks/Cole, 1988).
**25.** Amy S. Wharton and Rebecca J. Erickson, "Managing Emotions on the Job and at Home: Understanding the Consequences of Multiple Emotional Roles," *Academy of Management Journal,* September 1993, pp. 457–486.
**26.** Bobby J. Calder and Paul H. Schurr, "Attitudinal Processes in Organizations," in Larry L. Cummings and Barry M. Staw (eds.), *Research in Organizational Behavior* (Greenwich, Conn.: JAI Press, 1981), vol. 3, pp. 283–302.
**27.** Leon Festinger, *A Theory of Cognitive Dissonance* (Palo Alto, Calif.: Stanford University Press, 1957).
**28.** Patricia C. Smith, L. M. Kendall, and Charles Hulin, *The Measurement of Satisfaction in Work and Behavior* (Chicago: Rand-McNally, 1969).
**29.** Linda Grant, "Happy Workers, High Returns," *Fortune,* January 12, 1998, p. 81.
**30.** James R. Lincoln, "Employee Work Attitudes and Management Practice in the U.S. and Japan: Evidence from a Large Comparative Study," *California Management Review,* Fall 1989, pp. 89–106.
**31.** Frederick F. Reichheld, "Loyalty-Based Management," *Harvard Business Review,* March–April 1993, pp. 64–73.
**32.** Lincoln, "Employee Work Attitudes and Management Practice."
**33.** Leslie E. Palich, Peter W. Hom, and Roger W. Griffeth, "Managing in the International Context: Testing Cultural Generality of Sources of Commitment to Multinational Enterprises," *Journal of Management,* 1995, vol. 21, no. 4, pp. 671–690.
**34.** For research work in this area, see Jennifer M. George and Gareth R. Jones, "The Experience of Mood and Turnover Intentions: Interactive Effects of Value Attainment, Job Satisfaction, and Positive Mood," *Journal of Applied Psychology,* 1996, vol. 81, no. 3, pp. 318–325; Karl Aquino, Steven L. Grover, Murray Bradfield, and David G. Allen, "The Effects of Negative Affectivity, Hierarchical Status, and Self-Determination on Workplace Victimization," *Academy of Management Journal,* June 1999, pp. 260–272.
**35.** Quoted in Ronald B. Lieber, "Why Employees Love These Companies," *Fortune,* January 12, 1998, p. 73.
**36.** "One Man's Accident Is Shedding New Light on Human Perception," *Wall Street Journal,* September 30, 1993, pp. A1, A13.
**37.** William H. Starbuck and John M. Mezias, "Opening Pandora's Box: Studying the Accuracy of Managers' Perceptions," *Journal of Organizational Behavior,* 1996, vol. 17, pp. 99–117.
**38.** Frank E. Saal and S. Craig Moore, "Perceptions of Promotion Fairness and Promotion Candidates' Qualifications," *Journal of Applied Psychology,* 1993, vol. 78, pp. 105–110.
**39.** Quoted in Dan Seligman, "In Defense of Stereotypes," *Forbes,* December 1, 1997, p. 114.
**40.** Mark J. Martinko and William L. Gardner, "The Leader/Member Attribution Process," *Academy of Management Review,* April 1987, pp. 235–249; Jeffrey D. Ford, "The Effects of Causal Attributions on Decision Makers' Responses to Performance Downturns," *Academy of Management Review,* October 1985, pp. 770–786.
**41.** See Richard W. Woodman, John E. Sawyer, and Ricky W. Griffin, "Toward a Theory of Organizational Creativity," *Academy of Management Review,* April 1993, pp. 293–321.
**42.** See Thomas V. Busse and Richard S. Mansfield, "Theories of the Creative Process: A Review and a Perspective," *Journal of Creative Behavior,* January 1980, pp. 91–103.
**43.** Emily Thornton, "Japan's Struggle to Be Creative," *Fortune,* April 19, 1993, pp. 129–134.
**44.** Quoted in Ed Brown, "A Day at Innovation U.," *Fortune,* April 12, 1999, p. 164.
**45.** See Anne O'Leary-Kelly, Ricky W. Griffin, and David J. Glew, "Organization-Motivated Aggression: A Research Framework," *Academy of Management Review,* January 1996, pp. 225–253.
**46.** See Dennis W. Organ, "Personality and Organizational Citizenship Behavior," *Journal of Management,* 1994, vol. 20, no. 2, pp. 465–478, for a recent review of findings regarding this behavior.
**47.** Brian P. Niehoff and Robert H. Moorman, "Justice as a Mediator of the Relationship Between Methods of Monitoring and Organizational Citizenship Behavior," *Academy of Management Journal,* September 1993, pp. 527–556; see also Mark C. Bolino, "Citizenship and Impression Management: Good Soldiers or Good Actors?" *Academy of Management Review,* January 1999, pp. 82–98.

## Chapter 5

*Quoted in Shelly Branch, "You Hired 'Em. But Can You Keep 'Em?" *Fortune*, November 9, 1988, p. 248.

**1.** "Employers Give Creative Gifts to Reward Workers," *USA Today*, March 26, 1998, p. 1B; Shelly Branch, "You Hired 'Em. But Can You Keep 'Em?" *Fortune*, November 9, 1998, pp. 247–250; "Employees Who Value Time as Much As Money Now Get Their Reward," *Wall Street Journal*, September 22, 1999, p. B1; "Motivating Workers," *USA Today*, September 23, 1999, p. 1B.

**2.** Richard M. Steers, Gregory A. Bigley, and Lyman W. Porter, *Motivation and Leadership at Work*, 6th ed. (New York: McGraw-Hill, 1996). See also Ruth Kanfer, "Motivational Theory and Industrial and Organizational Psychology," in M. D. Dunnette and L. M. Hough (eds.), *Handbook of Industrial and Organizational Psychology*, 2nd ed. (Palo Alto, Calif.: Consulting Psychologists Press, 1990), vol. 1, pp. 75–170; Ruth Kanfer and Eric D. Heggestad, "Motivational Traits and Skills: A Person-Centered Approach to Work Motivation," in Larry L. Cummings and Barry M. Staw (eds.), *Research in Organizational Behavior* (Greenwich, Conn.: JAI Press, 1997), vol. 19, pp. 1–56.

**3.** Roland E. Kidwell Jr. and Nathan Bennett, "Employee Propensity to Withhold Effort: A Conceptual Model to Intersect Three Avenues of Research," *Academy of Management Review*, July 1993, pp. 429–456.

**4.** Jeffrey Pfeffer, *The Human Equation* (Boston: Harvard Business School Press, 1998).

**5.** See Jack W. Brehm and Elizabeth A. Self, "The Intensity of Motivation," in Mark R. Rosenzweig and Lyman W. Porter (eds.), *Annual Review of Psychology* (Palo Alto: Annual Reviews, 1989), vol. 40, pp. 109–132.

**6.** Craig Pinder, *Work Motivation in Organizational Behavior* (Upper Saddle River, New Jersey: Prentice-Hall, 1998).

**7.** Frederick W. Taylor, *Principles of Scientific Management* (New York: Harper, 1911).

**8.** Ibid., pp. 46–47.

**9.** See Charles D. Wrege and Amedeo G. Perroni, "Taylor's Pig-Tale: A Historical Analysis of Frederick W. Taylor's Pig-Iron Experiment," *Academy of Management Journal*, March 1974, pp. 6–27.

**10.** Pinder, *Work Motivation in Organizational Behavior.* See also Daniel Wren, *The Evolution of Management Thought*, 4th ed. (New York: Wiley, 1994).

**11.** Steers et al., *Motivation and Leadership at Work.*

**12.** Gerald R. Salancik and Jeffrey Pfeffer, "An Examination of Need-Satisfaction Models of Job Attitudes," *Administrative Science Quarterly*, September 1977, pp. 427–456.

**13.** Abraham H. Maslow, "A Theory of Human Motivation," *Psychological Review*, 1943, vol. 50, pp. 370–396; Abraham H. Maslow, *Motivation and Personality* (New York: Harper & Row, 1954). Maslow's most famous work includes Abraham Maslow, Deborah C. Stephens, and Gary Heil, *Maslow on Management* (New York: John Wiley & Sons, 1998); and Abraham Maslow and Richard Lowry, *Toward a Psychology of Being* (New York: John Wiley & Sons, 1999).

**14.** Quoted in "Living Overtime: A Factory Workaholic," *Wall Street Journal*, October 13, 1998, p. B1.

**15.** See Nancy Adler, *International Dimensions of Organizational Behavior*, 3rd ed. (Boston: PWS-Kent, 1997).

**16.** Mahmond A. Wahba and Lawrence G. Bridwell, "Maslow Reconsidered: A Review of Research on the Need Hierarchy Theory," *Organizational Behavior and Human Performance*, April 1976, pp. 212–240.

**17.** Howard S. Schwartz, "Maslow and Hierarchical Enactment of Organizational Reality," *Human Relations*, vol. 36, no. 10, 1983, pp. 933–956.

**18.** Clayton P. Alderfer, *Existence, Relatedness, and Growth* (New York: Free Press, 1972).

**19.** Ibid.

**20.** Frederick Herzberg, Bernard Mausner, and Barbara Synderman, *The Motivation to Work* (New York: Wiley, 1959); Frederick Herzberg, "One More Time: How Do You Motivate Employees?" *Harvard Business Review*, January–February 1968, pp. 53–62.

**21.** Herzberg, Mausner, and Synderman, *The Motivation to Work.*

**22.** Ibid.

**23.** Quoted in "Can Trees and Jogging Trails Lure Techies to Kansas?" *Wall Street Journal*, October 21, 1998, p. B1.

**24.** Herzberg, "One More Time"; Ricky W. Griffin, *Task Design: An Integrative Approach* (Glenview, Ill.: Scott, Foresman, 1982).

**25.** Pinder, *Work Motivation in Organizational Behavior.*

**26.** Frederick Herzberg, *Work and the Nature of Man* (Cleveland: World, 1966); Benedict Grigaliunas and Frederick Herzberg, "Relevance in the Test of Motivation-Hygiene Theory," *Journal of Applied Psychology*, February 1971, pp. 73–79; Valerie M. Bookman, "The Herzberg Controversy," *Personnel Psychology*, Summer 1971, pp. 155–189.

**27.** Pinder, *Work Motivation in Organizational Behavior.*

**28.** Marvin Dunnette, John Campbell, and Milton Hakel, "Factors Contributing to Job Satisfaction and Job Dissatisfaction in Six Occupational Groups," *Organizational Behavior and Human Performance*, May 1967, pp. 143–174; Charles L. Hulin and Patricia Smith, "An Empirical Investigation of Two Implications of the Two-Factor Theory of Job Satisfaction," *Journal of Applied Psychology*, October 1967, pp. 396–402.

**29.** Nathan King, "A Clarification and Evaluation of the Two-Factor Theory of Job Satisfaction," *Psychological Bulletin*, July 1970, pp. 18–31. See also Dunnette, Campbell, and Hakel, "Factors Contributing to Job Satisfaction," and R. J. House and L. Wigdor, "Herzberg's Dual-Factor Theory of Job Satisfaction and Motivation: A Review of the Evidence and a Criticism," *Personnel Psychology*, Summer 1967, pp. 369–389.

**30.** Adler, *International Dimensions of Organizational Behavior.*

31. Pinder, *Work Motivation in Organizational Behavior.*
32. Ibid.
33. David McClelland, *The Achieving Society* (Princeton, N.J.: Nostrand, 1961). See also David C. McClelland, *Human Motivation* (Cambridge: Cambridge University Press, 1988).
34. Quoted in "The Daddy Trap," *Business Week*, September 21, 1998, p. 62.
35. Michael J. Stahl, "Achievement, Power, and Managerial Motivation: Selecting Managerial Talent with the Job Choice Exercise," *Personnel Psychology*, Winter 1983, pp. 775–790.
36. "Larry Bossidy Won't Stop Pushing," *Fortune*, January 13, 1997, pp. 135–137.
37. McClelland, *The Achieving Society.*
38. Stanley Schachter, *The Psychology of Affiliation* (Stanford, Calif.: Stanford University Press, 1959).
39. David McClelland and David H. Burnham, "Power Is the Great Motivator," *Harvard Business Review*, March–April 1976, pp. 100–110.
40. McClelland and Burnham, "Power Is the Great Motivator"; Pinder, *Work Motivation in Organizational Behavior.*
41. For one recent approach to integrating needs, see Russell Cropanzano, Keith James, and Maryalice Citera, "A Goal Hierarchy Model of Personality, Motivation, and Leadership," in Larry L. Cummings and Barry M. Staw (eds.), *Research in Organizational Behavior* (Greenwich, Conn.: JAI Press, 1993), vol. 15, pp. 267–322.
42. Salancik and Pfeffer, "An Examination of Need-Satisfaction Models of Job Attitudes."
43. Pinder, *Work Motivation in Organizational Behavior.*

## Chapter 6

*Quoted in "Hire Now, Pay Later?" *Forbes*, August 23, 1999, p. 62.
1. "Hire Now, Pay Later?" *Forbes*, August 23, 1999, p. 62; "Painless Perks," *Forbes*, September 6, 1999, p. 138; "Net Start-Ups Pull Out Of the Garage," *USA Today*, October 1, 1999, pp. 1B, 2B.
2. For reviews, see Ruth Kanfer, "Motivational Theory and Industrial and Organizational Psychology," in M. D. Dunnette and L. M. Hough (eds.), *Handbook of Industrial and Organizational Psychology*, vol. 1, 2nd ed. (Palo Alto, Calif.: Consulting Psychologists Press, 1990), pp. 75–170; and Craig Pinder, *Work Motivation in Organizational Behavior* (Upper Saddle River, N.J.: Prentice-Hall, 1998).
3. J. Stacy Adams, "Toward an Understanding of Inequity," *Journal of Abnormal and Social Psychology*, November 1963, pp. 422–436. See also Richard T. Mowday, "Equity Theory Predictions of Behavior in Organizations," in Richard M. Steers and Lyman W. Porter (eds.), *Motivation and Work Behavior*, 4th ed. (New York: McGraw-Hill, 1987), pp. 89–110.
4. Paul S. Goodman, "Social Comparison Processes in Organizations," in Barry M. Staw and Gerald R. Salancik (eds.), *New Directions in Organizational Behavior* (Chicago: St. Clair, 1977), pp. 97–131.
5. Priti Pradham Shah, "Who Are Employees' Social Referents? Using a Network Perspective to Determine Referent Others," *Academy of Management Journal*, June 1998, pp. 249–268.
6. J. Stacy Adams, "Inequity in Social Exchange," in L. Berkowitz (ed.), *Advances in Experimental Social Psychology*, vol. 2 (New York: Academic Press, 1965), pp. 267–299.
7. Craig Pinder, *Work Motivation in Organizational Behavior* (Upper Saddle River, N.J.: Prentice-Hall, 1998).
8. Richard A. Cosier and Dan R. Dalton, "Equity Theory and Time: A Reformulation," *Academy of Management Review*, April 1983, pp. 311–319. See also Jerald Greenberg, "Cognitive Reevaluation of Outcomes in Response to Underpayment Inequity," *Academy of Management Journal*, March 1989, pp. 174–184.
9. Richard C. Huseman, John D. Hatfield, and Edward W. Miles, "A New Perspective on Equity Theory: The Equity Sensitivity Construct," *Academy of Management Review*, October 1987, pp. 222–234. See also Wesley C. King Jr., Edward W. Miles, and D. David Day, "A Test and Refinement of the Equity Sensitivity Construct," *Journal of Organizational Behavior*, 1993, vol. 14, pp. 301–317.
10. Quoted in "Holiday on Ice: Stuck at the Office," *USA Today*, November 18, 1998, p. B5.
11. Randall P. Settoon, Nathan Bennett, and Robert C. Liden, "Social Exchange in Organizations: Perceived Support, Leader-Member Exchange, and Employee Reciprocity," *Journal of Applied Psychology*, June 1996, pp. 219–227.
12. Edward C. Tolman, *Purposive Behavior in Animals* (New York: Appleton-Century-Crofts, 1932); Kurt Lewin, *The Conceptual Representation and the Measurement of Psychological Forces* (Durham, N.C.: Duke University Press, 1938).
13. Victor Vroom, *Work and Motivation* (New York: Wiley, 1964).
14. Quoted in "Perks That Work," *Time*, November 9, 1998, p. 86.
15. Lyman W. Porter and Edward E. Lawler, *Managerial Attitudes and Performance* (Homewood, Ill.: Dorsey Press, 1968).
16. See Terence R. Mitchell, "Expectancy Models of Job Satisfaction, Occupational Preference, and Effort: A Theoretical, Methodological, and Empirical Appraisal," *Psychological Bulletin*, 1974, vol. 81, pp. 1096–1112; and John P. Campbell and Robert D. Pritchard, "Motivation Theory in Industrial and Organizational Psychology," in Marvin D. Dunnette (ed.), *Handbook of Industrial and Organizational Psychology* (Chicago: Rand McNally, 1976), pp. 63–130, for reviews.
17. Pinder, *Work Motivation and Organizational Behavior.*
18. Ibid.
19. Campbell and Pritchard, "Motivation Theory in Industrial and Organizational Psychology."
20. Pinder, *Work Motivation and Organizational Behavior.*
21. Ibid.
22. Nancy Adler, *International Dimensions of Organizational Behavior*, 3rd ed. (Boston: PWS-Kent, 1997).

**23.** David A. Nadler and Edward E. Lawler, "Motivation: A Diagnostic Approach," in J. Richard Hackman, Edward E. Lawler, and Lyman W. Porter (eds.), *Perspectives on Behavior in Organizations*, 2nd ed. (New York: McGraw-Hill, 1983), pp. 67–78.
**24.** S. H. Hulse, J. Deese, and H. Egeth, *The Psychology of Learning*, 7th ed. (New York: McGraw-Hill, 1992). See also Gib Akins, "Varieties of Organizational Learning," *Organizational Dynamics*, Autumn 1987, pp. 36–48.
**25.** Ivan P. Pavlov, *Conditional Reflexes* (New York: Oxford University Press, 1927).
**26.** Hulse, Deese, and Egeth, *The Psychology of Learning*. For recent perspectives, see also Douglas F. Cellar and Gerald V. Barrett, "Script Processing and Intrinsic Motivation: The Cognitive Sets Underlying Cognitive Labels," *Organizational Behavior and Human Decision Processes*, August 1987, pp. 115–135; and Max H. Bazerman and John S. Carroll, "Negotiator Cognition," in L. L. Cummings and Barry M. Staw (eds.), *Research in Organizational Behavior*, vol. 9 (Greenwich, Conn.: JAI Press, 1987), pp. 247–288.
**27.** See Robert Wood and Albert Bandura, "Social Cognitive Theory of Organizational Management," *Academy of Management Review*, July 1989, pp. 361–384.
**28.** Harry Binswanger "Volition as Cognitive Self-Regulation," *Organizational Behavior and Human Decision Processes*, 1991, vol. 50, pp. 154–178.
**29.** B. F. Skinner, *Science and Human Behavior* (New York: Macmillan, 1953), and *Beyond Freedom and Dignity* (New York: Knopf, 1972).
**30.** Fred Luthans and Robert Kreitner, *Organizational Behavior Modification and Beyond* (Glenview, Ill.: Scott, Foresman, 1985).
**31.** Ibid.
**32.** "Workers: Risks and Rewards," *Time*, April 15, 1991, pp. 42–43.
**33.** Ibid.
**34.** See Richard Arvey and John M. Ivancevich, "Punishment in Organizations: A Review, Propositions, and Research Suggestions," *Academy of Management Review*, April 1980, pp. 123–132, for a review of the literature on punishment.
**35.** Ibid.
**36.** W. R. Nord, "Beyond the Teaching Machine: The Neglected Area of Operant Conditioning in the Theory and Practice of Management," *Organizational Behavior and Human Performance*, 1969, vol. 4, pp. 375–401.
**37.** Ibid.
**38.** Quoted in "Net Pro," *Profiles*, November 1996, p. 42.
**39.** Wood and Bandura, "Social Cognitive Theory of Organizational Management."
**40.** H. M. Weiss, "Subordinate Imitation of Supervisory Behavior: The Role of Modeling in Organizational Socialization," *Organizational Behavior and Human Performance*, 1977, vol. 19, pp. 89–105.
**41.** Albert Bandura, *Principles of Behavior Modification* (New York: Holt, 1969). See also Henry P. Sims Jr. and Dennis Gioia, *The Thinking Organization* (San Francisco: Jossey-Bass, 1986).
**42.** For an interesting example, see Gregory E. Prussia and Angelo J. Kinicki, "A Motivational Investigation of Group Effectiveness Using Social-Cognitive Theory," *Journal of Applied Psychology*, April 1996, pp. 187–198.
**43.** Fred Luthans and Robert Kreitner, *Organizational Behavior Modification* (Glenview, Ill.: Scott, Foresman, 1975); Luthans and Kreitner, *Organizational Behavior Modification and Beyond.*
**44.** See David A. Harrison, Meghna Virick, and Sonja William, "Working Without a Net: Time, Performance, and Turnover under Maximally Contingent Rewards," *Journal of Applied Psychology*, 1996, vol. 81, no. 4, pp. 331–345.
**45.** Luthans and Kreitner, *Organizational Behavior Modification and Beyond.*
**46.** Alexander D. Stajkovic, "A Meta-analysis of the Effects of Organizational Behavior Modification on Task Performance, 1975–95," *Academy of Management Journal*, October 1997, pp. 1122–1149.
**47.** "At Emery Air Freight: Positive Reinforcement Boosts Performance," *Organizational Dynamics*, Winter 1973, pp. 41–50; W. Clay Hamner and Ellen P. Hamner, "Organizational Behavior Modification on the Bottom Line," *Organizational Dynamics*, Spring 1976, pp. 3–21.
**48.** Hamner and Hamner, "Organizational Behavior Modification on the Bottom Line," ibid.
**49.** Quoted in Garry M. Ritzky, "Turner Bros. Wins Safety Game with Behavioral Incentives," *HRMagazine*, June 1998, p. 80.
**50.** Edwin Locke, "The Myths of Behavior Mod in Organizations," *Academy of Management Review*, April 1977, pp. 543–553.
**51.** H. H. Kelley, *Attribution in Social Interaction* (Morristown, N.J.: General Learning Press, 1971).
**52.** See E. L. Deci, "Effects of Externally Mediated Rewards on Intrinsic Motivation," *Journal of Applied Psychology*, 1971, vol. 18, pp. 105–115. See also Paul C. Jordan, "Effects of an Extrinsic Reward on Intrinsic Motivation: A Field Experiment," *Academy of Management Journal*, June 1986, pp. 405–412.


## Chapter 7


*Quoted in "These Six Growth Jobs Are Dull, Dead-End, Sometimes Dangerous," *Wall Street Journal*, December 1, 1994, p. A8.
**1.** "These Six Growth Jobs Are Dull, Dead-End, Sometimes Dangerous," *Wall Street Journal*, December 1, 1994, pp. A1, A8; *Hoover's Handbook of American Business 1999* (Austin: Hoover's Business Press, 1999), pp. 1418–1419.
**2.** Ricky W. Griffin and Gary C. McMahan, "Motivation Through Job Design," in Jerald Greenberg (ed.), *Organizational Behavior: State of the Science* (New York: Lawrence Erlbaum and Associates, 1994), pp. 23–44.
**3.** Adam Smith, *An Inquiry into the Nature and Causes of the Wealth of Nations* (New York: Modern Library, 1937). Originally published in 1776.
**4.** Charles Babbage, *On the Economy of Machinery and Manufactures* (London: Charles Knight, 1832).

**5.** Frederick W. Taylor, *The Principles of Scientific Management* (New York: Harper & Row, 1911).
**6.** Quoted in "These Six Growth Jobs Are Dull, Dead-End, Sometimes Dangerous," *Wall Street Journal*, December 1, 1994, p. A1.
**7.** C. R. Walker and R. Guest, *The Man on the Assembly Line* (Cambridge, Mass.: Harvard University Press, 1952).
**8.** Jia Lin Xie and Gary Johns, "Job Scope and Stress: Can Job Scope Be Too High?" *Academy of Management Journal*, 1995, vol. 38, no. 5, pp. 1288–1309.
**9.** Ricky W. Griffin, *Task Design: An Integrative Approach* (Glenview, Ill.: Scott, Foresman, 1982).
**10.** "These Six Growth Jobs Are Dull, Dead-End, Sometimes Dangerous," pp. A1, A8, A9.
**11.** H. Conant and M. Kilbridge, "An Interdisciplinary Analysis of Job Enlargement: Technoogy, Cost, Behavioral Implications," *Industrial and Labor Relations Review*, 1965, vol. 18, no. 7, pp. 377–395.
**12.** Frederick Herzberg, "One More Time: How Do You Motivate Employees?" *Harvard Business Review*, January–February 1968, pp. 53–62; Frederick Herzberg, "The Wise Old Turk," *Harvard Business Review*, September–October 1974, pp. 70–80.
**13.** R. N. Ford, "Job Enrichment Lessons from AT&T," *Harvard Business Review*, January–February 1973, pp. 96–106.
**14.** E. D. Weed, "Job Enrichment 'Cleans Up' at Texas Instruments," in J. R. Maher (ed.), *New Perspectives in Job Enrichment* (New York: Van Nostrand, 1971).
**15.** Griffin, *Task Design;* Griffin and McMahan, "Motivation Through Job Design."
**16.** Robert J. House and L. Wigdor, "Herzberg's Dual-Factor Theory of Job Satisfaction and Motivation: A Review of the Evidence and a Criticism," *Personnel Psychology*, 1967, vol. 20, pp. 369–389.
**17.** J. Richard Hackman and Greg Oldham, "Motivation Through the Design of Work: Test of a Theory," *Organizational Behavior and Human Performance*, 1976, vol. 16, pp. 250–279. See also Michael A. Campion and Paul W. Thayer, "Job Design: Approaches, Outcomes, and Trade-Offs," *Organizational Dynamics*, Winter 1987, pp. 66–78.
**18.** Ibid.
**19.** J. Richard Hackman, "Work Design," in J. Richard Hackman and J. L. Suttle (eds.), *Improving Life at Work: Behavioral Science Approaches to Organizational Change* (Santa Monica, Calif.: Goodyear, 1977).
**20.** Griffin, *Task Design.*
**21.** Griffin, *Task Design.* See also Karlene H. Roberts and William Glick, "The Job Characteristics Approach to Task Design: A Critical Review," *Journal of Applied Psychology*, 1981, vol. 66, pp. 193–217; and Ricky W. Griffin, "Toward an Integrated Theory of Task Design," in Larry L. Cummings and Barry M. Staw (eds.), *Research in Organizational Behavior*, vol. 9 (Greenwich, Conn.: JAI Press, 1987), pp. 79–120.
**22.** Ricky W. Griffin, M. Ann Welsh, and Gregory Moorhead, "Perceived Task Characteristics and Employee Performance: A Literature Review," *Academy of Management Review*, October 1981, pp. 655–664.
**23.** John L. Cordery and Peter P. Sevastos, "Responses to the Original and Revised Job Diagnostic Survey: Is Education a Factor in Responses to Negatively Worded Items?" *Journal of Applied Psychology*, 1993, vol. 78, pp. 141–143.
**24.** Roberts and Glick, "The Job Characteristics Approach to Task Design."
**25.** For a recent discussion of these issues, see Timothy Butler and James Waldroop, "Job Sculpting," *Harvard Business Review*, September–October 1999, pp. 144–152.
**26.** Gerald Salancik and Jeffrey Pfeffer, "An Examination of Need-Satisfaction Models of Job Attitudes," *Administrative Science Quarterly*, 1977, vol. 22, pp. 427–456; Gerald Salancik and Jeffrey Pfeffer, "A Social Information Processing Approach to Job Attitudes and Task Design," *Administrative Science Quarterly*, 1978, vol. 23, pp. 224–253.
**27.** Salancik and Pfeffer, "A Social Information Processing Approach."
**28.** Joe Thomas and Ricky W. Griffin, "The Social Information Processing Model of Task Design: A Review of the Literature," *Academy of Management Review*, October 1983, pp. 672–682. See also Griffin, "Toward an Integrated Theory of Task Design."
**29.** Charles A. O'Reilly and D. F. Caldwell, "Informational Influence as a Determinant of Perceived Task Characteristics and Job Satisfaction," *Journal of Applied Psychology*, 1979, vol. 64, pp. 157–165; Ricky W. Griffin, "Objective and Social Sources of Information in Task Redesign: A Field Experiment," *Administrative Science Quarterly*, June 1983, pp. 184–200. See also Griffin, "Toward an Integrated Theory of Task Design," and Donald J. Campbell, "Task Complexity: A Review and Analysis," *Academy of Management Review*, January 1988, pp. 40–52.
**30.** "Offenders Can Spread Ill Will from the Top Down," *USA Today*, September 9, 1998, pp. B1, B2.
**31.** David J. Glew, Anne M. O'Leary-Kelly, Ricky W. Griffin, and David D. Van Fleet, "Participation in Organizations: A Preview of the Issues and Proposed Framework for Future Analysis," *Journal of Management*, 1995, vol. 21, no. 3, pp. 395–421.
**32.** John A. Wagner III, "Participation's Effects of Performance and Satisfaction: A Reconsideration of Research Evidence," *Academy of Management Review*, 1994, vol. 19, no. 2, pp. 312–330.
**33.** See Putai Jin, "Work Motivation and Productivity in Voluntarily Formed Work Teams: A Field Study in China," *Organizational Behavior and Human Decision Processes*, 1993, vol. 54, pp. 133–155, for an interesting example.
**34.** Quoted in "Herb Kelleher Has One Main Strategy: Treat Employees Well," *Wall Street Journal*, August 31, 1999, p. B1.

**35.** "9 to 5 Isn't Working Anymore," *Business Week*, September 20, 1999, pp. 94–98.
**36.** A. R. Cohen and H. Gadon, *Alternative Work Schedules: Integrating Individual and Organizational Needs* (Reading, Mass.: Addison-Wesley, 1978).
**37.** Quoted in "Perks That Work," *Time*, November 9, 1998, p. 88.

## Chapter 8

*Quoted in "New Hires Win Fast Raises in Accelerated Job Reviews," *Wall Street Journal*, October 6, 1998, p. B1.
**1.** "Your Year-End Review Doesn't Have to Be Quite That Horrible," *Wall Street Journal*, December 23, 1997, p. B1; "New Hires Win Fast Raises in Accelerated Job Reviews," *Wall Street Journal*, October 6, 1998, pp. B1, B16; Dick Grote, "Performance Appraisal Reappraisal," *Harvard Business Review*, January–February 2000, p. 21.
**2.** Jon R. Katzenbach and Jason A. Santamaria, "Firing Up the Front Line," *Harvard Business Review*, May–June 1999, pp. 107–117.
**3.** A. Bandura, *Social Learning Theory* (Englewood Cliffs, N.J.: Prentice Hall, 1977).
**4.** See Edwin A. Locke, "Toward a Theory of Task Performance and Incentives," *Organizational Behavior and Human Performance*, 1968, vol. 3, pp. 157–189.
**5.** Gary P. Latham and Gary Yukl, "A Review of Research on the Application of Goal Setting in Organizations," *Academy of Management Journal*, 1975, vol. 18, pp. 824–845.
**6.** Gary P. Latham and J. J. Baldes, "The Practical Significance of Locke's Theory of Goal Setting," *Journal of Applied Psychology*, 1975, vol. 60, pp. 187–191.
**7.** Latham and Yukl, "A Review of Research on the Application of Goal Setting in Organizations."
**8.** Mark E. Tubbs, "Commitment as a Moderator of the Goal-Performance Relation: A Case for Clearer Construct Definition," *Journal of Applied Psychology*, 1993, vol. 78, pp. 86–97.
**9.** See Stephen J. Carroll and Henry L. Tosi, *Management by Objectives* (New York: Macmillan, 1973).
**10.** Robert Rodgers, John E. Hunter, and Deborah L. Rogers, "Influence of Top Management Commitment on Management Program Success," *Journal of Applied Psychology*, 1993, vol. 78, pp. 151–155.
**11.** Quoted in Jim Collins, "Turning Goals Into Results: The Power of Catalytic Mechanisms," *Harvard Business Review*, July–August 1999, p. 72.
**12.** H. John Bernardin and Richard W. Beatty, *Performance Appraisal: Assessing Human Behavior at Work* (Boston: Kent, 1984).
**13.** Michael M. Harris, David E. Smith, and Denise Champagne, "A Field Study of Performance Appraisal Purpose: Research Versus Administrative-Based Ratings," *Personnel Psychology*, Spring 1995, pp. 151–160.
**14.** Bernardin and Beatty, *Performance Appraisal: Assessing Human Behavior at Work.*
**15.** Quoted in "Performance Reviews: Some Bosses Try a Fresh Approach," *Wall Street Journal*, December 1, 1998, p. B1.
**16.** James M. Conway, "Analysis and Design of Multitrait-Multirater Performance Appraisal Studies," *Journal of Management*, vol. 22, no. 1, pp. 139–162.
**17.** Robert Hoffman, "Ten Reasons You Should Be Using 360-Degree Feedback," *HRMagazine*, April 1995, pp. 82–90; David A. Waldman, Leanne E. Atwater, and David Antonioni, "Has 360 Degree Feedback Gone Amok?" *Academy of Management Executive*, 1998, vol. 12, no. 2, pp. 86–94.
**18.** Vanessa Urch Druskat and Steven B. Wolff, "Effects and Timing of Developmental Peer Appraisals in Self-Managing Work Groups," *Journal of Applied Psychology*, 1999, vol. 84, no. 1, pp. 58–74.
**19.** Rhonda Reger, Loren Gustafson, Samuel DeMarie, and John Mullane, "Reframing the Organization: Why Implementing Total Quality Is Easier Said Than Done," *Academy of Management Review*, 1994, vol. 19, no. 3, pp. 565–584.
**20.** Jai Ghorpade and Milton M. Chen, "Creating Quality-Driven Performance Appraisal Systems," *Academy of Management Executive*, 1995, vol. 9, no. 1, pp. 32–40.
**21.** Forest J. Jourden and Chip Heath, "The Evaluation Gap in Performance Perceptions: Illusory Perceptions of Groups and Individuals," *Journal of Applied Psychology*, 1996, vol. 81, no. 4, pp. 369–379.
**22.** Bernardin and Beatty, *Performance Appraisal: Assessing Human Behavior at Work.*
**23.** Peter Senge, *The Fifth Discipline* (New York: Free Press, 1993).
**24.** See Edward E. Lawler, *Pay and Organization Development* (Reading, Mass.: Addison-Wesley, 1981).
**25.** Theresa M. Welbourne and Luis R. Gomez-Mejia, "Gainsharing: A Critical Review and a Future Research Agenda," *Journal of Management*, 1995, vol. 21, no. 3, pp. 559–609.
**26.** Quoted in "Tight Labor Market Squeezes Pay Raises," *USA Today*, November 23, 1998, p. B1.
**27.** Alfred Rappaport, "New Thinking on How to Link Executive Pay with Performance," *Harvard Business Review*, March–April 1999, pp. 91–105.
**28.** "Rich Benefit Plan Gives GM Competitors Cost Edge," *Wall Street Journal*, March 21, 1996, pp. B1, B4.
**29.** "Painless Perks," *Forbes*, September 6, 1999, p. 138.
**30.** John R. Deckop, Robert Mangel, and Carol C. Cirka, "Getting More Than You Pay For: Organizational Citizenship Behavior and Pay-for-Performance Plans," *Academy of Management Journal*, 1999, vol. 42, no. 4, pp. 420–428.
**31.** Ricky W. Griffin and Michael W. Pustay, *International Business—A Managerial Perspective*, 2nd ed. (Reading, Mass.: Addison-Wesley, 1999).

## Chapter 9

*Quoted in "Workplace Demands Taking Up More Weekends," *USA Today*, April 24, 1998, p. 1B.

**1.** "Workplace Demands Taking Up More Weekends," *USA Today*, April 24, 1998, p. 1B.
**2.** For a recent review, see Richard S. DeFrank and John M. Ivancevich, "Stress on the Job: An Executive Update," *Academy of Management Executive*, 1998, vol. 12, no. 3, pp. 55–65.
**3.** See James C. Quick and Jonathan D. Quick, *Organizational Stress and Preventive Management* (New York: McGraw-Hill, 1984), for a review.
**4.** Hans Selye, *The Stress of Life* (New York: McGraw-Hill, 1976).
**5.** Ibid.
**6.** For example, see Steve M. Jex and Paul D. Bliese, "Efficacy Beliefs as a Moderator of the Impact of Work-Related Stressors: A Multilevel Study," *Journal of Applied Psychology*, 1999, vol. 84, no. 3, pp. 349–361.
**7.** Meyer Friedman and Ray H. Rosenman, *Type A Behavior and Your Heart* (New York: Knopf, 1974).
**8.** Quoted in "Stress in the Valley," *Forbes*, September 6, 1999, p. 208.
**9.** Ibid.
**10.** Joshua Fischman, "Type A on Trial," *Psychology Today*, February 1987, pp. 42–50.
**11.** "Prognosis for the 'Type A' Personality Improves in a New Heart Disease Study," *Wall Street Journal*, January 14, 1988, p. 27.
**12.** Susan C. Kobasa, "Stressful Life Events, Personality, and Health: An Inquiry into Hardiness, "*Journal of Personality and Social Psychology*, January 1979, pp. 1–11; Susan C. Kobasa, S. R. Maddi, and S. Kahn, "Hardiness and Health: A Prospective Study," *Journal of Personality and Social Psychology*, January 1982, pp. 168–177.
**13.** Professor Cooper's findings were reported by Carol Kleiman, *Chicago Times*, March 31, 1988, p. B1.
**14.** Debra L. Nelson and James C. Quick, "Professional Women: Are Distress and Disease Inevitable?" *Academy of Management Review*, April 1985, pp. 206–218; Todd D. Jick and Linda F. Mitz, "Sex Differences in Work Stress," *Academy of Management Review*, October 1985, pp. 408–420.
**15.** "Complex Characters Handle Stress Better," *Psychology Today*, October 1987, p. 26.
**16.** Jeffrey R. Edwards, "An Examination of Competing Versions of the Person-Environment Fit Approach to Stress," *Academy of Management Journal*, 1996, vol. 39, no. 2, pp. 292–339.
**17.** Selye, *Stress of Life.* See also Stephan J. Motowidlo, John S. Packard, and Michael R. Manning, "Occupational Stress: Its Causes and Consequences for Job Performance," *Journal of Applied Psychology*, 1986, vol. 71, pp. 618–629.
**18.** "Corporate Mergers Take a Toll on Employees in Lost Jobs and Family Strain," *Wall Street Journal*, September 9, 1986, p. 1.
**19.** Robert I. Sutton and Anat Rafaeli, "Characteristics of Work Stations as Potential Occupational Stressors," *Academy of Management Journal*, June 1987, pp. 260–276.
**20.** Quoted in "Some Employers Find Way to Ease Burden of Changing Shifts," *Wall Street Journal*, March 25, 1998, p. B1.
**21.** See Edward R. Kemery, Arthur G. Bedeian, Kevin W. Mossholder, and John Touliatos, "Outcomes of Role Stress: A Multisample Constructive Replication," *Academy of Management Journal*, June 1985, pp. 363–375, for a recent examination of the effects of role demands.
**22.** Robert L. Kahn, D. M. Wolfe, R. P. Quinn, J. D. Snoek, and R. A. Rosenthal, *Organizational Stress: Studies in Role Conflict and Role Ambiguity* (New York: Wiley, 1964).
**23.** For recent research in this area, see Donna L. Wiley, "The Relationship Between Work/Nonwork Role Conflict and Job-Related Outcomes: Some Unanticipated Findings," *Journal of Management*, Winter 1987, pp. 467–472; and Arthur G. Bedeian, Beverly G. Burke, and Richard G. Moffett, "Outcomes of Work-Family Conflict Among Married Male and Female Professionals," *Journal of Management*, September 1988, pp. 475–485.
**24.** See Donna M. Randall, "Multiple Roles and Organizational Commitment," *Journal of Organizational Behavior*, 1988, vol. 9, pp. 309–317.
**25.** See Gary M. Kaufman and Terry A. Beehr, "Interactions Between Job Stressors and Social Support: Some Counterintuitive Results," *Journal of Applied Psychology*, 1986, vol. 71, pp. 522–526, for an interesting study in this area.
**26.** David R. Frew and Nealia S. Bruning, "Perceived Organizational Characteristics and Personality Measures as Predictors of Stress/Strain in the Work Place," *Academy of Management Journal*, December 1987, pp. 633–646.
**27.** Quick and Quick, *Organizational Stress and Preventive Management.*
**28.** Thomas H. Holmes and Richard H. Rahe, "The Social Readjustment Rating Scale," *Journal of Psychosomatic Research*, 1967, vol. 11, pp. 213–218.
**29.** Evelyn J. Bromet, Mary A. Dew, David K. Parkinson, and Herbert C. Schulberg, "Predictive Effects of Occupational and Marital Stress on the Mental Health of a Male Workforce," *Journal of Organizational Behavior*, 1988, vol. 9, pp. 1–13.
**30.** Quick and Quick, *Organizational Stress and Preventive Management.* See also John M. Ivancevich and Michael T. Matteson, *Stress and Work: A Managerial Perspective* (Glenview, Ill.: Scott, Foresman, 1980).
**31.** Quick and Quick, *Organizational Stress and Preventive Management.*
**32.** Ibid.
**33.** Ibid.
**34.** Quoted in "The New Paternalism," *Forbes*, November 2, 1998, p. 70.
**35.** Quick and Quick, *Organizational Stress and Preventive Management.* See also "Stress: The Test Americans Are Failing," *Business Week*, April 18, 1988, pp. 74–76.
**36.** "Employers on Guard for Violence," *Wall Street Journal*, April 5, 1995, p. 3A; Joel H. Neuman and Robert A. Baron, "Workplace Violence and Workplace Aggression: Evidence Concerning Specific Forms, Potential Causes, and Preferred Targets," *Journal of Management*, 1998, vol. 24, no. 3, pp. 391–419.

**37.** Raymond T. Lee and Blake E. Ashforth, "A Meta-Analytic Examination of the Correlates of the Three Dimensions of Job Burnout," *Journal of Applied Psychology*, 1996, vol. 81, no. 2, pp. 123–133.
**38.** See Susan E. Jackson, Richard L. Schwab, and Randall S. Schuler, "Toward an Understanding of the Burnout Phenomenon," *Journal of Applied Psychology*, 1986, vol. 71, pp. 630–640; and Daniel W. Russell, Elizabeth Altmaier, and Dawn Van Velzen, "Job-Related Stress, Social Support, and Burnout Among Classroom Teachers," *Journal of Applied Psychology*, 1987, vol. 72, pp. 269–274.
**39.** Quick and Quick, *Organizational Stress and Preventive Management.* See also John M. Kelly, "Get a Grip on Stress," *HRMagazine*, February 1997, pp. 51–57.
**40.** John W. Lounsbury and Linda L. Hoopes, "A Vacation from Work: Changes in Work and Nonwork Outcomes," *Journal of Applied Psychology*, 1986, vol. 71, pp. 392–401.
**41.** "Overloaded Staffers Are Starting to Take More Time Off Work," *Wall Street Journal*, September 23, 1998, p. B1.
**42.** "Eight Ways to Help You Reduce the Stress in Your Life," *Business Week Careers*, November 1986, p. 78.
**43.** Daniel C. Ganster, Marcelline R. Fusilier, and Bronston T. Mayes, "Role of Social Support in the Experiences of Stress at Work," *Journal of Applied Psychology*, 1986, vol. 71, pp. 102–110.
**44.** Quoted in "Workplace Hazard Gets Attention," *USA Today*, May 5, 1998, p. 1B.
**45.** Randall S. Schuler and Susan E. Jackson, "Managing Stress Through PHRM Practices: An Uncertainty Interpretation," in K. Rowland and G. Ferris (eds.), *Research in Personnel and Human Resources Management* (Greenwich, Conn.: JAI Press, 1986), vol. 4, pp. 183–224.
**46.** Quick and Quick, *Organizational Stress and Preventive Management.*
**47.** Ibid.
**48.** Richard A. Wolfe, David O. Ulrich, and Donald F. Parker, "Employee Health Management Programs: Review, Critique, and Research Agenda," *Journal of Management*, Winter 1987, pp. 603–615.
**49.** "Workplace Hazard Gets Attention," *USA Today*, May 5, 1998, pp. 1B, 2B.
**50.** Linda Thiede Thomas and Daniel C. Ganster, "Impact of Family-Supportive Work Variables on Work–Family Conflict and Strain: A Control Perspective," *Journal of Applied Psychology*, 1995, vol. 80, no.1, pp. 6–15; Victoria J. Doby and Robert D. Caplan, "Organizational Stress as Threat to Reputation: Effects on Anxiety at Work and at Home," *Academy of Management Journal*, 1995, vol. 38, no. 4, pp. 1105–1123.
**51.** Quoted in "The Daddy Trap," *Business Week*, September 21, 1998, p. 56.
**52.** "Work and Family," *Business Week*, September 15, 1997, pp. 96–99. See also Robert Levering and Milton Moskowitz, "The 100 Best Companies to Work For," *Fortune*, January 10, 2000, pp. 82–110

### Chapter 10

*Quoted in Leigh Muzslay, "Phoning from Home Keeps Placement Firm Up to Speed," *Houston Business Journal*, July 2, 1999, p. 30.
**1.** Leigh Muzslay, "Phoning from Home Keeps Placement Firm Up to Speed," *Houston Business Journal*, July 2, 1999, pp. 30–31; Richard Thomas, "The World Is Your Office," *Management Today*, July 1999, pp. 78–82; Jill McCullough, "With Phones and Fax Machines, HR Types Take on Telecommuters," *Business First—Columbus*, August 13, 1999, pp. 8A–10A.
**2.** Charles A. O'Reilly III and Louis R. Pondy, "Organizational Communication," in Steven Kerr (ed.), *Organizational Behavior* (Columbus, Ohio: Grid, 1979), p. 121.
**3.** Otis W. Baskin and Craig E. Aronoff, *Interpersonal Communication in Organizations* (Santa Monica, Calif.: Goodyear, 1980), p. 2.
**4.** "How Merrill Lynch Moves Its Stock Deals All Around the World," *Wall Street Journal*, November 9, 1987, pp. 1, 8.
**5.** William J. Seiler, E. Scott Baudhuin, and L. David Shuelke, *Communication in Business and Professional Organizations* (Reading, Mass.: Addison-Wesley, 1982).
**6.** Jeanne D. Maes, Teresa G. Weldy, and Marjorie L. Icenogle, "A Managerial Perspective: Oral Communication Competency Is Most Important for Business Students in the Workplace," *Journal of Business Communication*, January 1997, pp. 67–80.
**7.** Melinda Knight, "Writing and Other Communication Standards in Undergraduate Business Education: A Study of Current Program Requirements, Practices, and Trends," *Business Communication Quarterly*, March 1999, p. 10.
**8.** Robert Nurden, "Graduates Must Master the Lost Art of Communication," *The European*, March 20, 1997, p. 24.
**9.** Silvan S. Tompkins and Robert McCarter, "What and Where Are the Primary Affects? Some Evidence for a Theory," *Perceptual and Motor Skills*, February 1964, pp. 119–158.
**10.** Robert T. Keller and Winfred E. Holland, "Communicators and Innovators in Research and Develoment Organizations," *Academy of Management Journal*, December 1983, pp. 742–749.
**11.** See Everett M. Rogers and Rekha Agarwala-Rogers, *Communication in Organizations* (New York: Free Press, 1976), for a brief review of the background and development of the source-message-channel-receiver model of communication.
**12.** Charles A. O'Reilly III, "Variations in Decision Makers' Use of Information Sources: The Impact of Quality and Accessibility of Information," *Academy of Management Journal*, December 1982, pp. 756–771.
**13.** Quoted in Cynthia L. Kemper, "Sacre Bleu! English as a Global Lingua Franca? Why English Is Rapidly Achieving Worldwide Status," *Communication World*, June–July 1999, p. 41.

**14.** See Richard L. Daft and Robert H. Lengel, "Information Richness: A New Approach to Managerial Behavior and Organization Design," in Barry M. Staw and L. L. Cummings (eds.), *Research in Organizational Behavior*, vol. 6 (Greenwich, Conn.: JAI Press, 1984), pp. 191–233, for further discussion of media and information richness.
**15.** See Janet Fulk and Brian Boyd, "Emerging Theories of Communication in Organizations," *Journal of Management*, 1991, pp. 407–446, for a good review of the research on choice of medium for message transmission.
**16.** Anat Rafaeli and Robert I. Sutton, "The Expression of Emotion in Organizational Life," in Larry L. Cummings and Barry M. Staw (eds.), *Research in Organizational Behavior*, vol. 11 (Greenwich, Conn.: JAI Press, 1989), pp. 1–42.
**17.** See Jerry C. Wofford, Edwin A. Gerloff, and Robert C. Cummins, *Organizational Communication* (New York: McGraw-Hill, 1977), for a discussion of channel noise.
**18.** Donald R. Hollis, "The Shape of Things to Come: The Role of IT," *Management Review*, June 1996, p. 62.
**19.** Quoted in "Like It or Not, You've Got Mail," *Business Week*, October 4, 1999, p. 184.
**20.** Barbara Ettorre, "Communications Breakdown," *Management Review*, June 1996, p. 10.
**21.** Jeremy Main, "Computers of the World, Unite!" *Fortune*, September 24, 1990, pp. 115–122.
**22.** Kym France, "Computer Commuting Benefits Companies," *Arizona Republic*, August 16, 1993, pp. E1, E4.
**23.** Don Tapscott, "Investigating the Electronic Office," *Datamation*, March 1982, pp. 130–138.
**24.** Thomas, "The World Is Your Office."
**25.** Oren Harari, "Turn Your Organization into a Hotbed of Ideas," *Management Review*, December 1995, pp. 37–39.
**26.** Paul S. Goodman and Eric D. Darr, "Exchanging Best Practices Through Computer-Aided Systems," *Academy of Management Executive*, May 1996, pp. 7–18.
**27.** Jenny C. McCune, "The Intranet: Beyond E-Mail," *Management Review*, November 1996, pp. 23–27.
**28.** See Daniel Katz and Robert L. Kahn, *The Social Psychology of Organizations*, 2nd ed. (New York: Wiley, 1978), for more about the role of organizational communication networks.
**29.** For good discussions of small-group communication networks and research on this subject, see Wofford, Gerloff, and Cummins, *Organizational Communication;* and Marvin E. Shaw, *Group Dynamics: The Psychology of Small Group Behavior*, 3rd ed. (New York: McGraw-Hill, 1981), pp. 150–161.
**30.** Peter R. Monge, Jane A. Edwards, and Kenneth K. Kirste, "Determinants of Communication Network Involvement: Connectedness and Integration," *Group & Organization Studies*, March 1983, pp. 83–112.
**31.** See Michael J. Glauser, "Upward Information Flow in Organizations: Review and Conceptual Analysis," *Human Relations*, August 1984, pp. 613–644; and Irving S. Shapiro, "Managerial Communication: The View from the Inside," *California Management Review*, Fall 1984, pp. 157–172.
**32.** "GM Boots Perot," *Newsweek*, December 15, 1986, pp. 56–62; Bruce H. Goodsite, "General Motors Attacks Its Frozen Middle," *IABC Communication World*, October 1987, pp. 20–23.
**33.** See R. Wayne Pace, *Organizational Communication: Foundations for Human Resource Development* (Englewood Cliffs, N.J.: Prentice Hall, 1983), for further discussion of the development of communication networks.
**34.** David Krackhardt and Lyman W. Porter, "The Snowball Effect: Turnover Embedded in Communication Networks," *Journal of Applied Psychology*, February 1986, pp. 50–55.
**35.** Monge, Edwards, and Kirste, "Determinants of Communication Network Involvement."
**36.** Karl E. Weick and Larry D. Browning, "Argument and Narration in Organizational Communication," *Journal of Management*, Summer 1986, pp. 243–259.
**37.** "Small Is Beautiful Now in Manufacturing," *Business Week*, October 22, 1984, pp. 152–156.
**38.** Pace, *Organizational Communication.*
**39.** Losana E. Boyd, "Why 'Talking It Out' Almost Never Works Out," *Nation's Business*, November 1984, pp. 53–54.
**40.** Robert A. Snyder and James H. Morris, "Organizational Communication and Performance," *Journal of Applied Psychology*, August 1984, pp. 461–465.
**41.** Keith Davis and John W. Newstrom, *Human Behavior at Work: Organizational Behavior*, 7th ed. (New York: McGraw-Hill, 1985), pp. 314–323.
**42.** Thomas J. Peters and Robert H. Waterman Jr., *In Search of Excellence: Lessons from America's Best-Run Companies* (New York: Harper & Row, 1982), p. 121.
**43.** Shari Caudron, "Monsanto Responds to Diversity," *Personnel Journal*, November 1990, pp. 72–78; "Trading Places at Monsanto," *Training and Development Journal*, April 1993, pp. 45–49.
**44.** Charles A. O'Reilly, "Individual and Information Overload in Organizations: Is More Necessarily Better?" *Academy of Management Journal*, December 1980, pp. 684–696.
**45.** James L. McKenney and F. Warren McFarlan, "The Information Archipelago—Maps and Bridges," *Harvard Business Review*, September–October 1982, pp. 109–119.
**46.** Michael Brody, "Listen to Your Whistleblower," *Fortune*, November 24, 1986, pp. 77–78.

### Chapter 11

*Quoted in Joe Torre with Henry Dreher, *Joe Torre's Ground Rules for Winners* (New York: Hyperion Press, 1999).
**1.** David A Kaplan, "Warm and Fuzzy Pinstripes: Tough Times for Yankee Haters: They're Great—and Lovable," *Newsweek*, November 8, 1999, p. 80; Michael Knisley, "The Best in the

Business," *Sporting News*, November 8, 1999, p. 14; Roger Rosenblatt, "Damn Lovables: If You Don't Like the Yankees, It's Very Possible You Don't Really Like Sports," *Sports Illustrated*, November 18, 1999, p. 78; Joe Torre with Henry Dreher, *Joe Torre's Ground Rules for Winners* (New York: Hyperion Press, 1999).

**2.** Blake E. Ashforth and Fred Mael, "Social Identity Theory and the Organization," *Academy of Management Review*, January 1989, pp. 20–39.

**3.** Marvin E. Shaw, *Group Dynamics: The Psychology of Small Group Behavior*, 3rd ed. (New York: McGraw-Hill, 1981).

**4.** Ibid., p. 11.

**5.** Gerald R. Ferris and Kendrith M. Rowland, "Social Facilitation Effects on Behavioral and Perceptual Task Performance Measures: Implications for Work Behavior," *Group & Organization Studies*, December 1983, pp. 421–438; Jeff Meer, "Loafing Through a Tough Job," *Psychology Today*, January 1985, p. 72.

**6.** J. Paul Sorrels and Bettye Myers, "Comparison of Group and Family Dynamics," *Human Relations*, May 1983, pp. 477–490.

**7.** Alfred W. Clark and Robert J. Powell, "Changing Drivers' Attitudes Through Peer Group Decision," *Human Relations*, February 1984, pp. 155–162.

**8.** Joseph P. Shapiro, "You Guys Are Outta Here!" *U.S. News & World Report*, September 13, 1999, p. 55.

**9.** Francis J. Yammarino and Alan J. Dubinsky, "Salesperson Performance and Managerially Controllable Factors: An Investigation of Individual and Work Group Effects," *Journal of Management*, 1990, vol. 16, pp. 87–106.

**10.** William L. Sparks, Dominic J. Monetta, and L. M. Simmons Jr., "Affinity Groups: Developing Complex Adaptive Organizations," working paper, The PAM Institute, Washington D.C., 1999.

**11.** "Detroit vs. the UAW: At Odds over Teamwork," *Business Week*, August 24, 1987, pp. 54–55.

**12.** Brian Dumaine, "Who Needs a Boss?" *Fortune*, May 7, 1990, pp. 52–60.

**13.** Shawn Tully, "The Vatican's Finances," *Fortune*, December 21, 1987, pp. 28–40.

**14.** Dominic J. Monetta, "The POWER of Affinity Groups," *Management Review*, November 1998, p. 70.

**15.** "Women at Work," *Business Week*, January 28, 1985, pp. 80–85.

**16.** Bernard M. Bass and Edward C. Ryterband, *Organizational Psychology*, 2nd ed. (Boston: Allyn & Bacon, 1979), pp. 252–254.

**17.** John P. Wanous, Arnon E. Reichers, and S. D. Malik, "Organizational Socialization and Group Development: Toward an Integrative Perspective," *Academy of Management Review*, October 1984, pp. 670–683.

**18.** Quoted in Charles Fishman, "Whole Foods Is All Teams," *Fast Company*, September 1998, p. 105.

**19.** Susan Long, "Early Integration in Groups: A Group to Join and a Group to Create," *Human Relations*, April 1984, pp. 311–332.

**20.** Wanous, Reichers, and Malik, "Organizational Socialization and Group Development."

**21.** Steven L. Obert, "Developmental Patterns of Organizational Task Groups: A Preliminary Study," *Human Relations*, January 1983, pp. 37–52.

**22.** Bass and Ryterband, *Organizational Psychology*, pp. 252–254.

**23.** Bernard M. Bass, "The Leaderless Group Discussion," *Psychological Bulletin*, September 1954, pp. 465–492.

**24.** Jill Lieber, "Time to Heal the Wounds," *Sports Illustrated*, November 2, 1987, pp. 86–91.

**25.** Connie J. G. Gersick, "Marking Time: Predictable Transitions in Task Groups," *Academy of Management Journal*, 1989, vol. 32, pp. 274–309.

**26.** James H. Davis, *Group Performance* (Reading, Mass.: Addison-Wesley, 1964), pp. 82–86.

**27.** Shaw, *Group Dynamics*.

**28.** Charles A. O'Reilly III, David F. Caldwell, and William P. Barnett, "Work Group Demography, Social Integration, and Turnover," *Administrative Science Quarterly*, March 1989, vol. 34, pp. 21–37.

**29.** Nancy Adler, *International Dimensions of Organizational Behavior*, 3rd ed. (Boston: PWS-Kent, 1997), pp. 132–133.

**30.** P. Christopher Earley, "Social Loafing and Collectivism: A Comparison of the United States and the People's Republic of China," *Administrative Science Quarterly*, 1989, pp. 565–581.

**31.** Shaw, *Group Dynamics*, pp. 173–177.

**32.** Davis, *Group Performance*, p. 73; Steven E. Markham, Fred Dansereau Jr., and Joseph A. Alutto, "Group Size and Absenteeism Rates: A Longitudinal Analysis," *Academy of Management Journal*, December 1982, pp. 921–927.

**33.** Nigel Nicholson (ed.), *The Blackwell Encyclopedic Dictionary of Organizational Behavior* (Cambridge, Mass.: Blackwell, 1995), p. 522.

**34.** Davis, *Group Performance*, p. 82.

**35.** Bass and Ryterband, *Organizational Psychology*, pp. 252–254.

**36.** Quoted in Todd Balf, "Wanna Score?" *Fast Company*, January 1999, p. 164.

**37.** Shaw, *Group Dynamics*, pp. 280–293.

**38.** Daniel C. Feldman, "The Development and Enforcement of Group Norms," *Academy of Management Review*, January 1984, pp. 47–53.

**39.** J. Richard Hackman, "Group Influence on Individuals," in Marvin D. Dunnette (ed.), *Handbook of Industrial and Organizational Psychology* (Chicago: Rand McNally, 1976), pp. 1455–1525.

**40.** John Tower, Edmund Muskie, and Brent Skowcroft, *The Tower Commission Report* (New York: joint publication of Bantam Books and Times Books, 1987); *Taking the Stand: The Testimony of Lieutenant Colonel Oliver L. North* (New York: Pocket Books, 1987).

**41.** Tower, Muskie, and Skowcroft, *The Tower Commission Report*, pp. 37–38.

**42.** L. Festinger, "Informal Social Communication," *Psychological Review*, September 1950, p. 274.

**43.** William E. Piper, Myriam Marrache, Renee Lacroix, Astrid M. Richardson, and Barry D. Jones, "Cohesion as a Basic Bond in Groups," *Human Relations,* February 1983, pp. 93–108.
**44.** Davis, *Group Performance,* pp. 78–81.
**45.** Joseph P. Shapiro, "You Guys Are Outta Here!"
**46.** Tower, Muskie, and Skowcroft, *The Tower Commission Report; Taking the Stand.*
**47.** Robert T. Keller, "Predictors of the Performance of Project Groups in R&D Organizations," *Academy of Management Journal,* December 1986, pp. 715–726.
**48.** Ibid.
**49.** Irving L. Janis, *Groupthink,* 2nd ed. (Boston: Houghton Mifflin, 1982), p. 9.
**50.** Blake E. Ashforth and Fred Mael, "Social Identity Theory and the Organization," *Academy of Management Review,* January 1989, pp. 20–39.
**51.** "Now That It's Cruising, Can Ford Keep Its Foot to the Gas?" *Business Week,* February 11, 1985, pp. 48–52; Reed E. Nelson, "The Strength of Strong Ties: Social Networks and Intergroup Conflict in Organizations," *Academy of Management Journal,* June 1989, pp. 377–401, reprinted by permission.
**52.** See Stephen P. Robbins, *Managing Organizational Conflict* (Englewood Cliffs, N.J.: Prentice Hall, 1974), for a good review.
**53.** Charles R. Schwenk, "Conflict in Organizational Decision Making: An Exploratory Study of Its Effects in For-Profit and Not-for-Profit Organizations," *Management Science,* April 1990, pp. 436–448.
**54.** Robbins, *Managing Organizational Conflict,* 1974.
**55.** Kenneth Thomas, "Conflict and Conflict Management," in Marvin Dunnette (ed.), *Handbook of Industrial and Organizational Psychology* (Chicago: Rand McNally, 1976), pp. 889–935.
**56.** Robert R. Blake, Herbert A. Shepard, and Jane S. Mouton, *Managing Intergroup Conflict in Industry* (Houston: Gulf, 1964).
**57.** Alfie Kohn, "How to Succeed Without Even Vying," *Psychology Today,* September 1986, pp. 22–28.
**58.** Andrew S. Grove, "How to Make Confrontation Work for You," *Fortune,* July 23, 1984, pp. 73–75.
**59.** "Ford of Canada Reaches Tentative Pact with Union Similar to Chrysler Contract," *Wall Street Journal,* October 2, 1987, p. 5; "What's Throwing a Wrench into Britain's Assembly Lines?" *Business Week,* February 29, 1988, p. 41.
**60.** Quoted in Joe Torre with Henry Dreher, *Joe Torre's Ground Rules for Winners* (New York: Hyperion Press, 1999), p. 89.
**61.** Janis, *Groupthink.*
**62.** Robbins, *Managing Organizational Conflict.*
**63.** Ibid.

## Chapter 12

**1.** Eric L. Trist and K. W. Bamforth, "Some Social and Psychological Consequences of the Longwall Method of Goal-Getting," *Human Relations,* February 1951, pp. 3–38; Jack D. Orsburn, Linda Moran, and Ed Musselwhite, with John Zenger, *Self-Directed Work Teams: The New American Challenge* (Homewood, Ill.: Business One Irwin, 1990).
**2.** Charles C. Manz and Henry P. Sims Jr., *Business Without Bosses: How Self-Managing Teams Are Building High-Performance Companies* (New York: Wiley, 1993), pp. 12–14.
*Quoted in Polly Labarre, "The Company Without Limits," *Fast Company,* September 1999, p. 170.
**3.** Polly Labarre, "The Company Without Limits," *Fast Company,* September 1999, pp. 160–186; Anthony Dovkants, "Global Corporate Report: P&O to Sell Bovis Arm to Lend Lease," *Wall Street Journal,* Europe Edition, October 5, 1999, p. 9; "Australia's Lend Lease on Track for 25th Year of Growth," *AsiaPulse News,* October 29, 1999, p100830u6329.
**4.** *The American Heritage Dictionary of the English Language,* 3rd ed. (Boston: Houghton Mifflin, 1992), pp. 800, 1842.
**5.** See Jon R. Katzenbach and Douglas K. Smith, *The Wisdom of Teams: Creating the High-Performance Organization* (Boston: Harvard Business School Press, 1993), p. 45.
**6.** Manz and Sims, *Business Without Bosses,* p. 1.
**7.** Katzenbach and Smith, *The Wisdom of Teams,* 3.
**8.** Richard S. Wellins, William C. Byham, and George R. Dixon, *Inside Teams* (San Francisco: Jossey-Bass, 1994), p. 327.
**9.** Ibid., p. 328.
**10.** Ibid., p. 329.
**11.** Quoted in John A. Byrne, "The Global Corporation Becomes the Leaderless Corporation," *Business Week,* August 30, 1999, p. 90.
**12.** Orsburn, Moran, Musselwhite, and Zenger, *Self-Directed Work Teams,* p. 15.
**13.** Wellins, Bynham, and Dixon, *Inside Teams,* p. 335.
**14.** Manz and Sims, *Business Without Bosses,* pp. 10–11.
**15.** Wellins, Bynham, and Dixon, *Inside Teams,* pp. 335–336.
**16.** Katzenbach and Smith, *The Wisdom of Teams,* pp. 184–189.
**17.** Manz and Sims, *Business Without Bosses,* pp. 74–76.
**18.** Nigel Nicholson (ed.), *Encyclopedic Dictionary of Organizational Behavior* (Cambridge, Mass.: Blackwell, 1995), p. 463.
**19.** Brian Dumaine, "The Trouble With Teams," *Fortune,* September 5, 1994.
**20.** Ibid.
**21.** Ibid.
**22.** Ibid.
**23.** Quoted in John A. Byrne, "The Global Corporation Becomes the Leaderless Corporation," *Business Week,* August 30, 1999, p. 90.
**24.** Ellen Hart, "Top Teams," *Management Review,* February 1996, pp. 43–47.
**25.** Dan Dimancescu and Kemp Dwenger, "Smoothing the Product Development Path," *Management Review,* January 1996, pp. 36–41
**26.** Orsburn, Moran, Musselwhite, and Zenger, *Self-Directed Work Teams,* p. 37.

**27.** Ibid.
**28.** Ibid., pp. 92–108.
**29.** Manz and Sims, *Business Without Bosses,* pp. 27–28.
**30.** Ibid., pp. 29–31.
**31.** Orsburn, Moran, Musselwhite, and Zenger, *Self-Directed Work Teams,* pp. 107–122.
**32.** Quoted in "Make Yourself a Leader," *Fast Company,* June 1999 (insert following p. 128).
**33.** Ibid., p. 130.
**34.** Manz and Sims, *Business Without Bosses,* p. 200.
**35.** Quoted in Polly Labarre, "The Company Without Limits," *Fast Company,* September 1999, p. 165.
**36.** Manz and Sims, *Business Without Bosses,* p. 200.

### Chapter 13

*Quoted in "The Boss," *Business Week,* August 2, 1999, pp. 76–84.
**1.** "The Boss," *Business Week,* August 2, 1999, pp. 76–84; *Hoover's Handbook of American Business 1999* (Austin: Hoover's Business Press, 1999), pp. 616–617.
**2.** Ralph M. Stogdill, *Handbook of Leadership* (New York: Free Press, 1974). See also Bernard Bass, *Bass and Stogdill's Handbook of Leadership,* 3rd ed. (Riverside, N.J.: Free Press, 1990); and "In Search of Leadership," *Business Week,* November 15, 1999, pp. 172–176.
**3.** See Gary Yukl and David D. Van Fleet, "Theory and Research on Leadership in Organizations," in M. D. Dunnette and L. M. Hough (eds.), *Handbook of Industrial and Organizational Psychology,* vol. 3 (Palo Alto, Calif.: Consulting Psychologists Press, 1992), pp. 148–197.
**4.** Arthur G. Jago, "Leadership: Perspectives in Theory and Research," *Management Science,* March 1982, pp. 315–336.
**5.** John W. Gardner, *On Leadership* (New York: Free Press, 1990).
**6.** Jay A. Conger, "Leadership: The Art of Empowering Others," *Academy of Management Executive,* August 1989, pp. 17–24.
**7.** See John P. Kotter, "What Leaders Really Do," *Harvard Business Review,* May–June 1990, pp. 103–111. See also Abraham Zaleznik, "Managers and Leaders: Are They Different?" *Harvard Business Review,* March–April 1992, pp. 126–135.
**8.** Quoted in "Some Managers Are More Than Bosses—They're Leaders, Too," *Wall Street Journal,* November 16, 1999, p. B1.
**9.** David D. Van Fleet and Gary A. Yukl, "A Century of Leadership Research," in D. A. Wren and J. A. Pearce II (eds.), *Papers Dedicated to the Development of Modern Management* (Chicago: Academy of Management, 1986), pp. 12–23.
**10.** Bass, *Bass and Stogdill's Handbook of Leadership,* 1990.
**11.** Shelly A. Kirkpatrick and Edwin A. Locke, "Leadership: Do Traits Matter?" *Academy of Management Executive,* May 1991, pp. 48–60; see also Robert J. Sternberg, "Managerial Intelligence: Why IQ Isn't Enough," *Journal of Management,* 1997, vol. 23, no. 3, pp. 475–493.
**12.** Russell L. Kent and Sherry E. Moss, "Effects of Sex and Gender Role of Leader Emergence," *Academy of Management Journal,* 1994, vol. 37, no. 5, pp. 1335–1346.
**13.** For example, see Sheila Puffer, "Understanding the Bear: A Portrait of Russian Business Leaders," *Academy of Management Executive,* 1994, vol. 8, no. 1, pp. 41–49.
**14.** "Korea's Samsung Plans Very Rapid Expansion into Autos, Other Lines," *Wall Street Journal,* March 2, 1995, pp. A1, A14.
**15.** Dong I. Jung and Bruce J. Avolio, "Effects of Leadership Style and Followers' Cultural Orientation on Performance in Group and Individual Task Conditions," *Academy of Management Journal,* 1999, vol. 42, no. 2, pp. 208–218.
**16.** Philip M. Podsakoff, Scott B. MacKenzie, Mike Ahearne, and William H. Bommer, "Searching for a Needle in a Haystack: Trying to Identify the Illusive Moderators of Leadership Behaviors," *Journal of Management,* 1995, vol. 21, no. 3, pp. 422–470.
**17.** Quoted in "In Search of Leadership," *Business Week,* November 15, 1999, p. 172.
**18.** Rensis Likert, *New Patterns of Management* (New York: McGraw-Hill, 1961).
**19.** Edwin Fleishman, E. F. Harris, and H. E. Burtt, *Leadership and Supervision in Industry* (Columbus: Bureau of Educational Research, Ohio State University, 1955).
**20.** See Edwin A. Fleishman, "Twenty Years of Consideration and Structure," in Edward A. Fleishman and James G. Hunt (eds.), *Current Developments in the Study of Leadership* (Carbondale: Southern Illinois University Press, 1973), pp. 1–40.
**21.** Fleishman, Harris, and Burtt, *Leadership and Supervision in Industry.*
**22.** See Robert R. Blake and Jane S. Mouton, *The Managerial Grid* (Houston: Gulf, 1964); Robert R. Blake and Anne Adams McCanse, *Leadership Dilemmas—Grid Solutions* (Houston: Gulf, 1991).
**23.** See L. L. Larson, J. G. Hunt, and R. N. Osborn, "The Great Hi-Hi Leader Behavior Myth: A Lesson from Occam's Razor," *Academy of Management Journal,* 1976, vol. 19, pp. 628–641; P. C. Nystrom, "Managers and the Hi-Hi Leader Myth," *Academy of Management Journal,* 1978, vol. 21, pp. 325–331.
**24.** See Gary A. Yukl, *Leadership in Organizations,* 3rd ed. (Englewood Cliffs, N.J.: Prentice Hall, 1994).
**25.** Quoted in "She's Jump-Starting Saturn," *USA Today,* February 9, 1999, p. 3B.
**26.** See Fred E. Fiedler, *A Theory of Leadership Effectiveness* (New York: McGraw-Hill, 1967).
**27.** Fred E. Fiedler, "The Effects of Leadership Training and Experience: A Contingency Model Interpretation," *Administrative Science Quarterly,* December 1972, p. 455. Used by permission of *Administrative Science Quarterly.* Copyright © 1972 Cornell University. All rights reserved.
**28.** From Fred E. Fiedler, *A Theory of Leadership Effectiveness* (New York: McGraw-Hill, 1967). Reprinted by permission of the author.

**29.** See Chester A. Schriesheim, B. D. Bannister, and W. H. Money, "Psychometric Properties of the LPC Scale: An Extension of Rice's Review," *Academy of Management Review*, April 1979, pp. 287–294.
**30.** See Fred E. Fiedler, "Engineering the Job to Fit the Manager," *Harvard Business Review*, September–October 1965, pp. 115–122.
**31.** See Fred E. Fiedler, Martin M. Chemers, and Linda Mahar, *Improving Leadership Effectiveness: The Leader Match Concept* (New York: Wiley, 1976).
**32.** Chester A. Schriesheim, Bennett J. Tepper, and Linda A. Tetrault, "Least Preferred Co-Worker Score, Situational Control, and Leadership Effectiveness: A Meta-Analysis of Contingency Model Performance Predictions," *Journal of Applied Psychology*, 1994, vol. 79, no. 4, pp. 561–573.
**33.** See Martin G. Evans, "The Effects of Supervisory Behavior on the Path-Goal Relationship," *Organizational Behavior and Human Performance*, May 1970, pp. 277–298; Robert J. House, "A Path-Goal Theory of Leadership Effectiveness," *Administrative Science Quarterly*, September 1971, pp. 321–339; Robert J. House and Terence R. Mitchell, "Path-Goal Theory of Leadership," *Journal of Contemporary Business*, Autumn 1974, pp. 81–98.
**34.** See House and Mitchell, "Path-Goal Theory of Leadership."
**35.** See Terence R. Mitchell, "Motivation and Participation: An Integration," *Academy of Management Journal*, June 1973, pp. 160–179.
**36.** "Woman with a Mission," *Forbes*, September 25, 1995, pp. 172–173.
**37.** J. C. Wofford and Laurie Z. Liska, "Path-Goal Theories of Leadership: A Meta-Analysis," *Journal of Management*, 1993, vol. 19, no. 4, pp. 857–876.
**38.** See Victor H. Vroom and Philip H. Yetton, *Leadership and Decision Making* (Pittsburgh: University of Pittsburgh Press, 1973); Victor H. Vroom and Arthur G. Jago, *The New Leadership* (Englewood Cliffs, N.J.: Prentice Hall, 1988). *The New Leadership: Managing Participation in Organizations* by Vroom/Jago Eds. © 1988. Reprinted by permission of Prentice-Hall, Inc., Upper Saddle River, N.J.
**39.** Victor Vroom, "Leadership and the Decision-Making Process," *Organizational Dynamics* (Spring 2000).
**40.** Quoted in "Out of Tragedy at War, Lessons for Leaders on the Job," *Wall Street Journal*, August 15, 1999, p. B12.
**41.** Vroom and Jago, *The New Leadership.*
**42.** Vroom and Jago, *The New Leadership. The New Leadership: Managing Participation in Organizations* by Vroom/Jago Eds. © 1988. Reprinted by permission of Prentice-Hall, Inc., Upper Saddle River, N.J.
**43.** See R. H. George Field, "A Test of the Vroom-Yetton Normative Model of Leadership," *Journal of Applied Psychology*, February 1982, pp. 523–532; Madeline E. Heilman, Harvey A. Hornstein, Jack H. Cage, and Judith K. Herschlag, "Reaction to Prescribed Leader Behavior as a Function of Role Perspective: The Case of the Vroom-Yetton Model," *Journal of Applied Psychology*, February 1984, pp. 50–60.
**44.** George Graen and J. F. Cashman, "A Role-Making Model of Leadership in Formal Organizations: A Developmental Approach," in J. G. Hunt and L. L. Larson (eds.), *Leadership Frontiers* (Kent, Ohio: Kent State University Press, 1975), pp. 143–165; Fred Dansereau, George Graen, and W. J. Haga, "A Vertical Dyad Linkage Approach to Leadership Within Formal Organizations: A Longitudinal Investigation of the Role-Making Process," *Organizational Behavior and Human Performance*, 1975, vol. 15, pp. 46–78.
**45.** See Charlotte R. Gerstner and David V. Day, "Meta-Analytic Review of Leader-Member Exchange Theory: Correlates and Construct Issues," *Journal of Applied Psychology*, 1997, vol. 82, no. 6, pp. 827–844; Chester A. Schriesheim, Linda L. Neider, and Terri A. Scandura, "Delegation and Leader-Member Exchange: Main Effects, Moderators, and Measurement Issues," *Academy of Management Journal*, 1999, vol. 41, no. 3, pp. 298–318.
**46.** Paul Hersey and Kenneth H. Blanchard, *Management of Organizational Behavior: Utilizing Human Resources*, 3rd ed. (Englewood Cliffs, N. J.: Prentice Hall, 1977).

## Chapter 14

**1.** "Getting Off Their McButts," *Business Week*, February 22, 1999, pp. 84–88 (quote on p. 84); *Hoover's Handbook of American Business 1999* (Austin: Hoover's Business Press, 1999), pp. 940–941.
**2.** See Bernard Keys and Thomas Case, "How to Become an Influential Manager," *Academy of Management Executive*, November 1990, pp. 38–51.
**3.** Robert W. Allen and Lyman W. Porter (eds.), *Organizational Influence Processes* (Glenview, Ill.: Scott, Foresman, 1983).
**4.** Alan L. Frohman, "The Power of Personal Initiative," *Organizational Dynamics*, Winter 1997, pp. 39–48. See also James H. Dulebohn and Gerald R. Ferris, "The Role of Influence Tactics in Perceptions of Performance Evaluations' Fairness," *Academy of Management Journal*, 1999, vol. 42, no. 3, pp. 288–303.
**5.** Gary Yukl and J. Bruce Tracey, "Consequences of Influence Tactics Used with Subordinates, Peers, and the Boss," *Journal of Applied Psychology*, 1992, vol. 77, no. 4, pp. 525–535.
**6.** Quoted in Thomas A. Stewart, "Get With the New Power Game," *Fortune*, January 13, 1997, p. 61.
**7.** See James MacGregor Burns, *Leadership* (New York: Harper & Row, 1978); and Karl W. Kuhnert and Philip Lewis, "Transactional and Transformational Leadership: A Constructive/Developmental Analysis," *Academy of Management Review*, October 1987, pp. 648–657.
**8.** Francis J. Yammarino and Alan J. Dubinsky, "Transformational Leadership Theory: Using Levels of Analysis to Determine Boundary Conditions," *Personnel Psychology*, 1994, vol. 47, pp. 787–800.
**9.** Badrinarayan Shankar Pawar and Kenneth K. Eastman, "The Nature and Implications of Contextual Influences on Transformational Leadership: A Conceptual Examination,"

*Academy of Management Review*, 1997, vol. 22, no. 1, pp. 80–109.
**10.** Shelley A. Kirkpatrick and Edwin A. Locke, "Direct and Indirect Effects of Three Core Charismatic Leadership Components on Performance and Attitudes," *Journal of Applied Psychology*, 1996, vol. 81, no. 1, pp. 36–51.
**11.** Quoted in Curtis Sittenfeld, "Leader on the Edge," *Fast Company*, October 1999, p. 220.
**12.** See Robert J. House, "A 1976 Theory of Charismatic Leadership," in J. G. Hunt and L. L. Larson (eds.), *Leadership: The Cutting Edge* (Carbondale: Southern Illinois University Press, 1977), pp. 189–207. See also Jay A. Conger and Rabindra N. Kanungo, "Toward a Behavioral Theory of Charismatic Leadership in Organizational Settings," *Academy of Management Review*, October 1987, pp. 637–647.
**13.** Kenneth Labich, "Is Herb Kelleher America's Best CEO?" *Fortune*, May 2, 1994, pp. 44–52.
**14.** David A. Nadler and Michael L. Tushman, "Beyond the Charismatic Leader: Leadership and Organizational Change," *California Management Review*, Winter 1990, pp. 77–97.
**15.** David A. Waldman and Francis J. Yammarino, "CEO Charismatic Leadership: Levels-of-Management and Levels-of-Analysis Effects," *Academy of Management Review*, 1999, vol. 24, no. 2, pp. 266–285.
**16.** See Jay A. Conger and Rabindra N. Kanungo, "Charismatic Leadership in Organizations: Perceived Behavioral Attributes and Their Measurement," *Journal of Organizational Behavior*, 1994, vol. 15, pp. 439–452.
**17.** Daniel Sankowsky, "The Charismatic Leader as Narcissist: Understanding the Abuse of Power," *Organizational Dynamics*, Summer 1995, pp. 57–67.
**18.** See Steven Kerr and John M. Jermier, "Substitutes for Leadership: Their Meaning and Measurement," *Organizational Behavior and Human Performance*, 1978, vol. 22, pp. 375–403. See also Charles C. Manz and Henry P. Sims Jr., "Leading Workers to Lead Themselves: The External Leadership of Self-Managing Work Teams," *Administrative Science Quarterly*, March 1987, pp. 106–129.
**19.** Jon P. Howell, David E. Bowen, Peter W. Dorfman, Steven Kerr, and Philip Podsakoff, "Substitutes for Leadership: Effective Alternatives to Ineffective Leadership," *Organizational Dynamics*, Summer 1990, pp. 20–38. See also Philip M. Podsakoff, Scott B. Mackenzie, and William H. Bommer, "Transformational Leader Behaviors and Substitutes for Leadership as Determinants of Employee Satisfaction, Commitment, Trust, and Organizational Citizenship Behaviors," *Journal of Management*, 1996, vol. 22, no. 2, pp. 259–298.
**20.** Manz and Sims, "Leading Workers to Lead Themselves." See also Dean W. Tjosvold and Mary M. Tjosvold, *Leading the Team Organization* (New York: Lexington Books, 1991); and Susan G. Cohen, Lei Chang, and Gerald E. Ledford Jr., "A Hierarchical Construct of Self-Management Leadership and Its Relationship to Quality of Work Life and Perceived Work Group Effectiveness," *Personnel Psychology*, 1997, vol. 50, pp. 275–289.
**21.** Quoted in Keith H. Hammonds, "The Monroe Doctrine," *Fast Company*, October 1999, p. 232.
**22.** For reviews of the meaning of power, see Jeffrey Pfeffer, *Power in Organizations* (Marshfield, Mass.: Pitman Publishing, 1981); John Kenneth Galbraith, *The Anatomy of Power* (Boston: Houghton Mifflin, 1983); Henry Mintzberg, *Power in and Around Organizations* (Englewood Cliffs, N.J.: Prentice Hall, 1983); Gary A. Yukl, *Leadership in Organizations*, 3rd ed. (Englewood Cliffs, N.J.: Prentice Hall, 1994).
**23.** Stewart, "Get With the New Power Game," pp. 58–62.
**24.** John R. P. French and Bertram Raven, "The Bases of Social Power," in Darwin Cartwright (ed.), *Studies in Social Power* (Ann Arbor: University of Michigan Press, 1959, pp. 150–167. See also Philip M. Podsakoff and Chester A. Schriesheim, "Field Studies of French and Raven's Bases of Power: Critique, Reanalysis, and Suggestions for Future Research," *Psychological Bulletin*, 1985, vol. 97, pp. 387–411
**25.** Quoted in "Hard-Driving Boss," *Business Week*, October 5, 1998, p. 84
**26.** Jay A. Conger, "The Necessary Art of Persuasion," *Harvard Business Review*, May–June 1998, pp. 84–95.
**27.** Yukl, *Leadership in Organizations*, Chapter 10.
**28.** See also Thomas A. Stewart, "New Ways to Exercise Power," *Fortune*, November 6, 1989, pp. 52–64.
**29.** French and Raven, "Bases of Social Power."
**30.** Pfeffer, *Power in Organizations*.
**31.** Christopher P. Parker, Robert L. Dipboye, and Stacy L. Jackson, "Perceptions of Organizational Politics: An Investigation of Antecedents and Consequences," *Journal of Management*, 1995, vol. 21, no. 5, pp. 891–912.
**32.** Victor Murray and Jeffrey Gandz, "Games Executives Play: Politics at Work," *Business Horizons*, December 1980, pp. 11–23. See also Jeffrey Gandz and Victor Murray, "The Experience of Workplace Politics," *Academy of Management Journal*, June 1980, pp. 237–251.
**33.** See Stefanie Ann Lenway and Kathleen Rehbein, "Leaders, Followers, and Free Riders: An Empirical Test of Variation in Corporate Political Involvement," *Academy of Management Journal*, December 1991, pp. 893–905.
**34.** Gerald F. Cavanaugh, Dennis J. Moberg, and Manuel Valasquez, "The Ethics of Organizational Politics," *Academy of Management Review*, July 1981, pp. 363–374.
**35.** Pfeffer, *Power in Organizations*.
**36.** Robert H. Miles, *Macro Organizational Behavior* (Glenview, Ill.: Scott, Foresman, 1980). See also Carrie R. Leana, "Power Relinquishment Versus Power Sharing: Theoretical Clarification and Empirical Comparison of Delegation and Participation," *Journal of Applied Psychology*, 1987, vol. 72, pp. 228–233.

**37.** Timothy A. Judge and Robert D. Bretz Jr., "Political Influence Behavior and Career Success," *Journal of Management*, 1994, vol. 20, no. 1, pp. 43–65.
**38.** Pfeffer, *Power in Organizations;* Mintzberg, *Power in and Around Organizations.*
**39.** The techniques in Figure 13.5 are based on Pfeffer, *Power in Organizations;* Galbraith, *Anatomy of Power;* and Mintzberg, *Power in and Around Organizations.*
**40.** Michael Macoby, *The Gamesman* (New York: Simon & Schuster, 1976).
**41.** "How the 2 Top Officials of Grace Wound Up in a Very Dirty War," *Wall Street Journal,* May 18, 1995, pp. Al, A8.
**42.** See Elizabeth Wolf Morrison and Robert J. Bies, "Impression Management in the Feedback-Seeking Process: A Literature Review and Research Agenda," *Academy of Management Review,* July 1991, pp. 522–541; and William L. Gardner, "Lessons in Organizational Dramaturgy: The Art of Impression Management," *Organizational Dynamics,* Summer 1992, pp. 51–63.

## Chapter 15,

*Quoted in Patricia Sellers, "Crunch Time for Coke," *Fortune*, July 19, 1999, p. 74.
**1.** Dean Foust, Geri Smith, and David Ricks, "Man on the Spot," *Business Week,* May 3, 1999, pp. 142–151; William Echikson and David Rocks, "The Name Coke Now Scares People," *Business Week,* July 5, 1999, p. 32; Patricia Sellers, "Crunch Time for Coke," *Fortune,* July 19, 1999, pp. 72–78; and Dean Foust, David Rocks, Manjeet Kripalani, "Doug Daft Isn't Sugar-coating Things," *Business Week,* February 7, 2000, pp. 36–37.
**2.** Herbert Simon, *The New Science of Management Decision* (New York: Harper & Row, 1960), p. 1.
**3.** Simon, *The New Science of Management Decision.*
**4.** Quoted in Thomas A. Stewart, Alex Taylor III, Peter Petre, and Brent Schlender, "Henry Ford, Alfred P. Sloan, Tom Watson Jr., "Bill Gates: The Businessman of the Century," *Fortune,* November 22, 1999, p. 118.
**5.** Nandini Rajagopalan, Abdul M. A. Rasheed, and Deepak K. Datta, "Strategic Decision Processes: Critical Review and Future Directions," *Journal of Management,* vol. 19, no. 2, Summer 1993, pp. 349–384.
**6.** See Bernard M. Bass, *Organizational Decision Making* (Homewood, Ill.: Irwin, 1983), pp. 13–15, for a discussion of poorly structured and well-structured problems.
**7.** See George P. Huber, *Managerial Decision Making* (Glenview, Ill.: Scott, Foresman, 1980), pp. 90–115, for a discussion of decision making under conditions of certainty, risk, and uncertainty.
**8.** See Bass, *Organizational Decision Making,* pp. 83–89, for a discussion of uncertainty.
**9.** See Bass, *Organizational Decision Making,* pp. 27–31, on the economic theory of the firm.
**10.** Quoted in Anna Muoio, "Idea Summit," *Fast Company,* January–February 2000, p. 156.
**11.** "'90s Style Brainstorming," *Forbes ASAP,* October 25, 1993, pp. 44–61.
**12.** Henry Mintzberg, Duru Raisinghani, and Andre Thoret, "The Structure of 'Unstructured' Decision Processes," *Administrative Science Quarterly,* June 1976, pp. 246–275; Milan Zeleny, "Descriptive Decision Making and Its Application," *Applications of Management Science,* 1981, vol. 1, pp. 327–388.
**13.** See E. Frank Harrison, *The Managerial Decision-Making Process,* 5th ed. (Boston: Houghton Mifflin, 1999), pp. 55–60, for more on choice processes.
**14.** Ari Ginsberg and N. Ventrakaman, "Contingency Perspectives of Organizational Strategy: A Critical Review of the Empirical Research," *Academy of Management Review,* July 1985, pp. 412–434; Donald C. Hambrick and David Lei, "Toward an Empirical Prioritization of Contingency Variables for Business Strategy," *Academy of Management Journal,* December 1985, pp. 763–788.
**15.** Leon Festinger, *A Theory of Cognitive Dissonance* (Palo Alto, Calif.: Stanford University Press, 1957).
**16.** Patricia Sellers, "The Dumbest Marketing Ploys," *Fortune,* October 5, 1992, pp. 88–94.
**17.** See Harrison, *The Managerial Decision-Making Process,* pp. 74–100, for more on the rational approach to decision making.
**18.** See Paul C. Nutt, "The Formulation Processes and Tactics Used in Organizational Decision Making," *Organization Science,* 1993, vol. 4, no. 2, pp. 226–236.
**19.** Craig D. Parks and Rebecca Cowlin, "Group Discussion as Affected by Number of Alternatives and by a Time Limit," *Organizational Behavior and Human Decision Processes,* 1995, vol. 62, no. 3, pp. 267–275.
**20.** See James G. March and Herbert A. Simon, *Organizations* (New York: Wiley, 1958), for more on the concept of bounded rationality.
**21.** Herbert A. Simon, *Administrative Behavior: A Study of Decision Making Processes in Administrative Organizations,* 3rd ed. (New York: Free Press, 1976).
**22.** Richard M. Cyert and James G. March, *A Behavioral Theory of the Firm* (Englewood Cliffs, N.J.: Prentice Hall, 1963), p. 113; Simon, *Administrative Behavior.*
**23.** Kathleen M. Eisenhardt, "Making Fast Strategic Decisions in High-Velocity Environments," *Academy of Management Journal,* September 1989, pp. 543–576.
**24.** Irving L. Janis and Leon Mann, *Decision Making: A Psychological Analysis of Conflict, Choice, and Commitment* (New York: Free Press, 1977).
**25.** Quoted in "Internet Defense Strategy: Cannibalize Yourself," *Fortune,* September 6, 1999, p. 128.
**26.** Jerry Ross and Barry M. Staw, "Expo 86: An Escalation Prototype," *Administrative Science Quarterly,* June 1986, pp. 274–297.
**27.** Barry M. Staw, "Escalation of Commitment to a Course of Action," *Academy of Management Review,* October 1981, pp. 577–587.
**28.** Joel Brockner, Robert Houser, Gregg Birnbaum, Kathy Lloyd, Janet Dietcher, Sinaia Nathanson, and

Jeffrey Z. Rubin, "Escalation of Commitment to an Ineffective Course of Action: The Effect of Feedback Having Negative Implications for Self-Identity," *Administrative Science Quarterly*, March 1986, pp. 109–126.

**29.** Barry M. Staw and Jerry Ross, "Good Money After Bad," *Psychology Today*, February 1988, pp. 30–33.

**30.** M. A. Wallach, N. Kogan, and D. J. Bem, "Group Influence on Individual Risk Taking," *Journal of Abnormal and Social Psychology*, August 1962, pp. 75–86; James A. F. Stoner, "Risky and Cautious Shifts in Group Decisions: The Influence of Widely Held Values," *Journal of Experimental Social Psychology*, October 1968, pp. 442–459.

**31.** Dorwin Cartwright, "Risk Taking by Individuals and Groups: An Assessment of Research Employing Choice Dilemmas," *Journal of Personality and Social Psychology*, December 1971, pp. 361–378.

**32.** S. Moscovici and M. Zavalloni, "The Group as a Polarizer of Attitudes," *Journal of Personality and Social Psychology*, June 1969, pp. 125–135.

**33.** See Marvin E. Shaw, *Group Dynamics: The Psychology of Small Group Behavior* (New York: McGraw-Hill, 1981), pp. 68–76, for further discussion of group polarization.

**34.** Irving L. Janis, *Groupthink*, 2nd ed. (Boston: Houghton Mifflin, 1982), p. 9.

**35.** Gregory Moorhead, Christopher P. Neck, and Mindy West, "The Tendency Toward Defective Decision Making Within Self-Managing Teams: Relevance of Groupthink for the 21st Century," *Organizational Behavior and Human Decision Processes*, February/March 1998, pp. 327–351.

**36.** Gregory Moorhead, Richard Ference, and Chris P. Neck, "Group Decision Fiascoes Continue: Space Shuttle Challenger and a Revised Groupthink Framework," *Human Relations*, 1991, vol. 44, pp. 539–550.

**37.** Irving L. Janis, *Victims of Groupthink* (Boston: Houghton Mifflin, 1972), pp. 197–198.

**38.** Janis, *Groupthink*.

**39.** Moorhead, Ference, and Neck, "Group Decision Fiascoes Continue."

**40.** Janis, *Groupthink*, pp. 193–197; Gregory Moorhead, "Groupthink: Hypothesis in Need of Testing," *Group & Organization Studies*, December 1982, pp. 429–444.

**41.** Gregory Moorhead and John R. Montanari, "Empirical Analysis of the Groupthink Phenomenon," *Human Relations*, May 1986, pp. 399–410; John R. Montanari and Gregory Moorhead, "Development of the Groupthink Assessment Inventory," *Educational and Psychological Measurement*, Spring 1989, pp. 209–219.

**42.** Janis, *Groupthink*.

**43.** Fredrick W. Taylor, *The Principles of Scientific Management* (New York: Harper & Row, 1911).

**44.** Chris Argyris, *Personality and Organization* (New York: Harper & Row, 1957); Rensis Likert, *New Patterns of Management* (New York: McGraw-Hill, 1961).

**45.** Lester Coch and John R. P. French, "Overcoming Resistance to Change," *Human Relations*, 1948, vol. 1, pp. 512–532; N. C. Morse and E. Reimer, "The Experimental Change of a Major Organizational Variable," *Journal of Abnormal and Social Psychology*, January 1956, pp. 120–129.

**46.** See Marvin E. Shaw, *Group Dynamics*, pp. 57–68.

**47.** Quoted in Curtis Sittenfeld, "Powered by the People," *Fast Company*, July–August 1999, p. 189.

**48.** See Huber, *Managerial Decision Making*, pp. 140–148.

**49.** Victor Vroom, "Leadership and the Decision-Making Process," *Organizational Dynamics* (Spring 2000.)

**50.** See Carrie R. Leana, Edwin A. Locke, and David M. Schweiger, "Fact and Fiction in Analyzing Research on Participative Decision Making: A Critique of Cotton, Vollrath, Foggatt, Lengnick-Hall, and Jennings," *Academy of Management Review*, January 1990, pp. 137–146; John L. Cotton, David A. Vollrath, Mark L. Lengnick-Hall, and Mark L. Froggatt, "Fact: The Form of Participation Does Matter—A Rebuttal to Leana, Locke, and Schweiger," *Academy of Management Review*, January 1990, pp. 147–153.

**51.** See Bass, *Organizational Decision Making*, pp. 162–163, for further discussion of the nominal group technique.

**52.** See Huber, *Managerial Decision Making*, pp. 205–212, for more details on the Delphi technique.

**53.** J. Z. Rubin and B. R. Brown, *The Social Psychology of Bargaining and Negotiation* (New York: Academic Press, 1975).

**54.** R. J. Lewicki and J. A. Litterer, *Negotiation* (Homewood, Ill.: Irwin, 1985).

**55.** Howard Raiffa, *The Art and Science of Negotiation* (Cambridge, Mass.: Belknap, 1982).

**56.** K. H. Bazerman and M. A. Neale, *Negotiating Rationally* (New York: Free Press, 1992).

**57.** Ross R. Reck and Brian G. Long, *The Win-Win Negotiator* (Escondido, Calif.: Blanchard Training and Development, 1985).

### Chapter 16

*Quoted in Paul W. Beamish, "Sony's Yoshihide Nakamura on Structure and Decision Making," *Academy of Management Executive*, November 1999, p. 13.

**1.** Robert Triendl, "Sony Restructures to Embrace Digital Economy," *Research Technology Management*, September 1999, pp. 4–5; John Nathan, "Sony CEO's Management Style Wasn't 'Made in Japan,'" *Wall Street Journal*, Oct 7, 1999, Eastern edition, p. A30; Paul W. Beamish, "Sony's Yoshihide Nakamura on Structure and Decision Making," *Academy of Management Executive*, November 1999, pp. 12–16.

**2.** See Richard Daft, *Organization Theory and Design*, 2nd ed. (St. Paul, Minn.: West, 1986), p. 9, for further discussion of the definition of organization.

**3.** John R. Montanari, Cyril P. Morgan, and Jeffrey S. Bracker, *Strategic Management* (Hinsdale, Ill.: Dryden Press, 1990), pp. 1–2.

**4.** Quoted in Michael Moeller, Steve Hamm, and Timothy J. Mullaney, "Remaking Microsoft," *Business Week*, May 17, 1999, p. 106.

**5.** A. Bryman, A. D. Beardworth, E. T. Keil, and J. Ford, "Organizational Size and Specialization," *Organization Studies*, September 1983, pp. 271–278.
**6.** Joseph L. C. Cheng, "Interdependence and Coordination in Organizations: A Role System Analysis," *Academy of Management Journal*, March 1983, pp. 156–162.
**7.** See Henry Mintzberg, *The Structuring of Organizations* (Englewood Cliffs, N.J.: Prentice Hall, 1979), for further discussion of the basic elements of structure.
**8.** Max Weber, *The Theory of Social and Economic Organization*, trans. A. M. Henderson and Talcott Parsons (New York: Free Press, 1947).
**9.** Adam Smith, *An Inquiry into the Nature and Causes of the Wealth of Nations* (London: Dent, 1910).
**10.** Nancy M. Carter and Thomas L. Keon, "The Rise and Fall of the Division of Labour, the Past 25 Years," *Organization Studies*, 1986, pp. 54–57.
**11.** Glenn R. Carroll, "The Specialist Strategy," *California Management Review*, Spring 1984, pp. 126–137.
**12.** "Management Discovers the Human Side of Automation," *Business Week*, September 29, 1986, pp. 70–75.
**13.** See Robert H. Miles, *Macro Organizational Behavior* (Santa Monica, Calif.: Goodyear, 1980), pp. 28–34, for a discussion of departmentalization schemes.
**14.** Mintzberg, *The Structuring of Organizations*, p. 125.
**15.** Miles, *Macro Organizational Behavior*, pp. 122–133.
**16.** "Big Blue Wants to Loosen Its Collar," *Fortune*, February 29, 1988, p. 8; "Inside IBM: Internet Business Machines," *Business Week*, December 13, 1999, pp. EB20–28.
**17.** Ronald Henkoff, "Cost Cutting: How to Do It Right," *Fortune*, April 9, 1990, pp. 40–50.
**18.** Peggy Leatt and Rodney Schneck, "Criteria for Grouping Nursing Subunits in Hospitals," *Academy of Management Review*, March 1984, pp. 150–165.
**19.** Lyndall F. Urwick, "The Manager's Span of Control," *Harvard Business Review*, May–June 1956, pp. 39–47.
**20.** Dan R. Dalton, William D. Tudor, Michael J. Spendolini, Gordon J. Fielding, and Lyman W. Porter, "Organization Structure and Performance: A Critical Review," *Academy of Management Review*, January 1980, pp. 49–64.
**21.** Mintzberg, *The Structuring of Organizations*, pp. 133–147.
**22.** See David Van Fleet, "Span of Management Research and Issues," *Academy of Management Journal*, September 1983, pp. 546–552, for an example of research on span of control.
**23.** John R. Montanari and Philip J. Adelman, "The Administrative Component of Organizations and the Rachet Effect: A Critique of Cross-Sectional Studies," *Journal of Management Studies*, March 1987, pp. 113–123.
**24.** Quoted in Richard M. Hodgetts, "Dow Chemical's CEO William Stavropoulos on Structure and Decision Making," *Academy of Management Executive*, November 1999, p. 30.
**25.** D. A. Heenan, "The Downside of Downsizing," *Journal of Business Strategy*, November–December 1989, pp. 18–23.
**26.** Wayne F. Cascio, "Downsizing: What Do We Know? What Have We Learned?" *Academy of Management Executive*, February 1993, pp. 95–104.
**27.** Dalton et al., "Organization Structure and Performance."
**28.** See John Child, *Organization: A Guide to Problems and Practice*, 2nd ed. (New York: Harper & Row, 1984), pp. 145–153, for a detailed discussion of centralization.
**29.** Richard H. Hall, *Organization: Structure and Process*, 3rd ed. (Englewood Cliffs, N.J.: Prentice Hall, 1982), pp. 87–96.
**30.** "Can Jack Smith Fix GM?" *Business Week*, November 1, 1993, pp. 126–131; John McElroy, "GM's Brand Management Might Work," *Automotive Industries*, September 1996, p. 132.
**31.** Quoted in Alex Taylor III, "Compaq Looks Inside for Salvation," *Fortune*, August 16, 1999, p. 126.
**32.** Daniel R. Denison, "Bringing Corporate Culture to the Bottom Line," *Organizational Dynamics*, Autumn 1984, pp. 4–22.
**33.** Leonard W. Johnson and Alan L. Frohman, "Identifying and Closing the Gap in the Middle of Organizations," *Academy of Management Executive*, May 1989, pp. 107–114.
**34.** "The Selling of Acura—A Honda That's Not a Honda," *Business Week*, March 17, 1986, p. 93.
**35.** Brian S. Moskal, "Supervision (or Lack of It)," *Industry Week*, December 3, 1990, pp. 54–57; Roger Schreffler, "A Decade of Progress," *Automotive Industries*, November 1992, pp. 46–48; Alison Rogers, "GM vs. Honda: A Morality Tale," *Fortune*, February 8, 1993, pp. 11–12; "The Dangers of Running Too Lean," *Fortune*, June 14, 1993, pp. 114–116; Keith Naughton, "America's No. 1 Car Exporter Is Japan?" *Business Week*, February 26, 1996, p. 113.
**36.** Mintzberg, *The Structuring of Organizations*, pp. 83–84.
**37.** Arthur P. Brief and H. Kirk Downey, "Cognitive and Organizational Structures: A Conceptual Analysis of Implicit Organizing Theories," *Human Relations*, December 1983, pp. 1065–1090.
**38.** Jerald Hage, "An Axiomatic Theory of Organizations," *Administrative Science Quarterly*, December 1965, pp. 289–320.
**39.** Gregory Moorhead, "Organizational Analysis: An Integration of the Macro and Micro Approaches," *Journal of Management Studies*, April 1981, pp. 191–218.
**40.** J. Daniel Sherman and Howard L. Smith, "The Influence of Organizational Structure on Intrinsic Versus Extrinsic Motivation," *Academy of Management Journal*, December 1984, pp. 877–885.
**41.** John A. Pearce II and Fred R. David, "A Social Network Approach to Organizational Design-Performance," *Academy of Management Review*, July 1983, pp. 436–444.
**42.** Eileen Farihurst, "Organizational Rules and the Accomplishment of Nursing Work on Geriatric Wards," *Journal of Management Studies*, July 1983, pp. 315–332.

**43.** "Chevron Corp. Has Big Challenge Coping with Worker Cutbacks," *Wall Street Journal*, November 4, 1986, pp. 1, 25.
**44.** Neil F. Brady, "Rules for Making Exceptions to Rules," *Academy of Management Review*, July 1987, pp. 436–444.
**45.** Quoted in Patricia Sellers, "Crunch Time for Coke," *Fortune*, July 19, 1999, p. 78.
**46.** See Jeffrey Pfeffer, *Power in Organizations* (Boston: Pittman, 1981), pp. 4–6, for a discussion of the relationship between power and authority.
**47.** John B. Miner, *Theories of Organizational Structure* and Process (Hinsdale, Ill.: Dryden Press, 1982), p. 360.
**48.** "Management Lesson of Irangate," *Wall Street Journal*, March 24, 1987, p. 36.
**49.** Chester Barnard, *The Functions of the Executive* (Cambridge, Mass.: Harvard University Press, 1938), pp. 161–184.
**50.** Pfeffer, *Power in Organizations*, pp. 366–367.
**51.** Weber, *The Theory of Social and Economic Organization.*
**52.** For more discussion of these alternative views, see John B. Miner, *Theories of Organizational Structure and Process*, p. 386.
**53.** Quoted in Roger R. Klene, commentary on Paul S. Adler, "Building Better Bureaucracies," *Academy of Management Executive*, November 1999, pp. 36–47, 47–48.
**54.** Paul S. Adler, "Building Better Bureaucracies," *Academy of Management Executive*, November 1999, pp. 36–46.
**55.** This summary of the classic principles of organizing is based on Henri Fayol, *General and Industrial Management*, trans. Constance Storrs (London: Pittman, 1949); Miner, *Theories of Organizational Structure and Process*, pp. 358–381; and the discussions in Bedeian, *Organizations: Theory and Analysis*, 2nd ed. (Chicago: Dryden, 1984), pp. 58–59.
**56.** Miner, *Theories of Organizational Structure and Process*, pp. 358–381.
**57.** See Rensis Likert, *New Patterns of Management* (New York: McGraw-Hill, 1961); and Rensis Likert, *The Human Organization: Its Management and Value* (New York: McGraw-Hill, 1967), for a complete discussion of the human organization.
**58.** Miner, *Theories of Organizational Structure and Process*, pp. 17–53.

### Chapter 17

*Quoted in David Kirkland, "Superior Performance Is the Key to Independence," *Fortune*, August 16, 1999, p. 126.
**1.** Arik Hesseldahl, "Compaq Warns of Losses, Reorganizes," *Electronic News*, June 21, 1999, p. 16; Stewart Deck, "Compaq Counts Its Losses: Buildup of Enterprise Services Key in Rebound as Company Embarks on Major Reorganization," *Computerworld*, June 28, 1999, p. 30; "A Board Too Strong for Its Own Good?" *Business Week*, July 12, 1999, p. 36; David Kirkland, "Superior Performance Is the Key to Independence," *Fortune*, August 16, 1999, pp. 126–127; Alex Taylor III, "Compaq Looks Inside for Salvation," *Fortune*, August 16, 1999, pp. 124–127.
**2.** Quoted in "Sony Restructures to Embrace Digital Economy," *Research Technology Management*, September 1999, p. 4.
**3.** Lex Donaldson, "Strategy and Structural Adjustment to Regain Fit and Performance: In Defense of Contingency Theory," *Journal of Management Studies*, January 1987, pp. 1–24.
**4.** John R. Montanari, Cyril P. Morgan, and Jeffrey Bracker, *Strategic Management* (Hinsdale, Ill.: Dryden Press, 1990), p. 114.
**5.** See Arthur A. Thompson Jr. and A. J. Strickland III, *Strategic Management*, 3rd ed. (Plano, Tex.: Business Publications, 1984), pp. 19–27.
**6.** Alfred D. Chandler, *Strategy and Structure: Chapters in the History of the American Industrial Enterprise* (Cambridge, Mass.: MIT Press, 1962).
**7.** John R. Kimberly, "Organizational Size and the Structuralist Perspective: A Review, Critique, and Proposal," *Administrative Science Quarterly*, December 1976, pp. 571–597.
**8.** Peter M. Blau and Richard A. Schoenherr, *The Structure of Organizations* (New York: Basic Books, 1971).
**9.** The results of these studies are thoroughly summarized in Richard H. Hall, *Organizations: Structure and Process*, 3rd ed. (Englewood Cliffs, N.J.: Prentice Hall, 1982), pp. 89–94. For a recent study in this area, see John H. Cullen and Kenneth S. Anderson, "Blau's Theory of Structural Differentiation Revisited: A Theory of Structural Change or Scale?" *Academy of Management Journal*, June 1986, pp. 203–229.
**10.** "Small Is Beautiful Now in Manufacturing," *Business Week*, October 22, 1984, pp. 152–156.
**11.** Richard H. Hall, J. Eugene Haas, and Norman Johnson, "Organizational Size, Complexity, and Formalization," *American Sociological Review*, December 1967, pp. 903–912.
**12.** Catherine Arnst, "Downsizing Out One Door and in Another," *Business Week*, January 22, 1996, p. 41; Peter Elstrom, "Dial A for Aggravation," *Business Week*, March 11, 1996, p. 34; Alex Markels and Matt Murray, "Call It Dumbsizing: Why Some Companies Regret Cost-Cutting," *Wall Street Journal*, May 14, 1996, pp. A1, A5.
**13.** Robert I. Sutton and Thomas D'Anno, "Decreasing Organizational Size: Untangling the Effects of Money and People," *Academy of Management Review*, May 1989, pp. 194–212.
**14.** Joan Woodward, *Management and Technology: Problems of Progress in Industry*, no. 3 (London: Her Majesty's Stationery Office, 1958); Joan Woodward, *Industrial Organizations: Theory and Practice* (London: Oxford University Press, 1965).
**15.** Tom Burns and George M. Stalker, *The Management of Innovation* (London: Tavistock, 1961).
**16.** Charles B. Perrow, "A Framework for the Comparative Analysis of Organizations," *American Sociological Review*, April 1967, pp. 194–208.
**17.** James D. Thompson, *Organizations in Action* (New York: McGraw-Hill, 1967).

**18.** David J. Hickson, Derek S. Pugh, and Diana C. Pheysey, "Operations Technology and Organization Structure: An Empirical Reappraisal," *Administrative Science Quarterly*, September 1969, pp. 378–397.
**19.** Hickson, Pugh, and Pheysey, "Operations Technology and Organization Structure."
**20.** Andrew Kupfer, "How to Be a Global Manager," *Fortune*, March 14, 1988, pp. 52–58.
**21.** "Going Crazy in Japan—In a Break from Tradition, Tokyo Begins Funding a Program for Basic Research," *Wall Street Journal*, November 10, 1986, p. D20.
**22.** Quoted in Marc Gunther, "Eisner's Mouse Trap," *Fortune*, September 6, 1999, p. 114.
**23.** Richard L. Daft, *Organization Theory and Design*, 2nd ed. (St. Paul, Minn.: West, 1986), p. 55.
**24.** Robert B. Duncan, "Characteristics of Organizational Environments and Perceived Uncertainty," *Administrative Science Quarterly*, September 1972, pp. 313–327.
**25.** "Toy Makers Lose Interest in Tie-Ins with Cartoons," *Wall Street Journal*, April 28, 1988, p. 29.
**26.** Masoud Yasai-Ardekani, "Structural Adaptations to Environments," *Academy of Management Review*, January 1986, pp. 9–21.
**27.** John E. Prescott, "Environments as Moderators of the Relationship Between Strategy and Performance," *Academy of Management Journal*, June 1986, pp. 329–346.
**28.** Timothy M. Stearns, Alan N. Hoffman, and Jan B. Heide, "Performance of Commercial Television Stations as an Outcome of Interorganizational Linkages and Environmental Conditions," *Academy of Management Journal*, March 1987, pp. 71–90.
**29.** Thompson, *Organizations in Action*, pp. 51–82.
**30.** For more information on managerial choice, see John Child, "Organizational Structure, Environment, and Performance: The Role of Strategic Choice," *Sociology*, January 1972, pp. 1–22; John R. Montanari, "Managerial Discretion: An Expanded Model of Organizational Choice," *Academy of Management Review*, April 1978, pp. 231–241.
**31.** H. Randolph Bobbitt and Jeffrey D. Ford, "Decision Maker Choice as a Determinant of Organizational Structure," *Academy of Management Review*, January 1980, pp. 13–23.
**32.** "Thermos Fires Up Grill Lines," *Weekly Home Furnishings Newspaper*, August 24, 1992, p. 54; Brian Dumaine, "Payoff from the New Management," *Fortune*, December 13, 1993, pp. 102–110.
**33.** James W. Frederickson, "The Strategic Decision Process and Organization Structure," *Academy of Management Review*, April 1986, pp. 280–297.
**34.** Herman L. Boschken, "Strategy and Structure: Reconceiving the Relationship," *Journal of Management*, March 1990, pp. 135–150.
**35.** Quoted in John Huey and Geoffrey Colvin, "The Jack and Herb Show," *Fortune*, January 11, 1999, p. 164.
**36.** "Small Manufacturers Shifting to 'Just-In-Time' Techniques," *Wall Street Journal*, December 21, 1987, p. 25.
**37.** Elton Mayo, *The Human Problems of an Industrial Civilization* (New York: Macmillan, 1933); F. J. Roethlisberger and W. J. Dickson, *Management and the Worker* (Cambridge, Mass.: Harvard University Press, 1939).
**38.** Eric L. Trist and K. W. Bamforth, "Some Social and Psychological Consequences of the Longwall Method of Coal-Getting," *Human Relations*, February 1951, pp. 3–38.
**39.** "Small Manufacturers Shifting to 'Just-In-Time' Techniques."
**40.** Richard E. Walton, "How to Counter Alienation in the Plant," *Harvard Business Review*, November–December 1972, pp. 70–81; Pehr G. Gyllenhammar, "How Volvo Adapts Work to People," *Harvard Business Review*, July–August 1977, pp. 102–113; Richard E. Walton, "Work Innovations at Topeka: After Six Years," *Journal of Applied Behavioral Science*, July–August–September 1977, pp. 422–433.
**41.** Henry Mintzberg, *The Structuring of Organizations: A Synthesis of the Research* (Englewood Cliffs, N.J.: Prentice Hall, 1979).
**42.** See Harold C. Livesay, *American Made: Men Who Shaped the American Economy* (Boston: Little, Brown, 1979), pp. 215–239, for a discussion of Alfred Sloan and the development of the divisionalized structure at General Motors.
**43.** Anne B. Fisher, "GM Is Tougher Than You Think," *Fortune*, November 10, 1986, pp. 56–64.
**44.** Thompson and Strickland, *Strategic Management*, p. 212.
**45.** Kenneth Labich, "The Innovators," *Fortune*, June 6, 1988, pp. 51–64.
**46.** Henry Mintzberg, "Organization Design: Fashion or Fit," *Harvard Business Review*, January–February 1981, pp. 103–116.
**47.** Harvey F. Kolodny, "Managing in a Matrix," *Business Horizons*, March–April 1981, pp. 17–24.
**48.** Stanley M. Davis and Paul R. Lawrence, *Matrix* (Reading, Mass.: Addison-Wesley, 1977), pp. 11–36.
**49.** Lawton R. Burns, "Matrix Management in Hospitals: Testing Theories of Matrix Structure and Development," *Administrative Science Quarterly*, September 1989, pp. 355–358.
**50.** Ibid., pp. 129–154.
**51.** "The Virtual Corporation," *Business Week*, February 8, 1993, pp. 98–102; William H. Carlile, "Virtual Corporation a Real Deal," *Arizona Republic*, August 2, 1993, pp. E1, E4.
**52.** Thomas A. Stewart, "Reengineering: The Hot New Managing Tool," *Fortune*, August 23, 1993, pp. 41–48.
**53.** Robert Tomasko, *Rethinking the Corporation* (New York: AMA-COM, 1993).
**54.** Quoted in William J. Holstein and Susan Gregory Thomas, "Gateway Gets Citified," *U.S. News & World Report*, May 3, 1999, p. 42.
**55.** Rahul Jacob, "The Struggle to Create an Organization for the 21st Century," *Fortune*, April 3, 1995,

pp. 90–99; Gene G. Marcial, "Don't Leave Your Broker Without It?" *Business Week*, February 5, 1996, p. 138; Jeffrey M. Laderman, "Loading Up on No-Loads," *Business Week*, May 27, 1996, p. 138.
**56.** James R. Lincoln, Mitsuyo Hanada, and Kerry McBride, "Organizational Structures in Japanese and U.S. Manufacturing," *Administrative Science Quarterly*, September 1986, pp. 338–364.
**57.** "The Inscrutable West," *Newsweek*, April 18, 1988, p. 52.
**58.** Richard I. Kirkland Jr., "Europe's New Managers," *Fortune*, September 29, 1980, pp. 56–60; Shawn Tully, "Europe's Takeover Kings," *Fortune*, July 20, 1987, pp. 95–98.
**59.** Henry W. Lane and Joseph J. DiStefano, *International Management Behavior* (Ontario: Nelson, 1988).
**60.** William H. Davison and Philippe Haspeslagh, "Shaping a Global Product Organization," *Harvard Business Review*, July–August 1982, pp. 125–132.
**61.** John Child, *Organizations: A Guide to Problems and Practice* (New York: Harper & Row, 1984), p. 246.
**62.** Thomas J. Peters and Robert H. Waterman Jr., *In Search of Excellence: Lessons from America's Best-Run Companies* (New York: Harper & Row, 1982), pp. 235–278.
**63.** Thomas J. Peters and Nancy K. Austin, "A Passion for Excellence," *Fortune*, May 13, 1985, pp. 20–32.

### Chapter 18

*Quoted in Geoffrey Brewer, "Tom Siebel Is Bulking Up," *Sales & Marketing Management*, September 1998, p. 56.
**1.** "Tom Siebel," *Inc.*, May 1997, p. 105; Geoffrey Brewer, "Tom Siebel Is Bulking Up," *Sales & Marketing Management*, September 1998, p. 56; "Executive Profile: Thomas Siebel," *San Francisco Business Times*, November 27, 1998, p. 10; Nelson D. Schwartz, "Secrets of Fortune's Fastest-Growing Companies," *Fortune*, September 6, 1999, pp. 72–84.
**2.** See "Corporate Culture: The Hard-to-Change Values That Spell Success or Failure," *Business Week*, October 27, 1980, pp. 148–160; Charles G. Burck, "Working Smarter," *Fortune*, June 15, 1981, pp. 68–73.
**3.** Charles A. O'Reilly and Jennifer A. Chatman, "Culture as Social Control: Corporations, Cults, and Commitment," in Barry M. Staw and L. L. Cummings (eds.), *Research in Organizational Behavior* (Stamford, Conn.: JAI Press, 1996), vol. 18, pp. 157–200.
**4.** J. P. Kotter and J. L. Heskett, *Corporate Culture and Performance* (New York: Free Press, 1992).
**5.** Michael Tushman and Charles A. O'Reilly, *Staying on Top: Managing Strategic Innovation and Change for Long-Term Success* (Boston: Harvard Business School Press, 1996).
**6.** T. E. Deal and A. A. Kennedy, *Corporate Cultures: The Rites and Rituals of Corporate Life* (Reading, Mass.: Addison-Wesley, 1982), p. 4.
**7.** E. H. Schein, "The Role of the Founder in Creating Organizational Culture," *Organizational Dynamics*, Summer 1983, p. 14.
**8.** Thomas J. Peters and Robert H. Waterman Jr., *In Search of Excellence: Lessons from America's Best-Run Companies* (New York: Harper & Row, 1982), p. 103.
**9.** See M. Polanyi, *Personal Knowledge* (Chicago: University of Chicago Press, 1958); E. Goffman, *The Presentation of Self in Everyday Life* (New York: Doubleday, 1959); and P. L. Berger and T. Luckman, *The Social Construction of Reality* (Garden City, N.Y.: Anchor, 1967).
**10.** Louse Lee, "Tricks of E*Trade," *Business Week E.Biz*, February 7, 2000, pp. EB18–EB31.
**11.** Quoted in David Dorsey, "The New Spirit of Work," *Fast Company*, 1998, vol. 16, pp. 125–128.
**12.** Louse Lee, "Tricks of E*Trade," *Business Week E.Biz*, February 7, 2000, pp. EB18–EB31.
**13.** A. L. Kroeber and C. Kluckhohn, "Culture: A Critical Review of Concepts and Definitions," in *Papers of the Peabody Museum of American Archaeology and Ethnology*, vol. 47, no. 1 (Cambridge, Mass.: Harvard University Press, 1952).
**14.** C. Geertz, *The Interpretation of Cultures* (New York: Basic Books, 1973).
**15.** See, for example, B. Clark, *The Distinctive College* (Chicago: Adline, 1970).
**16.** E. Durkheim, *The Elementary Forms of Religious Life*, trans. J. Swain (New York: Collier, 1961), p. 220.
**17.** See Ouchi, *Theory Z;* and Peters and Waterman, *In Search of Excellence.*
**18.** See Ouchi, *Theory Z;* Deal and Kennedy, *Corporate Cultures;* and Peters and Waterman, *In Search of Excellence.*
**19.** E. Borgida and R. E. Nisbett, "The Differential Impact of Abstract vs. Concrete Information on Decisions," *Journal of Applied Social Psychology*, July–September 1977, pp. 258–271.
**20.** J. Martin and M. Power, "Truth or Corporate Propaganda: The Value of a Good War Story," in Pondy et al., pp. 93–108.
**21.** W. G. Ouchi, "Markets, Bureaucracies, and Clans," *Administrative Science Quarterly*, March 1980, pp. 129–141; A. Wilkins and W. G. Ouchi, "Efficient Cultures: Exploring the Relationship Between Culture and Organizational Performance," *Administrative Science Quarterly*, September 1983, pp. 468–481.
**22.** Peters and Waterman, *In Search of Excellence.*
**23.** J. B. Barney, "Organizational Culture: Can It Be a Source of Sustained Competitive Advantage?" *Academy of Management Review*, July 1986, pp. 656–665.
**24.** Daniel R. Denison, "What Is the Difference Between Organizational Culture and Organizational Climate? A Native's Point of View on a Decade of Paradigm Wars," *Academy of Management Review*, July 1996, pp. 619–654.
**25.** O'Reilly and Chatman, "Culture as Social Control."
**26.** Richard L. Osborne, "Strategic Values: The Corporate Performance Engine," *Business Horizons*, September–October 1996, pp. 41–47.
**27.** See Osborne, "Strategic Values: The Corporate Performance Engine";

and Gary McWilliams, "Dell's Profit Rises Slightly, As Expected," *Wall Street Journal*, February 11, 2000, p. A3.
**28.** Quoted in "The Jack and Herb Show," *Fortune*, January 11, 1999, p. 166.
**29.** Ouchi, *Theory Z.*
**30.** Catherine Reagor, "Wells Fargo Riding Roughshod in State, Some Say," *Arizona Republic*, September 8, 1996, pp. D1, D4; Catherine Reagor, "Wells Fargo to Cut 3,000 Additional Jobs," *Arizona Republic*, December 20, 1996, pp. E1, E2.
**31.** O'Reilly and Chatman, "Culture as Social Control."
**32.** John E. Sheridan, "Organizational Culture and Employee Retention," *Academy of Management Journal*, December 1992, pp. 1036–1056; Lisa A. Mainiero, "Is Your Corporate Culture Costing You?" *Academy of Management Executive*, November 1993, pp. 84–85.
**33.** Peters and Waterman, *In Search of Excellence.*
**34.** Kenneth Labich, "An Airline That Soars on Service," *Fortune*, December 31, 1990, pp. 94–96.
**35.** Quoted in Geoffrey Brewer, "Tom Siebel Is Bulking Up," *Sales & Marketing Management*, September 1998, p. 59.
**36.** Watts S. Humphrey, *Managing for Innovation: Leading Technical People* (Englewood Cliffs, N.J.: Prentice Hall, 1987).
**37.** Brian O'Reilly, "Secrets of the Most Admired Corporations: New Ideas and New Products," *Fortune*, March 3, 1997, pp. 60–64.
**38.** Laurie K. Lewis and David R. Seibold, "Innovation Modification During Intraorganizational Adoption," *Academy of Management Review*, April 1993, vol. 10, no. 2, pp. 322–354.
**39.** Quoted in Jerry Useem, "Internet Defense Strategy: Cannibalize Yourself," *Fortune*, September 6, 1999, p. 128.
**40.** Louise Lee, "Tricks of E*Trade."
**41.** Oren Harari, "Stop Empowering Your People," *Management Review*, November 1993, pp. 26–29.
**42.** W. Chan Kim and Renee A. Mauborgne, "Procedural Justice, Attitudes, and Subsidiary Top Management Compliance with Multinationals' Corporate Strategic Decisions," *Academy of Management Journal*, June 1993, pp. 502–526.
**43.** See Warren Wilhelm, "Changing Corporate Culture—Or Corporate Behavior? How to Change Your Company,"*Academy of Management Executive*, November 1992, pp. 72–77.
**44.** Quoted in Gary Silverman, Leah Nathans Spiro, John Rossant, and Owen Ullmann, "Is This Marriage Working?" *Business Week*, June 7, 1999, p. 134.
**45.** Socialization has also been defined as "the process by which culture is transmitted from one generation to the next." See J. W. M. Whiting, "Socialization: Anthropological Aspects," in D. Sils (ed.), *International Encyclopedia of the Social Sciences*, vol. 14 (New York: Free Press, 1968), p. 545.
**46.** J. E. Hebden, "Adopting an Organization's Culture: The Socialization of Graduate Trainees," *Organizational Dynamics*, Summer 1986, pp. 54–72.
**47.** J. B. Barney, "Organizational Culture: Can It Be a Source of Sustained Competitive Advantage?" *Academy of Management Review*, July 1986, pp. 656–665.
**48.** James R. Norman, "A New Teledyne," *Forbes*, September 27, 1993, pp. 44–45.

### Chapter 19

*Quoted in Neil Weinberg, "A Shock to the System," *Forbes*, May 31, 1999, p. 179.
**1.** Neil Weinberg, "A Shock to the System," *Forbes*, May 31, 1999, pp. 178–182; Nancy Williams, "EDS Unveils Leadership Teams as Company Completes New Business Approach," *PR Newswire*, November 30, 1999, p. 1488; "Fast and Unafraid," *Economist*, January 8, 2000, p. 68; Leah Beth Ward, "Electronic Data Systems Rounds Off Logo," *Knight-Ridder/Tribune Business News*, January 20, 2000, p. ITEM00021038.
**2.** "Baby Boomers Push for Power," *Business Week*, July 2, 1984, pp. 52–56.
**3.** "Americans' Median Age Passes 32," *Arizona Republic*, April 6, 1988, pp. A1, A5.
**4.** "Population Estimates Program," Population Division, U.S. Census Bureau, Washington, D.C. 20233.
**5.** Geoffrey Colvin, "What the Baby Boomers Will Buy Next," *Fortune*, October 15, 1984, pp. 28–34.
**6.** John Huey, "Managing in the Midst of Chaos," *Fortune*, April 5, 1993, pp. 38–48.
**7.** Peter Nulty, "How Personal Computers Change Managers' Lives," *Fortune*, September 3, 1984, pp. 38–48.
**8.** "Artificial Language Is Here," *Business Week*, July 9, 1984, pp. 54–62.
**9.** Thomas A. Stewart, "Welcome to the Revolution," *Fortune*, December 13, 1993, pp. 66–80.
**10.** Quoted in Andy Serwer, "There's Something About Cisco," *Fortune*, May 15, 2000, p. 116.
**11.** "Nokia's Restructured," *Television Digest*, September 4, 1995, p. 15; Rahul Jacob, "Nokia Fumbles, but Don't Count It Out," *Fortune*, February 19, 1996, pp. 86–88; Gail Edmondson, "At Nokia, A Comeback—and Then Some," *Business Week*, December 2, 1996, p. 106.
**12.** Kurt Lewin, *Field Theory in Social Science* (New York: Harper & Row, 1951).
**13.** Quoted in Neil Weinberg, "A Shock to the System," *Forbes*, May 31, 1999, p. 179.
**14.** Linda S. Ackerman, "Transition Management: An In-Depth Look at Managing Complex Change," *Organizational Dynamics*, Summer 1982, pp. 46–66; David A. Nadler, "Managing Transitions to Uncertain Future States," *Organizational Dynamics*, Summer 1982, pp. 37–45.
**15.** Noel M. Tichy and David O. Ulrich, "The Leadership Challenge—A Call for the Transformational Leader," *Sloan Management Review*, Fall 1984, pp. 59–68.
**16.** W. Warner Burke, *Organization Development: Principles and Practices* (Boston: Little, Brown, 1982).

**17.** Michael Beer, *Organization Change and Development* (Santa Monica, Calif.: Goodyear, 1980); Burke, *Organization Development.*
**18.** Quoted in Thomas A. Stewart, "How to Leave It All Behind," *Fortune*, December 6, 1999, p. 348.
**19.** Danny Miller and Peter H. Friesen, "Structural Change and Performance: Quantum Versus Piecemeal-Incremental Approaches," *Academy of Management Journal*, December 1982, pp. 867–892.
**20.** J. Lloyd Suttle, "Improving Life at Work—Problems and Prospects," in J. Richard Hackman and J. Lloyd Suttle (eds.), *Improving Life at Work: Behavioral Science Approaches to Organizational Change* (Santa Monica, Calif.: Goodyear, 1977), p. 4.
**21.** Richard E. Walton, "Quality of Work Life: What Is It?" *Sloan Management Review*, Fall 1983, pp. 11–21.
**22.** Daniel A. Ondrack and Martin G. Evans, "Job Enrichment and Job Satisfaction in Greenfield and Redesign QWL Sites," *Group & Organization Studies*, March 1987, pp. 5–22.
**23.** Ricky W. Griffin, *Task Design: An Integrative Framework* (Glenview, Ill.: Scott, Foresman, 1982).
**24.** Gregory Moorhead, "Organizational Analysis: An Integration of the Macro and Micro Approaches," *Journal of Management Studies*, April 1981, pp. 191–218.
**25.** James C. Quick and Jonathan D. Quick, *Organizational Stress and Preventive Management* (New York: McGraw-Hill, 1984).
**26.** Peter Petre, "Games That Teach You to Manage," *Fortune*, October 29, 1984, pp. 65–72.
**27.** Kenneth N. Wexley and Timothy T. Baldwin, "Management Development," *1986 Yearly Review of Management of the Journal of Management*, in the *Journal of Management*, Summer 1986, pp. 277–294.
**28.** Richard Beckhard, "Optimizing Team-Building Efforts," *Journal of Contemporary Business*, Summer 1972, pp. 23–27, 30–32.
**29.** Bernard M. Bass, "Issues Involved in Relations Between Methodological Rigor and Reported Outcomes in Evaluations of Organizational Development," *Journal of Applied Psychology*, February 1983, pp. 197–201; William M. Vicars and Darrel D. Hartke, "Evaluating OD Evaluations: A Status Report," *Group & Organization Studies*, June 1984, pp. 177–188.
**30.** Beer, *Organization Change and Development.*
**31.** Jerome L. Franklin, "Improving the Effectiveness of Survey Feedback," *Personnel*, May–June 1978, pp. 11–17.
**32.** Quoted in Anna Muoio, "Idea Summit," *Fast Company*, January/February 2000, p. 156.
**33.** Paul R. Lawrence, "How to Deal with Resistance to Change," *Harvard Business Review*, May–June 1954, reprinted in Gene W. Dalton, Paul R. Lawrence, and Larry E. Greiner (eds.), *Organizational Change and Development* (Homewood, Ill.: Irwin, 1970), pp. 181–197.
**34.** Daniel Katz and Robert L. Kahn, *The Social Psychology of Organizations*, 2nd ed. (New York: Wiley, 1978), pp. 36–68.
**35.** See Michael T. Hannah and John Freeman, "Structural Inertia and Organizational Change," *American Sociological Review*, April 1984, pp. 149–164, for an in-depth discussion of structural inertia.
**36.** Moorhead, "Organizational Analysis: An Integration of the Macro and Micro Approaches."
**37.** G. Zaltman and R. Duncan, *Strategies for Planned Change* (New York: Wiley, 1977); David A. Nadler, "Concepts for the Management of Organizational Change," in J. Richard Hackman, Edward E. Lawler III, and Lyman W. Porter (eds.), *Perspectives on Behavior in Organizations*, 2nd ed. (New York: McGraw-Hill, 1983), pp. 551–561.
**38.** Alfred M. Jaeger, "Organization Development and National Culture: Where's the Fit?" *Academy of Management Review*, January 1986, pp. 178–190.
**39.** Alan M. Webber, "Learning for a Change," *Fast Company*, May 1999, pp. 178–188.
**40.** Quoted in Alan M. Webber, "Learning for a Change," *Fast Company*, May 1999, p. 186.

### Appendix A

**1.** Jeffrey Pfeffer, "The Theory-Practice Gap: Myth or Reality?" *Academy of Management Executive*, February 1987, pp. 31–33.
**2.** Eugene Stone, *Research Methods in Organizational Behavior* (Santa Monica, Calif.: Goodyear, 1978).
**3.** Fred N. Kerlinger and Howard B. Lee, *Foundations of Behavioral Research*, 4th ed. (New York: Harcourt College Publishers, 1999).
**4.** Richard L. Daft, Ricky W. Griffin, and Valerie Yates, "Retrospective Accounts of Research Factors Associated with Significant and Not-So-Significant Research Outcomes," *Academy of Management Journal*, December 1987, pp. 763–785.
**5.** Richard L. Daft, "Learning the Craft of Organizational Research," *Academy of Management Review*, October 1983, pp. 539–546.
**6.** Larry L. Cummings and Peter Frost, *Publishing in Organizational Sciences* (Homewood, Ill.: Irwin, 1985). See also Ellen R. Girden, *Evaluating Research Articles From Start to Finish* (Beverly Hills, Calif.: Sage, 1996).
**7.** D. T. Campbell and J. C. Stanley, *Experimental and Quasi-Experimental Designs for Research* (Boston: Houghton Mifflin, 1966).
**8.** R. Yin and K. Heald, "Using the Case Study Method to Analyze Policy Studies," *Administrative Science Quarterly*, June 1975, pp. 371–381.
**9.** Kerlinger and Lee, *Foundations of Behavioral Research.*
**10.** Ramon J. Aldag and Timothy M. Stearns, "Issues in Research Methodology," *Journal of Management*, June 1988, pp. 253–276.
**11.** See C. A. Schriesheim et al., "Improving Construct Measurement in Management," *Journal of Management*, Summer 1993, pp. 385–418.
**12.** Cynthia D. Fisher, "Laboratory Experiments," in Thomas S. Bateman and Gerald R. Ferris (eds.), *Method and Analysis in Organizational Research*

(Reston, Va.: Reston, 1984); Edwin Locke (ed.), *Generalizing from Laboratory to Field Settings* (Lexington, Mass.: Lexington Books, 1986).
**13.** Stone, *Research Methods in Organizational Behavior.*
**14.** Phillip M. Podsakoff and Dan R. Dalton, "Research Methodology in Organizational Studies," *Journal of Management*, Summer 1987, pp. 419–441.
**15.** Stone, *Research Methods in Organizational Behavior.*
**16.** Kerlinger and Lee, *Foundations of Behavioral Research.*
**17.** Mary Ann Von Glinow, "Ethical Issues in Organizational Behavior," *Academy of Management Newsletter*, March 1985, pp. 1–3.

### Appendix B

**1.** Suneel Ratan, "Generational Tension in the Office: Why Busters Hate the Boomers," *Fortune*, October 4, 1993, pp. 56–70.
**2.** Julie Amparano, "Parents Cut Pay, Hours to Rear Kids," *Arizona Republic*, June 22, 1996, pp. A1, A19.
**3.** Bernard Wysocki Jr., "High-Tech Nomads Write New Program for Future Work," *Wall Street Journal*, August 19, 1996, pp. A1, A6.
**4.** Ray Marshall, "The Global Jobs Crisis," *Foreign Policy*, Fall 1995, pp. 50–68.
**5.** M. W. McCall and E. E. Lawler III, "High School Students' Perceptions of Work," *Academy of Management Journal*, March 1976, pp. 17–24.
**6.** D. T. Hall, *Careers in Organizations* (Santa Monica, Calif.: Goodyear, 1976), p. 4.
**7.** M. Breidenbach, *Career Development: Taking Charge of Your Career* (Englewood Cliffs, N.J.: Prentice Hall, 1988).
**8.** "Stable Cycles of Executive Careers Shattered by Upheaval in Business," *Wall Street Journal*, May 26, 1987, p. 31.
**9.** D. B. Miller, *Careers '79* (Saratoga, Calif.: Vitality Associates, 1979).
**10.** Amparano, "Parents Cut Pay, Hours to Rear Kids," pp. A1, A19.
**11.** U.S. Bureau of the Census, *1980 Census of the Population: Alphabetical Index of Industries and Occupations* (Washington, D.C.: U.S. Government Printing Office, 1981).
**12.** D. C. Feldman, *Managing Careers in Organizations* (Glenview, Ill.: Scott, Foresman, 1988), pp. 189–192.
**13.** P. M. Blau, J. W. Gustad, R. Jesson, H. S. Parnes, and R. C. Wilcox, "Occupational Choices: A Conceptual Hall, Careers in Organizations Framework," *Industrial and Labor Relations Review*, July 1956, pp. 531–543.
**14.** J. L. Holland, *Making Vocational Choices* (Englewood Cliffs, N.J.: Prentice Hall, 1973).
**15.** D. C. Feldman and H. J. Arnold, "Personality Types and Career Patterns: Some Empirical Evidence on Holland's Model," *Canadian Journal of Administrative Science*, June 1985, pp. 192–210.
**16.** E. Ginzberg, S. W. Ginzberg, W. Axelrod, and J. L. Herna, *Occupational Choice: An Approach to a General Theory* (New York: Columbia University Press, 1951); Hall, *Careers in Organizations.*
**17.** Holland, *Making Vocational Choices.*
**18.** T. R. Mitchell and B. W. Knudsen, "Instrumentality Theory Predictions of Students' Attitudes Toward Business and Their Choice of Business as an Occupation," *Academy of Management Journal*, March 1973, pp. 41–52; S. L. Rynes and J. Lawler, "A Policy-Capturing Investigation of the Role of Expectancies in Decisions to Pursue Job Alternatives," *Journal of Applied Psychology*, November 1983, pp. 620–631.
**19.** Michael B. Arthur and Denise M. Rousseau, "A Career Lexicon for the 21st Century," *Academy of Management Executive*, November 1996, pp. 28–39.
**20.** Brent B. Allred, Charles C. Snow, and Raymond E. Miles, "Characteristics of Managerial Careers in the 21st Century," *Academy of Management Executive*, November 1996, pp. 17–27.
**21.** P. A. Renwick, E. E. Lawler III, and staff, "What You Really Want from Your Job," *Psychology Today*, May 1978, pp. 53–65.
**22.** D. C. Feldman and H. J. Arnold, "Position Choice: Comparing the Importance of Job and Organizational Factors," *Journal of Applied Psychology*, December 1978, pp. 706–710.
**23.** Ellen F. Jackofsky and Lawrence H. Peters, "Part-Time Versus Full-Time Employment Status Differences: A Replication and Extension," *Journal of Occupational Behavior*, January 1987, pp. 1–9.
**24.** Courtney von Hippel, Stephen L. Mangum, David B. Greenberger, Robert L. Heneman, and Jeffrey D. Skoglind, "Temporary Employment: Can Organizations and Employees Both Win?" *Academy of Management Executive*, February 1997, pp. 93–104.
**25.** Andrew S. Grove, *Only the Paranoid Survive* (New York: Doubleday, 1999).
**26.** Douglas T. Hall, "Protean Careers of the 21st Century," *Academy of Management Executive*, November 1996, p. 8.
**27.** Hall, *Careers in Organizations.*
**28.** D. C. Feldman, "A Socialization Process That Helps New Recruits Succeed," *Personnel*, March–April 1980, pp. 11–23.
**29.** D. C. Feldman, "The Multiple Socialization of Organization Members," *Academy of Management Review*, April 1981, pp. 309–318.
**30.** R. A. Webber, "Career Problems of Young Managers," *California Management Review*, Summer 1976, pp. 19–33; E. Schein, *Career Dynamics: Matching Individual and Organizational Needs* (Reading, Mass.: Addison-Wesley, 1978).
**31.** D. C. Feldman, "A Practical Program for Employee Socialization," *Organizational Dynamics*, Autumn 1976, pp. 64–80.
**32.** "Should Companies Groom New Leaders or Buy Them?" *Business Week*, September 22, 1986, pp. 94–96.
**33.** Harvey Mackay, "Use Your Head in Leaving Job You Hate," *Arizona Republic*, January 5, 1997, p. D3.
**34.** T. P. Ference, J. A. F. Stoner, and E. K. Warren, "Managing the Career Plateau," *Academy of Management Review*, October 1977, pp. 602–612.
**35.** D. LaBier, "Madness Stalks the Ladder Climbers," *Fortune*, September 1, 1986, pp. 79–84.

**36.** F. Rice, "Lessons from Late Bloomers," *Fortune*, August 31, 1987, pp. 87–91.
**37.** R. C. Payne, "Mid-Career Block," *Personnel Journal*, April 1984, pp. 38–48.
**38.** J. Main, "Breaking Out of the Company," *Fortune*, May 25, 1987, pp. 81–88.
**39.** "Crushed Hopes: When a New Job Proves to Be Something Different," *Wall Street Journal*, June 10, 1987, p. 27.
**40.** D. T. Hall and F. S. Hall, "What's New in Career Management," *Organizational Dynamics*, Summer 1976, pp. 17–33.
**41.** Kerry D. Carson and Paula Phillips Carson, "Career Entrenchment: A Quiet March Toward Occupational Death?" *Academy of Management Executive*, February 1997, pp. 62–75.
**42.** Dan Hurley, "The Mentor Mystique," *Psychology Today*, May 1988, pp. 39–43.
**43.** Michael G. Zey, "A Mentor for All Reasons," *Personnel Journal*, January 1988, pp. 47–51.
**44.** "Guidelines for Successful Mentoring," *Training*, December 1984, p. 125.
**45.** Joy A. Schneer and Frieda Reitman, "Effects of Employment Gaps on the Careers of MBAs More Damaging for Men Than for Women," *Academy of Management Journal*, June 1990, pp. 391–406.
**46.** J. Walker, "Does Career Planning Rock the Boat?" *Human Resource Management*, Spring 1978, pp. 2–7.
**47.** C. S. Granrose and J. D. Portwood, "Matching Individual Career Plans and Organizational Career Management," *Academy of Management Journal*, December 1987, pp. 699–720.
**48.** M. A. Morgan, D. T. Hall, and A. Martier, "Career Development Strategies in Industry—Where Are We and Where Should We Be?" *Personnel*, March–April 1979, pp. 13–30.
**49.** T. A. DiPrete, "Horizontal and Vertical Mobility in Organizations," *Administrative Science Quarterly*, December 1987, pp. 422–444.
**50.** N. C. Hill, "Career Counseling: What Employees Should Do—and Expect," *Personnel*, August 1985, pp. 41–46.
**51.** J. C. Latack and J. B. Dozier, "After the Ax Falls: Job Loss as a Career Transition," *Academy of Management Review*, April 1986, pp. 375–392; W. Kiechel III, "Passed Over," *Fortune*, October 13, 1986, pp. 189–191.
**52.** E. H. Burack, *Creative Human Resource Planning and Applications: A Strategic Approach* (Englewood Cliffs, N.J.: Prentice Hall, 1988).
**53.** Ibid.
**54.** T. M. Camden, "Using Outplacement as a Career Development Tool," *Personnel Administrator*, January 1982, pp. 35–44.
**55.** See, for example, D. D. Van Fleet and J. Saurage, "Recent Research on Women in Leadership and Management," *Akron Business and Economic Review*, Summer 1984, pp. 15–24; E. M. Van Fleet and D. D. Van Fleet, "Entrepreneurship and Black Capitalism," *American Journal of Small Business*, Fall 1985, pp. 31–40; D. D. Bowen and R. D. Hisrich, "The Female Entrepreneur: A Career Development Perspective," *Academy of Management Review*, April 1986, pp. 393–407; "Male vs. Female: What a Difference It Makes in Business Careers," *Wall Street Journal*, December 9, 1986, p. 1; "In Dad's Footsteps: More Women Find a Niche in the Family Business," *Wall Street Journal*, May 28, 1987, p. 29.
**56.** "Cigarette Smoking Is Growing Hazardous to Careers in Business," *Wall Street Journal*, April 23, 1987, pp. 1, 19.
**57.** Adapted from Feldman, *Managing Careers in Organizations*, pp. 189–192. See also K. B. McRae, "Career-Management Planning: A Boon to Managers and Employees," *Personnel*, May 1985, pp. 56–61.
**58.** Z. B. Leibowitz and N. K. Schlossberg, "Training Managers for Their Role in a Career Development System," *Training and Development Journal*, July 1981, pp. 72–79.
**59.** Walker, "Does Career Planning Rock the Boat?"

# Glossary

**absenteeism** Failure to show up for work. (4)

**acceptance theory of authority** The theory that the manager's authority depends on the subordinate's acceptance of the manager's right to give directives and to expect compliance with them. (16)

**accommodation** Occurs when the parties' goals are compatible and the interaction between groups is relatively unimportant to the goals' attainment. (11)

**adhocracy** This structure is typically found in young organizations in highly technical fields. Within it, decision making is spread throughout the organization, power resides with the experts, horizontal and vertical specialization exists, and there is little formalization. (17)

**administrative hierarchy** The system of reporting relationships in the organization, from the lowest to the highest managerial levels. (16)

**affect** A person's feelings toward something. (4)

**affinity group** Collections of employees from the same level in the organization who meet on a regular basis to share information, capture emerging opportunities, and solve problems. (11)

**agreeableness** A person's ability to get along with others. (4)

**all-channel network** In this type of network, all members communicate with all other members. (10)

**applied research** Conducted to solve particular problems or answer specific questions. (Appendix A)

**assimilation** The process through which a minority group learns the ways of the dominant group. In organizations, this means that when people of different types and backgrounds are hired, the organization attempts to mold them to fit the existing organizational culture. (3)

**attitudes** A person's complexes of beliefs and feelings about specific ideas, situations, or other people. (4)

**attribution theory** Suggests that we attribute causes to behavior based on observations of certain characteristics of that behavior. Employees observe their own behavior, determine whether it is a response to external or internal factors, and shape their future motivated behavior accordingly. (4, 6)

**authoritarianism** The belief that power and status differences are appropriate within hierarchical social systems such as organizations. (4)

**authority** Power that has been legitimized within a particular social context. (16)

**autonomous work groups** Groups used to integrate an organization's technical and social systems for the benefit of large systems. (17)

**avoidance (negative reinforcement)** The opportunity to avoid or escape from an unpleasant circumstance after exhibiting behavior. Avoidance occurs when the interacting parties' goals are incompatible and the interaction between groups is relatively unimportant to the attainment of the goals. (6, 11)

**basic research** Involves discovering new knowledge rather than solving specific problems. (Appendix A)

**behavioral approach** Approach to leadership that tries to identify behaviors that differentiated effective leaders from nonleaders. It uses rules of thumb, suboptimizing, and satisficing in making decisions. (13, 15)

**benefits** An important form of indirect compensation. (8)

**"big five" personality traits** A set of fundamental traits that are especially relevant to organizations. (4)

**bounded rationality** The idea that decision makers cannot deal with information about all the aspects and alternatives pertaining to a problem and therefore choose to tackle some meaningful subset of it. (15)

**brainstorming** A technique used in the idea-generation phase of decision making that assists in the development of numerous alternative courses of action. (15)

**burnout** A general feeling of exhaustion that develops when an individual simultaneously experiences too much pressure and has too few sources of satisfaction. (9)

**career** A perceived sequence of attitudes and behaviors associated with work-related experiences and activities over a person's life span. (Appendix B)

Note: The number in parentheses after each entry refers to the chapter in which the term was discussed.

**career pathing** The identification of a certain sequence of jobs in a career that represents a progression through the organization. (Appendix B)

**career planning** Process in which individuals evaluate their abilities and interests, consider alternative career opportunities, establish career goals, and plan practical development activities. (Appendix B)

**career stages** The periods in which an individual's work life is characterized by specific needs, concerns, tasks, and activities. (Appendix B)

**career management** The process of implementing organizational career planning. (Appendix B)

**case study** An in-depth analysis of one setting. (Appendix A)

**centralization** A structural policy in which decision-making authority is concentrated at the top of the organizational hierarchy. (16)

**certainty** Condition under which the manager knows the outcomes of each alternative. (15)

**chain network** In this type of network, each member communicates with the person above and below, except for the individuals on each end who communicate with only one person. (10)

**change agent** A person responsible for managing a change effort. (19)

**channel noise** A disturbance in communication that is primarily a function of the medium. (10)

**charisma** A form of interpersonal attraction that inspires support and acceptance from others. (14)

**charismatic leadership** A type of influence based on the leader's personal charisma. (14)

**circle network** In this type of network, each member communicates with the people on both sides but with no one else. (10)

**classical conditioning** A simple form of learning that links a conditioned response with an unconditioned stimulus. (6)

**classical organization theory** An early approach to management that focused on how organizations can be structured most effectively to meet their goals. (1)

**coercive power** The extent to which a person has the ability to punish or physically or psychologically harm someone else. (14)

**cognition** The knowledge a person presumes to have about something. (4)

**cognitive dissonance** The anxiety a person experiences when he or she simultaneously possesses two sets of knowledge or perceptions that are contradictory or incongruent. (4, 15)

**collaboration** Occurs when the interaction between groups is very important to goal attainment and the goals are compatible. (11)

**collectivism** The extent to which people emphasize the good of the group or society. (3)

**command group** A relatively permanent, formal group with functional reporting relationships; usually included in the organization chart. (11)

**communication** The social process in which two or more parties exchange information and share meaning. (10)

**communication and decision-making** The stage of group development where members discuss their feelings more openly and agree on group goals and individual roles in the group. (11)

**communication networks** Networks that form spontaneously and naturally as the interactions among workers continue over time. (10)

**compensation package** The total array of money (wages, salary, commission), incentives, benefits, perquisites, and awards provided by the organization to an employee. (8)

**competition** Occurs when the goals are incompatible and the interactions between groups are important to meeting goals. (11)

**competitive strategy** An outline of how a business intends to compete with other firms in the same industry. (2)

**compressed work week** A situation in which employees work a full forty-hour week in fewer than the traditional five days. (7)

**compromise** Occurs when the interaction is moderately important to meeting goals and the goals are neither completely compatible nor completely incompatible. (11)

**conceptual skills** Used to think in the abstract. (2)

**configuration** An organization's shape, which reflects the division of labor and the means of coordinating the divided tasks. (16)

**conflict** A disagreement among parties. It has both positive and negative characteristics. (11)

**conflict model** A very personal approach to decision making because it deals with the personal conflicts that people experience in particularly difficult decision situations. (15)

**conflict resolution** Occurs when a manager resolves a conflict that has become harmful or serious. (11)

**conflict stimulation** The creation and constructive use of conflict by a manager. (11)

**conscientiousness** The number of goals on which a person focuses. (4)

**consideration behavior** Involves being concerned with subordinates' feelings and respecting subordinates' ideas. (13)

**contingency approach** An approach to organization design where the desired outcomes for the organization can be achieved in several ways. (17)

**contingency perspective** Suggests that, in most organizations, situations and outcomes are contingent on, or influenced by, other variables. (1)

**contingency plans** Alternative actions to take if the primary course of action is unexpectedly disrupted or rendered inappropriate. (15)

**continuous improvement** Perspective suggesting that performance should constantly be enhanced. (8)

**continuous reinforcement** With this type of reinforcement, behavior is rewarded every time it occurs. (6)

**contributions** An individual's contributions to an organization include such things as effort, skills, ability, time, and loyalty. (4)

**control and organization** The stage of group development where the group is mature; members work together and are flexible, adaptive, and self-correcting. (11)

**controlling** The process of monitoring and correcting the actions of the organization and its members to keep them directed toward their goals. (2)

**cosmopolite** Links the organization to the external environment and may also be an opinion leader in the group. (10)

**creativity** A person's ability to generate new ideas or to conceive of new perspectives on existing ideas. (4)

**cultural values** The values that employees need to have and act on for the organization to act on the strategic values. (18)

**decision making** The process of choosing from among several alternatives. (15)

**decision-making roles** There are four basic decision-making roles: the entrepreneur, the disturbance handler, the resource allocator, and the negotiator. (2)

**decision rule** A statement that tells a decision maker which alternative to choose based on the characteristics of the decision situation. (15)

**decoding** The process by which the receiver of the message interprets its meaning. (10)

**defensive avoidance** Entails making no changes in present activities and avoiding any further contact with associated issues because there appears to be no hope of finding a better solution. (15)

**delegation** The transfer to others of authority to make decisions and use organizational resources. (16)

**Delphi technique** A method of systematically gathering judgments of experts for use in developing forecasts. (15)

**departmentalization** The manner in which divided tasks are combined and allocated to work groups. (16)

**diagnostic skills** Used to understand cause-and-effect relationships and to recognize the optimal solutions to problems. (2)

**distress** The unpleasant stress that accompanies negative events. (9)

**division of labor** The way the organization's work is divided into different jobs to be done by different people. (16)

**divisionalized form** This structure is typical of old, very large organizations. Within it, the organization is divided according to the different markets served. Horizontal and vertical specialization exists between divisions and headquarters, decision making is divided between headquarters and divisions, and outputs are standardized. (17)

**downsizing** The process of purposely becoming smaller by reducing the size of the workforce or shedding divisions or businesses. (2)

**dual-structure theory** Identifies motivation factors, which affect satisfaction, and hygiene factors, which affect dissatisfaction. (5)

**dysfunctional behaviors** Those that detract from organizational performance. (4)

**effort-to-performance expectancy** A person's perception of the probability that effort will lead to performance. (6)

**employee-centered leader behavior** Involves attempting to build effective work groups with high performance goals. (13)

**empowerment** The process of enabling workers to set their own work goals, make decisions, and solve problems within their sphere of responsibility and authority. (7, 18)

**encoding** The process by which the message is translated from an idea or thought into transmittable symbols. (10)

**entry stage (exploration stage)** Characterized by self-examination, role tryouts, and occupational exploration. (Appendix B)

**environmental complexity** The number of environmental components that impinge on organizational decision making. (17)

**environmental dynamism** The degree to which environmental components that impinge on organizational decision making change. (17)

**environmental uncertainty** Exists when managers have little information about environmental events and their impact on the organization. (17)

**equity** The belief that we are being treated fairly in relation to others. (6)

**equity theory** Focuses on people's desire to be treated with what they perceive as equity and to avoid perceived inequity. (6)

**ERG theory** Describes existence, relatedness, and growth needs. (5)

**escalation of commitment** The tendency to persist in an ineffective course of action when evidence reveals that the project cannot succeed. (15)

**establishment stage (settling-down stage)** Stage in which the individual gets more recognition for improvement. (Appendix B)

**ethics** An individual's personal beliefs about what is right and wrong or good and bad. (2, 15)

**eustress** The pleasurable stress that accompanies positive events. (9)

**exit (withdrawal) stage** Characterized by a pattern of decreasing performance as individuals prepare to move on or retire. (Appendix B)

**expectancy theory** Suggests that people are motivated by how much they want something and the likelihood they perceive of getting it. (6)

**expert power** The extent to which a person controls information that is valuable to someone else. (14)

**extinction** Decreases the frequency of behavior by eliminating a reward or desirable consequence that follows that behavior. (6)

**extraversion** The quality of being comfortable with relationships; the opposite extreme, introversion, is characterized by more social discomfort. (4)

**feedback** The process in which the receiver returns a message to the sender that indicates receipt of the message. (10)

**fidelity** The degree of correspondence between the message intended by the source and the message understood by the receiver. (10)

**field experiment** Similar to a laboratory experiment but is conducted in a real organization. (Appendix A)

**field survey** Typically relies on a questionnaire distributed to a sample of people selected from a larger population. (Appendix A)

**fixed-interval reinforcement** Provides reinforcement on a fixed time schedule. (6)

**fixed-ratio reinforcement** Provides reinforcement after a fixed number of behaviors. (6)

**flexible reward system** Allows employees to choose the combination of benefits that best suits their needs. (8)

**flexible work schedules (flextime)** These schedules give employees more personal control over the hours they work each day. (7)

**formal group** Formed by an organization to do its work. (11)

**formalization** The degree to which rules and procedures shape the jobs and activities of employees. (16)

**friendship group** A group that is relatively permanent and informal and draws its benefits from the social relationships among its members. (11)

**gatekeeper** An individual who has a strategic position in the network that allows him or her to control information moving in either direction through a channel. (10)

**general adaptation syndrome (GAS)** Identifies three stages of response to a stressor: alarm, resistance, and exhaustion. (9)

**general environment** The broad set of dimensions and factors within which the organization operates, including political-legal, sociocultural, technological, economic, and international factors. (17)

**goal** A desirable objective. (8)

**goal acceptance** The extent to which a person accepts a goal as his or her own. (8)

**goal commitment** The extent to which a person is personally interested in reaching a goal. (8)

**goal compatibility** The extent to which the goals of more than one person or group can be achieved at the same time. (11)

**goal difficulty** The extent to which a goal is challenging and requires effort. (8)

**goal specificity** The clarity and precision of a goal. (8)

**grapevine** An informal system of communication that coexists with the formal system. (10)

**group** Two or more people who interact with one another such that each person influences and is influenced by each other person. (11)

**group cohesiveness** The extent to which a group is committed to staying together. (11)

**group composition** The degree of similarity or difference among group members on factors important to the group's work. (11)

**group performance factors** Composition, size, norms, and cohesiveness. They affect the success of the group in fulfilling its goals. (11)

**group polarization** The tendency for a group's average postdiscussion attitudes to be more extreme than its average prediscussion attitudes. (15)

**group size** The number of members of the group; it affects the number of resources available to perform the task. (11)

**groupthink** Occurs when a group's overriding concern is a unanimous decision rather than critical analysis of alternatives. (11, 15)

**hardiness** A person's ability to cope with stress. (9)

**Hawthorne studies** Conducted between 1927 and 1932, these studies led to some of the first discoveries of the importance of human behavior in organizations. (1)

**Hersey and Blanchard model** Identifies different combinations of leadership presumed to work best with different levels of organizational maturity on the part of followers. (13)

**hierarchy of needs theory** Maslow's hierarchy that assumes human needs are arranged in a hierarchy of importance. (5)

**human organization** Rensis Likert's approach that is based on supportive relationships, participation, and overlapping work groups. (16)

**human relations** Movement based on the assumption that employee satisfaction is a key determinant of performance. It marked the beginning of organizational behavior. (1)

**human relations approach** Suggested that favorable employee attitudes result in motivation to work hard. (5)

**human resource planning** Forecasting the organization's human resource needs, developing replacement charts (charts showing planned succession of personnel) for all levels of the organization, and preparing inventories of the skills and abilities individuals need to move within the organization. (Appendix B)

**hygiene factors** These factors are extrinsic to the work itself. They include factors such as pay and job security. (5)

**hypervigilance** A frantic, superficial pursuit of some satisficing strategy. (15)

**ideal bureaucracy** Weber's model that is characterized by a hierarchy of authority and a system of rules and procedures designed to create an optimally effective system for large organizations. (16)

**impression management** A direct and intentional effort by someone to enhance his or her own image in the eyes of others. (14)

**incentive systems** Plans in which employees can earn additional compensation in return for certain types of performance. (8)

**incremental innovation** Continues the technical improvement and extends the applications of radical and systems innovations. (18)

**incubation** A period of less intense conscious concentration during which a creative person lets the knowledge and ideas acquired during preparation mature and develop. (4)

**individual differences** Personal attributes that vary from one person to another. (4)

**individualism** The extent to which people place primary value on themselves. (3)

**inducements** The tangible and intangible rewards provided by organizations to individuals. (4)

**inequity** The belief that we are being treated unfairly in relation to others. (6)

**influence** The ability to affect the perceptions, attitudes, or behaviors of others. (14)

**informal group** A group that is established by its members. (11)

**informational roles** The monitor, the disseminator, and the spokesperson. (2)

**initiating-structure behavior** Involves clearly defining the leader-subordinate roles so that subordinates know what is expected of them. (13)

**innovation** The process of creating and doing new things that are introduced into the marketplace as products, processes, or services. (18)

**insight** The stage in the creative process when all the scattered thoughts and ideas that were maturing during incubation come together to produce a breakthrough. (4)

**intention** A component of an attitude that guides a person's behavior. (4)

**interactionalism** Suggests that individuals and situations interact continuously to determine individuals' behavior. (1)

**interest group** A group that is relatively temporary and informal and is organized around a common activity or interest of its members. (11)

**interpersonal demands** Stressors associated with group pressures, leadership, and personality conflicts. (9)

**interpersonal roles** There are three important interpersonal roles: the figurehead, the leader, and the liaison. (2)

**interpersonal skills** Used to communicate with, understand, and motivate individuals and groups. (2)

**intrapreneurship** Entrepreneurial activity that takes place within the context of a large corporation. (18)

**isolate** Individual who tends to work alone and to interact and communicate little with others. (10)

**isolated dyad** Two people who tend to work alone and to interact and communicate little with others. (10)

**jargon** The specialized or technical language of a trade, profession, or social group. (10)

**job analysis** The process of systematically gathering information about specific jobs to use in developing a performance measurement system, to write job or position descriptions, and to develop equitable pay systems. (8)

**job characteristics approach** Focuses on the motivational attributes of jobs. (7)

**job characteristics theory** Identifies three critical psychological states: experienced meaningfulness of the work, experienced responsibility for work outcomes, and knowledge of results. (7)

**job design** How organizations define and structure jobs. (7)

**job enlargement** Involves giving workers more tasks to perform. (7)

**job enrichment** Entails giving workers more tasks to perform and more control over how to perform them. (7)

**job hopping** Occurs when an individual makes fewer adjustments within the organization and moves to different organizations to advance his or her career. (Appendix B)

**job rotation** Systematically moving workers from one job to another in an attempt to minimize monotony and boredom. (7)

**job satisfaction** The extent to which a person is gratified or fulfilled by his or her work. (4)

**job sharing** A situation in which two or more part-time employees share one full-time job. (7)

**job specialization** Advocated by scientific management. It can help improve efficiency, but it can also promote monotony and boredom. (7)

**job-centered leader behavior** Involves paying close attention to the work of subordinates, explaining work procedures, and demonstrating a strong interest in performance. (13)

**laboratory experiment** Involves creating an artificial setting similar to a real work situation to allow control over almost every possible factor in that setting. (Appendix A)

**leader-member exchange (LMX)** This model of leadership stresses the fact that leaders develop unique working relationships with each of their subordinates. (13)

**leadership** Both a process and a property. As a process, leadership involves the use of noncoercive influence. As a property, leadership is the set of characteristics attributed to someone who is perceived to use influence successfully. (13)

**Leadership Grid** Evaluates leadership behavior along two dimensions, concern for production and concern for people, and suggests that effective leadership styles include high levels of both behaviors. (13)

**leadership substitutes** Individual, task, and organizational characteristics that tend to outweigh the leader's ability to affect subordinates' satisfaction and performance. (14)

**leading** The process of getting the organization's members to work together toward the organization's goals. (2)

**learning** A relatively permanent change in behavior or behavioral potential resulting from direct or indirect experience. (6)

**learning organization** An organization that works to facilitate the lifelong learning and personal development of all of its employees while continually transforming itself to respond to changing demands and needs. (8)

**least-preferred coworker (LPC) scale** Presumes to measure a leader's motivation. (13)

**legitimate power** Power that is granted by virtue of one's position in the organization. (14)

**liaison** An individual who serves as a bridge between groups, tying groups together and facilitating the communication flow needed to integrate group activities. (10)

**life change** Any meaningful change in a person's personal or work situation; too many life changes can lead to health problems. (9)

**life trauma** Any upheaval in an individual's life that alters his or her attitudes, emotions, or behaviors. (9)

**linking role** A position for a person or group that serves to coordinate the activities of two or more organizational groups. (11)

**locus of control** The extent to which people believe their circumstances are a function of their own actions versus external factors beyond their control. (4)

**long-term orientation** Focused on the future. (3)

**LPC theory of leadership** Suggests that a leader's effectiveness depends on the situation. (13)

**Machiavellianism** A personality trait. People who possess this trait behave to gain power and to control the behavior of others. (4)

**machine bureaucracy** This structure is typical of large, well-established organizations. Work is highly specialized and formalized, and decision making is usually concentrated at the top. (17)

**management by objectives (MBO)** A collaborative goal-setting process through which organizational goals cascade down throughout the organization. (8)

**management functions** Set forth by Henri Fayol; they include planning, organizing, command, coordination, and control. (16)

**management teams** Consist of managers from various areas; they coordinate work teams. (12)

**masculinity** The extent to which the dominant values in a society emphasize aggressiveness and the acquisition of money and material goods, rather than concern for people, relationships among people, and the overall quality of life. (3)

**mastery stage** The stage where individuals develop a stronger attachment to their organizations and lose some career flexibility; performance may vary. (Appendix B)

**matrix design** Combines two different designs to gain the benefits of each; typically combined are a product or project departmentalization scheme and a functional structure. (17)

**mechanistic structure** This structure is primarily hierarchical. Within it, interactions and communications are typically vertical, instructions come from the boss, knowledge is concentrated at the top, and loyalty and obedience are required to sustain membership. (17)

**medium** The channel or path through which the message is transmitted. (10)

**mentoring** Occurs when an older, more experienced person helps a younger employee grow and advance by providing advice, support, and encouragement. (Appendix B)

**Michigan leadership studies** These studies defined job-centered and employee-centered leadership as opposite ends of a single leadership continuum. (13)

**motivation** The set of forces that lead people to behave in particular ways. (5)

**motivation and productivity** The stage of group development in which members cooperate, help each other, and work toward accomplishing tasks. (11)

**motivation factors** These factors are intrinsic to the work itself. They include factors such as achievement and recognition. (5)

**motive** A factor that determines a person's choice of one course of behavior from among several possibilities. (5)

**multicultural organization** The multicultural organization has six characteristics: pluralism, full structural integration, full integration of informal networks, an absence of prejudice and discrimination, equal identification among employees with organizational goals for majority and minority groups, and low levels of intergroup conflict. (3)

**mutual acceptance** The stage of group development that is characterized by members sharing information about themselves and getting to know each other. (11)

**need** Anything an individual requires or wants. (5)

**need for achievement** The desire to accomplish a task or goal more effectively than in the past. (5)

**need for affiliation** The need for human companionship. (5)

**need for power** The desire to control the resources in one's environment. (5)

**need theories of motivation** These theories assume that need deficiencies cause behavior. (5)

**negative affectivity** People who possess this trait are generally downbeat and pessimistic, see things in a negative way, and seem to be in a bad mood. (4)

**negative emotionality** Characterized by moodiness and insecurity; those who have little negative emotionality are better able to withstand stress. (4)

**negative reinforcement (avoidance)** The opportunity to avoid or escape from an unpleasant circumstance after exhibiting behavior. (6)

**negotiation** The process in which two or more parties (people or groups) reach agreement even though they have different preferences. (15)

**noise** Any disturbance in the communication process that interferes with or distorts communication. (10)

**nominal group technique** Technique in which group members follow a generate-discussion-vote cycle until they reach an appropriate decision. (15)

**nonprogrammed decision** A decision that recurs infrequently and for which there is no previously established decision rule. (15)

**norm** A standard against which the appropriateness of a behavior is judged. (11)

**occupation** A group of jobs that are similar with respect to the type of tasks and training involved. (Appendix B)

**Ohio State leadership studies** These studies defined leader consideration and initiating-structure behaviors as independent dimensions of leadership. (13)

**open system** A system that interacts with its environment. (17)

**openness** The capacity to entertain new ideas and to change as a result of new information. (4)

**optimism** The extent to which a person sees life in relatively positive or negative terms. (9)

**organic structure** This structure is set up like a network. Within it, interactions and communications are horizontal, knowledge resides wherever it is most useful to the organization, and membership requires a commitment to the organization's tasks. (17)

**organization** A group of people working together to attain common goals. (16)

**organization chart** A diagram showing all people, positions, reporting relationships, and lines of formal communication in the organization. (16)

**organization climate** Current situations in an organization and the linkages among work groups, employees, and work performance. (18)

**organization culture** The set of values that helps the organization's employees understand which actions are considered acceptable and which unacceptable. (18)

**organization development** The process of planned change and improvement of the organization through application of knowledge of the behavioral sciences. (19)

**organization structure** The system of task, reporting, and authority relationships within which the organization does its work. (16)

**organizational behavior** The study of human behavior in organizational settings, the interface between human behavior and the organization, and the organization itself. (1)

**organizational behavior modification (OB mod)** The application of reinforcement theory to people in organizational settings. (6)

**organizational citizenship** The extent to which a person's behavior makes a positive overall contribution to the organization. (4)

**organizational commitment** A person's identification with and attachment to an organization. (4)

**organizational downsizing** A popular trend aimed at reducing the size of corporate staff and middle management to reduce costs. (17)

**organizational environment** Everything outside an organization. It includes all elements, people, other organizations, economic factors, objects, and events that lie outside the boundaries of the organization. (17)

**organizational goals** Objectives that management seeks to achieve in pursuing the firm's purpose. (16)

**organizational politics** Activities carried out by people to acquire, enhance, and use power and other resources to obtain their desired outcomes. (14)

**organizational socialization** The process through which employees learn about the firm's culture and pass their knowledge and understanding on to others. (18)

**organizational stressors** Factors in the workplace that can cause stress. (9)

**organizational technology** The mechanical and intellectual processes that transform inputs into outputs. (17)

**organizing** The process of designing jobs, grouping jobs into units, and establishing patterns of authority between jobs and units. (2)

**outcome** Anything that results from performing a particular behavior. (6)

**overdetermination** Occurs because numerous organizational systems are in place to ensure that employees and systems behave as expected to maintain stability. (19)

**participation** The process of giving employees a voice in making decisions about their own work. (7)

**path-goal theory of leadership** Suggests that effective leaders clarify the paths (behaviors) that will lead to desired rewards (goals). (13)

**perception** The set of processes by which an individual becomes aware of and interprets information about the environment. (4)

**performance behaviors** The total set of work-related behaviors that the organization expects the individual to display. (4)

**performance measurement (performance appraisal)** The process by which someone (1) evaluates an employee's work behaviors by measurement and comparison with previously established standards, (2) documents the results, and (3) communicates the results to the employee. (8)

**performance plan** An understanding between an employee and a manager concerning what and how a job is to be done such that both parties know what is expected and how success is defined and measured. (8)

**performance-to-outcome expectancy** An individual's perception of the probability that performance will lead to certain outcomes. (6)

**perquisites** Special privileges awarded to selected members of an organization, usually top managers. (8)

**personal power** Resides in the person, regardless of the position he or she fills. (14)

**personality** The relatively stable set of psychological attributes that distinguish one person from another. (4)

**person-job fit** The extent to which the contributions made by the individual match the inducements offered by the organization. (4)

**physical demands** Stressors associated with the job's physical setting, such as the adequacy of temperature and lighting and the physical requirements the job makes on the employee. (9)

**planning** The process of determining an organization's desired future position and the best means of getting there. (2)

**pluralistic organization** An organization that has diverse membership and takes steps to fully involve all people who differ from the dominant group. (3)

**position power** Resides in the position, regardless of who is filling that position. (14)

**positive affectivity** People who possess this trait are upbeat and optimistic, have an overall sense of well-being, and see things in a positive light. (4)

**positive reinforcement** A reward or other desirable consequence that a person receives after exhibiting behavior. (6)

**power** The potential ability of a person or group to exercise control over another person or group. (14)

**power distance** The extent to which less powerful persons accept the unequal distribution of power. (3)

**practical approach** The approach to decision making that combines the steps of the rational approach with the conditions in the behavioral approach to create a more realistic process for making decisions in organizations. (15)

**PRAM model** This model guides the negotiator through the four steps of planning for agreement, building relationships, reaching agreements, and maintaining relationships. (15)

**prejudices** Judgments about others that reinforce beliefs about superiority and inferiority. (3)

**preparation** Usually the first stage in the creative process. It includes education and formal training. (4)

**primary dimensions of diversity** Factors that are either inborn or exert extraordinary influence on early socialization: age, ethnicity, gender, physical abilities, race, and sexual orientation. (3)

**primary needs** The basic physical requirements necessary to sustain life. (5)

**problem solving** A form of decision making in which the issue is unique and alternatives must be developed and evaluated without the aid of a programmed decision rule. (15)

**problem-solving teams** Temporary teams established to attack specific problems in the workplace. (12)

**procedural justice** The extent to which the dynamics of an organization's decision-making processes are judged to be fair by those most affected by them. (18)

**process-based perspectives** These perspectives focus on how people behave in their efforts to satisfy their needs. (6)

**product development teams** Combinations of work teams and problem-solving teams that create new designs for products or services that will satisfy customer needs. (12)

**productivity** An indicator of how much an organization is creating relative to its inputs. (2)

**professional bureaucracy** This structure is characterized by horizontal specialization by professional area of expertise, little formalization, and decentralized decision making. (17)

**programmed decision** A decision that recurs often enough for a decision rule to be developed. (15)

**psychological contract** A person's set of expectations regarding what he or she will contribute to the organization and what the organization, in return, will provide to the individual. (4)

**punishment** An unpleasant, or aversive, consequence that results from behavior. (6)

**quality** The total set of features and characteristics of a product or service that determine its ability to satisfy stated or implied needs. (2)

**quality circles** Small groups of employees from the same work area who regularly meet to discuss and recommend solutions to workplace problems. (12)

**quality of work life** The extent to which workers can satisfy important personal needs through their experiences in the organization. (19)

**radical innovation** A major breakthrough that changes or creates whole industries. (18)

**rational decision-making approach** A systematic, step-by-step process for making decisions. (15)

**receiver** The individual, group, or organization that perceives the encoded symbols; the receiver may or may not decode them and try to understand the intended message. (10)

**reengineering** The radical redesign of organizational processes to achieve major gains in cost, time, and provision of services. (17)

**referent power** Exists when one person wants to be like or imitates someone else. (14)

**refreezing** The process of making new behaviors relatively permanent and resistant to further change. (19)

**reinforcement** The consequences of behavior. (6)

**reinforcement discrimination** The process of recognizing differences between behavior and reinforcement in different settings. (6)

**reinforcement generalization** The process through which a person extends recognition of similar or identical behavior-reinforcement relationships to different settings. (6)

**reinforcement theory** This theory is based on the idea that behavior is a function of its consequences. (6)

**reliability** The extent to which a measure is consistent over time. (Appendix A)

**research design** The set of procedures used to test the predicted relationships among natural phenomena. (Appendix A)

**responsibility** An obligation to do something with the expectation of achieving some act or output. (16)

**rethinking** Looking at organization design in totally different ways, perhaps even abandoning the classic view of the organization as a pyramid. (17)

**reward power** The extent to which a person controls rewards that another person values. (14)

**reward system** The system that consists of all organizational components, including people, processes, rules and procedures, and decision-making activities, involved in allocating compensation and benefits to employees in exchange for their contributions to the organization. (8)

**risk** Condition under which the decision maker cannot know with certainty what the outcome of a given action will be but has enough information to estimate the probabilities of various outcomes. (15)

**risk propensity** The degree to which a person is willing to take chances and make risky decisions. (4)

**role** A set of expected behaviors associated with a particular position in a group or organization. (9)

**role ambiguity** Arises when a role is unclear. (9)

**role conflict** Occurs when the messages and cues constituting a role are clear but contradictory or mutually exclusive. (9)

**role demands** Stressors associated with the role a person is expected to play. (9)

**role overload** Occurs when expectations for the role exceed the individual's capabilities. (9)

**satisficing** Examining alternatives only until a solution that meets minimal requirements is found. (15)

**schedules of reinforcement** Indicate when or how often managers should reinforce certain behaviors. (6)

**scientific management** One of the first approaches to management. It focused on the efficiency of individual workers and assumed that employees are motivated by money. (1, 5)

**scientific research** The systematic investigation of hypothesized propositions about the relationships among natural phenomena. (Appendix A)

**secondary dimensions of diversity** Factors that are important to us as individuals and to some extent define us to others but are less permanent and can be adapted or changed: educational background, geographic location, income, marital status, military experience, parental status, religious beliefs, and work experience. (3)

**secondary needs** The requirements learned from the environment and culture in which the person lives. (5)

**selective perception** The process of screening out information that we are uncomfortable with or that contradicts our beliefs. (4)

**self-efficacy** The extent to which we believe we can accomplish our goals even if we failed to do so in the past. (4, 8)

**self-esteem** The extent to which a person believes he or she is a worthwhile and deserving individual. (4)

**self-reactions** Comparisons of alternatives with internalized moral standards. (15)

**semantics** The study of language forms. (10)

**short-term orientation** Focused on the past or present. (3)

**simple structure** This structure is typical of relatively small or new organizations and has little specialization or formalization. Within this structure, power and decision making are concentrated in the chief executive. (17)

**social learning** Occurs when people observe the behaviors of others, recognize their consequences, and alter their own behavior as a result. (6)

**social loafing** The tendency of some members of groups to put forth less effort in a group than they would when working alone. (11)

**social responsibility** An organization's social responsibility is its obligation to protect and contribute to the social environment in which it functions. (2)

**social subsystem** Includes the interpersonal relationships that develop among people in organizations. (17)

**socialization** The process through which individuals become social beings. (18)

**sociotechnical systems approach** An approach to organization design that views the organization as an open system structured to integrate the technical and social subsystems into a single management system. (17)

**source** The individual, group, or organization interested in communicating something to another party. (10)

**span of control** The number of people who report to a manager. (16)

**stereotypes** Rigid judgments about others that ignore the specific person and the current situation. Acceptance of stereotypes can lead to the dangerous process of prejudice toward others. (3)

**stereotyping** The process of categorizing or labeling people on the basis of a single attribute. (4)

**strategic values** The basic beliefs about an organization's environment that shape its strategy. (18)

**strategy** The plans and actions necessary to achieve organizational goals. (17)

**stress** A person's adaptive response to a stimulus that places excessive psychological or physical demands on that person. (9)

**structural change** A systemwide organization development involving a major restructuring of the organization or instituting programs such as quality of work life. (19)

**structural imperatives** The three structural imperatives, environment, technology, and size, are the three primary determinants of organization structure. (17)

**suboptimizing** Knowingly accepting less than the best possible outcome to avoid unintended negative effects on other aspects of the organization. (15)

**superleadership** Occurs when a leader gradually and purposefully turns over power, responsibility, and control to a self-managing work group. (14)

**superordinate goal** An organizational goal that is more important to the well-being of the organization and its members than the more specific goals of interacting parties. (11)

**surface value** The objective meaning or worth a reward has to an employee. (8)

**symbolic value** The subjective and personal meaning or worth a reward has to an employee. (8)

**system** A set of interrelated elements functioning as a whole. (1, 17)

**systems innovation** Creates a new functionality by assembling parts in new ways. (18)

**task demands** Stressors associated with the specific job a person performs. (9)

**task environment** This environment includes specific organizations, groups, and individuals that influence the organization. (17)

**task group** A relatively temporary, formal group established to do a specific task. (11)

**team** A small number of people with complementary skills who are committed to a common purpose, common performance goals, and approach for which they hold themselves mutually accountable. (12)

**technical (task) subsystem** The means by which inputs are transformed into outputs. (17)

**technical skills** The skills necessary to accomplish specific tasks within the organization. (2)

**technology** The mechanical and intellectual processes used to transform inputs into products and services. (2)

**Telecommuting** A work arrangement in which employees spend part of their time working off-site. (7)

**Theory X** Concept described by Douglas McGregor indicating an approach to management that takes a negative and pessimistic view of workers. (1)

**Theory Y** Concept described by Douglas McGregor reflecting an approach to management that takes a positive and optimistic perspective on workers. (1)

**360-degree feedback** Performance management system in which people receive performance feedback from those on all sides of them in the organization: their boss, their colleagues and peers, and their own subordinates. (8)

**total quality management (TQM)** A form of management that focuses on the customer, an environment of trust and openness, working in teams, breaking down internal organizational barriers, team leadership and coaching, shared power, and continuous improvement. Use of this approach often involves fundamental changes in the organization's culture. (8)

**trait approach** This approach attempted to identify stable and enduring character traits that differentiated effective leaders from nonleaders. (13)

**transformational leadership** The set of abilities that allows the leader to recognize the need for change, to create a vision to guide that change, and to execute that change effectively. (14)

**transition management** The process of systematically planning, organizing, and implementing change. (19)

**transmission** The process through which the symbols that represent a message are sent to the receiver. (10)

**trial stage (socialization stage)** Stage in which individuals more specifically explore jobs and performance begins to improve. (Appendix B)

**turnover** When people quit their jobs. (4)

**type A** People who are extremely competitive, highly committed to work, and have a strong sense of time urgency. (9)

**type B** People who are less competitive, less committed to work, and have a weaker sense of time urgency. (9)

**Type Z firm** This type of firm is committed to retaining employees; evaluates workers' performance based on both qualitative and quantitative information; emphasizes broad career paths; exercises control through informal, implicit mechanisms; requires that decision making occur in groups and be based on full information sharing and consensus; expects individuals to take responsibility for decisions; and emphasizes concern for people. (18)

**uncertainty** Condition under which the decision maker lacks enough information to estimate the probability of possible outcomes. (15)

**uncertainty avoidance** The extent to which people prefer to be in clear and unambiguous situations. (3)

**unconflicted adherence** Continuing with current activities if doing so does not entail serious risks. (15)

**unconflicted change** Involves making changes in present activities if doing so presents no serious risks. (15)

**unfreezing** The process by which people become aware of the need for change. (19)

**universal approach** An approach to organization design where prescriptions or propositions are designed to work in any circumstance. (17)

**valence** The degree of attractiveness or unattractiveness a particular outcome has for a person. (6)

**validity** The extent to which a measure actually reflects what it was intended to measure. (Appendix A)

**valuing diversity** Means putting an end to the assumption that everyone who is not a member of the dominant group must assimilate. The first step is to recognize that diversity exists in organizations so that we can begin to manage it. (3)

**variable-interval reinforcement** Varies the amount of time between reinforcements. (6)

**variable-ratio reinforcement** Varies the number of behaviors between reinforcements. (6)

**verification** The final stage of the creative process where the validity or truthfulness of the insight is determined. (4) The feedback portion of communication in which the receiver sends a message to the source indicating receipt of the message and the degree to which he or she understood the message. (10)

**vigilant information processing** Involves thoroughly investigating all possible alternatives, weighing their costs and benefits before making a decision, and developing contingency plans. (15)

**virtual organization** A temporary alliance between two or more organizations that band together to undertake a specific venture. (17)

**virtual teams** Teams that work together by computer and other electronic communication utilities; members move in and out of meetings and the team itself as the situation dictates. (12)

**Vroom's decision tree approach to leadership** This model attempts to prescribe how much participation subordinates should be allowed in making decisions. (13)

**wheel network** In this type of network, information flows between the person at the end of each spoke and the person in the middle. (10)

**work teams** Include all the people working in an area, are relatively permanent, and do the daily work, making decisions regarding how the work of the team is done. (12)

**workforce diversity** The similarities and differences in such characteristics as age, gender, ethnic heritage, physical abilities and disabilities, race, and sexual orientation among the employees of organizations. (3)

**work-life relationships** The interrelationships between a person's work life and personal life. (9)

**workplace behavior** The pattern of action by the members of an organization that directly or indirectly influences organizational effectiveness. (4)

# Name Index

# Organization Index

# Subject Index

| | | | |
|---|---|---|---|
| 3/24/14 | | | |

## Supplements Designed to Aid Instructors and Students

### For Students:

**Student Web Site.** This site provides additional information, study aids, activities, and resources that help reinforce the concepts presented in the text.

- **Learning Objectives** for each chapter help guide students in their reading and studying.
- A brief **Chapter Outline** provides a quick framework for each chapter.
- The **Chapter Summary** helps students review key points.
- The **Developing OB Internet Skills** exercises from the text are repeated with relevant links and any necessary updates.
- **ACE Self-Tests** give students an opportunity to assess their knowledge.
- The **Glossary** from the main text is provided for easy reference.
- **Flash Cards** help students review the key terms that are boldfaced in the text.
- **Additional Cases** are provided for instructors and students who want extra opportunity to apply the concepts.
- Convenient **Chapter Links** to the organizations highlighted in the chapter-opening vignettes, boxes, and cases allow students to gain further insight into the practices of these businesses.
- A **Resource Center** provides links to various sites of general organizational behavior interest.

**OB in Action.** This book of exercises and cases provides hands-on experiential activities to help students bridge the gap between theory and practice. Working individually or in teams, students explore issues, tackle problems, and find solutions, using organizational behavior theories as their foundation.